D0984853

NAFTA AND FREE TRADE IN THE AMERICAS

A PROBLEM–ORIENTED COURSEBOOK

Second Edition

By

Ralph H. Folsom
Professor of Law
University of San Diego

Michael Wallace Gordon
Chesterfield Smith Professor of Law
University of Florida

David A. Gantz
Samuel M. Fegtly Professor of Law
University of Arizona
James E. Rogers College of Law

AMERICAN CASEBOOK SERIES®

Mat #40260057

American Casebook Series and West Group are trademarks
registered in the U.S. Patent and Trademark Office.

© West, a Thomson business, 2000
© 2005 Thomson/West
    610 Opperman Drive
    P.O. Box 64526
    St. Paul, MN 55164–0526
    1–800–328–9352

Printed in the United States of America

ISBN 0–314–15397–7

*TEXT IS PRINTED ON 10% POST
CONSUMER RECYCLED PAPER*

To our law faculty colleagues at Arizona, Florida, San Diego
and other institutions who have generously supported
our writing efforts and the production of the first
and second editions of this NAFTA coursebook.

*

Preface

Much has happened within and relating to NAFTA in the approximately five years since the first edition was published. However, NAFTA remains important and exciting after eleven years. No business lawyer practicing in North America, or representing foreign clients operating in North America, can escape NAFTA's significance. NAFTA also represents the future. After more than a decade, it is evident that NAFTA is the model for many newer free trade agreements, including but not limited to those concluded by the three NAFTA Parties with other nations both within and outside the Western Hemisphere.

Perhaps most significantly, in terms of NAFTA's general success, the vast majority of the originating goods traded within North America became duty-free and quota-free as of January 1, 2003; almost all the rest will follow suit by January 1, 2008. Extensive use of the Chapter 19 unfair trade dispute settlement mechanism has continued, with approximately one hundred actions having been filed with the NAFTA secretariats. Dispositive opinions have been issued in at least fifteen foreign investor-host state actions brought under Chapter 11, and many others are pending. The case load alone is adding significantly to the volume of jurisprudence with which a properly trained NAFTA lawyer must be familiar.

External factors are strongly affecting the continuing vitality of the Agreement. The full implementation of the Uruguay Round and Information Technology Agreement tariff reductions or eliminations by the United States in its "most favored nation" tariffs has narrowed the tariff advantage enjoyed by Mexico and Canada in the United States market. Mexico, in particular, is suffering from competition for foreign investment and jobs with China, India, Honduras and many other lower wage cost nations in the developing world. Mexico's NAFTA advantage has and will be further eroded under the regional free trade agreements being concluded by the United States and Canada with other countries in the Western Hemisphere and elsewhere, and by the expanded market access to the United States provided by the Caribbean Basin Initiative, the African Growth and Opportunity Act and the Andean Trade Preference Act. The current slow progress in the Doha Development Agenda at the WTO, and the virtual halt in the FTAA negotiations, seems likely to encourage further expansion of the United States' growing network of FTAs.

Similarly, the conclusion by Mexico of an FTA with the European Union in 2000, and with Japan in 2004, has reduced the competitive tariff advantage enjoyed by certain U.S. exporters to Mexico. Caterpillar, for example, no longer enjoys a 15% duty advantage when exporting tractors to Mexico; Volvo (in Sweden) now enjoys the same duty-free entry to the Mexican market, and Japanese competitors are not far behind.

While there has been some discussion among the NAFTA governments, private business interests and non-governmental organizations—principally relating to alleged deficiencies in the dispute settlement mechanisms, or in Mexico to deepening the level of regional integration—no proposals for amendment have achieved any significant level of consensus. Perhaps this is because formally amending NAFTA would be a very difficult process politically, requiring favorable actions by the Mexican and United States Congresses and the Canadian Parliament.

In this second edition, we have made a number of changes and additions, along with updating much of the original material. Most significantly, we have tried to expand the scope of the book to take into account other important regional trade agreements in the Western Hemisphere, including MERCOSUR, the Andean Group, the U.S.–Chile FTA, the U.S.–Central American FTA and the Mexico–European Union FTA, and to present an up-to-date view of the long-pending Free Trade Area of the Americas negotiations. We have also added many notes and comments throughout the book referring to the treatment of such issues as rules of origin, investment, labor rights and environmental protection in other FTAs. In the Documents Supplement, we have incorporated extensive excerpts from the United States–Chile FTA and the basic MERCOSUR instruments.

A new Chapter 1 has been added, focusing on the "globalism vs. regionalism" debate and GATT Article XXIV. This is followed by Chapters 2 and 3 with some background materials on the Canada–United States Free Trade Agreement of 1989 (CFTA) and its successor, the North American Free Trade Agreement of 1994 (NAFTA). We have added an historical introduction to economic integration in Central and South America (Chapter 4). Chapter 5 introduces four trade in goods problems: tariffs and rules of origin, non-tariff trade barriers, Canada's cultural industries exclusion and Mexico's energy sector. Chapter 6 concerns trade in services, with problems on legal services, trucking and buses, and financial services.

In Chapter 7, we move to NAFTA's investment law with problems centered on investor rights, obligations and remedies, including the now-common arbitration of investor-state claims. Chapter 8 selectively explores intellectual property law issues under NAFTA. Chapter 9 contains dispute settlement problems derived from Chapters 19 and 20 of NAFTA: panelist selection and conflicts of interest; binational panels addressing antidumping and injury issues, including extraordinary challenges; Chapter 20 inter-governmental arbitrations; and resolution of private commercial disputes.

Chapters 10 and 11 provide problems relating to NAFTA's "side" agreements, the North American Agreement on Labor Cooperation and the North American Agreement on Environmental Cooperation, respectively. These agreements deal with enforcement of the national laws of each NAFTA Party. They create unique regional procedures allowing individuals and non-governmental organizations to challenge the reality of environmental and labor enforcement.

Lastly, in Chapter 12, we look beyond NAFTA to other efforts to create free trade in the Western Hemisphere. The problems include issues relating to the long-delayed free trade relationship between the United States and Chile due to delays in Congressional authorization of "Trade Promotion Authority" (formerly "fast-track"); to the now-stalled negotiations toward a Free Trade Area of the Americas; and to other regional integration efforts in the region, with a focus on MERCOSUR.

NAFTA, however, remains the focus of our efforts. It continues to dominate Western Hemisphere trade. NAFTA has been the basis for more recent U.S. FTAs (as well as the FTAA drafts), with changes reflecting not only the different economic situations of the other parties, but also eleven years' experience applying the NAFTA legal provisions. This means, among other things, that a lawyer who is fully familiar with the operation of the NAFTA provisions should be able to understand and apply the parallel provisions of these more recent agreements without great difficulty.

The Documents Supplement especially prepared for use with this book has been revised and expanded to reflect developments in the past five years and to provide resources for the study of the United States–Chile Free Trade Agreement and MERCOSUR. References are made in each problem to those parts of the Documents Supplement which are essential to an analysis of the problem.

NAFTA and Free Trade in the Americas remains intended for a two or three semester-hour course. We expect some professors may want to expand upon Chapters 2 and 3, which are a very condensed introduction to CFTA and NAFTA, or the coverage of investment disputes (Chapter 7). The more than 20 problems that follow can be covered one per class session, but many could easily be extended to additional class hours. This is particularly true of those problems containing several parts, such as problem 12.2. The book is designed to facilitate faculty selection of those problems that fit their teaching goals, and enhancement with other readings of the problems which they feel are most important. We elaborate on different approaches to teaching from this coursebook in its revised Teacher's Manual.

As in the past, the authors welcome your comments, as lawyers, students or teachers, and suggestions for future editions.

RALPH H. FOLSOM
(rfolsom@sandiego.edu)
MICHAEL W. GORDON
(gordon@law.ufl.edu)
DAVID A. GANTZ
(gantz@law.arizona.edu)

January 2005

*

Acknowledgments

We wish to acknowledge that in preparing this second edition (and the first edition) we have been aided by numerous colleagues and students. These include Jorge Vargas of the University of San Diego, Davis Folsom of USC-Aiken, Jim Smith of UC-Davis, Baker & McKenzie, Ernesto Grihalva of San Diego, Stephen Zamora of the University of Houston, Robert Lutz of Southwestern University, Eduardo Bustamante of Tijuana, Kevin Kennedy of Michigan State University, Rafael Porrata-Dorata of Temple University, Jorge Ramirez of Texas Tech University, Nancy Fuller-Jacobs of La Jolla, Geoffrey Leibl of Del Mar, Alfredo Andere of Bonita and Tijuana, Jon Johnson of Toronto, Joseph Weiler of New York Unversity, Oliver Goodenough of Vermont law School, Alan Sykes of the University of Chicago, Jeffrey Atik of Loyola University (Los Angeles), Lars Noah of the University of Florida, Jose Luis Siqueiros of Mexico City, Alejandro Ogarrio of the Escuela Libre de Derecho, Leonel Pereznieto Castro of Mexico City, John E. Rogers of Mexico City, Sidney Picker of Case Western Reserve University, Franklin Gill of the University of New Mexico, Boris Kozolchyk of the University of Arizona, Carlos Loperena of Mexico City, James Holbein of Washington, DC, Thomas O'Keefe of Washington, DC, Daniel Magraw of Washington, DC, Lance Compa of Cornell University, Guadalupe Luna of Northern Illinois University, and Rosella Brevetti, Gary Yerkey and their colleagues with BNA's International Trade Reporter, Washington, D.C.

The authors owe a debt of gratitude to research assistants involved in this project, including Susanne Franke, Yohana Saucedo and Christie Villarreal for the first edition, and Lori Di Pierdomenico for this second edition. We also acknowledge the highly professional support of Thomson/West, particularly Roxanne Birkel, Jeff Becker and Staci Herr. The University of Arizona, James E. Rogers College of Law provided a 2004 summer research grant, and additional financial support, for David Gantz' work on the second edition.

The current authors are also extremely grateful for the work of the retiring first edition author, David Lopez. Much of the excellent material he prepared for the first edition remains in the second edition.

We also wish to thank our families for their support during this endcavor.

*

Summary of Contents

Table of Contents

PART THREE.   THE NAFTA SIDE AGREEMENTS

Table of Cases

The principal cases are in bold type. Cases cited or discussed in the text are roman type. References are to pages. Cases cited in principal cases and within other quoted materials are not included.

*

NAFTA AND FREE TRADE IN THE AMERICAS

A PROBLEM–ORIENTED COURSEBOOK

Second Edition

*

Part One

INTRODUCTION TO FREE TRADE IN THE AMERICAS

Chapter 1

THE THRESHOLD QUESTION: GLOBALISM VERSUS REGIONALISM

It is initially surprising to many students of international trade, particularly those familiar with the core principles of the General Agreement of Tariffs and Trade 1994, "most favored nation" treatment (Article I) and national treatment/non-discrimination (Article III), that members of the World Trade Organization, like the "Contracting Parties" of the 1947 GATT, may form "free trade agreements" or "customs unions" that are inconsistent with both of these principles, under the circumstances set out in Article XXIV of the GATT:

Territorial Application—Frontier Traffic—Customs Unions and Free-trade Areas

* * *

5.   ... [T]he provisions of this Agreement shall not prevent, as between the territories of contracting parties, the formation of a customs union or of a free-trade area or the adoption of an interim agreement necessary for the formation of a customs union or of a free-trade area; *Provided* that:

   (*a*) with respect to a customs union, or an interim agreement leading to a formation of a customs union, the duties and other regulations of commerce imposed at the institution of any such union or interim agreement in respect of trade with contracting parties not parties to such union or agreement shall not on the whole be higher or more restrictive than the general incidence of the duties and regulations of commerce applicable in the constituent territories prior to the formation of such union or the adoption of such interim agreement, as the case may be;

   (*b*) with respect to a free-trade area, or an interim agreement leading to the formation of a free-trade area, the duties and other regulations of commerce maintained in each of the constit-

2

uent territories and applicable at the formation of such free-trade area or the adoption of such interim agreement to the trade of contracting parties not included in such area or not parties to such agreement shall not be higher or more restrictive than the corresponding duties and other regulations of commerce existing in the same constituent territories prior to the formation of the free-trade area, or interim agreement as the case may be; and

(c) any interim agreement referred to in subparagraphs (a) and (b) shall include a plan and schedule for the formation of such a customs union or of such a free-trade area within a reasonable length of time.

* * *

7. (a) Any contracting party deciding to enter into a customs union or free-trade area, or an interim agreement leading to the formation of such a union or area, shall promptly notify the CONTRACTING PARTIES and shall make available to them such information regarding the proposed union or area as will enable them to make such reports and recommendations to contracting parties as they may deem appropriate.

* * *

8. For the purposes of this Agreement:

(a) A customs union shall be understood to mean the substitution of a single customs territory for two or more customs territories, so that

(i) duties and other restrictive regulations of commerce (except, where necessary, those permitted under Articles XI, XII, XIII, XIV, XV and XX) are eliminated with respect to substantially all the trade between the constituent territories of the union or at least with respect to substantially all the trade in products originating in such territories, and,

(ii) subject to the provisions of paragraph 9, substantially the same duties and other regulations of commerce are applied by each of the members of the union to the trade of territories not included in the union;

(b) A free-trade area shall be understood to mean a group of two or more customs territories in which the duties and other restrictive regulations of commerce (except, where necessary, those permitted under Articles XI, XII, XIII, XIV, XV and XX) are eliminated on substantially all the trade between the constituent territories in products originating in such territories.

* * *

10. The CONTRACTING PARTIES may by a two-thirds majority approve proposals which do not fully comply with the requirements of paragraphs 5 to 9 inclusive, provided that such proposals lead to the

formation of a customs union or a free-trade area in the sense of this Article.

* * *

Note on WTO Working Parties

There is a process under WTO rules, as para. 7, above, indicates, for Members contemplating FTAs and customs unions to notify the WTO of their intentions. The WTO's practice is to set up for each FTA or customs union a "working group" to analyze the agreement for consistency with GATT rules. However, despite the creation of dozens of such working groups in recent years, it is extremely rare for them to issue reports critical of Members' agreements. This is no doubt due in part to the requirement of consensus for WTO decision-making, and may also reflect the practical realization of WTO Member A sitting on a working party this year in the review of an FTA between Members B and C, that Member A may be in a situation in a year or two when Members B and C are sitting on a working group reviewing an FTA between Member A and some other Member!

Trade agreements—whether FTAs or customs unions—not falling within the global WTO umbrella are commonly referred to as "Regional trade agreements" (RTAs), even though many of them, such as the agreements between the United States and Israel or Singapore, and the agreement between Mexico and the European Union, are hardly "regional" by any normal interpretation of that term. There is a spirited debate among trade officials and economists regarding whether this enormous increase in RTAs is beneficial to the multilateral trading system ("MTS") and to the world economy, or whether RTAs simply detract from the (greater) desired goal of global free trade.

OVERVIEW OF DEVELOPMENTS IN THE INTERNATIONAL TRADING ENVIRONMENT

Annual Report (abridged), WTO Doc. WT/TPR/OV/9 Feb. 20, 2004, Part 10*

A GLOBAL VIEW OF RTAS

The rapid surge in RTAs, which began in the early 1990s, has been such that virtually all WTO Members are engaged in furthering their RTA trade strategy. As of January 2004, 281 RTAs have been notified to the GATT/WTO, of which 157 have been notified since January 1995. Over 190 notified agreements are currently in force, and 70 or more are estimated to be operational but have not yet been notified.

The apparent rush to negotiate RTAs may reflect a certain anxiety by countries of being left behind. This has been particularly noticeable in East and Southeast Asia, a traditional bastion for multilateral-only trade liberalization. The United States is also actively pursuing the regional path, and China has recently negotiated RTAs with Hong Kong, China and Macau, China. By contrast, the EU has decided not to negotiate any new RTAs before the conclusion of the Doha Round. However, the impending negotiation of Economic and Partnership Agreements (EPAs) with the African, Caribbean and Pacific countries (ACP) show that RTAs are still present on the EU policy agenda.

The traditional imperative of RTAs for the economic integration of geographically contiguous markets has considerably weakened. Today, most agreements link pairs of partners, and an increasing number link countries thousands of miles apart. At the same time, however, initiatives to establish large regional economic groupings, such as the Free–Trade Area of the Americas, the eastern enlargement of the EU, and ASEAN + 3 (China, Japan, and Korea), are also being pursued.

With regard to scope, earlier trends are being confirmed. Modern RTAs most often go far beyond traditional tariff-cutting exercises and even beyond existing multilateral rules by including regional rules on investment, competition, environment, and labour. Some WTO Members, as hubs of RTA networks, are increasingly taking advantage of RTA relations to break new ground in trade policy regulation.

Why RTAs?

Policy makers often emphasize the most conspicuous economic gains of RTAs, such as economies of scale, increased competition, and attraction of foreign direct investment, to advocate that bilateral or regional trade liberalization complements multilateral liberalization. By contrast, for RTA sceptics, preferential agreements encourage beggar-thy-neighbour trade practices and detract Members' focus and resources from multilateral liberalization and rule making.

Analytical research on the impact of RTAs has been unable to produce solid responses to those arguments. Building upon Jacob Viner's theoretical approach and the concepts of trade creation and trade diversion, most empirical research has focused on the economic costs and benefits of dismantling barriers within a specific RTA for the parties and those left outside. Assessments vary for different RTAs, sometimes even for the same RTA.

Even more difficult to assess are the economic effects of the increasing complexity of regulations introduced through these agreements. For instance, RTA rules of origin are usually quite stringent, the more so for products for which the margin of preference (difference between the MFN and the preferential tariff) is larger. Origin rules could then have an effect similar to that of a trade barrier protecting domestic production of final goods. Rules of origin may even be seen by traders as a factor of production *per se*, to be considered in the same manner as the availability and cost of inputs, labour costs, infrastructure, etc. In that sense, rules of origin can influence investment decisions, both with respect to input sourcing and location of production, and thus reinforce an RTA's investment diversion. In the absence of a decisive economic test in support of RTAs, and given that a plethora of RTA relations may entail a burden for business practice, why are countries currently putting so much energy into negotiating numbers of them?

Adherents to the political economy perspective would argue that, factors other than the expansion of trade and investment are at play. One such factor would be the use of RTAs to cement diplomatic ties and forge new geopolitical alliances. The economic side of this strategy is to deal with certain trade issues at the bilateral or regional level while leaving the most sensitive ones (such as agriculture) at the multilateral level. A "hub-and-spoke" RTAs web may be particularly effective in this respect as the leverage the hub has on the spokes at the bilateral level could be used to advance or resist specific issues at the multilateral level. Hence, webs of RTAs can be effective in promoting "competitive liberalization", but the setting of common standards and regulations among a group of countries may also produce vested interests and powerful constituencies that will resist advances at the multilateral level.

Also, market-access concerns may have become a compelling factor in RTA negotiations. By not adhering to the RTA "band-wagon", a country could find its products discriminated against by competitors in markets where it has no preferential access. Economies with a relatively small domestic market are particularly vulnerable to these pressures and often have no alternative than to conclude RTAs despite the strain this may place on their limited administrative resources.

MULTILATERALIZING REGIONALISM?

Do RTAs complement the MTS, helping to build and strengthen it, or do they undermine it? To ensure that regional initiatives are fully instrumental, alongside multilateral efforts, in furthering the development of world trade and balanced international trade relations, there is a need for rules and mechanisms capable of driving RTAs on a firm intersecting road with the multilateral trading system.

The principles identified in 1947 and enshrined in GATT Article XXIV (for customs unions and free-trade areas, in trade in goods), and in GATS Article V (for agreements on trade in services) remain sound. WTO provisions basically direct Members that conclude RTAs to promote deep intra-regional trade liberalization and facilitation (including for sensitive sectors), while maintaining the significance of multilateral liberalization and rule making.

These principles, however, are not always reflected in today's regional landscape. One example is with respect to scope, coverage, and depth of liberalization, where the spectrum of RTAs varies widely. A study by the Secretariat showed that, while RTAs have been effective in eliminating or substantially reducing tariffs on industrial products, they have not done the same for agricultural goods. Most often, agricultural trade, even on a preferential basis, remains subject to barriers. Another example is the increasingly broader regulatory framework of RTAs, which, while potentially useful in raising new trade issues on the international agenda, is, in effect, weakening the WTO regulatory function. The latitude enjoyed by parties to RTAs to set up their own regulatory frameworks could lead to a global patchwork of differing trade regulations. These may not only be difficult to harmonize at a later stage, but may also become effective trade barriers, ultimately adding to the costs of doing trade.

That the WTO basic principles governing RTA formation have often been only partially applied suggests that RTAs are unlikely to melt automatically into multilateralism in the name of systemic rationality. It also indicates that the WTO Membership is not adequately equipped to face the challenges that the proliferation of RTAs pose for the functioning of the rules-based MTS. Clearly there is a need to beef up the principles on RTAs with mechanisms that are effective and operational.

The decision by WTO Members, meeting at the Fourth Ministerial Conference in Doha, to launch negotiations aimed at clarifying and improving the disciplines and procedures under the existing WTO provisions on RTAs, reflects these concerns. It is premature to speculate on whether these negotiations will result in a redrafting of the WTO–RTA relationship or to a piecemeal re-interpretation and clarification of existing rules. However, the focus on transparency during the initial phase of the negotiations would seem to reflect a growing awareness of the need for closer surveillance and public scrutiny of RTAs, and to encourage greater adherence with the relevant WTO provisions.

* * *

Author's Note on NAFTA Partners' Other FTAs

What is now becoming a United States' network of free trade agreements began in the mid–1980s—very slowly and cautiously—with Israel and Canada, but the crown jewel is, of course, NAFTA. An agreement with Jordan was concluded in 2001, for political as well as economic reasons. The Clinton Administration began efforts near the end of its term to negotiate agreements with Singapore and Chile—comprehensive agreements based on NAFTA. The Singapore and Chile Agreements were completed by the Bush Administration and went into force January 1, 2004. An agreement with the Central American nations (Guatemala, El Salvador, Honduras, Nicaragua and Costa Rica) and the Dominican Republic—again based on NAFTA—was concluded in 2004, but was not been submitted to Congress in 2004. FTAs with Australia and Morocco were concluded and approved by Congress in 2004; the Australia FTA entered into force January 1, 2005, and the Morocco FTA was expected to be come effective early in 2005. Other FTAs are planned or under negotiation with Colombia, Ecuador, Peru, Bolivia and Panama in this hemisphere, and with Bahrain, Thailand and the nations of the South African Customs Union, and perhaps others, elsewhere. How quickly these more recent agreements can be concluded, and whether all or most of them will be approved by Congress, remains to be seen.

The United States is not alone among NAFTA Parties in its interest in FTAs. Canada currently has FTAs with Chile, Israel and Costa Rica, and is completing negotiations on an FTA with the other Central American nations. Canada has also been negotiating with the European Free Trade Association and Singapore, and is considering FTAs with the Andean Community (Venezuela, Colombia, Ecuador, Peru and Bolivia), the members of the Caribbean Common Market, and the Dominican Republic. Mexico at last count had FTAs with more than thirty countries, including Bolivia, Chile, the nations of Central America, Venezuela, Colombia, Israel, the European Free Trade Area, and the European Union. An FTA with Japan was concluded in 2004.

In South America, the nations of the Southern Cone Common Market (Brazil, Argentina, Paraguay and Uruguay), as the Mercosur group, have negotiated FTAs with Bolivia, Chile and the Andean Community, and are negotiating with the European Union (without much success in the case of the EU). In late 2003, Brazil proposed an FTA with the other members of the loose-knit "Group of 20," developing nations with a strong interest in an end to agricultural subsidies in the global trading context, led by Brazil, India, Egypt and South Africa.

The most ambitious Western Hemisphere FTA, the Free Trade Area of the Americas, is discussed in Chapter 12.

Questions and Comments

1. What is the principal difference between a customs union and a free trade area? Why is a customs union likely to be more difficult to negotiate than a free trade area?

2. What basic requirements must a free trade agreement meet in order to be consistent with the requirements of Article XXIV of the GATT?

3. According to the Uruguay Round Understanding on the Interpretation of Article XXIV, accepted as part of the WTO package in 1994, "The reasonable length of time referred to in paragraph 5(c) of Article XXIV should exceed 10 years only in exceptional cases." For schedule "C + " goods under NAFTA, tariffs are not eliminated for 15 years. The United States–Australia FTA provides for an 18 year phase-out of certain restrictions on sensitive agricultural products. Are these phase-out periods consistent with Article XXIV and the Uruguay Round Understanding?

4. The Agreement Establishing the World Trade Organization, April 15, 1994, the GATT 1994, the other multilateral trade agreements concluded under the "Uruguay Round" of trade negotiations, and most other GATT/WTO documents mentioned in this Chapter, can be found at http://www.wto.org. The U.S. free trade agreements mentioned above include U.S.-Israel Free

Trade Agreement, Apr. 22, 1985, 24 I.L.M. 653 (1985); Free Trade Agreement, Dec. 22–23, 1987 and Jan. 2, 1998 [Can.-U.S.] 27 I.L.M. 281 (1988); Agreement Between U.S. and Hashemite Kingdom of Jordan on the Establishment of a Free Trade Area, Oct. 24, 2000, 41 I.L.M. 63 (2002); United States—Chile Free Trade Agreement, Jun. 6, 2003, *entered into force Jan. 1, 2004*; United States—Singapore Free Trade Agreement, May 6, 2003, *entered into force Jan. 1, 2004.* Information and the official texts of current or recent FTAs to which the United States is a party may be found at http://www.ustr.gov. Information on Canadian FTA activity can be found on the website of the International Trade Canada, http://www.itcan-cican.gc.ca, "Regional and Bilateral Initiatives." Information on Mexican FTAs can be found at http://www.naftaworks.org/. Information on other Western Hemisphere trade agreements, including those concluded by Mexico, is available at http://www.sice.oas.org/TRADEE.ASP.

5. For additional information on the U.S. FTA program, *see U.S. & Central American Countries Conclude Historic Free Trade Agreement*, USTR Press Release, Dec. 17, 2003; *U.S. and Costa Rica Reach Agreement on Free Trade*, USTR Press Release, Jan. 25, 2004; Central American Free Trade Agreement [draft], Jan. 28, 2004; U.S. and Australia Complete Free Trade Agreement, USTR Press Release, Feb. 8, 2004, at ; Status of U.S. Trade Agreement Negotiations, 21 Int'l Trade Reptr. (BNA) 168, Jan. 4, 2004, *all available at* http://www.ustr.gov. For a hopefully complete list of Western Hemisphere Free Trade Agreements, *see* Chapter 3, Part B.

Chapter 2

CANADA AND THE UNITED STATES (FINALLY) AGREE ON FREE TRADE

R. FOLSOM AND W.D. FOLSOM, UNDERSTANDING NAFTA AND ITS INTERNATIONAL BUSINESS IMPLICATIONS

Chapter 3 (1996).*

FREE TRADE AS AN ALTERNATIVE TO ANNEXATION

One of the first acts of the American Revolution was to invade Canada. The goal was to unite Canadians with Americans against the British. After the Revolution, Benjamin Franklin led a delegation of Americans to Canada, but finding little support, went back to Philadelphia. Subsequently, in the Articles of Confederation (1781), the United States left open the possibility for Canada to be admitted to the union. What does this have to do with trade between the two countries? It initiated the idea of annexation of Canada to the United States, an idea that would influence relationships between the two countries for many years. At times fear of annexation has stimulated protectionist sentiments in Canada. At other times annexation has been seen as a positive economic alternative.

After the American Revolution, Alexander Hamilton proposed protective tariffs as a means to develop domestic manufacturing. His ideas were not implemented. Instead, during the 18th and early 19th centuries the United States used tariffs to generate revenue and for foreign policy purposes. During the same period in Canada, Great Britain controlled trade policy. When Britain decided in the 1830s to pursue free trade, it relinquished control of tariffs in Canada and at the same time Canada lost its protected access to British markets. Facing economic decline, a group of Canadian businessmen and journalists in 1849 signed the "Annexation Manifesto" asking that Canada become part of the United

States. Their motive was to gain access to U.S. capital and markets. An upturn in the Canadian economy during the following year ended calls for annexation, but Canadian political leaders recognized that sovereignty and trade with the United States were closely linked.

Lord Elgin, governor-general of Canada from 1847 to 1854, believed that a reciprocity agreement with the United States would reduce the likelihood of future calls for annexation. In the United States, a trade agreement with Canada was opposed by southerners who feared that it would lead to annexation and thus change the political balance in Congress on the slavery issue. Lord Elgin's visit to the United States in 1854 along with liberal quantities of champagne were apparently sufficient to convince U.S. politicians that a trade agreement would reduce the calls for annexation. The resulting Elgin–Marcy Treaty (1854) between the United States and Canada created free trade for almost all existing products and gave the United States access to Canadian fisheries.

FREE TRADE AFTER CANADIAN INDEPENDENCE

United States' manufacturing interests and a perception that Britain had been sympathetic to the Confederacy led to U.S. abrogation of the Elgin–Marcy Treaty in 1866. This in turn contributed to the creation of the Dominion of Canada the following year. The year 1866 had proven very prosperous for Canadians, in part due to increased U.S. imports in advance of the Treaty's end. This led the newly independent Canadian government to attempt a series of trade agreements. In 1869, Canada offered access to its fisheries and entry of U.S. manufactured goods if the United States would allow Canadian natural resources access to U.S. markets. With plenty of its own resources available at the time, the United States declined. Two years later Canada called for renewing the Elgin–Marcy Treaty, but U.S. politicians were not interested. In 1874 Canadian leaders negotiated a sectoral trade treaty with the United States, including natural resources and some manufacturing goods. The treaty was supported by U.S. President Grant, but died in the Senate. By 1879, Canadian nationalism and protection of Canadian manufacturing replaced an interest in increased trade with the United States.

In the 1890s the United States proposed a customs union with Canada. A customs union would have included a common set of tariffs with respect to other countries. But Canada had agreed to preferential tariffs for the British Empire and Commonwealth countries, and was unwilling to choose close ties with the United States over historic relations with Great Britain. The failure of these negotiations in 1896 led to the Fielding Tariffs in Canada and the Dingley Tariffs in the United States. These tariffs protected manufacturing in both countries and contributed to the development of "branch factories" in Canada by U.S. manufacturers.

While restrictions existed in the early 20th century, trade continually expanded. By 1911 over 60 percent of all Canadian imports came from the United States, and Canada was the second largest market for U.S. exports (after Great Britain). In 1911 it was the United States that suggested a free trade agreement with Canada. The two sides agreed to a series of schedules, reducing or eliminating tariff duties. The U.S. Congress ratified the treaty, but opposition from the Canadian Manufacturers Association and political concerns that it could lead to annexation contributed to its defeat in the Canadian Parliament. As a result of the intense opposition to this Treaty, Prime Minister Wilfrid Laurier's government fell.

Increased trade and economic relations between the two countries brought on by World War I led to new discussions of freer trade. President Woodrow Wilson factored into his decision to enter the war the goal of removing economic barriers and the establishment of an equality in trade conditions among all nations. Both scholars and politicians advocated trade as a path to greater world peace and understanding, but post-war recessionary concerns soon prevailed. Protectionist legislation in the United States (1922) and the Smoot–Hawley Tariff Act (1930) were matched by Canadian laws as each nation sought to preserve its economy. Such isolation contributed significantly to the economic depression that Canada and the United States encountered in the 1930s.

Franklin Roosevelt's election in 1932 and his "Good Neighbor Policy" meant changes in trade policy. The Reciprocal Trade Agreements Act (1935) was the first comprehensive trade agreement between Canada and the United States since Elgin–Marcy. The Act rolled back the protective tariffs of the previous fifteen years. Canadians received lower tariffs on agricultural and timber products and the United States gained concessions on machinery, autos and textiles entering Canada. In the next five years Canadian imports from the United States grew from 58 to 69 percent of total imports, while U.S. imports from Canada increased marginally from 36 to 37 percent of their total. Trade and investment increased during this period in part because the two nations signed another agreement in 1938.

World War II brought both countries out of the Depression and increased political and economic cooperation. Surprisingly, trade actually declined during World War II between the two countries as exports shifted to Europe. Defense sharing agreements coordinated war materials production between the two countries. Import and export controls and production quotas directed the two economies toward the war effort.

At the end of World War II United States and Canadian leaders held secret talks to develop a free trade agreement. This agreement would have allowed almost unrestricted entry of goods after a five-year transition period. Since good relations seemed a logical part of the emerging Cold War strategy, Canadian leaders generally supported the agreement. At the last minute Prime Minister William Mackenzie King, crediting divine intervention, reversed his support and the initiative died.

THE GENERAL AGREEMENT ON TARIFFS AND TRADE
(GATT): AN ALTERNATIVE TO FREE TRADE

The General Agreement on Tariffs and Trade (GATT) was signed in 1947. The GATT was part of the post-war reorganization of global economic relations including the International Monetary Fund (IMF) and the World Bank. The original GATT included 23 countries with Canada and the United States acting as major participants in efforts to reduce tariffs. Membership in GATT entitles countries to "most-favored-nation" status (the right to the lowest tariffs applied to another country's goods), to use the GATT dispute resolution procedures and to participate in GATT trade liberalization negotiations. Today, there are well over 100 members of the GATT and the newly formed World Trade Organization (WTO).

Over the years, a series of sessions or "Rounds" of GATT trade negotiations have dramatically reduced tariff levels among industrial nations and even begun to address more difficult non-tariff trade barrier issues. Steady progress within the GATT since World War II relieved past pressures for a Canadian–American free trade agreement. Indeed, Canadian opponents of free trade were generally delighted with GATT as an alternative.

This quiescent state of affairs lasted through the Tokyo Round GATT negotiations (1973–1979). While the Tokyo Round was initiated with predictions of benefits for developing countries, the principal results were tariff and non-tariff barrier reductions among developed countries. The protracted nature of the Uruguay Round (begun in 1986) and fear that it might fail spurred Canadian interest in negotiating a bilateral free trade agreement with the United States, as did its disenchantment with GATT trade dispute remedies. Likewise, Mexico's decision to join the GATT in 1986 represented a major change in its trade policy. Throughout its history, therefore, the GATT has significantly influenced trade in North America. This influence continues in various ways, perhaps most notably when GATT provisions are incorporated by reference into North American free trade agreements and by reservations of rights to pursue GATT [now WTO] remedies. More generally, as the GATT/WTO continues to bring down world tariff levels, the duty free margin of trade preference created by CFTA and NAFTA diminishes.

* * *

CANADIAN BRANCH FACTORIES

Economic nationalism in Canada and the threat of U.S. industrial dominance near the end of the 19th century resulted in the Fielding Tariffs of 1896. The "multinational" U.S. corporate response was the creation of "tariff or branch plants." The resulting change was overwhelming. In 1900, United States total investment in Canada represented less than 15 percent of all foreign investment (Great Britain provided 85 percent). By 1922 U.S. investors provided half of all foreign capital in

Canada, and by 1970 nearly 80 percent of foreign capital entering Canada came from the United States. Foreign firms now account for well over half of Canadian manufacturing output. As a result, Canada has been called the largest branch plant economy in the world.

U.S. firms established branch factories in Canada because of trade restrictions, but these subsidiaries have evolved into strategic elements in multinational business strategy. During the 19th century Canadian manufacturers resisted free trade agreements with the United States, but in the 1980s they supported [the Canada–U.S. Free Trade Agreement] CFTA. With the expansion of branch factories during this century, Canadian manufacturing has come to be dominated by MNC subsidiaries. This leads to an interesting political question. What was the role of multinationals in influencing the new direction in United States–Canadian trade relations?

United States multinationals came to Canada to jump tariff walls, but would they stay after trade restrictions ended? This was one of the major questions during the CFTA debate. By 1988 there had already been seven GATT Rounds reducing the importance of tariffs as an incentive for maintaining manufacturing subsidiaries in Canada, yet there were still many branch factories in the country. Why were they still there? Five reasons help explain this result. First, as noted earlier, the majority of exports from MNCs in Canada are intra-firm exchanges. As such, Canadian subsidiaries are part of a larger organizational strategy. Second, Canadian factories provide needed raw materials and intermediate goods in industries where Canadian producers have traditionally had a comparative advantage. Third, recognition of the sunk costs MNCs already have in their branch factories influence the decision to maintain these operations. Fourth, MNCs export as much as they import into Canada. United States multinationals are therefore not in Canada just to sell to Canadians. Lastly, while CFTA and NAFTA reduce or eliminate tariffs, there is always the potential for non-tariff barriers to be increased. Having factories in Canada reduces that danger.

* * *

LESSONS FROM CFTA

Since trade between the United States and Canada was already extensive and largely without restriction, CFTA did not significantly affect the level of trade between the two countries. Between 1989 and 1992 U.S. exports to Canada increased by 26 percent and U.S. imports from Canada expanded by 19 percent. Most of these increases are probably attributable to changes in GDP and exchange rates. Obviously, Canadian leaders perceive CFTA as benefitting their country, or why would they have participated in expanding CFTA into NAFTA? But Waverman reports that of five studies undertaken to assess the impact of CFTA, three show the agreement caused approximately 50,000 Canadian manufacturing job losses. Some of these losses were clearly linked to the closure of Canadian subsidiary plants by U.S. companies enjoying greater economies of scale by producing for Canada in their U.S. factories. Over 360,000 manufacturing jobs have been lost in Canada since 1989, but the major causes have been the recession during the period, general lack of competitiveness in a restructuring world and higher taxes, rather than CFTA.

* * *

R. FOLSOM, M. GORDON & A. SPANOGLE, INTERNATIONAL BUSINESS TRANSACTIONS, HORNBOOK
Chapter 21 (2001).*

Prior to the Canada–U.S. Free Trade Area Agreement (CFTA), about 70 percent of the trade between the two nations was already duty free. Tariffs on the remaining products averaged about 5 percent when entering the United States and about 10 percent when entering Canada. Annual trade between the two countries is valued at more than $200 billion U.S. dollars. This is more than three times U.S.–Japan trade. Roughly one-third of all Canada–U.S. trading concerns automotive goods, an industry still largely dominated by U.S. companies. As with the Israeli–U.S. Agreement, free trade between the United States and Canada was based upon reciprocity and could be terminated by either party with 6 months notice.

THE CFTA AGREEMENT IN OUTLINE

The CFTA covered manufactured and agricultural goods. It was generally oriented around the principle of national treatment and the Article III GATT rule to that effect was specifically incorporated in Chapter 1. Although the parties affirmed their existing trade agreements (including the GATT), if there was an inconsistency between CFTA and most of these agreements, it was agreed that the CFTA will prevail. The Provinces of Canada and the States of the U.S. must accord most-favored-treatment to goods that qualify under the CFTA. At Canadian insistence, "cultural industries" were specially treated, subject to a right in the other party to take measures of equivalent commercial effect in response to actions that would otherwise be inconsistent with the CFTA. Essentially, there was free trade in these goods, but ownership of them may be reserved to nationals and preservation of their Canadian character secured. Cultural industries are defined to include the publication, sale, distribution or exhibition of books, magazines, newspapers, films, videos, music recordings, and radio, television and cable dissemination. This exemption continues under NAFTA.

The CFTA did not repeal or directly amend the longstanding U.S.–Canadian Automotive Agreement (1965) under which the large majority of trading in autos and original equipment auto parts is undertaken duty free. However, a tougher 50 percent CFTA content rule was established for autos entering the U.S. Canada agreed to phase out its embargo on used autos by 1994. Government procurement contracts for $25,000 or more were opened to firms from both countries, but their goods must have at least a 50 percent U.S.–Canadian content. The CFTA expanded upon the GATT Procurement Code by creating common rules of origin, mandating an effective bid challenge system and improving the transparency of the bid process. Canada has created a Procurement Review Board before whom bid challenges based upon the CFTA may be made. An analysis of the decisions of this Board suggests that it provides open and effective relief.

The CFTA tariff removals were phased in over ten years through 1998. The most sensitive tariff reductions occurred later in the decade and these included duties on plastics, rubber, wood products, most metals, precision instruments, textiles, alcoholic beverages, consumer appliances, and agricultural and fish products. There was a petitioning procedure which permits private parties on either side of the border to seek to accelerate duty free entry in advance of 1999. This petitioning procedure was invoked to a significant degree, resulting in increased duty free trade between the United States and Canada. The CFTA terminated customs user fees and duty drawback programs by 1994, and duty waivers linked to performance requirements by 1988 (excepting the Auto Agreement). All quotas on imports and exports were removed unless allowed by the GATT or grandfathered by the CFTA.

The GATT Code on Technical Standards (1979) [replaced by the WTO Agreement on Technical Barriers to Trade in 1995] was reaffirmed by mutual pledges not to use product standards (health, safety and environment) as trade barriers. National treatment and mutual recognition of testing laboratories and certification bodies were required, and general commitments to harmonize federal standards as much as possible were made. A mandatory 60–day notice and comment period on proposed standards' regulations operated at all levels of government. An example was Canada's 1991 challenge of the upgrading of Puerto Rico's milk standards to existing federal requirements, as a violation of CFTA. The practical effect of this upgrading was to end Puerto Rican imports of long-life milk from Canada.

On agriculture, the CFTA eventually eliminated most bilateral tariffs and export subsidies, and selectively limited or removed quotas (including quotas on sugar, poultry, eggs and meat imports). The Canadians agreed to terminate import licenses for wheat, oats and barley whenever U.S. price supports for those commodities were equal or less than those in Canada. Wine and distilled spirits (but not beer) were generally opened to free and nondiscriminatory trade. Import and export restraints on energy products, including minimum export prices, were prohibited. Petroleum, natural gas, coal, electricity, uranium and nuclear fuels were covered. In short supply conditions, export quotas must be applied so as to proportionately share energy resources. There was permission to export 50,000 barrels per day of Alaskan oil to Canada, and a lengthy list of specific regulatory changes by both sides.

Either nation could invoke escape clause proceedings if there was a surge of imports resulting in injury to a domestic industry. Bilateral escape clause proceedings were eliminated after 1998. A "global" agreement altered traditional third party escape clause criteria to allow relief against CFTA goods only when these imports were substantial (over 10 percent of total) and contributed importantly to serious domestic injury or the threat thereof. Escape clause decisions were ultimately referred to binding arbitration if consultation between the United States and Canada did not result in a settlement.

The innovative rules of origin applicable under the Canadian–U.S. Agreement were established in Chapter 3. They differ from those found in United States legislation adopting the GSP program, the Caribbean Basin Initiative and the Israeli–U.S. Free Trade Area Agreement. There were general and product-specific rules of origin. Ordinarily, goods must be either wholly-produced in the United States or Canada or (if they contain materials or components from other countries) must have undergone a transformation sufficient to result in a new designation under the Harmonized Tariff Classification System employed by both countries. This was treated as the equivalent of "substantial transformation."

In addition, regarding certain assembled products, at least 50 percent of the cost of manufacturing the goods must be attributable to U.S. or Canadian material or the direct cost of processing in the United States or Canada. Note that these rules focus on production costs. The costs of advertising, sales, profit and overhead were excluded for purposes of determining Canadian or U.S. origin. The 50 percent local content test also served as a residual rule of origin applicable whenever the required change in tariff classification was absent in certain cases (notably textiles). The Canadian–U.S. rules of origin are found in Section 202 of the United States–Canada Free Trade Area Agreement Implementation Act. Special U.S.–Canada Free Trade Agreement Certificates of Origin (U.S. Customs Form 353 or Revenue Canada Form B151) had to be completed by exporters seeking duty free or reduced tariff entry. United States law required the retention of records, including these certificates, supporting CFTA preferential treatment for five years.

SERVICES AND INVESTMENT

Apart from reductions in tariffs, one notable feature of the Canadian–U.S. Free Trade Area Agreement was its application to services and investment. Many provisions of the Agreement sought to liberalize trade in services and investment capital flows between the two nations. In Chapter 16, traditional Canadian controls over foreign investment were substantially reduced for United States investors. In 1973 Canada enacted a restrictive investment law, the Foreign Investment Review Act (FIRA), and created a Foreign Investment Review Agency to pass upon new investment and acquisitions in Canada. The law was not as restrictive as those in the developing nations, but it did require substantial review. Joint ventures were not mandated, although the review agency often extracted local content promises before it approved new investment. That practice was condemned by the GATT panel after a request for review was submitted by the United States. The panel based its decision on Article III:4 national treatment requirements.

Canada replaced the FIRA with the Investment Canada Act in 1985. This Act continues the practice of reviewing proposed investment, but review is reserved for large investments [under NAFTA]. The Act is more investment encouraging and simplifies procedures. The CFTA changed the extensiveness of the restrictions that are placed on U.S. investment. Canada ended review of indirect acquisitions (U.S. firms buying U.S. firms with Canadian subsidiaries), but could still require divestiture of cultural subsidiaries to Canadian owners. For direct acquisitions, thresholds were increased, time for review shortened and procedures made easier. A general rule of national treatment in establishing, acquiring, selling and conducting businesses within CFTA was created. Transportation investments were notably excluded from this general rule. Most investment performance requirements were banned, and profits and earnings are freely transferable.

Not all services could be freely provided across the Canadian–U.S. border under the CFTA. A lengthy listing of covered services is found in Annex 1408 to Chapter 14 of the Agreement. These include agriculture and forestry, mining, construction, distribution, insurance, real estate, and various commercial and professional services. Engineering and accounting services were included but transportation, legal and most medical services were not. Covered services had to be accorded national treatment and a right of establishment, except as differences were required for prudential, fiduciary, health and safety and consumer protection reasons. State, provincial and local governments must grant most favored treatment to service providers. In addition, the U.S. and Canada agreed that their licensing and certification procedures must not be applied on a discriminatory basis and be based upon assessments of competence.

A general "standstill" on trade restraints applicable to services was agreed. This had the effect of grandfathering most existing restraints or discrimination. Special rules permitting temporary entry for business persons in either country supported free movement in services. Individual rules for architecture, tourism, computer services and telecommunications network services were detailed in separate annexes to the CFTA. Professionals, investors, traders, business visitors and executives also benefitted from a newly created temporary entry CFTA visa agreement.

Financial services were covered in Chapter 17 of the CFTA. Each side made specific commitments to alter or apply its regulatory regimes for the benefit of the other's financial services companies. For example, the U.S. promised not to apply less favorable treatment to Canadian banks than that in effect on October 4, 1987 and to grant them the same treatment accorded U.S. banks under the Glass–Steagall Act amendments. The continuation of multi-state branches of Canadian banks was also guaranteed. Canada, for its part, removed various statutory restraints on foreign ownership of financial institutions (including insurance and trust companies) and assets controls over foreign bank subsidiaries. Applications for entry into the Canadian financial market were treated on the same basis as Canadian applications, and U.S. banks could underwrite and deal in Canadian debt securities. All of these commitments were continued under NAFTA. Financial services' disputes were subject to formal consultation between the U.S. Treasury Department and the Canadian Department of Finance.

DISPUTE SETTLEMENT UNDER CFTA

Disputes under CFTA were handled in one of two ways. Disputes of a general nature were taken up under the GATT (now WTO) or addressed under Chapter 18, first by consultation and then by a binding arbitration panel of five independent experts. Each side chose two experts and those experts chose a fifth. Panels were formed in 1989 on salmon and herring and in 1990 on lobsters. Other trade disputes of special note focused on the allegedly low level of Canada's "stumpage fees" for timber (treated as a subsidy by the U.S.), mutual recriminations about trade restraints in beer, and a ruling of the U.S. Customs Service regarding the Canadian–U.S. content of Hondas manufactured in Canada. This ruling had the effect of disqualifying these automobiles from CFTA tariff treatment.

Special, unique dispute settlement rules applied to antidumping and countervailing duties under Chapter 19. Basically, both nations agreed to allow a binational panel to solve disputes of this kind, the governing law changing according to which is the importing country. The panels were drawn from a roster of at least 50 Canadian and United States citizens, a majority of whom were lawyers. Any final determination at the national level could be appealed by private or governmental parties to this panel using pleadings similar to those used in judicial proceedings. This binational panel replaced traditional judicial review of antidumping and countervailing duty orders. The only appeal from a binational panel decision in countervailing duty and antidumping cases was to the so-called "Extraordinary Challenge Committee." This Committee was composed of ten judges or former judges from the United States and Canada. Three of these judges were chosen to hear extraordinary challenges. These could be raised only if the panel was guilty of gross misconduct, made errors in procedure, or exceeded its authority. Numerous antidumping or countervailing duty determinations had been reviewed under Chapter 19 by the end of 1994 and the arrival of NAFTA. Most of these panel decisions were unanimous.

R. FOLSOM AND W.D. FOLSOM, UNDERSTANDING NAFTA AND ITS INTERNATIONAL BUSINESS IMPLICATIONS
Chapter 2 (1996).*

How can there be four legal traditions for three countries? The best answer is that Canada arguably brings two legal traditions into NAFTA, one from Quebec and one from the rest of Canada in which Quebec also participates.

* * *

NAFTA at its heart is about changing market forces, but law is the instrument and to a degree the guarantor of change. It is through legal enactments and proceedings that the new rules of the business game in North America are to be realized. Each legal system brings with it traditions that can be expected to influence how the NAFTA accords are interpreted, implemented and applied. These traditions go beyond the lawyer's headache created by legal texts that are authoritatively expressed in three different languages. They carry with them the history, politics, culture, and social and economic dynamics of Canada, Mexico and the United States.

The legal traditions of Quebec and Canada are difficult to understand. This results from the nation's fundamental lack of internal cohesion (or put more positively, its strained but remarkable ability to keep Quebec in Canada). With Quebec as a part of Canada, the nation partakes of both the Common Law (English) and Civil Law (French) traditions. Some of the fundamental differences in these traditions are explored below, but it is worth noting at the outset that a degree of cross-fertilization between them has taken place.

THE RECEPTION OF THE COMMON LAW IN CANADA

* * *

The Common Law, that is to say English legal traditions, prevails in nine of the ten Canadian provinces (excepting Quebec), in its [three] territories (Yukon, the Northwest Territories and Nunavut) and generally at the federal level. The dates of reception of English law into these provinces vary according to their histories and entry into the Canadian confederation. For the former territories of Alberta and Saskatchewan, for example, July 15, 1870 was the date when English law was received. This means that all English law as it stood as of that date became the law of these provinces. For Ontario, the date was October 15, 1792, and so forth.

As a rule, English law was supreme during Canada's colonial period. This supremacy embraced British legislation directed towards Canada as well as its historic body of Common Law as developed by the courts and

---

customary practices. Supremacy meant that no law adopted in Canada could alter any British statute or judicial doctrine. This subservient state of affairs lasted until 1931 when the British Parliament adopted the Statute of Westminster, eliminating its power to legislate for Canada unless requested to do so. Judicial subservience continued formally until 1949 when the Canadian Supreme Court finally became the court of last resort in the Canadian legal system. Prior thereto, the Judicial Committee of the British Privy Council served that function.

The reception of English legal traditions into Canada's legal system was broadly welcomed. Only in Quebec, where English criminal and civil law were imposed in 1763, was the reception hostile. So hostile, indeed, that French civil law was substituted rather quickly in 1774, but English criminal law continued to rule.

* * *

THE RECEPTION OF FRENCH CIVIL LAW IN QUEBEC

Quebec, or Nouvelle France as it was known prior to British conquest in 1760, is rich in French legal traditions. During its French colonial period, Nouvelle France initially followed the pattern prevailing in northern France. This was a splintered, feudalistic legal system employing customary law (droit coutumier) in hundreds of localities. In Nouvelle France, law and order were the responsibility of the commercial company exploiting it (La Compagnie des Cent Associes). In 1663, King Louis XIV dissolved this company and granted a degree of autonomy to the local Conseil Souverain. Just one year later, a royal edict applied one of the leading bodies of customary French law to Nouvelle France ... La Coutume de la Prevote et Vicomte de Paris. The customary law of Paris thus forms the historical basis for civil law in modern Quebec. To a surprising degree this body of law (derived significantly from Roman and Canon [Roman Catholic] legal principles) had already been organized in a logical format under numerous titles and articles of law. La Coutume de Paris was supplemented by royal edicts and the ordinances of Nouvelle France up until the British conquest.

Initially, the British sought to impose the laws and traditions of England upon Quebec in nearly all matters under a Royal Proclamation issued in 1763 by George III. This approach was the cause of enormous discontent and even the Governors of Quebec appointed by the King of England supported change. The Quebec Act of 1774 withdrew the Proclamation of 1763 and affirmed the rule of French civil law and civil procedure governing such matters as contracts, families, property, commerce and litigation, but retained British criminal law and procedure. The Act of 1774 thus supported the retention of French legal traditions which would have to co-exist with the Common Law prevailing elsewhere in Canada. This fundamental culturally-based division was solidified in the Constitutional Act of 1791 creating Upper (English) and Lower (French) Canada.

In actual operation, the French legal traditions of Quebec suffered from inroads by British legislative acts and internal social change. By the mid–19th century, the law of Quebec was a mishmash and increasingly incoherent. In France, meanwhile, Napoleon had introduced his famous law "Codes," exhaustive compilations of existing civil, commercial and criminal French legal principles. These "codifications," emulating those of Rome and a product of academic thinking, have since become France's greatest legal exports.

The codification movement reached Quebec in 1857 when a commission was established with the authority to draft a "Civil Code of Lower Canada" and a "Civil Procedure Code of Lower Canada." These Codes ended up quite like the Codes of Napoleon, drawing heavily on La Coutume de Paris as well as Roman and Canon law. The Civil Code of Lower Canada (CCLC) took effect (ironically by an Act of the British Parliament) in 1866, just prior to Canadian independence under the British North American Act of 1867. The Quebec Code of Civil Procedure, which also borrowed from Louisiana's code, became law in 1867. The CCLC, however, was replaced by the Civil Code of Quebec (CCQ), which came into effect on January 1, 1994. The CCQ superseded all prior conflicting Quebec law, and remains (as amended occasionally) in effect today.

* * *

In Quebec, the French legal traditions associated with Codes and deductive judicial reasoning have notably weakened as a result of cross-fertilization with the Common Law. Dissenting judicial opinions, for example, are a Common Law tradition that applies in Quebec. Professor Wolfgang Friedmann, writing as early as 1953, concluded that stare decisis is followed when the Supreme Court of Canada rules on Quebec civil law, that the courts of Quebec rarely fail to adhere to higher court rulings or reverse their own decisions, and that the Quebec courts are probably more intolerant of deviations from la doctrine and le jurisprudence than those of France. On balance, although the courts of Quebec and the rest of Canada operate from fundamentally different premises, the results are remarkably similar.

QUEBEC AND THE 1982 CONSTITUTION OF CANADA

Only Quebec did not accept the 1982 Canadian Constitution. Although its adoption by an Act of the British Parliament is said to bind Quebec to its terms, the province has not formally acceded to the Constitution. Negotiations aimed at keeping Quebec within the "constitutional family" of Canada began shortly after 1982. These negotiations eventually led to an agreement in 1987 known as the Meech Lake Accord. Perhaps the most controversial part of that Accord was a provision recognizing Quebec as a "distinct society" within Canada. Other provisions continued the drift towards greater provincial powers (a theme dear to the heart of western Canadian provinces) and changed the procedures for amending the Constitution.

The Meech Lake Accord was never consummated. While Quebec quickly ratified its contents, Newfoundland first approved and then withdrew its approval. Manitoba and New Brunswick never ratified the Accord. These rejections sent Canada back to square one. Further negotiations produced what became known as the Charlottetown Accord of 1992. This Accord also contained a "distinct society" clause referring specifically to the French-speaking majority, a unique culture and the Civil Law tradition in Quebec. The Charlottetown Accord was then put to a vote in a national referendum. The defeat was overwhelming: Six provinces, including Quebec, plus the Yukon territory voted no.

As a consequence, the forces long building within Quebec for separation from Canada have strengthened and its future as a part of Canada is by no means certain. In the Fall of 1994, the Parti Quebecois won control of the provincial government. A referendum on independence was scheduled for 1995. Late in October of 1995, the citizens of Quebec voted to remain part of Canada by a margin of only one percent. Independence would bring a host of legal issues, not the least of which would be Quebec's status (if any) under the North American Free Trade Agreement. It is conceivable that an independent Quebec might have to negotiate for membership in NAFTA and that Mexico, the United States or (English-speaking) Canada could veto Quebec's application. It is also conceivable that Quebec's "separation" may not be total and that it may therefore retain membership in NAFTA as part of a continuing relationship with Canada.

IN THE MATTER OF A REFERENCE BY THE GOVERNOR IN COUNCIL CONCERNING CERTAIN QUESTIONS RELATING TO THE SECESSION OF QUEBEC FROM CANADA

Supreme Court of Canada.
2 Can. S.C.R. 217 (1998).

PANEL: Lamer C.J. and L'Heureux–Dubé, Gonthier, Cory, McLachlin, Iacobucci, Major, Bastarache and Binnie JJ.

* * *

The following is the judgment delivered by THE COURT—

INTRODUCTION

This Reference requires us to consider momentous questions that go to the heart of our system of constitutional government. The observation we made more than a decade ago in *Reference re Manitoba Language Rights*, [1985] 1 S.C.R. 721, applies with equal force here: as in that case, the present one "combines legal and constitutional questions of the utmost subtlety and complexity with political questions of great sensitivity". . . .

The questions posed by the Governor in Council by way of Order in Council P.C. 1996–1497, dated September 30, 1996, read as follows:

1. Under the Constitution of Canada, can the National Assembly, legislature or government of Quebec effect the secession of Quebec from Canada unilaterally?

2. Does international law give the National Assembly, legislature or government of Quebec the right to effect the secession of Quebec from Canada unilaterally? In this regard, is there a right to self-determination under international law that would give the National Assembly, legislature or government of Quebec the right to effect the secession of Quebec from Canada unilaterally?

3. In the event of a conflict between domestic and international law on the right of the National Assembly, legislature or government of Quebec to effect the secession of Quebec from Canada unilaterally, which would take precedence in Canada?

* * *

SUMMARY OF CONCLUSIONS

As stated at the outset, this Reference has required us to consider momentous questions that go to the heart of our system of constitutional government. We have emphasized that the Constitution is more than a written text. It embraces the entire global system of rules and principles which govern the exercise of constitutional authority. A superficial reading of selected provisions of the written constitutional enactment, without more, may be misleading. It is necessary to make a more profound investigation of the underlying principles that animate the whole of our Constitution, including the principles of federalism, democracy, constitutionalism and the rule of law, and respect for minorities. Those principles must inform our overall appreciation of the constitutional rights and obligations that would come into play in the event a clear majority of Quebecers votes on a clear question in favour of secession.

The Reference requires us to consider whether Quebec has a right to unilateral secession. Those who support the existence of such a right found their case primarily on the principle of democracy. Democracy, however, means more than simple majority rule. As reflected in our constitutional jurisprudence, democracy exists in the larger context of other constitutional values such as those already mentioned. In the 131 years since Confederation, the people of the provinces and territories have created close ties of interdependence (economically, socially, politically and culturally) based on shared values that include federalism, democracy, constitutionalism and the rule of law, and respect for minorities. A democratic decision of Quebecers in favour of secession would put those relationships at risk. The Constitution vouchsafes order and stability, and accordingly secession of a province "under the Constitution" could not be achieved unilaterally, that is, without principled negotiation with other participants in Confederation within the existing constitutional framework.

The Constitution is not a straitjacket. Even a brief review of our constitutional history demonstrates periods of momentous and dramatic change. Our democratic institutions necessarily accommodate a continuous process of discussion and evolution, which is reflected in the constitutional right of each participant in the federation to initiate constitutional change. This right implies a reciprocal duty on the other participants to engage in discussions to address any legitimate initiative to change the constitutional order. While it is true that some attempts at constitutional amendment in recent years have faltered, a clear majority vote in Quebec on a clear question in favour of secession would confer democratic legitimacy on the secession initiative which all of the other participants in Confederation would have to recognize.

Quebec could not, despite a clear referendum result, purport to invoke a right of self-determination to dictate the terms of a proposed secession to the other parties to the federation. The democratic vote, by however strong a majority, would have no legal effect on its own and could not push aside the principles of federalism and the rule of law, the rights of individuals and minorities, or the operation of democracy in the other provinces or in Canada as a whole. Democratic rights under the Constitution cannot be divorced from constitutional obligations. Nor, however, can the reverse proposition be accepted. The continued existence and operation of the Canadian constitutional order could not be indifferent to a clear expression of a clear majority of Quebecers that they no longer wish to remain in Canada. The other provinces and the federal government would have no basis to deny the right of the government of Quebec to pursue secession, should a clear majority of the people of Quebec choose that goal, so long as in doing so, Quebec respects the rights of others. The negotiations that followed such a vote would address the potential act of secession as well as its possible terms should in fact secession proceed. There would be no conclusions predetermined by law on any issue. Negotiations would need to address the interests of the other provinces, the federal government, Quebec and indeed the rights of all Canadians both within and outside Quebec, and specifically the rights of minorities. No one suggests that it would be an easy set of negotiations.

The negotiation process would require the reconciliation of various rights and obligations by negotiation between two legitimate majorities, namely, the majority of the population of Quebec, and that of Canada as a whole. A political majority at either level that does not act in accordance with the underlying constitutional principles we have mentioned puts at risk the legitimacy of its exercise of its rights, and the ultimate acceptance of the result by the international community.

The task of the Court has been to clarify the legal framework within which political decisions are to be taken "under the Constitution", not to usurp the prerogatives of the political forces that operate within that framework. The obligations we have identified are binding obligations under the Constitution of Canada. However, it will be for the political actors to determine what constitutes "a clear majority on a clear question" in the circumstances under which a future referendum vote may be taken. Equally, in the event of demonstrated majority support for Quebec secession, the content and process of the negotiations will be for the political actors to settle. The reconciliation of the various legitimate constitutional interests is necessarily committed to the political rather than the judicial realm precisely because that reconciliation can only be achieved through the give and take of political negotiations. To the extent issues addressed in the course of negotiation are political, the courts, appreciating their proper role in the constitutional scheme, would have no supervisory role.

We have also considered whether a positive legal entitlement to secession exists under international law in the factual circumstances contemplated by Question 1, *i.e.*, a clear democratic expression of support on a clear question for Quebec secession. Some of those who supported an affirmative answer to this question did so on the basis of the recognized right to self-determination that belongs to all "peoples". Although much of the Quebec population certainly shares many of the characteristics of a people, it is not necessary to decide the "people" issue because, whatever may be the correct determination of this issue in the context of Quebec, a right to secession only arises under the principle of self-determination of peoples at international law where "a people" is governed as part of a colonial empire; where "a people" is subject to alien subjugation, domination or exploitation; and possibly where "a people" is denied any meaningful exercise of its right to self-determination within the state of which it forms a part. In other circumstances, peoples are expected to achieve self-determination within the framework of their existing state. A state whose government represents the whole of the people or peoples resident within its territory, on a basis of equality and without discrimination, and respects the principles of self-determination in its internal arrangements, is entitled to maintain its territorial integrity under international law and to have that territorial integrity recognized by other states. Quebec does not meet the threshold of a colonial people or an oppressed people, nor can it be suggested that Quebecers have been denied meaningful access to government to pursue their political, economic, cultural and social development. In the circumstances, the National Assembly, the legislature or the government of Quebec do not enjoy a right at international law to effect the secession of Quebec from Canada unilaterally.

Although there is no right, under the Constitution or at international law, to unilateral secession, that is secession without negotiation on the basis just discussed, this does not rule out the possibility of an unconstitutional declaration of secession leading to a de facto secession. The ultimate success of such a secession would be dependent on recognition by the international community, which is likely to consider the legality and legitimacy of secession having regard to, amongst other facts, the conduct of Quebec and Canada, in determining whether to grant or withhold recognition. Such recognition, even if granted, would not, however, provide any retroactive justification for the act of secession, either under the Constitution of Canada or at international law.

[In view of the answers to Questions 1 and 2, the Court determined that there was no conflict between domestic and international law to be addressed in the context of this Reference.]

The reference questions are answered accordingly.

Judgment accordingly.

BREBNER, THINGS FALL APART? NAFTA AFTER QUEBEC SECESSION
6 Dalhousie J. Legal Studies 287 (1997).*

The normal method for becoming a member of NAFTA is provided in Article 2204, the Agreement's accession clause:

1. Any country or group of countries may accede to this Agreement subject to such terms and conditions as may be agreed between such country or countries and the Commission and following approval in accordance with the applicable legal procedures of each country.

2. This Agreement shall not apply as between any Party and any acceding country or group of countries if, at the time of accession, either does not consent to such application.

That this clause does not allow for easy or automatic entry is demonstrated by the difficulties Chile has faced. If Quebec were to attempt to join by this mechanism it is likely that a protracted negotiation would ensue with all privileges suspended in the interim. Among the many problematic areas that Quebec negotiators might be forced to deal with in an accession negotiation are subsidies, investment, labour and the environment, and alcoholic beverages. From Quebec's point of view, such a negotiation immediately following separation would be doubly difficult because the existing power imbalance would be heightened by a desire to gain entry quickly. It is also probable that any negotiation with Canada conducted in the aftermath of separation would not be amicable, and it is possible that Canada would use its approval of Quebec's accession to the NAFTA to bargain concessions in other areas of the negotiation. All of which is to say that while eventual Quebec accession is a probable outcome, the likelihood of protracted uncertainty and delay militate in favour of exploring other options. If Quebec were not currently part of Canada, accession would be the only method by which it could join the agreement. Different considerations apply in the event of a secession. It is possible that Quebec could *succeed* to the NAFTA, either as of right, or, more likely, by agreement between the parties. This would mean that Quebec would, immediately upon attaining independence, become a national party to the agreement.

* * *

[T]he *Vienna Convention on Succession of States in Respect of Treaties* attempts to reconcile in a principled way. Article 16 provides that the clean slate doctrine forms the basis for the general rule applicable to former colonies, while separating states, such as Quebec, potentially are governed by Article 34(1):

> When a part or parts of the territory of a State separate to form one or more States, whether or not the predecessor State continues to exist:

> (a) any treaty in force at the date of the succession of States in respect of the entire territory of the predecessor State continues in force in respect of each successor State so formed. . . .

The reason this distinction is drawn is that in the case of separation, as opposed to decolonization, the separating territory is presumed to have played a role in the completion of the original agreement. The *Succession Convention* would appear to resolve the question of Quebec's rights to succeed to the NAFTA were it not for the fact that it is not in force and has attracted but a paucity of signatories, none of which are Canada, the U.S., or Mexico. Therefore, the question becomes whether its provisions are reflective of customary international law.

In the *Restatement (Third) of the Foreign Relations Law of the United States* the distinction drawn by the *Succession Convention* is explicitly rejected on the grounds that the status of the territory prior to independence is not determinative of the role it may have played in negotiating all or any of the treaties applicable to it. The *Restatement* holds that state practice is compatible with the application of the clean slate rule across the board.

* * *

The recent break-up of Czechoslovakia, Yugoslavia, and the Soviet Union provides further evidence of both the continuing use of the clean slate rule and the general practice of maintaining existing treaties. As P.R. Williams notes, following the dissolution of these countries the U.S. government initially formulated a policy designed to ensure treaty continuity: "as a matter of public international law [the successor states] were obligated to continue the treaties." The U.S policy also asked for a "commitment to be bound" from the governments in question, which suggests a weakness in the legal force of the presumption of continuity. And, as Williams notes, as time passed the U.S. became more interested in receiving political assurances rather than relying on any notion of legal obligation, thus undercutting the possibility of the emergence of a new customary rule of succession. The European Community maintained a similar position, asking for a commitment from the new states to "settle by agreement, including where appropriate by recourse to arbitration, all questions concerning state succession." In light of this, some commentators have gone so far as to suggest that there is a general, if still inchoate, "presumption of continuity." However, even if such a presumption exists, it is acknowledged that it is not "black-letter" law, and that any rules must be applied in a "reasoned, flexible manner." This would seem to suggest that if Quebec were to secede, it would, given its stated preference, in all likelihood succeed to the NAFTA, not as of right but in keeping with a general preference for continuity.

Chapter 3

MEXICO JOINS CANADA AND THE UNITED STATES IN FREE TRADE

R. FOLSOM AND W.D. FOLSOM, UNDERSTANDING NAFTA
AND ITS INTERNATIONAL BUSINESS IMPLICATIONS

Chapter 1 (1996).*

MEXICAN INDEPENDENCE

The Bourbon reforms of the 18th century and Napoleon's replacement of Spain's king with his brother Joseph in 1808 were two major factors leading to independence movements throughout Latin America. Mexico was influenced by this too, but a revolutionary "army" in Mexico in 1810, made up of poor mestizos and Indians led by Roman Catholic priests, slaughtered thousands of creoles and others, making Mexican elites fear independence. Nevertheless, Spanish liberals' insistence that the restored King Ferdinand adopt a liberal constitution in 1821 led Mexican creoles to support independence. Part of the 1821 declaration of independence asserted that Mexico would become a constitutional monarchy, but by 1822 it was a republic. The creoles stepped into the power vacuum created by the withdrawal of the presence of the Crown. The creoles were not interested in the ideas and institutions of democracy, but instead wanted to control the political and economic system without interference of Spanish decrees and officialdom. The early Mexican governments were chiefly comprised of generals (Santa Anna multiple times) and people trying to protect and maintain their economic and social interests. In reality, each region of Mexico had its own *caudillo* or military strongman, supported by very large landowners (*latifundistas*). If anything, the feudal strains in the Mexican economy got stronger.

The economy predictably declined after independence, creating more political instability and a series of military revolts. Each new central government borrowed funds abroad to finance their efforts. Instability resulted in high interest rates which increased costs and reduced funds available for infrastructure development and social needs.

In the 1830s, thousands of U.S. settlers began to arrive in Texas, which was then the Mexican state of Coahuila. Many U.S. settlers believed that Texas had been part of the Louisiana Purchase. Conflicts ensued, and the United States on several occasions offered to buy Texas from Mexico. The defeat of Santa Anna ended the conflict in 1836, but did not slow the westward movement of Americans into Mexican territory. This led to what is referred to by Mexicans as the "War of North American Invasion." U.S. forces occupied Veracruz, Monterey, and Mexico City. In the Treaty of Guadalupe Hidalgo (1848) Mexico ceded a vast area including California, Arizona, New Mexico and parts of Utah, Colorado and Nevada. A few years later (1853), the United States "purchased" additional Mexican lands in Arizona and New Mexico, completing the southwestern expansion of the United States into Mexican territory. Few U.S. citizens are aware of this history, but few Mexicans have forgotten the invasion and losses of Mexico. "American business people are advised to be aware of this event, and sensitive to the importance it continues to hold for Mexicans."

NINETEENTH CENTURY REFORMS AND RETRENCHMENT

In the 1850s Benito Juarez and other liberal Mexicans saw the opportunity to change many of the vestiges of colonialism. With the Reform movement and Constitution of 1857 slavery was abolished, the *fueros* system ended, and some church monopolies were terminated and church lands sold. The new Constitution also described Mexico as a representative, democratic nation. Needless to say neither church nor *fuero* groups in the country were pleased with these reforms. Civil War (1857–1867) ensued.

The liberal army won, but the economy was in disarray. The new Juarez government suspended all debt payments to Spain, France and Britain. In retaliation, France sent military forces and captured Mexico City (1863). Napoleon III named Maximilian von Hapsburg to rule Mexico, but his reign lasted only four years since French troops proved too costly, Napoleon needed the troops in Europe, and Maximilian did not have the good sense to leave. Juarez returned to lead Mexico, thus ending the idea of monarchy in Mexico. He initiated educational and economic improvements and adopted separation of church and state policies.

For 35 years (1876–1911) Porfirio Diaz dominated the history of Mexico. From a poor family in Oaxaca, Diaz studied law but joined the army in the movement against the French. In 1876 he led a revolt against the liberal successors to Juarez and assumed the presidency. Diaz surrounded himself with intellectuals of the era, positivists, who argued progress was only possible when there was order in society. Liberty was at first included as the third goal of the positivists, but the

Diaz years would strive for progress through order at the expense of liberty.

With firm control of society, foreign investment was encouraged and surged throughout the period. Foreign money built railroads with concessions from the government, and mining grew. Glass and textile industries were developed. Diaz brought modernization to the Mexican economy. In 1883, a new Diaz law eliminated the *ejido* system (communal lands owned by Native Americans). By the end of the Diaz regime few of Mexico's rural families owned land. Many of them were tied to haciendas through debt bondage. At the other extreme were several thousand haciendas, some of them millions of acres in size, owned by the Mexican elite. Foreign companies and the reassertive Roman Catholic Church also owned large areas of the country. The Diaz era thus brought economic change to Mexico, prosperity to a few, and discontent to many. One study found that at the end of the Diaz regime the Mexican peasant had less food than in 1520.

The Mexican Revolution and Its Aftermath

The Mexican Revolution (1910–1917) created major changes in society. Initially it was another in a series of revolts against the dictator, Diaz. During these seven years an estimated one million people died, Emiliano Zapata and Pancho Villa became legendary, and the Mexican people developed a sense of national identity. This new self-image would be expressed in the Constitution of 1917, one of the most socially progressive documents ever written.

* * *

The revolutionary character of the 1917 Constitution can be seen in its approach to land reform. By the early 1900s, a huge percentage of Mexico's land, water and mineral rights were owned by its leading families, the Roman Catholic Church and foreigners. The largest agricultural estates (latifundios) were run along feudal lines. Article 27 of the 1917 Constitution expresses the widespread discontent with this state of affairs. It authorizes expropriation to achieve more equitable land distribution, a power subsequently used to dismantle the latifundios and create communal lands (ejidos) for peasants.

The 1917 Constitution seizes control of all resources beneath the earth for the state. This includes oil and natural gas, subsequently nationalized in 1938 by Lazaro Cardenas (the father of Cuauhtemoc) and still controlled by the state-owned monopoly, PEMEX. Many consider this nationalization to be the beginning of Mexico's economic independence. To obtain property or mining concessions, foreigners (who enjoyed industrial and commercial dominance at the turn of the century) were forced to agree not to seek the protection of their home governments under what is known as the "Calvo clause." Moreover, in a constitutional clause that endures with limited exceptions today, foreigners are banned from direct ownership of land within 100 kilometers of Mexico's borders and 50 kilometers of its ocean shores.

The revolutionary character of the 1917 Constitution can also be seen in its protection of workers' rights. Article 123, at great length, details the rights of Mexican workers: an 8–hour day, a 7–hour night, housing and education benefits, limits on use of children and women workers, rest days, maternity leave, paid vacation, safety on the job, minimum and overtime wages, severance rights and dismissal only with cause, compensation for injuries on a no-fault basis, collective bargaining, the right to strike, and mandatory profit sharing. Mexico's Federal Labor Act reinforces these constitutional rights and a specialized system of Labor Courts exists to hear complaints.

Although the operational realities of these rights have not always matched their revolutionary origins, and the sums involved are not large when measured in U.S. dollars, one wonders whether the Mexicans might not teach U.S. labor unions a few things on workers' rights. The irony, of course, is that organized labor in the United States bitterly opposed NAFTA. This opposition led, in part, to a "side agreement" to NAFTA on labor cooperation negotiated by President Clinton.

More generally, the Mexican Constitution of 1917 is often perceived less as a set of foundational rules for the republic and more as a statement of aspirations or goals for society. This divorce between constitutional terms and every day living is reflected in the hundreds of amendments that have been made to the 1917 Constitution. The Mexican experience certainly suggests that it is a lot easier to amend a constitution when there is relatively little expectation that these amendments will lead to significant change in the near future.

* * *

SINGLE PARTY RULE

The 1917 Constitution supports a system of government in which the President, elected every 6 years with no reelection opportunity, is extremely powerful. Despite the attempt at separation of powers and a system of governmental checks and balances in the 1917 Constitution, Mexico's Presidents have characteristically had nearly absolute control over judicial and administrative appointments, state governorships, choice of their successors (tapado), the media, taxation, legislation, foreign policy and the military. Moreover, this control has remained in the hands of leaders from Mexico's self-proclaimed "revolutionary" party, the Partido Revolucionario Institucional (PRI) and its predecessors. In other words, Mexico has largely been run as a single party state since the late 1920s. So thorough has been the control that distinguishing between the PRI party apparatus and that of the state or government has not always been easy.

The PRI's power base consolidated over time around labor, peasant, military, civil service and to a lesser extent business supporters. Peasant support derived principally from periodic land distributions and subsistence living subsidies chiefly benefitting communal ejidos. Government and state enterprise (PEMEX, CFE) employee support for the PRI became nearly part of the job description. Labor support was and still is linked with the powerful Confederation of Mexican Workers (CTM) representing a large number of unionized Mexican workers. Non-unionized workers, such as street vendors and garbage pickers, also form part of the PRI power base. Indeed, one of the PRI's most salient characteristics has been its ability to absorb many groups into its camp. Pre-election spending, intimidation, corruption and the spoils of politics helped to keep this coalition together for many years.

A curious development in the last two decades has been the growing influence of highly educated "tecnicos." President Luis Echeverria (1970–76) marked something of a turning point in PRI party politics. The old line politicos and caciques were losing ground to younger technocrats. Echeverria and his chosen successor President Jose Lopez Portillo ruled in the era when Mexico was awash with oil money, its national debt mushroomed and hostility to foreign trade and investment reached its peak. Each ended their presidencies in a cloud of corruption. The party (but not "the Party") was clearly over when Lopez Portillo nationalized Mexico's banks and sharply devalued the peso late in his term of office.

By the time President Miguel de la Madrid took power in 1982, Mexico and the PRI were in crisis. De la Madrid, a public administrator by profession, scaled back the existing level of governmental/PRI corruption (which was extraordinary even by Mexican standards) and opened the national economy through membership in the GATT, debt renegotiations and early market reforms. Presidents Salinas (1988–1994) and Zedillo (1994–2000), both of whom obtained doctorates in economics from U.S. universities, cemented the rise to power of the technocrats. Privatization of state enterprises, reduced government spending, free market economics and NAFTA are largely their doing.

Only in recent times, with corruption from police officers to cabinet ministers endemic, has serious opposition to the PRI emerged from the left and right of Mexico's political spectrum. The left under the leadership of Cuauhtemoc Cardenas may well have won the 1988 presidential election, but electoral fraud assured continuing PRI control under Carlos Salinas. The conservative Partido de Accion Nacional (PAN) has assumed power over several state governorships, and the extreme left is conducting guerilla operations in the state of Chiapas. In the 1994 presidential elections, however, the PRI made a comeback of sorts when it polled about half the national vote in the most open and relatively honest presidential elections Mexico has ever had. PRI candidate Ernesto Zedillo (the substitute for the PRI's first candidate, Luis Donaldo Colosio, who was assassinated) prevailed over the PAN candidate and Cardenas. In July 2000, For the first time in over 70 years, an opposition (PAN) candidate, Vincente Fox, was elected president of Mexico, engendering great hopes for change among the Mexican people. Five years later, after 9/11, a serious recession and gridlock within the Mexican Congress, those hopes have largely diminished.

ZAMORA, THE AMERICANIZATION OF MEXICAN LAW: NON–TRADE ISSUES IN THE NORTH AMERICAN FREE TRADE AGREEMENT

24 Law & Policy Int'l Bus. 391 (1993)*

This Article has attempted to raise questions about using NAFTA as a vehicle for "americanizing" Mexican law—that is, as a means to pressure the Mexican government to adopt U.S.-style solutions to its own social and economic problems. These questions arise most significantly in the non-trade issues of NAFTA—services, foreign investment, protection of intellectual property rights, labor laws, environmental regulation—issues that deal only tangentially with the export or import of goods, but constitute important areas of domestic concern. In these areas in particular, U.S. leaders must pay particular attention to differences in culture that exist between U.S. and Mexican society. Placing new legal models on society without respect to cultural bases may not only be culturally imperialistic, it may also be counter-productive (the legal models are not likely to work as desired). This point was recently stressed by an editorial in one of Mexico City's most widely-read newspapers, the left-of-center daily *La Jornada*:

> ... [F]or Mexico, the operation of [NAFTA] ... cannot ignore the multicultural plurality that comprises the vastly diverse population of the three countries because [NAFTA] would simply be rendered unworkable. Respect for cultural differences, however, is not something that will occur automatically. In Mexico, we must continue to zealously keep guard so that the nation shall be preserved as the pluricultural historical unit that it is, in accordance with a collective desire for self-determination. Because that is our wish, the wish of the majority of Mexicans.

Using Mexico as a laboratory for U.S. legal ideas may not only prejudice Mexico, it could also bring negative results to U.S.-Mexican relations. Mexico will undergo important political and economic changes during this decade, with serious possibilities for destabilization. The challenge facing Mexico's political leaders will be to manage these changes while maintaining social control. U.S. leaders should be sensitive to this challenge, since an unstable Mexico is not in the U.S. interest.

Ironically, the United States does not need to take any action whatsoever to "americanize" Mexican law, since such a process is likely to occur anyway—but at a pace, and to the extent, that the Mexican government will attempt to dictate. As Mexico turns, after decades of autonomous economic policies, towards closer integration with the United States, it is likely to borrow legal models that fit with the larger, more dominant U.S. economy—an economy that constantly generates new products, new services, and even new industries, and must find new forms of legal regulation to deal with them. Since the advent of the economic *apertura* under President Salinas, the Mexican government, even without the heavy hand of U.S. pressure, has looked to U.S. legal models for new systems of regulation. Examples of this include the adoption of environmental laws and intellectual property laws that reflect (and even improve upon) U.S. legislation.

Luis Rubio, a Mexican political scientist and expert on political economy, recently noted that reform of the Mexican legal system will naturally occur by virtue of Mexico's adherence to NAFTA:

> ... [T]he treaty will require, out of convenience rather than obligation, important changes in the [Mexican] legal structure and, in particular, in the importance attributed to legal procedures.... [T]he dispute resolution mechanism adopted by the contracting parties requires not only the professionalization of governmental decision-making, but also the adoption of regulations and laws that are operational without the traditional level of governmental discretion.

If Rubio is correct, the flexibility of the Mexican legal system, which has served to enhance the paternalistic control of society by the government, will diminish in the wake of legal reforms that will proceed, either directly or indirectly, as a result of adherence to NAFTA. The corollary of Rubio's "professionalization of governmental decision-making" will be a reduction in the almost absolute control over economic activities that the political leadership has wielded—and a greater adherence to a transparent application of rules of law.

Adoption of U.S. legal models does not insure U.S.-style results, however. Mexican legal historian Guillermo Floris Margadant, for many years a teacher of law students in both the United States and Mexico, has observed that the formal differences in administrative law between the United States and Mexico are not great. "In administrative law," he notes, "there is no fundamental difference between the two systems. This area deals with practical solutions to problems that occur in everyday life.... On the other hand, the difference between the first world and the third world often becomes an important obstacle for Latin America to take advantage of the relevant U.S. experience. This distinction [i.e., the cultural difference] often turns out to be more important than the difference between neo-roman and Anglo–Saxon legal systems." It may be an overstatement, and politically incorrect as well, to describe the United States and Mexico as "first world" and "third world" countries. Even so, the statement, by a long-time observer of the U.S. and Mexican legal systems, correctly calls attention to the fact that cultural differences are more important in the application of laws than technical legal differences.

GORDON, ECONOMIC INTEGRATION IN NORTH AMER-ICA—AN AGREEMENT OF LIMITED DIMENSIONS BUT UNLIMITED EXPECTATIONS

56 Modern L. Rev. 157 (1993).*

Economic integration often is motivated less by economic interests than by social and political movements and pressures. The European Economic Community was founded on a blend of French ideas about addressing the 'German problem,' and British notions of creating a United States of Europe, nevertheless excluding Britain. Few observers doubted Germany's separate capacity to regain economic strength without economic integration. But in that strength lay the potential power to dominate, and possibly rule, Europe. Creation of a European Community might achieve the goal of 'Never Again War,' but it might be unable to avoid German economic dominance.

The proposed North American Free Trade Agreement also has an admixture of economic, social and political goals as its basis. It is of course intended to assist economic development, especially in less developed Mexico. But it is also intended to address the uncontrolled movement of millions of mostly unskilled, illegal Mexican immigrants entering the United States. If the NAFTA diminishes the rate at which Mexicans seek jobs in the United States, jobs which the restrictive Mexican economic policies of the 1970s and early 1980s failed to create at home, the NAFTA might achieve a goal of 'Never Again Echeverría.' President Luis Echeverría (1970–76), and his successor President José López Portillo (1976–82), moved Mexico towards substantial state ownership of the means of production and distribution. This 'mixed economy,' as the Mexican government euphemistically called it, was becoming increasingly identified with the centrally controlled non-market economies of Eastern Europe. Mexico bore little resemblance to the Asian market economies, although it envied their economic growth and expressed disdain at the movement of United States manufacturing to Asia rather than to Mexico.

This restrictive atmosphere and consequent immigration became the United States' 'Mexican problem.'

* * *

RELATIONSHIPS BEYOND TRADE

On its face NAFTA will appear to be exclusively about trading relationships, both freer trade in certain areas and more restricted trade in others. This probably will be no less so than the Treaty of Rome in giving life to the European Economic Community. But the NAFTA means much more than trade. It will be a document governing relationships. In its text will appear the new trade relationships among Canada, Mexico and the United States. But underlying the text are the relationships of East and West. The creation of a North American free trade area will bring into union some 357 million people with a total gross national product of some $5,932 billion, to deal with a Europe where the EC and EFTA nations comprise some 358 million people with a gross national product of some $5,784 billion. Economic Fortress Europe will confront Economic Fortress North America.

The relationships within the NAFTA extend outward to Asia. A NAFTA will return many United States owned but Asian based facilities, which produce for the United States market, to a location in North America—Mexico. Alongside the symbol of the 'Four Dragons' (Hong Kong, South Korea, Taiwan and Singapore) will be the symbol of an eagle clutching a snake. If the United States has its way, that snake will represent the Japanese. The United States views NAFTA as limiting Japanese use of Mexico as a base for 'screwdriver' operations, where low labour costs assist Japan in further increasing market shares in the United States.

If Mexican workers would stay at home, and the United States were to have current trade statistics common to those in the 1960s, there would be no talk of a NAFTA. But the reality of massive illegal immigration and trade deficits has caused the United States to shift its traditional East–West focus to North–South. To some degree, however, it was less the United States than Mexico which initiated the negotiations for a trade agreement. The United States had long been prepared to consider any discussions which would open Mexican markets to United States exporters, and increase opportunities for United States investment in Mexico. But the restrictive nature of the Mexican economy in the 1970s was inconsistent with a free trade agreement, and it was necessary for Mexico to initiate some relaxation of its rules before serious discussions could commence. Furthermore, Mexico and other Latin American nations have often had to initiate requests for increased trade linkage with the United States, since the principal focus of United States interests has always been Europe. That is reflected in much United States culture, including education. We are finally attempting to learn more about our North–South relationships, but we have many myths to overcome and many stereotypes to destroy.

Although there has been a greater concentration on Mexican issues in the past decade, when symposia are held concerning a Mexican topic, there is often an absence of Mexican participants. Even within the early stages of the negotiations for a NAFTA, concern was expressed by some United States parties involved with the negotiations that there could be no dispute panels with Mexico similar to the ones with Canada, because there were not sufficient trained and knowledgeable Mexicans who could serve on the panels. Yet Mexican attorneys have been helping United States attorneys and investors work through the maze of Mexican written laws and regulations as well as the unwritten laws and policies, the latter of which are so mysterious to foreigners. Mexican attorneys know far more about the United States legal system than United States attorneys know about the Mexican system. Numerous Mexican attorneys have graduate law degrees from United States law schools, while one can probably count on one hand the number of United States attorneys with a graduate law degree from Mexico. Far more Mexican attorneys are comfortable working in the English language than American attorneys are comfortable working in Spanish. This disparity reflects the lack of attention given to Mexico by the United States, and a more general lack of attention of the rich to the poor, whether individuals or nations.

* * *

THE ROLE OF CANADA

If the reader has noted an occasional reference to the NAFTA as a Mexican—United States agreement, it is not an intentional subordination of the role of Canada, but an acknowledgment that the NAFTA is a United States—Mexican solution to particular issues, with Canada an unnecessary but welcome third party. Canada is not a *de minimis* participant but rather a late entry, the absence of which would not have at all affected the development of a NAFTA. Canada, however, has obviously played an important role in the drafting process. Canada came into the NAFTA discussions only after Mexico and the United States had formally agreed to negotiate a trade agreement and the US President had notified Congress of such intent under the "fast track" procedure.

Because of the existence of a free trade agreement between Canada and the United States, the participation of Canada in the NAFTA reduces Canadian (and Mexican) concern over the development of bilateral trade agreements between the United States and Western Hemispheric nations with a resulting hub-spoke arrangement. Such an arrangement would mean that each participant in a bilateral agreement with the United States would have free trade with the US, but not with the other hub-spoke nations. Of course, the other nations could also develop bilateral agreements, such as Mexico and Canada, but there is little separate motivation for such agreements.

Canadian participation is also attributable to Canadian fear of business moving from Canada to Mexico to serve the United States market. Such moves will occur even without a NAFTA; Canadian participation allows Canada to play a role in setting the rules which may encourage or discourage such moves.

THE IMPACT OF NAFTA ON THE U.S. ECONOMY AND INDUSTRIES

USITC Pub. 332–381 (June 1997).

* * *

OVERVIEW OF NAFTA AND ITS EFFECTS

NAFTA took effect on January 1, 1994, after nearly a decade of rapidly growing U.S.-Mexican trade ties, and 5 years after the U.S.-Canada Free Trade Agreement (CFTA) entered into force. Three years later most of its tariff provisions are substantially in place, and their effects can be analyzed. NAFTA provided for immediate tariff reductions on 68 percent of U.S. exports to Mexico, and 49 percent of U.S. imports from Mexico. With respect to U.S.-Canada trade, virtually all tariffs on U.S.-Canadian trade have been eliminated as a result of the CFTA and NAFTA.

NAFTA also provides for reductions in nontariff barriers, including import prohibitions, quantitative restrictions, and import licensing requirements. For example, over a 10–year period Mexico will phase out trade and investment restrictions on autos and trucks. Upon implementing NAFTA, the United States immediately eliminated quotas for Mexican textile and apparel products that meet NAFTA rules of origin. Trade in energy is being liberalized. Numerous nontariff barriers on U.S.-Mexico agricultural trade have been replaced by tariff-rate quotas, which are being phased out by 2009. Most such reductions in nontariff barriers are proceeding on schedule.

In addition to reducing traditional trade barriers, NAFTA went beyond any previous trade agreement in obligating the NAFTA countries to establish rules governing the conduct of trade among the NAFTA partners. Nearly all of these "rulemaking" obligations are now in force. They govern such areas as the protection of direct investment, intellectual property, services trade, and government procurement. Furthermore, NAFTA includes dispute settlement provisions aimed at resolving conflicts over trade issues.

* * *

SECTORS WITH SIGNIFICANT NAFTA EFFECTS

Based on the industry sector analysis performed by Commission staff, NAFTA appears to have had a significant effect on the 1993–96 increase in U.S. trade flows for nine of the 68 sectors analyzed, specifically ITC Group Nos.—

1: Grains and oilseeds

2: Raw cotton

18: Textile mill products

19: Apparel and other finished textile products

34: Leather tanning and finishing

35: Women's footwear, except athletic

48: Household appliances

54: Motor vehicles

55: Motor vehicle parts

* * *

Sectors with Negligible NAFTA Effects

For 59 of the 68 sectors analyzed, NAFTA was determined to have had a negligible effect on increased trade flows because other factors predominated, including the strong U.S. economy. In about half of the sectors examined, the major trade increases were with Canada, and were primarily due to non-NAFTA factors; this is because U.S. import duties were already low and the removal of nontariff barriers had generally been accomplished prior to NAFTA under the CFTA. In some sectors, U.S. and Canadian industries are extensively interrelated, with the parent company and subsidiaries in different countries. Such integration occurs, for example, in industries producing certain processed foods, chemicals, engines and other automobile parts, and electronics.

* * *

NAFTA'S INTERACTION WITH THE URUGUAY ROUND
USITC Pub. 332–381 (June 1997).

Evaluating NAFTA's effect on U.S. trade is made more complex by the phase-in of a host of market-opening and rule-making agreements negotiated during the Uruguay Round of multilateral trade negotiations. The obligations are now embodied in the Agreement establishing the World Trade Organization (WTO) and the final Act of the Uruguay Round (hereafter, WTO Agreements). Indeed, the relationship between the two accords is a long and complex one, dating back to the launching of negotiations towards a CFTA in June 1986, which was widely seen as a U.S. effort to revive stalled efforts to launch an ambitious round of multilateral trade negotiations. Agreement to launch such a round quickly followed at the September 1986 Punta del Este GATT ministerial meeting. The Uruguay Round concluded on December 15, 1993, a year after NAFTA was signed. The WTO Agreements thus were being negotiated prior to, during, and after NAFTA's negotiation.

To a significant degree, NAFTA disciplines were both modeled on, and served as models for, the final WTO Agreements. Draft Uruguay Round texts were available on some topics when NAFTA negotiations were formally launched on June 12, 1991. In December 1991, GATT Director General Arthur Dunkel introduced the first comprehensive text on all topics under negotiation in the Uruguay Round, though participants were still far from consensus on the most controversial issues, such as agriculture, subsidies, and antidumping measures. This text generally served as a starting point for NAFTA negotiators since all three countries agreed that the Uruguay Round and the CFTA were the "floor" for NAFTA and strove to go beyond these accords to the greatest extent practicable.

The WTO Agreements entered into force on January 1, 1995. They address many of the same topics addressed by NAFTA. In addition, they address customs valuation and preshipment inspection, two areas not addressed in NAFTA, but which are not major issues in terms of market access in North America. NAFTA coverage includes state-trading and competition policy. These two topics are not addressed in the URAs but are particularly important for ensuring meaningful market access to Mexico, given Mexico's lack of prior history of antitrust enforcement, privatization of key sectors, and lingering government role in such fields as the purchase of staple foodstuffs.

To the extent there is an overlap between the accords, NAFTA disciplines generally go further and faster than their Uruguay Round counterparts, particularly in such areas as market access, investment and most services. For example, NAFTA involves complete elimination of tariffs. The Uruguay Round negotiations resulted in a 35–percent reduction in U.S. tariffs, with tariffs being lowered in stages starting Jan. 1, 1995. In the services area, NAFTA disciplines and commitments are generally more extensive than those in the Uruguay Round General Agreement on Trade in Services (GATS). NAFTA rules provide for unconditional MFN and national treatment, and for the right of establishment, for example. Mexico's and Canada's commitments under NAFTA are less restrictive than those under the GATS. Disciplines on such nontariff barriers as sanitary and phytosanitary measures, standards, and government procurement are largely the same in both accords, although coverage varies.

Some NAFTA innovations were ultimately incorporated into the final Uruguay Round accord, notably in the intellectual property area, where the final WTO provisions on trade-related intellectual property rights (TRIPs) are much stronger than those previously under discussion. The effect of the TRIPs changes is that within a relatively short period of time, standards for protection of intellectual property will be raised throughout the world to levels comparable to those existing in the United States and other developed economies. But NAFTA accomplishes this goal faster. Under NAFTA, Mexico was required to implement state-of-the-art IPR protection within NAFTA's first few years of operation. Under the WTO TRIPs Agreement, Mexico would have had until 2000 to make similar strides.

NAFTA disciplines on investment are regarded as much more far-reaching than those found in the Uruguay Round accord. They cover a range of matters affecting foreign direct investment generally, versus the more narrowly defined coverage of the WTO Agreement on Trade–Related Investment Measures (TRIMs). Unlike NAFTA, the TRIMs agreement does not address such basic issues for investors as the right of establishment, the right to fair and just compensation for expropriation, and the expeditious handling of investor-state disputes. Moreover, NAFTA's premise is that all flows of investment will be free of restrictions unless specifically exempted. These and other NAFTA disciplines have served as models in other trade-related forums. For example, they are forming the basis for U.S. pursuit of updated bilateral investment treaties with foreign partners, and for U.S. efforts to secure a Multilateral Agreement on Investment (MAI) in the OECD. [These negotiations were abandoned in 1998.]

* * *

JOHNSON, THE NORTH AMERICAN
FREE TRADE AGREEMENT
Chapter 1 (1994).*

BASIC RULE OF PREVALENCE

NAFTA 103 sets forth the basic rule governing the relationship between NAFTA and other agreements. In NAFTA 103(1), the Parties affirm their existing rights and obligations under the GATT and other agreements. NAFTA 103(2) provides that if there is an inconsistency between NAFTA and another agreement, NAFTA prevails to the extent of the inconsistency, unless otherwise provided. The rights and obligations covered by this rule are those in effect when NAFTA became effective on January 1, 1994.

INCORPORATION OF GATT AND [C]FTA PROVISIONS BY REFERENCE

NAFTA incorporates many provisions of both the GATT and the FTA by reference. Provisions of agreements incorporated by reference become part of the NAFTA text and are not subject to the rule of prevalence in NAFTA 103.

NAFTA 301 incorporates GATT Article III (the GATT national treatment provision) and its interpretative notes. NAFTA 309 incorporates GATT Article XI (import and export restrictions) and its interpretative notes. The FTA merely affirmed this GATT provision but did not incorporate it. NAFTA 603(1) incorporates the GATT provisions respecting prohibitions or restrictions on trade in energy and basic petrochemical goods. Article 2101 incorporates GATT Article XX (exceptions) and its interpretative notes. The application of these incorporated provisions is sometimes modified by NAFTA. For example, NAFTA 710 provides that incorporated GATT Articles III, XI and XX do not apply to sanitary or phytosanitary measures. NAFTA 315 restricts the application of GATT Articles XI:2(a), XX(g), XX(i) and XX(j), but NAFTA 2101 expands the meaning of the exceptions contained in GATT Articles XX(b) and (g).

Unlike the FTA, NAFTA does not incorporate the *GATT Agreement on Government Procurement* because of the enlarged scope of the NAFTA government procurement chapter.

As between Canada and the United States, NAFTA incorporates many FTA provisions. NAFTA Annex 302.2 incorporates the FTA Tariff Schedules of Canada and the United States for tariff elimination purposes. NAFTA Annex 302.2 also incorporates FTA 401(7) and 401(8) (concessionary rates and temporary reductions). NAFTA Annex 304.2 incorporates FTA 405 (duty waivers). Section A of NAFTA Annex 312.2

incorporates the FTA provisions respecting wine and distilled spirits. NAFTA Appendix 300–A.1 incorporates certain provisions of FTA Chapter Ten (automotive goods). Appendix 5.1 of NAFTA Annex 300–B incorporates FTA 407 (import and export restrictions) solely in respect of certain safeguard procedures respecting textile and apparel goods. NAFTA Annex 608.2 incorporates FTA Annexes 902.5 and 905.2 (import, export and certain regulatory measures respecting energy goods). NAFTA Annex 702.1 incorporates FTA 701, 702, 704, 705, 706, 707, 710 and 711 respecting agricultural goods. NAFTA Annex 801.1 incorporates FTA 1101 (safeguards). NAFTA Annex 1401.4 incorporates FTA 1702(1) and (2) (commitments of the United States respecting financial services). NAFTA Annex 2106 incorporates the entire FTA regime respecting cultural industries.

The technique of incorporating FTA provisions by reference can be convoluted. For example, NAFTA Appendix 300–A.1 states that notwithstanding the incorporation of certain FTA automotive provisions, the NAFTA rules of origin apply. NAFTA Annex 801.1, incorporating the safeguard provision in FTA 1101, also contains a clarification respecting origin. However, NAFTA Annex 702.1 incorporates virtually the entire FTA chapter on trade in agricultural goods but is silent as to whether the expression "originating" used in the incorporated provisions means "originating" under the FTA or NAFTA rules of origin. NAFTA Annex 801.1 is unclear as to whether the procedures set forth in NAFTA 803 to be followed in safeguard actions are to apply to safeguard actions to which the incorporated FTA 1101 applies.

NAFTA makes no specific reference to FTA 2006 (retransmission rights) or to FTA 2007 (print-in-Canada requirements). However the effect of the cultural exemption set forth in NAFTA Annex 2106 is to incorporate these FTA provisions.

Use by NAFTA of Other Agreements

Like the FTA, NAFTA 1902(2)(d)(i) requires that amendments to antidumping or countervailing duty laws not be inconsistent with the GATT, the *Agreement on Implementation of Article VI of the General Agreement on Tariffs and Trade* ("Antidumping Code") or the *Agreement on the Interpretation and Application of Articles VI, XVI and XXIII of the General Agreement on Tariffs and Trade* ("Subsidies Code"). Also like the FTA, but with greater precision, NAFTA requires that measures respecting balance of payments difficulties taken pursuant to the exception in NAFTA 2104 be consistent with the *Articles of Agreement of the International Monetary Fund* ("IMF Agreement").

However, NAFTA relies more than the FTA on other international agreements for its meaning and substance. Certain definitions in NAFTA depend for their meaning on other international agreements or the activities of international organizations. For example, the meaning of "nationals of another Party" in NAFTA 1721 depends upon a number of international intellectual property conventions. The definition of "international standard, guideline or recommendation" in NAFTA 724 means standards, guidelines or recommendations adopted by specifically identified international organizations.

NAFTA uses procedural rules and institutional structures established in other international agreements. The investor state dispute settlement procedures set forth in Section B of NAFTA Chapter Eleven are based upon the *Convention on the Settlement of Investment Disputes between States and Nationals of other States* ("ICSID Convention"), the *Inter–American Convention on International Commercial Arbitration* ("Inter–American Convention"), the *United Nations Convention on the Recognition and Enforcement of Foreign Arbitral Awards* ("New York Convention") and the arbitration rules of the United Nations Commission on International Trade Law ("UNCITRAL Arbitration Rules").

NAFTA requires that the NAFTA countries give effect to certain international agreements. For example, NAFTA 1701.2 requires the Parties to give effect to certain international conventions respecting intellectual property rights. NAFTA 1710 requires the Parties to protect integrated circuits in accordance with certain articles of the *Treaty on Intellectual Property in Respect of Integrated Circuits*.

None of these agreements is incorporated into the NAFTA and the NAFTA rule of prevalence is not reversed in respect of any of them. Accordingly, if any of these agreements is inconsistent with NAFTA, NAFTA prevails to the extent of the inconsistency.

THE FATE OF THE [C]FTA

The governments of Canada and the United States have agreed that upon NAFTA becoming effective, the FTA will be suspended. If NAFTA is terminated or if one of Canada or the United States withdraws, the FTA will resume. With the FTA suspended, there will be no question as to which of the FTA and NAFTA prevails. For all practical purposes, the FTA, except as incorporated into NAFTA or as continued by collateral agreement by Canada and the United States, will cease to exist.

* * *

SUBSEQUENT AGREEMENTS

Covered by specific NAFTA provisions

NAFTA recognizes that the GATT and certain other international agreements may be amended as a result of the Uruguay Round and takes into account some of these future changes. For example, NAFTA 301, NAFTA 309 and NAFTA 2101, which respectively incorporate GATT Articles III, IX and XX and their interpretative notes, also incorporate "any equivalent provision of a successor agreement to which all Parties are party". NAFTA 1902(2)(d) makes specific reference to successor agreements to the Antidumping Code and the Subsidies Code which are the *Agreement on the Implementation of Article VI* and the *Agreement on Subsidies and Countervailing Duties*. NAFTA Annex 300–B, Section 1(2) provides that NAFTA prevails if there is an inconsistency between NAFTA and the *Arrangement Regarding International Trade in Textiles* ("Multifibre Arrangement"). However, NAFTA Annex 300–B, Section 3(2) requires the NAFTA countries to eliminate any restriction respecting textile and apparel goods permitted by NAFTA, but required to be eliminated under any successor agreement to the Multifibre Arrangement. The Uruguay Round successor agreement to the Multifibre Arrangement is the *Agreement on Textiles and Clothing*. NAFTA 802 sets out rules respecting the application among the NAFTA countries of "any safeguard agreement" pursuant to GATT Article XIX. When the Uruguay Round agreements become effective, the safeguard agreement referred to in NAFTA 802 will be the *Agreement on Safeguards*. NAFTA 2005 sets out rules governing the relationship between the dispute settlement procedures in NAFTA Chapter Twenty and those under the GATT and its successor agreements, which will include the WTO Agreement and the *Understanding on Rules and Procedures Governing the Settlement of Disputes* when the Uruguay Round agreements become effective. The relationship between NAFTA and these Uruguay Round agreements will be governed by these NAFTA provisions.

* * *

NAFTA AND STATE AND PROVINCIAL GOVERNMENTS

Canada, the United States and Mexico are all federal states. Canada has ten provinces, each with its own legislature and exclusive areas of jurisdiction. The United States has fifty states and Mexico has thirty-one states. Each one of these states has its own government. NAFTA is an agreement among the federal governments of Canada, the United States and Mexico. No province or state is a party to it.

NAFTA 105 requires each of Canada, the United States and Mexico to ensure that all necessary measures are taken by provincial and state governments to ensure compliance with NAFTA. This is a stronger obligation than that contained in GATT Article XXIV:12. Provincial measures have been the subject of several GATT panels. Canada has never been successful in persuading a panel that it had satisfied GATT Article XXIV:12 in respect of the measure.

Provinces and states are exempt from some provisions of NAFTA, such as government procurement. In other instances, provinces and states are subject to a more lenient rule than their federal counterparts. For example, states and provinces have a period of time to list their reservations to the obligations under the investment, services and financial services chapters. In yet other instances, the federal government obligation to "ensure compliance" is replaced with the somewhat less onerous obligation to "seek, through appropriate measures, to ensure observance". The NAFTA text must be read carefully to determine whether an exemption for provinces and states applies or whether the obligation in NAFTA 105 has been modified.

* * *

TANGEMAN, NAFTA AND THE CHANGING ROLE OF STATE GOVERNMENT

20 Seattle U. Law. Rev. 243 (1996).*

NAFTA is the first treaty through which states have been guaranteed the right to be informed and to participate in trade matters affecting the states. In response to states' concerns about the potential legal threats raised by NAFTA, the NAFTA implementing legislation contains many specific provisions that guarantee states the ability to protect their laws: the right to be notified if a state law is challenged; the right to participate in the defense of state laws; and, the right to be notified of proceedings other than challenges that have the potential to affect states. The federal-state consultation provision contained within the Implementation Act, as well as provisions set out within the Statement of Administrative Action reflects the federal government's commitment to increasing communication with the States about trade-related matters that affect their interests.

The NAFTA consultative framework is codified under section 102(b)(1)(B)of the bill as the Federal–State Consultation Process. This consultative framework for communications with states in international trade matters reinforces the administration's goals and objectives contained within the Statement of Administrative Action and establishes procedures for the following:

1) grandfathering or revising state laws and regulations consistent with NAFTA to avoid conflicts with the agreement;

2) informing states on matters under the agreement affecting states;

3) providing opportunities for states to advise and inform the U.S. trade representative on agreement issues affecting states;

4) responding to the information and advice received from the states in developing the United States' positions on agreement issues affecting states; and,

5) involving states to the greatest extent practicable in developing the United States' positions regarding agreement issues affecting states.

The Federal–State Consultation Process affirmatively establishes the USTR's obligation to confer with states regarding NAFTA issues that "directly relate to or that may have a direct effect on [States]." Thus, in conformity with the established NAFTA consultative framework, the federal government is committed to carrying out U.S. obligations under NAFTA, as they apply to the States, through the greatest possible degree of federal-state consultation and cooperation.

* * *

Comment on Assessing NAFTA After Ten Years

As one might have expected, the ten year anniversary of NAFTA—January 1, 2004—brought a flood of assessments from various points of view. For example, one study concluded that Mexico's exports to the world would have been about 25% lower without NAFTA, and that foreign direct investment in Mexico would have been about 40% less.* A sampling of some of the more significant commentary is reproduced below, including the following excerpt by NAFTA Parties. Consider why a variety of experts has reached such diverse conclusions.

NAFTA: A DECADE OF STRENGTHENING A DYNAMIC RELATIONSHIP**

January 1, 2004 marks an important milestone in the trade and economic relationship between Canada, the United States and Mexico. This date marks the tenth anniversary of the launching of the North American Free Trade Agreement (NAFTA). Ten years ago the three countries formed a free trade area with a total gross domestic product (GDP), at present, of US$11.4 trillion. This makes North America the world's largest free trade area, with about one-third of the world's total GDP, significantly larger than that of the European Union. Even with the addition of ten new members next year, the EU's GDP will increase to US$8.3 trillion, still well behind the NAFTA region. Our three countries have enjoyed a thriving relationship derived from their decision to open doors and break down barriers. As we approach NAFTA's tenth anniversary, markets continue to open up for a freer flow of goods, services and investment, and our economies are integrating as never before. By expanding trade, investment and employment, the NAFTA is enhancing opportunities for the citizens of all three countries and has made our trilateral relationship more dynamic.

Looking forward, the Parties are committed to ensuring that the NAFTA strengthens this relationship. By maintaining the NAFTA rules-based framework for expanding the scope of North American business relationships, we are setting the conditions in which citizens of North America can excel.

STRENGTHENING TRILATERAL TRADE AND INVESTMENT

By strengthening the rules and procedures governing trade and investment on this continent, the NAFTA has allowed trade and investment flows in North America to skyrocket. According to figures of the International Monetary Fund, total trade among the three NAFTA countries has more than doubled, passing from US$306 billion in 1993 to almost US$621 billion in 2002. That's US$1.2 million every minute. In this same period:

* Lederman, Maloney & Luis Serven, Lessons from NAFTA for Latin America and the Caribbean Countries v (World Bank, 2004).

** Statement of Pierre S. Pettigrew, Minister of International Trade, Canada; Robert B. Zoellick, U.S. Trade Representative, United States; Fernando Canales, Secretary of the Economy, Mexico. Copyright © 2004.

· Canada's exports to its NAFTA partners increased by 87 percent in value. Exports to the United States grew from US$113.6 billion to US$213.9 billion, while exports to Mexico reached US$1.6 billion.

· US exports to Canada and Mexico grew from US$147.7 billion (US$51.1 billion to Mexico and US$96.5 billion to Canada) to US$260.2 billion (US$107.2 and US$152.9 billion, respectively).

· Mexican exports to the US grew by an outstanding 234 percent, reaching US$136.1 billion. Exports to Canada also grew substantially from US$2.9 to US$8.8 billion, an increase of almost 203 percent.

The NAFTA has allowed both Canada and Mexico to increase their exports to the United States, but not at the expense of each other's share in the U.S. merchandise import market. That's because substantial new trade has been generated throughout North America. Canada has consistently accounted for approximately 18 percent U.S. imports, while Mexico has seen its share of the U.S. imports increase from 6.8 percent in 1993 to 11.6 percent in 2002. The NAFTA has also boosted competitiveness at the global level. The Agreement has been instrumental in making North America one of the most active trading regions in the world. The NAFTA countries now account for almost 19 percent of global exports and 25 percent of imports. NAFTA fosters an environment of confidence and stability required to make long-term investments and partnering commitments. With a strong, certain and transparent framework for investment, North America has attracted foreign direct investment (FDI) at record levels. In 2000, FDI by other NAFTA partners in the three countries reached US$299.2 billion, more than double the US$136.9 billion figure registered in 1993. NAFTA has also stimulated increased investment from countries outside of NAFTA. North America now accounts for 23.9 percent of global inward FDI and 25 percent of global outward FDI.

STRENGTHENING PROSPERITY IN NORTH AMERICA

Liberalized trade provides advantages for businesses and consumers. Manufacturers in the NAFTA region benefit from a greater supply of inputs at lower prices. The result has been a rise in productivity that strengthens their competitiveness in global markets. For consumers in all three countries, NAFTA has provided more choices at competitive prices. Lower tariffs mean that families pay less for the products that they buy and they have a greater selection of goods and services, which increases their standards of living. The NAFTA has provided benefits in other, sometimes unexpected, ways as well. The movement of goods and people is creating growing linkages that facilitate the exchange of ideas and methods of addressing common challenges. People of the three countries are visiting each other in increasing numbers and are forming families and friendships that span the continent, which, in turn, promotes a deeper understanding of their respective cultures.

* * *

HUFFBAUER & SCHOTT, THE PROSPECTS FOR DEEPER NORTH AMERICAN INTEGRATION: A U.S. PERSPECTIVE*

NORTH AMERICAN TRADE AND INVESTMENT SINCE CUSFTA

Two-way U.S. merchandise trade with Canada jumped from C$186 billion (US$151 billion) in 1988 (the year before CUSFTA entered into force on January 1, 1989) to C$554 billion (US$353 billion) in 2002, an increase in U.S. dollar terms of 134 percent. (For the remainder of this *Commentary*, all currency figures are in U.S. dollars, unless otherwise stipulated.) By comparison, U.S. merchandise trade with non-NAFTA partners doubled in value during the same period. Two-way U.S. merchandise trade with Mexico soared from $79 billion in 1993 to $220 billion in 2002, a gain of 178 percent.

During that period, U.S. trade with non-NAFTA countries increased by 65 percent. Largely as a result of CUSFTA and NAFTA, U.S. exports to, and imports from, Canada and Mexico now account for one-third of total U.S. trade, compared with one-quarter in 1989.

CUSFTA and NAFTA have made less difference to services trade in North America. For some services, notably tourism, barriers were already very low before the trade agreements were ratified. For others, such as trucking and maritime transport, the barriers were not only high, they were almost impervious to liberalization. Moreover, the number of NAFTA temporary work visas for professional workers was very small, not enough to have much effect on the recorded flows of cross-border service income. Some service sectors, notably financial services and telecommunications, were greatly liberalized by CUSFTA and NAFTA, while others were little affected.

These cross-cutting forces show up in much weaker overall services trade growth between the NAFTA partners than merchandise trade growth. Two-way U.S.-Canada services trade increased to $66 billion in 2001 from $26 billion in 1989, an increase of 93 percent. During the same period, U.S. two-way services trade with non-NAFTA countries increased 129 percent. Two-way U.S.-Mexico services trade increased to $26 billion in 2001 from $18 billion in 1993, an increase of 43 percent. During the same period, U.S. two-way services trade with non-NAFTA countries increased by 66 percent. In other words, the statistics do not reveal a strong CUSFTA or NAFTA effect on overall services trade. Of course, particular segments of services trade—for example cross-border financial transactions and telecommunications—may have increased largely because of CUSFTA and NAFTA liberalization.

The CUSFTA/NAFTA story for foreign direct investment (FDI) has yet another aspect: not much for Canada, quite a bit for Mexico. Two-

* C.D. Howe Institute Commentary, no. 195, Jan. 2004. Copyright © 2004 C.D. Howe Institute. Reproduced with permission.

way FDI stocks between Canada and the United States increased to $244 billion by year-end 2001 from $104 billion in 1989, a gain of 135 percent. Two-way FDI stocks between Mexico and the United States (mainly U.S. investment in Mexico) rose to $64 billion by year-end 2001 from $16 billion in 1993, a gain of 288 percent. By contrast, two-way U.S. FDI stocks with the rest of the world, increased by 281 percent between 1989 and 2001, and 169 percent between 1993 and 2001.

Longitudinal data on private portfolio investment are unreliable, but a few inferences can be drawn from stocks of portfolio capital as of fiscal year 2001/2002. At the end of 2001, private U.S. holdings of foreign securities, including equities, long-term and short-term debt, totaled some $2,262 billion. Of this amount, $201 billion represented claims against Canadian issuers and $48 billion represented claims against Mexican issuers. In other words, claims against Canada were 9 percent of the global total, and claims against Mexico were 2 percent. Both figures were substantially less than the share of U.S. merchandise exports destined for NAFTA partners (23 percent and 14 percent respectively). Conversely, at the end of 2002, private portfolio investment in the United States totaled $4,338 billion. Of this amount, $208 billion represented claims held by Canadian investors, and $52 billion represented claims held by Mexican investors. As shares of the relevant totals, both Canadian and Mexican investors (5 percent and 1 percent, respectively) are much smaller than Canadian and Mexican exporters (18 percent and 12 percent, respectively).

To be sure, a great deal of financial integration has taken place within North America, including for example, the Manulife–John Hancock merger, the acquisition of Harris Bank by the Bank of Montreal, and the acquisition of Banamex by Citigroup. Even without massive cross-border portfolio flows, the mortgage security, equity and insurance markets should become more tightly linked—especially with the help of a pro-NAFTA regulatory environment in all three countries.

In summary, CUSFTA and NAFTA were very good for merchandise trade, while making little difference overall to services trade, though particular service industries benefited. FDI between the United States and Mexico got a clear boost from NAFTA, though the same cannot be claimed of FDI between the United States and Canada. Two-way U.S.-Canada FDI lagged significantly behind two-way U.S.-non-NAFTA FDI. If CUSFTA and NAFTA attracted FDI to Canada, it was from third countries, not the United States. Two-way U.S.-Canada and U.S.-Mexico portfolio investment stocks are not particularly large when contrasted with merchandise trade; however, the most meaningful financial integration has probably taken place through cross-border mergers and new corporate subsidiaries.

* * *

AUDLEY, PAPADEMETRIOU, POLASKI & VAUGHAN, NAFTA'S PROMISE AND REALITY*

Our Conclusions

NAFTA has not helped the Mexican economy keep pace with the growing demand for jobs. Unprecedented growth in trade, increasing productivity, and a surge in both portfolio and direct foreign direct investment have led to an increase of 500,000 jobs in manufacturing from 1994 to 2002. The agricultural sector, where almost a fifth of Mexicans still work, has lost 1.3 million jobs since 1994. Real wages for most Mexicans today are lower than they were when NAFTA took effect. However, this setback in wages was caused by the peso crisis of 1994–1995—not by NAFTA. That said, the productivity growth that has occurred over the last decade has not translated into growth in wages. Despite predictions to the contrary, Mexican wages have not converged with U.S. wages. NAFTA has not stemmed the flow of poor Mexicans into the United States in search of jobs; in fact, there has been a dramatic rise in the number of migrants to the United States, despite an unprecedented increase in border control measures. Historical migration patterns, the peso crisis, and the pull of employment opportunities in the United States provide better explanations for the increase in migration than NAFTA itself.

The fear of a "race to the bottom" in environmental regulation has proved unfounded. At this point some elements of Mexico's economy are dirtier and some are cleaner. The Mexican government estimates that annual pollution damages over the past decade exceeded US$36 billion per year. This damage to the environment is greater than the economic gains from the growth of trade and of the economy as a whole. More specifically, enactment of NAFTA accelerated changes in commercial farming practices that have put Mexico's diverse ecosystem at great risk of contamination from concentrations of nitrogen and other chemicals commonly used in modern farming. Mexico's evolution toward a modern, export-oriented agricultural sector has also failed to deliver the anticipated environmental benefits of reduced deforestation and tillage. Rural farmers have replaced lost income caused by the collapse in commodity prices by farming more marginal land, a practice that has resulted in an average deforestation rate of more than 630,000 hectares per year since 1992 in the biologically rich regions of southern Mexico.

Put simply, NAFTA has been neither the disaster its opponents predicted nor the savior hailed by its supporters. But while NAFTA's overall impact may be muddled, for Mexico's rural households the picture is clear—and bleak. NAFTA has accelerated Mexico's transition to a liberalized economy without creating the necessary conditions for the public and private sectors to respond to the economic, social, and environmental shocks of trading with two of the biggest economies in the world. Mexico's most vulnerable citizens have faced a maelstrom of change beyond their capacity, or that of their government, to control.

* * *

A NAFTA Timeline*

1986	Canada–U.S. free trade negotiations commence. Mexico joins the GATT.
	Uruguay Round of GATT negotiations launched.
1989	CFTA enters into effect.
1991	Congress extends fast track authority to NAFTA and Uruguay Round.
1992	NAFTA signed by Presidents Bush and Salinas, Prime Minister Mulroney.
1993 (August)	Side agreements on North American Labor and Environmental Cooperation concluded under President Clinton.
1993 (October)	Vice President Gore "defeats" Ross Perot in nationally televised NAFTA debate.
1993 (November)	U.S. Congress ratifies NAFTA.
1993 (December)	Uruguay Round agreements concluded.
1994 (January)	NAFTA enters into effect.
1994 (December)	Miami Summit supports creation by 2005 of a Free Trade Area of the Americas (FTAA).
1994–95	Mexican peso crashes, U.S. organizes rescue package.
1995 (January)	Uruguay Round agreements enter into effect. WTO created. Negotiations commence for Chile to join NAFTA. Quebec voters barely reject separation from Canada.
1995–2002	Congress refuses to provide "fast track" trade negotiating authority. Mexico concludes free trade agreements with Colombia, Venezuela, Costa Rica, Bolivia, Nicaragua, Guatemala, Honduras, El Salvador, Peru and Uruguay. Canada agrees to free trade with Costa Rica.
1997	Canada and Chile agree on free trade with side agreements. Mexico revises its free trade agreement with Chile.
2000 (July)	Mexico and European Union free trade agreement becomes effective.
2001 (November)	WTO Members launch Doha Development Round of negotiations.

2001 (December)	United States—Jordan free trade agreement enters into force.
2002 (August)	Congress provides "Trade Promotion Authority" to President Bush for bilateral and multilateral trade negotiations.
2003 (December)	United States completes free trade agreement negotiations with Central American nations (Costa Rica signs on in January 2004).
2004 (January)	United States–Chile and United States–Singapore free trade agreements enter into force.
2004 (February)	United States concludes negotiations of a free trade agreement with Australia.
2004 (March)	United States concludes negotiations of free trade agreements with Morocco and the Dominican Republic.
2004	United States completes or continues free trade agreement negotiations with the South African Customs Union, Ecuador, Bahrain, Colombia, Peru, Bolivia, Panama and Thailand.
2005 (January)	Original (unmet) deadline for completion of Doha Development Round and FTAA negotiations; U.S. FTA with Australia enters into force.

Questions and Comments

1. As you study the various legal and political issues raised in the following chapters on NAFTA, consider which, if any, NAFTA provisions should be improved after eleven years' experience. Which could be modified by understanding among the Parties—such as the "Interpretation" of Chapter 11 found in the Documents Supplement? Which would likely require a formal amendment or protocol to the Agreement, subject to approval by the Mexican and United States congresses and the Canadian Parliament? To what extent does harmonization of national legislation provide a partial solution?

2. A number of proposals have been made for modifications of the Chapter 11 investment obligations, and Mexican President Vicente Fox has suggested on a number of occasions that NAFTA should be more like the European Union, with freer movement of labor and, ultimately, removal of border controls. While many in the United States believe that these are worthy objectives for ten or twenty years hence, current opposition to increased immigration, and concerns over security against terrorists and drug traffic, make changes of this type unlikely in the short term.

Chapter 4

TOWARD FREE TRADE
IN THE AMERICAS

BAKER, INTEGRATION OF THE AMERICAS: A LATIN RENAISSANCE OR A PRESCRIPTION FOR DISASTER?

11 Temple Int'l & Comp. L.J. 309 (1997).*

In order to understand Latin America's failed attempts at integration, one must first appreciate the diversity of Latin America. Most U.S. citizens seem to believe that Latin America is homogeneous–similar in origin, culture, politics, history, and language. Contrary to this popular belief, Latin America is probably one of the most diverse of all continents. Several languages are spoken in Latin America, including Spanish, Portuguese, French, Maya, Quechua, Aymara, and numerous other Indian dialects. Furthermore, Latin America has four major cultures, "the Hispanic, French, West Indian, and Northern European," and within these four major cultures there exist numerous sub-cultures. In addition, Latin America also has several indigenous groups such as the Aztec, Araucanian, Inca, and Mayan Indians. Besides the cultural and linguistic differences, Latin America also has great diversity in geography, attitudes, politics, and history. Therefore, although most U.S. citizens believe that Latin America is dominated by the Hispanic culture, one must acknowledge the existence of other major cultures in the region in order to appreciate its diversity.

Furthermore, the colonial history of Latin American countries is quite different from that of the United States. In the United States, English mercantilism and then capitalism replaced the indigenous communal economic system. As a result, the current U.S. ideology of capitalism can be traced back to a single, dominant, and well-established free market economic tradition. Latin America, on the other hand, does not have a history of a single, dominant, and well-established economic tradition. Rather, its current economic ideology can be traced back to a dual tradition of indigenous communal societies and colonization that was more interested in exploitation of natural resources and religious conversion than mercantilism. Such a colonial philosophy is distinctly different than a capitalist system which relies upon market driven systems as suggested by Adam Smith's "invisible hand doctrine."

The social and economic systems of Latin America were not developed from capitalism. Throughout its history, Latin America has always been wary of foreigners. This fear stems from the conquests of the indigenous empires by the European conquistadors and the imperialism of the early 20th century. In analyzing what the "proper path" to development and economic growth in Latin America might be, its mercantile history cannot be disregarded. Today's Latin America is a reflection of both the new as well as the old. Modern skyscrapers tower above slums. Moreover, the legal system in Latin America is the "civil law or code law system as opposed to Anglo–Saxon law or the common law system. . . ." In addition, a majority of the world's Roman Catholics live in Latin America, with the largest national Church located in Brazil. Therefore, in order for a North American to understand Latin America, it is important to not have a myopic view of its situation when attempting to predict its future.

Diversity runs as a dominant motif in analyzing Latin American integration. Due to this diversity, Latin America has had a long history of unsuccessful attempts at political and economic integration, beginning as early as the first part of the 19th century. In their strive for independence, the former Spanish colonies attempted to form political and mutual alliances. In 1815, Simon Bolivar suggested the establishment of a confederation of Spanish American states. However, despite four attempts between 1826 and 1865, Bolivar's vision of a single entity never solidified. His dream, however, did not disappear from the minds of Latin leaders.

During the inter-war period, integration efforts were non-existent. On the contrary, Latin American social and political events would more appropriately be characterized as nationalistic.

Aside from the Mexican Revolution, Latin America produced no titanic upheavals during the first part of the century. There were numerous strikes, demonstrations, and governmental overthrows, but these insignificant events did not affect a large portion of the Latin American populations. The momentum during this period was the growth of major dictatorships which advocated for status quo rather than change. Despite the appearance of calmness, many Latin Americans were becoming restless. This restlessness helped to motivate the Latin American countries to pursue the economic integration efforts which followed.

The post-World War II period differed vastly from the first half of the century in that Latin Americans were generally more susceptible to change and reform. For example, the momentum toward Latin integration took on a different focus than that advocated by Simon Bolivar. Instead of emphasizing political integration, the Latin American nations focused on economic integration. Indeed, even before 1945, many agreements and conferences resulted from this movement such as the industrial cooperation and integration agreement between Argentina and Brazil in 1939 and the Regional Conference attended by Argentina, Bolivia, Brazil, Paraguay, and Uruguay in early 1941. These early attempts at economic integration ended in failure.

Although the European economies of the war-participating nations were devastated by World War II, Latin economies benefitted greatly by supplying raw materials to the war participants. At the same time that Latin American nations were attempting economic integration, European nations were also pursuing free trade agreements among themselves * * * Although the European and Latin approaches were similar, the results were completely opposite. Unlike the Latin attempts at integration, European attempts at integration resulted in increased trade and the burgeoning of European prosperity throughout the region. The essential question to ask is, how did the economies of these war-torn nations outperform the economies of the Latin nations?

The futile attempts at Latin American integration spurred the United Nations to sponsor studies of trade activity among Latin American nations. These United Nations proposals, specifically those of the Economic Commission for Latin America ("ECLA"), provided invaluable information for future attempts at Latin integration. At its first meeting in 1948, ECLA suggested that Latin integration should take place in the form of sub-regional groups. Some of these agreements came in the form of bilateral trade agreements such as those negotiated between El Salvador and four neighboring countries: Nicaragua and Guatemala in 1951, Costa Rica in 1953, and Honduras in 1954. Despite these sub-regional agreements, trade did not increase significantly among the Latin nations as expected.

ECLA changed its position in 1958 and suggested that Latin American nations should integrate in the form of a region or an association. The ECLA believed that the domestic industrialization would proceed at a quicker pace if import-substitution policies were based on a regional market rather than on national markets. The result was a conference in 1959, attended by representatives of Argentina, Bolivia, Brazil, Chile, Paraguay, Peru, Uruguay, and observers from Mexico and Venezuela. The Treaty of Montevideo was signed in February 1960, and established a free trade area called the Latin American Free Trade Association ("LAFTA"), which encompassed all the nations that had attended the 1959 conference except Venezuela. However, sub-regional agreements continued to expand. The Central American Common Market ("CACM"), the Andean Pact, and the Caribbean Community ("CARICOM") also came into existence in 1960, 1969, and 1973, respectively. These regional and sub-regional agreements began to breakdown during the late 1970s and 1980s. The difference in size and level of economic development made these three agreements difficult to coordinate. The "policy disparities resulting from widely different ideologies" also hindered the integration process. Most likely, the major reason for the breakdown of these integration agreements was the rise of nationalistic totalitarian regimes in the 1970s. During the early 1980s, regional integration arrangements continued to exist; however, most "survived in name only;" others ceased to exist.

These Latin American attempts at integration that resulted in failures were not accidents. These failures were deeply rooted in the history, culture, and diversity of these Latin states. In other words, the breakdown of these integration efforts occurred because of the "diversity motif" in Latin history. The first attempts at Latin American integration occurred less than thirty years after the United States Declaration of Independence, yet the degree of economic integration in the northern hemisphere is significantly different than in the southern hemisphere. One can also compare the progress of Latin American integration with that of European countries, which only began overt efforts to integrate their economies after World War II. What is the cause for the different results?

Latin America is an area composed of numerous unrelated states. There are giant economies such as Argentina, Brazil, Chile, and Mexico which comprise nearly eighty-five percent of the Latin economy today, and there are numerous small states whose economies are heavily dependent on a single commodity. Effective integration cannot occur when thirty-four different governmental policies are working against each other. Unlike the European Community, where the states have agreed to work closely together, the Latin nations have, in their actions and inactions, accentuated their differences. Instead of applying the European standard, Latin America must find a method which will work best under Latin conditions.

* * *

DEVLIN & ESTEVADEORDAL, WHAT'S NEW IN THE NEW REGIONALISM IN THE AMERICAS
Working Paper 6 (May 2001)*

* * *

THE NEW REGIONALISM

The Resurgence of Regionalism in the 1990s

The debt crisis of the 1980s and consequent balance of payments problems induced a deep recession in Latin America and with that a

* Inter–American Development Bank, Institute for the Integration of Latin America and the Caribbean (INTAL); Copyright © 2001 Inter–American Development Bank.

Reprinted with permission. (References omitted.) (Robert Devlin and Antoni Estevadeordal are economists with the IADB.)

severe contraction of imports. Since intraregional imports are the other side of intraregional exports, the collapse in the Latin American economy also induced a collapse of intraregional trade and open crisis in the already flagging formal integration agreements. The general economic paralysis in the region, coupled with the emergence of a new development strategy based on market opening, correct relative prices and privatization/deregulation seemed to some to be the final deathblow for regional integration. However, to the surprise of many observers, new regional initiatives began to appear in the second half of the 1980s and a true resurgence materialized in the decade of the 1990s.

While the earliest arrangements in this new wave were relatively unsophisticated and very limited in scope, the later accords of the 1990s were comprehensive, with some at the technological edge of regional integration.

The initial arrangements were negotiated as Economic Complementary Agreements (ACE in Spanish) under the framework of the Latin American Integration Association (ALADI in Spanish), which was created in 1980 as the successor to LAFTA. ALADI eschewed the grand objectives of the 1960s in favor of limited agreements confined to market access via the exchange of partial or full preferences on trade in specific products with accompanying rules for use of safeguards, rules of origin, etc.

The limited scope ACE agreements in the Southern Cone evolved into the birth of MERCOSUR (Brazil, Argentina, Paraguay and Uruguay) in 1991. The MERCOSUR customs union agreement began to evolve towards greater levels of integration, with the goal of becoming a common market. It also incorporated Bolivia and Chile as associate free trade area members. Meanwhile, a Presidential initiative in the Andean Group drove the member countries to free trade in the early 1990s and to form an imperfect customs union among the three of them (Colombia–Venezuela and Ecuador). The agreement changed its name to the Andean Community and set out the objective of a common market by 2005. A similar initiative relaunched integration in the Central American Common Market.

While the ACE Agreements in ALADI were being negotiated, Canada and the United States launched free trade negotiations in 1986 that would radically transform the landscape of international trade negotiations. * * * The subsequent NAFTA negotiations were built on the innovations of the Canada–U.S. accord. NAFTA was historic because it represented the first time a Latin American country would link up with an industrialized partner. Moreover, it became a prototype for other new initiatives in the Americas during the decade. A series of new Mexican bilateral free trade areas (FTAs) through the region as well as one between Chile and Canada followed the NAFTA model.

Other bilateral FTAs were promoted by Chile; they first followed a more traditional market access in goods approach, but later increasingly adopted many NAFTA-like characteristics. Meanwhile, the major subregions pursued "deep" integration involving large commitments in terms of loss of commercial sovereignty than one finds in an FTA. This renewed activity continues today. * * *

The Objective

The objective of regional integration in Latin America has shifted with the region's shift to a new overall strategy for development. In essence, the New Regionalism of the 90s is an integral part of the broad-based structural reforms that have been underway in Latin America since the mid–1980s. The central features of today's strategy include an opening to world markets, promotion of private sector initiative and withdrawal of the state from direct economic activity.

The New Regionalism's link to the structural reform process is most clearly observed in trade liberalization. In effect, regional integration is the third tier of a three-tiered process. As mentioned in the introduction, Latin America's average external tariff was radically reduced between 1985–1995 (>40% to <20%). The average maximum tariffs in the region fell from more than 80 percent to 40 percent with only two countries presently applying maximum tariffs of up to 100 percent on a small number of products. * * *

The second tier is at the multilateral level. A decade of multilateral Uruguay Round negotiations ended in April 1994 with the signature in Marrakesh of the Final Act. That Round was concerned with two basic issues regarding market access: (i) reducing obstacles to trade in goods and services and (ii) making the new levels of market access legally binding under tougher WTO regulations and procedures. In the area of tariff liberalization, this latest round of GATT negotiations implied a very substantial commitment on the part of Latin America to dismantle import barriers and adopt new disciplines. * * *

For a region with a modern history of closed economies, this two-level opening was clearly dramatic. While bringing benefits of more competition, lower input costs and enhanced consumption possibilities, the opening also introduced new difficulties. These included important fiscal costs, real resource costs from capital and labor made newly redundant, as well as political costs due to shifting domestic economic coalitions and the real or perceived threats of globalization. The large and rapid external liberalization during the decade could initially lean on considerable "water" in national tariff schedules, while needed fiscal adjustments were quite straightforward. But with tariffs having moved closer to differential margins of competitiveness between home and abroad and fiscal options narrowing, the political economy of trade liberalization became considerably more challenging during the course of the 1990s.

Government authorities have used support for regional integration as a signal of their continued commitment to liberalization even when political or economic conditions for further unilateral opening are difficult and when reciprocal multilateral initiatives are in a transitional phase, as has been the case since the end of the Uruguay Round.

In this context, regional integration has become a vital third tier of liberalization that has helped ensure continued momentum in the process. The fiscal implications of preferential liberalization among Latin American neighbors are less burdensome because typically levels of trade are initially small due to history as well as the legacy of protection. Political resistance to regional integration also can be less entrenched. It takes place within a delimited and familiar market space which reflects more symmetric competition than is found in the international arena. Moreover, there is a compensatory element of reciprocal exports in tandem with reciprocal imports, making for a potentially more balanced fallout of short costs and benefits. Regional opening can even be politically popular due to domestic receptiveness to "getting together" with certain neighbors. Hence, today regional integration is being used as an effective policy tool to deepen liberalization, further reduce average levels of protection, and reinforce the winds of competition. * * *

Regional based rules and peer pressure are also useful to "lock-in" liberalization commitments that under unilateral policy alone might be more easily reversed. It is true that some countries, largely in response to severe fiscal or balance of payments shocks, have temporarily increased protection during the 1990s. However, such measures have usually exempted regional integration partners, due to trade treaty obligations. Customs unions like that found in MERCOSUR have made it difficult (but not impossible) for any member country to raise tariffs on third parties since a plurilateral consensus must be reached. The lock-in effects of regional schemes (in combination with WTO [tariff] bindings) have contributed to anchoring the trade liberalization process and retard backpedaling.

From the above it is clear that, instrumentally, the new regional integration is dramatically different from the older schemes. However, the New Regionalism contrasts with the old in other dimensions as well.

- Attracting foreign direct investment (FDI). The old fears of dependence on FDI have evolved into an appreciation of FDI's contribution to enhanced international competitiveness and access to export markets. In an era of globalization there is an intensive world wide competition for this type of capital. Today the creation of a regional market like MERCOSUR are being deployed not as a way to restrict, or program, FDI as in the past, but rather as a way to distinguish countries from the world pack and attract FDI. Agreements which have successfully created a regional trademark, such as NAFTA and MERCOSUR, have become successful beacons for attracting this type of capital.

- Intraregional trade. The creation of a regional market has promoted trade and investment activity that is generating dynamic transformation effects in productive sectors. This is something that the old integration sought, but largely did not achieve due to, among other things, domestic price and regulatory distortions and the inability to open the regional market. With respect to international markets, the strong growth of intraregional exports reflects a more diversified product mix, a greater participation of differentiated, knowledge-based manufactured goods, and expanding specialization and scale economies through intra-industry trade. Firms have reoriented their marketing, investment and strategic alliances to exploit the regional market. Moreover, trade in some sectors, such as dairy and textiles, is a welcome outlet given severe protection in international markets. These dynamic transformation effects are contributing to more competitive economies which can face the challenges of globalization.

• Geopolitics. The outward orientation of Latin American policies has raised demand for more strategic participation in hemispheric and world forums. Regional integration has allowed countries to cooperate and be more effective global players. In the Free Trade of the Americans process, for example, the MERCOSUR, Andean and Caricom countries now each negotiate as a bloc, giving them more impact in the negotiations than if each country had acted alone. Regional integration and trade also has helped democratic countries seal hard won peace on frontiers with a tradition of military conflict. It moreover has set up a solidarity network (through democratic clauses) to protect the region's still young democracies. MERCOSUR's experience is a good example on both accounts: its formerly conflictive borders are now the most pacified and heavily trafficked in Latin America. The old integration was not able to achieve this because the primacy of protection blocked growth of commercial trade between neighbors, while many of the sponsors of the initiatives were often nationalistic authoritarian regimes with a vested interest in restricted borders, territorial disputes and non-democratic processes.

* * *

SICE, WESTERN HEMISPHERE CUSTOMS UNIONS AND FREE TRADE AGREEMENTS*

CUSTOMS UNIONS

Andean Community (1969)

Central American Common Market (1962–63)

Southern Cone Common Market (Mercosur) (1991)

Caribbean Community and Common Market (CARICOM) (1966)

FREE TRADE AGREEMENTS

Bolivia—Mercosur (1997)

Canada—Chile (1997)

* OAS Foreign Trade Information System, *available at* http://www.sice.oas.org; date of entry into force is indicated, except where the agreement has not entered into force; updated by the authors. Reprinted with permission.

Canada—Costa Rica (2002)

Canada—Israel (1997)

CARICOM—Costa Rica

CARICOM—Dominican Republic

Central America—Chile (2002)

Central America—Panama

Central America—Dominican Republic

Chile—European Free Trade Association

Chile—European Union

Chile—Korea (2004)

Chile—Mercosur (1996)

Mexico—Bolivia (1995)

Mexico—Chile (1999)

Mexico   Costa Rica (1995)

Mexico—Colombia—Venezuela (1995)

Mexico—European Free Trade Association (2001)

Mexico—European Communities (2000)

Mexico—Israel (2000)

Mexico—Japan (2004)

Mexico—Nicaragua (1998)

Mexico—Honduras—Guatemala—El Salvador (2001)

Mexico—Uruguay

NAFTA (Mexico, Canada, United States) (1994)

Panama—Taiwan (2004)

United States—Australia

United States-Chile (2004)

United States—Guatemala—El Salvador—Honduras—Nicaragua—Costa Rica—Dominican Republic (CAFTA)

United States—Israel (1985)

United States—Jordan (2001)

United States—Morocco

United States—Singapore (2004)

Preferential Trading Agreements

Latin American Integration Association (1981)

Columbia—CARICOM (1995)

United States—Vietnam (2001)

Venezuela—CARICOM

Part Two

NAFTA

Chapter 5

FREE TRADE IN GOODS

5.0 INTRODUCTION: TARIFFS AND TRADE*

With the implementation of NAFTA, the United States enjoys free trade with the two largest purchasers of U.S. goods. Canada was always the largest buyer of U.S. goods, and Mexico quickly surpassed Japan to become number two in the first year of NAFTA's operation. However, Japan regained its second place status in 2002, and it appears likely that by the end of 2004 China will surpass both Mexico and Japan as suppliers of goods to the United States, relegating Mexico to number four. This introduction outlines some of the reasons for growth in North American trading of goods. Our coverage here is centered on tariff and trade law that is not extensively analyzed in the problems that follow.

NAFTA combines with CFTA to create a North American free trade area for goods. Phased tariff removals are the means to this end. Article 302 of NAFTA prohibits all parties from increasing tariffs or establishing new tariffs on North American goods. This provision had the practical effect of ensuring that many Mexican goods could continue to enter the United States on a duty free basis. This most often occurred prior to NAFTA under the U.S. program of generalized tariff preferences (GSP). The GSP program, with many exceptions and controls, grants duty free entry to goods from over 100 developing nations. After President Reagan "graduated" Hong Kong, Singapore, South Korea and Taiwan from U.S. program in 1989, Mexico had ranked number one in GSP duty free imports until 1994.

TARIFFS AND CUSTOMS

NAFTA preserved the 1998 deadline for the elimination of tariffs on goods traded between Canada and the United States. This gave Canadian exporters short-term market access advantages compared to their Mexican competitors who did not get almost full duty-free access to the

* Adapted from R. Folsom, NAFTA and   2004). Copyright © 2004 West Group.
Free Trade in the Americas (West Group,

U.S. until 2003. NAFTA phased out most tariffs on North American goods by 2003. By 2008, essentially all North American trade in goods will be duty free. Four stages lead to this result, subject to agreement upon accelerated two-way or three-way tariff reductions.

The tariffs in effect on January 1, 1991 are the baseline. Tariffs on Schedule A goods, about half of all U.S. exports to Mexico, were dissolved immediately in 1994. Schedule B goods were subject to 20 percent annual tariff reductions to January 1, 1998. Schedule C goods were reduced 10 percent annually to January 1, 2003. Finally, tariffs on Schedule C+ goods are being removed at a 6.66 percent annual rate to January 1, 2008. Schedule C+ arrangements accommodate highly sensitive goods such as corn and beans into Mexico and orange juice and sugar into the United States. A few goods such as orange juice and furniture are not subject to straight-line tariff phase outs. Their tariffs are irregularly removed over time in so-called "kinky curves." Prior to NAFTA, Mexico's average applied tariff on U.S. goods was 10 percent, while the comparable U.S. tariff on Mexican goods was 4 percent.

General customs fees, which are quasi-tariffs, were eliminated under CFTA in 1994. Health and safety inspection fees can be collected. The U.S. customs user fee was eliminated on Mexican–United States trade in North American goods on July 1, 1999. As under CFTA, *export* taxes or tariffs are generally prohibited. However, Mexico can employ them to keep essential foodstuffs like corn, flour and milk in the country. Since these products have traditionally been subsidized in Mexico, United States or Canadian buyers might otherwise deplete them. Mexico can also apply export charges temporarily to foodstuffs in short supply.

Canada, Mexico and the United States have retained their national tariffs for purposes of third party trade. NAFTA does, however, move slightly in the direction of a common external tariff. For example, semiconductors and local area network data processing equipment have had a common external tariff of zero and been freely traded since 1994. Article 308 coordinates the external tariffs for automatic data processing goods and parts. As of 2004, these tariffs are uniform. This means that nearly all computer imports are treated as originating under NAFTA and can be freely traded.

Customs tariff refunds (drawback) and tariff waivers or remissions are addressed under NAFTA. Canada and the United States eliminated most such waivers on bilateral trade in 1996, a two year extension of the CFTA deadline. This CAFTA commitment had been altered by Article 303 of NAFTA. Waivers were similarly limited in 2001 for Mexico–United States trade. Essentially, NAFTA provides that duty waivers for parts and components from outside North America used to produce finished goods traded within North America are not authorized, regardless of whether the finished goods are originating goods subject to NAFTA tariff reductions or elimination, or non-originating goods subject to MFN tariffs when traded within the region. Waivers remain legal for imported parts and components that are used in the production of finished goods destined for third countries. Waivers can also be used with originating goods not yet subject to duty free treatment, or non-originating goods, up to the lesser of the amount of tariff due upon crossing a NAFTA border or the amount of duties originally paid upon importation of materials, parts and components. Article 303 does not apply to imports of originating materials, parts and components by one NAFTA member for production of finished goods exported to another NAFTA member, although by 2004 virtually all such materials, parts and components are duty free in any event under NAFTA.

The net result is that since 2003, when most originating goods circulate duty free within NAFTA, drawbacks or duty waivers are basically prohibited. This is having significant consequences. Canada and Mexico may ultimately lower their external tariffs on parts and components to those levels of the United States so as to avoid penalizing manufacturers in their countries who can no longer receive tariff refunds. If this eventually occurs, and there have already been unilateral tariff changes of this kind in Canada, a common NAFTA external tariff could evolve without the need for a formal agreement. However, to date at least, Mexican has taken a different approach, as discussed below.

NAFTA also bans new tariff waivers which are tied to performance requirements. The types of performance requirements that are prohibited include: 1) Export minimums; 2) local content; 3) local substitution or purchase minimums; 4) trade balancing export to import ratios; and 5) mandatory foreign exchange inflows. However, Mexico is not obliged to participate except by way of Annex 304.1. In that Annex Mexico promised not to disproportionately alter existing tariff waivers. Mexico also agreed to freeze the list of goods to which it traditionally grants such waivers. However, all Mexican tariff waivers were to be eliminated by 2001.

IMPACT ON MAQUILADORAS

The NAFTA regime on drawbacks and tariff waivers has been important to Mexico's export-driven maquiladora assembly plants. Most maquiladoras have historically relied on tariff refunds and waivers on inputs; typically, only 2%–3% of the maquiladoras' materials costs are incurred in Mexico. Under NAFTA, as of 2001, Mexico was required to cease the beneficial application of tariff refunds and waivers on imported materials, parts and components provided as a condition of exportation of the final product. Full Mexican tariffs would have applied to imported components originating outside of North America, which would have made it much more expensive to produce those goods in Mexico than before 2001.

Many Asian manufacturers using Mexican assembly plants are impacted. As the drafters of NAFTA intended, there should be no preferentially tariffed "export platforms" into Canada or the United States. Some such manufacturers had already switched to North American suppliers for their assembly plant inputs. Others, notably from Japan and Korea, have arranged for their home country suppliers to join them in production in Mexico. Components from these loyal affiliates generally avoid the origin problems created under NAFTA as Mexican customs refunds and waivers are eliminated. They also add to the North American content of the assembled goods, a key to meeting NAFTA rules of origin. However, in some industries, such as consumer electronics, reliance on some Asian parts and components is essential for cost and availability considerations.

Mexico essentially had three choices for dealing with this problem. They could have reduced their MFN tariffs across the board–often 12%–15% or more for components—to much lower levels, but this would have reduced overall tariff income. They could have retained the high tariffs, and hoped that maquiladoras would shift sourcing to North American from Asian sources. However, if such sources were unavailable, or high cost, the affected maquiladoras would likely close their operations in Mexico. Mexico chose a third option, a new "special sector" or PROSEC program, under which importations of certain materials, parts and components and essential machinery and equipment for producing goods in more than twenty industrial categories were made subject to zero or 5% duties, regardless of whether the finished products were exported, thus complying with Article 303. PROSEC greatly reduces the potential increased manufacturing costs for the covered industrial sectors, but with an additional layer of bureaucracy and greater uncertainties for business, since under PROSEC the government may change the list of imported products that benefit from preferential duty treatment.

Traditionally, sales of maquiladora products in Mexico have been limited. Starting in 1994, amendments to Mexico's Maquiladora Decree permitted such sales to increase based upon percentages of prior year individual maquiladora exports from Mexico. In 1994, for example, this percentage was 55%, rising 5% annually to 75% in 1998 and scheduled to be 85% in the year 2000. By 2001, maquiladoras were permitted sell their entire production in Mexico if they choose, although very few have done so. This schedule was coordinated with Mexico's phase-out of customs duty drawback and waivers on imported components.

REGULATORY AND TAX TREATMENT, QUOTAS

NAFTA, like CFTA, incorporates by reference the national treatment duties of Article III of the GATT 1947 agreement. Each federal government must generally treat North American goods in the same manner as its own goods. We consider national treatment issues in Problem 5.2. Article 301 further requires states, provinces and local governments to treat goods from other partners as favorably as they treat goods from anywhere, including their own jurisdiction. These treatment duties affect taxes, fees, sale or distribution requirements, usage regulations and a range of other laws. Specific exceptions, many of which are derived from GATT grandfather rights, are listed in Annex 301.3.

Incorporation of GATT Article III makes it a part of NAFTA. This means that the countries may pursue NAFTA versus World Trade Organization (WTO) dispute settlement. It seems likely that WTO and NAFTA panel reports on Article III issues will remain consistent, but to date there have been no Chapter 20 decisions on GATT Article III issues. Article III arbitration decisions under CFTA Chapter 18 suggest a close adherence to GATT principles.

The restrictive rules on use of trade quotas and price controls embodied in Article XI of the GATT 1947 agreement are also incorporated by reference into NAFTA. Under CFTA, they were simply affirmed. As with Article III, NAFTA dispute settlement is now an option on trade quota or price control issues. Mexico had 10 years from 1994 to eliminate its import licensing regime. Import and export quotas or restraints applied to goods from other nations will be honored by the NAFTA partners.

NAFTA provides for quota relief on a variety of specific goods. Textile quotas on originating goods are generally removed. On non-originating textile goods, quotas are gradually phased out. Agricultural and food product quotas are reduced in number, and energy quotas are discouraged. Quotas on motor vehicles and their parts are phased out. Most other traditional North American trade quotas are retained.

Export restraints justified under Articles XI or XX of the GATT are subjected to special additional rules applicable to CFTA (but not NAFTA) trade. These special rules require maintaining historically proportionate supplies, not pricing exports above domestic levels and not disrupting normal channels of supply. These rules are found in NAFTA, but do not apply to Mexico. Mexico can therefore apply trade quotas and other export restraints subject only to GATT 1947 rules. Canada and the United States may restrain exports to Mexico under those same rules.

RULES OF ORIGIN

Mexico has the highest average tariffs, the U.S. has the lowest, and Canada falls in the middle. Since free trade in goods only applies to goods that originate in North America, non-originating goods are subject to the normal MFN tariffs of Canada, Mexico and the United States. Origin determinations are thus critical to NAFTA traders. There are Uniform NAFTA Regulations governing rules of origin and customs procedures, including a common Certificate of Origin, which is reproduced in Problem 5.1.

EXCEPTIONS TO FREE TRADE

Every chapter of NAFTA has specific exceptions that accompany it. Chapter 21, labeled "Exceptions," is of wider application. For example, information flows adverse to law enforcement can be restrained under NAFTA. So can flows that affect personal privacy or financial information rights. Perhaps the best known exception is that for Canadian cultural industries which was extended to Canadian–Mexican trade. This exception does not apply to Mexico–United States trade. We take up this exception in Problem 5.3.

In addition, Chapter 21 incorporates by reference into NAFTA Article XX of the GATT 1947 (and its interpretative notes). Article XX authorizes restraint on international trade in the name of public morality, public health, protection of intellectual property, conservation of natural resources and so forth. Article 2101 of NAFTA seeks to clarify Article XX of the GATT. It declares environmental health protection a legitimate reason to restrain NAFTA trade. So is conservation of living and non-living exhaustible natural resources. The health protection exception contained in Article XX of the GATT is specifically replaced by NAFTA's provisions on sanitary and phytosanitary (SPS) regulations. We cover NAFTA's SPS rules in Problem 5.2. It was also agreed that all health, safety and consumer protection laws must be consistent with NAFTA. They may not be administered in arbitrary or unjustifiably discriminatory ways. Nor may they amount to a disguised restriction on NAFTA trade.

The NAFTA national security exceptions to free trade follow those created in CFTA. As a general rule, NAFTA does not impact national tax laws. However, Article 301 (national treatment) applies to tax regulations "to the same extent as does Article III of the GATT." Article III bans discriminatory taxation of imported goods and frequently applies to sales, excise and value-added taxes. Income, capital gains taxation, and corporate capital taxation, if applied to a particular service, must also be given national treatment.

Articles 2103.2 through 2103.6 indicate that international tax conventions prevail over NAFTA. This might, for example, authorize performance requirements that would otherwise be prohibited by NAFTA. The most recent relevant conventions are the 1980 Canada–United States Tax Convention, the 1992 Canada–Mexico Tax Convention, and the 1994 Mexico–United States Tax Convention.

NAFTA, with an eye towards Mexico, governs the extent to which balance of payments problems justify restraints of trade. Article 2104 legitimizes use of quotas, surcharges and the like only if authorized by the International Monetary Fund. This makes it unlikely that NAFTA nations can restrain payments on current transactions, dividends, royalties and the like. Capital transfers, on the other hand, are not subject to IMF controls. Mexico can therefore restrain major capital outflows.

Temporary Import Restraints (Escape Clauses)

Under CFTA, Canada and the United States severely limited their ability to bilaterally protect their markets against surging imports when the imports cause or threaten serious injury to a domestic industry. These limitations continue in force. Chapter 8 of NAFTA, applicable to all three parties, substantially reproduces the CFTA provisions on emergency import protection. Bilateral escape clause action was possible for serious injury or a threat of serious domestic industry injury until 2003;

as of the end of the "transition period" (January 1, 2003) it could be used only for Schedule C+ goods which become duty free in 2008. Bilateral relief can be applied for a maximum of four (not just three) years for Schedule C+ goods. Another variation from CFTA protective relief permitted advancing the scheduled NAFTA tariff reductions to later dates, but no later than final duty free dates under the Agreement. (To date, this authority has never been used.)

Article 802 of NAFTA applies to all three countries when global escape clause proceedings are pursued. To start, there is a rebuttable presumption that NAFTA goods will be excluded from global actions. Rebuttal is possible if the NAFTA imports are a "substantial share" of total imports, and those NAFTA imports "contribute importantly" to serious domestic industry injury or its threat. "Substantial share" is defined as "normally" including only the five largest supplier-nations. In other words, imports from Canada, Mexico or the United States must be in the top five for any global escape clause relief to apply. Furthermore, NAFTA imports with growth rates that are appreciably lower than the growth rate from all sources will "normally" not be considered to "contribute importantly" to injury. If initially excluded from escape clause global actions, NAFTA imports may later be included should a surge in NAFTA trade occur.

Any global escape clause remedies may not reduce the flow of goods across NAFTA borders below levels corresponding to a recent representative time period plus reasonable growth. The exporting NAFTA partner may in turn pursue substantially equivalent compensatory action. Lastly, NAFTA details in Article 803 and Annex 803.3 procedures that must be followed in bilateral or global emergency protective proceedings. These procedures do not differ substantially from those already used in United States law as administered by the U.S. International Trade Commission.

Presidents Bill Clinton and George W. Bush excluded the United States' NAFTA partners from global safeguard remedies applied under the WTO's Agreement on Safeguards in cases involving wheat gluten, lamb meat, line pipe and steel, even though in the steel case Canada and Mexico were among the major suppliers of steel to the United States. The WTO's Dispute Settlement Body ultimately determined that the safeguards in all three cases failed to comply with WTO rules, and that the US International Trade Commission (ITC) had insufficiently justified its exclusion of imports from Canada and Mexico.

THE CORN BROOM CASE

In its first (and only) application of Section 302 of the NAFTA Implementation Act and NAFTA Article 801, the ITC found in 1996 that the elimination of tariffs on Mexican corn brooms resulted in a surge of imports that were the substantial cause of serious injury or its threat to the U.S. broom industry. No. NAFTA–302–1. The ITC subsequently recommended tariff increases starting at 12 percent above the MFN level declining to 3 percent above that level in the fourth year of relief. This recommendation concerned brooms from Mexico and other nations excepting only Canada and Israel. No. TA–201–65, ITC Pub. 3984. Aug. 1996.

President Clinton decided against tariff increases, but instructed the USTR to attempt to negotiate solutions with Mexico and other countries while the Labor, Commerce and Agriculture Departments developed an adjustment plan for the U.S. corn broom industry. Mexico, meanwhile, requested consultations under NAFTA Chapter 20 dispute resolution. Late in 1996, President Clinton deemed the negotiations a failure and imposed substantial tariffs and tariff-rate-quotas (TRQs) on broom imports from Mexico and other countries for 3 years. Mexico, in turn, raised tariffs on U.S. wine, brandy, bourbon, whiskey, wood office and bedroom furniture, flat glass, telephone agendas and chemically-pure sugar, fructose and syrup products. This retaliation was deemed by Mexico "substantially equivalent" to the U.S. broom tariff surcharges valued at roughly $1 million.

Early in 1998, the NAFTA Chapter 20 arbitration panel ruled in Mexico's favor. USA–97–2008–01. Specifically, the panel ruled that the ITC had failed to explain why plastic brooms were not directly competitive with corn brooms, and therefore part of the U.S. domestic industry. U.S. officials indicated they would comply, but then took nine months to terminate the safeguards in a decision that does not cite the NAFTA arbitration as a reason for termination. Mexico subsequently removed its retaliatory tariffs.

SPECIAL ESCAPE CLAUSES

Textile and apparel goods, some agricultural goods, frozen concentrated orange juice and major household appliances benefit from special escapes from import competition under NAFTA. Many of these provisions were created to secure passage of NAFTA through the United States Congress. For example, textile and apparel goods are subject to a unique import protection scheme found in Annex 300–B. Standard bilateral escape clause relief on originating goods is possible under less demanding conditions until 2003. For non-originating goods, until 2003, quotas may be used as remedies by the United States or Mexico. The most important alteration probably concerns decision-making: the U.S. International Trade Commission does not participate. Instead, the Interagency Committee for the Implementation of Textile Agreements (CITA), thought to be more pro-industry, is the body that determines escape clause relief for textiles and apparel under NAFTA.

A special provision located in Article 703 benefits U.S.-grown chili peppers, eggplant, watermelons, tomatoes, onions and other agricultural goods. These may be protected using tariff-rate-quotas. The United States NAFTA Implementation Act, in Section 309, protects against imports of frozen concentrated orange juice from Mexico until 2007. Additional tariffs apply if the futures price for OJ falls below historic levels for five consecutive days. Once this happens, tariffs on Mexican OJ imports are "snapbacked" to the lower of the present or July 1, 1991 most-favored-nation GATT rates. These tariffs are eliminated when the average historic price level is exceeded for five days. This statistically driven protective mechanism, a monument to Florida politicians, has frequently been triggered.

The President's Statement of Administrative Action (SAA) accompanying the NAFTA Implementation Act contains yet another special escape from import competition. This time the beneficiaries are United States producers of major household appliances. It is thought that this statement, and its arcane rules of operation under Chapter 8 escape clause relief, secured critical votes in the House of Representatives for the passage of NAFTA.

AGRICULTURAL GOODS

Trade in agricultural goods and food products is always sensitive as we shall see in Problem 5.2. Canada and the U.S. undertook only token changes in CFTA, not the least because each has powerful farm lobbies. Mexico's large *ejido* communal land program is oriented towards subsistence farming and constitutionally protected. This makes change in agricultural hyper-sensitive. Nevertheless, agricultural free trade between the United States and Mexico was substantially advanced by NAFTA. Relatively little progress was made on the Northern front where the CFTA rules on agricultural trade were retained under NAFTA. These rules reduced quota, import license and other agricultural nontariff trade barriers in only a limited way.

Agricultural export subsidies are generally restrained under NAFTA. However, this restraint does not apply to Mexican–United States agricultural trade. Notice and consultation must precede any subsidization and a Working Group on Agricultural Subsidies monitors this volatile area. It is deemed "inappropriate" for one NAFTA partner to subsidize agricultural goods unless there are subsidized imports entering that market from a non-member country. The NAFTA partners have promised to collaborate on retaliatory measures against the offending third-party. It is significant that NAFTA reserves for all partners the right to apply countervailing tariffs against subsidized agricultural imports. Canada, for example, has assessed countervailing duties on United States corn.

Mexico and the United States undertook more diffuse agricultural trade reform. Approximately half of all Mexico–U.S. agricultural trade immediately became duty-free. The United States and Mexico also converted agricultural quotas, import licenses and other nontariff trade barriers into tariffs ("tariffication"). Equivalent restrictive tariffs or tariff-rate quotas (TRQs) replaced these restraints. Tariff rate quotas adjust the level of applicable tariffs according to the volume of imports, generally rising with import volume.

Duty free entry at lower import volumes often accompanies TRQs. The amount of duty free agricultural goods entering Mexico and the United States has been increased by 3 percent annually. Nearly all tariffs on Mexican–U.S. agricultural goods were eliminated by 2004. By 2009 tariffs for even the most sensitive agricultural items, such as corn and dry beans entering Mexico, become duty free. Government data indicates that trade in agricultural goods has been moderately expending in both directions, to the consternation of some Mexico chicken and hog farmers, among others.

The sensitivity of U.S.-Mexican agricultural trade is reflected in emergency protective measures that apply until 2004. Under this provision, Mexico and the United States may impose tariffs at designated import "trigger" levels. The lower of the tariff rate in effect on July 1, 1991 or the importing nation's current most-favored-nation tariff can be assessed when imports surge for the remainder of the growing season or calendar year. The trigger levels increase yearly until 2004 when they can no longer be invoked as temporary protection on agricultural trade. Use of this special provision forecloses the option of NAFTA's general "escape clause."

In pursuing a tariffication process, Mexico and the United States acted in advance of the WTO Agreement on Agriculture (1995). Under that Agreement, Canada and the United States were obligated to do likewise. When Canada tariffied (using TRQs) a number of agricultural quotas at levels measured in hundreds of percent, the United States filed a complaint under NAFTA. This complaint was the first under Chapter 20 to go to arbitration. A panel of five arbitrators unanimously ruled that Canada's tariffication and tariff levels were consistent with its treaty obligations. CDA–95–2008–01.

PROBLEM 5.1 NAFTA RULES OF ORIGIN: CUSTOMS CONDUCTS VERIFICATION PROCEEDINGS, ISSUES ADVANCE RULINGS AND RESOLVES ORIGIN DISPUTES

SECTION I. THE SETTING

The Canadian, Mexican and United States customs authorities acquired additional responsibilities under NAFTA. Indeed, Chapter 5 of the NAFTA agreement focuses exclusively on customs procedures, including origin verification proceedings and advance rulings.

For purposes of this problem, you are an attorney in the Office of Regulations and Rulings of U.S. Customs and Border Protection (CBP), formerly the U.S. Customs Service, in the Washington "Headquarters" office. Your job, *inter alia*, is to interpret and supervise the administration of the NAFTA Rules of Origin (Chapter 4). Your decisions, once affirmed at higher levels at CBP, may be appealed to the U.S. Court of

International Trade. (Essentially the same functions are performed by attorneys in the Canada Border Services Agency or Aduana Mexico and reviewed by the federal court in Canada and the Tribunal Fiscal in Mexico.) Rules of origin are critical to the operational reality of NAFTA. Unless goods or services are "originating" (North American as a matter of NAFTA law), they cannot be freely traded.

The following cases have come to your office:

1. Fresh tuna caught in Mexican waters and fresh salmon caught in Canadian waters are being imported into the United States. Their origin under NAFTA has been disputed in a verification proceeding.

2. Some of the tuna and salmon above are being fresh frozen on Mexican and Canadian ships, wrapped in packaging of Asian origin that adds four percent to total value, and imported into the United States. An advance ruling on the origin of these goods has been disputed.

3. An image projector, such as a device for projecting overhead transparencies (HTS Heading 9008) is being assembled in Mexico by a Mexican-owned company. All of its components originate exclusively from Canada or the United States. What is its origin?

4. Same projector with a housing made of steel imported from Europe/Asia/Brazil (you choose) which was fabricated into a housing in the United States. The projector has cleared customs but its NAFTA origin–and whether duties are owed–is disputed between CBP and the importer, possibly as the result of a "protest" filed against CBP. You must issue a ruling on the projector's origin for NAFTA purposes.

5. Same projector except that the housing was fabricated in Europe/Asia/Brazil (you choose) and imported into Mexico before assembly into a projector. Can you rule?

6. Same facts as in No. 5 except that the F.O.B. invoice price of the projector is $100.00. The steel housing cost the Mexican assembler $10.00. Can you rule and, if so, how? And if the housing cost is $50.00?

7. Same facts as in No. 5 except that the total cost of the projector to the Mexican assembler is $75.00 including a $5.00 royalty to a patent holder. The steel housing cost is $10.00. Can you rule and, if so, how? And if the housing cost is $50.00?

8. Combined facts as in Nos. 4, 5, 6 and 7. How do you rule?

9. Same facts as in No. 4 except the projector housing is made of Canadian steel fabricated into a housing in the U.S. How do you rule?

10. Chinese cotton fabrics have been imported in bulk by a Mexican shirt and blouse manufacturer. The fabric is cut, sewn and finished in Mexico. When exported to the U.S., customs duties

are assessed. The importer claims duty free NAFTA entry. How do you rule?

11. Chinese cotton has been imported into the U.S. where it has been spun into yarn and made into fabric. This fabric is shipped to Mexico for cutting, sewing and finishing into shirts and blouses which are exported to the Unites States. Customs duties are assessed and the importer claims duty free NAFTA entry. How do you rule?

12. Japanese and Korean electronics manufacturers have created numerous assembly plants in Mexico. They have used Asian-made components for years, but have recently persuaded some of their corporate family affiliates to produce key components in Mexico. These include picture tubes for color televisions and color computer monitors. U.S. customs assesses duties on these televisions and monitors. The importer claims duty free NAFTA entry. How do you rule?

13. Volkswagen Jettas (and all other models for the U.S. market) are made in Mexico. VW obtained an advance ruling on their origin under NAFTA which suggested duty free status. But U.S. customs assesses duties, which VW challenges. Are advance rulings binding on customs authorities? What special rules apply to automobile origin disputes?

SECTION II. FOCUS OF CONSIDERATION

NAFTA, like all free trade areas, faces a fundamental problem. Unlike the European Union, there is no common external NAFTA tariff. Canada, Mexico and the United States apply their own tariffs to goods entering their markets. Goods from outside the region could enter the country with the lowest tariff (almost always the U.S.) and attempt free entry into the other member states. Or parts and components could be imported into Mexico duty-free from Asia, subjected to final ("screwdriver") assembly in Mexico, and imported into the United States duty-free. Obviously, this cannot be allowed. The solution is to designate which goods can be freely traded within the region. This solution comes in the form of "rules of origin". That is why it is said that the NAFTA rules of origin are the key to unlocking free trade.

It is noteworthy that the CFTA/NAFTA rules of origin broke with longstanding U.S. "substantial transformation" doctrine governing the origin of goods. *See Anheuser–Busch Brewing Association v. United States*, 207 U.S. 556, 28 S.Ct. 204, 52 L.Ed. 336 (1908). The NAFTA approach, focusing on the "tariff-shift approach" instead, is expected to become globally important as a similar WTO agreement on (non-preferential rules of origin is eventually agreed upon in Geneva.

The purpose of the NAFTA rules of origin is to benefit the region economically, i.e. to benefit North American goods and services by assuring that only goods which undertake a significant manufacturing operation in the region, or use a high portion of regional inputs, qualify for duty-free treatment. In this problem, we focus on some of the trade impact that has accompanied the tariff reductions under CFTA and NAFTA. We then turn to an understanding of which goods and services may be freely traded and why. Lastly, we study common customs procedures adopted under NAFTA to facilitate trade and resolve origin and other disputes.

Chapters 4 and 5 of the NAFTA agreement are essential to an analysis of this problem. These materials are found in the Documents Supplement.

SECTION III. READINGS, QUESTIONS AND COMMENTS

McCALL, WHAT IS ASIA AFRAID OF? THE DIVERSIONARY EFFECT OF NAFTA'S RULES OF ORIGIN ON TRADE BETWEEN THE UNITED STATES AND ASIA
25 Cal. West. Int'l L.J. 389 (1995).*

THE NAFTA'S RULES OF ORIGIN

The NAFTA rules of origin raised some of the more controversial and difficult issues in the NAFTA negotiations. The governments involved, as well as those representing economic and political interests in the three countries, wanted the reduced duties available under NAFTA to benefit only products that involve significant manufacturing and other economic activity in the three countries. Most particularly, the NAFTA members did not want Mexico, with its lower wage rates and other costs, to be used as an "export platform" for entry into the United States of goods that consisted largely of third-country materials.

Consequently, the NAFTA rules of origin are detailed, complex, and comprehensive. NAFTA includes a twenty-six page Rules of Origin section, including express definitions of thirty terms, a seventeen page Customs Procedure section, two pages of a Notes section, and a 169 page annex with specific rules of origin for individual Harmonized System chapters.

* * *

TARIFF-SHIFT RULES

A good may qualify as an originating good only when each nonoriginating material used to produce the good undergoes an applicable "change in tariff classification" as a result of production in one or more of the NAFTA countries. The particular change required depends on the tariff classification of the good involved. A change in origin based on a shift in tariff classification is a relatively recent development resulting from the adoption by most countries of the International Convention on the Harmonized Commodity Description and Coding System ("Harmonized System").

* * *

The following illustration is an example of the tariff-shift rules of origin under NAFTA: Canada produces bread, pastries, cakes, and biscuits, which come under Harmonized System Number 1905.90, with flour imported from Europe. The flour is categorized as Harmonized System Chapter 11. These items are then shipped to the United States. The applicable rule of origin states: "A change to heading 19.02 through 19.05 from any other chapter." Thus, for all products classified in Harmonized System Headings 1902 through 1905, all non-North American inputs must be classified in an Harmonized System chapter other than Harmonized System Chapter 19 in order to be considered "originating goods." These baked goods would qualify for NAFTA benefits because the non-originating material, the flour, is classified outside of Chapter 19.

VALUE-CONTENT RULES

Where the non-originating part or parts do not qualify as originating goods under the change in tariff classification test, the product can still be treated as originating in NAFTA if it meets the required regional value-content test.

Regional value-content rules require a percentage of the value of the good to be North American. A good will qualify as an originating good if the assembly of such parts and components within NAFTA accounts for sixty percent of the value of the finished product or fifty percent of the net cost of the product. Under Article 402 of NAFTA, the regional value content can be calculated by either the transaction value or the net-cost method.

THE TRANSACTION-VALUE METHOD

The transaction-value method generally means the price actually paid or payable for the good. The transaction-value method is generally easier to calculate than the net-cost method. A manufacturer may choose whichever method is most advantageous to his goods with certain exceptions.

The transaction-value method calculates regional content by: (1) subtracting the price paid for non-NAFTA-origin materials used in the production of the good from the price charged the consumer for the finished good and (2) dividing that figure by the price charged the consumer. If the product contains more than sixty percent regional value content, it qualifies as an originating good. Put simply, the assembly of parts and components within the NAFTA zone must account for at least sixty percent of the value of the finished product. For example, a Mexican manufacturer produces electric hair curling irons from Japanese hair curler parts. Each curling iron is sold for U.S. $4.40. The value of the non-originating hair curler parts is U.S. $1.80.

The hair curling iron is not an originating good because its regional value content is below 60% using the transaction value method.

THE NET-COST METHOD

The net-cost method is based on the total cost of the good minus sales promotion, marketing, after-sales service, royalties, shipping, packing, and non-allowable interest costs. The net-cost method calculates regional content by subtracting the price paid for non-NAFTA-origin materials from the net cost to the producer of the good and dividing that figure by the net cost to the producer. If the product contains more than fifty percent regional content, it will qualify as an originating product.

For example, assume the Mexican manufacturer above uses the net cost method for the hair curling irons imported into the United States. The total cost for the hair curler is U.S. $3.90. This figure includes U.S. $0.25 for shipping and packing costs. There are no other costs. The net cost therefore is U.S. $3.65.

The hair curling iron would be considered an originating good using the net cost method because the regional value content is a little over 50%.

* * *

DEPARTMENT OF THE TREASURY
UNITED STATES CUSTOMS SERVICE

NORTH AMERICAN FREE TRADE AGREEMENT
CERTIFICATE OF ORIGIN

Please print or type   19 CFR 181.11, 181.22

1. EXPORTER NAME AND ADDRESS	2. BLANKET PERIOD *(DD/MM/YY)*
	FROM
	TO
TAX IDENTIFICATION NUMBER:	
3. PRODUCER NAME AND ADDRESS	4. IMPORTER NAME AND ADDRESS
TAX IDENTIFICATION NUMBER:	TAX IDENTIFICATION NUMBER:

5. DESCRIPTION OF GOOD(S)	6. HS TARIFF CLASSIFICATION NUMBER	7. PREFERENCE CRITERION	8. PRODUCER	9. NET COST	10. COUNTRY OF ORIGIN

I CERTIFY THAT:

• THE INFORMATION ON THIS DOCUMENT IS TRUE AND ACCURATE AND I ASSUME THE RESPONSIBILITY FOR PROVING SUCH REPRESENTATIONS. I UNDERSTAND THAT I AM LIABLE FOR ANY FALSE STATEMENTS OR MATERIAL OMISSIONS MADE ON OR IN CONNECTION WITH THIS DOCUMENT;

• I AGREE TO MAINTAIN, AND PRESENT UPON REQUEST, DOCUMENTATION NECESSARY TO SUPPORT THIS CERTIFICATE, AND TO INFORM, IN WRITING, ALL PERSONS TO WHOM THE CERTIFICATE WAS GIVEN OF ANY CHANGES THAT COULD AFFECT THE ACCURACY OR VALIDITY OF THIS CERTIFICATE;

• THE GOODS ORIGINATED IN THE TERRITORY OF ONE OR MORE OF THE PARTIES, AND COMPLY WITH THE ORIGIN REQUIREMENTS SPECIFIED FOR THOSE GOODS IN THE NORTH AMERICAN FREE TRADE AGREEMENT, AND UNLESS SPECIFICALLY EXEMPTED IN ARTICLE 411 OR ANNEX 401, THERE HAS BEEN NO FURTHER PRODUCTION OR ANY OTHER OPERATION OUTSIDE THE TERRITORIES OF THE PARTIES; AND

• THIS CERTIFICATE CONSISTS OF _____ PAGES, INCLUDING ALL ATTACHMENTS.

11.	11a. AUTHORIZED SIGNATURE	11b. COMPANY
	11c. NAME *(Print or Type)*	11d. TITLE
	11e. DATE *(DD/MM/YY)*	11f. TELEPHONE NUMBER ▷ *(Voice)* *(Facsimile)*

Customs Form 434 (121793)

PAPERWORK REDUCTION ACT NOTICE: This information is needed to carry out the terms of the North American Free Trade Agreement (NAFTA). NAFTA requires that, upon request, an importer must provide Customs with proof of the exporter's written certification of the origin of the goods. The certification is essential to substantiate compliance with the rules of origin under the Agreement. You are required to give us this information to obtain a benefit.

Statement Required by 5 CFR 1320.21: The estimated average burden associated with this collection of information is 15 minutes per respondent or recordkeeper depending on individual circumstances. Comments concerning the accuracy of this burden estimate and suggestions for reducing this burden should be directed to U.S. Customs Service, Paperwork Management Branch, Washington DC 20229, and to the Office of Management and Budget, Paperwork Reduction Project (1515-0204), Washington DC 20503.

NORTH AMERICAN FREE TRADE AGREEMENT CERTIFICATE OF ORIGIN INSTRUCTIONS

For purposes of obtaining preferential tariff treatment, this document must be completed legibly and in full by the exporter and be in the possession of the importer at the time the declaration is made. This document may also be completed voluntarily by the producer for use by the exporter. Please print or type:

FIELD 1: State the full legal name, address (including country) and legal tax identification number of the exporter. Legal taxation number is: in Canada, employer number or importer/exporter number assigned by Revenue Canada; in Mexico, federal taxpayer's registry number (RFC); and in the United States, employer's identification number or Social Security Number.

FIELD 2: Complete field if the Certificate covers multiple shipments of identical goods as described in Field # 5 that are imported into a NAFTA country for a specified period of up to one year (the blanket period). "FROM" is the date upon which the Certificate becomes applicable to the good covered by the blanket Certificate (it may be prior to the date of signing this Certificate). "TO" is the date upon which the blanket period expires. The importation of a good for which preferential treatment is claimed based on this Certificate must occur between these dates.

FIELD 3: State the full legal name, address (including country) and legal tax identification number, as defined in Field #1, of the producer. If more than one producer's good is included on the Certificate, attach a list of additional producers, including the legal name, address (including country) and legal tax identification number, cross-referenced to the good described in Field #5. If you wish this information to be confidential, it is acceptable to state "Available to Customs upon request". If the producer and the exporter are the same, complete field with "SAME". If the producer is unknown, it is acceptable to state "UNKNOWN".

FIELD 4: State the full legal name, address (including country) and legal tax identification number, as defined in Field #1, of the importer. If the importer is not known, state "UNKNOWN"; if multiple importers, state "VARIOUS".

FIELD 5: Provide a full description of each good. The description should be sufficient to relate it to the invoice description and to the Harmonized System (H.S.) description of the good. If the Certificate covers a single shipment of a good, include the invoice number as shown on the commercial invoice. If not known, indicate another unique reference number, such as the shipping order number.

FIELD 6: For each good described in Field #5, identify the H.S. tariff classification to six digits. If the good is subject to a specific rule of origin in Annex 401 that requires eight digits, identify to eight digits, using the H.S. tariff classification of the country into whose territory the good is imported.

FIELD 7: For each good described in Field #5, state which criterion (A through F) is applicable. The rules of origin are contained in Chapter Four and Annex 401. Additional rules are described in Annex 703.2 (certain agricultural goods), Annex 300-B, Appendix 6 (certain textile goods) and Annex 308.1 (certain automatic data processing goods and their parts) NOTE: In order to be entitled to preferential tariff treatment, each good must meet at least one of the criteria below.

Preference Criteria

A   The good is "wholly obtained or produced entirely" in the territory of one or more of the NAFTA countries as referenced in Article 415. **Note: The purchase of a good in the territory does not necessarily render it "wholly obtained or produced".** If the good is an agricultural good, see also criterion F and Annex 703.2. *(Reference: Article 401(a) and 415)*

B   The good is produced entirely in the territory of one or more of the NAFTA countries and satisfies the specific rule of origin, set out in Annex 401, that applies to its tariff classification. The rule may include a tariff classification change, regional value-content requirement, or a combination thereof. The good must also satisfy all other applicable requirements of Chapter Four. If the good is an agricultural good, see also criterion F and Annex 703.2. *(Reference: Article 401(b))*

C   The good is produced entirely in the territory of one or more of the NAFTA countries exclusively from originating materials. Under this criterion, one or more of the materials may not fall within the definition of "wholly produced or obtained", as set out in Article 415. All materials used in the production of the good must qualify as "originating" by meeting the rules of Article 401(a) through (d). If the good is an agricultural good, see also criterion F and Annex 703.2. *Reference: Article 401(c).*

D   Goods are produced in the territory of one or more of the NAFTA countries but do not meet the applicable rule of origin, set out in Annex 401, because certain non-originating materials do not undergo the required change in tariff classification. The goods do nonetheless meet the regional value-content requirement specified in Article 401 (d). This criterion is limited to the following two circumstances:

    1 .The good was imported into the territory of a NAFTA country in an unassembled or disassembled form but was classified as an assembled good, pursuant to H.S. General Rule of Interpretation 2(a), or

    2 .The good incorporated one or more non-originating materials, provided for as parts under the H.S., which could not undergo a change in tariff classification because the heading provided for both the good and its parts and was not further subdivided into subheadings, or the subheading provided for both the good and its parts and was not further subdivided.

    NOTE: This criterion does not apply to Chapters 61 through 63 of the H.S. *(Reference: Article 401(d))*

E   Certain automatic data processing goods and their parts, specified in Annex 308.1, that do not originate in the territory are considered originating upon importation into the territory of a NAFTA country from the territory of another NAFTA country when the most-favored-nation tariff rate of the good conforms to the rate established in Annex 308.1 and is common to all NAFTA countries. *(Reference: Annex 308.1)*

F   The good is an originating agricultural good under preference criterion A, B, or C above and is not subject to a quantitative restriction in the importing NAFTA country because it is a "qualifying good" as defined in Annex 703.2, Section A or B (please specify). A good listed in Appendix 703.2B.7 is also exempt from quantitative restrictions and is eligible for NAFTA preferential tariff treatment if it meets the definition of "qualifying good" in Section A of Annex 703.2. **NOTE 1: This criterion does not apply to goods that wholly originate in Canada or the United States and are imported into either country. NOTE 2: A tariff rate quota is not a quantitative restriction.**

FIELD 8: For each good described in Field #5, state "YES" if you are the producer of the good. If you are not the producer of the good, state "NO" followed by (1), (2), or (3), depending on whether this certificate was based upon: (1) your knowledge of whether the good qualifies as an originating good; (2) your reliance on the producer's written representation (other than a Certificate of Origin) that the good qualifies as an originating good; or (3) a completed and signed Certificate for the good, voluntarily provided to the exporter by the producer.

FIELD 9: For each good described in field #5, where the good is subject to a regional value content (RVC) requirement, indicate "NC" if the RVC is calculated according to the net cost method; otherwise, indicate "NO". If the RVC is calculated over a period of time, further identify the beginning and ending dates (DD/MM/YY) of that period. *(Reference: Articles 402.1, 402.5).*

FIELD 10: Identify the name of the country ("MX" or "US" for agricultural and textile goods exported to Canada; "US" or "CA" for all goods exported to Mexico; or "CA" or "MX" for all goods exported to the United States) to which the preferential rate of customs duty applies, as set out in Annex 302.2, in accordance with the Marking Rules or in each party's schedule of tariff elimination.

For all other originating goods exported to Canada, indicate appropriately "MX" or "US" if the goods originate in that NAFTA country, within the meaning of the NAFTA Rules of Origin Regulations, and any subsequent processing in the other NAFTA country does not increase the transaction value of the goods by more than seven percent, otherwise "JNT" for joint production. *(Reference: Annex 302.2)*

FIELD 11: This field must be completed, signed, and dated by the exporter. When the Certificate is completed by the producer for use by the exporter, it must be completed, signed, and dated by the producer. The date must be the date the Certificate was completed and signed.

Customs Form 434 (121793)(Back)

WRIGHT, HTS PRODUCT CLASSIFICATION SHIFTS AND NET COST REGIONAL CONTENT, A PRACTICAL EXAMPLE

Baker & McKenzie (San Diego).*

To be sure, the analysis of whether a product qualifies as "originating" under Preference Criterion B can be complicated. On the other hand, it is the method by which most products will qualify as "originating" under NAFTA. One such example is provided here:

Assume a company in Canada known as Company A imports unfinished bearing rings from Japan. In Canada, Company A processes the rings into finished bearing rings. The unfinished bearing rings are classified under HTS Subheading 8482.99.11.

The finished bearing rings are also classified under HTS Subheading 8482.99.11. Company A's costs per unit are:

Non-originating materials	$0.75
Originating materials	$0.15
Labor (originating)	$0.35
Overhead (originating)	$0.05
	$1.30

The Annex 401 specific rule of origin for HTS Subheading 8482.99.11 is:

"A change to subheading 8482.91 through 8482.99 from any other heading."

As the unfinished bearing rings and the finished bearing rings are classified in the same heading, the finished bearing rings do not qualify as originating. Note that the above Annex 401 specific rule of origin does not contain a RVC [regional value content] requirement.

Then, assume that Company A sells the finished bearing rings to a company in the United States known as Company B for $1.45. Further assume that Company B incorporates the finished bearing rings into ball bearings. As stated above, the finished bearing rings are classified under HTS Subheading 8482.99.11. The ball bearings are classified under HTS Subheading 8482.10. Company B's costs of production are:

Non-originating materials (finished rings)	$1.45
Originating material	$0.45
Labor (originating)	$0.75
Overhead (originating)	$0.05
	$2.70

Company B wishes to sell the ball bearings to a related company in Mexico known as Company C, but Company C will only purchase the ball bearings if they qualify for favorable duty treatment under the NAFTA upon importation into Mexico. Do the ball bearings qualify as originating under the NAFTA?

The Annex 401 specific rule of origin for HTS Subheading 8482.10 is:

A change to subheading 8482.10 through 8482.80 from any other subheading outside that group, except from Canadian tariff item 8482.99.11 or 8482.99.91, U.S. tariff item 8482.99.10A, 8482.99.30A,

8482.99.50A, or 8482.99.70A, or Mexican tariff item 8482.99.01 or 8482.99.03; or A change to subheading 8482.10 through 8482.80 from Canadian tariff item 8482.99.11 or 8482.99.91, U.S. tariff item 8482.99.10A, 8482.99.30A, 8482.99.50A, 8482.99.70A, or Mexican tariff item 8482.99.01 or 8482.99.03, whether or not there is also a change from any subheading outside that group, provided there is a regional value content of not less than:

(a) 60 percent where the transaction value method is used,

or

(b) 50 percent where the net cost method is used.

As the non-originating components (the finished rings) constitute more than seven percent (7%) of the total cost of the ball bearings, the rings must satisfy one of the two above-mentioned tariff shift requirements. As the finished rings are classified under Canadian HTS Subheading 8482.99.11, the rings do not meet the first tariff shift requirement. However, they do meet the second tariff shift requirement, but then the stated RVC requirement must be met with respect to the ball bearings. Furthermore, as Company B and Company C are related, only the net cost method of determining the RVC is available.

The formula, for determining the RVC of a product, using the net cost method, again, is:

$$RVC = \frac{NC - VNM}{NC} \times 100$$

[Where VNM = value of non-originating materials]

Therefore, with respect to the ball bearings:

$$RVC = \frac{\$2.70 \ (NC) - \$1.45 \ (VNM)}{\$2.70 \ (NC)} \times 100 = 46\%$$

As 46% is less than 50%, the ball bearings are not "originating" and NAFTA favorable duty treatment cannot be claimed under Preference Criterion B upon importation of the ball bearings into Mexico.

However, the producer can accumulate the value of the originating material in the non-originating finished rings. If the value of the originating material in the $1.45 *non*-originating finished ring can be accumulated, perhaps the RVC will be 50% or higher.

Assuming that the information provided by Company A is accurate, the originating value of the non-originating finished ring is $0.15 for originating material, $0.35 for labor, and $0.05 for overhead. The sum of these figures is $0.55. Utilizing the option of accumulation, Company B's costs would then be as follows:

Non-originating value of rings	$0.75
Originating value of rings	$0.55
Originating material	$0.45
Labor (originating)	$0.75
Overhead (originating)	$0.05
	$2.55

And the RVC of the ball bearings would then be:

$$RVC = \frac{\$2.55 \ (NC) - \$0.75}{\$2.55 \ (NC)} \times 100 = 71\%$$

By utilizing the accumulation option, the RVC of the ball bearings is 71%, and the bearings therefore can be considered to be "originating" under Preference Criterion B. Hence, Company B can now so certify the ball bearings for their importation into Mexico by Company C.

RAMIREZ, RULES OF ORIGIN: NAFTA'S HEART, BUT FTAA'S HEARTBURN

29 Brook. J. Int'l L. 617, 650–51 (2004)*

Even though the NAFTA rules of origin serve the three NAFTA partners well, the rules are not without their detractors. Chief among the complaints is that the rules are far too complex, and that paradoxically, the rules actually form a barrier to trade more than they dismantle trade barriers. The complexity of the rules and the cost of resources needed to identify, understand, track and comply with these rules are especially costly for developing nations and their industries. In fact, NAFTA's rules of origin are so complex that they are accompanied by a two hundred page Annex that explains many of the intricate technical details an exporter must examine to determine the origination of a particular product. Studies that have evaluated administrative costs associated with rules of origin compliance reveal that companies spend anywhere from 1.4% to 5.7% of the value of the goods exported. Applying these same percentages to the combined trade between the United States and Canada reveals that the total administrative costs of NAFTA's rules of origin could amount to anywhere from $8 billion to $31 billion a year. There is some evidence that importers and exporters are opting to forgo NAFTA's free trade benefits simply because the costs of compliance with the rules of origin are too high. Both critics and supporters of the FTAA continue to raise concerns that the rules of origin themselves may form obstacles to trade.

* * *

* Copyright © 2004 Brooklyn Journal of International Law. Reprinted with Permission. (Jorge Alberto Ramirez is Associate Professor of Law and Director, International Programs, Texas Tech University School of Law.)

WRIGHT, CUSTOMS SERVICE VERIFICATIONS OF NAFTA PRODUCT ORIGIN
Baker & McKenzie (San Diego).*

As stated in 19 C.F.R Section 181.74, et seq. (1996), a NAFTA Verification conducted by U.S. Customs is a proceeding in which U.S. Customs determines whether a good imported into the U.S. from Mexico or Canada qualifies as a NAFTA-originating good. Note that a Verification can involve a U.S. importer, exporter, or producer or a foreign exporter or producer. It may also involve the verification of the origin of a *material* that is used in the production of a finished good.

Typically, however, U.S. Customs investigates the NAFTA claims of the foreign producer upon whose NAFTA Certificate of Origin (Customs Form ("CF") 434) or other proof of NAFTA-origin a foreign exporter and then a U.S. importer have relied in making their NAFTA claims. In other words, in order to establish that an imported product is not originating under NAFTA, U.S. Customs ultimately must determine that the foreign producer's NAFTA certification is unfounded.

How is a NAFTA Verification Conducted by U.S. Customs?

U.S. Customs may utilize several different methods of conducting a NAFTA Verification. The first method of verifying whether a good is originating under NAFTA is by written questionnaire. As indicated above, this questionnaire is usually sent to the foreign exporter or producer for its completion. The U.S. Customs officials conducting the NAFTA Verification can obtain additional information by telephone, facsimile or any other means agreed to by the entity whose NAFTA claims are the subject of the NAFTA Verification.

U.S. Customs' favored method of conducting a NAFTA Verification, however, is a visit to the offices of the foreign exporter and/or producer. During their visit, the U.S. Customs officials conducting the Verification are entitled to review any and all import/export, manufacturing, and financial records which are relevant to the NAFTA claims at issue. As will be explained in greater detail below, the most important documents in a NAFTA Verification are the NAFTA Certificates of Origin prepared by the exporter and/or producer and a printout of the costed bill of material for the finished product in question. The latter document should indicate the country of origin, the tariff classification, and the cost of each component contained in the finished product. Note that the U.S. Customs officials are also entitled to receive a tour of the manufacturing facility and a detailed description of the manufacturing process regarding the product(s) in question.

Finally, as long as all of the interested parties, including the foreign exporter, the foreign consulate, and the foreign Customs Service agree,

U.S. Customs can use any other method available to obtain the desired information. However, if U.S. Customs bases a negative NAFTA qualification determination on such information, the information must be in writing and must be signed by the party whose NAFTA claims are under review.

* * *

How Should a Company Prepare For a NAFTA Verification?

Each importer and exporter involved in a NAFTA claim is required to maintain in its files for five years each NAFTA Certificate of Origin, or CF 434, which it prepared or upon which it is relying. Therefore, any entity which is the subject of a NAFTA Verification first and foremost should make sure to have on hand for U.S. Customs' inspection the relevant NAFTA Certificates of Origin.

In addition, the exporter and/or producer in a NAFTA Verification is usually asked to provide any and all supporting documentation for each NAFTA Certificate of Origin which it has prepared. Note that U.S. Customs can also ask the importer or exporter to obtain the desired supporting information from the producer.

Most products qualify as originating under NAFTA pursuant to "Preference Criterion B," which is the specific rule of origin for the finished product set forth in Annex 401 of NAFTA. Furthermore, the specific rule of origin for most products requires only that the tariff classifications of the non-NAFTA-originating components contained in the finished product fall outside of the range of tariff classifications stipulated in Annex 401. Therefore, in order to determine whether a product meets a tariff shift requirement, a company should print and review a costed bill of material for the product in question, upon which the cost, country of origin, and tariff classification of each component listed in the bill of material is indicated. Note that this review should take place *prior* to the producer's completion of a NAFTA Certificate of Origin.

Review of such a costed bill of material will reveal whether any of the tariff classifications of the components contained in the product fall within the prohibited range of tariff classifications. If the classification of a component does in fact fall within the prohibited range of tariff classifications, the producer can then prove that the component in question is itself originating under NAFTA and therefore does not have to meet the tariff shift requirement. In order to prove that such a component is originating under NAFTA, however, the producer will have to produce a copy of the NAFTA Certificate of Origin provided by the supplier for that component or other proof that the component is NAFTA-originating.

Finally, the de minimis rule provides that seven percent (7%) or less of the value of the finished product may be composed of non-NAFTA-originating components which do not meet the tariff shift requirement.

If the exporter and/or producer is relying on the de minimis rule to qualify its products for NAFTA favorable duty treatment, however, it should be prepared to document the cost of each component of the finished product, using financial documents, such as purchase orders, invoices, the producer's books of account, inventory reports, and purchase price variance records.

If the specific rule of origin for a product, according to Annex 401 to NAFTA, provides that, in order to be originating under NAFTA, the product must meet a NAFTA content, or "regional value content" ("RVC") requirement rather than, or in addition to, a tariff shift requirement, the producer in a NAFTA Verification should be prepared to prove to U.S. Customs the RVC of the product in question. As is further explained below in Section III, there are two methods of ascertaining the RVC of a product: the transaction value method and the net cost value method. Most maquiladora operations, however, are required to utilize the net cost method of determining the RVC of a product. In any case, in order to document that a product meets a RVC requirement, the producer should be prepared to support its analysis with actual purchase orders, invoices, and other such financial information regarding the value of the finished product and the NAFTA origin and cost of each component contained therein.

NAFTA AND THE AUTOMOTIVE INDUSTRY
USTR Study on the Operation and Effect of NAFTA (July, 1997).

TARIFF CUTS
As required by NAFTA, Mexico reduced its car and light truck tariffs from 20 percent to 10 percent at the beginning of 1994. The remaining duties on light trucks will be phased out by January 1, 1998; duties on cars will be eliminated by January 1, 2003. By January 1, 1998, 75 percent of U.S. automotive parts exports will enter Mexico duty free, with the remaining duties eliminated by January 1, 2003.

The United States eliminated its 2.5 percent tariff on Mexican-built passenger vehicles in 1994. At the same time, the United States cut its 25 percent tariff on Mexican light (pick-up) trucks to 10 percent. The remaining tariff will be eliminated by January 1, 1998. The U.S. 4 percent tariff on cab chassis and the 25 percent tariff on other completed trucks are being phased out over ten years. The majority of Mexican automotive parts entered the United States duty free before NAFTA and remained duty free; remaining duties were either eliminated immediately or will be phased out over five or ten years.

The NAFTA also established stronger North American rules of origin to ensure that automotive products benefitting from tariff reductions are substantially manufactured within the region.

ELIMINATION OF NON-TARIFF BARRIERS
On implementation of NAFTA, Mexico immediately eliminated or reduced significant trade restrictions which had previously served as

incentives to investment in Mexico. For example, Mexico eliminated its trade balancing requirement (from $1.75 of exports for every $1.00 of imports to $0.80 of exports for every $1.00 imported), lowered its local content requirement, and eliminated import quotas on new cars and light trucks. The NAFTA established two transitional import quotas for heavy trucks and buses, one for manufacturers in Mexico and one for companies not manufacturing in Mexico; this sector of the vehicle market will be totally open by January 1, 1998.

TRADE FLOWS

U.S. Exports to Mexico

Intra-company shipments by the Big Three and U.S. parts suppliers account for most of U.S.-Mexican trade. Between 1993 and 1996, the dollar value of U.S. exports of motor vehicles to Mexico increased by 548.7 percent, to $1.3 billion. Exports grew from roughly 17,000 units in 1993 to about 91,000 units in 1996. Had the peso devaluation and resulting dramatic drop in Mexican economic output and domestic consumption not caused the Mexican automotive market to collapse in 1995, it is likely that U.S. exports to Mexico in that year alone would have reached 87,000 units and might have reached well over 100,000 units, with even greater volumes in 1996. Export volume is up 40 percent to a total of 28,721 units for the first quarter of 1997 compared to the first quarter of 1996. The increase in U.S. motor vehicle exports to Mexico reflected the gradual elimination of Mexican tariff and non-tariff trade restrictions, as required by NAFTA, that had previously limited vehicle imports.

U.S. exports of automotive parts to Mexico fell by 3.5 percent from 1993 to 1996. The decline was directly attributable to the sharp retraction of the Mexican economy in 1995. As the Mexican market improves, U.S. parts exports should continue the recovery that began in 1996. Indeed, first quarter 1997 exports of U.S. auto parts grew to $2.2 billion, a 25 percent increase over first quarter 1993. Moreover, with the growth in U.S.-made vehicle sales to Mexico, the opportunities for sales of U.S. aftermarket parts in Mexico should rise.

The U.S. share of the Mexican imported parts market rose 2.4 percentage points in 1994 to 68.7 percent, and rose again in 1995 to 71.2 percent, and increased slightly in 1996 to 71.7 percent. The increases over the first two years were largely due to NAFTA provisions permitting U.S.-assemblers to source a greater percentage of automotive parts from outside Mexico.

U.S. Imports from Mexico

U.S. imports of motor vehicles from Mexico increased from $3.7 billion in 1993 to $11.3 billion in 1996. On average over 50 percent of the content of vehicles exported to the United States from Mexico is U.S.-made, according to industry analysts. Increased U.S. demand for popular sport utility vehicles and pick-up truck models (made in both Mexico and the United States) contributed to the surge in imports during the period. Increased demand for these products generated capacity constraints in the United States that were relieved through increased imports.

U.S. automotive parts imports from Mexico increased from $7.4 billion in 1993 to $11.6 billion in 1996, an increase of 58.4 percent. The growth in imports was largely due to a 6.8 percent increase in U.S. motor vehicle production between 1993 and 1996 reflecting strong U.S. domestic demand for automobiles.

U.S. Trade with Canada

* * *

Total U.S. automotive exports to Canada were $27.5 billion in 1993, rising to $34.4 billion in 1996, an increase of 24.9 percent. Total U.S. automotive imports from Canada were $37.1 billion in 1993 and $46.3 billion in 1996, an increase of 25 percent. The U.S. dollar value of parts exports to Canada grew 20.7 percent from 1993 to 1996. Parts imports from Canada grew 22.4 percent during the period. The value of U.S. motor vehicle exports to Canada grew 33.1 percent from 1993 to 1996, while the value of motor vehicle imports grew 25.9 percent.

INVESTMENT

Big Three major manufacturing plant investments in the United States from 1993 to 1996 totaled $39.1 billion. During the same time, the Big Three invested $3 billion in Mexican facilities.

Big Three passenger vehicle and light truck operating capacity grew by 490,000 units between 1993 and 1996 to a total of 11,037,000 units. In the same period, their capacity in Mexico grew by 241,000 units, reaching a total of 838,000 units. (Operating capacity is a factor of both plant investment and employment levels.) The three companies added 394,000 units to their combined U.S. pick-up truck capacity during the period, compared with 144,000 units in Mexico—even though NAFTA reduces and then eliminates the U.S. 25 percent duty rate on pick-up trucks imported from Mexico.

The U.S. continues to be an alternative market for investment in the automotive sector. Foreign investment in the automotive sector continues to flow into the United States, including: BMW's investment in South Carolina to assemble passenger vehicles; Chrysler's reopening of its St. Louis, Missouri plant to produce minivans; GM's conversion of its Arlington, Texas plant to produce sport utility vehicles; the Mercedes plant in Alabama to assemble vehicles; Nissan's relocation of the production of its Altima engines from Mexico to a new plant in Decherd, Tennessee; and Toyota's construction of a new plant in Princeton, Indiana to build full-size pickups and a new plant in Buffalo, West Virginia to build engines.

While the vast majority of investment in North America is in the United States, some auto manufacturers have invested in Mexico prior to and following the implementation of NAFTA. This investment in Mexico reflects a number of factors. Expanded investments in Mexico by Nissan and VW were aimed at accommodating increased sales in Mexico as well as the addition of new model production. In 1994, BMW and Honda began construction of plants in Mexico to serve the growing Mexican market because Mexican automotive decrees effectively require the two companies to produce in Mexico if they want to sell there. The NAFTA requires Mexico to eliminate this local manufacturing requirement by January 1, 2004.

The NAFTA has created synergies in the North American automotive market that will help ensure a globally competitive U.S. automotive industry. U.S. parts manufacturers have been restructuring their investments in order to rationalize their production in all three countries. Most major parts producers now have plants in all three NAFTA countries. By lowering Mexican local content and trade balancing requirements during the period, NAFTA automotive provisions have stimulated investment in the U.S. market that might otherwise have gone to Mexico.

Note on the Mexican Auto Industry Today*

By the end of 2000, Mexico had become the tenth largest automotive manufacturing nation in the world, with automobile production of almost two million units, representing 2% of world-wide production. . . . Production is expected to increase to approximately 2.5 million vehicles annually by 2005. Dow Jones reported in December 2002 that exports of automobiles from Mexico to Canada grew from about 180,000 vehicles in 1990 to 1.23 million in the first eleven months of 2002. The firms involved in automobile and light truck production, largely for the domestic or the United States markets, included BMW, Daimler–Chrysler, Ford, General Motors, Honda, Mercedes–Benz, Nissan, Toyota and Volkswagen. There are also seventeen heavy-duty truck and bus producers; eight engine producers are also located in Mexico. The approximately 600 firms in the auto parts sector, roughly three fourths of which manufacture for the OEM market, represented approximately $13.5 billion worth of production in 2000.

The Mexican domestic auto market is the second largest in Latin America, after Brazil. There are about 11.3 million vehicles on the road, with an average age of 9.4 years. The automotive industry alone accounted for $32 billion in exports in 2000, and over $23 billion in imports. By 2002, seventy-four percent of total Mexican automotive production was exported, compared to thirty-four in 1990.

Note on Textile and Electronics Origin**

Textiles and apparel have unique rules of origin. Special production requirements are created that protect North American manufacturers. There

---

* Adapted from David A. Gantz, NAFTA, Article 303, PROSEC and the New *Maquiladora* Regime in Mexico, *in* The Auto Pact, Investment, Labour and the WTO 137 (Maureen Irish, ed., 2004). Copyright © 2004 David A. Gantz and Kluwer Law International. Reprinted with permission.

** Adapted from R. Folsom, NAFTA and Free Trade in the Americas (2nd Ed., 2004). Copyright © 2004 West Group. Reprinted with permission.

is a "yarn forward" rule. This requires: (1) use of North American spun yarns; (2) to make North American fabrics; (3) that are cut and sewn into clothing in North America. Similarly, cotton and man-made fiber yarns have to be "fiber forwarded" for North American free trade.

These "triple transformation" rules of origin have already had substantial impact. Mexican imports (heavily comprised of U.S. content) have increasingly displaced East Asian apparel, though less so since 2001, as production shifted to China in particular. Furthermore, Mexico raised its tariffs on non-NAFTA textiles in the wake of its 1995 financial crisis, while continuing NAFTA tariff reductions. The margin of preferential access to Mexico for Canadian and United States textiles was thus magnified. Exports of U.S. textile components to Mexico have also been enhanced by greater allowance under NAFTA of maquiladora apparel sales inside Mexico.

Silk, linen and other fabrics that are scarce in North America are excepted from NAFTA's triple transformation rules, but must still be cut and sewn in North America. Textile products with less than 7 percent non-originating material measured by weight can also be freely traded. This amount is treated as *de minimis*. Some non-qualifying textiles and clothing may be preferentially traded under quotas within NAFTA. U.S. manufacturers have complained about Canadian exports of wool suits under preferential quotas.

Electronics

NAFTA created some unique rules of origin for consumer electronics products. These rules are based on changes in tariff classifications that contain particular components. For example, in order to qualify for free trade, color television sets with screens over fourteen inches must contain a North American-made color picture tube. Since 1999 such color television sets must also contain, among other things, North American amplifiers, tuners and power supplies.

For a video cassette recorder to qualify for preferential treatment under NAFTA, it must contain a North American circuit board. For a microwave oven, all the major parts, except the magnetron, must be made in the North American countries. Computers must contain a North American motherboard.

The initial impact of NAFTA on the electronics and computer industries was significant. United States, Japanese and Korean investment in electronics production facilities in Mexico has grown, especially in the manufacture of those components that convey NAFTA origin. Mexican purchases of U.S. electronic components and finished goods produced in maquiladoras are up substantially. However, since 2001, there has actually be some disinvestment from Mexico as firms move their electronic plants to China and other low cost manufacturing centers.

NAFTA AND THE TEXTILE INDUSTRY
USTR Study on the Operation and Effect of NAFTA (July, 1997).

* * *

To qualify for special tariff and quota treatment, goods generally must be produced from yarn made in a NAFTA country ("yarn forward"). The NAFTA includes exceptions to this general rule, however, intended to give producers flexibility to import products when needed. One example is a system of "tariff preference levels" established in NAFTA under which yarn, fabric, and apparel that is made in North America but does not meet the yarn forward test may nevertheless be accorded preferential duty treatment up to agreed annual import levels.

TRADE FLOWS

* * *

The NAFTA has prompted a shift in the growth of textile and apparel trade from the Far East to NAFTA countries. The NAFTA has made Mexico and Canada the top two suppliers of textiles and apparel for the United States, benefitting U.S. producers whose fiber, yarn, and fabric is incorporated in their products. Between 1993 and 1996, total U.S. imports of textile and apparel products from China, Taiwan, Hong Kong and Korea—the major Far East suppliers—declined by 13 percent on a quantity basis while imports of textiles and apparel from Canada and Mexico more than doubled. Because NAFTA's strict rules limiting preferential duty and quota treatment to products made in North America—and given growing regional integration in the sector—these imports contain increasing amounts of U.S. textile components. This is not the case with imports from Asia, which use very limited quantities of U.S. components.

* * *

NAFTA, ARTICLE 303 AND PROSEC*

NAFTA ushered in significant changes in the *maquiladora* regime, beginning January 1, 1994. On the positive side, the most important of these changes included the reduction and elimination of customs duties and non-tariff restrictions on "originating goods" made in Mexico and exported to the United States, and a new regime for protection of foreign investment. On the negative side, NAFTA Article 303 required the elimination of the Mexican duty waiver for items imported from non-NAFTA sources that are used to manufacture goods for export to the United States and Canada.

* * *

Elimination of Duty Waiver Programs Tied to Exports. Most significantly, as of January 1, 2001, NAFTA imposed significant restrictions on duty waiver or remission programs in Mexico. These restrictions affected the importation of non-NAFTA items used in production of goods for

* Adapted from David A. Gantz, NAFTA, Article 303, PROSEC and the New *Maquiladora* Regime in Mexico, *in* The Auto Pact, Investment, Labour and the WTO 137 (Maureen Irish, ed., 2004). Copyright © 2004 David A. Gantz and Kluwer Law International. Reprinted with permission.

export to the other NAFTA countries. At the same time, NAFTA also eliminated the restrictions on *maquiladora* sales in the domestic market. One major rationale for the elimination of duty waiver programs is that they create unfair competition between Mexican goods produced for the U.S. market and goods produced in the United States, also for the U.S. market.

For example, suppose that identical color television receivers are manufactured at two plants, one in San Diego, the other in Tijuana, Baja California, seventeen miles away. Assume that the entire production for both plants is for the U.S. market; that the manufacturing cost (exclusive of duties on parts and components) is $100 (the same in both plants); and that parts imported from Asia represent $20 worth of total manufacturing costs. If the duty on Asian parts is 10% in both Mexico and the United States, the total manufacturing cost would be $102 ($100 plus 10% x $20) in each plant. However, if the $2 in Mexican duties are remitted under the *maquiladora* regime, the television made in Tijuana will enjoy a production cost advantage of $2 when competing against the television made in San Diego.

This is a perfectly logical scenario if one assumes that, under normal circumstances, competition in the United States market is between U.S. made goods and Mexican goods. However, in many instances, this is not the case. For all practical purposes, there are no televisions made in the United States, and most apparel and footwear are also imported. Thus, in many sectors, the competition within the United States market is between Mexico and China or Mexico and the Dominican Republic. While goods from China and the Dominican Republic may be dutiable when entering the U.S. market (although many such products, such as most consumer electronics and computers are not), Chinese and other foreign manufacturers continue to enjoy duty waiver programs in their own countries. Where U.S. most-favored-nation duties are low or zero (effectively eliminating any tariff benefit as a result of manufacturing in Mexico), Mexican firms risk a loss of their competitive position. Their competitors in those countries do not have to pay the duties on imported components, e.g., the $2.00 for customs duties on the non-NAFTA television set parts in the previous example.

The other major rationale for Article 303 is to increase the North American, particularly Mexican, content of goods made in Mexico. As noted earlier, the NAFTA rules of origin are also designed to facilitate this objective. One reason for the seven-year grace period for the ban on duty waivers was to permit major Mexican producers and their suppliers to establish materials, parts and components production facilities in Mexico. It was anticipated that rules of origin requiring a high regional value, coupled with an elimination of duty waiver with the corresponding penalty (in import duties) for continuing to import parts and components from outside North America, would be a powerful double incentive for regional sourcing.

Moreover, waiver of duties for imported machinery and equipment, if such importations are tied to the exportation of finished goods, would be a violation of Mexico's obligations under the WTO Agreement on Subsidies and Countervailing Measures. The SCM Agreement generally prohibits export and import substitution subsidies, as of January 1, 2003, for developing country Members such as Mexico. This requirement has precluded Mexico from continuing its long-standing practice of permitting indefinite deferral of customs duties on imported machinery and equipment for use in the *maquiladoras*. However, under GATT, there is an explicit exception for "[t]he exemption of an exported product from duties or taxes borne by the like product when destined for domestic consumption, or the remission of such duties or taxes in amounts not in excess of those which have accrued...." Thus, the elimination of duty waivers for imported materials, parts and components used in the manufacture of goods for export—as distinct from machinery and equipment—is dictated by Mexico's NAFTA obligations, not by GATT 1994 or the SCM Agreement.

* * *

These restrictions do *not* apply to originating materials, parts and components; or machinery and equipment imported from other NAFTA nations; or to items used in the production of finished goods exports to non-NAFTA nations. This is a very large percentage, since by some estimates 90% of the materials, parts, and components used by the *maquiladoras* are sourced in the NAFTA region. The impact of Article 303 primarily falls on those important sectors that depend extensively on non-NAFTA exports, particularly textiles and apparel and electronics. However, auto parts are also affected where non-NAFTA sources for items used in their manufacture are significant. On the one hand, as noted earlier, automobiles require a high (62.5%) regional value content, and the origin of the parts of specific subassemblies is also traced. Nevertheless, 37.5% of the content of automobiles need *not* originate in North America, giving the automobile and auto parts manufacturers some leeway in sourcing parts and components from outside North America if costs are significantly lower.

Because of these requirements the Mexican Government was faced with a very serious dilemma. First, Mexico was obligated under NAFTA, as of January 1, 2001, and the WTO's Agreement on Subsidies and Countervailing Measures, as of January 1, 2003, to eliminate the most significant element of the *maquiladora* program, the connection between duty waiver or remission programs, and the obligation to export, as indicated above. Secondly, Mexico did not want to take any steps that would encourage the *maquiladoras* to move their operations out of Mexico, either to areas of the Caribbean or Central America where the limitation on duty waivers would not apply, or to Asia, with its generally lower wage costs *and* the absence of duty waiver limitations. The United States had every reason to share this second objective.

Mexico's third dilemma relates to the fact that the elimination of duty waivers was designed in part, as noted earlier, to encourage investment and job creation in parts and components production. If fewer non-NAFTA parts and components are imported, this would lead to a higher North American (read "Mexican") content of goods assembled in Mexico for the United States and Canadian markets.

Mexico's Solution. There is no public information relating to whether the governments of the United States, Canada and Mexico seriously considered the possibility of *de facto* acceptance by the United States and Canada of even a temporary suspension of the requirements of Article 303. Some groups in Mexico pressed this option with the Mexican government. The Border Trade Alliance, a group representing border interests in the United States and Mexico, even lobbied the U.S. Trade Representative's office, requesting "that the three NAFTA partners reevaluate Article 303 as to its original intent per the NAFTA agreement versus its actual impact," and urging Article 303's suspension during this study process.

Similarly, there is no indication that Mexico considered reducing its MFN tariffs—averaging over 10% and peaking at 35%—to or near zero across the board, as Canada had earlier. The *maquiladora* sector is broad, but it is not the entire economy. An across-the-board reduction or elimination of MFN duties might have been costly in terms of lost customs revenues. Ultimately, Mexico's preparations for the selective duty reduction program that took effect January 1, 2001 began by November 14, 1998, when the first proposed special sector (PROSEC) decree was published. However, this initially promising early start was followed by months of silence, and the final rules for the PROSEC regime were not published until the last minute, on December 31, 2000.

* * *

Most significantly, this special sector program–PROSEC–severed the connection between the availability of duty waivers and any requirement that all or a portion of finished goods production be exported. The favorable tariff rates applied to designated import items whether the finished goods were exported or sold on the domestic market. The *maquiladora* sector was preserved as a separate regime, but without the benefits of duty free importation of materials, parts and components and machinery and equipment. Those benefits, to the extent available, are now available only under the separate, PROSEC mechanism. Presumably, such duty waivers would be legal under NAFTA and the SCM Agreement, so long as they were not conditioned on exports. This solution, as noted above, is in two parts.

* * *

The PROSEC regime is probably most logically viewed as a replacement system with many of the same features as the prior duty waiver regime, without the connection to exports *per se*. However, PROSEC does possess a few very important differences and imposes a totally new layer of administrative requirements. First, until January 1, 2001, a *maquiladora* could be assured that essentially all of its non-NAFTA import items would be subject to duty waivers. Under the prior rules, the principal incentive for purchasing some materials, parts and components in North America was to comply with the NAFTA rules of origin and, thus, enjoy reduced duty or duty free entry into the United States or Canadian markets. However, under the PROSEC Decree, most *maquiladoras* can import most of their non-NAFTA import items duty-free, or at 5%, but *only* if they are properly registered for the PROSEC program and *only* if the non-NAFTA import items and their finished products are specifically listed in the PROSEC Decree as amended.

Thus, there are two lists under the Decree, one for finished products, the second for specific parts and components and machinery and equipment. (PROSEC Decree, D.O., Dec. 30, 2000, arts. 4, 5.) The twenty-two sectors subject to the PROSEC Decree are the following:

electrical industry	electronics	furniture
toys and sporting goods	footwear	mining and metallurgy
capital goods	photographic equipment	agricultural machinery
chemicals	rubber and plastics	iron and steel
transportation (exc. auto-motive)	pharmaceutical products	paper and cartons
wood	leather and fur	automotive and auto parts
textiles and garments	chocolate and candy	coffee
miscellaneous		

However, in order for a firm to qualify for PROSEC benefits, its specific product or products must be listed in Article 4, and import items must be listed in Article 5. In each case, the listing is by harmonized tariff number (e.g., under item 8528.10 for television receivers).

Second, as noted earlier, eligibility for PROSEC benefits is not automatic, even for firms in the industrial sectors specified. Each firm seeking the benefits of the Decree must register and be approved by the Secretariat of Economy (SECON), with the concurrence of the Secretary of the Treasury and Public Credit (SHCP). SECON is required to issue an authorization within twenty days of application. An annual report and certain other administrative steps are also required.

Initially, some (including the author) were skeptical that the only firms seeking PROSEC benefits would be the *maquiladoras*, making the legal separation of the *maquiladora* regime and the PROSEC regime largely a sham. However, November 2001 data indicates that of the 2,963 firms registered for PROSEC benefits, 1456 are *maquiladoras*, 1,159 are registered under the other, similar *Pitex* export regime, and 348, or approximately 12%, are non-exporters whose products are presumably confined to the domestic market. The significant number of non-exporting firms benefitting from PROSEC obviously helps Mexican authorities demonstrate publicly that the new, bifurcated system is not a ruse that complies with the letter, but not with the spirit, of Article 303.

* * *

Firms that import many parts and components were initially concerned that SECON would take a long time to fine-tune the import lists subject to favorable tariff treatment. In the meantime, such *maquiladoras* would see their manufacturing costs rise significantly because of customs duty liabilities. While, as noted earlier, most of these concerns have not been realized, the uncertainty of a system where the government could, with little notice, make imported parts and components subject to import duties simply by removing the items from the PROSEC list is a significant concern. In September 2002, the Mexican authorities determined to review the PROSEC tariff codes for the electronics industry at least annually; when modifications are to be made, they will not become effective until 180 days after they have been published in the *Diario Oficial*. This change in procedure decreases the level of uncertainty faced by firms operating under PROSEC, but does not eliminate it entirely.

The willingness of SECON to add or delete items from the list is extremely important, but may represent difficult choices for the government. SECON is caught in a "Catch–22": if SECON willingly grants all requested additions of import items to the reduced-duty/duty free list under PROSEC, they will please the finished goods manufacturers, but may hurt Mexican (or U.S.) parts and components manufacturers who produce items that compete with Asian imports, although often at slightly higher prices. Favoring the finished goods manufactures helps to encourage them to maintain or expand their facilities in Mexico, but jeopardizes existing and future investment in materials, parts and components production, with the corresponding loss of jobs, technology transfer, etc. On the other hand, if SECON is unduly restrictive in approving items for inclusion in PROSEC, even when the items of the requisite quality and price cannot reasonably sourced in Mexico or elsewhere in North America, SECON risks encouraging those firms to move their manufacturing operations elsewhere.

GRUBEN, BEYOND THE BORDER: HAVE MEXICO'S MAQUILADORAS BOTTOMED OUT?*

Recent changes in the dollar cost of doing business in Mexico may explain not only some recent problems of the maquiladoras, but also their recent upturn. Between October 1998 and March 2002, the inflation-adjusted value of the dollar weakened against the Mexican peso by 28 percent. At the same time, the dollar strengthened against the currencies of Malaysia, Singapore, Sri Lanka, Thailand and the Philippines. These changes in the real exchange rate lowered the dollar cost of buying products in the five Asian countries, while raising it in Mexico. In Mexico, average manufacturing wages in dollar terms rose 45 percent between 1998 and 2002 but fell in Singapore and Sri Lanka. Since March 2002, however, the real value of the dollar has strengthened 17 percent

* Southwest Economy, Jan/Feb 2004.   Dallas. Reprinted with permission.
Copyright © 2004 Federal Reserve Bank of

against the peso, lowering the cost of doing business in Mexico. Meanwhile, the dollar has appreciated only slightly against the currencies of China, Malaysia and the Philippines and declined against those of Sri Lanka, Singapore and Thailand.

SECTORAL DIFFERENCES

More than 80 percent of the Mexican maquiladora employment declines in 2001 and 2002 can be explained by changes in U.S. aggregate demand and increases in the cost of doing business in Mexico. Eighty percent, however, is not 100 percent. Clearly, more is required to explain maquiladora fluctuations than U.S. industrial production, the real exchange rate and wage rate fluctuations.

Employment in both electronics and textiles and apparel maquiladoras grew faster than the *all other* group [1998–2000], but it also fell harder after reaching its peaks. By October 2003, employment in both industries was markedly below September 1998 levels. Although October 2003 employment in all other industries was also well below its peak, it was well above September 1998—farther above it, in fact, than employment in textiles and apparel and electronics was below it. Moreover, total maquiladora employment seems to have bottomed out. The relevant question here is whether the recovery of *all other* and perhaps electronics will offset the continued fall off in textiles and apparel.

Much of what made the two industries sink farther than *all other* reflects government policy. For textiles and apparel, the big policy change came in January 1994, when the North American Free Trade Agreement gave this industry a new set of rules for trade with the United States and Canada. Before NAFTA, China was the United States' principal source of textiles and apparel products. The special tariff breaks textiles and apparel received under NAFTA pushed Mexico past China to become the United States' No. 1 supplier. But in 2000, the United States gave some of the same trade openings to Caribbean Basin Initiative countries (which include the nations of Central America). In 2001, the United States extended other openings to China when it joined the World Trade Organization. Both China and the Caribbean Basin Initiative countries overtook Mexico in textile and apparel exports to the United States. Mexico seems unlikely to be able to compete again in the lowest wage, low-skill labor markets that much of this industry occupies. [Authors' note: Assuming that the United States—Central American Free Trade Agreement enters into force January 1, 2006, the five Central American nations and the Dominican Republic, all of which have a thriving apparel industry, will enjoy access to the U.S. textile, electronics and other markets similar to that of Mexico.]

The story of the electronics maquiladora employment fluctuations is more convoluted. The U.S. recession of 2000–2001 began with a downturn in U.S. electronics-related industries associated with a worldwide slump in these industries. The relation between the downturn in U.S. industries and their Mexican counterparts is clear. Compounding the industry downturn, changes in real exchange rates and dollar-denominated manufacturing wages in Mexico during October 2000 through March 2002 were affecting the cost of doing business.

In 2001, a new NAFTA rule went into effect that made maquiladora operations more difficult, costly and uncertain in Mexico. NAFTA Article 303 outlawed tariff rebates for imports from non-NAFTA countries. For firms that imported from Asia for assembly in Mexico and subsequent export to the United States—a long-time practice of special importance to the electronics maquiladoras. Article 303 made Mexican operations more expensive overnight. Firms began to take their operations elsewhere.

The Mexican government attempted to counteract these tariff cost increases with subsidies administered through a program known as Prosec. Some maquiladora managers, complaining that Prosec's policies were mercurial and ad hoc, relocated their operations in spite of the program. Also, because electronics maquiladoras are especially sensitive to exchange rate fluctuations, the real exchange rate appreciation of 1998–2002 may have affected these plants more than others. Finally, the development of input supply chains in electronics made China a stronger competitor.

Outlook for Maquiladoras

While most of Mexico's maquiladora downturn in 2001 and 2002 can be explained by reductions in U.S. demand and cost-of-doing-business changes expressed through wage and exchange rate fluctuations, a significant share of the downturn is due to changes in trade policy and increased competition abroad in terms of supply networks and input costs. As the U.S. recovery continues apace in the wake of its 2000–2001 recession, so should the resuscitation of Mexico's maquilas. The recent softening of the Mexican peso has not done much so far to make maquiladoras come back, but it helped to stanch their decline, and its more positive effects may still be ahead.

Policy changes raise questions as to when or whether the maquiladoras will soon regain their peak levels of employment or output, but it is hard not to think that Mexico's maquiladoras have already bottomed out, even with further declines in Mexico's garment industry.

Note on the Harmonized System

The Harmonized System is described by the World Customs Organization as follows:

> The Harmonized Commodity Description and Coding System, generally referred to as "Harmonized System" or simply "HS", is a multipurpose international product nomenclature developed by the World Customs Organization (WCO). It comprises about 5,000 commodity groups, each identified by a six digit code, arranged in a legal and logical structure and is supported by well-defined rules to achieve uniform classification. The system is used by more than 190 countries and economies as a basis

for their Customs tariffs and for the collection of international trade statistics. Over 98% of the merchandise in international trade is classified in terms of the HS.

The HS contributes to the harmonization of customs and trade procedures, and the non-documentary trade data interchange in connection with such procedures, thus reducing the costs related to international trade. It is also extensively used by governments, international organizations and the private sector for any other purposes such as internal taxes, trade policies, monitoring of controlled goods, rules of origin, freight tariffs, transport statistics, price monitoring, quota controls, compilation of national accounts, and economic research and analysis. The HS is thus a universal economic language and code for goods, and an indispensable tool for international trade.*

The general nomenclature for the HS as adopted in the United States (HTSUS) is provided in NAFTA, Annex 401, reproduced below. Of particular interest here is the "Special" sub-column of Column 1, which includes, e.g., the preferential tariff rates for goods imported from Mexico ("MX") and Canada ("CA") under NAFTA and Chile under the FTA ("CL"), as well as those imported under special programs such as the Generalized System of Preferences ("A"), the Caribbean Basin Economic Recovery Act ("E") and the Andean Trade Preference Act ("J"). (The "General" sub-column provides "MFN" tariffs; column 2 tariffs, charged on imports from the handful of nations that are not WTO members or parties to bilateral trade agreements with the United States (e.g., North Korea), are the notorious "Hawley—Smoot" tariffs of 1930.)

HARMONIZED TARIFF SCHEDULE of the United States (2004)

Heading/ Subheading	Stat. Suffix	Article Description	Units of Quantity	Rates of Duty 1 General	Rates of Duty 1 Special	2
9008		Image projectors, other than cinematographic; photographic (other than cinematographic) enlargers and reducers; parts and accessories thereof:				
9008.10.00	00	Slide projectors	No.	7%	Free (A, CA, CL, E, IL, J, JO, MX) 5.2% (SG)	45%
9008.20		Microfilm, microfiche or other microform readers, whether or not capable of producing copies:				
9008.20.40	00	Capable of producing copies ..	No.	Free		35%
9008.20.80	00	Other	No.	3.5%	Free (A, CA, CL, E, IL, J, JO, MX, SG)	45%
9008.30.00	00	Other image projectors	No.	4.6%	Free (A, CA, CL, E, IL, J, JO, MX, SG)	45%
9008.40.00	00	Photographic (other than cinematographic) enlargers and reducers	No.	Free		20%
9008.90		Parts and accessories:				
9008.90.40	00	Of image producers, other than cinematographic	X	Free		35%
9008.90.80	00	Other	X	2.9%	Free (A, CA, CL, E, IL, J, JO, MX, SG)	20%

* Copyright © 1997–2000 World Customs Organization. Reprinted with permission.   See http://www.wcoomd.org/ie/En/Topics_Issues/topics_issues.html.

NAFTA, ANNEX 401

SPECIFIC RULES OF ORIGIN

Section A—General Interpretative Note

For purposes of interpreting the rules of origin set out in this Annex:

(a) the specific rule, or specific set of rules, that applies to a particular heading, subheading or tariff item is set out immediately adjacent to the heading, subheading or tariff item;

(b) a rule applicable to a tariff item shall take precedence over a rule applicable to the heading or subheading which is parent to that tariff item;

(c) a requirement of a change in tariff classification applies only to nonoriginating materials;

* * *

(g) the following definitions apply:

chapter means a chapter of the Harmonized System;

heading means the first four digits in the tariff classification number under the Harmonized System;

section means a section of the Harmonized System;

subheading means the first six digits in the tariff classification number under the Harmonized System; and

tariff item means the first eight digits in the tariff classification number under the Harmonized System as implemented by each Party.

Section B—Specific Rules of Origin

* * *

9008.10–40   A change to subheadings 9008.10 through 9008.40 from any other heading; or

A change to subheadings 9008.10 through 9008.40 from subheading 9008.90, whether or not there is also a change from any other heading, provided there is a regional value content of not less than:

(a) 60 percent where the transaction value method is used, or

(b) 50 percent where the net cost method is used.

9008.90   A change to subheading 9008.90 from any other heading.

Questions and Comments

1. Tariff-shift rules of origin depend upon the International Convention on the Harmonized Commodity Description and Coding System, known as the "Harmonized System"(HS). Canada, Mexico and the United States have adopted this classification of goods system, which is why the excerpt on image projectors is titled the "Harmonized Tariff Schedule of the United States". What are the HS classification headings for image projectors? For parts thereof?

2. Tariff-shifts concern "non-originating material". What material is that? *See* Article 415 and 401. If all the material in a good is NAFTA "originating", do tariff-shifts matter? *See* Article 401 (a) and (c).

3. What is a tariff-shift rule of origin? *See* Article 401(b), Annex 401 and the NAFTA Certificate of Origin Preference Criterion B. Why are tariff-shifts the core NAFTA rule for non-originating materials? *See* McCall.

4. Read the NAFTA Annex 401 rules of origin for image projectors and parts thereof (which are identified by their HS headings). What tariff-shifts are required for non-originating materials in these rules?

5. When image projector parts are tariff-shifted to image projectors (say by assembly), what *additional* NAFTA rule of origin applies? *See* Annex 401.

6. Now let's examine value-content rules. What does "regional value content (RVC)" mean? *See* Article 402. There are two methods of calculating RVC, the transaction value method and the net cost method. Do you understand the differences between these methods? *See* also Article 415 (Definitions). Note that generally speaking the exporter or producer of the goods get to choose between these two methods of calculating RVC. *See* Article 402(1). Which would you generally choose and why?

7. Why does NAFTA Annex 401 sometimes, as with image projectors, require RVC in addition to a tariff-shift to qualify goods as originating? For some goods, RVC alone is the test of origin. *See* Article 401(d).

8. What de minimis non-originating content rule is established in Article 405? Does this rule override Article 401 (Originating Goods)?

9. Examine the NAFTA Certificate of Origin in the materials. This is the United States version of the common certificate contemplated by Article 501. *See* particularly the Preference Criteria A through F. Do these criteria correspond to your understanding of Chapter 4 of the NAFTA agreement?

Note that you will need the HS Tariff Classification Number to complete this Certificate. Why are the addresses and tax identification numbers of the exporter, importer and producer required? Which of these three parties is in the best position to know the origin of the goods? Who signs the Certificate and why? *See* Article 501. Who relies on its veracity? *See* Article 502.

10. Proving that goods are originating for NAFTA purposes involves a lot of record keeping. Who is responsible for maintaining those records and for how long? *See* Article 505. Ramirez suggests that sometimes the costs of record keeping and origin compliance may exceed NAFTA's free trade benefits. When is this most likely to be true?

11.   What is a NAFTA "verification of origin" proceeding? *See* Article 506 and the second excerpt by Wright. What powers do the customs authorities have in conducting such proceedings? What rights do exporters and producers have? *See* also Article 510.

12.   What is an "advance ruling"? *See* Article 509. When might advance rulings on NAFTA origin prove advantageous? For Volkswagen's exports of Beetles from Mexico to the U.S., who issues the advance ruling? Are advance rulings binding on the relevant customs authority? *See* Article 509 (4) and (6). Can they be revoked or modified? *See* Article 509(9).

13.   As a customs official, you will want to pay special attention to Article 510 (Review and Appeal), since your decision may well be appealed to the Court of International Trade. Note that there are Uniform NAFTA Regulations on interpreting, applying and administering Chapters 4 and 5. *See* Article 511.

14.   Please issue your rulings in the cases that have come before you in this problem.

15.   NAFTA's rules of origin have had a major impact on Asian-owned Mexican maquiladoras. Why is the impact on Asian owned maquiladoras more significant than on U.S. or Canadian owned firms? If you are Mexican legal counsel for Japanese electronics firms in Tijuana, Baja California, what strategy would you recommend for dealing with NAFTA Article 303 and PROSEC? See second Gantz excerpt.

16.   Perhaps because of the difficulties faced by Mexican *maquiladoras* (and their U.S. owners) in complying with the Article 303 requirements and the new administrative hurdles imposed by PROSEC at a time when Mexican competitiveness vis a vis China is declining, the Chile FTA and CAFTA contain no provision similar to NAFTA Article 303. Thus, as long as they meet their obligations under the WTO Agreement on Subsidies and Countervailing Duties (which permits duty remission for materials, parts and components but not for machinery and equipment), the United States does not require the FTA members to eliminate this important competitive benefit.

17.   Mexico presently has free trade agreements with Bolivia, Chile, Colombia, Peru, Venezuela, the Central American nations and the European Union, and has completed negotiations with Japan. It is negotiating others within Latin America. These agreements create an opportunity for producers of goods in Mexico, especially in maquiladoras, to enjoy duty free status for their exports to Latin American as well as for North American trade. The key to seizing this opportunity are the rules of origin under Mexico's free trade agreements. These rules are complex and not uniform. Many of them roughly track the NAFTA rules of origin with most transaction value regional content requirements ranging between 45 and 55 percent.

18.   The NAFTA rules of origin are subject to modification by agreement of the NAFTA Parties. Rules of origin relating to alcoholic beverages, petroleum and topped crude, pearl jewelry, headphones with microphones, chassis fitted with engines, photocopiers an certain food additive emulsifiers were modified in 2003. Those relating to spices and seasonings, precious metals, speed dry controllers, printed circuit assemblies, household appli-

ances (except televisions), loudspeakers, thermostats and toys were modified in 2004. The reasons given were to permit more foreign content and streamline administrative procedures that are required of importers to demonstrate that a product is entitled to NAFTA duty benefits. A NAFTA Working Group is pursuing further rules of origin liberalization in the areas of chemicals, pharmaceuticals, plastics and rubber, motor vehicles and their parts, footwear and copper, and for items where the three NAFTA Parties have a common MFN rate of duty of zero (including most electronic products). (The current NAFTA rules of origin are incorporated in the "General Notes" section of the Harmonized Tariff Schedules of the United States (updated in January and July each year), available at http://www.usitc.gov/taffairs.htm#HTS.)

19. In May 2004, the U.S. government imposed anti-dumping duties of between 5.22 percent to 78.45 percent on color television imports from China. Almost immediately, several Chinese producers announced that they would move their television production for the U.S. market from China to Mexico (where there are no AD duties outstanding against televisions). What factors, other than anti-dumping duties, should have influenced this decision? (Ironically, the establishment of a thriving color television industry in Mexico—at least 3–4 years prior to NAFTA—owned by Korean and Japanese firms was stimulated in significant part by anti-dumping duty orders then in effect in the United States against televisions imported from Korea and Japan!)

PROBLEM 5.2 NONTARIFF TRADE BARRIERS AND NAFTA: PRODUCT STANDARDS AND TRADER JANE

SECTION I. THE SETTING

Trader Jane, Inc. is a California-based import-export trading company. Trader Jane does not sell to the public. Its specialty is moving goods across borders and delivering them to retailers. The profit margins are thin, so volume is the key to success for Trader Jane.

NAFTA has opened up new trading opportunities which Trader Jane has been quick to seize. It is generally pleased with the removal of nearly all tariffs on trade between Canada and the United States (although it is concerned that some high tariffs remain on agricultural goods formerly subject to quotas). Lately, Trader Jane has turned its focus to Mexico where almost all tariffs have now been eliminated, again with some exceptions for agricultural products (corn, beans). What impacts Trader Jane critically are nontariff trade barriers (NTBs). These barriers are most often encountered in product standards, i.e., regulatory rules governing the production and sale of goods. As Trader Jane sees it, NTBs are more pernicious then tariffs. If an importer has an NTB problem, the goods can be seized and removed from the market. Unfortunately, of late, Trader Jane has been confronted with several NTB problems.

First, in its exporting role, Trader Jane recently shipped to Mexico several containers of cellular phones made in the USA. This equipment conforms to all U.S. product standards regarding safety and technical operation. But the goods have been withdrawn from sale in Mexico and their importation is now prohibited because (it is alleged) they do not meet the requirements of Mexico's federal telecommunications equipment "norma" (regulation). Mexico seems particularly concerned with health hazards associated with "electromagnetic fields" (EMF), sometimes referred to as "electrosmog."

This is a very technical dispute, with the Mexican authorities asserting that several of the parameters for such equipment have not been met. You would have to be an engineer to know whether this is true or not. Trader Jane does not employ any engineers, but it may lose a big client if it cannot get this problem solved. The U.S. manufacturer of the cell phones, one of world's largest, is equally upset. Each had thought that NAFTA had taken care of these types of problems.

Second, in its importing role, Trader Jane has just bought several containers of long-life milk from a Quebec manufacturer. Long-life milk is produced by subjecting regular milk to ultra-high temperatures and then, once cooled, packaging it in hermetically sealed containers. Long-life milk lasts 6 to 12 months at room temperature. In the United States, many campers and boaters use long-life milk.

There are Quebec regulations governing the production and handling of long-life milk. These regulations are particularly strict since, obviously, milk is a food product. In the United States, production of milk is jointly controlled by the federal government and the states. This is done principally through an organization known as the National Conference on Interstate Milk Shipments (NCIMS). This voluntary organization is comprised of all state and local milk control agencies and the federal Food and Drug Administration (FDA). Any member of NCIMS must adopt the "Pasteurized Milk Ordinance" (PMO). This model ordinance was developed after extensive scientific research and studies by the Public Health Service of the FDA. It has been incorporated into the laws of the 50 U.S. states, the District of Columbia and Puerto Rico. It is administered by those jurisdictions through a milk certification program.

Under a cooperative program with the Food and Drug Administration which governs interstate milk shipments, all milk certified as meeting the PMO can be sold freely throughout the United States, the District of Columbia and Puerto Rico. Trader Jane's problem is that the long-life milk it bought in Quebec at a very good price in Canadian dollars is said to fail the PMO standards. Once again, Trader Jane thought that NAFTA had taken care of all that.

You are an attorney with a law firm known for its international trade expertise. Trader Jane turns to you for advice and counsel.

SECTION II. FOCUS OF CONSIDERATION

In this problem, we focus upon nontariff trade barriers. Such barriers are commonly found in product or service standards relating to safety, health, consumer protection or the environment. Regulatory laws of this kind are often adopted with little or no consideration given to their external impact. The authorities believe they are acting in the public interest and proceed accordingly. As regionalization and globalization have expanded economic activity, nontariff trade barrier restraints have become the premier problem.

The negotiators of NAFTA were well aware of NTBs. Section B of Chapter 7 of the NAFTA agreement focuses on health regulations associated with pests, diseases, food additives and food contaminants. These are known as NAFTA's provisions on "Sanitary and Phytosanitary Measures" (SPS). Trader Jane's problems with long-life milk fall within their scope. Chapter 9 of the NAFTA agreement is concerned with product safety, health, environmental or consumer protection regulations other than SPS. Thus Chapter 9, titled "Standards–Related Measures" (SRM), covers a much broader range of goods and services, including the cell phones exported by Trader Jane to Mexico.

Section B of Chapter 7 and Chapter 9 of the NAFTA agreement are essential to an analysis of this problem. These materials are found in the Documents Supplement.

SECTION III. READINGS, QUESTIONS AND COMMENTS

PART A. SPS STANDARDS

FOLSOM, GORDON AND SPANOGLE, INTERNATIONAL BUSINESS TRANSACTIONS HORNBOOK
Chapter 14 (2nd Ed. 2001)*

There are numerous nontariff trade barriers applicable to United States imports. Many of these barriers arise out of federal or state safety and health regulations. Others concern the environment, consumer protection, product standards and government procurement. Many of the relevant rules were created for legitimate consumer and public protection reasons. They were often created without extensive consideration of their international impact as potential nontariff trade barriers. Nevertheless, the practical impact of legislation of this type is to ban the importation of nonconforming products from the United States market. Thus, unlike tariffs which can always be paid and unlike quotas which permit a certain amount of goods to enter the United States market, nontariff trade barriers have the potential to totally exclude foreign exports.

The diversity of regulatory approaches to products and the environment makes it extremely difficult to generalize about nontariff trade barriers. The material below concerns health restrictions relating to food, safety restrictions relating to consumer products, environmental auto emissions standards and selected other NTBs. These areas have been chosen merely as examples of the types of NTB barriers to the United States market, and are by no means exhaustive. Special NTB rules apply in the context of the Canada–U.S. Free Trade Agreement and the NAFTA. Sanitary and phytosanitary measures (SPS) dealing with food safety and animal and plant health regulations are the subject of a WTO Uruguay Round accord.

FOOD PRODUCTS

All foods imported into the United States are subject to inspection for their wholesomeness, freedom from contamination, and compliance with labeling requirements (including the 1993 nutritional labeling rules). This examination is conducted by the Food and Drug Administration using samples submitted to it by the United States Customs Service. If these tests result in a finding that the food products cannot be imported into the United States, they must be exported or destroyed. Milk and cream imports are the subject of special permit requirements administered by the Department of Health and Human Services. Basically, the Department certifies that foreign producers operate under sanitary conditions. There is a broad web of federal rules governing food products, including food imports. These involve, for example, the Federal Insecticide, Fungicide and Rodenticide Act, the Perishable Agricultural Commodities Act, and the Food, Drug and Cosmetic Act. Food which is admitted into the United States under surety bond pending FDA inspection and later found inadmissible must be exported or destroyed. If this does not occur, an action by the Customs Service against the importer and the surety for liquidated damages will typically follow. A strict six-year statute of limitations applies to government complaints seeking liquidated damages running from the importer's breach of the bond.

WIRTH, THE ROLE OF SCIENCE IN THE URUGUAY ROUND AND NAFTA TRADE DISCIPLINES
27 CORNELL INT'L L.J. 817 (1994)*

SCIENCE AND THE NATIONAL REGULATORY PROCESS

The Uruguay Round and the NAFTA texts on sanitary and phytosanitary measures purport to apply scientifically-based trade disciplines to the domestic process of adopting regulatory measures in the area of public health and food and drug safety. Because these new trade disciplines establish constraints on domestic regulatory processes designed to preclude protectionist abuse of national measures, the effects of those new requirements in turn depend on the role of science in regulatory processes in these areas.

RISK ASSESSMENT, RISK MANAGEMENT, AND SCIENCE POLICY

One fundamental axiom admonishes that regulations to protect public health involve social policy choices. Because the regulatory process is not wholly scientific, science does not have all the answers. There is no way to infer regulatory outcomes solely on the basis of scientific data, especially when most regulations are implicitly or explicitly crafted to respond to a particular social, economic, or political context. While scientific analysis can provide assistance in attaining a given public health goal, the choice of that goal reflects societal values as to which science may provide little, if any, guidance. In other words, science may inform the regulatory process but cannot, by itself, determine the result with particularity. For instance, a risk assessment may help in setting a standard designed to limit the probability that an individual will develop cancer after a lifetime of exposure to a particular chemical substance to no more than one chance in a million. By contrast, the choice of the one-in-a-million goal—as opposed to, say, zero or one-in-a-thousand—is one of public policy.

Although by no means universally accepted, one approach that expressly acknowledges this dichotomy prescribes a bifurcation of the regulatory process into two phases: "risk assessment," which in principle establishes the strictly scientific basis for regulatory action, and "risk management," which is the multidisciplinary process of choosing regulatory measures:

> Risk assessment is an exercise that combines available data on a substance's potency in causing adverse health effects with information about likely human exposure, and through the use of plausible assumptions, it generates an estimate of human health risk. Risk management is the process by which a protective agency decides what action to take in the face of such estimates. Ideally the action is based on such factors as the goals of public health and environmental protection, relevant legislation, legal precedent, and application of social, economic, and political values.

In this two stage methodology, scientific questions can be isolated and addressed in an objective matter through risk assessment methodologies at the beginning of the regulatory process. But the allegedly scientific process of risk assessment necessarily requires inferences, choices, and assumptions that themselves reflect policy preferences, an area sometimes known as "science policy."

Pure policy choices are supposedly confined to the second place, risk management. At this stage, science may be relevant for such tasks as evaluating technical options. Risk management decisions, however, also engage other considerations, most notably social values. Regulatory policy, then, is not exclusively the domain of scientists, but of public authorities who make judgments about how to achieve social goals that are informed by scientific data and scientific inferences.

Because the recently adopted texts on sanitary and phytosanitary measures and technical barriers to trade in the Uruguay Round and the

NAFTA echo these themes, the risk assessment/risk management duality provides a useful vehicle for analyzing the new trade disciplines. Thus, both the Uruguay Round and the NAFTA texts on sanitary and phytosanitary measures specify that domestic regulations must be based on a risk assessment. Both these texts, as well as the NAFTA technical barriers text (under which, as discussed above, a risk assessment is optional rather than mandatory), then specify certain elements that must characterize the risk assessment methodology employed. The Uruguay Round SPS Agreement requires "sufficient" scientific evidence. The texts require that regulators consider, respectively, "available" or "relevant" scientific evidence. Both the Uruguay Round and NAFTA texts on sanitary and phytosanitary measures state that national regulatory authorities must take into account international risk assessment methodologies. Neither the Uruguay Round nor the NAFTA text appears, at least as an explicit matter, to accommodate measures that are not adopted by technically expert regulatory authorities, but that instead are enacted directly by legislatures or as a result of popular referenda without a formal risk assessment.

In the risk management phase, the texts expressly recognize the importance of social value choices. This is somewhat clearer in the two NAFTA passages, which explicitly identify each party's right to establish its own levels of protection. Similarly, the Uruguay Round SPS Agreement repeatedly acknowledges the significance of an appropriate level of sanitary or phytosanitary protection in excess of that implicit in international standards. In contrast to the scientific process of risk assessment, which is subject to trade disciplines of varying degrees of rigor in the Uruguay Round and the NAFTA texts, those passages by and large leave the choice of a national level of protection—*i.e.*, the endpoint of the regulatory process reflecting social value choices—to each contracting party. But both texts specify that the choice of level of protection should be responsive to the objective of minimizing negative trade effects.

* * *

Overall, a number of generalizations can be made concerning the Uruguay Round and NAFTA TBT and SPS texts. First, the disciplines in the Uruguay Round TBT Agreement are not based on science. Second, while the analogous text in the NAFTA does allude to scientific principles concerning risk assessments, the performance of risk assessments is optional under that agreement. Of the two texts that require mandatory risk assessments grounded in science as an express condition of the validity of a national regulatory measure, the Uruguay Round and NAFTA SPS texts,

- both express a preference for internationally harmonized standards, which are presumptively valid if applied by a party to the agreement;

- both apply scientific tests to national measures more stringent than international standards; however, the NAFTA SPS passage is somewhat clearer on the absolute right of a party to adopt more stringent measures by reference to its chosen level of protection;

- both appear to segment the scientific underpinnings for a standard (risk assessment) from the choice of regulatory measure (risk management), with the NAFTA text being somewhat clearer in this regard by comparison with the Uruguay Round's juxtaposition of "scientific justification" and appropriate level of protection;

- both require consideration of applicable international risk assessment methodologies;

- only the Uruguay Round Agreement articulates a requirement that a national measure be based on "sufficient" scientific evidence;

- both define a level of protection reflecting social value judgments as a public policy choice made by each individual contracting party, with the NAFTA text somewhat more explicit that the choice of level is to be independent of scientific considerations;

- both require the consideration of adverse trade effects in the national choice of level of sanitary and phytosanitary protection;

- neither, as a general matter, purports to subject the risk management phase of the regulatory process to science-based disciplines;

- the NAFTA text, by comparison with the Uruguay Round SPS Agreement's definition of "scientific justification," is somewhat more explicit in confining the scientific disciplines strictly to the risk assessment process and establishing that the choice of level of protection and selection of regulatory measures are independent of scientific considerations.

SCIENTIFIC UNCERTAINTY

The tasks of both risk assessment and risk management are complicated by uncertainty and lack of data that characterize much of the scientific basis for regulation. According to a former Administrator of the United States Environmental Protection Agency:

> From its earliest days, [the United States Environmental Protection Agency] was often compelled to *act under conditions of substantial scientific uncertainty.*

> . . . .

> [T]he problem of uncertainty was moved from the periphery to the center.

> . . . .

> For [some] substances—and these are the ones that naturally figure most prominently in public debate—the data remain ambiguous.

Because science is incomplete, the scientific data set underlying any regulation is necessarily incomplete. That, however, does not diminish the scientific nature of the inquiry. Indeed, the appropriate handling of uncertainties is part of the scientific process of risk assessment.

In response to the challenge of prescribing regulatory requirements under conditions of uncertainty, a precautionary approach has begun to gain fairly wide acceptance on the supranational and international levels. The "precautionary principle" counsels governmental authorities to err on the side of environmental protection in formulating public policy in contexts characterized by conditions of scientific uncertainty. Precautionary approaches can be interpreted as a counterweight to, if not an outright rejection of, "wait and see" philosophies that emphasize a high degree of scientific certainty as a precondition to adopting policy responses.

MARTIN, SOVEREIGNTY AND FOOD SAFETY IN A NAFTA CONTEXT
24 Can.–U.S. Law J. 369 (1998).*

The principle of equivalence is becoming increasingly important because, aside from the legal plane on which governments retain considerable sovereignty over food safety decisions, there is a more practical reality of how food safety regulation is actually done in an increasingly globalized economy.

Particularly in Canada and the United States after NAFTA, there has been a significant trend in larger and fewer food processing establishments making specialized products for a global or at least a North American market. With the removal of tariffs on processed food, companies with operations on both sides of the Canada/U.S. border have increasingly rationalized production by assigning North American product mandates to plants situated in one country or the other. Contrary to the predictions of some Canadian nationalists at the time of the Free Trade Agreement, a sizeable number of these plants are in Canada, so rationalization has been accompanied by a huge increase in two-way trade in agri-food products.[5] As a practical matter, neither Canada nor the United States is in any position to inspect the high volume of products crossing the border. In any case, to do so is not the most effective way of ensuring the food safety status of products. In the past several years, efforts have focused on more efficient ways to deal with these volumes of trade, and assure the safety of the food supply. The main innovation has been a focus on processed-based food safety systems, whereby standards concentrate on how the product is processed, rather than on assessing the safety of the final product at the end of the

* Copyright © 1998 U.S.–Canada Law Journal. Reproduced with permission. (At the time this article was written, Paul Martin was the Acting Director of the Multilateral Trade Policy Division of Agriculture and Agri–Food Canada.)

5. According to Agri–Food Canada, Canadian agri-food exports to the United States were $3.6 billion in 1989 and $10.3 billion in 1996. Imports for the same years were $4.3 billion and $7.9 billion, respectively. Similar growth has occurred in Canadian trade with other countries over the same time frame.

production line. Of course, if regulations are to focus on what happens in a processing plant and the processing plant is in another country's jurisdiction, some level of coordination between national inspection authorities is required. In general, this takes the form of mutual recognition of the equivalence of the systems in the two countries.

This situation continues to accord full sovereignty to the importing party, which ultimately must be convinced that the system under which a product is produced is adequate and reliably implemented. However, it puts a significant market pressure on regulatory systems in both countries to evolve in ways that are compatible. Essentially, food businesses that have been established on one side of the international border or the other with a view to serving both markets need to be able to secure the necessary food safety approvals in both markets without fail, or the investment that has gone into making North American scale plants in each country will be lost.

Fortunately, both Canada and the United States have long histories of fairly compatible approaches to food safety regulation, and both are moving in similar directions with more focus on Hazard Analysis Critical Control Point (HACCP) plans at the plant level, and in the horticulture area, back to the farm level. Both have been using their government resources in more of a monitoring and audit role to ensure that the necessary process controls are actually observed. This is both more resource-efficient and more effective in terms of reliable food safety results than the old end-point product inspection model. In order to allow plants to effectively meet standards in both countries, the specific requirements for HACCP programs in the countries need to be broadly consistent, and the regulatory authorities in both countries must be willing to recognize equivalence in situations where differences in some of the details of manufacturing and control procedures do not have significant food safety implications.

BREDAHL AND HOLLERAN, TECHNICAL REGULATIONS AND FOOD SAFETY IN NAFTA

www.andes.missouri.edu (3–2–99).

THE US–MEXICO AVOCADO DISPUTE

Background

A recent longstanding, high profile dispute between the US and Mexico over US phytosanitary regulations was resolved this February [1999] after eighty-one years. In 1914, US officials first established a quarantine prohibiting the importation of Mexican avocados when they identified avocado seed weevils in Mexican avocados. Fearing pest infection, US officials implemented the quarantine which has remained on the books ever since. In the 1970s, Mexico twice petitioned for approval to export avocados to the US. USDA/APHIS rejected the Mexican requests citing 1) the apparent ease with which seed weevils were recovered in the Mexican state of Michoacan and 2) that seed weevils and

Mexican fruit flies were frequently intercepted in fruit contraband at the border.

In the 1980s, Mexico expanded its avocado groves and improved its production processes. Again in the 1990s, Mexico issued several requests for approval to export the avocados to the US. One of the requests led APHIS in July 1993 to allow Hass avocados grown in Michoacan to be imported into Alaska under certain conditions. Mexico is the world's largest producer of avocados and Michoacan produces over two-thirds of Mexico's total avocado production. Growers and packers in Michoacan adopted sophisticated grove management techniques, packing practices and shipping practices in order to export their avocados. (Roberts and Orden)

Inspired by NAFTA negotiations in 1994, Mexico requested extended entry for Hass avocados to be imported into the northeastern states. APHIS acted on the request, drew up a proposal to allow fresh Hass avocados from Michoacan to enter certain areas of the US, and then solicited comments as the process requires. Finally, on February 5, 1997, APHIS published its final science-based rule allowing Mexican Hass avocados to enter certain US states under a systems approach.

Issues

- US Avocado Growers. On one side, the US avocado growers from California and Florida voiced their discontent about lifting the quarantine on Mexican avocados citing fear over the pest risk to the US industry. Domestic producers also expressed concern about Mexico's ability to guarantee pest mitigation procedures as called for in the proposal.

- On the other side, growers and others voiced concern that the continued prohibition on Mexican avocados could result in a third country regulatory standard that would affect US products. The concern, for example, was that Mexico would impose standards against US wheat, apples, peaches and cherries.

- SPS Elements at issue. Mexico maintained that there was no scientific reason to reject the systems approach proposal; with the quarantine, Mexico argued, the US had established a high standard of protection. Mexico also argued that surveys indicated that host-specific pests had been eradicated from avocado export producing areas and that the fruit fly populations were low in these areas. Mexico challenged the US that it was not complying with trade agreement provisions and allowing trade from low pest prevalent areas. Additionally, Mexico argued that pre-harvest, packing, transport and shipping practices had been implemented to minimize the risk of pests in avocado export shipments.

- The US Restrictive Quarantine "Q56". "The PPQ (Plant Protection and Quarantine Program) administers the Fruit and Vegetables Quarantine 7 CFR 319.56 which establishes the terms under which fruits and vegetables can gain entry into the United States." (Roberts and

Orden, p.10) The restrictive quarantine, under which the Mexican avocado quarantine falls, is referred to as "Q56".

According to Q56, APHIS can grant an import permit if the fruit or vegetable:

1.   is not attacked in the country of origin by injurious insects;

2.   has been treated or is to be treated for all injurious insects that attack it in the country of origin;

3.   is imported from a definite area or district in the country of origin that is free from all injurious insects; or

4.   is imported from a definite area or district that is free from certain injurious insects that all other injurious insects have been eliminated by treatment or any other approved procedures. (Code of Federal Regulations, p.220.)

- Rulemaking Process. USDA/APHIS issued a proposal in 1995 to allow fresh Hass avocados grown in Michoacan be imported into the US under certain conditions. Following that, USDA provided 105 days of comment period for scientists and independent scientific panels to present their views on the proposed rule. The comment period included five public hearings across the country and collected over 2,000 comments; over half of the comments came from the avocado industry; 85% of the comments opposed the rule. The final rule was based on a thorough scientific risk assessment which recommended that a "systems approach" would be appropriate.

Resolution Mechanism: "Systems Approach"

On February 5, 1997, USDA/APHIS published a new rule that allows the importation of avocados from Michoacan, Mexico under certain conditions. The rule is based on scientific risk assessments that include a series of interrelated restrictions termed a "systems approach". The rule contains APHIS' requirements which were devised to prevent the entry of any exotic plant pests which attack avocados into the US. Under the systems approach, commercial shipments of fresh Hass avocados grown in approved orchards in the Mexican state of Michoacan may be imported into 19 northeastern states and the District of Columbia from November through February.

The systems approach safeguards are designed to progressively reduce risk to an insignificant level. The safeguards make up what is termed a "fail-safe" system which means that if one of the mitigating measures should fail, there are others in place to ensure that the risk is managed and reduced. It is a system of safeguards which occur consecutively in stages. The nine mitigating measures consist of: 1) natural host plant resistance to fruit flies; 2) field surveys; 3) pest trap and bait measures in the orchards; 4) field sanitation measures; 5) post-harvest safeguards; 6) winter shipping; 7) packinghouse instructions; 8) port-of-arrival inspections; 9) limited US distribution. USDA oversees and supervises all of these stages. Should pests in the avocados be detected at any stage in the system, avocado imports may be suspended from affected areas. Clearly, the final rule does not imply guaranteed entry for the Michoacan avocado growers; avocados can only enter if all the safeguards are met.

Systems approach resolution mechanisms are not novel in agricultural trade. Systems approach requirements are also used to allow the US to export fruits and vegetables from areas that are not free of certain pests, including citrus from Florida to Japan and apples from Washington State to China and Japan. The US also uses the systems approach to import products like Japanese Unshu oranges, Spanish tomatoes, and Israeli peppers.

Implications

To address the concern that Mexican avocados are diverted from approved destinations to California and Florida, each imported avocado must be individually labeled with a sticker of origin. Additionally, each shipment must be made in a sealed container with the Northeast destinations labeled. States in other areas have instituted a look-out for diverted avocados.

From an economic perspective, USDA estimates that approximately eight percent of the US avocado production is sold in the 19 states where the Hass Mexican avocados will be imported. As a result, it is estimated that the rule will only have a limited impact on US producers. APHIS believes that consumers stand to benefit from the systems approach.

The US–Mexico avocado trade dispute over US phytosanitary regulations illustrates the issue that resolution of SPS issues can be complex, even when national SPS measures are science-based. One means countries have for addressing SPS issues is to adopt relevant standards or regulations such as ISO 9000 or HACCP. That said, the trade agreements allow countries' standards to be more stringent than international standards. Since trading partners may have different food safety concerns, they may therefore have differing food safety strategies. How these strategies coexist can be important.

Rapprochement Strategies

There are various strategies countries can adopt to address food safety. Jacobs proposed three strategies for reducing international trade conflicts arising from differences in non-tariff barriers to trade, of which technical regulations and voluntary standards are a subset:

• Harmonization: standardization of regulations in identical form.

• Mutual Recognition: acceptance that alternative technical regulations, systems and standards can lead to the same level of food safety and quality. Hooker and Caswell equate this approach to "reciprocity" in the Canadian–US Free Trade Agreement or "equivalency" as used in GATT.

● Coordination or alignment: the gradual narrowing of difference between alternative technical regulations, systems and standards, perhaps based on voluntary international codes of practice.

Questions and Comments

1. Virtually every government regulates food products. Prior to CFTA and NAFTA, Canada, Mexico and the United States had a wealth of such regulations. Does NAFTA require *any* alteration of national, or state or provincial, SPS rules? *See* Article 712.

2. Trader Jane's SPS problem concerns the Pasteurized Milk Ordinance (PMO), a uniform set of state regulations cooperatively developed with federal authorities through the NCIMS organization. Does NAFTA require that the states of the United States comply with Section B of Chapter 7? *See* Article 105 and Article 709. Does NAFTA require that organizations such as NCIMS comply with Section B? *See* Article 711.

3. Article 712 contains NAFTA's basic SPS rights and obligations. What basic rights are there? What basic obligations? Who decides whether the PMO is "necessary" and "appropriate"?

4. Article 712(3) requires SPS measures to be based on "scientific principles" and a "risk assessment." What does that mean? *See* Articles 715 and 724. Suppose Trader Jane wants to challenge the PMO on the grounds that these requirements have not been met. How would you proceed to evaluate such issues? *See* Wirth.

5. Article 712(4) bars arbitrary or unjustifiable SPS discrimination between "like goods" where "identical or similar conditions" prevail. Suppose that the Quebec long-life milk regulations ensure perfectly healthy milk production and for decades there has never been a health problem identified with Quebec long-life milk. Is that enough for Trader Jane to prove a breach of Article 712(4)? What about Article 712(5) concerning "unnecessary obstacles"? And Article 712(6) concerning "disguised restrictions"?

What insights do you draw from Bredahl and Holleran's study of the U.S.–Mexico avocado dispute? On May 24, 2004, the U.S. Department of Agriculture proposed new rules which would permit avocados grown in Mexican state of Michoacan to be exported to all U.S. states year round, eliminating the current restrictions to 31 northern states and then only from October 15 to April 15. See 69 Fed. Reg. 29466 (May 24, 2004).

6. Assume that there are international SPS standards for long-life milk. Must the United States adhere to them? *See* Article 713. Should Trader Jane care? *See* the excerpt by Martin.

7. Upon consulting with the Quebec milk authorities, Trader Jane is told that this problem is really an illusion. The Quebec authorities are ready to prove that their regulations are the equivalent of the PMO. Should Trader Jane take up their offer? *See* Article 714.

8. Suppose that the NAFTA Committee on Sanitary and Phytosanitary Measures established in Article 722 has been meeting to discuss SPS equivalency generally and, specifically, milk products regulatory equivalency. Would that fact help Trader Jane? *See* Article 722 and 723.

Do Quebec and Trader Jane have the burden of proving the inconsistency of an SPS measure with NAFTA? *See* Article 723(6).

9. On balance, does Section B of Chapter 7 deal effectively with SPS measures as potential NTB problems?

PART B. STANDARDS RELATED MEASURES

COFFIELD, COMMONALITY OF STANDARDS— IMPLICATIONS FOR SOVEREIGNTY—A U.S. PERSPECTIVE

24 Can.–U.S. Law J. 235 (1998).*

The tension in the standards area is between that right of a country to regulate in the area of safety and the health of its animals, plants, and humans against their commitment to minimize barriers to trade. That great tension is what leads to agreements to find a mutual accommodation of those two goals. In the NAFTA SRM agreement, the explicit issue of sovereignty is addressed at the beginning in Article 904, which establishes the right of each Party to adopt, maintain, or apply any SRM related to the protection of human, animal, or plant life or health, the environment, or consumers, and any measure to ensure its enforcement and implementation, including the right to prohibit imports. I would maintain that, on the face of it, that dispenses with the issue of sovereignty as we know it in the case of a trade agreement. That Article also provides that each Party may, in pursuing its legitimate objectives of safety in the protection of human, animal, or plant life, establish the levels of the protection that it considers appropriate, so long as it is nondiscriminatory, provides national treatment, and is on an MFN basis.

One concern which arose involving internal federal/state/provincial separation of powers, which is a very sensitive issue as we all know, was also addressed in Article 901. Article 901 makes it clear that the federal government can always mandate compliance by sub-federal governments and non-governmental organizations (NGOs). Thus, the Parties themselves, all subject to the overall obligations to comply, would only seek through appropriate measures to ensure observance of Articles of this agreement by states, provinces, or NGOs. Each one of those words was painfully negotiated. They seek, through appropriate measures, to ensure observance. In order to exactly protect the sensitivities of that particular concern, I cite these provisions affecting internal jurisdiction, not as questions of sovereignty, but to demonstrate that, in the context of the SRM agreement, the Parties had to be sensitive to even more delicate issues than was the case in most other aspects of the NAFTA. As regards SRMs, however, the concern over sovereignty has arisen essentially, as in the case of most trade agreements, and how people interpret the details, concerning the interpretation of this agreement is played in the media as having potential intrusions on sovereignty.

Do any of these provisions really affect sovereignty? Product standards, certifications, labeling requirements, and similar requirements by individual countries are increasingly becoming a main source of trade disputes and are a potential and a real obstacle to trade. As tariffs continue downward worldwide, and as trade thus increases, products are faced with a growing array of regulatory requirements when entering export markets. We may ask, why did this not happen twenty years ago? It is not as though the standards were not there twenty years ago. It is because a lot of trade did not move due to tariff barriers; the standards were really never implemented. You could not get into the market because the tariff was twenty or thirty percent. Now you find that there are other things in that market that may affect your trade even more than a barrier, because they are not price-related. They are related to a physical obstacle in terms of the standards with which the product must comply. As a private practitioner, I found that my own practice has shifted in the last seven or eight years. It now consists of dealing with regulatory issues for the most part, primarily those involving food or product standards. Obviously, it is in the private sector where we know that issues are real issues. If that has happened in my practice, I assume it has happened in a lot of other people's practices as well.

Product standards are necessary. They need not be trade barriers. They can be fully justified in many instances. However, with growing globalization and the increasing number of markets, confusion in setting standards, and in enforcing them has increased. In the international trade establishment, the goal has been to prevent standards from operating as unnecessary obstacles to trade. The standards-related measures in Chapter 9 cover three different kinds of measures, including what the parties term as standards, technical regulations, and conformity assessment procedures. Standards, under Chapter 9, are defined as providing:

> [F]or common and repeated use, rules, guidelines, or characteristics for products, or related processes and production methods, or for services or related operating methods with which compliance is not mandatory ... [including] terminology, symbols, packaging, marking or labeling requirements as they apply to a product, process, or production or operating method."

This is the important part of the term "standards." Under the NAFTA, standards by definition are not mandatory, and are most frequently set by private standardizing bodies.

An example would be the standards developed by the American Society of Testing, which has issued over eight thousand five hundred voluntary standards. Governments can also set voluntary standards. An example in the United States would be the Consumer Products Safety Commission (CPSC). There is, in the United States, a proliferation of private standard-setting organizations. According to a study by the Organization for Economic Cooperation and Development (OECD), in

1991, the number of standards set in the United States by private organizations numbered thirty-five thousand. The U.S. government frequently relies on these private voluntary standards. It is especially important, therefore, that both the GATT agreement and the NAFTA cover this particular area. This is one part of the NAFTA that covers a private action, not a government action. To the extent that a country can ensure that its voluntary standards do not operate as trade barriers, it would have to have a great deal of control over these non-governmental standard-setting bodies.

Once again, as noted earlier, the obligation in the NAFTA is that the governmental Parties to the agreement seek to ensure that these private standard-setting bodies conform to the obligations in the agreement. This is a lesser obligation than in other parts of the NAFTA, simply because it is dealing with a private entity, rather than something over which the government has direct control through its regulatory process. However, it is important to note that the consequence of violating the agreement is the same for a private body as it is for a government. If a government undertakes the obligation, if there is a private standard-setting organization that has, in fact, impeded trade through the way it set its standard or because the standard is unreasonable, the government pays for that.

That is not unusual in the case of a federal, provincial, or a federal/state relationship both in the WTO and NAFTA, as well. The agreement does not require the federal government to do what they cannot do, which is mandate certain things. It does require the government to be responsible in terms of their "payment" if their entities have not complied. Technical regulations under the NAFTA cover the mandatory government product standards. These include the same definitions of standards as the voluntary ones, except that these are mandatory. They may first have been developed by a private standard-setting body and then have been adopted and been made mandatory by the government, which is frequently the case.

The U.S. government, for example, increasingly relies on the private sector to develop standards which are adopted. One example that I can give you is in the area of government procurement. This can be positive, in that it relieves the government from a long process of having to set the standard. It lets the industry that is most knowledgeable about the product or the process set the standards. It also, however, can be a problem. I just give one example in the case of government procurement, when the company bidding on the contract sets the standard. There is something to be said here about fairness. And in that particular case, I looked very closely at the standard, and it was very hard for anybody else to meet that standard except for the company that had been bidding on it. The U.S. Department of Defense thought that it was a good standard, so they adopted it. That contract went out for bid, and, frankly, nobody else could meet that standard. So there does need to be some checks and balances on this issue of voluntary standards, particularly when they are set by a particular company, rather than being set industry-wide.

Conformity of assessment procedure is any procedure used directly or indirectly to determine that a technical regulation or standard is fulfilled, including sampling, testing, inspection, evaluation, verification, monitoring, auditing, assurance of conformity, accreditation of registration, or approval, et cetera. But on the strong lobbying of the Food & Drug Administration during the course of these negotiations, the United States has interpreted this to mean that issues that are country-sensitive, such as registration or approval of a pharmaceutical, would not be a conformity assessment procedure. One of the success stories in the NAFTA is the mutual recognition of the Underwriters' Laboratories and the Canadian Testing Standards. These bodies have now become competitors in North America because a manufacturer can go to either one of them and get a stamp of approval which is good in either country. It is what is most convenient, what is most cost-effective. It is what I would call one of the confirmations that these kinds of agreements can positively increase trade, not just be an obstacle.

In determining how best to police or enforce agreements, it is necessary to look at voluntary and mandatory standards and conformity assessment procedures together. This is not always easy to do, as internal compliance as to how these are treated may vary. However, to the extent that each can be used as an obstacle to trade, they must be addressed similarly as involves the commitments of the governments to minimize trade barriers.

The basic obligation in the NAFTA is that SRMs are to be nondiscriminatory, and that no Party may prepare, adopt, or apply any SRM with a view to, or with the effect of, creating an unnecessary obstacle to trade. This obligation basically reflects the GATT–WTO technical barriers to trade agreement principles. The critical detail in the obligation is that Parties may have SRMs that restrict trade, so long as a demonstrable purpose of the measure is to achieve a legitimate objective, and the measure does not operate to exclude goods that meet the objective. The legitimate object activities are further described, not exclusively, as those involving safety, protection of human, animal, or plant life or health, and the environment, including matters involving quality and identifiability of goods and services and parenthetical sustainable development, considering a number of factors in sustainable development, such as climate, but not including the protection of domestic production. So, once again, you have a series of attempts to define what is legitimate. But still, you put in the caveat that, if somebody can prove that this is a protection of domestic production, it is not, in fact, within that discretion.

These obligations contain a fairly broad opt-out provision for those concerned about the sovereignty of the Parties to develop social goal standards, especially when, ultimately, the Parties initially determine which SRMs that Party considers appropriate. If the Parties do set SRMs which would otherwise be inconsistent, for example, mandating a stricter standard than that promulgated by an international body, then under the provisions of the code, they can do a risk assessment to justify the legitimacy of the standard. Risk assessments are otherwise voluntary.

However, if a Party does use a risk assessment in determining the legitimacy of its objectives, the agreement requires that certain conditions be met; most importantly, that the higher standard is not a disguised restriction on trade and does not discriminate or result in an arbitrary or unjustifiable distinction between similar goods with similar risk levels in the degree of the restriction.

* * *

The NAFTA does go beyond the GATT Technical Barriers to Trade (TBT) agreement, in that it commits the Parties, to the extent practicable, to make their respective SRMs compatible, so as to facilitate trade between the Parties. The idea of the compatibility of the standard can be addressed in a regional agreement far more readily than it can in a multilateral agreement. In addition, each Party must treat technical regulations adopted or maintained by the other Party as equivalent to its own, when the exporting Party in cooperation with the importing Party demonstrates to the satisfaction of the importing Party that its technical regulations adequately fulfill the important Party's legitimate objectives.

This was written by lawyers, and what it means is that, if you can convince the other guy that what you have done is to make your products basically equivalent, they are going to let it in. Sometimes, your tongue kind of trips over this language. What it really represents is a very practical approach to setting and enforcing standards in the NAFTA countries.

Under the agreement, the Parties also agree to accept the results of a conformity assessment procedure of another Party whenever possible. That is, once again, if you can convince the other guy that this has been done in a way that, in fact, meets your legitimate objectives. Unfortunately, despite the passage of several years, there are still a lot of potential disputes, ambiguity, and language of compatibility in North America. All sides seem to be determined not to change one iota of their own regulations and to assume that any change they would have to make would be a step downward.

One example dealing with food is nutrition labeling. I use this example because it is something in which, to my great frustration, I get involved in quite a bit between the United States and Canada. The United States has made its own determination as to what it considers necessary on a food label, and that is mandatory. If you pick up a head of lettuce which is in shrink wrap, it has something on the back. Canada, on the other hand, has determined that, if you label, you have to include things which are different than the things included on the U.S. label, and it has to be in both English and French. Therefore, you have a natural trade barrier determined by market size for selling these products in both markets. You defeat economies of scale, which the agreement was supposed to encourage. I have always felt that we can put the information in English and French, and we could have one nutrition label. Surely we ought to be able to come up with something on which both Parties can agree. This has been going on for years, and I am told that, until a certain person in the Canadian government retires, it is unlikely that it will be resolved.

SYKES, PRODUCT STANDARDS FOR INTERNATIONALLY INTEGRATED GOODS MARKETS
Chapter 4 (1995).*

MARKET MECHANISMS AND MULTILATERALLY SUBSIDIZED STANDARDIZATION

Given the staggering variety of standards and regulations in the international economy, it is perhaps surprising that technical barriers are not more of a problem in international markets and that much trade occurs without serious attention to them. This was true even before important international initiatives such as those of the General Agreement on Tariffs and Trade (GATT). Market activity alone suffices to avoid many technical barrier problems. When decentralized markets alone are not enough, firms move toward cooperative efforts undertaken by international organizations that resemble, in many respects, the private and public-private standardization entities that operate domestically in most trading nations. It would be misleading to characterize these organizations as affording a strictly "market" solution to technical barriers, for they are typically supported by a mixture of public and private funding, and their members include both governmental and private sector entities. But they operate without benefit of much legal formality, drawing recommendations from technical expert groups and thereafter striving for "consensus" defined in one way or another. In this respect, their functioning is difficult to distinguish from many entirely private entities.

The international organizations develop standards addressing the entire range of issues discussed in this book—compatibility, health and safety, product quality, labeling, testing, and certification. The mere existence of such standards sometimes ensures (or reflects) their widespread adoption. Equally clearly, however, the international standards organizations cannot alone provide a complete solution to the technical barrier problem.

OVERVIEW OF INTERNATIONAL STANDARDIZATION ORGANIZATIONS

Of the important international standardization organizations still operating, the first was the International Electrotechnical Commission (IEC), established in 1908. It resulted from the rapid technical progress in electrical technology at the time and the perception that standards were necessary to maintain a reasonable level of compatibility among electrical products. It remains the most important international standardization body for electrical and electronic goods.

The IEC is now affiliated with the International Organization for Standardization (ISO), formed in 1947, the same year as GATT. The impetus for its establishment came from the United Nations, following a breakdown of certain earlier standards organizations during World War II. The "jurisdiction" of the ISO is unlimited, and in principle, the ISO may undertake standardization initiatives relating to any product or service market. In practice, the ISO tends to defer to the more specialized entities such as the IEC when they exist.

The members of both the ISO and the IEC are country representatives. Each nation may designate its own representative, with the result that some members are government agencies and others are private sector entities (the American National Standards Institute is a private entity that represents the United States). They are funded by dues collected from their members.

In the years after the creation of the ISO, particular concern over the trade effects of food standards led to initiatives before the United Nations Food and Agriculture Organization (FAO) and the World Health Organization (WHO) to reform them. The result was the creation of the Codex Alimentarius Commission, founded in 1962. The Codex develops standards for all manner of food safety and labeling issues. Its members are also country representatives, and its funding has been largely through the FAO and WHO. Interestingly, when the budgets of those agencies proved inadequate for a time, private sector organizations with an interest in the activities of the Codex stepped forward to contribute.

This listing of organizations is hardly exhaustive. A few of the many other international bodies with significant interest in standardization activities include the International Telecommunications Union (ITU), the International Conference on Weights and Measures, the International Labor Organization, the International Bureau for the Standardization of Man–Made Fibres, the International Commission on Illumination, the International Air Transport Association, the International Institute of Refrigeration, and the International Institute of Welding.

The detailed operation of each organization is slightly different, but the essence of what goes on is similar for most of them. The organization usually draws on interested members to form a working group or committee to consider the possibility of standards in a particular area. If this group can come to a reasonable "consensus" (the precise meaning of that term is variable), it will make a proposal for a standard. In one way or another, the member nations will then vote on whether to make the proposal into a "standard." In the ISO, for example, committees of technical experts develop "recommendations," which are sent to member bodies for approval. A recommendation becomes a standard after a sufficient number of member bodies accept it—in the 1970s, the ISO moved from a unanimity rule to a 75 percent rule for determining when to convert a recommendation into a standard.

To be sure, member nations are not obligated to follow or adopt these standards in their national markets, even if they vote in favor of adopting them in the international body. The decision to create a standard, however, typically suggests that widespread (although not necessarily universal) adherence will follow.

MEXICO—PROCESS OF STANDARDIZATION/CERTIFICATION

U.S. Dept. of Commerce (March 14, 1997).

This industry sector analysis includes information on compliance to Mexican official product, systems, processes and service industry standards. The official Mexican title for mandatory standards is Normas Oficiales Mexicanas (NOMs). This report outlines the issuing bodies, procedures, basic requirements, certification and compliance.

* * *

The system is divided into mandatory NOMS and voluntary standards called NMXs. There are currently 559 NOMs, 316 proposed NOMs and 5,443 NMXs. Further, under the North American Free Trade Agreement (NAFTA) Mexico, the United States and Canada are working to make their standards-related measures compatible to the greatest extent possible by 1998.

NOMs are issued by various Mexican Government Secretariats according to the jurisdiction of each one. Annually, the Mexican Secretariat of Commerce publishes the Program of Standardization listing the Mandatory and Voluntary Mexican Standards that are to be created or to be revised.

Only test laboratories accredited by the government can test products subject to NOM compliance. Accredited calibration laboratories also exist to assure precision in the transfer of the reference standards to measurement instruments for commercial or industrial use.

Nine private sector organizations are accredited to develop standards and/or certify products and/or services in specific fields. Some of these organizations have their own laboratories and perform the entire certification process, or they may work in conjunction with other entities and subcontract third-party laboratories. Other government agencies have their own laboratories in which products are tested to certify compliance with the appropriate NOMs.

The Government of Mexico had traditionally been the primary actor in determining product standards, labeling and certification policy, with little input from the private sector and less from consumers. As a result, independent standards and certification organizations like those in the U.S. were virtually non-existent in Mexico. The Secretariat of Commerce and Industrial Promotion (SECOFI) [now the Secretariat of the Economy, or SECON] has initiated efforts to reverse this situation, shifting the responsibility for the formulation of voluntary standards to the private sector or to mixed commissions.

In 1992, the Mexican Government undertook an ambitious project to revamp its entire system for formulating product standards, testing, labeling and certification regulations. The cornerstone of this review is the 1992 Standardization and Metrology law, which provides for greater transparency and access by the public and interested parties to the standards development process. This exercise has resulted in a reduction of obligatory product standards to less than six hundred. The process is not without its problems, as poorly drafted regulations and inadequate communication between enforcement agencies, such as customs, have occasionally led to trade disruptions. In such instances the Mexican Government has been receptive to U.S. concerns and willing to resolve problems.

Under the NAFTA, Mexico has re-affirmed its prior General Agreement on Tariffs and Trade (GATT) via the World Trade Organization (WTO) obligations to meet international standards. In addition, Mexico has taken tentative steps toward reciprocal recognition of foreign standards and accreditation of foreign test laboratories.

Mexico, the United States and Canada will, to the greatest extent possible, make their standards-related measures compatible. By 1998, conformity assessment bodies located in the United States will be able to apply for accreditation to test products to Mexican standards.

[SECOFI/SECON] is the organization with the authority to manage and to coordinate the standardization activities in the country. Its authority derives from the Federal Law on Metrology and Standardization (Ley Federal de Metrologia y Normalizacion–LFNM) enacted on January 26, 1988 and updated in 1992.

The Mexican Standardization System follows international guidelines and is compatible with the purposes of GATT's Code of Standards. The Mexican Standardization System consists of about 559 mandatory NOMs (Norma Official Mexicana–NOM) by which products must be certified for compliance and 5,443 voluntary standards NMX (Norma Mexicana–NMX) that improve and assure the quality of Mexican products.

The Mexican Government has three major areas of concern in setting mandatory standards:

        A.   Protection of health and safety of consumers

        B.   Commercial information

        C.   Protection of environment and ecology

which affect different products and services, such as:

Measuring instruments

Terms, expressions and symbols

Sizes of wearing apparel, shoes, etc.

Industrial and medical gas equipment

Equipment and apparatus for the conduction and use of electricity

Environmental protection

Pollution Control

Standardization of telecommunication networks

SYKES, PRODUCT STANDARDS FOR INTERNATIONALLY INTEGRATED GOODS MARKETS
Chapter 3 (1995).*

MARKET SOLUTIONS AND MARKET FAILURES

The process of ensuring product compatibility and policing aspects of quality has always entailed a mixture of public sector and private sector initiatives. Yet great variation exists across nations in the matters that have been left to the market and those that have been subjected to regulation, and debates continue both in political assemblies and in the academy as to the appropriate role of government in regulating product characteristics.

Whatever the appropriate scope of government intervention, it is indisputable that the market alone regularly generates solutions to compatibility problems and quality problems within industries. These private sector efforts are by no means confined to national boundaries. The International Organization for Standardization (ISO), the International Electrotechnical Commission (IEC), and other international organizations regularly produce global standards as a result of private sector initiatives. For some technical barrier "problems," therefore, the best public policy response may be to leave the matter to the private sector, perhaps with some government encouragement in the form of subsidy to overcome collective action problems. In other cases, however, market failure may be anticipated. The issues tend to divide, with some overlap, between compatibility measures and quality measures.

COMPATIBILITY AND THE MARKET

Because only *in*compatibilities give rise to "technical barriers," the emphasis here is on the causes of incompatibilities and the question whether they are economically inefficient. The possibility that inefficient compatibility may arise is largely ignored here. The central question, then, is what inference to draw when the market has not produced compatibility on its own, at least to the degree that some observers believe appropriate and within a time frame that they believe appropriate. One possibility is that the absence of greater compatibility in the marketplace reveals that it is undesirable. The other possibility is that market failure in the economic sense has arisen. Which is the case in a given instance may be unclear. Consider first the various welfare issues that arise with incompatibilities, and next the question of whether the market will sort things out optimally.

WELFARE EFFECTS OF INCOMPATIBILITY. The economic consequences of any product incompatibility, whether market-or government-generated, turn on much the same issues—the extent to which incompatibility is a result of valuable product heterogeneity in the market or an impediment to it, the extent to which the incompatibility affects costs of production, the extent to which it affects competition, the extent to which it precludes the attainment of "network externalities," and the extent to which efforts to eliminate it would prove costly for reasons other than an attendant reduction in product variety. Regarding the first set of issues, much of what is regarded as choice in the marketplace entails a lack of compatibility and may, in some sense, create technical barriers to commerce. As an example, consider the introduction of the compact audio disc (CD) technology. It immediately resulted in several incompatibilities between long-playing records and CD players, between analog recording equipment and CD production, and so on. Yet these incompatibilities lay at the heart of the difference between the new and old technologies, and it was not possible to avoid them and still embrace the benefits of the new technology. Likewise, the availability of choice among different makes and models of televisions, automobiles, washing machines, and innumerable other products logically necessitates incompatibility between at least some of their components—if the components were all identical, the products would not be different. When incompatibility is of this type, efforts to reduce it will obviously entail a significant cost in the form of restrictions on consumer choice.

These sorts of incompatibilities, however, are rarely viewed as technical barriers. When incompatibility necessarily results from product differentiation by manufacturers driven by the development of superior technology, by heterogeneity in consumer preferences, and so on, it tends to emerge within nations as well as across them. Therefore any problems that it creates are typically not perceived as international trade problems.

When incompatibility does become an issue in international trade, the usual concern is that nations or national industries will converge or have converged on a particular compatibility standard for convenience or for strategic reasons and that resulting international incompatibilities serve little or no useful function. Examples include the international divergence between the metric and imperial systems, the present difference in color television broadcast formats between the United States and Europe, the divergence between left-hand drive and right-hand drive vehicles, divergence in railroad gauge standards, and differences in voltage standards.

In such cases, the likely effect of incompatibilities is to *reduce* variety in the marketplace. Many electrical appliance manufacturers that might otherwise be inclined to export may be discouraged from doing so by the difference in voltage standards. Television manufacturers that serve the U.S. and Japanese markets, with the NTSC broadcast format, may not attempt to manufacture for the French market with its SECAM format or other European markets with their PAL formats. The reduction in choice that these international incompatibilities can produce, therefore, is one of their welfare costs.

Similarly, incompatibilities can increase production costs and thus prices. Costs can rise, for example, because the need to produce different products for different markets prevents the realization of economies of scale in manufacturing. It may also necessitate costly changes in inventory policies and distribution systems. In some cases, the increase may be trivial, and incompatibility may not pose much of a problem, whereas in other cases, market segmentation may have a significant effect on costs.

The segmentation of markets due to incompatibilities may also create competition problems. If a market is small relative to the minimum efficient scale of operation for producers, only one or a few firms may serve it. Incompatibilities may thus function as a barrier to entry, with the possibility of welfare losses due to the exercise of market power.

Incompatibilities can also prevent the attainment of network externalities. When a new user joins a telephone or computer network, for example, other users may receive a nonpecuniary benefit. To the extent that compatibility standards facilitate larger networks, the existence of network externalities in some settings suggests an additional benefit to these standards. This issue has obvious significance for telecommunications and computers.

For a variety of reasons, therefore, most of the incompatibilities that are viewed as technical barriers in the trading community are likely to have some significant economic costs associated with them, rarely offset by any valuable heterogeneity in the product market that incompatibility facilitates. It does not follow that these incompatibilities should be eliminated, however, for at least two reasons. First, to eliminate incompatibilities, a choice must be made among the competing options. Often it will not be clear which option is superior. Second, once incompatibilities emerge, it is not costless to correct them. The divergence in television broadcast formats is a useful example once again. If the world as a whole, or even Europe alone, were to convert to a single format, broadcast facilities using the discarded format would have to incur significant costs to replace equipment, and consumers with television receivers incompatible with the new format would have to purchase new ones. Such difficulties of conversion are sometimes referred to as the "installed base" problem, and it is an empirical question whether the costs of conversion would exceed the benefits.

This last point suggests the importance of distinguishing incompatibilities that already exist from those that may arise in the future. It may, at times, be worth avoiding incompatibilities in the first instance but not be worth fixing them after they have arisen.

VIABILITY OF MARKET SOLUTIONS. If product incompatibilities result in a significant increase in production costs and prevent firms from taking advantage of profitable opportunities to sell to consumers in other markets, an incentive to eliminate incompatibility will arise at least on the part of some market participants. Even when profits will be competed down to a competitive level in the long run, opportunities to expand sales and reduce costs yield at least transitory gains that justify efforts to attain them.

Incompatibilities may be eliminated in various ways. Firms may elect on their own to make their products compatible with those of the industry leader (the decision to make IBM-compatible software and hardware by firms in the computer industry was largely a "follow the leader" approach). Alternatively, the developer of a proprietary technology may license it cheaply with the objective of making it the industry standard (the triumph of the VHS standard for video-cassettes is said to be an example). Yet another alternative is merger among the firms with the need to cooperate on compatibility matters (the history of the railroad industry in the United States is suggestive). Incompatibilities may also be remediable through various forms of interfaces or adapters, a familiar item in the suitcases of world travelers who must cope with voltage differences.

A further way that the private sector eliminates undesirable incompatibilities is through cooperative efforts to promulgate compatibility standards. The creation of standards organizations such as the American Society of Testing and Materials, the American Society of Mechanical Engineers, the American Society of Automotive Engineers, and others, established and funded privately, reflects effective market responses to profitable opportunities for standardization.

GENERAL AGREEMENT ON TARIFFS AND TRADE (1994)

ARTICLE III. NATIONAL TREATMENT ON INTERNAL TAXATION AND REGULATION

* * *

1. The contracting parties recognize that internal taxes and other internal charges, and laws, regulations and requirements affecting the internal sale, offering for sale, purchase, transportation, distribution or use of products, and internal quantitative regulations requiring the mixture, processing or use of products in specified amounts or proportions, should not be applied to imported or domestic products so as to afford protection to domestic production.

* * *

Ad *Article III*

Paragraph 1

The application of paragraph 1 to internal taxes imposed by local governments and authorities within the territory of a contracting party is subject to the provisions of the final paragraph of Article XXIV. The term "reasonable measures" in the last-mentioned paragraph would not require, for example, the repeal of existing national legislation authorizing local governments to impose internal taxes which, although technically inconsistent with the letter of Article III, are not in fact inconsistent with its spirit, if such repeal would result in a serious financial hardship for the local governments or authorities concerned. With regard to taxation by local governments or authorities which is inconsistent with both the letter and spirit of Article III, the term "reasonable measures" would permit a contracting party to eliminate the inconsistent taxation gradually over a transition period, if abrupt action would create serious administrative and financial difficulties.

---

2. The products of the territory of any contracting party imported into the territory of any other contracting party shall not be subject, directly or indirectly, to internal taxes or other internal charges of any kind in excess of those applied, directly or indirectly, to like domestic products. Moreover, no contracting party shall otherwise apply internal taxes or other internal charges to imported or domestic products in a manner contrary to the principles set forth in paragraph 1.

* * *

Paragraph 2

A tax conforming to the requirements of the first sentence of paragraph 2 would be considered to be inconsistent with the provisions of the second sentence only in cases where competition was involved between, on the one hand, the taxed product and, on the other hand, a directly competitive or substitutable product which was not similarly taxed.

---

3. With respect to any existing internal tax which is inconsistent with the provisions of paragraph 2, but which is specifically authorized under a trade agreement, in force on April 10, 1947, in which the import duty on the taxed product is bound against increase, the contracting party imposing the tax shall be free to postpone the application of the provisions of paragraph 2 to such tax until such time as it can obtain release from the obligations of such trade agreement in order to permit the increase of such duty to the extent necessary to compensate for the elimination of the protective element of the tax.

4. The products of the territory of any contracting party imported into the territory of any other contracting party shall be accorded treatment no less favourable than that accorded to like products of national origin in respect of all laws, regulations and requirements affecting their internal sale, offering for sale, purchase, transportation, distribution or use. The provisions of this paragraph shall not prevent the application of differential internal transportation charges which are based exclusively on the economic operation of the means of transport and not on the nationality of the product.

5. No contracting party shall establish or maintain any internal quantitative regulation relating to the mixture, processing or use of products in specified amounts or proportions which requires, directly or

indirectly, that any specified amount or proportion of any product which is the subject of the regulation must be supplied from domestic sources. Moreover, no contracting party shall otherwise apply internal quantitative regulations in a manner contrary to the principles set forth in paragraph 1.

* * *

Paragraph 5

Regulations consistent with the provisions of the first sentence of paragraph 5 shall not be considered to be contrary to the provisions of the second sentence in any case in which all of the products subject to the regulations are produced domestically in substantial quantities. A regulation cannot be justified as being consistent with the provisions of the second sentence on the ground that the proportion or amount allocated to each of the products which are the subject of the regulation constitutes an equitable relationship between imported and domestic products.

* * *

8.   (a) The provisions of this Article shall not apply to laws, regulations or requirements governing the procurement by governmental agencies of products purchased for governmental purposes and not with a view to commercial resale or with a view to use in the production of goods for commercial sale.

(b) The provisions of this Article shall not prevent the payment of subsidies exclusively to domestic producers, including payments to domestic producers derived from the proceeds of internal taxes or charges applied consistently with the provisions of this Article and subsidies effected through governmental purchases of domestic products.

9.   The contracting parties recognize that internal maximum price control measures, even though conforming to the other provisions of this Article, can have effects prejudicial to the interests of contracting parties supplying imported products. Accordingly, contracting parties applying such measures shall take account of the interests of exporting contracting parties with a view to avoiding to the fullest practicable extent such prejudicial effects.

* * *

Note on NAFTA and Telecommunications*

Cross-border services and investment in basic telecommunications and public networks are not authorized by NAFTA. Nevertheless, the privatization of TELMEX (with a 10 percent U.S. partner) and Mexico's participation in the WTO agreement on basic telecommunications have made a difference. Mexico now allows 49 percent foreign ownership in wireline services, and 100 percent ownership in cellular and private leased-line services. AT & T, MCI and other long distance U.S. carriers have invested heavily in the Mexican market.

One key issue is what local network connection rates TELMEX can charge these carriers. This issue was first subject to intense private negotiations which failed. In 1996, the Mexican Ministry of Communications and Transport (SCT) set rates following "international norms." These rates were viewed by U.S. companies as providing TELMEX with a subsidy for its inexpensive local phone services. Likewise, they increased the incentive to invest in new telecommunications infrastructure so as to be able to avoid connecting through TELMEX entirely. The rates were reduced significantly in 1998, but not before TELMEX had turned the competitive tables by establishing very effective long distance services in the United States targeted at Mexicans and Mexican–Americans calling "home."

Chapter 13 of NAFTA creates North American rules for much of the "enhanced" telecommunications industry. Enhanced or value-added telecommunications services are defined in the agreement as those employing computer processing applications that act on customer-transmitted information, provide customers with information or involve customer interaction with stored information. Such services include, for example, voice mail, cellular phone, fax, paging systems and electronic mail services. It is noteworthy that the enhanced telecommunications provisions of NAFTA are supreme if inconsistencies with any other part of the agreement arise.

The NAFTA rules on enhanced telecommunications can be summarized as follows. Domestic and international public telecommunications networks and services must be made available on reasonable, nondiscriminatory terms and conditions. Providers of enhanced or value-added telecommunications services, information services, and internal corporate communication systems specifically benefit from this provision. Access terms must generally be reasonable and allow leasing private lines, attachment of equipment to public networks, switching, signaling and processing functions, and selection of operating protocols. All national licensing rules and procedures governing NAFTA telecommunications providers must be transparent, expeditiously applied and nondiscriminatory. A review of the financial solvency and ability of providers to meet technical regulations is anticipated. Furthermore, unlike many utilities, enhanced telecommunications providers need not cost-justify their rates, make mandatory interconnections, nor provide services to the public. Investment by North Americans in enhanced telecommunications companies has been essentially free of restrictions since 1995.

NAFTA also sets some general rules for public telecommunications networks. Transport rates, for example, must be based on actual economic costs, but cross-subsidization between services is permissible. A flat-rate basis must be used to price privately leased circuits. Standards for equipment attached to public networks are authorized only to prevent technical damage or interference, to prevent billing problems, or to guarantee safety. Mutual reciprocity for equipment test results undertaken in each NAFTA country is the rule and there is agreement on promoting international standards for compatibility. In this regard, the delayed arrival of Mexico's telecom standards was discussed in Chapter 4. Mexico's acceptance of U.S. telecommunications test data was also delayed until 1997.

Public telecommunications monopolies are not prohibited by NAFTA provided they do not engage in anticompetitive conduct regarding enhanced services. The agreement specifically prohibits cross-subsidization, predatory behavior and discriminatory access terms in the enhanced telecommunications sector. Each NAFTA government must provide effective access to the information necessary for companies and users to benefit from NAFTA's enhanced telecommunications regime. Specifically, information on public network tariffs and contract terms, interface requirements, standards organizations, attachment conditions and licensing controls must be provided.

Questions and Comments

1. What exactly are "standards-related measures"? How do "standards" differ from "technical regulations". *See* Article 915. Is the Mexican cell phone norma a standard or a technical regulation?

Does NAFTA require *any* alteration of national, or state or provincial, SRM rules? What about local government SRMs such as municipal code requirements?

2. Trader Jane's SRM problem concerns a federal Mexican norma governing technical specifications for cell phones. Does NAFTA require that this norma meet the rules established in Chapter 9? *See* Article 901. Suppose the norma originated in one or more of the Mexican states. Does Chapter 9 apply? *See* Article 902. And if the norma originated in a Mexican non-governmental standardizing body? *Id.* Contrast your answers to the same questions regarding SPS measures in Part A.

3. What is the significance of the "affirmation" in Article 903 of the GATT Agreement on Technical Barriers to Trade (1979)? In 1995, after NAFTA, a new GATT/WTO Agreement on Technical Barriers to Trade (TBT) became effective. All three NAFTA members adhere. Is a breach of the 1995 TBT Agreement a breach of NAFTA? The 1979 TBT Agreement?

In other parts of NAFTA, provisions of the GATT agreement were incorporated by specific reference. *See* Article 301 incorporating Article III of the GATT 1947 agreement "or any equivalent provision of a successor agreement to which all parties are party", i.e., Article III of the GATT 1994 agreement. *See* also Article 309 incorporating GATT Article XI (Quotas) and Article 2101 similarly incorporating GATT Article XX (Exceptions). Do these examples help us understand the significance of Article 903?

As to whether the GATT provisions cited above apply to SPS measures, see Article 710.

4.　Article 904 contains NAFTA's basic SRM rights and obligations. What basic rights are there? What basic obligations? Must the Mexican norma be "necessary" and "appropriate"?

5.　Read carefully the second sentence in Article 904(1). What does this sentence suggest for Trader Jane? Is there a comparable provision regarding SPS measures? *See* Article 712(1).

6.　Must Mexico have a "legitimate objective" for its norma? *See* Article 904(2). If so, what might that be? *See* Article 915. Suppose Mexico says that its norma is designed to protect cell phone users from electromagnetic field (EMF) injury. Is that a legitimate objective? Must Mexico conduct an "assessment of risk" in establishing its SRMs? *See* Article 907. If not, why? Recall that such assessments *are* required for SPS measures.

7.　Mexico's norma applies to all cell phones sold in that country. Suppose Trader Jane argues that it is only being enforced against U.S.-made cell phones. What does Article 904(3) suggest? What is "national treatment"? What is "most favored nation" treatment? Might we now have a GATT dispute on our hands? *See* Article III of the GATT 1994. Or is it a NAFTA dispute? Is it both?

Are there likely to be any "market solutions" to Trader Jane's problem? *See* the second Sykes excerpt.

8.　Has Mexico created an "unnecessary obstacle" to NAFTA trade? *See* Article 904(4). How would you argue on behalf of Trader Jane that it has? How would you argue on behalf of Mexico that is has not?

9.　How are international SRMs created? *See* the first Sykes excerpt. Suppose there are international cell phone standards. Must Mexico adopt them? *See* Article 905. Suppose Mexico argues that it has a high percentage of cell phone users and cell phones therefore pose greater societal risks than in the United States. Does that matter? Does Article 905 tell us a bit more about "legitimate" SRM objectives?

10.　Suppose that the cell phones meet all U.S. standards, including EMF safety. Trader Jane argues that the U.S. standards are equivalent. Equivalent to what? *See* Article 906. Is this the same as the SPS test of equivalence? *See* Part A and Article 714.

Suppose Trader Jane offers independent test results certifying compliance with the U.S. standards to the Mexican authorities as proof of "conformity" with Mexican law. Must Mexico entertain such an offer of proof? *See* Articles 906(6) and (7). Must it accept such proof?

11.　What is a "conformity assessment" and why are they important to SRMs? *See* Articles 908 and 915, and the excerpt by Coffield.

12.　Note that Article 913(5)(a)(ii) and Annex 913.5.a–2 create a NAFTA Telecommunications Standards Subcommittee. What does this Subcommittee do? Might its work affect Trader Jane's problem?

13.　Note also that Chapter 13 of the NAFTA agreement is exclusively devoted to Telecommunications. This problem has been designed to minimize Chapter 13 issues, which primarily concern the provision of enhanced or value-added telecommunications services. You may wish to explore NAFTA's impact on this vital industry, where annual long distance traffic services are worth over $2 billion annually. Certain Mexican commitments made not under NAFTA but under the WTO's General Agreement on Trade in Services (GATS) were, in the view of the United States, breached through the failure of Telmex to provide "cost-oriented and reasonable" interconnect rates between the local phone system and competing long-distance providers in Mexico. *See Mexico—Measures Affecting Telecommunications Services,* WT/DS204/R, Panel Report (Mar. 12, 2004), *available at* http://www.wto.org. In June 2004, the United States and Mexico announced that they had settled the dispute, with Mexico agreeing to modify its restrictions on commercial negotiation of international settlement rates (charged for connections into Mexico's telecommunications network).

14. Chapter 9 standards issues were raised in one NAFTA Chapter 20 dispute, but the decision was based on violations of Chapters 11 and 12. *See Cross–Border Trucking Services,* Secretariat File No. USA–MEX–98–2008–01 (Feb. 6, 2001), discussed in Chapter 6, *infra.*

PROBLEM 5.3 MEDIA MOGUL ENCOUNTERS THE CANADIAN CULTURAL INDUSTRY EXCLUSION

SECTION I. THE SETTING

Your client, MEDIA MOGUL, is a Hollywood legend. It always seems to be ahead of the industry when it comes to making money on media products (films, music, videos, TV programs, etc.). MEDIA MOGUL is neither "culturally oriented" nor "culturally sensitive." It takes pride and profit in producing for mainstream U.S. audiences.

One of MEDIA MOGUL's best selling products is a TV sitcom "Nights of Your Life". Another hot product is a video called "Nightlife". A third more focused product is a radio program called "Kountry Night Music". It has plans to produce a film titled, you guessed it, "Nights". All of these products are featured in a monthly magazine it owns called MEDIA MOGUL Illustrated.

MEDIA MOGUL has done well in the United States market. Its sales and licensing department believes that MEDIA MOGUL's products will appeal to foreign audiences. For starters the department wants to target Canada and Mexico because these are thought to be "easy". Most MEDIA MOGUL products are manufactured in the Hollywood area using stock actors, musicians, directors, technicians and the like. But with its emphasis on the bottom line, MEDIA MOGUL would be willing to produce just about anywhere conditions and technology permit, especially if its costs are noticeably lower.

MEDIA MOGUL approaches you for advice on its prospects in the Canadian and Mexican markets.

SECTION II. FOCUS OF CONSIDERATION

Trade in media products has expanded enormously in recent years. For the United States, media-related exports rank second behind only defense-oriented goods, services and technology. Part of the boom can be explained by the ever increasing number of channels available on cable and satellite broadcast systems, and by the widespread availability of home entertainment devices like VCRs. The Internet promises an expansion in demand for and trade in media products that is mind boggling.

There is no international agreement governing trade in media products. Considerable effort was made to reach such an accord in the Uruguay Round of WTO agreements, but these efforts failed. Many say that this failure was primarily the result of a late withdrawal of support by the United States. In the absence of an international agreement, regional law has become important to trade in media products. The most (in)famous example is the European Community Broadcasting Directive No. 89/552. This 1989 law provides that "when practicable" European broadcasters should reserve a majority of their air time for programs of "European origin" (defined in terms of economic not cultural content). *See* R. Folsom, *European Union Law in A Nutshell,* Chapter 5.

Less well known are the NAFTA rules governing trade in "cultural industry" goods. These rules originated in the Canada–U.S. Free Trade Agreement of 1989 (CFTA) and were expressly retained under NAFTA. (The cultural industry rules do not apply at all to U.S.—Mexico trade relations; why not?) As we shall see, MEDIA MOGUL and their attorneys will learn all about the Canadian cultural industry exclusion.

ROBINSON, THE INFORMATION REVOLUTION—CULTURE AND SOVEREIGNTY—A CANADIAN PERSPECTIVE
24 Can.–U.S. Law J. 147 (1998).*

This session is unusual in at least two respects: it is a rematch from 1997, and it is your entertainment for today. We are going to do it in a debate/drama style. You have heard of the "Thrilla from Manila," and there was the "Rumble in the Jungle." Well, this is the "Clash in Cleveland on Culture."

* * *

I am both a free trader and a cultural protectionist, and that dichotomy is very hard for our American colleagues to understand. Kim Campbell, the Consul General of Canada, is similarly bifurcated. She is a former Prime Minister of Canada. In an address to the U.S. film industry out at a university in southern California, she made that apology (or boast, depending on your point of view) and said she used to try to apologize to Bill Clinton. He did not understand her either because, from the Canadian prospective, Americans characterize culture as a business. Canadians characterize it as quite a bit more. Whether that characterization is merely self-serving by my American colleagues, I do not know. In the case of Mr. Jack Valenti it is,[1] but there are others who I am sure have more genuinely objective views on this subject.

* * *

Let me rattle off the usual statistics. The United States controls ninety-five percent of Canadian movie screens. That does fluctuate. Some say it is ninety-two percent; some say it is ninety-six percent, but let us say it is ninety-five percent. The United States controls eighty percent of Canadian news and television broadcasts. U.S.-published books take up sixty percent of Canadian bookshelf space, and U.S. magazines make up eighty percent of the English-language market.

(What I really wanted, for a personal reason, when we defined culture in the Canada/United States Free Trade Agreement, was for football to be added to the definition of culture. I could not get anywhere with that proposal. I am from Hamilton, Ontario, a dirty steel town down the lake from Toronto. It is like your Pittsburgh; it has steel mills and rough, tough football. The town's football team is over 120 years old. Of course, we invented the game in Canada and sent it, by way of the annual Harvard–McGill rugby match, to you in the United States. Now Canadian football needs protection from the inundation of this degraded, four-down, small-field version that you play in this country. But my friends in Ottawa said we were going to have enough trouble with this cultural exemption, without putting football in it.)

I think it is important to realize when we start this discussion that this is not a legal issue; this is a socio-political issue. There is an exemption in the Canada–United States Free Trade Agreement (FTA) which was carried over to NAFTA. When it comes to culture, we do not have to give Mexicans or Americans anything in the nature of national or most-favored-nation (MFN) treatment. It is not covered by the law. Of course, there are some exceptions, like the *Periodicals* case,[2] which ultimately defined magazines as goods under the WTO. In essence, however, this is not a legal issue. Let us not get bogged down on this. Canada has the right to discriminate all it wants. Saying that this is a legal issue is a red herring.

In John Ragosta's article last year,[3] he talked a good deal about balance. I feel that it is helpful to understand the issue to appreciate that there is no balance between the Canadian and American markets for culture, and by that I mean things that are particularly Canadian as contrasted with pop culture.

What is an example of that? We have a company in Toronto called LiveEnt, Inc., which was controlled until two days ago by a Canadian

---

1. Jack Valenti is the President and Chief Executive Officer of the Motion Picture Association of America.

2. *See Canada—Certain Measures Concerning Periodicals*, Panel Report, WT/DS31/R Mar. 14, 1997; Report of the Appellate Body, (WT/DS31/AB/R), June 30, 1997.

3. See John Ragosta, The Cultural Industries Exemption from NAFTA—*Its Parameters—A U.S. Perspective*, 23 Can.–U.S. L.J. 165 (1997).

named Drabinski. He builds and operates live theaters in New York, among other things. People might say that Canadian culture has been successfully marketed in the United States because Drabinski has a theater in New York and is building a theater in Chicago. What are Canadians complaining about? (Drabinski was just taken over by Michael Ovitz two days ago, so that will be end of it as a Canadian company.)

But in any event, what LiveEnt sells is pop culture, nicely packaged. *Ragtime* is a perfect example.[4] It has nothing to do with Canadian culture. So, in that sense, one has to realize that things particularly Canadian—and my definition of Canadian culture is Canadians talking to Canadians about things Canadian—have no market in the United States. Why is that? Because Americans do not care what goes on in Canada.

* * *

My point about balance is that there can never really be free trade or fair trade in culture between the United States and Canada if you accept my assumption that culture is not a commodity. If that is the case, that our distinctive Canadian culture can never be sold south of the border, even though the U.S. popular culture can be and is sold north of the border, then my thesis is that we Canadians have to take some steps to protect that small market of twenty-five million people spread out over three thousand miles who are going to receive the inundation of U.S. culture. They will receive it because of our geographical proximity, one of our languages is in common, and there is a relative absence of trade and investment barriers between our two countries.

* * *

One can argue forever about what is distinctive about Canada's culture. Is there a distinctive Canadian culture? Canadians debate this as a blood sport. The three things people can get into bar fights about in Canada are Quebec's sovereignty, hockey, and the question, are we really a culturally distinct people? The secondary issue is, assuming our culture is distinctive, is it worth protecting?

These issues are not relevant to this debate, I submit, because it is simply not open to Americans to question the existence of a distinctly Canadian culture. If Canadians believe they have a Canadian culture which needs protection, that must be the end of the discussion.

My submission is that, to have a genuine belief in one's own separate cultural identity carries with it the right to defend that belief, which is an entirely legitimate use of sovereignty.

* * *

I am sure John will make the point, and I will have to agree with him on this one, that all of the Canadian efforts to protect culture may

---

4. RAGTIME (Frank Galati, dir. 1997).

be futile because of what is happening technologically. He would then say, so why bother? I would say we have to try harder. We will just have to invent something like radar, as the British did just before the Second World War to protect themselves from the Luftwaffe.

I do not think the American people or the U.S. Congress would tolerate for a nanosecond the level of domination of its cultural industries by foreigners that Canadians are forced to tolerate. Congressmen speaking in the House complained that the Japanese were buying the U.S. movie industry when Sony brought its business to the United States. They lamented that it would be horrible if foreigners owned U.S. industries. Well, in this case, the foreigners are you. You own our cultural industries. The Canadian government is attempting to put up some minimal protections to keep what we Canadians have. We are not trying to chase it all away.

If you look at the market shares of Canadian cultural industries held by Americans, the United States has a clearly dominant position which is certainly open to abuse, if not abusive in itself. Now, if you took your own standards of the Sherman Act and the Clayton Act and applied them, would this conduct be legal? I suggest it might not be. They used to call the big Hollywood studios the seven thieves. Now it is the six sisters. The film industry is a pretty tightly controlled business in the United States, let alone in Canada, where the six sisters totally dominate.

* * *

One more thing, and I will sit down. There is an interesting additional argument that I heard recently. English language dominance in Canada is being aided and abetted by U.S. dominance of films, print, and television in Canada, and this is encouraging Anglo-phobia in Quebec, which is furthering the separatist cause. I think there is some merit in that analysis, and even more merit in Canada being allowed to use its perfectly legal right to throw up cultural protectionist barriers.

In the final analysis, I believe the best way to the look at the issue is simply this; our countries share the world's largest (maybe the second largest, if you count the E.U. as one entity) bilateral trading relationship at one billion dollars a day. We have heard for centuries that we share the world's longest undefended border, and that is not a small thing. We have supported each other in war, peace, and foreign policy since the War of 1812, which was the last time we had to chase you Yanks back south of the border. Ever since then, it has been sweetness and light between us. We have also been shoulder-to-shoulder with the United States in peaceful pressures right up until the latest confrontation with Iraq, where we sent a couple of tiny boats, which is about half of our Navy, to the Persian Gulf.

Why is it that many Americans cannot see the forest of this outstanding relationship for the trees of this relatively minor trade barrier and just back off? Surely, you have enough serious trade problems with other countries. Canadian culture is a peanut in terms of U.S.-Canada and U.S.-world trade and political relationships. Since Canadians feel strongly about this issue, and John certainly acknowledges that they do, and indeed complains that they shout about it too much, and since the United States already has such a large, dominant (some would say abusively dominant) share of Canadian cultural industries in the business sense, why not have a little more common sense and common courtesy in this area and just leave it alone?

Canadian culture is no threat whatsoever to U.S. cultural industries. Canadian culture is already mainly in the hands of U.S. business, and excessive greed is a poor basis for continuing our trade relations in the good state that they are now, and have been in for a long time.

RAGOSTA, THE INFORMATION REVOLUTION—CULTURE AND SOVEREIGNTY—A U.S. PERSPECTIVE
24 Can.–U.S. Law J. 155 (1998).*

Today, I do not want to talk primarily about the legality, the existence, or even the advisability of Canadian cultural restrictions. Rather, I have been asked to address a topic that is perhaps less interesting in terms of the heat of the debate, but ultimately far more important to Canadians, as it is to the United States—the development of technology, and whether technology is going to undermine the ability to protect so-called "cultural industries" in the manner in which Canada and other countries have sought to do.

Before turning to that topic, however, I must respond to some of Mr. Robinson's efforts to justify Canadian protectionism allegedly in the defense of Canadian culture.

* * *

Canadian culture is not nearly so fragile, nor of so little interest, as Mr. Robinson's plea for special protection suggests.

As Mr. Robinson was kind enough to send me his notes beforehand, I had one of my legal assistants get on the Internet and pull down a list of names of leading pop artists in the United States who are Canadian nationals. These artists include Sarah MacLachlan, Shania Twain, Alanis Morisette, k.d. lang, Bryan Adams, Crash Test Dummies, Men Without Hats, Barenaked Ladies, and Celine Dion, just to name a few. (I did not mention Anne Murray, Neil Young, or Rush because I know who they are.)

Mr. Robinson may dismiss these artists as "pop culture" (a cultural discrimination in itself), but Canadian influence goes well beyond that. Canadian movies have been increasingly successful, as evidenced by the recent success of *The Sweet Hereafter* and the consistent popularity of the *Anne of Green Gables* series among young people. In fact, *USA Today, the Weekend Edition* last week (and I have to explain that I was on vacation, which is why I was reading *USA Today*) talked about the fact that key movie and television filming sites are moving away from Hollywood. Two of the top ten sites in North America, I believe, are Vancouver and Toronto. As for actors, the list is too long to read. Canadian authors include Margaret Atwood, Douglas Coplin, and Michael Ondaatje, the latter having written a novel later made into an Academy Award-winning movie.[1] Therefore, I do not agree that Americans have no interest in what Canadians have to say.

The second thing that strikes me about Mr. Robinson's presentation is his statement that Canadian culture is really just "Canadians talking to Canadians about things Canadian." I have to tell you that this is the best straight line I have ever been handed ... but I am going to resist. You can fill in what I might say. It strikes me, however, that were I Canadian and I cannot speak personally to that view, I would be offended by this definition. (I was also offended last year at this conference when Canadian culture was defined as things not-American). I would think that Canadian culture is Canadians speaking from a Canadian perspective about things of greater value: about life, about love, about death, about compromise, about hope, and about fear, etc.

And, of course, The United States has an interest, as does the world, in hearing a Canadian perspective on those transcendent values, just as Canadians are interested in an American perspective or a Japanese perspective or a French perspective on those things.

* * *

Finally, I want to address the question of balance and Mr. Robinson's criticism of my call for balance in Canada's cultural policies. I do not mean to suggest, nor did I mean to suggest last year, that the question of balance for Canada involves balancing U.S. interests versus Canadian interests. Quite the contrary; I would not suggest that Canada do that. I think the issue of balance is a question of balancing the protection of real cultural interests with that of purely commercial interests that are currently being protected by many Canadian cultural policies. Canada may be willing to pay the price for the former, but should not pay the price for the latter. The balance is what is going to be greatly affected by the development of technology.

* * *

Before I continue, let me briefly mention a list of current cultural issues and disputes among the United States, Canada, and Europe. As we go through these, think about them in terms of balance and technology. With respect to each matter, we might ask: Has Canada reached the proper balance between protecting Canadian commercial interest and the Canadian cultural interest? Second, is the underlying "cultural"

---

1. Michael Ondaatje, The English Patient: A Novel (Vintage Books, 1992).

restriction that caused this dispute one which is going to be viable, or maintain a reasonable balance as technology develops?

The first is Polygram, which will prove to be an interesting case to monitor. Polygram's complaint is that the current Canadian film distribution policy limits a European Union company's ability to distribute films in Canada that did not have at least a fifty-one percent stake in producing, while American producers are exempt from this policy. An interesting aspect, and one on which we will touch later, is that this debate has not stemmed from a debate on cultural protection *per se,* but from a violation of MFN status. The E.U. has repeatedly stated that the Polygram case is not to be viewed as a challenge to Canadian cultural restrictions.

The second issue is that of cable restrictions, which have still not been eliminated since our the conference last year. I am not going to go through the Canadian Radio–Television and Telecommunications Commission (CRTC) process this past year. It did somewhat liberalize Canadian access to U.S. cable service last summer and still continues to preclude access for MTV, HBO, and others. In fact, in January of this year, the CRTC talked about adding a new "cultural" protection by requiring that five percent of a cable service's revenue go to the creation and presentation of Canadian programming.

Sports Illustrated and the split-run issue in magazines remains an area of great importance.[6] The *Sports Illustrated* case is interesting. There, Canada argued with some persuasiveness that it was only regulating a service not covered by Canada's GATS obligations and thus a service that the WTO could not reach. GATT obligations, on the other hand, focus on goods; to have GATS disciplines, you have to have something that you can get your hands on. But what does that mean? The panel took a very broad view that all it needed to have authority to address Canadian restrictions was to find something tangible crossing the border in competition with a Canadian product. This view can greatly expand the WTO's ability to reach so-called cultural restrictions.

Ignoring *Sports Illustrated* for the moment, let us briefly think again about Canadian restrictions on split-runs. The primary restriction is Chapter 19 of the Canadian Income Tax Act. The second clause of Chapter 19 states that even if a publication is published, edited, printed, staffed in Canada, and all of its graphic arts are done in Canada, it cannot take a tax deduction for advertising revenues if it is owned by a U.S. citizen. Is that protecting Canadian culture? Is that balanced? Will that survive technological innovation?

The fourth example relates to a recent complaint of the MPAA [Motion Picture Association of America] about Canadian director requirements to have a film certified as Canadian. Consider a film made in Vancouver, having Canadian actors and technicians, that is printed in Canada, and uses a U.S. director. On the other hand, consider a film

---

6. *See Canada—Certain Measures Concerning Periodicals,* Panel Report, WT/ DS31/R, Mar. 14, 1997; Report of the Appellate Body, WT/DS31/AB/R, June 30, 1997.

made in New York, having U.S. actors and technicians, that is printed in the United States, and uses a Canadian director. Which film would appear to promote Canadian culture? Canada's current scheme appears to provide protection to the latter, not to the former.

* * *

Some of these practices are legitimate, and some are illegitimate. Today's question is, what, over the long run, will survive the development of technical knowledge? What is technology capable of overriding in this area? I am not a technological expert, but I have seen enough, talked with enough people, and read enough to realize that unfortunately, the revolution is coming.

For those of us who are slow to learn about the Internet and all of its different capabilities, learn now. On the Internet, you can dial up a movie or a broadcast of a small college's homecoming football game. You are able to communicate by e-mail. You can subscribe to magazines and order books. While on-line subscription services have yet to catch on fully, in another few years, when high-quality computer printers are a household item, you will wake up in the morning to your issue of *Time* or *Newsweek* in full color (perhaps on glossy paper) on your home printer.

We are undeniably in the midst of a technology revolution that may have an enormous impact on a country's ability to regulate its cultural industries. Where will the limits lie?

I think that cultural restrictions which seek to regulate distribution rather than content is where regulators, in Canada and elsewhere, are going to run into trouble technologically. Distribution now comes through technology, such as Amazon.com, satellite distribution, digitized music, and Internet access to magazines and movies, just to name a few. Regulation of cable will quickly become irrelevant, because access to the Internet via telephone lines and satellites is becoming ever more popular.

How can Canada seek to regulate this new, burgeoning method of distribution? One could put a bug on every telephone line going into every Canadian's house and try somehow to filter out things lacking in "cultural purity," assuming that one can figure out what to filter out. One can deny Canadians access to the Internet, or try to restrict it. I will tell you this, though, there is not a single parent in this room who would accept being denied access to U.S. Internet sites. The French tried that, and they got run over. In fact, my law firm experimented with this notion. We allowed some New York attorney to set our Internet policy for a few months. The firm restricted access to the Internet because it feared attorneys were wasting their time and were messing around on the Internet instead of doing research. They tried to filter out what they viewed to be commercial or entertainment sites. We ultimately had to dump the policy. We could not live with it because our researchers required access to the Internet. So, if you cannot regulate every phone line and every broadcast, how can you restrict access? It seems to me you cannot.

Canada seems to have given up on restricting satellite dishes, especially as they have become much smaller. The only thing that really prevented satellite dishes from entirely taking over the Canadian cable service was a very clever Canadian regulation, one which I used to think would solve the problem for Canada. This very clever regulation says to the Canadian cable services that if you permit your signal to be broadcast over a satellite not authorized by the Canadian government, they will remove you completely from Canadian cable. So, if a company already has substantial access to Canadian cable, like The Nashville Network or Country Music Television does, they would not want to sign a contract that would permit their signal to be used on a "rogue" satellite. This regulation, too, will be taken over by technology. When you reach the point where people will have access to TV through either their telephone lines, which is coming, or through a satellite, cable regulation will be out the window.

That brings me to a point where Mr. Robinson and I do not disagree; perhaps we even agree. Some of these technological advances are going to undermine the ability to restrict distribution. What does Canada do if they want to protect their culture? The first option is to continue to restrict distribution at their own peril, in the way they have been, and watch revolutionary developments in technology pass them and their restrictions by. Maybe they can get lawyers and technicians who are clever enough to figure out all of this and develop new methods to restrict access. I used to think this was possible, but I am no longer sure. I think that, at best, it is a rear-guard action.

The second option is just to rise out from under the restrictions and let the market take over. On the one hand, I think that Canadian culture would thrive far better in such a system than some in Canada might think. Indeed, it was former Canadian Minister of Foreign Affairs Andre Ouellette who said that to "protect" culture, Canada must "project" culture. On the other hand, I suspect this would not be a very welcome suggestion in Canada. In fact, even though numbers indicate that Canadians prefer to watch U.S. movies, Canadians continue to hate themselves for doing so. Studies repeatedly show that Canadians want cultural protectionism.

The third option is to get out of the business of trying to regulate distribution, and get into the business of trying to promote Canadian culture and cultural values more directly. I would suggest that many of the current restrictions have nothing to do with protecting Canadian culture. The *Country Music Television* case, with which I am very familiar because we represented Country Music Television, had nothing to do with protecting Canadian culture. The United States made it very clear that it was willing to live with any Canadian content requirement, any Canadian investment requirement, and any broadcast regulation which required it to put money back into Canada. But that was not sufficient for Canadian regulators. The only difference between Country Music Television and the New Country Network, for which CMT was summarily replaced, was where the dividend check went. That is what mattered to Canadian regulators.

* * *

There are alternatives to promote culture. One example would be to encourage investment in cultural interests. Canada has been very successful in this regard. Canada is the second largest exporter of films and TV shows in the world and makes billions of dollars of revenue per year.

* * *

I continue to believe that there is a balance for Canada to strike and I do not think it is inconsistent with the protection of Canadian culture. Fortunately or unfortunately, I have come to the conclusion that technology will force the establishment of balance as well as a movement toward increasingly legitimate cultural regulation as restrictions on distribution become increasingly irrelevant. In any case, technology is going to force the balance to be struck in a very different place than where it is now.

JOHNSON, THE NORTH AMERICAN FREE TRADE AGREEMENT
Chapter 10 (1994).*

Canada has a variety of measures relating to cultural industries that affect the right of establishment and impose performance requirements as a condition of receiving advantages in the form of grants from federal and provincial funding agencies. The primary purpose of these measures is not to insulate Canadians from American cultural products but to ensure that at least some of the cultural products available to Canadians are created by Canadians and involve Canadian talent and Canadian themes. The following briefly describes certain Canadian measures affecting television, films, book publishing and magazines.

TELEVISION AND CABLE

Free television is television programming that can be received by an antenna. There are three television networks in Canada, the publicly owned Canadian Broadcasting Corporation (CBC) and privately owned CTV and Global. Most television stations in Canada are owned or affiliated with the networks. However some, like CITY in Toronto, are independent. To operate, the operator of a television station must receive a licence from the Canadian Radio–Television and Telecommunications Commission ("CRTC"). The declaration of policy in the *Broadcasting Act* includes a statement that the Canadian broadcasting system must be "effectively owned and controlled by Canadians". Accordingly, a licence will not be granted unless the operator is Canadian-owned.

The declaration of policy in the *Broadcasting Act* also requires that the Canadian broadcasting system, "through its programming and the employment opportunities arising out of its operations, serve the needs and interests, and reflect the circumstances and aspirations, of Canadian men, women and children". Accordingly, television stations are subject to quota requirements in their broadcasting in that a certain amount of the programming broadcast by a station must be Canadian. The rules regarding Canadian content for CRTC purposes are set forth in a public notice issued by the CRTC in April, 1984. Points are awarded for particular aspects of a production being Canadian (such as the director or lead actor or actress) and the production must accumulate six points. Also, with certain exceptions at least 75% of total remuneration must be paid to Canadians and at least 75% of post-production costs must be incurred in Canada.

Cable television is delivered to subscribers through coaxial cable by a cable company. The programming may be either from free television through signals gathered by the cable company or from a cable service like TSN or CNN. Cable companies and cable services are licensed by the CRTC and must be Canadian-owned. The CRTC regulates the channels that cable companies can deliver to subscribers. For example, while Rogers Cable is permitted to carry the U.S.-operated CNN, it is not permitted to carry the U.S.-operated ESPN because it competes with Canadian-owned TSN. Cable services licensed in Canada are subject to quota requirements regarding Canadian programming similar to the free television stations.

FILM AND VIDEO PRODUCTION AND DISTRIBUTION

* * *

[S]everal Canadian programs clearly impose content-based performance requirements as conditions of receiving benefits. Income tax write-offs in the form of enhanced capital cost allowances are available for films that are certified by the Canadian Audio–Visual Certification Office ("CAVCO") on behalf of the applicable federal government minister as a "certified production". For a film or tape to be a "certified production", it must be produced by a Canadian and earn a minimum of six units of production on a prescribed point system similar to that described above. Also, the 75% expenditure tests described above must be met. Certified productions automatically qualify as Canadian for CRTC quota purposes but a production certified as Canadian under the CRTC rules will not necessarily qualify as a "certified production" for income tax benefits.*

Film productions that meet CRTC content requirements command premiums because they can be used by television broadcasters and cable

---

* Authors' Note: While the Canadian tax credit has changed somewhat since this article was written, the points system described is still very much operational in terms of determining who qualifies for the credit.

services in meeting Canadian quota requirements. Government funding through federal agencies such as Telefilm Canada or the National Film Board Co–Production Fund or the various provincial agencies are based on criteria which relate to nationality or content.

Canada has entered into co-production agreements with over twenty-five countries including Mexico, but not the United States. Co-production agreements are individually negotiated and vary from country to country. However, a co-production agreement will describe the production media covered (such as film and television), the minimum financial and creative participation by each party, the terms of participation for third parties and procedures for entry and exit of creative and technical personnel and equipment. A qualifying co-production film will be entitled to the full benefit of government incentives that are accorded to Canadian films. Co-ventures (international co-productions with countries that do not have a treaty with Canada) may none the less qualify as 100% Canadian content if certain criteria are met.

The major exhibitors of films in Canada are Cineplex–Odeon (partly Canadian-owned) and Famous Players (owned by Paramount, a U.S. corporation). There are no ownership restrictions on film exhibitors but Investment Canada would likely exercise its jurisdiction to prevent further erosion of Canadian ownership of the Canadian exhibition industry. There is nothing in Canada corresponding to the Mexican requirement referred to in § 7.9(3)(d)(v) that a certain portion of screen time be reserved for domestically produced films. In fact, most films exhibited in Canadian theatres are produced in the United States.

Distribution of films in Canada is done principally through the U.S. majors such as Twentieth Century Fox, Tristar, Columbia and Warner. These entities acquire distribution rights to films and control distribution to exhibitors and to the video market and television. Some of the U.S. majors have Canadian subsidiaries. There are two particularly significant Canadian-owned film distributors in Canada, namely Alliance and Astral. There are no ownership restrictions in Canada respecting distributors and the proposed film distribution legislation which was contemplated in 1988 and which would have placed limitations on the ability of foreign-owned film distribution companies to operate in Canada was never passed. However, Investment Canada could exercise its jurisdiction to prevent the further expansion in Canada of foreign-owned film distribution companies.

BOOK PUBLISHING

In 1985, the Canadian government announced the so-called "Baie Comeau Book Publishing Policy" (the "Baie Comeau Policy") following the acquisition of Prentice–Hall Inc. and its Canadian subsidiary, Prentice–Hall Canada by Paramount (then Gulf & Western). The policy was designed to raise the level of Canadian ownership in publishing, which was then about 27%. The Baie Comeau Policy provided that a foreign investor could only establish or acquire an interest in a Canadian book publishing or distribution business in the form of a joint venture under Canadian control. A direct or indirect acquisition of a foreign-controlled Canadian business had to be accompanied by an undertaking to divest control of the business to a Canadian at a fair market price within two years. Paramount was permitted to keep Prentice–Hall Canada but was required to sell Ginn Publishing Canada Inc., an educational publishing house that it had subsequently acquired, together with another smaller publishing house called GLC Publishing. No buyer for the companies appeared and the Canadian government, through the Canada Development Investment Company ("CDIC"), bought a controlling interest in the two companies in February, 1989. * * *

In early 1992 the Canadian government decided to discontinue the Baie Comeau Policy and the concept of forced divestiture. A revised book publishing policy announced in January, 1992, provides that acquisition of existing Canadian-controlled businesses by non-Canadians will not be permitted. Exceptions can be made if the business is in financial distress and Canadians have been given a full and fair opportunity to purchase. Non–Canadians wishing to sell existing businesses must give Canadians a full and fair opportunity to purchase and acquisitions by non-Canadians, as well as indirect acquisitions, are subject to the "net benefit to Canada" test. The policy sets out a number of commitments that Investment Canada would typically require from a foreign investor.

In February, 1994, CDIC sold Ginn Publishing Canada Inc. to Paramount. The government approved the transaction after receiving several undertakings from Paramount and also approved the sale of another Canadian publishing company, Maxwell Macmillan Canada Inc., to Paramount. The Ginn transaction was widely criticized in the Canadian press as a sellout to U.S. corporate interests. Whether the Ginn situation was unique on its own facts or represents a further shift in Canadian government policy remains to be seen.

MAGAZINES AND PERIODICALS

The Canadian government has used a combination of tax and border measures to encourage the development of the Canadian magazine industry. Section 19 of the *Income Tax Act* (Canada) does not permit the deduction of outlays of expenses for advertising space in a newspaper or periodical which is not a qualified "Canadian issue" of a Canadian-controlled newspaper or periodical. Tariff code item 9958 prohibits the importation of special editions, including split runs and regional editions, of periodicals with advertisements directed to a market in Canada that do not appear in editions distributed in the country of origin. Split runs are issues of a periodical using substantially the same editorial content but differing in some local content and advertising. This tariff code item also prohibits the importation of issues of periodicals with more than 5% of the advertising space indicating sources of availability or terms or conditions for the sale of goods in Canada. The objective of these measures is to encourage advertisers to place advertisements in Canadian periodicals and to discourage the U.S. magazine industry from serving the Canadian market with "Canadian" editions with advertising directed at Canadian consumers but with minimal Canadian content.

These measures have encouraged the development of a domestic magazine industry which has come a long way since the 1950s when the magazine market in Canada was dominated by the Canadian editions of *Time* and *Readers Digest*. As the former Minister of Communications, Perrin Beatty, said in March, 1993: "Canada has produced a vibrant, home-grown magazine industry whose livelihood depends on Canadian advertising revenues." However these measures have failed to stop split runs, which the Canadian Magazine Publishers Association views as a serious competitive threat. Multinational businesses have little difficulty in achieving the benefit of a deduction for advertisements placed in U.S. magazines. Canadian editions of magazines such as *Sports Illustrated* are designed and laid out in the United States and beamed electronically to Canada for printing. As a result, they never cross the border physically and therefore are not subject to tariff code item 9958. In July, 1993, the government issued new guidelines respecting the administration of the *Investment Canada Act* indicating that it would treat any new title launched in Canada by a non-Canadian publisher as a new business rather than the expansion of an existing business and therefore subject to full review. These guidelines do not affect split run editions such as *Time* or *Sports Illustrated* published in Canada before the new guidelines were issued.

In 1993 the Canadian government appointed a task force to review federal measures supporting the Canadian magazine industry. The task force report, which was released in March, 1994, concluded that an increase in split-run editions would threaten the viability of the Canadian magazine industry because significant advertising revenues would be diverted from Canadian magazines. The task force recommended that each issue of a split-run edition be subject to an excise tax of 80% of the amount charged for all advertising in that issue. * * *

GOODENOUGH, DEFENDING THE IMAGINARY TO THE DEATH? FREE TRADE, NATIONAL IDENTITY, AND CANADA'S CULTURAL PREOCCUPATION

15 Ariz. J. Int'l & Comp. Law 203 (1998).*

THE LAWS OF CANADA

Canada has employed a broad range of legal measures in its efforts to promote and protect its cultural autonomy across most of these categories. These measures include a variety of direct and tax-based subsidies for Canadian cultural industries, from magazine and book publishing to film and television production. Quotas for work containing significant Canadian content, and penalties and outright prohibitions

* Copyright © 1998 Arizona Journal of International and Comparative Law. Reproduced with permission. (Oliver R. Goodenough is Professor of Law, Vermont Law School.)

against the import and distribution of certain classes or percentages of external cultural production have also been imposed. Finally, there are rules regulating the foreign ownership of Canadian-based cultural industries. This essay does not include a complete catalog of these Canadian and provincial laws. Instead, it will examine a few national examples chosen from each category, providing a background for the wider discussion.

A Policy Divide: Exclusion or Choice

A certain policy schizophrenia underlies these measures. No consistent choice has been made between an *exclusionary* goal (i.e., keeping U.S. product out), which might be called *strong* protection, and a choice goal (i.e., keeping Canadian product in existence), which might be called *weak* protection. Strong protection, such as keeping things out, provides the greatest short-term help to Canadian providers. It also gives the greatest comfort to those who view U.S. cultural products as appalling stuff. Flat prohibitions, negative quotas, and other significant barriers on imports and foreign ownership are weapons of the exclusionary policy. Weak protection, by contrast, seeks only "to ensure Canadians have a choice of cultural materials from which to choose, including Canadian." The weapons for preserving choice include economic subsidies and affirmative quotas for Canadian production. Canada's measures fall on both sides of this strong/weak divide.

Subsidies and Incentives

The subsidies and incentives provided to Canadian culture producers have been significant and varied, although the recent crisis in Canadian government finance has led to some reduction in this area. Among the continuing pieces of government support have been highly-subsidized postage rates for many Canadian magazine publishers. Since the establishment of the Canada Post Corporation as a separate Crown corporation in 1981, there has been a set of special "funded" rates of postage available to eligible Canadian publications, including periodicals, mailed in Canada for delivery in Canada. * * *

The Canadian film and television industries also receive significant support, both from direct grants and investment from Telefilm Canada, and in the form of accelerated tax depreciation for qualifying productions. While the level of support has varied over the years, at some times the combined federal and provincial effect has been to provide as much as thirty percent of the production budget, a huge advantage in the capital-starved world of production.

Prohibitions, Penalties and Quotas on Foreign Product

There are a number of prohibitions, penalties and quotas that restrict the importation of cultural material. For instance, in recent years Canadian television broadcasters have faced quotas for "Canadian content" programming. Under the current regulations promulgated by the Canadian Radio-television and Telecommunications Commission

(CRTC) pursuant to the Canadian Broadcasting Act of 1991, private television broadcasters in Canada are required to air a minimum of fifty percent Canadian content programming in the evening time slots from six p.m. to midnight. The traditional tests for Canadian content have depended both on a point system, requiring that the producer be Canadian and that at least six of ten key creative positions be filled by Canadians, and on a cost basis requiring that at least seventy-five percent of expenditures be made to Canadians. United States and Canadian production companies involved in Canadian-content programming give a great deal of attention to the bona-fide meeting of these requirements.

In the area of direct broadcast satellite television, Canada has imposed a fifty percent Canadian content requirement on services distributed in Canada. Because Canada was slow in starting its own satellite services, there has been a thriving "grey market" in dishes aimed at U.S. satellites using a dummy U.S. address for billing. For awhile, estimates of the numbers of Canadians who signed up ranged as high as 20,000 a month, for a total of 500,000 subscribers. In November 1996, the Canadian Industry Ministry mailed out a brochure for Canadian retailers and importers to distribute a warning to consumers that "[r]etailers cannot legally sell such equipment, and everyone involved—pirate, retailer, and purchaser—could be charged with a criminal offence." The availability by the end of 1997 of planned Canadian satellite services has presented the possibility of law-abiding small-dish television. As such service gains acceptance, it will probably decrease, but not eliminate, the trans-border trade.

In the magazine field, Tariff Code 9958, enacted in 1965, flatly prohibited the importation into Canada of an issue of a periodical that is a special edition. This includes the prohibition of a split-run or regional edition that contains an advertisement that is primarily directed to a market in Canada and that does not appear in identical form in all editions of that issue of the periodical that were distributed in the periodical's country of origin. The intended effect is to prevent the issuance of a special Canadian advertising edition of what is otherwise a U.S. periodical. With a somewhat elitist aesthetic niceness, and emphasizing the fact that "high" culture is *not* at the center of this dispute, there are exceptions for periodicals whose principal function is the encouragement, promotion or development of the fine arts, letters, scholarship or religion.

In 1993, Time Warner thought that it had discovered a loophole in this provision. Rather than importing the magazine physically across the U.S.-Canadian border, it sent the editorial content for a special Canadian edition of the unequivocally mass-market SPORTS ILLUSTRATED by electronic transfer to Canadian printing facilities. As a result, Bill C–103, which added "Part V.I—Tax on Split-run Periodicals" to the Excise Tax Act, was adopted. This provision imposed an excise tax of 80 percent on the value of all advertisements contained in the split-run edition. The amendment defined a split-run edition as one that (i) is distributed in

Canada; (ii) has more than twenty percent of editorial material which is the same or substantially the same as editorial material that appears in one or more excluded editions of one or more issues of one or more periodicals; and (iii) contains an advertisement that does not appear in identical form in all the excluded editions. There are exemptions for split-run editions, portions of which are sold in Canada but which are not aimed at Canada, and for certain grandfathered editions that were distributed prior to March 26, 1993.

INVESTMENT REGULATION

Canada heavily regulates the ownership of its cultural industries. This was initially part of an overall regulation of foreign investment, first under the relatively restrictive Foreign Investment Review Act of 197[4] and, since 1985, by the more lenient Investment Canada Act. [See Chapter 5] Cultural investments of as little as five million Canadian dollars are scrutinized by Investment Canada, which has the power to turn them down if they are not of "net benefit to Canada."

One relatively recent example of these policies in action was the flap over the denial of permission for the U.S.-based Borders, Inc. to open an affiliated "superstore" in Toronto. On the one hand, Borders had played by the rules, finding Canadian partners who would own fifty-one percent of the enterprise. The ostensible problem was that the Toronto Borders would purchase its books through the U.S. company's centralized book-buying system. One might assume that an astute book seller—even one with otherwise hopeless U.S. ownership—would ensure that a bookstore in Toronto contained a large number of Canadian-market titles, thus meeting the "choice" policy concern. Nonetheless, some Canadians feared that this arrangement would give effective control over the book selection process to the United States.

Another problem, however, was the "strong" protectionist concern that the economies of scale of the big U.S.-based operation would allow it to out-compete the locals. The Canadian book retailing industry was worried that if Borders and other U.S. retailers, such as Barnes and Noble Inc. and Tower Records, imported books from the United States for sale in Canada, they would have a significant cost advantage over Canadian retailers. Preserving Canadian booksellers, at least as much as Canadian books, seems at the heart of this dispute.

Satellite television has also been subject to investment control. In addition to trying to prevent Canadians from signing up with U.S.-based and U.S. programmed direct-broadcasters, the opportunity to establish Canadian-based, Canadian programmed services has been largely limited to Canadian companies.

In the area of film, in March 1997, Canada used its investment restrictions to prevent the Dutch firm PolyGram, NV from using a Canadian subsidiary to distribute foreign-made films other than those in which it was the principal investor. The European Union declared its intention to challenge this holding through the WTO, in part because

Hollywood distributors continue to operate massively on a "grandfathered" basis.

* * *

CANADA–UNITED STATES FREE TRADE AGREEMENT (1989)

Article 2005. Cultural Industries

1. Cultural industries are exempt from the provisions of this Agreement, except as specifically provided in Article 401 (Tariff Elimination), paragraph 4 of Article 1607 (divestiture of an indirect acquisition) and Articles 2006 and 2007 of this Chapter.

2. Notwithstanding any other provision of this Agreement, a Party may take measures of equivalent commercial effect in response to actions that would have been inconsistent with this Agreement but for paragraph 1.

Article 2006. Retransmission Rights

1. Each Party's copyright law shall provide a copyright holder of the other Party with a right of equitable and non-discriminatory remuneration for any retransmission to the public of the copyright holder's program where the original transmission of the program is carried in distant signals intended for free, over-the-air reception by the general public. Each Party may determine the conditions under which the right shall be exercised. For Canada, the date on which a remuneration system shall be in place, and from which remuneration shall accrue, shall be twelve months after the amendment of Canada's *Copyright Act* implementing Canada's obligations under this paragraph, and in any case no later than January 1, 1990.

* * *

Article 2007. Print-in-Canada Requirement

Canada shall repeal section 19(5)(a)(i)(A) and (B) and section 19(5)(a)(ii)(A) and (B) of the *Income Tax Act,* which define a Canadian issue of a newspaper or a periodical for purposes of deduction from income of expenses of a taxpayer for advertising space, as one that is printed or typeset in Canada.

* * *

Article 2012. Definitions

For purposes of this Chapter:

"cultural industry" means an enterprise engaged in any of the following activities:

    (a) the publication, distribution, or sale of books, magazines, periodicals, or newspapers in print or machine readable form but not including the sole activity of printing or typesetting any of the foregoing,

(b) the production, distribution, sale or exhibition of film or video recordings,

(c) the production, distribution, sale or exhibition of audio or video music recordings,

(d) the publication, distribution, or sale of music in print or machine readable form, or

(e) radio communication in which the transmissions are intended for direct reception by the general public, and all radio, television and cable television broadcasting undertakings and all satellite programming and broadcast network services;

JOHNSON, THE NORTH AMERICAN FREE TRADE AGREEMENT
Chapter 10 (1994).*

NAFTA Annex 2106 reads as follows:

Notwithstanding any other provision of this Agreement, as between Canada and the United States, any measure adopted or maintained with respect to cultural industries, except as specifically provided in Article 302 (Market Access—Tariff Elimination), and any measure of equivalent commercial effect taken in response, shall be governed under this Agreement exclusively in accordance with the provisions of the *Canada—United States Free Trade Agreement.* The rights and obligations between Canada and any other Party with respect to such measures shall be identical to those applying between Canada and the United States.

NAFTA Annex 2106 has the effect, as between Canada and the United States, of incorporating into NAFTA the entirety of the FTA provisions as they affect cultural industries. While the FTA does not apply as between Canada and Mexico, the effect of the last sentence of NAFTA Annex 2106 is to apply the FTA provisions as they affect cultural industries as between Canada and Mexico. Thus the provisions of the FTA and not those of NAFTA govern measures affecting cultural industries as between Canada and each of the United States and Mexico. As between the United States and Mexico, measures affecting cultural industries will be governed by the provisions of NAFTA.

* * *

The sole exception in NAFTA Annex 2106 is in respect of NAFTA 302 which eliminates tariffs. In so far as goods which are the products of cultural industries (such as books, newspapers, periodicals, films, videos and sound recordings) are concerned, the elimination of tariffs will proceed in the manner prescribed in NAFTA 302 and NAFTA Annex 302.2.

* * *

The effect of requiring that cultural industries be governed exclusively by the FTA provisions is to incorporate into NAFTA not only the exemption in FTA 2005(1) and the retaliation provision in FTA 2005(2), but all the provisions of the FTA affecting cultural industries. These include the FTA trade-in-goods provisions and the FTA services and investment chapters, including the grandfathering provisions and the exclusion from the FTA definition of "covered services" of most activities carried on by cultural industries. As under the FTA, the retaliation right in FTA 2005(2) will apply only to measures affecting cultural industries that are not inconsistent with the FTA solely because of FTA 2005(1). The retaliation right will not apply to measures that are grandfathered under the FTA or are excluded by reason of not being covered services. As NAFTA Annex 2106 provides that the rights and obligations between Canada and other NAFTA countries are to be "identical" to those applying between Canada and the United States, the relevant date for grandfathering as between Canada and Mexico is the date that the FTA became effective, which was January 1, 1989.

NAFTA does not make any reference to the forced divestiture requirement in FTA 1607(4), the retransmission rights provision in FTA 2006 or the print-in-Canada provision in FTA 2007. However, as all these provisions relate to cultural industries, the effect of NAFTA Annex 2106 is that these FTA provisions will continue to apply as between Canada and the United States, and will also apply as between Canada and Mexico.

The NAFTA Annex 2106 requirement that cultural industries be governed exclusively by the FTA has the effect of exempting cultural industries from NAFTA provisions that were not in the FTA. While the FTA prohibited performance requirements such as content requirements as conditions to establishing a business, NAFTA 1106(3) also prohibits such performance requirements as conditions of receiving advantages like subsidies. Telefilm Canada's Canadian content requirements for production grants would contravene NAFTA 1106(3) were it not for NAFTA Annex 2106. NAFTA Annex 2106 prevents the most-favoured-nation obligations in NAFTA 1103 and NAFTA 1203 from requiring Canada to extend the same benefits to the United States as it presently extends to other countries under its co-production agreements. Another significant effect of NAFTA Annex 2106 is that the intellectual property provisions of NAFTA Chapter Seventeen, including those respecting copyright, do not apply as between Canada and either the United States and Mexico in so far as cultural industries are concerned. The retaliation right in FTA 2005(2) will not apply to any measure respecting a cultural industry that is inconsistent with any of these NAFTA provisions.

* * *

By preserving the FTA grandfathering provisions for cultural industries, NAFTA 2106 represents a departure from the general attempt under NAFTA to achieve transparency through the specific identification of non-conforming measures through reservations. The approach taken to cultural industries in NAFTA 2106 as between Canada and Mexico is particularly convoluted because the two countries will be applying between them the provisions of a treaty to which Mexico was never a party. It must be emphasized that the NAFTA 2106 operates bilaterally. While Canada has preserved the right to take measures to protect its cultural industries without regard to the obligations imposed by NAFTA, the United States and Mexico have each preserved an identical right as against Canada.

COUNTRY MUSIC TELEVISION DISPUTE
USTR Press Release (June 22, 1995).

BACKGROUND

In late 1993 and early 1994, the Canadian Radio-television and Telecommunications Commission (CRTC) held a regulatory proceeding to consider new applications for authority to distribute programs over cable television in Canada. In that proceeding, at the request of New Country Network, the Commission on June 6, 1994 revoked CMT's authorization to be distributed in Canada once New Country Network began distribution. The Canadian-owned licensee began distribution on January 1, 1995 and, at that time, CMT was evicted from the Canadian market. On February 6, USTR accepted CMT's Section 301 petition and initiated an investigation of certain practices of the CRTC—specifically, the investigation focuses on the CRTC's practice of denying market access to foreign-owned television programming services which are determined to be directly competitive with Canadian-owned services (the so-called competitive services policy).

PRESS RELEASE

USTR Mickey Kantor announced today that Nashville-based Country Music Television and New Country Network (a Canadian network) have reached a tentative agreement to form a single Canadian country music network to be called CMT: Country Music Television (Canada). Kantor stated, "I am tremendously pleased to be announcing today support for this tentative agreement." Kantor had set yesterday as the deadline by which USTR would publish a list of proposed retaliation targets if progress was not made toward resolving the issues in the Country Music Television section 301 investigation.

In a press release issued today by the firm's U.S. and Canadian partners—Gaylord Entertainment Company and Group W Satellite Communications (U.S.) and Rogers Communications and Rawlco (CDN)—it was announced that the parties would allow an additional 45 days to conclude the final details of the arrangement. Approval of the partnership is then required from the Canadian Government. The partners also announced that under this arrangement CMT Canada will be available to six million Canadian homes, 4 million more homes than CMT had reached in Canada prior to their eviction from the Canadian market on January 1, 1995, and will renew broadcasting of Canadian artists.

Kantor went on to say that, "We hope that the agreement, upon final implementation, which includes any necessary approval from the Government of Canada, will provide a sufficient basis to terminate the section 301 investigation." If the investigation is terminated, the USTR will closely monitor, under section 301 authority, the operation of the CMT commercial settlement.

However, Kantor further stated that the United States Government remains extremely concerned that Canada's competitive services policy remains in place. "This policy continues, by its very existence, to threaten the security of other U.S. services currently authorized for distribution in Canada and discourages other U.S. services from seeking such authorization." Therefore, USTR will also closely monitor, under section 301 authority, the experience of other U.S. services that have, or may choose to seek, authorization for distribution in Canada. Should any adverse action be taken on the part of the Government of Canada with respect to the granting or termination of such authorizations for U.S. services, the USTR, in consultation with U.S. industry, will examine whether further action under section 301 is appropriate.

SCHWANEN, A MATTER OF CHOICE: TOWARD A MORE CREATIVE CANADIAN POLICY ON CULTURE

C.D. Howe Institute Commentary No. 91
April, 1997

THE PUBLIC PURPOSE OF CULTURAL POLICY

The aims and instruments of cultural policy depend in large part on whether Canadian culture can be considered a "public" good and on whether public intervention is required to correct features of the market that might lead to an underprovision of, or underexposure to, Canadian cultural output.

Culture as a Public Good

Public goods possess characteristics that make it difficult for the private sector to produce them profitably in quantities that the public would prefer to have, for two reasons.

First, any individual within the community can consume a public good without there being less of it available to everyone else. Second, in most cases, no one can be excluded from a public good's benefit; indeed, everyone benefits from it whether one pays for it or not. If contributions to the cost of such goods were left to individual choice, some people would be tempted not to make them, in the expectation that the good would be available regardless of their financial support. This, in turn, would lead to an underfunding and underprovision of public goods (the "free-rider" problem), which is why they are usually funded out of the public purse. Examples of such public goods include national defense, vaccination programs to combat epidemic diseases, crime prevention, and the justice system itself. Thus, if certain Canadian cultural products have the characteristics of a public good, they are probably underprovided, even by a fairly and efficiently functioning private market, and a case could be made for considering public policies to encourage the increased provision of these products.

The desirability of such public goods does not, in itself, automatically justify public intervention, however. Implementing any type of policy—and collecting the taxes to pay for it—is inherently costly, can make matters worse if the policy is badly implemented, and contains the risk that mechanisms instituted for public intervention will be captured by special interests seeking to use state funds and protective regulations to sustain them at the public's expense.

This being said, I review here some possible purposes of Canadian cultural activities that give them the characteristic of a public good.

Shared Experience and Information

In some cases, the public-good aspect of a cultural activity comes in the form of information about, and representations of, other Canadians and of what is of interest to them. The public good of concern to the community here, while not necessarily (and often not desirably) flowing from the state, is comprised of information with a Canadian content. Of course, non-Canadian information and representations could become the basis for a common understanding among Canadians, but only at the cost of a lessening of the functioning or the relevance of the Canadian community.

What is important in this context, therefore, is the ability to access products and services that transmit the cultural and informational signals individuals need to ensure their informed participation in the community and, ultimately, the community's continued survival (which one presumes is a goal held sufficiently strongly in common).

Specifically, Canadians' ability to be informed about other Canadians enhances everyone's ability to make the best possible decisions in both the public and the private spheres, given that Canadians live in a particular political community, separate in many ways from other countries. In that sense, information that incorporates certain assumptions and reflects institutions and situations that distinguish the Canadian community from others can be viewed as a public good.

In this respect, Nobel Prize winner Kenneth Arrow observes:

> If it is valuable for two people to meet without being able to communicate with each other during their trips, the meeting-place must be agreed on beforehand. It may not matter much where the meeting is to be. But a person who learned one meeting-place is not much use to an organization which has selected another.

The relevant parallel is that, if a commonly agreed "trip"—belonging to a separate political entity called Canada—yields valuable results, but Canadians have trouble communicating with each other, then a commonly agreed-on meeting place is a valuable public good. Ensuring that there is such a meeting place in the form of channels of exchange between Canadians therefore becomes a valid goal of cultural policy. It is important to note, however, that the public-good aspect here is not that of enforced uniformity of views or forced preservation of the state, but the element that allows one to make informed public decisions as long as one is attached to a particular community.

"Merit Goods"

Another form of public good is the "merit" good—that is, a good that the public at large should be especially encouraged to consume, or an activity in which they should participate. The view here is that the public would not do so adequately at unsubsidized prices. Whether it be a national art gallery, the symphony, or the opera, the assumption is that the community should help preserve and display exemplars of a particularly rich cultural heritage.

Many analysts find it difficult to justify subsidies for such goods, however, arguing, in particular, that they are hard to reconcile with the usual assumption that individuals are informed enough to make their own choices, and that if they choose not to patronize a certain activity, then there is no reason the state should do it for them at their expense. Indeed, studies have shown that individuals who most enjoy subsidized "merit" goods are also those with above-average income, while many taxpayers will not exhibit much interest in them, regardless of price and accessibility.

Merit goods can, however, fulfill a public purpose in other ways, perhaps akin to the benefits provided by insurance or a diverse ecosystem. One may never encounter a calamitous event or visit a rainforest but still regard the existence of collective mechanisms to ensure against one or preserve the other as important to one's well-being. Hence, one would want to participate in a collective (private or public) effort to pay for such mechanisms.

Another point worth noting is that much of the state's support for merit goods actually comes in the form of tax deductions afforded individuals who make the effort to maintain the good or activity through charitable contributions or contributions to a variety of artistic, political, or other endeavors. Clearly, such support encourages the direct involvement of individuals in their community and, in reflecting the tastes and preferences of at least some segment of the public, this support may encourage the building of "social capital" in ways direct intervention by the state does not.

* * *

DEAD ENDS: BASELESS GROUNDS FOR CULTURAL POLICY

To sharpen one's view of the aims of cultural policy, it is useful to identify reasons that are sometimes invoked for intervention and protectionism in the cultural sector but that ought not to form the basis of a sound cultural policy (although they may have a role to play in other policy contexts). Two that are often mentioned are cultural industries as job creators, and cultural industries as export generators.

Cultural Industries as Job Creators

By some accounts, since the 1970s, Canada has been moving away from a cultural policy rationale based on fundamental concepts of art and culture, with their unpredictable implications for economic activity and employment, and toward one geared to cultural "industries." One often-stated reason for the desirability of this trend is that the public will be more supportive of measures that help these industries grow if it can be shown that they create some visible "bang for the buck"—that is, if many jobs are created in return for the funds poured into them and for the protection they are afforded.

Indeed, it is probably easier to define a policy to protect cultural "industries" than one to promote Canadian "culture." And precise definitions of "industries" are often necessary when attempting to explain how a general framework will apply to specific endeavors, or for analytical purposes. For example, the clear definition of "cultural industry" in the Canada–US Free Trade Agreement, and reproduced in the NAFTA, has determined which specific activities are exempt from these agreements, and has effectively sheltered Canada's protectionist measures for these industries from NAFTA challenges (to such an extent that the United States had to make its case in the WTO on the magazine issue). But, as Dowler notes, "[a]lthough a sector-by-sector analysis can be valuable . . . the genesis of the cultural policy apparatus and its logic cannot be derived in this manner."

More fundamentally, those who favor protection for cultural "industries" because they "create jobs" seem to believe that such a policy will succeed here even though it has failed for other products or services. Of course, protectionism can sustain some jobs in any sector, but many others will be lost because, for example, state subsidies reduce taxpayers' disposable income, or because encouraging growth in a particular sector redirects resources, such as capital, that could have been better used elsewhere. Indeed, many of those who support the idea of a state-sponsored policy on culture concede this point. For example, political scientist Franklyn Griffiths defends the argument that cultural policies are essential to the ability of a sovereign people to make independent choices, but says "[t]hose who conceive of Canadian culture primarily in terms of cultural industries and employment potential will be asked [in his study] to think again."

In short, given protectionism's poor historical record in promoting economic growth, there is no justification to use it for public intervention in the cultural industries.

Cultural Industries as Export Generators

As noted earlier, Canada's exports of cultural goods and services have increased at a remarkable rate in recent years, a development from which Canadians can derive satisfaction. But many of these products are tailored for international audiences, and export markets by themselves ought to be large enough to support Canadian cultural products that do not particularly speak to a Canadian audience. In other words, export promotion of cultural or any other products is a matter for trade or industrial policy. While the selling of cultural products abroad is to be welcomed, it should not be the basis of cultural policy *per se*, nor should it be the basis on which Canadian cultural products are subsidized or protected.

SUPPORTING THE CHOICE OF A CANADIAN CULTURE

As we have seen, there are important public and private benefits in Canadians' having continued access to cultural products with significant Canadian content. This means that cultural policy should support the creation of such content where necessary, and improve the functioning of both public and private markets in such a way that Canadian cultural products remain on Canadians' "information agenda." Indeed, cultural policy should be judged to have failed if Canadian cultural production, taken as a whole, fails to find or sustain an audience.

Equally, cultural policy should be judged to have failed if it requires the increasing use of devices that limit the public's exposure to foreign cultural products, particularly in a world in which such measures are becoming increasingly costly or impractical.

GOODENOUGH, DEFENDING THE IMAGINARY TO DEATH? FREE TRADE, NATIONAL IDENTITY AND CANADA'S CULTURAL PREOCCUPATION

15 Ariz. J. Int'l & Comp. Law 203 (1998).*

CULTURE TRANSMISSION THEORY AND THE RESILIENCE OF CULTURES

Earlier, this article suggested that surviving cultural patterns have built-in mechanisms of self-protection, and that this may give some justification to legal regimes that implement trade protection. The other side of this argument, however, first asks whether or not the threat of imports is as large as it is made out to be, and second whether the legally mandated protective measures are likely to be effective against whatever threat may exist. It is time to re-open the question of how much effect the exposure to creative works has on who people are and how they behave. Is the link between culture as a product and culture as a belief system really a strong one?

Much of what makes us behave as we do comes through learning that occurs at a very young age, based in large part on the interactions we have with our parents and other care-givers. The next important factor is the repeat interactions which the youth has with members of the local community. Most of our cultural patterns propagate themselves not at the level of intentional national policy, but through smaller, more localized and spontaneous contacts. The astonishing resilience which many culture traits display is rooted in the difficulty which later, more external influences have in disrupting or superceding the role of these interactions. That said, the huge industry of media-based advertising depends for its existence on the ability of the media to influence choices and preferences, and as television watching becomes a substitute for personal contact in the young, this resilience may be under new attack. The effect of exposure to outside cultural industries in homogenizing cultural distinctions cannot be fully dismissed. As one Canadian scholar and diplomat recently declared:

> The [Canadian] magazine issue is a kind of microcosm of a much larger issue, which is, "Do we want to live in a world in which there are no differences?"

There is evidence, however, that most people deal not in a single cultural milieu, but at a number of different, carefully distinguished levels. For instance, the Dutch have for years been open to a wide variety of cultural influences, and are notorious for speaking many different languages. Nonetheless, in their domestic dealings, the Dutch language, the Dutch culture, and the Dutch character have preserved themselves. Nearer to home, the ability of French Canada to preserve its language and character in the face of a history of oppression from the English-speaking community argues for the potential resilience of minority cultural traits in a multicultural world. Indeed, the presence of a widely accepted "lingua franca" for use across differing groups, whether in language or other aspects of culture, may actually allow for the *strengthening* of localized in-group patterns.

Culture transmission theory also suggests that truly invasive ideas will be almost impossible to keep out. For instance, the French struggle over preserving the French language from modest invasion by English terms is notable largely for its futility. United States efforts to institutionalize English are equally short-sighted and reflect some of the same kinds of jingoistic nationalism which underlie Canada's protectionism. In areas where cultural invasion is likely, draconian measures are required to prevent it. If the foreign approach is appealing enough to be taken up as a broadly adopted replacement for a prior local pattern, then only total embargo is likely to succeed. The cultural equivalents of zebra mussels, kudzu, Dutch elm disease and killer bees only need a little exposure to eventually triumph. The country must be a North Korea, or an Albania under the old regime, excluding almost all foreign contacts, for prohibition to have its desired effect. Such cultural autarchy is not only a terrible way to live, it is extremely difficult to maintain these days.

In summary, cultural transmission theory suggests that most foreign influences will "bounce off" of a healthy culture without government intervention, or at the very least will be compartmentalized for use in contexts separate from the hearth and home. Where the link between exposure to foreign product and a change in domestic values is weak, there is little to worry about. On the other hand, the penetrating ability of those that do not "bounce off" will be little affected by government-level efforts to keep them under quota. Where the link between exposure and change is strong, there is little to be done. Tariff walls are poor substitutes for consumer preferences.

CULTURAL PROTECTION'S REAL POINT: RALLYING ROUND THE FLAG

* * *

The Canadian side is both right and wrong in arguing that the culture war is at the center of the battle to preserve Canadian sovereignty. For Anglophone Canada, at least, the argument is not important for its factual logic—the battle was in fact lost or won, depending on the context, years ago—but rather for its symbolic logic. As one noted Canadian Studies scholar stated, "the story of Canada is the story of a people attempting to create a unified and distinct nation in North America. This is the very essence of the Canadian National experience." Nations organize themselves as much in opposition to external threat as they do out of shared internal conviction. In part, this reflects a deeply rooted set of human social principles; part of why we are willing to follow leadership is because the leaders will protect us from threat.

* * *

It is in this context that the anti-Americanism of the culture protectors is sensible, at least as a starting point. The description by Canadian officials of Canada's loss on the magazine front as a "cultural invasion" is in fact valid in this context, as well. The repeated use, in many contexts, of the language of war to describe this set of disagreements is rooted not just in metaphorical license but in a deep reflection of their real nature.

At this symbolic level of reality, the thing protected, at least as to Anglophone Canada, may often be imaginary. The implementation may often be over-broad, tainted by self-indulgence and self-interest, and redolent of censorship. But at this level of deeper logic, the importance of protection may be critical. The cost is not simply a "rent" diverting the nation's resources into the pockets of a self-selected national cultural elite. Nor is the patent ongoing failure of many of the measures of protection a matter of droll self-delusion. Rather, it is a perfect element in a recurring pageant of threat and defense. In the end, it is not necessary to win the cultural "war" with the United States; indeed such a win, if possible, would only create the need to invent some less plausible "boogie-man" to replace it. The issue's very intractability gives it a useful longevity. Hollywood is not a flimsy threat like the Soviet Union, which will collapse from internal incompetence.

But even here, at this deeper level, the policy of defending the imaginary to the death is fatally flawed. If Canada continues to press this logic, it will indeed be to the death, a death brought about not by "invasion" from the south, but by the incomparably better claims to culturally-based nationhood possessed by Francophone Quebec and by the First Nation Peoples. Rather than acting as a rallying cry for national preservation, cultural protection provides the intellectual basis for a break-up of Canada. Instead of supporting a pan-Canadian society, it threatens it. The defense may lead to the death of the very ideal it is invoked to protect.

Questions and Comments

1. What is a "cultural industry"? Compare CFTA Article 2012 with NAFTA Article 2107. Do these definitions differ? Which is the controlling definition?

2. What types of Canadian laws and policies are sheltered by the cultural industry exclusion? See the Johnson excerpts. MEDIA MOGUL would like to know whether the Canadians are protecting their "culture" or their "industries". What is your reply?

3. Does the cultural industry exclusion apply to trade in goods? Trade in services? Investment? Intellectual property? Dispute settlement? Are your answers to be found in the NAFTA agreement? In the CFTA agreement?

4. Where do your answers leave MEDIA MOGUL? Does the cultural industry exclusion apply as between Canada and Mexico? If so, why? Between Mexico and the United States? If not, why? (As Spanish radio and television programming, and print media, expand in Canada, this is not simply an academic issue.) What do your answers suggest for MEDIA MOGUL?

5. Canadian cultural industry laws and policies in effect on Jan. 1, 1989 were grandfathered. This grandfathering was extended to Mexico through NAFTA Annex 2106. Suppose Canada adopts a new cultural industry protection law. What can Mexico or the United States do? *See* CFTA Article 1607.4. Might this "remedy" help MEDIA MOGUL?

6. When Canada adopted its "split-run" periodicals tax in 1995, why did the U.S. elect to challenge it before the WTO Dispute Settlement Body rather than under NAFTA? In July 1997, the DSB confirmed an Appellate Body finding that the Excise Tax Act was inconsistent with GATT rules. See Case no. WT/DS31/AB/R, *available at* http://www.wto.gov. What was the likely basis of the Appellate Body decision? (Review GATT, Article III:2 and the ad article in Problem 5.4.)

As a sequel to *Sports Illustrated*, a Bill was introduced in the Canadian parliament that would have prohibited foreign magazine publishers from selling advertising aimed primarily at the Canadian market. In May of 1999, an intergovernmental settlement was reached. U.S. publishers may now wholly-own Canadian magazines. In addition, Canada will permit U.S. split-run editions without Canadian editorial content. Such editions may contain Canadian advertisements not in excess of 12 percent by lineage (rising to 18 percent in several years).

7. Robinson asserts that he is both a free trader and a cultural protectionist. When Robinson refers to culture as "Canadians talking to

Canadians about things Canadian" what does he mean? Is it akin to Schwanen's argument that culture is a "public good"? Are either of these ideas reflected in the CFTA/NAFTA cultural industry exclusion?

8. Robinson would no doubt be appalled by the plans of MEDIA MOGUL. He asserts that Canadian culture is threatened by "excessive [U.S.] greed." Do you agree? Does Ragosta? How do you explain the dominance of U.S. media products in the Canadian market?

9. Ragosta believes that technology will (if it has not already) seriously undermine Canadian cultural industry protectionism, especially distribution restraints. Schwanen seems to agree. That sounds like good news for MEDIA MOGUL. What technological strategies should MEDIA MOGUL pursue?

10. Does the *Country Music Television* dispute and its resolution suggest that culture or economics is really driving Canadian law? What about the *Borders Bookstore* dispute? And *Polygram?* What do these examples suggest for MEDIA MOGUL?

11. Do you agree with Schwanen's analysis of the public purpose of cultural policy? Do Canadian content rules foster a Canadian identity and a sense of community? How do we know a "merit good" when we see one? Are MEDIA MOGUL's goods meritorious? Who gets to decide that question? Is there an element of censorship in Canadian cultural policy?

12. Goodenough introduces us to some interesting culture transmission theory. Do you think that MEDIA MOGUL's products, if allowed in Canada, would "bounce off" Canadian culture? Might your answer vary depending upon whether MEDIA MOGUL's products are in Quebec versus English-speaking Canada?

13. Does "rallying around the flag" help you understand Canada's cultural industry laws and policies? In the "war" against Hollywood, would MEDIA MOGUL make a "perfect enemy" with which to do battle?

What do you think of Professor Goodenough's provocative conclusion: "Rather than acting as a rallying cry for national preservation, cultural protection provides the intellectual basis for a break-up of Canada [into Anglophone Canada, Francophone Quebec and the First Nation Peoples]."

14. Suppose MEDIA MOGUL decides to take advantage of the decline in the value of the Canadian dollar and some Ontario subsidies by producing its film, "Nights", in Toronto. The film qualifies as Canadian content and therefore commands a premium in Canada. Having made the film and enjoyed a successful opening night in Toronto, the Canadian authorities suddenly ban "Nights" as offensive to Canadian culture. No further distribution is allowed.

MEDIA MOGUL files a complaint under the NAFTA Chapter 11 investor-state arbitration procedures. What result? You do not need to look at Chapter 11 to reply.

15. The first edition of this textbook was by West Publishing, of St. Paul, MN. This second edition is published by Thomson West, a subsidiary of Thomson Corporation, a Canadian publishing conglomerate with media subsidiaries on five continents. Should this acquisition have been considered a "cultural industries" issue?

PROBLEM 5.4 MONOPOLY STATE ENTERPRISES: PEMEX AND CFE

SECTION I. THE SETTING

The title to Chapter 6 of the NAFTA agreement is "Energy and Basic Petrochemicals". The opening sentence in Article 601 reads as follows: "The Parties confirm their full respect for their Constitutions". If you are confused, you are not alone.

Energy Resources, Inc. (ENRES) is a Texas corporation set up in the 1980s to take advantage of U.S. energy deregulation. ENRES does not produce energy. Rather, it likes to think of itself as an "energy entrepreneur". ENRES's specialty is bringing together energy suppliers and users, which is not always easy. For its efforts, and ENRES has a lot of happy clients, it charges substantial fees.

ENRES has followed CFTA and NAFTA with great interest. It has opened Canadian and Mexican offices and now advertises itself as "the" North American energy entrepreneur. ENRES has several clients who would like to get profitably involved with the Mexican energy market. Historically, this market has been almost totally closed to foreigners for reasons that relate to the first sentence in Article 601 of NAFTA. But the winds of change are blowing in Mexico, and ENRES is committed to navigating those winds as well as anyone.

Your assignment, as corporate counsel, is to explain to management the law and policies of Mexico regarding oil, petrochemicals, electricity and natural gas. Management particularly wants to know what opportunities are available to its Canadian and U.S. clients. Your budget has been increased to allow for the retention of Mexican attorneys as needed.

SECTION II. FOCUS OF CONSIDERATION

Petróleos Mexicanos (PEMEX) is more than just a state-owned monopoly. For many Mexicans, PEMEX symbolizes the spirit of its Revolution, embodied forcefully in Article 27 of the 1917 Mexican Constitution. PEMEX was created when Mexico nationalized its oil and gas industry (entirely owned by foreigners) in 1938. For many Mexicans, this nationalization was the equivalent of declaring economic independence. In the years that followed, PEMEX and its powerful unions were intimately allied with Mexico's ruling political party, the PRI. PEMEX became more than Mexico's number one employer, often providing housing, schools and health clinics as well. For the Mexican government and the PRI, PEMEX became the ultimate cash cow.

The Comisión Federal de Electricidad (CFE) shares much of the same revolutionary inspiration and Constitutional history as PEMEX. CFE is state-owned and possesses a near monopoly over electricity production and distribution in Mexico. CFE buys most of its fuel from PEMEX.

Chapter 6 of the NAFTA and its appendices are essential to an analysis of this problem. These materials are found in the Documents Supplement.

SECTION III.   READINGS, QUESTIONS AND COMMENTS

1917 CONSTITUTION OF THE UNITED MEXICAN STATES
Article 25

The public sector shall be exclusively in charge of strategic areas defined in Article 28, paragraph 4 of the Constitution, the Federal Government shall always have ownership and control on the organizations created for this purpose.

* * *

ARTICLE 27

3.   In the Nation is vested the direct ownership of all natural resources of the continental shelf and the submarine shelf of the islands; of all minerals or substances, which in veins, ledges, masses or ore pockets, form deposits of a nature distinct from the components of the earth itself, such as the minerals from which industrial metals and metalloids are extracted; deposits of precious stones, rocksalt and the deposits of salt formed by sea water; products derived from the decomposition of rocks, when subterranean works are required for their extraction; mineral or organic deposits of materials susceptible of utilization as fertilizers; solid mineral fuels; petroleum and all solid, liquid, and gaseous hydrocarbons; and the space above the national territory to the extent and within the terms fixed by international law.

* * *

5.   In those cases to which the two preceding paragraphs refer, ownership by the Nation is inalienable and imprescriptible, and the exploitation, use, or appropriation of the resources concerned, by private persons or by companies organized according to Mexican laws, may not be undertaken except through concessions granted by the Federal Executive, in accordance with rules and conditions established by law. The legal rules relating to the working or exploitation of the minerals and substances referred to in the fourth paragraph shall govern the execution and proofs of what is carried out or should be carried out after they go into effect, independent of the date of granting the concession, and their nonobservance will be grounds for cancellation thereof. The Federal Government has the power to establish national reserves and to abolish them. The declarations pertaining thereto shall be made by the Executive in those cases and conditions prescribed by law. In the case of petroleum, and solid, liquid, or gaseous hydrocarbons or radioactive minerals, no concessions or contracts will be granted nor may those that have been granted continue, and the Nation shall carry out the exploitation of these products, in accordance with the provisions indicated in the

respective regulatory law. It is exclusively a function of the Nation to generate, conduct, transform, distribute, and supply electric power which is to be used for public service. No concessions for this purpose will be granted to private persons and the Nation will make use of the property and natural resources which are required for these ends.

ARTICLE 28

* * *

The functions exercised exclusively by the State in the strategic areas referred herein shall not constitute monopolies: the coinage of money; the postal system; telegraph; radiotelegraph; radiotelegraphy and communications via satellites; the issuance of money by a single bank to be controlled by the Federal Government; petroleum and other hydrocarbons; basic petroleum chemistry; radioactive minerals and nuclear power production; electricity; railroads; and the activities expressly provided for in the laws issued by the Congress of the Union.

SMITH, CONFRONTING DIFFERENCES IN THE UNITED STATES AND MEXICAN LEGAL SYSTEMS IN THE ERA OF NAFTA

1 U.S.-Mexico Law J. 85 (1993).*

New Spain (colonial Mexico) was not well prepared either for self government or democracy at the time of its independence in 1821 after centuries of highly centralized Spanish colonial administration. Moreover, the Mexican creole (Spanish born in Latin American) population was bitterly divided over the continuing domination of the church, army, and large landowners. Also, the population was markedly heterogeneous because of the large native population that was not acculturated to European or democratic values. In the century preceding the Mexican Constitutional Convention of 1917, Mexico was dominated by *caudillismo* (charismatic political and military chieftains) and political chaos. Porfirio Díaz assumed the presidency in 1876, bringing political stability to Mexico until 1910. He united the conservative factions (clergy, army, landowners, rural chieftains) and foreign interests. However, the constituencies of Father Miquel Hidalgo y Costillo, General José María Morelos, and the liberals, who had fought for a century for religious toleration and for an end to the domination of the army, rural bosses, and foreign interests, were not to be denied. The simmering social tensions exploded in the revolution of 1910. The coup d'etat and assassination of the recently elected President Francisco I. Madero, accomplished with the complicity of the United States Embassy, unleashed the revolutionary forces led by Venustiano Carranza, Alvaro Obregón, Pancho Villa, and Emiliano Zapata.

The Mexican Constitution of 1917, like previous Mexican constitutions, was written and promulgated in a time of war and religious and

---

* Copyright © 1993 U.S.-Mexico Law Journal. Reproduced with permission.   (James F. Smith is Senior Lecturer, School of Law, University of California, Davis.)

political strife. The Constitution is ideological, even dogmatic. It includes statements of broad principles as well as detailed prescriptive provisions. Although the Querétero Convention was called by Carranza to restore the liberal Constitution of 1857 and to make modest political reforms, revolutionary goals were incorporated into the document as well. Carranza called the Constitutional Convention of Querétero to isolate his political enemies, which included both the old order and his former revolutionary allies. All factions hostile to the cause of his "Constitutional Army" were excluded from the convention, including not only the forces of Victoriano Huerta but Pancho Villa (who called his own constitutional convention in Aguascalientes) and Emiliano Zapata. It appears that Carranza thought of the convention as more of a symbolic than a deliberative event. He set a time limit of sixty days to "discuss, approve and modify" the draft constitution, which was essentially the Constitution of 1857. The Querétero delegates, however, represented the social conscience of the revolution. The revolutionary articles, Article 27 (agrarian reform and national ownership of the subsoil, coastland, etc.) and Article 123 (labor protection), were drafted by committees meeting outside of the main assembly and were overwhelmingly approved by the convention. The Mexican Constitutional Convention, unlike the Philadelphia Convention over a century earlier, addressed economic and social goals and rights, equating social justice with—if not elevating it over—individual liberty.

Dr. Guillermo F. Margadant, a noted legal historian of Mexico, has described the promulgation of the Mexican Constitution of 1917 in the following terms:

> The Constitution of 1917 was a multilateral declaration of war, directed against the large land holders, the bosses, the clergy, and mining companies (that lost their rights to the subsoil). The potentially threatening effect of the Constitution was softened by the fact that Venustiano Carranza calmed the Church and oil companies by promises that under his regime the Constitution would not have total effect.

The Mexican Constitution has been consistently characterized by Mexican constitutional scholars as a project to be accomplished, a statement of revolutionary ideals that is nominal in that there is no intended immediate congruency between its stated aspirations and reality.

AMENDING THE CONSTITUTION

Ulysses Schmill, the current president of the Mexican Supreme Court, has noted that Mexico's Constitution may be classified as "rigid" in that it may not be amended by ordinary legislation. In practice, however, it has proven to be quite easily amended. Under Article 135 of the Mexican Constitution, amendments (*reformas*) may be proposed by a two-third vote of each legislative house and then must be accepted by an absolute majority of the state legislatures. In the United States, two-thirds of the Congress are required to initiate an amendment, but three-fourths of the states must ratify the proposal. Mexico has amended its Constitution 359 times in less than half the time that the United States has accepted twenty-six amendments. The amendments to the Mexican Constitution are incorporated in the text rather than listed at the end, as in the United States Constitution. There are three reasons for the relative frequency of amendments to the Mexican Constitution as compared with the United States Constitution: (1) the amendment process is less restrictive in Mexico and this is especially true given the political reality of a dominant political party and a powerful presidency; (2) the Mexican Constitution provides not only a broad outline of the form of government but a prescriptive government code which is quite detailed, thereby requiring more amendments; and (3) the Mexican Supreme Court has limited power to render binding interpretations of the Constitutions, whereas the United States Supreme Court has effectively "amended" the United States Constitution hundreds of times. Mexico has on occasion processed an amendment in less than one month.

LEVY, NAFTA'S PROVISION FOR COMPENSATION IN THE EVENT OF EXPROPRIATION: A REASSESSMENT OF THE "PROMPT, ADEQUATE AND EFFECTIVE" STANDARD
31 Stanf. J. Int'l L. 423 (1995).*

The two principal aims of the Mexican Revolution of 1910–20 were agrarian reform and land redistribution. The Revolution's rallying cry of *"tierra y libertad"* ("land and liberty") carried particular force given that, by 1910, approximately 1000 families controlled the vast majority of Mexican land, leaving most of the population in the serf-like state of *peones*. Article 27 of the 1917 Constitution represents a fulfillment of the revolutionary promise, providing the basis for agrarian reform, destruction of concentrated landholdings, and expropriation of property. More profoundly, Article 27 embodies the idea of property in Mexico as "a right belonging to all of the nation . . . a function of society." A drafter of the Mexican Constitution explained Article 27 as an assurance that "Mexican law will establish fully as a basic, solid and unalterable principle that above the rights of individuals to property there were superior rights of society, represented by the State, to regulate its distribution as well as its use and conservation." Indeed, the Mexican Supreme Court of Justice followed this rationale when it interpreted Article 27 as an effort to:

> eliminate the classical concept which defined the right of property as an absolute untouchable right, and to replace it with a concept which recognizes private property as a social function. Thus, private property would not be the exclusive right of one individual, but a right subordinated to the common welfare.

* * *

Concurrent with the agrarian expropriations, Mexico expropriated its oil industry. Unlike the land expropriations, where foreigners and Mexican nationals suffered equally, this action harmed only foreign oil companies, since oil concerns were entirely foreign-owned. The surface land and the oil rights were primarily owned by British and U.S. citizens who had invested in the exploration for oil at the invitation of the pre-revolutionary Mexican government. The oil expropriations were motivated by a desire to ensure that Mexicans controlled Mexican oil, and had their basis in Article 27 of the 1917 Constitution, which vested ownership of minerals and subsoil in the Mexican government. This Article 27 provision contradicted the original oil concessions of the early 1900s, under which Mexican mining codes "put the exploitation of oil at the disposal of the owner of the surface land." In 1938, the Mexican government expropriated all oil companies through a decree which placed the government in complete control of the production and distribution of oil products. To achieve that end, the decree ordered the expropriation of the machinery, installations, storage tanks, and other assets of the oil companies then operating in Mexico.

Mexico's expropriation of its oil industry prompted another exchange of diplomatic correspondence in 1940, in which Secretary Hull echoed previous assertions: "[T]he right to expropriate property is coupled with and conditioned on the obligation to make *adequate, effective and prompt compensation.* The legality of an expropriation is in fact dependent upon the observance of this requirement." The Secretary disputed the Mexican government's previous assertion that the two governments were in agreement: "[I]t is incorrect to state that there is 'no divergence of opinion between the Government of the United States and that of Mexico' on the subject of expropriation." Secretary Hull suggested that the U.S. claims be submitted to arbitration, but the Mexican government insisted on the doctrine of exhaustion of local remedies and countered that any delay was the fault of U.S. companies which had refused to submit to Mexican valuation of the expropriated property. Thus, in the case of the oil expropriations, the Mexican government insisted that it was willing to compensate—but only on its own terms in accordance with its own laws.

Indeed, according to Professor Kunz, the two governments *were* in agreement about the oil expropriations. Professor Kunz focuses on the fundamental difference between the agricultural and oil expropriations: The former harmed Mexicans and foreigners alike, while the latter harmed only foreign nationals. The agrarian expropriations led to a divisive controversy which "concerns the existence or non-existence of an international norm requiring compensation in cases of expropriations of a general and impersonal character." In contrast, Professor Kunz argues, with respect to the oil expropriations "we need not discuss, whether compensation is due under international law, whether the international norm in question does or does not exist, but only *whether the conditions of expropriations*, laid down by an international norm, *fully recognized*, have been fulfilled...."

Thus, contentious issues centered around what would be compensated—just the machinery and surface rights, or the loss suffered by the expropriation of the subsoil resources—and how much would be paid. As with the agrarian expropriations, the settlement ultimately left disputes about the international law of compensation for expropriation unresolved. The U.S. oil companies and the Mexican government disagreed on the level of appropriate compensation for the expropriated properties. The United States assessed the value of the property at $200 million, while the Mexican government argued that a payment of $10 million would suffice. Ultimately, a mixed claims commission set the compensation at almost $24 million, with an additional interest payment of three percent from the date of expropriation.

As illustrated by the 1938 and 1940 disputes over land and oil compensation, the historical positions of the United States and Mexico have seemed irreconcilable. Instead of resolving their respective differences on the international law of compensation for expropriation, they chose to settle claims on an ad hoc basis. The fact that some fifty years later, in NAFTA, the two governments have finally agreed to a provision addressing compensation for expropriation is therefore particularly significant.

HOMANT, MEXICO: CONSTITUTIONAL AND POLITICAL IMPLICATIONS OF THE 1995 NATURAL GAS REGULATIONS

4 Tulsa J. Comp. & Int'l L. 233 (1997).*

HISTORY OF THE OIL INDUSTRY IN MEXICO

Modern foreign investment in natural gas is inevitably influenced by the development and present condition of Mexico's oil industry. To understand the basis on which the Mexican government makes natural gas foreign investment decisions, an understanding of the special relationship between oil, gas and the government is essential.

It was foreign enterprise, not domestic entities, that began to develop Mexican oil when it was first discovered in 1901. The Mining Law of 1884 gave surface owners the right to own subsurface oil, the Petroleum Law of 1901 authorized the Mexican government to grant oil concessions in public lands, and the Mining Law of 1909 reaffirmed the subsoil rights of surface owners. Protected by these acts, foreign companies (mainly American and British) significantly owned and controlled oil production in Mexico until 1938.

The leaders of the government, after the Mexican Revolution, sought to reduce the influence of foreign investors over Mexico's wealth, through the Constitution of 1917, specifically Article 27, which declared that the Mexican nation owned Mexican subsoil resources. Foreign oil companies attempted to protect their investments through the intervention of their home governments, even though forbidden by Mexico's Petroleum Law of 1925. The United States government insisted that disputes such as labor troubles, tax disputes, resistance to retail price increases, and wasteful drilling practices had to be settled by international arbitration.

When the foreign oil companies refused to abide by domestic Mexican laws, the Mexican government responded by expropriating the strike-bound companies and creating the government owned Petróleos Mexicanos (PEMEX). The 1938 expropriation of foreign owned oil concessions in Mexico was the world's first major expulsion of foreign oil companies from a developing country in the name of national sovereignty. Foreign owned natural gas concessions were also banned. This was a defining moment in Mexican history, that gave rise to national passions strongly held in the hearts of Mexicans today. The resulting "creation of PEMEX has long been a matter of national heritage, pride and wealth."

Mexico has the potential to be a major natural gas and oil player. Over the years, Mexico has exported about half its oil. PEMEX's rising petroleum output has allowed Mexico to overtake Venezuela as Latin America's leading oil-producing nation, making Mexico the sixth-largest producer in the world, after Saudi Arabia, the United States, Russia, Iran and China. Mexico does not belong to the Organization of Petroleum Exporting Countries (OPEC), and its growing crude oil output is part of a worldwide pattern of production increases by nonmembers that is dampening OPEC efforts to increase oil prices.

In 1995, President Zedillo and PEMEX's Director General announced the sale of sixty-one PEMEX petrochemical plants located mainly in ten petrochemical complexes to domestic and foreign investors. Given Mexico's understandable ongoing fear and mistrust of United States investors, this was a controversial proposal. PEMEX was to take a minority position in each plant for several years, at least until labor conditions and contractual terms had been stabilized to the satisfaction of the new investors, the Mexican government, and the labor union. A total of seventy domestic and foreign companies announced intentions to bid for the petrochemical facilities, which are located mostly in Veracruz and other southeastern states.

The private investment initiative was immediately questioned by Mexican workers, and in succeeding months the labor union's opposition grew to include full page ads and rallies. During a rally attended by five thousand PEMEX workers, protestors carried signs that read: "To sell PEMEX is to sell Mexico" and "We reject the sale of our national patrimony." The constitutional question has become so significant that some opponents have asked President Zedillo to hold a voter's referendum.

* * *

The attempted privatization of Mexico's state-owned petrochemical sector has been a prolonged affair. After months of controversy and public protest, the first sale is still pending. The Energy Ministry is postponing the sale of the first complex, a group of ammonia plants in Veracruz at Cosoleacaque, due to the magnitude of social protests and possible labor union actions.

Additionally, used chemical plants such as the Cosoleacaque complex will sell for only about US $150 million, which will provide little or no profit to Mexican government. Much money has been spent preparing and promoting private foreign investment, and the government does not wish to take a loss after so much publicity.

HISTORY OF THE ELECTRICAL INDUSTRY IN MEXICO

The history of the electricity industry in Mexico is also inextricably tied to natural gas foreign investment because natural gas fuels the electrical plants. The Mexican government not only owns and operates PEMEX, one of the world's largest oil and gas companies, but also owns and operates the Comisión Federal de Electricidad (CFE). CFE supplies a minimum of twenty million of Mexico's ninety million citizens with electricity through a system whose capacity has grown to about 32,000 megawatts.

In 1992 the private sector was allowed to invest in new electrical generation facilities, as long as the energy produced was for self-supply or was sold to the state owned CFE. However, progress was slow because of an ineffective regulatory framework on tariff policy and difficulties resolving disputes between the CFE and suppliers.

The Mexican government is encouraging the CFE, which operates its own facilities, to move from fuel oil to the more environmentally friendly natural gas. Additionally, more than half the country's industry uses fuel oil, and only a third natural gas. By the year 2000 the Mexican government hopes this ratio will be reversed.

In February of 1995, a ten-year Electricity Plan (implementing the revised Electricity Law of December 1992) forecasted electricity annual growth between 2.5 and 4.5 percent. The Electricity Plan predicts Mexico will require 14,639 megawatts of new electric generating capacity by the year 2004. CFE has plans to build 6,479 megawatts of generating capacity, leaving a deficit of 8,160 megawatts to be covered by the private sector.

The nation's supply of electricity is generated mainly by outdated oil-burning power plants that are harmful to the environment. Money raised from private investment will be used by the Mexican government to increase the exploration of natural gas and to switch from fuel burning to natural gas generated electrical plants. It is estimated that between US $20 to $28 billion is needed over the coming decade for new investment in Mexico's electric power generation, transmission and distribution network.

The economically and environmentally preferred method to meet the expected growth in the demand for electric energy, and comply with future environmental legislation, is to significantly increase the natural gas-fired electricity generation from twenty to forty percent and reduce the other types of generation, according to the Electricity Plan. Combined-cycle, gas-fired power plants are expected to play a major role in satisfying electricity demand in the future.

In May 1996, U.S. and Mexican investors signed a long awaited agreement with the Mexican government to build the first privately funded natural gas generated electrical power plant, which will be fueled by US $300,000 a day of Texas natural gas. The US $647 million Samalayuca II plant is being built thirty miles south of Ciudad Juarez, across the border from El Paso, Texas. The Samalayuca II plant will play a key role in the continued development of the booming border region, as well as providing jobs in Texas. The Ciudad Juarez region, with a population of more than 1.5 million, continues to grow rapidly and is home to half of Mexico's booming maquiladora assembly plants. Construction of the new power plant is expected to be complete by the fall of 1998.

El Paso Energy Corporation, in a consortium with three U.S. partners, is putting up twenty percent of the US $132 million equity investment and the other US $515 million will come from debt financing, mostly from the Export–Import Bank of the United States. The agreement between the U.S. companies and Mexico is a watershed event in United States participation in the rapidly growing Mexican energy sector.

The complex deal calls for the consortium to lease the plant for twenty years to the CFE, which will operate it. This arrangement is referred to as a "Build–Lease–Transfer (BLT)," which allows foreign investors to be able to own the Mexican electric power plants and earn profits by selling electric power back to CFE for the life of the facility.

* * *

History of the Natural Gas Industry in Mexico

With PEMEX senior management intensely involved in planning for private foreign investment in petrochemical plants and dealing with prospective electric power investors that want long term natural gas supply contracts, the Mexican government has changed the rules in the area of natural gas transportation and distribution. As a result, foreign investors are considering whether the new Natural Gas Regulations provide enough protection against PEMEX's overwhelming presence in Mexico's industrial fuels market to justify an investment in natural gas pipelines or local distribution. Mexico is the Western Hemisphere's fourth richest country in natural gas reserves. Mexico's 68 trillion cubic feet rank fourth after the United States: 162 trillion cubic feet, Venezuela: 129 trillion cubic feet, Canada: 95 trillion cubic feet.

PEMEX is a potent symbol of national identity: it is Mexico's biggest company and the sixth largest oil company in the world. Despite PEMEX's size and power, low capital investment has slowed development of new refining facilities and severely reduced natural gas exploration. The Mexican government has taxed PEMEX so onerously over the years that little revenue is left for capital investment to drill new oil or gas wells or maintain old ones. Traditionally, PEMEX has been Mexico's lead employer, as well as a generous civil benefactor. It has often built and operated housing, schools and health clinics in poorer areas with weak and equally poor governments. Reflecting the Mexican government's new efficiency philosophy, in 1994 PEMEX had revenues of US $31 billion and was required to contribute twenty-eight percent of federal government revenues.

Until the recent legal changes, PEMEX was solely responsible for natural gas activities. Although the state-owned company developed a barely adequate 6200–mile pipeline network, the concepts of natural gas storage and marketing are virtually unknown in Mexico. Budgetary constraints limit pipeline construction, and the consequent lack of infrastructure has contributed to an underutilization of natural gas in industrial processes, as well as in residential and commercial markets. The private distribution networks are also very concentrated and not responsive to market demands.

* * *

There are two basic problems regarding natural gas and PEMEX. First, eighty-seven percent of Mexico's gas production of approximately 3.6 billion cubic feet per day in 1995 was "associated" with oil. That is, most of this production is a by-product of oil fields located in PEMEX's southern region and offshore in the Bay of Campeche. Unless non-associated reserves in the north are developed, natural gas production will remain secondary to oil. PEMEX did drill and develop natural gas in the north near Reynosa and Monterrey in the 1980s, but this is inadequate and there is no natural gas service at all in Western and Northwestern Mexico. About twenty percent of Mexico, including the entire Yucatán and Baja California peninsulas and about twenty cities including Tiajuana, Mexicali, Merida, San Luis Potosi and Aguascalientes, have no access to natural gas. There is a clear potential for developing gas, but it is an investment-intensive area which also requires the construction of a gas pipeline infrastructure.

Second, "Mexico's gas transmission network has excess capacity in some places and severe bottlenecks in others." The main 48–inch PEMEX trunkline is carrying only a third of its capacity, while PEMEX imports natural gas from the United States to serve customers in the north.

There is speculation that PEMEX is reluctant to develop natural gas, partly due to the 1992 gas pipeline explosion in Guadalajara which killed more than two hundred people. Additionally, the electrical power plants, which would be the largest market for natural gas, are currently the main purchasers of PEMEX's high sulphur crude oil that is below export quality. In other words, large investments will be required to develop natural gas, with a slow return. PEMEX has relatively easy access to the associated supplies of natural gas in the southeast and Gulf of Mexico, because that natural gas is located alongside reserves of crude oil. Natural gas in the north is located deep in the ground, and the extraction of natural gas in the northern states will require a significant commitment of capital.

* * *

NORTH AMERICAN FREE TRADE AGREEMENT (NAFTA)

NAFTA establishes a "free trade" area between Mexico, the United States and Canada; its primary objectives are to break down barriers to trade, promote fair competition, and to increase foreign investment opportunities. When NAFTA took effect January 1, 1994, it reaffirmed Mexico's constitutional monopoly on the exploration, development, transportation and First Hand Sales of natural gas. Article 601(1) of NAFTA provides that "the parties confirm their full respect for their constitutions."

The most important reservation in NAFTA's chapter on energy is Annex 602.3, which provides that:

> The Mexican State reserves to itself the following strategic activities and investment in such activities: (a) exploration and exploitation of crude oil and natural gas; refining or processing of crude oil and natural gas; and production of artificial gas, basic petrochemicals and their feedstocks; and pipelines; and (b) foreign trade; transportation, storage and distribution, up to and including first hand sales of the following goods: crude oil; natural and artificial gas; goods covered by this Chapter obtained from the refining or processing of crude oil and natural gas; and basic petrochemicals.

Although NAFTA affords its signatories the protection of the national treatment principle for investments across the borders of the parties, private investment is not permitted in the activities in which reservations apply. Since the reservation is essentially a unilateral act accepted by the other parties to the Treaty, Mexico is free to modify or withdraw its reservation at any time.

* * *

There are various reasons why, even though at face value NAFTA appears to discourage foreign investment in natural gas in Mexico, this has not turned out to be the case. The reality of the situation follows the lead of the Preamble of NAFTA, which states that one of NAFTA's fundamental principles is the sustained and gradual liberalization of trade in energy and basic petrochemical goods. For example, NAFTA allows, subject to the approval of the Mexican Foreign Investment Commission, one hundred percent foreign ownership in Mexican companies that provide natural gas well drilling services. Up to forty nine percent foreign ownership is permitted without the need for approval. As to minerals generally, after five years the present forty-nine percent ceiling on foreign ownership will be increased to permit one hundred percent foreign ownership, without Foreign Investment Commission approval, of an enterprise "engaged in extraction or exploitation of any mineral."

* * *

Article 1102 of the Investment Chapter of NAFTA requires Mexico to open up petrochemicals, those not classified as basic, to foreign investment. There are only eight petrochemicals classified as basic petrochemicals by the Mexican government.

The Mexican Energy Ministry had decided it would not have applied a NAFTA clause restricting foreign ownership to only forty nine percent to the Cosoleacaque petrochemical complex, had the sale been completed. It announced, however, it will apply the clause in the sale of other petrochemical complexes to be sold. Invoking the NAFTA clause would have allowed the government to restrict production of the eight basic petrochemicals to companies that are majority-owned by Mexicans. The NAFTA clause was not part of the original guidelines released when the privatization of the petrochemical plants were first announced. Obviously, the government's decision to apply a NAFTA clause to ensure majority Mexican capital in later sales of petrochemical complexes has greatly diminished foreign interest in them.

The government's decision to invoke the NAFTA clause may mean that the petrochemical complexes will not be sold as one massive unit. The plants may need to be privatized individually, ushering in a cumbersome process of breaking the complexes into separate entities for sale. This option is considered impractical, because plants within each complex are connected to each other and share common connections to gas, power, water, and other utilities. Many observers think the clause will complicate the divestiture and make them virtually unsalable. However, others think that foreign investor interest may pick up again, if the Mexican government can somehow offer the necessary legal security. At this point, however, sales of all of the petrochemical complexes are postponed indefinitely.

Another obstacle to foreign investment posed by Article 27's directive is that neither concessions nor contracts regarding oil exploitation may be granted. That directive suggests that, even if PEMEX prefers to hire out hydrocarbon exploitation activity, rather than perform the activity itself, PEMEX may not constitutionally do so by means of "concessions" or "contracts."

In the Annex 602.3 reservation to NAFTA, Mexico exempted a broad range of "strategic activities." Mexico also made exceptions to NAFTA which incorporate various legislative restrictions on hydrocarbon operations by foreigners. Those exceptions declare that foreigners may not have interest in a Mexican enterprise that stores, transports, or sells liquified petroleum gas or installs "fixed deposits," or sells at retail gasoline, diesel, lubricants, oils or additives, and that authorization by the Foreign Investment Commission is required for foreign ownership of more than forty-nine percent of a Mexican enterprise "involved in 'non-risk sharing' contracts for the exploration and drilling works of petroleum and gas wells" or in "construction of means for the transportation of petroleum and its derivatives."

* * *

In June 1996, U.S. natural gas companies contended that with the Mexican government's opening of the natural gas market, the import duty tax on natural gas should be terminated. NAFTA established a base duty of ten percent on natural gas imported into Mexico with a one percent decrease each year for ten years. PEMEX's natural gas is cheaper than U.S. imported gas and the U.S. natural gas companies are requesting a more rapid phase-out of the duty tax than NAFTA requires.

In July 1996, the Mexican government denied the United States' request to lower its tariff on natural gas, but offered to consider the issue in exchange for concessions from the U.S. in other areas of NAFTA. The Mexican government insists that the speeding up or elimination of the now seven percent tariff on natural gas is an issue that should be negotiated in exchange for similar reductions in tariffs on Mexican exports with Canada and the United States. Mexican officials maintain that they are flexible about negotiating a lower gas tariff so as not to jeopardize government plans to promote foreign investment in natural gas storage and transportation. They contend, however, that the era of unilaterally and inappropriately lowering tariffs is over.

REGULATORY LAW TO ARTICLE 27 OF THE CONSTITUTION IN THE PETROLEUM SECTOR

1958, as amended; Mexican Law Library, Vol. 4, 1998 Supp.*

Article 1. The Nation shall have direct, inalienable, and interminable control of all hydrocarbons found in national territory, including the continental shelf, in strata or deposits, whatever their physical state, including intermediate states, and which may compose, accompany, or derive from crude oil.

Article 2. Only the Nation may carry out the various methods of exploiting hydrocarbons which may constitute the petroleum industry within the terms of the following article.

In this law the word "petroleum" shall include all natural hydrocarbons referred to in Article 1.

Article 3. The petroleum industry includes:

I. The exploration, exploitation, refining, transportation, storage, distribution, and first-hand sales of petroleum and the products which may be obtained from its refining;

II. The exploration, exploitation, processing, and first-hand sales of gas, as well as the transportation and storage which may be indispensable and necessary to interconnect its exploitation and processing; and

III. The processing, transportation, storage, distribution, and first-hand sales of derivatives of petroleum and gas capable of being used as basic industrial raw materials, and which constitute the basic petrochemicals enumerated as follows:

1. Ethane;

2. Propane;

3. Butane;

4. Pentane;

5. Hexane;

6. Heptane;

7. Raw material for carbon black;

8. Napthas; and

9. Methane, when it arises from hydrocarbons, is obtained from deposits located in national territory, and is used as a raw material in petrochemical industrial processes.

Article 4. The Nation shall carry out the exploration and exploitation of petroleum and the other activities referred to in article 3 which are considered strategic within the terms of Article 28, fourth paragraph, of the Political Constitution of the United Mexican States, through Petróleos Mexicanos and its subsidiary organisms.

Except as provided in Article 3, the transportation, storage and distribution of gas may be carried out, with prior permission, by the social and private sectors which may construct, operate, and own the pipelines, installations and equipment within the terms of regulatory and technical provisions which may be issued.

The transportation, storage and distribution of methane gas is included in the activities, and in the regime, referred to in the preceding paragraph.

When, in the processing of petrochemical products other than the basic petrochemicals enumerated in section III of article 3 of this law, petroliferous products or basic petrochemicals are obtained as sub-products, such sub-products may be used in the productive process within plants of the same unit or complex, or be delivered to Petróleos Mexicanos or its subsidiary organisms, under contract and within the terms of such administrative provisions as the Secretariat of Energy may issue.

Enterprises which fall within the case referred to in the preceding paragraph shall be obligated to provide notice to the Secretariat of Energy, which shall be empowered to verify compliance with the above-cited administrative provisions and, if applicable, impose the sanctions referred to in article 15 of this Law.

Article 5. The Secretariat of Energy shall assign to Petróleos Mexicanos such land as such institution may request of it, or which the Federal Executive may consider it expedient to assign to it, for the purposes of petroleum exploration and exploitation.

The Regulations to this law shall establish the cases in which the Secretariat of Energy may refuse or cancel such assignments.

Article 6. Petróleos Mexicanos may enter into such construction and service contracts with physical or moral persons as may be required for the better performance of its activities. Remuneration which may be established in such contracts shall always be in money, and percentages in products or participation in the return from exploitation may never be granted in exchange for services provided or construction performed.

Article 7. The surface inspection and exploration of land for the purpose of researching its petroleum potential shall only require the permission of the Secretariat of Energy. If there is any opposition by the owner or holder of the land, when such land is private, or by the legal representatives of the ejidos or rural communities, when such land is subject to an ejidal or communal regime, the Secretariat of Energy, after hearing the parties, shall grant the permission through an acknowledgment which Petróleos Mexicanos shall make of its obligation to indemnify the affected parties for damage or injuries which may be caused, in accordance with the expert report which the Commission for the Appraisal of National Assets shall perform within six months. Petróleos Mexicanos may pay an advance, in consultation with the same Commission. The rest of the payment shall be finalized once the expert report has been concluded.

Article 8. The Federal Executive shall establish zones for petroleum reserves on lands which, due to their petroleum potential, may merit such designation, for the purpose of guaranteeing the future supply of the country. The incorporation of land into the reserves, and its disincorporation therefrom, shall be made by presidential decree, based on the respective technical reports.

Article 9. The petroleum industry and the activities referred to in article 4, second paragraph, are subject to exclusive federal jurisdiction. Consequently, only the Federal Government may issue technical provisions, regulatory laws, and regulations which may govern such activities.

Article 10. The petroleum industry is a public utility with priority over any other use of the surface or subsurface of lands, including over the possession of lands by ejidos or rural communities, and the provisional or definitive occupation or expropriation of such lands may proceed through legal indemnification in all cases in which the Nation or its petroleum industry may so require.

Activities relating to the construction of pipelines constitute a public utility. Petróleos Mexicanos, its subsidiary organisms, and enterprises in the social and private sectors shall be obligated to provide transportation and distribution of gas services to third parties through pipelines within such terms and conditions as may be established in the regulatory provisions.

Article 11.   The Federal Executive shall issue rules related to the oversight of petroleum-related employment and the technical rules which shall govern the exploitation of such employment.

Article 12.   To the extent not provided in this law, the acts of the petroleum industry and the activities referred to in article 4, second paragraph, shall be considered commercial and shall be governed by the Code of Commerce and, to the extent not provided therein, by the provisions of the Civil Code for the Federal District in ordinary matters and for the entire Republic in federal matters.

Article 13.   Parties interested in obtaining the permits referred to in the second paragraph of article 4 of this law must present an application to the Secretariat of Energy which shall contain: the name and domicile of the applicant, the services it desires to furnish, the technical specifications of the project, investment programs and commitments and, as the case may be, any documentation which may evidence its financial capacity.

Permits may be assigned with the previous authorization of the Secretariat of Energy, and provided the assignee meets the requirements to be a holder thereof and obligates itself to comply, within the terms thereof, with the obligations prescribed in such permits. In no case may the permit, the rights granted in such permit, or the assets subject to such rights, be assigned, encumbered or sold to a foreign government or state.

The permits may be revoked for any of the following reasons:

I.   For not exercising the rights conferred therein during the time period set forth in the permits;

II.   For interrupting the services which are the subject of the permit, without justified cause and the authorization of the Secretariat of Energy;

III.   For carrying out discriminatory practices in prejudice of users, and violating the prices and rates, if any, which may be established by a competent authority;

IV.   For assigning, encumbering or transferring the permits in violation of that provided in this law;

V.   For not complying with Official Mexican Norms, or the conditions established in the permit.

Permittees shall be obligated to allow examiners of the Secretariat of Energy access to their installations, as well as to provide the Secretariat of Energy all information which may be required to confirm compliance with their obligations.

Article 14. The regulation of the activities referred to in article 4, second paragraph, and of the first-hand sale of gas, shall have as their purpose to ensure its efficient supply and shall include:

I.   The terms and conditions for:

(a) The granting, transfer, and revocation for noncompliance of the permit;

(b) First-hand sales;

(c) The furnishing of transportation, storage and distribution services;

(d) Access, under non-discriminatory and competitive conditions, to services relating to transportation, storage and distribution through pipelines;

(e) The presentation of sufficient and adequate information for the purposes of regulation;

II.   The determination of applicable prices and rates when, in the judgment of the Federal Competition Commission, conditions of effective competition do not exist. The social and private sectors may request such Commission to declare the existence of competitive conditions;

III.   Procedures for public consultation in defining regulatory criteria, if any;

IV.   The inspection and oversight of compliance with conditions established in the permits and applicable Official Mexican Norms;

V.   Conciliation and arbitration procedures to resolve disputes relating to the interpretation and compliance of contracts, and procedures to challenge the refusal to enter into them;

VI.   Such other means of regulation as may be set forth in applicable provisions.

Article 15. Violations of this law and its regulatory provisions may be sanctioned with fines from 1,000 to 100,000 times the amount of the general minimum wage effective in the Federal District on the date the violation is committed, in the judgment of the competent authority, taking into account the importance of the violation.

In the event of a violation of that provided in the fourth and fifth paragraphs of article 4 of this Law, and without prejudice to the sanctions prescribed in the preceding paragraph, the violator shall forfeit to Petróleos Mexicanos the petroliferous sub-products or basic petrochemicals obtained.

In applying this article, the procedure prescribed in the Federal Law of Administrative Procedure shall be followed.

Article 16. The Secretariat of Energy shall be responsible for enforcement of this law, with such participation as may be given to the

Energy Regulatory Commission within the terms of regulatory provisions.

* * *

TRANSITORY ARTICLES

(Published in the Official Gazette of Mexico of May 11, 1995)

* * *

THIRD. Petróleos Mexicanos shall maintain ownership of, and shall maintain in operating condition, pipelines and the accessory equipment and installation for the transportation of gas referred to in article 4, second paragraph, which form part of its current holdings, subjecting their operation to this law and to regulatory, technical and regulatory provisions which may be issued.

Petróleos Mexicanos shall also continue to carry out activities of transporting gas with other equipment which may form part of its holdings, subjecting them to applicable provisions.

* * *

TRANSITORY ARTICLES

(Published in the Official Gazette of Mexico of November 23, 1996)*

* * *

SECOND. Petróleos Mexicanos shall preserve ownership of and shall maintain in operating condition the pipelines and their accessory equipment and installations for the transportation of methane, within the terms of the third transitory article to the Decree containing amendments to the Regulatory Law to Article 27 of the Constitution in the Petroleum Sector, published in the Official Gazette of the Federation on May 11, 1995.

Historical Record:

Original Publication: November 29, 1958.

Amendments: Appearing in the Official Gazette of the Federation on: December 30, 1977; May 11, 1995, November 13, 1996.

* Authors' note: as of late 2004, there had been no further amendments to the Regulatory Law to Article 27.

HOMANT, MEXICO: CONSTITUTIONAL AND POLITICAL IMPLICATIONS OF THE 1995 NATURAL GAS REGULATIONS

4 Tulsa J. Comp. & Int'l L. 233 (1997).*

MEXICO'S 1992 PEMEX ORGANIC LAW

After the tragic explosion of the sewer line in Guadalajara, PEMEX was re-established by the Mexican Congress as a business through the passage of the 1992 Pemex Organic Law. To increase efficiency and decrease risk of accidents, a restructuring plan for PEMEX was devised in 1992. PEMEX was divided into four subsidiaries consisting of (1) production and exploration, (2) refining, (3) natural gas and basic petrochemicals, and (4) secondary petrochemicals. The plan also included reducing the work force to 53,000 employees. However, the present workforce of PEMEX is still 130,000.

Since 1992, PEMEX has aggressively sought private partners for some of its non-energy business units. For example, partners from the private sector undertook majority positions in the areas of air transportation, lubricants, and bunker fuel. In addition, PEMEX sought strategic partners in selected areas of its energy business, mainly the joint venture with Shell U.S.A., to construct a new refinery at Deer Park, Texas. However, the 1992 PEMEX Organic Law still did not define the sectors of the oil industry that were constitutionally open to privatization.

MEXICO'S 1995 NATURAL GAS REGULATIONS

Mexico has traditionally maintained an exclusive monopoly franchise, PEMEX, for natural gas transportation, storage and distribution. The changing of the implementing regulations to Article 27 of the Constitution, through passage of the 1995 Natural Gas Regulations (NGRs), to allow direct foreign investment in these areas was partly in response to NAFTA. Enactments that privatize natural gas in Mexico are significant because of the hyper-sensitivity of the state hydrocarbons monopoly exercised by PEMEX. To begin the privatization of natural gas, in May 1995 the Mexican Congress amended the 1958 Regulatory Law, the prior implementing instrument, by defining the "strategic area" of the oil industry so that transportation, storage and distribution of natural gas is no longer a state monopoly. The 1958 Regulatory Law originally defined the hydrocarbons monopoly created by Article 27 of the Mexican Constitution.

Article 27 has been amended fifteen times since its promulgation in the 1917 Constitution, almost twice the number of all amendments of the United States Constitution during the same period. Some of those Article 27 amendments were as revolutionary as the original text itself: effectuating the right of needful communities to have land expropriated for use as communal lands, creating state monopolies in hydrocarbons and electric power, and allowing religious organizations to own land.

Thus, it is not unusual to re-interpret the meaning of the words of Article 27 through the use of implementing regulations.

The new Regulatory Law of Article 27 of the Constitution on Petroleum and the Regulation of Natural Gas passed in May 1995 allows that for natural gas derivatives that are basic petrochemicals, transportation, storage and distribution continue as a state monopoly, but for natural gas those activities do not. The amendment distinguishes between "natural gas derivatives" and "natural gas."

* * *

The May 1995 enactment called for its own implementing regulations to be issued within 180 days. By November 9, 1995, the Mexican Congress issued those regulations. Composed of 110 Articles and 10 Transitory provisions, the new Natural Gas Regulations (NGRs) operate as a "transparent and precise framework which gives economic and legal certainty to investors, workers, consumers and users" of natural gas. The NGRs formally codify, in a federal statute, the controversial policies created in this area by the conflicting prior amendments to Article 27 of the Constitution of Mexico.

* * *

The new regulations are designed fundamentally to promote development of the natural gas industry while protecting users and limiting market power. Five principal participants operate in the natural gas industry: PEMEX is responsible for First Hand Sales and operation of its existing transportation network; transporters construct, own, and operate new pipelines; storage companies develop storage systems; distributors supply and market natural gas in defined geographic regions; and marketers buy and sell and may act as intermediaries to transportation, storage and distribution services. All of the parties are free to market natural gas.

Under the new regulations, PEMEX retains control of natural gas exploration, drilling and refining, but will likely sell off the distribution side of the business hoping that private investors will expand delivery to unserved areas. The NGRs are consistent with NAFTA in that they allow those private investors to hold up to a forty-nine percent stake in transportation, storage and distribution of natural gas. As spelled out in NAFTA, investors can petition the Mexican National Foreign Investment Commission for ownership of up to one hundred percent.

The regulations also provide that the changes will be administered by the Energy Ministry and a new Energy Regulatory Commission (CRE). Thus, PEMEX is stripped of some of the regulatory functions it had in the past, such as the responsibility for approving supply contracts for imported natural gas. Thus, the regulatory functions PEMEX previously exercised over natural gas imports, transportation, distribution and marketing will be taken over by those other entities.

* * *

The CRE will issue permits for transportation, storage and distribution of natural gas, with these functions subjected to many of the same regulatory tenets operative in the United States. Operators may deny access to their facilities only when there is no available capacity or when the access or interconnection is not technically feasible.

The CRE also sets regulated prices when competitive conditions are found not to exist in the market, acts as mediator for resolving controversies, and applies administrative sanctions. For example, PEMEX is the leading consumer of natural gas in Mexico, using it for petrochemical feedstock, refinery fuel, gas pipeline compression, and its own power generation operations. Similarly, the Mexican Federal Electricity Commission (CFE) is the second leading consumer of natural gas. The CRE will now act as a mediator in dealings between the two state agencies and foreign private suppliers. The Mexican Congress further put limits on PEMEX by attaching an amendment to the new regulations stating that the price of natural gas supplied by a monopoly supplier may not exceed prevailing international prices.

* * *

Mexico is unlikely to develop an urban underground natural gas network like the United States. Mexico's main interest appears to be in cross-country pipelines to supply industries and power plants. The present natural gas system in Mexico serves only the Gulf coast, central and north-central regions, leaving the entire Northwest, Pacific Coast, and Yucatán without service. Mexican officials are concerned that the western half of the country does not become strategically dependent on the United States, so authorities are more likely to require that United States companies hook up at least partially with existing Mexican gas pipelines rather than import more U.S. gas.

Under the new legislation, the government will grant concessions to domestic or foreign companies to transport, distribute, and store natural gas. Now, private companies can import gas, bid for and be granted thirty-year permits to construct, own and operate new pipelines and distribution networks, thereby bypassing PEMEX entirely. An open market is expected to develop in northern Mexico when customers have credible supply options due to their proximity to the United States.

* * *

CASE STUDY: 1996 NATURAL GAS CONCESSION IN MEXICALI

The choice to launch natural gas privatization from Mexicali, President Zedillo's hometown, is symbolic of his commitment to liberalize Mexico's entire energy sector. Since about 1980, the Mexican state of Baja California Norte has been asking Mexico City for natural gas service for its principle cities, Mexicali and Tijuana. A number of international companies have chosen to establish businesses in other Mexican cities because they have access to natural gas service, meanwhile ignoring the cities of Baja California Norte.

Because of extreme weather conditions and accelerated commercial and industrial growth, northern Mexican cities, including those in Baja California Norte, have high levels of energy consumption and are ripe for a natural gas distribution system. In the next five years, natural gas distribution in Baja California Norte could require US $100 million in capital investments and more than US $500 million for the construction of power plants.

Northwestern Mexico, where the state of Baja California Norte is located, is a natural first area for United States and other foreign gas companies to invest in Mexican energy operations. This part of the country is far removed from Mexico's own developed natural gas reserves in the south. Baja California Norte in particular is a relatively narrow, barren peninsula of 70,000 square kilometers extending eight hundred miles southward from the California border. Its industrial development is in the northern portion of the region in the cities of Tijuana, Ensenada, Mexicali and Rosarito Beach where there is a fast growing population and a booming maquiladora industry.

Natural gas is especially needed in Mexicali and Tijuana, cities with more than two million people combined and thousands of maquiladoras. Natural gas is also needed in the power generation plant at Rosarito Beach through construction of a pipeline from the U.S. border to the town twenty minutes away.

The Mexican government awarded its first natural gas privatization license in August 1996, about two weeks after the Cactus complex obliteration, to a bi-national partnership composed of two U.S. companies and a Mexican company, called Distribuidora de Gas Natural de Mexicali (DGN). The award was a monumental step for economic progress in Mexico and a milestone for United States companies attempting to move into the Latin American market. The Mexican government indicated during the bidding process that the license would go to the company that offered the lowest distribution rate for customers.

American, French, Canadian, Spanish and Mexican companies registered for bidding on the natural gas distribution contract in Mexicali. The winner was ultimately selected on the basis of the lowest natural gas transmission costs and on skills in market analysis and planning. DGN's winning bid of US $1.14 per gigacalorie was the lowest bid. Their license allows DGN to build and operate a natural gas distribution system in Mexicali, a city that now relies on propane and fuel oil.

The partnership will initially invest US $25 million during the first five years, providing service to major commercial and industrial users and 25,000 residents. Natural gas is expected to be available in Mexicali by 1997. Although the Mexicali project calls for an investment of only US $25 million, it marks the opening of Mexico's entire energy market. DGN is the first private operation to ship natural gas for retail sale in Mexico. The company will have a thirty-year operating permit that provides exclusive distribution rights for twelve years.

Presently, Mexicali has no natural gas distribution system, relying on bottled propane for space heating and cooking in the residential sector. Mexicali has 2,500 homes already linked to propane gas pipelines, which can easily be switched over to natural gas service. The partnership has until the end of the year 2002 to bring 25,000 Mexicali customers on line, approximately one of every four homes in this desert city. With temperatures averaging over one hundred degrees during summer months, and residential electric air-conditioning bills sometimes topping US $1,000 per month, the partnership should find a ready market for an alternative energy source.

The system will have an initial capacity of about ten million cubic feet per day, but it would be economically feasible with initial sales of less than half that level. As industrial loads increase, developers will install distribution branches to serve residential and commercial demand. The natural gas supply will come through a pipeline from the United States to Mexicali. Initially, the project will provide natural gas to steel, glass, cement, truck, food and maquiladora factories. Eventually, it will also serve the 700,000 residents of the bustling border city nearly a hundred miles southeast of San Diego, California. Predictions put the minimum cost of between US $40 and $50 million overall to build the fifteen-mile long pipeline from the U.S. border to Mexicali, linking with the United States distribution system. The natural gas will come from either Alberta, Canada, Texas, Oklahoma, New Mexico or other U.S. states.

Until the award was made, Mexico's natural gas distribution was mostly controlled by PEMEX; only a few private domestic operators have been allowed to distribute natural gas to customers. If a foreign company owned a factory and wanted to use natural gas, it would have to pay for the pipeline and give it away to PEMEX because it was not possible to own the pipeline. Under the new award system, PEMEX, which previously had natural gas distribution as an exclusive business, is not eligible to bid on any of these contracts for natural gas concessions.

There is a concern that in Mexicali, as is the case throughout Mexico, natural gas providers must compete against a tradition of cheap propane fuel. Long subsidized by PEMEX, liquid propane gas sells at below market rates. While that subsidy is expected to be phased out by the year 1998, the partnership has to price its domestic natural gas service cheaply in order to compete now. The exclusive twelve-year concession to serve the border city of Mexicali begins a privatization process that will open the entire country to natural gas providers, creating an estimated US $3 billion-a-year market for private utilities over the next decade. The Mexicali Project is the first of twenty-two natural gas distribution systems being offered to private companies throughout Mexico. Ten of the areas to be opened up next are Mexico City, Bajio, Cuernavaca, Hermosillo, La Laguna, Northeast of Baja California, Pachuca, Querétaro, Tampico and Toluca, many of which include urban zones already connected to a network of transportation pipelines or that already have access to imported natural gas.

Mexico is quickly advancing private foreign investment in an effort to offset the economic difficulties caused by the devaluation of the peso in 1995, causing the legislature to promulgate new laws allowing private companies to build, own or operate power plants, storage facilities and natural gas or electricity distribution systems. The money is needed not only to recover and resume growth, but to prime the flow of money back into the country and to build a market for PEMEX natural gas output.

Mexico's first wave of privatization saw the nation's banks, telephone monopoly and other entities pass from government to private control with little difficulty. Mexico's privatization drive is one of the most ambitious in the world, reducing state-run companies from 1,239 in 1984 to 221 in 1994. The privatization of just eight hundred public companies, including Mexico's four main ports, raised US $21 billion. The creation of the new Comisión Reguladora de Energia (CRE) and the promulgation of the NGRs in 1995 constitute a critical ingredient in Mexico's strategy for promoting the expansion of the use of natural gas and the generation of electricity with natural gas.

This landmark law broke the oligopoly that about fifteen Mexican firms held on Mexico's gas distribution sector. The Mexican companies can still make offers for new projects, but under the new legislation, overseas firms also can bid. The legislation also freed the domestic companies from the obligation to buy gas from Mexico's state-owned petroleum monopoly, PEMEX. Under the old rules, the Mexican suppliers had to purchase from PEMEX, but now both they and the foreign competitors can get gas from the cheapest source.

Most United States gas companies are not concerned that the CRE will favor domestic companies or combinations that include Mexican companies when evaluating proposals. However, some potential U.S. investors have noted that the new NGRs may not allow the Mexican regulatory commission to play an independent role in settling disputes between parties; that the regulations lack provisions granting exclusivity to transporters for services for a five-year term; and they lack a grant of exclusivity to distributors for natural gas sales in a specific location.

LOPEZ–VELARDE, SOME CONSIDERATIONS ON THE NEW FOREIGN INVESTMENT POSSIBILITIES IN THE MEXICAN OIL AND GAS INDUSTRY

Mexican Law Library, Vol. 4, 1998 Supp.*

PRESENT AND UPCOMING BIDS

The Plan for National Development for the period from 1995–2000 and the Program for the Development and Restructuring of the Energy Sector establish that the energy sector must evolve efficiently with the participation of the private sector, in those activities in which the law enables it to participate. In accord with the these two plans, the first international public call regarding distribution of natural gas in Mexico was published, on March 1, 1996, in the Official Gazette of the Federation. Such bid set forth the development of the geographic zone encompassing Mexicali, Baja California. This permit was granted to a group formed by Pacific Enterprises International, San Diego Gas & Electric and Grupo Mexicano Próxima (the "Group"), on August 12, 1996.

Pursuant to petitions on behalf of the government of the state of Chihuahua and the principal consumers of natural gas of this state, the CRE published another geographic zone for distribution of natural gas on May 21, 1996. Such zone encompasses Chihuahua, Cuauhtemoc–Anahuac, and Delicias (the "Chihuahua zone"). The Chihuahua zone was also won by the Group.

Furthermore, the CRE also published on November 29, 1996, a public call for the natural gas distribution in the geographic zone composed by the cities of Hermosillo, Guaymas and Empalme located in the Mexican State of Sonora (the "Sonora zone"). Said zone was won by the U.S. company "KN Energy."

In addition to the above mentioned geographic zones, the CRE published on December 16, 1997, one of the most important geographic zones for natural gas distribution in Mexico, the municipalities of Lerma, Metepec, Ocoyoacac, San Mateo Atenco, Toluca, Xonacatlan and Zinacantepec, in the State of Mexico ("Toluca").

On July 2, 1997, the CRE published the denial of the proposed geographical zone submitted to said Commission by Distribuidora de Gas Natural del Estado de Mexico, S.A. ("Diganamex"). Thus, the Commission commenced the procedure to allow private participation in the distribution of natural gas by publishing a Resolution in the Official Gazette of the Federation designating two of the most awaited geographical zones known as the Federal District and the Cuautitlan–Texcoco Valley zones.

* * *

The CRE will grant two distribution permits; one for the Mexico City Metropolitan Zone and the other one for the Cuautitlán-Texcoco Zone.

It is expected that, in 1997, besides the Mexicali, Chihuahua, Sonora, Toluca, Panuco River (located in the State of Tamaulipas), Mexico City, and Cuautitlán-Texcoco geographic zones, the CRE will publish public calls for the cities and municipalities of (i) the Bajío region composed of the municipalities of Leon, Celaya, Salamanca and Irapuato; (ii) the Laguna region composed of the municipalities of Torreon, Gomez Palacio and Ciudad Lerdo; (iii) the Baja California region composed of the municipalities of Tijuana, Rosarito, Ensenada and Tecate; (iv) Pachuca (located in the State of Pachuca); (v) Querétaro and San Juan del Rio (located in the State of Querétaro); (vi) Cuernavaca (located in the State of Morelos); (vii) Puebla (located in the State of Puebla); and (viii) Reynosa (located in the State of Tamaulipas).

Due to the lack of pipeline distribution infrastructure in the north and middle part of the Mexican Republic, public calls are also expected for the cities of Guanajuato and Durango. At the same time, in the southeast of the Mexican Republic, public calls are expected for the states of (i) Veracruz; and (ii) Yucatán.

TRANSPORTATION

In general, Mexican or foreign corporations with a presence in Mexico can obtain permits from the CRE through the application process. However, in some cases, and upon the request of the federal or state governments, the CRE may call for a public bidding process. Transportation permits will be issued for defined routes and capacities. Such permits will provide the permittee with a non-exclusive right to build, install and operate natural gas transportation systems.

The CRE has located transportation projects in (i) Ciudad Pemex–Mérida; (ii) Rosarito; (iii) Mérida-Valladolid; (iv) San Agustín Valdivia–Samalayuca–Chihuahua; (v) Palmillas–Toluca; and (vi) Hermosillo–Guaymas.

Questions and Comments

1. Read carefully Articles 25, 27 and 28 of the 1917 Mexican Constitution. What do they require for Mexico's oil, gas, petrochemical and electricity industries? What are their implications for ENRES? Might these provisions be amended? *See* the Smith excerpt.

2. Professor Margadant has referred to the 1917 Constitution as a "declaration of war" against the oil companies, among others. Do you agree? If so, why did Mexico wait 21 years before creating PEMEX? What events triggered Mexico's nationalization of its oil and gas industry in 1938?

3. How did Mexico and the United States resolve the issue of compensation for the oil and gas assets expropriated in 1938? As Levy notes, NAFTA finally brought an historic agreement on rules for compensation of foreign investors in the event of expropriation. We take up those rules in Chapter 5.

4. With all of its energy resources, most people think of Mexico as an energy exporter. Is that an accurate picture? Would you advise ENRES to focus on exporting to or importing from Mexico? What about investing in Mexico's energy sector?

5. Do you now understand the first sentence in Article 601 of NAFTA? Does Annex 602.3 conform to the Mexican Constitution? Does it exceed that Constitution? Does it conform to or exceed the Regulatory Law to Article 27 of the Mexican Constitution in the Petroleum Sector (hereinafter "Regulatory Law 27")? What is the relationship between Article 27 and this Law?

6. Does NAFTA Annex 602.3 suggest any opportunities for ENRES? In oil? In natural gas? In petrochemicals? In electricity?

7. Chapter 6 of NAFTA applies to "basic" petrochemicals? How do we know what that means? *See* NAFTA Article 602.2 and Regulatory Law 27,

Article 3(III). Should ENRES focus its clients' attention on basic or non-basic petrochemicals?

8. Is privatization of non-basic petrochemical plants required by NAFTA? Why has the privatization announced in 1995 stalled? *See* the excerpt by Homant. Would you advise ENRES clients to bid on the Cosoleacaque plants in Veracruz? Can foreigners obtain majority control?

9. What opportunities were created in 1992 (pre-NAFTA) for foreigners to invest in electrical generation facilities in Mexico? *See* Homant. Does NAFTA create additional opportunities? *See* Annex 602.3(5).

10. What does the Samalayuca II plant example (*see* Homant) suggest for ENRES's clients? Must the foreign owners of this plant sell their power to CFE? What is a "Build–Lease–Transfer" (BLT) agreement?

11. Does NAFTA create opportunities for ENRES clients regarding natural gas? *See* Annex 602.3. Does Regulatory Law 27 (as amended)? *See* Article 4 para. 2, Article 10 and Article 14. And the 1995 Natural Gas Regulations? *See* Homant.

12. What does the Mexicali natural gas concession case study suggest for ENRES's clients? *See* Homant. And its successors? *See* López-Velarde.

13. Does NAFTA create opportunities for ENRES clients regarding oil? *See* Annex 602.3. Does Regulatory Law 27 (as amended)? *See*, Articles 1–10. Did the 1992 PEMEX Organic Law? *See* Homant.

14. Recently, Pemex has developed the "Multiple Service Contract"–supposedly consistent with Article 27 of the Mexican Constitution–which will permit private companies to finance 100% of gas field development. They will be paid for works performed and services rendered, but the natural gas produced in the field will remain the property of Pemex. Bidding for the first seven blocks was opened in July 2003; as of February 2004 five of the seven blocks had been awarded, to U.S. Argentine, Japanese and Mexican firms. However, this first group of contracts is not likely to significantly increase Mexico's natural gas production. (*See* U.S. Department of Energy, Country Analysis Briefs—Mexico, Mar. 2004, *available at* http://www.eia.doe.gov.) Notwithstanding these recent, and limited, steps, many observers believe that high fossil fuel and electrical energy costs–twice those in some parts of the United States–are among the factors that are encouraging some potential investors to establish manufacturing facilities in Asia instead. There is also some irony in the fact that Mexico must import 20% to 25% of the gasoline it consumes domestically, due to insufficient refining capacity.

15. According to the U.S. Department of Energy, demand for electricity in Mexico is expected to grow at an annual rate of 5.6% between 2003 and 2012, and will require $50 billion in investment to meet this demand. In 1999, the Mexican government announced plans for a major structural reform of its electricity sector, including privatization of power companies, but the Zedillo Administration was unable to implement the changes. The Fox Administration (December 2000–2006) has also sought to implement the substantial privatization of the electricity sector several years later, only to be frustrated by political opposition in the Mexican Congress and at the Supreme Court. Shortages of electric power in Northern Mexico have led to *ad hoc* solutions in

a few cases. For example, Arizona Public Service, the utility serving Phoenix and Yuma, Arizona, has made arrangements, presumably with CFE's blessing, to deliver electricity at the Southwestern Border directly to several large *maquiladoras* located in an industrial part in San Luis del Rio Colorado, Sonora, Mexico. CFE is not involved in the transaction. Are such arrangements legal under Annex 602.3(5)?

Chapter 6

TRADE IN SERVICES

6.0 INTRODUCTION

NAFTA accomplished most of what the Canada–U.S. Free Trade Agreement (CFTA) had begun, the adoption of provisions intended to remove restrictions on various services.* CFTA had adopted an eight article services chapter, many provisions of which are mirrored in NAFTA Chapter 12 on Cross–Border Trade in Services. But as in the case of most areas governed by CFTA, NAFTA constituted not only a development of ideas first contained in the CFTA, but an application of those ideas to a very different nation, Mexico. CFTA did not have an international agreement to draw upon for guidelines in establishing principles for the trade of services. For such areas as dumping, subsidies, government procurement, safeguards, and standards, the GATT rules offered not only a good starting point, but rules to which both countries adhered, and which probably would not be deviated from in a significant manner in any regional free trade agreement such as the CFTA . But the GATT did not address services. The WTO would do so in its General Agreement on Trade in Services (GATS), but the WTO was not adopted until after the NAFTA, and the discussion of services during the WTO negotiations was much more contentious than during the NAFTA negotiations.

As noted in Chapter 2, CFTA included Annex 1408, which listed the services covered by the CFTA Articles. Within the definition of professional services, legal services was notably missing. NAFTA would change that omission, and make limited progress in the integration of legal services within the free trade area. CFTA also omitted trucking transportation, indeed it included no forms of transportation within its services rules, although the U.S.—Canada order was generally open to cross-border trucking services for years before CFTA. NAFTA would also change that omission, except for the exclusion of domestic and international air transportation and maritime transportation services. In both

---

* There was some attention to services in the 1985 U.S.–Israel Free Trade Agreement.

CFTA and NAFTA financial services were excluded from the general services chapter, but *included* in special, separate chapters.

The NAFTA approach to services is referred to as a "negative list" approach. If a sector is not excluded or made subject to a reservation, the sector comes within the NAFTA rules. Civil aviation is specifically excluded, for example, and each Party has taken exceptions, which appear in the extensive annexes to the Agreement.

The OAS overview of NAFTA Chapter 12 illustrates that chapter's evolution from CFTA to NAFTA. NAFTA Chapter 12 includes thirteen articles, plus a three section Annex 1210.5 including twenty sections, and an Appendix 1210.5–C governing civil engineers. Furthermore, the Parties have made, in Annexes I and II, extensive reservations to national treatment, most-favored nation treatment and local presence commitments. In Annex V, they have also preserved various quantitative restrictions. Finally, each Party is required to set out in Annex VI its commitments to liberalize quantitative restrictions, licensing requirements, performance requirements or other non-discriminatory measures.

NAFTA trade in services provisions, as in other sectors addressed to opening trade, place the greatest burden of change on Mexico. Professor Zamora notes some of that burden.

OAS OVERVIEW OF THE NORTH AMERICAN FREE TRADE AGREEMENT*

Chapter Twelve: Cross-Border Trade in Services

The Canada–US FTA marked the first time that cross-border services were addressed in a general trade agreement and subjected to the traditional trade principles of nondiscrimination and transparency. Since then, the Uruguay Round of multilateral trade negotiations has succeeded in concluding a General Agreement on Trade in Services (GATS). It establishes the equivalent for traded services to what the GATT has provided for trade in goods for the past 45 years.

As set out in Article 1201, chapter twelve applies to all measures affecting cross-border trade in all non-financial services not otherwise falling within the ambit of chapter eleven and not specifically excluded from coverage (e.g., procurement, air services other than specialty air services).

The NAFTA requires each Party to list in the Agreement's annexes those sectors, subsectors and activities where it wishes to retain full flexibility to enact new non-conforming measures.

Chapter twelve applies to laws and regulations affecting the provision of services across NAFTA borders. This includes measures affecting the production, distribution, marketing, sale and delivery of a service, as well as those related to the purchase or use of a service. The chapter also

* Available at http://www.sice.oas/summary/NAFTA.

applies to measures requiring a service provider to post a bond, while the treatment of the bond or security is subject to chapter eleven.

The chapter does not apply to a number of matters dealt with in other parts of the Agreement, including government procurement (chapter ten), financial services (chapter fourteen), air services (other than aircraft repair and maintenance services during which an aircraft is withdrawn from service and specialty air services) and subsidies and grants provided by a Party. Additionally, each Party maintains the right to take action necessary to enforce measures of general application that are consistent with the Agreement.

Chapter twelve does not require Parties to provide individuals from other NAFTA countries access to their labour market. The chapter affirms that each government may provide public services or perform public functions (e.g., law enforcement, correctional services and public education), in a manner that is not inconsistent with its obligations.

Articles 1202 and 1203 require that each government accord nondiscriminatory treatment to cross-border service providers within NAFTA. Under Article 1202, Parties may not discriminate in favour of domestic service providers. Accordingly, Article 1202 commits each Party to treat service providers of the other Parties no less favourably than it treats its own service providers in like circumstances. With respect to measures of a state or provincial government, national treatment means treatment no less favourable than the most favourable treatment the state or province accords to the service providers of the country of which it forms a part.

Article 1203 requires that each Party accord to service providers of another Party treatment no less favourable than it accords service providers from other countries (including non-NAFTA countries) in like circumstances.

Each NAFTA country is committed under Article 1204 to providing the better of the treatment required by Articles 1202 and 1203. The no-less-favourable standard applied in Articles 1202 and 1203 requires that service providers from other Parties be accorded treatment no less favourable than that accorded, in like circumstances, to domestic and non party service providers. Further, while a Party may impose different legal requirements on other NAFTA service providers to ensure that domestic consumers are protected to the same degree as they are in respect of domestic firms.

Article 1205 prohibits a Party from imposing a territorial (e.g., local, state, federal) residency requirement for cross border NAFTA service providers. Specifically, under Article 1205, a Party may not require a service provider of another NAFTA country to establish or maintain a residence, representative office, branch, or any other form of enterprise in its territory as a condition for the cross-border provision of a service.

Under Article 1206, each Party can lodge reservations aimed at maintaining existing non-conforming measures or preserving the ability to enact new non-conforming measures in specific sectors, sub-sectors, or activities. Existing non-conforming federal, provincial and state measures will be listed in Annex I to the NAFTA. Each Party will have up to two years after the entry into force of NAFTA (i.e., until January 1, 1996) to complete its list of existing non-conforming provincial and state measures. All non-conforming measures currently in force at the municipal and other local government level may be retained and need not be listed. [Authors' note: notwithstanding this obligation, the NAFTA Parties did not formally incorporate lists of specific non-conforming state and provincial practices in the NAFTA annexes.]

While Articles 1202, 1203 and 1205 do not apply to amendments to existing non-conforming measures set out in Annex I, and existing local government measures, this is so only to the extent that such amendments do not decrease the conformity of a measure, as it existed immediately before the amendment, with Articles 1202, 1203 and 1205 of the NAFTA. Further, each Party has retained the right to enact new non-conforming measures in respect of those sectors, sub-sectors or activities set out in Annex II (including aboriginal affairs and social affairs such as income security or insurance, social security or insurance, social welfare, public education, public training, health, and child care).

Under Article 1207, the Parties may maintain existing quantitative restrictions and adopt new ones in the future respecting the number of service providers in a particular sector. However, to increase transparency, Article 1207 does require the Parties to list any quantitative restriction at the federal, provincial or state level in Annex V. While quantitative restrictions maintained at the federal level are set out in Annex V, the Parties have one year in which to list existing provincial or state quantitative restrictions. The Parties are also required to notify other Parties when adopting a quantitative restriction at the federal, provincial or state level and to periodically endeavour to negotiate the liberalization or removal of the restrictions set out in Annex V. Parties are not required to list existing local measures or notify other Parties of new measures adopted at the local level.

Under Article 1208, each Party is to set out in its schedule to Annex VI its commitments to liberalize quantitative restrictions, licensing requirements, performance requirements or other non-discriminatory measures.

To ensure that the existing or future measures of a Party relating to the licensing or certification of nationals of another Party do not constitute an unnecessary barrier to trade, each Party shall endeavour to ensure under Article 1210 that its licensing and certification requirements and procedures are based on objective and transparent criteria such as competence; are no more burdensome than necessary to ensure the quality of the service; and are not in themselves a restriction on the provision of a service. However, paragraph three of Article 1210 makes clear that the MFN treatment provisions of Article 1203 do not require a

Party, which recognizes the education, experience, licenses or certifications of professional service providers obtained in the territory of a Party or non-Party, to recognize the credentials of the professional service providers of another NAFTA country.

Within two years of entry into force, Parties are required to remove any citizenship or permanent residency requirements, set out in its schedule to Annex I, that they maintain for the licensing and certification of professional service providers of another Party. However, failure to do so does not give rise to recourse under the dispute settlement procedures of chapter twenty. Rather, governments may respond by maintaining or reinstating an equivalent requirement in the same sector. Governments will consult periodically to determine the feasibility of removing any citizenship or permanent residency requirements for each others' service providers not eliminated within two years.

Annex 1210.5 has three sections: general provisions for licensing and certification, foreign legal consultants and the temporary licensing of engineers.

* * *

Under Article 1211, a Party may deny the benefits of chapter twelve to service providers of another NAFTA country where the Party establishes that the service is being provided by an enterprise owned or controlled by nationals of a non-Party with which it does not have diplomatic relations or to which it is applying economic sanctions. A Party may also deny benefits to cross-border providers of transportation services covered by this chapter if they provide such services with equipment not registered by any NAFTA country. Parties may also withhold the benefits of chapter twelve if the services involved are provided through an enterprise that is owned or controlled by persons of a non-NAFTA country and the enterprise has no substantial business activity in the territory of any Party. In this case, the denying government is to first give prior notification and to consult in accordance with Articles 1803 and 2006.

Annex 1212 addresses matters related to cross-border land transportation services. Each Party is to establish contact points to provide information published by that Party pertaining to several areas including safety requirements and taxation. During the fifth year after the date of entry into force of the Agreement (i.e., 1998) and periodically thereafter, the Commission will consider reports from the Parties assessing their respective liberalization of bus and truck transportation services as set out in the Parties Schedules to Annex I. Within seven years after the NAFTA comes into effect (i.e., by 2000), the Parties will consult to consider further liberalization commitments.

ZAMORA, THE AMERICANIZATION OF MEXICAN LAW: NON–TRADE ISSUES IN THE NORTH AMERICAN FREE TRADE AGREEMENT

24 Law & Policy in Int'l Bus. 391 (1993).*

* * *

TRADE IN SERVICES

NAFTA includes three chapters that deal with trade in services: Chapter 12 (Cross-border Trade in Services), Chapter 13 (Telecommunications) and Chapter 14 (Financial Services). In addition, Chapter 11 (Investment) and related Annexes set forth rules that govern foreign investment in service industries. Chapter 6 sets forth special rules for investments and services associated with production of energy and basic petrochemicals.

Chapter 12 is extremely broad, covering all services other than financial services, energy-related services, and air transport services. Service sectors of particular interest to U.S. providers include construction, land transportation, and professional services (legal, medical, engineering, etc.). U.S. companies are also heavily interested in energy services covered by Chapter 6 (and reservations contained in NAFTA Annex I). Chapter 14 (financial services) covers every type of financial institution, including commercial banks, securities firms, insurance companies, finance companies, and financial leasing companies.

In general, these are all areas in which Mexican law has traditionally allowed little room for foreign participation. For example, with the exception of Citibank, which benefits from a grandfather clause, no foreign bank is allowed to offer banking services in Mexico. The Mexican insurance market has been effectively closed to foreign insurance providers since 1935. Land transportation (passenger and freight) has traditionally been reserved to exclusively Mexican carriers (i.e., Mexican companies with no foreign participation), as have domestic air transport and telecommunications. The provision of legal services in Mexico by foreign lawyers has similarly been severely restricted, even though the situation is clouded by uncertainties in Mexican law. When one adds immigration laws that limit the number of resident foreigners who are entitled to seek employment, it is easy to see why the Mexican services sector has been even more protected from competition—through direct investment or by provision of services from abroad—than the manufacturing sector. As a consequence, Mexico has been an insignificant customer for U.S. service providers.

NAFTA sets forth general rules of national treatment and most-favored-nation treatment, as well as a general rule against requiring a service provider of another Party from establishing or maintaining an office in the other Party's territory as a condition for providing cross-border services. Notwithstanding these and other liberalizing measures, the seven annexes and related schedules that are part of the NAFTA agreement contain numerous reservations that allow Mexico to maintain restrictions on foreign service providers. The telecommunications sector remains particularly restricted, since the provision of public telecommunications services have not been made subject to NAFTA. Foreign provision of energy-related services is also strictly limited because of Mexican government domination of this sector. As a result, the overall effect of NAFTA will be to open immediately new windows of opportunity for U.S. and Canadian companies, with continued phasing out of certain restrictions built into the agreement, and the possibility of future liberalizing agreements after an initial transition period.

* * *

Mexico's commitments under NAFTA will require changes in Mexican laws, primarily in eliminating or softening prohibitions on foreign involvement in service industries. Overall, however, the entry into force of NAFTA will not per se require fundamental reform of the legal regimes governing each service sub-sector....

Nevertheless, as restrictions on foreign service providers are phased out, the eventual effect may be to change the way these industries are regulated in Mexico ... trade in services involves a more intrusive involvement in the economy of another country than trade in goods. The company or individual offering the service will usually have an intensive, ongoing relationship, often through permanent offices, with the foreign country. The Mexican government, both federal and state agencies, has legitimate concerns over the quality of such services to local buyers. In addition, most of the industries under discussion in NAFTA—insurance, legal services, banking, medical services—are highly regulated, especially in comparison with manufacturing industries. As foreign service providers bring with them new ways to do business, not to mention new types of services, they are bound to present new challenges for Mexican regulators. The result will likely be not only to change the type and quality of services provided in Mexico, but also the legal regime surrounding those services.

* * *

PROBLEM 6.1 PROFESSIONAL SERVICES: A TORONTO LAWYER WISHES TO PRACTICE IN FLORIDA/ FLORIDA LAWYERS WISH TO PRACTICE AND OPEN FIRM BRANCH IN MEXICO

SECTION I.　THE SETTING

Canadian lawyers to the U.S.

Nelson Eddy has spent the past three years practicing Canadian and international law in a large Toronto law firm's London office. He previously practiced tax and estate planning law for many years in Toronto. He formed a new Toronto law firm with Janet Macdonald just a few months ago. Eddy & Macdonald represents a Canadian corporation which has opened a resort hotel in Orlando near Disney World. Eddy received an LL.B. from McGill years ago, and a year later an LL.M. in Comparative Law from the University of Florida. That did not entitle him to sit for the Florida Bar exam. (Mr. Eddy could have taken the bar with an LL.M. from an ABA accredited law school in a number of other states, such as New York, California and Illinois, probably would have been permitted to take the New York bar exam based on his Canadian LL.B. degree, without any further legal studies. In some states, such as Arizona, he probably could have successfully petitioned the state bar examiners for permission to sit for the bar, again based solely on his Canadian LL.B.)

Eddy has a home near Orlando. He plans to phase into retirement over a period of about 10 years, spending two months in Florida each winter (when he would work on the Florida hotel's legal business), and flying back and forth every month to do the hotel's work the rest of the year. He would like to be able to practice law *while in* Florida. Specifically, he would like to be able to do the following:

1.　Advise the Toronto company's Florida hotel on *Canadian tax law*. The hotel is willing to make him a part-time employee and appoint him in-house counsel if that would help.

2.　Advise the hotel on *international law* issues, such as the hotel's various rights under the Canada–U.S. Treaty of Friendship, Commerce & Navigation, and the NAFTA.

3.　Advise the hotel on *Florida corporation and hotel business law*.

4.　Begin accepting some general legal work for neighbors in Florida, such as estate planning for some fellow Canadians.

5.　Become a Florida Foreign Legal Consultant if that will entitle him to do all of the above.

6.　Be admitted to the Florida Bar based on his admission to practice in Canada, without taking the Florida Bar.

7. Just go ahead and give any legal advice he wishes and ignore the consequences as a cost of doing business.

U.S. lawyers to Mexico

Fitzgerald & Sam, a Tampa, Florida, law firm specializing in international business and trade law, represents Transco, Inc., a Tampa based ocean shipping company. Transco has recently formed Transco de México, a joint venture affiliate in Veracruz, Mexico. Both Fitzgerald & Sam have J.D.s from U.S. law schools. Fitzgerald has a Maestria en Derecho (master's degree in law) from Iberoamericana in Mexico City, which he obtained as a Fulbright Scholar a decade ago. Sam has a LL.M. from the London School of Economics in Shipping Law. Fitzgerald & Sam would like to be able to do the following:

1. Open a law office in Veracruz or Mexico City and represent Transco de México with regard to *U.S. shipping law*.

2. Do the same and represent Transco de México on *international shipping law* issues, such as Hague and Hague–Visby Convention rules.

3. Do the same and represent Transco de México on *Mexican law* pertaining to ocean transportation.

4. Become Mexican Foreign Legal Consultants if that will entitle them to do all of the above.

5. Merge with a two person Mexican law firm to become Hernandez, Fitzgerald, Sanchez and Sam. All four would share equally in earnings from work undertaken in Mexico. The firm in Tampa would remain separate.

6. Fitzgerald would like to be admitted to the Mexican Bar. As noted above, he has a master's degree from a Mexican law school.

7. Just go ahead and give any legal advice they wish and ignore the consequences as a cost of doing business.

SECTION II. FOCUS OF CONSIDERATION

Increased trade within NAFTA has meant an increased need for many professional services, including accountants, financial advisors, architects, and, of course, *lawyers*, the focus of this problem. Lawyers drafted the NAFTA. They thus had personal interests when it came time to discuss providing legal services across borders. Canada and Mexico were concerned with the possible extensive influx of U.S. lawyers, especially large U.S. law firms entering and taking over or merging with (and likely dominating) local law firms.

What is it that these foreign lawyers want to do? Practice the law of their own country but in the foreign nation? Practice the law of the foreign nation where they are not admitted? Practice international law? Perhaps they want to be admitted in the foreign nation so they may practice in both nations. The U.S. has already experienced some of this, on a state-to-state basis as well as with Canadians. "Snowbird" destinations such as Florida have made it difficult for "northerners" to become members of the bar if they decide to take the exam in their later years, so they might winter over and practice a little law on the side while they are there. They might even build a successful Florida law practice to retire to later. Canadian snowbirds would certainly like to have the same opportunity. But they have greater hurdles, because they do not have U.S. law degrees and may not take the Florida bar exam. Mexico also has some experience with foreign lawyers. Many Americans have tried to live and practice in Mexico. A fair number have succeeded, but only after successfully running the Mexican gauntlet to acquire a Mexican law degree and, in most instances, bring an *amparo* constitutional challenge after being denied the right to practice under the Mexican federal law of the professions, which prohibits foreign citizens from practicing law in Mexico.[1] This law has been repeatedly held in violation of Article 5 of the Mexican Constitution.

The movement of lawyers across borders was underway when NAFTA was in negotiation. NAFTA accelerated this movement both by its provisions and the natural inertia of services following trade and investment. There are many possible examples. Our two hypotheticals represent several of the interests.

The enactment of NAFTA was not driven by a desire to increase the "trade" in professionals, but rather trade in goods and other services. But the latter begets the former; more trade of goods means the need for more professional advice of many forms. Thus NAFTA included Chapter 12 on services. Professional services are defined in Art. 1213 to include, although not specifically by name, legal services. The complexity begins with Annex 1210.5 on Professional Services, which under Section A governs licensing and certification, and the development of professional standards for services, and under Section B requires each Party to adopt "Foreign Legal Consultant" rules. Certification and licensing are and will remain at the heart of opening professional services.

These NAFTA provisions are complex, and obviously reflect a mix of not always certain proportions of (1) protection of local lawyers against an influx of foreign lawyers, and (2) assuring the adequacy of legal services offered to the public. Considering the expectations and interests of Eddy & Macdonald, and of Fitzgerald & Sam, we are introduced to the world of NAFTA annexes. It is a world of reservations, restrictions and reciprocity.

Part A of this problem considers the cross-border provision of legal services under the NAFTA, concentrating on the two hypotheticals. Part B inquires about the possible lessons to be learned from the experience of the member states of the European Union.

Reference to Chapter 12 of NAFTA, Annex 1210.5 and several portions of Annexes I, II, V and VI, and the Florida and ABA Model Rules on

---

1. Ley Reglamentaria del Articulo 5o. Constitucional, relativo al ejercicio de las profesiones en el Distrito Federal, Diario Oficial, 26 May 1945.

Foreign Legal Consultants are needed for a discussion of this problem. They are included in the Documents Supplement.

SECTION III. READINGS, QUESTIONS AND COMMENTS

PART A: NAFTA RULES

Comment on Professional Services and NAFTA

The focus of NAFTA professional services provisions is to apply a Party's licensing and qualification requirements to other Party's nationals in a manner no more burdensome than necessary, and so that they do not constitute a disguised trade restriction. Art. 1210(1). The focus of professional licensing and certification under NAFTA rules is to limit each nation's requirements to those required to maintain the quality of the services rendered. Each Party is to eliminate any citizenship or permanent residency requirement noted in Annex I, and if a Party fails to so act, other affected Parties may maintain equivalent restrictions. Art. 1210(3). Automatic recognition of admission to practice in another Party is not required, but each Party is given an opportunity to demonstrate that its "education, experience, licenses or certifications" should be recognized. Each Party is required to allow Foreign Legal Consultants to practice or advise on the law of any country in which the person is admitted to practice. Annex 1210.5 Section B (1). Special to the professional provisions in Chapter 12 are those in Annex 1210.5, Section B, which includes seven provisions outlining legal services in the form of the admission of Foreign Legal Consultants (FLC).

In the overall NAFTA annexes, the Parties made various agreements to remove citizenship and residence requirements. For example, Mexico agreed to allow Canadian (not U.S.) lawyers to form a partnership with Mexican lawyers, but with Mexican lawyers in control. Annex I–Mexico, I–M–46. Mexico also stipulated that Canadian and U.S. lawyers would be subject to Annex VI–Mexico, VI–M–2, which allows them (1) to become FLCs in Mexico if the applicable provinces within Canada and states within the United States reciprocate, and (2) to open law firms in Mexico to provide services permitted by FLCs, also based on reciprocity. See also Annex 1210.5 Section B. But any foreign lawyer from a Canadian province or U.S. state which tries to join a qualified (i.e., reciprocity conditions met) FLC firm in Mexico will be denied entry if that person's province or state does not have a FLC law. For example, if a New York law firm opened in Mexico (N.Y. allowing Mexican FLCs), it could not hire a Utah admitted lawyer who worked for the N.Y. firm *if* Utah did not allow Mexican FLCs. Mexico also adopted rules in Annex II–Mexico, II–M–10, which are only applicable to the U.S. They allow Mexico to reserve the right to "adopt or maintain any measure relating to the provision of legal services and foreign legal consultancy services by persons of the United States." Why are these special restrictions only applicable to the U.S.? The U.S. disagreed with the requirement that a U.S. firm opening in Mexico would have to have a majority of Mexican owners who would control the firm. The 1993 Investment Law may have altered this limitation.

Canada and the U.S. have agreed to reciprocally license FLCs, but only in the described provinces for Canada and states for the United States, meaning where there are FLC rules. Annex VI–Canada, VI–C–1; Annex VI– United States, VI–U–3. Additionally, both Canada and the U.S. agreed to remove citizenship and residency requirements on patent attorneys. Annex I–Canada, I–C–22; Annex I–United States; I–U–9.

Before we proceed with a principal focus on Chapter 12, we must note the relationship of Chapter 16: Temporary Entry for Business Persons. Lawyers may wish to enter either *temporarily* or *permanently*. Chapter 16 includes rules allowing the temporary movement of business persons without meeting a labor market test. While many *business* travelers have used *tourist* visas, very frequent visits under a tourist visa may raise suspicion as to the real purpose. Furthermore, unless the tourist visa is for multiple entries, there may be long waits to obtain each visa, as in the case of Mexicans going to the U.S. The NAFTA is intended to accommodate temporary business travelers, and Annex 1603 in Sections A–D identifies four categories of travelers who are eligible for temporary entry. They are Business Visitors, Traders and Investors, Intra–Company Transfers, and Professionals. Professions are listed in Appendix 1603.D.1, which includes Lawyers (and Notaries in Quebec) with an "LL.B., J.D., LL.L., B.C.L., or Licenciatura Degree (five years); or membership in a state/provincial bar." Section 1603(D) allows a Party to set a numerical limitation on the number of professionals entering their territory. The U.S. limited the number of professionals admitted on an annual basis from Mexico to 5,500 (Appendix 1603.D.4–U.S.). Canada has not set a quota. Although these NAFTA rules may increase the ease of entry of lawyers as temporary business travelers, these rules in no way affect *what* the lawyers are permitted to do once in the other Party's nation.

So much of what might be accomplished by the NAFTA parties in integrating the legal profession calls for an understanding of the current status of legal education and cross border admission, the subject of the reading by Attorney Barker.

BARKER, THE NORTH AMERICAN FREE TRADE AGREEMENT AND THE COMPLETE INTEGRATION OF THE LEGAL PROFESSION: DISMANTLING THE BARRIERS TO PROVIDING CROSS–BORDER LEGAL SERVICES

19 Houston J. Int'l L. 95 (1996).*

A.   CANADIAN LEGAL EDUCATION SYSTEM

In Canada, there exists a mixture of two distinct legal systems: civil law as practiced in Quebec and common law as practiced in the balance of the provinces and territories. Federal law in Canada, however, is standard, employing common law traditions throughout the country.

* * *

Legal studies are normally pursued after a first university degree. Admission to Canadian common law schools are based on undergraduate grades, Law School Admission Test (LSAT) scores and other requested information such as personal qualifications and accomplishments, ethnic background, letters of recommendation and any graduate or professional records. After three years of full time study in a common law institution, the degree of Bachelor of Laws (LL.B.) is awarded.[74]

As in the United States, professors both lecture and use the Socratic method of questioning; eliciting both the facts and legal principles of the case, as well as analyzing the legal reasoning used by the court.... The students' examinations ... emphasize the writing component of law school, as the examinations are almost uniformly written, and seminar classes are often required.

* * *

B.   CANADIAN LEGAL CERTIFICATION REQUIREMENTS

1.   Domestic Candidate Regulations

Upon graduation and the awarding of the LL.B. degree, an attorney-candidate must be admitted to, or "called to the bar," of the law society of the province in which the person elects to practice law. Specific powers are conferred upon these law societies by provincial legislation to regulate bar admissions, as they are the sole governing bodies of the legal profession in each province. Thus, these standards for admission are regulated by each of these provincial law societies, and differ between provinces.

Provincial law societies are responsible for approving law school programs, operating bar admission courses, and offering continuing education lectures and seminars....

Once the candidate's degree has been recognized by the provincial law society, a period of internship as articling clerks under the supervision of a qualified member of the law society is required.... Finally, before a candidate may be admitted to practice in the province, a bar admissions course or professional training course must be successfully completed. Much like in the United States, there is a bar admission examination at the end of the bar admissions course. However, since the bar admission course is required before the bar admission examination, failure rates on the examination are extremely low—about one percent.*

---

74. McGill University, an institution in Montreal, offers a four year program which grants a dual degree (B.C.L. and LL.B.) in both Canadian civil and common law. [Authors' note: by 2005, some Canadian law facilities were considering a change in the basic law degree from the LL.B. to the J.D., as most U.S. law schools did some thirty years ago. Also, since Mr. Barker's article was written, Ottawa began offering the LL.L. or the LL.B. as a one-year add on to the basic degree. Laval and the University of Montreal currently offer both common and civil law degrees, but not as a joint program, such as McGill's.

* Authors' note: In Quebec, the failure rate is said to be much higher.

2. *Foreign Candidate Regulations*

Citizenship has traditionally been a requirement to admittance to the various law societies, but this requirement was struck down in British Columbia as a violation of the equality and anti-discrimination provisions of the Canadian Charter of Rights and Freedoms. . . .

All of the common law provinces except Alberta require that a candidate graduate from an approved Canadian university or obtain specific approval from the Joint Committee on Foreign Accreditation (JCFA) if the candidate received a degree from a foreign law school. . . .

Once a foreign candidate receives approval from the JCFA, the candidate is then able to qualify under the same domestic regulations as graduates from Canadian law schools—by articling and participating in the appropriate bar review course. However, the only foreign law degrees that are generally recognized are those from common law legal institutions. As a result, many instances exist where civil law graduates are excluded from becoming fully integrated into the Canadian legal system.

* * *

A. Mexican Legal Education System

In Mexico, as well as most of Latin America, immediately after twelve years of formal education, students as young as seventeen or eighteen enter law school. Many of these students are merely seeking to obtain an undergraduate degree or a liberal education. In reality, the only liberal arts training occurs during the first two years of a five year program, when political science, economics, history, and sociology courses may be mixed in with their legal course work. The actual practice of law is not the goal of many Mexican law students. Instead, their legal education is used as a vehicle to explore careers in politics, business, or government. Accordingly, the legal curriculum remains basically academic and practical skills and application of law in context are generally not taught.

Full-time professors are rare, as most of the law faculty will be active practitioners who generally only come to campus for lectures. Unfortunately, these adjunct professors take a theoretical and philosophical approach—seeking to emulate the full-time professors—rather than bringing a pragmatic, practice-oriented approach to their lectures.

Classes are usually extremely large, possibly ranging from 400–500 students, and attendance is often not required, leading to a large percentage of absenteeism. Mexican legal textbooks are generally treatises, written by professors or practicing attorneys—comparable to hornbooks in the United States. . . . Examinations are usually oral, although written work is also generally required for graduation. Separate oral examinations on a written thesis, comprehensive examinations and legal internships or practicums may be required after the completion of all courses. There is no separate or independent bar examination as a prerequisite to practice.

B. Mexican Legal Certification Requirements

1. Domestic Candidate Regulations

Once the law student obtains his *Licenciado en Derecho*, the student applies to the state's Bureau of Professions for recognition of his diploma. This automatically makes the student eligible to practice law.

* * *

Unlike Canada and the United States, a Mexican lawyer who has received his license may practice in any state in the country....

2. Foreign Candidate Regulations

Foreigners are allowed to become Mexican attorneys only if they receive a Mexican legal education and their immigration status qualifies them for a professional license. Prior to the NAFTA, foreign attorneys without these qualifications were limited to consulting or teaching.

Under the NAFTA, there are two requirements that limit a foreign attorney from becoming fully integrated in Mexico. The first requirement, lasting for a period of two years, requires a person to be of Mexican nationality before obtaining a professional certificate. The NAFTA dictates that two years after the date of entry into force the Mexican nationality requirement is no longer valid and the only remaining restriction is that the applicant must have a Mexican address.

Therefore, as of 1996, foreign professionals should be allowed to become fully integrated in Mexico. Nonetheless, until formal reciprocity is achieved by NAFTA member states, attorneys from the United States who desire to become fully integrated in Mexico must still complete the five years of studies at a Mexican law school, and register their diploma with the Bureau of Professions.

In short, the requirements remain the same for foreigners as their domestic counterparts; no provision has been made for the recognition of a foreign law degree. Moreover, the non-Mexican attorney must also obtain special authorization from the Ministry of the Interior before entering into practice.

Another NAFTA restriction regarding foreigners is the Mexican reservation that only attorneys licensed in Mexico may have an ownership interest in a law firm established in the territory of Mexico. However, Mexico's most recent foreign investment law permits foreign attorneys to own up to forty-nine percent of a Mexican law firm. Despite this liberalization of the law, there are still benefits to becoming a fully integrated Mexican attorney, as only attorneys licensed in Mexico can own up to 100% of a Mexican law firm.

* * *

A. United States' Legal Educational System

Law school in the United States is a three-year full-time program, normally attended after the applicant receives his first university degree.

Similar to Canadian admissions, admissions to legal institutions in the United States are based on undergraduate grades, Law School Admission Test (LSAT) scores and other requested information such as personal qualifications and accomplishments, ethnic background, letters of recommendation and any graduate or professional records. Upon graduation, the degree of Juris Doctor (J.D.) is awarded.

* * *

Legal education in the United States is dominated by the Socratic method and the intensive study of case materials. . . .

* * *

B. United States' Legal Certification Requirements

1. Domestic Candidate Regulations

Each state in the United States regulates its own legal profession and sets its own bar admission requirements. . . .

Therefore, for most jurisdictions, the requirement for professional licensure includes a written bar examination and a J.D. degree from an approved law school in the United States. . . .

2. Foreign Candidate Regulations

In the United States, law and attitudes have been and continue to be fairly restrictive against foreign attorneys. . . . Although citizenship may no longer be used as a requirement for admission to the bar, many states require foreign lawyers to complete three years of law school in the United States and pass the bar examination before allowing them to fully integrate into practice.

In 1980, New York amended its rules to permit full integration by graduates from foreign law schools. The New York rules now require that the foreign candidates for admission to the state bar must graduate from a law school recognized by the competent accrediting agency of the government of the candidate's country, and the candidate must have completed a period of law study at least substantially equivalent in duration to the three years required in the United States.

If the candidate meets these criteria and has studied in a common law jurisdiction, the candidate is automatically eligible to sit for the New York bar examination. Before graduates from civil law jurisdictions are eligible to sit for the New York bar examination, they must complete a program of twenty-four semester hours at an accredited law school in the United States or, alternatively, have been accepted for study towards an LL.M. or S.J.D. law degree by an American law school.

Other states have followed New York's example in permitting foreign law graduates to sit for their bar examinations. California, Georgia, Massachusetts, Michigan, New Jersey, Ohio, Pennsylvania, Texas, and the District of Columbia all permit foreign law graduates to sit for their bar examinations once certain requirements have been met.

Generally, once lawyers are admitted in one state in the United States, they are permitted to give legal advice on all law, whether state or federal, regardless of the jurisdiction in which the lawyer was admitted. So long as an attorney does not appear in court, imply local admittance, or practice primarily in the law of the jurisdiction in which not admitted, problems should not arise. This does not mean that one can formally practice law in a jurisdiction in which that individual is not admitted. Nevertheless, it is not unusual to find integrated foreign attorneys, usually admitted in New York, practicing in another jurisdiction within the United States. [Authors' note: but see the discussion of *Bluestein v. State Bar of California* in the following article.]

NEEDHAM, THE LICENSING OF FOREIGN LEGAL CONSULTANTS IN THE UNITED STATES
21 Fordham Int'l L.J. 1126 (1998).*

* * *

In the twenty-one jurisdictions in the United States that have adopted provisions permitting foreign legal consultants to give legal advice, the specific contours of the regulations differ widely. The lack of uniformity in the treatment of foreign legal consultants causes difficulties, especially when representatives of the United States are negotiating with representatives of other countries to hammer out reciprocal agreements under which the lawyers which each has licensed can be permitted to practice in the other country. Crucial to successful negotiations is the concept that each country's attorneys will be able to become authorized to give legal advice in the other country under similar conditions.... As the financial and commercial markets move beyond national boundaries to become global markets, lawyers practicing in the United States will increasingly be called upon to analyze and understand international law and the laws of countries outside the United States. Adopting regulations allowing foreign legal consultants to practice law will permit U.S. lawyers to better serve their current clients. In addition, U.S. lawyers will more easily obtain access to markets for legal services in other countries once reciprocal access is available for the lawyers from those countries. Therefore, each of the jurisdictions within the United States should adopt regulations permitting foreign legal consultants to practice law. Ideally, the requirements should be made uniform throughout all fifty states and the District of Columbia.

I. THE CURRENT OPERATION OF THE FOREIGN LEGAL CONSULTANT STATUS

Upon compliance with the requirements of a particular state's rules, foreign legal consultants are granted an official status in that state for the limited purpose of giving legal advice regarding the laws of jurisdictions other than the United States. In even the most narrowly worded regulations, the foreign legal consultants are permitted to give advice regarding the laws of the country in which they were originally licensed. The regulations address common topics, but there is a good deal of variation from state to state.

A. Scope of Permitted Legal Work

All of the regulations in the United States predictably prohibit the foreign legal consultant from giving advice regarding the state's local law. This is not surprising, given the political realities surrounding any relaxation of the prohibition on the unauthorized practice of law. Locally licensed attorneys are likely to urge that their monopoly be protected. The narrowest regulations, ... restrict the foreign legal consultant to giving legal advice only on the laws of the country in which the attorney was originally licensed. [A few] jurisdictions permit foreign legal consultants licensed there to give legal advice regarding international law and third country law, as long as they do not give advice on U.S. law.

[Some] jurisdictions ... also permit the foreign legal consultant to pass along to a client advice regarding the law of the state granting the foreign legal consultant status as well as federal law, as long as the advice originates with a lawyer who holds a law license in that state.

* * *

A majority of the regulations ... contain similar language specifying that the foreign legal consultant cannot prepare any papers to be filed with, or appear before, any court or administrative agency in the state granting the status, and cannot prepare any instrument affecting title to real estate located in the United States, prepare any wills or trust instruments, or prepare any instrument with respect to marital rights or custody of a child of a resident of the United States. . . .

In [a few] states, the wording of the regulation permits the foreign legal consultants to engage in additional activities. In addition to the same list of prohibitions, the regulations [two states] explicitly permit a foreign legal consultant to prepare documents relating to personal property in situations in which the instrument affecting title to the property is governed by the law of a jurisdiction in which the foreign legal consultant is admitted to practice. The rules in [two states] expressly prohibit foreign legal consultants only from appearing in court and preparing court pleadings, but omit any prohibition of preparation of documents related to real estate, wills, and marital rights or child custody. . . .

B. Experience in the Active Practice of Law

The most conservative foreign legal consultant regulations require that for five of the seven years immediately preceding the application, the applicant must have been engaged in the active practice of law while located in the applicant's home jurisdiction. This disadvantages applicants who have been practicing law in countries outside their home jurisdiction, a common practice, during some of the time that they have been admitted as attorneys. . . .

More liberal regulations permit the applicant to meet the time in practice requirement while working in a location outside his home jurisdiction, typically requiring only that the applicant's practice "substantially involve or relate to" the laws of his home jurisdiction.

C. Reciprocity

The concept of reciprocity underlies decisions about the enactment and wording of regulations governing cross-border entry into legal services markets. In a number of states, locally licensed lawyers have been denied entry to practice law in a country that demanded reciprocal treatment of its attorneys. The locally admitted attorneys' desire to enter the other country's market provided the impetus that prompted the enactment and liberalization of foreign legal consultant regulations. . . . [I]n states which have long recognized the foreign legal consultant status, the desire for reciprocal recognition has prompted expansion of the powers granted under the regulations. New York licensed attorneys advocated that foreign legal consultants be permitted to become partners and shareholders in New York law firms, in part because the New York attorneys wanted to obtain reciprocal treatment in other countries.

Some jurisdictions within the United States . . . require reciprocity. In those states, if the applicant's home country does not allow members of its bar the opportunity to render legal services as foreign legal consultants under "substantially similar circumstances," then the applicant will not be approved as a foreign legal consultant.

Whether reciprocity is required, or simply factored into the decision to grant foreign legal consultant status, the applicant must provide a translated summary of the rules in the applicant's country permitting members of the state's bar to establish offices there to give legal advice to clients in that country. Some jurisdictions, allow the candidate to submit additional documentation, including "a summary of the law and customs of the foreign country that relate to the opportunity afforded to members of the Bar of this Court [D.C.] to establish offices for the giving of legal advice to clients in such foreign country." The benefits of this approach are obvious. A more realistic decision can be made by taking into account as much information as possible regarding the circumstances facing members of the states' bar when they attempt to practice in the applicant's home country.

D. Application and Renewal Fees

In most states, the fee charged for the initial application for foreign legal consultant status appears to be about the same as that required of applicants for full membership in the state's bar. . . .

* * *

F. *Utilization*

New York has by far the most lawyers who have registered as foreign legal consultants,.... In most other states, ... fewer than a dozen lawyers have registered as foreign legal consultants.

* * *

... [O]ther requirements in some states operate to dissuade applicants. In California, for example, applicants are required to provide the admission committee with evidence of an insurance policy, letter of credit, or other form of security to guarantee payment of malpractice claims and losses to clients caused by dishonest conduct. Very few malpractice insurers are willing to write policies requiring payment of claims caused by intentional wrong-doing, and those which are willing to provide coverage charge expensive rates for the additional exposure.

Some requirements may appear innocuous, but become insurmountable in practice. For example, in some countries in which a government has been overthrown, attorneys who were licensed under the previous regime may be unable to obtain a certificate of good standing from the new authorities. The lack of the certificate in this situation does not indicate any negative disciplinary history, client dissatisfaction, or other improprieties in the attorney's previous legal career. The regulations in effect in all states, other than California, explicitly permit the courts to exercise discretion in their application of the admission requirements. In some cases, a court might waive the required good standing certificate. A court, however, is also free to reject an applicant who fails to supply all of the required documentation.

It is important to note that the discussion about foreign legal consultants in both academic journals and practitioner-oriented materials focuses almost exclusively on one type of law practice engaged in by foreign legal consultants—the representation of clients that are large multinational corporations. The sophisticated transactions entered into by well-informed business clients indeed constitute an important category of work performed by foreign legal consultants. A significant number of foreign legal consultants, however, advise individuals as their primary clients, ... Anecdotal information from those involved in the registration process in various states indicates that this type of practice occupies at least one fourth of the foreign legal consultants working in some states. These practitioners provide legal advice which would otherwise be impossible for their clients to obtain in a cost-effective manner....

II. THE NEW YORK RULE AUTHORIZING FOREIGN LEGAL CONSULTANTS

New York was the first jurisdiction in the United States to create an official status for non-U.S. licensed lawyers. Following the U.S. Supreme Court's 1973 decision *In re Griffiths*[160] striking down the requirement that applicants for regular admission to a state bar be U.S. citizens, the

---

160. 413 U.S. 717 (1973).

New York statute provides that the status of legal consultant is to be conferred "without examination and without regard to citizenship."

* * *

Once a person is licensed as a foreign legal consultant, he is free to give advice regarding the law of the country in which he was originally licensed or on international law, but he can only give advice on New York law or federal law on the basis of prior advice from an attorney licensed in New York. At least one attorney admitted as a legal consultant has been disciplined for advertising his services as though he were licensed to practice law in New York and for failing to disclose his status as a legal consultant on signs at his office and to his law partner before entering into a partnership to practice law. The Peruvian lawyer's status as a legal consultant in New York was revoked as a consequence of his failure to make the required disclosures.

* * *

In November 1993, New York's rule governing foreign legal consultants was amended to make the requirements more liberal in a number of areas. The required time in active practice was changed from five of the preceding seven years to three of the preceding five years. The time in practice can now take place outside the country which originally admitted the applicant. And, although the applicant must "intend to practice as a legal consultant in [New York] and to maintain an office [there] for that purpose," he is no longer required to reside in New York.

In addition, a new provision was added in 1993 which explicitly allows a foreign legal consultant to become a partner in any partnership which includes members of the New York bar as well as to employ or be employed by members of the New York bar. This ended a controversy over whether such partnership or employment was ethically proper for the full members of the New York bar. . . .

III.   THE CALIFORNIA RULE AUTHORIZING FOREIGN LEGAL CONSULTANTS

The California Rules of Court were amended in 1987 by the state's Supreme Court to include a new Rule 988[161] which permits a lawyer admitted to practice in a foreign country to provide advice in California regarding the law of the country in which he is admitted after he complies with the requirements of the rule to be granted the as a status of a "Registered Foreign Legal Consultant."

Rule 988 has been described as overly restrictive and as presenting a formidable barrier to the foreign attorney who seeks to be admitted under its terms. However, the restrictions on the Registered Foreign Legal Consultant's practice in California closely track those imposed in New York and Washington D.C. Another principal limitation imposed in California is that the legal consultants in that state are not permitted to

161.   Authors' note: Rule 988, which received minor modifications December 1, 1993, remains in force as of 2004.

give legal advice on the law of any jurisdiction other than those in which he is admitted to practice law. This contrasts with the foreign lawyer's freedom under the rules in New York and Washington D.C. to at least pass along legal advice regarding issues of U.S. federal and state law which is being given by other lawyers.

Before the adoption of Rule 988, the California Supreme Court had reached a conclusion similar to that reached by the New York Court of Appeals in *Roel*. In *Bluestein v. State Bar of California*, the court held that a person not admitted in California who purported to give advice on the law of Spain was thereby committing the unauthorized practice of law. The facts in *Bluestein* suggested the need to protect clients who sought legal advice from the person for, unlike the lawyer in *Roel*, he was not licensed to practice as a lawyer in Spain, or in any other country.... The California court cited the reasoning in *Roel*, and echoed the concern expressed in the New York case about the ability to discipline all lawyers who give advice to clients in the state.

* * *

Decision-makers in other states that have not yet adopted a foreign legal consultant status may have some continuing interest in the reasoning of a formal opinion of a California ethics committee that was rendered prior to the adoption of Rule 988. A lawyer licensed in California asked the Los Angeles County Bar Association Ethics Committee whether he could properly employ, as a consultant on Iranian law, an attorney admitted in Iran who was not licensed to practice law in California.

The Ethics Committee decided that, at least concerning matters of Iranian law, the Iranian lawyer could "render assistance" to the lawyer licensed in California and that the lawyer licensed in Iran would not be considered to be engaging in the unauthorized practice of law in California as long as,

> his role is to assist and advise the employer's clients, the employer does not communicate in any way that his employee is acting as a lawyer admitted to practice in the state, the employer is assured of his employee's competence and takes steps to verify the accuracy of his work, and the employee does not receive a percentage of profits or compensation for referrals. Additionally, the employee may serve as a foreign language translator or interpreter.

Moreover, if the lawyer licensed in California did not take the steps outlined in the opinion, he could be regarded as acting as a mere conduit facilitating the practice of law by the foreign lawyer, which would expose the California licensed lawyer to malpractice liability and to charges that the California lawyer had assisted the unauthorized practice of law.

NOTE ON THE ABA FOREIGN LEGAL CONSULTANT RULES

In August 1993, the American Bar Association's ("ABA") House of Delegates adopted a "Model Rule for the Licensing of Legal Consultants" sponsored by the ABA's Section of International Law and Practice and its Committee on Transnational Legal Practice, based on the New York rule. In 1193 and again in 2002, The House of Delegates recommended that those states which had not adopted a foreign legal consultants' rule (27 as of mid–2004) do so promptly; others with non-conforming rules had been urged to modify such rules "in the interest of uniformity and clarity." Progress is slow; only one state (Massachusetts) has adopted a foreign legal consultant rule since January 1, 2000. Nor is there evidence to date, that states with non-conforming rules have made revisions in accordance with the Model Rule.*

* * *

NELSON, LAW PRACTICE OF U.S. ATTORNEYS IN MEXICO AND MEXICAN ATTORNEYS IN THE UNITED STATES: A STATUS REPORT
6 U.S.–Mexico L.J. 71 (1998)**

The first principal barrier to the rendition of legal services by lawyers qualified in other countries is found in the prerequisite education and examination requirements extended to those already qualified in another country. In the United States, certain commercially-important states, such as New York, have made it relatively easy for lawyers qualified in other countries to become full members of the host state bar. This is achieved through the completion of a one-year Master of Laws (LL.M.) degree program and passage of the bar examination. Many foreign lawyers, including substantial numbers from Canada and Mexico, have become members of the New York bar in this way. Under the Diplomas Directive, European Union (EU) member states must allow lawyers qualified in other EU member states the opportunity to practice locally. Qualified lawyers must either complete a period of adaptation or a limited examination designed to reconcile the differences between the legal systems of the two member states. Also the countries of the former British Commonwealth mutually recognize the qualifications of members of their respective legal professions.

With these limited exceptions, the vast majority of countries generally do not permit a foreign lawyer to qualify as a member of the local legal profession without completing the same educational requirements as someone with no prior education or training. The length of the educational requirement renders it impractical for most lawyers to interrupt their careers long enough to qualify in another country. This seriously impairs the mobility of the legal profession, which is vital to its globalization.

---

* See ABA, Report 201 H, August 1993; Foreign Legal Consultant Rules [status of adoption], Mar. 17, 2003, *available at* http://abanet.org.

** Copyright © 1998 U.S.-Mexico Law Journal. Reprinted with permission.

The second principal barrier is the prohibition found in many countries against the formation of partnerships between lawyers and anyone other than another lawyer of that country. This barrier results from a very strict application of the rule, common to most lawyers' codes of ethics, that a lawyer must not share fee income with non-lawyers. This barrier does not exist in the United States because foreign lawyers are recognized as lawyers for purposes of partnerships. Thus, in all states, members of their respective bars are permitted to practice in partnership with foreign lawyers, with no limitations on foreign ownership of law firms.[14] Accordingly, it is possible for a foreign law firm to establish and operate under its own name by associating with lawyers admitted to practice. However, the widespread existence of this kind of prohibition in countries other than the United States is a major obstacle to the formation of multinational partnerships. This is unfortunate because multinational partnerships offer the best overall solution to the problems posed by the education/examination barrier.

* * *

The second approach to eliminate the education/examination barrier is to accord a degree of recognition to the education, training and experience of the foreign lawyer. This would require reduction of the education and examination requirements to specific areas. These areas would be limited to those necessary to adapt the lawyer's experience to the host country's legal system. Upon satisfaction of the abbreviated requirements, the lawyer would be admitted to full membership in the host country's legal profession. This is the approach adopted in the European Community under the Diplomas Directive and, in principle, in France since the merger of the professions of *avocat* and *conseiller juridique*.[15] The difficulty with this approach from the standpoint of liberalization is that it lacks transparency. The degree of liberalization is a function of the extent to which the educational and examination requirements are reduced to those that are objectively required to ensure effective adaptation of the lawyer's pre-existing skill and knowledge to a different legal system.

The third approach is the basis for the American Bar Association's (ABA) policy in this area.

* * *

14. Despite the Supreme Court's ruling in *Application of Fre Le Poole Griffiths for Admission to the Bar*, 413 U.S. 717 (1973), that requiring U.S. citizenship for admission to practice law violates the Equal Protection Clause of the Fourteenth Amendment, eleven states (Arkansas, Iowa, Maryland, Montana, Nebraska, New Hampshire, Ohio, Rhode Island, South Dakota, Utah, and West Virginia) still had this qualification in 1992 according to the Office of the U.S. Trade Representative.

Connecticut, the state whose rule was held unconstitutional in *Griffiths*, requires bar applicants to show either U.S. citizenship or reciprocal access in the applicant's country of citizenship.

15. The *conseil juridique* title was abolished in 1991. All conseils juridiques and trial lawyers [*avouets*] became attorneys [*avocats*] on January 1, 1992, regardless of their nationality. Law No. 90–1259 art. 1(1).

Comment on U.S. Law Firms Opening Offices in Mexico

As of 2004, there are only a handful of U.S. law firms operating in Mexico City under their own names, three headquartered in New York, two in Texas, and one each in Florida and Illinois. Baker & McKenzie has several offices in Mexico, several of which at least pre-dated NAFTA; the vast majority of their lawyers are Mexican licenciados.

However, many U.S. firms appear to have some sort of "correspondent relationship" (which may have many meanings) with Mexican law firms. Also unclear is whether the arrangements have been successful, however that is to be measured. The U.S. firm usually goes to Mexico to serve its U.S. clients, and thus to keep the business within the firm. It is not interested in giving away anything to the Mexican firm, but it needs the base of operations. If the Mexican firm has exceptionally good clients, that is all the better.

Major Mexican law firms tend to be much smaller than U.S. firms. The largest is apparently Bryan, Gonzalez Vargas y Gonzalez Baz, S.C., with some 85 lawyers in its Mexico City headquarters and seven other offices, including Madrid and New York. Gonzalez Baz believes that the NAFTA is a stage in the ultimate development of huge multinational law firms, and his firm has considered expansion throughout Latin America. Many of its attorneys have U.S. LL.M. degrees, and spend much of their time serving U.S. or other foreign clients. At least two large multinational accounting firms, Deloitte Touche and PriceWaterhouseCooper, provide Mexican legal services through Mexican lawyer-employees or partners.

There was certainly some fear among Mexican lawyers at the outset of NAFTA that they would be invaded and taken over by the litigious American firms. Litigation is a small part of the work of most Mexican firms, but it is growing, as Problem 9.5 illustrates. Many excellent Mexican firms are small, perhaps three or four partners, with one in control. That partner may have taken over the firm from his father, and views the firm as something to pass on to his children. But large multinationals often have anti-nepotism policies, and a merger of the Mexican firm may ends its historic practice and its character. The merged firms are little threat to most general practices; they are interested in serving clients which have also crossed borders. Whether or not the merger experience has been successful is debated. Some Mexicans suggest the practice is not successful, but American reaction suggests that such comments are intended to keep more U.S. firms out of Mexico.

DEL DUCA & SCIARRA, DEVELOPING CROSS–BORDER PRACTICE RULES: CHALLENGES AND OPPORTUNITIES FOR LEGAL EDUCATION
21 Fordham Int'l L.J. 1109 (1998).*

With respect to professional services, Article 1210 sets forth some additional assurances. Article 1210 provides that individual licensing decisions should be based upon objective and transparent criteria, such as competence, and that they should not be unnecessarily burdensome or purely protectionist in nature. It addresses the prospect of unilateral or mutual recognition agreements, whereby a licensing body determines that a class of individuals licensed outside the host country will be able to use their foreign license to practice in the host country. Finally, it requires that the opportunity to negotiate such agreements be open to all NAFTA jurisdictions who show an interest in negotiating such agreements.

The licensing of professional services providers is further addressed in Annex 1210.5 to Chapter 12 (the "Annex"). The Annex addresses a procedural issue and provides that, in processing an application for a professional license, the host country government should render a decision on the application without undue delay. This provision complements Article 1210(1) and the concern expressed in that Article about disguised restrictions on trade in services. The Annex also provides a road-map to guide the NAFTA governments and their sub-national governments in their negotiation of mutual recognition agreements or other forms of trade liberalization.

Section A of the Annex applies to the various professions which require licensure as a prerequisite to practice of the profession. Section A recognizes that some professions may be self-regulating and that the appropriate relevant body charged with addressing the issue of licensure may not be a governmental entity, but may be a professional association or board. The negotiators intended to allow these groups to meet on a trilateral basis, develop proposals for mutual recognition or temporary licensure, and submit these proposals to the NAFTA governments, which together comprise NAFTA's governing body (the "NAFTA Commission"). Once the NAFTA Commission reviews the proposals to ensure consistency with the agreement, the NAFTA governments agreed to have the relevant regulatory bodies adopt the proposals.

While the approach outlined by this road-map may appear to be cumbersome, it actually reflects a delicate balance that the negotiators had to strike between the desire for further liberalization of barriers to professionals and the recognition that much of the regulatory authority was not, strictly speaking, in the hands of the federal governments of the three NAFTA members. As a practical matter, this approach appears to be working well. Groups of professionals, among them engineers, architects, accountants, and nurses, have formed trilateral NAFTA committees for their respective professions in response to the Annex and have made varying degrees of progress towards developing proposals for submission to the NAFTA Commission.

Technically speaking, the legal profession falls within the scope of Section A of the Annex. However, the task for the legal profession is complicated by an additional component of the road-map set forth in Section B of the Annex. This additional section was added to the Annex due to the importance the negotiators attached to the issue of legal services and in recognition of the fact that the treatment of foreign legal consultants ("FLCs") was not uniform among the United States, Canada, and Mexico.

Section B of the Annex aims to accomplish the goal of ensuring that FLCs can effectively practice the law of their home country in the host country. Section B also contemplates that the regulators and practitioners in the legal profession will meet trilaterally to address two main concerns which were raised during the NAFTA negotiations. These concerns address the types of associations forged between FLCs and locally-licensed lawyers and the development of mutually-acceptable standards for the FLC licensing process. Any proposals resulting from this trilateral process are to be forwarded to the NAFTA Commission to ensure consistency with NAFTA as a whole. In addition, Section B charges the NAFTA governments with the task of developing common procedures throughout their respective territories for the licensure of FLCs.

* * *

After NAFTA went into effect on January 1, 1994, members of various professional associations began to act under the provisions of Annex 1201.5. In the legal services area, members of the profession and regulators from the three NAFTA countries agreed to meet in the form of a working group to address the Annex 1201.5 directives (the "Trilateral Lawyers Working Group" or "TLWG"). While the composition of each country delegation to the TLWG varied somewhat, each delegation was comprised of members representing state, provincial, or federal bar associations, some representation on behalf of the regulatory authorities, and some federal government representation.

* * *

CORTÉS ROCHA, TRANSNATIONAL PRACTICE OF THE LEGAL PROFESSION IN THE CONTEXT OF THE NORTH AMERICAN FREE TRADE AGREEMENT (NAFTA)

15–AUT Int'l. Practicum 111 (Autumn, 2002)*

Developments under NAFTA. Although we are far from a consensus on the issue, some small but significant advances have been made in recent years. The North American Free Trade Agreement (NAFTA), signed by the United States, Canada and Mexico in 1993 and effective as of 1 January 1994, dealt for the first time with matters relating to the transborder practice of law, as well as the association of foreign attorneys and firms with local firms of the NAFTA countries. This has been a landmark in international law and treaties.

NAFTA recognized the need for close cooperation to eliminate barriers and to facilitate the cross-border delivery of legal services, and encouraged the development of joint recommendations by the relevant professional bodies of the three countries for the licensing of FLCs and the establishment of forms of association or partnership between fully licensed lawyers of a country and FLCs of the other countries. The Treaty established that attorneys licensed in any of the three countries may act as FLCs in the territory of the other member countries with respect to the law in which they are licensed to practice. NAFTA also provided for a work program for future liberalization regarding foreign legal consulting services. Evidently, NAFTA followed the ABA's preference for the FLC approach for the provision of transborder legal services.

* * *

The Treaty also established that the scope of such associations, as well as the licensing and practice of FLCs, should be negotiated by the relevant professional bodies of the three NAFTA countries, with the view to developing joint recommendations. For such purposes, the representatives of the legal profession of Canada (the Federation of Law Societies of Canada in collaboration with the Canadian Bar Association), of Mexico (the Mexican Committee on the International Practice of Law (COMPID), lead by Barra Mexicana), and of the U.S. (the ABA through its Sections of International Law and Practice and Legal Education of Admissions to the Bar) met regularly in the course of four years, in more than eight rounds of intensive negotiations in different cities of the three countries. The result was an accord on the cross-border delivery of legal services, consisting of a Joint Recommendation and a Model Rule respecting Foreign Legal Consultants (the "NAFTA–FLC Accord"), which was signed by the Chairman of the Delegations of the three countries in Mexico City (in the historic San Idelfonso College) in the evening of 19 June 1998.

Features of the Accord and Model Rule. The NAFTAL–FLC Accord recognizes that it is in the interest of the public and of their legal professions to facilitate the cross-border delivery of timely, competent and economical legal services among the Parties within a regulatory regime which protects the public of the Parties, while recognizing the significant differences among them as to the regulation of the practice of law. The NAFTA–FLC Accord also recognizes that the international practice of law, as required by international relations and under NAFTA, extends beyond the services provided by FLCs, and that, as a matter of public policy, licensing of FLCs cannot be equated to the licensing systems applicable to fully licensed lawyers.

The Model Rule on foreign legal consultants provides the licensing requirements for FLCs, which include good standing in the applicant's home country; reciprocity; good character and reputation; previous practice experience (five years); liability insurance and defalcation coverage, if required in the host country; and submission to the jurisdiction of the regulatory body in the host country. The scope of practice of the FLC under the Model Rule comprehends the practice of and advice on the law of any country in which the FLC is licensed to practice, or on international law. The FLC may not represent a client in court or in any administrative procedure, except as permitted by the laws of the host country. The FLC may act as an arbitrator or as counsel in arbitration. The FLC could only practice or advise on the law of the host country if so permitted by the host country, which is not the case in Mexico.

A law firm based in any NAFTA country may establish itself in any other NAFTA country to provide legal consultancy services through its members holding FLC licenses issued by the host country. According to the Model Rule, a lawyer licensed or a firm headquartered in a home country may enter into a partnership or form a law firm with one or more lawyers licensed or with a firm licensed in the host country, except that, in the case of Mexico being the host country: (i) all the partners of the firm must be fully licensed or licensed as FLCs in Mexico, (ii) the FLC licensed partners may not outnumber the partners licensed in Mexico; and (iii) the management of the firm must be entrusted to the partners licensed in Mexico. A lawyer licensed or a law firm headquartered in any NAFTA country may employ a lawyer licensed in any other NAFTA country, except that, in the case of Mexico being the host country, no lawyer licensed in Mexico may be employed by a non-licensed lawyer in Mexico, or by a non-qualified law firm. An FLC in the host country may be employed by another FLC licensed by the host country, or by a lawyer licensed or a firm headquartered in the host country.

A law firm of any NAFTA country may enter into an alliance or other form of economic arrangement, other than a partnership, with a lawyer licensed or a firm headquartered in another NAFTA country. An FLC practicing in a host country may continue to be an employee of or associated with a lawyer or law firm in the FLC's home country. The Model Rule also included provisions on marketing of foreign legal consultancy services, professional rights and duties, immigration matters, license term and renewals.

Discussion. The Canadian and the Mexican delegations delivered the Joint Recommendation and Model Rule on FLCs to their respective governments, immediately after being signed, in order that it could be discussed in the Free Trade Commission established by the Treaty, with the recommendation that the Model Rule be implemented to facilitate the practice by FLCs from the other countries in their territories. Unfortunately, this Joint Recommendation, although it was signed by the Chair of the American Delegation, apparently has never been formally presented to the U.S. government, nor has it been submitted for discussion in the NAFTA Commission, presumably due to late opposition by the U.S. Delegation. Consequently, until the rules of the Model Rule with respect to the trans-border practice of law through foreign legal consultants are implemented, the basic provisions established in NAFTA will continue to apply with the reservations made by each country.

* * *

Questions and Comments

It ought not be difficult to address alternative number 7 in each of the above hypotheticals in Section I. The Canadian and U.S. lawyers should fully understand the serious consequences of the unauthorized practice of law in any jurisdiction. We assume they do and are looking to the options of becoming Foreign Legal Consultants, or members of the foreign bar, or refraining from practice. That does not answer the question of what legal work a foreign lawyer might do while in another country without admission as a FLC or member of the bar. If the answer *none* is assumed to be correct, then the thousands of trips lawyers make across borders every day to undertake legal business must be improper.

Presumably, it is not unlawful for a Mexican lawyer to fly to Aspen where a Los Angeles client is vacationing and discuss a few final provisions of and execute a contract for the sale of a Mexico City office building. Or for a Canadian lawyer to be vacationing in Miami, Florida, and talk on the telephone to a New York client in Tampa, Florida, about a Canadian legal issue. Or for a U.S. lawyer to meet in London with lawyers from Moscow and Cairo, to work out a joint venture oil exploration agreement. Thus, what Eddy from Canada and Fitzgerald and Sam from the U.S. wish to do in the U.S., and Mexico, respectively, may not be absolutely prohibited, even if they do not even become FLCs or gain admission to the bar. Our interest remains nevertheless not what the thresholds are for undertaking legal work without being admitted, but how NAFTA seeks (1) to assist a lawyer in being admitted, either as a FLC or full member of the bar, and (2) to allow law firms from one Party to open law offices in another Party.

The interests of Eddy with regard to practice in Florida.

Eddy's concerns are directed to both what the Florida rules state regarding the unauthorized practice of law, and what they allow Foreign Legal Consultants to do, if Eddy qualifies. Our interest is principally in the Foreign Legal Consultant rules, and whether the Florida rules, as an example of the rules of U.S. states, meet NAFTA Chapter 12 obligations.

The first four items relate to rendering legal advice *while in* Florida. Some of the four questions are answered if Eddy becomes a Foreign Legal Consultant. They are all answered if Eddy is admitted to the Florida Bar.

1. May Eddy provide any of the advice in the first four categories without either becoming a Foreign Legal Consultant, or being admitted to practice in Florida? Does it matter whether Eddy gives advice while on a one day business trip to the Florida hotel, versus while on vacation at his Orlando home? If Eddy is advising the Florida hotel on Canadian tax obligations he might properly do so *from* Canada by memos and telephone calls. Is the problem the rendering of advice by a non-admitted lawyer while physically located in Florida, or the giving of advice by anyone anywhere to a person or entity which is located in Florida? Does the Florida law have any extraterritorial effect?

When the Toronto company was considering whether to locate its hotel in Florida, California, Cuba or Mexico, Eddy might have prepared a memo comparing each jurisdiction's corporations laws. That is not the unauthorized practice in these jurisdictions—or is it? Although the Florida Bar might not want anyone not admitted to Florida to give advice on Florida law, no matter where that person is located and renders the advice, the Florida parties in charge of the unauthorized practice of law obviously have a limited reach to enforce their demands. Eddy & Macdonald could remain comfortably in Toronto sending frequent memos to the Florida hotel corporation which constitute advice on various aspects of Florida corporation, tax and product liability law. Only if the corporation needed representation in a Florida court would an admitted Florida lawyer need be present.

The fourth item involves some general estate planning work for fellow Canadians living or vacationing in Florida. Might Eddy gain information and discuss their estate planning needs, but do the paper work when back in Toronto?

2. If Eddy is appointed in-house counsel for the Canadian corporation, does it change giving advice in any of the first three categories?

3. If Eddy wishes to become a Foreign Legal Consultant in Florida, does he qualify?

Assume Eddy is allowed to become a Foreign Legal Consultant in Florida, may he render advice in each of the four areas noted? He plans to add on the Toronto firm letterhead that he is "admitted to practice foreign and international law in Florida." Is that allowed? He would like to have some separate letterheads using his Orlando house address. It will list his status as member of the Canadian firm, and that he is a "Foreign Legal Consultant" Is that allowed? That raises another question-is a FLC expected or required to reside in and have an office in Florida? Does Eddy's admission to be a FLC in Florida depend on Canada's (or Ontario's) admission of Florida lawyers as FLCs (a reciprocity requirement)?

4. Would these answers be different under the ABA Model Rule?

5. If the answers are different, is Florida in violation of the NAFTA Chapter 12 because it has not amended its rules to follow the ABA rules?

6. There are other FLC requirements, such as the fee, which may constitute a barrier if unrealistic. The state of Georgia has required a fee of $3,000 for a FLC, compared to $75 for admission to practice. The Model Rules suggest the fees ought to be comparable. Florida charges an annual fee comparable to that charged to members of the Bar.

7. Eddy may perform all of the four services if he is admitted to the Florida Bar. We do not explore the different state's admission rules in this problem, but Eddy will have to have a J.D. from a U.S. law school to sit for the Florida Bar, a common requirement in the U.S. His LL.M. might allow him to receive a J.D. in two years, but he needs the J.D. to practice.

Attorney Steven Nelson discusses how New York has made it easier for foreign lawyers, including those with civil rather than common law training, to be admitted after receiving a one year LL.M. degree and passing the bar examination, rather than requiring the three year J.D. Couldn't Eddy expect Florida to treat him the same way, after all he already has a University of Florida LL.M.? Should it make a difference if Eddy were a Mexican lawyer, with only civil law training? Currently, Canadian lawyers with common law degrees are permitted to take the New York Bar, and some others (e.g., Arizona on a case-by-case basis), without any further legal training, given the strong similarity of the U.S. and Canadian legal education systems. See Barker.

The extract by Attorney Barker outlining the Canadian legal profession suggests Canadian graduates may be ready to sit for any U.S. state bar, without further study. But the Mexican process is quite different. What more ought to be required for Mexican law graduates to practice in Canada or the U.S.—an LL.M. in U.S. law, or the full J.D. or LL.B.? There are few courses on Canadian or Mexican law offered in U.S. law schools. Should there be more? Should completion of such courses help satisfy cross-border admission? Would increased exchange programs across-borders help?

8. NAFTA calls for the elimination of barriers to cross-border professional services. The readings illustrate the significant differences among the Parties, especially differences between Mexico on the one hand, and Canada and the U.S. on the other. They include not only substantive elements of legal education, but the problematic regulation of lawyers in Canada and the U.S. by often very protective states. But there are significant differences between Canada and the U.S., the U.S. is more restrictive, and most states require no apprenticeship period. Perhaps the adoption of an apprentice period in the remaining states is a way of admitting foreign graduates, but will enough law firms be willing to take on apprentices to meet the demand?

9. If Eddy in our Canada–U.S. hypothetical may practice Canadian law in Florida as a FLC, why can't a New York lawyer become a Florida FLC and practice New York law? If New York law includes federal law, and international law, that might give the New York lawyer a basis for a practice. But if the New York lawyer is denied such right, is there any Constitutional violation by according special privileges in Florida to an alien (meaning only the Canadian, notwithstanding that Floridians consider New Yorkers to be truly "aliens", and much less apt to be understood when speaking than Canadians)?

The interests of Fitzgerald & Sam in opening an office in Mexico, and of Fitzgerald in being admitted to the Mexican Bar.

1. To the extent that Fitzgerald or Sam wish to render legal advice *in* Mexico, they will do so lawfully only as Mexican FLCs, or after admission to practice in Mexico. FLC licensing in Mexico is federal, not state or provincial as in the U.S. and Canada, respectively. The NAFTA allowed sub-jurisdictions (states and provinces) which had adopted FLC rules to maintain them, but they could not become more restrictively applied. Because Mexico had no FLC rules, federal or state, the matter becomes federal. Does Mexico's Annex VI entry limit application on reciprocity?

2. If Fitzgerald & Sam wish to have an office in Mexico, after having become Mexican FLCs, but with no persons in the office as members of the Mexican bar, this would seem much like Eddy from Canada opening an office in Florida. Indeed, Fitzgerald has just learned that Eddy & Macdonald from Toronto have "opened" an office in Veracruz, where the Toronto company is building a new hotel. Fitzgerald therefore feels comfortable that Fitzgerald & Sam will be able to have a Veracruz office.

3. U.S. firms have been practicing Mexican law for some time out of "client offices" in Mexico. Perhaps it is Transco's Veracruz corporate office

where Fitzgerald & Sam lawyers admitted only in the U.S. will function and give advice while in Mexico. Is that lawful? Does "lawful" mean what Mexico can control, rather than what Mexican rules permit? Where do the Baker & McKenzie "branches" fit into the rules? Although what U.S. lawyers may do regarding opening branch offices in Mexico may be restricted under rules permitted under NAFTA, the 1993 Mexican Foreign Investment Act which liberalizes permissible foreign investments, may allow an "investment" by a foreign law firm in the form of establishing a Mexican office, with approval of the Mexican Foreign Investment Commission.

One Houston firm (Butler & Binion) decided several years ago not to open a Mexico City office. A partner said the reason is that "we know too much." What do you suppose they know which has discouraged them? They suggest high overhead, pollution in Mexico City, and that Mexico already has "a very good bar"? Aren't many cities polluted? Many other major cities have high overhead? Most major cities have very good bars. What do you suppose their reason really was? Why does Shearman & Sterling maintain offices in four U.S. cities, Toronto, seven European cities, Tokyo, Hong Kong, Beijing and Singapore, but suggest a Mexican office is unnecessary because "you can jump on a plane" to do business in Mexico. Isn't there direct plane service between New York City and Toronto, Frankfurt, London and Paris? Is this all a little posturing between and among U.S. law firms? Is Baker & McKenzie's approach—with semi-autonomous offices in many Mexican and other foreign cities—more likely to prevail in the long run?

4.   For Fitzgerald to be admitted in Mexico, Attorney Barker explains the obstacles. The two years have passed for Mexico to require citizenship. NAFTA Art. 1210(3). But it is not clear that Mexico has eliminated this requirement. Fitzgerald may thus face bringing an *amparo* constitutional challenge if he is denied registration as a lawyer under the old law of the professions. If Fitzgerald must complete the five year program, starting off with 18 year olds at the age of at least 24–25, can he expect *any* credit towards the five years from a Mexican law school for his three years of U.S. legal study? (Under American Bar Association rules, an ABA approved U.S. law school may give a foreign lawyer up to one year's credit for his foreign legal study toward the JD degree. Some U.S. lawyers have worked *ad hoc* arrangements with individual Mexican law schools to obtain their Mexican law degrees in three or three and a half years of Mexican study, effectively receiving a year or two of credit for their U.S. J.D. degrees.)

5.   An area unexplored is the issue of professional responsibility. It arises in many contexts. For example, are national norms of professional ethics similar in the three Parties? What should be required as to proof of good moral character for admission as a FLC? Admission to the Bar? Should the matter simply be left to each admitting jurisdiction?

PART B. ARE THERE LESSONS TO BE LEARNED FOR THE NAFTA PARTIES FROM THE EXPERIENCE IN THE EUROPEAN UNION?

Although our interest is in the NAFTA, the current domestic rules within the NAFTA Parties may be viewed as overly restrictive. As economic integration increases in this hemisphere, perhaps we need to consider how a larger economic union (in terms of number of nations and different cultures) has addressed legal services across national borders. Law firm mergers are occurring within the EU, and with U.S. firms, a pattern which may influence activities within the NAFTA, and any further regional integration in the Western Hemisphere. The 1999 merger of Clifford Chance from the UK, Pünder Volhard Weber & Axter from Germany, and Rogers & Wells from the U.S., created the largest law firm to date, some 2,700 lawyers in 40 offices worldwide, with more than US$1 billion income. Keith Clark, senior partner of Clifford Chance, assumed the chairmanship of the firm and stated that the reason for the merger is that:

> Law firms that service global business and finance must respond to clients' needs for global legal services. That requires mergers of like-minded, high-quality firms. Interview in The Times, Law Reports at 7 (Sept. 7, 1999)

Clark also noted that in ten years' time he expected his firm to have "leading operations across the Americas, Europe, Asia and Africa." Note that "Americas" is plural.

DEL DUCA & SCIARRA, DEVELOPING CROSS–BORDER PRACTICE RULES: CHALLENGES AND OPPORTU-NITIES FOR LEGAL EDUCATION
21 Fordham Int'l L.J. 1109 (1998).*

* * *

DIFFERENCES BETWEEN EC AND NAFTA PROCESSES

Member States have surrendered a significant amount of sovereignty to the EC. Primarily because of this surrender of sovereignty, the EC has achieved a degree of harmonization over a broad area of subject matter unequaled by any other international organization. This is illustrated in the area of cross-border practice by:

(1) The 1977 Provision of Services Directive which permits EC lawyers, under specified conditions, to render services on an occasional basis throughout the EC;

(2) The 1989 Mutual Recognition of Diplomas Directive which permits lawyers to obtain the lawyers' local title in any host Member State and provides compensation for objective differences between training in the state of origin and the host state by

    (a) going through an "adaptation" of up to three years in the host country; or

(b) passing an aptitude test in the host country's law and language; and

(3) The ... Right of Establishment Directive, which ... will allow EC lawyers to establish themselves in other EC countries under their home title. It would thereby abolish the need for lawyers to become certified to practice under the host country's title.

R. FOLSOM, EUROPEAN UNION LAW IN A NUTSHELL
156–161 (4th ed., 2004).*

RIGHT OF ESTABLISHMENT—PROFESSIONALS

The right to go into business as a self-employed person in another member state is secured by Article 52 of the Treaty of Rome. This is known as the "right of establishment." ...

Implementation of the right of establishment for professionals is anticipated in Article 47 by the issuance of legislation mutually recognizing diplomas and national licenses. Medical doctors, dentists, veterinarians, architects and many others have benefitted from these provisions and the substantial implementing law that now accompanies them. For example, the Council has adopted directives about freedom to supply services in the case of travel agents, tour operators, air brokers, freight forwarders, ship brokers, air cargo agents, shipping agents, and hairdressers. It has been relatively easy to deal with those professions (e.g., medicine and allied professions) in which diplomas and other evidence of formal qualification relate to equivalent competence in the same skill. It did, however, take 17 years to negotiate the directive on free movement of veterinarians. And litigation over the implementation of these directives continues. It took a Commission prosecution to remove the French requirement that doctors and dentists give up their home country professional registrations before being licensed in France.

Typically, European law on the right of establishment creates minimum professional training standards which, if met, will result in mutual recognition. Substantial variations in training may trigger special admissions requirements, such as time in practice, an adaptation period or an aptitude test. A major single market directive applies this approach to virtually all professionals receiving diplomas based upon a minimum of three years of study. Mutual recognition in this instance means that access is gained to host country professional bodies. This is different from the home country licensing method of mutual recognition used for banking, insurance and investment advisors. Even in the absence of such legislation, professional disqualification on grounds of nationality is prohibited.

LEGAL SERVICES

Considerable difficulty has been encountered in lifting restrictions within member states on the freedom to provide legal services. For example, within the legal profession there may be only a small amount of training or required knowledge held in common by a "lawyer" from a civil law jurisdiction (e.g., an *avocat* from France) and a "lawyer" from a common law jurisdiction (e.g., a solicitor from England). As a result, the initial directive relating to lawyers' services took a delicate approach to the question of freedom to provide legal services and stopped short of dealing with a right of establishment.

This 1977 directive allows a lawyer from one member state, under that lawyer's national title (e.g., abogado, rechtsanwalt, barrister), to provide services in other member states. This includes the right to appear in court without local co-counsel unless representation by counsel is mandatory under national laws. Once retained, a local lawyer need not actually conduct the litigation. It is sufficient that the local attorney is retained to "act in conjunction with" the proceedings. But the legal services directive cannot be used so as to circumvent national rules on professional ethics, particularly where a dual nationality lawyer has been disbarred and then moves to another state.

Directive 77/249 gave rise to lawyer identity cards issued under the auspices of *Commission Consultative des Barreaux Européans* (C.C.B.E.), which was charged to propose a specific directive about a right of establishment for lawyers. However, the mutual recognition of diplomas accomplished in Council Directive 89/48 applies to lawyers. The maximum adaptation or training period allowed under this directive is three years. In 1997, the long-awaited right of establishment directive was adopted. It mirrors much of the prior law, but makes it easier (than under the diploma directive) to join the local bar after three years of sustained practice in the host state.

The C.C.B.E. adopted a common Code of Conduct for lawyers in 1988. It is hoped that this Code will ultimately become binding in all member states. It seeks to harmonize rules of conduct on confidentiality, conflicts of interest, segregation of client funds and malpractice insurance. In other areas, the Code does not harmonize, but rather provides choice of law rules to resolve conflicting national approaches to advertising, contingent fees and membership on boards of directors. The host country rules in these areas will apply to lawyers providing services across borders under Directive 77/249. Home country rules apply as to general fee arrangements.

Admission to the practice of law is still governed by the rules of the legal profession of each member state. Several European Court judgments have upheld the right of lawyer applicants to be free from discrimination on grounds of nationality, residence or retention of the right to practice in home jurisdictions. For example, a Greek lawyer who had a doctorate in German law and had worked for some time advising on Greek and European law in Munich was denied admission to the German bar. On appeal, the Court of Justice held that Article 43 obligates member states not to impede the movement of lawyers. The member state must compare an applicant's specific qualifications with those detailed by national law. Only if the applicant does not meet all the necessary qualifications may the host state require additional courses or training.

By joining the bar in another country, lawyers acquire the right to establish themselves in more than one nation. See Directive 98/5 on rights of establishment for lawyers. The multinational law firm, pioneered by Baker and McKenzie in the United States, has had relatively few regional counterparts in Europe until very perhaps ten years ago. Attorneys from member states are establishing affiliations and sometimes partnerships which reflect and service the economic, political and social integration of Europe. These "European law firms" often compete with existing branches of North American multinational firms for the lucrative practice of Common Market law.

In professional fields, the real barrier to movement of people across borders is language. In some instances, linguistic requirements for jobs are lawful despite their negative impact on free movement rights. As much as Europe may succeed in its campaign for truly establishing an integrated market, the language barriers will remain. Although younger generations are increasingly multilingual, a professional who cannot speak to his or her clients or students is unlikely to succeed in another member state.

* * *

FREEDOM TO PROVIDE AND RECEIVE SERVICES ACROSS EUROPEAN BORDERS

The freedom of nonresidents to provide services within other parts of Europe is another part of the foundations of the Treaty of Rome. The freedom to provide services (including tourism) implies a right to receive and pay for them by going to the country of their source. Industrial, commercial, craft and professional services are included within this right, which is usually not dependent upon establishment in the country where the service is rendered. In other words, the freedom to provide or receive services across borders entails a limited right of temporary entry into another member state.

The Council has adopted a general program for the abolition of national restrictions on the freedom to provide services across borders. This freedom is subject to the same public policy, public security and public health exceptions applied to workers and the self-employed. The Council's program has been implemented by a series of legislative acts applicable to professional and nonprofessional services. As with the right of self-establishment, discrimination based upon the nationality or non-residence of the service provider is generally prohibited even if no implementing law has been adopted.

HARTLEY, THE FOUNDATIONS OF EUROPEAN COMMUNITY LAW
211 (4th ed. 1998).*

* * *

The starting-point for the principle of mutual recognition is a higher education diploma awarded on completion of professional education and training of at least three years' duration, or the equivalent period part time. Where, in the host State, the taking up and pursuit of a regulated profession is subject to the possession of a diploma, the competent authority of that State may not refuse to authorise a national of a member State to take up and pursue that profession on the same conditions as apply to its own nationals, provided the applicant holds a diploma required in another State for the pursuit of the profession in question, *or* has pursued that profession for at least two years in a State which does not regulate that profession (Article 3).

Where the applicant's education and training is at least one year shorter than that which is required by the host State, or where there is a shortfall in the period of supervised practice required by the host State, the applicant may be required to provide *evidence of professional experience*. This may not exceed the shortfall in supervised practice, nor twice the shortfall in duration of education and training, required by the host State; in any event, it may not exceed four years (Article 4(1)(a)).

The host State may also require an *adaptation period* not exceeding three years:

> (a) where matters covered by the applicant's education and training differ substantially from those covered by that of the State; or

> (b) where the activities regulated in the host State are not regulated in the applicant's State of origin; or

> (c) where the profession regulated in the host State comprises activities which are not pursued in the State from which the applicant originates,

provided, in the latter two situations, the difference corresponds to *specific* education and training required in the host State and covers matters which differ *substantially* from those covered by the evidence of formal qualification (Article 4(1)(b)).

Instead of the adaptation period the applicant may opt for an aptitude test. However, for professions whose practice requires precise knowledge of national law and in which the giving of advice on national law is an essential and constant aspect of that activity, a State may stipulate either an adaptation period or an aptitude test (Article 4(1)(b)).

The requirements of periods of professional experience *and* adaptation cannot be applied cumulatively. Thus the total period cannot exceed four years.

In addition, the host State may allow an applicant to undertake in the host State, on a basis of equivalence, that part of his training which consists of supervised professional practice (Article 5).

* * *

Questions and Comments

1. Professor Del Duca and attorney Sciarra note three Directives addressed to cross-border legal services within the EU. Do any of the directives reflect the approach of NAFTA?

2. The third Directive, dealing with the right of establishment, is further outlined in the Folsom extract. Would it be possible for the NAFTA Parties to recognize the law diplomas of each other and allow any graduate to sit for any bar examination? Is it likely that an average law graduate from British Columbia, with the addition of a bar exam prep course, could pass any state bar in the U.S.? Would such passage make them *qualified* to practice law? What about a Mexican or Quebec graduate, coming from a civil law system? Or a U.S. graduate such as Fitzgerald or Sam taking a bar exam in Mexico?

Mexico does not require a bar exam, but one could be established. Perhaps certain courses might have to be taken during the law degree program if one planned to sit for another Party's bar exam? Would receiving an LL.M. or Maestria degree be a satisfactory compromise between having to start all over and do the original law degree, or just taking the bar with recognition of the first degree? Prof. Folsom also notes Directive 77/249, which is the first noted by Del Duca and Sciarra, allowing a lawyer to provide some services. Is it the same as being a Foreign Legal Consultant? Folsom also mentions the third item in the list of Del Duca and Sciarra, Directive 89/48, which is the mutual recognition of diplomas mandate. What about the Canadian approach, at Ottawa, for example, where a civil law graduate can obtain a common law certification for a year's additional study, and vice-versa? Could that work among the NAFTA Parties? Note that in the United States, most jurisdictions do not permit foreign lawyers with U.S. LL.M. degrees to sit for the bar.

In the *Van Binsbergen* case in the EC, (case 33/74), a Dutch lawyer, Van Binsbergen, qualified as an advocate in the Netherlands. He moved to Belgium, but wished to represent persons in the Netherlands, but was blocked by a Dutch Bar rule that required persons representing clients before certain tribunals (i.e., social security) to live in the state where the service was provided. The EU Court of Justice held he was entitled to rely upon Articles 59(1) and 60(3), which were directly effective, even though recognition and harmonization had not yet been achieved under Directives issued under Article 57.

In another significant decision, *Thieffry v. Conseil de l'Ordre des Avocats à la Cour de Paris* (Case 71/76), Thieffry, a Belgian national with a Belgian law degree wanted to undertake training to be admitted to the French bar.

His Belgian degree was recognized by the University of Paris, and he obtained a qualifying certificate in France for the profession of *avocat*. The European Court held he could not be refused admission. Note the role the European Court plays in these cases. There is no such court in NAFTA, but a Chapter 20 panel might be convened if Chapter 12 rights are denied.

3.   Professor Hartley of the London School of Economics outlines the concept of mutual recognition in the EU. Could this work in NAFTA? If you say no because of the differences between the civil and common law, and the different languages, the same differences exist in the EU, with many more languages.

4.   Canada doesn't show much flexibility with regard to American J.D. graduates. In general, they are required to complete 30–45 credit hours in a Canadian law school—2–3 semesters—although the actual rules provide a discretionary alternative, writing 8–10 examinations on different subjects in Canadian law. (Federation of Law Societies of Canada, Evaluation Guidelines for Foreign Lawyers.) As of 2003, Canada has moved toward reciprocity among provinces for lawyers who relocate, without requiring a bar examination. Eight provinces have signed the National Mobility Agreement (NMA) as of October 2003, British Columbia, Alberta, Saskatchewan, Manitoba, Ontario, Quebec, Nova Scotia and Newfoundland. The NMA indicates considerably more flexibility than among U.S. states, where there is virtually no recognition in one jurisdiction of bar membership in another, except under limited circumstances in which the District of Columbia permits those who have passed the bar in one of the states to waive into the D.C. bar.

PROBLEM 6.2 CROSS–BORDER TRANSPORTATION SERVICES: SERVICIOS DE MONTERREY OF MEXICO (TRUCKS) AND GREENHOUND OF THE U.S. (BUSES)

SECTION I.   THE SETTING

Servicios de Monterrey is a large trucking transportation firm located in Monterrey, Mexico, and wholly-owned by Mexicans. It transports goods throughout Mexico, and wishes to be able to send its trucks with Mexican drivers to locations throughout Canada and the United States. It has hundreds of trucks, of many sizes, including the largest currently allowed in Mexico, which are 48 foot trailer trucks (the norm in the U.S. is becoming 53 feet). Servicios has many full-time drivers, and has hired many new inexperienced drivers to handle the increased traffic generated by the NAFTA. Under current rules, for most truckload shipments, Servicios' tractors (the cab unit) haul the loaded trailers into the border area, where they are transferred to a short-haul tractor or "mule" which hauls the trailer across the border, where it is turned over to a U.S. trucking firm to haul the trailer to its U.S. destination. Truckloads of smaller shipments (less than truckload, or "LTL") are unloaded in the border area and reloaded on a trailer destined for the United States. Servicios' tractors may haul other trailers back to Monterrey, or may return empty. Servicios is one of some 500 Mexican motor carriers that have filed applications for registration with the U.S. DOT. Servicios is considered the most modern and efficient Mexican trucking organization, and it has received numerous awards from the Mexican government, chambers of commerce and trucking associations for its commitment to full compliance with Mexican safety regulations applicable to both its trucks and drivers.

Greenhound is a major bus company incorporated in Delaware with its principal offices in St. Louis. It is one of the largest bus companies in the U.S., and provides bus service throughout the U.S. It wishes to commence bus service throughout Canada and Mexico. Greenhound has an excellent reputation for transporting persons with disabilities, having refitted their bus fleet with expensive equipment to accommodate these persons. Mexican buses are generally without such accommodations. Canadian buses are better, but not yet the level of U.S. Greenhound buses. Greenhound is also suspicious that its problems in extending service throughout Mexico are somehow related to fears of increased illegal immigration from Mexico.

SECTION II. FOCUS OF CONSIDERATION

Borders create obstacles to the movement of goods as well as people. If a load of furniture from Monterrey destined to Home Depot in Atlanta is stopped short of the Nuevo Laredo/Laredo border crossing for transfer to a short-haul mule, and then transferred a second time to a long-haul U.S. trucking firm, before it may proceed through the U.S. to Atlanta, the additional costs will be passed on to the consumer and may constitute a sufficient additional cost to discourage the trade. Additionally, the goods may have to be warehoused at the border, causing further delays and costs. Of further concern are the two legal systems rules applicable to bills of lading, insurance policies, etc.

Bus companies receive numerous complaints from their customers when they have to change buses at the borders. It is inconvenient, time consuming, and leads to increased costs. Persons who travel on buses are often from the poorer sectors of society, and additional costs are a significant financial burden to them. Of further concern are the three legal systems rules applicable to ticketing, service to disabled persons, insurance, etc.

It is not only access to transportation services that is covered in NAFTA, but also foreign investment in transportation services. NAFTA includes several provisions relating to commercial air, land and water transportation. Most appear in Annexes I, II and V of the Agreement. *Access to Mexico* by Canadian and U.S. companies, and vice-versa, is in stages—international charter and bus service immediately, international truck service to border states and international scheduled bus service in 1997, and international truck service to anywhere in Mexico in 2000. The staging process also applies to *ownership of Mexican companies* providing inter-city bus service, truck transportation service, and domestic transportation of international truck cargo within Mexico. Forty-nine percent ownership is allowed immediately, fifty-one percent in 2001, and total ownership in 2004. Mexico, which formerly prohibited any foreign ownership of companies providing domestic inter-city bus service, trucking services, or tourist transportation services, has been required to make the most significant concessions.

Mexican trucks have long been prohibited from *access to the U.S.* beyond the "Border Commercial Zone", which is the area generally close to each port of entry. The Bus Regulatory Reform Act of 1982 imposed a four-year moratorium on trucks, and has been renewed every two years. Bus owners are not always pleased that they are considered the same as trucks in some legislation. The former Interstate Commerce Commission (ICC) issued operating permits to foreign carriers, but the president could override ICC decisions if in the national interest. Under NAFTA, the following activities were to be permitted by the United States for Mexican companies:

U.S. activities by international charter and tour bus companies	January 1994
cross-border trucking services (border states only)	December 1995
Mexican investment in trucking services for distribution of international cargo	December 1995
international scheduled bus service	January 1997
cross-border trucking services (all states)	January 2000
Mexican investment in U.S. bus services	January 2001

Only the rules relating to international charter and tour bus companies were implemented on schedule. Although NAFTA is supposed to allow "international cargoes" to be transported directly from one NAFTA state to another any location in another NAFTA state, without changing trucking companies at the border, the 1995 and 2000 deadlines were not met. These reciprocal rights were indefinitely delayed by unilateral action of the Clinton administration, for expressed reasons of concern regarding safety of Mexican trucks and drivers. By January, 1997, the Parties were to establish standards for tires, brakes, vehicle weights, dimensions, engine emissions and road signs. It has not been accomplished. The provisions governing Mexican investment in the United States, scheduled for implementation in December 1995 and 2001, which would, for example, have permitted 100 percent ownership of a U.S. trucking company by Servicios de Monterrey, and 100 percent ownership of a Mexican bus company by Greenhound, were also delayed. (President Bush authorized this cross-border investment by Mexicans in U.S. trucking and bus companies in 2001.)

NAFTA provisions govern access to North American cross-border transportation. That means the right of a truck and driver from one Party to deliver goods to any location in another Party. But NAFTA does not open purely *domestic* transportation to these vehicles. In other words, a Servicios truck might be able to deliver the furniture from Monterrey to Atlanta, and take a cargo back to Mexico from anywhere in the U.S., for example Topeka, Kansas. But it could not take a cargo from Atlanta to Topeka. Annex–I–Canada, at I–C–37; annex I–Mexico, at I–M–66, I–M–68; annex I–United States, at I–U–18. But Servicios might invest in a U.S. carrier which does carry goods between Atlanta and Topeka.

The issue is not solely one of vehicles, but who drives those vehicles. For example, Mexico retained the right to exclude foreign drivers, a rather unusual concession and not one to the liking of U.S labor unions. Annex I–Mexico, at I–M–68. Some U.S. labor unions have objected to all foreign trucks entering the U.S., allegedly because foreign trucks are not as safe, their drivers are not as skilled and obtain licenses more easily than in the U.S., many foreign drivers will not understand traffic signs in English, and driving rules differ in Canada and Mexico. The International Brotherhood of Teamsters has for the most part been opposed to any opening of the U.S. border to Mexican *trucks*, although they really are opposed to Mexican *drivers*. Their opposition would cease abruptly were U.S. drivers to be required to drive Mexican trucks in the U.S. The unions have also stated that unless goods are thoroughly checked, Mexico will become an even greater transshipment location for drugs.

The truck transportation issue has divided U.S. unions and trucking companies. The larger U.S. trucking companies, represented by the American Trucking Association (ATA), are interested in increasing business by being able to operate in Mexico. They do not feel as threatened by Mexican trucking companies as U.S. drivers feel threatened by Mexican drivers. But the ATA does object to Mexican trucks which do not meet U.S. safety standards, and insists that Mexican trucks should not be admitted until the DOT has adequate means to enforce safety standards. A different view has been expressed in California, where the highway patrol has stated that most Mexican carriers are as safe as their U.S. counterparts. The unsafe Mexican vehicles are the short-haul "drayage" carriers which operate along the border, especially to haul cargo across the border for transfer to a long-haul carrier. Many of the drayage truckers will likely go out of business when direct access is achieved. Few Mexican trucking companies presently in existence are likely to be able to compete with U.S. trucking firms for long-haul carriage.

Motor carriers and drivers entering the U.S. are required to comply with the U.S. Federal Motor Carrier Safety Regulations (FMCSR). That requires Mexican drivers to have a Mexican Licencia Federal, or a non-resident commercial driver's license issued by a U.S. state; to maintain records of driver's duty status; to comply with U.S. driver hours-of-service regulations; to mark vehicles with the company name, Mexican city and state, and ICC MX number; to secure the cargo properly; to prepare daily vehicle inspection reports; and to comply with all local and state laws, including those relating to air pollution. Local and state laws may address weight and size limits, fuel permits, special inspection requirements, vehicle licensing and hazardous materials/waste permits. If the truck is carrying hazardous materials, it must comply with the U.S. Federal Hazardous Materials Regulations (FHMR), which require shipping papers to be readily accessible/visible in English; include emergency response information; comply with Research and Special Programs Administration (RSPA) of the U.S. DOT; proper marking and packaging of the materials; and display of a vehicle placard. Compliance with these requirements is necessary to obtain a Certificate of Registration to operate in the Commercial Zone, which is the immediate area surrounding the port of entry, as described in the U.S. Code of Federal Regulations. Additionally required are an insurance form, and immigration permit.

Bus transportation shares some of the problems of truck transportation, but has some unique issues. It does not have the load weight problem, although some newer double deck buses may create weight issues. It does have driver problems, since the cargo is people and not goods.

We first try to identify some of the issues that have caused the delay in opening the borders to trucks and buses. In doing so we ought to ask whether stated reasons (i.e., safety) are really a mask for unstated reasons (i.e., union fear of lower paid drivers, company fear of competition). We also consider the NAFTA rules, and discover that unlike many areas of the NAFTA where there are rather extensively detailed provisions, the cross-border provisions essentially open up the border but then imposes numerous restrictions in the annexes. We then turn to litigation, first to the Chapter 20 *Cross Border Trucking Services* decision (Feb. 6, 2001), and then to U.S. domestic litigation designed to frustrate Bush Administration and Congressional efforts to comply with NAFTA obligations, ending (for now at least), with the unanimous 2004 U.S. Supreme Court decision discussed in this section.

NAFTA Chapter 12 and its annexes, Annex 913.5a1, portions of general annexes I, II, V and VI, and of the DOT legislation, are required for this problem. They are included in the Documents Supplement.

SECTION III. READINGS, QUESTIONS AND COMMENTS

NAFTA AND THE BORDER: TRANSPORTATION INFRASTRUCTURE, ACCESS AND RECIPROCITY

5 Mexico Trade & Law Reporter, January, 1992.*

* * *

RESTRICTIONS ON U.S. MOTOR CARRIERS' ACCESS TO MEXICO

The Mexican constitution prohibits foreigners from operating commercial vehicles in Mexico. However, in 1955 the Mexican government issued a declaration, known as the "Ruiz Cortines Decree," which established the legal basis for the operation of U.S. motor carriers within Mexico's border area. While the decree provided legal precedent for U.S. motor carrier access to Mexico, it has not been uniformly applied across the border, and U.S. commercial motor carriers are effectively denied access to most areas of Mexico.

Since 1987 the U.S. Department of Transportation, in discussions with Mexico's Secretaria de Comunicaciones y Transporte, has sought to expand border access for motor carriers. However, pressure from truckers' unions has so far prevented the Mexican government from liberalizing laws on access for foreign commercial carriers into Mexico.

Currently, the only Mexican community along the border where U.S. motor carriers enjoy reciprocal treatment is the city of Nuevo Laredo across from Laredo, Texas. Laredo is the major motor carrier crossing point in Texas. A local informal agreement between U.S. and Mexican carriers in Laredo and Nuevo Laredo allows each side's tractors (truck cabs) to deliver trailers across the border, but they must return without a load or with an empty trailer. Local officials and truckers and shippers on both sides of the border hail this arrangement as a model solution for other border entry port problems. However, U.S. federal authorities consider the arrangement to be inefficient.

Despite overall lack of reciprocal access for U.S. commercial motor carriers, in recent years Mexican authorities have granted access to some U.S. commercial vehicles. In July 1989 Mexico deregulated its trucking industry. One of the effects of the deregulation was to allow U.S. maquiladora plants in Mexico to use their own fleet of motor carriers to transport their inputs and final products across the border. On December 7, 1990, the U.S. Department of Transportation and the Mexican Secretaria de Comunicaciones y Transporte reached an agreement that gave U.S. tourist buses the same access to Mexico enjoyed by Mexican tourist buses in the United States.

According to a Department of Transportation official, in October 1990 a high level official in Mexico's Secretaria de Comunicaciones y Transporte announced that Mexico would grant U.S. truckers access into Mexican border communities. However, on March 6, 1991 at the semiannual meeting of the U.S.–Mexico Transportation Working Group, representatives of the Mexican federal government retracted this promise.

RESTRICTIONS ON MEXICAN MOTOR CARRIERS' ACCESS TO THE UNITED STATES

In retaliation for Mexico's refusal to grant access to U.S. commercial motor carriers, the United States has sought to limit access by Mexican carriers to specified commercial zones. Section 226 of the 1984 Motor Carrier Safety Act sets forth two provisions that restrict access by foreign motor carriers to the United States.

Section 226 requires that foreign commercial motor carriers operating in the United States remain within designated commercial zones along the U.S.–Mexico border as defined by the Interstate Commerce

Commission (ICC). The limits of the ICC commercial zones generally encompass the border port of entry and contiguous municipalities or areas that are commercially a part of such a port of entry. Section 226 also requires that all foreign motor carriers obtain a certificate of registration from the ICC to operate within these commercial zones.

In order to obtain a certificate of registration from the ICC, Mexican motor carriers must have insurance to operate in the United States. The Mexican motor carriers must also have paid all applicable U.S. highway taxes to the Internal Revenue Service and have agreed to comply with U.S. equipment safety standards for vehicles' brakes, lighting, and electrical systems. Enforcement of the certificate requirement is the responsibility of the ICC and the U.S. Customs Service. State highway patrols are primarily responsible for enforcing the commercial zone restriction as well as safety standards.

According to researchers at the University of Texas at El Paso, U.S. Customs has had difficulties enforcing the complex certificate requirement. Moreover, local and federal officials at the border report that most Mexican motor carriers are still unable to meet federal motor carrier safety requirements. Although the Motor Carrier Safety Act was passed in 1984, Mexican motor carriers were exempt from federal motor carrier safety regulations until January 1, 1990. A front wheel brake requirement officially took effect for Mexican motor carriers on January 1, 1991. Currently, Mexican motor carriers do not meet that requirement, according to U.S. officials interviewed.

U.S. authorities have met significant resistance when they have attempted to enforce federal motor carrier safety requirements and have imposed penalties on Mexican motor carriers at some ports of entry. At such times, Mexican Customs, local law enforcement agencies, and motor carriers' unions have reportedly retaliated by limiting the access of U.S. vehicles into Mexico at these ports of entry. These disruptions in the flow of commercial and passenger traffic have caused considerable hardship for communities on the U.S. side of the border. Consequently, local officials in these communities have pressured state and federal agencies to limit enforcement of the motor carrier safety regulations.

* * *

Another U.S. restriction is expected to affect Mexican motor carriers in the United States. Under the Motor Commercial Vehicle Safety Act of 1986 (P.L. 99–570, Title 12 of the Anti–Drug Abuse Act) Mexican commercial drivers will be required to obtain commercial driver licenses that meet standards set by the U.S. Department of Transportation.

CAZAMIAS, THE U.S.—MEXICAN TRUCKING DISPUTE: A PRODUCT OF A POLITICIZED TRADE AGREEMENT (NOTE)

33 Texas Int'l L.J. 349 (1998).*

The passage of the North American Free Trade Agreement (NAF-TA) opened a new era of friendly relations between the United States and Mexico. After years of mutual distrust, the United States and Mexico, along with Canada, bound their political and economic futures by forming a free trade bloc. With 85 percent of previous U.S. and Mexican trade conducted by land transportation, the opening of the international trucking market was to be a critical component of NAF-TA's future.

* * *

Many expressed concerns regarding the envisioned transportation system. With increased commercial traffic would come increased risks in the areas of public safety, the environment, and illegal drug transport. The International Brotherhood of Teamsters (IBT) and Citizens for Reliable and Safe Highways (CRASH) took a tough stance against the phase-out provisions, arguing that opening the border would compromise U.S. safety standards and put U.S. citizens at risk. Joan Claybrook, co-chair of CRASH, warned that the trade agreement would result in "a compromising down on [U.S.] requirements."

The groups' efforts to stymie the trucking provisions paid off. On the scheduled day of the opening, U.S. Department of Transportation (DOT) Secretary Federico Peña announced that the United States would not process Mexican applications for operating authority. Peña said that safety concerns and inadequate harmonization between U.S. and Mexican trucking standards compelled the administration to override NAF-TA's trucking provisions. The secretary declared the years of preparation for the border opening to be insufficient, telling reporters that the administration wanted to "implement NAFTA correctly."

The Clinton administration's legal authority for violating the NAF-TA timetable is a result of the absence of any provisions for opening land transportation in the NAFTA Implementation Act. The Bus Regulatory Reform Act of 1982 imposed a moratorium on Mexican truck operations in the United States. Under the moratorium, Mexican trucks were expressly prohibited from conducting U.S. operations. The president possessed sole authority to remove or modify the moratorium if he determined "that such removal or modification is in the national interest." Mexican trucks, however, may operate inside U.S. "commercial zones."[13] On January 1, 1994, the president partially modified the

---

13.   See 49 U.S.C. § 10530 (1994). Mexican trucks have been allowed to obtain "Certificates of Registration" allowing them to operate only within certain "com-

moratorium to allow Mexican motor carriers to carry passengers between Mexico and the United States. He gave Congress written notice on November 4, 1993, as the statute required. Apparently, the safety concerns over commercial freight vehicles that so agitated the administration in December 1995 were not a concern two years earlier when it approved bus traffic liberalization. Because the president gave no notice in anticipation of the December 18, 1995 liberalization phase for motor carriers, the moratorium on Mexican trucks remains in effect.

U.S. and Mexican leaders have made little progress in reopening the border. Some have claimed that the president was catering to the unions on the eve of an election year. The Mexican Commerce secretary publicly decried the U.S. action as a violation of the treaty and requested consultations with the United States under NAFTA Article 2006. Because U.S. law does not provide a deadline for U.S. action on foreign driving applications, the administration denied violating the accord. The United States agreed to hold informal consultations under Chapter 20, but neither country [as of 1998 had] yet requested a panel to resolve the dispute. U.S. and Mexican negotiators continue to hold "informal" discussions on the closed border.

* * *

HISTORY OF THE TRUCKING DISPUTE

Jointly and individually, the United States and Mexico took extensive measures in preparing for the border opening. The DOT, along with state agencies, increased the resources available to the border area prior to the border opening. Texas added 109 officers to handle more border inspections. California spent thirty million dollars on inspection centers. The DOT granted the border states two million dollars for inspection in 1994 and 1995, and promised another one million dollars in 1997. In addition, Mexico earmarked a portion of the World Bank's loans to improve border infrastructure, including the improvement of its weighing stations.

U.S. and Mexican leaders met extensively to discuss border infrastructure renovation. Transportation Secretary Federico Peña and Mexican Minister of Transportation and Communication Emilio Gamboa conducted the first-ever North American Transportation Summit on April 29, 1994. The conference resulted in a Memorandum of Understanding (MOU) between the United States and Mexico. The MOU set forth the blueprints for cooperation between U.S. and Mexican officials at the federal, state, and local level. It was designed to facilitate coordination between U.S. and Mexican transportation officials.

mercial zones" inside U.S. border cities. The requirements for a certificate of registration are more lax than those for operating authority inside the United States because certificates of registration do not give drivers of Mexican motor carriers authority to drive beyond the commercial zones into the state's interior. Commercial zones vary in size according to the border city's area and population. Rarely do they extend beyond the border town's city limits.

The United States and Mexico reached agreement on a range of other issues during the summit. Mexico granted U.S. truckers access to northern border terminals and facilities. Both nations agreed to standardize safety operations regarding hazardous materials and to set up an electronic communication system to more efficiently exchange information on commercial drivers. Summit leaders negotiated a science and technology agreement that would use new and highly advanced technologies for border inspections. Mexico agreed to participate in Roadcheck 1994, a U.S. program designed to ensure safety on U.S. roads and highways.

Outside the summit, the United States and Mexico attempted to harmonize their inspection methods and step up safety precautions. Officials from the DOT and Texas Department of Public Safety (DPS) conducted workshops in Mexico to educate Mexican truckers about the border opening and the heightened inspections that would accompany it. The Clinton Administration called for the creation of the Land Transportation Safety Subcommittee (LTSS), a group consisting of transportation experts from the federal and state level, as well as private sector representatives. The expressed purpose of the LTSS was to harmonize safety standards between the United States and Mexico by January of 1997. It would work closely with state transportation officials to ensure consistency between their standards and Mexican standards regarding vehicle weight and dimensions, tires, brakes, parts and accessories, cargo securement, maintenance, and emission levels.

For its part, Mexico joined the Commercial Vehicle Safety Alliance (CVSA). The CVSA is an organization comprised of U.S. and Canadian officials working to ensure consistent roadside inspection procedures between the various Canadian and U.S. jurisdictions. Funded by both federal governments, the CVSA spent US$6.27 million on the U.S. border state inspection posts. Mexico also upgraded the standards of its commercial driver's license and cooperated with U.S. officials in conducting training sessions for Mexican truckers and inspection officials.

On the day of the scheduled border opening, the DOT director for motor carriers met with reporters to discuss the historic event. The director explained that the DOT had put tough safety enforcement programs in place and promised that Mexican trucks would be held to U.S. standards. Later in the day, however, DOT Secretary Federico Peña called his own press conference with an entirely different message for reporters. He announced a freeze on Mexican applications for trucking permits due to inadequate harmonization between U.S. and Mexican safety standards.

The secretary's announcement may have been motivated by political rather than safety considerations. The IBT had been lobbying against the border opening since NAFTA's passage. It opposed competition with the less-regulated Mexican trucking industry. Revealingly, a few hours before the secretary's press conference, the IBT issued a press release announcing the U.S. decision to stop processing Mexican applications for operating authority. Coupled with the contradictory remarks of Peña and Martin, the untimeliness of the IBT's press release suggested a more political nature to the U.S. decision.

Opponents of the border opening raised genuine challenges to U.S. readiness for international trucking, however. They noted that the United States and Mexico had agreed to recognize each other's commercial driver's licenses (CDL) despite a three-year minimum age requirement difference: U.S. drivers must be twenty-one to obtain a CDL, while Mexican drivers need only be eighteen. While the United States would enforce its own law by restricting access to Mexican drivers under twenty-one, the age discrepancy would force inspectors to guard against underaged Mexican drivers using false identification. Additionally, neither U.S. nor Mexican CDLs contained a foreign language requirement. Leaders from the IBT noted that safety is compromised when the English skills of foreign truckers are insufficient to converse with the general public or read highway and traffic signs. With regard to inspection procedures, the IBT and CRASH questioned U.S. and Mexican capability to exchange information efficiently.

Regardless of U.S. motivations to delay the border opening, the Mexican response appeared calculated to gain political leverage. The Mexican Commerce Secretary took a reproachful posture against the United States, calling for Chapter 20 consultations immediately. The Zedillo administration, however, had been under substantial pressure from its trucking industry to postpone the border opening another year. Taking a hard stance against the United States provided Mexico with a bargaining chip. At the time the trucking provisions were to take effect, the United States was challenging the Mexican treatment of a U.S. company, the United Parcel Service. The United States was also exploring an antidumping suit against Mexican tomato distributors. An aggressive posture on trucking gave Mexico rhetorical ammunition against the United States in these areas as well as in future areas of trade dispute.

Mexico would have violated its own law if it had refused to act on the U.S. trucking applications. Unlike the U.S. law, Mexican law prescribes time limits to approve or reject applications for trucking permits. Understandably, Mexican truckers would have been angered by U.S. competition in their own market without reciprocal Mexican operations in the United States. Mexican officials thus were compelled to find a legal excuse to bar U.S. trucking operations in Mexico. The oddest part of the Mexican dilemma was that it arrived at its solution with the help of the United States. The United States sent legal trade experts to Mexico to "craft language that would provide [Mexico] the legal vehicle they need[ed] to treat U.S. carriers in reciprocal fashion." The Clinton Administration thus had a major role in keeping U.S. truckers from competing in Mexico.

The trucking dispute grew more contentious and more visible in the months following the secretary's announcement. Senators Alfonse D'Amato (R–N.Y.) and Diane Feinstein (D–Calif.) wrote a bill that would tie

U.S. approval of Mexican trucker applications to enhanced Mexican efforts to fight cross-border drug smuggling. Republican representatives, on the other hand, wrote a public letter to the President asking him to honor the NAFTA trucking provisions and end the delay. Ineffective bilateral consultations continued while the number of applications on both sides of the border multiplied.

Tensions mounted on the border as well. The DPS and DOT escalated inspections due to the secretary's rhetoric about safety concerns. Mexican truckers reacted bitterly to tougher border inspections, blockading the international bridges in several Mexican border cities. The protest interfered with tourism and cross-border trade, forcing a meeting between U.S. and Mexican officials. The meeting, however, yielded no solutions.

* * *

LEMING, INSURERS JOIN MEXICAN BORDER TRAFFIC SNARL
Journal of Commerce (January 27, 1999).*

An unlikely coalition of insurance organizations, labor unions and consumer groups has emerged to oppose opening U.S. highways to Mexican truck traffic.

The problem is twofold: On the one hand, Mexico's own truck safety systems are below par, and on the other, U.S. border inspection programs to detect substandard equipment are woefully lacking, insurance industry sources say.

* * *

"Without adequate safety programs at the border, we run the risk of one or more preventable serious or even catastrophic accidents involving Mexican vehicles, which could undermine the support for NAFTA," said David Snyder, assistant general counsel for the American Insurance Association in Washington.

... A study released late last year by the Office of the Inspector General surveyed Mexican trucks crossing the border under the current regime of limited access to certain zones and found that of the trucks inspected, 44 percent did not meet U.S. safety requirements.

However, critics of the report contend it is misleading. Most of the trucks crossing into commercial zones from Mexico into the U.S. are owned by transfer companies shuttling freight to warehouses across international bridges.

These trucks are usually old and unreliable because long-haul truckers are not keen to tie up a $100,000 rig for five hours at bridge crossings. Critics note also that U.S. brand-name truck makers like

Freightliner and Kenworth manufacture in Mexico for the long-haul market.

* * *

"We have to throw more bodies at the enforcement task," Mr. Bell said, but the federal government and the states are at loggerheads about who should provide the additional personnel.

"Of all the border states," said Mr. Bell, "California has done the best job, going so far as to install electronic scales that can weigh moving trucks."

Differing national standards are another issue. Mexico allows 130,-000–pound trucks on its highways, vs. the 80,000–pound U.S. standard. He said the California scales have detected Mexican trucks loaded well above even the Mexican limits. Mr. Bell commended Mexico for the progress it has made on truck-safety issues, but said, "It's not a matter that they need more laws, they need more enforcement," and need to address the problem of bribery of law-enforcement officials to ignore violations.

* * *

Gloria Leal, general counsel, Texas insurance department, said there are 19 border entry points in Texas from Mexico. For trucks from Mexico to operate in Texas, they must have insurance written by a U.S.-licensed insurer, she said. ASEMEX, or Aseguradora Mexicana, a state-owned Mexican insurer, established a branch in Texas in 1994 and obtained permission to write all lines, except workers compensation. ASEMEX, now owned by Seguros Comercial, is still licensed to write all lines. "At first availability of insurance was a problem for Mexican truckers entering the U.S.," Ms. Leal said, but then it became a question of affordability.

Michael Scippa, executive director of Citizens for Reliable and Safe Highways (CRASH), a San Francisco consumer group that pushes truck safety, said the United States already has enough problems with truck safety. "In 1997, there were 444,000 large-truck (more than 10,000 pounds) crashes in this country," he said. "The number of deaths caused by those crashes in 1997, according to DOT figures, was 5,355, and 133,000 injuries. About 20 percent of those injuries are catastrophic," including loss of limbs, paralysis and brain damage, which require lifelong care.

* * *

Mr. Scippa expressed concern that the U.S. trucking industry is trying to use NAFTA to have its own restrictions eased in the name of "harmonization." Both Canada and Mexico have higher weight limits, he said, and Canadian drivers are allowed to log 30 percent more successive hours behind the wheel than their American counterparts, while Mexico has no hours-of-service limits at all.

* * *

The third leg of this unlikely alliance comes from the International Brotherhood of Teamsters, which fought NAFTA all along on the grounds that it would destroy American jobs, but now opposes any further authority for Mexican trucks to operate beyond the border zones.

"It's been a huge safety concern for us. We don't want these unsafe trucks sharing the roads with our members," said Fred McLuckie, legislative coordinator in the Teamsters' government affairs department. Mr. McLuckie said the report "confirms what we've been saying for the last couple of years"—that enforcement mechanisms at the border are lacking and that Mexico hasn't implemented an adequate internal inspection program to improve the safety of Mexican truck fleets.

For instance, he said, the crossing at Laredo, Texas, sees 4,500 trucks inbound from Mexico every weekday, but is staffed by only four full-time federal safety inspectors, backed up by four state inspectors who are there on a part-time basis. On weekends, when traffic climbs to 5,000 trucks a day, inspections are "virtually nonexistent," he said.

Congressional Testimony

STATEMENT BY: JIM LA SALA, INTERNATIONAL PRESIDENT AMALGAMATED TRANSIT UNION, AFL–CIO ON THE FUTURE OF THE OFFICE OF MOTOR CARRIERS (OMC) AND IMPROVING INTERCITY BUS SAFETY BEFORE THE GROUND SUBCOMMITTEE TRANSPORTATION COMMITTEE UNITED STATES HOUSE OF REPRESENTATIVES, MAY 26, 1999.

The Amalgamated Transit Union, AFL–CIO, (ATU) is pleased to testify on behalf of more than 165,000 transportation workers in the United States and Canada, employed in the mass transit, over-the-road, school bus and paratransit industries on "The Future of the Office of Motor Carriers (OMC)."

* * *

Overall, the motor coach industry has an amazingly safe record of operations. During the decade of 1987–1996, the National Safety Council, accounted for an average of 4.3 fatalities per year compared with 44,080 persons per year killed in all highway fatalities during this period. The motor coach fatality rate for this ten-year period was .018 per 100 million passenger miles. According to the Department of Transportation's (DOT) Bureau of Transportation Statistics, the 1996 fatality rate for passenger cars was .96 per 100 million passenger miles or more than 50 times higher than the average rate for motor coaches. While this record is impressive, more can and should be done to ensure the safety employees and passengers in the over the road bus industry.

As we now turn to the debate over the Office of Motor Carriers, one overriding but simple point must be made and kept in mind: A truck is not a bus. All of our concerns, and those expressed by our counterparts in the truck and bus industries over the federal regulatory scheme, including the role of the OMC and the priorities governing the expenditure of DOT resources are driven by this simple distinction.

Given the vast differences in equipment, travel and transport functions, training, and operating environment, the federal Office of Motor Carriers should establish a separate regulatory and enforcement division with responsibilities over intercity bus operations.

To date, the inspection, investigative, and other enforcement resources of the OMC have been targeted in the trucking sector, rendering bus operation a mere stepchild in their oversight role. By way of example, the current effort to consider revisions to the hours of service regulations has, as in the past, begun with a unified set of alternative options governing both truck and bus operators. Yet, given the substantial difference in day-to-day operations and scheduling, any proposed changes should begin with a separate inquiry concerning the current rules effects on safe bus operations to determine whether AU changes are warranted.

* * *

Increasing resources for effective enforcement is critical in the years ahead. Perhaps no more compelling argument for expanding such resources can be made than with reference to the potential safety risks that may arise from full implementation of the North American Free Trade Agreement (NAFTA). Under its provisions, both Mexican truck and bus operators are to be permitted full access throughout the United States. Fortunately, in December 1995, given widespread concerns over the potential safety risks of such expanded operations, the Clinton Administration suspended efforts to open the border. Current plans call for expanded cross-border operations in January 2000. Already, according to an August 1997 Government Accounting Office report, from January to May 1997 an estimated 90,000 commercial passenger vehicles crossed the border, yet only 528 buses were inspected, and 22 percent of those inspected were placed out of service. In comparison, about 10 percent of the U.S. commercial passenger vehicles inspected from October 1996 through June 1997 were placed out of service. While commendable efforts have been undertaken by both countries to ensure comparable safety and training standards and effective enforcement of those laws, no one can question the necessity for additional resources to meet the challenges of increased cross-border operations.

STATEMENT OF NORMAN Y. MINETA BEFORE THE U.S. HOUSE OF REPRESENTATIVES; COMMITTEE OF TRANSPORTATION AND INFRASTRUCTURE SUBCOMMITTEE ON GROUND TRANSPORTATION, ON OVERSIGHT OF THE OFFICE OF MOTOR CARRIERS AND OVERSIGHT OF BUS SAFETY

MAY 26, 1999.

I would like to thank you for your invitation to appear before the Subcommittee on Ground Transportation's Oversight of the Office of

Motor Carriers and Oversight of Bus Safety. As a former member of Congress, and chairman of this Committee, it is ... a pleasure ... to talk about a very important subject, motor carrier safety.

Earlier this year, in February 1999, Federal Highway Administrator Ken Wykle and Secretary Rodney Slater asked that I undertake an independent review of the Motor Carrier Safety functions and operations within the Department of Transportation. My charge was to review what was working, or not working as the situation might be, and to identify actions and strategies necessary to reduce both the number of highway traffic fatalities and injuries as well as reductions in highway traffic fatality/injury rates....

* * *

Substantial increases in motor carrier transport activities at the U.S. border crossings with Canada and Mexico were brought about by the North American Free Trade Agreement (NAFTA). The General Accounting Office reported in 1997, as did the Department of Transportation's Office of Inspector General in December 1998, that trucks entering the US through border crossings in Arizona, New Mexico and Texas were not meeting U.S. safety standards and four U.S. border states' readiness for enforcement varied significantly. The primary problems reported are too few qualified safety inspectors, and there are deficient or non-existent truck inspection facilities at the main border crossings. Also, of those trucks inspected, in-bound Mexican trucks operating within the free trade zones had a much higher out-of-service rate than U.S. trucks, indicating a need for much higher inspection and enforcement activity. While the three border states have increased their inspection activities, it does not appear adequate to assure safe operating compliance by January, 2000 when NAFTA will allow motor carriers to operate throughout the U.S. Some of the states consider border crossing safety to be a primary Federal responsibility. The Department sought and the Congress approved additional funding ... for safety and corridor improvements.

Recommended Actions:

1. Increase the number of Federal safety inspectors (minimum of 50 new Federal Inspectors) at the southern border crossings for roadside inspections of inbound vehicles and drivers.

2. Increase targeted ... funding for border states to assume and increase roadside safety inspections of vehicles and drivers.

3. Accelerate roadside safety inspection infrastructure development and improvements....

* * *

Effective, consistent and reliable motor carrier safety programs depend on timely issuance of motor carrier safety rules consistent with existing statutes, new legislation, new research and technology, safety and economic incentives, and proven safety management and operating practices. The public safety interests are best served when safety regulations and operating rules are well defined, understood, and firmly but fairly administered. Over the course of several years, several major rules have been in the process of being written, reissued or delayed for a number of reasons. With the enactment of major surface transportation legislation and other related legislation in the past 8 years, a backlog of implementing regulations has developed. To some extent, the problems have been magnified by: (a) complexity and enormity of some rules; (b) different interest of the manifold stakeholders; (c) lack of complete scientific research; (d) shortage of qualified skills and abilities within the rulemaking organization itself; (e) cautionary approach brought on by potential legal challenges and bureaucratic entanglements during the process; and (f) decision making processes or apparent reluctance to give priority, make hard choices and move on.

Recommended Actions:

1. Streamline the rulemaking process within the Department of Transportation by establishing clear priorities, schedules and accountability at each phase/step, by conducting concurrent rulemaking processes and reviews, and by eliminating redundant and non-value added steps.

2. Increase the staff resources devoted to motor carrier rulemaking activities with additional qualified personnel (minimum 10 to 12 new FTE technical, human factors, economists and legal).

KOZOLCHYK, FOREWORD, NORTH AMERICAN STANDARD TRANSPORTATION PRACTICES—A GUIDE TO TRUCK TRANSPORTATION

(Edited by Gary T. Doyle, National Law Center
for Inter–American Free Trade (1998)).*

FOREWORD

... The North American Standard Transportation Practices (NAS-TRAPS) are the product of a painstaking process of gathering and selecting the practices involved in the transportation of merchandise by truck in the three NAFTA countries. They incorporate the practices of the most experienced, knowledgeable and respected participants in the transportation business in the NAFTA region. These practices, therefore, are not mere expressions of what respected transportation practitioners or the National Law Center for Inter–American Free Trade (NLCIFT) would like to see in place. They are exercised with the intent to bind the practitioners, a requirement of customary law almost since Roman times (*opinio juris sive necessitatis*).

The process of gathering motor transportation practices in the NAFTA region started virtually with the creation of the NLCIFT.... I

* Copyright © 1998 National Law Center for Inter–American Free Trade. Reproduced with permission. (Boris Kozolchyk is Director of the National Law Center and a law professor at the University of Arizona.)

asked Meredith Munger, a research volunteer at the NLCIFT, to prepare a description of the "legal" journey of goods shipped southward from Arizona to Mexico and northward from Mexico to the United States. Shortly thereafter, Gary Doyle, Esq., became the coordinator of the NLCIFT's North American Committee on Surface Transportation Law and Practice (NACST). One of this committee's goals was to draft a set of practices to guide shippers, carriers, forwarding agents, freight forwarders, customs brokers, bankers, insurers and consignees through the process of transporting goods by road in the NAFTA region. . . .

The primary goal of NACST tri-national committee work was to develop a uniform North American regime for carrier liability for merchandise loss or damage and to create a standardized format for a North American truck and rail bill of lading that would obviate the problems found in the disparities study. A single example illustrates the range of disparate practices: under Canadian law, a carrier is liable for damage or loss to the extent of CA$2 per pound; under United States law he is liable for the value of the shipment; and under Mexican law, a carrier is liable to the extent of 2 cents per pound.

In 1995 the committee created a paper-based and electronic format for a truck bill of lading and carriers began using the NACST format in the NAFTA region. The negotiations on the liability regime have reached an impasse on the limits acceptable to shippers and carriers, however, and the Mexican and United States governments have deadlocked on the reciprocal rights of transnational trucking. Thus, the NACST work on a uniform liability regime presently awaits resolution of the disagreements between the Mexican and United States governments on the interpretation of NAFTA provisions on the liberalization of motor transportation services, and between shippers and carriers on the limits of liability for loss or damage to shipped goods.

The disparities uncovered in our study plus the increased number of risks, such as the truck hijackings associated with Mexico's (fortunately waning) economic crisis, make the adoption of NASTRAPS all the more necessary. Because governmental action on reciprocal trucking rights may still be years away, there is much to be gained by a healthy exercise of what the three legal systems defer to as "party autonomy." . . .

By incorporating these standard practices into their NAFTA region truck bills of lading, freight bills, interline or interchange agreements, truck manifests and delivery receipts, shippers, carriers, brokers, agents and consignees will insure that *their* law will be the applicable law. This can be accomplished by adopting simple wording, such as: "The parties to this contract, bill, receipt or transportation document agree that it will be governed, where applicable, by NASTRAPS." By incorporating NASTRAPS into the above transactions, the parties will insure that, eventually, uniform practices and documentation will also develop, among other uses, for notices to the various participants, claim forms, and insurance policies or certificates.

These standard practices were collected during a five-year process that included seven tri-national meetings. This process was preceded by surveys, interviews and exhaustive research of legal and business literature. . . . To qualify for selection, practices had to fulfill three objectives: prove cost effective for businessmen or providers of professional services, satisfy the lawyers as lawful and all the participants as fair.

The widespread observance of selected practices typically undergoes at least two stages of development. During the first stage, the key parties or participants in the transaction or activity must be identified and properly labeled, and their relationship with other participants must be established. In the second stage, a system of informal or extra-judicial remedies is added to the enumeration of rights and duties.

A participant relying on these practices must know, first of all, who the key parties are. Thus, he or she must be able to identify, for example, who is deemed a "carrier," and, within the category of carrier, who is a "drayage" or a "connecting" carrier. Similarly, he must also know the difference between a "forwarding agent" and a "freight forwarder," what services and responsibilities each of these parties should expect from the other, and so on. This is why a significant effort went into the preparation of NASTRAPS' glossary; its purpose is not only descriptive or educational, but also prescriptive, as each term entails an assumption of rights and duties. After the key parties and their functions are defined, the rights and duties of all the participants are articulated in chronological fashion, from the time of packaging the goods to that of claiming the damages or losses following delivery (or lack thereof).

The drafting of these practices has been inspired, in some measure, by the International Chamber of Commerce's highly influential INCO-TERMS and UCP. As with INCOTERMS, the transportation practices are set forth along a time line that commences when the buyer or his agent picks up the goods for transport from the seller's/exporter's warehouse, and ends with the carrier's delivery of the goods to the buyer's place of business. As with the UCP, the transportation contract is given independence from the underlying transaction and its enforceability is made to depend upon its own set of documents, whether on paper or in electronic form.

Yet a significant distinction exists between the UCP and the NAS-TRAPS: the latter, unlike the former, do not have their own set of sanctions or extra-judicial remedies. . . . Because the NASTRAPS is still in its first stage of formulation, it does not contain extra-judicial remedies. In order to get to this second (extra-judicial sanction) stage, the present set of directive expressions will have to prove itself. . . .

The above-described system of directives is believed to incorporate the best practices. Despite our concerted efforts, however, what we have selected as best practices may be displaced by other practices and directives Therefore, a reasonable trial time in the NAFTA marketplace is needed before extra-judicial sanctions can be attached to a violation of the NASTRAPS directives.

IN THE MATTER OF CROSS–BORDER TRUCKING SERVICES*

(Secretariat File No. USA–MEX–98–2008–01)

I. INTRODUCTION

A. THE DISPUTE

1. The Panel in this proceeding must decide whether the United States is in breach of Articles 1202 (national treatment for cross-border services) and/or 1203 (most-favored-nation treatment for cross-border services) of NAFTA by failing to lift its moratorium on the processing of applications by Mexican-owned trucking firms for authority to operate in the U.S. border states. Similarly, the Panel must decide whether the United States breached Articles 1102 (national treatment) and/or 1103 (most-favored-nation treatment) by refusing to permit Mexican investment in companies in the United States that provide transportation of international cargo. Given the expiration on December 17, 1995 of the Annex I reservation that the United States took to allowing cross-border trucking services and investment, the maintenance of the moratorium must be justified either under the language of Articles 1202 or 1203, or by some other provision of NAFTA, such as those found in Chapter Nine (standards) or by Article 2101 (general exceptions).

The Parties' views are summarized as follows:

2. **Mexico** contends that the United States has violated NAFTA by failing to phase out U.S. restrictions on cross-border trucking services and on Mexican investment in the U.S. trucking industry, as is required by the U.S. commitments in Annex I, despite affording Canada national treatment. Mexico believes such failure is a violation of the national treatment and most-favored-nation provisions found in Articles 1202 and 1203 (cross-border services) and Articles 1102 and 1103 (investment).

3. Mexico also contests the U.S. interpretation of Articles 1202 and 1203, without arguing that the Mexican regulatory system is equivalent to those of the United States and Canada. According to Mexico, Mexican trucking firms are entitled to the same rights as U.S. carriers under U.S. law, that is "(i) consideration on their individual merits and (ii) a full opportunity to contest the denial of operating authority." Any other approach is a violation of Articles 1202 and 1203. During the NAFTA negotiations, both governments understood that "motor carriers would have to comply fully with the

---

* Excerpts from Final Report of the [NAFTA Chapter 20] Panel, Feb. 6, 2001, http://www.NAFTA-sec-alena.org/

standards *of the country in which they were providing service.*" However, the obligations of the Parties were "not made contingent upon completion of the standards-capability work program" or the adoption of an identical regulatory system in Mexico.

4. Mexico asserts that the U.S. conduct must be reviewed in light of Article 102(2) of NAFTA, which requires that the "Parties shall interpret and apply the provisions of the [NAFTA] Agreement in the light of its objectives set out in paragraph 1." Among others, the objectives include eliminating barriers to trade in services and increasing investment opportunities "in accordance with applicable rules of international law." Mexico contends that the U.S. conduct does not further these objectives.

5. According to Mexico, "There are no exceptions to the relevant NAFTA provisions that could even potentially be applicable." Mexico contends that the U.S. failure to implement its cross-border trucking services and investment obligations is not justified by the standards provisions contained in Chapter Nine (standards) nor by Article 2101 (general exceptions), particularly in light of the fact that when NAFTA was negotiated the United States was well aware that Mexico's regulatory system was significantly different from those operating in the United States and Canada.

6. Mexico charges that the U.S. inaction is motivated not by safety concerns but by political considerations relating to opposition by organized labor in the United States to the implementation of NAFTA's cross-border trucking obligations.

7. The **United States** argues that because Mexico does not maintain the same rigorous standards as the regulatory systems in the United States and Canada, "the in like circumstances" language in Article 1202 means that service providers [from Mexico] may be treated differently in order to address a legitimate regulatory objective. Further, since the Canadian regulatory system is "equivalent" to that of the United States, it is not a violation of the most-favored-nation treatment under Article 1203 for the United States to treat Canadian trucking firms which are "in like circumstances" vis-a-vis U.S. trucking firms in a more favorable manner than Mexican trucking firms.

8. According to the United States, the inclusion in NAFTA Articles 1202 and 1203 of the phrase "in like circumstances" limits the national treatment and most-favored-nation obligations to circumstances with regard to trucking operations which are like, and that because "adequate procedures are not yet in place [in Mexico] to ensure U.S. highway safety," NAFTA permits "Parties to accord differential, and even less favorable, treatment where appropriate to meet legitimate regulatory objectives."

9. The United States believes its interpretation is confirmed by Article 2101, which provides that:

nothing in . . . Chapter Twelve (Cross–Border Trade in Services) . . . shall be construed to prevent the adoption or enforcement by any Party of measures necessary to secure compliance with laws or regulations that are not inconsistent with the provisions of this Agreement, including those relating to health and safety and consumer protection.

10. The United States also rejects Mexico's contention that the U.S. failure to implement Annex I with regard to cross-border trucking services and investment was politically motivated. At best, the United States contends, political motivation is "only of marginal relevance" to this case in the sense that highway safety has generated controversy in the United States. Moreover, the United States asserts that WTO practice is to avoid inquiring into the intent of parties accused of WTO violations. The issue, rather, is "whether Mexico has met its burden of proving a violation by the United States of its NAFTA obligations."

11. **Canada**, which exercised its right to participate in accordance with Article 2013, insists that the major issue in interpreting Article 1202 is a comparison between a foreign service provider providing services cross-border (here, from Mexico into the United States), and a service provider providing services domestically. Canada also contends that a "blanket" refusal by the United States to permit Mexican carriers to obtain operating authority to provide cross-border trucking services would necessarily be less favorable than the treatment accorded to United States' truck services in like circumstances. Canada also asserts that the United States is precluded from relying on Chapter Nine because levels of protection established under Chapter Nine must still be consistent with the national treatment requirements of Article 1202 and other NAFTA provisions.

* * *

VII. FINDINGS, DETERMINATIONS AND RECOMMENDATIONS

A. FINDINGS AND DETERMINATIONS

295. On the basis of the analysis set out above, the Panel unanimously determines that the U.S. blanket refusal to review and consider for approval any Mexican-owned carrier applications for authority to provide cross-border trucking services was and remains a breach of the U.S. obligations under Annex I (reservations for existing measures and liberalization commitments), Article 1202 (national treatment for cross-border services), and Article 1203 (most-favored-nation treatment for cross-border services) of NAFTA. An exception to these obligations is not authorized by the "in like circumstances" language in Articles 1202 and 1203, or by the exceptions set out in Chapter Nine or under Article 2101.

296. The Panel unanimously determines that the inadequacies of the Mexican regulatory system provide an insufficient legal basis for the United States to maintain a moratorium on the consideration of applications for U.S. operating authority from Mexican-owned and/or domiciled trucking service providers.

297. The Panel further unanimously determines that the United States was and remains in breach of its obligations under Annex I (reservations for existing measures and liberalization commitments), Article 1102 (national treatment), and Article 1103 (most-favored-nation treatment) to permit Mexican nationals to invest in enterprises in the United States that provide transportation of international cargo within the United States.

298. It is important to note what the Panel is not determining. It is not making a determination that the Parties to NAFTA may not set the level of protection that they consider appropriate in pursuit of legitimate regulatory objectives. It is not disagreeing that the safety of trucking services is a legitimate regulatory objective. Nor is the Panel imposing a limitation on the application of safety standards properly established and applied pursuant to the applicable obligations of the Parties under NAFTA. Furthermore, since the issue before the Panel concerns the so-called "blanket" ban, the Panel expresses neither approval nor disapproval of past determinations by appropriate regulatory authorities relating to the safety of any individual truck operators, drivers or vehicles, as to which the Panel did not receive any submissions or evidence.

B. RECOMMENDATIONS

299. The Panel recommends that the United States take appropriate steps to bring its practices with respect to cross-border trucking services and investment into compliance with its obligations under the applicable provisions of NAFTA.

300. The Panel notes that compliance by the United States with its NAFTA obligations would not necessarily require providing favorable consideration to all or to any specific number of applications from Mexican-owned trucking firms, when it is evident that a particular applicant or applicants may be unable to comply with U.S. trucking regulations when operating in the United States. Nor does it require that all Mexican-domiciled firms currently providing trucking services in the United States be allowed to continue to do so, if and when they fail to comply with U.S. safety regulations. The United States may not be required to treat applications from Mexican trucking firms in exactly the same manner as applications from U.S. or Canadian firms, as long as they are reviewed on a case by case basis. U.S. authorities are responsible for the safe operation of trucks within U.S. territory, whether ownership is U.S., Canadian or Mexican.

301. Similarly, it may not be unreasonable for a NAFTA Party to conclude that to ensure compliance with its own local standards by service providers from another NAFTA country, it may be necessary to implement different procedures with respect to such service providers. Thus, to the extent that the inspection and licensing requirements for Mexican trucks and drivers wishing to operate in the United States may not be "like" those in place in the United States, different methods of ensuring compliance with the U.S. regulatory regime may be justifiable. However, if in order to satisfy its own legitimate safety concerns the United States decides, exceptionally, to impose requirements on Mexican carriers that differ from those imposed on U.S. or Canadian carriers, then any such decision must (a) be made in good faith with respect to a legitimate safety concern and (b) implement differing requirements that fully conform with all relevant NAFTA provisions.

302. These considerations are inapplicable with regard to the U.S. refusal to permit Mexican nationals to invest in enterprises in the United States that provide transportation of international cargo within the United States, since both Mexico and the United States have agreed that such investment does not raise issues of safety.

[signatures omitted]

Note on the Aftermath of the Panel Decision

The Bush Administration announced immediately that it would comply with the Panel decision, reversing Clinton Administration policy, although timing remained uncertain. As a result, protests also began immediately. Bert Cadwell, a spokesman for the Teamsters Union, promised that "We will continue to fight the opening of the border until the Mexican government can guarantee their standards are higher and the U.S. can guarantee that we have the inspection facilities to keep unsafe trucks out." Joan Claybrook argued that "It is imperative that we continue to limit access for these dangerous trucks even if it means paying trade sanctions ... It is impossible to inspect every truck, and we cannot knowingly put drivers at risk by inviting dangerous rigs onto U.S. highways."* In May 2001, the Department of Transportation proposed rules "to Ensure Safety of Mexican Trucks and Buses Operating in the U.S." Those proposed rules included the establishment of a safety monitoring and compliance initiative to determine whether Mexican carriers operating in the United States were complying with applicable safety regulations. (DOT Press Release, May 1, 2001, FMCSA, 08–01.)

The debate between the Bush Administration and U.S. trucking interests, on one side, and the unions and citizens' groups, on the other, continued throughout most of 2001. A transportation funding bill passed by the Senate in August, over administration objections, and threats of a veto by the President and a filibuster by Senators McCain and Gramm, would have excluded Mexican trucks until a series of stringent inspection requirements had been met, a process the administration feared would take two

* See New York Times, Feb. 7, 2001, at A–12.

years or more. Ultimately, a compromise was struck in November 2001, resulting in legislation that in the absence of litigation would have permitted certification of Mexican trucking firms in 2002, after the safety obligations of the legislation were met. Litigation ensued, (see *infra*), but as of November 2004, the DOT appeared ready to begin issuing operating permits to a number of the hundreds of Mexican trucking firms that had applied for U.S. operating authority. (See DOT Appropriations Act, reproduced in the Document Supplement; Justice Thomas' opinion excerpts, *infra*.)

U.S. TRANSPORTATION DEPARTMENT IMPLEMENTS NAFTA PROVISIONS FOR MEXICAN TRUCKS, BUSES

(FEDERAL MOTOR CARRIER SAFETY ADMINISTRATION, NEWS RELEASE DOT 107–02, NOV. 27, 2002)

U.S. Transportation Secretary Norman Y. Mineta today directed the U.S. Department of Transportation's Federal Motor Carrier Safety Administration (FMCSA) to act on the 130 applications received thus far from Mexico-domiciled truck and bus companies seeking to transport international cargo in cross-border services in the United States or to provide regular route services between Mexico and the United States.

Secretary Mineta's action was prompted today when President Bush modified the moratorium on granting operating authority to Mexican motor carriers. The President's action means that the United States has fulfilled its obligations under the North American Free Trade Agreement (NAFTA) and that Mexican truck and regular-route bus service into the U.S. interior can begin. As a practical matter, this service will begin only after the FMCSA reviews Mexican carrier applications and grants provisional operating authority to qualified Mexican truck and bus companies seeking this authority.

"By modifying the moratorium, President Bush has made good on his commitment to open the border to international trucking and cross-border regular route bus service. This will help increase trade between our countries," Secretary Mineta said. "Mexican carriers and drivers must meet the same standards as U.S. operators. I have made a lifelong commitment to equality under the law and will not, however, tolerate discriminatory enforcement. In this matter of trucking, as in all the modes of transportation, the pervasive issue is safety."

Secretary Mineta added, "We look forward to working with Mexico, in the same way that we already are cooperating with the Canadians, as we synchronize our activities in advance of opening the border for expanded passenger bus and truck operations."

Kenneth M. Mead, the Inspector General of the Department of Transportation, stated: "The Department has worked diligently and aggressively to fulfill the requirement for establishing a strong safety program before the southern border was opened to long-haul Mexican truck traffic. This objective has been met by having in place a sufficient number of inspectors, adequate facilities and space for inspections, measures to ensure that licenses are valid and that motor carrier firms pass safety and compliance reviews. These actions are testimony that this Secretary and the Department place a high value on safety. As mandated by Congress, we will continue to review and report on the implementation of these requirements."

Mexican trucking firms that receive operating authority as a result of this process will be permitted to deliver and back-haul cargo to and from the United States. Similarly, Mexico-domiciled bus companies will be permitted to schedule regular passenger service to and from points in Mexico and the United States. Mexico is obligated under NAFTA to provided expanded access for U.S. carriers.

The change in the moratorium today affects only international cargo and service between the United States and Mexico. It left in place the moratorium on permits to Mexico-domiciled motor carriers for providing truck or bus services between points in the United States.

The FMCSA, which regulates interstate truck and bus safety, will be granting operating authority only to Mexican motor carriers that comply with all U.S. safety standards and insurance requirements. The agency has established a detailed application process and a comprehensive safety monitoring program, which are intended to ensure that only Mexican carriers capable of fully complying with U.S. safety regulations operate in the United States. Individual applications are being reviewed and as soon as all the administrative steps are completed, including completion of on-site safety audits, qualified motor carriers will be granted provisional operating authority.

The Department will continue to work closely with the Department of Justice, the Office of Homeland Security, and other relevant federal agencies to help ensure the security of the border and prevent potential threats to national security.

* * *

Mexican drivers will be subject to U.S. drug and alcohol requirements. They also must follow U.S. hours of service rules to ensure that they have sufficient rest to drive safely, and they must maintain logs to prove it to safety inspectors. To drive in the United States, commercial drivers from Mexico must have a Licencia Federal, the Mexican equivalent of a U.S. commercial driver's license. In a 1991 memorandum of understanding, the United States and Mexico established reciprocity between the Mexican Licencia Federal and the U.S. commercial driver's license. The 1991 memorandum includes recognition by the United States that Mexican truck drivers who possess a Licencia Federal also meet U.S. medical requirements. U.S. and Mexican truck inspectors can access federal and state databases in the United States and Mexico during an inspection to check whether a driver's license is valid.

To receive operating authority, all Mexico-domiciled carriers must undergo a safety audit by the FMCSA. During these audits, inspectors assess a carrier's safety posture and assist applicants with information concerning U.S. safety regulations and help ensure that these carriers have methods in place to comply with the safety regulations. The United States and Mexico will share safety data generated on both sides of the border in such audits by U.S. officials. Of the 130 Mexico-domiciled motor carriers that have applied to begin cross-border long-haul cargo service into the United States, approximately half are ready for safety audits.

To help ensure safety, Mexican carriers granted authority to operate in the United States beyond the border commercial zones also will receive a formal compliance review within the first 18 months of operation. Carriers that receive and maintain satisfactory compliance ratings will be awarded permanent operating authority at the end of the 18–month period of operating under provisional operating authority.

All Mexican trucks and buses operating in the United States will be required to display a valid Commercial Vehicle Safety Alliance (CVSA) inspection decal. These decals, valid for 90 days, indicate a vehicle has passed a safety inspection by a qualified inspector. Likewise, Mexican truck and bus companies will be required to carry U.S. insurance while operating in the United States.

In addition to the 130 Mexico-domiciled motor carriers that have applied to operate beyond the border commercial zones in the United States, 854 Mexico-domiciled motor carriers have applied to the Federal Motor Carrier Safety Administration for provisional certificates of registration to operate in the border commercial zones. Of these 854 applicants, the FMCSA has issued provisional certificates to 459.

* * *

DEPARTMENT OF TRANSPORTATION ET AL v. PUBLIC CITIZEN ET AL.
124 S.Ct. 2204, 541 U.S. 752 (2004).

Justice Thomas delivered the opinion of the [unanimous] court.

* * *

The Government of Mexico challenged the United States' implementation of NAFTA's motor carrier provisions under NAFTA's dispute-resolution process, and in February 2001, an international arbitration panel determined that the United States' "blanket refusal" of Mexican motor carrier applications breached the United States' obligations under NAFTA. Shortly thereafter, the President made clear his intention to lift the moratorium on Mexican motor carrier certification following the preparation of new regulations governing grants of operating authority to Mexican motor carriers.

In May 2001, FMCSA [Federal Motor Carrier Safety Administration] published for comment proposed rules concerning safety regulation of Mexican motor carriers. One rule (the Application Rule) addressed the establishment of a new application form for Mexican motor carriers that seek authorization to operate within the United States. Another rule (the Safety Monitoring Rule) addressed the establishment of a safety-inspection regime for all Mexican motor carriers that would receive operating authority under the Application Rule.

In December 2001, Congress enacted the Department of Transportation and Related Agencies Appropriations Act, 2002, 115 Stat. 833. Section 350 of this Act, *id.,* at 864, provided that no funds appropriated under the Act could be obligated or expended to review or to process any application by a Mexican motor carrier for authority to operate in the interior of the United States until FMCSA implemented specific application and safety-monitoring requirements for Mexican carriers. Some of these requirements went beyond those proposed by FMCSA in the Application and Safety Monitoring Rules. Congress extended the § 350 conditions to appropriations for Fiscal Years 2003 and 2004.

In January 2002, acting pursuant to NEPA's [National Environmental Policy Act] mandates, FMCSA issued a programmatic EA [Environmental Assessment] for the proposed Application and Safety Monitoring Rules. FMCSA's EA evaluated the environmental impact associated with three separate scenarios: where the President did not lift the moratorium; where the President did but where (contrary to what was legally possible) FMCSA did not issue any new regulations; and the Proposed Action Alternative, where the President would modify the moratorium and where FMCSA would adopt the proposed regulations. The EA considered the environmental impact in the categories of traffic and congestion, public safety and health, air quality, noise, socioeconomic factors, and environmental justice. Vital to the EA's analysis, however, was the assumption that there would be no change in trade volume between the United States and Mexico due to the issuance of the regulations. FMCSA did note that § 350's restrictions made it impossible for Mexican motor carriers to operate in the interior of the United States before FMCSA's issuance of the regulations. But, FMCSA determined that "this and any other associated effects in trade characteristics would be the result of the modification of the moratorium" by the President, not a result of FMCSA's implementation of the proposed safety regulations. App. 60. Because FMCSA concluded that the entry of the Mexican trucks was not an "effect" of its regulations, it did not consider any environmental impact that might be caused by the increased presence of Mexican trucks within the United States.

The particular environmental effects on which the EA focused, then, were those likely to arise from the increase in the number of roadside inspections of Mexican trucks and buses due to the proposed regulations. The EA concluded that these effects (such as a slight increase in emissions, noise from the trucks, and possible danger to passing motorists) were minor and could be addressed and avoided in the inspections process itself. The EA also noted that the increase of inspection-related emissions would be at least partially offset by the fact that the safety requirements would reduce the number of Mexican trucks operating in the United States. Due to these calculations, the EA concluded that the issuance of the proposed regulations would have no significant impact on the environment, and hence FMCSA, on the same day as it released the EA, issued a FONSI.

On March 19, 2002, FMCSA issued the two interim rules, delaying their effective date until May 3, 2002, to allow public comment on provisions that FMCSA added to satisfy the requirements of § 50. In the regulatory preambles, FMCSA relied on its EA and its FONSI to demonstrate compliance with NEPA. FMCSA also addressed the CAA [Clean Air Act] in the preambles, determining that it did not need to perform a "conformity review" of the proposed regulations under 42 U. S. C. § 7506(c)(1) because the increase in emissions from these regulations would fall below the Environmental Protection Agency's (EPA's) threshold levels needed to trigger such a review.

In November 2002, the President lifted the moratorium on qualified Mexican motor carriers. Before this action, however, respondents filed petitions for judicial review of the Application and Safety Monitoring Rules, arguing that the rules were promulgated in violation of NEPA and the CAA. The Court of Appeals agreed with respondents, granted the petitions, and set aside the rules. 316 F. 3d 1002 (CA9 2003).

The Court of Appeals concluded that the EA was deficient because it failed to give adequate consideration to the overall environmental impact of lifting the moratorium on the cross-border operation of Mexican motor carriers. According to the Court of Appeals, FMCSA was required to consider the environmental effects of the entry of Mexican trucks because "the President's rescission of the moratorium was 'reasonably foreseeable' at the time the EA was prepared and the decision not to prepare an EIS [Environmental Impact Statement] was made ..." Due to this perceived deficiency, the Court of Appeals remanded the case for preparation of a full EIS.

The Court of Appeals also directed FMCSA to prepare a full CAA conformity determination for the challenged regulations. It concluded that FMCSA's determination that emissions attributable to the challenged rules would be below the threshold levels was not reliable because the agency's CAA determination reflected the "illusory distinction between the effects of the regulations themselves and the effects of the presidential rescission of the moratorium on Mexican truck entry."

We granted certiorari, 540 U.S. ___ (2003) and now reverse.

* * *

We hold that where an agency has no ability to prevent a certain effect due to its limited statutory authority over the relevant actions, the agency cannot be considered a legally relevant "cause" of the effect. Hence, under NEPA and the implementing CEQ [Commission on Environmental Quality] regulations, the agency need not consider these effects in its EA when determining whether its action is a "major Federal action." Because the President, not FMCSA, could authorize (or not authorize) cross-border operations from Mexican motor carriers, and because FMCSA has no discretion to prevent the entry of Mexican trucks, its EA did not need to consider the environmental effects arising from the entry.

* * *

Unlike the regulations implementing NEPA, the EPA's CAA regulations have defined the term "[c]aused by." *Ibid.* In particular, emissions are "[c]aused by" a Federal action if the "emissions ... would not ... occur in the absence of the Federal action." *Ibid.* Thus, the EPA has made clear that for purposes of evaluating causation in the conformity review process, some sort of "but for" causation is sufficient.

Although arguably FMCSA's proposed regulations would be "but for" causes of the entry of Mexican trucks into the United States, the emissions from these trucks are neither "direct" nor "indirect" emissions. First, the emissions from the Mexican trucks are not "direct" because they will not occur at the same time or at the same place as the promulgation of the regulations.

Second, FMCSA cannot practicably control, nor will it maintain control, over these emissions. As discussed above, FMCSA does not have the ability to countermand the President's decision to lift the moratorium, nor could it act categorically to prevent Mexican carriers from being registered or Mexican trucks from entering the United States. Once the regulations are promulgated, FMCSA would have no ability to regulate any aspect of vehicle exhaust from these Mexican trucks. FMCSA could not refuse to register Mexican motor carriers simply on the ground that their trucks would pollute excessively.

* * *

The emissions from the Mexican trucks are neither "direct" nor "indirect" emissions caused by the issuance of FMCSA's proposed regulations. Thus, FMCSA did not violate the CAA or the applicable regulations by failing to consider them when it evaluated whether it needed to perform a full "conformity determination."

* * *

Questions and Comments

1. What is the problem? Is the issue one regarding the "foreign" *trucks and buses*, or the "foreign" *drivers*? Or does it not matter because it is really unions demanding no access? Or are there other concerns, such as crime (truck and cargo hijacking, drug trafficking), immigration or customs delays? Are trucks very different than buses for purposes of regulation and cross-border access?

2. Cross-border *bus* and *truck* transportation are usually *considered* separately, but in rules and regulations often *treated* the same. *Truck* transportation from Mexico to the U.S. phases in with such transportation first allowed (in 1997–but delayed) only to the four border states, and later (in 2000–also delayed) throughout the U.S. Bus transportation to *all* locations in the U.S. was to be allowed by 1997 (but delayed). The U.S. did not establish such reservations with regard to trucks from Canada. Why? Mexico agreed to allow Canadian and U.S. trucking companies to operate cross-border services to the six Mexican border states in 1997 (delayed), bus services to anywhere in Mexico in 1997 (delayed), and truck service to anywhere in Mexico in 2000 (delayed). Mexico's delays are mostly because of U.S. delays. Canada has no limitations on U.S. trucks or buses. Which means that U.S. trucks and buses enter Canada. Canada also has no limitations on

Mexican trucks and buses, and Mexican trucks are able to transit the U.S. without U.S. operating authority. (They are presumably subject to U.S. safety and insurance requirements while in the United States.)

Tour or charter buses obtained full cross-border permission at the inception of NAFTA. Why are they treated differently than scheduled bus service? There have been a number of cross-border bus operators calling themselves tour or charter carriers, but effectively operating scheduled services.

3. *Vehicle and driver safety issues.* According to a 2001 General Accounting Office report (GAO), quoting DOT figures, the number of northbound truck crossings increased from 2.7 million in 1994 to over 4.3 million in 2001. About 80,000 trucks crossed the border in 2000; 63,000 of those were estimated to be of Mexican origin. (Most of these, of course, were the short-haul "mules," hauling trailers from the Mexican side of the border zone to the U.S. side.) An earlier (1998) report uses GAO statistics to compare inspection failure rates at the border of both Mexican and U.S. trucks. It raises one matter which seems easily corrected, the failure of Mexico to require records of drivers' hours, to limit drivers' hours, to mandate front wheel brakes, and Mexico's allowance of heavier (97,000 pound gross weight, but Leming notes 130,000 pound) trucks than the U.S. (80,000 pound gross weight). But it also notes that Mexico bars 53 foot trailers allowed in the U.S., limiting Mexican trucks to 48 feet. When common grounds are reached, will it be a race for the bottom, meaning that all trucks will be at least 53 feet, have gross weight limits of 97,000 pounds, and no front wheel brake requirements? For example, unsuccessful in increasing work hours up to 80 hours per week in the U.S., U.S. trucking firms apparently have urged that Canadian rules be changed to allow 80 hours (from the current 60), with the hope that once established, the Canadian rules would have to be adopted by the U.S. to make the rules standard throughout the NAFTA area.

AFL–CIO Transportation Trades Department head Hall is "horrified" about the deaths in the industry each year in the U.S., and that opening the borders to Mexican trucks will increase these dismal statistics. Should he be concentrating on improving the U.S. record? The testimony of Amalgamated Transit Union (AFL–CIO) President La Sala focuses on the lack of very extensive inspection of Mexican buses entering the U.S. Note how the U.S. bus industry emphasizes that a bus is not a truck. The U.S. bus industry (owners and drivers) is concerned that the rules applicable to driving *trucks* are imposed on bus drivers. Trucks appear to cause far more accidents than buses, as the comments of the Director of Highway Safety Osterman emphasize. The U.S. truck *industry* has succeeded in increasing the size of trucks, which appears directly related to the increased number of fatal accidents. Would the U.S. truck and bus industry be more successful by working together in establishing international regulations? One might suggest that they have been very successful to date; cross-border truck and bus transportation from Mexico to the U.S. has been blocked by these industries. To some degree, the industry is in a quandary, it tries to forestall the adoption of new regulations (which will cost the industry money), but the adoption of such regulations, and their application to Mexican trucks and buses and their drivers will very likely further delay opening the border, as Mexico tries to catch up to the changing U.S. standards. Shouldn't the standards be NAFTA standards, and not separate member state standards?

Truck and driver safety issues (and now pollution) appear to be the principal unresolved issues. Causing a delay in implementation of full cross-border service. Mexican drivers are not required to maintain logbooks, for example. The GAO reported in 2001 that Mexico had taken many steps to improve both commercial vehicle safety and emissions, but opined that compliance with U.S. safety standards remained "unclear." (See GAO, "Coordinated Operational Plan Needed to Ensure Mexican Trucks" Compliance with U.S. Standards," Dec. 2001; Congressional Research Service Report on Trucking Problems at the U.S.–Mexico Border (1998).

4. *Border inspections.* The testimony of Mineta, and the November 2002 press statement, seem to place the focus on border inspections. If there are fair standards and inspections, the problem will be much reduced. Thus, the border is where some changes are being made so that the U.S. opens to Mexican trucks without jeopardizing U.S. highway safety. Even when the safety issues are resolved, there will be some continuing process of inspection at the border; it is an integral element of the 2001 legislation. On paper, at least, the legislation and the funding demonstrates the readiness of the U.S. to undertake adequate inspections of trucks and checking status (especially proper licensing) of drivers at the border. Cazamias mentions this, and also that Mexico was opening its border to U.S. vehicles, and when the U.S. did not, it was the U.S. government which helped Mexico find a justification for reconsidering and stopping the entry—essentially using an argument of reciprocity.

5. *Customs issues.* Even if trucks were able to move freely across the borders due to safety concerns, there remains a problem with customs. In a free trade area, shouldn't goods move through the borders without customs checks? Corruption within the Mexican customs service, and the under invoicing of imports, has been a serious problem for Mexico. Customs officials routinely allow imports in exchange for bribes, and often subject Mexicans returning to Mexico with cash earnings to extortion demands. Mexico adopted a new customs law on May 1, 1999, which allows further checking of invoice prices with average prices of similar imports. Post 9/11 concerns over terrorism have led to a variety of new security measures at the U.S.–Mexican and U.S.–Canadian borders, and the introduction of a host of new electronic measures for cargo and personal inspection. (See the U.S. Customs and Border Protection website, http://www.customs.treas.gov.)

6. *Records.* To some degree the reason for retaining the moratorium shifted from a blanket accusation that Mexican trucks are unsafe and drivers are inadequate, to the lack of sufficient enforcement procedures in the U.S. to undertake an adequate review of records which monitor the fulfillment of safety standards. Mexican trucks have successfully entered the U.S. and been stopped in two dozen *non*-border states. Some have even gone on to Canada; legally, the DOT does not have authority to regulate Mexican trucks carrying cargo directly to Canada. Mexico does not require the trucking form of records mandated in the U.S., but Mexico is trying to establish a database of truck information, and is re-licensing Mexican trucks. The U.S. insists on

having the history of the trucks, especially maintenance records, before U.S. operating licenses are granted.

7. *Truck hijacking.* Truck hijacking is a serious problem in Mexico, as outlined in the Congressional Research Service Report. There is evidence that organized groups involved in drugs have switched to hijacking because the profits are high and risk of severe penalties is very low. There are ongoing attempts to develop a uniform cargo liability regime which would more fairly distribute the losses due to cargo thefts. Is the threat to U.S. trucks and drivers a justification for delaying implementation of the NAFTA provisions?

8. *Immigration.* To what extent does the U.S. concern for illegal immigration from Mexico affect the opening of U.S. borders to trucks and buses?

9. *Politics.* The Cazamias comment gives us the history of the trucking dispute between the U.S. and Mexico, with opposition by U.S. unions and highway safety organizations causing the U.S. DOT to oppose opening the U.S. border according to the NAFTA schedule. This opposition was most successful in Congress and in the federal court litigation, which delayed implementation of the NAFTA rules for over six years before and nearly three and a half years after the panel decision. See also Hale E. Sheppard, *The NAFTA Trucking Dispute: Pretexts for Noncompliance and Policy Justifications for U.S. Facilitation of Cross Border Services,* 11 Minn. J. Global Trade 235 (2002).

10. Why did Public Citizen and the Teamsters litigate on the basis of alleged environmental concerns, rather than safety issues? The Supreme Court decision hardly mentions NAFTA; it is an exercise in statutory interpretation, with a very narrow holding. Post-decision, the Department of Transportation should proceed to certify Mexican applications.

11. *Role of NAFTA.* The above illustrates the main problems with cross-border transportation. The January, 1992, comments in the Mexico Trade & Law Reporter outline the status then of restrictions on U.S. motor carriers access to Mexico, and Mexican access to the U.S. Mexican access to the U.S. effectively may include access to Canada. How many of the noted problems has NAFTA resolved?

Annex 913.5 establishes a framework for the development of technical and safety trucking standards by 2000. Areas to address include vehicle weights and dimensions, maintenance and repair, driver's medical standards, non-medical testing and licensing, and hazardous materials transportation. The standards have not been developed.

12. *Solutions.* Could Servicios prior to certification of Mexican trucks, have established a distribution center in Laredo where it would warehouse all goods for sale in the U.S.? It would own a fleet of U.S. trucks driven by U.S. drivers for the transportation throughout the U.S. If the first stage (access to the four U.S. border states) had been achieved, why couldn't access have been extended a little more so that the distribution centers could be in Houston or Dallas, perhaps a better location for business reasons? Some observers believe that the volume of Mexican trucks entering the United States will be modest. Assume that Servicios has obtained certifica-

tion from the Department Transportation, satisfying DOT that it will be able to meet the safety and monitoring requirements imposed by the law and regulations, what additional problems will it face in making a successful international freight business? Note the requirement of obtaining U.S. insurance and the difficulties of finding another "international cargo" in the U.S. destination city to avoid having to return to Mexico empty. (NAFTA does not authorize Mexican trucking firms to carry cargo from one U.S. city to another U.S. city.) Are problems with drivers–immigration restrictions and English language fluency–likely to be easy to resolve? How do these same issues affect American trucking firms interested in serving Mexico?

13. The different legal systems have led to different transportation documents, such as bills of lading. This means a different bill of lading for each national segment of the shipment. The National Law Center for Inter–American Free Trade (NLCIFT) in Tucson, Arizona, has been working on a uniform bill of lading for use throughout the NAFTA area for almost a decade. The Center is developing North American Standard Transportation practices (NASTRAPS), as explained in the foreword by Professor and Center President Kozolchyk. Further harmonization is needed in insurance policies, hazard waste/materials manifests, and secured lending instruments, some of which are also projects of this excellent Center. Servicios, for portions of its carriage in the United States, will of course be subject to U.S. rules regarding carrier liability for lost or damaged cargo.

Note that the NASTRAPS are designed to be similar to INCOTERMS and the UCP, two products of the International Chamber of Commerce in Paris, which are commonly used in documentary sales and letters of credit, respectively. They are accepted and applied by courts as rules chosen by the parties to agreements. Are the NASTRAPS likely to receive such acceptance? But Professor Kozolchyk is careful to explain that gaining the standing of INCOTERMS and the UCP will take time and acceptance. The NLCIFT is also working on developing a uniform regime for carrier liability for merchandise loss or damage. Carrier liability limits are very different in the three NAFTA nations, and have been the most important factor blocking further progress.

14. Many groups are interested in the trucking issue. For example, the Florida tomato growers have challenged Mexico for dumping tomatoes, but have also noted the lack of safety of their trucks. If tomatoes must be handled at the border, there is both an added cost and an added possibility of damage or spoilage for this fragile fruit. See John J. Van Sickle, A Compromise in the Fresh Tomato Trade Dispute, 11 Fla. J. Int'l L. 399, 400 (1997).

15. Another dimension of the problem is foreign investment in the trucking and bus industry. The final extract from the Mexico Trade & Law reporter briefly notes where investment is headed. How did the NAFTA panel treat the investment issues? Could the United States reasonably cite safety concerns as grounds for preventing a Mexican firm from purchasing a U.S. registered trucking company? Will increased investment help to eliminate the vehicle and driver problems discussed above? Note that President Bush eliminated the bar to Mexican investment in U.S. trucking firms and bus companies in June 2001. See "Bush Kills Mexican Investment Moratorium for Trucking, Buses," Inside US Trade, Jun. 8, 2001.

PROBLEM 6.3 FINANCIAL SERVICES: BANKWEST PLANS NEW FULL SERVICE OFFICES IN CANADA AND MEXICO

SECTION I. THE SETTING

Mergers of banks in a dozen western states resulted in the creation of BankWest (BW), with headquarters in San Francisco. Now the bank wishes to have "West" mean Western Hemisphere rather than Western U.S., by extending its activities to Canada and Mexico.

Mexico

BankWest would like to either acquire a major Mexican bank which already has many branches, or begin to establishes branches or subsidiaries by acquisition or new investments.

Canada

BankWest would like to acquire the Commonwealth Bank group in Canada. The Commonwealth Bank group includes many banks throughout Canada, and would almost double the size of the BW. The Commonwealth Bank group is considered a Schedule I bank in Canada. The weak Canadian dollar makes an acquisition all the more attractive at this time. A second possibility is for BankWest to begin to acquire or open smaller local banks and operate them either as subsidiaries or branches.

You have been retained as a lawyer to help the expansion of the BankWest into Mexico and Canada, having been on the NAFTA committee that drafted Chapter 14 on Financial Services.

SECTION II. FOCUS OF CONSIDERATION

Chapter 12 of NAFTA, which is entitled Cross–Border Trade in Services, does not cover financial services. Chapter 14 addresses these special services, just as Chapter 13 is a special chapter governing telecommunications services. Chapter 14 includes only 16 articles, plus six annexes. But it covers a broad range of financial services issues, including special provisions which govern financial services dispute resolution. Furthermore, General Annex VII to NAFTA, which contains reservations to the free trade commitments, includes 14 pages of U.S. reservations, 4 pages of Canadian reservations, and 22 pages of Mexican reservations.

NAFTA Chapter 14, as is the case for much of the NAFTA, has its origins in CFTA. Although CFTA provided a sound base for the drafters of NAFTA to build upon, the financial provisions of the CFTA addressed very different issues than the provisions of NAFTA, recognizing that Canada and the United States each had separately developed a complex regulatory process for financial institutions. Each system included some protectionist features, but each nation was for the most part committed to deregulation, although Canada continued to protect its largest, or

Schedule I, banks. Neither nation sought meaningful new financial services trade advantages in the CFTA negotiations, both wanted some assurances that they would not be disfavored by new rules, or amendments to current regulatory rules, and both affirmed that the provisions would only provide a temporary stage in a process that would liberalize financial services.

Chapter 17 of CFTA governed financial services. Five articles plus definitions covered principally separate, specific commitments of each nation. When NAFTA was negotiated, the financial services provisions assumed a different focus than in the earlier CFTA. The NAFTA financial services provisions are mainly about obtaining specific commitments from Mexico to open its previously closed banking system to participation by U.S. and Canadian banks. As Ewell Murphy, frequent writer on Mexican investment laws, has appropriately noted, "Where FTA whispered hopeful ambiguities, NAFTA articulates explicit promises."[1]

For Mexico, addressing the financial services sector in negotiating the NAFTA was a challenge to its historic resistance to foreign investment in financial services, and the turmoil of the banking industry in the 1980s. NAFTA is an especially significant commitment for Mexico, which had at least until the mid–1980s possessed a general framework of laws and regulations which were trade and investment restrictive. Notably restrictive have been Mexican financial laws. The financial sector was essentially closed to foreign participation under the 1973 foreign investment law. Banking was largely in private, Mexican ownership. But lame-duck President López Portillo nationalized the banks in August, 1982, at a time of crisis for Mexico when the nation defaulted on its debt and implemented currency controls.

In 1990, under the Salinas de Gortari administration, banks were re-privatized, and the Act to Regulate Financial Groups was passed to allow Mexico to meet commitments it intended to make in the preparation for NAFTA. NAFTA and the new Mexican legislation added something to Mexican financial services it had never confronted—foreign competition. The 1993 Mexican Foreign Investment Law, and amendments in 1996, further liberalized foreign investment in financial institutions, likely assisting in the recovery from the December, 1994, peso devaluation in the first month of the Zedillo administration, a financial crisis outgoing President Salinas refused to address in his final months in office, concerned that it would harm his chances at becoming the first head of the new WTO. Disclosures of his corruption in office soon foreclosed that opportunity. Under President Zedillo, with pressures from the 1994 crisis and the need to attract foreign capital continuing, further liberalization toward foreign participation occurred in 1998, with the elimination of most of the remaining restrictions on foreign ownership of banks operating in Mexico (permitting 100% foreign ownership).

1. Ewell E. Murphy, Jr., "Access and Protection for Foreign Investment in Mexico under Mexico's New Foreign Investment Law and the North American Free Trade Agreement," 10 ICSID Review: Foreign Investment L.J. 54 (1995).

Whatever has been the motivation for financial services liberalization in Mexico since NAFTA began, the changes in Mexico in opening its financial services sector to foreign participation is quite the opposite from the continued refusal of the U.S. to open its borders to the trucking services sector, as discussed in the previous problem.

BankWest has been pleased to learn that investment in the Mexican banking industry has been facilitated by NAFTA and further post-NAFTA liberalization, and that the Central Bank under Guillermo Ortiz since 1998 has greatly reduced inflation and fluctuations in interest rates. Despite the acquisition of major Mexican banks by U.S. and Spanish financial services conglomerates, BankWest is hopeful that there is room for expansion into Mexico at this time, and that Mexico's financial services will continue to become less restrictive–and more profitable–in the next decade. BankWest is impressed with the recent changes, but remains concerned with continuing risk factors in the Mexican banking sector, including but not limited to executing against collateral for loans that go bad. At minimum, BankWest wants to know what it is permitted to do now in expanding to Mexico. BankWest has a sense that while financial services legislation has been a dynamic process in Mexico in recent years, change has slowed due to disagreements between President Fox and the PRI opposition in Congress. Also, the Bank is aware that stability in banking in developing nations is affected by many actions, both internal and external, including, in the case of Mexico, competition with China and other countries for the foreign investment dollar, and dependence on the United States for most trade in goods and services.

The devaluation of the Mexican peso in December, 1994, was difficult for the Mexican banking industry to survive. Mexico required several years and a US$40 billion U.S. loan program (all repaid early with interest) to recover from this crisis. The Asian and Russian banking crises of 1997–1998 were not helpful to Mexican banking stability, but did not have a major adverse impact. Other foreign banks have voted confidence in the Mexican banking system through their pocketbooks. The Bank of Montreal and Bank of Nova Scotia in Canada, Bilbao and Santander in Spain, and Citibank in the United States, have all purchased controlling interests in Mexican banks. The Citibank acquisition of Banamex, in May 2001, involved an investment of US$12.5 billion.

In mid–1999 a new financial crisis in Mexico was not out of the question, but was averted, in the view of many, by the Central Bank's insistence on maintaining high interest rates to control inflation. Since that time, the Mexican peso has been highly stable, depreciating only in 2002 by a modest amount at a time when it was considered overvalued by international traders and government officials. These actions have given BankWest considerable confidence in Mexico's banking and financial stability, but it is aware that there will be a presidential election in July 2006, with the usual uncertainties, as well as a history in Mexico of the ruling party manipulating the economy for political means in the runup to the election.

Part A explores opening banks in Canada and Mexico by BankWest. Part B focuses on dispute resolution in financial services under NAFTA.

NAFTA Chapters 11 and 14 are essential to an analysis of this problem. They are found in the Documents Supplement.

SECTION III. READINGS, QUESTIONS AND COMMENTS

PART A. CROSS–BORDER EXPANSION OF BANKING SERVICES WITHIN NAFTA

Comment on Foreign Banking in Mexico in 1999

The banking crisis of 1994 has disclosed a banking system with serious weaknesses, and especially deficiencies in effective government regulation. Corruption has not missed the banking sector, allegations have been made that since closed banks illegally financed the ruling party's (PRI) presidential campaign in 1994. The World Bank has tried to impress upon Mexico the need for reform, but reform tends to follow banking disasters, rather than rational planning. Banks nearing insolvency sometimes take on high risks as a bailout gamble. Professor Charles Calomiris of the Columbia Business School, commented that one effect of the 1994 crisis:

> was the commitment to allow greater foreign entry into the system. This, the most meaningful banking reform during crisis, was expanded in December 1998 with the lifting of remaining barriers to foreign ownership. Before the crisis, only Citibank and Santander operated banks in Mexico, with limited size and activities. But today new foreign entry has transformed Mexican banking. The competitive pressure from that entry, more than anything else, is driving the push for reform of the domestic banking system. Incompetent and corrupt domestic banks are faced with the choice of either losing customers or transforming themselves into viable banks.

Wall Street Journal, July 16, 1999, at A15.

ROGERS AND ZUBIKAIRI ARRIOLA, FOREIGN BANKS IN MEXICO: ON THE VERGE OF A NEW ERA?
7 U.S.–Mexico L.J. 11 (1999).*

By 1882 foreign investors had established significant stakes in the Mexican banking system. It has been estimated that at that time foreign investors controlled as much as 94% of the capital of the Mexican system. Of the total foreign investment, 60% was from France, 21% from the United States, 11% from England, 7% from Germany and 1% from the Netherlands. Banco Nacional de México ("Banamex") was then controlled by French investors who owned 70% of its stock. Investors from France also owned 46% of the capital of Banco de Londres, Sudamérica y México ("Banco de Londres"), 60% of Banco Central Mexicano, 50% of the Banco del Estado de México and 34% of Banco Peninsular Mexicano. Major institutional investors included the Société

Financière pour l'Industrie au Mexique, the Société Franco–Suisse pour l'Industrie Électrique and the Société Financière Franco–Suisse. The investments were in both commercial banks and in specialized mortgage banks around the country.

U.S. investors had minority interests in Banamex, Banco de Londres and others, and controlled the Banco Internacional Hipotecario de México. There was a U.S.-owned institution called "American Bank" with offices in Mexico City and in Torreón, and trust companies such as "United States and Mexico Trust Company" and "International Bank and Trust Company of America." Other interests were scattered around Mexico, in various regional and small banks. British investment seems to have been concentrated initially in the Banco de Londres, but British investors evidently relinquished control of that bank to French and U.S. investors at some point. Clearly the foreign investment during this period was overwhelmingly European in nature, with European investors having 79% of the total; U.S. investors were a relatively small factor, with only 21% of the total.

Banco de Londres (founded in 1864) and Banamex (founded in 1881) were by far the largest banks in Mexico during most of the administration of the dictator/President Porfirio Díaz (often called the "Porfiriato"), particularly from 1890 to 1911. Many of the other banks were based outside of Mexico City. In 1875 the Chihuahua state legislature chartered the Banco de Santa Eulalia, and in 1878 a similar charter was granted to the Banco Mexicano by such legislature; each bank was owned by U.S. investors. The Banco de Nuevo León was founded in 1891 and grew rapidly during the Porfiriato; by 1910 it had taken the place of Banco de Londres as the second largest bank in the country.

During this period two key laws were enacted affecting the banking system, the Commercial Code of 1884 and the General Law of Credit Institutions adopted in 1897, which established a set of general rules to replace a system of concessions and privileges that greatly favored the largest banks. Nevertheless the 1897 law ratified the position of Banamex and Banco de Londres as the only banks authorized to issue banknotes in the Federal District.

Domestic investment in the banking sector gradually increased during the Porfiriato, and the reduction of British investment in Banco de Londres in favor of local investors was encouraged or forced by President Díaz. The other foreign-owned banks were also increasingly encouraged to accept Mexican investors as joint-venture partners. The Mexican Revolution began in 1910, and the revolutionary turmoil sharply affected the foreign-owned banks; a number of them became insolvent, and others became Mexican-owned with the sale of controlling interests to Mexican shareholders. The only new foreign entrant into the banking sector was National City Bank of New York (later called First National City Bank and then Citibank), which established a branch office in 1929 primarily to finance trade between Mexico and the U.S.

From the end of the Revolution until 1965, it seems to have been legally possible for additional foreign banks to establish a presence in Mexico, but economic and political conditions were not sufficiently encouraging to foreign banks to want to establish more than representative offices, and thus Citibank continued to be the only foreign bank with branches in Mexico. There were, however, investments by Banque Nationale de Paris in Banco del Atlántico and by Banco Popular Español in Banco del Valle de México (later absorbed by Banco del Atlántico). Then, just as Mexico began to be a more attractive place for foreign investment in the early 1960's because of the rapid economic growth it had enjoyed, the General Law of Credit Institutions was amended in 1965 to exclude foreign investment in the banking sector. Citibank's operations were permitted to continue as before, but they accounted for less than one percent of the assets of the Mexican banking system as a whole and the branches were prohibited from taking savings deposits or engaging in trust operations.

Over the years, a large number of foreign banks came to have representative offices in Mexico. By 1970, there were over 30 such offices in Mexico City, representing U.S., British, Canadian, German, Spanish, French, Italian and Swiss banks. These offices were (and still are) strictly limited as to the activities they may perform in Mexico. One of the activities that such offices are often suspected by the government of engaging in is that of illegally soliciting or taking deposits from Mexicans, whether through the foreign banks' private banking units or otherwise.

When the Mexican debt crisis erupted in August of 1982, the Mexican government took the dramatic step of nationalizing the Mexican banking system. The López Portillo administration took this action on the ground that the owners of the banks had contributed to causing the crisis, but many viewed the government as attempting to make the owners scapegoats for the government's own policy failures. In any event, for the next eight or nine years, the issue of foreign bank participation in the Mexican banking system was blunted by the fact that the system was controlled by the government. It seemed unlikely to many during that period that privately-held foreign banks would be permitted to participate in the Mexican banking system if Mexican banks in general were not permitted to be owned by private investors. However, once the Mexican banking system began to be returned to private ownership during the administration of Carlos Salinas de Gortari in the early 1990's, the barriers to foreign participation in the system began to weaken as well.

During the negotiation of NAFTA during the early 1990's, as the re-privatization of the Mexican banks was occurring, one of the key objectives of the U.S. negotiating team was to open up Mexico to investment by U.S. banks. This issue seems to have been fiercely contested by the Mexican negotiators, who were concerned that Mexican banks, which were just returning to private ownership after almost a decade of government control, were not prepared to compete directly with their counterparts in the U.S. and Canada. The outcome of this part of the negotiation was Chapter Fourteen of NAFTA on Financial Services, which liberalized cross-border financial services between the three signatories of NAFTA, and, more specifically, Annex VII(B) to NAFTA, which sets forth the reservations and commitments of Mexico with respect to the establishment and operation in Mexico of foreign-owned financial institutions.

Under Annex VII(B), Mexico agreed to a gradual opening of its financial system to foreign investment on the condition that (among other things) such investment would have to be through Mexican subsidiaries rather than branches. One of the arguments for this requirement was that it was necessary to ensure the Mexican government's control over the country's money supply. However, because it meant that a foreign bank's Mexican subsidiary's operations would be limited by the subsidiary's capital rather than by the capital of its parent bank, the requirement had the effect of substantially reducing the capacity and usefulness of a foreign bank's Mexican operations, at least until such time as the limitations on the size of such subsidiary might be loosened. Citibank would have been permitted to continue operating through branches, but if it had done so it would not have been entitled to any of the benefits of Annex VII(B), including the eventual elimination of the size restrictions. Evidently for this reason, Citibank eventually decided to convert its Mexican branches into a subsidiary operation.

The gradual opening under Annex VII(B) to foreign commercial banks, securities firms, insurance companies and nonbank banks was structured so that during a six-year transition period their capital participation would be limited to specified percentages of the total capital of the corresponding part of the financial system. In the case of commercial banks, the maximum capital that would be authorized for a Mexican subsidiary of a foreign bank organized under the laws of the U.S. or Canada was to be 1.5% of the total capital of the Mexican banking system. In addition, the aggregate capital of all of the Mexican subsidiaries of U.S. and Canadian banks was not to exceed 8% of the total capital of the Mexican commercial banking system, with this aggregate limit to gradually increase to 15% of such total capital by the end of the transition period (i.e., by January 1, 2000).

* * *

NAFTA became effective on January 1, 1994, but in anticipation of it coming into force, Mexico enacted amendments (also effective on January 1, 1994) to its *Ley de Instituciones de Crédito* (Credit Institutions Law or CIL) which gave effect to the provisions of Annex VII(B) with respect to commercial banks (or *instituciones de banca múltiple*, as commercial banks are called under that law). The new Mexican subsidiaries of foreign banks would be permitted to be formed as Foreign Financial Affiliates of foreign financial institutions, and could either be stand-alone banks or operate as members of foreign-owned financial groups formed under amended provisions of the Financial Groups Law

(*Ley de Agrupaciones Financieras*). Each of these laws now contains a chapter on "Affiliates" or "Holding Company Affiliates" of Foreign Financial Institutions, prescribing the rules for investment by such institutions in their Mexican bank subsidiaries or financial group holding company subsidiaries. Such subsidiaries must be organized under Mexican law and have at least 99 percent of their capital stock held by the foreign financial institution.

To implement these new provisions, on April 21, 1994 the Ministry of Finance and Public Credit (the *Secretaría de Hacienda y Crédito Público* or "SHCP") of Mexico published its Rules for the Establishment of Affiliates of Foreign Financial Institutions, prescribing the procedures for applications by foreign financial institutions for authorizations by the SHCP to establish Affiliates or Holding Company Affiliates under the CIL, the LRFG, the Securities Market Law and related laws. Since that date over 100 applications were made to the SHCP and many of such applications were approved. By September 1996, 69 Affiliates had been authorized and were operating, of which there were 17 banks, 9 securities firms, 11 financial leasing companies, 5 financial factoring companies, 10 nonbank banks, 15 insurance companies and 2 bonding companies.

Based on the membership of the Association of International Financial Institutions (*Asociación de Instituciones Financieras Internacionales S.C.* or AIFI) in mid-August 1998, at least seventeen Mexican bank subsidiaries of foreign banks were operating, including at least four as members of financial groups. Ten of the banks were owned by U.S. institutions, and of the remainder, two are owned by French banks, two by Dutch banks, one by a Spanish bank, one by a Japanese bank and one by a German bank, although it appears that the European and Japanese institutions utilized subsidiaries in the U.S. or Canada as vehicles for their investments. Interestingly, so far no Canadian bank has established a subsidiary as an Affiliate under the NAFTA-inspired provisions of the CIL. However, a couple of Canadian banks have acquired significant interests in existing banks, pursuant to 1995 amendments to the CIL and LRFG (see part III below),[22] which may at some point convert into Affiliates.

AIFI members also included two Mexican securities firms or *casas de bolsa* (owned by Bankers Trust and Goldman Sachs), seven nonbank banks and 64 bank representative offices, representing banks from Germany (9), the United States (7), Spain (7), France (7), Japan (5), Canada (4), the United Kingdom (4), Switzerland (3), Italy (2), Belgium

---

22. As of August 13, 1998, such bank subsidiaries were said to be those of ABN AMRO Bank, American Express Company, Bank of Boston, Banco Santander de Negocios, Bank of America, Bank of Tokyo–Mitsubishi, Banque Nationale de Paris, Chase Manhattan Bank, Citibank, Comerica Bank, Dresdner Bank, First Chicago Bank NBD, GE Capital, ING Barings, J.P. Morgan, Republic National Bank of New York and Société Générale. Of these, according to the AIFI, membership list the four that are members of Mexican financial groups formed under the LRFG were Chase, Citibank, ING Barings and J.P. Morgan. Affiliates of Nations Bank, Fuji Bank and Banco Bilbao Vizcaya appear not to be members of the AIFI.

(2), South Korea (2), multilateral institutions (2), Israel (2), Netherlands (1), Australia (1) and various countries in Latin America and the Caribbean (6). In addition, four foreign securities firms have representative offices that are AIFI members.

III. THE FEBRUARY 1995 OPENING

When it had become clear that the December 1994 devaluation, and the financial crisis that resulted therefrom, would imperil the solvency of the Mexican banking system, the government determined to go beyond its NAFTA commitments and make it possible for foreign banks to provide additional capital to the system. Further amendments to the CIL were enacted in February 1995, which made it possible for foreign banks to acquire up to 100% of the capital of existing Mexican banks through "programs approved by the [SHCP] for the purpose of converting the respective multiple banking institution into an Affiliate." However, these 1995 Amendments excluded any bank with capital exceeding 6% of the total capital of the banking system—then meaning the three largest banks, Banamex, Bancomer and Banca Serfín—from eligibility for any such foreign takeover. This would change under the amendments proposed by the Zedillo administration in March of 1998 (see part IV below).

* * *

IV. THE 1998 PROPOSALS

In early 1998, the Zedillo administration developed a financial reform package which it proposed to the Mexican Congress.... With regard to the issue of foreign investment in the banking sector, the package would eliminate most remaining restrictions on such investment. The proposed changes would, in large part, focus on changes in the classifications of the shares of capital stock issued by Mexican banks (the portion of the package that would affect the supervision of the banking system and foreign investment in the banks is herein sometimes referred to as the "Reform Bill").

* * *

The key change in this regard would be the elimination of the limitation in the current law that prevents a foreign financial institution from obtaining approval of the authorities for acquiring a Mexican bank which has a capital stock that exceeds 6% of the total capital of all of the Mexican commercial banks. In other words, the Reform Bill would open up the possibility of foreign banks acquiring any of the three largest banks in Mexico, i.e., Banamex, Bancomer or Serfín. Of the three, Serfín seems the most likely to acquire a foreign owner, in that it has been the one in the greatest financial difficulty and it already has two foreign shareholders with significant stakes who have indicated an interest in increasing their shares.

Under the proposed changes to the CIL and LRFG, the board of directors of a bank would have to consist of 15 members, instead of the

11 members required by current law.... As under the current law, all board members would have to reside within Mexico, although they may be foreigners. [Authors' note: as indicated earlier, this legislation authorizing 100% foreign ownership in Mexican banks without the earlier limitations was enacted in 1998.]

GOUVIN, CROSS–BORDER BANK BRANCHING UNDER THE NAFTA: PUBLIC CHOICE AND THE LAW OF CORPORATE GROUPS

13 Conn. J. of Int'l L. 257 (1991).*

* * *

How the NAFTA Changed the Landscape

In many ways it seems that the NAFTA banking provisions have been *much ado about nothing*. Despite the exaggerated claims, both positive and negative, that accompanied the passage of the NAFTA, the empirical data since the passage of the Agreement suggests that the North American financial services market is not radically different.

The NAFTA was intended to give the member nations broad access to each other's markets. The banking provisions of the NAFTA are based in large part on the banking provisions of United States–Canada Free Trade Agreement (FTA). The foundational ideas of both treaties are national treatment and most favored nation status. As between the United States and Canada, the NAFTA added little to the existing relationship memorialized in the FTA, but it did add important provisions framing the relationship of the two countries with the Mexican banking system. What follows is a summary of the changes the NAFTA brought about within the confines of the existing banking regimes in the three signatory countries.

A. The United States

Under the NAFTA, Canada and Mexico's access to the United States banking market did not change in any material way. The United States already extended national treatment to all foreign banking organizations doing business in the United States. Before the treaty both Canadian and Mexican banks had access to the U.S. market on terms similar to those available to all other countries. Under the FTA, however, the United States granted Canada a concession under the Glass–Steagall Act to treat Canadian government securities as "bank eligible" securities. Under the NAFTA, however, the United States did not extend that same treatment to Mexican government securities.

On the other hand, Mexican financial holding companies that, as of January 1, 1992, owned a Mexican bank with U.S. operations and also owned a Mexican securities firm that owned or controlled a U.S. securities firm were grand-fathered to offer both brokerage and banking in the United States for five years without being a violation of Glass–Steagall. Otherwise, Mexican banks entering the U.S. market are treated as any other foreign bank doing business in the United States.

B. *Canada*

Under the FTA, U.S. banks gained preferential access to the Canadian banking market. Although the FTA did not make any meaningful changes in the access of Canadian banks to the U.S. market, it did provide U.S. banks with rights not shared by non-Canadian banks generally. In effect, it provided national treatment in Canada for U.S. banks that were established there. As a result of the FTA changes, U.S. banks were no longer subject to the foreign ownership restrictions of the Bank Act. The Bank Act now makes special provision for "NAFTA country residents." The policy of national treatment as embodied in the NAFTA also liberalized the treatment of U.S.-owned Schedule II banks. Specifically, U.S. Schedule II banks are permitted to branch across Canada in the same streamlined fashion that Canadian banks may.

Canada has not, however, become the 51st state. For many purposes, U.S. and Mexican banks are still foreign banks. For example, they may not branch directly into Canada, but may operate in Canada only through a Canadian-chartered Schedule II subsidiary. Canadian bank regulators apparently insisted on requiring a Canadian-chartered subsidiary in order to ensure that Canadian law would apply.

* * *

C. *Mexico*

Prior to the NAFTA, Mexico's banking market essentially was closed to American banks. The NAFTA changed that by permitting U.S. and Canadian banks to establish wholly-owned banking subsidiaries in Mexico. Given the relative weakness of Mexico's banking system compared to its two imposing northern neighbors, however, Mexico negotiated for some protections in the NAFTA to prevent foreign domination of the Mexican banking industry. Specifically, Mexico set out aggregate capital limits for foreign subsidiaries. In the wake of the 1994 peso crisis, Mexico modified, but did not abandon, its foreign ownership rules to permit greater foreign influence in the banking system.

After the transition period, U.S. and Canadian institutions will be permitted to acquire outright existing Mexican banks, subject to the limitation that the sum of the capital of the acquired bank and any affiliate of the foreign acquirer not exceed four percent of the aggregate capital of all commercial banks in Mexico. Barring unforeseen circumstances, this restriction will prevent the unfriendly acquisition of Mexico's six largest banks since they all exceed the capital limit.

CROSS-BORDER BRANCHING: PUBLIC POLICY AND LEGAL THEORY

International banking is now a fact of life. Some U.S. banking organizations now report that a majority of their productive assets are located abroad. As the North American market for goods and services becomes more integrated, there will be increasing pressure on the NAFTA countries to rationalize cross-border banking. Under the terms of the NAFTA, the time is now at hand to re-examine the issue of cross-border branching. Section 1403(3) of the NAFTA states:

> at such time as the United States permits commercial banks of another Party located in its territory to expand through subsidiaries or direct branches into substantially all of the United States market, the parties shall review and assess market access provided by each party ... with a view to adopting arrangements permitting investors of another Party to choose the juridical form of establishment of commercial banks.

Section 1403(1) stipulates that investors of a Party should be free to establish financial institutions in the other countries "in the juridical form chosen by such investor." The import of that provision is that banks should be able to expand across borders by establishing either branches or subsidiaries as dictated by their business plan rather than by banking law.

A. Methods of Engaging in Cross-Border Banking

1. Subsidiaries

All three NAFTA countries permit banks from the other NAFTA countries to expand into their territory by establishing separately chartered subsidiaries in the host country. The subsidiary must comply with all licensing and regulatory requirements, including capital requirements. The subsidiary approach to expansion suffers from several weaknesses. The costs of establishing a subsidiary can be considerable. A free standing bank must have a complete internal infrastructure, capital base and management team. In addition, subsidiaries are limited somewhat in their lending capacity, since loan limits are typically a function of the amount of the bank's capital. The problem of a low lending limit can often be avoided through the use of loan participation agreements. Perhaps owing to the expense of establishing and operating subsidiaries, it appears that subsidiaries are less attractive than branches.

On the other hand, if subsidiaries are respected as legal persons separate and distinct from their corporate parents, they may be an effective method for insulating the parent from liabilities arising out of the subsidiary's banking activities. Indeed, the limitation of the parent's liability is frequently the most important reason for forming subsidiaries. . . .

... [I]n modern practice, corporations form subsidiaries for any number of reasons, including, in addition to the desire to limit liability, the need to comply with regulatory ownership requirements, a desire to establish certain procedural benefits, such as venue and jurisdiction, or in the case of banking in the NAFTA countries because present law does not permit cross-border branching. Regardless of the reasons for the use of subsidiaries, it may be said that despite their separate legal existence they form a cohesive economic unit with their parent and related corporations.

* * *

2. *Branching*

In general, from the point of view of the parent banking organization, branching should be more economically attractive than setting up an independent subsidiary since capital, accounting, and legal costs can be shared more easily. In the United States, operations would be more easily integrated because the prohibitions of §§ 23A and 23B [Federal Reserve Act restrictions on transactions among affiliates within a holding company organization] will not apply to transactions between branches, but they would restrict transactions between commonly controlled subsidiaries. In addition, loans generated by a branch can be made based on the capital of the home bank in the home country instead of on the branch's capital. On the other hand, liabilities of the branch will likely be imposed on the home office more readily than the obligations of a separately organized subsidiary would be. Although local regulators are likely to have less control over a branch because the regulator in the home country will have primary responsibility, the branch is likely to be more stable because of the greater worldwide capital of the bank.

3. *Other Ways of Accessing Foreign Markets*

Another way to do business with a foreign country is through a "representative office" which does not solicit loans or take deposits, but which acts as a liaison to make it easier for potential borrowers or depositors in the host country to transact business with the foreign bank in the bank's home country. In addition to these three common approaches, the United States permits banking activities to be carried out through "agencies" chartered by a state or the federal government, which are in effect special purpose banks.

* * *

B. *Problems of Cross–Border Regulation*

Regulation is an inescapable fact of modern banking. Cross-border regulation, however, is awkward. Both the home and host countries have legitimate claims to full and accurate information on banks operating in or from their jurisdiction, and both regulators have a legitimate concern to prevent the threat of systemic risk brought about by bank failure. In an ideal world, bank regulators in different countries would be comfortable if they knew that a fellow regulator in another country was supervising the other aspects of an international bank's operations by applying rigorous standards. Such an ideal scheme would require at least two preconditions: (1) regulators would have to agree on acceptable standards that would pass international muster, and (2) regulators would have to have confidence in the competence and integrity of the regulators in other countries. Unfortunately, the NAFTA countries do not meet these conditions. It will be extraordinarily difficult for trade negotiators to make agreements about cross-border branching without also making a commitment to harmonize North American banking law. For example, the United States would legitimately want to know whether the source of strength doctrine would allow the Federal Reserve Board to pursue the holding companies of Mexican and Canadian banks operating in this country. Canada and Mexico would legitimately want to know whether Glass–Steagall will prohibit their banks from operating freely in the United States while also being part of an organization that owns a securities company. But the NAFTA does not contain any meaningful commitment to harmonization of the banking regulatory schemes of the three countries.

On the second point, it is not at all clear that the regulators in the three countries have the mutual respect necessary for a successful cooperative regulation effort. For example, Canadians resent what they consider to be the propensity of U.S. regulators to seek extraterritorial application of U.S. law. During the negotiation of the FTA and the NAFTA, it was understood that a significant part of Canada's opposition to cross-border branching was based on Canadian banking regulators' desire that there be a Canadian bank doing business in the country that they could regulate. Similarly, there was some concern in the United States that the Mexican banking regulators were not up to the task of supervising a modern banking system.

Given the lack of harmonization and the lack of mutual respect, it was inevitable that the NAFTA banking structure would default to a system requiring subsidiaries instead of one that permitted branching. Therefore, under current law, all three NAFTA countries permit expansion by establishment of subsidiaries, but only the United States permits foreign banks, including Canadian and Mexican banks, to expand into our market through branching. The fact that the U.S. law permits branching, however, is not the end of the story. Foreign banks seeking to establish a presence in the United States must comply with a labyrinth of federal regulations which seem to treat foreign banks less favorably than U.S. banks. The Foreign Bank Supervision Act of 1991 tightened U.S. supervision of foreign branches and agencies operating in the United States. The law provides for increased sharing of information between home and host country regulators; mandates deposit insurance for all deposits under $100,000; requires the Federal Reserve to approve all applications for any branch, agency or representative office; and permits the Federal Reserve Board to examine and close all such international banking facilities.

* * *

From a regulator's point of view, in a modern world where one banking organization might act across the country and around the world through dozens of wholly owned subsidiaries, the fiction of separate corporate personality for each subsidiary in a corporate group does not reflect reality. Because in the real world there is little practical difference between a wholly owned subsidiary and a traditional branch, it seems overly formalistic that the legal treatment of one should differ from the other. In order to accommodate complex corporate groups, international law will have to jettison traditional ideas about corporate personality, but when the corporate actors operate across national borders the challenge of harmonizing concepts of enterprise liability is a daunting one.

If a workable solution to the moral hazard can be devised, and if home and host country regulators can coordinate their efforts in a mutually agreeable manner, there should be no real difference between a subsidiary and a branch, and financial services providers should be free to set up their corporate structures as they see fit. Therefore, if one were writing on a clean slate to devise the optimal North American legal framework for structuring the financial services industry one would probably enact a plan that permits the individual players in the market to determine the corporate structure they prefer, be it branching or holding company form. Unfortunately, the NAFTA negotiators are not writing on a clean slate. They have political, historical, and economic factors unique to their individual countries that they need to pay attention to. These factors make the public choice perspective on trade agreements a more useful tool for understanding the cross-border branching issue than the arguments based on the law of corporate groups.

———

OAS OVERVIEW OF THE NORTH AMERICAN FREE TRADE AGREEMENT

CHAPTER FOURTEEN: FINANCIAL SERVICES

Article 1401 states that chapter fourteen covers the rights of financial services institutions, the investors in those institutions, and cross-border providers and consumers under the Agreement. Certain articles from the investment chapter are brought forward to also apply to chapter fourteen. Under Annex 1401.4, specific commitments between Canada and the US under the FTA are incorporated into the NAFTA. Paragraph 3 ensures that government-owned entities such as insurance and workers' compensation programs fall outside the scope of the Chapter. Article 1401 also provides that a Party may grant a monopoly right to a private concern in order to carry out any activity that is a part of a public retirement plan or statutory system of social security.

Article 1402 makes clear that self-regulatory organizations are covered by the chapter where membership is required by the party.

Under Article 1403, the Parties accept the principle that an investor should be permitted to establish a financial institution in the territory of another Party in the juridical form chosen by such an investor. Under paragraph 4, financial institutions have a right to establish in each other's territory, but a Party may require a subsidiary or impose prudential requirements consistent with national treatment as defined in Article 1405.

Article 1404 places a freeze on restrictions governing the provision of cross-border trade in financial services. Article 1404 also establishes a right to purchase which allows a consumer of financial services to purchase cross-border financial services. Providers have no right to do business or solicit cross-border financial services without having first established in the territory in question.

Article 1405 provides that investors, financial institutions and cross-border providers must be given national treatment, further defined by equality of competitive opportunity. Equal competitive opportunities allow for different treatment as long as it does not disadvantage the foreign institutions or investors in comparison with their domestic counterparts.

Article 1406(1) makes the concept of MFN applicable to financial services. However, the article provides that mutual recognition of regulation can result in preferential treatment of one NAFTA partner's institutions or investors, so long as any other Party is given the opportunity to demonstrate that it qualifies for similar treatment, and given an adequate opportunity to negotiate such recognition.

Under Article 1407, a financial institution has the right to introduce any new financial service, already provided elsewhere in a Party's territory, to another part of the NAFTA territory. Article 1408 provides that a Party cannot require that senior managerial or other essential personnel engaged by a financial institution be of any particular nationality. A Party may require that a simple majority (and not more) of the board of directors of a financial institution be composed of nationals, residents, or a combination of those.

Article 1410 ensures that reasonable measures may be taken for prudential reasons to protect the integrity of the financial system or the consumers of financial services. Article 1411 specifies that all new measures must be made publicly available through a recognized enquiry point. Measures of general application must be published or made public. All applications for financial institutions should be resolved within 120 days except where regulatory hearings need to be held or where it is not practical.

Under Article 1412, a Financial Services Committee, composed primarily of officials of the respective Party's Finance or Treasury departments will report to the Free Trade Commission. The Committee will supervise the chapter's implementation, play a specific role in the dispute settlement process, and meet annually to discuss the state and functioning of the Agreement as it relates to financial services.

Consultations and dispute settlement mechanism are available under Article 1413 for Parties that consider that a measure of another Party is inconsistent with the Agreement. The general dispute settlement provisions of chapter twenty, with modifications, applies to this chapter. Modifications include a separate roster of fifteen financial services experts who can be called upon to mediate financial services-related dispute. No cross-sector retaliation affecting financial services is permitted under the Agreement. Investment-related disputes will be resolved as under chapter eleven, except that any case involving prudential measures must be examined by the Financial Services Committee and if there is no agreement, the prudential consideration is resolved by the government-to-government panel process. Investment-related disputes are the only cases in which an individual may bring a case against another Party.

Article 1413 also includes a clause to assist in dealing with problems of extraterritoriality. Paragraph 3 allows a Party to request the presence at consultations of regulatory authorities of another Party, in order to discuss general measures affecting the operation of financial institutions or the cross-border provision of services.

Annex 1413.6 provides that Mexico can request consultations or an arbitral panel to determine the existence of threats to the essential nature of the Mexican Market and payments system, should foreign banks reach 25 percent of the aggregate capital of the Mexican market following the transition clause. The panel decision is not binding, and any action Mexico takes as a result of it could be open to dispute by Canada or the US.

In order to be eligible for exemption from foreign ownership exemptions, NAFTA firms must be ultimately controlled by Party residents.

Mexico is granted the same exemptions from Canadian laws affecting foreign-owned financial institutions that were given to the United States under the FTA.

The schedule of Mexico describes the transition process, including temporary capital limits for banks, securities firms, and insurance companies. All limits die at the end of the transition period, but Mexico can freeze group capital limits once during the four years following the end of transition, for a period of three years only, if capital limits of 25 percent for banks and 30 percent of securities firms are reached.

The schedule also sets out Mexico's permanent commitments. Acquisition of an established Mexican bank would be prohibited if it would give the purchaser more than 4 percent of aggregate commercial bank capital in Mexico.

The schedule of the United States describes the derogation with respect to Canada and cross-border trade in securities. The United States has given Mexican firms that do banking and securities, prior to entry into force of the Agreement, a five-year ability to continue to function as per status quo ante, but not to grow by acquisition. The concession does not apply to Canadian firms because they already have section 20 subsidiaries and operate under that rule.

GOUVIN, CROSS–BORDER BANK BRANCHING UNDER THE NAFTA: PUBLIC CHOICE AND THE LAW OF CORPORATE GROUPS

13 Conn. J. of Int'l L. 257 (1999).*

* * *

CANADA

Canada's banking industry presents a radical contrast to the U.S. banking scene. All banks are federally chartered and fall into one of two categories: "Schedule I" or "Schedule II" banks. So-called Schedule I banks are subject to the "widely-held" rule: no person or group may control more than ten percent of the voting stock of a Schedule I bank. Instead of the thousands of independent banks found in the United States, Canada is dominated by six large Schedule I institutions with nationwide branching networks. Schedule II banks, on the other hand, may be closely held and owned by non-Canadians.

In addition, unlike American banks but similar to their Mexican counterparts, Canadian banking organizations are not constrained by the artificial product line distinctions found in the Glass–Steagall Act. Under present Canadian law, banks, insurance companies, and securities firms are permitted to own one another and to provide services to the public through separate subsidiaries in a holding company structure. While the separate subsidiary requirement provides some financial insulation for the bank, the operational insulation required by U.S. law is lacking.

The lines of command in the Canadian bank regulatory scheme are much clearer than in the American regulatory system. In Canada, a federal banking supervising agency whose head is appointed by the cabinet and who reports directly to the Minister of Finance, is the chief banking regulator. The federal supervisor is responsible for all federally chartered financial institutions including banks, insurance companies and trust companies, while sharing responsibility with the provinces for oversight of securities firms. The Canadian federal deposit insurer plays a secondary role in bank oversight, while the Bank of Canada maintains data on the financial system generally and on banks individually.

Another big difference between U.S. banks and their Canadian competitors is the weight of the regulatory burden shouldered by each. Although it is an imprecise measure, the differing volume of banking legislation in the two countries speaks to the difference in regulatory attitudes. In the early 1990s, U.S. federal banking laws and regulations totaled approximately 220,000 pages, while in Canada the entire Bank Act and associated regulations amounted to no more than 530 pages. This might not be surprising in light of the deep concern in U.S. banking policy over branching and activities, both of which are not important issues in Canada.

BERZIEL, CANADIAN BANK ACT AND ITS IMPLEMENTATION UNDER THE NAFTA

3 NAFTA: Law and Bus. Rev. of the Americas 135 (1996).*

* * *

CANADIAN BANKING SYSTEM

In 1792, Montreal businessmen attempted to establish the first Canadian bank. While their attempt was unsuccessful, it stimulated the development of Canada's modern banking system. The Bank of Montreal, founded in 1817 by nine local merchants, still operates today. In fact, the Canadian banking industry continued to rapidly expand throughout Canada's provinces. Each province incorporated and governed the new banks by their own set of laws until the British North America Act of 1867. This act removed the governing power from the provinces and gave the new federal government exclusive jurisdiction over the banking system. The new federal government inherited a banking system that consisted of 35 banks with 164 branches.

Originally, the Canadian banking system consisted of a large number of locally-owned banks. Through the years, the system has evolved and is now comprised of relatively few banks with extensive branches totaling over 7,400. The major commercial banks in Canada at present are the Bank of Montreal, the Bank of Nova Scotia, Canadian Imperial Bank of Commerce, Canadian Western Bank, the National Bank of Canada, the Royal Bank of Canada and [T.D. Canada Trust]. Six of these seven banks control more than 80% of the financial market in Canada. Canada's extensive branching system allows its banks to serve 1,600 communities in the ten provinces and both territories. As a result, Canada boasts a higher ratio of full service banking branches per person than any other major industrialized nation. Canada has one bank branch for every 3,578 people. This extensive banking system gives Canadians the flexibility of having both neighborhood convenience and nationwide access for their financial needs.

Commercial banks are Canada's primary source of monetary deposits which comprise the major component of the nation's official money supply. Consequently, Canadian banks are highly regulated. The Bank Act is the Canadian federal legislative act that governs Canadian chartered banks and foreign banks operating in Canada. The Bank Act is subject to parliamentary review every ten years. This policy of periodic review is due to the fear Canadians have of powerful banks. The review forces bank regulators and parliament to consider both innovative and technological changes in the dynamic banking industry.

In addition to the Bank Act, Canada's banks are subject to provincial legislation which affects the operations of banks. This legislation differs depending on the province where the bank is located. The dual regulation of banks through federal and provincial statutes creates overlap and makes Canadian banking highly complex.

To further complicate the banking industry, banks are also regulated by several national departments. For example, the Department of Finance controls the types of financial services that can be offered and the types of investments permitted. The Office of the Superintendent of Financial Institutions (OSFI) administers regulation and supervision of banks, loan and investment companies and cooperative credit associations. The OSFI supervises 10 domestic banks, 55 subsidiaries of foreign banks, and approximately 80 trusts and loans, credit unions and investment companies registered with the federal government. The regulatory scheme is completed with the Bank of Canada which acts as the fiscal agent for the federal government. The Bank of Canada, a separate corporation, acts independently of the government but is responsible for formulating and implementing monetary policies.

The Bank Act creates two types of banks: Schedule I and Schedule II. Schedule I banks are both majority Canadian-owned and widely held by the public. No person may own more than ten percent of any class of shares and non-residents may not own more than 25 percent of the total number issued and outstanding shares. Canada has seven active Schedule I banks.

Schedule II banks are usually closely held with their shares held by only a few parties and generally not offered to the public. Canadian residents or those nations who have been accorded residency status can own up to 100 percent of the bank's shares for the bank's first ten years. However, after the first ten years, this percentage must be reduced to ten percent unless the bank is an approved subsidiary of a foreign bank. If it is an approved subsidiary, a foreign bank may own up to a 100% of a Schedule II bank with no dilution requirement.

* * *

RESERVATIONS AND COUNTRY-SPECIFIC LIMITATIONS IN CHAPTER 14

Chapter 14 provides a system of reservations to exempt certain laws and regulations in the NAFTA countries that are inconsistent with its provisions. The reservations are organized for each NAFTA government into schedules with three sections. In section A, each government lists the federal, state or provincial, and local laws or regulations which are exempt from Chapter 14. These exempt laws are automatically "grandfathered". A "rachet" provision provides "that once a reserved law is liberalized it cannot later be made more restrictive." In section B, financial service sectors reserve the right to maintain existing inconsistent federal regulations and to implement new non-conforming regulations. Section C of the governments' schedules lists specific country commitments undertaken by each of the individual NAFTA countries.

Canada's schedule of reservations lists three significant federal law exemptions from NAFTA requirements. First, Canada reserves a retention requirement for re-insurance services in accordance with the Canadian Insurance Companies Act. The Act requires that no more than 25% of re-insurance can be purchased abroad. Second, in section B, Canada reserves the right to introduce new restrictions on cross-border security trade. Finally, Canada limits NAFTA's benefits to firms in the United States and Mexico that are ultimately controlled by residents of these nations. This is contrary to the general rule which allows any company resident in a NAFTA country, regardless of ultimate ownership, to be considered a NAFTA firm. In addition to the three exemptions, Canada specifically commits to exempt Mexico from the "10/25" rules in which the United States were exempted under the FTA.

The United States' schedule also lists three main exemptions. In the first exception, the United States has grand-fathered all restrictions in federal law which are inconsistent with Chapter 14 obligations. The United States parallels Canada's second exemption by permitting new restrictions on cross-border securities trade. The third exemption specifically commits the United States to provide Mexican firms with a five year transition period to conform their activities in the United States to the Bank Holding Company Act of 1956.

Mexico's schedule differs from the United States' and Canada's schedules by establishing market share and capital limits instead of exemptions. Until January 1, 2000, the individual market share of commercial banks owned by the United States or Canada cannot exceed 1.5% of Mexican banking system. Thereafter, these commercial banks cannot exceed 4% of the total capitalization of Mexico's domestic banking system. Moreover, the aggregate market share of all Canadian and United States bank subsidiaries is limited to 8% as of 1994 with rising annual increments until reaching 15% in 1999. The aggregate market share limitation is eliminated in 2000. However, the Mexican government reserves the right to reimpose the cap should foreign market share reach 25% before 2004.

Amending Canada's Bank Act to Comply With NAFTA

To implement the provisions of NAFTA's Chapter 14, Canada amended its Bank Act with the NAFTA Implementation Act §§ 22–29. The purpose of these amendments was to exclude NAFTA residents and foreign bank subsidiaries controlled by NAFTA residents from the Bank Act's strict provisions governing non-residents. The amendments fulfill the goals of Chapter 14 by granting national treatment and most-favored nation treatment to NAFTA nations.

Sections 22 and 23 begin the amendments by defining a NAFTA country resident. "NAFTA country residents are natural persons ordinarily resident in a NAFTA country other than Canada and corporations and other entities incorporated ... in a NAFTA country other than Canada that are controlled by one or more natural persons ordinarily resident in a NAFTA country other than Canada." Section 25 revises the definition of non-resident to exclude NAFTA residents.

Section 24 permits residents and NAFTA residents to own a significant interest in a Schedule II bank for a period of ten years beginning the date the bank came into existence. A significant interest is defined as more than 10% of any class of outstanding shares. Section 24 also authorizes the Minister of Finance to consider the non-financial activities of a resident or a NAFTA resident in deciding whether such a person should be allowed to incorporate or acquire a significant interest in a Schedule II bank.

Section 28 grants foreign bank subsidiaries controlled by Mexican residents the same treatment granted under the FTA to subsidiaries controlled by United States' residents. The section also governs the conduct of a non-NAFTA country bank subsidiary. A non-NAFTA country bank is defined as "a foreign bank subsidiary that is not controlled by a NAFTA country resident."

Non–NAFTA country bank subsidiaries are limited to locating one branch and their head office in Canada. Furthermore, no non-NAFTA country bank subsidiary can have average domestic assets exceeding an amount fixed by the Minister of Finance for that subsidiary for any three month period. Non–NAFTA country bank subsidiaries are prohibited from owning more than 12% of the total domestic assets held by all banks. Thus, the Minister of Finance cannot fix the amount of a non-NAFTA country bank subsidiary's average domestic assets above 12%.

Section 29 addresses section 508 of the Bank Act which prohibits foreign banks from conducting business in Canada. The 1992 Bank Act allowed foreign banks to enter into agreements with Canadian banks to permit United States' residents access to their bank accounts through the use of an automated bank machine operated by a Canadian financial institution. The Amendment now allows Mexican residents to receive these same benefits by changing "United States residents" to NAFTA residents.

* * *

Canadian Expansion into the United States

Canadian banks have conducted business in the United States since 1850 and continue to have strong presence in the United States' financial sector today. Canadian banks now have 51 subsidiaries, branches, agencies or offices in the United States. The top six banks in Canada all operate uninsured branches and agencies in the United States. The Bank of Montreal is the only Canadian bank with a United States banking subsidiary.[266] Canadian banks are the second largest source of foreign bank loans in the United States. Canadian banks in the United States employ 8500 people and have 17% of their assets in the United States.

In 1984, the Bank of Montreal acquired Harris Bank in Chicago. Since the passage of NAFTA, the Bank of Montreal has embarked on a plan to use Harris Bank to establish the Bank of Montreal as the first North American bank with continent-wide reach. The Harris bank ranks fifth out of sixty United States institutions for its expertise in foreign exchange transactions. By the year 2002, Harris aims to capture 12% of the Chicago market which would produce half of the Bank of Montreal's income in the United States alone. Through the acquisition of Harris, the Bank of Montreal acquired 72 branches which will help the Bank of Montreal reach its goal of 120 branches and 1 million customers in the United States.

NAFTA has also fostered the expansion of other Canadian banks into the United States. [T.D. Canada Trust] opened a trade services office in Houston on March 1, 1995. The trade services office offers core trade finance products with the hope of capitalizing on business with United States exporters. National Bank of Canada has also expanded into the United States by providing financing to small and medium-sized businesses. The Royal Bank of Canada, the fourth largest bank in North America, is also taking advantage of NAFTA by planning to expand into the United States in the area of electronic banking.

CANADIAN EXPANSION INTO MEXICO

NAFTA has also opened opportunities for Canadian banks to expand into Mexico. Four of the six leading Canadian banks already have representative offices in Mexico. The National Bank of Canada uses its representative office to help its Canadian and United States' customers in Mexico. In addition, the National Bank of Canada has signed a cooperation agreement with the Mexican bank Confia. Both banks will offer their services and business contacts to the clients of the other institution in both countries and around the world.

The Bank of Montreal is also taking advantage of Mexico's resources. Nesbitt Burns Inc., a subsidiary of the Bank of Montreal, signed an agreement with Casa de Bolsa Bancomer, Mexico's second-largest banking group, to exchange business between Canada and Mexico. Nesbitt Burns Inc. will sell Mexican equities and fixed-income products in Canada while Casa de Bolsa Bancomer will sell Canadian securities in Mexico.

In addition, the Bank of Montreal joined forces with Grupo Financiero Bancomer SA, Mexico's second largest financial group, to create the First Canadian NAFTA Advantage Fund. The mutual fund is designed to

---

266. The Bank of Montreal is the tenth largest bank in North America and [as of 1996] the only Canadian bank listed on the New York Stock Exchange.

achieve long-term capital growth by investing in NAFTA-oriented companies in the United States, Canada and Mexico. The First Canadian NAFTA Advantage Fund invests 20% of its assets in each of the three NAFTA countries with the remaining 40% allocated based on investment opportunities.

* * *

Questions and Comments
The extension of U.S. banking services to Mexico

1.   Attorney Rogers and Licenciado Zubikairi provide a history of Mexican banking. It is a history which parallels that of productive industry—substantial foreign ownership in the 1800s, extending until the revolution in 1910, and followed by nearly a century of fluctuating concepts of foreign ownership. Has NAFTA provided any stability to the Mexican banking system? Could you possibly have predicted the course of events had you been asked the initial questions in the problem a century ago? Can you do any better now?

2.   Rogers and Zubikairi note that a key objective of the U.S. in the NAFTA negotiations was to open up Mexican banking. Did they succeed enough for the Bank of the West to be able to profit from expansion into Mexico? The thrust of NAFTA is to establish an open financial services sector, with specific reservations and exceptions spelled out.

3.   The 1995 amendments to the Mexican Banking system, described by Rogers and Zubikairi, open up the acquisition route to our client, and to its many competitors in the United States, Canada and Spain. Mexico needed more capital in its banks after the late 1994 peso devaluation. The amendments allow the Ministry of Finance and Public Credit to permit foreign acquisition of 100 percent of all but the three largest banks, and even that latter prohibition was the subject of 1998 changes, paving the way, *inter alia*, for Citibank's acquisition of Banamex in 2001. Our client is not in the position to acquire one of the largest Mexican banks, but it might acquire one of the remaining smaller banks. The decision seems now to be where we wish to commence business in Mexico, and whether or not there is a reasonably sound local bank which might be a good target. If there is, it is off to the Ministry of Finance and Public Credit that we will go, seeking approval.

4.   If we have at this point decided that our Mexican investment will be by way of opening foreign financial affiliates, the process is explained in the Rogers and Zubikairi article. They indicate that this has been the practice followed by many financial services companies, not only banks. But there is a choice. Our subsidiaries may be stand-alone banks or parts of foreign–owned financial groups. Note that the two Canadian banks entering Mexico have not followed this route of using foreign financial affiliates, but have acquired interests in Mexican banks. One took over control of a Mexican bank, the other assumed a minority position in Bancomer, which under Mexican law could not be controlled by foreigners, as the authors explain. Why do you suppose these two Canadian banks have followed the acquisition/participation route?

5. Article 1404 disallows restrictions on cross-border trade in financial services, unless they are set out in Annex VII. Banks engage in many forms of transactions, and in many currencies. BankWest expects to engage in transactions in U.S. dollars and pesos. The BankWest plans to allow Mexicans to convert pesos to dollars, with the dollars credited to accounts in the U.S. This is viewed by Mexicans as useful in times of threats to the value of the Mexican peso. Of course BankWest may refuse to make such conversions if it believes that Mexico will not redeem the pesos for dollars. Should BankWest be worried?

6. The Bank sees references to establishing "a" foreign financial affiliate in Mexico. But it wants numerous banks throughout Mexico, starting in the north. Does it create a single foreign financial affiliate and branch through that entity, or must it (and may it) establish numerous unrelated (horizontally) foreign financial affiliates?

7. It seems our client effectively will have to choose *subsidiaries* over *branches* for Mexican expansion. Branches may only engage in transactions with non-residents under Art. 7 of the Credit Institutions Law. What is the reason for the Mexican preference for subsidiaries rather than branches?

8. Should BankWest be concerned that Fuji Bank, a main competitor chartered in Japan with subsidiaries in California, has shown interest in expanding to Mexico? BankWest thought that NAFTA offered benefits only to the NAFTA Parties. What other evidence suggests that this is not the case?

The extension of U.S. banking services to Canada

1. Professor Gouvin and Ms. Berziel each outline the Canadian banking industry, which illustrates a greater federal control and limitations of ownership by single persons than in the U.S. Ms. Berziel further relates how the Canada Bank Act has been amended to comply with NAFTA. Does it matter whether the target group of BankWest in Canada is one of the few Schedule I bank groups, or a group of Schedule II banks? Will the "widely held" rule prevent BankWest from "taking over" the Commonwealth Bank group in Canada, assuming it is a Schedule I bank?

2. The annexes additionally outline part of the relationship between the U.S. and Canada. Annex 1401.4 incorporates Art. 1702(1) and (2) of the CFTA, which outlines the commitments of the U.S. to Canada. Those commitments granted to foreign and domestic banks in the U.S. the ability to deal in certain debt obligations backed by Canada or its political subdivisions to the same extent as those backed by the U.S. (Art. 1702(1)) and gave national treatment under federal law to Canadian controlled banks rights to establish branches and subsidiaries (Art. 1702(2)). But the Art. 1703 commitments of Canada to the U.S. are not incorporated in NAFTA. How, then, is the BankWest interest in expanding to Canada governed?

The piecemeal approach of somewhat vague ambitions in the CFTA is not followed in the NAFTA. NAFTA contains promises, and extends those promises to attempt to govern actions of states and provinces. Banking services are opened subject to the limited exceptions of Art. 1410, first to protect recipients of financial services, to maintain responsible financial institutions, and to ensure the integrity and stability of the system (Art. 1410(1)); and second to allow non-discriminatory actions to achieve "monetary and related credit policies or exchange rate policies." (Art. 1410(2)) Article 1409 also allows non-conforming measures to be listed in Annex VII. The Annex VII measures show Canada's unrestrictive federal system, which appears to have little more effect on BankWest than to require the residency in Canada of the controlling persons. Annex VII(A)-Canada, at VII–C–2. What more is expected of BankWest if it only targets Schedule II banks?

Does BankWest qualify in Canada as a "NAFTA country resident?" Assuming it does, how much of a Schedule II bank may it own? For how long? Is the reputation of BankWest in the U.S. at all important?

3.   Annex 1409.1 allows Canada to set forth existing non-conforming measures of Canadian provinces. But Canadian banks are federally chartered; no restrictions of provinces were noted in Annex VII. So should BankWest worry about provincial banking legislation?

4.   Does Canada seem content with the current NAFTA structure?

5.   If BankWest has opportunities in Quebec, should it take advantage of them, in view of the final comments of Ms. Berziel. Whose position sounds more plausible, that of the Canadian Finance Minister or that of the Quebec Deputy Premier? Do you think Roger & Wells has important clients in Quebec?

6.   Should BankWest be concerned that Fuji Bank, a main competitor chartered in Japan with subsidiaries in California, has shown interest in expanding to Canada as well as to Mexico? Are the answers the same as asked above regarding Fuji Bank's interest in Mexico?

Harmonization of Currency Within the NAFTA—Why Not Adopt the U.S. Dollar?

The U.S. dollar has been the strongest currency in NAFTA, although it depreciated significantly against the Canadian dollar, the Euro and the Japanese yen in 2002—2004. From time to time there have been occasional suggestions that Canada and Mexico ought to adopt the dollar. Other countries have given the idea some thought, including Argentina (which maintained peso—dollar parity until 2001). Panama actually uses the dollar (bills, not coins) as its official currency, and has very low inflation. Ecuador and El Salvador have both pegged their currencies to the U.S. dollar.

President Carlos Menem of Argentina in early 1999 asked his finance ministry to consider the adoption of the U.S. dollar. Argentines were not aghast at the idea, as they have suffered from sometimes five digit inflation in the past. The nation had already taken severe steps to limit the powers of its central bank from inflationary actions, including prohibiting the central bank from (1) lowering interest rates to reduce recession, or (2) infusing capital into the regular banks for lending. Alan Blinder, former Federal Reserve vice chairman, believed that Argentina had effectively delegated to the U.S. Federal Reserve much of Argentina's monetary policy. After Mexico devalued its peso in December, 1994, Argentina asked the U.S. for an immediate shipment of four hundred million dollars in cash, because the Argentine people were worried about a devaluation of the Argentine currency and the demand for U.S. dollars increased dramatically. It may be hard for someone in the U.S. to consider even momentarily giving up the U.S. dollar, but Argentines have lived with terrible inflation. The Wall Street Journal noted that:

> Argentina's history makes talk of adopting the U.S. dollar as its own more than idle chatter. Disgusted by its central bank's inability to prevent hyperinflation, Argentina eight years ago put the central bank out of the business of printing money, created a new peso worth $1 each and passed a "currency board" law requiring the government to hold enough dollars in reserves so that every peso can be exchanged for a U.S. dollar. Inflation went from a peak of 5,000% in 1989 to roughly 1% today, an achievement as popular in Argentina as a World Cup victory in Soccer.

> The walls of El Portugues, a Buenos Aires steakhouse, offer a quick course in the country's sorry economic history. Framed on the wall are one-million peso bills from the late 1980s that are worthless today, a 1,000 peso bill stamped "1 austral" on its face from an unsuccessful 1985 attempt to stabilize the currency, and the austral bills themselves, bitter reminders of the hyperinflation of the late 1980s. Mariano Gutierrez–Walker, the restaurant's 28 year old manager says it does seem strange to think of using American dimes in Argentina. "But," he says, pointing to one of the framed bills on the wall, "I used to buy things with this bill here and it doesn't even exist anymore." Wall St. J., Jan. 18, 1999.

Any possibility of dollarizing the Argentine economy disappeared with the devaluation in 2001 and the resulting financial crisis. President Kirchner's administration has been unable to agree with the IMF on an economic recovery strategy, and appeared to have effectively defaulted on $82 billion in private bonds, notwithstanding an 8.7% annual growth rate in 2003 and a predicted 7.1% in 2004, with inflation below 3% annually.

The Argentine experience (both good and bad), and that of Panama, Ecuador and El Salvador, must influence thinking in Canada and Mexico. Three alternatives appear plausible. One is the adoption of the dollar by Canada and Mexico. The second is the adoption of a NAFTA currency, following the practice in the EU. The third is essentially the status quo, where most international trade transactions are denominated in U.S. dollars, and U.S. financial institutions are lending to businesses and individuals (mortgages) in dollars, to select clients buying homes from certain projects where U.S. builders are involved. (In Canada, in contrast, the use of U.S. currency is frowned upon, and conversion rates at retail establishments tend to greatly favor their Canadian owners.)

Several Northwest Mexican states, including Sonora, Baja California, and Baja California del Sur, are effectively dollarized, in that many transactions even on the street are paid in dollars.

In March, 1999 (pre Argentina collapse), the prestigious Mexican Businessmen's Council suggested dollarization to the president. To some degree Mexico is dollarized, like Argentina. But much less so, and only unofficially. Curiously, Mexican politicians have argued that such action would harm Mexico's traditional experiences of high inflation and more irregular growth.

That would seem an argument in favor, rather than against, dollarization. A middle-of the road course is also suggested, which is similar to the former Argentine practice. That would involve using both currencies with official approval, and would not mean the end of the Mexican peso, which is not likely for political reasons. In many ways, private Mexican banks are acting with more restraint than the government. The banks have stopped mortgage lending because of unpredictable inflation, and even car loans are hard to obtain without extremely high interest rates.

There is more talk of a NAFTA currency than dollarization in Mexico. But a NAFTA "euro" seems most unlikely. Because of the immense size of the U.S. economy compared to Canada or Mexico, any NAFTA currency would look very much like a dollar. Canadian support for a NAFTA currency has traditionally been led by Quebec, which tends to favor free trade, and de-linkage with English speaking Canada. Canada officially appears opposed to a NAFTA currency, but a leading think tank openly supports dollarization, which many in Canada view inevitable. *See* Courchene and Harris, From Fixing to Monetary Union: Options for North American Currency Integration, C.D. Howe Institute (June, 1999). Probably the most significant barrier is political: neither Canada nor Mexico is anxious for its monetary policy to be determined by actions of the Federal Reserve Board, which rarely if ever take Canadian or Mexican economic considerations into account when determining monetary policy.

FOLSOM, EUROPEAN UNION LAW IN A NUTSHELL
166 (4th Ed. 2004).*

ECONOMIC AND MONETARY UNION, A COMMON CURRENCY

The legal basis for the European Monetary System (EMS) and European Currency Units (ECUs) was substantially advanced by the addition to the Treaty of Rome of Article 98 in the Single European Act of 1987. This article committed the member states to further development of the EMS and ECU, recognized the cooperation of the central banks in management of the system, but specifically required further amendment of the Treaty if "institutional changes" were required. In other words, a common currency managed by an EU central bank system was *not* part of the campaign for a Europe without internal frontiers. Draft plans for such developments surfaced in the Commission using the U.S. Federal Reserve Board as a model. Britain, always concerned about losses of economic sovereignty (what greater loss is there?), proposed an alternative known as the "hard ECU." This proposal would have retained the national currencies but added the hard ECU as competitor of each, letting the marketplace in most instances decide which currency it preferred.

In December of 1989, the European Council (outvoting Britain) approved a three stage approach to economic and monetary union (EMU). Stage One began July 1, 1990. Its focus was on expanding the power and influence of the Committee of Central Bank Governors over monetary affairs. This Committee was a kind of EuroFed in embryo. It was primarily engaged in "multilateral surveillance." Stage One also sought greater economic policy coordination and convergence among the member states. Stage Two anticipated the creation of a European Union central banking system, but functioned with the existing national currencies in the context of the EMS and ERM. Stage Two was a learning and transition period. In October of 1990, it was agreed (save Britain) that Stage Two would commence January 1, 1994. This deadline was actually met, and the European Monetary Institute was installed in Frankfurt. It was the precursor to the European Central Bank. Stage Three involved the replacement of the national currencies with a single currency, the EURO, managed by a European Central Bank. In December of 1991, agreement was reached at Maastricht to implement Stage Three no later than Jan. 1, 1999 with a minimum of seven states. Britain and Denmark reserved a right to opt out of Stage Three.

All member states had to meet strict economic convergence criteria on inflation rates, government deficits, long-term interest rates and currency fluctuations. To join the third stage, a country was supposed to have an inflation rate not greater than 1.5 percent of the average of the three lowest member state rates, long-term interest rates no higher than 2 percent above the average of the three lowest, a budget deficit less than 3 percent of gross domestic product (GDP), a total public indebtedness of less than 60 percent of GDP, and no devaluation within the ERM during the prior two years. These criteria likewise govern admission of the new member states in May 2004, subject to certain grace periods.

It was also agreed at Maastricht that in the third stage the European Central Bank (ECB) and the European System of Central Banks (ECSB) would start operations. The ECB and ECSB are governed by an executive board of six persons appointed by the member states and the governors of the national central banks. The ECB and the ECSB are independent of any other European institution and in theory free from member state influence.

* * *

The main functions of the ECB and ECSB are: (1) define and implement regional monetary policy; (2) conduct foreign exchange operations; (3) hold and manage the official foreign reserves of the member states; and (4) supervise the payments systems. The ECB has the exclusive right to authorize the issue of bank notes within the Common Market and must set interest rates to principally achieve price stability. The Court of Justice may review the legality of ECB decisions. The ECB works closely with the Ecofin Council's broad guidelines for economic policy, such as keeping national budget deficits below 3 percent of GDP in all but exceptional circumstances (2 percent decline in annual GDP). If the Ecofin considers a national government's policy to be inconsistent with that of the region, it can recommend changes including budget cuts. If appropriate national action does not follow such a warning, the Ecofin can require a government to disclose the relevant information with its bond issues, block European Investment Bank credits, mandate punitive interest-free deposits, or levy fines and penalties. By 2003, Portugal, France, Italy and Germany were under threat of sanctions for failure to comply with the 3 percent budget deficit rule.

The economic performance of member states in 1997 became the test for admission to the economic and monetary union. Since both France and Germany had trouble meeting the admissions criteria, this opened a window for much more marginal states such as Belgium, Italy and Spain to join immediately. Greece also subsequently qualified for the EURO zone. As expected, Denmark, Britain and Sweden opted out of initial participation in the common currency. The Danes did so by voting No in a national referendum. The Swedes voted similarly in 2003.

On January 1, 1999, the participating states fixed the exchange rates between the EURO and their national currencies. National notes and coins were removed from the market by July 2002 as the EURO was installed. The EURO has been used for most commercial banking, foreign exchange and public debt purposes since 1999. It has also been adopted (voluntarily) by the world's securities markets, and by Monaco, San Marino, the Vatican, Andorra, Montenegro and Kosvo.

The arrival of the EURO has important implications for the United States and the dollar. For decades, the dollar has been the world's leading currency, although its dominance has been declining since the early 1980s. Use of the Deutsche Mark and Yen in commercial and financial transactions, and in savings and reserves, has been steadily rising. The EURO is likely to continue the dollar's decline in all of these markets. It is certainly the hope of many Europeans that they have successfully created a rival to the dollar.

Questions and Comments

1. The Canadian dollar had been declining in value against the U.S. dollar for many years, but increased from about $0.61 to $0.78 in 2002–2004. The Mexican peso has declined very significantly against the dollar over the past few decades, but has been much steadier since the collapse of the peso in December, 1994. Should Canada and/or Mexico adopt the U.S. dollar? Would it assist in cross-border financial transactions? What are the principal obstacles (economic and political)? Panama uses the U.S. dollar and thus has decades of experience; is the experience of an economy the size of Panama's relevant for Canada and Mexico. What lessons does the failed parity experiment hold? Would not use of the dollar control inflation in Mexico? Isn't the U.S. dollar already a "semi-official" currency in Mexico? If California has no control over U.S. monetary policy, why should Canada or Mexico expect to have any control? Might the U.S. government attempt to influence political decisions in Canada and Mexico were they to adopt the dollar? Is Brazil realistic in its dreams of having one of the four major world currencies? What should it aspire to?

2. The European Union has harmonized the European currency. The EU did not adopt any one member state's currency, but created a new currency, the "Euro," and, very importantly, a European Central Bank to

replace the national central banks. (However, the 3% limit on budget deficits is not being met by Germany, France and some other Euro–zone members.) Would the U.S. be willing to adopt a common currency and relinquish monetary policy to a board where only one of three votes was U.S.? Should a common currency be on the agenda for the Free Trade Area of the Americas negotiations? What is the difference between a NAFTA currency and dollarization by Canada and Mexico?

3.   What would be the impact on the U.S. if Mexico and Canada adopted the dollar, with or without the blessing of the U.S.? Some two-thirds of all U.S. currency already circulates *outside* the U.S. If the U.S. is asked by Canada to provide it with enough U.S. dollars to replace all the Canadian currency, what does Canada have to give up in return? Since the U.S. will receive items of value, and it costs about four cents to make a bill ($1 or $50), wouldn't the U.S. be receiving an interest free loan?

PART B. RESOLUTION OF FINANCIAL SERVICES DISPUTES

Articles 1414 and 1415 of Chapter 14 govern financial services dispute resolution. But they do not provide the framework for dispute resolution, but rather act as a conduit for the transfer of non-investment financial services disputes to Chapter 20 dispute resolution, and for financial investment disputes to Chapter 11 arbitration. But it is not that simple. Chapter 14 allows the Parties to keep some of the procedure within Chapter 14, such as the composition of a Chapter 20 dispute panel.

Assume that BankWest acquired Banco del Norte, a family owned group of banks in the state of Tamaulipas, just south of the Texas border. The banks were acquired for $27 million from the owner Hector Gomez, the sole owner. Hector Gomez' grandfather started the banks, and passed them to Hector's father. Hector has a brother Roberto who inherited one-half the banks, and who sold his half to Hector during the peso crisis in December, 1994, for about $2 million. Roberto was angry at the fact that his brother Hector has made so much money. Roberto used his $2 million to finance his campaign which has made him governor of the state. He has demanded that our client BankWest resell controlling interest in Banco del Norte for about one-tenth of its value. After BankWest refused, Governor Gomez began a campaign against the bank, also opening another bank which he owns with some political friends. Banco del Norte has been refused permission to open new branches, and when they have applied, the Governor's bank has quickly followed the rejection with an opening of one of his bank's branches at the planned location of Banco del Norte. The Governor has had bank examiners in every Banco del Norte branch, making demands that have interfered with the branches' work. Last week, several of the branches were locked shut because inspectors found "problems" with the bank branches, including litter in front of the bank, too dim exit sign lights, hiring away an employee of the Governor's new bank, and other alleged faults. Banco del Norte and BankWest believe that all of the charges are false, and the

Governor has said they will be withdrawn as soon as BankWest sells him Banco del Norte.

BankWest wants to know if they have any action against Mexico under the NAFTA for the above actions.

GORDON, NAFTA AND FINANCIAL DISPUTE RESOLUTION*

The NAFTA financial services dispute resolution provisions are quite modest, but constitute a further evolution from the brief provisions in the CFTA. The NAFTA Chapter 14 financial services provisions generally fully incorporate NAFTA Chapter 20 dispute resolution procedures, unless the parties wish to use special Chapter 14 financial services panels. When the dispute involves foreign *investment* in financial services, however, there are additional special provisions in the NAFTA Chapter 14, which may engage Chapter 11 investment dispute processes. Chapter 14 acknowledges the uniqueness of financial services disputes, or perhaps the political influence of the financial sector in demanding special provisions.

NON-INVESTMENT FINANCIAL SERVICES DISPUTE SETTLEMENT

For non-investment financial services disputes, Chapter 14 Articles 1413 and 1414 govern the process of consultation and dispute panel, respectively. Where the dispute involves a financial services investment, Article 1415 is applicable. Because investment disputes come within the Chapter 11 investment provisions, Article 1415 integrates financial services investment dispute resolution concepts with the provisions of Chapter 11, rather than Chapter 20.

Consultations: When a financial dispute involves a dispute other than an investment dispute, Articles 1413 and 1414 of Chapter 14 govern the process for consultations, and, if the consultations fail, effectively send the proceeding to a Chapter 20 dispute panel proceeding. Article 1413 provides for consultations on any issue of financial services at the request of any party. The Party to whom the request is addressed need only "give sympathetic consideration to the request." Art. 1413(1). There is no mandate that the Parties even agree to consult. Any consultation requested by a Party is to be conducted so as to include, if Canada is a Party, the Canadian Department of Finance; if Mexico is a Party, the Secretaría de Hacienda y Crédito Público; and if the United States is a Party, the Department of the Treasury (for banking and other financial services), and the Department of Commerce (for insurance services). There is no provision for the participation in, or even attendance at, a consultation by any person other than government officials of the Parties. The language of Article 1413 refers exclusively to certain government officials. However, because consultation is an informal process, the Parties could agree on the procedures to be followed, including participation by affected private persons and institutions in the financial

---

*Adapted from a paper presented at a conference on Non–Judicial Dispute Settlement in International Financial Transactions at the Law Centre for European and International Cooperation, Köln, Germany, March 22–23, 1999.

institutions which have given rise to the conflict, or which may be affected by the outcome of the consultation.

There are no specific procedures in the NAFTA governing how Article 1413 consultations are to be conducted. Presumably, the parties may decide how they are to proceed. There are, however, some rules regarding information disclosure. A Party may request, from the competent regulatory authority in another Party, information for *supervisory* purposes about a financial institution (or cross-border financial services provider) in the latter Party's territory. Art. 1413(5). Where information is needed for a consultation proceeding, a Party may request the regulatory authorities in another Party to participate in the consultations and provide information about the latter Party's "measures of general application" which affect the operations of either financial institutions or cross-border financial service providers located in the requesting Party's territory. Art. 1413(3). But the regulatory authorities are not required to disclose any information or take any action that might "interfere with the regulatory, supervisory, administrative or enforcement matters." Art. 1413(4). Thus, the challenged Party may reduce the effectiveness of a consultation proceeding by refusing to present needed information. It does not need to refuse to consult, but to appear and express with the deepest regret that disclosure of the requested and essential information would interfere with the Party's regulation of its financial services. Consultations will be effective only when all parties believe that there is sufficient information before all the parties present to lead to an effective resolution. But ineffective consultations are likely to be a prelude to the aggrieved Party initiating the more formal dispute panel process.

When there is a consultation, the results are to be reported to the Financial Services Committee at its annual meeting. Presumably each Party may report its own opinion of the results, or they might agree on a joint report. The report seems to be required whether or not the consultation proceeded to a successful agreement, although it is unlikely that failure of a Party to report a consultation is likely to lead to sanctions, which are not provided for in the Agreement.

Dispute Settlement Panel: Separate dispute resolution provisions for financial services disputes were included in order to assure that dispute panels addressing issues under Chapter 14—"Financial Services"— might be composed of persons with "expertise or experience in financial services law or practice, which may include the regulation of financial institutions." Art. 1413(3)(a). The make-up of financial services panels may vary depending upon the demands of the Parties.

The essential feature of the financial services dispute panel selection process is that the Chapter 20, Article 2011, panel selection procedures apply unless (1) the disputing Parties agree to a panel composed entirely of Chapter 14 roster members, or (2) where there is no such agreement but either disputing Party wishes to choose panel members from the Chapter 14 roster, and the Party complained against wishes to have the chair of the panel appointed from the Chapter 14 roster and is able to invoke the Article 1410 exception. Art 1414(4).

Each Party must maintain a Chapter 14 roster of up to 15 persons "willing and able" to serve. They are appointed by consensus for three year terms, and may be reappointed. The members must be persons with "expertise or experience in financial services law or practice, which may include the regulation of financial institutions." While a financial services dispute panel may be selected under the Article 2011 process (using Chapter 20 roster members), a dispute panel under Chapter 14 may be formed exclusively from Chapter 14 roster members if the disputing Parties agree. But such a panel is constituted only when the disputing Parties agree to have the panel composed entirely of persons from the Chapter 14 roster. A disputing Party may decide to select Chapter 14 roster panelists, **or** select some or all of them from the Article 20 roster, which consists of persons with "expertise or experience in law, international trade, other matters covered by this Agreement or the resolution of disputes arising under international trade agreements." Such use of Chapter 20 rosters is not mandatory when the parties do not agree to exclusively use Chapter 14 roster members; **either** disputing party may choose to select persons from either Chapter 14 or Chapter 20 rosters. Furthermore, if the Party complained against invokes the Article 1410 exception, the chair of the panel must meet the expertise or experience requirements of Article 1414, not Article 2009. The Article 1410 exception allows a Party to have measures which may be inconsistent with its obligations under NAFTA, if adopted or maintained for several reasons related to the protection of various persons involved in or owed a fiduciary duty by a financial institution; to maintain the safety, soundness, integrity or financial responsibility of financial institutions; or to ensure the integrity or stability of a Party's financial system.

Because the Article 1414 provisions applicable to financial services panels address only the composition of the panel, and remedies, the procedures of the panel hearings are the same as for Chapter 20 dispute panels. With regard to remedies, if the panel finds a measure of a Party to be inconsistent with the Agreement obligations, the remedy depends on the impact of the measure. First, if the measure affects *only* the financial services sector, benefits may only be suspended in that sector. Art. 1414(5)(a) Second, if the measure affects that sector *and* any other sector, benefits may be suspended in the financial services sector that have an equivalent effect to the effect in the other Party's financial sector which were the subject of the dispute. Third, the panel does not have the authority to suspend benefits where the questioned measures affect only a sector other than the financial services sector. The latter limitation would certainly seem appropriate when the panel is a financial services dispute panel which includes all or some Chapter 14 roster members. What if the parties to what seemed mostly or exclusively to be a financial services matter, had appointed **only** Chapter 20 roster members, who have the experience and authorization to deal with complaints in other sectors? But while the matter may deal with financial services issues, they are likely to contain broader issues, and the originator of the complaint would be likely to charge violations under several theories, and would have been unwise to choose dispute resolution under Chapter 14. Chapter 20 would be preferred. The composition of the panel ought to mirror the composition of the dispute.

The Chapter 20 report process both for initial and final reports applies to financial services disputes, unless it involves certain investment disputes, which have been submitted to arbitration, and are thus subject to special provisions. Art. 1415. Chapter 14 includes some limitations on the order of the panel, and thus what might be implemented. When the panel has found a measure inconsistent with obligations under the NAFTA, but it affects only the financial services sector, benefits may be suspended only in the financial services sector. Art. 1414(5). If it involves that sector and another sector, benefits in the financial services sector may be suspended which have an equivalent effect. If only another sector is involved, benefits in the financial services sector may not be suspended.

Chapter 14 issues which use Chapter 20 panels are subject to the rules of Chapter 20, and there is no appeal of a Chapter 20 decision. If a Party against whom a Chapter 20 arbitral panel has ruled believes that the decision was incorrect, it is likely to refuse to abide by the decision, accepting permissible countermeasures taken by the successful Party. Attempting to appeal the decision into the nation's court system would violate NAFTA obligations, which view the arbitral process as final, and would serve to diminish the overall effectiveness of the Agreement. That would be true no matter what the outcome of a court decision. A ruling upholding the arbitral panel would be meaningless and viewed as an unnecessary and improper interference with the NAFTA process. A ruling against the arbitral panel would be rejected by the affected Party and likely criticized by the third (non-participating) Party.

FINANCIAL SERVICES INVESTMENT DISPUTE SETTLEMENT.

When the financial services dispute involves an investment, Article 1415 incorporates Chapter 11 arbitration procedures. The financial services investment must meet the investment definition of Article 1416, which refers to an investment as defined by Article 1139. The focus of Chapter 11 is on the use of international arbitration to settle investment disputes. For a financial services investment dispute under Article 1116 (Claim by an Investor of a Party on Its Own Behalf) or 1117 (Claim by an Investor of a Party on Behalf of an Enterprise), submitted as a claim for arbitration under Section B of Chapter 11 (Investment—Settlement of Disputes between a Party and an Investor of Another Party), the disputing Party may invoke the Article 1410 exception, which causes the matter to be shifted from the arbitration tribunal to the Financial Services Committee for a decision regarding whether Article 1410 provides a valid defense. Art. 1415. Once the exception has been invoked, the arbitration tribunal may only proceed after receipt of a decision or report. If the defense is valid, the matter goes no further as a financial services process. If the defense is rejected, the matter will continue to be processed under the Article 1116 or 1117 arbitration provision. If no decision on the validity of the Article 1410 defense is made by the Committee within 60 days of receipt of the referral, either party may request the establishment of an arbitral panel under Article 2008 to hear the principal dispute. The membership of that panel is governed by the same Article 1414 provisions that govern non-investment financial services disputes, allowing a panel of Chapter 14 roster members, or of Chapter 20 roster members, or a mix of both.

However, there are other limitations on the use of the Chapter 11 investment provisions by investors in financial services. Article 1401:2 limits Chapter 11 actions to those charging violations of Articles 1109 (financial transfers), 1110 (expropriation), 1111 (special formalities and information requirements), 1113 (denial of benefits for certain third-country controlled enterprises), and 1114 (environmental measures). This means, most significantly, that alleged violations of Articles 1102 (national treatment), 1103 (most favored nation treatment) and 1105 (fair and equitable treatment) cannot be brought to a Chapter 11 arbitral tribunal. Rather, violations of national treatment or most favored nation treatment under Chapter 14 (there is no fair and equitable treatment provision) could be raised only by the home government under the provisions of Chapter 20. A Chapter 11 tribunal has already made a preliminary decision in a dispute regarding the purchase of dollar denominated Mexican bank debentures by a U.S. company that the company's national treatment and fair and equitable treatment claims are barred, effectively leaving only the expropriation claim (which remains in litigation). See Fireman's Fund Insurance Co. v. United Mexican States, Decision on the Preliminary Question ICSID Case No. ARB(AF)/02/01 (July 17, 2003).

Perhaps one ought to be hesitant in writing about a Chapter 14/20 dispute resolution system that is yet to be used. But the above outline of the system should illustrate a wise consideration of resolution of disputes in an extremely important sphere of activity. The NAFTA provisions serve a dual function, first to open financial markets, and second to provide a framework for the disputes which will inevitably arise once those markets are opened on paper, but perhaps not in actuality. It seems reasonable to predict that the financial dispute settlement provisions will not remain dormant indefinitely. When disputes do arise, it will become possible to test their value. In view of the general sense that Chapters 19 and 20 have functioned effectively, financial disputes coming under Chapter 20 ought to be resolved successfully when and if any arise. But financial *investment* disputes may be more problematic, as noted above.

Questions and Comments

1. The first decision when a conflict arises in the financial services industry is to determine whether or not it involves an investment dispute. Does it really make any difference whether the problem of Banco del Norte

and BankWest is characterized as an investment dispute or something else, such as a denial of national treatment in opening new branches? (See the discussion of Fireman's Fund, above.)

2.　For non-investment disputes, what factors would determine whether to use the provisions of Chapter 14 in selecting a panel, as opposed to using Chapter 20?

3.　If the dispute is an investment dispute, what form of arbitration would apply, UNCITRAL or one of the ICSID forms? How will the panel be selected? (See Chapter 7.)

4.　Is the dispute between BankWest and Banco Norte, and Mexico, the kind of *investment* suit Chapter 11 was intended to allow? How would a dispute between BankWest and Banco Del Norte be resolved if there were no involvement by Government Gomez or other Mexican state or federal officials? (See NAFTA, Article 2022.)

5.　There have been no financial services disputes thus far under NAFTA, Chapter 14 (except for the Fireman's Fund Case, discussed in Professor Gordon's note, which is really a Chapter 11 investment dispute). Why do you suppose such disputes have been so rare?

Chapter 7

FOREIGN INVESTMENT

7.0 INTRODUCTION: THE CONVERGENCE OF FOREIGN IN-VESTMENT LAWS AND RESOLUTION OF INVESTMENT DISPUTES IN THE NAFTA NATIONS

There are two schemes of foreign investment rules which must be addressed. The first are the foreign investment laws and regulations of the individual NAFTA Parties. The current respective foreign investment laws of Canada, Mexico and the United States are not only very different, but have reached their current status by means of quite separate histories. The second scheme is that of NAFTA, which establishes common laws in some areas, and seeks to extend that harmonization to nearly all foreign investment, with minimum exceptions. These are important provisions; the prior Canada–United States Free Trade Agreement (CFTA) included a few very modest provisions governing investment, only one of which addressed dispute settlement. But investment between Canada and the United States was considerably less restricted at the time CFTA was negotiated than between Mexico and the CFTA Parties at the time NAFTA was negotiated. What little groundwork was provided by CFTA for the later development of the NAFTA investment rules was nevertheless a helpful start. The GATT offered no such help, from its beginning it had not been intended to govern investment. Nor did the WTO offer guidelines; the WTO was still in the process of negotiation when the NAFTA was signed in 1992, and the investment provisions finalized in the WTO are of far more limited scope (largely dealing with performance requirements) than those of NAFTA.

CFTA should not be viewed as a harmonization of similar attitudes towards foreign investment, with NAFTA as adding a nation with a restrictive tradition towards such investment. In some respects, Canada and Mexico held similar views towards foreign investment, based on their experience with U.S. investment. Both nations were concerned with dominance by U.S. investment. Both were concerned that they would become the site for foreign (mainly U.S.) investment to extract natural resources for shipment abroad for manufacture. Both were concerned with the impact of dividends returned abroad to the parent corporate owners, and their impact on the nation's balance of payments. And finally, both were concerned that having so many foreign centers of decision-making would lead to few professional managerial positions in Canada and Mexico for host nation citizens, where the best jobs would be the supervision of the extraction of natural resources. This parallel concern of the U.S.'s north and south neighbors is partly why both Canada's and Mexico's foreign investment laws, outlined below, have been quite restrictive. But the Canadian laws have often been more sophisticated, addressing more closely acquisitions than greenfields (starting from scratch in a green field) investment.

There is more to NAFTA, however, than a common scheme of laws governing foreign investment. The Agreement also seeks to assure that a foreign investment is secure, and that treatment accorded foreign investment meets requirements of international law, including national treatment and "fair and equitable treatment". (Arts. 1102, 1105(1).) Because international law has been disappointing in its deficiencies regarding rules governing both the responsibility of the foreign investor towards the host state, and the host state towards the investor, this may be deceptive protection. The nature of international law governing takings of property, for example, has long been a major subject of debate. The NAFTA Parties have addressed this debate, and have included a substantial article governing "Expropriation and Compensation." (Art. 1110.)

The NAFTA Parties were often accused of failing to consider environmental issues in drafting the Agreement. This is certainly true in many areas covered in the Agreement, and the criticism and debate led to the adoption of the environmental side agreement.[1] Chapter 11 contains a provision stating that nothing "shall be construed to prevent a Party from adopting, maintaining, or enforcing any measure otherwise consistent with this Chapter that it considers appropriate to ensure that investment activity in its territory is undertaken in a manner sensitive to environmental concerns." (Article 1114(1).) However, this somewhat circular language would not necessarily preclude a finding by an arbitral panel that an otherwise legal environmental regulation required payment of compensation to a foreign investor whose business was damaged as a result. The fact remains, however, no NAFTA tribunal to date has reached such a conclusion.

The importance of the resolution of investment disputes is evident by the attention given such issue in NAFTA. While the general investment provisions are covered in the first 14 articles of Chapter 11, which comprise Section A, the next 24 articles, which comprise Section B, govern dispute settlement, as do the four annexes to Chapter 11. Chapter 11 was unique in a free trade agreement at the time of the

---

1. The NAFTA environmental provisions are the subject of Chapter 11 of this textbook.

negotiations, as it provides the rules governing foreign investment, the methods to settle disputes involving foreign investment, with the standing of *individual* investors of a Party to challenge the actions of another Party, rather than requiring the government of the investor to bring the claim. In all of these respects, Chapter 11 closely resembles the many bilateral investment treaties ("BITs") concluded by the United States, Canada and many other countries during the past 25 years, more than 1500 as of 2004, 45 by the United States alone. (There are over 2100 BITs, but some do not provide for binding investor-state arbitration.)

Although Chapter 11 is entitled "Investment", all investment is not necessarily governed by its provisions. As previously discussed, the notable exception is investment in financial services,[2] covered in Chapter 14, which includes rules both governing the investment, and outlining a procedure for the settlement of disputes. The dispute settlement provisions of Chapter 14 (see Art. 1415), however, are integrated with those of Chapter 11.

Comment on the Investment Laws of Canada, Mexico and the United States

Nations, including the United States, have seldom welcomed *all* foreign investment. Investment which offers the nation something it lacks, such as technology, or sufficient numbers of jobs, may be so welcome it is offered incentives. But foreign investment which competes with domestic investment may face very complex obstacles, or absolute prohibitions. Thus each nation has its own history of foreign investment rules. The respective histories of Canada, Mexico and the United States in developing each nation's current laws illustrates the struggle with balancing restrictions and incentives.

Canada. Although U.S. persons often view Canada through a mirror and see themselves, thus assuming that Canadians and the Canadian government will be very receptive to foreign investment, the policies of Canada over the years reflect an ambivalent attitude towards investment. Canada has long regulated foreign investment by both federal and provincial laws. Soon after its creation as a federation in 1867, Canada established high tariffs to protect infant industries from exports from the U.S. This caused U.S. manufacturers to invest in Canada to surmount the tariff wall. Soon the U.S. was the principal source of foreign investment, and for U.S. industries Canada was a natural location for the first foreign investments of many U.S. companies.

Most Canadian investment laws have focused on specific sectors, such as financial institutions, transportation, natural resources[3] and, quite importantly, publishing.[4] Canada was always a natural target for investment from

---

2. Financial services are discussed in Problem 6.3.

3. Oil and gas acquisitions were prohibited until the *Masse Policy* adopted in 1992 was rescinded, leaving such regulation to the Investment Canada Act, which allowed such investment, but with approval required of some acquisitions. The thresholds before approval was required were quite high, making the law less restrictive than it otherwise appeared.

4. Canada considers publishing to be a cultural industry. Until restrictions in the Canadian *Baie Comeau Policy* on ownership

the United States, especially since so much of the industrial development of the United States occurred relatively near the Canadian border. Canada's attitude toward foreign investment remained quite receptive until nationalistic forces in the 1960s began to challenge an open investment policy. The first measure of significance was the creation of the Foreign Investment Review Agency (FIRA) in 1974, which allowed the federal government to review proposed foreign investment, especially acquisitions of Canadian companies, and in some cases deny their development. The National Energy Program in 1980 was intended to *reduce* foreign ownership in the oil and gas industry. Most of that foreign ownership was by United States companies. A Conservative government elected in 1984 replaced the FIRA with the Investment Canada Act (ICA)(1985),[5] which governs foreign investment in Canada and especially acquisitions. When the CFTA was adopted, it incorporated part of the ICA, providing that a review of an acquisition under the ICA would not be subject to the CFTA dispute settlement provisions. (CFTA Art. 1608(1).) The ICA was to be amended to comply with the CFTA, but considerable definitional language in the ICA was retained by reference. When NAFTA was adopted, excluded from NAFTA dispute settlement provisions were decisions by Canada following a review under the ICA. This, plus the exclusion of "cultural industries" of Canada by incorporation of the CFTA provisions (Art. 2106, Annex 2106.), indicate that Canada has insisted in retaining some domestic control over foreign investment, especially the acquisition of Canadian owned industries, and most especially "cultural" industries.

Mexico. The U.S. has never viewed Mexico through the same mirror as Canada, seeing itself in the reflection. Despite all the differences between Canada and the U.S., Canada usually has been viewed an equal by the U.S. Not so with Mexico. The U.S. has traditionally viewed Mexico as something less than a partner. The U.S. views Mexico as needing the U.S., but the U.S. had not viewed the U.S. as needing Mexico, at least until NAFTA raised the prospects of a low wage platform to assist U.S. manufacturers in competing more effectively with their counterparts in the European Union and Japan. Mexico had responded accordingly, with suspicion and deliberation. While Canada never really flirted with socialism, substantially increasing national ownership of the means of production and distribution, Mexico did so in the 1970s. The Mexican investment law, the transfer of technology law, and the trade names and inventions law, all enacted in the 1970s, were models of restrictive laws of developing nations adopted during the tense and often bitter North–South dialogue, when developing nations argued that they were poor because the developed nations were rich, and that there had to be a transfer of wealth from the latter to the former. The 1973 Mexican investment law was such a product.

Several government actions reducing foreign ownership of investment brought considerable industrial production and distribution into government ownership long before the 1973 law. Mexico opened to foreign investment with few restrictions during the *Porfiriato,* the 1876–1911 reign of Porfirio

---

of publishing were relaxed, foreign investment in publishing was very difficult.

5. R.S.C. 1985, ch. 28 (1st Suppl.), *as amended* by 1988 ch. 65 and Investment Canada Regulations SOR/85–611, *as amended* by SOR/89–69.

Díaz. But the state assumed a more restrictive role with the new 1917 Constitution, which followed the revolutionary turmoil beginning in 1910. It soon became apparent that the state would begin to intervene in many areas where there was established foreign investment. After an unsuccessful attempt by Mexico to participate in the foreign owned petroleum industry in 1925, a labor dispute led to the total nationalization of the industry in 1938, reducing in the minds of many Mexicans the apparent conflict with Article 27 of the Mexican Constitution, which decreed all natural resources to be owned by the nation. Two years later, the government severely limited foreign participation in the communications sector. A 1944 Emergency Decree was the first broad attempt to regulate foreign investment, and limited certain investments to joint ventures. The joint venture concept was extended by a Mixed Ministerial Commission established in 1947, although it was of limited effectiveness. The 1950s saw some limited control of specific industries introduced, and electric power was nationalized in 1960. Mining was controlled by an act in 1961, but the next dozen years were relatively free of significant changes.

The 1973 Law to Promote Mexican Investment and Regulate Foreign Investment,[6] to some degree pulled together the policies of encouraging but limiting foreign investment, which had been introduced during the past several decades, and were clearly part of the Echeverrían Administration policy, which began in 1970. A strict 1972 Law for the Registration of the Transfer of Technology and the Use and Exploitation of Patents and Marks,[7] forewarned the coming restrictiveness towards foreign investment. The 1973 Investment Law classified investments, limiting some to state ownership, some to private ownership exclusively by Mexican nationals, and most of the rest where foreign ownership was limited to 49%. The law did not apply retroactively, but if a company expanded into new lines of products or new locations, it was expected to Mexicanize, that is to sell majority ownership to Mexicans. But escape provisions and the operational code in Mexico (the way things really work), resulted in few existing companies converting to Mexican majority ownership. What the laws did accomplish was to curtail significant new investment. A new institution, the National Commission on Foreign Investment, assumed substantial discretionary power to carry out the new rules.

What President Echeverría started, his successor José López Portillo continued when he entered office in 1976. His final year in office in 1982 saw first the amendment of the 1972 Transfer of Technology Law, retaining its restrictiveness and extending its scope, and second, the nationalization of the banking industry. His successor Miguel de la Madrid assumed control of a nation with a defaulted national debt, a plunging currency, and diminished interest by foreign investors. He realized that Mexico must change its policies. De la Madrid issued investment regulations in 1984 which partly relaxed the restrictiveness of the 1970s. Further regulations were issued in the following years, and in 1989, the first year of Carlos Salinas de Gortari's presidency, new Regulations were issued that were so inconsistent with the clear philosophy of the restrictive 1973 law that their Constitutionality was questioned. The direction was turned—Mexico's ascension into the strato-

6. Diario Oficial, Mar. 9, 1973.
7. Diario Oficial, Dec. 30, 1972.

sphere of developing nation restrictiveness towards foreign investment had reached its apogee in 1982, and was coming back to earth. Foreign investment was returning. It was further encouraged by Mexico's admission to the GATT in 1985, after years of internal debate. The replacement of the 1973 Investment Law twenty years after its introduction ended an unsettling era of Mexican foreign investment policy.

The 1993 Investment Act[8] was a highlight of the Salinas Administration, an encouragement to the many investors who had made commitments to Mexico during his administration, and a pre-requisite to participation in and compliance with NAFTA. The 1993 law improved access to investment in Mexico, containing investment attracting provisions absent from the earlier law. Abandoned was the mandatory joint venture focus, although that was never successful in stimulating foreign investment, and–over nine years–the elimination of the requirement of government approval for most foreign investments. Moreover, the new law permitted foreign ownership of property in the "prohibited zones"—100 km. from the borders and 50 km. from the seacoasts—for "commercial" purposes. But some significant restrictions remained, including control over natural resources, reservation of some areas for Mexican nationals, and retention of the Calvo Clause doctrine (in likely conflict with the international arbitration obligations of Mexico in NAFTA Chapter 11, Section B), which attempted to limit a foreign investor's use of its own nation's diplomatic efforts in the event of an investment conflict with Mexico. But the law nevertheless was a huge reversal of the policies of the 1970s, and it both established a more efficient National Registry of Foreign Investment, and allowed proposals to be assumed to have been approved if they were not acted upon within the established timeframe. (Regulations adopted 1999 are consistent with both the 1993 law, and its investment encouraging philosophy.) Mexico under NAFTA is not quite as open to foreign investment as are Canada and the United States, but with the 1993 law it had established a sufficiently respectful base from which to participate in NAFTA's foreign investment framework. It was quite a remarkable transformation, and a credit to several of Mexico's leaders.

United States. The United States has no "foreign investment law", or "foreign investment review agency", as have been discussed above with regard to Canada and Mexico, but it is incorrect to suggest that foreign investment is fully and freely admitted in the United States.[9] The U.S. has restrictions on foreign participation in facilities that produce or use nuclear materials. Domestic airlines are subject to a maximum 25 percent foreign equity (voting shares) ownership. Just as many foreign investment laws of other nations, including those discussed above of Canada and Mexico, have caused consternation in the U.S. about allegedly ambiguous provisions, the Exon–Florio amendment provisions have often proven to be unwelcome abroad. They especially include the absence of any definition of national security; decisions under Exon–Florio and similar legislation are excluded from arbitral review under NAFTA Chapters 11 and 20.(Art. 1138.1.) But for the most part the review process has not discouraged acquisition of U.S.

---

8. Diario Oficial, Dec. 27, 1993; see Documents Supplement.

9. But the U.S. Committee on Foreign Investment in the U.S. (CFIUS), under the authority in the Exon–Florio amendment to the Defense Production Act, does review a very few proposed acquisitions, where there are national security implications.

businesses, although there have been several instances where proposed acquisitions have been halted, and even reversed.

Comment on Foreign Investment and NAFTA

The NAFTA investment provisions in Chapter 11 are included in two major Sections. Section A covers investment rules, and Section B the settlement of investment disputes.

Section A includes several general rules which require each Party to offer specific treatment to each other Party. The most important is "national treatment," requiring treatment to another Party "no less favorable than that it accords" to the Party's own investors. (Art. 1102) This is similar to the provision that follows, that a Party accord investors of another Party treatment no less favorable than that it accords to any other Party or non-Party. (Art. 1103) There is also a requirement that the treatment of investors of another Party meet a minimum standard, incorporating a rule of "international law, including fair and equitable treatment and full protection and security." (Art. 1105) The "fair and equitable treatment" provisions has been the subject of enormous debate and at least half a dozen NAFTA arbitral tribunal decisions. These provisions are a kind of boiler-plate framework, and they have roots in the GATT treatment applicable to the sale of goods and in the bilateral investment treaties ("BITs") concluded by the United States with various developing countries since 1980. The national treatment concept in NAFTA applies equally to goods, services, technology and investment. But foreign investment has some special requirements, and several NAFTA provisions attempt to deal with them.

One ongoing concern of foreign investors has been *performance requirements*, local mandates that a certain percentage of the goods or services be exported, or be of domestic content, or meet a balance between import needs and exports, or link local sales to the volume of exports, or contain certain technology transferred from abroad, or mandate meeting certain exclusive sales targets. Each of these is addressed in NAFTA, with certain exceptions. (Art. 1106) Perhaps the second most disliked domestic restriction on foreign investment are mandated levels of local equity, the *involuntary joint venture*. A prohibition against a minimum level of domestic equity is included in the national treatment provision. (Art. 1102(4)) There is also a prohibition against a minimum number of local persons being appointed to senior management. (Art. 1107(1)) But there may be a local requirement that a majority of the board of directors (or a board committee) be nationals or residents, as long as the investor is not therefore impaired in controlling the investment. (Art. 1107(2)) A fourth investor concern is free transferability of profits, royalty payments, etc., both during the operation and upon liquidation of the investment. The Agreement attempts to assure this right, with some exceptions dealing with such issues as bankruptcy, securities trading, criminal offenses (money laundering), etc. (Art. 1109)

The above areas of concern deal mostly with the ability to commence and operate an investment free from certain restrictions. There is another time in the life of a corporation which has long been perhaps the most significant risk for foreign investors. That is when the business is nationalized or expropriated. NAFTA includes an eight part article outlining rules for both the taking, and the compensation. (Art. 1110) Nowhere do the words "prompt, adequate and effective" appear, the standard the United States government has long argued to be the mandate of international law, but constituting a standard specifically rejected by Mexico subsequent to the nationalization of petroleum in 1938. The language of NAFTA addresses each of these areas, however, in detail. Compensation "shall be paid without delay and be fully recognizable." But there have been disputes over whether an expropriation has occurred, particularly where the taking is indirect or "creeping." The adequacy of compensation issue is covered by the NAFTA requirement of "fair market value" appraised "immediately before" the expropriation occurs, and the adequacy by the requirement of payment in a "G7 currency", or one convertible to such currency. The expropriation article has also been the subject of considerable debate during the past ten years, and Article 1110 has been used on a number of occasions to challenge actions which are not traditional nationalizations, but more impediments to effective operation of an investment which significantly reduce its value (discussed in Problem 7.2).

Chapter 11 applies to all investments, as defined in Article 1139. But exempted are financial services investments covered in Chapter 14, and the numerous exemptions contained in Annex III,[10] and where special social services are performed (police, public health, etc.). (Art. 1101) But if the provisions of Chapter 11 conflict with provisions in other chapters, the latter prevails. (Art. 1112)

Section B governs the settlement of investment disputes between a Party and an investor of another Party. This part of Chapter 11 establishes a procedure for claims. It proceeds first by consultation or negotiation (Art. 1118), and then moves directly to arbitration under the ICSID Convention, the latter's Additional Facility Rules, or the UNCITRAL Arbitration Rules. Arbitration may be brought under the ICSID Convention where both the disputing Party and the Party of the investor are parties to the Convention; since neither Canada or Mexico are ICSID parties, the standard ICSID mechanism is not available at present for Chapter 11 disputes. However, the ICSID Additional Facility Rules apply if either the disputing Party or the Party of the investor is a party to the Convention, which makes the Additional Facility Rules available for U.S. and Mexico or U.S. and Canada disputes. The UNCITRAL arbitration rules are also available for such disputes, and for disputes between Canada and Mexico. But the matter is not fully shifted to these forms of arbitration; such issues as the selection of arbitrators, the place of arbitration, and enforcement are covered in NAFTA. (Arts. 1123–1124, 1130, 1136.)

The investment provisions of Chapter 11 are a major step in the multilateral agreement process. They are far more developed than those contained in the earlier CFTA, and the more recent WTO agreement on Trade–Related Investment Measures (TRIMS). As noted above, they follow U.S. practice with BITs, and after ten years, have served as a model for the investment provisions in the U.S.–Singapore and U.S.–Chile FTAs, the U.S.–Central American FTA ("CAFTA"), other bilateral FTAs currently being negotiated by the United States, and the 2004 U.S. Model BIT. They will

---

10. The Annex III Mexican reservations do not affect this problem.

likely be the model for the investment provisions of the FTAA as well if and when such an agreement is concluded.

However rational the progress in the development of the NAFTA investment rules may appear, these rules are not without their critics. The absence of serious attention to the environment and labor issues led to the adoption of NAFTA-saving environmental and labor side agreements. The negotiations for the FTAA and the various U.S. FTAs are also addressing both of these issues. But that is not enough to satisfy some critics. The rhetoric of the North–South dialogue of the 1960s and 1970s, reflected to some extent in the failure of the "Multilateral Agreement on Investment" at the OECD in 1998, has never really gone away. Turning their attention to NAFTA, some scholars and many NGOs suggest that NAFTA is little more than a way for the United States to further dominate investment in Mexico, by establishing rules which for the most part govern the conduct of Mexico in admitting investment, but omitting any consideration of the responsibilities of the foreign investor. Whether these concerns have some rational basis or are largely misplaced remains to be seen. After ten years, only four investors have recovered under Chapter 11, and expropriation has been found in only one case, *Metalclad*, discussed *infra*. The concerns about Chapter 11 as a mechanism to dominate Mexico may also have been misplaced. Of the 38 actions filed under Chapter 11 as of mid–2004, 13 were against Mexico, 11 against Canada, and 14 against the United States! In fact, many of the critics have done an about-face, and complain that Chapter 11 gives foreign investors in the United States greater rights than they would enjoy under U.S. law. The NAFTA jurisprudence, including a lengthy excerpt from the tribunal decision in *S.D. Myers v. Government of Canada*, is discussed under Problem 7.2.

PROBLEM 7.1 RESTRICTIONS ON INVESTMENT: PHOTO–MAT™ OF DALLAS EXPANDS ITS RETAIL STORES TO CANADA AND MEXICO

SECTION I. THE SETTING

Photo–Mat™, Inc. is incorporated in Texas, with its principal offices in Houston. It has more than 1,400 small, free standing photo development and film sales buildings in many mall parking lots, resort hotels, and on university campuses. They are concentrated in the Southwest, but have recently spread as far as Florida and Washington. All are called Photo–Mat™ Labs, and have very distinct architecture in the form of an old view camera with an open bellows. Photo–Mat™ owns about half of the locations, and franchises the remainder. Photo–Mat™ is interested in investing in both Mexico and Canada. It wishes to build as many as 100 company owned stores in several northern Mexico cities. Additionally, it wishes to build about 60 company owned stores in British Columbia, to be managed by the Northwest Region offices in Seattle.

Mexico

Photo–Mat™ is impressed with what it has learned about investing under NAFTA rules, after its officers and legal staff attended the annual conference of the U.S.-Mexico Law Institute in Santa Fe, New Mexico. But as proceeds with its planned investments in Mexico, valued at $30 million, it has encountered a number of questions which require resolution before the investment moves forward.

Photo–Mat™ believes it has properly complied with the provisions of the Mexican Foreign Investment Law of 1993, and its Regulations. It has put together a detailed investment plan, which will involve a wholly owned subsidiary incorporated in Mexico under the name Photo–Mat™ de México. Photo–Mat™ will retain ownership of the film processing machines which it will send to Mexico. The management of Photo–Mat™ is aware that NAFTA has "opened" investment in Mexico. Consequently, it is surprised by Mexico's proposed conditions on the offered tax incentives in the course of ongoing negotiations with the Mexican authorities. Moreover, Photo–Mat™ has learned that a smaller, Mexican-owned photo finishing firm, Una Hora Foto de Mexico, S.A. ("UHFM") has received a number of benefits that do not appear to be available to Photo–Mat™ under Mexican law. Most important, UHFM is permitted to import film, paper and chemicals from low cost sources in Asia, without paying any Mexican import duties or value added taxes. This benefit could give UHFM a significant cost advantage in competition with Photo–Mat™ .

The company's vice-president and counsel have a number of specific questions including whether the proposed conditions are consistent with Mexican law and with Mexico's obligations under the NAFTA:

1. Apart from any special arrangements for Mexican tax breaks, is approval of the National Foreign Investment Commission required for Photo–Mat's™ planned investments? Under what circumstances would new investments in Mexico require government approval?

2. May Photo–Mat™ staff its Mexican headquarters with six non-Mexican top managers? May it designate 8 (out of a total of 9) members of the Board of Directors of Photo–Mat de México from its U.S. (national) management? May it bring in a non-Mexican employee from its United States or other foreign operations to manage each of the 100 company owned stores in Mexico?

3. Does Mexican law require Photo–Mat™ to institute any particular type of training program to educate Mexican employees in the technical skills required to process the film, retail selling, and management?

4. Is Photo–Mat™ obligated to equip its stores in Mexico with the same level of technology for processing film as it uses in its United States stores?

5. May Photo–Mat™ use U.S.–produced photographic chemicals and print paper for all processing in Mexico, or is Photo–Mat™ obligated to use Mexican source chemicals, including those produced by Mexican or foreign owned companies located in Mexico?

6. If the Government of Mexico (or the states in which Photo–Photo–Mat™ operates) agree to provide tax incentives in the form of property and income tax relief or job training benefits—a proposal now under negotiation—may Mexico (or its states) require as a condition of those benefits that Photo–Mat™ locate ten of the 100 planned stores in several smaller cities and towns which were not originally planned locations for Photo–Mat™, require a specific training program that goes beyond what Photo–Mat™ has planned (no. 3, above), or demand the use of Mexican source chemicals (no. 4, above)?

7. Does it matter if any of these requirements are to be imposed not by the Mexican federal government, but by one or more of the Mexican states, based on state legislation that was in force as of January 1, 1994, and has not been modified?

8. May Mexico condition these incentives upon opening new locations in other parts of those towns as soon as the annual sales of the existing stores reaches a certain level? On requiring that Photo–Mat™ after ten years' operation in Mexico have a public offering on the Mexican stock exchange, to allow public participation in the acquisition of a minimum of ten percent of its shares? That all of its advertising in Mexico be undertaken by Mexican advertising companies (Mexican or foreign owned)? That all persons appearing in promotional photographs used in Mexico appear to "be" Mexican?

9. May Mexico condition the offered incentives upon Photo–Mat's™ agreeing that it will accept whatever treatment is accorded Mexican owned stores; will not seek the assistance of the United States government in the event of conflicts; and will accept the Mexican domestic courts as the exclusive forum for the resolution of disputes regarding the investment?

10. Assuming the project goes forward, would Photo–Mat™ have any basis for objecting to the more favorable treatment provided to UHFM, or demanding the same treatment for its operations in Mexico?

Canada

Photo–Mat™ has assumed that since it is not *acquiring* any companies in Canada (considered in Problem 7.2), it merely has to comply with Canadian and British Columbian provincial rules regarding forming and operating corporations. But it has run into some trouble with British Columbian provincial law. Photo–Mat™ has been told it will not be allowed to build its typical small processing building, in the form of a camera (one enters through the lens), because it is "incompatible" with Canadian architecture. Furthermore, the usual large signs located on the roof of Photo–Mat™ buildings will not be allowed, also because of provincial laws. The signs will be limited to signs over, or to the side of, the main entry doors, and of quite small size.

Photo–Mat™ hopes to be able to process films for local professional photographers, as well as the major part of its business, amateur photographers, but a Canadian federal law requires that all licensed, professional photographers must have their work processed within Canada by Canadian owned processors. This law is justified under the rules allowing Canada to protect Canadian cultural industries. Canadian processors are required to inform the Canadian National Tourist Commission of photographs which appear to depict Canada in an unfavorable manner.

Photo–Mat's™ legal division vice-president has also asked you to advise her on the consistency of these Canadian and local rules which will restrict Photo–Mat's™ proposed Canadian investment.

SECTION II.   FOCUS OF CONSIDERATION

While we have often stereotyped Mexico as a difficult nation in which to invest, and Canada as easy, we are to learn that stereotypes are often mythical. The Introduction in 7.0 outlines the development of investment laws in Canada and Mexico. Although NAFTA does not require each Party to repeal all laws governing foreign investment, it does require is that each Party treat investors of other Parties in certain ways. But there are also exceptions which allow the continuation of some vestiges of earlier restrictionist policies. Whether or not justified, they are part of NAFTA, and they are effective insofar as the are consistent with Chapter 11, and with the reservations of Annexes I and II. Our interest is principally in the way in which NAFTA affects our investment, rather than in whether or not national or local laws of the Parties are violated by the acts of the Canadian and Mexican governments.

The focus of this problem is mostly on the provisions in Section A of Chapter 11 of NAFTA. We reserve the articles of Section A dealing with expropriation, much of our discussion of fair and equitable treatment and national treatment, and all of Section B dealing with the settlement of investment disputes, for consideration in the following problem. Our principal focus here will be to consider the various restrictions applicable to the planned investments in Mexico and Canada. We will briefly consider whether the Mexican and Canadian government demands upon Photo–Mat™ violate Mexican and Canadian domestic law, respectively, as well as whether the demands are in conflict with commitments under NAFTA. This will work us through many of the provisions of Section A of Chapter 11, especially the performance requirements in Article 1106. Because NAFTA has just completed its first decade, and because only a few of the recorded investment conflict cases brought under NAFTA have involved the conditions of operation in Mexico or Canada, we do not have the wealth of jurisprudence now available on issues such as national treatment, fair and equitable treatment and expropriation.

Secondly, we will consider some criticisms of the overall approach of the NAFTA investment provisions, that the provisions are Canadian and

U.S. driven and offer little to Mexico, especially since they overlook the needs of Mexico as a developing nation.

The 1993 Mexican Foreign Investment Law, Chapter 11 and Annex I of the NAFTA are essential to this problem. They are included in the Documents Supplement.

SECTION III.   READINGS, QUESTIONS AND COMMENTS

PART A. THE MANDATES IMPOSED BY MEXICO AND CANA-DA

Comment on the Development of Investment Rules

Attempts to develop an International Trade Organization under the failed Havana Charter after WWII (when the successes included the creation of the IMF and World Bank, but only the bare-bones GATT in lieu of the ITO), left an investment rule abyss until bilateral investment treaties began to be used by European nations in the late 1950s. The U.S. joined in their use in the late 1970s. While rules for investment were not successfully developed on a multilateral basis by the UN's Code of Conduct attempts during the 1970s, the issue of the *settlement* of investment disputes took a major step with the 1965 conclusion of the Convention on the Settlement of Investment Disputes Between States and Nationals of Other States. Mar. 18, 1965; 17 U.S.T. 1270; T.I.A.S. 6090, 575 U.N.T.S. 159. The Convention established within the World Bank an affiliated institution called the International Centre for the Settlement of Investment Disputes (ICSID), located in Washington, D.C.

The GATT was never intended to include investment rules, which were to be in the failed ITO. Although one of the later GATT rounds might have addressed the issue, there were many obstacles, not the least being the problem with U.S. Congressional approval of such a major change or addition to the GATT. When the Uruguay Round negotiations began, intended to result in a major expansion of GATT coverage, in accordance with the Congressionally-mandated negotiating objectives, investment rules (along with trade in services, trade in agricultural products, intellectual property and dispute settlement) were a major focus of the U.S. negotiators. By the time the Agreement Establishing the WTO was approved in 1994, with its subsidiary agreement on Trade Related Investment Measures (TRIMs), the NAFTA, with its Chapter 11, was already in place. The Canada–U.S. Free Trade Agreement had covered investment in a modest manner, but with little attention to investment dispute settlement. The November 2001 WTO decision launching the "Doha Development Round" of WTO trade negotiations left open the possibility of negotiating a comprehensive agreement on investment (at the insistence of the European Union), but the topic was dropped from the agenda in July 2004.

One other organization requires mention. It is the Organization for Economic Cooperation and Development (OECD), formed essentially as a group of rich European NATO nations plus the U.S. and Canada, Australia, New Zealand, and Japan, with Finland and Turkey. The OECD has expanded its membership significantly, especially following the breakup of the USSR, with South Korea, Mexico, the Czech Republic, Hungary, Slovenia and Poland. The OECD issued Guidelines for Multinational Enterprises (1976) as a kind of non-binding code of conduct for its member states. The OECD sought to negotiate a Multilateral Agreement on Investment (MAI), which ultimately failed in 1998 over such issues as extraterritoriality, exceptions for the EU, the right to protect culture, and concerns that investment protection would erode the governments' ability to protect the environment and public health. Even the UN is back in the mix, working with the International Chamber of Commerce on investment rules which if successful–a very big "if"–would moderate the restrictiveness of the UN's earlier abortive efforts on "permanent sovereignty over natural resources" and the "Charter of Economic Rights and Duties of States."

VARGAS, MEXICO'S FOREIGN INVESTMENT ACT OF 1993

Mexican Law (Vargas ed. 1998).*

THE NEW FOREIGN INVESTMENT ACT 1993

* * *

The most distinctive feature of the 1993 Act is its clear policy to promote, not regulate, foreign investment. Although the new federal statute breaks away from the legal and administrative rigidity imposed by the 1973 Act, it shares some of the traditional policies of the old Act. At the same time, the 1993 Act advances some of the policies of liberalization and flexibility already contained in the 1989 Regulations to a higher legal plateau. Overall, the 1993 Act unquestionably represents the most progressive legal framework ever formulated in Mexico to govern foreign investment.

* * *

Provisions Contrary to the 1973 Act

The 1993 Act contains a number of innovative features. First, the new Act liberalizes access to, and participation in, foreign investment in Mexico by streamlining and expediting the corresponding administrative procedures. The most marked departure from the 1973 Act is the abandonment of its traditional "forty-nine to fifty-one percent" rule.

Second, the new Act adopts a clear promotional attitude aimed at attracting foreign capital to Mexico. . . .

Finally, the 1993 Act eliminates the imposition of performance requirements upon foreign investors, thus reducing to a minimum the exercise of discretionary powers on the part of competent Mexican authorities, including the Commission.

The elimination of performance requirements, including export requirements, capital controls, and domestic content percentages, were included in order to place the 1993 Act, especially Articles 8 and 9, in symmetry with the pertinent NAFTA provisions.

Provisions in Consonance with the 1973 Act

Despite its relative progress and openness, the 1993 Act continues to maintain a number of traditional legal policies and institutions. It is not difficult to understand why the drafters of the new statute lacked the courage to break away from past molds. One of the strongest arguments in favor of retaining certain traditional policies in an area as delicate as foreign investment, must be couched in historic and economic terms rather than legal concepts. For example, notwithstanding the recent emergence of a climate of intergovernmental cooperation and mutual respect that seeks to modify the difficult relations of the past, Mexico continues to have inherent reservations about its unavoidable situation as neighbor of the most powerful nation in the world. Thus, from an historic and economic perspective, this new warmer climate may be superficial rather than substantive.

Additionally, because of this chronic distrust, Mexico may feel more secure if it continues to keep exclusive control over certain natural resources and activities, such as petroleum, electricity, nuclear energy, and satellite communications. This approach is enunciated in Articles 5 and 6 of the 1993 Act, and is said to be for strategic and security considerations.

A number of years will have to pass before Mexico will even consider eliminating the most drastic of the restrictive policies of the 1993 Act. These policies consist of the activities exclusively reserved to the Mexican government and those restricted to Mexican nationals. If these restrictions are ever eliminated, it may be a gradual exercise in close consonance with the economic recovery that NAFTA is expected to trigger. It is likely to take place only as a direct result of a strong economy and a sound democratic system with respect for human rights and for the environment, however, and not as a proposition initiated by a country plagued with socio-economic and political problems principally caused by an unfair distribution of wealth.

The 1993 Act incorporates into its new text important traditional policies that were originally included in the 1973 Act.

Activities Reserved to the Government

The new Act continues to maintain a large number of activities reserved exclusively to the Mexican government as enumerated in Article 5. These activities involve: (1) petroleum, (2) basic petrochemicals, (3) electricity, (4) nuclear energy, (5) radioactive minerals, (6) satellite communications, (7) telegraph services, (8) radiotelegraphic and postal services, (9) railroads, (10) issuance of paper money and minting of money, and, (11) control, supervision, and surveillance of ports, airports, and heliports.

The activities enumerated in Article 5 of the 1993 Act are actually more extensive than those listed in Article 4 of the 1973 Act. In other words, there are *more activities* reserved exclusively to the government of Mexico in the current Act than in the old Act....

In consonance with Mexico's modern policy of deregulation, the 1993 Act slightly relaxes the traditional monopolistic intrusion of the Mexican Government in some activities previously considered strategic, such as mining, railroads, and wireless communications. The new statute, consistent with the 1989 Regulations, allows a variable degree of foreign investment in these areas.

* * *

A few words about the notion of economic activities reserved exclusively to the Mexican State are relevant. There is no question that, under international law, Mexico, as well as any other nation-state, has the sovereign right to reserve certain activities to its exclusive and absolute control. Traditionally, this approach has been applied to a select number of activities perceived to have a direct impact upon national security or other vital interest of the state. This basic concept may explain why, for example, petroleum and other hydrocarbons, nuclear energy, radioactive minerals, the issuance of paper money, and the minting of money, have always been under the exclusive control of the Government of Mexico. The national perception of what a strategic interest is, or even the definition of a vital interest, is subject to change, depending on time and progress made in science and technology.

* * *

Activities Reserved to Mexican Nationals

As enumerated in Article 6, the new Act perpetuates the existence of a number of activities exclusively reserved to Mexicans or to Mexican corporations with an Exclusion of Foreigners Clause.

These activities consist of the following: (1) national land transportation for passengers, tourism, and freight, not including messenger and package-delivery services; (2) retail gasoline sales and liquefied petroleum gas; (3) radio broadcasting services and other services in radio and television, other than cable television; (4) credit unions; (5) development banking institutions; and (6) rendering of professional and technical services.

The 1973 Act lists only five activities in this category. Surprisingly, the 1989 Regulations were quite prolific in this area, listing thirty-two economic activities exclusively reserved to Mexican nationals. Because Article 4 of the 1993 Act provides that, until the new Regulations to the new statute are published, the 1989 Regulations "shall continue to be in force in everything not inconsistent with this Act", it is valid to assume that most, if not all, of the thirty-two activities appearing in the 1989 Regulations continue to be in force.

In order to avoid any possible circumvention of the restrictions imposed on foreign investors by Article 6 of the new Act, this Article explicitly establishes in its final part:

> Foreign investment cannot participate in a direct manner in the activities and corporations mentioned in this article, nor through trusts, agreements, social or statutory covenants, pyramid schemes or any other mechanism granting them any control or participation, save what is provided in Title V of this Act.

Article 6 of the new Act establishes a schedule allowing foreign investment to have gradual, but increasing, participation in economic activities exclusively reserved to Mexicans; these activities include international ground transportation for passengers, tourism and freight between points within the territory of Mexico, and the service of administering bus terminals for passengers and related services. According to this article, foreign investment may participate in up to forty-nine percent of the capital stock of Mexican corporations as of December 1995; up to fifty-one percent as of January of 2001, and up to one hundred percent, as of January 1, 2004.

Activities with Fixed Maximum Percentages

Article 7 of the new Act maintains a limitation on foreign investment by preserving four categories with fixed maximum foreign investment percentages:

1) Up to 10%, in cooperatives;

2) Up to 25% of the capital stock of Mexican corporations in national transportation, air taxi transportation, and specialized transport;

3) Up to 30% of the capital stock of Mexican corporations that are corporations controlling financial groupings, credit institutions of multiple banking services, and brokerage houses; and

4) Up to 49% of the capital stock of Mexican corporations that are involved in insurance, bonds, money exchange, general deposit warehousing, manufacturing and selling of explosives, firearms and cartridges, printing and publication of domestic newspapers, cable television, basic telephone services, freshwater and coastal fishing in Mexico's exclusive economic zone, or shipping corporations.

* * *

SANDRINO, THE NAFTA INVESTMENT CHAPTER AND FOREIGN DIRECT INVESTMENT IN MEXICO: A THIRD WORLD PERSPECTIVE

27 Vanderbilt J. of Transnat'l L. 259 (1994).*

The NAFTA Investment Chapter and Mexico: New Rules on Governing Foreign Direct Investment

... The NAFTA investment obligations, particularly with respect to treatment, protection against dispossession, and compensation for expropriation of alien property, represent a significant shift in Mexico's position regarding traditional rules governing foreign investment. Since the nineteenth century, Mexico has contested vehemently the traditional principles of international law governing the protection of foreigners and foreign property. As previously discussed, the Mexican Constitution embodies the Calvo Doctrine, a direct challenge to the international minimum standard doctrine advocated by industrialized states in international economic relations. Furthermore, in the international arena, Mexico has led the Third World in a call for restructuring international law to support the sovereignty of every state in the treatment of foreign investment located in its territories.

A. Scope and Coverage: General Overview

The principles regarding scope and coverage application are found in the NAFTA provisions defining "investors" of the signatories. Under the treaty, an investor of a NAFTA party is defined to include "a NAFTA party or state enterprise thereof, or a national or an enterprise of such [p]arty, that seeks to make, is making or has made an investment." An enterprise of a NAFTA party includes all forms of business entities "constituted or organized" under the laws of that NAFTA party. The provisions of the Investment Chapter cover not only investors from a NAFTA party, but also investors with substantial business activities in NAFTA states. Investment is defined to include ownership and all interests in an enterprise, such as certain loans to an enterprise and equity and debt security of an enterprise. Investment covers interests that entitle an owner to share in income or profits of the enterprise, assets of the enterprise on dissolution, real estate, and tangible or intangible property, including intellectual property.

* * *

B. General Treatment Standards

1. National and Most–Favored–Nation Treatment

The Investment Chapter provides that each NAFTA party must treat NAFTA investors and their investments no less favorably than its own investors and investments. This principle, called a national treatment obligation, ensures the equality of treatment between foreigners and nationals. Furthermore, NAFTA provides that each NAFTA party treat NAFTA investors and their investments no less favorably than it treats investors or investments from third parties. This principle, known as Most Favored Nation, guarantees that treaty-protected investments will be treated at least as favorably by the NAFTA state as nationals and firms from any third state. To illustrate, if Mexico extends a particular benefit to investments from a state like Brazil, it must offer the same benefit to investors from the United States and Canada. These treatment principles apply to all measures relating to the "establishment, acquisition, expansion, management, conduct, operation, and sale or other disposition of investments." Subject to the agreed exceptions in the annexes, these obligations ensure that a NAFTA party may not subject enterprises to different or more onerous operating conditions simply by virtue of foreign ownership.

NAFTA provides that a NAFTA party must accord the better of either national or Most Favored Nation treatment. This allows the foreign investor to take advantage of whichever standard of treatment is more beneficial, ensuring that the foreign investor will suffer no disadvantage in relation to either host state nationals or to investors from third states. NAFTA expressly prohibits certain commonly encountered impediments to investment, such as requiring that a minimum level of equity be held by nationals or that certain senior management positions be reserved to local nationals.

For Mexico, the national treatment standard is clearly a departure from the requirement of minority ownership and control of the 1973 FIL....

2. *Minimum Standard of Treatment*

NAFTA requires that the host state accord to investments of a NAFTA party "treatment in accordance with international law, including fair and equitable treatment and full protection and security." The reference to international law in NAFTA signifies a recognition by the parties that customary principles of international law exist external to the treaty. "Fair and equitable" treatment is a classic formulation of international law. While the precise meaning of the phrase is open to a variety of interpretations, an important aspect of this standard is that foreign investors should not lack the protection and security afforded to nationals. Another important implication of the standard is that foreign investors should not, in comparison with nationals, be put at a competitive disadvantage in obtaining permits or authorizations necessary to conduct business operations in the state concerned.

C. *Prohibition of Performance Requirements*

NAFTA prohibits the imposition of performance requirements "in connection with the establishment, acquisition, expansion, management, conduct or operation of an investment of an investor of a Party or a nonparty in its territory." The list of performance requirements includes export performance, domestic content, domestic sourcing, trade balancing, product mandating, and technology transfer requirements. In addition to prohibiting these requirements, NAFTA prohibits a party from conditioning receipt of incentives in connection with an investment in its territory by requiring the investors of a NAFTA party or a nonparty to (1) give preference to domestic sourcing, (2) achieve a certain level of domestic content, or (3) achieve a certain trade balance by restricting domestic sales to some proportion of exports or foreign exchange earnings. NAFTA allows the NAFTA states, however, to condition the receipt of investment incentives on the location of production facilities, employment, employee training, or expansion of facilities in the NAFTA territory.

* * *

In the last decade, a number of Third World states have adopted more flexible foreign investment policies, partly because of their need for additional foreign capital to fuel economic growth. The incentive policies to attract foreign capital often were coupled with controls on foreign direct investment as a means of curbing the practices of TNCs. Industrialized states maintain that these performance requirements limit foreign participation in these markets and can be as injurious as restrictive tariffs. In their view, these performance requirements, if left to multiply, could become a serious impediment to a liberal world trading environment.

The issue of restrictive and distorting effects of performance requirements has reemerged in the Uruguay Round of GATT. Although performance requirements have been discussed on several occasions in past GATT rounds, in the Uruguay Round, the United States and some contracting parties to GATT offered certain "proposals" aimed at expanding GATT's institutional structure. One of these new issues, connected with issues of trade-related investment measures (TRIMs), seeks to link investment policy with trade policy and thereby bring within the framework of GATT rules those government investment measures that have a serious trade restrictive and distorting effect. The objective of the Uruguay Round with respect to TRIMs is to liberalize international investment so that it operates on the same basis as the conduct of international trade.

After having sought input from the business community, the United States offered an illustrative list of TRIMs in its negotiating plan. This extensive plan listed the kinds of TRIMs to be prohibited and basic principles for an agreement. The initial list of TRIMs submitted by the United States was rejected by developing states because it constrained the ability of developing states to control TNCs in their own territory. The coverage of TRIMs accorded in the draft Uruguay Round text has been limited primarily to domestic content and trade balancing requirements.

The performance requirements in the Investment Chapter of NAF-TA, which parallel the original United States proposals during the Uruguay Round, are much broader than the GATT TRIMs. Because the Uruguay Round ended without the contracting parties extending GATT to TRIMs, the performance requirements in NAFTA will give the United States a significant amount of leverage during the next Uruguay Round negotiations.

D. Transfers Relating to Investments

A foreign investment would be seriously impeded without the ability to transfer capital and profits out of the host state. Consequently, the transfer provision is one of the most important provisions in NAFTA. The NAFTA monetary transfer provision covers five basic issues relating to an investment of a NAFTA party in the territory of another NAFTA party. NAFTA provides that all of these transfers be made "freely and without delay," in "a freely usable currency at the market rate of exchange." This includes transfers to the investor, such as remittance of profits and dividends, the payment of interest and capital gains, management fees, and proceeds from the sale of liquidation of an investment. Transfer provisions in NAFTA also apply to payments under contract for goods or services in an investment to a third party, such as a subsidiary.

Industrialized states consider the ability to make monetary transfers one of the most important provisions in an investment treaty. Nevertheless, chronic balance-of-payment difficulties of most host states, and the host states' need to conserve foreign exchange to pay for essential goods and services, often make them unwilling or unable to grant investors the unrestricted right to make monetary transfers. Most Third World states have exchange control laws to regulate the conversion and currency abroad. For further protection, Third World states either have stipulated a rate of exchange in bilateral arrangements or have referred to IMF exchange regulations. The monetary transfers dilemma exemplifies the conflicting goals of the industrialized and Third World states. While industrialized states seek broad, unrestricted guarantees on monetary transfers, Third World states seek more restrictive options.

The NAFTA provision regarding monetary transfers echoes the guarantees that industrialized states and their investors and firms seek in order to maximize their investment projects. Under NAFTA, foreign investors will be able to make any transfers relating to an investment in a NAFTA state with broad and unrestricted guarantees [unless the Party is experiencing serious balance of payments difficulties–Article 2104].

* * *

THE SIGNIFICANCE OF THE NAFTA INVESTMENT PROVISIONS FOR THE THIRD WORLD

The foregoing assessment of the investment provisions in Chapter 11 of NAFTA demonstrates that Mexico's attitude towards foreign direct investment and the role of international law in its regulation have changed significantly. Since the nineteenth century Mexico persistently has challenged the traditional principles of state responsibility, asserting the sovereign interests of the host state. Inspired by the profound transformation in the political structure of the world in the 1960s and 1970s, Mexico led the Third World in challenging the traditional principles that had been established without the Third World's participation and consent. Third World states, contending that political developments had not been followed by economic and social transformation, called for a restructuring of international law. The emergence in the mid–1970s of the proposals for a NIEO [New International Economic Order] was one of the many indicators of the development of a consensus among the developing states on the rules governing North–South economic relations. The purpose of these new legal rules was to replace the structure of international economic relations with a fairer system, in an attempt to close the widening gap between Third World and industrialized states to remove international disequilibria and disparities.

More than two decades after the attack by Third World states on the traditional concept of state responsibility, the Third World is experiencing changing attitudes about foreign investment. Debt-burdened Third World states, in need of capital, have begun to re-open their economy to foreign investment. Like Mexico, these states are entering into arrangements with industrialized states that are reinvigorating traditional rules for international investment protection. But none of these arrangements have the broad scope of protection for foreign investment found in the investment provisions in NAFTA. These provisions reaffirm the traditional principles of international law. The negotiation of NAFTA by a Third World state and two industrialized states is significant for future North–South international economic relations.

* * *

Comment on Chapter 11 as a Model for Other Agreements

It was anticipated that NAFTA Chapter 11 might serve as a model for other, more broadly based agreements on foreign investment. This has been the case, but only recently, and probably not in the manner initially expected. Eleven years after NAFTA, and almost seven years after the failure of the MAI negotiations at the OECD, there is currently no broad ongoing multilateral effort to negotiate investment protection. To some extent, this must be traced not only to NGO but to governmental dissatisfaction with the constraints actually or hypothetically imposed on governmental actions, or on the national court process, particularly in areas affecting the environment and public health. Many of these concerns have arisen, not in disputes between U.S. and Mexican investors, but in the two dozen or so Chapter 11 investment disputes filed by U.S. investors against the Canadian government, and vice versa. Given that all prior U.S. experience with BIT type provisions has been in treaties with developing countries, the ability of developed country investors in other developed countries to bypass the local court system for resolution of investment disputes *in other developed countries* is essentially unique under NAFTA. (A great expansion of such developed-country-investor to developed country disputes, to the consternation of many both within and outside the governments, might well have occurred had the MAI negotiations been successfully concluded, and an OECD investment treaty ratified by its members.) While all of the U.S. BITs with various developing countries were fully reciprocal, there is relatively little investment by, say, Argentine nationals in the United States, and to the best of our knowledge, no foreign investor (other than in Canada under NAFTA) has ever sought international arbitration against the United States Government under a BIT.

Paradoxically, there has been an explosion in the conclusion of bilateral investment treaties (BITs), to a total of over 2000 world-wide by 2004. This presumably reflects the importance that individual developing countries, including many that in the past supported permanent sovereignty and "Charter of Economic Rights and Duties of States" (CERDS) resolutions in the United Nations, place on improving their "investment climate" so as to attract foreign capital for economic development purposes, with the jobs, exports and technology benefits that often result. A few major holdouts—Brazil and China, among others—has not stemmed the tide for the rest. The OAS, which provides technical support to the FTAA process, prepared a compendium of investment treaties in the Western Hemisphere for the working group. This compendium shows that the nations have already adopted quite similar approaches to regulating foreign investment, in such areas as the scope of the agreement, the treatment of foreign investment, transfers capital and earnings, expropriation, and dispute settlement.

The United States has negotiated more than 45 BITs, of which about 40 are in force, and after a multi-year moratorium is now concluding others, beginning in mid–2004 with Uruguay. Equally, NAFTA— Chapter 11 like provisions—with some significant modifications discussed in Part B—are finding their way into the many FTAs completed or under negotiations initiated by USTR Ambassador Zoellick. These include, *inter alia*, the U.S. FTAs already in force with Chile and Singapore; those for which negotiations have been completed (Central America, Dominican Republic, Morocco, Bahrain); and those under negotiations or soon to be negotiated (Colombia, Ecuador, Peru, Bolivia, South African Customs Union states). (The Australia FTA has Chapter 11, Section A–like provisions but no mandatory dispute settlement obligations). Should there be a comprehensive Free Trade Area of the Americas (FTAA) which includes an investment chapter—an exceedingly unlikely possibility at this writing—much of the same language would likely appear there as well. Thus, it is not unreasonable to assume that within 3–5 years the United States could have in force, through its FTAs and BITs, investment protection arrangements with 70–80 countries. These multiple agreements will not have the uniformity that would have been achieved in an MAI or similar broad multilateral agreement, but they will likely share many more similarities than differences.

MACDONALD, CHAPTER 11 OF NAFTA: WHAT ARE THE IMPLICATIONS FOR SOVEREIGNTY?
24 Canada–U.S. L. J. 281 (1998).*

In entering into Chapter 11 of the North American Free Trade Agreement (NAFTA), the chapter relating to investment, the government of Canada was confirming its departure from two long-established treaty-making customs. . . .

What are the two changes? The first is the undertaking to make comprehensive international commitments to protect foreign investment. . . . [t]he government of Canada in the past has been loath to enter into either bilateral or multilateral treaties guaranteeing investment. The second is that Canada has adhered to the more traditional view that nation-states, and, under some circumstances, international organizations, are the appropriate persons to make claims based on international law in international tribunals, but that nationals, either individual or corporate, are not. . . .

Over the past thirty years, there has been a clear trend towards protecting the rights of investors in other states by bilateral international treaties. Some, but not all of that process, was driven by international organizations such as the Organization for Economic Cooperation and Development (OECD), of which Canada is a member. Relative to other developed countries, Canada has been slow to accept the obligations of such treaties.

Canadian reluctance was in no sense because of hostility to international investment. From the very beginnings of European settlement in our part of North America, Canadian prosperity has been driven by investment from abroad, both public and private. It is not investment itself which has been the source of the Canadian reluctance, although there has always been a spirited national debate as to the potential risk of loss of control that investment might bring. Rather, it is the structure of the Canadian constitution, specifically the distribution of powers between the national and provincial governments, which has caused the government of Canada to hesitate in making international commitments to protect foreign investment.

. . . The constitutional changes of 1982 put important restraints on the freedom of action of both the federal and provincial governments in the field of civil rights. But, they did not impose rights comparable to those of American constitutional law in favour of the owners of property. The Canadian Charter of Rights, section 7, assures that "everyone has

* Copyright © 1998 Canada U.S. Law Journal. Reprinted with permission. (Donald Macdonald is a Canadian lawyer and diplomat who has held many government positions. He was the author of the *Macdonald Report*, which preceded Canada's entry into the CFTA and later the NAFTA.)

the right to life, liberty and security of the person ... ," but it does not go on, as do the Fifth and Fourteenth Amendments of the United States Constitution with respect to the powers of Congress or the States, to assure the right to "property."

... For a variety of reasons, political ideology, history, or just plain parochialism, the provincial governments that met with the federal government to negotiate the 1982 amendments were not able to agree on the protection of property rights....

An American listener may comment that, whatever the limitations on the protection of property within Canada, surely the government of Canada must be able, under its treaty-making power, to carry out treaty obligations to foreign countries to protect property as the United States could do under Article II, section 2 of the U.S. Constitution. The answer is that there was no provision for a domestic treaty ratification process comparable to that of the United States included in the Canadian constitutional arrangements of 1867, and governments in Canada have been unable to agree to include one since then, even though in the interval there has been an important change in Canada's place within the world. The Canadian government has the power to enter into treaties with foreign states on behalf of Canada as a whole, but the Canadian Parliament has no power to carry such treaties into effect within the country where the subject matter of the treaty and the enactment falls within the jurisdiction of the provincial governments. As the presiding judge in the leading case on this matter stated in his reasons for judgment:

> While the ship of state now sails on larger ventures and into foreign waters she still retains the water-tight compartments which are an essential part of her original structure....
>
> . . .
>
> In other words, the Dominion [as the national government was then described] cannot, merely by making promises to foreign countries, clothe itself with legislative authority inconsistent with the constitution which gave it birth.

It was because of those constitutional limitations that the government of Canada was reluctant to enter into international agreements which would require enforcement within the provincial area of jurisdiction....

Why then, it might be asked, did the cautious bureaucrats and Ministers from two successive Canadian Ministries throw caution to the winds and commit Canada to NAFTA to the wholehearted protection of foreign investment? ... I think that the government of Canada was prepared to take its constitutional chances because the investment provisions were included within a trade agreement. To continue the constitutional discussion, section 91(2) of the Canada Act of 1867 gives to the Parliament of Canada the power to make laws in relation to "the regulation of trade and commerce." The scope of that otherwise extensive phrase has been much cut down by judicial interpretation within Canada, but there has not, so far as I know, ever been an effective challenge of a trade agreement with a foreign country, an agreement negotiated and signed by the government of Canada pursuant to its executive powers and justified on the basis of the trade and commerce power. . . .

* * *

Questions and Comments

Mexico

1. One of the principal benefits of Chapter 11 and the 1993 FIL is the absence of the requirement of the specific approval of the Mexican Government for foreign investments under most circumstances. (See FIL, Article 8. Foreign investments must still be registered with the Foreign Ministry, FIL, Article 32.) What is the maximum dollar amount of investment permitted in Mexico without Commission approval? (See NAFTA, Annex I–4.) How is Photo–Mat™ affected, if at all? Suppose the investment had been made in 1995 instead of in 2005?

2. The restrictions proposed by the Mexican government and/or the states in exchange for tax incentives have not been received with enthusiasm at the home office of Photo–Mat™ in Houston. Photo–Mat™ fully planned to hire and, when and where needed, train Mexicans to work in its stores. But it had not given much thought to the *management* staff in Mexico. Photo–Mat™ de México is to have a board of directors, which Photo–Mat™ expects to control from the United States, Mexican law will govern the composition of that board of directors, and Photo–Mat™ has no problem complying with that law. It planned to send several U.S. employees to run the Mexican operation, at least for the time being. Are the individual store managers "senior management" such that the positions could be filled by expatriates?

3. To what extent are these conditions consistent with Articles 1106 and 1107 of NAFTA? Suppose the proposed restrictions on Photo-Mat's™ operations would apply *only* if Photo-Mat™ accepts the various tax and worker training incentives being offered by the federal and/or state government? Is there anything to prevent Photo-Mat™ from contracting for such benefits, giving up something in return? After all, Photo-Mat™ can refuse the proffered extra benefits and elect to enjoy all Mexican obligations to it under NAFTA Chapter 11 and the 1993 FIL.

4. Photo–Mat™ has several different processors in its various stores. Which one is used depends on the demand. Photo–Mat's™ interest in Mexico partly is because it believes it can use modern technology to reduce costs of, and speed-up the time for, processing. But it would always be likely to first test new technology in stores in the Houston area, near the company headquarters, before introducing it throughout the company's territories, including the rest of the United States, and abroad. What does the Mexican investment law require, if anything, regarding such technology choices by foreign investors?

5. Photo–Mat™ expects to save money on its North American operations by purchasing chemicals, paper and other supplies in large quantities

to supply its stores in all three countries. (It has contracts with Kodak in New York to supply all of its outlets, and receives both high quality products and volume discounts.) Photo–Mat™ estimates that it would increase its costs about 15 percent to use local products. Isn't this the same as requiring an automobile company to have 30 percent local content? May Mexico demand use of local supplies, either as a condition of tax benefits or otherwise?

6. Photo–Mat™ does not want to litigate before Mexican courts. It intends to use commercial arbitration for contracts with any Mexican suppliers, as do many Mexican businessmen in Mexico. And it thought it had a *right* to arbitration of any investment conflicts with the Mexican government under NAFTA. The *Calvo Clause* has long been a problem for foreign investors, although there are no apparent instances where a foreign investor forfeited property for seeking its home nation's government assistance. Is this a *Calvo Clause* requirement, or simply a permissible extension of national treatment to say that Photo–Mat™ is entitled to the same treatment as a Mexican investment, *but nothing more*? Would that be subject to challenge on the "fair and equitable" requirement of Article 1105's minimum requirements? For the *Calvo Clause* response of NAFTA, you have to shift over to Section B, Articles 1116–1117. The extract by Murphy might help with this analysis. Do his comments help Photo–Mat™?

7. Would a Mexican government requirement, again as a quid pro quo for tax incentives, that Photo–Mat™ make a public stock offering, violate the elimination of limits on majority ownership? Suppose Photo–Mat™ intends to have its Mexican employees participate in the company stock option plan. That would allow Mexicans to buy shares in the parent Photo–Mat™ company. It does not plan to relinquish any of the shares of Photo–Mat™ de México to any other parties.

8. Photo–Mat™ has a contract with a Los Angeles advertising agency, and it is very pleased with its work. The agency does not have a location in Mexico, but it might open one in the next few years if a few of its other clients invest in Mexico. But for now, Photo–Mat™ must argue that this is merely another NAFTA prohibited restriction. Is it? Is it a restriction with a basis in the Mexican investment law?

9. Note how some of these concerns of Mexico, as reflected in the proposal for tax benefits, may be consistent with what Prof. Alvarez discusses in the extracts in Part B. Do these address issues which some NAFTA critics believe ought to be covered in the Agreement, under some rules of responsibility of the foreign investor? Aren't the benefits of foreign investment significantly reduced if Photo–Mat™ can bring in large numbers of expatriate employees to service its stores, or transfer second level technology, or fail to purchase supplies from local sources? Part B may help answer some of these above questions, or at least offer a different perspective.

Canada

10. Is Photo–Mat™ correct in assuming that since it is not acquiring any companies in Canada, but opening new locations, it is not subject to any special reservations under NAFTA made by Canada? Were Photo–Mat™ involved in an acquisition, would NAFTA Chapter 11 Annex 1138.2 provisions prohibit a NAFTA review of a Canadian decision taken under the Investment Canada Act?

With respect to the British Columbian provincial laws restricting architecture and signs, Photo–Mat™ needs to know both whether these are prohibited under NAFTA, and whether the prohibitions extend to provincial laws, or just to federal laws. Canadian lawyer and government official Macdonald offers a perspective from Canada about the conflict over federal and provincial authority to regulate investment. The ability of the federal government, and therefore the applicability of NAFTA, in regulating subdivisions such as states, provinces, counties, cities, towns, etc., has constitutional dimensions. The federal government will probably argue that investment barriers are really trade barriers and are given to the federal government under the Canadian Constitution. British Columbia will argue that as a province it has rights over property in the province and that includes foreign investment. Who wins?

Perhaps we should first address what NAFTA says, and then consider, if need be, whether such a NAFTA restriction or obligation is in violation of the applicable Party's constitution. NAFTA Article 1101 suggests that its provisions apply to all "measures adopted or maintained by a Party relating to (a) investors of another Party." But we are not dealing with a measure of a Party, if the Party is only the federal government. Article 105 requires each Party to ensure that "state and provincial governments" observe the Agreement, so it would seem that British Columbia must comply with the Agreement, unless NAFTA is in violation of the Canadian Constitution. In any event, is this necessary to decide if we discover that the same rules are applied to all buildings in the province, not only ones owned by foreigners? But see Article 1108:1. What about Art. 1105 minimum standards—are they met even if national treatment is not violated? Some of the same considerations we worked through in the Mexican portion above apply to the first question, *if* NAFTA governs. But what do you tell the Photo–Mat™ legal vice-president about the architecture and sign requirements of British Columbia? Does it matter if the B.C. requirements were in force as of January 1, 1994?

11.   The federal laws which limit processing to Canadian processors seems clearly to be a violation of Art. 1102's national treatment obligations, and perhaps Art. 1106's prohibitions of certain performance requirements. If that is the conclusion, Canada might try to justify the action on cultural grounds. We have already explored some of the Canadian rules applying to culture, in Problem 5.3. Perhaps we might limit the inquiry here to whether Photo–Mat™ is a "cultural industry" under CFTA Art. 2012 definitions, which are incorporated into NAFTA.

Franchises in Mexico

12.   What if Photo–Mat™ planned 60 franchises in Mexico City. Are they "foreign investments" and thus governed by Chapter 11? The definition of an investment in Article 1139 is extensive. A Photo–Mat™ franchise in Mexico is considered an "enterprise" under (a) of Art. 1139, if it is organized under Mexican law, and includes corporations, partnerships, joint ventures and other associations (Art. 201), or if it is a branch. It is clearly not a branch of the U.S. company. But it certainly seems to be a partnership, joint venture or at least an "other association." Even if it can be argued that it is not an enterprise, Art. 1139 (h) may apply. We do not know whether Photo–Mat™ intends to commit "capital", but it is committing "other resources" in

the form of technology, and thus comes with Art. 1139(h). But under (i) of the same article, if the franchise is only a claim to money from a commercial contract for sale of services it is not covered. A franchise is a sale of services. If it is a sale of services, however, doesn't NAFTA Chapter 12, Cross–Border Trade in Services, become applicable? See, John M. Vernon and Carole A. Azulaye, *A Guide to Implementing Mexico's New Foreign Investment Law*, 13 Franchise L.J. 105 (1994).

Of course, even if NAFTA is not applicable, Mexican domestic law will apply to the franchise, especially the 1991 Law for the Protection and Promotion of Industrial Property (which may have implications under the NAFTA's intellectual property provisions, Chapter 17). Much of what the franchiser Photo–Mat™, Inc., and its Mexican franchisees, will be concerned with will be importing into Mexico all the requirements of a franchise, and the applicable tariff treatment under NAFTA. That is considered under other problems, especially Problem 5.1.

The Mexican Maquiladora Program

13.   Although Photo–Mat™'s investment in Mexico will not involve assembly, an important part of foreign investment in Mexico is the maquiladora program. The maquiladora program is discussed in Problem 5.1. See also, Panel Discussion, The Mexican Maquiladora: Rumors of its Death Are Premature, 7 U.S.-Mexico L.J. 203 (1999). Perhaps Photo–Mat™ might benefit from the maquila program. For film dropped at Photo–Mat™ stores along the border in the U.S., it might be taken across into a "twin-plant" in Mexico for processing, and returned to the United States store. U.S. duty would be paid only on the value of the processing. But that is only useful if the Mexican processing is fairly labor intensive, and most of Photo–Mat™'s processing is done by one person working at a large, highly automated machine. If Photo–Mat™ undertakes more labor intensive processing, for example specialized development and enlargement, it might even be worth air shipments to a Mexican border plant. But for now, Photo–Mat™ is interested in locating film processing stores in Mexico to serve *Mexican* photographers.

Special Industries

14.   Some industrial sectors are subject to special rules. For example, Annex 300–A: Trade and Investment in the Automotive Sector, includes provisions applicable both to exports of parts and finished vehicles, and to investment. With regard to investment, and consistent with Chapter 11, Mexico immediately allowed Canadian and U.S. investors to own up to 49 percent in an autoparts enterprise. That increased to 100 percent in 1999. The three principal U.S. automobile manufacturers (Ford, Chrysler and General Motors), have long been in Mexico with wholly owned subsidiaries (Chrysler is just less than 100%); it was the penetration of the auto*parts* industry that was of interest to Canadian and U.S. investors.

Investment Related Rule Developments in Other Forums

15.   NAFTA does not address other investment-related issues that have been discussed at the OECD negotiations such as tax harmonization and the existence of stock markets allowing takeovers by stock purchases, institutional obstacles to takeovers (such as the *keiretsu* structure in Japan, bank

holdings of equity in Germany, and measures in Quebec intended to retain provincial control of important enterprises), restrictions on privatized government companies which allow retention of local control by "golden shares", anti-takeover statutes in some U.S. states, use of non-voting shares in Canada to maintain local control, use of merger law to block takeovers, and administrative approval which may delay and discourage acquisitions (U.S. Exon–Florio law, Canadian review, etc.). Double taxation treaties are in force among the NAFTA Parties separately from NAFTA, and there is a broad exclusion of taxation from NAFTA coverage, in Article 2103.

PART B. NAFTA INVESTMENT RULES FROM A DIFFERENT PERSPECTIVE

ALVAREZ, CRITICAL THEORY AND THE NORTH AMERICAN FREE TRADE AGREEMENT'S CHAPTER ELEVEN

28 Inter–American L. Rev. 303 (1996–97)*

The rhetorical power of the NAFTA investment chapter—its perceived legitimacy among traditional international lawyers—needs to be compared to some troublesome realities on the ground. The rhetoric of the NAFTA investment chapter is that of scrupulous neutrality and equal protection. Its text is grounded in symmetrical and reciprocal rights as between the NAFTA parties and their investors. This befits the treaty's claim that it is a "fair" contract between "sovereign equals." The reality is quite different. There is no actual symmetry of direct benefits to the national investors of all three NAFTA parties—at least not for the foreseeable future. As few Mexican investors are likely to be in the position to penetrate the U.S. market, it is almost exclusively U.S., not Mexican, nationals that get the benefit of the investment chapter. In reality, U.S. firms, not Mexican companies, will be demanding national and most-favored-nation treatment; they, not Mexican firms, will be the ones relying on the NAFTA to renege on their prior promises to litigate in local courts; they, not small-or medium-sized Mexican firms, will be reaching for supposedly "impartial" international arbitration to resolve investor-state disputes; they, not Mexican nationals, will be able to challenge local ordinances as de facto confiscatory measures or as breaches of the NAFTA prohibition on performance requirements. U.S. firms will be the ones claiming the direct benefits of free unencumbered repatriation of profits. Thanks to guaranteed arbitration, U.S. multinationals, who have been largely responsible for the promulgation and entrenchment of the doctrine of state responsibility to aliens, will henceforth be in a strengthened position to claim the benefits of that doctrine as well as the growing body of "lex mercatoria" so favorable to their interests.

... The predictable consequences of investment liberalization within Mexico were scarcely considered, much less addressed, by the negotiators

* Copyright © 1996–97 Inter–American Law Review. Reprinted with permission.   (Jose Alvarez is professor of law at Columbia University.)

of the investment chapter. The social, cultural, and political costs of investment liberalization were not factored into the economists' models that produced this treaty. Yet, in the unmodelled real world, the Mexican people, especially those on the bottom of Mexican society, are now facing severe economic dislocations, which range from sectorial unemployment to a rising tide of bankruptcies for small-and medium-sized Mexican firms. For now, what the vast majority of the Mexican population has witnessed are the social costs of investment liberalization and not its presumed longer term benefits. . . .

The economic models that produced the NAFTA investment chapter focus on Mexican GNP, not equity. Even assuming that the sanguine estimates of economists prove correct with respect to the growth of the Mexican economy as a whole, no one knows whether the widening gap between Mexican elites and the desperately poor, along racial and ethnic lines, will only be exacerbated by FDI nor what the resulting social and political costs will be if the gap increases. Furthermore, investment liberalization, NAFTA-style, has been pursued without regard for the need to legitimize FDI to the Mexican people, and not merely to those in Chiapas. In Mexico and elsewhere, investment liberalization has been pursued without a vision of social justice, without real democratic legitimacy, and without concern for the historical record of FDI. NAFTA negotiators from all sides pretended that free trade and free investment were interchangeable phenomena—as if the import of a Sony television and the sale to a foreign investor of a treasured cultural icon are as indistinguishable politically as they are under economic theory. Many real world effects of incoming FDI flows were not addressed, at least not for Mexico.

* * *

The rhetoric of the investment chapter suggests a narrow economic treaty dealing with a limited set of protections for a defined group. The drafters of the NAFTA, as well as the commentators who have addressed it, tend to see it as a treaty within the self-contained sphere of "private" international law or, even more narrowly, "international economic law." In reality, this is a treaty that has an impact on the civil, political, economic, and social rights of a variety of individuals—from national investors driven out of business to those employed and unemployed by the changing fortunes and preferences of foreign multinational enterprises, especially in those sectors of the Mexican economy most likely to be dominated by foreign investors such as commercial agriculture and export manufacturing. But, if viewed as the human rights treaty that, in fact, it is, the NAFTA investment chapter is the most bizarre human rights treaty ever conceived.

Under the NAFTA investment chapter, corporate and natural investors have gained direct access to binding denationalized adjudication of any governmental measure that interferes with their ample rights. Many of the NAFTA investor protections echo human rights contained in the Universal Declaration of Human Rights and the principal human rights conventions, including rights against discrimination, to security, to recognition as a legal person, to nationality, to freedom of movement, and to own property and not be arbitrarily deprived of it. Interestingly, the United States has only managed to agree on such a potentially effective regime for human rights enforcement in the context of one type of legal person, the foreign investor, and not for any other human being.

Seen from this perspective, the NAFTA investment chapter is a human rights treaty for a special-interest group. Except for relatively weak side agreements, which deal with environmental and labor issues, this is a treaty that is effectively silent with respect to the rights of others, who may be affected by FDI flows, and that ignores many of the other rights also contained in the Universal Declaration of Human rights. In the chapter protecting the rights of businesses, there is no mention of a human being's right to "economic" rights "indispensable for . . . dignity and the free development of . . . personality." Similarly, there is no mention of a right to work, of free choice of employment, of just and favorable conditions of work, or of protection against unemployment. Neither is there mention of rights of "equal pay for equal work" and "just and favourable remuneration ensuring . . . an existence worthy of human dignity," or of the "right to form and to join trade unions." No one, not even the foreign investor's employees, are given enforceable rights to "rest and leisure, including reasonable limitations of working hours and periodic holidays with pay." No one is given a right to an "adequate" standard of living or a "right to education," and, of course, there is no discussion of a "social and international order" in which all of these human rights can be fully realized for all persons, not merely foreign investors. What is perhaps most striking in a treaty whose essential goal is economic development is that there is no attempt to connect the rights it so lavishly bestows on its investors to the needs of the collective; there is no real attempt to put flesh on concepts such as a "right to development" or "sustainable development."

* * *

Furthermore, the NAFTA investment chapter does not purport to impose any corresponding duties on the U.S. multinationals it privileges. The NAFTA chapter contains scarcely one word about the many duties that multinationals should owe host states under international law. These duties have been canvassed, for example, in the Draft Code on the Conduct of Transnational Corporations, which has been under discussion at the United Nations for years. There is no mention of duties to respect the national sovereignty of the states in which they operate; to contribute towards the achievement of national economic goals and development objectives; to implement contracts in good faith and to renegotiate contracts subject to a fundamental change in circumstances; to adhere to socio-cultural objectives and values; to respect human rights; to abstain from corrupt practices; to cooperate in the allocation of decisionmaking powers among their entities such as to enable them to contribute to economic development, local equity participation, and the managerial and technical training of nationals; and to give priority to the employ of nationals. Moreover, there is no mention of duties to avoid transfer pricing practices, which have the effect of modifying the tax base on which their entities are assessed or of evading exchange control measures; to cooperate with host state's transfer of technology goals; to perform their activities with due regard to relevant international standards of consumer protection; and to disclose financial information. While many of these duties are not regarded as controversial in the abstract, the prospect of making them as enforceable as the rights recognized in the NAFTA would have seemed heretical to NAFTA negotiators.

The bottom line is that instead of the comprehensive, balanced, and truly reciprocal investment regime that it purports to be, the NAFTA investment chapter is merely a short-sighted, one-way ratchet to reward and attract U.S. capital. Even those who assume that the attraction of foreign capital provides its own reward ought to be concerned should this treaty's imbalances undermine its promise to supply *stable* and *enduring* rights for foreign investors.

* * *

Once we use critical insights to "deconstruct" and "reconstruct" the NAFTA investment chapter, we may become aware that investment liberalization, NAFTA-style, is not what it appears to be: a manifestation of neutral or impersonal "market" forces. We may realize just how much the NAFTA investment chapter reflects U.S. laws and perspectives.

At the same time, it is important that race critics not be seen as mere naysayers. The challenge for race critics, as well as other critics of the NAFTA, is to help construct alternative models for "sustainable investment liberalization." As the United States strives for hemisphere-wide investment liberalization through a Free Trade Agreement for the Americas, or even globally, through negotiations in the Organization of Economic Cooperation and Development and the World Trade Organization, race critics may usefully remind government negotiators of the need to keep investment liberalization responsive to the desperate plight of the underclass in both FDI sending and receiving states as only this kind of liberalization is likely to survive the pressures of representative government. What everyone, on both sides of the North/South divide, *should* want are investment rules of the road that endure because they are perceived as, and are, fair.

Questions and Comments

1. Professor Sandrino's comments are positive regarding the direction taken by investment rules in NAFTA, but become less so as she discusses a new framework for the regulation of foreign investment. Compare the extract by Prof. Alvarez, who reminds us that the investment upon which NAFTA is focused is largely U.S. investment in Mexico, never mind that investment flows between the United States and Canada are much larger. Professor Alvarez emphasizes that quite forcefully. Does Prof. Alvarez offer

any new ideas that were not debated at length in the 1960s and 1970s under the North–South dialogue? Have the "legal crits" picked up the flag of the South in that dialogue? The literature of critical legal studies regarding U.S. trade and investment abroad is filled with stories about the way large multinational corporations function abroad, including treatment of labor, bribery of foreign officials, withdrawal of plants without considering the social impact, etc.

2. Are Professor Alvarez and others suggesting that the multinationals ought to stay at home? He notes that foreign investment in Mexico "has been pursued without regard for the need to legitimize FDI to the Mexican people ... without a vision of social justice, without real democratic legitimacy, and without concern for the historical record of FDI." Is he careful to follow up these serious charges with exactly how a company, for example our Photo–Mat™, should structure its investment and consider all these omissions? When he later reiterates some of the demands of the UN from the 1970s, can you develop these into concrete policies for Photo–Mat™ to follow in Mexico?

For a specific example, how can Photo–Mat™ "adhere to socio-cultural objectives and values" when it opens in Mexico? By translating its name and any logos to Spanish? By using Mexicans in advertising photographs? By adopting a trademark for use in Mexico which is clearly Mexican? By adapting its hours to the Mexican norm, even though it may not be required to do so under law? Are these legal issues, or issues that will be business decisions? With all the rhetoric that Professor Alvarez suggests is practiced by the investing nations, how can Photo–Mat™ translate the rhetoric of the developing nations into identifiable desires that may lead to the adoption of business practices that are profitable to Photo–Mat™, and appealing to the host nations? Who should determine whether traditional Mexican "values"– such as living in small cramped homes without paved floors, electricity, indoor plumbing or running water–should be jeopardized by exposure to the changes which may be brought about by foreign investment? More specifically, who should decide whether the disadvantages of foreign investment are outweighed by the advantages? Does it matter whether the Mexican government which made the decision to conclude NAFTA was effectively a one party system (governed by the PRI since the Mexican revolution) which could hardly be described as representative of the people? (Note that the Vincente Fox Administration, chosen by Mexico in a free election in 2000, has emphatically ratified Mexico's participation in NAFTA.)

3. Professor Alvarez suggests that although the NAFTA investment provisions are grounded in "scrupulous neutrality and equal protection", he adds that the "reality is quite different." What proof does he offer that Mexican investments in the United States are denied the investment rights in section A? Were Photo–Mat™ originally a Mexican corporation which wanted to invest in Canada and the United States, would it be denied national treatment, MFN, and the other benefits of Chapter 11? If NAFTA is based on "scrupulous neutrality and equal protection", doesn't that sound good to the Mexican entrepreneur planning to expand into Canada and the United States? Prof. Alvarez says there is no "actual symmetry of direct benefits"; what he must mean is that there is no symmetry of *quantity* of investment, rather than of *application* of the NAFTA rules. His article could

be written about the European Union, from the perspective of Spain or Greece, or any new developing nation additions. Considering the way nations are standing in the queue to join the EU, or to conclude FTAs with the United States, Canada or Japan, it does not appear that his arguments are discouraging economic unions between disparate economies, based on these principles of "scrupulous neutrality and equal protection". The Alvarez article was written in 1996, before any of the now voluminous NAFTA Chapter 11 jurisprudence was available. Does Professor Alvarez (like most of the NAFTA drafters) assume that Mexico would be the respondent in all or almost all of the Chapter 11 cases? There is in fact some significant Mexican investment in the United States, particularly in the cement industry: Cementos Mexicanos is now the largest cement producer in the United States. There will probably be some significant Mexican investment in the trucking business, now that the U.S. moratorium has been lifted. (See Chapter 6.)

4. When Professor Alvarez turns to some of the areas earlier addressed by the UN in the 1970s, he repeats a long list of grievances of the developing world. All may be addressed in specific rules, whether host nation, home nation or through multinational institutions. (For example, Mexican law prohibits their officials from receiving bribes, U.S. Foreign Corrupt Practices Act prohibits U.S. persons from making them to Mexican officials, and the recent OECD Convention affirms and develops these rules. However, corruption in Mexico remains a serious problem.) But many such rules are vague, and would create wonderment on the part of Photo–Mat™ if presented without explanation. For example, what are Mexico's transfer of technology goals? Are they as expressed in the restrictive 1972 Mexican transfer of technology law, or in the current technology protection laws? Is Photo–Mat™ to comply with the view often expressed by developing country nationalists, that all technology is the patrimony of mankind, and not subject to exploitation for profit?

5. Assume Mexico totally discouraged all foreign investment. What would be its prospects for economic development? Many Mexican businessmen complain that the *lack* of available tax and other incentives in Mexico, along with relatively high cost labor in parts of Mexico, act as a disincentive to investment, and actually favor countries such as China that have more extensive incentive programs for foreign investment.

6. Who ought to govern investment, the nation in which the investment capital originates, the host nation for the investment, or perhaps some international organization? Or a mix of the three? We need to remember that nearly all foreign investment capital is *private* capital, which usually has choices. But being *private* does not necessarily mean being socially responsible, whether the investment is at home or abroad. Is the social responsibility of a corporation, whether it acts at home or abroad, solely to make profits, and the responsibility of the host nation to see that it also acts socially responsible according to host nation norms? Does that put a burden on Mexico as a host nation that it is unable to assume? If the officers of Photo–Mat™ are listening, how much more do we need to say before they will decide it is much easier to stay home, or divert the proposed Mexican investment to Canada, or to the developed nations of Western Europe, or the emerging market economies of Eastern Europe, or China? The 1960s and 1970s saw

much investment stay north of the border, or flow into other developed countries, principally in Europe.

7. To date, there have been only two NAFTA Chapter 11 tribunal decisions interpreting Article 1106, both involving investments in Canada, not Mexico. In *S.D. Myers v. Canada* (Nov. 12, 2000), 40 ILM 1408 (2001), the investor argued that Canada's ban on the exportation of hazardous waste (PCBs), forcing their disposal in Canada, constituted a prohibited performance requirement. The tribunal disagreed, essentially holding unless a measure was expressly prohibited under Article 1106 it was not actionable as a performance requirement. (That tribunal ultimately found a compensable denial of national treatment under Article 1102.) In *Pope & Talbot v. Canada* (Interim Award, Jun. 26, 2000), the investor argued that Canada's restriction of softwood lumber exports to the United States through the use of an export licensing scheme was an unlawful performance requirement. That tribunal also adopted a narrow reading of Article 1106, holding that the seven express requirements of Article 1106(1) and four in Article 1106(3) "are limiting in each case." See Rajeev Sharma, *The Jurisprudence Interpreting NAFTA Article 1106: The Prohibition Against Performance Requirements, in* NAFTA Investment Law and Arbitration: Past Issues, Current Practice, Future Prospects 77, 83–87 (Todd Weiler, ed., Transnational Publ. 2004). Chapter 11 pleadings and decisions, many of which are not formally published even in ILM, are with a few exceptions found at http://www.NAFTAlaw.org, a privately managed website by Professor and frequent Chapter 11 litigator Todd Weiler. See also the official government websites, http://international.gc.ca (Government of Canada); http://www.state.gov/documents/ (U.S. Government); http://www.economia-snci.gob.mx (Mexico).

PROBLEM 7.2 THE SETTLEMENT OF INVESTMENT DISPUTES UNDER CHAPTER 11: U.S.–OWNED HAZARDOUS WASTE TRANSFER STATION AND LANDFILL OPERATOR PREVENTED FROM OPERATING CANADIAN FACILITY

SECTION I. THE SETTING

You are a lawyer for International Trade Canada—the government agency that is responsible for defending Canada in investment disputes—and have been asked to prepare an analysis for your superior of the case brought under Chapter 11 by Waste Disposal, Inc. (WDI).

Four years ago the Canadian federal government authorized WDI to construct and operate a transfer station for hazardous waste in a sparsely populated area 200 miles north of Toronto on some 400 acres. Approximately 800 people live within six miles of the site. Some make their living as hunting guides because the area is teeming with numerous varieties of ducks. The Canadian environmental ministry (Environment Canada) issued WDI a federal permit to construct a hazardous waste landfill. Shortly thereafter, the Ontario government granted WDI a provincial land use permit to operate the landfill. The provincial permit was issued subject to the condition that the project adapt to the specifications and technical requirements indicated by the corresponding authorities, meaning the federal, provincial and municipal governments.

One month later, WDI officials met with the Premier of Ontario to discuss the project. WDI asserts that at this meeting it obtained the Premier's support for the project. The Premier has denied this repeatedly since learning of WDI's assertions.

WDI further asserts that it was told by the Premier of Ontario that all necessary permits for the landfill had been issued with the exception of the federal permit for *operation* of the landfill. A written statement submitted by the head of the responsible Environment Canada agency suggests that a hazardous waste landfill could be built if all permits required by the corresponding federal and provincial laws were acquired. WDI admits that it was never clear that the responsibility for obtaining project support in the province and local municipality lay with the federal government, but it believed that to be the case.

Environment Canada granted WDI the federal permit for operation of the landfill. Shortly after the issuance of the federal permit, the Premier of Ontario, believed to be considering a campaign for Prime Minister of Canada, joined a public campaign to denounce and prevent the operation of the landfill. WDI had believed that after months of negotiation it had secured Ontario's agreement to support the project. WDI began construction of the landfill. Canada denies the alleged Ontario agreement or support had ever been obtained.

Construction continued openly and without interruption and federal and provincial officials inspected the construction site during this period, and WDI provided them with written status reports of its progress. But just before completion of the construction, Ontario and the local municipality encompassing the project ordered the cessation of all construction activities due to the absence of a municipal construction permit. Construction was abruptly terminated.

WDI asserts that it was once again told by federal officials that it had all the authority necessary to construct and operate the landfill; that federal officials said it should apply for the municipal construction permit to facilitate an amicable relationship with the municipality; that federal officials assured it that the municipality would issue the permit as a matter of course; and that the municipality lacked any basis for denying the construction permit. Canada denies that any federal officials represented that a municipal permit was not required or that the federal government would obtain the permit for WDI, and affirmatively states that a permit was required and that WDI knew, or should have known, that the permit was required. WDI resumed construction and submitted an application for a municipal construction permit. Meanwhile, the federal government granted WDI an additional federal construction permit to construct the final disposition cell for hazardous waste and other complimentary structures such as the landfill's administration building and laboratory. At about the same time, the Provincial University of Ontario issued a study reversing earlier findings and stating that the proposed landfill was geographically unsuitable for a hazardous waste landfill, creating great health risks for the 800 people living in the area. This supported an earlier private study commissioned by Environment Canada that had made similar conclusions. WDI was never told of the latter report.

WDI completed construction of the landfill, and held an "open house," or "inauguration," of the landfill which was attended by a number of dignitaries from the United States and from Canada's federal, provincial and local governments. Demonstrators impeded the "inauguration," blocked the exit and entry of buses carrying guests and workers, and employed tactics of intimidation against WDI. WDI asserts that the demonstration was organized at least in part by the provincial and local governments, and that provincial and local police assisted in blocking traffic into and out of the site. WDI was thenceforth effectively prevented from opening the landfill.

After months of negotiation, WDI and the federal government of Canada, entered into an agreement that provided for and allowed operation of the landfill. The Premier of Ontario, however, denounced the agreement shortly after it was publicly announced.

One year after WDI's application for the municipal construction permit was filed, the application was denied. In doing this, the municipality noted the "impropriety" of WDI's construction of the landfill prior to receiving a municipal construction permit. There is no indication that the municipality gave any consideration to the construction of the landfill and the efforts at the operation during the year during which the application was pending.

WDI has pointed out that there was no evidence of inadequacy of performance by WDI of any legal obligation, nor any showing that WDI violated the terms of any federal or provincial permit; that the federal government had preempted governance of the construction and operation of landfills and that WDI therefore had no need to obtain a municipal permit; that the environmental studies were a sham and politically motivated; and that most of the specific construction requirements had been met.

WDI, Ontario and the municipality continued to attempt to resolve their issues with respect to the operation of the landfill. These efforts failed. A month before the expiry of his term, the Premier of Ontario issued an Ecological Decree declaring a Natural Area for the protection of the beloved and endangered Loon, a bird of great national pride. The Natural Area encompasses the area of the landfill. WDI relies in part on this Ecological Decree as an additional element in its claim of expropriation, maintaining that the decree effectively and permanently precluded the operation of the landfill. WDI also alleges, on the basis of reports by Canadian media, that the Premier of Ontario stated that the Ecological Decree "definitely cancelled any possibility that exists of opening the disputed industrial waste landfill". WDI also asserts that a high level Ontario official, with respect to the Ecological Decree and as reported by Ontario media, "expressed confidence in closing in this way, all possibility for the U.S. firm WDI to operate its landfill in this zone, independently of the future outcome of any claim it might bring before any tribunal, including an arbitral panel the NAFTA treaty." The landfill remains dormant. WDI has not sold or transferred any portion of it. WDI initiated the present arbitral proceeding against the Government of Canada under Chapter Eleven of the NAFTA.

SECTION II. FOCUS OF CONSIDERATION

This problem concentrates principally on the process of dispute settlement in Chapter 11, outlined in Introduction 7.0. NAFTA provisions carry further the investment provisions of the CFTA. Adding Mexico to form NAFTA meant addressing several investment law problems that had not been at issue in relations between Canada and the United States. One was the impact of the Mexican *Calvo Clause* concept, as discussed in problem 7.1. Mexico was additionally reluctant to accept international law as applicable law to determining compensation subsequent to an expropriation, or restricting government actions with regard to its treatment generally of foreign investment. Mexico had long rejected the U.S. view that international law requires prompt, adequate and effective compensation. Mexico believed the applicable law was domestic law, and the standard more "appropriate" or "just", than the U.S. view. However, as indicated earlier, during the first eleven years of NAFTA about 60% of the NAFTA Chapter 11 cases filed were against the government of Canada and the United States, not Mexico.

In most "traditional" expropriation cases, the issue is not whether the conduct constitutes an expropriation, as there usually is a fairly clear intervention, if not confiscation, of the property. The conflict usually is over the proper method of determining compensation. Our Canadian–U.S. conflict is different, like most of the expropriation-related litigation between NAFTA investors and NAFTA governments (including those against Mexico). The dispute will likely include a question of proper compensation, if there has been an expropriation. But more importantly, the Waste Disposal International case raises questions as to the definition of expropriation which are dealt with imperfectly in Chapter 11, with terms such as "indirect" or "tantamount to expropriation" used but not defined. In our problem we must address the takings issue. We must also consider other grounds under NAFTA for compensation, including national treatment (probably very weak here but the basis for a finding of a violation in *S.D. Myers*) and violation of the internationally required minimum standard of treatment, including denial of fair and equitable treatment, which has been used as a basis of attack in *S.D. Myers, Loewen* and *Mondev* in similar NAFTA cases. These issues, plus the process of referring the matter to arbitration under Chapter 11 section B, are the central areas of focus of this problem.

The materials raise other questions in addition to what constitutes an expropriation. Given that Chapter 11 does not explicitly require the exhaustion of local remedies before turning to international arbitration, we must also assess the effect of a domestic court decision, if any, on the arbitral process. Another question is whether the use of Chapter 11 by WDI and in some of the cases brought to date, is consistent with the intent expressed in Chapter 11. Finally, there is an overriding issue that is the subject of much controversy today in Canada and the United States: is Chapter 11, in which international arbitration is substituted for domestic court litigation, or supplements such litigation, appropriate for countries such as Canada and the United States, which have administrative and judicial systems which are generally considered to be independent, expert and non-corrupt, particularly if Chapter 11 provides recoveries to foreign investors that would not be available to their domestic counterparts under similar circumstances.

Chapter 11 of NAFTA is essential to an analysis of this problem. It appears in the Documents Supplement.

SECTION III. READINGS, QUESTIONS AND COMMENTS

GANTZ, RESOLUTION OF INVESTMENT DISPUTES UNDER THE NORTH AMERICAN FREE TRADE AGREEMENT

10 Ariz. J. of Int'l & Comp. L. 335 (1993).*

A. HISTORICAL BACKGROUND

There is surely great irony in the fact that the most comprehensive framework for the settlement of investment disputes ever embodied in a multilateral agreement is incorporated in an agreement in which Mexico and the United States are the leading parties. Certainly, the development of international law relating to state responsibility for economic injuries to aliens, a necessary precondition to international settlement of related disputes, has been greatly affected by bilateral disputes between the United States and Mexico.

Mexican law and jurisprudence has long incorporated the "Calvo Clause," which stipulates that foreign persons operating in Mexico should be considered in all respects as Mexicans, thus limiting the resolution of disputes to local courts adjudicating under domestic law provisions and prohibiting any intervention by the home government. In effect, the Calvo Clause standard, at least in theory, is one of non-discriminatory national treatment. Predictably, one of the earliest invocations of the United States' opposing view that a taking of alien property anywhere in the world requires the payment of "prompt, adequate and effective compensation" is found in an exchange of diplomatic notes in 1938 between U.S. Secretary of State Cordell Hull and the Minister of Foreign Relations of Mexico.

Efforts to establish widely accepted rules of international law relating to the treatment of aliens has been a significant element of U.S. international economic policy throughout most of the twentieth century. Limited successes in resolving expropriation disputes with various countries, including those of Latin America, were achieved, but international agreement on the applicability of international law as the basis for international dispute settlement proved elusive. A United Nations Resolution on "Permanent Sovereignty Over Natural Resources," adopted after extensive compromise between the United States and the developing nations, endorsed a requirement that expropriation must be followed by the payment of "appropriate" compensation, with references made both to national legislation and international law.

The trends in the 1970s and early 1980s in the international arena were also mixed. The vast majority of the members of the United Nations asserted in the "Charter of Economic Rights and Duties of States" ("CERDS") a right to nationalize, with compensation to be determined under domestic law alone, exclusively in local courts. A 1977 arbitral award stated that the earlier U.N. resolution reflected customary international law while the "CERDS" did not, but this statement probably was not convincing to most nations outside the developed world. The Iranian Claims Tribunal that resolved the many disputes between nationals of the United States and the government of Iran concluded in 1977 that customary international law established a standard that is essentially "prompt, adequate and effective compensation." However, these decisions were based in significant part on the existence of an extensive and detailed "just compensation" provision in the Treaty of Amity, Economic Relations and Consular Rights of August 15, 1955 between the United States and Iran, which was ruled applicable in many of the claims.

* * *

The influence of Chapter 16 of the U.S.-Canada Free Trade Agreement ("CFTA") on Chapter 11 of the NAFTA must also be noted, even though Chapter 16 of the CFTA is only one-half the length of Chapter 11 of the NAFTA. Like NAFTA, the CFTA contains provisions relating to national treatment, performance requirements, transfers of funds and expropriation, the latter with due reference to "payment of prompt, adequate and effective compensation" at fair market value. While there is no specific reference in Chapter 16 to "international law," the official U.S. government analysis of the provision states, correctly, that the standard of expropriation is "in accordance with generally accepted international law standards."

More significantly, the CFTA contains no provision for international arbitration of investment disputes between private parties and governments. However, disputes relating to the provisions of Chapter 16 may be brought within the government-to-government dispute settlement mechanisms provided in Chapter 18 of the CFTA, with arbitration of such disputes under Chapter 18 conducted before panelists selected for their experience in the field of international investment. At the time of the negotiations, U.S. government and private concerns regarding investment in Canada related to restrictions on investment in Canada under the Investment Canada Act. Given the similarity of the U.S. and Canadian court systems, and mutual confidence in their impartiality, it seems likely that the U.S. negotiators, at least, felt that the inclusion of the appropriate standard of compensation, along with the possibility of dispute resolution through government-to-government arbitration under Chapter 18 of the CFTA, provided the needed level of protection.

* * *

Chapter 11—Framework for Settlement of Disputes

Section B of Chapter 11 provides a multi-tiered mechanism for resolution of investment disputes between foreign investors and the host country or host country state enterprises. However, Chapter 11 has no applicability to disputes between foreign investors and nationals of the host country, although such disputes may be subject to commercial arbitration.

Conciliation and Negotiation

Before there is any resort to arbitration, "disputing parties" are encouraged to seek a solution to their dispute through consultation or negotiation. The requirement of 90 days notice to the other party prior to the filing of a claim for arbitration is apparently designed to encourage such consultation or negotiation.

Arbitral Jurisdiction

Once such notice is provided, an investor may demand binding arbitration for a variety of claims, on his own behalf or on behalf of an enterprise that he controls, directly or indirectly. These include (1) a claim that the government of another NAFTA party has breached an obligation under Section A of Chapter 11; (2) a claim that a state enterprise of another NAFTA party has acted in a manner inconsistent with the party's obligations under Chapter 11 (investment) or Chapter 14 (financial services) in the exercise of its regulatory, administrative or other governmental authority; or (3) a claim that a state monopoly has acted in a manner inconsistent with a party's obligations under Chapter 11 where the entity "exercises any regulatory, administrative or other governmental authority that the Party has delegated to it . . . ."

This broad statement of jurisdiction creates an apparent dichotomy. If a state enterprise violates its government's obligations under the financial services chapter, arguably the matter is subject to binding arbitration. However, if the government itself violates those Chapter 14 obligations, the matter must be referred to the government-to-government dispute settlement provisions of Chapter 20.

Disputes under Chapter 11 are subject to a three year statute of limitations. Actions not brought within three years from the "date on which the investor first acquired, or should have acquired, knowledge of the alleged breach" are barred. If "creeping" expropriation is alleged, i.e., where government actions over time are challenged as being equivalent to a taking, disagreement may arise over the date of the breach of Chapter 11, and, therefore, the time at which the statute of limitations begins to run.

When submitting a claim to arbitration, an investor must consent in writing to arbitration, on his own behalf and on behalf of any enterprise owned or controlled by him that is a party to the arbitration. Further, he must waive the right to initiate or continue administrative or judicial actions in the courts of the affected government, except in proceedings for injunctive, declaratory or other extraordinary relief. The three governments that are parties to the agreement have included as part of the agreement a "blanket" prior written consent to arbitration. Under the "blanket" prior consent rule, in the event an investor demands arbitration under Chapter 11, no further consent by his government is required. Moreover, this "blanket" prior consent also applies to the consent requirements of the ICSID Convention, including consent to the jurisdiction of the Center under the Convention or the Additional Facility Rules, the New York Convention on the Recognition and Enforcement of Foreign Arbitral Awards,[46] and the Inter–American Convention on International Commercial Arbitration.[47] This reference to the ICSID Convention and the Additional Facility Rules is crucial. Because Canada and Mexico are not parties to the Convention, it is this prior consent to arbitration under the auspices of the ICSID Additional Facility Rules that makes the arbitral provisions binding on the governments of Mexico and Canada.

Procedural Rules

Section B provides the procedural rules to be used in the absence of agreement by the parties. These include the number and appointment of arbitrators (normally three), the consolidation of multiple claims involving common issues of law or fact, notice, participation and documentary requirements, the place of arbitration and the use of experts. None of these provisions is particularly unusual, but by specifying explicit rules to be used in the absence of agreement between the arbitrating parties, a possible source of delay in the proceedings is avoided.

46. June 10, 1958; 21 U.S.T. 2517, T.I.A.S. 6997, 330 U.N.T.S. 38, art. II. Mexico, the United States and Canada are all parties to this accord, which requires the recognition and enforcement of foreign arbitral awards in the domestic courts of the parties, upon proper application of the prevailing party, through summary proceedings.

47. January 30, 1975; KAV. 2215, T.I.A.S.___, 14 I.L.M. 336 (1975). The United States and Mexico are parties to this convention providing a framework for arbitration between private parties of different nationality.

In most instances the Secretary General of ICSID serves as the appointing authority, when the parties fail to agree on the choice of arbitrators. Chapter 11 contemplates arbitration under the ICSID Convention or the ICSID Additional Facility Rules using the widely accepted UNCITRAL Arbitration Rules, as modified by Chapter 11. The governing law is "this Agreement and applicable rules of international law."

Limitations and Exclusions

It is recognized that, in some instances, a Chapter 11 dispute may relate to the interpretation of one or more of the parties' reservations under Annexes I–IV of the NAFTA. The arbitral tribunal does *not* have jurisdiction over such issues. Instead, such questions are to be referred to the Free Trade Commission created under Chapter 20, which must provide its interpretation in writing to the arbitral tribunal within 60 days. That interpretation is binding on the Tribunal.

In addition, certain types of governmental decisions are excluded from arbitration. These include the decision to exclude an investment based on national security grounds, and the decision by Canada under its Investment Canada Act or by Mexico's National Commission on Foreign Investment not to approve an investment. Since the national security exclusion is reviewable under Chapter 20 procedures, a decision by the United States under its Exon–Florio procedures to review foreign acquisitions that have national security implications would presumably be subject to Chapter 20 procedures.

Other exceptions reflect the continuing influence of the Mexican "Calvo Clause" despite its extreme narrowing under the NAFTA. For example, under the NAFTA an investor in Mexico may not submit a claim for breach of obligations by the Mexican government or state enterprises both to arbitration *and* to the national courts or administrative agencies. Similarly, once a Mexican enterprise owned or controlled by a foreign investor has submitted a claim to the national courts or administrative agencies asserting a breach of rights covered by the NAFTA investment provisions, the same matter may not subsequently be referred to arbitration under Chapter 11. These limitations, particularly the latter one, will require foreign-owned Mexican enterprises to carefully weigh the pros and cons of initially referring a matter to the Mexican internal legal process. The submission of what appears at the time to be a minor matter to the Mexican courts could preclude later arbitration of the same issue, should it be demonstrated that the claim against the government in fact comes within the NAFTA's protections.

Remedies and Enforcement

An arbitral tribunal established under Chapter 11 may order an "interim measure of protection" to protect the rights of the parties pending resolution of a dispute. The final award may provide monetary damages and interest and/or restitution of property, provided that the disputing (NAFTA government or state enterprise) party will have the option of paying monetary damages and interest in lieu of restitution.

The detailed listing of permitted variations to the award is definitely unusual by U.S. BIT standards.

The rate of interest to be awarded from the date of a taking to date of compensation is not specified, but is instead left to the discretion of the arbitrators. While costs may also be awarded, punitive damages are expressly barred.

As is typical of such arbitrations, awards are limited in their effectiveness to the parties at hand (Article 1136:2) , but are final and binding. However, under certain conditions arbitral awards under Chapter 11 may be made public. Furthermore, the awards are enforceable under any of the three conventions mentioned earlier and in the national courts of the three parties if the offending party fails to pay the award. Also, if one does not comply with the arbitral award to the complaining investor, the investor's government can bring the matter to government-to-government dispute settlement under Chapter 20, charging that the failure to abide by the award is inconsistent with the offending government's obligations under the NAFTA.

* * *

SANDRINO, THE NAFTA INVESTMENT CHAPTER AND FOREIGN DIRECT INVESTMENT IN MEXICO: A THIRD WORLD PERSPECTIVE
27 Vanderbuilt J. of Transnat'l L. 259 (1999).*

EXPROPRIATION AND COMPENSATION

The United States and other industrialized states have maintained that the most dangerous risk to a foreign investment is the expropriation of his property without compensation or with inadequate compensation. In their view, the fear of expropriation and nationalization always has constituted a serious impediment to foreign investment in Third World states. For their part, Third World states, particularly Mexico and the rest of Lain America, as an expression of economic self-determination, have called for a reappraisal of norms of customary international law governing expropriation and nationalization issues. The result has been an international community divided along North–South boundaries that is unable to formulate an effective legal mechanism to deal with this conflict. In the absence of an international consensus, industrialized states have sought to establish legal regimes for protecting foreign investments of their nationals and firms through bilateral arrangements and now through NAFTA. At the same time, they have sought to reaffirm in these agreements traditional principles of international law of nationalization and expropriation, including standards of compensation that reflect the customary international law of an earlier era.

In this context, the NAFTA agreement on expropriation and compensation clearly has fulfilled the United States objectives. NAFTA provisions represent a significant shift from Mexico's longstanding challenge to these principles—a challenge that originated in the nineteenth century and is embedded in the very fiber of Mexico's legal structure. To fully understand the significance of these NAFTA provisions, one must look at various elements of the treaty's expropriation and compensation article, from an historical perspective, with an emphasis on Mexico and the Third World.

Article 1110 of the NAFTA Investment Chapter provides for the protection of foreign investments against nationalization, expropriation, and other forms of interference that are "tantamount to nationalization or expropriation." The Article covers direct, indirect, and "creeping expropriation." In accordance with traditional principles of international law, the Article provides that investments may not be expropriated except: for a public purpose; on a nondiscriminatory basis; in accordance with due process of law; and upon payment of compensation as specified in the Article.

Generally, the right of a sovereign nation to expropriate foreign property in its territory has not been disputed by Third World and industrialized states. The dispute usually involves one or more of the four specified conditions. The condition most often the source of controversy between the United States and Mexico in particular, and Third World and industrialized states in general, is the condition requiring payment of compensation.

NAFTA provides that adequate compensation is a condition for lawful expropriation or nationalization and that compensation must be paid without delay, equal to the fair market value of the investment immediately before the expropriation took place, including interest from the date of expropriation, and be fully realizable. The compensation must also be fully transferable, as provided by the transfer article.

The NAFTA standard for compensation, providing that the compensation be made "without delay," "equal to the fair market value of the investment," and "fully realizable," is the United States modern version of the [Secretary of State Cordell] Hull formula. Most Third World states oppose such high standards of valuation, and instead argue for "appropriate compensation ... taking into account ... all circumstances that the State considers pertinent." In order to understand fully the significance of the compensation standard in light of North–South differences, it is important to discuss each element of the formula.

The NAFTA element "fair market value" for compensation by an expropriating state is the standard advocated by the United States and other industrialized states. The combination of "fair market value in freely transferable dollars" provides the foreign investor the highest value for the expropriated property. In recent years, the United States and other industrialized states have attempted to incorporate the "fair market value" standard in their BITs.

Third World states challenged the traditional stand in the Charter of Economic Rights and Duties of States, which provides for compensation that is "appropriate" to the circumstances giving rise to the expropriation. Mexico's special standard for compensation employed during the oil nationalizations, excusing expropriations that were "inspired by legitimate causes and the aspirations of social justice," has also challenged the traditional rules. In addition, Latin American states that support the Calvo Doctrine allow their domestic courts to determine the appropriate standard of compensation.

Third World opposition to the fair market value standard has focused on the "ability to pay." Third World states have argued that the problem with the fair market value standard, which reaffirms the traditional rules of customary international law, is that it would "thwart their efforts to carry out badly needed social and economic reforms.

* * *

The NAFTA investment dispute settlement mechanism represents a significant departure for Mexico with respect to the role of international law in international economic relations. Mexico's distrust of private-state arbitration stems from the Calvo Doctrine, which denies that the state of the owner can intervene on his behalf against the host state. Investment contracts between states and foreign investors commonly include a Calvo Clause under which a foreign investor agrees, as part of his submission to local law, not to seek the diplomatic intervention of his government in any matter arising out of the contract. The Mexican interpretation of these clauses is that the foreign investor is bound by the local rule of law, even in the face of a violation of international law. When foreign investment is concerned, the import of the Calvo Doctrine is that arbitration is an unacceptable yielding of sovereignty. The arbitral procedures in the dispute settlement mechanism in NAFTA will have a significant impact on international economic relations between Third World and industrialized state.

MURPHY, ACCESS AND PROTECTION FOR FOREIGN INVESTMENT IN MEXICO UNDER MEXICO'S NEW FOREIGN INVESTMENT LAW AND THE NORTH AMERICAN FREE TRADE AGREEMENT

ICSID Review Foreign Investment L.J. 54 (1998).*

FOUR INNER BASTIONS

Repudiation of Echeverrían economic policies by the Salinas Administration did not leave an unobstructed pathway for foreign enterprise. There remained four inner bastions of resistance: a compulsory Calvo

Clause, restrictions on foreign ownership of Mexican real property, and Mexican state monopolies in hydrocarbons and electric power. These bastions were inspired, not by mere Mexican conviviality with the "New International Economic Order," but by deep convictions of Mexican history. They were constructed, not only of statutes and regulations, but from impassioned provisions of the Mexican Constitution.

* * *

Of the four bastions, the Calvo Clause and restrictions on foreign ownership of Mexican real property were written into the original Article 27 as drafted in Querétaro and adopted with the 1917 Constitution. . . .

Article 27 imposed the Calvo Clause as a condition to granting Mexican real property to foreigners:

> Only Mexicans by birth or naturalization and Mexican companies have the right to acquire ownership of lands, waters and their appurtenances, or to obtain concessions for the exploitation of mines, waters or mineral fuels, in the Mexican Republic. The State may grant the same right to foreigners provided that they agree before the Ministry of [Foreign] Relations to consider themselves as nationals with respect to said properties and accordingly not to invoke the protection of their Governments in regard to them; under penalty, in case of breaches of the agreement, of losing to the benefit of the Nation the properties they may have acquired thereby.

* * *

Although Article 27 has been amended fifteen times since its adoption, its real property restrictions remain essentially as originally written. The general restriction (including the Calvo Clause) was amended only to eliminate concessions for mineral fuels from the categories of properties that may be acquired by private interests, whether Mexican or foreign. . . .

* * *

INVESTMENT PROVISIONS OF NAFTA

For Mexico, the substantive and procedural commitments to investment protection expressed in NAFTA constitute an historic break with the Calvo Doctrine, the "New International Economic Order," and past Echeverrían economic policies. That is particularly true of Mexico's accepting the enforcement mechanism of transnational arbitration. Although for many years Mexico has adhered to multinational treaties that make transnational arbitration agreements and awards enforceable among private parties, even among Latin American nations Mexico has been conspicuous for its unwillingness to adhere to international agreements that require investment-receiving nations to arbitrate foreign investment disputes.[292] As regards investors of other NAFTA Parties,

---

292. For example, Mexico does not adhere to either the Convention on the Settlement of Investment Disputes of 1965 (the "ICSID Convention") or the Convention

with NAFTA that unwillingness is decisively reversed. As one analyst concluded, NAFTA "represents the first time Mexico has entered into an international agreement providing for investor-state arbitration"[293] and constitutes "a significant departure for Mexico with respect to the role of international law in international economic relations."

THE BASTIONS REVISITED

For the reasons detailed above, it is clear that the 1993 Law and Mexico's adherence to NAFTA are effective commitments to access and protection for foreign investment in Mexico. For foreign investors generally, the 1993 Law provides investment access to all sectors the Law does not reserve for present or future state monopolies, or for present exclusivities or priorities of Mexican nationals. For foreign investors of other NAFTA Parties, NAFTA elevates that investment access to the level of national and most-favored-nation treatment, waives future state monopolies in sectors not presently specified, and adds significant undertakings of investment protection enforcement by transnational arbitration and, ultimately, by the suspension of NAFTA benefits from the investor's own NAFTA Party.

These commitments of access and protection represent a fundamental reorientation of Mexican public policy toward foreign investment. If Article 27 of the post-Revolutionary Constitution converted private property from an absolute right to one limited by the public interest, the 1993 Law and NAFTA reconverted the interests of foreign investors to absolute rights. Where the 1973 statute reserved Mexico's prerogatives to create additional state monopolies and future exclusivities and priorities of Mexican nationals, the 1993 Law waived the latter and, for investors of other NAFTA Parties, NAFTA relinquished both. Most significantly, NAFTA's mechanism for resolving investment disputes effectively abandons, for investors of other NAFTA Parties, a century of Mexican adherence to the Calvo Doctrine.

Nevertheless, when we re-examine the four inner bastions of Mexico's resistance to foreign investment in their historical context, from Article 27 of the Mexican Constitution through the 1993 Law and NAFTA, we see that each of the bastions has survived with remarkable vitality. The Calvo Clause is deftly waived for investors of other NAFTA Parties, but it remains firmly institutionalized for foreign investors generally. Although the restrictions on foreign ownership of Mexican real property are applied with sophisticated accommodation, they contin-

Establishing the Multilateral Investment Guarantee Agency of 1985 (the "MIGA Convention"), and has not signed with the United States either a bilateral investment treaty or a bilateral agreement supporting investment insurance programs of the U.S. Overseas Private Investment Corporation, although as of April 1, 1994 negotiations were pending for such an agreement regarding the Overseas Private Investment Corporation. *See id.* at S–3.

293. Gloria L. Sandrino, The NAFTA Investment Chapter and Foreign Direct Investment in Mexico: A Third World Perspective, 27 Vand. J. Transnat'l L. 259, 319 (1994).

ue in effect. The state monopolies in hydrocarbons and electric power persist, industrially enormous and juridically intact.

We have seen that Article 27 imposed the Calvo Clause as a condition to granting Mexican real property to foreigners; that the 1973 statute expanded it to cover, *ipso facto*, the acquisition by foreigners of "properties of any kind"; and that the 1989 Regulations described those properties in more detail and institutionalized the Calvo Clause as a requirement for the constitutive documents of every Mexican company that has no "exclusion-of-foreigners" clause. The 1993 Law follows Article 27 and maintains, essentially unchanged, the Regulations on that point. As so applied, the Calvo Clause obligates foreign investors, on penalty of losing their Mexican investments, to consider themselves as Mexican nationals, and not invoke the protection of their governments, concerning them.

For foreign investors of other NAFTA Parties, the imposition of the Calvo Clause contradicts the investment protection provisions of NAFTA, which afford those foreign investors a recourse (namely, the resolution of investment disputes by transnational arbitration) not available to Mexican nationals and, if Mexico refuses to pay an arbitral award, allows those foreign investors to invoke the protection of their governments (for Party-to-Party arbitration to suspend NAFTA benefits commensurate with the refusal). That contradiction, however, is deftly resolved by the Mexican Law Concerning the Making of Treaties,[297] which contemplates treaties that establish "international mechanisms for the solution of legal controversies" between foreigners and Mexico, and makes enforceable in Mexico the awards rendered by such "mechanisms." In other words, although all foreign investors in Mexico are still subject to the Calvo Clause, Mexico has agreed to honor arbitral awards resulting from the exercise by foreign investors of treaty rights (e.g., NAFTA's investment protection provisions) that are inconsistent with a Calvo Clause.

INTRODUCTION TO THE ICSID CONVENTION*

The Convention on the Settlement of Investment Disputes between States and Nationals of Other States was opened to signature on March 18, 1965 on behalf of all the States members of the International Bank for Reconstruction and Development. On October 14, 1966, thirty days after the deposit with the Bank of the twentieth instrument of ratification, the Convention entered into force in accordance with its Article 68(2). As of November 2003, a total of 154 States had signed the Convention. Of these, 140 had become Contracting States by depositing instruments of ratification, including Switzerland which, although not a member of the Bank, was invited to sign the Convention under Article 67 thereof on February 2, 1967.

* * *

---

297. Ley Sobre la Celebración de Tratados, Diario Oficial, Jan. 2, 1992, at 2.

* Adapted from the ICSID website, http://www.worldbank.org/icsid/, an excellent source for descriptive materials, text of the Convention and arbitral rules, and case information.

ICSID Additional Facility

Besides providing facilities for conciliation and arbitration under the ICSID Convention, the Centre has since 1978 had a set of Additional Facility Rules authorizing the ICSID Secretariat to administer certain types of proceedings between States and foreign nationals which fall outside the scope of the Convention. These include conciliation and arbitration proceedings where either the State party or the home State of the foreign national is not a member of ICSID. Additional Facility conciliation and arbitration are also available for cases where the dispute is not an investment dispute provided it relates to a transaction which has "features that distinguishes it from an ordinary commercial transaction." The Additional Facility Rules further allow ICSID to administer a type of proceedings not provided for in the Convention, namely fact-finding proceedings to which any State and foreign national may have recourse if they wish to institute an inquiry "to examine and report on facts."

Administration of Ad Hoc Arbitration Under UNCITRAL

A third activity of ICSID in the field of the settlement of disputes has consisted in the Secretary–General of ICSID accepting to act as the appointing authority of arbitrators for ad hoc (i.e., non-institutional) arbitration proceedings. This is most commonly done in the context of arrangements for arbitration under the Arbitration Rules of the United Nations Commission on International Trade Law (UNCITRAL), which are specially designed for ad hoc proceedings.

* * *

The Arbitration (Additional Facility) Rules

The Arbitration (Additional Facility) Rules are based on the ICSID Arbitration Rules, and provisions of the Convention which lend themselves to inclusion in an instrument of a contractual nature, and include some provisions derived from the UNCITRAL Rules and the ICC Rules. The reference table following the text of the Arbitration (Additional Facility) Rules shows the origin of their provisions.

As under the ICSID Rules, the majority of the members of a tribunal are required to be nationals of third countries, and the Chairman of the Centre's Administrative Council is the residual appointing authority. However, the Chairman is not restricted in his choice to a Panel of Arbitrators. Arbitrators are explicitly required to disclose any past and present professional business and other relevant relationships with the parties (Art. 14).

In order to assure the widest possible international recognition and enforcement of awards arbitration proceedings may be held only in States that are parties to the 1958 UN Convention. Subject thereto the Tribunal determines the place of arbitration and the award must be made at that place (Art. 20, 21).

Following UNCITRAL Article 1.2 the Rules provide that they shall govern the proceedings "save that if any of these Rules is in conflict with a provision of the law applicable to the arbitration from which the parties cannot derogate, that provision shall prevail" (Art. 1). As regards the law applicable to the dispute in the absence of its designation by the parties "the Tribunal shall apply (a) the law determined by the conflict of laws rules which it considers applicable and (b) such rules of international law as the Tribunal considers applicable" (Art. 55). Paragraph (a) follows UNCITRAL Article 33.1 while paragraph (b) is derived from Article 42 of the Convention.

S.D. Myers, Inc. [SDMI] v. Government of Canada

November 12, 2000*

[Authors' note: The *S.D. Myers* decision provides a good example of how NAFTA Chapter 11 tribunals analyze the various issues; it is unusual in that all four major Chapter 11 substantive protections, under Articles 1102, 1105, 1106 and 1110, are addressed. S.D. Myers is an Ohio corporation engaged, inter alia, in remediation of hazardous waste known as PCBs. It entered the Canadian market with the objective of obtaining PCB wastes for treatment in the Ohio facilities, and ultimately established an affiliate, Myers Canada. During the entire period, there was only one Canadian competitor, Chem–Security, located in Alberta. S.D. Myers enjoyed a significant cost advantage because it was cheaper for Ontario PCB producers to ship their waste a few hundred miles to Ohio rather than 1500 miles to Alberta. In 1995, the Canadian Minister of the Environment issued interim and final orders that had the effect of banning PCB exports from Canada. Various documents before the tribunal strongly indicated that the purpose of such ban was to force Canadian companies to have their PCB wastes treated at Chem–Security. However, S.D. Myers' export-import opportunities were only temporary, limited to about 18 months, due to U.S. import restrictions on PCB wastes. On October 30, 1998, S.D. Myers filed its Chapter 11 notice of arbitration against Canada, charging violations of national treatment, fair and equitable treatment, the ban against performance requirements, and expropriation.]

* * *

Chapter X: Did Canada Comply With Its NAFTA Chapter 11 Obligations?

237. In this Chapter the Tribunal reviews the merits of SDMI's claims under four separate provisions of Chapter 11 of the NAFTA.

Article 1102 (National Treatment)

238. SDMI claims that CANADA denied it "national treatment," contrary to Article 1102. Article 1102(1) states:

---

* 40 I.L.M. 1408 (2001).

Each Party shall accord to investors of another Party treatment no less favorable than it accords, in like circumstances, to its own investors, with respect to the establishment, acquisition, expansion, management, conduct, operation, and sale or other disposition of investments.

* * *

241. CANADA argues that the Interim Order merely established a uniform regulatory regime under which all were treated equally. No one was permitted to export PCBs, so there was no discrimination. SDMI contends that Article 1102 was breached by a ban on the export of PCBs that was not justified by bona fide health or environmental concerns, but which had the aim and effect of protecting and promoting the market share of producers who were Canadians and who would perform the work in Canada.

242. CANADA's submission is one dimensional and does not take into account the basis on which the different interests in the industry were organized to undertake their business.

Like Circumstances

243. Articles 1102(1) and 1102(2) refer to treatment that is accorded to a Party's own nationals "in like circumstances." The phrase "like circumstances" is open to a wide variety of interpretations in the abstract and in the context of a particular dispute.

244. WTO dispute resolution panels, and its appellate body, frequently have been required to apply the concept of "like products." The case law has emphasized that the interpretation of "like" must depend on all the circumstances of each case. The case law also suggests that close attention must be paid to the legal context in which the word "like" appears; the same word "like" may have different meanings in different provisions of the GATT. . . .

245. In considering the meaning of "like circumstances" under Article 1102 of the NAFTA, it is similarly necessary to keep in mind the overall legal context in which the phrase appears.

246. In the GATT context, a prima facie finding of discrimination in "like" cases often takes place within the overall GATT framework, which includes Article XX (General Exceptions). A finding of "likeness" does not dispose of the case. It may set the stage for an inquiry into whether the different treatment of situations found to be "like" is justified by legitimate public policy measures that are pursued in a reasonable manner.

247. The Tribunal considers that the legal context of Article 1102 includes the various provisions of the NAFTA, its companion agreement the NAAEC and principles that are affirmed by the NAAEC (including those of the Rio declaration). The principles that emerge from that context, to repeat, are as follows:

— states have the right to establish high levels of environmental protection. They are not obliged to compromise their standards merely to satisfy the political or economic interests of other states;

— states should avoid creating distortions to trade;

— environmental protection and economic development can and should be mutually supportive.

248. As SDMI noted in its Memorial, all three NAFTA partners belong to the OECD. OECD practice suggests that an evaluation of "like situations" in the investment context should take into account policy objectives in determining whether enterprises are in like circumstances. The OECD Declaration on International and Multinational Enterprises, issued on June 21, 1976, states that investors and investments should receive treatment that is ... no less favorable than that accorded in like situations to domestic enterprises. In 1993 the OECD reviewed the "like situation" test in the following terms:

As regards the expression "in like situations," the comparison between foreign-controlled enterprises is only valid if it is made between firms operating in the same sector. More general considerations, such as the policy objectives of Member countries could be taken into account to define the circumstances in which comparison between foreign-controlled and domestic enterprises is permissible inasmuch as those objectives are not contrary to the principle of national treatment.

249. The Supreme Court of Canada has explored the complexity of making comparisons as it has developed its line of decisions on discrimination against individuals. In the Andrews case, the Court stated that the question of whether or not discrimination exists cannot be determined by applying a purely mechanical test whether similarly situated individuals are treated in the same manner. Whether individuals are "similarly situated," and have been treated in a substantively equal manner, depends on an examination of the context in which a measure is established and applied and the specific circumstances of each case.

250. The Tribunal considers that the interpretation of the phrase "like circumstances" in Article 1102 must take into account the general principles that emerge from the legal context of the NAFTA, including both its concern with the environment and the need to avoid trade distortions that are not justified by environmental concerns. The assessment of "like circumstances" must also take into account circumstances that would justify governmental regulations that treat them differently in order to protect the public interest. The concept of "like circumstances" invites an examination of whether a non-national investor complaining of less favourable treatment is in the same "sector" as the national investor. The Tribunal takes the view that the word "sector" has a wide connotation that includes the concepts of "economic sector" and "business sector."

251. From the business perspective, it is clear that SDMI and Myers Canada were in "like circumstances" with Canadian operators such as

Chem–Security and Cintec. They all were engaged in providing PCB waste remediation services. SDMI was in a position to attract customers that might otherwise have gone to the Canadian operators because it could offer more favourable prices and because it had extensive experience and credibility. It was precisely because SDMI was in a position to take business away from its Canadian competitors that Chem–Security and Cintec lobbied the Minister of the Environment to ban exports when the U.S. authorities opened the border.

National Treatment and Protectionist Motive or Intent

252. The Tribunal takes the view that, in assessing whether a measure is contrary to a national treatment norm, the following factors should be taken into account:

— whether the practical effect of the measure is to create a disproportionate benefit for nationals over non-nationals;

— whether the measure, on its face, appears to favour its nationals over non-nationals who are protected by the relevant treaty.

253. Each of these factors must be explored in the context of all the facts to determine whether there actually has been a denial of national treatment.

254. Intent is important, but protectionist intent is not necessarily decisive on its own. The existence of an intent to favour nationals over non-nationals would not give rise to a breach of Chapter 1102 of the NAFTA if the measure in question were to produce no adverse effect on the non-national complainant. The word "treatment" suggests that practical impact is required to produce a breach of Article 1102, not merely a motive or intent that is in violation of Chapter 11.

255. CANADA was concerned to ensure the economic strength of the Canadian industry, in part, because it wanted to maintain the ability to process PCBs within Canada in the future. This was a legitimate goal, consistent with the policy objectives of the Basel Convention. There were a number of legitimate ways by which CANADA could have achieved it, but preventing SDMI from exporting PCBs for processing in the USA by the use of the Interim Order and the Final Order was not one of them. The indirect motive was understandable, but the method contravened CANADA's international commitments under the NAFTA. CANADA's right to source all government requirements and to grant subsidies to the Canadian industry are but two examples of legitimate alternative measures. The fact that the matter was addressed subsequently and the border re-opened also shows that CANADA was not constrained in its ability to deal effectively with the situation.

256. The Tribunal concludes that the issuance of the Interim Order and the Final Order was a breach of Article 1102 of the NAFTA.

* * *

Article 1105

258. SDMI submits that CANADA treated it in a manner that was inconsistent with Article 1105(1) of the NAFTA. Entitled "Minimum Standard of Treatment," it reads as follows:

Each Party shall accord to investments of investors of another Party treatment in accordance with international law, including fair and equitable treatment and full protection and security.

259. The minimum standard of treatment provision of the NAFTA is similar to clauses contained in BITs. The inclusion of a "minimum standard" provision is necessary to avoid what might otherwise be a gap. A government might treat an investor in a harsh, injurious and unjust manner, but do so in a way that is no different than the treatment inflicted on its own nationals. The "minimum standard" is a floor below which treatment of foreign investors must not fall, even if a government were not acting in a discriminatory manner.

260. The U.S.-Mexican Claims Commission noted in the Hopkins case that:

It not infrequently happens that under the rules of international law applied to controversies of an international aspect a nation is required to accord to aliens broader and more liberal treatment than it accords to its own citizens under its municipal laws ... The citizens of a nation may enjoy many rights which are withheld from aliens, and conversely, under international law, aliens may enjoy rights and remedies which the nation does not accord to its own citizens.

261. When interpreting and applying the "minimum standard," a Chapter 11 tribunal does not have an open-ended mandate to second-guess government decision-making. Governments have to make many potentially controversial choices. In doing so, they may appear to have made mistakes, to have misjudged the facts, proceeded on the basis of a misguided economic or sociological theory, placed too much emphasis on some social values over others and adopted solutions that are ultimately ineffective or counterproductive. The ordinary remedy, if there were one, for errors in modern governments is through internal political and legal processes, including elections.

262. Article 1105(1) expresses an overall concept. The words of the Article must be read as a whole. The phrases ... fair and equitable treatment ... and ... full protection and security ... cannot be read in isolation. They must be read in conjunction with the introductory phrase ... treatment in accordance with international law.

263. The Tribunal considers that a breach of Article 1105 occurs only when it is shown that an investor has been treated in such an unjust or arbitrary manner that the treatment rises to the level that is unacceptable from the international perspective. That determination must be made in the light of the high measure of deference that international law generally extends to the right of domestic authorities to regulate matters within their own borders. The determination must also take into account any specific rules of international law that are applicable to the case.

264. In some cases, the breach of a rule of international law by a host Party may not be decisive in determining that a foreign investor has been denied "fair and equitable treatment," but the fact that a host Party has breached a rule of international law that is specifically designed to protect investors will tend to weigh heavily in favour of finding a breach of Article 1105.

265. The breadth of the "minimum standard," including its ability to encompass more particular guarantees, was recognized by Dr. Mann in the following passage:

... it is submitted that the right to fair and equitable treatment goes much further than the right to most-favored-nation and to national treatment ... so general a provision is likely to be almost sufficient to cover all conceivable cases, and it may well be that provisions of the Agreements affording substantive protection are not more than examples of specific instances of this overriding duty.

266. Although modern commentators might consider Dr. Mann's statement to be an over-generalisation, and the Tribunal does not rule out the possibility that there could be circumstances in which a denial of the national treatment provisions of the NAFTA would not necessarily offend the minimum standard provisions, a majority of the Tribunal determines that on the facts of this particular case the breach of Article 1102 essentially establishes a breach of Article 1105 as well.

267. Mr. Chiasson considers that a finding of a violation of Article 1105 must be based on a demonstrated failure to meet the fair and equitable requirements of international law. Breach of another provision of the NAFTA is not a foundation for such a conclusion. The language of the NAFTA does not support the notion espoused by Dr. Mann insofar as it is considered to support a breach of Article 1105 that is based on a violation of another provision of Chapter 11. On the facts of this case, CANADA's actions come close to the line, but on the evidence no breach of Article 1105 is established.

268. By a majority, the Tribunal determines that the issuance of the Interim and Final Orders was a breach of Article 1105 of the NAFTA. The Tribunal's decision in this respect makes it unnecessary to review SDMI's other submissions in relation to Article 1105.

* * *

Article 1106—Performance Requirements

270. SDMI contends that CANADA's export ban breached Article 1106 of NAFTA because, in effect, SDMI was required, as a condition of operating in Canada, to carry out a major part of its proposed business, the physical disposal of PCB waste in Canada. In doing so, SDMI effectively would have been required to consume goods and services in Canada.

271. Article 1106 states:

No party may impose or enforce any of the following requirements, or enforce any commitment or undertaking, in connection with the establishment, acquisition, expansion, management, conduct or operation of an investment of an investor of a Party or a non Party in its territory:

(b) to achieve a given level or percentage of domestic content

(c) to purchase, use or accord a preference to goods produced or services provided in its territory or to purchase goods or services from persons in its territory;

272. Article 1106(5) states:

Paragraphs 1 and 3 do not apply to any requirement other then the requirements set out in those paragraphs

273. The export ban imposed by CANADA was not cast in the form of express conditions attached to a regulatory approval but, in applying Article 1106 the Tribunal must look at substance, not only form.

274. The 1947 GATT agreement contained no specific provisions on performance requirements. One dispute was brought before a GATT panel. The USA challenged CANADA's FIRA. Under that statute, non-Canadian investors in some circumstances had to obtain regulatory approval before operating or expanding in CANADA. The regulator could attach conditions to its approval. For example, a factory operator might be required to purchase 50% of its supplies from local suppliers, rather than from abroad. The GATT panel accepted some aspects of the U.S. complaint and rejected others, but the GATT panel looked at the substance of the measure notwithstanding the fact that the GATT did not contain any express provision equivalent to Article 1106 of the NAFTA.

275. Although the Tribunal must review the substance of the measure, it cannot take into consideration any limitations or restrictions that do not fall squarely within the "requirements" listed in Articles 1106(1) and (3).

276. The only part of the definition that might apply to the current situation is ... conduct or operation of an investment ... but in the opinion of the majority of the Tribunal, subparagraph (b) clearly does not apply and, neither does subparagraph (c).

277. Looking at the substance and effect of the Interim Order, as well as the literal wording of Article 1106, the majority of the Tribunal considers that no "requirements" as defined were imposed on SDMI that fell within Article 1106. Professor Schwartz considers that the effect of the Interim Order was to require SDMI to undertake all of its operations in Canada and that this amounted to a breach of subparagraph (b).

278. By a majority, the Tribunal concludes that this is not a "performance requirements" case.

Article 1110–Expropriation

279. SDMI claims that the Interim Order and the Final Order were "tantamount" to an expropriation and violated Article 1110 of the NAFTA.

280. The term "expropriation" in Article 1110 must be interpreted in light of the whole body of state practice, treaties and judicial interpretations of that term in international law cases. In general, the term "expropriation" carries with it the connotation of a "taking" by a governmental-type authority of a person's "property" with a view to transferring ownership of that property to another person, usually the authority that exercised its *de jure* or *de facto* power to do the "taking".

281. The Tribunal accepts that, in legal theory, rights other than property rights may be "expropriated" and that international law makes it appropriate for tribunals to examine the purpose and effect of governmental measures. The Interim Order and the Final Order were regulatory acts that imposed restrictions on SDMI. The general body of precedent usually does not treat regulatory action as amounting to expropriation. Regulatory conduct by public authorities is unlikely to be the subject of legitimate complaint under Article 1110 of the NAFTA, although the Tribunal does not rule out that possibility.

282. Expropriations tend to involve the deprivation of ownership rights; regulations a lesser interference. The distinction between expropriation and regulation screens out most potential cases of complaints concerning economic intervention by a state and reduces the risk that governments will be subject to claims as they go about their business of managing public affairs.

283. An expropriation usually amounts to a lasting removal of the ability of an owner to make use of its economic rights although it may be that, in some contexts and circumstances, it would be appropriate to view a deprivation as amounting to an expropriation, even if it were partial or temporary.

284. In this case the closure of the border was temporary. SDMI's venture into the Canadian market was postponed for approximately eighteen months. Mr. Dana Myers testified that this delay had the effect of eliminating SDMI's competitive advantage. This may have significance in assessing the compensation to be awarded in relation to CANADA's violations of Articles 1102 and 1105, but it does not support the proposition on the facts of this case that the measure should be characterized as an expropriation within the terms of Article 1110.

285. SDMI relied on the use of the word "tantamount" in Article 1110(1) to extend the meaning of the expression "tantamount to expropriation" beyond the customary scope of the term "expropriation" under international law. The primary meaning of the word "tantamount" given by the Oxford English Dictionary is "equivalent". Both words require a tribunal to look at the substance of what has occurred and not only at form. A tribunal should not be deterred by technical or facial considerations from reaching a conclusion that an expropriation or conduct tantamount to an expropriation has occurred. It must look at

the real interests involved and the purpose and effect of the government measure.

286. The Tribunal agrees with the conclusion in the Interim Award of the *Pope & Talbot* Arbitral Tribunal that something that is "equivalent" to something else cannot logically encompass more. In common with the *Pope & Talbot* Tribunal, this Tribunal considers that the drafters of the NAFTA intended the word "tantamount" to embrace the concept of so-called "creeping expropriation", rather than to expand the internationally accepted scope of the term expropriation.

287. In this case, the Interim Order and the Final Order were designed to, and did, curb SDMI's initiative, but only for a time. CANADA realized no benefit from the measure. The evidence does not support a transfer of property or benefit directly to others. An opportunity was delayed.

288. The Tribunal concludes that this is not an "expropriation" case.

* * *

[Authors' note: In a separate award dated October 21, 2002, the tribunal ultimately found damages based on the Articles 1102 and 1105 violations in the amount of CDN$6,050,000, plus interest. Canada appealed the award to the courts in Ontario, the situs of the arbitration (under the UNCITRAL Rules); that tribunal rejected the challenge, and Canada and S.D. Myers settled the case.]

*Comment on Additional NAFTA Chapter 11 Jurisprudence**

The NAFTA investment protection provisions have produced a significant volume of litigation in ten years, primarily relating to national treatment (Article 1102), fair and equitable treatment (Article 1105) and expropriation (Article 1110). These provisions, in particular, have proved difficult for tribunals to apply in practice, and the governing law–the NAFTA agreement and "applicable rules of international law–has not always been clear. More than a dozen Chapter 11 actions brought by foreign investors against NAFTA host governments have resulted as of mid–2004 in decisions on the merits or other dispositive or partially dispositive opinions, and another twenty or so are in various stages of proceedings. A handful—*Metalclad v. United Mexican States, Loewen Group. v. United States, Pope & Talbot v. Canada, S.D. Myers v. Canada, Methanex v. United States*—have generated considerable attention

* This comment draws on Gantz, Dispute Resolution Under the North American Free Trade Agreement, © David A. Gantz, 1999, 2003, 2004; Gantz, An Appellate Body for Review of Arbitral Decisions In Investor—State Disputes: Problems and Prospects, for a conference, The Two Faces of Court–Arbitrator Interaction Under Investment Trea ties, Washington, D.C., March 31, 2004 © David A. Gantz, 2004; and Gantz, *The Evolution of U.S Views on Investment Protec-*

tion: From NAFTA to the United States Chile Free Trade Agreement, 19 Am. U. Int'l L. Rev. 679 (2004), Copyright © 2004 David A. Gantz and the American University International Law Review. The cases are most easily available at http://www.NAFTAlaw.org. Most can also be found on the official governments websites, http://www.dfait-maeci.gc.ca/tnanac/disp/SDM_archive-en.asp or http://www.state.gov/s/l/c3439.htm.

among the NAFTA member governments (which appreciate losing cases no more than any private defendant), the foreign investment bar, and non-governmental organizations that are concerned with environmental protection, alleged erosion of national sovereignty or other problems, real or imagined. Only four cases—*Metalclad, S.D. Myers, Pope & Talbot* and *Feldman Karpa v. United Mexican States*—have resulted in monetary damages awards against Canada or Mexico, but there have been no monetary damages awarded to date against the United States. Another group of cases—*Azinian v. United Mexican States, UPS v. Canada, Mondev v. United States, ADF v. United States and Loewen Group v. United States*—has resulted in a dismissal of all allegations against the respondent governments. Several of the most important cases are discussed below; this summary is not intended to be comprehensive. Most intermingle issues under Articles 1102, 1105 and 1110.

The first NAFTA Chapter 11 case involved an action by the U.S. Virginia based Ethyl Corporation against Canada. Ethyl is the sole North American producer of the gasoline additive MMT. MMT produced in the U.S. is exported to Canada where a wholly owned subsidiary further processes the fuel additive and distributes it to Canadian gasoline refineries. MMT is used to increase octane in unleaded gasoline. There are studies suggesting that MMT increases toxic emissions in gasoline powered vehicles. The Ethyl company claimed a 1997 Canadian ban on importation or interprovincial transport of the product constituted an expropriation of the goodwill and other value of Ethyl's investment in Canada. Furthermore, the Canadian action gave to Canadian producers of other octane increasing fuel additives (i.e., corn based ethanol) an advantage. Ethyl initiated a claim against Canada for $250 million. Canada lifted the ban, but only after a parallel challenge by Alberta was made to the ban as excessively trade restrictive and in violation of the Canadian Agreement on Internal Trade. Canada canceled the ban, noting the lack of scientific evidence that MMT is harmful, paid Ethyl $13 million, and the claim was withdrawn.

Metalclad concerned the alleged expropriation of it's investment in a hazardous waste disposal facility in Mexico. The publicly-traded U.S. firm obtained all the necessary federal permits for its facility, relying on the federal government's assurances (which the tribunal concluded were accurate) that no state or municipal permits were required. However, the municipality denied the local permits required by Metalclad to legally operate the facility. According to the tribunal, the municipality by so doing exceeded its authority, and "effectively and unlawfully prevented the Claimant's operation of the landfill." This, said the tribunal, was an indirect expropriation. The Tribunal also found that the Mexican government had violated Article 1105 by its failure to provide a "transparent and predictable framework" for the investor in the latter's efforts to comply with Mexican laws regarding the siting of a hazardous waste disposal facility. In the tribunal's words, Mexico had failed "to ensure a transparent and predictable framework for Metalclad's business planning and investment." While the fair and equitable treatment and indirect expropriation violations based on denial of transparency were ultimately reversed by the British Columbia Supreme Court, the expropriation award was sustained on other grounds, i.e., the decision of the state government to treat the site as an ecological reserve, permanently excluding Metalclad from the site. [The similarity of the facts in Metalclad to those in the WDI hypothetical in Problem 7.2 is not entirely coincidental!]

For *S.D. Myers*, see the decision, *supra.*

Pope & Talbot concerned allegations that Canada's implementation of its obligations under the 1996 Softwood Lumber Agreement with the United States violated NAFTA's requirements of national treatment and fair and equitable treatment, among others, and also constituted a compensable arbitration. Although the tribunal rejected claims of violation of national treatment and of an expropriation, it ultimately found a violation of fair and equitable treatment, as discussed below. After more than three years and five major opinions, the tribunal awarded Pope & Talbot approximately $462,000, roughly 0.1 percent of the initial $509,000,000 original claim!

The concerns of the NAFTA Parties over *Pope & Talbot, S.D. Myers* and other assumed deviations from the customary international law standard prompted the first and to date only binding "Interpretation" of NAFTA Chapter 11, which, *inter alia*, stated that "The concepts of 'fair and equitable treatment' and 'full protection and security' do not require treatment in addition to or beyond that which is required by the customary international law minimum standard of treatment of aliens." The Interpretation (which is reproduced in the Supplement) was extensively criticized by the *Pope & Talbot* Tribunal in a later opinion, and the tribunal suggested that the Interpretation might really be an amendment (which would be subject to constitutional processes in the three countries). However, in the end the Tribunal grudgingly accepted that the action was an Interpretation. Language in the United States—Chile FTA attempts to resolve at least some of this confusion by including the term "customary international law" in the fair and equitable treatment provision, and defining that term in much greater detail (see Document Supplement).

In *Methanex*, the Canadian firm challenged the action of the State of California in banning the gasoline additive, MTBE, because of the perceived risks of MTBE pollution of the underground water supply. Methanex manufactures methanol, which is the principal ingredient in MTBE, and argued that the measures taken by California constituted a "substantial interference and taking of Methanex US' business and Methanex's investment in Methanex US. These measures were characterized both directly and indirectly tantamount to expropriation." However, the original tribunal did not reach the question of whether California's action constituted a compensable taking under Article 1110. Rather, the original complaint was dismissed on grounds that the connection between the California MTBE ban and Methanex' operations was not "legally significant" so as to satisfy the "relating to" language in NAFTA, Article 1101. The action remains pending.

Of course, whether the regulatory actions are "valid" under Article 1110 is to be determined by the adjudicatory process. It is notable that the recently concluded United States—Chile Free Trade Agreement, the investment provisions of which are generally similar to those found in NAFTA, Chapter 11, contains an annex designed to restrict, perhaps significantly, the scope of the "indirect" expropriation provisions as they may apply to government regulatory activities:

> Except in rare circumstances, nondiscriminatory regulatory actions by a Party that are designed and applied to protect legitimate public welfare objectives, such as public health, safety, and the environment, do not constitute indirect expropriation.

In *Loewen*, a Mississippi state court trial alleged to have been conducted in an intentionally prejudicial manner had resulted in a verdict against Loewen (a Canadian operator of funeral homes) of approximately $100 million in actual damages and $400 million in punitive damages, in a commercial transaction worth less than $5 million. Because the claimant allegedly could not meet bonding requirements for an appeal, set at $625 million, Loewen settled the case for $175 million, "under conditions of extreme duress" and brought a Chapter 11 claim. Among Loewen's contentions was that actions of the trial court, the excessive judgment and the bonding requirements were violations of NAFTA, Article 1105, in that Loewen was denied justice and denied fair and equitable treatment by the Mississippi courts.

In partial response, the United States argued, *inter alia*, that the treatment accorded to Loewen by the courts of Mississippi could not be shown by claimant to be "below the international minimum standard required by Article 1105." The United States had contended that the fact that "the Tribunal must consider the entirety of the United States' system of justice stems from the nature of the *customary* international law obligation that gives rise to State responsibility for denial of justice." The United States ultimately prevailed. The tribunal agreed that the Mississippi court decision was "a disgrace"; it was "clearly improper and discreditable and cannot be squared with minimum standards of international law and fair and equitable treatment." However, the tribunal agreed with the United States that Loewen had failed to adequately pursue available domestic remedies, preventing Loewen from prevailing on its denial of justice/denial of fair and equitable treatment under international law claims.

Loewen was ultimately dismissed on procedural grounds, with the Tribunal holding that availability of the Chapter 11 mechanism was lost when Loewen, in bankruptcy, transferred its interests to a U.S. firm.

This has not prevented anti-NAFTA groups in the United States from seizing on *Loewen* as "an all-out attack on democracy. If successful, it would undermine the jury system, which is fundamental to our system of justice."

In *Mondev v. United States*, the Claimant directly challenged the Interpretation, the meaning of fair and equitable treatment and the requirements of customary international law. However, since Mondev had chosen to invoke the protection of local courts, which had decided against the firm, the tribunal limited its review to "that aspect of the Article 1105(1) which concerns what is commonly called denial of justice, that is to say, with the standard of treatment of aliens applicable to decisions of the host State's courts or tribunals." Like Pope & Talbot, Mondev also argued that the Interpretation was effectively an amendment to NAFTA, permitted only "with the applicable legal procedures of each Party." If the appropriate standard was found to be customary international law, Mondev argued that "that law had to be given its current content, as it has been shaped by the conclusion of hundreds of bilateral investment treaties, including NAFTA, and by modern international judgments and arbitral awards."

The United States, in defending the Interpretation and criticizing the *Pope & Talbot* Tribunal, contended that "customary international law" meant just that, and the BITs were not relevant unless it could be shown that they reflected *opinio juris*– evidence of a general practice, agreement in the literature or previous court cases. The United States also sought to discredit arbitral decisions that attempted to apply standards of customary international law based on a specific treaty. Both Mexico and Canada admitted that the customary international law standard could evolve over time. However, both countries still argued that the threshold for finding a violation of customary international law in this area was high, or required evidence of an "arbitrary action substituted for the rule of law" for a violation. In *Mondev,* the tribunal examined whether the content of customary international law providing for fair and equitable treatment and full protection and security in investment treaties was any different than it was in the 1920s. The tribunal held that the "substantive and procedural rights of the individual in international law have undergone considerable development," "to the modern eye, what is unfair or inequitable need not equate with the outrageous or egregious," and that "a State may treat foreign investment unfairly and inequitably without necessarily acting in bad faith."

The tribunal also recognized that dozens of nations' BITs had influenced the content of the rules governing the treatment of foreign investment in current international law by obligating parties to accord foreign investment fair and equitable treatment. While the United States conceded the significance of the jurisprudence of state practice and arbitral tribunals, it also contended that a tribunal still could not "adopt its own idiosyncratic standard of what is 'fair or equitable' without reference to established sources of law." The tribunal reasoned that the reference to "customary international law" in the Interpretation must mean that status of that body of law no earlier than 1994, when the NAFTA came into force. As a result, where the tribunal found no denial of justice, there could be no violation of Article 1105, and the tribunal dismissed Mondev's claim.

A somewhat similar analysis of Article 1105 and customary international law occurred in *ADF Group v. United States*, where the tribunal focused on the key question of whether the enforcement of a federal "Buy American" provision precluded ADF from fabricating steel for guardrails to be sold in Virginia, and was therefore a violation of Article 1105. Thus, customary international law is the standard applicable in Article 1105. However, the tribunal recognized that Article 1105 is something more than a rule against discrimination between domestic and foreign investors. Presently, the United States, Mexico, and Canada all agree that the Interpretation refers to customary international law as it exists today, although Mexico and Canada continue to remind tribunals that "the threshold remains high" for a violation of that standard. However, this does not mean that the investor had demonstrated that there exists, "a general and autonomous requirement (autonomous, that is, from specific rules addressing particular, limited, contexts) to accord fair and equitable treatment and full protection and security to foreign investments" in today's customary international law. In *ADF Group*, the investor simply did not make his case that such U.S. domestic measures as domestic content and performance requirements in the peculiar context of government procurement are violations of fair and equitable treatment as that term is used in NAFTA.

Several other cases have shed further light on the proper application of the international law standard for fair and equitable treatment. In *Waste Management v. United Mexican States* [Waste Management II, Apr. 2004], a dispute involving the failure of a Mexican municipality to pay its contractual obligations to the U.S. operator of a sanitary landfill, the tribunal concluded, based on the factual record as a whole, that the government's failure to "fulfil contractual obligations did not suffice to create liability under Article 1105." Nor would there be a violation unless it amounted to "an outright and unjustified repudiation of the transaction" and some sort of domestic remedy was available to the creditor to deal with the non-payment. Similarly, in *Gami Investments v. United Mexican States,* the tribunal again rejected a claim of denial of fair and equitable treatment, in this instance arising out of Mexico's administration of its sugar production and export regime. (Gami was a minority U.S. shareholder in a Mexican sugar mill operator.) That tribunal refused to conclude that the "failures in the Sugar Program were both directly attributable to the government and directly causative of GAMI's alleged injury," and denied Article 1105 relief on that ground. (Neither Waste Management nor GAMI prevailed on any other ground under Chapter 11, Section A.)

Transparency Issues

A related concern regarding the Chapter 11 process has been the lack of transparency. Under the ICSID Additional Facility Rules—to date the preferred mechanism under Chapter 11—the process is not transparent, as neither the written nor the oral proceedings were open to the public. NAFTA itself provides that the final award may be made public if either the government or the private party wishes to do so (in the case of Canada or the United States), or subject to the applicable arbitration rules (Mexico). Even the formal notice initiating arbitration may not be public if neither party decides to release it. None of this was particularly surprising when NAFTA was negotiated, given that the private investor's interests are considered paramount, and that international commercial arbitration is normally a confidential process. The difficulty arises when the particular cases raise important public law and policy concerns, as with the potential impact of the Chapter 11 mechanism on the national or local government's ability to enact environmental or other regulations.

However, the degree of transparency of the process has increased significantly in recent years. In July 2001, the NAFTA Parties, in the Interpretation mentioned above, stated that "nothing in NAFTA imposes a general duty of confidentiality" and agreed that they would "make available to the public in a timely manner all documents submitted to, or issued by, Chapter 11 tribunals" subject to certain exceptions for confidential or privileged information. In October 2003, Canada and the United States, but not Mexico, issued statement indicating that they would consent—and request disputing investors and tribunals to consent—to holding hearings that are open to the public, subject to measures to protect confidential business information. At the same time, a statement was issued setting forth procedures for non-disputing party (*amicus curiae*) participation in Chapter 11 proceedings, and a questionnaire which claimants are requested to (but not required to) complete was also published. (See Documentary Supplement.) Open hearings are now the rule; for example, the hearing on the merits on *Methanex* the week of June 7, 2004, was open to the public.

CONGRESSIONAL REACTION TO CHAPTER 11: TRADE PROMOTION AUTHORITY

Many of the concerns, and some aspects of the decisions noted above are reflected in the "Trade Promotion Authority" negotiating guidelines for subsequent free trade agreements. The resulting negotiating authority text reflected, *inter alia,* such concerns and compromises:

> [T]he principal negotiating objectives of the United States regarding foreign investment are to reduce or eliminate artificial or trade-distorting barriers to foreign investment, *while ensuring that foreign investors in the United States are not accorded greater substantive rights with respect to investment protections than United States investors in the United States,* and to secure for investors important rights comparable to those that would be available under United States legal principles and practice. . . . *

---

* 19 U.S.C. § 3802(b)(2002) (emphasis added); see Document Supplement.

The rationale was explained in the Senate Report:

> The negotiating objective on foreign investment reflects the [Senate Finance] Committee's view that it is a priority for negotiators to seek agreements protection the rights of U.S. investors abroad and ensuring the existence of an investor-state dispute settlement mechanism. It also reflects the view that in entering into investment agreements, negotiators must seek to protect the interests of the United States as a potential defendant in investor-state dispute settlement. In other words, there ought to be a balance. Protecting the rights of U.S. investors abroad should not come at the expense of making Federal, State and local laws and regulations unduly vulnerable to challenges by foreign investors.*

COURT REVIEW OF NAFTA ARBITRAL DECISIONS?

Arbitral decisions under NAFTA are not immediately final; Article 1136:3 explicitly contemplates the possibility of requests for revision or annulment. To date, under NAFTA, three arbitral decisions have been reviewed by a court of the "situs" of arbitration. In *United Mexican States v. Metalclad*, before the British Columbia Supreme Court [a court of first instance], the court concluded that the Tribunal acted beyond the scope of the submission to arbitration by finding a transparency requirement in Chapter 11 as the basis for determining that Mexico had violated Articles 1105 (fair and equitable treatment) and 1110 (expropriation) of NAFTA. (The tribunal's finding of indirect expropriation was upheld on other grounds.) In *S.D. Myers v. Mexico*, a federal court sitting in Ottawa upheld the arbitral tribunal. The court declined to review a jurisdictional challenge based on Canada's allegation that there was no "investment" by S.D. Myers, and applied what it said was a "correctness" standard of review for legal issues (such as the meaning of the word "investor") and a "reasonableness" standard for application of facts to legal issues, reflecting Article 34 of the UNCITRAL Model Code as adopted in Canada. Finally, in *United States v. Feldman Karpa*, the Ontario Superior Court of Justice dismissed the appeal of the tribunal's decision, Judge Chilcott stated: "In my view, a high level of deference should be afforded to the Tribunal, especially in cases where the Appellant Mexico is really challenging a finding of fact. The panel who has heard the evidence is best able to determine issues of credibility." (A further appeal to Ontario's highest court was dismissed on similar grounds.)

The idea of a single Appellate Body, perhaps modeled after the WTO's Appellate Body, has received support from diverse sources. NGOs and some government agencies have been concerned about the lack of appeals, so that *ad hoc* arbitrators cannot be controlled, and any legal errors are made cannot be effectively corrected for the current or future cases. The use of the Commission's power to issue binding Interpretations (noted above), is plagued by uncertainties. Moreover, despite the

---

* Bipartisan Trade Promotion Authority Act of 2002, S. Rep. No. 107–139, at 13 (2d Sess. 2002).

lack of formal precedential value of earlier arbitral decisions—NAFTA, Art. 1136:1 states that "An award made by a Tribunal shall have no binding force except between the disputing parties and in respect of the particular case"—prior decisions *are* being regularly cited by parties to arbitrations, which effectively requires tribunals to discuss, distinguish and/or follow those earlier decisions. This increases the risk for concerned governments, NGOs or private investor groups in leaving an allegedly erroneous decision unchallenged. There is obviously some dissatisfaction with court review (particularly in recent Canadian NAFTA cases), either because courts have only limited experience with the issues or themselves make flawed interpretations of complex treaty provisions or principles of international law, or because the courts are giving too much (or too little) deference to the tribunals.

However, agreeing on the proper standard of review may not be easy. The possible range of standards of review runs the gamut from the high degree of deference incorporated in the ICSID and UNCITRAL (or New York Convention) standards, in theory, at least, providing only very limited review to de novo review. Presumably, the NGO and government supporters of the appellate body concept have in mind a broad scope of review. One possibility is the WTO Appellate Body standard for review of Panel decisions, empowering the Appellate Body to review "issues of law covered in the panel report and legal interpretations developed by the panel" (DSU, art. 17:6). The *Chevron v. Natural Resources Defense Council** standard, with deference to an expert tribunal below, affirmation even where reviewing court might have reached a different determination, but reversal where the tribunal below makes legal errors, is certainly one which could be adapted to an appellate body for investment disputes, as it has been under Article 17:6 of the WTO's Antidumping Agreement. Finally, at least in theory, a de novo review of law and facts could be permitted, although it seems unlikely than any of the interested groups would want to impose the time, expense and uncertainties of such review, even for public policy related issues.

Finally, The legal and practical challenges to the idea are significant. Separate appellate bodies for every FTA or BIT are impractical. Therefore, from a practical and financial point of view only a single appellate body makes sense. ICSID or the OECD are probably the only logical fora, with participation available (but optional) for ICSID or OECD members alike. (The vast majority of WTO Members have shown a strong aversion to an agreement on foreign investment. The FTAA, where the draft of the investment chapter contains appellate body language, is moribund; if revived, it may not include an investment chapter. A free-standing investment appellate body is unlikely both for cost reasons and because of the reluctance of many countries, including the United States, to create new international entities). ICSID, because both developed and developing countries are parties, is likely the preferred forum.

* 467 U.S. 837 (1984).

Procedurally, should the appellate body have authority to confirm, set aside and remand? Should there be permanent members (as with the WTO Appellate Body) or an *ad hoc* tribunals formed from a standing roster (like the ICSID Annulment Committee)? Who has input into the selection of the members? Should party nationals be permitted to serve, as on investment tribunals under ICSID and NAFTA, or excluded, as with ICSID Annulment Committee and with WTO panels (but not with the Appellate Body)? Would 5–7 of the world's outstanding investment arbitrators be willing to serve on an appellate body, which would likely foreclose their continued work as arbitrators, at least where the AB had review jurisdiction? Incorporating an appellate body would require amendment of bilateral investment treaties, the investment provisions of NAFTA and other FTAs. In most instances, changes in domestic law would also be required. The amendment of BITs would be easier politically than amending investment provisions of NAFTA and FTAs, since it could be difficult, if reopening NAFTA or FTAs, to limit the modifications to inclusion of an appellate body. It seems unlikely, for example, that any of the NAFTA Parties would be interested in reopening NAFTA.

The first serious attempt in creating an appellate body for investment disputes has arisen under the Central American Free Trade Agreement, which provides that such a mechanism for CAFTA will be developed through a negotiating group appointed within three months of the entry into force of the Agreement. (Annex 10–F; see Documents Supplement.) However, late in 2004, the ICSID Secretariat was consulting with member governments and the private sector on a proposal for an ICSID "Appellate Facility." This would be submitted for approval to the Administrative Council (membership) as "Rules" (like the Additional Facility Rules) rather than as a protocol to the Convention, which would require ratification by all of the member states.

Questions and Comments

1. The comments note that NAFTA Chapter 11 is now being used as the basis for investment protection provisions in recent FTAs and the new 2004 model BIT. How has the Trade Promotion Authority (comments and supplement) changed the NAFTA provisions for subsequent agreements? Who will likely benefit from these changes? How would you expect an Appellate Body (for NAFTA, CAFTA, other FTAs or a single entity for many investment treaties) to influence arbitral panels?

2. Professor Sandrino comments on expropriation, which has become a focus of many investment disputes filed under NAFTA (along with national treatment and fair and equitable treatment). But her expropriation discussion follows traditional routes, and could hardly have contemplated how investors have interpreted expropriation in some of the cases discussed in the Comment above. She concludes that the NAFTA dispute settlement procedure is a significant departure for Mexico because of its history with the Calvo Clause, which Attorney and Professor Murphy develops in the subsequent comment. Has the Calvo Clause been a toothless bastion, given

there appears to have been no instance in Mexico where a foreign company forfeited its investment for violating the Calvo Clause? What remains of the Calvo Clause for U.S. and Mexican investors in light of Chapter 11, Section B?

3. What would be the basis of the claim by WDI under Chapter 11?

4. What legal rules must the Chapter 11 arbitral tribunal follow? (The procedure of arbitration which WDI will follow is briefly outlined in the Gantz extract, but one ought to read through Articles 1115 through 1139 of Chapter 11.) Consider the following:

a. Which arbitration rules apply? Only the United States is a party to the ICSID Convention. ICSID arbitration is described in the readings. What are the differences between arbitration under the ICSID Convention and under the Additional Facility Rules of ICSID? Why did the NAFTA Parties include arbitration under the ICSID Rules, even though those rules could not be used because Mexico and Canada aren't parties to the ICSID Convention? Why do you think Canada, a developed country and a major capital exporting country, hasn't ever ratified the ICSID Convention?

b. Appointment of the arbitrators is obviously important. Articles 1123 through 1125 outline the process. ICSID's Secretary General acts as the appointing authority. He will ask WDI and Canada to each appoint an arbitrator. Who may be appointed? Nationals of their own nation? If they make such appointments, they go on to try to agree on the presiding arbitrator. What if they fail to agree? Where will the arbitration be conducted? WDI would prefer in the United States, but it wants the arbitral decree enforced if it wins. Perhaps it would be best to have it in some nation which has the respect of Canada? Are there limitations?

c. Who decides the place of arbitration—does Article 1130 help? Note that even if the situs or seat of the arbitration is agreed to be Canada (as in *Metalclad, S.D. Myers, Feldman Karpa* and others) if the arbitration is under the ICSID Additional Facility Rules the hearing and most or all of the tribunals' meetings will likely be in Washington, D.C. at ICSID headquarters. (The *S.D. Myers* arbitration, under the UNCITRAL Rules, was held in Canada, but some UNCITRAL cases are now utilizing the secretariat services of ICSID in Washington as well.)

d. What law does WDI want applied in the arbitration? What does Chapter 11 provide? Is there any basis for the tribunal to apply national (Canadian) law in the arbitration? How might Canadian law be relevant to the decision?

5. Is Canada responsible for the acts of its provinces and municipalities?

6. Did Canada violate the fair and equitable treatment mandate of Article 1105? Is *S.D. Myers* helpful to WDI in making its case? Note that Article 1105 requires that treatment of foreign investors meet a minimum standard, which is "treatment in accordance with international law, including fair and equitable treatment and full protection and security." Is there any language in the Interpretation (see Supplement) that assists or hinders

WDI's claim? Would WDI be in a better or worse position if the United States—Chile FTA version of the "minimum standard of treatment" (Article 10.4, reproduced in the Supplement) were applicable to NAFTA? Some enterprising NAFTA litigants may argue that this Chilean language simply explains what minimum standard of treatment/fair and equitable treatment/full protection and security means under customary international law. Others may argue that it is a different standard, and proves that the NAFTA language means something different.

7. Might WDI successfully argue that Canada knew or should have known of the misunderstanding as to what permits were needed and whether or not the federal government would obtain provincial and municipality approval?

8. Is it clear from the facts that a municipal permit for the construction of the landfill was in fact required?

9. Assume that the Canadian law actually grants to the federal government the power to authorize construction and operation of hazardous waste landfills, stating that: "the powers of the federal government extend to the regulation and control of activities considered to be highly hazardous, and of the generation, handling and final disposal of hazardous materials and wastes for the environment of ecosystems, as well as for the preservation of natural resources, in accordance with the law, other applicable ordinances and their regulatory provisions." Assume Canadian law also limits the environmental powers of the municipalities to issues relating to non-hazardous waste, and the same law also limits provincial environmental powers to those not expressly attributed to the federal government. How would this help WDI pursue its Chapter 11 claim?

10. Isn't there an issue of reasonable reliance by WDI? If so, is this a violation of Canada's obligation to provide fair and equitable treatment under Article 1105 of NAFTA?

11. But doesn't NAFTA Article 1114 allow a Party to ensure that investment activity is undertaken in a manner sensitive to environmental concerns? How is a tribunal to deal with the language "otherwise consistent with this Chapter" if there appears to be coverage under Article 1102 or 1105, and also under 1114?

12. What about WDI's claim under NAFTA Article 1110: Expropriation? Article 1110 provides that "[n]o party shall directly or indirectly . . . expropriate an investment . . . or take a measure tantamount to . . . expropriation . . . except: (a) for a public purpose; (b) on a non-discriminatory basis; (c) in accordance with due process of law and Article 1105(1); and (d) on payment of compensation. . . . " "A measure" is defined in Article 201(1) as including "any law, regulation, procedure, requirement or practice." First, must the expropriation be open, deliberate and acknowledged takings of property, such as outright seizure or formal or obligatory transfer of title in favor of the host State? Do the actions of the Canadian authorities, federal, provincial and local, rise to the level of expropriation? Would your answer be different if the Premier of Ontario had not issued the ecological decree? Is the *S.D. Myers* analysis of expropriation helpful or harmful to WDI?

13. What should the damages be? Are damages and compensation under NAFTA articles 1105 and 1110 to be calculated in the same manner?

Is it generally easier to prove a violation of Article 1105 than 1110? (See S.D. Myers.) Do the damages provisions of Article 1110 apply only to expropriation losses or to losses under Articles 1102, 1105 or other provisions as well? WDI proposes two alternative methods for calculating damages. One is a discounted cash flow analysis of future profits to establish the fair market value of the investment. Two is to value WDI's actual investment in the landfill (considerably less than under the first method). Does it matter that WDI never operated, making calculation of future profits somewhat speculative? What should the tribunal allow?

14. What might some alternatives to a Chapter 11 claim have been? Would a Chapter 20 claim be appropriate? What about a suit in the Canadian federal courts? Doesn't the Canadian legal system have a high reputation for impartiality and fairness? (After all, in the *S.D. Myers* appeal, the Ontario court found against the Canadian government.) Could the matter be settled in the International Court of Justice in the Hague? Are any decisions of the ICJ helpful, such as *Barcelona Traction*, 1970 ICJ Rep. 3, or *Elettronica Sicula S.p.A. (ELSI)*, Judgment (U.S. v. Italy), 1989 ICJ Rep. 15?

15. *Loewen* and *Mondev* both involved situations in which the claimant was challenging the validity of a NAFTA Party's court decisions. In *Loewen*, the tribunal found that the claimant had not fully exhausted its local remedies (appeals within Mississippi or in the federal system) and because of that concluded that there had been no breach of the United States' fair and equitable treatment obligation. In *Mondev*, the shortcomings of the Massachusetts court system, and limits on its jurisdiction, were insufficient to convince the tribunal that there had been a violation of Article 1105. Effectively, a denial of justice is required (even though those words do not appear in NAFTA). Under what circumstances is a national court decision a violation of Chapter 11?

16. *Loewen* has gained the support of some formidable comment, including former president and judge of the International Court of Justice at the Hague, Professor Sir Robert Jennings, who has suggested the Mississippi judgment speaks for itself, and is an "international flouting of the most ordinary requirements of justice."(He made these comments in the course of a paid expert opinion submitted on behalf of *Loewen*.) A commentator of Public Citizen's Global Trade Watch—the same group that litigated against the implementation of cross-border trucking services—stated that the case raised freedom of speech issues, that O'Keefe (local funeral home owner and plaintiff in Mississippi case) was merely stressing the value of local ownership, and that the claim was a misuse of a fatally flawed investment chapter which needs to be replaced. Also criticized was the secrecy of the arbitral proceedings, and the threat to the civil justice system in the U.S. Do you agree? Is the NAFTA intended to address fundamental characteristics of a Party's legislative, executive or judicial branches?

17. A successful award is one enforced. Canada, the United States and Mexico are signatories to the New York Convention regarding the enforcement of arbitral awards. But that does not ensure enforcement. Do you believe Canadian courts—which are considered independent from the executive branch of the government would enforce an award against the Government? If not, what other alternatives does WDI have to seek enforcement? (In *S.D. Myers* and *Pope & Talbot*, Canada paid the awards to the claimant once the arbitral process and review were completed. Mexico paid the claimant in *Metalclad*; *Feldman* remains in the Canadian judicial system.) Professor Michael Reisman has written about the breakdown of some of the

systems of control intended to assure the enforcement of arbitral awards. Among the institutions he attributes some failures to both the ICSID and the New York Convention. See W. Michael Reisman, Systems of Control in International Adjudication & Arbitration (1992). Consider the situation of Argentina. As of mid–2004, there were more than 30 ICSID cases brought against Argentina arising out of steps taken by the Argentine government and/or provinces after the financial collapse of 2002, totaling billions of dollars. Collection could be a significant issue if some or most of the claimants ultimately prevail.

18.   Is the Chapter 11 dispute settlement process being misused, as many suggest, especially environmental groups that believe legitimate environmental regulation is threatened? Have investors confused the meaning of "regulation" with "expropriation"? Many of the cases discussed in the comments seem to involve regulatory actions by the foreign government. Should NAFTA Chapter 11 be available for use by Canadian citizens unhappy with U.S. restrictions on Canadian beef imports as a result of concerns over Mad Cow Disease? By U.S. citizens objecting to Mexico refusing to release stored water from the Rio Grande? Review the Commission Interpretation, the excerpt from TPA, Annex 10–D and Article 10.4 of the U.S.–Chile FTA in the Documents Supplement. What considerations in Congress and the Executive Branch led to these changes with regard to regulatory takings and "customary international law" as it limits "fair and equitable treatment"? How would the new treaty language (similar to that in the Singapore FTA and CAFTA) affect your clients if they are involved in an investment dispute under one of those agreements?

19.   A major criticism of the arbitration process generally, and thus as used by the NAFTA, is its secrecy. Arbitration is not subject to the openness that prevails in the courts, although as one of the comments indicates, NAFTA arbitral tribunal proceedings are now open to the public in most instances, and most of the pleadings are available on the Internet, either on government or private websites. How might public arbitration help? Or hurt? (See the Commission declarations in the Documents Supplement.)

20.   The explosion of litigation between foreign investors and host governments has not been limited to NAFTA, Chapter 11; it has increased dramatically under BITs and other investment agreements during the past decade. The United Nations Commission on Trade and Development (UNCTAD) reported in 2004 that at least 160 claims have been made under such treaties (including NAFTA). Of the 106 cases that have been brought under the World Bank's International Centre for the Settlement of Investment Disputes (ICSID), 103 have been submitted since 1994, 37 against Argentina alone. (Most of the rest have been brought under the UNCITRAL Arbitration Rules.)

21.   After eleven years there is a rapidly growing body of literature discussing Chapter 11 issues. See, e.g., NAFTA Investment Law and Arbitration: Past Issues, Current Practice, Future Prospects (Todd Weiler, ed., Transnational Publ. 2004).

Chapter 8

INTELLECTUAL PROPERTY

8.0 INTRODUCTION: INTERNATIONAL INTELLECTUAL PROPERTY RIGHTS*

Chapter 8 covers NAFTA and intellectual property rights. We focus primarily on patents and trade secrets, and introductory material for both can be found in Problems 8.1 and 8.2. NAFTA was notably the first international trade agreement to include coverage of trade secrets. We also consider in these problems NAFTA law on gray market trading and counterfeiting.

In this introduction, our goal is to survey those areas of intellectual property law that space has not allowed us to treat more extensively in Problems 8.1 and 8.2. We review some fundamentals concerning trademarks, copyrights, their international and regional recognition, franchising, Special 301 procedures under U.S. law, and the WTO Trade–Related Intellectual Property Rights Agreements (TRIPs).

TRADEMARK PROTECTION

Virtually all countries offer some legal protection to trademarks, even when they do not have trademark registration systems. Trademark rights derived from the use of marks on goods in commerce have long been recognized at common law and remain so today in countries as diverse as the United States and the United Arab Emirates. The latter nation, for example, had, no trademark registration law in 1986, but this did not prevent McDonald's from obtaining an injunction against a local business using its famous name and golden arches without authorization. However, obtaining international trademark protection requires separate registration under the law of each nation. Roughly 50,000 trademark applications are filed each year by United States citizens with the appropriate authorities in other countries.

* Adapted from R. Folsom, M. Gordon, J. Spanogle, International Business Transactions Hornbook (West Group, 2001).

In the United States, trademarks are protected at common law and by state and federal registrations. Federal registration is permitted by the U.S. Trademark Office for all marks capable of distinguishing the goods on which they appear from other goods. Unless the mark falls within a category of forbidden registrations (e.g. those that offend socialist morality in the People's Republic of China), a mark becomes valid for a term of years following registration. In some countries (like the U.S. prior to 1989), marks must be used on goods before registration. In others, like France, use is not required and speculative registration of marks can occur. It is said that ESSO was obliged to purchase French trademark rights from such a speculator when it switched to EXXON in its search for the perfect global trademark. Since 1989, United States law has allowed applications when there is a bona fide intent to use a trademark within 12 months and, if there is good cause for the delay in actual usage, up to 24 additional months. Such filings in effect reserve the mark for the applicant. The emphasis on bona fide intent and good cause represent an attempt to control any speculative use of U.S. trademark law.

The scope of trademark protection may differ substantially from country to country. Under U.S. federal trademark law, injunctions, damages and seizures of goods by customs officials may follow infringement. Other jurisdictions may provide similar remedies on their law books, but offer little practical enforcement. Thus, trademark registration is no guarantee against trademark piracy. A pair of blue jeans labeled "Levi Strauss made in San Francisco" may have been counterfeited in Israel or Paraguay without the knowledge or consent of Levi Strauss and in spite of its trademark registrations in those countries. Trademark counterfeiting is not just a third world problem, as any visitor to a United States "flea market" can tell. Congress created criminal offenses and private treble damages remedies for the first time in the Trademark Counterfeiting Act of 1984. In many countries trademarks (appearing on goods) may be distinguished from "service marks" used by providers of services (e.g., The Law Store), "trade names" (business names), "collective marks" (marks used by a group or organization), and "certification marks" (marks which certify a certain quality, origin, or other fact).

Although national trademark schemes differ, it can be said generally that a valid trademark (e.g., a mark not "canceled," "renounced," "abandoned," "waived" or "generic") will be protected against infringing use. A trademark can be valid in one country (ASPIRIN brand tablets in Canada), but invalid because generic in another (BAYER brand aspirin in the United States). A trademark can be valid, e.g., CHEVROLET NOVA brand automobiles in the U.S. and Mexico, but diminished in value for reasons of language. If you were Mexican, would you buy a CHEVROLET promising to "no va"?

Unlike patents and copyrights, trademarks may be renewed continuously. A valid mark may be licensed, perhaps to a "registered user" or it may be assigned, in some cases only with the sale of the goodwill of a business. A growing example of international licensing of trademarks can be found in franchise agreements taken abroad. And national trademark law sometimes accompanies international licensing. The principal U.S. trademark law, the Lanham Act of 1946, has been construed to apply extraterritorially (much like the Sherman Antitrust Act) to foreign licensees engaging in deceptive practices. See especially Scotch Whiskey Association v. Barton Distilling Co., 489 F.2d 809 (7th Cir.1973).

Foreigners who seek a registration may be required to prove a prior and valid "home registration," and a new registration in another country may not have an existence "independent" of the continuing validity of the home country registration. Foreigners are often assisted in their registration efforts by international and regional trademark treaties.

INTERNATIONAL RECOGNITION OF TRADEMARKS

The premium placed on priority of use of a trademark is reflected in several international trademark treaties. These include the Paris Convention, the 1957 Arrangement of Nice Concerning the International Classification of Goods and Services, and the 1973 Trademark Registration Treaty done at Vienna. The treaties of widest international application are the Paris Convention and the Arrangement of Nice, as revised to 1967, to which the United States is signatory. The International Bureau of WIPO plays a central role in the administration of arrangements contemplated by these agreements.

The Paris Convention reflects an effort to internationalize some trademark rules. In addition to extending the principle of national treatment and providing for a right of priority of six months for trademarks, the Convention mitigates the frequent national requirement that foreigners seeking trademark registration prove a pre-existing, valid and continuing home registration. This makes it easier to obtain foreign trademark registrations, avoids the possibility that a lapse in registration at home will cause all foreign registrations to become invalid, and allows registration abroad of entirely different (and perhaps culturally adapted) marks. Article 6 bis of the Paris Convention requires the member nations to refuse to register, to cancel an existing registration or to prohibit the use of a trademark which is considered by the trademark registration authorities of that country to be "well known" and owned by a person entitled to the benefits of the Paris Convention. This provision concerns what are called "famous marks" and prevents their infringement even if there has been no local registration of the mark.

The Nice Agreement addresses the question of registration by "class" or "classification" of goods. In order to simplify internal administrative procedures relating to marks, many countries classify and thereby identify goods (and sometimes services) which have the same or similar attributes. An applicant seeking registration of a mark often is required to specify the class or classes to which the product mark belongs. However, not all countries have the same classification system and some lack any such system. Article 1 of the Nice Agreement adopts, for the purposes of the registration of marks, a single classification system for goods and services. This has brought order out of chaos in the field. The 1973 Vienna Trademark Registration Treaty (to which the United States is a signatory) contemplates an international filing and examination scheme like that in force for patents under the Patent Cooperation Treaty. This treaty has not yet been fully implemented, but holds out the promise of reduced costs and greater uniformity when obtaining international trademark protection. At least twenty-nine European and Mediterranean countries are parties to the Madrid Agreement for International Registration of Marks (1891, as amended). This agreement already permits international filings to obtain national trademark rights and is administered by WIPO. A Common Market Trademark can now be obtained in the European Community. The 1994 Trademark Law Treaty substantially harmonized trademark registration procedures.

COPYRIGHT PROTECTION

Nearly one hundred nations recognize some form of copyright protection for "authors' works." The scope of this coverage and available remedies varies from country to country, with some uniformity established in the roughly 80 nations participating in the Berne and Universal Copyright Conventions, infra. In the United States, for example, the Copyright Act of 1976 protects all original expressions fixed in a tangible medium (now known or later developed), including literary works, musical works, dramatic works, choreographic works, graphic works, audiovisual works, sound recordings and computer programs. It is not necessary to publish a work to obtain a U.S. copyright. It is sufficient that the work is original and fixed in a tangible medium of expression. Prior to 1989, to retain a U.S. copyright, the author had to give formal notice of a reservation of rights when publishing the work. Publication of the work without such notice no longer dedicates it to free public usage.

U.S. copyright protection now extends from creation of the work to 70 years after the death of the author. The author also controls "derivative works," such as movies made from books. Only the author (or her assignees or employer in appropriate cases) may make copies, display, perform, and first sell the work. Registration with the U.S. Copyright Office is not required to obtain copyright rights, but is important to federal copyright infringement remedies. Infringers are subject to criminal penalties, injunctive relief and civil damages. Infringing works are impounded pending trial and ultimately destroyed. But educators, critics and news reporters are allowed "fair use" of the work, a traditional common law doctrine now codified in the 1976 Copyright Act. The marketing of copyrights is sometimes accomplished through agency "clearinghouses." This is especially true of musical compositions because the many authors and potential users are dispersed. In the United States, the American Society of Composers, Authors and Publishers (ASCAP) and Broadcast Music, Inc. (BMI) are the principal clearing houses for such rights. Thousands of these rights are sold under "blanket licenses" for fees established by the clearing houses and later distributed to their members. Similar organizations exist in most European states. Their activities have repeatedly been scrutinized under United States and European antitrust law. See Broadcast Music, Inc. v. Columbia Broadcasting System, Inc., 441 U.S. 1, 99 S.Ct. 1551, 60 L.Ed.2d 1 (1979); Re GEMA, 10 Common Mkt. L. Rep. D35 (1971), 11 Common Mkt.L.Rep. 694 (1972).

Copyright protection in other countries may be more or less comprehensive or capable of adaptation to modern technologies. The copyrightability of computer programs, for example, is less certain in many jurisdictions. In some developing countries, "fair use" is a theme which is expansively construed to undermine copyright protection. But these differences seem less significant when contrasted with the worldwide problem of copyright piracy, ranging from satellite signal poaching to unlicensed CDs, tapes and books. A Joint International Copyright Service run since 1981 by WIPO and UNESCO is designed to promote licensing of copyrights in the third world. This Service does not act as an agency clearinghouse for authors' rights, a deficiency sometimes said to promote copyright piracy.

In the United States, the Copyright Felony Act of 1992 criminalized all copyright infringements. The No Electronic Theft Act of 1997 (NET) removed the need to prove financial gain as element of copyright infringement law, thus ensuring coverage of copying done with intent to harm copyright owners or copying simply for personal use. The Digital Millennium Copyright Act of 1998 (DMCA) brought the United States into compliance with WIPO treaties and created two new copyright offenses; one for circumventing technological measures used by copyright owners to protect their works ("hacking") and a second for tampering with copyright management information (encryption). The DMCA also made it clear that "webmasters" digitally broadcasting music on the internet must pay performance royalties.

INTERNATIONAL RECOGNITION OF COPYRIGHTS

Absent an appropriate convention, copyright registrations must be tediously acquired in each country recognizing such rights. However, copyright holders receive national treatment, translation rights and other benefits under the Universal Copyright Convention (UCC) of 1952 (U.S. adheres). Most importantly, the UCC excuses foreigners from requirements provided notice of a claim is adequately given (E.g., © 2005, Folsom, Gantz and Gordon). Some countries like the U.S. took an option *not* to excuse registration requirements. The exercise of this option had the effect at that time of reinforcing the U.S. "manufacturing clause" requiring local printing of U.S. copyrighted books and prohibiting importation of foreign copies. This protectionist clause finally expired under U.S. copyright law in 1986. The UCC establishes a minimum term for copyright protection: 25 years after publication, prior registration or death of the author. It also authorizes compulsory license schemes for translation rights in all states and compulsory reprint rights and instructional usage in developing countries.

National treatment and a release from registration formalities (subject to copyright notice requirements) can be obtained in Pan–American countries under the Mexico City Convention of 1902 and the Buenos Aires Convention of 1911, the U.S. adhering to both. Various benefits can be had in many other countries through the Berne Convention of 1886 (as revised). Like the UCC, the Berne Convention suspends registration requirements for copyright holders from participating states. Unlike the UCC, it allows for local copyright protection independent of protection granted in the country of origin and does not require copyright notice. The Berne Convention establishes a minimum copyright term of the life of the author plus 50 years, a more generous minimum copyright than that of the UCC. It also recognizes the exclusive translation rights of authors. The Berne Convention does not contemplate compulsory licensing of translation rights. Most U.S. copyright holders previously acquired Berne Convention benefits by simultaneously publishing their works in Canada, a member country.

In 1989, the United States ratified the Berne Convention. U.S. ratification of the Berne Convention creates copyright relations with an additional 25 nations. Ratification has eliminated U.S. registration requirements (reserved under the UCC) for foreign copyright holders and required protection of the "moral rights" of authors, i.e., the rights of integrity and paternity. The right of paternity insures acknowledgment of authorship. The right of integrity conveys the ability to object to distortion, alteration or other derogation of the work. It is generally thought that unfair competition law at the federal and state levels will provide the legal basis in U.S. law for these moral rights. A limited class of visual artists explicitly receive these rights under the Visual Artists Rights Act of 1990.

* * *

Special 301 Procedures

Extensive negotiations were conducted within the GATT under the Uruguay Round on trade-related intellectual property rights (TRIPs). The developed nations sought an Anti–Counterfeiting Code and greater patent, copyright and trademark protection in the third world. The developing nations within GATT resisted on nearly all fronts. The TRIPs negotiations failed to reach a conclusion as scheduled in December 1990, as the Uruguay Round negotiations stalled over intellectual property, services and other issues. Meanwhile, faced with massive technology transfer losses, "Special 301" procedures were established unilaterally by the United States in the 1988 Omnibus Trade and Competitiveness Act. These procedures are located in Section 182 of the Trade Act of 1974. They can lead to initiation of Section 301 proceedings under that Act. Section 301 proceedings are generally used to obtain market access for U.S. exporters of goods and services, but are also capable of being used to pressure and perhaps sanction other nations whose intellectual property policies diverge from U.S. standards.

Special 301 requires the U.S. Trade Representative (USTR) to identify those countries that deny "adequate and effective protection of intellectual property rights" or deny "fair and equitable market access to United States persons who rely upon intellectual property protection." The USTR must also identify "priority foreign countries" whose practices are the most "onerous or egregious" and have the greatest adverse impact on the United States, and who are not entering into good faith negotiations or making significant progress in negotiations towards provision of adequate and effective protection of intellectual property rights.

The USTR has developed "watch lists" and "priority watch lists" under Special 301 while pursuing negotiations with the many nations on those lists. These negotiations have had some success. Argentina agreed, as a result of Special 301 negotiations, to modify registration procedures for and improve protection of pharmaceuticals under its patent law. Mexico was removed from priority status on the Special 301 watch list after it announced new patent legislation. This legislation increased the term of Mexican patents to 20 years, offered protection for chemical and pharmaceutical products as well as biotechnology processes, restricted use of compulsory licenses and made improvements to the Mexican law of trademarks and trade secrets. Intellectual property reforms in Korea, Taiwan and Saudi Arabia have also removed them from the USTR's priority watch list.

THE TRIPs AGREEMENT

The Uruguay Round accords of April 1994 include an agreement on trade-related intellectual property rights (TRIPs) binding upon the over 146 nations that are members of the World Trade Organization. In the United States, the TRIPs agreement was ratified and implemented by Congress in December of 1994 under the Uruguay Round Agreements Act. There is a general requirement of national and most-favored-nation treatment among the parties. The TRIPs covers the gamut of intellectual property. On copyrights, there is protection for computer programs and databases, rental authorization controls for owners of computer software and sound recordings, a 50–year motion picture and sound recording copyright term, and a general obligation to comply with the Berne Convention (except for its provisions on moral rights). On patents, the Paris Convention (1967) prevails, product and process patents are to be available for pharmaceuticals and agricultural chemicals, limits are placed on compulsory licensing, and a general 20–year patent term from the date of application is created. United States law has been altered to create patent terms of 20 years from the date of filing, not 17 years from the date of issuance, as it was previously. For trademarks, service marks become registrable, internationally prominent marks receive enhanced protection, the linking of local marks with foreign trademarks is prohibited, service marks become registrable, and compulsory licensing is limited. In addition, trade secret protection is assisted by TRIPs rules enabling owners to prevent unauthorized use or disclosure. Integrated circuits are covered by rules intended to improve upon the Washington Treaty. Lastly, industrial designs and geographic indicators of alcoholic beverages (e.g., Canadian Whiskey) are also part of the TRIPs regime. Infringement and anti-counterfeiting remedies are included in the TRIPs, for both domestic and international trade protection. There are specific provisions governing injunctions, damages, customs seizures, and discovery of evidence.

Comment on TRIPS and Pharmaceutical Products

One of the most controversial aspects of TRIPs is protection of patents of pharmaceutical products, particularly for diseases which raise major public health issues for poor countries, such as HIV/AIDs, tuberculosis and malaria. (In a different context, discussed *infra*, pharmaceutical prices have significantly affected U.S.–Canada and U.S.–Mexico trade.) In these areas intellectual property protection for pharmaceutical products (under TRIPs and otherwise), recognized as important for the development of new medicines, conflicted with the objective of protecting public health, usually, in the case of poor countries, through the manufacture or importation of far cheaper generic drugs. Many of the countries in most need of such drugs, such as the countries of Sub–Saharan Africa facing an HIV/AIDs epidemic, had no pharmaceutical manufacturing facilities, and thus would need to import generics, making this a major trade as well as intellectual property issues. The dispute over the right of poor countries to manufacture and distribute generic drugs internationally in such situations, with Brazil and India leading the developing country group, threatened to derail the initiation of a new round of WTO trade negotiations, which effort had already failed once, in Seattle in 1999. The first steps were taken by the Ministers in November 2001, but pharmaceutical patent issues continued to plague the Doha Round until August 2003, when the United States capitulated and WTO's General Council adopted additional "compulsory licensing" and trade rules to facilitate the manufacture and export of critical pharmaceutical products. Canada, but not the United States, has adopted such rules. Mexico has agreed not to seek benefits under the WTO Medicines Agreement. How well these provisions will satisfy either developing country governments or the pharmaceutical industries in developed nations remains to be seen.

PROBLEM 8.1 GRAY MARKET TRADING AND TRADE SECRET MISAPPROPRIATION: COCA–COLA IN NORTH AMERICA

SECTION I. THE SETTING

PART A. TRADE SECRETS

Late in the nineteenth century an entrepreneurial Georgia soft drink manufacturer mixed together some common ingredients to produce Coca–Cola. The rest, as they say, is history.

COKE, now available in virtually every part of the globe, is still manufactured under strict secrecy. It is said that only a handful of persons inside the company at any given moment have knowledge of the formula for producing COKE. The production process is segmented so that workers are aware of only one segment. Coca–Cola exclusively manufactures the syrup that is the base of the drink. Bottling companies around the world, some owned by Coca–Cola and some not, add water to create the beverage.

Chemists can dissect the contents of a can of COKE and tell us precisely what are its ingredients. But they cannot tell us how those ingredients are put together to produce the taste associated with COKE. That taste is the "real thing" and worth a fortune. Indeed, when Coca–Cola changed the formula slightly a few years ago consumers demanded and got "Classic" COKE back on the market.

In Canada, there is an independently owned bottling company located in Quebec. It does business under the name of Quebec Soft Drinks (QSD) and is properly licensed by Coca–Cola. QSD also bottles other brands of soft drinks, including some generics. QSD and Coca–Cola have had longstanding profitable business relations.

There are many employees at QSD, but for our purposes the most important is Xavier, a computer specialist. Xavier is, politically speaking, a separatist. In other words, he supports Quebec independence and generally all things Québécois. COKE is decidedly not French and symbolizes for some Québécois an unwanted invasion of American lifestyle and culture.

Xavier takes all this quite seriously and has spent months trying to hack Coca–Cola's computers to get "the formula." Then one night, with a glass of vin rouge at his side, Xavier hits gold and downloads the COKE production formula. With not too much deliberation, he posts the formula on QSD's website, an act that very shortly gets him fired. QSD removed the formula from its website several days after its posting.

Coca–Cola, to put it mildly, is outraged. It wonders what, if any, protection and remedies it is entitled to under NAFTA, the very first international agreement to cover trade secrets.

PART B. GRAY MARKET TRADING

Meanwhile, down Mexico way, there are several bottling plants run as wholly owned subsidiaries of Coca–Cola. These plants, like their Canadian counterparts, have made excellent COKE for many years. They meet all of Coca–Cola's technical product specifications and have always cooperated fully in protecting Coca–Cola's trademarks and copyrights.

In Mexico, COKE is a very popular drink. But the peso's 1994–95 devaluation, followed by a long downward float against the U.S. dollar, has made COKE relatively expensive for the average Mexican, even though retail prices are lower than in the United States. One reason is because the COKE syrup is invoiced in U.S. dollars. Even a decade after the devaluation, major Mexican COKE bottlers have excess production capacity. Retailers and wholesalers of the beverage in cans can easily obtain more COKE than they are likely to be able to sell in Mexico. One such large retailer is the U.S. discount chain PRICECORP. PRICECORP is one of several U.S. retail chains that have opened stores throughout Mexico since NAFTA. It has purchased huge quantities of COKE in the past and can obtain pretty much as much COKE as it wants from several Mexican bottlers.

Because of the peso's decline against the U.S. dollar—from about 3.3 pesos/$1 in late 1994 to over 11 pesos/$1 at the end of 2004, a "gray market" trading opportunity exists. In other words, COKE can be bought at wholesale prices in Mexico well below wholesale prices in the United States. PRICECORP, which has a bevy of gray marketeers, has decided to ship container loads of COKE from Mexico to its retail outlets in the U.S. border states. It has already run some ads promoting "a special" on COKE.

Coca–Cola has seen those ads. It wants the containers seized at the border by U.S. Customs and is ready to do whatever it takes to protect its U.S. distribution system. You might find it noteworthy in all of this to remember that Coca–Cola and its bottlers have friends in Congress. In 1978, the U.S. Federal Trade Commission decided that agreements between Coca–Cola and its bottlers that prohibited sales by the bottlers outside assigned territories unreasonably restrained trade. In 1980, under the Carter administration, Congress negated this ruling by providing a very special antitrust law exemption for "trademark soft drink" manufacturing licenses designating exclusive geographic areas. 94 Stat. 939 (1980). The beer industry tried but failed to get a similar exemption. With the United States essentially carved up among Coca–Cola and its bottlers, no wonder they are hostile to gray market competition.

But what can Coca–Cola do? Perhaps NAFTA will enlighten us.

SECTION II.   FOCUS OF CONSIDERATION

The law of trade secrets is not extensively studied. It is a hybrid of intellectual property, tort, contract and (sometimes) criminal law principles. Unlike patents, copyrights and trademarks, the "owner" of trade secrets cannot register them with government authorities and obtain statutory exclusivity. About all an owner can do is surround the secret with trusted employees, promises of safekeeping, nondisclosure clauses and the like. Former, disgruntled and retired employees are classic sources of trade secret leaks. And once the secret is out, it is irretrievably in the public domain. No amount of damages, penalties or fines are likely to make the former owner feel whole.

Gray market trading represents one of the "cutting edges" of international trade law. Such trading involves genuine (not counterfeit) goods. These goods lawfully bear the patents, trademarks and copyrights of the owner of those intellectual property rights. From the owner's perspective, gray market goods are often a problem when traded without authorization across international borders because established distribution patterns and markets are disrupted. From the perspective of many consumers and free traders, however, the price competition offered by gray market goods is a blessing. Cameras, electronic goods, cosmetics, footwear, designer apparel and sports gear are just some of the most commonly traded gray market items. Moreover, most gray market issues are controlled by national law rather than under global or regional international trade agreements.

Chapter 17 of NAFTA is essential to an analysis of this problem. It is found in the Documents Supplement.

SECTION III.　READINGS, QUESTIONS AND COMMENTS

PART A. TRADE SECRETS

R. FOLSOM AND W.D. FOLSOM, UNDERSTANDING NAFTA AND ITS INTERNATIONAL BUSINESS IMPLICATIONS
Chapter 8—Matthew Bender & Co. (1996).*

Intellectual property rights are embodied for the most part in patents, trademarks, copyrights and trade secrets. Such rights were not covered in the Canada–United States Free Trade Agreement. NAFTA, in Chapter 17, establishes basic rules for North American intellectual property rights. Even the European Union, which has had over 40 years to harmonize intellectual property rights, does not rival NAFTA's accomplishments. Chapter 17 was negotiated in the midst of the Uruguay Round GATT negotiations which eventually produced agreement on Trade–Related Aspects of Intellectual Property Rights (TRIPs). The TRIPs agreement took effect in 1995. It overlaps substantially with the NAFTA provisions on intellectual property rights. Both TRIPs and NAFTA provide that consistent agreements conveying more extensive intellectual property rights protection prevail.

Why are intellectual property rights so controversial? From the perspective of the industrial world (including Canada and the United States), patents, copyrights, trademarks and trade secrets are essential to their modern technology-driven economies. Such rights are used as incentives and rewards for innovative research, development and progress. Needless to say, this perspective corresponds with a very high degree of ownership of intellectual property rights around the world.

From the perspective of the developing world (including Mexico), patents, copyrights, etc. are often expensive barriers to economic improvement. Third world nations are basically technology importers, and done legally this means paying royalties to owners of intellectual property rights. The stream of royalty payments from the developing to the industrial world is in fact huge, with much smaller sums headed the other way. Such payments add to the costs of development, and in some cases are quite simply unaffordable.

In many Latin American countries, including Mexico until 1991, technology transfer commissions were established and given the power to veto nearly all intellectual property licensing and franchising agreements. These commissions traditionally have controlled in great detail the terms and conditions of technology transfer agreements, even to the point determining what royalties were acceptable. Absent commission approval, no such agreements could be validly concluded. Mexico's elimination in 1991 of its technology transfer control system means that intellectual property owners and their licensees are once again free to bargain over the terms and conditions of their agreements.

These competing perspectives on intellectual property rights have resulted in certain patterns of law and behavior. The industrial nations have pushed hard at every opportunity for recognition in the laws of developing nations of the right to obtain intellectual property protection.

* * *

It is easy to understand why the United States and Canada (to a lesser extent) as technology exporters share the common goal of obtaining effective protection for intellectual property rights around the world. In NAFTA, Mexico promises to meet (if not exceed) their greatest expectations. For Mexico, building upon its 1991 Law for the Fostering and Protection of Industrial Property, joining NAFTA is a coming of age on intellectual property rights.

* * *

COPYRIGHTS

In terms that sometimes exceed the TRIPs agreement, the NAFTA nations have promised extensive protection of copyrights, sound recordings, program-carrying satellite signals and industrial designs. Article 1705 protects copyrights on all works of original expression including books, articles, choreography, photographs, paintings, sculpture, films, videos, records, tapes, CDs and other traditionally copyrighted materials. Article 1705 also makes computer programs and data compilations (whose selection or arrangements constitute intellectual creations) copyrightable. This protection is at least coextensive as that granted by Article 2 of the Berne Convention for the Protection of Literary and Artistic Works (1971). In most cases, copyrights must be granted either for the author's life or 50 years from the work's genesis. Sound recordings also get a 50–year term.

NAFTA copyright holders get all of the rights enumerated in the Berne Convention (the basic right is protection against copying of the work) plus others that are more contentious. Article 1704.2 specifically gives NAFTA copyright holders control over importation of unauthorized copies, first public distribution rights over the work (whether by sale, rental or otherwise), control over communication of the work to the public and over commercial rental of computer programs. Bringing the original or a copy of a computer program on the market does not exhaust this rental right. In a provision targeted at Mexico, mandatory translation and reproduction licenses authorized by the Berne Convention are not to be permitted where these needs could be fulfilled by the copyright holder but for a NAFTA partner's laws and regulations.

In general, NAFTA holders may freely and separately transfer their copyright and related rights and the recipient enjoys all of these rights and their economic benefits (royalties). This covers, for example, employment contracts whereby employees assign works of their creation to their employers. It also covers copyright licensing agreements. However, in language a little less open-ended than that on patents, Article 1705.5 allows NAFTA states to limit or create exceptions to copyright and related rights in "special cases" that do not conflict with "normal exploitation" of the work. Such exceptions may not unreasonably prejudice the legitimate interests of the owner.

TRADEMARKS

Many business enterprises may not have patents or copyrights, but nearly all have trade or service marks. Most companies doing business in NAFTA use marks in connection with their goods or services. Protection of these marks is important to their business reputations and marketing. Trade and service marks also perform important information signaling functions that enable markets to work efficiently and consumers to reach informed purchasing decisions. We all, for example, associate products with their qualities (and sometimes prices) through trademarks.

The TRIPs and NAFTA provisions on marks are quite similar, but fall short of creating (as in Europe) a common regional trademark. Article 1708 of NAFTA ensures that Canada, Mexico and the United States will provide for the registration of trademarks (generally on goods), service marks, collective (organizational) marks and certification marks that are capable of distinguishing goods or services from one another. Although each country must provide a reasonable opportunity for interested persons to petition to cancel trademark registrations, they need not allow for a reasonable opportunity to oppose registration before it happens. The nature of the goods or services to which a mark is applied cannot form the basis of a denial of registration. Internationally "well-known" marks are given special rights as against prior unauthorized users (pirates) of such marks. For these purposes, whether a mark is well-known focuses upon knowledge of it in the sector of public normally dealing with the goods or services to which it applies. COCA–COLA™, for example, epitomizes internationally well-known marks and could take advantage of these prerogatives.

The ability to seek trademark registrations cannot depend upon prior actual usage on goods or services in the NAFTA country of application. But, if actual usage does not occur within 3 years, such applications may be denied. And registration itself can depend on use. By requiring actual use of marks on goods or services prior to registration, the opportunities for speculating in marks are reduced. There is also agreement among the NAFTA partners to refuse to register immoral, deceptive, scandalous and disparaging marks, and those that falsely suggest a connection with or contempt of persons, institutions, beliefs or national symbols. Registration of words in English, French or Spanish that generically designate goods or services or types thereof is prohibited. And there is agreement not to allow registration of marks indicating the geographic origin (appellation) of goods if they are "deceptively misdescriptive." Initial trademark registrations must be valid for at least 10 years and must be renewable indefinitely provided use is maintained (unless circumstances beyond the owner's control justify non-use). Use is maintained when undertaken by persons subject to the trademark owner's control, such as NAFTA franchisees.

Registered trademark owners in NAFTA countries have the right to prevent all other persons from using in commerce identical or "similar" signs on identical or similar goods or services when this would cause a "likelihood of confusion." While the "fair use" of descriptive terms may be allowed as an exception to such infringement rights, mandatory use of a second "local" trademark (Mexico once legislated this) and any other use that reduces the function of trademarks as source indicators cannot be required. Compulsory licensing of trademarks is banned, but contractual licensing and assignment of trademarks can be conditioned in the laws of each NAFTA partner.

Much of the content of NAFTA regarding trade and service marks was already law in Canada and the United States. Only in Mexico were there relatively major alterations in trademark law because and in anticipation of NAFTA.

TRADE SECRETS

Trade secrets, unlike patents, copyrights and trademarks, are not a formally recognized category of intellectual property rights that can be registered, protected and enforced. Indeed, public registration of trade secrets is an oxymoron. Whereas the registration of patents, copyrights and trademarks brings with it well established rights and obligations, protection of trade secrets is mostly a matter of less formal private industry practices and efforts. If a trade secret is successfully kept, however, it can last forever ... long after patents and copyrights have expired and gone into the public domain. For example, the formula for COCA–COLA is often cited as one of the world's best kept trade secrets. It is known at any given moment by only a handful of company personnel. But if a trade secret is lost due to a disgruntled employee or retiree, through industrial espionage or otherwise, it is equally gone forever. Trade secrets are thus a high stakes environment.

Prior to NAFTA, no international or regional (European Union) agreement on trade secret protection existed. NAFTA and TRIPs, in nearly identical terms, seek to assist those businesses that wish to protect their legitimate trade secrets. Each government must provide the legal means for any person to prevent trade secrets from being disclosed, acquired or used without consent "in a manner contrary to honest commercial practices." NAFTA even defines what this means: "Practices such as breach of a contract, breach of confidence and inducement to breach. . . ." Persons who acquire (but not those who use) trade secrets knowing them to be the product of such practices or who were grossly negligent in failing to know this also engage in dishonest commercial practices.

For NAFTA purposes, information is secret if it is not generally known or readily accessible to persons who normally deal with it, has commercial value because of its secrecy, and the person who controls the information has taken reasonable steps to keep it secret. However, in order to qualify for protection, the trade secret holder may be required to produce evidence documenting its existence.

If a trade secret holder wishes to license its information, generally called "know-how licensing," this option (however risky) is up to the holder. No NAFTA government may discourage or impede the voluntary licensing of trade secrets by imposing excessive or discriminatory conditions on such licenses. And in testing and licensing the sale of pharmaceutical and agricultural chemical products, two industries where trade secrets can be critical, each government has a general duty to protect against disclosure of proprietary data submitted by those industries.

FOLSOM, GORDON AND SPANOGLE, INTERNATIONAL BUSINESS TRANSACTIONS IN A NUTSHELL
Chapter 6 (2004).*

KNOWHOW

Knowhow is commercially valuable knowledge. It may or may not be a trade secret, and may or may not be patentable. Though often technical or scientific, e.g., engineering services, knowhow can also be more general in character. Marketing and management skills as well as simply business advice can constitute knowhow. If someone is willing to pay for the information, it can be sold or licensed internationally.

Legal protection for knowhow varies from country to country and is, at best, limited. Unlike patents, copyrights and trademarks, you cannot by registration obtain exclusive legal rights to knowhow. Knowledge, like the air we breathe, is a public good. Once released in the community, knowhow can generally be used by anyone and is almost impossible to retrieve. In the absence of exclusive legal rights, preserving the confidentiality of knowhow becomes an important business strategy. If everyone knows it, who will pay for it? If your competitors have access to the knowledge, your market position is at risk.

Protecting knowhow is mostly a function of contract, tort and trade secrets law. Employers will surround their critical knowhow with em-

ployees bound by contract to confidentiality. But some valuable knowledge leaks from or moves with these employees, e.g., when a disgruntled
retired or ex-employee sells or goes public with the knowhow. The
remedies at law or in equity for breach of contract are unlikely to render
the employer whole. Neither is torts relief likely to be sufficient since
most employees are essentially judgment proof, though they may be of
more use if a competitor induced the breach of contract. Likewise, even
though genuine trade secrets are protected by criminal statutes in a few
jurisdictions, persuading the prosecutor to take up your business problem is not easy and criminal penalties will not recoup the trade secrets
(though they may make the revelation of others less likely in the future).

Despite all of these legal hazards, even when certain knowhow is
patentable, a desire to prolong the commercial exploitation of that
knowledge may result in no patent registrations. The international
chemicals industry, for example, is said to prefer trade secrets to public
disclosure and patent rights with time limitations. Licensing or selling
such knowhow around the globe is risky, but lucrative.

UNIFORM TRADE SECRETS ACT

(with 1985 amendments).

§ 1. [Definitions]

As used in this Act, unless the context requires otherwise:

(1) "Improper means" includes theft, bribery, misrepresentation,
breach or inducement of a breach of a duty to maintain secrecy, or
espionage through electronic or other means;

(2) "Misappropriation" means:

(i) acquisition of a trade secret of another by a person who
knows or has reason to know that the trade secret was acquired by
improper means; or

(ii) disclosure or use of a trade secret of another without
express or implied consent by a person who

(A) used improper means to acquire knowledge of the trade
secret; or

(B) at the time of disclosure or use, knew or had reason to
know that his knowledge of the trade secret was

(I) derived from or through a person who had utilized
improper means to acquire it;

(II) acquired under circumstances giving rise to a duty
to maintain its secrecy or limit its use; or

(III) derived from or through a person who owed a
duty to the person seeking relief to maintain its secrecy or
limit its use; or

(C) before a material change of his position, knew or had reason to know that it was a trade secret and that knowledge of it had been acquired by accident or mistake.

(3) "Person" means a natural person, corporation, business trust, estate, trust, partnership, association, joint venture, government, governmental subdivision or agency, or any other legal or commercial entity.

(4) "Trade secret" means information, including a formula, pattern, compilation, program, device, method, technique, or process, that:

(i) derives independent economic value, actual or potential, from not being generally known to, and not being readily ascertainable by proper means by, other persons who can obtain economic value from its disclosure or use, and

(ii) is the subject of efforts that are reasonable under the circumstances to maintain its secrecy.

§ 2. [Injunctive Relief]

(a) Actual or threatened misappropriation may be enjoined. Upon application to the court, an injunction shall be terminated when the trade secret has ceased to exist, but the injunction may be continued for an additional reasonable period of time in order to eliminate commercial advantage that otherwise would be derived from the misappropriation.

(b) If the court determines that it would be unreasonable to prohibit future use, an injunction may condition future use upon payment of a reasonable royalty for no longer than the period of time the use could have been prohibited.

(c) In appropriate circumstances, affirmative acts to protect a trade secret may be compelled by court order.

§ 3. [Damages]

(a) In addition to or in lieu of injunctive relief, a complainant may recover damages for the actual loss caused by misappropriation. A complainant also may recover for the unjust enrichment caused by misappropriation that is not taken into account in computing damages for actual loss.

(b) If willful and malicious misappropriation exists, the court may award exemplary damages in an amount not exceeding twice any award made under subsection (a).

§ 4. [Attorney's Fees]

If (i) a claim of misappropriation is made in bad faith, (ii) a motion to terminate an injunction is made or resisted in bad faith, or (iii) willful and malicious misappropriation exists, the court may award reasonable attorney's fees to the prevailing party.

§ 5. [Preservation of Secrecy]

In an action under this Act, a court shall preserve the secrecy of an alleged trade secret by reasonable means, which may include granting protective orders in connection with discovery proceedings, holding in camera hearings, sealing the records of the action, and ordering any person involved in the litigation not to disclose an alleged trade secret without prior court approval.

§ 6. [Statute of Limitations]

An action for misappropriation must be brought within 3 years after the misappropriation is discovered or by the exercise of reasonable diligence should have been discovered. For the purposes of this section, a continuing misappropriation constitutes a single claim.

§ 7. [Effect on Other Law]

(a) This Act displaces conflicting tort, restitutionary, and other law of this State pertaining to civil liability for misappropriation of a trade secret.

(b) This Act does not affect:

(1) contractual or other civil liability or relief that is not based upon misappropriation of a trade secret; or

(2) criminal liability for misappropriation of a trade secret.

§ 8. [Uniformity of Application and Construction]

This Act shall be applied and construed to effectuate its general purpose to make uniform the law with respect to the subject of this Act among states enacting it.

* * *

KEWANEE OIL CO. v. BICRON CORP.

416 U.S. 470, 94 S.Ct. 1879, 181 U.S.P.Q. (BNA) 673 (1974).

We granted certiorari to resolve a question on which there is a conflict in the courts of appeals: whether state trade secret protection is pre-empted by operation of the federal patent law. Harshaw Chemical Co., an unincorporated division of petitioner, is a leading manufacturer of a type of synthetic crystal which is useful in the detection of ionizing radiation. In 1949 Harshaw commenced research into the growth of this type crystal and was able to produce one less than two inches in diameter. By 1966, as the result of expenditures in excess of $1 million, Harshaw was able to grow a 17–inch crystal, something no one else had done previously. Harshaw had developed many processes, procedures, and manufacturing techniques in the purification of raw materials and the growth and encapsulation of the crystals which enabled it to accomplish this feat. Some of these processes Harshaw considers to be trade secrets. The individual respondents are former employees of Harshaw who formed or later joined respondent Bicron. While at Harshaw the individual respondents executed, as a condition of employment, at least one agreement each, requiring them not to disclose confidential information or trade secrets obtained as employees of Harshaw. Bicron was formed in August 1969 to compete with Harshaw in the production of the crystals, and by April 1970, had grown a 17–inch crystal.

[T]he Court of Appeals reversed the District Court, finding Ohio's trade secret law to be in conflict with the patent laws of the United States. We hold that Ohio's law of trade secrets is not preempted by the patent laws of the United States, and, accordingly, we reverse.

The subject of a trade secret must be secret, and must not be of public knowledge or of a general knowledge in the trade or business. This necessary element of secrecy is not lost, however, if the holder of the trade secret reveals the trade secret to another "in confidence, and under an implied obligation not to use or disclose it." These others may include those of the holder's "employees to whom it is necessary to confide it, in order to apply it to the uses for which it is intended." Often the recipient of confidential knowledge of the subject of a trade secret is a licensee of its holder. The protection accorded the trade secret holder is against the disclosure or unauthorized use of the trade secret by those to whom the secret has been confided under the express or implied restriction of nondisclosure or nonuse. The law also protects the holder of a trade secret against disclosure or use when the knowledge is gained, not by the owner's volition, but by some "improper means," Restatement of Torts § 757(a), which may include theft, wiretapping, or even aerial reconnaissance. A trade secret law, however, does not offer protection against discovery by fair and honest means, such as by independent invention, accidental disclosure, or by so-called reverse engineering, that is by starting with the known product and working backward to divine the process which aided in its development or manufacture. Novelty, in the patent law sense, is not required for a trade secret. However, some novelty will be required if merely because that which does not possess novelty is usually known; secrecy, in the context of trade secrets, thus implies at least minimal novelty.

* * *

The maintenance of standards of commercial ethics and the encouragement of invention are the broadly stated policies behind trade secret law. "The necessity of good faith and honest, fair dealing, is the very life and spirit of the commercial world." *National Tube Co. v. Eastern Tube Co.*, 3 Ohio Cir. Cr. R., N.S. at 462.

* * *

Since no patent is available for a discovery unless it falls within one of the express categories of patentable subject matter of 35 U.S.C. § 101, the holder of such a discovery would have no reason to apply for a patent whether trade secret protection existed or not. Abolition of trade secret protection would, therefore, not result in increased disclosure to the public of discoveries in the area of nonpatentable subject matter. Also, it is hard to see how the public would be benefitted by disclosure of customer lists or advertising campaigns; in fact, keeping such items secret encourages businesses to initiate new and individualized plans of operation, and constructive competition results. This, in turn, leads to a greater variety of business methods than would otherwise be the case if privately developed marketing and other data were passed illicitly among firms involved in the same enterprise.

The question remains whether those items which are proper subjects for consideration for a patent may also have available the alternative protection accorded by trade secret law. Certainly the patent policy of encouraging invention is not disturbed by the existence of another form of incentive to invention. In this respect the two systems are not and never would be in conflict. Similarly, the policy that matter once in the public domain must remain in the public domain is not incompatible with the existence of trade secret protection. By definition a trade secret has not been placed in the public domain.

The more difficult objective of the patent law to reconcile with trade secret law is that of disclosure, the quid pro quo of the right to exclude. We are helped in this stage of the analysis by Judge Henry Friendly's opinion in *Painton & Co. v. Bourns, Inc.*, 442 F.2d 216 (C.A.2 1971). There the Court of Appeals thought it useful, in determining whether inventors will refrain because of the existence of trade secret law from applying for patents, thereby depriving the public from learning of the invention, to distinguish between three categories of trade secrets:

> (1) the trade secret believed by its owner to constitute a validly patentable invention; (2) the trade secret known to its owner not to be so patentable; and (3) the trade secret whose valid patentability is considered dubious.

Id. at 224. Trade secret protection in each of these categories would run against breaches of confidence—the employee and licensee situations—and theft and other forms of industrial espionage.

* * *

If a State, through a system of protection, were to cause a substantial risk that holders of patentable inventions would not seek patents, but rather would rely on the state protection, we would be compelled to hold that such a system could not constitutionally continue to exist. In the case of trade secret law no reasonable risk of deterrence from patent application by those who can reasonably expect to be granted patents exists. Trade secret law provides far weaker protection in many respects than the patent law. While trade secret law does not forbid the discovery of the trade secret by fair and honest means, e.g., independent creation or reverse engineering, patent law operates "against the world," forbidding any use of the invention for whatever purpose for a significant length of time. The holder of a trade secret also takes a substantial risk that the secret will be passed on to his competitors, by theft or by breach of a confidential relationship, in a manner not easily susceptible of discovery or proof. Where patent law acts as a barrier, trade secret law functions relatively as a sieve. The possibility that an inventor who believes his invention meets the standards of patentability will sit back, rely on trade secret law, and after one year of use forfeit any right to patent protection, 35 U.S.C. § 102(b), is remote indeed.

Nor does society face much risk that scientific or technological progress will be impeded by the rare inventor with a patentable invention who chooses trade secret protection over patent protection. The ripeness-of-time concept of invention, developed from the study of the many independent multiple discoveries in history, predicts that if a particular individual had not made a particular discovery others would have, and in probably a relatively short period of time. If something is to be discovered at all very likely it will be discovered by more than one person. Even were an inventor to keep his discovery completely to himself, something that neither the patent nor trade secret laws forbid, there is a high probability that it will be soon independently developed. If the invention, though still a trade secret, is put into public use, the competition is alerted to the existence of the inventor's solution to the problem and may be encouraged to make an extra effort to independently find the solution thus known to be possible. The inventor faces pressures not only from private industry, but from the skilled scientists who work in our universities and our other great publicly supported centers of learning and research.

We conclude that the extension of trade secret protection to clearly patentable inventions does not conflict with the patent policy of disclosure.

* * *

ECONOMIC ESPIONAGE ACT OF 1996
18 U.S.C. § 1831 et seq.

§ 1832. Theft of trade secrets

(a) Whoever, with intent to convert a trade secret, that is related to or included in a product that is produced for or placed in interstate or foreign commerce, to the economic benefit of anyone other than the owner thereof, and intending or knowing that the offense will, injure any owner of that trade secret, knowingly—

(1) steals, or without authorization appropriates, takes, carries away, or conceals, or by fraud, artifice, or deception obtains such information;

(2) without authorization copies, duplicates, sketches, draws, photographs, downloads, uploads, alters, destroys, photocopies, replicates, transmits, delivers, sends, mails, communicates, or conveys such information;

(3) receives, buys, or possesses such information, knowing the same to have been stolen or appropriated, obtained, or converted without authorization;

(4) attempts to commit any offense described in paragraphs (1) through (3); or

(5) conspires with one or more other persons to commit any offense described in paragraphs (1) through (3), and one or more of such persons do any act to effect the object of the conspiracy,

shall, except as provided in subsection (b), be fined under this title or imprisoned not more than 10 years, or both.

(b) Any organization that commits any offense described in subsection (a) shall be fined not more than $5,000,000.

§ 1834. Criminal forfeiture

(a) The court, in imposing sentence on a person for a violation of this chapter, shall order, in addition to any other sentence imposed, that the person forfeit to the United States—

(1) any property constituting, or derived from, any proceeds the person obtained, directly or indirectly, as the result of such violation; and

(2) any of the person's property used, or intended to be used, in any manner or part, to commit or facilitate the commission of such violation, if the court in its discretion so determines, taking into consideration the nature, scope, and proportionality of the use of the property in the offense.

(b) Property subject to forfeiture under this section, any seizure and disposition thereof, and any administrative or judicial proceeding in relation thereto, shall be governed by section 413 of the Comprehensive Drug Abuse Prevention and Control Act of 1970 (21 U.S.C. 853), except for subsections (d) and (j) of such section, which shall not apply to forfeitures under this section.

§ 1837. Applicability to conduct outside the United States

This chapter also applies to conduct occurring outside the United States if—

(1) the offender is a natural person who is a citizen or permanent resident alien of the United States, or an organization organized under the laws of the United States or a State or political subdivision thereof; or

(2) an act in furtherance of the offense was committed in the United States.

§ 1839. Definitions

As used in this chapter—

* * *

(3) the term "trade secret" means all forms and types of financial, business, scientific, technical, economic, or engineering information, including patterns, plans, compilations, program devices, formulas, designs, prototypes, methods, techniques, processes, procedures, programs, or codes, whether tangible or intangible, and whether or how stored, compiled, or memorialized physically, electronically, graphically, photographically, or in writing if—

> (A) the owner thereof has taken reasonable measures to keep such information secret; and

> (B) the information derives independent economic value, actual or potential, from not being generally known to, and not being readily ascertainable through proper means by, the public; and

(4) the term "owner", with respect to a trade secret, means the person or entity in whom or in which rightful legal or equitable title to, or license in, the trade secret is reposed.

Questions and Comments

1. What exactly is a "trade secret"? Do trade secrets differ from the wealth of "knowhow" or "confidential information" that most businesses possess? Does NAFTA make those distinctions? See Articles 1711.1 and 1721.1.

2. Prior to Xavier, are you sure that Coca–Cola's production process was a trade secret under NAFTA Article 1711? Why? And after Xavier?

3. What "steps" did Coca–Cola take to protect its production process information? Were they "reasonable"? Could it have done more? If so, does that fact remove its information from NAFTA trade secret protection? See Article 1711.1(c).

4. What is the significance of the requirement that to qualify for protection a trade secret must be "evidenced"? See Article 1711.2. Does this requirement affect your analysis of whether Coca–Cola took reasonable steps to protect its secret? Xavier might think so.

5. Suppose Coca–Cola had the option of obtaining a "process patent" way back when it first invented COKE. Why did it not do so? Was that a mistake?

6. Suppose you are a U.S. federal prosecutor and there is a Canada–U.S. Extradition Treaty. Coca–Cola comes to you with its Xavier problem and an awareness of the Economic Espionage Act of 1996. Would you undertake a criminal prosecution? Does the Act's jurisdiction reach Xavier's conduct?

7. Does the definition of a trade secret in the Economic Espionage Act of 1996 differ from that in NAFTA Article 1711? If so, does that difference matter?

8. The 1996 Act authorizes seizures of all proceeds from the theft of trade secrets as well as property used or intended for use in the misappropriation. In the context of this problem, what might such a remedy mean?

9. Suppose that a U.S. bottling company (not affiliated with QSD or Coca–Cola) found the recipe on the web. It expertly brews the "real thing" which it sells as Cool–Cola. There is no trademark or copyright infringement, nor any attempt at passing off Cool–Cola as COKE. Might this amount to "misappropriation" supporting injunctive and damages relief? See the Uniform Trade Secrets Act.

10. Forget Xavier for the moment. Suppose Cool–Cola ingeniously "reverse engineers" a can of COKE and thereby obtains the production process formula. It then produces and sells the same tasting beverage under its Cool–Cola label. Does NAFTA speak to the legality of reverse engineering? Is reverse engineering an "honest commercial practice"? See Article 1721.2.

11. Does *Kewanee Oil* shed some light on whether reverse engineering is an honest commercial practice? We will revisit this issue in a developing world context in Problem 5.2.

Kewanee Oil affirms the validity of state trade secrets law. The more than forty states that have adopted the Uniform Trade Secrets Act will be glad to hear that. Do you agree with the Supreme Court that there is no reasonable risk that extending trade secret protection to clearly patentable subject matter will deter patent applications and public disclosure? The chemical and bio-tech industries are said to frequently prefer trade secret protection to process patents. Why?

12. Remembering how much COKE symbolizes a part of American culture, is it conceivable that Canada's cultural industry exclusion might apply to this problem? Does that exclusion extend to NAFTA's intellectual property rights provisions? If so, does Xavier have an "out"? Review Problem 5.3.

13. What types of disputes are likely to arise in the application of the August 30, 2003, WTO General Council Decision on the TRIPS Agreement and Public Health? Does it strike a reasonable balance between developing country health concerns and the developed country pharmaceutical firms' objectives?

PART B. GRAY MARKET TRADING

TREATY ESTABLISHING THE EUROPEAN COMMUNITY

(Rome, 1957, as amended).

ARTICLE 30

The provisions of Articles 28 and 29 shall not preclude prohibitions or restrictions on imports, exports or goods in transit justified on grounds of public morality, public policy or public security; the protection of health and life of humans, animals or plants; the protection of national treasures possessing artistic, historic or archaeological value; or the protection of industrial and commercial property. Such prohibitions or restrictions shall not, however, constitute a means of arbitrary discrimination or a disguised restriction on trade between Member States.*

FOLSOM, EUROPEAN UNION LAW IN A NUTSHELL
Chapter 4 (2004).**

INTELLECTUAL PROPERTY RIGHTS AS EUROPEAN TRADE BARRIERS

A truly remarkably body of case law has developed around the authority granted national governments in Article 30 (formerly 36) to protect industrial or commercial property by restraining imports and exports. These cases run the full gamut from protection of trademarks and copyrights to protection of patents and know-how. There is a close link between this body of case law and that developed under Article 81 (formerly 85) concerning restraints on competition.

Trade restraints involving intellectual property arise out of the fact that such rights are nationally granted. Owners of intellectual property rights within Europe are free under most traditional law to block the unauthorized importation of goods into national markets. There is thus a strong tendency for national infringement lawsuits to serve as vehicles for the division for the Common Market. Although considerable energy has been spent by the Commission on developing Common Market patents that would provide an alternative to national intellectual property rights, these proposals have yet to be fully implemented. In 1993, however, the Council reached agreement on a Common Market trademark regime. And the Council has adopted Directive 89/104, which seeks to harmonize member state laws governing trademarks. In the copyright field, several directives have harmonized European law, perhaps most importantly on copyrights for computer software (No. 91/250).

The European Court of Justice has addressed these problems under Article 30 and generally resolved against the exercise of national intellectual property rights in ways which inhibit free internal trade. In many of these decisions, the Court acknowledges the existence of the right to block trade in infringing goods, but holds that the *exercise* of that right is subordinate to the Treaty of Rome. The Court has also fashioned a doctrine which treats national intellectual property rights as having been *exhausted* once the goods to which they apply are freely sold on the market. One of the few exceptions to this doctrine is broadcast performing rights which the Court considers incapable of exhaustion. Records, CDs, and cassettes embodying such rights are, however, subject to the exhaustion doctrine once released into the market. Such goods often end up in the hands of third parties who then ship them into another member state.

The practical effect of many of the rulings of the Court of Justice is to remove the ability of the owners of the relevant intellectual property rights to successfully pursue infringement actions in national courts. When intellectual property rights share a common origin and have been

---

* See also GATT 1994, Article XX.   ** Copyright © 2004 West Group. Reprinted with permission.

placed on goods by consent, as when a licensor authorizes their use in other countries, then infringement actions to protect against trade in the goods to which the rights apply are usually denied. This may not be the case, however, when voluntary trademark assignments that are not anticompetitive are involved. In such cases, the ECJ has demonstrated some concern for consumer confusion when trade in parallel goods occurs.

It is only when intellectual property rights do not share a common origin or the requisite consent is absent that they stand a chance of being upheld so as to stop trade in infringing products. Compulsory licensing of patents, for example, does not involve consensual marketing of products. Patent rights may therefore be used to block trade in goods produced under such a license. But careful repackaging and resale of goods subject to a common trademark may occur against the objections of the owner of the mark. And compulsory licensing cannot be conditioned upon import bans applicable to the beneficiary licensee. Such bans offend the free movement of goods law and unfairly create investment incentives.

An excellent example of the application of the judicial doctrine developed by the Court of Justice in the intellectual property field under Article 30 can be found in *Centrafarm BV and Adriann de Peipjper v. Sterling Drug Inc.* (1974) Eur.Comm.Rep. 1147. The United States pharmaceutical company, Sterling Drug, owned the British and Dutch patents and trademarks relating to "Negram." Subsidiaries of Sterling Drug in Britain and Holland had been respectively assigned the British and Dutch trademark rights to Negram. Owing in part to price controls in the UK, a substantial difference in cost for Negram emerged as between the two countries. Centrafarm was an independent Dutch importer of Negram from the UK and Germany. Sterling Drug and its subsidiaries brought infringement actions in the Dutch courts under their national patent and trademark rights seeking an injunction against Centrafarm's importation of Negram into The Netherlands.

The Court of Justice held that the intellectual property rights of Sterling Drug and its subsidiaries could not be exercised in a way which blocked trade in "parallel goods." In the Court's view, the exception established in Article 30 for the protection of industrial and commercial property covers only those rights that were specifically intended to be conveyed by the grant of national patents and trademarks. Blocking trade in parallel goods after they have been put on the market with the consent of a common owner, thus exhausting the rights in question, was not intended to be part of the package of benefits conveyed. If Sterling Drug succeeded, an arbitrary discrimination or disguised restriction on regional trade would be achieved in breach of the language which qualifies Article 30. Thus the European Court of Justice ruled in favor of the free movement of goods within the Common Market even when that negates clearly existing national legal remedies. While the goal of creation of the Common Market can override national intellectual property rights where internal trade is concerned, these rights apply fully to the importation of goods (including gray market goods) from outside the Common Market. See especially, *Silhouette International v. Hartlauer,* No. C–355/96 (July 16, 1998) (Austrian manufacturer's trademark rights block imports of its sunglasses from Bulgaria). North American exporters of goods subject to rights owned by Europeans may therefore find entry challenged by infringement actions in national courts. On the other hand, Levi Strauss successfully cited *Silhouette* to keep low-price out of the EU.

MILLER, NAFTA: PROTECTOR OF NATIONAL INTELLECTUAL PROPERTY RIGHTS OR BLUEPRINT FOR GLOBALIZATION? THE EFFECT OF NAFTA ON THE FIRST SALE DOCTRINE IN COPYRIGHT LAW

16 Loyola L.A. Entertainment L.J. 475 (1996).*

CBA v. RECORD STORE, A HYPOTHETICAL

CBA Records, Inc. ("CBA") is a United States company that manufactures compact discs and cassette tapes for sale in the United States and abroad. In anticipation of increased business dealings between the United States and Mexico as a result of the North American Free Trade Agreement ("NAFTA"), CBA authorized Grupo Musica, S.A., a Mexican company, to produce and sell certain recordings exclusively in Mexico under a licensing agreement.

Some time later, a CBA employee in the United States was browsing in a local record store and noticed a CBA compact disc that was manufactured in Mexico. Upon further investigation, it was determined that a third party had bought several thousand recordings from Grupo Musica in Mexico, brought them into the United States, and sold them to various retail outlets around the country. CBA sued the retailer and the third party importer (collectively "Record Store") for copyright infringement, under 17 U.S.C. §§ 106(3) and 602(a).

Record Store's defense is based on 17 U.S.C. § 109(a), commonly known as the "first sale doctrine." Under this doctrine, once a legally manufactured, copyrighted product is placed on the market for the first time with the copyright owner's authority, that owner's subsequent distribution rights in the product are extinguished, and he or she cannot control any future sales of that physical copy of the product.

CBA believes that the first sale doctrine applies only to products manufactured in the United States. It asserts that because the recordings at issue were made in Mexico, they have not been "lawfully made" for purposes of United States law, and the first sale defense does not avoid liability for copyright infringement. Record Store maintains, however, that because the United States and Mexico have entered into a free trade agreement (NAFTA), that agreement governs and should act to expand the first sale territory to allow the defense regardless of the place of manufacture, as long as the manufacture was authorized and was within the NAFTA territories. Record Store cites recent European case law that reached this result. In the European Community, the Treaty of Rome was found to override national law so that a first sale in one member state was found to act as a first sale in any other member state.

* * *

NAFTA contains specific sections for copyright, trademark and patent. Articles 1705 (regarding copyright) and 1706 (regarding sound recordings) provide to authors (or producers of sound recordings) the right to authorize or prohibit, inter alia, "(a) the importation into the Party's territory of copies of the work made without the right holder's authorization; (b) the first public distribution of the original and each copy of the work by sale, rental or otherwise."

Most notable is the inclusion of a provision in NAFTA embodying the first sale doctrine. We also see, as in the United States Code, a juxtaposition of the first sale doctrine with the importation right. Clearly, the territoriality of the importation right of subsection (a) is national, and can be seen as a multilateral extension of the United States' importation right of 17 U.S.C. § 602(a). Subsection (b) does not explicitly address territoriality. However, it does address the first sale and is therefore open to interpretation. One may infer territoriality from the proximity of the subsections and a desire for consistency. On the other hand, the omission of a territorial definition for the first sale provision could also facilitate application of the European model of territorial expansion.

Subsection (a) prohibits the importation of copies "made" without the right holder's authorization. It does not address the issue of copies "re-sold" without authorization. Therefore, referring back to the hypothetical, recordings made and first sold in Mexico with CBA's authorization, then imported into the United States without CBA's authorization, might slip through the cracks of NAFTA's copyright provisions.

In general, however, NAFTA is seen as "a watershed in the history of protection of intellectual property rights ... vastly increasing the level of protection afforded to holders of such rights." It is viewed by some as a United States initiative creating high standards of intellectual property protection and enforcement. Indeed, one of the major objectives of NAFTA is to "provide adequate and effective protection and enforcement of intellectual property rights in each Party's territory."

NAFTA begins its section on intellectual property with the following statement regarding the nature and scope of obligations: "Each Party shall provide in its territory to the nationals of another Party adequate and effective protection and enforcement of intellectual property rights, while ensuring that measures to enforce intellectual property rights do not themselves become barriers to legitimate trade." Thus, NAFTA defers to national laws for the enforcement of intellectual property rights, directing each Party to "ensure that enforcement procedures . . . are available under its domestic law." It also includes the very significant caveat of non-interference with free trade objectives; the text goes on to say that "[s]uch enforcement procedures shall be applied so as to avoid the creation of barriers to legitimate trade and to provide safeguards against abuse of the procedures."

This language is comparable to Article 30 of the EEC Treaty which provides the two part balancing test used by the ECJ in its exhaustion cases. On one hand, the first sentence of the EEC Treaty provision includes a national intellectual property exception to the free movement principle, analogous to the rights allowed by NAFTA Article 1705 regarding copyright, as discussed above. On the other hand, the second sentence of Article 30 states that the exceptions "shall not, however, constitute a means of arbitrary discrimination or a disguised restriction on trade between Member States."

Thus, in both trade agreements we find the perennial balancing of the two objectives: protection of intellectual property and free trade. This balancing in the EC led to a result in which the ultimate principle of free trade prevailed. It is possible that a similar weighing of these objectives under NAFTA might have a similar result, the purpose of both agreements being the elimination of trade barriers and facilitation of movement between member states.

QUALITY KING DISTRIBUTORS, INC. v. L'ANZA RESEARCH INTERNATIONAL, INC.

Supreme Court of the United States, 1998.
523 U.S. 135, 118 S.Ct. 1125, 140 L.Ed.2d 254.

Justice STEVENS delivered the opinion of the Court.

Section 106(3) of the Copyright Act of 1976(Act), 17 U.S.C. § 106(3), gives the owner of a copyright the exclusive right to distribute copies of a copyrighted work. That exclusive right is expressly limited, however, by the provisions of §§ 107 through 120. Section 602(a) gives the copyright owner the right to prohibit the unauthorized importation of copies. The question presented by this case is whether the right granted by § 602(a) is also limited by §§ 107 through 120. More narrowly, the question is whether the "first sale" doctrine endorsed in § 109(a) is applicable to imported copies.

Respondent, L'anza Research International, Inc. (L'anza), is a California corporation engaged in the business of manufacturing and selling shampoos, conditioners, and other hair care products. L'anza has copyrighted the labels that are affixed to those products. In the United States, L'anza sells exclusively to domestic distributors who have agreed to resell within limited geographic areas and then only to authorized retailers such as barber shops, beauty salons, and professional hair care colleges. L'anza has found that the American "public is generally unwilling to pay the price charged for high quality products, such as L'anza's products, when they are sold along with the less expensive lower quality products that are generally carried by supermarkets and drug stores." App. 54 (declaration of Robert Hall). L'anza promotes the domestic sales of its products with extensive advertising in various trade magazines and at point of sale, and by providing special training to authorized retailers.

L'anza also sells its products in foreign markets. In those markets, however, it does not engage in comparable advertising or promotion; its prices to foreign distributors are 35% to 40% lower than the prices charged to domestic distributors. In 1992 and 1993, L'anza's distributor in the United Kingdom arranged the sale of three shipments to a distributor in Malta; each shipment contained several tons of L'anza products with copyrighted labels affixed. The record does not establish whether the initial purchaser was the distributor in the United Kingdom or the distributor in Malta, or whether title passed when the goods were delivered to the carrier or when they arrived at their destination, but it is undisputed that the goods were manufactured by L'anza and first sold by L'anza to a foreign purchaser.

It is also undisputed that the goods found their way back to the United States without the permission of L'anza and were sold in California by unauthorized retailers who had purchased them at discounted prices from Quality King Distributors, Inc. (petitioner). There is some uncertainty about the identity of the actual importer, but for the purpose of our decision we assume that petitioner bought all three shipments from the Malta distributor, imported them, and then resold them to retailers who were not in L'anza's authorized chain of distribution.

After determining the source of the unauthorized sales, L'anza brought suit against petitioner and several other defendants.[5] * * *

This is an unusual copyright case because L'anza does not claim that anyone has made unauthorized copies of its copyrighted labels. Instead, L'anza is primarily interested in protecting the integrity of its method of marketing the products to which the labels are affixed. Although the labels themselves have only a limited creative component, our interpretation of the relevant statutory provisions would apply equally to a case involving more familiar copyrighted materials such as sound recordings or books.

* * *

Section 109(a) provides:

"Notwithstanding the provisions of section 106(3), the owner of a particular copy or phonorecord lawfully made under this title, or any person authorized by such owner, is entitled, without the authority of the copyright owner, to sell or otherwise dispose of the possession of that copy or phonorecord. . . ."

* * *

---

5. L'anza's claims against the retailer defendants were settled. The Malta distributor apparently never appeared in this action and a default judgment was entered against it.

The most relevant portion of § 602(a) provides:

"Importation into the United States, without the authority of the owner of copyright under this title, of copies or phonorecords of a work that have been acquired outside the United States is an infringement of the exclusive right to distribute copies or phonorecords under section 106, actionable under section 501 . . . . ''

* * *

It is significant that this provision does not categorically prohibit the unauthorized importation of copyrighted materials. Instead, it provides that such importation is an infringement of the exclusive right to distribute copies "under section 106." Like the exclusive right to "vend" that was construed in Bobbs–Merrill, the exclusive right to distribute is a limited right. The introductory language in § 106 expressly states that all of the exclusive rights granted by that section—including, of course, the distribution right granted by subsection (3)—are limited by the provisions of §§ 107 through 120. One of those limitations, as we have noted, is provided by the terms of § 109(a), which expressly permit the owner of a lawfully made copy to sell that copy "[n]otwithstanding the provisions of section 106(3)."

After the first sale of a copyrighted item "lawfully made under this title," any subsequent purchaser, whether from a domestic or from a foreign reseller, is obviously an "owner" of that item. Read literally, § 109(a) unambiguously states that such an owner "is entitled, without the authority of the copyright owner, to sell" that item. Moreover, since § 602(a) merely provides that unauthorized importation is an infringement of an exclusive right "under section 106," and since that limited right does not encompass resales by lawful owners, the literal text of § 602(a) is simply inapplicable to both domestic and foreign owners of L'anza's products who decide to import them and resell them in the United States.

* * *

The parties and their amici have debated at length the wisdom or unwisdom of governmental restraints on what is sometimes described as either the "gray market" or the practice of "parallel importation." In K Mart Corp. v. Cartier, Inc., 486 U.S. 281, 108 S.Ct. 1811, 100 L.Ed.2d 313 (1988), we used those terms to refer to the importation of foreign-manufactured goods bearing a valid United States trademark without the consent of the trademark holder. Id., at 285–286, 108 S.Ct., at 1814–1815. We are not at all sure that those terms appropriately describe the consequences of an American manufacturer's decision to limit its promotional efforts to the domestic market and to sell its products abroad at discounted prices that are so low that its foreign distributors can compete in the domestic market.[29] But even if they do, whether or not we

---

29. Presumably L'anza, for example, could have avoided the consequences of that   competition either (1) by providing advertising support abroad and charging higher

think it would be wise policy to provide statutory protection for such price discrimination is not a matter that is relevant to our duty to interpret the text of the Copyright Act.

U.S. TARIFF ACT OF 1930
19 U.S.C. § 1526.

MERCHANDISE BEARING AMERICAN TRADEMARK

(a) Importation prohibited. Except as provided in subsection (d) of this section, it shall be unlawful to import into the United States any merchandise of foreign manufacture if such merchandise, or the label, sign, print, package, wrapper, or receptacle, bears a trade-mark owned by a citizen of, or by a corporation or association created or organized within, the United States, and registered in the Patent Office [Patent and Trademark Office] by a person domiciled in the United States, under the provisions of the Act entitled "An Act to authorize the registration of trade-marks used in commerce with foreign nations or among the several States or with Indian tribes, and to protect the same," approved February 20, 1905, as amended, and if a copy of the certificate of registration of such trade-mark is filed with the Secretary of the Treasury, in the manner provided in section 27 of such Act, unless written consent of the owner of such trade-mark is produced at the time of making entry.

(b) Seizure and forfeiture. Any such merchandise imported into the United States in violation of the provisions of this section shall be subject to seizure and forfeiture for violation of the customs laws.

(c) Injunction and damages. Any person dealing in any such merchandise may be enjoined from dealing therein within the United States or may be required to export or destroy such merchandise or to remove or obliterate such trade-mark and shall be liable for the same damages and profits provided for wrongful use of a trade-mark, under the provisions of such Act of February 20, 1905, as amended.

K MART CORP. v. CARTIER, INC.
Supreme Court of the United States, 1988.
486 U.S. 281, 108 S.Ct. 1811, 100 L.Ed.2d 313.

OPINION OF THE COURT

JUSTICE KENNEDY announced the judgment of the Court and delivered the opinion of the Court with respect to Parts I, II–A, and II–C, and an opinion with respect to Part II–B, in which WHITE, J., joined.

A gray-market good is a foreign-manufactured good, bearing a valid United States trademark, that is imported without the consent of the United States trademark holder. These cases present the issue whether the Secretary of the Treasury's regulation permitting the importation of

prices, or (2) if it was satisfied to leave the promotion of the product in foreign mar- kets to its foreign distributors, to sell its products abroad under a different name.

certain gray-market goods, 19 CFR § 133.21 (1987), is a reasonable agency interpretation of § 526 of the Tariff Act of 1930 (1930 Tariff Act), 46 Stat. 741, as amended, 19 USC § 1526.

The gray market arises in any of three general contexts. The prototypical gray-market victim (case 1) is a domestic firm that purchases from an independent foreign firm the rights to register and use the latter's trademark as a United States trademark and to sell its foreign-manufactured products here. Especially where the foreign firm has already registered the trademark in the United States or where the product has already earned a reputation for quality, the right to use that trademark can be very valuable. If the foreign manufacturer could import the trademarked goods and distribute them here, despite having sold the trademark to a domestic firm, the domestic firm would be forced into sharp intrabrand competition involving the very trademark it purchased. Similar intrabrand competition could arise if the foreign manufacturer markets its wares outside the United States, as is often the case, and a third party who purchases them abroad could legally import them. In either event, the parallel importation, if permitted to proceed, would create a gray market that could jeopardize the trademark holder's investment.

The second context (case 2) is a situation in which a domestic firm registers the United States trademark for goods that are manufactured abroad by an affiliated manufacturer. In its most common variation (case 2a), a foreign firm wishes to control distribution of its wares in this country by incorporating a subsidiary here. The subsidiary then registers under its own name (or the manufacturer assigns to the subsidiary's name) a United States trademark that is identical to its parent's foreign trademark. The parallel importation by a third party who buys the goods abroad (or conceivably even by the affiliated foreign manufacturer itself) creates a gray market. Two other variations on this theme occur when an American-based firm establishes abroad a manufacturing subsidiary corporation (case 2b) or its own unincorporated manufacturing division (case 2c) to produce its United States trademarked goods, and then imports them for domestic distribution. If the trademark holder or its foreign subsidiary sells the trademarked goods abroad the parallel importation of the goods competes on the gray market with the holder's domestic sales.

In the third context (case 3), the domestic holder of a United States trademark *authorizes* an independent foreign manufacturer to use it. Usually the holder sells to the foreign manufacturer an exclusive right to use the trademark in a particular foreign location, but conditions the right on the foreign manufacturer's promise not to import its trademarked goods into the United States. Once again, if the foreign manufacturer or a third party imports into the United States, the foreign-manufactured goods will compete on the gray market with the holder's domestic goods.

Until 1922, the Federal Government did not regulate the importation of gray-market goods, not even to protect the investment of an independent purchaser of a foreign trademark, and not even in the extreme case where the independent foreign manufacturer breached its agreement to refrain from direct competition with the purchaser. That year, however, Congress was spurred to action by a Court of Appeals decision declining to enjoin the parallel importation of goods bearing a trademark that (as in case 1) a domestic company had purchased from an independent foreign manufacturer at a premium. See A. Bourjois & Co. v. Katzel, 275 F. 539 (C.A.2 1921), rev'd, 260 U.S. 689, 43 S.Ct. 244, 67 L.Ed. 464, 26 A.L.R. 567 (1923).

* * *

A majority of this Court now holds that the common-control exception of the Customs Service Regulation, 19 CFR §§ 133.21(c)(1)–(2) (1987), is consistent with § 526. * * * A different majority, however, holds that the authorized-use exception, 19 CFR § 133.21(c)(3) (1987), is inconsistent with § 526. * * *

In determining whether a challenged regulation is valid, a reviewing court must first determine if the regulation is consistent with the language of the statute. "If the statute is clear and unambiguous 'that is the end of the matter, for the court, as well as the agency, must give effect to the unambiguously expressed intent of Congress.' * * * The traditional deference courts pay to agency interpretation is not to be applied to alter the clearly expressed intent of Congress." Board of Governors, FRS v. Dimension Financial Corp., 474 U.S. 361, 368, 106 S.Ct. 681, 88 L.Ed.2d 691 (1986). * * *

Following this analysis, I conclude that subsections (c)(1) and (c)(2) of the Customs Service regulation, 19 CFR §§ 133.21(c)(1) and (c)(2) (1987), are permissible constructions designed to resolve statutory ambiguities. All Members of the Court are in agreement that the agency may interpret the statute to bar importation of gray-market goods in what we have denoted case 1 and to permit the imports under case 2a. * * * As these writings state, "owned by" is sufficiently ambiguous, in the context of the statute, that it applies to situations involving a foreign parent, which is case 2a. This ambiguity arises from the inability to discern, from the statutory language, which of the two entities involved in case 2a can be said to "own" the United States trademark if, as in some instances, the domestic subsidiary is wholly owned by its foreign parent.

A further statutory ambiguity contained in the phrase "merchandise of foreign manufacture," suffices to sustain the regulations as they apply to cases 2b and 2c. This ambiguity parallels that of "owned by," which sustained case 2a, because it is possible to interpret "merchandise of foreign manufacture" to mean (1) goods manufactured in a foreign country, (2) goods manufactured by a foreign company, or (3) goods manufactured in a foreign country by a foreign company. Given the imprecision in the statute, the agency is entitled to choose any reasonable definition and to interpret the statute to say that goods manufactured by a foreign subsidiary or division of a domestic company are not goods "of foreign manufacture."[4]

Subsection (c)(3), 19 CFR § 133.21(c)(3) (1987), of the regulation, however, cannot stand. The ambiguous statutory phrases that we have already discussed, "owned by" and "merchandise of foreign manufacture," are irrelevant to the proscription contained in subsection (3) of the regulation. This subsection of the regulation denies a domestic trademark holder the power to prohibit the importation of goods made by an independent foreign manufacturer where the domestic trademark holder has authorized the foreign manufacturer to use the trademark. Under no reasonable construction of the statutory language can goods made in a foreign country by an independent foreign manufacturer be removed from the purview of the statute.

* * *

It is so ordered.

Questions and Comments

1. What exactly is a gray market good? Are such goods counterfeit?

2. Who, in this problem, is manufacturing gray market COKE? Who is trading the gray market COKE?

3. For *internal* purposes, can gray market goods (often called "parallel goods") be free traded inside Europe? See, for example, the discussion of *Centrafarm* in the readings. What about for *external* trade purposes? See *Silhouette.*

4. I disagree with Justice Scalia's reasons for declining to recognize this ambiguity. * * * First, the threshold question in ascertaining the correct interpretation of a statute is whether the language of the statute is clear or arguably ambiguous. The purported gloss any party gives to the statute, or any reference to legislative history, is in the first instance irrelevant. Further, I decline to assign any binding or authoritative effect to the particular verbiage Justice Scalia highlights. The quoted phrases are simply the Government's explanation of the practical effect the current regulation has in applying the statute, and come from the statement of the case portion of its petition for a writ of certiorari.

Additionally, I believe that agency regulations may give a varying interpretation of the same phrase when that phrase appears in different statutes and different statutory contexts. There may well be variances in purpose or circumstance that have led the agency to adopt and apply dissimilar interpretations of the phrase "of foreign manufacture" in other regulations implementing different statutes.

I also disagree that our disposition necessarily will engender either enforcement problems for the Customs Service or problems we are unaware of arising out of our commercial treaty commitments to foreign countries. Initially, it is reasonable to think that any such problems or objections would have arisen before now since it is the current interpretation of the regulations we are sustaining. Second, I believe that the regulation speaks to the hypothetical situation Justice Scalia poses, and that the firm with the United States trademark could keep out "gray-market imports manufactured abroad by the other American firms," * * * because the regulation allows a company justifiably invoking the protection of the statute to bar the importation of goods of foreign or domestic manufacture. 19 CFR § 133.21(a) (1987). In this instance, the domestic firm with the United States trademark could invoke the protection of the statute (case 1) and bar the importation of the other domestic firm's product manufactured abroad even though our interpretation of the phrase "of foreign manufacture" would characterize these latter goods to be of domestic manufacture.

4. Does Chapter 17 say anything about gray market trading inside NAFTA? If not, what law governs such trading?

5. Do you agree with Miller's argument that Chapter 17 (like Article 30 of the EC Treaty) can be read to promote free trade at the expense of national intellectual property rights? See especially Articles 1701.1, 1705 and 1714.1.

What is the "first sale doctrine"? Do you agree with Miller that NAFTA's copyright provisions "embody" the first sale doctrine?

6. If NAFTA embodies the first sale doctrine, what are the implications for Coca–Cola of the Supreme Court's decision in *Quality King*? What business interest was L'anza trying to protect in *Quality King*? And what business interest is Coca–Cola trying to protect? In *Quality King*, the goods were made in the USA and imported back into the United States. In our problem, the COKE syrup comes from the USA, but COKE in cans comes from Mexico. Should that matter? See, e.g., *Parfums Givenchy v. Drug Emporium, Inc.*, 38 F.3d 477 (9th Cir. 1994).

7. Section 1526 of the Tariff Act of 1930 was adopted as the "Genuine Goods Exclusion Act". What does Section 1526 prohibit? What remedies are provided?

The history of Section 1526 is recounted by Justice Kennedy in *K Mart*. In his terms, is our problem a Case 1, 2 or 3 scenario?

8. The *K Mart* opinion contains a 5 to 4 affirmation of the U.S. Customs Service's "common control" exception to Section 1526 and a 5 to 4 rejection of the "authorized use" exception. What are these exceptions and why did the Customs Service adopt them? Are they consistent with the legislative origins of the Act? With the Act's ambiguous language?

Can Coca–Cola invoke Section 1526 to block gray market trade in COKE from Mexico? From Canada, assuming QSD is its source? What is the impact of *K-Mart* on gray market trading?

9. One of the Chapter 11 investment cases against Mexico involved "gray market" exports. A U.S. owned company sought to purchase Mexican Marlboro® cigarettes in Mexico (which were priced lower in Mexico than in the United States, presumably for the same reasons that Mexican COKE was sold at lower prices) from large retailers such as Sam's Club and export them to the United States and other destinations. The business plan foundered because Mexican authorities, ostensibly on technical legal grounds, refused to refund to the exporter the 85% excise taxes assessed on cigarettes for the Mexican market, making the exported cigarettes prohibitively expensive. The claimant was unsuccessful in demonstrating to the Tribunal that the denial of the tax rebates was expropriatory, noting, *inter alia*, that "NAFTA and principles of customary international law do not, in the view of the Tribunal, *require* a state to permit cigarette exports by unauthorized resellers (gray market exports)." (The tribunal did find a denial of national treatment under Article 1102, based on evidence in the record that some domestic cigarette resellers were receiving the tax rebates that made the business feasible.) *Feldman v. Mexico*, 42 I.L.M. 625 (2003) (Dec. 16, 2002).

PROBLEM 8.2 COMPULSORY LICENSING AND COUNTERFEITING: PHARMACEUTICALS AND NAFTA

SECTION I. THE SETTING

PART A. COMPULSORY LICENSING

Canada, alone in North America, has a national health care system. This system is tax supported, not perfect and relatively expensive, but it provides nearly universal health care benefits to Canadian society. While there are critics, especially when the quality of care is debated, many if not most Canadians are proud of their national health care system. If they head south to Florida for the winter, one of their biggest fears is the cost of a medical emergency in the United States.

One benefit under the Canadian system is prescription drugs. Practically speaking, this means that the Canadian government pays for most pharmaceuticals. The government is always under pressure to contain drug costs. One way it has traditionally done so is through "compulsory licensing" of patented pharmaceuticals. Compulsory licensing forces the patent owner to license others to make, use and sell the invention. It is a provision found in the patent laws of most developing societies, like Mexico, and many industrial nations such as Germany, Japan, Britain and Canada. The United States is very nearly unique in not permitting compulsory licensing of its patents. However, even in the United States, the idea is not unknown. In the immediate aftermath of 9/11 and the anthrax scare in October 2001, when the U.S. Government was seeking a supply of the anti-anthrax antibiotic Cipro to distribute widely in the U.S., the inability of the patent-holder, Bayer AG, to provide the necessary supplies led to discussion in the Bush Administration and Congress of possible compulsory licensing of Cipro to allow generic production. (The idea was quickly dropped.)*

The low cost of Canadian (and Mexican) pharmaceutical products compared to the United States has contributed to a serious political problem for U.S. drug companies and the FDA. Under U.S. law, it is technically illegal to import prescription drugs from Canada, Mexico or other nations to the United States, with the principal rationale being that the U.S. Food and Drug Administration has not determined that such products are safe and effective (even in circumstances when U.S. origin pharmaceuticals are exported to Canada or Mexico and re-exported to the United States.) Do NAFTA's rules on product safety standards affirm this approach? See Problem 5.2. For many years, persons living near the borders, particularly retirees on fixed incomes who regularly use prescription drugs for chronic ailments, have periodically crossed the border to purchase their drug needs at prices from 20% to 50% of U.S.

---

* See Vanessa Fuhrmans and Ron Winslow, The Treatment: It's Image Under Fire, Bayer AG Scrambles to Meet Cipro Demand, Wall St. J., Oct. 22, 2001, at A–1.

prices. By and large, U.S. customs officials have not interfered with returning citizens who carry quantities obviously intended for personal use. Also, enterprising travel services have organized bus trips for U.S. citizens to Mexico and Canada for the same purpose, and a number of Internet based pharmacies in Canada have been created to provide mail order sales to the United States. More recently, the issue has escalated by the decisions of municipalities such as Worcester, MA and states such as Illinois, who have announced their intention to purchase Canadian source drugs through their health plans, with potential savings of millions of dollars. Pharmaceutical companies and the Bush Administration have strongly resisted these actions, with the pharmaceutical companies threatening to restrict sales to pharmacies in Canada who sell to U.S. citizens, and the head of the FDA threatening prosecution. However, the partial legalization at least of such transactions seems inevitable; a number of bills are pending in Congress, and (former) Health and Human Services Secretary Tommy Thompson has recognized such legislation will eventually be enacted.*

SKBD, Inc. is a major U.S. producer of pharmaceuticals. It operates globally and owns the Canadian, Mexican and U.S. patents on DOLA-MINE™, the leading prescription medication for seizure disorders. People who need DOLAMINE tend to take it for life. Unfortunately, DOLA-MINE is expensive. There are 10 more years to run on its patents, which means that generic drug producers have yet to enter this market. Other less expensive patented pharmaceuticals can be substituted for DOLA-MINE, but they tend to have more unwanted side effects and may be less beneficial to people with seizure disorders.

SKBD has always "serviced" the Canadian and Mexican markets by exporting DOLAMINE from its Maryland production facility. For reasons of cost, the Canadian government has proposed compulsory licensing of SKBD's DOLAMINE patent to a Canadian manufacturer. This private manufacturer is a big low cost supplier of pharmaceuticals under the Canadian national health plan. The government was about to issue a compulsory licensing order when some bright young attorney thought to have a look at NAFTA.

PART B. COUNTERFEITING

In Mexico, the cost of DOLAMINE is prohibitive for most patients, although cheap when compared to U.S. prices. Some Mexicans have made do with the substitute patented pharmaceuticals which are less expensive. Others have simply gone without effective drug care or purchased "dolaminazine", a bootleg nonprescription version of DOLA-MINE whose origins are obscure. Perhaps dolaminazine is Hecho en Mexico, perhaps not. There have been reports that dolaminazine may be entering Mexico from Brazil where even allowing pharmaceutical patents has been controversial for decades.

* See Tamsin Carlisle, Pfizer Pressures Canadian Sellers of Drugs to U.S., Wall St. Journal, Jan. 14, 2004, at A–6; Bush Aide Expects Drug Imports, Wall St. Journal, May 5, 2004, at D–2.

SKBD, which spent millions developing DOLAMINE, is not a happy camper. It thought that the 1991 Mexican Law of Industrial Property and NAFTA had cemented its exclusive patent rights. Mexican patent grants to foreigners have soared since the 1991 Law. SKBD is ready to aggressively assert its Mexican patent rights to DOLAMINE.

SECTION II. FOCUS OF CONSIDERATION

Compulsory licensing needs to be viewed against an historic policy in much of the developing world against granting any pharmaceutical patents. For reasons of health and cost, many nations understandably prefer not to import patented pharmaceuticals. Since pharmaceuticals are fairly easy to reverse engineer, a policy of patent denial tends to foster "home-made" pharmaceutical industries. United States unilateral pressures (associated with the heavy hand of Section 301 of the Trade Act of 1974), NAFTA and TRIPs all move in the direction of granting and protecting pharmaceutical patents. Against this backdrop, compulsory licensing is a less restrictive alternative to limiting or denying patent rights. (See comment on TRIPS and the Doha declaration earlier in this Chapter.) Neither NAFTA nor TRIPs bars compulsory licensing, as we will learn in Part A of this problem.

Part B moves to Mexico (and Brazil?) in its exploration of patent remedies. Counterfeiting, not just of pharmaceuticals, is a growth industry around the globe. Mexico has, it would seem, all the right laws on the books. But what about their operational realities? It helps to remember that Mexico is a developing country not just economically, but also in terms of its legal system. You might want to consider in reading these materials whether and how SKBD can pragmatically assist Mexico in enforcing its patent and trade laws.

Chapter 17 of NAFTA is essential to an analysis of this problem. It is found in the Documents Supplement.

SECTION III. READINGS, QUESTIONS AND COMMENTS

PART A. COMPULSORY LICENSING

FOLSOM, GORDON AND SPANOGLE, INTERNATIONAL BUSINESS TRANSACTIONS IN A NUTSHELL
Chapter 6 (2004)*

Issues surrounding the transfer of knowledge across national borders have provoked intense discussions during the last decade. The discussions promise to continue unabated. At the core is the desire of third world countries (often advanced developing countries like Brazil, South Korea, Taiwan and Singapore) to obtain protected information quickly and affordably irrespective of the proprietary rights and profit motives of current holders (usually persons from the most developed countries). Developing countries want production processes which maximize uses of abundant, inexpensive labor but which result in products that are competitive in the international marketplace. Capital intensive production processes (e.g., robot production of automobiles) may be of less interest. MNEs may be willing to share (by way of license or sale) a good deal of proprietary information, but are reluctant to part with their "core technology."

Among the industrialized countries, efforts often occur to acquire (even by way of stealing) "leading edge" technology. One example involved attempted theft of IBM computer technology by Japanese companies ultimately caught by the F.B.I. In the United States, the Office of Export Administration uses the export license procedure to control strategic technological "diversions." But in 1984 falsification of licensing documents by prominent Norwegian and Japanese companies allowed the Soviets to obtain the technology for making vastly quieter submarine propellers. In the ensuing scandal, "anti-Toshiba" legislation was adopted in the U.S. Congress. See Section 2443 of the 1988 Omnibus Trade and Competitiveness Act. Leading Japanese executives resigned their positions, which is considered the highest form of apology in Japanese business circles.

The predominant vehicle for controlling technology transfers across national borders is the "license" or "franchise" contract. The holder of information in one country first acquires the legally protected right to own the information in another country. The holder then licenses the right, usually for a fee, to a person in that other country. The very sharing of information raises a risk that proprietary control of the technology may be lost or, at a minimum, that a competitor will be created. Absent authorized transfers, piracy of intellectual property is increasingly commonplace. Indeed, in some countries such theft has risen to the height of development strategy.

The developing nations (as a "Group of 77"), the industrialized nations and the nonmarket economy nations have tried to agree in UNCTAD upon an international "Code of Conduct" for the transfer of technology. Wide disparities in attitudes toward such a Code, have been reflected by the developing nations' insistence that it be an "internationally legally binding Code," and the industrialized nations' position that it consist of "guidelines for the international transfer of technology." Some economics of the debate are illustrated by the fact that persons in the United States pay about one-tenth in royalties for use of imported technology than they receive in royalty payments from technology sent abroad. * * *

PATENT PROTECTION

For the most part, patents are granted to inventors according to national law. Thus, patents represent *territorial* grants of exclusive rights. The inventor receives Canadian patents, United States patents, Mexican patents, and so on. Since over one hundred countries have laws regulating patents, there are relatively few jurisdictions without some form of patent protection. However, legally protected intellectual property in one country may not be protected similarly in another country. For example, many third world nations *refuse* to grant patents on pharmaceuticals. These countries often assert that their public health needs require such a policy. Thailand has traditionally been one such country and unlicensed or compulsory licensed "generics" have been a growth industry there, and in Brazil and India as well.

Nominal patent protection in some developing nations may lack effective forms of relief—giving the appearance but not the reality of legal rights. Since international patent protection is expensive to obtain, some holders take a chance and limit their applications to those markets where they foresee demand or competition for their product. Nevertheless, U.S. nationals continue to receive tens of thousands of patents in other countries. But the reverse is also increasingly true. Residents of foreign countries now receive over 50 percent of the patents issued under United States law. In many countries, persons who deal with the issuance and protection of patents are called patent agents. In the United States, patent practice is a specialized branch of the legal profession. Obtaining international patent protection often involves retaining the services of specialists in each country.

What constitutes a "patent" and how it is protected in any country depends upon domestic law. In the United States, a patent issued by the U.S. Patent Office grants the right for 20 years to exclude everyone from making, using or selling the patented invention without the permission of the patentee. The United States grants patents to the "first to invent," not (as in many other countries) the "first to file." Patent infringement can result in injunctive and damages relief in the U.S. courts. "Exclusion orders" against foreign-made patent infringing goods are also available. Such orders are frequently issued by the International Trade Commission under Section 337 of the Tariff Act of 1930, and are enforced by the U.S. Customs Service. A U.S. patent thus provides a short-term legal, but not necessarily economic, monopoly. For example, the exclusive legal rights conveyed by the patents held by Xerox on its photocopying machines have not given it a monopoly in the marketplace. There are many other producers of non-infringing photocopy machines with whom Xerox competes.

There are basically two types of patent systems in the world community, registration and examination. Some countries (e.g., France) grant a patent upon "registration" accompanied by appropriate documents and fees, without making an inquiry about the patentability of the invention. The validity of such a patent grant is most difficult to gauge until a time comes to defend the patent against alleged infringement in an appropriate tribunal. In other countries, the patent grant is made following a careful "examination" of the prior art and statutory criteria on patentability or a "deferred examination" is made following public notice given to permit an "opposition." The odds are increased that the validity of such a patent will be sustained in the face of an alleged infringement.

The United States and Germany have examination systems. To obtain U.S. patents, applicants must demonstrate to the satisfaction of the U.S. Patent Office that their inventions are novel, useful and nonobvious. Nevertheless, a significant number of U.S. patents have been subsequently held invalid in the courts and the Patent Office has frequently been criticized for a lax approach to issuance of patents. In 1998, over 150,000 U.S. patents were issued, an increase of 33 percent above 1997. Much of this growth is centered in high-tech industries, including computer software patents.

The terms of a patent grant vary from country to country. For example, local law may provide for "confirmation," "importation," "introduction" or "revalidation" patents (which serve to extend limited protection to patents already existing in another country). "Inventor's certificates" and rewards are granted in some socialist countries where private ownership of the means of production is discouraged. The state owns the invention. This was the case in China, for example, but inventors now may obtain patents and exclusive private rights under the 1984 Patent Law. Some countries, such as Britain, require that a patent be "worked" (commercially applied) within a designated period of time. This requirement is so important that the British mandate a "compulsory license" to local persons if a patent is deemed unworked. Many developing nations have similar provisions in their patent laws ... the owner must use it or lose it.

INTERNATIONAL RECOGNITION OF PATENTS

The principal treaties regarding patents are the 1970 Patent Cooperation Treaty and the 1883 Convention of the Union of Paris, frequently revised and amended. To some extent, the Paris Convention also deals with trademarks, servicemarks, trade names, industrial designs, and unfair competition. Other recent treaties dealing with patents are the European Patent Convention (designed to permit a single office at Munich and The Hague to issue patents of all countries party to the treaty), and the European Community Patent Convention (designed to create a single patent valid throughout the EC).

The Paris Convention, to which over 140 countries including Canada, Mexico and the U.S. are parties, remains the basic international agreement dealing with treatment of foreigners under national patent laws. It is administered by the International Bureau of the World Intellectual Property Organization (WIPO) at Geneva. The "right of national treatment" (Article 2) prohibits discrimination against foreign holders of local patents and trademarks. Thus, for example, a foreigner granted a Canadian patent must receive the same legal rights and remedies accorded Canadian nationals. Furthermore, important "rights of priority" are granted to patent holders provided they file in foreign jurisdictions within twelve months of their home country patent applications. But such rights may not overcome prior filings by others in "first to file" jurisdictions. Patent applications in foreign jurisdictions are not dependent upon success in the home country. Patentability criteria vary from country to country. Nevertheless, the Paris Convention obviates the need to file simultaneously in every country where intellectual property protection is sought. If an inventor elects not to obtain patent protection in other countries, anyone may make, use or sell the invention in that territory. The Paris Convention does not attempt to reduce the need for individual patent applications in all jurisdictions where patent protection is sought. Nor does it alter the various domestic criteria on patentability.

The Patent Cooperation Treaty (PCT), to which about 120 countries including Canada, Mexico (recently) and the U.S. are parties, is designed to achieve greater uniformity and less cost in the international patent filing process, and in the examination of prior art. Instead of filing patent applications individually in each nation, filings under the PCT are done in selected countries. The national patent offices of Japan, Sweden, Russia and the United States have been designated International Searching Authorities (ISA), as has the European Patent Office at Munich and The Hague. The international application, together with the international search report, is communicated by an ISA to each national patent office where protection is sought.

Nothing in this Treaty limits the freedom of each nation to establish substantive conditions of patentability and determine infringement remedies. However, the Patent Cooperation Treaty also provides that the applicant may arrange for an international preliminary examination in order to formulate a non-binding opinion on whether the claimed invention is novel, involves an inventive step (non-obvious) and is industrially applicable. In a country without sophisticated search facilities, the report of the international preliminary examination may largely determine whether a patent will be granted. For this reason alone, the Patent Cooperation Treaty may generate considerable uniformity in world patent law. In 1986 the United States ratified the PCT provisions on preliminary examination reports, thereby supporting such uniformity.

* * *

NOAH, NAFTA'S IMPACT ON TRADE IN PHARMACEUTICALS

33 Houston L. Rev. 1293 (1997).*

The international market in drug products is dominated by multinational enterprises. Large pharmaceutical companies headquartered primarily in the United States and Europe have subsidiaries in Canada and, to a lesser extent, Mexico. These multinationals account for the bulk of new drug research and development. In contrast, manufacturers headquartered in Mexico are relatively small enterprises. Foreign investment in Canadian and Mexican companies may increase in the future, especially with improvements in intellectual property protection, but the bulk of future research and development (R & D) seems destined to remain in the United States, Europe, and Japan.

The pharmaceutical industry depends heavily on patent and other intellectual property rights (IPR) to recoup the significant investments necessary for new drug R & D. In many countries, especially third-world nations, intellectual property protection tends to be weak, and the United States government has aggressively sought modifications in the patent laws of its trading partners. Indeed, the lack of meaningful patent protection for pharmaceutical products has become a flashpoint over the last decade, most notably in an ongoing trade dispute with Brazil. As more fully discussed below, NAFTA represents a major success in this respect. In contrast, the Agreement does not address parallel imports in violation of a company's trademark rights.

ENHANCED PATENT PROTECTION FOR PHARMACEUTICALS

Among the numerous IPR provisions of particular importance to the drug industry, NAFTA provides "pipeline protection," ensuring that pharmaceutical products under patent in one country but not another will be protected by the other signatories for the unexpired patent term remaining after July 1, 1991. NAFTA also accords trade secret protection for testing data submitted to government agencies. Some of the Agreement's specific effects on the domestic laws of the different member countries are summarized below, but NAFTA's enhanced intellectual property protections may have broader importance to the extent that other Latin American nations eventually join the accord or that NAFTA serves as a model for other regional trade agreements in the future.

Modifications in Canadian Law. NAFTA prohibits discrimination by the Parties on the basis of either the field of technology or whether the product was produced domestically instead of imported from one of the other Parties. For a number of years, Canada discriminated in its treatment of pharmaceutical products. Until 1993, Canada used a compulsory licensing system as a mechanism to control the pricing of pharmaceuticals. Although modified in various respects over the years, this law had been in place since 1969.

Initially, Canadian companies were permitted to market, upon payment of minimal royalties to the patent holder (generally four percent of the net sales price), generic copies of drugs patented in other countries even if their patent terms had not yet expired. After 1987, Canada limited such compulsory licensing by granting market exclusivity to the foreign patent holder for the first seven years of the patent term. In contrast, generic drugs may not be approved in the United States until after the expiration of the entire patent term or a separate statutory period of market exclusivity, whichever occurs later. By allowing for faster generic competition, the Canadian compulsory licensing system served to depress domestic prices, making it more difficult for foreign manufacturers of new drugs to recoup their substantial R & D investments.

The Free Trade Agreement negotiated in 1987 between Canada and the United States had failed to resolve these and other contentious intellectual property issues. In 1993, however, Canada enacted legislation to eliminate this form of compulsory licensing and extended the patent life to twenty years, notwithstanding that overall drug costs were expected to increase substantially. NAFTA ratifies this modification in Canadian law, which of its own terms became retroactive to December 20, 1991. * * * The Agreement, therefore, prevents Canada from re-instituting the compulsory licensing system that it previously had applied to pharmaceutical products.

Modifications in Mexican Law. Until recently, Mexico had one of the weakest intellectual property regimes in the world. For example, Mexican law authorized compulsory licensing, and it did not recognize product patents for pharmaceuticals. Moreover, differences in available remedies, especially the inability to seek preliminary injunctions, and weak enforcement further reduced the meaningful level of intellectual property protection for manufacturers of innovative products.

In 1991, Mexico enacted its new Industrial Property Law to address a number of these shortcomings. Serious trade negotiations would not have been possible without Mexico's decision to modernize its patent laws, and NAFTA requires continued adherence to those modifications. In addition, the Agreement calls on the Parties to make injunctive relief available in appropriate cases, thereby importing a common-law judicial remedy into the Mexican legal system.

Modifications in American Law. In contrast with the significant changes in Canadian and Mexican patent protection laws for pharmaceuticals, now codified by NAFTA, the Agreement requires only a fairly modest alteration in the intellectual property laws of the United States.

PARIS CONVENTION FOR THE PROTECTION OF INDUSTRIAL PROPERTY
(Stockholm revision, 1967).

ARTICLE 5

A.1. Importation by the patentee into the country where the patent has been granted of articles manufactured in any of the countries of the Union shall not entail forfeiture of the patent.

2. Each country of the Union shall have the right to take legislative measures providing for the grant of compulsory licenses to prevent the abuses which might result from the exercise of the exclusive rights conferred by the patent, for example, failure to work.

3. Forfeiture of the patent shall not be provided for except in cases where the grant of compulsory licenses would not have been sufficient to prevent the said abuses. No proceedings for the forfeiture or revocation

of a patent may be instituted before the expiration of two years from the grant of the first compulsory license.

4.   A compulsory license may not be applied for on the ground of failure to work or insufficient working before the expiration of a period of four years from the date of filing of the patent application or three years from the date of the grant of the patent, whichever period expires last; it shall be refused if the patentee justifies his inaction by legitimate reasons. Such a compulsory license shall be non-exclusive and shall not be transferable, even in the form of the grant of a sub-license, except with that part of the enterprise or goodwill which exploits such license.

* * *

HALEWOOD, REGULATING PATENT HOLDERS: LOCAL WORKING REQUIREMENTS AND COMPULSORY LICENSES AT INTERNATIONAL LAW

35 Osgoode Hall L.J. 243 (1997).*

This article seeks to establish that domestic patent legislation that requires "local working," and creates relatively wide powers for granting compulsory licences, would not be in contravention of the *Agreement on Trade–Related Aspects of Intellectual Property Rights* or the *North American Free Trade Agreement*.

The argument is a timely one, because all around the globe, governments are changing—or being pressured to change—their domestic patent legislation in favour of foreign patentees, including loosening or eliminating local working requirements, and severely restricting their use of compulsory licences. Working requirements and compulsory licences are important mechanisms by which a patent granting country can compel foreign patentees to transfer technology to within its jurisdiction. "Local working" refers to the condition some countries impose on patentees that their patented product or process must be used or produced in the patent granting country. This condition has the effect of forcing foreign patentees to situate production facilities within the patent granting country. Such transfers of technology are desirable from the patent granting country's point of view because they contribute to a variety of public policy goals such as employment creation, industrial and technological capacity building, national balance of payments, and economic independence. "Compulsory licensing" refers to the practice of governments allowing parties other than the original patentees to exploit patented products and processes. In such cases, the patentee is forced to grant a licence to a third-party licensee to exploit the patented product or process, in return for which the patentee generally receives a royalty payment at a rate set by legislative fiat. Justifications for the grant of compulsory licences vary considerably between countries. Perhaps the most important use of compulsory licences is as a remedy for patent-holder abuses such as "non-working," or the maintenance of artificially high prices for patent protected commodities. As far as their effect on the transfer of technology is concerned, the immediate advantage of compulsory licensing is obvious: compulsory licences allow third parties to exploit on a local basis that technology which the original patentees failed to introduce into the country in the first place, or failed to use once it was introduced. In the absence of controls such as compulsory licensing and mandatory local working, patent granting countries are left in the unenviable position of having to trust that foreign patent holders will decide *on the basis of their own self interests* to transfer technology to within their jurisdictions.

Despite the evident advantages of compulsory licensing and mandatory working requirements from a nation-building point of view, many commentators take the position that signatory states to *NAFTA* and/or *TRIPS* have forfeited, or severely limited their ability to invoke these two mechanisms. The notion that *NAFTA* and *TRIPS* have this effect is generally based on two claims.

The first claim is that *NAFTA* and *TRIPS* preclude any legislation that requires national "working" of patents. Accordingly, "working" can be satisfied completely by importing the patented product into the patent granting country. "Working" therefore, has been redefined and diminished to the extent that it no longer serves to guarantee the transfer of anything but finished commodities.

The second claim is that *NAFTA* and *TRIPS* drastically restrict the conditions under which states may grant compulsory licences. Many commentators and patent rights advocates propound that compulsory licensing is now governed exclusively by articles 1709:10 and 31 of *NAFTA* and *TRIPS* respectively and that under those articles, compulsory licensing must be severely constrained. If they are correct, the ability of states to utilize compulsory licensing in order to foster technology transfers is undermined.

I will argue that both claims are inaccurate.

* * *

[LOCAL WORKING]

In 1883, the Union for the Protection of Industrial Property, produced the *Paris Convention*. This was the first multilateral treaty negotiation to standardize the treatment of intellectual property on an international scale. For the purposes of this paper, however, the most important development was the correlative treatment of 1) the local working requirement, and 2) the importation of patented material.

Article 5(1) of the *Paris Convention, 1883* stated that importation of patented articles "shall not entail forfeiture of the patent." Article 5(2), however, stated: "Nevertheless, the patentee shall remain under the obligation to exploit his patent in accordance with the laws of the country into which he introduces the patent.''

Prior to the recognition that importation would not entail forfeiture, some countries' legislation stipulated that a patentee was not allowed to import *any* of the patented material, despite the fact that the patent was for the most part being worked locally. In such cases, the patent was revoked * * *

The *Paris Convention* was subject to six subsequent revisions over the course of 115 years. At the most recent revision conference, held in Stockholm, in 1967, article 5(A)(2) was altered to read, "Each country . . . shall have the right to take legislative measures providing for the grant of compulsory licences to prevent the abuses which might result from the exercise of the exclusive rights conferred by the patent, for example, failure to work.'' Georg Bodenhausen, who was the Director of the United International Bureau for the Protection of International Property at the time of the 1967 revision, confirmed that "work" in the 1967 version meant the actual use of the patent within the patent granting country:

> The member states are also free to define what they understand by 'failure to work.' Normally, working a patent will be understood to mean working it industrially, namely, by manufacture of the patented product, or industrial application of a patented process. Thus, importation or sale of the patented article, or of the article manufactured by a patented process, will not normally be regarded as 'working' the patent.

Throughout the 114 years of the *Paris Convention*, two fundamental principles have remained virtually unchanged: 1) that importation will not entail forfeiture; and 2) that member countries may pass legislation to mandate local working within the patent granting country.

THE RELATIONSHIP OF THE PARIS CONVENTION TO TRIPS AND NAFTA

* * *

NAFTA article 17:2 is somewhat more ambiguous in its commitment to respect the *Paris Convention*. Article 2 states: "each party shall, *at a minimum*, give effect to this chapter and to the substantive provisions of . . . the *Paris Convention* [1967].'' It is possible to argue that any protection extended to patentees in *NAFTA* complies with article 2 as long as it does not involve the extension of *less* patent protection than was set out in the *Paris Convention*. Consequently, any new, and *stronger* protection provided for in *NAFTA*—even if it contravened the substantive provisions of the *Paris Convention, 1967*—might comply with article 2. At the very least, however, article 2 suggests that *NAFTA* should be interpreted, if and where possible, in accordance with the *Paris Convention, 1967*. Certainly, if *NAFTA* is silent, or ambiguous, with respect to an issue that is clearly set out in the *Paris Convention*, the *Paris Convention* should be used as a guide for interpreting *NAFTA*.

* * *

In this section, I analyze the parallel frameworks that exist in *NAFTA*, articles 1709:7, 1709:8 and 1709:9 and *Paris Convention, 1967,* articles 5(A)(1) and 5(A)(2). Like *TRIPS*, article 27:1, *NAFTA*, article 1709:6 recognizes that imports are patentable subject matter. *NAFTA* article 1709:6 is almost identical to *TRIPS* article 30 * * *

There are only two significant differences between the relevant *NAFTA* and *TRIPS* provisions. First, *NAFTA*, article 1709:8 provides that: "a party may revoke a patent only when ... (b) the grant of a compulsory license has not remedied the lack of exploitation." Second, *NAFTA* does not include an equivalent to *trips* article 8. Consequently, the argument in favour of importing the substantive provisions of article 5(A) of the *Paris Convention* into *NAFTA* is little different from that set out in the previous section regarding *TRIPS*.

In short, the argument is weakened by the absence in *NAFTA* of the explicit mention of "abuses" and "practices which affect the international transfer of technology," which were included in article 8 of *TRIPS*. The argument is strengthened however, by the language of *NAFTA* article 1709:8, which is extremely similar to *Paris Convention*, article 5(A)(2) which states that a state must only revoke (or forfeit) a patent after having attempted to remedy abuses with compulsory licensing.

* * *

CONCLUSION WITH RESPECT TO LOCAL WORKING

Based on the foregoing analysis, it is evident that legislation requiring local working of patents would not be in contravention of either *TRIPS* or *NAFTA*. The argument is perhaps marginally stronger with respect to *TRIPS*, given the inclusive reference to the *Paris Convention* in *TRIPS* article 2. On the other hand, there is nothing in *NAFTA*, that either directly, or implicitly, contradicts the *Paris Convention*. Consequently, the significance of the weaker language with which *NAFTA* makes reference to the *Paris Convention* is minimal.

Finally, it is important to note that the interpretation urged upon us by patent rights advocates—that articles 27:1 and 1709:7 redefine "working" to permit 100 per cent importing—effectively reverses the historical function of patents. Patents were originally granted to promote the domestic application of foreign technologies, with little protection for the rights of the original foreign patentees. The interpretation advanced by patent advocates emphasizes protection of foreign patentees, to the exclusion of any consideration of local interests in technology transfers.

COMPULSORY LICENSING

* * *

It was established in the previous section that *if* compulsory licenses were to be allowed within *NAFTA* and *TRIPS*, they would fall under articles 30 and 1709:6. It still remains to be determined however, under what circumstances those articles will actually allow compulsory licensing. Unfortunately, articles 30 and 1709:6 are rife with ambiguous phrases, the meanings of which are critical to this analysis. Consequently, I have dedicated the following analysis to determining the meaning of four crucial phrases found in articles 30 and 1709:6: 1) "limited exceptions;" 2) "normal exploitation of a patent;" 3) "legitimate interests of patent owners" (which I shall treat as synonymous with "normal exploitation"); and 4) "legitimate interests of third parties."

* * *

Article 1709:8 of *NAFTA*, read together with article 1709:6, likewise clarifies what the *NAFTA* drafters may have intended by "limited exceptions" in article 1709:6. Article 1709:8 states that a "party may revoke a patent only when . . . *the grant of a compulsory license* has not remedied the lack of exploitation." Article 1709:8 juxtaposes the remedies of compulsory licensing and forfeiture; it is clear from the context that, of the two remedies, the drafters considered compulsory licensing to represent the more limited exception to patent rights. I argue, therefore, that compulsory licensing should be considered as one of the "limited exceptions" to be considered in article 1709:6.

* * *

Having exhausted the interpretive resources within the *TRIPS* and *NAFTA* agreements (*i.e.*, other provisions within the respective treaties) to discern the ambit of articles 30 and 1709:6, I will now rely on outside sources, specifically the history of the *Paris Convention*. Ultimately, I argue that whatever ambiguity remains with respect to the meaning of 1) "normal exploitation," and patentees' "legitimate interests"; 2) "limited exceptions"; and 3) interests of third parties is clarified by reading those phrases in harmony with article 5 of the *Paris Conventions, 1883 to 1967*.

* * *

Prior to 1925, the only remedy available for non-working, pursuant to the *Paris Conventions, 1883, 1900,* and *1911* was forfeiture. Article 5(3) of the *Hague Revision, 1925* of the *Paris Convention*, substituted compulsory licensing for forfeiture as a remedy for patentee abuses (including non-working). Forfeiture was still an available remedy, but only after attempts through compulsory licensing had failed.

The introduction of mandatory licensing was not achieved without controversy. Mandatory licensing represented a compromise between the most industrialized countries, led by the United States, who were pushing for the complete eradication of "working," and less industrialized countries (the most vocal being Japan, Yugoslavia, and Poland) who preferred the *status quo*. One of the primary fears of the latter group was that the right to grant compulsory licences to domestic licensees would be useless because the potential local licences lacked sufficient technical capability to "take on" the patented production or application in the first place.

While the less developed countries' resistance to the introduction of compulsory licensing was defeated, they were not entirely disappointed with the outcome of the 1925 Hague Revision Conference. While they lost direct access to their most forceful remedy for non-working (forfeiture), the *Convention* did extend the application of the new remedy (compulsory licensing) to a broader range of actionable "abuses."

"Abuse" has been widely interpreted across a number of judicial jurisdictions, including situations where patents were being worked, but not sufficiently to satisfy local demand, or at exorbitant prices. The British *Patents and Designs Act, 1949* for example, allowed for the grant of compulsory licenses when demand for a patented article was not being met on reasonable terms, or when the demand was being met "to a substantial extent by importation," or when the commercial working of a patent was hindered by the importation of the article.

Many countries have also developed laws whereby they may grant compulsory licences—despite there being no evidence of abuse by the patentee—if they consider it is in the public interest to do so. In Germany, for example, in the early and middle part of this century, compulsory licences were granted to reduce the cost of vital goods, ensure adequate supply to the domestic market, prevent plant failures, and to improve the balance of trade by encouraging domestic, export industries. Until 1991, Canadian patent legislation allowed for compulsory licences for pharmaceuticals in the absence of proof of abuse by the original patentee. Between 1987 and 1991 the Canadian *Patent Act* provided for a longer grace period during which time patentees were free from the threat of compulsory licenses if the patented pharmaceuticals contained active compounds manufactured in Canada. This extra protection was afforded by way of incentive to further public policy goals and was independent of any other criterion for judging patentee behaviour.

* * *

CONCLUSION REGARDING COMPULSORY LICENSING

On the basis of the above analysis, it is reasonable to conclude that *NAFTA* and *TRIPS* allow compulsory licensing as a remedy for non-local working and other, more broadly defined abuses (such as insufficient working, and inadequate supply of local market). Compulsory licensing in these instances would fall within the meaning of *TRIPS*, article 30 and *NAFTA*, article 1709:6. Neither of these two provisions sets out concrete guidelines with respect to the conditions under which such licenses could be granted. Consequently, national legislation passed with respect to these two classes of compulsory licences could be relatively broad.

It is not so clear however, whether compulsory licensing in the public interest, without proof of abuse, would similarly fall within the meaning of the same articles. It is more likely that this third class of compulsory licensing would fall within the aegis of *TRIPS* article 31 and *NAFTA* article 1709:10. Consequently, compulsory licensing in the public interest, in the absence of proof of patentee abuse, would be subject to the limitations set out in that article.

PATENT ACT OF CANADA
R.S.C. Chapter P–4.

65. (1) The Attorney General of Canada or any person interested may, at any time after the expiration of three years from the date of the grant of a patent, apply to the Commissioner alleging in the case of that patent that there has been an abuse of the exclusive rights thereunder and asking for relief under this Act.

(2) The exclusive rights under a patent shall be deemed to have been abused in any of the following circumstances:

(*a*) if the patented invention, being one capable of being worked within Canada, is not being worked within Canada on a commercial scale, and no satisfactory reason can be given for that non-working;

(*b*) if the working of the invention within Canada on a commercial scale is being prevented or hindered by the importation from abroad of the patented article by the patentee or persons claiming under him, by persons directly or indirectly purchasing from him or by other persons against whom the patentee is not taking or has not taken any proceedings for infringement;

(*c*) if the demand for the patented article in Canada is not being met to an adequate extent and on reasonable terms;

(*d*) if, by reason of the refusal of the patentee to grant a licence or licences on reasonable terms, the trade or industry of Canada or the trade of any person or class of persons trading in Canada, or the establishment of any new trade or industry in Canada, is prejudiced, and it is in the public interest that a licence or licences should be granted;

(*e*) if any trade or industry in Canada, or any person or class of persons engaged therein, is unfairly prejudiced by the conditions attached by the patentee, whether before or after the passing of this Act, to the purchase, hire, licence or use of the patented article or to the using or working of the patented process; or

(*f*) if it is shown that the existence of the patent, being a patent for an invention relating to a process involving the use of materials not protected by the patent or for an invention relating to a substance produced by such a process, has been utilized by the patentee so as unfairly to prejudice in Canada the manufacture, use or sale of any materials.

* * *

(4) For the purpose of determining whether there has been any abuse of the exclusive rights under a patent, it shall be taken, in relation to every paragraph of subsection (2), that patents for new inventions are granted not only to encourage invention but to secure that new inventions shall so far as possible be worked on a commercial scale in Canada without undue delay.

* * *

66. (1) On being satisfied that a case of abuse of the exclusive rights under a patent has been established, the Commissioner may exercise any of the following powers as he may deem expedient in the circumstances:

(*a*) he may order the grant to the applicant of a licence on such terms as the Commissioner may think expedient, including a term precluding the licensee from importing into Canada any goods the importation of which, if made by persons other than the patentee or persons claiming under him, would be an infringement of the patent, and in that case the patentee and all licensees for the time being shall be deemed to have mutually covenanted against that importation;

(*b*) if the Commissioner is satisfied that the invention is not being worked on a commercial scale within Canada, and is such that it cannot be so worked without the expenditure of capital for the raising of which it will be necessary to rely on the exclusive rights under the patent, he may, unless the patentee or those claiming under him will undertake to find that capital, order the grant to the applicant, or any other person, or to the applicant and any other person or persons jointly, if able and willing to provide that capital, of an exclusive licence on such terms as the Commissioner may think just, but subject to this Act;

(*c*) if the Commissioner is satisfied that the exclusive rights have been abused in the circumstances specified in paragraph 65(2)(*f*), he may order the grant of licences to the applicant and to such of his customers, and containing such terms, as the Commissioner may think expedient;

(*d*) if the Commissioner is satisfied that the objects of this section and section 65 cannot be attained by the exercise of any of the foregoing powers, he shall order the patent to be revoked, either forthwith or after such reasonable interval as may be specified in the order, unless in the meantime such conditions as may be prescribed in the order, with a view to attaining the objects of this section and section 65, are fulfilled, and the Commissioner may, on reasonable cause shown in any case, by subsequent order extend the interval so specified, but the Commissioner shall not make an order for revocation that is at variance with any treaty, convention, arrangement or engagement with any other country to which Canada is a party; or

(c) if the Commissioner is of opinion that the objects of this section and section 65 will be best attained by not making an order under the provisions of this section, he may make an order refusing the application and dispose of any question as to costs thereon as he thinks just.

FAUVER, COMPULSORY PATENT LICENSING IN THE UNITED STATES: AN IDEA WHOSE TIME HAS COME

8 N.W.J. Int'l Law & Bus. 666 (1988).*

When a business decides whether to compete in today's world marketplace, it must consider the extent to which its ideas and designs will be protected from misappropriation around the world. Despite its international ramifications, however, patent protection is territorial, operating only within the jurisdiction granting the patent. Companies wishing to compete overseas must obtain patents from each country in which protection is sought. While several treaties and international congresses have been successful in creating fundamental equity and uniformity among national patent laws, complete uniformity is difficult to achieve due to different philosophies regarding free enterprise, monopoly rights, and technological development.

* * *

The practical arguments against compulsory licensing in the United States—that such licenses are unnecessary, reduce incentives to develop new technology, are unconstitutional, and increase foreign competition— are relatively weak. However, opponents of compulsory licenses may gain more support from theoretical positions on contract and property rights, as well as from general attitudes regarding the United States position in world trade. As a matter of contract theory, patent grants constitute an agreement between the government and the inventor, wherein the inventor agrees to reveal the discovery and the means to use it in return for the government's promise of a [twenty] year monopoly on the production of the idea. Under this view, compulsory licensing may be interpreted as a failure of consideration on the part of the government, or even a breach of contract should a compulsory license be granted retroactively. If contract principles are highly valued, then this theory emerges as a strong theoretical basis for opposing compulsory licenses. If a patent is considered the property of its owner, the patentee becomes free to use or not use, or license or assign, at will. Under this theory, compulsory licenses may constitute a taking. Even if compulsory licenses do not acquire the constitutional dimensions of a taking, they still have been considered "a totally inappropriate expropriation of private property."

The United States attitude towards its role in the world market also vitiates the need for a compulsory license system. United States companies historically have been more successful exploiting overseas markets than foreign firms have been in the United States. While general protectionist legislation has often been helpful, much of the United States success can be attributed to its dominant role in the development of technology. Developing nations may need compulsory licenses to help bring technology into the country, but up to this point the United States has not perceived a similar need.

Today, however, the situation is changing. The United States consumer markets are being exploited with great success by the Japanese, West Germans, and others. The United States trade deficit was $171 billion in 1987, compared with a $79.8 billion surplus in Japan's trade balance for the same period. Foreign companies are also assuming a more dominant position in United States patent holdings. In 1969, for example, 25% of United States patents granted went to foreign investors. By 1987 this figure had risen to 47%.

A particular example of the need for compulsory licensing is found in our relations with Japan. In 1980, the top ten Japanese patent-holding companies held 1,916 United States patents; by 1985, that figure had more than doubled to 4,018. The relatively infrequent granting of compulsory licenses may not be a fair measure of their true effect. It is a largely prophylactic provision, one which might incline a patent holder to license voluntarily even where he might otherwise have preferred to maintain his exclusive right. Any voluntary licensing, however, does not provide total protection from a compulsory license, because the extent of its use is still subject to review whether the use is exclusive or not. That review would fall under the adequacy of supply, public interest, or "worked in the country" categories of compulsory licensing. Otherwise, a patent holder could easily defeat the provision by creating a dummy licensee.

Perhaps the most persuasive argument lies in the comparative advantage created in other countries by the effective patent protection in the United States. It appears that foreign companies holding United States patents have more freedom to exploit their inventions in the United States than United States citizens do overseas. Largely due to the recent creation of the Federal Circuit Court of Appeals to adjudicate patent appeals, more patents have been recently held valid in the United States than ever before, and United States patent holders have been receiving higher damage awards in infringement suits. By contrast, no similar strengthening of patents systems has occurred in other countries. Thus, "[f]oreign competitors seem to get a better shake in the United States than American companies do abroad." The inequities in patent infringement enforcement reflect a larger pattern of abuse of United States intellectual property rights in general, a problem of serious magnitude in international trade. If the recent crisis-level political rhetoric about international "competitiveness" is to be believed, perhaps compulsory licensing is an idea whose time has come.

* * *

While most countries provide for compulsory patent licensing, the United States does not. An analysis of the rationales given for many compulsory licensing systems may suggest the United States position to be a mistake, because compulsory licensing advances a nation's technological development. In accordance with the broad objectives of patent laws, compulsory licensing encourages the production and use of patented goods and increases access to advanced technology.

Carefully constructed compulsory licensing laws would help restore a balance between the patent system of the United States and those of other countries. To avoid issuance of a compulsory license, foreign holders of United States patents would be encouraged by these laws to grant licenses to domestic producers. Even if foreign producers choose to import, a compulsory license granted under appropriate circumstances would still result in a domestic producer. Either way the United States economy benefits. Further, as this Comment has suggested, such provisions would not significantly reduce the rewards and incentives currently offered to inventors, particularly when applied to domestic patentees.

The tendency of the United States to supply the world with technology made its access to foreign technology unimportant in the past. Today, however, the growing technological capabilities of many foreign countries warrant renewed consideration of not only this shift in scientific ability, but of compulsory patent licensing as well.

Questions and Comments

1. What is "compulsory licensing?" What is a "local working requirement?" How are these concepts treated under NAFTA? See Articles 1709.6, 1709.7, 1709.8 and 1709.10. In what sense might they be "takings"?

2. Do you agree with Halewood that Article 5 of the Paris Convention should be used to interpret Article 1709 of NAFTA? See Article 1701.2 and note its language: "each party shall, at a minimum, give effect to this Chapter *and* to [the Paris Convention]" (emphasis added).

3. Are the Paris Convention and NAFTA consistent on the legality of working requirements and compulsory licensing? Is either clear on the legality of such provisions? If compulsory licensing is not legal under NAFTA, what in the world is Article 1709.10 all about? And what about the express reference to compulsory licensing in Article 1709.8?

4. SKBD is exporting, not producing, DOLAMINE in Canada. After NAFTA, may Canada require production of DOLAMINE within its territory? Either way, may Canada compulsorily license DOLAMINE? Halewood's

arguments are a little difficult to follow. Read him carefully before responding.

5.　Noah tells us that Canada enacted legislation in 1993 (before NAFTA) to eliminate compulsory licensing of pharmaceuticals. He asserts that NAFTA "ratifies" this result and prevents Canada from "reinstituting" such licensing. Is he right? Halewood would surely disagree.

6.　Suppose, for reasons of exploding costs, Canada reinstitutes compulsory licensing for pharmaceuticals and follows very precisely the terms of NAFTA Article 1709.10. Must Canada approach SKBD and first seek a voluntary license? Who gets to decide what will be the terms and conditions of such a license and whether they are "reasonable?"

7.　Suppose a compulsory license for DOLAMINE is ordered. Is there a duty to remunerate SKBD? If so, how much? Can SKBD seek judicial review of the order? Of the level of remuneration? Would a compulsory license of SKBD's patent be a taking of an investment under NAFTA, Chapter 11, subject to international arbitration under Part B?

8.　Why not ignore compulsory licensing and simply regulate the price of pharmaceuticals in Canada? If the regulated price of DOLAMINE is "too low," what can SKBD do? Must it export to Canada?

9.　Suppose SKBD stops exporting DOLAMINE to Canada. What then? Might its Canadian patent be forfeited? See again Article 5 of the Paris Convention. In Japan, by the way, some part of the invention must be made in Japan. Otherwise, it is not "worked," and therefore possibly forfeited.

What about compulsory licensing after SKBD stops exporting ? Is the refusal to export, as Halewood discusses, an "abuse?" Does that matter? See Sections 65 and 66 of the Canadian Patent Act.

10.　With considerably more than half of all new U.S. patents going to foreigners, should the United States adopt a compulsory licensing system? Fauver thought this was an idea whose time had come in 1988. What about now?

11.　Halewood suggests that compulsory licensing is permissible under NAFTA for non-local working of a patent, "abuses," and when in the public interest. Would the threat of chemical warfare (anthrax in the United States), coupled with the lack of sufficient production capacity for Cipro with Bayer AG, justify compulsory licensing?

12.　Compare Mexico's provisions on obligatory and public utility patent licensing in Articles 70 and 77 of its 1991 Industrial Property Law:

> Article 70. In the case of inventions, after three years from the date the patent is granted, or after four years from the date the patent request is presented, whichever is later, any person may request the Institute to grant an obligatory license to exploit such invention, when such exploitation has not been carried out, except for duly justified reasons.
>
> An obligatory license will not be granted when the owner of the patent or the person who is the grantee of a contractual license has been importing the patented product or the product obtained through the patented process.

Article 77. For reasons of emergency or national security, as long as such conditions exist, the Institute, by declaration published in the Official Gazette, may determine that certain patents be exploited through the granting of public utility licenses, if failure to do so may impede delay, or increase the cost of producing, providing or distributing basic consumer necessities.

The concession of these licenses shall proceed within the terms of the second paragraph of article 72, and be neither exclusive nor transferable.

PART B. COUNTERFEITING

FOLSOM, GORDON AND SPANOGLE, INTERNATIONAL BUSINESS TRANSACTIONS IN A NUTSHELL
Chapter 6 (2004)*

INTERNATIONAL PATENT AND KNOWHOW LICENSING

This section concerns the most common form of lawful international technology transfer—patent and knowhow licensing. Before any patent licensing can take place, patents must be acquired in all countries in which the owner hopes there will be persons interested in purchasing the technology. Even in countries where the owner has no such hope, patent rights may still be obtained so as to foreclose future unlicensed competitors. Licensing is a middle ground alternative to exporting from the owner's home country and direct investment in host markets. It can often produce, with relatively little cost, immediate positive cash flows.

International patent and knowhow licensing is the most critical form of technology transfer to third world development. From the owner's standpoint, it presents an alternative to and sometimes a first step towards foreign investment. Such licensing involves a transfer of patent rights or knowhow (commercially valuable knowledge, often falling short of a patentable invention) in return for payments, usually termed royalties. Unlike foreign investment, licensing does not have to involve a capital investment in a host jurisdiction. However, licensing of patents and knowhow is not without legal risks.

From the licensee's standpoint, and the perspective of its government, there is the risk that the licensed technology may be old or obsolete, not "state of the art." Goods produced under old technology will be hard to export and convey a certain "second class" status. On the other hand, older more labor intensive technologies may actually be sought (as sometimes done by the PRC) in the early stages of development. Excessive royalties may threaten the economic viability of the licensee and drain hard currencies from the country. The licensee typically is not in a sufficiently powerful position to bargain away restrictive features of standard international licenses. For all these reasons, and more, third world countries frequently regulate patent and knowhow licensing agreements. Such law is found in the Brazilian Normative Act No. 17 (1976) and the Mexican Technology Transfer Law (1982) (repealed 1991), among others. Royalty levels will be limited, certain clauses prohibited (e.g., export restraints, resale price maintenance, mandatory grantbacks to the licensor of improvements), and the desirability of the technology evaluated.

Regulation of patent and knowhow licensing agreements is hardly limited to the third world. The European Community, for example, after several test cases before the European Court of Justice, issued "block exemption" regulation controlling patent licensing agreements. Many of the licensing agreement clauses controlled by EU technology transfer regulations are the same as those covered by third world technology transfer legislation.

* * *

The licensor also faces legal risks. The flow of royalty payments may be stopped, suspended or reduced by currency exchange regulations. The taxation of the royalties, if not governed by double taxation treaties, may be confiscatory. The licensee may produce "gray market" goods which eventually compete for sales in markets exclusively intended for the licensor. In the end, patents expire and become part of the world domain. At that point, the licensee has effectively purchased the technology and becomes an independent competitor (though not necessarily an effective competitor if the licensor has made new technological advances).

Licensing is a kind of partnership. If the licensee succeeds, the licensor's royalties (often based on sales volumes) will increase and a continuing partnership through succeeding generations of technology may evolve. If not, the dispute settlement provisions of the agreement may be called upon as either party withdraws from the partnership. Licensing of patents and knowhow often is combined with, indeed essential to, foreign investments. A foreign subsidiary or joint venture will need technical assistance and knowhow to commence operations. When this occurs, the licensing terms are usually a part of the basic joint venture or investment agreement. Licensing may also be combined with a trade agreement, as where the licensor ships necessary supplies to the licensee, joint venturer, or subsidiary. Such supply agreements have sometimes been used to overcome royalty limitations through a form of "transfer pricing," the practice of marking up or down the price of goods so as to allocate revenues to preferred parties and jurisdictions (e.g., tax havens).

Protection From Piracy

Theft of intellectual property and use of counterfeit goods are rapidly increasing in developing and developed countries. Such theft is not limited to consumer goods (Pierre Cardin clothing, Rolex watches). Industrial products and parts (e.g., automotive brake pads) are now being counterfeited. Some developing countries see illegal technology transfers as part of their economic development. They encourage piracy or choose not to oppose it. Since unlicensed producers pay no royalties, they often have lower production costs than the original source. This practice fuels the fires of intellectual property piracy. Unlicensed low cost reproduction of entire copyrighted books (may it not happen to this book) is said to be rampant in such diverse areas as Nigeria, Saudi Arabia, and China. Apple computers have been inexpensively counterfeited in Hong Kong. General Motors estimates that about 40 percent of its auto parts are counterfeited in the Middle East. Recordings and tapes are duplicated almost everywhere without license or fee. And the list goes on.

Legal protection against intellectual property theft and counterfeit goods is not very effective. In the United States, trademark and copyright holders may register with the Customs Service and seek the blockade of pirated items made abroad.* Such exclusions are authorized in the Lanham Trademark Act of 1946 and the Copyright Act of 1976. Patent piracy is most often challenged in proceedings against unfair import practices under Section 337 of the Tariff Act of 1930. Section 337 proceedings traditionally involve some rather complicated provisions in Section 1337 of the Tariff Act of 1930. Prior to 1988, the basic prohibition was against: (1) unfair methods of competition and unfair acts in the importation of goods, (2) the effect or tendency of which is to destroy or substantially injure (3) an industry efficiently and economically operated in the U.S. Such importation was also prohibited when it prevented the establishment of an industry, or restrained or monopolized trade and commerce in the U.S.

The Omnibus Trade and Competitiveness Act of 1988 revised Section 337. The requirement that the U.S. industry be efficiently and economically operated was dropped. The importation of articles infringing U.S. patents, copyrights, trademarks or semiconductor chip mask works is specifically prohibited provided a U.S. industry relating to such articles exists or is in the process of being established. Proof of injury to a domestic industry is not required in intellectual property infringement cases. Such an industry exists if there is significant plant and equipment investment, significant employment of labor or capital, or substantial investment in exploitation (including research and development or licensing).

Determination of violations and the recommendation of remedies to the President under Section 337 are the exclusive province of the International Trade Commission (ITC). Most of the case law under Section 337 concerns the infringement of patents. While not quite a per

---

* See 19 U.S.C. § 1526, reproduced earlier in this Chapter. Sec. 526 is not ideal, but it is far better than the remedies available in most other countries. For example, the United States for years has tried to convince Canada to adopt equivalent legislation to block counterfeit goods at the border, to no avail.

se rule, it is nearly axiomatic that any infringement of United States patent rights amounts to an unfair import practice for purposes of Section 337. Section 337 proceedings result in general exclusion orders permitting seizure of patent counterfeits at any U.S. point of entry. However, the Customs Service finds it extremely difficult when inspecting invoices and occasionally opening boxes to ascertain which goods are counterfeit or infringing. Many counterfeits do look like "the real thing."

For most seizure remedies to work, the holder must notify the customs service of an incoming shipment of offending goods. Use of private detectives can help and is increasing, but such advance notice is hard to obtain. Nevertheless, the Customs Service seized $7.6 million worth of counterfeit goods in the first six months of fiscal 1987. More than one-third of the goods seized were toys and the three major sources were Taiwan, Korea and Hong Kong.

Infringement and treble damages actions may be commenced in United States courts against importers and distributors of counterfeit goods, but service of process and jurisdictional barriers often preclude effective relief against foreign pirates. Even if such relief is obtained, counterfeiters and the sellers of counterfeit goods have proven adept at the "shell game," moving across the road or to another country to resume operations. Moreover, the mobility and economic incentives of counterfeiters have rendered the criminal sanctions of the Trademark Counterfeiting Act of 1984 largely a Pyrrhic victory. Ex parte seizure orders are also available under the 1984 Act and the Lanham Trademark Act when counterfeit goods can be located in the United States. Goods so seized can be destroyed upon court order.

International solutions have been no less elusive. The GATT agreement on TRIPS addresses these problems, but its effectiveness remains to be tested. Various United States statutes authorize the President to withhold trade benefits from or apply trade sanctions to nations inadequately protecting the intellectual property rights of U.S. citizens. This is true of the Caribbean Basin Economic Recovery Act of 1983, the Generalized System of Preferences Renewal Act of 1984, the Trade and Tariff Act of 1984 (amending Section 301 of the 1974 Trade Act), and Title IV of the 1974 Trade Act as it applies to most favored nation tariffs. Slowly this carrot and stick approach has borne fruit. Under these pressures for example, Singapore drafted a new copyright law, Korea new patent and copyright laws, and Taiwan a new copyright, patent, fair trade and an amended trademark law. Brazil introduced legislation intended to allow copyrights on computer programs. Though these changes have been made, there is some doubt as to the rigor with which the new laws will be enforced when local jobs and national revenues are lost.

EDGE, PREVENTING SOFTWARE PIRACY THROUGH REGIONAL TRADE AGREEMENTS: THE MEXICAN EXAMPLE

20 N.C. J. Int'l Law & Com. Reg. 175 (1994).*

One reason developing countries may have an economic incentive to emphasize the short term when evaluating the costs of implementing an intellectual property system is that they face significant initial costs in its establishment. First, the government must write laws and expend resources on their enforcement. Second, "costs may arise due to the increased economic activity within a country. For example, new plants may require new roads or may cause environmental problems." Third, the country loses low cost access to expensive products. Pirated versions are usually cheaper than a legitimate version. Finally, the country's consumer surplus declines when purchasers are required to pay a higher price for the product.

Another reason that developing countries are less likely to implement these intellectual property protections is that a different attitude towards public and private property is often found in these countries. Developing countries do not have a history of recognizing intellectual property protection because in the past, these countries did not engage in the production of innovative products or information that required such protection. Furthermore, because these products benefit the society as a whole, the countries believe that information found in protected products, such as pharmaceuticals, should be a public good. Developing countries, therefore, are hostile to raising the expense of a product with a high public benefit by granting the developer a monopoly on its use or distribution.

A third reason why developing countries have weak intellectual property protections is that these countries often emphasize their need for the protected items to generate economic growth. They argue that with access to innovative products and information at a low cost, their economic condition would improve, and ultimately, the rest of the world would benefit from their economic growth.

An additional reason why developing countries frequently ignore intellectual property protection is that they tend to emphasize the short-term benefits of weak intellectual property protection. By using pirated technology, the developing country can acquire the materials needed for industrialization, but at a lower cost. The country can also allow the pirating of products to become a domestic industry employing local workers. Finally, by misappropriating foreign goods, a developing country can maintain its balance of trade by retaining resources, such as money, in the domestic economy.

To avoid the costs of an intellectual property system, developing countries often look for cheaper routes of obtaining technology. "Free riding" is one tactic for acquiring technology cheaply. Essentially, the country relies on piracy as a resource.

MEXICO'S MODIFICATION OF ECONOMIC POLICIES AND INTELLECTUAL PROPERTY PROTECTION

In response to the economic difficulties of the 1980s, the Mexican government began pursuing policies which encouraged international trade and provided stronger intellectual property protection for high technology products. The initial stages [1989–90] of this process involved lowering trade barriers and modifying the copyright laws. For computer goods, the Mexican government lowered the tariffs and licensing restrictions which had acted as a barrier to trade. It also [in 1991] revised the copyright law to provide express protection for software. In its most recent efforts, Mexico pursued the NAFTA, an agreement that will ultimately eliminate all trade barriers between the three signatories and provide strong intellectual protection for high technology products.

* * *

DESIGNATION AS A PRIORITY WATCH COUNTRY

While Mexico's economy was a substantial factor in leading to the modifications in its trade and intellectual property policies, another factor which should not be discounted was Mexico's placement on the priority watch list in 1989 by the USTR. Mexico was targeted under Section 301 for the weak intellectual property protection given to U.S. products. After the Mexican government took significant steps to strengthen its intellectual property laws, Mexico was removed from the priority watch list. The threat of trade sanctions under Section 301 appears to have been a significant impetus for the changes in Mexican law; it has also been credited with encouraging Mexico's participation in the NAFTA.

LAW FOR THE PROMOTION AND PROTECTION OF INDUSTRIAL PROPERTY*

Diario Official June 27, 1991.

(Amended D.O. Aug. 2, 1994).

Article 1. The provisions of this law are public in nature and of general observance throughout the Republic, without prejudice to that provided in international treaties to which Mexico is a party. Its administrative enforcement is vested in the Federal Executive acting through the Mexican Institute of Industrial Property.

* * *

* © West Group.

Article 6. The Mexican Institute of Industrial Property, which is the administrative authority in the area of industrial property, is a decentralized organ with juridical personality and its own property * * *

Article 199Bis. In administrative declaration proceedings relating to the violation of any of the rights protected under this law, the Institute may adopt the following measures:

I.   Order that merchandise which infringes the rights of those protected by this law be withdrawn from circulation, or that such circulation be restricted;

II.   Order the withdrawal from circulation of:

(a) Objects which are made or used illegally;

(b) Objects, packages, wrapping, paper, advertising material and the like, which infringe any of the rights protected by this law;

(c) Announcements, signs, billboards, paper and the like which infringe any of the rights protected by this law; and

(d) Utensils or instruments used in the manufacture, preparation or acquisition of any of the items described in the foregoing sub-sections (a), (b) and (c);

III.   Prohibit immediately the sale or use of products used to violate rights protected by this law;

IV.   Order the seizure of goods, in accordance with the provisions of articles 211 and 212Bis 2;

V.   Order the alleged violator or third parties to suspend or cease the activities constituting a violation of the provisions of this law; and

VI.   Order the suspension of services or the closure of an establishment when the measures prescribed in the foregoing sections are not sufficient to prevent or avoid a violation of the rights protected by this law.

If a product or service is already in the flow of commerce, those persons who sell such products or provide such services shall be obliged to abstain from their sale or provision from the date on which they are notified of the order.

Such obligations shall also apply to producers, manufacturers, importers, and their distributors, who shall have the responsibility of recovering immediately those products which are already in commerce.

Article 199Bis 1. In considering the application of the measures referred to in the preceding article, the Institute shall require the applicant to:

I.   Provide evidence that he is the owner of such right, and provide evidence of any of the following:

(a) The existence of a violation of his rights;

(b) That such violation is imminent;

(c) The possibility that he will suffer irreparable harm; and

(d) The existence of a well-based fear that evidence will be destroyed, hidden, lost or altered.

II. Produce a bond sufficient to cover damages which may be caused to the person against whom such measure has been requested; and

III. Provide the information necessary to identify the goods, services, or establishments, with which or in which the violation of industrial property rights may have been committed.

* * *

Article 211. If during the inspection there is credible evidence of the commission of any of the acts or circumstances described in articles 213 and 223, the inspector may impose a precautionary sequestration of the products involved in the presumed commission of such violations or crimes. An inventory of the sequestered assets shall be made and appear in the minutes of the inspection. The person in charge or the owner of the establishment in which the goods are located shall be designated as the depositary thereof, if such establishment is at a fixed place; otherwise, the products shall be held at the Institute.

In the case of facts or circumstances indicating the possible commission of crimes, the Institute shall mention such fact in the resolution which is issued for such purpose.

* * *

Article 212Bis 2. In event that the final resolution on the substance of the controversy declares that an administrative infraction has been committed, the Institute, with hearing given to the interested parties, shall decide upon the disposition of the sequestered assets in accordance with the following rules:

I. It shall place the sequestered goods at the disposition of a competent judicial authority as soon as it has been notified of the commencement of an action before such authority to remedy any physical damage or for the payment of damages;

II. It shall place such assets at the disposition of the arbitrator, in the event that arbitral proceedings have been elected;

III. It shall proceed, as the case may be, within the terms prescribed in any agreement executed by the affected owner and the alleged violator regarding the disposition of such goods;

IV. In cases not included in the foregoing sections, each one of the interested parties shall present in writing, within the five days following the hearing, his proposal regarding the disposition of the sequestered goods which have been withdrawn from circulation or whose sale has been prohibited;

V.   Each of the parties must be given an opportunity to respond to the proposals presented for the purposes of coming to a common agreement regarding the disposition of such goods and to communicate such agreement to the Institute within the five days following the date such opportunity was given; and

VI.   If the parties do not indicate their agreement in writing regarding the disposition of the goods within the time period conferred, or if none of the cases referred to in section I to III apply, within a time period of ninety days after the final resolution has been determined, the Board of Governors of the Institute may decide upon:

(a)   The donation of the goods to agencies or entities of the Federal Public Administration, federative entities, municipalities, public institutions, or to charitable or welfare institutions, when the public interest will not be affected; or

(b)   The destruction of the same.

Chapter II—Administrative Violations and Sanctions

Article 213. Administrative violations consist of:

I.   Carrying out acts contrary to good industrial, commercial or service sector usages and customs, which involve unfair competition and which are related to the subject matter regulated under this law;

II.   Making products which are not patented appear as products which are patented. If a patent has lapsed or has been declared null, such violation shall be incurred after one year from the date of lapsing or, as the case may be, from the date of final declaration of nullity;

* * *

XI.   To manufacture or prepare products covered by a patent or by a registration of a utility model or industrial design without the consent of its owner, or without its respective license;

XII.   To offer for sale or to place in circulation products covered by a patent or by a registration of a utility model or industrial design, knowing that they were manufactured or elaborated without the consent of the owner of the patent or registration or without the corresponding license;

XIII.   To use patented processes, without the consent of the owner of the patent or its respective licensee;

XIV.   To offer for sale or to place in circulation products which result from the utilization of patented processes, knowing that they were used without the consent of the owner of the patent or of the person who has a license for their exploitation;

* * *

Article 214. Administrative violations of this law or any other provisions arising therefrom shall be sanctioned with:

    I.   A fine up to the amount of 20,000 times the general minimum daily wage effective in the Federal District;

    II.   An additional fine up to the amount of 500 times the general minimum daily wage effective in the Federal District for each day in which the violation persists;

    III.   Temporary closure of up to 90 days;

    IV.   Permanent closure;

    V.   Administrative arrest of up to 36 hours.

Article 215. The investigation of administrative violations shall be carried out by the Institute on its own motion or at the request of an interested party.

* * *

Article 221. The sanctions established in this law and related legislation may be imposed in addition to compensation for damages suffered by those affected, under the general provisions of civil law, and without prejudice to that provided in the following article.

Article 221Bis. The repair of physical damages or compensation for damages for violation of rights conferred by this law shall in no case be less than 40% of the price of sale to the public of each product or service involving a violation of one or more rights of industrial property regulated under this law.

* * *

Chapter III—Crimes

Article 223. It shall be a crime to:

    I.   Repeat the activities prescribed in sections II to XXII of article 213 of this law, once the first administrative sanction imposed thereon has become final;

    II.   To intentionally falsify marks on a commercial scale;

    III.   To reveal to a third party an industrial secret obtained as a result of one's work, post, charge, professional undertaking, business relationship, or by the granting of a license for its use, without the consent of the person who holds such industrial secret, having been advised of its confidential nature, for the purpose of obtaining an economic benefit for himself or for a third party, and with the purpose of causing injury to the person holding the secret;

IV. To take possession of an industrial secret to use it or to disclose it to a third party, without authority and without the consent of the person who holds it or of its authorized user, for the purpose of obtaining an economic benefit for oneself or for a third party and with the objective of causing damage to the person who holds the industrial secret or to its authorized user; and

V. To use the information contained in an industrial secret which one has obtained by virtue of his work, charge, post, professional undertaking, or business relationship, without the consent of the holder thereof or of its authorized user, or to whom it has been disclosed by a third party, with the knowledge that such third party did not have the consent of the person who holds the industrial secret or its authorized user, for the purpose of obtaining an economic benefit and with the objective of causing damage to the person who holds the industrial secret or its authorized user.

The crimes prescribed in this article shall be prosecuted through criminal complaint brought by the injured party.

Article 224. Two to six years of prison and a fine of one hundred to ten thousand times the general minimum daily wage effective in the Federal District may be imposed on the person who commits the crimes described in the preceding article.

USTR, 2004 SPECIAL 301 REPORT*

Mexico

During the past year, Mexico took significant steps to improve IPR protection. The United States commends Mexico for resolving the "linkage" issue between the Mexican Institute of Industrial Property and the Ministry of Health by implementing in September 2003 a Presidential decree that requires applicants for safety and health registrations to show proof of a patent and proof that test data were obtained in a legitimate manner. In addition, Mexico enacted legislation classifying piracy as an organized crime, and has created a special IPR prosecutor within the Office of the Attorney General(PGR). However, lax enforcement at both the criminal and administrative level, and particularly against copyright piracy and trademark counterfeiting, remains a serious problem. Companies continue to report high rates of counterfeiting of trademarked products. Despite continuing to raise long-standing concerns over these issues, many trademarks owners in Mexico still have problems with enforcement and case administration. When counterfeit items are discovered, injunctive relief measures issued against trademark infringers are often unenforceable.

Copyright piracy remains a major problem in Mexico, with U.S. industry loss estimates growing each year and totaling $712 million in

2003—the second largest level of losses in the hemisphere. Pirated sound recordings and motion pictures are widely available throughout Mexico, crippling legitimate copyright–related businesses. Strong concerns remain over the amendments to Mexico's copyright law passed by the Congress in July 2003 and still in the process of implementation. These amendments failed to address the comprehensive reforms needed by Mexico to (1) effectively implement the obligations of the WIPO Copyright Treaty and the WIPO Performances and Phonograms Treaty (Mexico is a member of both treaties); and (2) address deficiencies in Mexico's copyright law, such as the failure to provide for national treatment and inadequate provisions regarding the scope of exclusive rights. The United States urges Mexico to take the necessary steps to resolve the current deficiencies.

Enforcement against piracy and counterfeiting in Mexico remains weak, and the few raids by Mexican authorities result in convictions of or deterrent penalties against pirates or counterfeiters. To strengthen enforcement, the United States urges Mexico to expand anti-piracy and anti-counterfeiting efforts against commercial distribution, street piracy and counterfeiting in all major cities; impose strong criminal penalties and destroy seized products, and increase the speed of administrative and judicial actions. In addition, the recently adopted organized crime law should be aggressively used to combat IPR infringements. We hope that previously held bilateral discussions on IPR can be revitalized to provide a constructive and productive forum to address and resolve these IPR concerns in an effective manner.

CAMP, IP PROTECTION IN MEXICO

Inter–American Trade Report (Sept. 5, 1997).*

Far and away, the greatest need for further improvement of the Mexican law relates to enforcement. There is no private right to injunctive relief for the infringement of either trademarks, trade secrets or patents. There are administrative remedies, including closure and temporary imprisonment, which may be carried out by IMPI [Instituto Méxicano de la Propriedad Industrial]. These administrative remedies are based upon investigations by IMPI inspectors and are ordered and carried out by IMPI officials. These procedures are increasingly effective for trademark protection, but are of doubtful effectiveness for the enforcement of patents or trade secrets.

The reason for this perceived disparity in enforcement of the administrative procedures, as between trademarks on the one hand and patents and trade secrets on the other, is the shortage of qualified inspectors for patent and trade secret violations. IMPI has succeeded in employing inspectors sufficiently qualified to verify trademark violations, but has not been able to employ inspectors who are qualified to make definitive determinations on patent infringements or trade secrets. Violations of patent rights or trade secret violations are not evaluated and judged exclusively by inspectors; such violations must also pass the inspection and evaluation of the IMPI legal department (Dirección de Protección a la Propiedad Industrial). Thus, while closure or imprisonment following trademark inspections is often immediate and, therefore, effective in controlling infringement, the same is not true for patents and trade secrets.

The evaluation of the inspector's report in the legal department of IMPI can last indefinitely, thus rendering completely ineffective the administrative provisional remedies available under existing law designed to suspend what is probably illegal use of others' intellectual property. The practical impact is that the infringer continues to profit from the stolen patent or trade secret and, indeed, is able to use part of his profits to finance the defense of the infringement claim. The prospect of such delay concerns property owners and can have a chilling effect on the desire of owners to transfer technology to Mexico or to invest in the development of that technology in Mexico.

Many owners believe that the private right to injunctive relief should be made available to them. The injunction itself is not broadly available under Mexican law. While it exists with respect to copyrights under articles 145 and 146 of the copyright law, it is seldom exercised.

KIRCHANSKI, PROTECTION OF U.S. PATENT RIGHTS IN DEVELOPING COUNTRIES: U.S. EFFORTS TO ENFORCE PHARMACEUTICAL PATENTS IN THAILAND

16 Loyola L.A. Int'l & Comp. L. J. 569 (1994).*

Although a number of studies have questioned whether it is beneficial for developing countries to adopt Western-type systems for intellectual property protection, many developing countries have adopted such systems. This choice probably has been motivated by a belief in the predicted benefits of an intellectual property system, as well as a belief that having an intellectual property system reflects a certain level of status. Now, the threats of trade retaliation employed by the United States are providing additional reasons for Third World countries to adopt an intellectual property system. Yet, adopting an intellectual property system, either by free choice or under compulsion, does not mean necessarily that the adoption of the system is in the country's best interest. The level of a country's development alters the cost-benefit ratio of granting patents. As a country develops, it will pass through a number of stages, each of which presents a different cost-benefit picture for the granting of patents. Several authors have suggested different versions of a model of economic evolution. The following scenario is a summary of their views.

The first stage is that of a country at a very low level of economic development. A completely under-developed country has little technological capacity and infrastructure, and will make few, if any, internationally patentable inventions. Such a country would not benefit from a patent system because, as an under-developed country, it would not be limited by a shortage of inventions but by the ability to utilize readily available technology. Whereas the economy of a developed country depends on new inventions, an under-developed country needs to expand its economy by implementing older inventions that are already available in the public domain.

As the country's economy develops, markets and the infrastructure necessary for innovation will also develop, and the country will reach the second stage. The country becomes capable of using more advanced technology and may become an intellectual property pirate. Such a country is often rapidly developing and fuels the growth of its economy through intellectual property theft.

Eventually, a country will reach the third stage of development, where its businesses can create world-class inventions. At that point, it becomes profitable for the country to grant patent protection so as to protect its own innovators. Profits from piracy of international intellectual property are outweighed by losses to the country and its inventors caused by failure to protect their own inventions. Because international intellectual property protection is on a *quid pro quo* basis, the country must provide strong patent protection so that other advanced countries will reciprocate and respect its patents. WICs, including the United States, reached this third stage over a century ago. Many of the difficulties with international intellectual property protection may be caused by a failure of WICs to recognize the evolutionary stages of patent protection.

* * *

These same observations, however, can be interpreted in a different way. First, pirating intellectual property has produced strong, growing economies. This supports the idea that countries at a certain level of development (the second stage) benefit greatly from pirating. Second, there is a wide range in the economic status of the pirate countries. Third, only the richest, most developed of the pirate countries (Korea and Taiwan) have been successfully "persuaded" to strengthen their intellectual property laws.

In other words, intellectual property pirating fuels development until the country reaches the point where intellectual property protection becomes economically advantageous. At that point in the development, represented by the transition from stage two to stage three in the model, an intellectual property system either develops or can be imposed successfully from the outside. This supports the interpretation that a country naturally adopts a comprehensive system of intellectual property protection only when it reaches an adequate level of development. Attempts to force a country to adopt an intellectual property scheme will be successful only if the country is sufficiently developed to benefit from the scheme. If the country has not reached this point, the costs of intellectual property protection will outweigh its benefits, and the protection scheme, if adopted, will be enforced only sporadically.

This interpretation could explain the results of the Pharmaceutical Manufacturers Association's efforts to promote worldwide patent protection for pharmaceuticals. Korea, Taiwan, and Canada have recently amended their patent laws to give improved protection to pharmaceuticals. The gross national product per capita, the number of scientific publications, the number of domestic patents, and the number of U.S. patents for these countries are quite high. These factors are consistent with the notion that these countries have already reached stage three of development. The success of the Pharmaceutical Manufacturers Association's efforts could indicate that these countries were simply ready to adopt pharmaceutical patent protection. An analysis of these same factors also suggests that Thailand ranks below the average of the pirate countries on most indicators of development. This would mean that, while the Thai economy is expanding rapidly, it has not yet reached stage three. It may be useless, or even counter-productive, to try to force a complete intellectual property system on a country before the country is adequately developed. It is too early to determine whether the system of pharmaceutical patent protection that the United States has forced on Thailand will be successful.

Proposed Alternatives to Current U.S. Practices

If strengthening intellectual property protection harms rather than benefits developing countries, the wisdom of the U.S. policy is questionable. A mechanism should be created that will protect a developing country from economic damage and promote development until that country reaches the stage at which it is profitable for the country to strengthen its intellectual property laws. One possible solution is to use economic incentives to alleviate potential damage.

There are three reasons why WICs should grant incentives to the least developed nations. First, unrestricted aid is necessary to develop the infrastructure of these countries so that the economy can improve to the point where protection of intellectual property is beneficial. Much of the current U.S. foreign aid to under-developed countries is granted with this goal in mind. Second, incentive aid should be aimed specifically at reducing the costs of the imposed intellectual property systems. Because, initially at least, WICs would be the major benefactors of the intellectual property system, they should help to defray the costs. Fortunately, the costs of operating a patent system in the poorest countries would be low; these countries represent such poor markets that the United States and other WICs do not bother to protect most of their intellectual property there. Thus, the volume of patents (and, therefore, the administrative costs of the system) will be low. Third, aid is needed to overcome the damage to developing economies caused by the increased costs of protected technologies—particularly those involving food production or health-care.

* * *

The form that the incentive aid should take must still be decided. Certainly, foreign aid payments to fund-development projects should continue. Direct aid payments should also be made to defer the operational expenses of fledgling patent systems until they can be supported by user fees. The problems surrounding the payment of royalties on pharmaceuticals and similar health/food items are more troubling. There are two competing goals. On one hand, it is in the interest of the United States to stimulate the economies of developing nations and to ensure their welfare. Not only would vigorous economies in the Third World provide a market for U.S. products, but peace and prosperity in the Third World would allow the United States to reduce its own internal military expenditures. On the other hand, the U.S. Government is also under considerable political pressure to guarantee the profitability of U.S. pharmaceutical companies by allowing them to collect royalties on the international use of their patents. Perhaps, this second goal is now less cogent than it was during the Reagan and Bush Administrations, considering the Clinton Administration's efforts to lower the domestic costs of pharmaceuticals.

Nevertheless, both goals could be met by making pharmaceuticals available to developing nations without royalty costs and having the U.S. Government rebate to the manufacturers a royalty payment based on the number of units shipped. Alternatively, the United States could allow its pharmaceutical companies to collect its foreign royalties, but then rebate the royalties as foreign aid to the lesser-developed countries. The drawback of this latter approach is that drug prices might increase unconscionably, and there is no guarantee that the foreign governments would share the rebates with their poorest citizens. It should be remembered that if the power of the United States is used to further retaliatory trade policies that force protection of pharmaceutical patents, the U.S. Government will effectively be subsidizing the pharmaceutical industry anyway. One unfortunate aspect of such policies is that the rest of the United States' foreign trade must bear the costs of the subsidy when the retaliatory tariff costs are passed on as higher prices on exports from developing countries. Nevertheless, this is the approach sanctioned by the current statutes. Once the royalty costs are covered by a subsidy, it might become economically viable for U.S. companies to undertake pharmaceutical production in the foreign country. In this way, the promised benefits of an intellectual property system would be obtained more rapidly.

The key to the subsidy system would be to end (perhaps gradually) the subsidy once the country reaches an adequate level of economic development. It is also possible for the exact criteria for ending the subsidy to be negotiated on a country-by-country basis. It is highly unlikely that a country could (or would want to) retard economic development artificially, simply to keep receiving a subsidy on pharmaceuticals. Thus, the goal of worldwide intellectual property protection could be achieved while ensuring the developing countries that such a system would necessarily be to their benefit.

Questions and Comments

1.   Does NAFTA require patents on pharmaceuticals? See Articles 1709.1, 1709.2, 1709.3 and 1709.4.

2.   What makes a good "counterfeit"? If dolaminazine is made in Mexico, is it counterfeit? Assuming Brazil does not allow pharmaceutical patents, if dolaminazine is made there is it counterfeit? And when Brazilian-made dolaminazine arrives in Mexico is it counterfeit?

3.   Suppose the dolaminazine is being made in Mexico in violation of SKBD's patent, what remedies must Mexican law provide? See Articles 1714, 1715, 1716 and 1717. Does the 1991 Mexican Industrial Property Law (as amended) meet these NAFTA requirements? See Articles 199 Bis, 212 Bis 2, 214 and 223.

Recall that Noah (excerpted in Part A) cited NAFTA as requiring the creation of injunctive remedies hitherto unknown in Mexico's intellectual property law tradition. Are such remedies found in the 1991 Industrial Property Law? Camp does not think so. Are they both right?

4.   Suppose the Mexican "pirate" producer of dolaminazine has been located and identified. *Which* remedies do you recommend SKBD pursue and why?

5.   Now let's assume that the source of the dolaminazine in Mexico is Brazilian. Does NAFTA address that possibility and, if so, how? See Articles 1716 and 1718. Does the Mexican Industrial Property Law cover imports of patent infringing articles? Assuming so, what must SKBD do to invoke these provisions? See the Note on Counterfeiting in Mexico and Article 199 Bis of the Mexican Law.

6.   Millions of containers of goods are shipped to Canada, Mexico and the United States each year. Less than one percent are ever opened. What does that suggest about the odds that authorities will uncover a shipment of counterfeit goods? How might SKBD improve those odds?

7.   Suppose Mexican officials have identified and seized a container load of Brazilian-made dolaminazine. What are the possible outcomes? Will the goods be destroyed? See NAFTA Article 1718.12 and Article 212 Bis 2 of the 1991 Mexican Industrial Property Law.

8.   Japan and Switzerland provide prominent examples of nations that chose to develop while limiting patent rights. The Swiss actually refused to grant *any* patents. Such policies allowed them to "borrow" liberally from the world's technological base. Why should not Mexico and Brazil be allowed to take a similar free ride? See the excerpt by Edge.

9.   Following Kirchanski's analysis, is Mexico a first, second or third stage country? Mexico clearly has strengthened its intellectual property laws. Was that done as a matter of self-interest or "persuasion" by the United States?

Kirchanski suggests that if a country has not reached stage three, where the benefits of intellectual property protection outweigh its costs, then it will enforce its IP laws "only sporadically." Is that true of Mexico? Of Canada? Of the United States?

10. What do you think of Kirchanski's proposal that the United States adopt financial incentive programs to encourage patent protection for pharmaceuticals? Is there any such program in NAFTA? Why not?

11. In addition to trademarks, copyrights, patents and trade secrets, NAFTA, Chapter 17 also covers geographical indications, layout designs of semi-conductor integrated circuits, and encrypted program-carrying satellite signals. Intellectual property coverage is somewhat expanded in Chapter 17 of the United States–Chile FTA, and Chapter 15 of CAFTA. In particular, both of the newer agreements provide protection for domain names on the Internet, and expanded protection for all types of digital products (software, music, text and videos).

12. According to USTR, protection for copyrights, trademarks and patents is also strengthened in these agreements. With regard to pharmaceuticals, rules restrict generic drug patent application approvals for five years if, as is often the case, the application relies on test data compiled by the manufacturer of the original drug. In effect, such rules will create short-term exclusive rights for branded drugs, which may be very valuable. Drug patent issues became a contentious issue in Congress with regard to approval in the United States and Australia of the U.S.–Australia Free Trade Agreement, and in the FTA negotiations between the U.S. and the Andean countries, and with Panama in late 2004.

Chapter 9

DISPUTE SETTLEMENT

9.0 INTRODUCTION

It is very difficult to overemphasize the importance of the various NAFTA dispute settlement processes. While today the efficiency and fairness of the WTO's Dispute Settlement Body are largely unquestioned (despite some Members' unhappiness with specific decisions), this was not the case with the GATT process prior to 1995. The experience under the GATT too often illustrated that an inadequate dispute settlement process significantly diminishes the value of the entire trade agreement. The NAFTA drafters were well aware of the deficiencies of the GATT, and tried to avoid them during the NAFTA negotiations in 1991–1992. They were also aware of the general acceptance of the dispute settlement experience under the CFTA, and tried to replicate their most successful features. No part of the NAFTA experience has received more attention from the press, from scholars, and sometimes from those directly involved, than the settlement of disputes under Chapters 11, 19 and 20 of NAFTA. In part, this results from the substantial number of cases brought under the NAFTA provisions, more than 35 under Chapter 11, over 100 under Chapter 19 and more than a dozen under Chapter 20.

This chapter deals primarily with dispute settlement under NAFTA Chapters 19 and 20. Chapter 7 of this book, on foreign investment, addresses investment dispute settlement under NAFTA Chapter 11. Dispute settlement under NAFTA's labor and environmental side agreements is covered in Chapters 10 and 11 of this book, respectively.

GORDON, NAFTA DISPUTE PANELS: STRUCTURES AND PROCEDURES

R. Folsom, M. Gordon and J.A. Spanogle, Handbook
on NAFTA Dispute Settlement (1998).*

THE CFTA AND THE NAFTA

NAFTA dispute resolution provisions have roots in the CFTA, an agreement which created new ties to the largest bilateral trading relationship in the world. The dispute resolution process created in the CFTA is much the result of Canadian dislike for what it viewed as an overly aggressive U.S. use of antidumping and countervailing duty laws. But the CFTA dispute resolution *experience* illustrates a general satisfaction both with the dumping and subsidy dispute resolution process as carried out under Chapter 19 of the CFTA, and also with the separate process for more general issues under Chapter 18 of the CFTA. Panel processes proved faster than the time experiences of national courts. Also, panel procedures operated smoothly, and the panelists were for the most part thought to have conducted their reviews professionally, and performed thorough analyses of the facts and arguments. The CFTA dispute resolution framework was nevertheless less comprehensive than that agreed to in the subsequent NAFTA negotiations. The ability to carry forward the dispute resolution concepts in the two-nation CFTA to the three-nation NAFTA, and indeed expand them, owes much to the success of the CFTA, even though it predates the NAFTA by only five years.

The CFTA included several specific dispute settlement provisions. Chapter 16 of the CFTA, on Investment, included dispute resolution provisions which incorporated parts of the previous Investment Canada Act, the Canadian laws regulating foreign investment. The Chapter 16 provisions of the CFTA were precautionary, exempting from CFTA investment dispute resolution decisions made under the Investment Canada Act with respect to reviewable acquisitions; reserving rights under customary international law to investments not covered in the chapter; preserving rights under the GATT and under any other international agreement to which the two parties belonged; and requiring full consideration to arbitration or Chapter 18 panels with panelists "experienced and competent in the field of international investment." Investment dispute resolution provisions in the NAFTA are less protective of domestic investment than in the CFTA; there are fewer exemptions than under the CFTA. The NAFTA sets forth an elaborate scheme for the settlement of investment disputes, with consultation, negotiation, arbitration and, in the event of continued dispute, a tribunal. The provisions for the settlement of investment disputes are quite different from other NAFTA dispute resolution processes, including dispute resolution involving financial services (except financial services *investment* issues), allegations of subsidies and dumping, and the broad, general provisions of Chapter 20.

The broadest dispute settlement provisions in the CFTA, parallel in context but far fewer in number of provisions to Chapter 20 of the NAFTA, were included in Chapter 18 of the CFTA. Entitled Institutional Provisions, they covered all disputes under the Agreement except those involving financial services under Chapter 17, and antidumping and countervailing duty cases under Chapter 19. The Agreement created the Canada–United States Trade Commission as, among other things, the dispute resolving body for Chapter 18 issues. The Commission was given the power to establish its own rules and procedures. Where the Commission failed to resolve a dispute, it would be referred to Chapter 11 (Emergency Action), or to an arbitration process which involved the use of special panels, with detailed procedures.

A general reference to Chapter 19 dispute resolution may mean either the CFTA or the NAFTA. Chapter 19 in each agreement was the chapter assigned for rules relating to dispute settlement of antidumping and countervailing duty cases. The structure of these two chapters is nearly identical. The NAFTA Chapter 19 is a development of the briefly functional but quite successful experience of the CFTA Chapter 19 panel process. The CFTA Chapter 19 process was intended to be short-lived; the parties were supposed to develop alternative processes for dumping and subsidies. During its brief lifetime, none were developed. The CFTA Chapter 19 thus was present and active when the NAFTA was being negotiated, and played an important role in the fashioning of Chapter 19 of the NAFTA.

As previously noted, the CFTA did not include special dispute resolution provisions beyond Chapter 17 consultations for *financial services* disputes. As discussed below, the NAFTA financial services dispute resolution provisions are quite modest, but constitute a further step from those in the CFTA. The NAFTA Chapter 14 financial services provisions generally fully incorporate NAFTA Chapter 20 dispute resolution procedures, unless the parties wish special Chapter 14 financial services panels. When the dispute involves foreign *investment* in financial services, however, there are additional special provisions in the NAFTA Chapter 14, discussed in detail in the context of problem 6.3. The CFTA financial services provisions allowed only for consultations, and this minimal reference to financial services disputes illustrated the sensitivity of financial services, further supported by the exclusion of matters under CFTA Chapter 17 from the Chapter 18 dispute resolution processes.

The creation of a government-to-government dispute resolution mechanism in the form of the Commission in the CFTA was one of the major accomplishments of the CFTA negotiating process. There was some comparable experience with the GATT procedures, but the GATT dispute process had some evident shortcomings. Sessions of the GATT Contracting Parties initially heard informal complaints. Later, a system of panels with independent experts developed. However, both the establishment of a panel and reaching a decision were often easily blocked by a GATT Contracting Party. This consensus approach soon made evident its inherent weaknesses. The Uruguay Round, leading to the creation of the WTO and its Understanding on Rules and Procedures Governing the Settlement of Disputes, attempted to improve the dispute resolution processes, especially by changing the practice of reaching a decision by consensus, with one of the disputing parties consequently able to block the decision. The CFTA did not build upon the GATT processes, partly because of the difference between a multi-nation and a bilateral agreement. The CFTA created the Chapter 18 binational trade Commission to resolve, or at least commence the process of resolution of, most disputes. Significantly, the CFTA, like the GATT and the later NAFTA, did not allow individuals standing to challenge other government's actions under the Agreement. CFTA Chapter 18 differed from the GATT, however, by allowing a party receiving a favorable decision from a panel to take action, even though the Commission did not agree on the resolution of the dispute.

THE DISPUTE SETTLEMENT PROVISIONS OF THE NAFTA

1. The Settlement of General Disputes Under Chapter 20

Chapter 20 dispute resolution may prove to be the process that will endure as the most important dispute resolution part of the NAFTA.* While it is thus far little used, and not very clear in many respects, it is the process for settling disputes for nearly all areas except principally (1) subsidy and dumping issues, and investment conflicts. If subsidy and dumping provisions are ever eliminated, which currently does not seem likely, Chapter 19 dispute resolution would be rendered obsolete. Many observers believe that if the NAFTA is to reach the level of success in free trade that has been achieved by the European Union, which does not recognize subsidy or dumping actions between Member States, actions based on subsidies or dumping must be ended within NAFTA. Were Chapter 19 dispute resolution eliminated, that would leave Chapter 20 as the principal interpretive process for most disputes. If a formal court with jurisdiction to interpret NAFTA provisions is ever to develop, as in the European Union, it will likely evolve from Chapter 20, or at least from the Chapter 20 experience, but certainly also influenced by the history of Chapter 19 proceedings.

* * *

2. The Settlement of Subsidy and Dumping Disputes Under Chapter 19

Chapter 19 of NAFTA builds upon the generally agreed upon success of Chapter 19 of the CFTA. It is very limited in scope, applying only to

* Authors' note: While Chapter 20 has not produced extensive litigation between the NAFTA governments—only three decisions in ten years—and in that sense has proven less important that Chapters 11 and 19, Chapter 20 has served as a model for government-to-government dispute settlement in the FTAA drafts, and in the U.S. FTAs with Singapore, Chile, CAFTA and others.

unfair trade (dumping and countervailing duty) actions. During the brief period of the CFTA there were 49 panels initiated, with decisions rendered in 30, and only three decisions leading to an extraordinary challenge procedure. Although there is some sense that the experience under the CFTA was more successful for Canadian rather than United States exporters, the general support for the process led the NAFTA negotiators to adopt nearly the same panel and extraordinary challenge committee framework.

* * *

The success of the CFTA Chapter 19 panels made the formulation of the NAFTA Chapter 19 process relatively easy. CFTA panels had the reputation for complying with the time schedule, rendering impartial and high quality decisions, and rendering decisions which brought forth compliance.

* * *

3. The Settlement of Emergency Action Disputes Under Chapter 8

This perhaps ought to be titled the *prohibition* of the establishment of an arbitral panel in response to a proposed emergency action. Emergency actions are allowed under Chapter 8, but only during the transition period. After the ten year transition period, an emergency action may be initiated only with the consent of the Party whose goods are challenged, essentially ending the effective use of the action. But even during the transition period, the use of the action is limited.

If a Party against which the emergency action is taken, or possibly the third Party, is opposed to the proposed emergency action, a request may be made for consultations under Chapter 20. If consultations are not successful, use of the Commission's good offices, conciliation or mediation is also available under Chapter 20. Article 804, however, prohibits the next step a Party might take under Chapter 20, a request for the establishment of an arbitral panel under Article 2008. This essentially eliminates the use of Chapter 20's legal adjudication, the adopted process based on a preference that the matter be settled by a more consensus based procedure short of appointment of a panel. But the prohibition is only for a panel regarding a proposed emergency action, and may not apply for one to rule on the interpretation of NAFTA safeguard language.

The Article 804 prohibition is a perhaps the most significant exclusion provision of the NAFTA, although there are some exclusions for certain investment related issues in Article 11. There are also Chapter 21 exceptions, which are not specific exceptions to the initiation of a process of dispute settlement, but defenses which may be used if a Party does initiate a process....

4. The Settlement of Investment Disputes Under Chapter 11

There is no binational panel system for investment disputes. The focus of Chapter 11 is on the use of international arbitration. While nothing prevents an investor and a Party from using arbitration in the event of an investment dispute in the absence of Chapter 11, it provides a procedure calling for consultations and subsequently, if unsuccessful, more formal arbitration using a combination of ICSID or UNCITRAL and NAFTA rules.

Mexico's experience with the Calvo Clause long posed some problems when a private investor's government assisted the investor in a dispute with Mexico. The United States has always rejected the Calvo Clause, but it remained as a partial obstacle in the NAFTA negotiations of investment provisions. If a Party (Canada or the United States) could not take up the cause of one of its citizens with an investment in Mexico, who was aggrieved at the action of the government of Mexico, Party-to-Party dispute settlement would be impossible. Mexico agreed to change its view, leading to the structure of Articles 1116 and 1117. . . .

* * *

5. *The Settlement of Financial Services Disputes Under Chapter 14*

Chapter 14 acknowledges the uniqueness of financial services disputes, or perhaps the political power of the financial sector in demanding separate provisions. It provides for a two-part process, and has a cross-relationship with the Chapter 11 investment dispute settlement provisions. It further draws upon Chapter 20 for certain arbitral panel procedures.

* * *

Separate dispute resolution provisions for financial services disputes were included in order to assure that dispute panels addressing issues under Chapter 14—"Financial Services"—could be composed of persons with "expertise or experience in financial services law or practice, which may include the regulation of financial institutions." As discussed in the section dealing with the selection of the panels, the formation of financial services panels may vary depending upon the demands of the Parties.

If the financial services issue constitutes an *investment* dispute, the rules are different and governed by Article 1415. Since investment disputes come within the Chapter 11 investment provisions, Article 1415 integrates financial services investment dispute resolution concepts with the provisions of Chapter 11, rather than Chapter 20.

* * *

THE CHOICES OF DISPUTE SETTLEMENT UNDER THE NAFTA AND/OR THE WORLD TRADE ORGANIZATION (WTO)

When the NAFTA was concluded, the Uruguay Round was in its final stages. But because the new WTO was not yet in existence, references in the NAFTA are to the GATT, and sometimes also to "any agreement negotiated thereunder, or any successor agreement." One ought to read GATT to mean WTO unless otherwise noted.

* * *

Choices Under the NAFTA

The NAFTA, like the CFTA, has numerous references to the GATT to affirm existing rights under GATT, or incorporate provisions and procedures of the GATT. The NAFTA provisions which govern NAFTA and GATT dispute settlement procedures are in the seven-part Article 2005. The basic premise in this Article is similar to that in the CFTA, that disputes may be settled in either forum at the discretion of the complaining party. The complaining Party is likely to choose the forum best suited to its claim. Exceptions of qualifications to complaining Party discretion in choosing the forum are the subject of three sections of the article. First, before one NAFTA Party initiates a proceeding in the WTO against a second Party to the NAFTA, where the action could also be brought under the NAFTA dispute resolution procedures, the initiating Party must notify the third NAFTA Party of its intention. Thus a complaint by Canada against the United States must be preceded by notification to Mexico by Canada. If the third Party, in this case Mexico, would also like to be a complaining Party, but would prefer that the matter be settled under NAFTA dispute settlement procedures, it must consult with the original complaining Party and, unless that original complaining Party is successful in convincing the third Party that the WTO is the better forum, the matter will "normally" be settled under the NAFTA.

In three cases the responding party may cause a matter to be held exclusively under the NAFTA. First, in any action where the responding Party claims the matter is subject to Article 104 ("Relation to Environmental and Conservation Agreements"), second, where the responding Party claims the matter is subject to Section B of Chapter Seven ("Sanitary and Phytosanitary Measures"), and third, where the responding Party claims the matter is subject to Chapter Nine ("Standards–Related Measures"). In each case the responding Party must make the demand for consideration under the NAFTA in writing, and deliver it to the other Parties and to the Party's Section of the Secretariat. The delivery must be no later than 15 days after the complaining party has initiated dispute settlement proceedings. If these procedures are followed, the complaining Party must withdraw the proceeding from the other forum, now the WTO, and commence a proceeding under NAFTA Article 2007.

Once a proceeding has been initiated under Article 2007 in NAFTA, the WTO is no longer available as a forum. Similarly, except for the exceptions noted above, once a proceeding has been initiated under the WTO, that forum is exclusive. The initiation of a proceeding under the GATT is deemed to be a request for a panel, which continues under the

WTO (Understanding on Rules and Procedures Governing the Settlement of Disputes).

* * *

This Chapter contains five problems, but covers only part of the full NAFTA dispute resolution structure and process. This Chapter concentrates on the dispute resolution processes of Chapters 19 and 20 of NAFTA, and on private commercial disputes only briefly referred to in Article 2022 of Chapter 20 of NAFTA, and left for resolution by means of traditional judicial and non-judicial (NAFTA preferred) methods.

Any reference to the resolution of disputes in NAFTA ought not omit comment on the resolution of *labor* and *environmental* disputes. The substantive rules of these two important spheres, and the procedures for the resolution of disputes, have been left to two separate side agreements outside the main NAFTA. Labor and the environment, respectively, are the subjects of Chapters 10 and 11 of this book.

Within this chapter, Problem 9.1 discusses two important issues. The first is the process of panel selection, which is quite different depending upon whether the panel is formed under Chapter 19 or 20. The second is the conduct expected from the panel members, especially the issue of conflicts of interest. The participants in a Chapter 14 financial services dispute may be selected under Chapter 20 rules, or using provisions of Chapter 14 which assure participation by persons with expertise in financial services. Chapter 11 investment disputes have panels selected in a very different manner, because Chapter 11 refers matters to ICSID or UNCITRAL arbitration.

Problem 9.2 inquires into the role of a Chapter 19 panel in a dumping case. The majority of Chapter 19 cases under CFTA and NAFTA have involved the review of dumping determinations.

Problem 9.3 covers Chapter 19's review of injury determinations in unfair trade cases, and the use of Extraordinary Challenge Committees.

Problem 9.4 turns to Chapter 20, which covers a much broader range of issues than Chapter 19, essentially governing all NAFTA disputes not otherwise specifically covered, such as the dumping and subsidy issues under Chapter 19. A Chapter 20 challenge may be brought against many different actions of a Party, actual or proposed.

Lastly, Problem 9.5 draws upon the very few provisions of NAFTA which focus upon the settlement of private commercial disputes, and which emphasize the use of arbitration. NAFTA has generated considerable private commercial litigation because of the increased volume of trade. While arbitration is often used, much is left to judicial resolution under national court systems.

PROBLEM 9.1 PANEL SELECTION AND THE CODE OF CONDUCT: ATTORNEYS AS PROSPECTIVE PANELISTS

SECTION I. THE SETTING

Growing up in El Centro, California, along the U.S.-Mexico border, was not always easy but gave attorney Francisco ("Frank") Puente many of the bilingual and intercultural skills necessary to prosper in the new North American legal market spawned by NAFTA in the mid 1990s. Frank attended law school in New York City in the late–1970s and received an advanced degree in international law from Georgetown Law School in the 1980s.

Frank spent nearly a decade as an associate and, later, as a partner at a prominent Washington, D.C. law firm specializing in international law. During the early–1990s, he served as a consultant to the Government of Mexico on matters related to the negotiation of NAFTA. On several occasions, Frank has represented Canada, Mexico and other governments in various transactions with U.S. corporations.

A few years ago, as his NAFTA-related practice began to thrive, Frank joined a colleague in opening his own firm, Puente & Wilson, L.L.P., in the District of Columbia. Frank's practice involves mostly international transactional work but, increasingly, involves representing foreign companies in litigation, arbitrations and mediations in the United States. Since 1995, he has represented Mexican companies in two proceedings challenging final antidumping duty determinations by the International Trade Administration (ITA) of the U.S. Department of Commerce. Although Frank expects the demand for this type of legal service to remain stable for the foreseeable future, his partner, Pamela Wilson, is likely to handle all such matters that come to their firm in the future.

At least once a year, Frank teaches an international trade course as an adjunct professor at the American University, Washington College of Law. Several of his law review articles on NAFTA and especially dispute resolution under NAFTA have been well-received in academic circles and are cited frequently. Somehow, Frank also manages to make six or seven presentations a year at conferences throughout North America on NAFTA-related topics.

Shortly after NAFTA entered into force, Frank applied for membership on the NAFTA Chapter 19 roster of eligible panelists. Despite his occasional representation of foreign governments, Frank was placed on the roster in 1996, and has been reappointed annually (after completing a fresh application) ever since.

As you consider the readings and answer the questions which follow, assume that you are an intern in the Office of the United States Section of the NAFTA Secretariat. Periodically, the Secretariat receives a new

Request for Panel Review from a Canadian or Mexican company seeking review of a final antidumping or countervailing duty determination of the Commerce Department's International Trade Administration (ITA) or a final injury determination by the U.S. International Trade Commission. Less frequently, the Secretariat receives a request that a Chapter 20 arbitral panel be convened. Your objective is to learn the procedures for forming Chapter 19 and 20 panels and what roster members such as attorney Frank Puente must disclose to ensure that there are no conflicts of interest or ethical concerns with their service on such panels.

SECTION II.　FOCUS OF CONSIDERATION

This problem examines the processes set forth in Chapters 19 and 20 for the selection of panelists. The processes under each Chapter differ somewhat but are relatively straightforward. The NAFTA Parties' experience since 1994 with the panel selection provisions reveals a number of significant concerns, including delay in the selection process, the Parties' disregard of the stated deadlines for making panelist choices, and the failure of the Parties to establish a roster of eligible panelists for Chapter 20 disputes. Although panel proceedings have not moved as swiftly as under CFTA, and almost never meet the deadlines specified under either Chapter 19 or Chapter 20, many of the Chapter 19 proceedings–particularly during the first five years of NAFTA—have been completed more quickly than domestic proceedings in trade matters in the United States, before the Court of International Trade and the Court of Appeals for the Federal Circuit.

Another major concern focuses on the panelists themselves. At the time they negotiated NAFTA, the Parties understood that the success of the Chapter 19 and 20 dispute settlement mechanisms would hinge in large part on the integrity and impartiality of those who serve as decision-makers in such proceedings. To ensure the integrity and impartiality of panelists, the Parties adopted the Code of Conduct for Dispute Settlement Procedures Under Chapters 19 and 20 of NAFTA ("the Code"). The Code stipulates a variety of obligations owed by panelists, including responsibilities to the dispute resolution process, disclosure obligations, duties relating to the performance of panel duties, the independence and impartiality of panelists, and the maintenance of confidentiality. The Code expressly applies to persons who are panelists, potential panelists or former panelists as well as to persons who work as assistants to the panelists.

A number of controversies regarding the Code have arisen in recent years. One issue relates to the ambiguity of certain terms in the Code, such as "appearance of impropriety" and "interest, relationship or matter that is likely to affect the candidate's independence or impartiality." Another point of contention is that the Code requires the disclosure of all possible conflicts without limitation as to time or materiality. Finally, some commentators have argued that consistency in the application of the Code is elusive because Mexican, Canadian and U.S. cultures have differing interpretations of what constitutes a "conflict of interest." These controversies will be touched on below.

NAFTA Annex 1901.2, Articles 2009 through 2011, and the Code of Conduct for Dispute Settlement Procedures Under Chapters 19 and 20 of the North American Free Trade Agreement are essential to an analysis of this problem. They are included in the Documents Supplement.

SECTION III. READINGS, QUESTIONS AND COMMENTS

PART A. CHAPTER 19

CHAPTER 19'S DISPUTE RESOLUTION PROCESS*

Dispute resolution under Chapter 19, unlike Chapter 20, begins with a request for an arbitral panel. No prior consultations or Free Trade Commission review are necessary because Chapter 19 cases, in essence, are appeals of prior rulings by a government agency that dumping has occurred [or an actionable subsidy has been furnished] and has injured a domestic industry. The steps leading to the agency's final determination include the information-gathering, complaint, and response opportunities that Chapter 20's initial stages (of consultation and Commission intervention) are designed to provide.

Chapter 19 panels consist of five panelists who are drawn from a preformed roster of a minimum of twenty-five judges, former judges, and lawyers from each NAFTA Party. (As of mid–2004, there were 40 plus persons listed on the Canadian roster, 38 on the Mexican roster, and 70 on the U.S. roster.) Within thirty days of a panel request, the involved NAFTA Parties each select two panelists and, within twenty-five days thereafter, agree on the selection of the fifth panelist. In practice, the fifth panelist rotates by nationality. If, for example, there are three U.S. panelists and two Mexican panelists on case no. 1, there will be three Mexican panelists and two U.S. panelists on case no. 2, and so on. A majority of the panelists and the chair of the panel must be lawyers in good standing. Unfortunately, the selection process is often delayed (probably through indifference rather than bad faith), and it is not uncommon today for completion of the panel selection process to require three years or more. The NAFTA governments have discussed the delay problem at high levels periodically in recent years, but the situation has not measurably improved. The Parties still decline to select panelists by lot from the rosters as provided in Chapter 19, defeating one of the major purposes of having standing rosters. However, not all Chapter 19 cases have been delayed. For example, in the several actions involving the United States' decision to impose antidumping and countervailing duties on softwood lumber from Canada in 2002, the initial panel decisions (subject to remands) were issued in approximately one year.

* * *

* Adapted and updated from Lopez, Dispute Resolution Under NAFTA: Lessons From the Early Experience, 32 Tex. Int'l L.J. 163 (1997). Copyright © 1997 Texas International Law Journal and David Lopez. Reprinted with permission.

HOLBEIN & GREENIDGE, NAFTA CODE OF CONDUCT PROVIDES INTERNATIONAL GUIDELINES FOR ETHICAL BEHAVIOR

1 NAFTA: L. & Bus. Rev. Am. 50 (1995).*

PERSONS GOVERNED BY CODE OF CONDUCT

In accordance with the requirements of Articles 1909 and 2009 of NAFTA, the governments of Canada, Mexico, and the United States have negotiated a Code of Conduct. The Code applies specifically to members and former members of panels established to review ... AD/CVD determinations under Article 1904 or general disputes under Article 2008.... The Code also applies to members and former members of special committees established pursuant to Article 1905 or extraordinary challenge committees formed under Annex 1904.13 of the Agreement. In addition, the Code sets forth disclosure obligations for members of rosters established pursuant to Article 1414 (financial services), Article 2009 (general issues) or Annex 1901.2 (AD/CVD) or 1904.13 (special or extraordinary challenge committees) and for individuals not on a roster who are under consideration for appointment to a panel or committee. Assistants and staff members of covered individuals are also bound by certain obligations. The Code is based on the Code of Conduct existing under the CFTA, "with certain changes made to better ensure the integrity and impartiality of the proceedings under the Agreement."

NAFTA SECRETARIAT

The NAFTA Secretariat is a unique organization created under Chapter 20 to administer binational panel review procedures to settle disputes under the NAFTA. Consisting of "mirror image" offices in Washington, Ottawa and Mexico City, the three Secretariat sections work together to provide administrative support to panels and maintain a file system for all case documents, functioning much like the Clerk of the Court in judicial reviews. It has no substantive role in panel deliberations or the outcome of decisions.

THE SECRETARIAT'S ROLE UNDER THE CODE

The Secretariat acts as a buffer between the Parties, participants, the public and panelists to ensure that *ex parte* communications and political pressures do not influence panel actions. To that end, the Secretariat handles all interactions among the participants, Parties, panelists and candidates concerning the Code of Conduct including:

● obtaining disclosure information from potential panelists;

● obtaining supplementary information once a panel is named;

● informing participants of the composition of the panel;

- receiving inquiries from panelists concerning changes in their circumstances and the possible impact on their further participation;

- referring questions to panelists from the Parties and funneling responses back for consideration;

- referring allegations from participants against panelists to the Parties for further instructions; and

- when a panelist withdraws from an active review, providing notice to all participants that the matter is suspended until a replacement panelist is named.

INDEPENDENCE AND IMPARTIALITY GENERALLY

The Preamble to the Code states that "the Parties place prime importance on the integrity and impartiality of proceedings" under the dispute settlement provisions of the Agreement. The general obligations are outlined below:

- Each member must avoid impropriety and the appearance of impropriety and must be independent and impartial.

- Members must also avoid entering into any relationship or acquiring any financial or personal interest likely to affect his or her impartiality or that might reasonably create an appearance of impropriety or apprehension of bias.

- Members of Article 1904 panels are prohibited from representing a participant in an administrative proceeding, domestic court proceeding or another Article 1904 panel proceeding involving the same goods.

TEST FOR APPEARANCE OF IMPROPRIETY OR APPREHENSION OF BIAS

The NAFTA Code further builds on the CFTA Code by supplying a test for the principle of appearance of impropriety or bias found in the U.S. and Mexico and in Canada (as "apprehension of bias"). The governing principle of the Code of Conduct is that a candidate under consideration for service on a panel or committee or a member of a panel or committee must disclose the existence of any interest, relationship or matter that is likely to affect the candidate's or member's independence or impartiality or that might reasonably create an appearance of impropriety or an apprehension of bias. An appearance of impropriety or an apprehension of bias is created ... where a reasonable person, with knowledge of all the relevant circumstances that a reasonable inquiry would disclose, would conclude that a candidate's or member's ability to carry out the duties with integrity, impartiality and competence is impaired.

The test is drawn from the "reasonable person" or "objective observer" test enunciated in the Code of Conduct for United States Judges, which was considered by the NAFTA Parties to reflect appropriate elements of the test found in the jurisprudence of each country. Panels and committees in Chapter 19 proceedings replace judicial review in the courts of competent jurisdiction in the NAFTA countries. Like those under the CFTA, even though members serving on Chapter 19 panels should be generally familiar with international trade law, they are held to the standard articulated in Chapter 19 and the Code of Conduct. By adopting the reasonable person test, the NAFTA Parties emphasized the need for the public and litigants, particularly with respect to Chapter 19 proceedings, to have the same degree of confidence in the integrity and impartiality of the panel system as they would a court. Similarly, the U.S. Judicial Conference commented in its Code of Conduct for United States Judges that " ... violation of [the] Code diminishes public confidence in the judiciary and thereby does injury to the system of government under law." NAFTA requires that the roster include judges and former judges "to the fullest extent practicable."

GOVERNING PRINCIPLE OF DISCLOSURE

The Code includes an Introductory Note to help clarify the duty of candidates for inclusion on a panel or members of existing panels. As this Note states:

> The governing principle of the Code is that candidates and members must disclose any interest or relationship or matter likely to affect their independence or impartiality or that might create an appearance of bias.

DISCLOSURE OF FINANCIAL INTERESTS

Specific requirements include disclosure of any financial interests of a candidate in a proceeding or in its outcome and in an administrative proceeding, a domestic court proceeding or another panel or committee proceeding that involves issues that may be decided in the proceeding for which the candidate is under consideration. Additionally, a candidate must disclose such financial interests of a candidate's employer, partner, business associate or family members as well as past or existing financial, business, professional, family or social relationships with any interested parties in the proceeding, or their counsel, involving the candidate or a candidate's employer, partner, business associate or family member.

DUTY TO DISCLOSE IN WRITING

Candidates in Chapter 19 and 20 proceedings must make disclosures in writing by completing an initial disclosure statement. This form is agreed upon by the three Parties to the agreement and is forwarded to the candidates by the Secretariat as part of the process for consideration of a candidate for appointment to a panel. After examining the complaint, members selected to review a final antidumping or countervailing duty determination must also complete a supplementary disclosure statement.

CONTINUING OBLIGATION TO DISCLOSE

Candidates are required to become aware of and continue to disclose relevant interests. These disclosure obligations continue throughout the course of a proceeding once a candidate is appointed to serve on a panel or committee. Candidates affirm in their initial disclosure that they will, once appointed, become aware of and continue to disclose relevant interests by submitting the disclosure in writing to the responsible Secretariat for consideration by the Parties which are represented by the United States Trade Representative, the Canadian Department of Foreign Affairs and International Trade [now International Trade Canada] and the Mexican Secretaría de Comercio y Fomento Industrial (SECOFI) (The Secretaria de Economia—SECON—in recent years).

Issue Conflicts

The Code requires disclosure of any interests that a member, his or her employer, partner, business associate or family member has in an administrative proceeding, domestic court proceeding or another panel or committee proceeding involving issues that may be before the panel to which he or she has been selected. Additionally, members must disclose public advocacy, legal or other representation on an issue disputed in the proceeding or involving the same goods. The requirement that all members appointed in Chapter 19 proceedings review the complaints and complete a supplementary disclosure statement is imposed to ascertain at the earliest stage possible whether a panelist could be disqualified. One basis for such possible disqualification may be that the panelist representing a client in a matter before the agency whose determination is under review by the panel then advocates a position on an issue before the panel.

Frequent Suspensions for Issue Conflicts

A dozen panelists have withdrawn and panels have been suspended pending the selection of replacement panelists under the CFTA. This problem with issues forcing the withdrawal of panelists has occurred more frequently than one might expect because so many of the panelists are active members of the trade bar. They are prohibited from sitting on a panel while they are appearing in an administrative proceeding, a domestic court proceeding or another panel or committee proceeding that involves issues that may be decided in the proceeding for which the panelist has been selected. NAFTA allows panelists to engage in other business during the proceeding, but they may not do so in contravention of the Code of Conduct.

Performance of Duties

Panelists, committee members and their assistants are required by the Code to fairly and diligently perform their panel duties, including being available or easily contacted, avoiding *ex parte* communications, maintaining the confidentiality of the proceeding and participating fully in the process. For a period of one year after the completion of an Article 1904 proceeding, a former member shall not personally advise or represent any participant in the proceeding with regard to antidumping or countervailing duty matters. A former member must also avoid actions that may create the appearance that the member was biased in carrying out the member's duties or would benefit from the decision of the panel or committee.

INDEPENDENCE AND IMPARTIALITY OF MEMBERS

The Code requires panelists and committee members to be independent, impartial, act in a fair manner, and to not be influenced by self-interest, outside pressure, political considerations, public clamor, loyalty to a Party or fear of criticism. In addition, they must avoid, directly or indirectly, incurring any obligation or accepting any benefit that would in any way interfere, or appear to interfere, with the proper performance of their duties. They may not use their positions on panels or committees to advance any personal or private interests. A member cannot allow past or existing financial, business, professional, family or social relationships or responsibilities to influence the member's conduct or judgment. Finally, a panelist or committee member must avoid entering into any relationship, or acquiring any financial interest, that is likely to affect the member's impartiality or that might reasonably create an appearance of impropriety or an apprehension of bias.

MAINTENANCE OF CONFIDENTIALITY

The Code contains specific provisions concerning member and former member obligations for maintaining the confidentiality of non-public information, including the NAFTA requirement that members not disclose which members are associated with majority or minority opinions. This duty extends to maintaining the confidentiality of a panel or committee decision until its release by the Secretariat.

DUTIES OF FORMER MEMBERS

After completion of an Article 1904 proceeding, former members of such proceeding may not for a period of one year advise or represent any participant in the proceeding on antidumping or countervailing duty issues. Like members, former members of Article 1904 panels may not represent a participant in an administrative proceeding, domestic court proceeding or another 1904 proceeding involving the same goods. Former members must avoid any actions that might create the appearance that he or she was biased while serving on a panel or committee.

ASSISTANTS AND STAFF

The Code provisions concerning responsibilities to the process, disclosure obligations and maintenance of confidentiality also apply to assistants and staff. Members have an additional duty to ensure that their assistants and staff observe those obligations.

DISQUALIFICATION AND VIOLATIONS OF THE CODE

The NAFTA provides that if a disputing Party believes that a panelist has violated the Code of Conduct, the disputing Parties must consult. If the disputing Parties are in agreement that there has been a violation, the panelist must be removed and a new panelist selected....

The NAFTA Chapter 19 rules also provide that where a participant believes that a panelist or assistant has violated the Code they must make the allegation in writing to the responsible Secretary. The responsible Secretary will then promptly notify the Parties of the allegation for further investigation.

As noted earlier, candidates or members are not required to disclose "trivial" matters and the Code does not determine under what circumstances the Parties will disqualify a candidate or member based on a particular disclosure made. Under CFTA practice, the Parties generally agreed on the removal and replacement of panelists, or conversely on the retention of panelists, after evaluating a disclosed conflict or appearance of conflict. In most instances where panels were suspended and new panelists selected, panelists recused themselves sua sponte once a conflict or appearance of bias arose.

* * *

CONCLUSION

The CFTA and NAFTA Codes of Conduct establish a high standard for professional and ethical conduct of individuals serving as nongovernment experts in politically sensitive trade disputes. The area of conflict of interest and appearance of bias or misconduct is problematic for all individuals involved in these systems. The definition of appearance of bias or misconduct is sometimes difficult to apply to individuals explicitly permitted to perform other business while serving on NAFTA panels or committees. The depth of the search conducted by candidates and the ability to identify actual or perceived conflicts on often sketchy information is both difficult and expensive for many candidates, especially those in large firms. The system is functioning due in no small part to the integrity of those individuals who have served and the detailed requirements of the Code of Conduct. In the drafting process of the NAFTA Code of Conduct, the Parties intended to tighten existing central CFTA Code provisions concerning impartiality, disclosure, appearances of bias and issue conflicts. To provide guidance and further clarify candidate and member obligations, the Parties added a test for appearance of bias, emphasized issue conflict prohibitions, revised the disclosure statement and added a supplementary disclosure statement requirement for Article 1904 proceedings. Because the NAFTA Parties were interested in continuing the CFTA dispute settlement procedures as an efficient and effective mechanism, the Code of Conduct was prepared to foster that goal. It is incumbent upon candidates, members and former members of Chapter 19 and 20 panels or committees to adhere to the letter of the Code of Conduct, particularly the Code's disclosure obligations. The Parties rely on such disclosures in order to exercise their right under the NAFTA dispute settlement mechanism to accept or reject a candidate. Since Chapter 19 dispute settlement replaces judicial review of antidumping and countervailing duty cases in Canada, Mexico and the United States, it is imperative that all safeguards to ensure that panelists adhere to the principle of impartiality and the appearance of impartiality in the conduct of those proceedings. The Code of Conduct is a central safeguard of that principle. Only time and experience under this intense form of scrutiny of those serving in dispute settlement roles will tell whether this mechanism will be applicable to other international agreements.

———

NAFTA SECRETARIAT U.S. Section

14th Street & Constitution Avenue., N.W. Washington, D.C. 20230

May 18, 1999

Prof. David Lopez
St. Mary's Law School
One Camino Santa Maria
San Antonio, TX 78228

Professor Lopez:

CONSIDERATION FOR APPOINTMENT AS PANELIST USTR has advised me that you are being considered for appointment to a binational panel to be convened under Article 1904 of the NAFTA. The panel will review the final antidumping duty Investigation respecting Certain Stainless Steel Round Wire From Canada made by the International Trade Administration, U.S. Department of Commerce. The Request for Panel Review was filed with the U.S. Section of the Secretariat on May 7, 1999, and has been assigned Secretariat File No. USA/CDA–99–1904–04.

ENCLOSURES: Please disclose any affiliation with the steel industry or any of the NAFTA governments in your disclosure form. I am enclosing several documents to aid in your conflicts search in this matter, as follows:

         1) disclosure statement

         2) availability form

         3) tentative time line

         4) service list of interested parties

         5) request for panel review

         6) final determination

         7) code of conduct

RESPONSE: If at all possible, please return your completed disclosure statement and availability form to me by fax not later than Monday June 21, 1999. If you do not choose to fax your disclosure statement, please send it by courier to me at the address above by the same date. I will relay them to USTR for final selection.

SELECTION INFORMATION: For your information, five panelists must be agreed upon by USTR and External Affairs by Wednesday, July 7, 1999 for both cases. I will contact you, if you are selected, with further instructions. Should you have any questions concerning the selection process or the panel review process, please call me.

Sincerely yours,

United States Secretary

    cc: Office of the General Counsel, USTR Denis Fortier, Acting Canadian Secretary Rafael Serrano Figueroa, Mexican Secretary

Enclosures as stated

NORTH AMERICAN FREE TRADE AGREEMENT

In the Matter of Stainless Steel Round Wire From Canada

Secretariat file No. USA/CDA–99–1904–04

INITIAL DISCLOSURE STATEMENT

I have read the *Code of Conduct for Dispute Settlement Procedures under Chapters 19 and 20 of the North American Free Trade Agreement* (Code of Conduct). I am fully aware that Part II of the Code of Conduct requires that I disclose any interests, relationships and matters that are likely to affect my independence or impartiality or that might reasonably create an appearance of impropriety or an apprehension of bias in the matter cited above.

I have read the request for panel or committee review filed in the matter cited above and have made all reasonable efforts to determine whether there are any such interests, relationships or matters. I make the following statement fully aware of my duties and obligations under the Code of Conduct.

1. I do not have any financial or personal interest in the matter cited above or in its outcome, except as follows:

2. I do not have any financial or personal interest in an administrative proceeding, a domestic court proceeding or another panel or committee proceeding that involves issues that may be decided in the matter cited above, except as follows:

3. Neither my employer, partner, business associate or family member has a financial or personal interest in the matter cited above or in its outcome, except as follows:

4. Neither my employer, partner, business associate or family member has a financial or personal interest in an administrative proceeding, a domestic court proceeding or another panel or committee proceeding that involves issues that may be decided in the matter cited above, except as follows:

5. I do not have any past or existing financial, business, professional, family or social relationship with any interested parties in the matter cited above, or their counsel, nor am I aware of any such relationship involving my employer, partner, business associate or family member, except as follows:

6. I have not publicly advocated, nor have I provided legal or other representation, concerning any issue in dispute in the matter cited above or involving the same goods, except as follows:

7. I do not have any interests or relationships, other than those described above, nor am I aware of any matters, that are likely to affect my independence or impartiality or that might reasonably create an appearance of impropriety or an apprehension of bias, except as follows:

I recognize that, once appointed, I have a continuing duty to make all reasonable efforts to become aware of any interest, relationship or matter within the scope of Part II of the Code of Conduct that may arise during any stage of the matter cited above and to disclose it in writing to the Secretariat, as and when I become aware of it.

[typed name, signature and date]

SUPPLEMENTARY DISCLOSURE STATEMENT
(ARTICLE 1904 PROCEEDINGS)

I am fully aware that Part II of the Code of Conduct requires that I disclose any interests, relationships and matters that are likely to affect my independence or impartiality or that might reasonably create an appearance of impropriety or an apprehension of bias in the matter cited above. I have read the complaint in the matter cited above. I have made all reasonable efforts to determine whether there are any such interests, relationships or matters. I make the following statement fully aware of my duties and obligations under the Code of Conduct.

1.   I do not have any financial or personal interest in an administrative proceeding, a domestic court proceeding or another panel or committee proceeding that involves issues that may be decided in the matter cited above, except as follows:

2.   Neither my employer, partner, business associate or family member has a financial or personal interest in an administrative proceeding, a domestic court proceeding or another panel or committee proceeding that involves issues that may be decided in the matter cited above, except as follows:

3.   I have not publicly advocated, nor have I provided legal or other representation, concerning any issue in dispute in the matter cited above, except as follows:

[typed name, signature and date]

NAFTA SECRETARIAT ORIGINAL TIME LINE FOR REQUEST FOR PANEL REVIEW NAFTA ARTICLE 1904 AS OF 1999/05/10

STAINLESS STEEL ROUND WIRE FROM CANADA

USA–CDA–99–1904–04

FINAL DETERMINATION PUBLISHED: / /

R. 34	Request for Panel Review filed in USA on - 1999/05/07	Day 0
R. 39	Complaint to be filed by - 1999/06/07	Within 30 days after Request for Panel Review
R. 40	Notice of Appearance to be filed by - 1999/06/21	Within 45 days after Request for Panel Review
Annex 1901.2(3)	Panel Selection to be completed by Parties by - 1999/07/01	Day 55
R. 41	Final Determination and Reasons Index, Admin. Record to be filed by - 1999/07/06	Within 15 days after Notice of Appearance
Annex 1901.2(3)	Parties to select 5th Panelist by - 1999/07/07	Day 61
R. 57(1)	Briefs by complainants to be filed by - 1999/09/07	Within 60 days after filing of Admin. Record.
R. 57(2)	Briefs by Investigating Authority or Participant in support filed by - 1999/11/08	Within 60 days after Complainants' Briefs
R. 57(3)	Reply Briefs to be filed by - 1999/11/23	Within 15 days after Authority's Briefs
R. 57(4)	Appendix to the Briefs to be filed by - 1999/12/03	Within 10 days after Reply Briefs
R. 67(1)	Oral Argument to begin by - 1999/12/23	Within 30 days after Reply Briefs
Article 1904.14	PANEL DECISION DUE BY - 2000/03/17	Within 90 days after the Oral Arguments

HOLBEIN, NAFTA CHAPTER 19: THE U.S. SECRETARIAT'S PERSPECTIVE

Practicing Law Institute, 1075 PLI/Corp 769 (1998).*

An occasional problem for some panelists is the lifetime prohibition on representing participants in the panel review in administrative proceedings, domestic court proceedings or another Article 1904 proceeding. Other panelists have expressed concern about the prohibition for one year on representing participants in the panel proceeding in any other antidumping or countervailing duty proceeding. Additionally, the broad disclosure requirements in the Code of Conduct make it difficult for many roster members to be completely certain that all relevant facts have been discovered and disclosed. This uncertainty is compounded when the panel review concerns such items as steel and cement. It is often difficult for the Secretariat to provide detailed lists of the members of coalitions of firms in a given industry. Without lists of members, it is difficult for roster members to review computer runs of clients to ensure that the law firm is not representing a client in a given industry.

* * *

GANTZ, RESOLUTION OF TRADE DISPUTES UNDER NAFTA'S CHAPTER 19: THE LESSONS OF EXTENDING THE BINATIONAL PANEL PROCESS TO MEXICO

29 L. & Pol'y Int'l Bus. 297 (1998).**

Even though panelists serve part-time, with only token compensation, they are subject to a detailed code of conduct. The code requires disclosure of any circumstances that raise a conflict or appearance of conflict. For example, the code requires disclosure of "[a]ny past or existing financial, business, professional, family or social relationship with any interested parties in the proceeding, or their counsel, or any such relationship involving a candidate's employer, partner, business associate or family member...." The provision is extremely expansive. There are no time limits or materiality requirements with regard to these relationships. If a prospective panelist's law firm worked for an interested party in a matter unrelated to trade law twenty years ago, or another member of the firm had a social relationship with an interested party or its counsel, disclosure would technically be required and failure to disclose would be a violation of the code. If a binational panelist were hired by a law firm as a consultant for a specific case unrelated to the panel matter or any of the interested parties, that consulting relationship arguably would make the law firm the candidate's "business associate," and any possible conflicts of the law firm would have to be disclosed. The result is that the code could be interpreted to preclude a panelist or his or her law firm from accepting any legal business that presents a conflict or appearance of conflict, however remote, without the consent of the two affected NAFTA governments.

While there is a need for a code of conduct, the situation inevitably generates conflicts or the appearance thereof, because most panelists are practicing attorneys who continue their professional activities during the panel process. Panelists have on occasion faced the choice of withdrawing from a proceeding or asking their firm to forego new business, or even faced delays in changing firms because of the time required to seek the governments' views on potential conflicts, however remote. Avoidance of conflicts is essential to the functioning of the panel process. However, the problem is exacerbated by delays that ironically are caused periodically when a panelist is required to resign because of a conflict that has developed after the panel has been convened.

In addition, the perception of what constitutes a conflict of interest or an appearance of a conflict may vary among attorneys of different cultures. The U.S. concept of "appearance of conflict" is probably broader than the Mexican concept. It can be argued that the potential disqualification of a prospective panelist for any possible appearance of conflict, however remote and after full disclosure to the parties, operates as a significant bottleneck in the panel process. Difficulties on the part of the NAFTA governments in forming panels—due in part to actual or perceived conflicts—have caused a suspension of the panel process on at least nine occasions. Despite the rule that panel selection is to be completed within 55 days of the request for a panel, the average panel selection has required 108 days. The practical need for attorney panelists to appear before their respective administering authorities at the same time they are serving as panelists on unrelated matters may also raise questions as to whether such ongoing adversary relationships are colored by panel service, or vice versa.

Actual, rather than apparent, conflicts have been a serious problem for some panels. Logically enough, candidates for panel positions "shall not be affiliated with a Party . . . ." While undefined in the NAFTA, this bars government employees and presumably anyone with a paying consulting relationship with the government from serving as a panelist. One extraordinary challenge under the CUSFTA was based on alleged conflicts that had not been disclosed. In one of the initial Mexican NAFTA cases, two Mexican panelists resigned at different times as a result of actual or alleged conflicts.[5] In another, two Canadian panelists resigned and had to be replaced, one because of conflicts.[6] In each

---

5. *See Flat Coated Steel Products from the United States*, MEX–94–1904–01, Opinion at 8 (1996). One panelist inexplicably accepted a position with the Mexican Government, despite the NAFTA requirement that "candidates shall not be affiliated with a Party [government]" . . . and was forced by the government to resign. The other left the panel after a series of public and private allegations of conflicts or appearances of conflicts, and several mysterious office break-ins during which data and computer equipment were stolen.

6. *See Rolled Steel Plate from Canada*, MEX–96–1904–02 . . . . One panelist resigned for lack of time; the other because he

instance these resignations caused delays ranging from several to many months. In the first case, when the resignations occurred after a public hearing, the remaining panelists, along with the two replacements, concluded that a second public hearing should be convened in order to avoid any question as to whether the interested parties had an appropriate opportunity to present their positions to all panelists who would be participating in the decision.

* * *

... the NAFTA Code of Conduct for panelists should be revised to soften the catch-all provision that requires disclosure of "[a]ny past or existing financial, business, professional, family or social relationship with any interested parties in the proceeding, or their counsel, or any such relationship involving a candidate's employer, partner, business associate or family member...." At a minimum, the NAFTA governments should consider issuing guidelines with examples of conflicts or appearances of conflicts that would be considered material or significant, and those which could be ignored after disclosure. The conflicts problem for sitting panelists would also be reduced somewhat if there were fewer, but better paid, panelists, and if the NAFTA governments cooperate in facilitating prompt appointment of panelists under existing regulations. Although full disclosure of potential conflicts, already required under NAFTA rules, must continue, national government policies that disqualify panelists only for significant conflicts or appearances of conflicts rather than for irrelevant ones, along with guidelines for prospective panelists, should be emphasized. Also, the use of isolation techniques, so that panelists can be insulated from knowledge of matters on which other law firm members are working that might raise conflict issues, should be considered in appropriate circumstances.

LUTZ, LAW, PROCEDURE AND CULTURE IN MEXICO UNDER THE NAFTA: THE PERSPECTIVE OF A NAFTA PANELIST
3 Sw. J. L. & Trade Am. 391 (1996).*

Failure of some binational Panelists from both the United States and Mexico to adequately examine and disclose existing and potential conflicts of interest have led to a number of problems, namely untimely suspensions of Panels extending the time for resolution of disputes well beyond the prescribed 315 days. Such delays and the inability of Panelists, once selected, to adequately serve risks the loss of both public confidence in the system and questions its integrity. One of the persistent criticisms of the binational process regards the time it takes. Many of the delays that have been experienced in the process with Mexico can be directly traced to suspensions of Panels due to the recusal or withdrawal of Panelists.

took a consultancy position with the Canadian government.

Since Panelists that serve on Panels are drawn from the private sector, the NAFTA required that they not be "affiliated" with any country and that they abide by a Code of Conduct for Panelists. The fact that one of the only three grounds for review of a Panel's decision under the Extraordinary Challenge Committee process includes conflicts of interest and misconduct of a Panelist underscores the importance of strict adherence by Panelists to the Code of Conduct.

In my experience, the most troublesome issues arising in the binational Panel process—generally collected under the rubric of "conflicts of interest"—are: conflicts arising from personal relationships; the meaning of "affiliated with a Party"; general (or group) financial and other bias (e.g., partner in law firm, professor in university); and "appearance of impropriety or an apprehension of bias". Each of these issues is problematic in practice either because it is inadequately defined, or because there is a lack of general understanding among potential panelists of the meaning of the proscribed conflict, due largely to differing legal cultures.

With the assistance of the national NAFTA Secretariat in defining terms and clarifying institutional expectations under the Code of Conduct, panelists should be certain that they are, and will be able to remain, "conflict-free" for the duration of the Panel review. While the Code does a fairly good job of providing a checklist of conflict categories for panelists, a few key concepts may be helpful to focus on when doing one's self-evaluation for conflicts: 1) when in doubt, disclose; 2) anything that might affect a panelist's independence or impartiality should also be disclosed; 3) anything that might reasonably create an appearance of impropriety or an apprehension of bias should be disclosed; and 4) all of the above continue in effect from beginning to the end of any service on a Panel.

Questions and Comments

1. What qualifications are required for a person to serve as a Chapter 19 panelist? See Annex 1901.2(1). Is Frank eligible to serve as a Chapter 19 panelist? How many potential panelists ("candidates") is the Chapter 19 roster supposed to include?

2. What is the process for selecting the five members of a panel? See Annex 1901.2(2)–(3). In choosing panelists, are the Parties limited to individuals listed on the roster of eligible panelists? How is the chair of a panel selected? See Annex 1901.2(4).

3. According to Annex 1901.2, what is supposed to happen if a Party delays more than 30 days in making its two initial appointments to a panel? See Annex 1901.2(2). What is supposed to happen if, by the 55th day after the request for a panel, the Parties cannot agree on the selection of a fifth panelist? See Annex 1901.2(3).

4. Based on your review of the letter from the NAFTA Secretariat—U.S. Section to Professor Lopez, is it realistic, in practice, to expect that the disputants can select any panelists within 30 days after the request for a

panel? Assuming that the 30–day deadline for initial panel selections is unrealistic and, further, that the deadlines for panel selection normally have not been met in practice, does this suggest that the Chapter 19 panel selection process is defective? See Holbein.

5. What general responsibilities do candidates, panelists and former panelists owe to the dispute settlement process? See Code of Conduct, Section I; Holbein & Greenidge. What disclosures are such persons obligated to make? See Code of Conduct, Section II; Initial Disclosure Statement; Gantz. What duties do panelists assume once they are selected to serve on a panel? See Code of Conduct, Sections III, IV & VI. What obligations do former panelists possess? See Code of Conduct, Sections V & VI; Holbein & Greenidge.

6. Chapter 19 panelists must disclose the existence of any interest, relationship or matter that might reasonably create an "appearance of impropriety" or an "apprehension of bias." What is the test for "appearance of impropriety" and "apprehension of bias"? See Holbein & Greenidge.

7. One day while you are working at the Secretariat, a new request for a Chapter 19 panel arrives. In this case, a Mexican steel company is challenging a final countervailing duty determination of the ITA. The Secretariat soon will mail a letter to Frank Puente informing him that he is being considered for appointment as a panelist in this case. Which of the following interests, relationships or matters must Frank disclose in the Initial Disclosure Statement:

   a. that Frank and the attorney representing the Mexican steel company met one another when they were both attending Georgetown Law School;

   b. that the attorney representing the Mexican steel company was a student in one of Frank's international trade classes at American University;

   c. that Frank and the attorney representing the Mexican steel company spoke on panels together at a number of NAFTA-related conferences in 1999? 1997? 1995?

   d. that the attorney representing the United States was a partner at Frank's former law firm during the time Frank was a junior associate;

   e. that the Mexican steel company was a client of Frank's former firm in the mid–1980s, although not one of the clients for whom Frank provided legal services;

   f. that, in a recently published law journal article, Frank argues that antidumping and countervailing duty determinations by the ITA are inappropriately influenced by interest groups representing the U.S. steel industry;

   g. that Frank has served as a consultant to the Mexican and Canadian governments;

   h. that Frank's partner, Pamela Wilson, is representing a U.S. steel company in a Chapter 19 panel proceeding filed in Mexico;

    i.   that Frank is serving as a consultant to the United States government on domestic issues completely unrelated to Chapter 19 proceedings; and

    j.   that $500,000 Frank has set aside in retirement investments includes $3,000 worth of U.S. steel industry stocks.

    8.   Are there reasons why the United States might be unlikely to select a candidate like Frank for service on a NAFTA panel? If so, what are those reasons?

    9.   Assume that Frank makes all appropriate disclosures on the Initial Disclosure Statement and is appointed to the Chapter 19 panel that will decide the Mexican steel company's complaint. Six months into the panel proceedings, Frank's partner, Pamela Wilson, is retained (at the rate of $125 per hour) by the United States government to assist it in connection with matters relating to the World Trade Organization (WTO). Does the Code of Conduct require Frank to disclose the relationship between Pamela and the United States? See Section II.C. Does the relationship between Puente & Wilson and the U.S. government render Frank a person "affiliated with a Party," in contravention of Annex 1901.2(1)? What do attorneys such as Frank sacrifice in serving as Chapter 19 panelists?

    10.   Same as in 9, above, but assume that Pamela Wilson is retained at $300 per hour to represent a client in a non-steel antidumping case before the Commerce Department, in which one of the legal issues before Commerce is identical to one of the legal issues before Frank's panel. Assume that Frank is being compensated at the now standard rate for Chapter 19 and Chapter 20 panelists, CDN$800 per day, up from CDN$400 up to 2001, currently about US$80 per hour. If the choice is between Pamela's foregoing her new representation, or Frank's resigning from the panel, what is the likely result? Note that when a panel proceeding drags on for several years rather than being completed in or near the requisite 315 days, the likelihood that one or more panelists will be forced to retire because of such conflicts increases, resulting in further delays in completing panel reviews.

    11.   Chapter 19 does not expressly authorize or mention that the NAFTA governments are to conduct background checks of each potential panelist or of the panelist's business and personal interests. Chapter 19 does not empower the governments to subpoena documents from prospective panelists or review their income tax records to determine panelists' sources of income. In what ways, then, might a panelist's violation of the Code of Conduct be discovered?

    12.   What happens if a Chapter 19 panelist is disqualified for violating the Code of Conduct? See Annex 1901.2(9); Rules 81 & 82 of the Rules of Procedure for Article 1904 Binational Panel Reviews.

PART B. CHAPTER 20

GANTZ, DISPUTE SETTLEMENT UNDER THE NAFTA AND THE WTO: CHOICE OF FORUM OPPORTUNITIES AND RISKS FOR THE NAFTA PARTIES

14 Am. U. Int'l L. Rev. 1025 (1999).*

The arbitral panel process contemplates the use of a standing roster limited to thirty persons designated by the NAFTA Parties, with experience in "law, international trade, other matters covered by this Agreement or the resolution of disputes arising under international trade agreements" who are independent of the governments and comply with an applicable code of conduct. Thus, the panelists need not be lawyers, and presumably, the "independent of the governments" requirement means that they cannot be government employees. Where there are no more than two disputing Parties, a group of five arbitrators will be chosen, normally from the roster. Interestingly, in a unique "reverse selection process," one Party chooses the two national arbitrators of the other Party. For example, in the *Dairy Products* case, the United States selected the two Canadian panelists from a list of candidates offered by Canada, and Canada selected the American panelists from a list of candidates offered by the United States. The two governments choose the chairperson of the panel by agreement; if there is no agreement, a Party chosen by lot selects the chair of the panel, who may not be a citizen of the disputing Parties. Thus, in the normally contemplated situation—and in fact in the two cases that have reached arbitration under Chapter 20—the panels consist of two nationals from each of the disputing Parties, and a chairperson from a neutral country. Where all three NAFTA Parties are involved in the proceeding, the chairperson will be chosen in the same manner, but the Party complained against chooses two panelists, one national each from the complaining Parties, and the complaining Parties will choose two panelists who are nationals of the party complained against.

Despite the flexible criteria for panelists, eight of the ten panelists who have served on the two cases under Chapter 20 to date [now 11 of 15 in the three cases] have been law professors.[9] Of the remaining [four]

9. *See In re Tariffs Applied by Canada to Certain U.S.-Origin Agricultural Products*, CDA–95–2008–01, Report of the Panel (Dec. 2, 1996) (appointing American law professors Sidney Picker, Jr. and Stephen Zamora, Canadian professors Ronald C.C. Cuming and Donald M. McRae, and British professor Elihu Lauterpacht to the binational review panel).... In [*In re U.S. Safe-guard Action Taken on Broom Corn Brooms from Mexico*, USA–97–2008–01], the panelists were American law professors John H. Barton and Robert H. Hudec, Mexican law professor and attorney Dionisio Kaye, Mexican attorney Raymundo Enriquez, and a non-lawyer Australian government official, Paul O'Connor. [Authors' note: In the third case, *Cross-Border Trucking Services*, USA–98–2008–1, all five panelists, J. Martin Hunter, Luis Miguel Diaz, David A. Gantz, C. Michael Hathaway and Alejandro Ogarrio were lawyers.]

panelists, three are attorneys, while the other is a non-lawyer (non–Party) government official.

Ideal Timeline for NAFTA Chapter 20 Panel Selection Process
(Two Disputing Parties)

Request for Arbitral Panel by Party filed on	Day 0
Selection of Chair to be completed	within 15 days after Request for Arbitral Panel
Panel Selection to be completed	15 days after selection of Chair

PICKER, THE NAFTA CHAPTER 20 DISPUTE RESOLUTION PROCESS: A VIEW FROM THE INSIDE
23 Can.-U.S. L.J. 525 (1997).*

There have been, to date, two cases [three as of 2004] brought under Chapter 20 of NAFTA. The one on which I served has proceeded through the entire process; the other is still at the beginning stage. The first one is the dairy/poultry case, which has caused some (not altogether surprising) reaction among at least some of the government personnel.

* * *

As a dispute proceeds along in the arbitral process, it should be noted that it is considered, once elected, to be almost entirely confidential. . . .

In practice, confidentiality is extended straight through to the names of the panelists during the process itself so that when the appointment is made, no one is supposed to know who we are. Only after that final report does anyone else ever know the names of the five people who have participated, regardless of how they voted. That confidentiality aspect was violated in our case. If any of you are familiar, we were appointed in January of 1996, and within twenty-four hours, the committee and the press posted a full list of who we were, along with our nationalities. . . .

When that occurred, we never did know who was responsible for the leak. It had not happened before. But it did not appear to us to create any substantial problem. As far as we were concerned, there seemed to be something of a star chamber quality about the process where you do not know who the decision makers are supposed to be. We had suggested to the secretariats that the names should have been made public, anyway. It is prohibited by the rules under which they operate which interpret the agreement, and they would not do so. Thereafter, we could not even confirm or deny if we were actually panelists for the remainder of the almost year that we served.

It did not seem to disrupt the process in any way. Perhaps the reason for trying to keep our identities confidential was so we would not be harassed by interested parties. Perhaps it had no effect on us because we were law professors, after all. Who could harass a law professor, but another law professor or a dean?

* * *

Once an arbitral panel is requested, a panel must be established. In preparation for this, Canada, Mexico, and the United States were obliged to create a roster of thirty persons. It does not specifically state that they must be balanced, ten from each nation, but since they must be agreed to by consensus, that would have been the normal assumption. That was to have been done by January 1, 1994, but it has never happened. We have heard that comment before. It has not been established. Does it affect the process? Yes and no.

There was never a requirement under NAFTA that a panel must be drawn exclusively, or even at all, from the roster. Under the agreement the three countries are free to assemble the panel from anybody outside the roster that they wish; however, the hooker is if you draw from the roster, then there can be no complaint about the person drawn. If each country selects a person who is on the roster, there is no veto. If a person is put forward who is not drawn from the roster, there is a system of what is virtually unlimited peremptory challenges. Each opposing party may cast as many vetoes as it wishes. That is one of the problems of not having a roster, and that is one of the reasons why you ended up with five professors. Many of the people who would be put forward are likely to be vetoed by one government or another for political or other reasons.

There is a second problem that is created by not having the roster in place, and that is the conflict-of-interest provisions. NAFTA has fairly rigid conflict-of-interest provisions, and I am not questioning the reasons for them. But there should be no conflicts of interest with respect to the panelists, nor should there be the appearance of conflicts of interest. But the fact that these very strong provisions are in place makes it very difficult to put together a panel without either a conflict or an appearance of a conflict, especially when the matter is so broad as dealing with so much of the dairy and poultry industry, and much of agriculture was actually affected by that decision.

As a result, with most people and most of those who were not academic types, there would tend to be a conflict of interest. If you do not have a roster in place, which would have been a pre-clearance process, then what you end up with is having a relatively small pool of people from which you can draw where that conflict is not present.

It is interesting to note that those conflict-of-interest provisions, incidentally, apply to assistants as well. While the agreement itself does not say so, each panelist is entitled to an assistant, like a clerk. Actually it is not limited to one, and one of our panelists had two assistants, making eleven people altogether. It comes as no surprise that, of the eleven people who participated in the process, five panelists and six assistants, ten of them were drawn from academia. I am not saying that that is good, bad, or indifferent; it was a fact of life. The eleventh person was an assistant who was a young law clerk in a law firm. He had to withdraw halfway through the process because his firm engaged a client where there could have been the appearance of a conflict of interest. This is a continuing problem that one needs to address. It would be minimized if the roster process had been in place.

And as long as I have touched on the question of law professors, let me say that Robert Cassidy's suggestive professorial prescriptions last Friday may have some basis in the agreement. There is nothing in the agreement that says you should be appointing professors. I am not the slightest bit ashamed of that in my profession. But if you examine the qualifications of a panel participation under Article 2009, Section 2, you do not find anything about academics.

* * *

However, again you have this problem because of the conflict-of-interest provisions that those who tend to qualify would be professors. The rest of the group who qualify under the criteria that I have mentioned would likely be precluded as long as there is no roster under the conflict of interest provisions, although they are experts in international law and international trade and may have participated in the panel process. I think that contributes to some of this difficulty of how one ended up not only on our panel, but on many of the panels that have existed under the Chapter 18 predecessor with a collection of academics.

* * *

Under NAFTA, the panel chair is selected first. Under the Canada/U.S. Free Trade Agreement, the panel chair was selected last. I am not sure whether this makes any difference. It probably does as a strategic matter. If the parties who are supposed to come to an agreement can agree on a chair, then knowing who that person is, they can decide what kind of a panel they would like to assemble and to see to what degree that person would or would not be influenced by the chair. But they would know who would, generally, be in charge of having control of the process.

The chair is chosen by mutual agreement. There is no nationality requirement with respect to a chair. Anybody can be chosen, and in this case the person chosen, as I mentioned, was Professor Lauterpacht who was British. He was not a national of either party. It could have been a Mexican; it could have been anybody. If they fail to agree on a chair, the person is chosen by a lottery. You can contrast this, if you want, with the Canada/U.S. Free Trade Agreement, where the chair was selected by the commission. The commission was involved in that process, and the chair was the last person chosen. So, under the Canada/U.S. Free Trade Agreement, the four panelists came first, and not the parties but the commission could look over these four panelists and then say, we think we can control this group. The commission would make the selection, and if they could not do it, then the four previously selected got to choose their own chair. The NAFTA process, therefore, transfers greater control to the disputing parties under the FTA system.

The selection of the remaining four roster members is somewhat unique, although it may be a distinction without substantive difference. Under the NAFTA process, each disputing party puts forward the name of a person who is not its own national but a national of the other disputing party. In effect then, because, I guess, notwithstanding the Canadian press, I was really an American, I must have been put up by the Canadians. Because I was not a roster member, I was, clearly, subject to a peremptory challenge, and somehow I survived. I am not sure I will survive it again. But the United States could have passed a veto.

The same thing applied to the Canadians. There were two Canadians and two Americans who were put forward. It was a reversal of the usual procedure where a country would put forward its own national. Had there been a roster in place, and if I were on the roster, Canada would still have been obliged to put forward the name of a person who was not its national, but if they chose someone from the roster, then there is no peremptory challenge process in place.

Why the nationality requirements? There are a number of different reasons for having it. First, I do not think the reverse nationality process really makes any substantive difference. It is interesting, but I do not think it makes any substantive difference from the old system where there was still a nationality requirement. The reasons for imposing these nationality requirements may rest on the assumption that a national arising from his or her own country's legal culture will best understand and interpret that legal culture and explain it to the other parties. We heard yesterday about the aspects of legal culture, and that may be one of the reasons why this was imposed. . . .

Will the panelists, in fact, support their own country? There seems to be no evidence that that actually occurs in either the Chapter 18 or Chapter 20 processes. If you look at other panel decisions in Chapter 18, or if you look at the Chapter 19 processes and the countervailing duty, for a surprising number of cases, decisions were unanimous. There may be a number of other reasons as to why that may be unanimous, but the point is that there does not seem to be, with one or two exceptions, any real likelihood that the nationality of the panel actually affects the process. I think the significance is that it is important politically. It may make the decision more credible and more acceptable to governments when you have nationals present, and I do not think it actually affects the process.

* * *

That leads me to institutionalization. You all heard the prior participants ... commenting on the fact that NAFTA lacks in institutional permanency and organizational core. Suggestions were made for consideration of a permanent tribunal to replace the present panel system. Henry King pointed out that such an institution, which was, by the way, called for and recommended in the joint working group on dispute settlement of the ABA, the CBA, and the Barra Mexicana, would provide any institutional memory, that was important. I concur in those recommendations. I think there is a need for some form of permanent or ongoing tribunal. It would probably better serve what the objectives of the dispute resolution process are about.

The panel dispute resolution mechanisms, which are built into the FTA and the later NAFTA, are not the equivalent court or a similar tribunal. They are ad hoc, and I suspect they were intended to be so. The panels are hand-tailored to each dispute. There is no reason that any panel member will have the opportunity to participate in any later panel. Each panel then, in other words, will face the problem of substantially indulging in the cliche in re-inventing its own grief.

* * *

A second aspect that I think would be a problem is precisely what was referred to, I think by Mr. Cassidy the other day. That was the suggestion that the panelists themselves will be the institutional memory. I believe in the Chapter 19 discussion, and I cannot recall which person had made the statement, the panelists who are reappointed will come with their own memory and that will be a countervailing effect and we do not really need a formal tribunal. I disagree. I think that that is precisely a reason for a tribunal.

In the Chapter 19 process, if you actually look at the people who are appointed, statistically, many of them have been appointed many times. So you have multiple appointments, and it is true that the person who served before will bring to the process his or her memories of prior cases and that will influence the process. If everyone has done it before, I suppose we would all cancel each other out.

But in the Chapter 18–20 process, that is not true. Only one person has served on more than one panel, if you put Chapters 18 and 20 together. ...you have only one or two panels who may have been there before, those persons will also provide memory. They provide institutionalization, and that may give them a greater than one-fifth influence over the process. That I would in due course of time find trouble if that process continued....

... I think that the establishment of a permanent panel or a tribunal would avoid not only many of the distortions to which I have referred, but it will also provide for more opportunities for establishing procedures and related processes on its own as the parties come together on a regular and an ongoing basis. Increasing familiarity with processes if you have an ongoing tribunal and interaction between the same tribunal members would establish an institutional culture that courts normally provide. And eventually that will create a more independent and, I think, a more professional formal dispute resolution mechanism. That may be one of the very reasons why it is not there because I believe that the parties never intended that to happen. Nevertheless, I think it's worth noting.

I will give you some pragmatic reasons why I think it would also help if there were a tribunal, and I will try to list them very briefly. First, if you had an ongoing tribunal of permanently appointed people, you would avoid the conflict of interest problems we talked about. You would just go through that headache once for each of the appointments of these people on an ongoing tribunal and you do not have to repeat that.

Second, it would save a lot of time. The loss of time in establishing panels is unavoidable. In the case of the dairy/poultry case, for the year-and-a-half the process took place, at least one-third of it was merely putting the panel together. That could have been saved. You also would not have had so many professors on that, if you had this process in place.

Third, for panelists who, inevitably, have to juggle a number of conflicting schedules and obligations because they have other career paths, you avoid what is a de facto kind of conflict of pressures on your time and on your career. This is particularly true when, as happened in the dairy/poultry case, the time limits specified in the agreement or in the model were slick. In theory, we thought, the last panelist was appointed in January. We should have finished in April of last year, a year ago. We did not finish until December of last year. And that meant for everyone involved a practical problem of juggling one's schedule and trying to figure out how to compete with commitments that had been made for the periods of the summer and the fall and so forth, and that adversely influences how the process is going to work.

I think also if you had a more permanent tribunal, there would be less pressure on worrying about the time limits. I think when you loosen the time limits and give more time for the appropriate consideration as required in these cases, an ongoing tribunal would not have competing interests in order to try to juggle the schedule.

* * *

They would also make it much easier to control the security problems. Everyone would be in a single place. You would have greater control over your materials. It is rather cumbersome when you are a panelist and you are scattered all over North America or, in our case, substantial parts of the world and you are responsible for the security of the materials, for the receipt of materials, for being able to communicate and interact with each other, and it becomes difficult. As a practical matter, just working out the schedules when we can get together and when we can deliberate and where we can deliberate, we had to resort to telephone conferences.

In one case, and I do not think I am breaching my obligation, we had an extraordinary combination of people scattered from Ottawa; Saskatoon; Houston; Mexico City; Washington; London; Cambridge, England; St. Petersburg, Russia; and New Haven, Connecticut, trying to figure out how to communicate across twelve time zones with conference calls or trying to figure out for our schedules what is the most convenient city to come together and talk. These would all be eliminated if there were a panel process.

* * *

These are my views on a permanent tribunal versus the panel process. I will now close by saying it ain't gonna happen. I do not see in the reasonably foreseeable future that the parties are going to amend the agreement in any way in order to establish an ongoing tribunal. I think they intended the results that they have here. It does give them greater control. If that is what the parties intended, well, that is the agreement, and that is what we have. I do think that without any amendment, you can, nevertheless, do a better job institutionalizing than is now being done.

For example, . . . we need to start with the establishment of a roster. If one puts together the thirty-person roster and uses that as the basis for institutionalization, one can find perhaps a better de facto institution develop than merely the Secretariat or past panelists.

Questions and Comments

1. What qualifications are required for a person to serve as a Chapter 20 panelist? See Art. 2009–2010. How do Chapter 20 qualifications differ from Chapter 19 qualifications, in theory and in actual practice? Does it matter that under Chapter 19 panelists are applying the national antidumping or countervailing duty laws of the responding Party, while under Chapter 20 they are applying the law of NAFTA? Assuming that he is objective, reliable, of sound judgment and independent of the NAFTA governments, does Frank Puente otherwise qualify to serve as a Chapter 20 panelist?

2. Article 2011 provides for one panel selection process where there are two disputing Parties and another process where there are more than two disputing Parties. What is the process for selecting a Chapter 20 panel in a two-party dispute? in a three-party dispute? See Article 2011; Gantz.

3. Why does Chapter 20 contain two distinct panel selection processes—one for disputes involving two Parties and another for disputes involving more than two Parties—but Chapter 19 contains only one selection process for all Chapter 19 disputes?

4. Can a Party appoint a person not on the Chapter 20 roster to a panel? See Article 2011.3; Picker. Why are appointments from outside the Chapter 20 roster subject to unlimited peremptory challenges? Why, after more than eleven years, have the NAFTA Parties been unable to agree on designating the members of the Chapter 20 Roster?

5. Chapter 20 involves a so-called "reverse selection" process in the sense that the parties select the chair of the panel first and then the four remaining panelists. As you will recall, the process is different under Chapter 19. There, the Parties begin by selecting four panelists and then agree upon a fifth panelist. The chair of the Chapter 19 panel is selected by the panelists, not the Parties. In what ways does the Chapter 20 reverse selection process give the Parties greater control over panel formation? See Picker. All three Chapter 20 panel chairmen have been chosen from outside North America, two British and one Australian citizen(s). (Does this suggest concerns over the dominance of common law lawyers or law professors, even in cases involving Mexico? Mexico probably isn't concerned: it won both *Broom Corn Brooms* and *Cross-Border Trucking* by unanimous decisions.)

6. In the first Chapter 20 proceeding (the 1995 dairy/poultry case), it took over 190 days, not 30, to select all five panelists. In the third (the 1998 cross-border trucking case), panel selection required over a year. At what specific point(s) in the Chapter 20 panel selection process is delay by a Party possible? See Article 2011. What can be done to reduce delays in Chapter 20 panel selection? See Picker. Why has the panel selection process been quicker in the WTO's Dispute Settlement Body, where panelists are appointed by the Secretariat in consultation with the Members? Note that in the WTO, the Dispute Settlement Body is a committee of the entire 148 country membership, and the WTO is a separate international organization, while the NAFTA Secretariat is a creature of the NAFTA governments under the Free Trade Commission (Articles 2001, 2002).

7. As of late 2004, only three Chapter 20 panels had been convened, with the most recent decision rendered in 2001. As the Gantz article notes, in these three cases, (the dairy/poultry, broom corn brooms, cross-border trucking services), eleven out of fifteen panelists were law professors. Why have so many of the Chapter 20 panelists to date been law professors? See Picker. Assuming Mexico nominated Frank Puente to serve as a panelist in a Chapter 20 dispute with the United States, would you recommend that the United States exercise a peremptory challenge against him?

8. Although, as Professor Picker concludes, the creation of a permanent tribunal to resolve NAFTA disputes may not be realistic for the foreseeable future, in what ways would the establishment of such a court be an improvement over the existing, ad hoc panel selection process? See Picker. In what ways is the existing panel selection process superior? Would a permanent tribunal encourage the NAFTA governments to utilize the Chapter 20 process more frequently, overcoming their (apparent) preference for WTO dispute settlement where both alternatives are available?

PROBLEM 9.2 CHAPTER 19: DUMPING DISPUTES; NEW ENGLAND APPLES TO MEXICO— MEXICAN PEACHES TO GEORGIA

SECTION I.   THE SETTING

CONVEG, INC., is a large United States fruit and vegetable conglomerate, substantially vertically integrated from production on numerous large farms which it owns, processing facilities, and distribution to retailers. It produces many different fruit and vegetable products. During early 1999, CONVEG acquired about half of the Georgia peach production. The remaining Georgia peach farms are owned by family business entities. Most of them are quite small. Georgia peach growers have about 30 percent of the annual peach market in the U.S., but 90 percent of the May to September market in the Southeast. The Southeast for fruit growers includes Florida, Georgia, and the Carolinas.

CONVEG and the other Georgia peach growers discovered that after the signing of the NAFTA, Mexican peach growers were continuing to gain increased shares in the markets served by the Georgia peach growers, which included much of the U.S., but with the major incursions in the Southeast. CONVEG is unhappy because except for the sale of peaches, the company is very profitable.

CONVEG and the other Georgia growers have met to consider what they might do to lessen the impact of Mexican peaches in the Georgia growers' traditional markets, especially the Southeast. With the aid of in-house counsel from CONVEG, and outside counsel, they have listed the following as possible actions:

1. Initiate a "Section 201" action (also referred to as a safeguard or escape clause action) under Section 201 of the Trade Act of 1974. Perhaps also urge federal legislation which will alter the definition of "industry" in Section 202, to include as an industry any group of four or more states.

2. Initiate an antidumping duty action under Section 731 of the Tariff Act of 1930.

3. Initiate a countervailing duty action under Section 701 of the Tariff Act of 1930.

4. Seek the initiation of a Section 301 action under the Trade Act of 1974.

5. Seek the blockage of the peaches on the grounds that they threaten United States agriculture and consumers because of the likelihood of their carrying diseases.

6. Urge federal legislation which would require inspection of peaches in Mexico before exporting, comparable to the 1957 Poultry Products Inspection Act regarding inspection of chickens. This would bar the importation of peaches which are not "healthful, wholesome [and] fit for human food," and require Mexico to adopt sanitary inspection facilities which are the "same as" those in the United States.

7. Urge federal legislation requiring all states to inspect all produce entering any state for sale from abroad for compliance with labeling, packaging, sanitary and phytosanitary (diseases and pests) and other rules. Require a mandatory inspection fee.

8. Urge all states, especially Georgia, to adopt state laws requiring inspection of all peaches at the state border for compliance with federal and state labeling, packaging, sanitary and phytosanitary, and other rules. Require a mandatory inspection fee.

9. Urge the United States Trade Representative to adopt administrative requirements requiring Mexican peaches to be shipped in the same kind of boxes as are used in the United States. Mexican peaches are shipped in egg-like boxes, with each peach separately wrapped, while United States peaches are shipped in ordinary cartons.

10. Urge similar changes to labeling laws so that each individual peach from Mexico would have to have a permanent, indelible label designating Mexico as the place of origin.

11. Urge all states, especially Georgia, to adopt a program for frequent inspections in supermarkets for proper identification of the country of origin. Impose substantial fines and requirements for the destruction of any noncomplying goods.

After considerable discussion, CONVEG and its attorneys decided to pursue number 2 above, the initiation of a dumping action. It was filed with the International Trade Administration of the Department of Commerce, which rendered both preliminary and final determinations that the peaches were sold at less than fair value in the Southeast market. The International Trade Commission rendered both preliminary and final determinations finding injury to the peach industry in the four-five month, four state Southeast market, and antidumping duties were duly imposed.

The Mexican peach growers, acting as a trade association of growers called AGMEX, are very concerned about these final determinations. AGMEX has commenced proceedings under Chapter 19. It claims that the U.S. ITA improperly calculated less than fair value because of the information on which the ITA relied was not accurate. The Mexican peach growers and AGMEX had refused to supply the ITA with considerable requested information, and the ITA mainly used information provided by CONVEG. AGMEX also challenges first, the ITC determination of the U.S. market, claiming that it incorrectly found the Southeast region of only four states to constitute the industry, and second, the injury determination. The ITC role will be considered in the following problem, addressing countervailing duties and subsidies.

AGMEX has retained you to advise it on the panel procedures, including how AGMEX can assure sufficient Mexican representation on the binational panel, the ability to challenge the ITA findings because they were based on data obtained from unreliable sources (the Mexican growers refused to provide accurate data), and what avenues of appeal are available if the panel decision is unfavorable to Mexico.

Ironically, at the same time the above peaches from Mexico dispute was evolving, Mexican apple growers were complaining about New England apples.

INDUSTRIA MANZANA, S.A., is a large Mexican fruit conglomerate, substantially vertically integrated from production on numerous large orchards which it owns, processing in several facilities, and distribution to retailers. It produces numerous fruit products. During early 1998, INDUSTRIA MANZANA acquired a large number of northern Mexico fruit orchards which produce both red and golden delicious apples, leaving the remaining orchards primarily owned by family enterprises. Most are quite small orchards.

INDUSTRIA MANZANA and the other Mexican apple growers discovered that their share of the Mexican market was diminishing because of imports from the United States, mainly from the state of Washington and from New England. Under NAFTA, tariffs on apples entering Mexico have been declining. At 18 percent in 1994, they were eliminated entirely in 2003. A quota system allowed 55,000 tons of apples into Mexico from the United States in 1994, with that number increasing three percent annually until 2002, with all restrictions then eliminated.

A dumping action was initiated under Articles 28–36, 62–71 of the Mexican Foreign Trade Law. The Secretaría de Economia (SECON), determined that the New England apples were being sold in Mexico at less than fair value, and also that the Mexican apple industry in northern Mexico was materially injured.

INDUSTRIA MANZANA had also considered other actions similar to those considered by CONVEG, such as safeguard or countervailing duty actions, seeking the blockage of the apples on the grounds that they threaten Mexican agriculture and consumers because of the likelihood of their carrying diseases, urging federal legislation which would alter the Mexican law to favor the Mexican industry and require inspection of apples in the United States before exporting, urging administrative requirements mandating that U.S. apples to be shipped in the same cartons used in Mexico which U.S. apple growers believe will cause damage to their apples, and urging similar changes to labeling laws so that each individual apple from the U.S. will have a permanent, indelible label designating the U.S. as the place of origin. These mirror the ideas noted above considered by CONVEG. Like the U.S. peach growers, the Mexican Apple growers have decided to concentrate on a dumping action.

The United States apple growers, acting as a trade association of growers called GROWSAP, are obviously concerned about the determinations of SECON. GROWSAP had warned the Mexican growers that it will respond to each Mexican or Chihuahua initiative. GROWSAP has initiated a petition before the NAFTA to challenge the conclusions of SECON, presenting arguments very much the same as in the NAFTA challenge by the Mexicans in the Georgia peach case.

SECTION II.   FOCUS OF CONSIDERATION

If the above facts appear familiar, they should be. For nearly two decades, Florida tomato and winter vegetable growers have been concerned about the increasing volume of imports from Mexico, both to Florida specifically, and to other parts of the United States where Florida growers have long had a significant market share. The Florida growers' concern accelerated with the creation of NAFTA, which opened trade and allowed even more Mexican tomatoes to enter the United States market.

For a lesser period, Mexican apple growers have been concerned about the increasing volume of apple imports from the United States, especially from the state of Washington. Mexican growers have long had a significant market share. The Mexican growers' concern accelerated with the creation of NAFTA, which opened trade and allowed even more United States apples to enter the Mexican market. Other agricultural products which have been subject to trade disputes under NAFTA include pork, beef, wheat, avocados and shrimp, among others.

Are tomatoes and apples examples of how successful NAFTA has been as an expression of principles of comparative advantage, or an example of unfair trade practices in action?

The concern about apple imports from the United States is mainly by the Mexican growers of red delicious apples, which represent about 73 percent of the apples grown in Mexico, the remainder being golden delicious, both of which are largely produced in the northern border state of Chihuahua.

While the tomato conflict might be labeled a conflict between the United States and Mexico, the principal if not exclusive protagonist in the United States is the Florida industry. This is important because to the extent that the Florida growers are able to have the United States government adopt and pursue their position, it shifts a share of the costs from the Florida growers to the United States. The peach conflict may be viewed in the same form, as more a Georgia–Mexico than United States–Mexico issue.

While the apple conflict also might be labeled a conflict between the United States and Mexico, the principal if not exclusive protagonist in Mexico is the Chihuahua apple industry, and the principal protagonist in the United States is the apple industry in Washington. This is important because to the extent that the Chihuahua growers are able to have the Mexican government adopt and pursue their position, it shifts a share of the costs from the Chihuahua growers to Mexico.

The ongoing tomato dispute with Florida, and the apple dispute with Mexico, are both currently dormant, attributable to two, separate suspension agreements reached between the two governments. These suspension agreements might be useful to resolve the peach and apple disputes in our hypothetical.

The facts of the hypothetical illustrate how domestic producers of any goods or services might react to increasing imports which threaten the existence of the respective nation's entity or industry. Often business clients know only that they are being harmed by imports. They do not know the range of actions which might be available to them on a state, federal, or international level, nor the degree of difficulty in successfully pursuing these separate courses of action.

This problem principally explores the role of a binational dispute panel formed according to NAFTA when there are complaints of dumping. We enter the conflict only *after* affirmative determinations have been made in each respective case. Our interest is in the process under NAFTA reviewing the affirmative administrative agency decisions, not in the process of those agencies outside of the scope of a NAFTA review. The Mexican complaint initially was heard by SECOFI [now SECON], which makes both the "Less Than Fair Value" (LTFV) *and* injury determinations. In the United States, there is a bifurcated process which is more the result of history than reason, although now preferred by many observers. The International Trade Administration (ITA) in the Department of Commerce makes the LTFV determination, and the International Trade Commission (ITC) makes the injury determination. The procedures of each of these three organizations (SECOFI, ITA and ITC) are to be considered by binational panels. In our hypothetical both the LTFV and injury determinations of each nation have been challenged, but we will save consideration of injury for the following problem, which addresses both injury determinations and the process of appeal under an Extraordinary Challenge Committee (ECC). In this problem we will address panel selection, the role of the panel, and the responsibilities and limitations of each panel as it reviews the national administrative LTFV determinations in the two cases.

Chapter 19 of NAFTA, and portions of the U.S North American Free Trade Agreement Implementation Act (1993), are essential to an understanding of this problem. They are set forth in the Documents Supplement.

SECTION III.   READINGS, QUESTIONS AND COMMENTS

Comment on the Chapter 19 Binational Panel Dispute Resolution Process

Each nation retains its own dumping law, although that law ought to be consistent with NAFTA obligations and consistent with GATT/WTO obligations since each is a member. Thus, SECON applies Mexican law, and the ITA and ITC apply United States law. That is essential to an understanding of what a Chapter 19 binational panel does. It first replaces national judicial review with binational panel review. It secondly determines whether or not the Party's administering agency made its determination "in accordance with the antidumping or countervailing duty law of the importing Party." It must follow the "general legal principles" that a court in the importing Party would apply in reviewing the administering authority's determination. The binational panel is limited in what it may do. It may not write a new determination (i.e., reverse the Authority's decision), but either remand a decision for action not inconsistent with the panel's determination, or uphold the determination. The action of the panel may not be appealed in a Party's courts, but may be reviewed in the "Extraordinary Challenge Committee" procedure (The ECC process is one subject of the following problem). That procedure is very limited, and is not the same as a general judicial review.

Chapter 19 is unique to the CFTA and NAFTA. Unlike the Chapter 11 and Chapter 20 provisions, Chapter 19 type provisions have not been exported to newer trade agreements concluded by the United States, Canada or Mexico. Nor does a Chapter 19 appear in the FTAA drafts. However, like the rest of NAFTA—because of the extreme difficulty of amending the Agreement—Chapter 19 is likely to remain a permanent fixture of NAFTA dispute settlement.

PART A. PEACHES FROM MEXICO TO THE U.S.

This part will address the process in general, and the cases which involved imports to the U.S. of Mexican tomatoes and winter vegetables.

POWELL AND BARNETT, THE ROLE OF UNITED STATES TRADE LAWS IN RESOLVING THE FLORIDA–MEXICO TOMATO CONFLICT

11 Florida J. of Int'l L. 319 (1997).*

ANTIDUMPING LAW

The term "dumping" is generally used to describe price discrimination in which a producer charges a higher price in its home market than in an export market. Article VI of GATT 1947, and the Agreement on Implementation of Article VI of GATT 1994 (Antidumping Agreement), authorize WTO Members to impose antidumping duties when products are dumped and cause material injury to, threaten material injury to, or materially retard the establishment of a domestic industry in the export market. The dumping aspects of these international agreements have been incorporated into U.S. law at Subtitle B of Title VII of the Tariff Act of 1930, as amended.

In most cases, an antidumping investigation is commenced by the filing of a petition requesting relief on behalf of the domestic industry producing the domestic like product. In substance, the petition must contain evidence "reasonably available" to the petitioners to support their claims of material injury and dumping. In other words, it should contain information about the condition of the domestic industry, prices of the imported products with which they are concerned, foreign (home market or third country) prices of comparable products, and in some cases, the cost of producing the products.

Before initiating an investigation, Commerce must confirm that there is sufficient industry support for the petition. Sufficient industry support exists when more than fifty percent of those members of the industry expressing either support for or opposition to the petition (excluding those with no opinion) favor the investigation, and the supporters account for no less than twenty-five percent of total domestic production.

* * *

The Commerce investigation involves the collection of information needed to calculate U.S. prices and normal value for the products under investigation. Commerce makes adjustments to these prices to put them on a comparable, ex-factory basis and compares them to determine whether dumping is occurring. To obtain this information, Commerce issues questionnaires to the foreign producers of the subject merchandise (respondents), requesting detailed information on their corporate structure and affiliations, distribution and sales processes, accounting and financial practices, and the specifications of the products they sell that are subject to the investigation. In addition, Commerce normally requires respondents to report, on a transaction-specific basis, twelve months of both their home market and their U.S. sales. These sales reports must include all relevant expenses on a transaction-specific basis, from price, quantity, and customer name to a complete physical description of the merchandise sold to the movement, packing, and direct selling expenses associated with the sale.

The twelve-month period for which data are collected is referred to as the period of investigation. The period of investigation typically is the four fiscal quarters most recently completed prior to the filing of the antidumping petition, although Commerce has discretion to vary this period in appropriate circumstances. The period of investigation precedes the filing of the petition in order to ensure that foreign producers cannot artificially revise their pricing after the investigation begins solely to reduce or eliminate their actual rates of dumping.

"Normal value" is the term used to denote the comparison point for determining whether the U.S. price is dumped. Normal value may be based on home-market sales, third-country sales, or constructed value.

The statutory preference is to base normal value on home-market sales, provided that home-market sales have been made in sufficient quantities to form a basis for comparison; normally at least five percent, by volume, of sales to the United States. When home-market sales do not meet this standard, the home market is not considered "viable," and the statute directs Commerce to examine third-country sales if they form an adequate basis for comparison.

If there are insufficient or no sales in either the home market or in third countries, Commerce uses constructed value as the basis for normal value. . . .

* * *

Depending upon the manner in which normal value is calculated, that figure may need to be adjusted to place it on an ex-factory basis for comparison to the U.S. price. Adjustments include substituting U.S. packing costs for home-market packing costs, deducting movement expenses, and deducting any taxes imposed on home-market sales that are rebated or not collected on U.S./export sales. In addition, when the comparison is made with the U.S. price, Commerce may make other adjustments to the normal value to account for differences in quantity, circumstances of sale (for example, credit, warehouse, and other expenses), level of trade, and physical differences in the merchandise being compared.

The U.S. price that Commerce uses to determine whether dumping is occurring may be calculated as either an "export price" or a "constructed export price." As described in Section 772(a) of the Tariff Act of 1930, an export price calculation is appropriate when the first sale of the merchandise to an unaffiliated purchaser, either in the United States or for exportation to the United States, is made prior to the importation of the merchandise into the United States.... Constructed export price situations typically occur in one of two situations. Most constructed export price transactions occur when the producer or exporter has an affiliated sales agent in the United States. Constructed export price transactions also may occur when the U.S. sales agent is unaffiliated, such as in the case of consignment sales, in which the U.S. sales agent is simply the consignee and does not take title to the merchandise.

Regardless of whether the U.S. price is based on the export price or constructed export price, the price is adjusted, if necessary, to include U.S. packing, home-market import duties that were rebated because of exportation, and any countervailing duties imposed to offset export subsidies. The price also will be adjusted to exclude any U.S. import duties and any movement expenses incurred in bringing the merchandise into the United States. When the U.S. price is a constructed export price, additional adjustments will be made to exclude any commissions, direct and indirect selling expenses, selling expenses incurred on behalf of the buyer, and further manufacturing expenses. Additionally, Commerce must now allocate profit to these "constructed export price expenses" and reduce the constructed export price accordingly.

Within 140 days of initiating an antidumping investigation, Commerce must issue a preliminary determination as to "whether there is a reasonable basis to believe or suspect" that dumping is taking place. If the preliminary determination is affirmative, Commerce will instruct the U.S. Customs Service to impose a bonding requirement on the subject merchandise in the amount of the estimated antidumping duties to ensure payment if duties ultimately are imposed. Regardless of whether Commerce's preliminary determination is affirmative or negative, Commerce must complete its investigation and issue a final determination.

Between the preliminary and final determinations, Commerce conducts a verification of the data submitted by each respondent. This verification consists of an on-site visit by Commerce analysts, and in some cases, accountants, to spot-check the respondent's submitted data. Respondents are asked to provide documentation for the sales-specific data submitted and to reconcile that data to the company's audited books and records. Verification of sales data often lasts a full week, while a cost verification (when below-cost sales are being investigated) often lasts a second full week.

Following verification, but prior to the final determination, both petitioners and respondents have an opportunity to submit briefs and participate in a public hearing. New factual information may not be submitted at this time; rather, this is an opportunity for parties to make arguments regarding Commerce's interpretation of respondents' data and its analysis of those data.

Commerce has limited authority to "settle" an antidumping investigation prior to completing its investigation. This authority is rarely used. In fact, at present, Commerce has more than 400 antidumping duty orders in place and only thirteen antidumping suspension agreements.

* * *

Section 734(b) provides Commerce the authority to suspend an investigation pursuant to an agreement with companies representing substantially all (at least eighty-five percent) exports to the United States that they will either cease dumping, or less frequently, cease exports to the United States. . . .

Section 734(c) provides Commerce with the authority to suspend an investigation pursuant to an agreement with companies representing substantially all (at least eighty-five percent) exports to the United States that will "eliminate" completely the injurious effect of their exports to the United States. In addition, such an elimination of injury agreement must prevent price suppression or undercutting of U.S. prices and eliminate at least eighty-five percent of the dumping margin found in the investigation. Because such an agreement does not completely eliminate the dumping that has been found to be occurring, Commerce may only enter into such agreements when there are extraordinary circumstances. "Extraordinary circumstances" have been defined as meaning that the case is complex and that suspension would be "more beneficial" to the domestic industry than continuation of the investigation.

* * *

In the case of an agreement pursuant to Section 734(b) or (c), before entering into the agreement, Commerce must first determine that the agreement is in the public interest and can be effectively monitored. If Commerce finds that the terms of a suspension agreement are being violated, it must terminate the agreement and resume the investigation from the point of the preliminary determination. Rarely, a domestic producer or respondent will request "continuation" following the conclusion of a suspension agreement. When continuation is requested, both

Commerce and the ITC proceed to their final determinations; however, assuming both determinations are affirmative, no antidumping duty order is issued. Instead, the proceeding continues to be suspended pursuant to the agreement, and if the agreement is violated, Commerce immediately issues the antidumping duty order.

* * *

THE 1980 WINTER VEGETABLES CASE

... In September of [1978], several groups representing Florida growers of fresh cucumbers, eggplant, peppers, squash, and tomatoes filed an antidumping petition against imports of those products from Mexico. Significantly, that case was limited to "vegetables shipped during the winter vegetable season and cover[ed] entries during the period November 1 in any year through the last day of the following April."

The investigation was limited both in terms of the specific vegetables covered and as to the time period during which they were shipped and entered into the United States. There is, however, no discussion of these limitations in Commerce's determination. The 1980 case is of limited value in explaining temporal limitations in the scope of an antidumping investigation.

THE 1996 TOMATOES INVESTIGATION

Following the negative determination in 1980, dumping claims against Mexico by the Florida industry lay dormant for sixteen years. On March 29, 1995, the Florida tomato industry sought relief from increasing imports of fresh winter tomatoes from Mexico under Section 201 of the Trade Act of 1974, which permits the President to impose restrictions on imports to provide time for a domestic industry to adjust to import competition. This claim was limited to tomatoes imported during the months of January through April. In April 1995, the ITC rejected Florida's claim for provisional relief, finding, among other things, that the like product could not properly be limited to winter tomatoes, and that the provisional relief, even if granted, could not have had a significant impact on that season (that is, that the injury could be timely prevented through an ordinary Section 202 investigation). The Florida industry subsequently withdrew its request for full relief under Section 202.

A year later, the domestic industry returned with a two-pronged approach. On March 11, 1996, they filed a petition with the ITC again seeking full relief under Section 202 of the Trade Act of 1974. This time, however, the petition virtually abandoned its claim that the like product should be limited to winter production. In addition, the request for relief was filed on behalf of the bell pepper industry as well as the tomato industry. Once again, however, on July 2, 1996, the ITC found that the domestic tomato and bell pepper producers were not suffering "serious injury" by substantially increased imports of tomatoes and bell peppers.[104]

On April 1, 1996, the domestic industry filed an antidumping petition with Commerce and the ITC. This petition contained sufficient information regarding the condition of the U.S. tomato growers and the prices of Mexican tomatoes in the United States and in Mexico to justify Commerce's initiation of an antidumping investigation. The petition contained production information for the entire U.S. industry (based on USDA statistics), including the production of the petitioners and others supporting the petition. These data established that the petitioners and the supporters represented more than fifty percent of U.S. fresh tomato production, thus establishing sufficient industry support to meet the statutory requirements.

* * *

Commerce issued its preliminary determination on November 1, 1996. In contrast to the 1980 investigation, in which no margins of dumping were found, Commerce found that there was a reasonable indication that dumping was occurring in the 1996 investigation. . . .

Commerce, however, did not complete the 1996 investigation. Instead, shortly after making its preliminary determination, it signed a suspension agreement with Mexican tomato growers, who accounted for substantially all imports of fresh tomatoes from Mexico into the United States. In this agreement, each signatory agreed to revise its prices to eliminate completely the injurious effects of its tomato exports to the United States.

Consistent with the requirements of Section 734(c) of the Tariff Act of 1930, the agreement established a reference price below which the signatories agreed not to sell tomatoes in the United States. The agreement also provided that no entry by any exporter would be dumped at greater than fifteen percent of the estimated dumping margin for that exporter from the investigation. Commerce found that the combination of these requirements would completely eliminate the injurious effect of Mexican tomato imports and prevent the suppression or undercutting of domestic price levels by Mexican tomato imports.

For the Mexican growers, the signing of the suspension agreement eliminated (at least for the time being) a major source of uncertainty in the market: the existence and extent of antidumping duties. The agreement replaced that uncertainty with a need to change how they did business. The reference price requirements of the agreement meant that Mexican growers could no longer simply ship their product to the United States, accept whatever price the consignment agent received, and hope to come out ahead at the end of a growing season. Instead, their consignment contracts had to be revised to ensure that consignees could

104. Fresh Tomatoes and Bell Peppers, USITC Pub. 2985, Inv. No.TA–201–66, at 1– 5 (Aug. 1996).

not sell tomatoes on behalf of the signatories for less than the agreed reference price. Equally important, the consignees had to ensure that their sales contracts, on behalf of the signatories, contained appropriate language such that the buyer could not make claims for post-sale price adjustments, which would have the effect of lowering the price below the reference price.

* * *

IMPROVEMENTS MADE BY NAFTA TO THE U.S.-CANADA MODEL

... First, it should be noted that despite the addition of a third party, the system did not become one of trinational panels....

One improvement introduced by NAFTA is a preference for judges, either sitting or retired, from the federal courts of the three countries. This change emphasizes that a panel's task is to apply existing law as a court would, not to create a new body of law. This change also will have the effect of reducing the potential for a conflict of interest by trade practitioners who also represent clients in other trade matters pending before the administering authorities of the countries involved.

* * *

The third change, the corrective mechanism added by Article 1905, is quite substantial. The parties recognized that some risk attended the melding of Mexico's civil law system, together with its recently enacted antidumping and countervailing duty law, with the common law system, and the more mature antidumping and countervailing duty laws of the other two NAFTA parties. The principal protection against an adverse clash of systems was to ensure sufficient change to Mexico's laws that the exporters of all three countries would be in a roughly equivalent position. Essentially, this combination of changes shifts Mexico several steps closer to a common law system for antidumping and countervailing duty.

Article 1905 then provides that if a party's laws prevent a panel from being established, or have the effect of rendering its decisions non-binding, or if these laws fail to provide a meaningful opportunity for judicial review, and a special committee agrees that one of these situations exists, the complaining party may suspend operation of the binational panel system, or suspend equivalent benefits to the other party. This is, of course, a remedy reminiscent of GATT. Article 1905 goes on to provide that when and if the problem is eliminated, any suspension of operation of the binational panel system would be terminated. This snapback provision, while potentially draconian in its impact, is an effective and fair method for ensuring that Chapter 19 continues to operate as the Parties anticipated it would.

FOLSOM, GORDON & SPANOGLE, HANDBOOK OF NAFTA DISPUTE SETTLEMENT
BINATIONAL PANEL SUMMARY*

Gray Portland Cement and Clinker from Mexico USA–95–1904–02, September 13, 1996

NAFTA Chapter 19 Binational Panel

This is a review of the third annual review conducted by the Department of Commerce International Trade Administration (ITA) of an antidumping duty order.

The ITA review was challenged by CEMEX (a Mexican company), the Department of Commerce, the Ad Hoc Committee of AZ–NM–TX–FL Producers of Gray Portland Cement, and the National Cement Company of California, with leave to intervene granted to Cementos de Chihuahua (CdC)(a Mexican company), and the Government of Mexico granted permission to file an amicus brief. The panel unanimously ruled that the final determination of Commerce in its third administrative review was based on substantial evidence and in accordance with law.

Commerce issued an antidumping order on July 18, 1990, after the required less than fair value (LTFV) investigation, but with no comments filed opposing the initial petition commencing the investigation. [Aug. 13, 1990] In October, 1990, the Government of Mexico initiated consultations with the United States under provisions of the GATT Antidumping Code to consider Mexico's concern that Commerce had improperly initiated the dumping investigation by failing to determine that a proper party had petitioned for the investigation. Mexico believed the petition was not filed "on behalf of the industry affected". A GATT panel issued a report on July 9, 1992, that supported Mexico's position, but the report was blocked by the United States and thus was an unadopted report.

While GATT was deliberating, Commerce conducted two annual reviews of the antidumping order. CEMEX challenged the results of the second review's results. A third review covered only one Mexican manufacturer/exporter-CEMEX. For the first time, CEMEX challenged Commerce's original 1989 investigation. CEMEX argued that the GATT report constituted an international obligation requiring Commerce to void the original antidumping order. Commerce completed its third review on May 19, 1995, and determined that CEMEX failed to provide the agency with adequate information needed to complete the review. Commerce therefore assigned duties on the basis of the best information available, and imposed the highest rate found for any firm in the LTFV determination, 61.85 percent. Commerce rejected the GATT report argument.

The panel outlined the proper scope and standard of review for a binational panel, noting that the panel could only review the administrative record compiled during the third administrative review, and that the panel's decision could only apply prospectively to final determinations made after January 1, 1994, the date of entry into force of the NAFTA. The panel stated that the ultimate question was whether Commerce's findings in the third administrative review were based upon substantial evidence and made in accordance with law.

CEMEX and CdC argued that the 1989 decision to initiate an investigation was not in accordance with law. It argued that because the petitioner Ad Hoc Committee defined the industry as a regional industry, Commerce had to "poll" the domestic industry to determine its support.

The panel determined (1) that CEMEX's and CdC's claims were barred by the statute of limitations and also barred by the doctrine of res judicata, (2) that the panel lacked authority to review or alter either the decision to initiate an investigation or the final determination, (3) that the unadopted GATT panel report did not bar the panel, nor require the conclusion demanded, and (4) that Commerce acted within its authority in using best information available in assigning a dumping margin.

The statute of limitations applicable was found to be in § 516a of the Tariff Act of 1930, which limited challenges to final determinations in antidumping investigations to 30 days after notice of a determination (in this case of LTFV sales) or of an antidumping order. That statute would apply for any appeal in the United States, which would lie to the Court of International Trade (CIT). CEMEX and CdC did not identify any challenge to the third review which differed from any decision in the 1989 initiation decision. All the annual review did was to seek to calculate the proper duty assessment, accepting as a given the existence of the antidumping duty order. U.S. law does not permit Commerce to rescind an antidumping duty order in a review based upon a reconsideration of the LTFV determination.

The panel further barred the claim under the doctrine of res judicata, because that doctrine prevents the litigation of grounds and defenses that were available to the parties, whether or not they were asserted.

The panel next ruled that it lacked the authority to review or alter Commerce's final LTFV determination, or to grant the parties prospective relief. The panel relied upon Article 1906 of the NAFTA, which states that Chapter 19 shall only apply prospectively to final determinations made after the entry into force of the agreement.

The argument that the GATT report, which had been blocked, constituted an international obligation of the United States, was held by the panel to be incorrect. Although CEMEX, CdC and Mexico agreed that the report was not binding on the panel, they suggested it was the "best available interpretation of what GATT requires." They also argued that it created an "international obligation" which must be complied with by the United States. The panel gave a lengthy review of the nature of international obligations as part of U.S. law, and concluded that there was no such obligation binding upon the United States arising from the unadopted GATT report, and nothing in U.S. law, GATT law or international law required Commerce to retroactively revoke the 1990 order.

This left the panel to consider the issue of Commerce's application of the best information available standard to determine the dumping margin. Such use was held proper because the opposing parties failed to provide information requested which would have allowed a more accurate calculation. During the review Commerce had made a series of requests to CEMEX for certain sales information. CEMEX argued that such information was not needed. The panel disagreed. Furthermore, the panel held Commerce to have properly exercised its discretion when implementing best information available by deciding to apply its two-tier methodology. That methodology had been used previously and was supported by sufficient evidence. The panel decided it unnecessary to address the argument of Commerce and the Ad Hoc Committee that U.S. law required the use of the best information available that is most adverse or unfavorable to a non-complying respondent, because the panel believed Commerce had not acted arbitrarily or without substantial evidence in selecting the rate.

Addressing several additional motions, the panel first allowed the Government of Mexico to file an amicus curiae brief because the panel has authority to adopt procedures not covered in the rules. Secondly, the panel accepted a memorandum of law from a law professor offered by CEMEX, although agreeing in principle with Commerce that such a memorandum prepared by a non-party might be improper. The panel suggested a sworn affidavit or appearance by the professor would have been more appropriate, but accepted the memorandum because it could find no rules prohibiting such documents, and there are no limits on the lengths of briefs. The panel found weight to the fact that the memo was supported by the professor's previously published views on international law. Finally the panel denied the motion by Commerce and the Ad Hoc Committee to strike the brief of CdC. The panel believed the arguments of CdC were much the same as those in the brief of CEMEX, and the arguments to be within the limits of permissible intervention.

DECISION OF THE BINATIONAL PANEL

Gray Portland Cement and Clinker from Mexico USA–95–1904–02,
September 13, 1996 NAFTA Chapter 19 Binational Panel

* * *

E.   COMMERCE'S APPLICATION OF BIA [BEST INFORMATION AVAILABLE]

The next set of issues we address concerns the Department's application of the BIA standard to arrive at a dumping margin for Types II and V cement in the third annual administrative review. The threshold issue we must decide is whether the DOC acted within its authority when it chose to use BIA in assigning a dumping margin to imports from CEMEX. The second issue is whether, in its choice of BIA to apply to CEMEX, Commerce acted within its authority.

1. *Commerce Properly Used BIA for CEMEX's Imports*

The antidumping statute of the United States provides that the DOC "shall [use BIA] whenever a party . . . refuses or is unable to produce information requested in a timely manner and in the form required." 19 U.S.C. s 1677e(b) (1992). This provision applies to requests for information made during administrative reviews pursuant to Section 751 of the antidumping statute, as well as during LTFV determinations. See Allied–Signal Aerospace Co. v. U.S. 996 F.2d 1185 (Fed.Cir.1993).

In premising resort to BIA on the provision of requested information in a manner and time satisfactory to the Department, the statute vests Commerce with broad authority as to whether to use BIA in any particular case. While not binding upon this panel, we find the reasoning of a recent binational panel under the U.S.-Canada Free Trade Agreement (USCFTA) persuasive on this issue: the DOC's

> discretion to resort to BIA stems not only from the variety of statutory grounds for the use of BIA—refusal to produce information, inability to produce information in the required form, significantly impeding an investigation—but also from the need for [Commerce] to control the fact-gathering process. The courts have viewed [Commerce]'s authority to resort to BIA as essential to the fulfillment of [Commerce]'s responsibility to determine in a timely manner an accurate dumping margin, both in antidumping investigations and in administrative reviews.

Certain Cut-to-Length Carbon Steel Plate from Canada, USA–93–1904–04, 1994 FTAPD, LEXIS 14, October 31, 1994, at 68, quoting Replacement Parts for Self–Propelled Bituminous Paving Equipment from Canada, USA–90–1904–01, 1992 FTAPD, LEXIS 2, May 15, 1992, at 74 (footnote omitted).

Commerce's discretion to use BIA is, of course, not unbounded. A reviewing court—and hence, this panel—is not obligated to sustain a decision by Commerce to use BIA should said decision be unsupported by substantial evidence on the record or otherwise not in accordance with law. 19 U.S.C. s 1516a(b)(1)(B) (1988). Applying this standard, the Department's use of BIA has been upheld, save for the unusual situation in which its requests for information from respondents have been unreasonable under the circumstances—as where, for example, the information did not exist or the Department failed adequately to notify respondent of what it was seeking. See, e.g., Olympic Adhesives, Inc. v. United States, 899 F.2d 1565 (Fed.Cir.1990); Mitsui & Co., Ltd. v. United States, 1994 Ct. Int'l. Tr. LEXIS 59, Slip Op. 94–44; NTN Bearing Corp. v. United States, 17 CIT 713, 826 F. Supp. 1435 (1993); Daewoo Electronics Co., Ltd. v. United States, 13 CIT 253, 712 F. Supp.

931 (1989), aff'd in part and rev'd in part, remanded, 6 F.3d 1511 (Fed. Cir. 1993). Stated differently, where the Department's requests for information have been reasonable in view of the circumstances, both courts and USCFTA panels have upheld the use of BIA when such information has not been provided in a form and at a time acceptable to the DOC. See, e.g., Allied–Signal, 996 F.2d 1185; Koyo Seiko Co., Ltd. v. United States, 898 F. Supp. 915 (Ct. Int'l Tr. 1995); Certain Cut-to-Length Carbon Steel Plate from Canada, U.S.A.–93–1904–04, 1994 FTAPD, LEXIS 14 (Oct. 31, 1994).

In the instant case, the DOC made a series of requests for information concerning CEMEX's home market sales of Type I cement. These requests had two principal bases. One concerned Commerce's need to determine whether sales of Types II and V cement occurred "within the ordinary course of trade," as was claimed by CEMEX. Given that the ordinary course of trade is defined at least in part through comparison with the terms and conditions for sales of similar products, the DOC was of the view that it could not evaluate this claim absent the data it sought from CEMEX regarding sales of Type I cement. Final Results of Third Review, 60 Fed. Reg. at 26,869. The record is quite clear that CEMEX did not provide such data to the Department, thereby impairing the DOC's ability to complete a comparative investigation. Id.

A second, independently sufficient basis for Commerce's request for sales information concerning Type I cement lay in the possibility that sales of Types II and V cement might, indeed, be found to be outside the ordinary course of trade, thereby necessitating the DOC's reliance on sales of Type I cement, as similar merchandise, in order to determine Fair Market Value ("FMV"). In this regard, it should be noted that in the second administrative review, Commerce determined that CEMEX's home market sales of Types II and V cement were outside the ordinary course of trade, and that the CIT affirmed that finding, in so doing instructing the DOC to collect Type I sales information rather than resort to a constructed value methodology. CEMEX, S.A. v. United States, CIT Slip Op. 95–72 (April 24, 1995). In the words of the CIT,

> There is a statutory preference for the use of similar merchandise in determining FMV. . . . Constructed value should only be used where Commerce has made a determination that the exporter's home market prices are inadequate or unavailable for the purpose of calculating FMV.

Id. at 31–32 (citation omitted). To be sure, Commerce's finding in the second administrative review is not binding on subsequent reviews and the above-cited CIT decision was not handed down until well after the third administrative review began. Nonetheless, Commerce's finding in the second administrative review of the need for Type I sales data, and its affirmation by the CIT, lends support to the DOC's position in the instant case that its requests for Type I sales data in the third administrative review were not unreasonable.

CEMEX argues that the Department did not need information on sales of Type I cement because CEMEX had submitted information demonstrating that sales of Types II and V were in the ordinary course of trade for the period of review of the third administrative review. Based on this, CEMEX argues that the DOC's requests for information on Type I sales were unreasonable, and that, therefore, its resort to BIA should be overturned by this panel. We do not find that argument persuasive. As has been stressed previously, Commerce's discretion here is broad, with requests for information being subject to the general reasonableness standard described above. Believing that the DOC gave adequate consideration to the evidence of changed circumstances submitted by CEMEX, we find no basis for CEMEX's assertion that the Department acted unreasonably during the third administrative review in requesting information on Type I sales for FMV purposes.

Although we are sensitive to the risks involved in allowing the DOC too free a hand in requesting information, lest it lead to a de facto barrier to imports, that was not the case here. Commerce's requests for Type I sales information clearly came within the range of discretion implied by the reasonableness standard, and we, therefore, hold that the DOC was justified in applying BIA when those requests for information were not answered. This decision is made easier by the fact that CEMEX had provided information on Type I sales during the LTFV investigation and during the first and second administrative reviews. In addition, over the course of its requests to CEMEX, the Department (i) warned CEMEX that BIA might be applied if the requested information were not forthcoming (Letter of 2/4/94, supra note 24); (ii) narrowed the scope of its requests to reduce the burden which supplying the requested information would place on CEMEX (Letter of 11/29/93, supra note 24); and (iii) granted a time extension requested by CEMEX (Letter of 11/29/93, supra note 24). For this panel to hold otherwise would be to sanction CEMEX's tactic of answering routine requests for information with substantive objections to the appropriateness of those requests, a practice that would render it impossible for Commerce to administer the antidumping statute in the manner intended by Congress. See Ansaldo Componenti, S.p.A. v. United States, 628 F. Supp. 198 (Ct. Int'l Tr. 1986); Mitsubishi Heavy Industries, Ltd. v. United States, 833 F. Supp. 919 (Ct. Int'l Tr. 1993).

* * *

Questions and Comments

1. Stephen Powell (formerly Chief Counsel for Import Trade Administration in the Department of Commerce, now a law professor at the University of Florida), and Mark Barnett (attorney in the same office), define dumping and note the role of the ITA in determining sales at less than fair value (LTFV). In our peach case, the Mexican peach growers and their association AGMEX, have not responded to requests for information from the ITA. What are the consequences of this failure, which certainly makes it difficult for the ITA to reach an accurate conclusion?

2. The NAFTA panel will review the ITA determination to determine whether the ITA properly applied U.S. law. It will review the manner in which the ITA reached its LTFV determination, and whether four states constitute an industry and three-four months of sales is adequate, rather than the entire U.S. as the market, and twelve months as the proper time. As Powell and Barnett explain, the calculation of "normal value" and the U.S. price has variables. The method selected by the ITA may be challenged. Perhaps home market sales were not sufficient, and either a third market or a constructed value ought to have been used. For the U.S. price, did the ITA use an "export price" or a "constructed export price", and was the choice justified? Also, there may be challenges to the various adjustments which were, or should have been, made. If during the ITA's considerations, the Mexican government indicated its dislike for what appeared to be forthcoming and impliedly threatened to ask for a binational panel, would that influence the ITA? Was that why a suspension agreement was reached in the tomato case?

3. Most of the binational panel reviews of U.S. administrative agency decisions concern the antidumping or subsidies margins determined by Commerce rather than injury determinations of the ITC. In an initial investigation, Commerce determines dumping and subsidization and the ITC, injury. However, many of the cases—including ten involving Mexican cement (several of which are discussed in this problem)—are annual "administrative reviews" in which Commerce recalculates the dumping or subsidy margins using more recent data. While annual reviews can be requested by any party, normally there are no corresponding reviews of injury determinations, until the five-year "Sunset" reviews.

4. If we assume, as the facts suggest for CONVEG, that there has been a final determination of dumping by the ITA (and of injury by the ITC), a panel will be formed. Who do you want on the panel if you represent CONVEG? In the second extract by Powell and Barnett, they suggest the NAFTA's preference for judges is an improvement over the CFTA. Why? Do you agree? (In fact, judges have seldom if ever been willing to serve as Chapter 19 panelists.) What about practicing attorneys? Professors? Economists? Someone who has already served on a prior panel (and is willing to serve on another)? The authors also make no apologies for Mexico's admission being conditioned on changes in Mexican law so that it is "closer to a common law system for antidumping and countervailing duty." Why do they believe that was necessary? Finally, they applaud the suspension rights of a Party under specific circumstances. Are the circumstances sufficient to justify such possibly drastic measures?

5. For the most part the Chapter 19 process has been viewed positively, but different nations have viewed dumping from different lenses. One trade lawyer has commented:

> During the NAFTA negotiations I never heard anybody on the Canadian side complaining that they were not being given fair access to the U.S. courts or that the U.S. courts were in any way biased. The criticism always was of the structure of the dumping system or the bias of the administrators, so if you have a flawed structure and biased administrators, what do you do? Of course, you fix the courts, which

have nothing to do with a flawed structure or the biased administration. That is what we got. It was clearly a political decision, something that had to be done in order to close. It was never presented on the American side as an interim measure, and I am quite sure it is not likely to be an interim measure, but it is something that has, I think, generally worked. This has had some interesting consequences. First of all, I should say I am not a panelist, so aside from the cases in which I have served, you have had often better-articulated decisions out of panels than you would have gotten out of the international trade or the court of appeals of the federal circuit. That is because the panelists, by and large, know a great deal more about the law than do the judges who typically hear the cases. The panelists also have more time to think about the cases, typically, than do judges. So that, I think, has been a benefit.

Robert Cassidy, Dispute Resolution Under NAFTA: A U.S. Perspective, 23 Canada–U.S. L.J. 147,148 (1997).

Although the intention expressed in CFTA was that dumping actions would disappear after five years, that expression did not appear in the NAFTA. Cassidy thinks Chapter 19 of NAFTA is more than an interim measure; ten years' experience after his article was written only confirms that view. Although exploration of the economic theory of dumping is far beyond the scope of our problem, some believe that dumping ought to be abolished and dealt with under antitrust laws, or at least restricted to the relatively rare situation of predatory pricing. For political reasons in many WTO Member countries, this simply isn't going to happen.

6.   A major conflict continues over the extent to which a panel, whether a panel under NAFTA or the WTO, ought to "defer" to the expertise of the administering authority in applying national law. That conflict also exists with regard to the review in the U.S. Court of International Trade (CIT). A fair number of the decisions of the CIT, NAFTA and the GATT/WTO have indeed rejected the conclusions of the ITA and ITC. If NAFTA panels (or the CIT or GATT/WTO panels) could not overturn national administrative agency determinations, what role would the panels play? Note that under NAFTA, Article 1904:3 and Annex 1911 the panel must apply the same standard of review would a national court reviewing an antidumping or countervailing duty determination. In the United States, for example, the standard is narrow and provides substantial deference to the ITA or ITC: "unsupported by substantial evidence on the record, or otherwise not in accordance with law." (19 U.S.C. § 1516a.)

On the other hand, if substantial deference is not given to the very considerable experience of the applicable administrative agency, isn't the role of the panel excessive? Could it be that there is some suspicion, justified or not, that the ITA and/or ITC (and their equivalents in Canada and Mexico), may be subject to political influence? Which would be more subject to such influence, the ITA or the ITC? If U.S. nationals suspect the independence of the ITA and/or ITC, is it fair to expect Canadians and Mexicans to accept without question their determinations?

7.   One area of conflict is when the ITA uses the "best information available" (BIA) ("facts available" under the WTO's 1994 Antidumping Agreement) to determine export prices and normal values in the LTFV

analysis. If the foreign exporters do not provide the information requested by the administering authority, it may use information from other sources, most likely from the complaining domestic industry. The extract from the *Gray Portland Cement from Mexico* panel decision shows how part of a panel decision reads. It also illustrates the developing jurisprudence of the NAFTA, by its citations to previous binational panel decisions, and U.S. cases. In addition to ruling that the ITA properly used BIA for the cement imports, the panel went on to find the methodology in applying BIA also proper. The *Gray Portland Cement* panel decision is part of a long dispute between Mexico and the U.S. The Binational Panel Summary, which precedes the BIA extract, outlines the earlier conflict. It has not ended. After the panel upheld the imposition of dumping duties, subsequent annual administrative reviews continued to find even higher dumping margins. Mexico (and the U.S. producers in two cases) asked for new panels to review several of the annual administrative reviews.

8.   What if the best result in the view of the panel is to provide injunctive relief? Is the fact that the Court of International Trade may not grant such relief binding? Or does the answer lie in what NAFTA allows, not in what national courts may or may not do? Why shouldn't the panels have the authority to reverse national administrative determinations, rather than only to affirm or remand them? Note that the WTO panels have authority to affirm or reverse, but not to remand.

9.   What if the peach industry in the Southeast obtained legislation in each state that mandated that all peaches be packed in a way that made it difficult for Mexican growers to comply, but easy for U.S. growers? (Hint: see GATT, Article III, incorporated in NAFTA by Article 301:1.) For an interesting discussion of the packing methods the Florida tomato industry tried to impose on Mexico, see Patrick F.J. Macrory, U.S. Restrictions on Imports of Winter Vegetables From Mexico, 11 Fla.J.Int'l L. 299, 315 (1997); Comments of John van Sickle, Patrick Macrory and Michael W. Gordon, Agricultural Disputes: Mexican Tomatoes to Florida and Washington Apples to Mexico, 6 U.S.-Mex. L.J. 117, 141 (1998).

10.   The tomato case ended in a suspension agreement. Is the peach case another dispute where a suspension agreement might be the best solution? Would it parallel that of the tomato suspension agreement?

11.   Because many of the NAFTA panel decisions involve long standing trade disputes, a single panel decision is often neither the beginning nor the end of the conflict. Steel cases have been a frequent subject for panels, and are likely to be in the future. The softwood lumber dispute between Canada and the U.S. (discussed in the following problem) was the subject of five CFTA panel decisions and one ECC decision in the early to mid–1990s. The 1996 settlement agreement which followed this litigation expired in 2001, and was immediately followed by the filing of new anti-dumping and countervailing duty cases by the U.S. lumber interests. As of late 2004, after three NAFTA Chapter 19 panel decisions and three decisions at the WTO, the duties imposed by the United States, may have to be lifted—eventually. Few observers believe that the end of the dispute has arrived!

PART B. APPLES FROM THE U.S. TO MEXICO

Part A considered a Chapter 19 NAFTA binational panel reviewing an agency determination by the U.S. ITA. This part considers the use of a NAFTA panel to review Mexican SECOFI determinations.

SYMPOSIUM, AGRICULTURAL DISPUTES: MEXICAN TOMATOES TO FLORIDA AND WASHINGTON APPLES TO MEXICO*

6 U.S.–Mexico L.J. 117 (1998).**

GORDON: Is the apple dispute an issue throughout Mexico, or is it specific to Chihuahua? In other words, is it predominantly a state issue?

HURTADO: It is certainly a regional issue. The State of Chihuahua is one of the largest in Mexico, and the production of apples is very highly concentrated in that area. In addition, the Minister of Commerce, Herminio Blanco, is from Chihuahua. So political factors may come into play here as everywhere.

GORDON: I assume that Chihuahua apple producers and Sinaloa tomato producers hold very different views as to whether or not Mexico should get tough on the apple issue. A tough stance on apples in Mexico could exacerbate the tomato issue in the United States.

HURTADO: Absolutely. The same principle applies in all trade disputes. Whenever an industry prevails in a particular case, there is a fear that retaliation will affect that country's other products. The current controversy over high fructose corn syrup has been of great concern to Mexican tomato producers, for instance, because of the possibility of U.S. retaliation. A commercial war injures everybody. No one wishes to provoke one, or to be blamed for one.

* * *

GORDON: In Mexico, the *Secretaría de Comercio and Fomento Industrial* (SECOFI) [now SECON] handles both [LTFV and injury]. Is that correct?

HURTADO: Yes. After ten years of practice, I am not sure which system is more effective or appropriate. Few cases have been tried in Mexico so far, because we are relative newcomers in this area. In 1987, when we joined the General Agreement on Tariffs and Trade (GATT), we also adopted the antidumping code, but the law was not finalized until 1993. Only since then has our law been truly comparable to that of the United States. From that date on there have been only about 200

---

* These comments were part of a discussion about the tomato and apple cases. Extracted are questions by the moderator, Prof. Michael W. Gordon, responses by David Hurtado, a practicing attorney in Mexico City and comments by Steven J. Powell, Chief Counsel for Import Administration, U.S. Department of Commerce.

** Copyright © 1998 the U.S.–Mexico Law Journal. Reprinted with permission.

cases. Approximately eighty of them have been resolved by imposing antidumping or countervailing duties.

The Mexican system is indeed more unitary than that of the United States: the cases are handled entirely within SECOFI, particularly the *Unidad de Prácticas Comerciales Internacionales* [International Commercial Practices Unit]. This unit, in turn, has two subsidiary departments. One deals with dumping, and the other with injury. The analysis of dumping and injury occurs simultaneously, however. The conclusion reached by each department is subsequently analyzed by the head of the unit. If dumping margins have been found, and if that dumping has been found to be the principal or sole cause of the injury, then a resolution is issued linking the two activities, and dumping duties are imposed. This would seem to be a less democratic system, but I am personally unfamiliar with the political nuances of the process. Certainly there have been many cases where the head of the unit favors, or allegedly favors, one sector of the industry. Because there is only one final decision maker, our system is potentially more expeditious. That decision maker is more exposed to political influence or to directives from his superiors within SECOFI, however.

* * *

GORDON: David, what is the struggle going on to define injury in dumping cases in Mexico? How is this problem approached?

HURTADO: For the petitioner to prevail in a dumping case, according to the law, the dumped products have to be the direct cause of the injury. Every case involves an analysis of the particular domestic industry. Very thorough analyses and verifications are conducted, and evidence is very important to determine whether dumping or some other factor such as natural competition or advantage is the direct cause of the displacement of a product's sales. It is a very thoughtful analysis along the lines of the GATT. I think the SECOFI has done a good job in every resolution of isolating the injury aspect, analyzing other possible causes of the injury in accordance with the guidelines specified by law.

GORDON: Do the regulations to the Foreign Trade Law go into injury in some depth?

HURTADO: Absolutely. The regulations expand the general provisions of the law and give more detailed guidelines on how to analyze dumping and injury.

POWELL: You mentioned that SECOFI has to find that the dumped imports are the direct cause of the harm. Does that mean that SECOFI will look at other causes and determine whether or not they are more important than dumping? In other words, will it engage in a weighing of different causes? The importers in the apple situation, for instance, were arguing that the apple growers in Chihuahua were having difficulties for a whole variety of other reasons, rather than dumped imports. The Secretary has rejected those arguments, at least at the preliminary stages. But have there been cases where SECOFI has said that other causes were more important than the dumped imports?

HURTADO: Absolutely, there have been many of them. I would think that in about thirty percent if not more of the cases that have been dismissed, the reason has been that there was no connection between the dumping margin and the injury, even when SECOFI recognized that the import prices constituted dumping. The burden is on the parties to offer economic analysis and a worldwide view of a specific product's market, in order to prove that non-dumping elements may need to be considered.

The high-fructose corn syrup case is, in many respects, illustrative of SECOFI's approach. It is believed by some that the sugar industry has been injured by a variety of factors other than fructose. I have teams researching that. The sugar industry was at first state-owned; then it was privatized; then came the devaluation. Many factors caused it to become a deeply indebted industry. Fructose did not really enter the market until the sugar industry was already deeply in trouble. We are trying to prove that the injury was produced by many elements other than fructose.

GORDON: Although time pressure is certainly an important factor, recent [dumping] cases suggest that resorting to "best information available" does not necessarily yield satisfactory determinations. In the United States, for example, a great deal of criticism has been levied at Mexico's preliminary determination in the apple case, which was based partly on "best information available." Is there a likelihood that we might reevaluate the time frames for ITA and SECOFI investigations, so that they need not resort to such limited sampling?

HURTADO: I do not think so. An important feature of Mexican antidumping law is that the final resolution in a dumping case imposes separate duties for the companies that appeared in the case versus the ones that did not. The duties imposed on those who appeared in the case are based on the actual dumping margin found. Industry members who do not offer a defense in the case become subject to a residual or "pseudo-dumping" duty, which is essentially the highest dumping margin found.

This is what happened in the apple cases. Approximately ten exporters were named in the initial investigation, but only two of them made an appearance during the resolution phase. This surprised us, given the importance of the apple industry to the state of Washington. There are many other pitfalls in this case, but it is a simple fact that information from two companies is not statistically representative of an entire industry. Furthermore, the importers presented invoices inconsistent with those submitted by the two exporters. SECOFI was forced to resort to the "best information available" at the preliminary stage.

POWELL: Accuracy and expediency have always been at war in trade cases. I seriously doubt that respondents would wish these cases to last more than a year. Our investigations take place during a time of trouble in the market. Importers do not know from whom to buy;

exporters do not know who their buyers are going to be. Although such investigations are part of doing business in the international sector, it is probable that most countries are pushing for shorter investigations. It is important to keep in mind that deadlines were added to the GATT for the first time in the Uruguay Round. Some countries were taking a great deal longer than a year or so to complete their investigations. I do not believe that the desire for accuracy will lead to the restoration of longer investigation periods. Instead, I think that it will encourage countries to invest more resources in each investigation.

David mentioned the youth of SECOFI's unfair practices law. It is still relatively new. Nonetheless, the Mexicans have become the second most active users of dumping laws in the entire world, following only the United States. In just a few years, they have surpassed the Europeans, the Canadians, and the Australians. This has been done with the addition of a substantial number of staff. We used to go to Geneva and people would laugh at us when we told them that the ITA and the ITC each had about two hundred people conducting investigations. They would say, "My God, why do you need that many people?" We need them because we have about five hundred active investigations pending at any given moment, either in the initial or the review stage. Lawsuits number about the same. I think other countries are beginning to realize that if they want to administer an antidumping law successfully, they have to commit adequate resources. In a sense, the themes of the WTO Anti-Dumping Agreement are accuracy and transparency. These very important goals, in which we think the United States is already a leader, require creativity and investigative resources.

Turning to the specific question of apples, I would like to make a some observations. As I understand the facts, the two U.S. companies that chose to respond submitted their questionnaire responses on time and in proper form. Both of those facts were confirmed by SECOFI in its preliminary determination. SECOFI also asked importers for their information about pricing of apples; at the same time, they obtained invoices from those importers to double-check the responses that they were getting. It is somewhat unusual to go into records at this stage. Usually this is not done until the on-site verification phase, after the preliminary determination, although the investigating body is entitled to review a company's records when it sees fit. In this case, SECOFI found discrepancies between the pricing reported by importers and the pricing reported by exporters in regard to the same transactions. It consequently asked the two U.S. producers to supply invoices as well. Needless to say, those invoices matched the numbers given by the producers in their questionnaire response. Some discrepancies nonetheless remained. It is unclear how many of these there were. Either three out of 120 invoices did not match, or the three that SECOFI was able to trace did not match. In any event, SECOFI decided at that point that the information from both the exporters and the importers was unreliable as a basis to calculate margins. As a result, it discarded all of that information and used the numbers the petitioner had supplied. Such figures are, to put it mildly, sometimes generous to the petitioner. In this case, the petitioner had alleged a dumping margin of 101%. This margin became the "best information" or "facts available" margin, and SECOFI assigned it to the apple exporters in its preliminary determination.

What I find most interesting is the question of why SECOFI would assume that the U.S. exporter was lying. In my opinion, that would be the only basis for disregarding all the information that had been supplied, rather than just the three invoices in which there was an observed discrepancy. Why were all 120 invoices discarded from the analysis? There are many possible explanations for the invoice discrepancies. Clearly, one of them could be dumping engaged in by the U.S. trading company serving as an intermediary between the exporter and the importer. Another possibility is that the importer was trying to avoid paying regular tariffs on apples. There is still a tariff on apples going into Mexico, although it is trending down with the NAFTA.

These are not accusations. My point is simply that there are a number of possible explanations for the discrepancies that SECOFI found, not necessarily attributable to the exporters. The troubling fact here is not that SECOFI resorted to the "best information available." When other data are unusable, this is the only alternative. What disturbs me is that the data supplied by the exporters could only be considered unusable if SECOFI found that they did not cooperate to the best of their ability. In other words, SECOFI's investigators assumed that the exporters were lying to them.

HURTADO: That is not my understanding of the case. To the best of my knowledge, what SECOFI said was that the two exporters were not representative of the aggregate exports from the country. This is why they disregarded the information.

POWELL: That is not what SECOFI said in its preliminary findings. It said that the invoices did not match, that the figures on both sides were thus unreliable, and that it would not use any of those numbers. This is especially troubling because of another fact: at the "disclosure conference" held by SECOFI, the investigators refused to share the disputed invoices with the U.S. producers. Perhaps this was based on confidentiality reasons.

HURTADO: Mexican law has strict rules regarding access to confidential information in a dumping procedure. This does not mean that access is impossible to obtain, however. The party seeking the information must provide a valid reason for doing so, and must post a bond. I have personally requested information regarding the sugar industry on behalf of importers of high fructose corn syrup. This was more or less easily managed, as long as those conditions were met.

* * *

REYNA, NAFTA CHAPTER 19 BINATIONAL PANEL
REVIEWS IN MEXICO: A MARRIAGE OF TWO
DISTINCT LEGAL SYSTEMS

5 U.S.–Mexico L.J. 65 (1997)*

An issue that invariably arises in discussions concerning NAFTA
binational panel reviews is whether foreign panelists can adequately
apply the national law of the importing country. . . .

The initial Mexican binational panel reviews have raised a number
of interesting issues related to whether panels apply the appropriate
standard of review. As the *Steel Plate* and *Polystyrene* reviews demonstrate, the application of Mexican law by binational panels has been
problematic, primarily due to the differences between the legal systems
of the United States (and Canada) and Mexico and because Mexico's
experience in trade matters is not as developed as that of the United
States and Canada.

One of Mexico's principal NAFTA negotiating objectives was the
adoption of the trade dispute resolution mechanism established under
Chapter 19 of the FTA which was structured in accordance with the U.S.
and Canadian common law legal systems. As the FTA mechanism was
incorporated in the NAFTA with little change, Mexico was obligated to
make significant substantive revisions to its antidumping laws and
regulations in order to implement the binational process. Those revisions, however, were not sufficient to account for all the nuances that
would arise as a result of the fundamental differences between the
Mexican civil law code system and the common law structure of the
binational panel review process.

It is no surprise, therefore, that the initial panel reviews have
involved important issues novel under both Mexican law and the binational panel process. When Mexico revised its domestic laws, it adopted a
number of foreign legal concepts that have no basis under the Mexican
legal system. In addition, while NAFTA Chapter 19 was designed to limit
the range of law applied in panel reviews, the Mexican legal system
requires the application of a significantly broader range of law than
applied in U.S. or Canadian reviews, a factor that has the potential to
create a perception that Mexican reviews are inconsistent with the letter
and spirit of NAFTA Chapter 19.

In the *Steel Plate* review, the panel ruled that the final antidumping
duty determination was null and void on grounds that, among other
reasons, the *Secretaría de Comercio y Fomento Industrial* [Secretariat of
Commerce and Development] (SECOFI) was not competent in the early
stages of the underlying antidumping investigation. This ruling raised a
number of important and complex issues of first instance.

First, the panel had to determine the significance of competency in
the context of a binational panel review in Mexico. The term "competent

investigating authority" is used throughout NAFTA Article 1904. Its meaning with respect to the United States and Canada is simple; in the case of the United States, "competent investigating authority" means the U.S. Department of Commerce International Trade Administration or the U.S. International Trade Commission, and in the case of Canada it means the Canadian International Trade Tribunal or the Deputy Minister of National Revenue for Customs and Excise. Under U.S. trade law, the legal concept of "competency" is not a significant issue and, apparently, no antidumping duty determination has been remanded (or reversed) on the basis that the investigating authority was not competent.

In Mexico's case "competent investigating authority" means the designated authority within SECOFI, a definition which appears the same as that for Canada and the United States. Its apparent simplicity, however, belies the significance of "competency" under Mexican law,[17] and the complexity involved in its interpretation and application. The extent of that complexity, in addition to the formalism inherent in Mexican law, is evident in the majority opinion in the *Steel Plate* review which held that the authority within SECOFI that conducted the initial stages of the underlying investigation had not been legally established and, therefore, did not legally exist.[18]

. . . The panel's decision regarding the competency of the investigating authority had the effect of rendering the final determination null and void, and of terminating the investigation and revoking the related outstanding antidumping duty orders, an outcome not envisioned under the NAFTA.

Second, the panel had to determine the extent, if any, of its authority to apply Articles 237, 238 and 239 of the Mexican Federal Fiscal Code in order to give effect to its competency decision. . . . The Steel panel decided that, in order to provide a remedy consistent with its decision, it was required to apply the judgement guidelines contained in Articles 237 and 239 of the Federal Fiscal Code. . . .

The *Steel Plate* panel decision generated considerable public attention in Mexico as it was widely perceived to have resulted from an application of foreign legal concepts, *i.e.* American, to a Mexican proceeding. In reality, the *Steel Plate* review involved the interpretation and application of Mexican, not American, law. To astute observers of binational proceedings, the real interest concerned the effect of the decision within the context of the NAFTA binational structure.

* * *

17. Generally, "*competencia*" refers to capacity of an authoritative organ to undertake or conduct certain functions or legal acts. The legal interests of a person (or entity) may be affected only by a written order by a competent authority.

18. In *Steel Plate*, the dissenting opinion contends that the NAFTA definition of "competent authority" limits the scope of review on competency matters to the single issue of whether the final determination was issued by a designated authority within SECOFI.

The difficulty inherent in the resolution of the issues presented in the *Steel Plate* and *Polystyrene* cases was compounded by the (understandable) lack of administrative determinations and judicial opinions which the panelists and parties could rely for meaningful guidance. Compared to the United States and Canada, whose unfair trade systems date back to the turn of this century, Mexico's unfair trade system is relatively young. Mexico acceded to the GATT in 1986 at which time it adopted the GATT Antidumping Code. Since its accession to the GATT, the number of trade cases brought in Mexico increased steadily, and by the mid–1990's Mexico had become one of the world's leading countries in the use of antidumping duty remedies.

In U.S. reviews, the panelists and parties typically have an abundance of judicial opinions and administrative cases to apply and interpret. This is not the case in Mexican reviews. Despite the large number of antidumping investigations brought in Mexico during the 1990's, by the end of 1996, the *Tribunal Fiscal* had yet to complete a review of an antidumping duty determination. Moreover, because the NAFTA entered into effect in 1994, there is nominal administrative and judicial experience in Mexico with respect to the NAFTA requirement that final antidumping duty determinations be based on the administrative record and that reviews of final determinations be made on the basis of the administrative record.

In any event, Article 1904 provides that a panel must apply the applicable standard of review, the antidumping duty law, and the general legal principles that a court of the importing party would apply to a review of the final determination. The term "antidumping duty law" includes legislative histories, administrative practices, and judicial precedents, all concepts that have a rich application in common law.

In Mexico, "legislative histories" are not as expansive as in the United States or Canada, and courts do not generally rely on legislative histories for statutory construction purposes. The concept of "administrative practices" as understood under U.S. administrative law does not exist in Mexican administrative law, and a judicial "precedent" is established when the Mexican Supreme Court, or the Federal Circuit Courts, consistently decide the same point in five consecutive separate cases. This means that there is little judicial "precedent" in trade matters.

In view of the foregoing, Mexico's initial experience under the binational process may support a perception that panel reviews in Mexico involve an irreconcilable conflict of two distinct legal systems. This renders the binational panel process meaningless. Such a perception, however, would be erroneous. While the Mexican reviews may appear aberrant to persons unfamiliar with civil code legal systems, it is unreasonable to expect Mexican reviews to mirror U.S. (or Canadian) reviews, or otherwise involve familiar sounding issues. There is no indication that different results would have been obtained had the reviews been conducted by the *Tribunal Fiscal*. Indeed, that the initial reviews involved difficult and novel issues demonstrates the characteristics of integrity and independence desired of panels, and are factors that strengthen and lend credibility to the binational panel review process.

PRACTICE BEFORE U.S.–MEXICO BINATIONAL PANELS UNDER CHAPTER NINETEEN OF NAFTA: A PANEL DISCUSSION
5 U.S.–Mexico L.J. 73 (1997)*

EDUARDO DAVID: The case in which my firm was involved, *In re Flat Coated Steel Products From the United States*, was the first final determination of the *Secretaría de Comercio y Fomento Industrial* (SECOFI) to be reviewed by a binational panel under Chapter 19.....

SECOFI determined that U.S. steel producers were selling flat coated steel products below the home market price into the Mexican market. As a result, antidumping duties were imposed. On October 3, 1994, U.S. steel producers presented a petition before the Mexican NAFTA Secretariat requesting the formation of a binational panel to review this determination. A panel was formed, and written and oral arguments were presented by all interested parties. Notwithstanding the fact that the case had been fully briefed and argued, the panelists needed to spend substantial time in resolving several unexpected practical problems during the proceeding.

Many conflicts exist because of the differences between the Mexican civil code legal system and United States and Canada common law tradition.... A threshold problem for the Mexican panelists in *Flat Coated Steel* was applying their understanding of NAFTA procedural rules which differ substantially from the general procedural rules that have historically applied to litigation in Mexico.

Another problem arose when Mexican lawyers representing the parties cited principles of Mexican law or used Mexican legal terms. It is very difficult to present an argument which is intended to target both Mexican and North American panelists when Mexican attorneys feel compelled in their briefs to cite basic principles of Mexican law such as those found in Articles 14 and 16 of our Constitution.

As an example, the Mexican legal principle of *motivación* [motivation] and *fundamentación* [foundation] is basic to and clearly understood by a Mexican attorney. However, if such a principle were to be translated literally, "motivation and foundation for application" would not make any sense to a North American attorney. It must be remembered that this principle of law is one of the pillars of Mexican constitutional law, and its legal implications are drilled into the heads of Mexican law students from the beginning of their studies. Therefore, even if translated into English, the lack of Mexican legal foundation and rationale makes it difficult for non-Mexican panelists to fully understand the possible consequences of finding a violation of this important Mexican legal principle.

Another major issue involves the authority and powers of the panel. As established by Article 1904, Paragraph 1 of NAFTA, the panel replaces the competent judicial authority which normally would have reviewed the case. In Mexico, such judicial authority would be the Tax Courts. This raises the issue of whether the Mexican Tax Courts have the power to determine the competence of the binational panel, and of course if the binational panel would have the same powers as the Mexican Tax Courts would have. In interpreting Mexican law, one should rely not only on one article, but on the entire jurisprudential legal system of Mexico. The standard of review is established by Article 238 of the *Código Fiscal de la Federación* [Federal Fiscal Code]. This explains when a procedure is considered null and void. The options of the panel are either to confirm the determination or to remand it to the authority which would have to implement a determination.

Confirmation of the determination does not create a problem. But Article 238 only establishes what is to be considered as null and void, not what the authority should do in case the Fiscal Court declares the determination null and void. Therefore, Article 238 must be interpreted in conjunction with Article 239 of the C.F.F. which establishes what effects a determination may have if it is declared *"lisa y llana."* There is no adequate translation for certain Spanish terms which I will explain. Depending upon the case, Article 239 states that a determination could be declared *"nula lisa y llana"* or *"para efectos."* *"Nula lisa y llana"* means that the determination is simply null and void; the authority may not remand the proceeding. *"Para efectos"* means that the authority must remand the proceeding. The problem was that if the panel declared a determination issued by the Mexican authority *lisa y llana*, the determination could not be remanded to restart the procedure. Only if the determination were declared *"para efectos"* could the determination be remanded to restart the procedure. In my opinion, the panel is empowered to declare an administrative determination completely null and void, *lisa y llana*, because it is supposed to act as the judicial authority of Mexico where the determination was issued.

The translations also created some problems during the filings of briefs and in the public hearings. Parties were supposed to provide the panel English versions of their briefs. Translating was difficult and in certain cases, burdensome. The problem was translating the documents so they could be understood by a U.S. panelist.... During the hearing, translation was even more difficult despite having professional translators. Several times it was necessary to correct the translator because of terms that were very difficult to translate. Once again, a wrong translation might create confusion and perhaps misinterpretation by the panelists.

* * *

Hearings presented another problem. Hearings in Mexico are ...
conducted only to resolve questions of evidence, and the judge may make
decisions about evidentiary questions without actually questioning the
parties. On the other hand, the panel is permitted to interrupt the
attorneys during presentations in order to resolve doubts or ask questions.

* * *

Not only were there problems relating to procedures and interpretation of law; but there were also other practical problems that arose
during the presentation of our briefs at the hearing. For instance, my
law firm works as co-counsel with a U.S. firm. Explaining the Mexican
law and drafting the brief with U.S. attorneys was very complicated.
Because of differences in legal systems and jurisprudence, a Mexican
attorney's approach to interpreting an issue of law is considerably
different than that of a U.S. attorney. It is difficult to make oneself
understood by a U.S. attorney who does not have a similar legal
background, and it is equally difficult to understand a U.S. attorney
whose manner of thinking is completely different. As a result, drafting
the briefs was time consuming and not cost-effective. . . .

The empowerment of Mexican attorneys over non-Mexican attorneys
also presented a problem. Only Mexican attorneys could appear before
the panel. The panel members decided that only Mexican attorneys who
are empowered to appear before the panel could participate in the
proceeding, however, co-counsel were designated in our briefs.

The Mexican translation of the NAFTA rules were entirely literal
and difficult to understand. Consequently, the U.S. translation of the
record was used rather than the Mexican version. It is amazing how a
word can change the whole meaning of an article.

There were also external problems, for example, the pressure from
the media during the entire procedure. Many attorneys and panelists felt
the pressure. The media was permitted to publish comments suggesting
SECOFI lacked competence and was not empowered to issue the resolution. This generated tension and led to the resignation of several
panelists. More confusion was created, and that is why a new hearing
was required. Everybody had to prepare once again, and the case was not
resolved for two years.

 ... The use of both U.S. and Mexican attorneys in this kind of
procedure is advisable, even essential, because the panel will always be
composed of panelists from Mexico and the United States or Canada.
Also, it is very important for attorneys who will be involved in NAFTA
panels to try to understand the legal systems of the other countries.
Because of the difference between legal systems, the current procedures
will tend to be longer than they may be in the future once better
understanding is acquired. I think that it is important to have this kind
of conference in order to improve the understanding of our respective
laws which should eventually expedite the panel process.

Questions and Comments

1. The panel discussion extracts by David Hurtado and Stephen Powell offer some comparison of the practices of SECOFI/SECON and the ITA/ITC in addressing trade cases. Hurtado, a Mexico City attorney, does not seem bothered that Mexico has adopted trade laws and procedures from the U.S. and GATT/WTO nations. He explains the unitary nature of the Mexican system, which contrasts with that in the U.S. (and Canada), but is similar to the unitary European Commission system. He views the tradeoffs as a more expeditious system, but more likely to be subject to political influences. Both the Mexican SECON and the U.S. ITA are government departments (or parts thereof), while the U.S. ITC is intended to be separate from any department (like the SEC or FCC), with ITC commissioners appointed by the President with the advice and consent of the Senate for nine year terms. Would the efficiency gained by absorbing the ITC's functions by the Department of Commerce be offset by greater potential political influence? Is there any real evidence of political influence affecting the work of the ITA? (Consider recent cases involving goods from China and Vietnam.)

Hurtado notes the use of best information available (BIA) by SECON, but he does not believe that additional time for making a decision would help reduce the use of BIA. What do you tell the various U.S. apple growers with regard to cooperating with SECON and producing whatever information is requested?

Powell outlines Mexico's rise to a major world player in using dumping actions to address trade issues. He is concerned with the manner in which SECON asked for price information, and disagrees with Hurtado that the information produced by the two of ten U.S. exporters who responded was not sufficient to use, causing SECON to turn to BIA. Do Hurtado and Powell give you enough information to agree with one of them?

2. Jimmie Reyna, who served on the second Chapter 19 panel to review a Mexican SECOFI determination, the *Steel Plate* dispute, introduces us to the panel's need to understand some complex characteristics of another legal system, the civil law system of Mexico, and especially the issue of "competency". He also notes problems attributable to Mexico's relatively recent entry into the world of sophisticated trade issues, such as dumping. SECON initially was finding its way through the process, and it should have been expected to occasionally stumble. After all, no one suggests the Canadian and U.S. administrative agencies have a perfect record of following the Canadian and U.S. laws, respectively.

A very important comment of Reyna is that Mexicans may misconceive the process, and believe the panel applied U.S. legal concepts. He believes it did not, but other critics believe that the whole process of dispute resolution in the NAFTA, not only Chapter 19, but also Chapters 20 and 11, is a U.S. product. Or, are they simply features routinely found in common law jurisdictions, but seldom in civil law jurisdictions? On whose side do you stand? You may wish to wait until you have finished this Chapter, and especially read the next three problems, before you make your decision. If you believe that there are irreconcilable conflicts between the two legal systems, how would you resolve them? You may again wish to wait and view the dispute resolution process at the end of this Chapter.

Reyna also reinforces the limitations of a panel; it has quite clear guidelines about its role. Is it really any different than a domestic court of review, such as the Court of International Trade in the U.S.?

3. Mexican attorney Eduardo David adds to this theme of lack of understanding of the Mexican legal system, with comments from his experience with several cases, including the same *Steel Plate* case Reyna served on as a panelist. In addition to a lack of understanding of such concepts as motivación and fundamentación, he notes problems with translations both in the briefs and in the oral hearings. Those hearings, he notes, are quite new in procedure to Mexican lawyers.

4. What if the Mexican government or the Mexican apple growers trade association, in an attempt to protect the domestic apple market, initiates a "Buy Mexican Apples" campaign directed to Mexican restaurants, institutions and consumers. The campaign is neither misleading nor untruthful, attempting only to foster nationalism in purchasing habits of Mexicans. The U.S. and the Georgia peach growers might also consider a similar campaign, "Buy U.S. Peaches." The peach growers might try to obtain legislation that requires the government to only buy U.S. peaches for the school lunch programs throughout the U.S. Mexico might reciprocate regarding apples. There are thus other avenues of attack. But Chapter 19 is only for dumping and subsidy (countervailing duty) cases. Other restrictive practices may give rise to a Chapter 20 challenge, the subject of Problem 9.4.

5. The facts are adapted from the apple case of Mexico and the tomato and winter vegetable cases of the U.S. They never went to NAFTA panels, because of the use of a suspension agreement, where the growers agreed not to sell below a floor price. Might not that be the best way for our case to be settled? But is a suspension agreement a *final* settlement of such a dispute? Or does it just buy time?

6. The issue of apples to Mexico also involves labor. The Teamsters represent some U.S. apple pickers, and in December, 1998, the union filed a NAFTA complaint about allegedly unsafe working conditions at Washington orchards (the first challenge to U.S. working conditions). The labor side agreement is the subject of Chapter 10. The U.S. New England apple growers might face the same problem raised by the teamsters in 1998.

7. U.S. apple growers are also concerned about Asian imports, partly because of the financial crisis, and particularly due to cheap apple juice concentrate imports from China. Thus, conflicts within the NAFTA area may reflect or be affected by much larger competitive factors.

8. In a pending Chapter 11 case, *Canfor Corp. v. United States,* filed July 9, 2002, a Canadian lumber producer has challenged the 2002 U.S. antidumping and countervailing duty orders against softwood lumber from Canada under NAFTA's *investment* provisions, alleging violations of NAFTA Articles 1102, 1103, 1105 and 1110. (See Notice of Arbitration and Statement of Claim, *available at* http://www.naftlaw.org.) Canfor and other Canadian producers also brought Chapter 19 actions against the Commerce Department and ITC.

PROBLEM 9.3 CHAPTER 19: MATERIAL INJURY AND EXTRAORDINARY CHALLENGE PROCEEDINGS—APPLES AND PEACHES, PART II

SECTION I.   THE SETTING

Problem 9.2 introduced you to CONVEG (Georgia's largest peach producer), AGMEX (a Mexican peach growers' association), INDUSTRIA MANZANA (the large Mexican apple growing concern) and GROWSAP (a U.S. apple growers' association). To stem imports from rival foreign growers, CONVEG and INDUSTRIA MANZANA elected–from the multiple choices available to them–to initiate dumping actions with their respective governments. Affirmative dumping determinations and the imposition of antidumping duties by each government spawned two separate Chapter 19 proceedings, one initiated by AGMEX and the other by GROWSAP. Working through Problem 7.2, you saw how a Chapter 19 panel works in reviewing final antidumping determinations of the ITA and SECON.

However, in order to impose anti-dumping (or countervailing duties), a government's administering authority–SECOFI/SECON in Mexico, the U.S. International Trade Commission in the United States– must also have found that the dumping and/or subsidization also resulted in material injury or the threat to the domestic industry. For purposes of this problem we assume that the ITC in the United States has found evidence of material injury by Mexican peaches.

Shortly after the ITA and ITC's final determinations are published in the *Federal Register*, AGMEX requests review under Chapter 19 in a proceeding that will be separate from the review of the dumping determination. A binational panel is duly convened and issues a final decision (by a vote of three to two) remanding the ITC's injury determination with instructions that the antidumping duty be rescinded and all funds collected from Mexican peach exporters be refunded to them. Soon after the panel concludes its work, the affected U.S. government agencies conclude that the panel effectively ignored the applicable standard of review, and decided on its own that there really wasn't strong evidence of material injury. In the context of this "peach" dispute, assume that you are the Assistant U.S. Trade Representative responsible, in consultation with the ITC's General Counsel, for making an initial assessment of whether to pursue relief under Chapter 19's extraordinary challenge procedure. You will be asked to present the matter, including options available under Chapter 19 and your recommendation, to the USTR for final decision.

SECTION II.   FOCUS OF CONSIDERATION

Here we examine the work of Chapter 19 panels in injury cases. As emphasized in Problem 9.2, the role of binational panels is to determine whether the investigating authority has properly applied those portions of its antidumping or countervailing duty laws relating to material injury determinations. This finding by the panel must be "based solely on the record created during the administrative process and on the standard of review and the general legal principles that would apply in that country's courts."[1]

Because the governmental process in the United States is bifurcated, a Chapter 19 panel may be called upon to assess whether the ITA's antidumping or subsidy determination, and the ITC's injury determination were in accordance with U.S. unfair trade laws. In Mexico, determinations on dumping, subsidy and injury are all made by SECON; thus, the potential issues before a Chapter 19 panel in cases challenging Mexican action will be whether SECON's rulings were in accordance with Mexican unfair trade laws.

Finally, Article 1904.9 provides that the decisions of NAFTA binational panels shall be "binding on the involved Parties with respect to the particular matter between the Parties that is before the panel." Further, Article 1904.11 prohibits the Parties from providing, in domestic legislation, for "an appeal from a panel decision to its domestic courts." However, this does not mean that Chapter 19 panel proceedings are beyond all forms of review. Article 1904.13 authorizes involved Parties to assert an "extraordinary challenge" against a panel or panelist under very limited circumstances such as when a panel "manifestly" exceeds its jurisdiction. Three ECC proceedings occurred under the CFTA, and as of mid–2004 two have been brought under NAFTA. This Problem examines the CFTA origins of NAFTA's extraordinary challenge mechanism, and the extraordinary challenge proceedings and Extraordinary Challenge Committees (ECCs) operating under NAFTA.

You will need to refer to the following materials in working through this Problem: NAFTA Article 1904, Annex 1904.13, Annex 1911, the Rules of Procedure for Article 1904 Binational Panel Reviews, and the Rules of Procedure for Article 1904 Extraordinary Challenge Committees. All of these items are set forth in the Documents Supplement.

SECTION III. READINGS, QUESTIONS AND COMMENTS

PART A. PANEL REVIEW OF INJURY DETERMINATIONS

GALLAGHER, CUSTOMS DUTIES AND IMPORT REGULATIONS
21A Am. Jur. 2d (West Group 1998/1999).*

The U.S. International Trade Commission, formerly called the U.S. Tariff Commission, is composed of six commissioners appointed by the

---

1. Stephen Powell & Mark Barnett, *The Role of United States Trade Laws in Resolving the Florida–Mexico Tomato Conflict*, 11 FLA. J. INT'L L. 319, 356 (1997).

President with the advice and consent of the Senate. Not more than three of the commissioners may be members of the same political party. The President designates one of the commissioners as chairman and one as vice chairman of the Commission. . . .

The Commission has its principal office in Washington, D. C., with another at the Port of New York, but may, by one or more of its members or by such agents as it may designate, prosecute any inquiry necessary to its duties in any part of the United States or in any foreign country.

* * *

Upon receipt of the petition [for antidumping or countervailing duties], the Secretary of Commerce will notify the governments of the exporting countries involved, examine the readily available information, and determine whether the petition alleges the elements necessary for the imposition of a countervailing, or antidumping determination. At this time, the Secretary of Commerce will also determine if the petition has been filed by, or on behalf of, the domestic industry affected by the trade practices.

If these determinations are affirmative, the Secretary of Commerce will initiate an investigation to determine whether a countervailable subsidy is being provided or if the subject merchandise is being, or is likely to be sold in the United States at less than its fair value. If these determinations are negative, the Secretary of Commerce will dismiss the petition, terminate the proceeding, and notify the petitioner in writing of its reasons for the determination. Finally, the Secretary of Commerce will also notify the International Trade Commission (ITC) regarding its decision, and will provide the ITC with information available to it if the decision is affirmative.

. . . The International Trade Commission then conducts an investigation to determine whether there is a reasonable indication of injury.

If the International Trade Commission determines that there is a reasonable indication of injury, the Secretary of Commerce will make a preliminary determination of whether there is a reasonable basis to believe that injury has occurred. If this determination is affirmative, the Secretary will determine an estimated countervailable subsidy rate. . . .

Within a statutorily specified time period after the date of the preliminary determination, the Secretary of Commerce will make a final determination of whether a countervailing duty [or antidumping duty, in an antidumping duty petition] is appropriate. . . . The International Trade Commission will then determine . . . whether an industry in the United States is materially injured, or is threatened with material injury, or that the establishment of an industry in the United States is materially retarded, by reason of imports, or sales (or the likelihood of sales) of the merchandise that the Secretary found [to be benefitting from a subsidy or dumped]. . . .

* * *

Customs Service determinations involving countervailing and anti-dumping duties, which are reviewable on the petition of an interested party under 19 USCA § 1516a, are final and conclusive upon all parties unless a civil action contesting the denial of a protest is commenced in the U.S. Court of International Trade, or reviewed by a binational panel of determination commenced pursuant to 19 USCA § 1516a(g) and NAFTA Article 1904.

VICTOR, INJURY DETERMINATIONS BY THE UNITED STATES INTERNATIONAL TRADE COMMISSION IN ANTIDUMPING AND COUNTERVAILING DUTY PROCEEDINGS

16 N.Y.U. J. Int'l L. & Pol. 749 (1984).*

Whether or not one agrees with the [International Trade Commission (ITC)] in any given case, the Agency is to be applauded generally for its improved performance in recent years. Despite the severe statutory deadlines under which the Commission must operate, the ITC and its staff are trying very hard to render well investigated and thoughtful determinations. The staff reports and written opinions of the Commission have improved tremendously over the last four years. One has the sense that the facts and the law, as intended by Congress, control the outcome of the investigation. This was not always the case in the past, and reflects both the improved quality of the Commission generally and the fact that the Court of International Trade looms in the background as a citadel to ensure that fair proceedings and well reasoned opinions in accordance with the law are the order of the day.

* * *

MATERIAL INJURY

Material injury is defined by the Act as "harm which is not inconsequential, immaterial, or unimportant." The Act sets forth with particularity the indicia of injury the ITC must examine in determining whether a domestic industry is materially injured by reason of imports. These indicia are: (1) the volume of imports; (2) the effect of imports on prices in the United States for like products; and (3) the impact of imports on domestic producers of like products. The presence or absence of any of these factors is not determinative of the Commission's decision with regard to injury. The legislative history of the Act makes clear that the "significance of the various factors affecting an industry depends upon the facts of each particular case."

* * *

THREAT OF MATERIAL INJURY

In contrast to the detailed criteria set forth in the statute for the determination of material injury, the statute is devoid of any guidelines to be considered by the ITC in its determination of a threat of material injury. The legislative history, however, instructs the Commission to "consider any economic factors it deems relevant," and stresses that the law should be "administered in a manner so as to prevent actual injury from occurring" and that "relief should not be delayed if sufficient evidence exists for concluding that the threat of injury is real and imminent."

The landmark case in this area is the often cited CIT decision in *Alberta Gas Chemicals, Inc. v. United States.* There, the court struck down as unsupported by substantial evidence, the Commission's affirmative determination of threat which was based partly on a finding of expanding supplies from Canada, the exporting country in that case.

The court found that the Commission's analysis was "flawed with supposition and conjecture" because the expansion plans cited by the Commission as a basis for its finding of threat were uncertain and subject to several contingencies. The court noted that the financing had not even been arranged. The court concluded that the mere possibility that injury might occur at some remote future time did not meet the "real and imminent" standard enunciated by Congress.

* * *

The House Report to the Act identifies four demonstrable trends to be considered by the Commission in its determination of whether a threat of injury exists: (1) the rate of increase of the dumped or subsidized exports to the United States market; (2) capacity in the exporting country to generate exports; (3) the likelihood that such exports will be directed to the United States market, taking into account the availability of other export markets; and (4) the nature of the subsidy in question (*i.e.*, is the subsidy the sort that is likely to generate exports to the United States).

* * *

CAUSATION

Causation is a complex issue. Any injury suffered by the domestic industry must, under the language of both the antidumping and countervailing duty laws, be "by reason of" imports. Legislative history indicates that the standard for finding the requisite causal link between imports and injury is not high. Imports need not be the "principal," "substantial," or "significant" cause of material injury. Rather, they need only be a contributing cause of injury to the domestic industry. Moreover, in making this determination, Congress admonished the Commission not to weigh the effects of less than fair value imports against the effects associated with other factors, *e.g.*, the volume and prices of imports sold at less than fair value, contraction in demand or changes in patterns of consumption, trade restrictive practices of and competition between the foreign and domestic producers, development in technology, and the export performance and productivity of the domestic industry.

Despite this prohibition, the legislative history allows the Commission, in examining the overall injury to a domestic industry, to consider information indicating that the harm is caused by factors other than less than fair value imports.

The ITC has followed this statutory mandate. For example, in *Snow Grooming Vehicles*, the ITC based its negative determination, in part, on finding that poor ski conditions had reduced the demand for snow grooming vehicles and that the imports did not compete with the domestically produced items but rather with other imports. In *Portable Electric Typewriters from Japan*, the evidence demonstrated that the injury was caused by the domestic industry's inability to compete with fair-priced imports. Additionally, in *Galvanized Carbon Steel Sheet from West Germany, Chlorine from Canada*, and *Secondary Aluminum Alloy in Unwrought Form from the United Kingdom*, the Commission determined that economic conditions in U.S. markets were responsible for the difficulties experienced by both U.S. and foreign producers, and that if imports were removed from the market, the domestic industry would be unchanged.

There are two important and as yet unsettled issues in the causation area. The first issue is whether, to find that the injury was caused by "reason of imports," the ITC is required to find a causal connection between the amount of subsidy or dumping margin and the injury, or merely a causal link between the sales of the subsidized or dumped imports and the injury. The second issue is whether, assuming dumping has occurred, the fact that the U.S. price of the imported good exceeds the price of the domestic "like" product means that only technical dumping and, hence, no injury per se, exists.

VENKATARAMAN, BINATIONAL PANELS AND MULTILATERAL NEGOTIATIONS: A TWO-TRACK APPROACH TO LIMITING CONTINGENT PROTECTION

37 Colum. J. Transnat'l L. 533 (1999).*

POLITICIZATION OF THE ITA

The politicized nature of the International Trade Administration (ITA), the division of the Commerce Department that conducted AD and CVD investigations, compounded the bias inherent in the law itself. The ITA was responsible for determining whether foreign goods had been sold at less than fair market value in the United States (in AD cases), or whether a foreign government had subsidized the firm under investigation (in CVD cases). As a component of an executive department, however, with its senior officials appointed by the President and confirmed by the Senate, the ITA lacked insulation from the protectionist forces in Congress which may control or have significant influence over the agency's funding and its very existence. The politicization of the ITA may best be understood in contrast to the International Trade Commission (ITC), which is responsible for a final injury determination. The ITC is an independent agency with commissioners serving nine-year terms, and although they, too, are Presidential appointees who must be confirmed by the Senate, no more than three of the six commissioners may be of the same political party. Furthermore, ITA officials are political appointees who serve at the discretion of the President and, as a result, are more likely to be perceived as responsive to protectionist demands of domestic industry. ITC Commissioners, on the other hand, generally may not be removed from office on the basis of Presidential disapproval of their decisions under the trade remedy laws. It is not surprising, therefore, that the protectionist bias of the ITA is reflected in its antidumping record: 97% of companies the agency investigates are found to have dumped goods on the American market. Even the CIT has expressed an awareness of the ITA's unabashed bias in favor of domestic industry, with one judge noting that the ITA's "predatory 'gotcha' policy does not promote cooperation or accuracy or reasonable disclosure by cooperating parties intended to result in realistic dumping determinations." The inevitably politicized nature of AD and CVD findings by the Commerce Department therefore contributed to Canadian perceptions of unfairness.

* * *

JUDICIAL REVIEW

Finally, the credibility of the U.S. government in its application of the trade remedy laws was further undermined by foreign producers' lack of faith in the domestic judiciary to evaluate objectively the AD/CVD findings of the Commerce Department. Particularly as a result of what Canadians viewed to be "extreme deference" to determinations of administrative agencies in the post-*Chevron* era, Canadians often perceived a lack of serious attention given to Canadian arguments by American judges. Although judicial deference to a reasonable agency interpretation was mandated under the *Chevron* doctrine, it is possible, and perhaps even likely, that judges addressing complaints of Canadian exporters considered those parties' arguments with equal weight as those of the U.S. industry. Because fairness inevitably involves a subjective assessment, however, the perception of Canadians resorting to the American judicial system is of greater significance in understanding Canadian concerns during the free trade negotiations than the actual impartiality of judges. This view of the American judiciary, in addition to the actions of U.S. agencies that favored domestic industry claims, encouraged the Canadians to seek a mechanism which would ensure fairness in trade relations with the United States.

DUHNE, MEXICO, IN ANTI–DUMPING UNDER THE WTO: A COMPARATIVE REVIEW
(Steele, ed. 1996)*

LEGISLATIVE SCHEME

Mexican anti-dumping administrative procedure is basically regulated by the Foreign Trade Law (the "Law"), enacted on 27 July 1993, and by the Regulations of the Foreign Trade Law (the "Regulations"), published in the Official Gazette of the Federation on 30 December of the same year. . . .

* * *

REGULATORY PRACTICE AND ADMINISTRATION

The Ministry of Commerce and Industrial Development ("Secretaría de Comercio y Fomento Industrial", or "the Ministry") [now SECON] is responsible for conducting administrative investigations on unfair international trade practices, such as dumping and countervailing, and on safeguards, in accordance with Article 5 of the Law. The Ministry conducts such investigations through its Unit for International Trade Practices ("the Unit"), which is an administrative agency belonging to the Ministry.

* * *

PRACTICE AND PROCEDURE

The application for anti-dumping duties shall be filed before the Ministry by local producers of identical or like products. However, the Ministry has the authority to start *ex officio* an anti-dumping investigation.

The application shall be supported by the evidence required to demonstrate the dumping practice, the material injury and the causal link between both.

The Ministry usually screens the applications before they are filed. Although not legally required, it is an extended practice for the applicants to have one or several meetings with the authorities before filing an application, in order to convince them of its merits. Once it has been filed, the Ministry may either accept the application, and officially declare the beginning of the investigation, publishing the initial resolution in the Official Gazette of the Federation, or request additional information from the complainant (which shall be filed within a 20–day term), or reject the application. This means that the Ministry will not start an official investigation unless it is convinced of its merits, and that anti-dumping duties should be established to protect the local producers.

As mentioned above, after accepting an application, the Ministry issues, and publishes in the Official Gazette of the Federation, an "Initial Resolution accepting the application and declaring the start of an anti-dumping investigation" (the "initial resolution"). A copy of the resolution is sent, along with the public version of the application, to the importers and exporters mentioned in the application, together with the applicable questionnaires, and an official communication notifying the investigation has begun, and requesting specific information.

* * *

The exporters and importers have 30 days to file their defense. All information submitted by all parties, including evidence, must be submitted in Spanish, or with a Spanish translation enclosed.

INTERIM RESOLUTION

Between 30 and 130 days of the "initial resolution", and once the Ministry has analyzed the information and evidence filed by the exporters and importers in their defense, the Ministry issues an "interim resolution". In said interim resolution, the Ministry may conclude the investigation, if it is convinced, after the preliminary findings, that there is insufficient evidence of the existence of dumping or of material injury caused by said dumping. If the Ministry does find sufficient evidence, it may (and practically always does) continue the investigation. If the interim resolution is published at least 45 days after the initial resolution, the Ministry may establish provisional anti-dumping duties, if it deems it necessary (again, it almost always does) in order to prevent material injury from being caused in the course of the investigation.

VERIFICATION

The Ministry will normally verify the information submitted by the local producers, and by foreign producers. The most relevant procedure used in order to verify the information submitted, is through *"in-situ* inspections". The Ministry verifies the information filed by local producers, as well as the information filed by some (and, in some investigations, all) the foreign producers and exporters. ... A typical visit lasts from two to five days.

* * *

PUBLIC HEARING

Between the interim and the final resolutions, a "public hearing" will be held, in which all parties may be present to interrogate other parties on the evidence or information filed in the course of the investigation. Although attendance at the public hearing is not mandatory, it represents a unique opportunity for the parties to try to discredit the information or evidence filed by other parties, and to refute their arguments, before the Ministry concludes the investigation. Each party would be represented at the hearing by its legal representative and by the officers and experts that may fully understand and debate the technical issues being argued. Public hearings are very formal, and usually take all day.

* * *

Final Resolution

Once the term for submitting the final arguments and conclusions elapses, the investigation is concluded, and the Ministry prepares a draft of its final resolution, which is sent to the Foreign Trade Commission. Finally (within 260 business days from the publication of the initial resolution), the Ministry will issue its final resolution, publish it in the Official Gazette of the Federation and notify it to every party.

* * *

Material Injury Determination

Local producers must prove that they have suffered material injury (or that there is a threat of material injury), as a result of the dumping practice. Articles 39 and 41 define injury and causation, as follows.

ARTICLE 39.—For the purposes of this Law, injury is the patrimonial loss or deprivation of any licit and ordinary profit suffered or that may be suffered by the domestic production of the merchandise in question or an obstacle to the establishment of new industries. Threat of injury is the imminent and clearly foreseen risk of injury to domestic production. The determination of threat of injury shall be based on facts and not simply on allegations, surmises or remote possibilities.

During the administrative investigation, it must be proven that the injury or threat of injury to domestic production is a direct consequence of imports under price discrimination or subsidy conditions, under the terms of this Law.

* * *

The causal link between dumping and injury is essential, and the Ministry is becoming increasingly rigorous on this, having concluded several investigations without establishing any anti-dumping duties for lack of sufficient evidence supporting this element. . . .

The Ministry also examines if there are other factors that caused the material injury, other than the dumped imports, including:

(a) volume and value of imports (from the same or from other countries) not made at dumping prices;

(b) contraction in demand or changes in the pattern of the national consumption;

(c) trade restrictive practices of the local and foreign competitors; and

(d) developments in technology, productivity and/or export performance of the local producers.

* * *

REVIEW

There are four procedures that might be used against a resolution issued by the Ministry in an anti-dumping investigation.

THE ADMINISTRATIVE APPEAL FOR REVERSAL

This is a procedure before the Ministry itself, in order to revoke, modify or confirm the corresponding resolution. . . .

JUDICIAL PROCEEDINGS FOR ANNULMENT

These proceedings are regulated by the Federal Fiscal Code. . . . The Federal Fiscal Court might either: (a) confirm the appealed resolution, (b) annul the resolution, or (c) partially annul the resolution, instructing the Ministry to modify its resolution in a certain form.

ALTERNATIVE MECHANISMS IN INTERNATIONAL TREATIES OR AGREEMENTS

Currently, Mexico is a Party to several free trade agreements that establish alternative review procedures, replacing the regular administrative or judicial review. This presents the possibility of alternative mechanisms for the solution of controversies regarding unfair practices, contained in international treaties or agreements.

* * *

THE *AMPARO* PROCEEDINGS

In general terms, the *amparo* is a constitutional lawsuit (it is not technically an appeal), through which the Federal Courts (such as the District Judge or the Collegiate Circuit Courts) review the constitutionality or the legality of a final resolution or decision, adopted by an administrative or judicial authority, or the constitutionality of a Law, a Regulation, an International Treaty or the like.

The *amparo* procedure may only be used against definitive resolutions that might not be reviewed through another procedure, for example, against a final decision adopted by the Federal Fiscal Court in a Judicial Proceeding for Annulment, or against a resolution adopted by the Ministry, implementing a final decision adopted by an international panel in the above-mentioned alternative mechanisms for the solution of controversies.

DECISION OF THE PANEL–GREY PORTLAND CEMENT AND CLINKER FROM MEXICO
[Fifth Annual Review] USA–97–1904–01 (June 18, 1999)*

* * *

In appreciation of the large number of issues presented to the Panel and upon careful consideration of the record in this Fifth Administrative

* Footnotes omitted. This and other Chapter 19 decisions are available from the NAFTA Secretariat website, http://www.NAFTA-sec-alena.org.

Review, the briefs of the parties submitted in this matter, and the oral hearings conducted on December 14 and 15, 1998 in Washington, D.C., the Panel provides the following summary of its decision:

A. Whether the Department's refusal to revoke the antidumping order based upon alleged defects in the initiation of the original LTFV investigation is supported by substantial evidence on the record and is otherwise in accordance with law.

The Panel affirms the decision of the Department to refuse to revoke said order.

B. Whether the Department's determination that CEMEX's home market sales of Type II cement were outside the "ordinary course of trade" is supported by substantial evidence on the record and is otherwise in accordance with law.

The Panel upholds the Department's finding that home market sales of Type II cement were outside the ordinary course of trade.

C. Whether the Department's decision to treat CDC and CEMEX as a single entity (*i.e.*, to "collapse" both producers and calculate a single dumping margin) is supported by substantial evidence on the record and is otherwise in accordance with law?

The Panel upholds the Department's decision to collapse CDC and CEMEX.

D.1. Whether the Department's determinations with respect to normal value ("NV") are supported by substantial evidence on the record and are otherwise in accordance with law, as respects certain claims made by CEMEX and CDC, specifically—

D.1.a. Whether the Department's determination that bagged Type I cement should be included in the calculation of NV as part of the foreign like product is supported by substantial evidence on the record and is otherwise in accordance with law.

A Panel majority determines that bagged Type I cement should not have been included within the foreign like product and remands the issue to the Department for a determination consistent with this opinion.

* * *

STANDARD OF REVIEW

The manner in which this Panel performs the reviewing function prescribed by the NAFTA is defined by the standard of review. Not only does the application of the proper standard of review guide the work of the Panel, it appropriately confines its function. "Panels must conscientiously apply the standard of review," "must follow and apply the law, not create it," and "must understand their limited role and simply apply established law." Since this case involves the exercise of the Panel's reviewing function with respect to a myriad of issues, a clear elucidation of the Panel's reviewing standard and its limits will explain how the Panel has exercised its reviewing authority. The standard of review required for U.S. Chapter 19 cases is dictated by § 516A(b)(1)(B) of the Tariff Act of 1930, which requires the Panel to "hold unlawful any determination, finding, or conclusion found ... to be unsupported by substantial evidence on the record, or otherwise not in accordance with law. . . ."

1. Substantial Evidence

In assessing such "substantiality," courts and binational panels must consider "the record in its entirety, including the body of evidence opposed to the [agency's] view." Thus, the Panel's role is "not to merely look for the existence of an individual bit of data that agrees with a factual conclusion and end its analysis at that." Rather, the Panel must also take into account evidence in the record that detracts from the weight of the evidence relied on by the agency in reaching its conclusion. However, it is clear that the substantial evidence standard does not entitle courts or binational panels to "reweigh" the evidence or substitute its judgment for that of the original finder of fact, the agency. It is well settled that "the possibility of drawing two inconsistent conclusions from the evidence does not prevent an administrative agency's finding from being supported by substantial evidence." The reviewing authority therefore may not "displace the [agency's] choice between two fairly conflicting views, even though [it] would justifiably have made a different choice had the matter been before it *de novo*."

* * *

In undertaking its review function in U.S. antidumping and subsidy cases, the courts often employ the vocabulary of "deference," making it clear that the substantial evidence standard generally requires the reviewing authority to accord deference to an agency's factual findings, its statutory interpretations, and its methodologies. Specifically, with respect to their review of agency fact-finding, courts and binational panels have noted that "deference must be accorded to the findings of the agency charged with making factual determinations under its statutory authority." However, the application of the substantial evidence standard and deference to agency decision-making does not mean abdication of the Panel's authority to conduct a meaningful review of the agency's determination. The reviewing function is not superfluous, nor a rubber-stamp. Accordingly, deference has its bounds. An agency's decision must have a reasoned basis. The reviewing authority may not defer to an agency determination premised on inadequate analysis or reasoning.

* * *

2. In Accordance With Law

With respect to whether an agency has acted according to law, a reviewing tribunal may have greater latitude than in the case of agency fact-finding, depending on the particular of law and facts involved. On issues of statutory interpretation, "deference to reasonable interpretations by an agency of a statute that it administers is a dominant, well-settled principle of federal law." The Supreme Court has stated that "when a court is reviewing an agency decision based on a statutory interpretation, if the statute is silent or ambiguous with respect to the specific issue, the question for the court is whether the agency's answer is based on a Permissible construction of the statute." Moreover, the CAFC [Court of Appeals for the Federal Circuit] has emphasized that "[d]eference to an agency's statutory interpretation is at its peak in the case of a court's review of Commerce's interpretation of the antidumping laws." As a result of Congress' "entrust[ing in the antidumping field] the decision making authority in a specialized, complex economic situation to administrative agencies," reviewing courts acknowledge that "the enforcement of the antidumping law [is] a difficult and supremely delicate endeavor [for which] [t]he Secretary of Commerce . . . has broad discretion in executing the law."

* * *

Questions and Comments

1. What will you tell your boss about the role of the International Trade Commission in this countervailing duty matter. Again, you may want to review the excerpt by Gallagher. What is "material injury"? *See* Victor. What is "threat of material injury"? In what ways and at what stages of its investigation can politics influence ITC determinations of injury? *See* Victor, Venkataraman. Is the ITC less susceptible to political influence than the ITA?

2. Attorney Paul Victor attributes improved performance by the ITC, in part, to the fact that "the Court of International Trade looms in the background as a citadel to ensure that fair proceedings and well-reasoned opinions in accordance with the law are the order of the day." Is the possibility of judicial review of final CVD determinations by U.S. courts sufficient to ensure the integrity of countervailing duty decisions by the ITA and ITC? *See* Venkataraman. Does the answer to this question explain, at least in part, why the NAFTA Parties agreed to allow binational panels to review AD/CVD determinations by domestic agencies?

3. A panelist has asked you to assist her on a Chapter 19 binational panel (at the princely wages of CDN$400 per day, or about US$40 per hour.)

She is interested in your advice with respect to several issues: What is the proper role of a binational panel in reviewing a final determination by SECON, such as the determination in our *Apples* hypothetical? How does it differ from that applicable to panel reviews of U.S. panel decisions, as reflected in *Cement*? Why is the "standard of review" so important to a panel's work? In what body of law can one find the standard of review that governs SECON's final determinations? Assuming the panel in *Apples* finds that SECON did not properly apply Mexican law, what relief is the panel authorized to order? *See* Decision of the Panel in *Cement.*

4. Are Chapter 19 binational panels free from the same political influences that lead some observers to question the ability of domestic judicial systems to render objective countervailing duty determinations? Will a U.S. lawyer who makes her living representing clients before the ITA and ITC be objective when she is being asked in a panel proceeding to those agencies' actions in another case to be unlawful or not supported by the administrative record?

5. Note, for purposes of Part B, that the panel in *Cement* upheld Commerce with respect to ten of the fourteen challenges raised under Chapter 19 by the Mexican cement interests.

PART B. EXTRAORDINARY CHALLENGE COMMITTEES

GESSER, WHY NAFTA VIOLATES THE CANADIAN CONSTITUTION
27 Denv. J. Int'l L. & Pol'y 121 (1998).*

NAFTA allows a limited right of appeal to the ECC that reviews certain Panel decisions. However, appeals are only permitted when: (1) there has been gross misconduct, bias, serious conflict of interest, or other material misconduct on the part of a panelist; (2) there has been a serious departure from a fundamental rule of procedure; or (3) a Panel manifestly exceeds its powers, authority or jurisdiction, for example, by failing to apply the appropriate standard of judicial review. It must also be established that the action materially affected the Panel's decision, and that the decision threatens the integrity of the Binational Panel review process.

Each NAFTA country selects five sitting or retired judges as potential ECC members. From this roster, the two opposing countries in a dispute pick a committee of three. After each country selects one member, the two countries draw lots to determine which side gets to choose the third member. The ECC either affirms the Panel decision or vacates it for remand to a new Panel. The ECC's rulings are binding with respect to the matter and the parties involved. As is the case for the Binational Panels, Chapter 19 of NAFTA expressly prohibits any Party to the Agreement from establishing legislatively a procedure to challenge ECC determinations in their respective court systems.

MERCURY, CHAPTER 19 OF THE UNITED STATES–CANADA FREE TRADE AGREEMENT 1989–95: A CHECK ON ADMINISTERED PROTECTION?

15 Nw. J. Int'l L. & Bus. 525 (1995).*

A second significant alteration to the [CFTA] Chapter 19 system concerns amendment of the Extraordinary Challenge Committee procedures. Under the [CFTA], an Extraordinary Challenge Committee's responsibilities ended with ensuring that a panel articulated and applied the correct standard of review. Under NAFTA, an Extraordinary Challenge Committee's mandate has been broadened in two important respects.

First, an Extraordinary Challenge Committee under NAFTA is explicitly authorized to examine a panel's analysis of substantive law and underlying facts. Again, Canada and the United States have offered disparate interpretations of this amendment. Where the Canadian government has asserted that this amendment only makes "explicit" what was already "implicit" under the [CFTA], the United States sees this expansion as an "important change." When combined with the fact that Extraordinary Challenge Committees now are entitled to 90 days to undertake their review, as opposed to 30 days under the [CFTA], it becomes evident that the Extraordinary Challenge Committee procedures have been modified in order to resemble those applicable to appellate courts.

Apart from procedural changes made to the ECC process, there has been another, more important, and potentially problematic, alteration to the [CFTA] system. During the FTA years, panel decisions were effectively non-reviewable except under a narrow list of unusual circumstances which included gross misconduct, bias, breach of fundamental procedures, or action that "manifestly" exceeded a panel's mandate. The decisions of the three Extraordinary Challenge Committees confirmed the notion that panels were to have considerable latitude when examining final determinations.

Under NAFTA Article 1904.13(iii), an Extraordinary Challenge Committee can now vacate or remand a panel opinion if it finds that the panel "failed to apply the appropriate standard of review." Yet again, the two countries have offered different interpretations of this amendment. Where Canada has stated that this alteration "does not expand the scope of an extraordinary challenge proceeding from what had been negotiated under the [CFTA]," the United States considers this change to be "significant."

Merely articulating and faithfully applying the United States standard of review may no longer be sufficient to immunize a panel decision from successful extraordinary challenge. Given the fact that there has been, at times, considerable disagreement between panelists as to what constitutes the appropriate "standard of review," judges on Extraordinary Challenge Committees may now be invited to examine how a binational panel both articulated and applied the relevant standard. ...

OPINION AND ORDER OF THE EXTRAORDINARY CHALLENGE COMMITTEE GRAY PORTLAND CEMENT AND CLINKER FROM MEXICO

ECC–2000–1904–01USA (Oct. 30, 2003)

* * *

1. ... Under the provisions of Chapter 19 of the NAFTA, an extraordinary challenge proceeding is not the equivalent of a legal appeal in which the parties with a direct stake in the outcome brief and argue the issues. Rather, under the streamlined process created under the NAFTA, an extraordinary challenge review has a more limited and specific purpose, namely, to consider allegations that action taken by a particular binational panel are outside the scope of the panel's authority, and pose a threat to the integrity of the panel review system. As such, the extraordinary challenge process by definition implicates the interests of all States–Parties, including Canada.

The States–Parties to the NAFTA selected a specific process for resolving disputes as an alternative to the standard court appeal process of the nation whose law governs the particular dispute. Under the alternative process adopted under the NAFTA, the binational panel review system is the mechanism for appeal of specific claims and agency determinations involving the antidumping and countervailing duty laws. By contrast, the extraordinary challenge process, as its name suggests, is reserved for extraordinary situations where there are substantial allegations of legal error, such as gross misconduct, serious departure from fundamental rules of procedure, action that manifestly exceeds a panel's authority or similar acts that threatens the integrity of the panel review process. As one of the States–Parties to the NAFTA, Canada has a fundamental interest in any threats to the integrity of the NAFTA decision-making process.

2. The ECC will not dismiss the extraordinary challenge petition filed by the United States on April 13, 2000 for lack of jurisdiction. Under NAFTA Article 1904. a party may invoke an extraordinary challenge committee review as follows:

> "Where, within a reasonable time after the Panel decision is issued, an involved Party alleges that:

(a)(i) A member of the Panel was guilty of gross misconduct, bias, or a serious conflict of interest, or otherwise materially violated a rule of conduct;

(ii) the Panel seriously departed from a fundamental rule of procedure;

(iii) the Panel manifestly exceeded its powers, authority or jurisdiction set out in this Article, for example by failing to apply the appropriate standard of review, and

(b) any of the acts set out in subparagraph (a) has materially affected the Panel's decision and threatens the integrity of the Binational Panel review process, that Party may avail itself of the extraordinary challenge procedure set out in Annex 1904.13."

No extraordinary challenge committee has ever been convened under the NAFTA prior to this ECC, so there is no direct guidance as to how to interpret the provisions defining the minimum pleading requirements for invoking an ECC.

The parties acknowledge that three extraordinary challenge committees were convened under a predecessor to the NAFTA, namely, the Canadian Free Trade Agreement ("FTA"), and that the standards outlined in the opinions issued by these three ECCs are persuasive on the issue of jurisdiction. Our review of the statutory provisions of the NAFTA, and the guidance provided by the ECCs convened under the FTA, lead us to conclude that the United States has satisfied the minimum requirements for seeking ECC review. The United States has asserted:

(1) that the Binational Panel violated Article 1904.13(a)(iii) in that it "manifestly exceeded its powers" in rejecting the definition of the like foreign product" made by the Department of Commerce in the Final Results for purposes of calculating the amount of the antidumping duty to be applied for the POR [Period of Review], because the agency's product definition was supported by substantial evidence;

(2) that in so doing, the Binational Panel violated Article 1904.13(b), because its error has "materially affected the Panel's decision;" and

(3) that in so doing, the Binational Panel's decision "threatens the integrity of the Binational Panel review process" because the Panel did not sustain the agency definition at issue, as the United States maintains it was required to do under the substantial evidence rule, and instead determined that there was not substantial evidence to support the agency definition. Because the United States petition for extraordinary challenge review alleges the requirements for such review, and supports these legal claims with substantial factual allegations tied to the record, the ECC will not dismiss the petition for lack of jurisdiction.

3. The ECC determines that this is not an appropriate case in which to reverse or modify the decision of the Binational Panel on the merits of the petition filed by the United States. Under Article 19 of the NAFTA, the Binational Panel must apply the law of the importing country, here the United States, in reviewing appeals from an administrative agency determination. In its extraordinary challenge petition, the United States argues that the Binational Panel violated two key principles of United States statutory and decisional law regarding judicial review of agency determinations: the "substantial evidence" test and the rule of "great deference" to agency decision-making.

The United States argues that the Panel, in rejecting the determination of the "foreign like product" set forth in the Final Results, failed to follow the "substantial evidence" test, under which a reviewing court must uphold the agency's findings so long as they are based on "such relevant evidence as a reasonable mind might accept as adequate to support a conclusion...." The court (or as here, the Binational Panel) must uphold such findings even if there is other substantial evidence in the record that might support different findings. In addition, the reviewing court must not conduct a *de novo* review of the evidence in the record. The United States argues that there was more than sufficient evidence to support the product definition set forth by the Department of Commerce in the Final Results.

The United States also argues that the Panel violated the principle that courts must show great deference to agency decision-making. Under the well-known standard for judicial review of actions taken by administrative agencies set forth in *Chevron U.S.A. v. National Resources Defense Council*, 467 U.S. 837 (1984), a reviewing court may reverse or modify an agency determination only if it is clearly contrary to applicable law, or the intent of Congress as clearly set forth in the law. Generally speaking, the United States Supreme Court declared in *Chevron* that agency determinations should be given "great deference" if they are made as to an issue about which the governing statute is silent or ambiguous, or if the issue is one as to which Congress had clearly delegated decision-making authority to an administrative agency. Courts in the United States have recognized this principle in the context of international trade, declaring that the Department of Commerce has "special expertise" with regard to U.S. antidumping laws.

In opposing the extraordinary challenge petition, CEMEX sharply disputes the position of the United States on both principles. First, CEMEX asserts that the Binational Panel was correct in finding that there was insufficient evidence in the record to support the definition of the "foreign like product" announced in the Final Results, arguing that the evidence in the record was substantially similar to the product definition used in earlier administrative reviews of the antidumping order at issue, and that nonetheless the Department of Commerce adopted a different product definition in the Final Results without support in the record. On the principle of deference to agency decision-making, CEMEX argues that the *Chevron* decision and subsequent decisions of United States courts make clear that there are limits to deference to agency decisions, and that "[n]o deference is due to agency interpretations at odds with the plain language of the statute itself." ... CEMEX argues that the Panel was well aware of, and discussed at length, its obligations to review interpretations of the antidumping statutes under the *Chevron* principles, and that the Panel reversed the Department of Commerce definition in part on purely legal grounds in that the Department of Commerce failed to apply several portions of the applicable statute, and impermissibly misinterpreted the one portion it did apply.

After careful review, the ECC has determined that it will not disturb the decision of the Binational Panel because the United States petition fails to establish a substantial violation of an extraordinary nature sufficient to authorize the ECC to reverse the Binational Panel's decision. The ECC fails to find evidence of "gross misconduct," "serious conflict of interest" or other wrongdoing that might justify invoking the ECC process and reversing the Panel's decision. The United States petition, while raising serious issues with regard to the particular determination by the Panel which it has challenged, has failed to demonstrate that the Panel "manifestly exceeded its powers" or that the decision of the Panel in any way "threatens the integrity" of the binational panel review process.

As the Government of Canada has outlined, and as the parties acknowledge, the Binational Panel review process is intended to replace regular appellate court review with a streamlined process for reviewing agency determinations, and Panel review is intended to be the final appeal of determinations, absent the "extraordinary" circumstances required for an ECC to be convened pursuant to NAFTA Article 1904.13. All parties also acknowledge the persuasive, If not binding, interpretations by the three ECC panels convened under the FTA. All of these ECC panel decisions declare that ECC review is much more circumscribed and exceptional than a legal appeal of a court decision.

* * *

The ECC concludes that, even if the Binational Panel may have erred in its determination that the product definition in the Final Results was not supported by substantial evidence and that the agency failed to apply all the factors set forth in the relevant statutory provision, the Binational Panel did not act in a manner that violates the provisions of NAFTA Annex 1904.13. Rather, the ECC determines that the Panel proceeded in precisely the manner contemplated by the NAFTA binational panel review provisions. The ECC concludes that it is apparent that the Panel understood and applied the substantial evidence standard, as well as the *Chevron* doctrine of great deference to agency decisions, in its analysis, even if the manner in which it applied those standards to the factual issue that is the subject of this petition appears to be erroneous from the perspective of the United States and the STCC.

The extraordinary challenge process is not a typical appellate court review of a decision, either by an agency or a lower court. Rather, the process is clearly reserved for extraordinary situations which reflect a systemic problem that threatens the overall panel review process. Even if the Panel erred in its legal determination that the Department of Commerce product definition was not supported by substantial evidence, and that the agency did not apply all the relevant statutory factors, nothing in the Panel's conduct rises to the level of "manifestly exceeding its powers, authority or jurisdiction," and above all nothing in the Panel's handling of its review of the Final Results appears to "threaten[] the integrity of the Binational Panel Review process" as required by NAFTA Annex 1904.13 in order for the ECC to reverse or modify the Binational Panel's decision. The ECC therefore declines to do so.

4. Although the ECC finds, after a careful examination of the record and the briefs on the petition of the United States, that the petition fails to establish the kind of gross misconduct, serious conflict of interest or other impropriety, and further that the petition fails to establish conduct that "manifestly exceeded [the] powers, authority or jurisdiction" of the Binational Panel or that "threatens the integrity of the Binational Panel review process," the members of the ECC do note, as dicta, that in their view the dissenting opinion of panelist Harry B. Endsley with regard to the specific issue that gave rise to the petition for extraordinary challenge review reflects the better-reasoned approach.

* * *

LUTZ, LAW, PROCEDURE AND CULTURE IN MEXICO UNDER THE NAFTA: THE PERSPECTIVE OF A NAFTA PANELIST

3 Sw. J. L. & Trade Am. 391 (1996).*

Applying the standard of review is a matter that has occasionally confounded non-national Panelists reviewing U.S. and Canadian decisions. But in the Mexican context, the task of application required substantial interpretation because there was no history of Fiscal Tribunal application or other judicial gloss with respect to review of AD/CVD determinations. Moreover, the designated standard of review (Article 238 of the Federal Fiscal Code [*Código Fiscal de la Federación*]) was originally for review of administrative decisions relating to taxation and other fiscal matters (*e.g.*, reviews of assessments of customs duties). These typically involve a government claim against an individual with respect to the individual's obligation to pay a tax to the government. On their face, AD proceedings are much more complex, usually involving multiple parties and interests. They are multidimensional in nature, involving, *inter alia*, the national economy, the trade relations of at least two

(Professor Lutz was a member of the majority in the *Cement* panel decision subject to ECC review.)

countries, domestic producers and their employees, importers of foreign goods and the exporters of those goods. Thus, one might say that in this regard the binational panel process under Chapter 19 does not replace judicial review of AD/CVD cases in Mexico, rather it creates a fundamentally different sort of review.

* * *

Standards of review, generally speaking, refer to the degree of deference reviewing tribunals are entitled to give to agency decisions. They also proscribe what the tribunal may do when it finds the agency action inadequate or wrong. Non–Mexican Panelists may find marked differences on both these grounds between their own country's standard of review and the one they are required to apply in reviewing Mexican AD determinations.

The standard of review enunciated in Article 238 provides:

An administrative determination shall be declared illegal when any one of the following grounds is established:

I.   Lack of jurisdiction or authority of the agency or official issuing the challenged determination or ordering, initiating or carrying out the proceeding in which the challenged determination was issued;

II.   An omission of formal legal requirements by the agency or official issuing the challenged determination which affects the person's right of proper defense as well as the scope or meaning (outcome) of the challenged determination, or a failure of the agency or official to provide a reasoned determination based upon the record;

III.   A violation or defect of procedure by the agency or official issuing the challenged determination, which affects the person's right of proper defense as well as the scope or meaning (outcome) of the challenged determination;

IV.   If the facts which underlie the challenged determination do not exist, are different from the facts cited by the agency, or were considered by the agency in an erroneous way; if the challenged determination was issued by the agency in violation of the applicable laws or rules; or if the correct laws or rules were not applied by the agency;

V.   Whenever a discretionary determination by an agency falls outside the lawful scope of that discretion.

When applying this standard, Panels must also, according to *jurisprudencia*, follow what has been called the "logical order" rule. That is, they should apply each paragraph of Art. 238 in a consecutive and hierarchical order. Thus, the Panel may examine a ground argued under Art. 238(2) only after it is satisfied that the ground under Art. 238(1) is not established.

UNITED STATES TARIFF ACT OF 1930
19 U.S.C. § 1516a(b)(1)(B) (1999).

The court shall hold unlawful any determination, finding, or conclusion found ... to be unsupported by substantial evidence on the record, or otherwise not in accordance with law ....

FEDERAL COURT ACT OF CANADA
R.S.C. 1985, ch. F–7, s. 18.1(4).

GROUNDS OF REVIEW

The Trial Division may grant relief under subsection (3) if it is satisfied that the federal board, commission or other tribunal

(a) acted without jurisdiction, acted beyond its jurisdiction or refused to exercise its jurisdiction;

(b) failed to observe a principle of natural justice, procedural fairness or other procedure that it was required by law to observe;

(c) erred in law in making a decision or an order, whether or not the error appears on the face of the record;

(d) based its decision or order on an erroneous finding of fact that it made in a perverse or capricious manner or without regard for the material before it;

(e) acted, or failed to act, by reason of fraud or perjured evidence; or

(f) acted in any other way that was contrary to law.

Questions and Comments

1. How does NAFTA's extraordinary challenge process differ from the prior, CFTA extraordinary challenge process? *See* Gesser and Mercury. What were some of the perceived shortcomings in the CFTA process? How were these shortcomings addressed in NAFTA? In particular, how was the scope of ECC review expanded under NAFTA?

2. What do you understand to be the appropriate role of an ECC? Do you agree with the very circumscribed characterization of its authority set out in *Gray Portland Cement*? Under what circumstances, if any, would such an ECC be willing to overturn a panel decision? Are you concerned that in this instance, apparently, the panel itself got by with exceeding its powers of review, but there was no effective remedy for the United States because the ECC followed its own scope of review scrupulously?

3. If the ECC had been provided a somewhat broader scope of review, would the ECC have nevertheless upheld the *Cement* panel? Note that the ECC made it very clear that its indication of agreement with the panel dissent was only dicta.

4. In an earlier ECC under CFTA, the ECC majority upheld a panel decision in a softwood lumber countervailing duty determination by Com-

merce, resulting in a famous, blistering dissent by retired U.S. Circuit Judge Malcolm Wilkey. (Extraordinary Challenge Committee–Softwood Lumber Products from Canada, ECC–94–1904–01 USA (Aug. 3, 2004)) In his dissent, Judge Wilkey writes that the role of an ECC is "roughly comparable to that of the Supreme Court in the administrative review process." He continued, "In summary, I believe that this Binational Panel Majority opinion may violate more principles of appellate review of agency action that any opinion by a reviewing body which I have ever read. . . . The two dissenters likewise are "experts" in the field of trade law and their analysis, which supported in every major detail that of Commerce, was persuasive. . . . They were sensible of their position, *i.e.*, that their responsibility was *not* to redo the whole analysis which had been done by Commerce, but to find any major flaws in Commerce's evidence or reasoning which, if established, would negate the substance of the Department's findings. The dissent recognized that, where reasonable minds might differ and Commerce had a point supported by substantial evidence, then the result achieved by Commerce should be sustained. Even if another reasonable conclusion could be reached on the same evidence, the agency is entitled to have its interpretation validated. This is a fundamental point reiterated in literally decades of United States law, but it is a point lost upon the Panel majority, and I fear, on my two Canadian colleagues." Are these comments helpful in clarifying the function of ECCs in NAFTA's dispute resolution scheme?

5. The result in *Softwood Lumber* was sufficient to cause Judge Wilkey to reject the panel/ECC system in its entirety: "Reflecting on all the above, I submit that the well intentioned system of Extraordinary Challenge Committees, as a substitute for the standard appellate review under United States law, has failed. It has failed both at the Panel and the Committee level to apply United States law, substantively, and most clearly in regard to the United States standard of review of administrative agency actions. The system runs the risk, not only of producing egregiously erroneous results as in the instant three to two Panel decision, but also of creating a body of law—even though formally without precedential value—which will be divergent from United States law applied to countries not members of NAFTA."

6. Judge Wilkey's dissent includes a serious indictment of the "substitute appellate review system" constructed first in the CFTA and later in NAFTA. Do you agree with Judge Wilkey's claim that one country's standards of review cannot be understood and applied by judges and lawyers of a foreign country? (Before you answer this question, review the Mexican, U.S. and Canadian standards of review set forth above.) Why does Judge Wilkey expect that the deficiencies he asserts will be magnified by expansion of the "substitute appellate review system" to include Mexico and possibly other Civil Law countries in Latin America?

7. Is the ground for ECC review in *Gray Portland Cement* similar to that which will be involved in your presentation to the USTR in the "peach" dispute? How would the evidence considered by a *Peaches from Mexico* ECC differ from the material considered by the *Gray Portland Cement* ECC?

8. Article 1904.13 requires that a request for an ECC be made "within a reasonable time after the panel decision is issued." Suppose that instead of an alleged violation of the standard of review by the panel—presumably

evident at the time the decision of the panel is released—the Office of the USTR (and, therefore, you) just learned of possible misconduct by two panelists in the "peach" dispute—four months after the panel concluded its work. Does the United States still have time within which to file a request for an ECC? *See* ECC Rule 37.

9. What qualifications must a person possess to be eligible to serve on an ECC? *See* Annex 1904.13. If the United States decides to request an ECC in the "peach" dispute, what process will be followed in selecting the three members of the ECC? The three ECC members in *Gray Portland Cement* were all active or retired federal judges. In the "peach" dispute, can either the United States or Mexico choose an ECC member from outside the fifteen-person roster? (Only the U.S. has appointed a full roster of ECC committee members. Canada has appointed only two, and Mexico, none.) Are ECC members subject to the NAFTA Code of Conduct? *See* ECC Rule 22.

10. After the *Peaches from Mexico* ECC is selected, what tasks will it undertake in the extraordinary challenge proceeding? *See* Annex 1904.13(3). What substantive law will govern the ECC's decisions? *See* ECC Rule 6. Once the *Peaches from Mexico* ECC is ready to render a decision, will its decision be made by consensus or majority vote? *See* ECC Rule 61. What possible actions may the ECC take in its final decision? *See* ECC Rule 63. What is supposed to happen if the ECC vacates the original panel decision? *See* Annex 1904.13(3).

11. Assume that the *Peaches from Mexico* ECC makes the findings necessary to vacate the decision of the original panel, orders that the decision is vacated, and that the Mexican government becomes extremely upset about the decision. Can Mexico appeal the ECC's decision to any tribunal?

12. Compare the three standards of review applicable to local courts (and binational panels) reviewing national dumping and subsidy determinations? Which gives the binational panel the broadest latitude during review?

13. Early in 2003, the United States filed ECC–2003–1904–01USA, arising from an October 2002 panel decision in *Pure Magnesium from Canada*. In October 2004, the ECC concluded that:

> "(a) the Panel manifestly exceeded its powers by failing to apply the correct standard of review and

> (b) such action materially affected the Panel's decision, but

> (c) that the Panel's action did not threaten the integrity of the binational panel review process.

Accordingly, this challenge is dismissed and by virtue of section 3 of NAFTA Annex 1904.13 the challenged panel decision stands affirmed."

14. In September 2004, a NAFTA binational panel remand (the third such remand) effectively required the International Trade Commission to reverse its threat of material injury determination in the most recent U.S. antidumping and countervailing duty cases against Canadian softwood lumber. In so doing, the ITC commented:

> The Commission has undertaken the responsibilities explicitly delegated to it by Congress to weigh the evidence, make the complex determina-

tions required by law, and ensure that its determinations are supported by substantial evidence. The Commission rejects the Panel's branding such actions as "an effort to preserve its finding of threat of material injury." It is the Panel that has preordained the outcome as negative determinations and ignored the Commission's analysis and exposition of record evidence that addressed the Panel's concerns in its prior decisions.

In October 2004, the United States filed an extraordinary challenge in this softwood lumber case. The United States is presumably arguing that the panel's action meets all three of the criteria set out in Annex 1904.13.

PROBLEM 9.4 CHAPTER 20 DISPUTE PROCE-DURES: U.S. TIGHTENS THE EMBARGO AND SANCTIONS CANADIAN AND MEXICAN FIRMS DOING BUSINESS IN CUBA

SECTION I. THE SETTING

Pressure from several senators who were holding up numerous ambassadorial appointments led the United States President to list several new Canadian and Mexican companies under Title IV of the Cuban Liberty and Democratic Solidarity (LIBERTAD) Act (better known as Helms–Burton), 22 U.S.C. §§ 6021–6091. This meant that a number of their officers, and their family members (specifically named), were denied visas to enter the U.S., because the Canadian and Mexican companies were determined by the U.S. to be "trafficking" in property expropriated by the Cuban government without compensation. Two consequences of the listing under Title IV have caused considerable embarrassment to the President.

First, the son of the president of one of the listed Canadian companies is married to the daughter of the Canadian Prime Minister, and the listing caused the young couple to return to Canada from Washington, where he was a first year law student at George Washington University, and she was a part-time aide to a senator who had strongly opposed the President's actions. They are both minors.

Second, one of the listed Mexican companies had planned its annual company outing at Disney World in Florida. Some 40 persons had prepaid reservations, including the listed officers and their families. The entire trip has been canceled.

The actions of the U.S. have caused Canada and Mexico to ask that a Chapter 20 panel be formed. Canada and Mexico had considered asking for such a panel soon after the enactment of the Helms–Burton law in 1996, but withheld partly because the European Union had asked for a panel to be formed under the WTO dispute settlement procedures. (That panel was suspended by mutual agreement between the United States and the EU.) You work with the Washington law firm representing both Canada and Mexico in this Chapter 20 proceeding. Your job will be to discuss with your partners and clients (and their Canadian and Mexican lawyers as well) the procedure that will be followed, and to try to predict the defenses raised by the U.S., as well as their validity as defenses under NAFTA.

SECTION II.   FOCUS OF CONSIDERATION

Chapter 20 serves a much broader dispute resolution role than Chapter 19. Article 2004 allows recourse to a panel:

> with respect to the avoidance or settlement of all disputes between the Parties regarding the interpretation or application of this Agreement or wherever a Party considers that an actual or proposed measure of another Party is or would be inconsistent with the obligations of this Agreement or cause nullification or impairment in the sense of Annex 2004.

The full scope of Chapter 20 is yet to be tested, especially the meaning of "measure", but a challenge to the Helms–Burton legislation certainly seems to work along the edges of panel jurisdiction. The three Chapter 20 challenges to reach the panel stage were not quite as surprising, involving first, Canadian tariffs on several U.S. agricultural products, second, a safeguard action by the U.S. against Mexican broom corn brooms and, third, the U.S. failure to implement NAFTA obligations regarding Mexican trucks that wished to carry international cargo into the United States.

Part A of this Problem outlines Chapter 20 proceedings, including the various stages leading to a panel. Some experience of a Chapter 20 panelist is provided, including the preparation of the initial and final reports. Finally, some contrasts between using the NAFTA and the WTO process are considered.

Part B includes material on the Helms–Burton law which is the subject of the Chapter 20 challenge. This part considers a fuller scope of a panel's activities than in Broom Corn Brooms, such as a violation of international law, and also the response of the U.S. that the matter is beyond the reach of the NAFTA dispute process because it is an issue which the U.S. labels "national security."

Chapter 20, Article 803 and Annex 803.3, plus § 302(b) of the U.S. NAFTA Implementation Act, are necessary for an analysis of Part A of this problem. Chapter 20 and Art. 2102 are necessary for Part B. They are included in the Documents Supplement.

SECTION III. READINGS, QUESTIONS AND COMMENTS

PART A. THE CHAPTER 20 PANEL PROCESS

LOPEZ, DISPUTE RESOLUTION UNDER NAFTA: LESSONS FROM THE EARLY EXPERIENCE

32 Texas Int'l L.J. 163 (1997)*

* * *

CHAPTER 20'S DISPUTE RESOLUTION PROCESS

Chapter 20 constructs a three-stage dispute resolution process involving: (1) consultations, (2) a meeting of the Commission, and (3) non-binding arbitration. The first step in resolving a dispute over the interpretation, application, or alleged breach of NAFTA is for a complaining party to formally request consultations with the offending party. If the consulting parties fail to arrive at a mutually satisfactory resolution to the dispute within thirty days of the request for consultation, any of the parties may request a meeting of the Free Trade Commission. The Commission shall convene within ten days of the request and "shall endeavor to resolve the dispute promptly." To resolve the dispute, the Commission may use technical advisers or experts and make recommendations as appropriate.

If the Free Trade Commission has not resolved a dispute within thirty days after convening (or within another period agreed to by the parties), any disputant may request that an arbitral panel be formed. "On delivery of the request, the Commission shall establish an arbitral panel." These panels consist of five arbitrators who are drawn from a preformed roster of thirty individuals having expertise in law, international trade, or the resolution of disputes arising under international trade agreements. In controversies involving two parties, the parties are to agree on the chair of the panel within fifteen days of the request for a panel and, within fifteen days thereafter, are each to designate two panelists who are citizens of the other disputing party.[22]

The panel's formal charge is "[t]o examine, in light of the relevant provisions of the Agreement, the matter referred to the Commission ... and to make findings, determinations and recommendations...." Subject to the agreement of the disputants, the panel may seek advice from experts or request a formal written report from a scientific review board. Further, Chapter 20 guarantees the disputants the right to at least one hearing before the panel and the right to make written submissions.

---

* Copyright © 1997 the Texas International Law Journal and David Lopez. Reprinted with permission.

22. The panel selection process is slightly different in a dispute involving all three NAFTA countries. In those cases, the three disputants agree on the chair of the panel, then the party complained against selects two panelists (a citizen of each of the two complaining parties) and, finally, the complaining parties jointly select two panelists who are citizens of the party complained against.

Within ninety days after the last panelist is selected, the panel is to present to the disputing parties an initial report containing the panel's findings of fact, legal determinations, and recommendations.[26] Any disputant within fourteen days may submit written comments to the panel on its initial report. By no later than thirty days after presentation of the initial report, the panel shall deliver its final report to the disputing parties for transmission to the Free Trade Commission. "Unless the Commission decides otherwise, the final report of the panel shall be published 15 days after it is transmitted to the Commission."

The last aspect of Chapter 20's dispute resolution system is implementation of the panel's final report. Upon receiving the panel's final report, the disputing parties are required to agree on a resolution to the controversy, "which normally shall conform with the determinations and recommendations of the panel." If within thirty days after receiving the panel's final report the disputants have not reached a "mutually satisfactory resolution," the complaining party may suspend NAFTA benefits to the offending party until such time as an agreed resolution is reached. The suspended benefits should be roughly equivalent to the harm incurred as a result of the offending party's misconduct and should be in the same trade sector or sectors as those affected by the offending measure.

* * *

In view of Chapter 20's breadth, one might expect that a substantial number of the disputes that arise between the NAFTA countries will fall within the province of Chapter 20. It is possible to isolate those disputes that are true Chapter 20 conflicts (as opposed to disputes more appropriately handled under one of NAFTA's other dispute settlement systems) because the Agreement requires that a party who formally invokes the Chapter 20 processes must simultaneously notify the NAFTA Secretariat of that action. Article 2006 mandates that a country requesting Chapter 20 consultations shall deliver a written request to its own section of the NAFTA Secretariat. In the same way, NAFTA requires the disputants to formally notify the Secretariat of any escalation of the dispute to the later Chapter 20 stages and of any agreed resolution to the conflict.[34] In theory, the NAFTA Secretariat keeps track of each conflict that formally enters the Chapter 20 dispute resolution system. In practice, the Secretariat tends to report to the public only those Chapter 20 disputes that reach the arbitral panel review stage of dispute settlement; consequent-

26. Chapter 20 permits panelists to issue minority opinions in addition to a majority opinion, but it does not allow the identity of which panelists are associated with majority or minority opinions to be disclosed. [Authors' note: all three Chapter 20 decisions to date have been unanimous.]

34. If consultations do not resolve a dispute, Article 2007 requires a country requesting a meeting of the NAFTA Free Trade Commission to notify the Secretariat of that request. If the Commission is unsuccessful in settling the controversy, Article 2008 requires a country requesting an arbitral panel to formally notify the Secretariat of that request. Finally, Article 2018 requires that the disputants notify their respective Sections of the Secretariat of any resolution of any dispute.

ly, little is known publicly about dispute settlement experience in the early Chapter 20 stages.

* * *

GANTZ, DISPUTES AMONG THE NAFTA GOVERNMENTS*

There have been only three decisions under Chapter 20 to date.[1] In the first, the United States charged that NAFTA required Canada to eliminate duties on certain dairy products. Under the WTO Agreement on Agriculture, Canada had agreed to "tarification" of dairy products (conversion of quantitative restraints to tariffs), but there is no obligation under the WTO to eliminate tariffs. Under NAFTA, in contrast, all tariffs must be eliminated within no more than 15 years. Canada took the position that these items are exempt from the NAFTA tariff reductions; the United States disagreed. Although NAFTA does not specify the use of a neutral country fifth arbitrator, a panel consisting of two Canadian and two U.S. law professors was chosen, with a British law professor as chairperson. The panel ultimately determined unanimously that Canada's actions were consistent with NAFTA.[2]

In a second action, Mexico challenged the United States' application of safeguards to broom corn brooms from Mexico. Mexico argued that the application of the safeguards was inconsistent with NAFTA, Chapter 8 and with the WTO Agreement on Safeguards. The panel, chaired by an Australian government official, found unanimously in favor of Mexico, holding that the U.S. International Trade Commission had failed to explain adequately its "domestic industry" determination in violation of NAFTA. Unfortunately, the United States declined to comply with the panel ruling immediately, maintaining the safeguards in place for nine months after the issuance of the panel decision. The Presidential Proclamation lifting the safeguards cited only the failure of the U.S. industry to make a positive adjustment to import competition; the NAFTA decision was not mentioned. Mexico continued to apply high tariffs to a series of U.S. products as retaliation permitted under NAFTA and the GATT until the U.S. lifted the safeguards.

* Adapted from Dispute Resolution Under the North American Free Trade Agreement, Copyright © 2000, 2004, David A. Gantz. Used with permission.

1. The Softwood Lumber Agreement, May 29, 1996, 35 I.L.M. 1195, which seeks to resolve a long-running dispute between Canada and the United States over Canadian lumber exports to the United States, contains an *ad hoc* dispute settlement mechanism that is based in part on NAFTA Chapter 20 (Art. V). An arbitral panel was convened in November 1998 to address an alleged violation of the agreement as a result of British Columbia's reduction of certain charges for harvesting timber from government-owned lands, "In the Matter of British Columbia's June 1, 1998 Stumpage Reduction." The panel, operating generally under the NAFTA Chapter 20 Rules of Procedure, reviewed briefs submitted by the Parties, held a hearing and began the preparation of a decision, but the case was settled by the Parties before the panel process was completed. *See* Exchange of Diplomatic Notes dated Aug. 26, 1999 (on file with author).

2. Tariffs Applied by Canada to Certain U.S.-Origin Agricultural Products, Case no. CDA–95–2008–01 (Dec. 2, 1996).

The third proceeding involved the refusal of the United States to implement a NAFTA provision requiring the United States and Mexico, as of December 1995, to permit each other's trucking firms to carry international cargoes between the ten Mexican and four U.S. border states.[3] Investment by Mexican firms in U.S. trucking companies had also been precluded. Mexico had charged that the United States had violated the national treatment and most-favored nation treatment provisions of Chapter 11 (investment) and Chapter 12 (cross-border services), as well as the specific provisions of Annex I imposing such obligations. The Panel ultimately agreed with Mexico, although in recognition of legitimate safety concerns in the United States, it held that "to the extent that the inspection and licensing requirements for Mexican truckers and drivers wishing to operate in the United States may not be 'like' those in place in the United States, different methods of ensuring compliance with the U.S. regulatory regime may be justifiable." In this respect, the Bush Administration made every effort to comply with its NAFTA obligations, but was thwarted by a recalcitrant Congress, as well as the lower federal courts—until the Supreme Court decision of June 2004.

In addition, the NAFTA governments have brought a variety of other disputes to the NAFTA Commission for consultations, and in some instances, to convening of NAFTA dispute resolution panels. A non-exhaustive list (due to the secrecy of consultation requests) includes:

(A) Uranium Exports (U.S. v. Canada, 1994), in which bilateral consultations under Chapter 20 apparently resolved Canadian concerns over a suspension agreement between the United States and Russia concerning dumping of uranium, through U.S. assurances that Canadian interests would be taken into account;

(B) Import Restrictions on Sugar (Canada v. U.S., 1995), involving a dispute over American import restraints on Canada and a Canadian antidumping action against U.S. sugar, ultimately resolved when the U.S. and Canada negotiated revised sugar quotas;

(C) Restrictions on Small Package Delivery (U.S. v. Mexico, 1995), where the United States protested on behalf of United Parcel Service regarding alleged discriminatory regulations limiting truck size for local delivery, with the case abandoned *de facto* when UPS discontinued business activities in Mexico;

(D) Restrictions on Tomato Imports (Mexico v. United States, 1996), in which Mexican objections to a U.S. tariff rate quota on Mexican tomatoes were ultimately resolved without Chapter 20 dispute settlement in accordance with an agreement by the United States government and Mexican tomato growers suspending application of U.S. antidumping duties;

3. In the Matter of Cross–Border Trucking Services, Case no. USA–MEX–98–2008– 01 (Feb. 6, 2001). This case is excerpted and discussed in detail in Problem 6.2.

(E) Helms–Burton Act (Mexico and Canada v. United States, 1996), in which Mexico and Canada challenged the U.S. Helms–Burton Act provisions restricting travel and facilitating lawsuits against foreign companies that invested in Cuba, ultimately suspending the complaint when the United States and the European Union agreed to suspend a parallel WTO complaint;

(F) Restrictions on Sugar (Mexico v. U.S., 1998), involving U.S. quotas on Mexican sugar and a Mexican antidumping order against U.S. high fructose corn syrup. The Chapter 20 case remains technically pending, although no action has been taken, apparently due to the United States' refusal to agree on the composition of the panel. Parallel actions in the WTO and before NAFTA Chapter 19 have been concluded, and the United States recently brought a second WTO action challenging an allegedly discriminatory Mexican excise tax on beverages sweetened with HFCS; the problem remains unresolved;

(G) Farm Products Blockade (Canada v. United States, 1998), involving a challenge of U.S. state actions physically blocking imports of Canadian agricultural products, resulting in a suspension of Chapter 20 action pending ongoing bilateral discussions;

(H) Bus Service (Mexico v. United States, 1998), similar to Truck Transport, with Mexico seeking Chapter 20 action to force the United States to comply with provisions relating to cross-border long distance bus service. While the dispute was never formally consolidated with the dispute in Cross–Border Trucking Services before Chapter 20 panel (as Mexico had requested), it is assumed that final resolution of the trucking dispute will also result in a favorable conclusion of this proceeding as well; and

(I) Sportfishing Laws (United States v. Canada, 1999), in which the U.S. charged that certain Ontario restrictions on U.S. residents and guides (requiring tourists to spend the night in Canada and U.S. citizen guides obtain Ontario fishing licenses) are discriminatory under NAFTA. Consultations under Chapter 20 were initiated, and resulted in a settlement between the two Governments in which Ontario revoked the discriminatory practices that were at issue.

As evidenced by the various Chapter 20 proceedings discussed above, the NAFTA governments were not reluctant to raise their constituents' interests to the level of Chapter 20 dispute resolution during the first five or six years of NAFTA. To the extent that Chapter 20 is viewed primarily as a mechanism for consultations and conciliation, the mechanism has been successful in a number of instances in resolving or at least diffusing the issue politically. Moreover, the affected private interests have had no or only very limited alternative means for seeking redress of their claims. Also, at least two cases—Brooms and Sportfishing—involve what could be considered small industries with limited political influence, although issues relating to major trade in goods by significant industries (dairy products) and services (cross-border trucking) were also resolved under the mechanism.

However, since 2001, The NAFTA Parties have from all public indications made little use of Chapter 20. There are probably several reasons for this. First, some of the major trade related issues within the region—post 9/11 security and immigration—are not dealt with under NAFTA. Second, issues involving dumping and subsidies, including but not limited to high fructose corn syrup, softwood lumber and HFCS, effectively require resolution by the WTO's Dispute Settlement Body because they typically raise issues under the WTO Agreements on Dumping and Subsidies, and such issues are explicitly excluded from Chapter 20 jurisdiction[4]. Also, there appears to be a preference among all three NAFTA Parties for the DSB over Chapter 20. Undoubtedly, this is at least partially a result of the inordinate delays in several cases—notably *Cross-Border Trucking Services*—which indicate significant procedural imperfections in the system, particularly with regard to the apparent inability of the Parties to agree promptly on panelists. (The four year delay in appointing a Chapter 20 panel to deal with an ongoing dispute over high fructose corn syrup exports to Mexico and sugar exports to the United States has apparently soured the Mexican government on the Chapter 20 process.) Those who expect adjudicatory systems to follow set time limits and strict procedural rules are likely to find the NAFTA Chapter 20 system wanting. Some NAFTA Government officials may also believe that to ensure objectivity it is preferable to have as panelists individuals who are not nationals of any of the disputing Parties. Also, as all aspects of the panel process, except the final decision, are confidential,[5] those with an interest in the substantive aspects of the dispute, but who are not Parties, may not be able to assess fully the implications of a particular case. Nor is there any provision for *amicus curiae* briefs or participation of experts, except, in the latter instance, at the request of the Parties or at the Panelists' initiative.

* * *

PICKER, THE NAFTA CHAPTER 20 DISPUTE RESOLUTION PROCESS: A VIEW FROM THE INSIDE

23 Canada–U.S. L.J. 525 (1997)

[See excerpt in Problem 9.1, *supra*.]

4. NAFTA, art. 1901(3) provides that, " . . . [N]o provision of any other Chapter of this Agreement shall be construed as imposing obligations on a Party with respect to the Party's antidumping law or countervailing duty law."

5. NAFTA, Art. 2012(1)(b) (making hearings, interim report and all submissions confidential); Art. 2017(1) (calling for publication of the final report within 15 days of its issuance, unless otherwise agreed by the Free Trade Commission); NAFTA Chapter 20 Model Rules of Procedure, Art. 25, (restricting those present at a hearing to representatives and advisers of the Parties, Secretariat personnel, and panelists' assistants). The WTO's dispute settlement process, of course, is similarly non-transparent.

PICKER, NAFTA CHAPTER TWENTY—REFLECTIONS ON PARTY-TO-PARTY DISPUTE RESOLUTION
14 Ariz. J. of Int'l & Comp. L. 465 (1997).*

INITIAL REPORT/FINAL REPORT PROCESS

NAFTA Chapter 20, like CUSFTA Chapter 18 before it, and similar to the new dispute resolution provisions of the WTO, provides that the panel within specified time limits shall issue an Initial Report to the disputing parties who thereafter have fourteen days to comment. The panel may thereafter consider such comments and make whatever revisions it deems appropriate before issuing its Final Report which is due thirty days after the issuance of the Initial Report. The entire process is confidential.

The Final Report is precisely what its name indicates, final and hence non-appealable. It is presented to the disputing parties who are required to transmit it to the Commission within an unspecified but reasonable period of time. While the disputing parties are free to attach to the Final Report any separate views they may have, the Commission is not an appeal organ and hence may not reject the Final Report on the basis of any such views. Rather, the disputing parties may agree on the resolution of the dispute, in which case they are expected but not required to conform to the Report's determinations or recommendations. If the disputing parties do not agree on the resolution the complaining party may within thirty days suspend equivalent benefits to which the party complained against would otherwise be entitled, if the Report determines that a measure is inconsistent with NAFTA obligations or causes nullification or impairment.

What is the purpose of the Initial Report/Final Report process? The Initial Report appears to offer the disputing parties an opportunity to assess the panel's thinking and to provide whatever comments they deem appropriate. The panel is thereafter free to make whatever change, correction, or modification it deems appropriate. Furthermore, by receiving what is effectively a preview of the panel's coming determination, the disputing parties have some time to take such steps as they deem necessary to prepare the public for whatever consequences may follow from the eventual publication of the Final Report. It may also have been the intention of the parties that the Initial Report, as with conciliation, might prompt the parties to settle the dispute, although there is no evidence that an Initial Report has ever done so either under CUSFTA Chapter 18 or NAFTA Chapter 20.

Thus, the Initial Report/Final Report process can be seen in either of two ways. First, it may be the rough equivalent of a lower court/appeal court process, or perhaps more accurately, a court determination followed by a rehearing. The Initial Report is released for publication, and the parties may present arguments in support of and in opposition to the published opinion. Thus, a court may consider both the Initial Report and the subsequent arguments to determine whether the Initial Report is correct, or should be modified or reversed. Second, it may be seen as a part of the work product producing the opinion, allowing the panel to prepare an interim opinion reflecting its thinking, submit it to the interested parties for their commentary, which the panel may then take into account as part of its effort in producing the final opinion.

Are these two processes different? They may be. If the process is intended to enhance the quality of the work by providing outside, albeit interested, feedback, then the panel may be freer in preparing the Initial Report either to test ideas or language without fear of public scrutiny. If, on the other hand, the process is an equivalent of an appeal or rehearing process, then the Initial Report must be more critically and carefully constructed. In practice, there may not be any significant difference between these two processes provided confidentiality is maintained. However, in the case of the first NAFTA Chapter 20 dispute, the Initial Report was leaked by unknown persons to the public and immediately published.

Without suggesting that such publication in any way affected or influenced the Final Report, it is likely to present the appearance of having done so. Publication of an Initial Report, like publication of a lower court opinion, invites public scrutiny and calls for interpretation of any difference between it and the Final Report (or in the case of the lower court analogy, the appellate court's opinion), investing nuance if not substantial meaning in each such difference. Thus, if the Initial Report/Final Report process is roughly similar to an appeal or rehearing process, then publication, though unfortunate, is unlikely to tarnish the Final Report or its integrity. If, on the other hand, the purpose is "work product," then publication of the Initial Report could have a chilling effect on the willingness of a panel to revise an opinion, thereby frustrating the purpose of the project, and such publication may therefore warrant consideration of declaring the proceedings to be null and void. While the NAFTA does not clearly indicate the purpose of the process, its confidentiality requirements strongly suggest that "work product" is the more appropriate reason. In any event, the leak clearly suggests the need for tighter security control by everyone concerned. Perhaps the three NAFTA parties or the Commission should consider setting specific consequences in the event of future leaks.

INSTITUTIONALIZATION AND THE NAFTA CHAPTER TWENTY PROCESS

The panel dispute resolution mechanism built into the CUSFTA and later the NAFTA is not equivalent to that of a court or similar tribunal. It is essentially ad hoc and apparently intended to be so. Panels are hand-tailored to each dispute; there is no reason that any panel member will have the opportunity to participate in a later panel, although establishment of a roster would make subsequent participation more likely. Each panel must therefore establish its own manner of addressing what may become related issues of process. As the cliché suggests, the wheel must be reinvented with each dispute. By contrast, a permanent body hearing periodic disputes inevitably will develop an institutional mentality and approach to dispute resolution. Procedures and related processes are likely to develop or be established as needed. Increasing familiarity with the processes and with fellow tribunal members would establish an institutional culture which could create an independent dispute resolution mechanism of increasing substance. Such an ongoing mechanism was suggested by the Joint Working Group on Dispute Settlement of the American Bar Association, the Canadian Bar Association, and the Barra Mexicana when considering the NAFTA. The Group specifically criticized the Chapter 18 panel process of the CUSFTA, stating that, "[a] stronger and more elaborate system . . . is required."

In addition to institution-building, an ongoing permanent tribunal could offer practical benefits, including the following: (1) A permanent tribunal of members with reasonably long-term tenure would eliminate the present tedious process of selecting panelists. As stated earlier in this Article, the increasing difficulty of finding panel members who are satisfactory to all parties concerned, qualified, and most important, free of conflicts of interest, makes the process cumbersome. Over one-third of the time between the initiation of the panel process in the first NAFTA Chapter 20 dispute, and the issuance of the panel's Final Report, was devoted to the selection of the panelists. (2) It is increasingly likely that panelists, as in the first case, will be academics who as a group are most likely to be free of conflict of interest problems. Whether or not academics otherwise make the best panelists is problematic, but it is doubtful, given the qualifications provisions of NAFTA Article 2009, that academics were the principal intended panelists. (3) The logistics of distributing materials to panelists and their assistants (who inevitably live in widely scattered locations across North America and abroad) as well as scheduling and assembling them for hearings and deliberation sessions would be eliminated while simultaneously providing more effective control over confidential material. (4) For panelists who inevitably juggle panel obligations with their ongoing career commitments, conflicts of time, and professional interests would be avoided. Furthermore, such competing commitments may conflict with the NAFTA's relatively rigid time limits which in turn could jeopardize the quality of panel decisions. Such time restraints would be less necessary with a permanent tribunal composed of long-term career-committed judges who hold no competing positions.

Whatever ideological or practical benefits it might otherwise offer, whether or not such a permanent and relatively independent tribunal would contribute to the goals of the NAFTA, remains problematic. Perhaps the parties, as sovereign states recognizing different socio/cultural backgrounds, require greater political control in order to determine more effectively for themselves the nature and extent of international institution building.

While it is unlikely that the NAFTA in the near future will consider substitution of a permanent tribunal for the panel process, nevertheless some form of institution building process will take place even under the present system. The NAFTA Secretariat is obligated to provide "administrative assistance'' to Chapter 20 panels. Inevitably, given the necessary supervision of panel processes by the permanent Secretariats, they will provide ad hoc panels with institutional memory and continuity. Their influence over the process therefore will inevitably increase. Such influence, however, may present the Secretariats with conflicting interests because they are created and overseen by NAFTA's Free Trade Commission, and obligated to assist it, which may, or may appear to, conflict with a developing institutional service provided to independent panels.

Institutionalization can also result from repeated assignment of the same panelists. The more they serve, the more familiar each becomes with the process, and inevitably, they bring to the process their own de facto institutional memories. Substantial repetition has taken place in the CUSFTA/NAFTA Chapter 19 panels. In the six CUSFTA Chapter 18/NAFTA Chapter 20 cases to date, only one person has been a repeat panelist. Such multiple appointees are inevitably valuable resources to fellow panelists, but whether or not the influence this sort of institution substitution provides was intended by the parties is questionable.

Within the framework of the present panel process, greater institutionalism may be created first by finally establishing the thirty person roster called for in the Agreement, and then by periodically bringing all roster members together for two to three days in a retreat atmosphere. They could meet and become familiar with Secretariat personnel and processes, and, without ever disclosing classified aspects of individual cases, discuss institutional problems panels generally might encounter. Annual federal judicial conferences held by the federal circuits in the U.S. could provide a rough model for such retreats. By getting to know each other the thirty roster members would also have a better chance of creating a framework of collegiality. Hence, once any five roster members found themselves on a designated panel, they could undertake the process with a wheel already invented and spinning.

GANTZ, DISPUTE SETTLEMENT UNDER THE NAFTA AND THE WTO: CHOICE OF FORUM OPPORTUNITIES AND RISKS FOR THE NAFTA PARTIES

14 Am. U. Int'l L. Rev. 1025 (1999).*

THE NAFTA AND WTO DISPUTE SETTLEMENT MECHANISM

* * *

The NAFTA Chapter 20 and WTO DSU provide similar mechanisms for dispute resolution, but the process differs in significant respects, particularly in execution. The WTO process is managed by the DSB, constituting the full membership of the WTO, and administered by the WTO Secretariat in Geneva. While NAFTA incorporates a Free Trade

Commission and a secretariat that on paper appear similar to the DSB and WTO Secretariat, both are creatures of the disputing parties when they are administering dispute settlement procedures. At least two members of the NAFTA Free Trade Commission are necessarily officials of the governments that are parties to a NAFTA Chapter 20 dispute. In contrast, only two or a few WTO Members are parties to any single dispute under the WTO. Because the vast majority of the members of the DSB are not involved in the matter, they should be more or less impartial implementers of the dispute settlement process. Consequently, the existence of the independent DSB and the Secretariat appears somewhat more likely to assure the proper application and enforcement of the DSU's strict time limits.

* * *

Both the WTO and the NAFTA mechanisms are at least nominally legalistic or "rule oriented" systems, which incorporate a formal adjudicatory decision-making process and effective enforcement mechanisms, as distinct from more pragmatic and flexible models that rely upon diplomatic negotiations between treaty partners—or political power—to resolve conflicts over the interpretation and application of international agreements. The choice between a mechanism designed to provide compromise settlements, at the expense of specific norms, and rule-based decisions that will serve the goals of long-term predictability and efficiency, has been decisively resolved in favor of the latter.

* * *

THE CHALLENGES OF DISPUTE SETTLEMENT OPTIONS: AN ASSESSMENT

Factors Influencing Party Choices

The cases brought before the NAFTA and WTO mechanisms can be divided into three categories: (1) no effective choice of forum; (2) apparent choice, with legal or political considerations in some instances dictating one forum over the other; and (3) availability of parallel fora.

1. No Effective Choice of Forum

For two of the three matters actually resulting in final panel reports there was effectively no choice of forum. With regard to Agricultural Products Tarification, the Canadian measures under dispute were clearly consistent with the WTO Agreement on Agriculture; only the issue of NAFTA legality was in doubt. In Split–Run Periodicals, the reverse was true; while the Canadian measures were covered by the "cultural industries" exception of NAFTA, they were held illegal under GATT/WTO rules.

Also, in many of the cases that have not gone beyond consultations, a forum choice did not effectively exist. In several cases the NAFTA Parties could seek dispute resolution only under NAFTA because no GATT/WTO violation can be alleged to provide DSU jurisdiction. Small Package Delivery, Truck Transport, and Bus Service all fall within this category. Similarly, the Dairy Products Exports Subsidies WTO case, because it turns on interpretation of the WTO Subsidies Agreement, appears to raise no NAFTA violations that could be the basis of Chapter 20 jurisdiction.

2. *Effective Choice of Forum*

Of the three disputes among the NAFTA parties that have resulted in final panel reports, only one, Brooms, raised a clear choice of forum issue. In addition, the Helms–Burton Act case ultimately referred to the NAFTA mechanism, logically could have been brought by Mexico or Mexico and Canada, respectively, under the WTO DSU as well. The same is probably true with Restrictions on Sugar and Uranium Exports. In all instances, however, there were subtle reasons that dictated the complaining Party's choice.

In Brooms, Mexico had colorable arguments that the United States' safeguards were invalid under specific provisions of both the NAFTA and the WTO. Why, then, did Mexico choose Chapter 20 rather than the DSU? There is some evidence of a disagreement within the Mexican government. Some officials apparently argued that the WTO was a more efficient process in which the appointment of panels was more automatic and less subject to delay. Moreover, interpretation of the NAFTA safeguard provisions applicable to "global" safeguards actions and the "emergency action" raised technicalities that might be difficult to resolve and did not exist under WTO Safeguards Agreement. Other officials favored NAFTA Chapter 20 because of their view that it would operate more quickly and that prompt compliance by the United States was more likely. Also, since Mexico had already exercised its right to retaliate by suspending trade benefits under NAFTA Article 803.6, the prospect of delays in the panel selection process under Chapter 20 was not as daunting as it might have been had relief been deferred until the final panel report. In retrospect, the time required for the Chapter 20 panel decision in Brooms, even with the delay in compliance, was comparable to that normally experienced in the WTO. There may also have been a belief among the Parties that avoiding a WTO precedent on safeguards was desirable.

The Helms–Burton matter presented Mexico and Canada with several options. They could have joined a WTO action brought against the United States by the European Union, challenging the legality of the legislation under various provisions of the GATT and the General Agreement on Trade in Services. In this particular instance, however, the arguments that the legislation violated NAFTA may have been stronger than the GATT arguments, because the NAFTA includes extensive provisions on investment and limited rights regarding business travel. The "national security" GATT exception upon which the United States expected to rely in defense of Helms–Burton at the WTO is reproduced in substantially identical form in the NAFTA. Thus, Canada and Mexico might have pursued violations of both sections of the NAFTA much more effectively under Chapter 20 than in a WTO panel proceeding. Moreover, in retrospect, the settlement of the WTO case—in which President Clinton agreed to continue to defer the availability of the private right of action provisions of the Act and seek modification of the immigration provision—benefitted Canada and Mexico equally even though they were not parties to the WTO action, as both might reasonably have anticipated.

In Import Restrictions on Sugar, the Canadian government believed that the United States actions in implementing the WTO Agreement on Agriculture violated both the Agreement and the NAFTA and requested consultations. The NAFTA forum appears to have been chosen because the solution was perceived to be political rather than strictly legal, since from the American point of view the sugar matter was linked to United States' concerns over Canadian policies on wheat and other agricultural products, and possibly to other disputes.

In Uranium Exports, Canada's 1994 consultation request under Chapter 20 could have been made just as easily under the GATT Article XXIII procedures because the dispute raised national treatment obligations under both the NAFTA and the GATT. It is important to note that at that time the WTO DSB was not yet available. There appear to be two main reasons why Canada chose Chapter 20, both of which are speculative. First, since the NAFTA had only recently gone into force, Canada might have been interested in testing the new Chapter 20 proceedings. Second, the then-existing GATT Article XXIII alternative offered few advantages over Chapter 20 in terms of time required and implementation of panel reports. As noted earlier, those procedures did not assure prompt panel action, and a single GATT Contracting Party could effectively block GATT implementation of a panel report.

Existence of Substantive Law Advantages

Due to the parallel nature of most NAFTA chapters and specific WTO agreements, the NAFTA Parties may have the luxury in many instances of choosing the provisions that are most favorable to their cases. . . .

Advantages and Disadvantages of Differing Procedures

While the NAFTA Chapter 20 and WTO DSU procedures significantly differ as written, both processes are still evolving, and the actual differences in some cases are more apparent than real, . . . Moreover, the WTO is undertaking a "review" process which may result in changes to the WTO system that make it more effective. No similar review is contemplated with regard to Chapter 20, although, if and when a permanent roster is appointed by the NAFTA Parties, some of the delays relating to selection of panelists may be reduced. The most significant procedural considerations are summarized as follows:

1. Delays in the process are probably less likely in the WTO than under Chapter 20, due to the existence of an independent secretariat and a mechanism for choosing panelists from a permanent roster, despite the

existence of an appeal. As long as there is no permanent NAFTA roster, a Party has some control over the proceedings simply by drawing out the selection process, including, but not limited to, the fifth arbitrator, who traditionally has not been a North American national, and for which there is no mandatory choice mechanism. Thus, a NAFTA Party that wishes to go slow initially—perhaps in the hope that the matter may be settled—may wish to encourage dispute resolution under Chapter 20 rather than at the WTO, where it is more difficult for a Party to delay the initial proceedings.

2. In practice, panel decisions are equally binding, with one exception. The NAFTA lacks a detailed mechanism for implementation and lacks provisions to encourage the Parties to comply within a reasonable time. . . .

3. Whether NAFTA or WTO panelists are preferred as arbitrators, and whether five is preferable to three, depends on the particular circumstances of the case. If the issue relies on knowledge of the GATT, whether directly or indirectly, a WTO panel is more likely to have expertise, given that most of the panelists are present or former government official representatives to the GATT/WTO. If certain aspects of the case require knowledge of the North American economic or legal situation—as in Farm Products Blockade—or environmental law expertise, however, it may be easier to find NAFTA nationals with the desired expertise, particularly where each Party may choose two panelists. On the other hand, if the presence of the other Party's nationals is believed to jeopardize the fairness and objectivity of the process, the WTO, with its rule against nationals of the disputants on the panel except at the Appellate Body level, may be preferred.

4. Theoretically, the Appellate Body of the WTO should produce a higher degree of predictability and consistency than the single-stage Chapter 20 process. It is not yet clear that this record will be the norm, at least until the WTO Review defines the scope of responsibility of and the use of precedent by Appellate Body members more explicitly. Nor is it clear that NAFTA panelists are less likely to follow relevant GATT/ WTO panel and Appellate Body decisions than future WTO panels, given that prior GATT or WTO panel decisions are not binding on future panels. . . .

Political Considerations

Politics is likely to be a factor in some cases, in the sense that the Parties seek to place maximum pressure on each other toward settlement. This may well lead to multiple filings, . . . Where a NAFTA Party believes that it is desirable to do so, it may be able to follow the Canadian approach in Farm Products Blockade, and avoid the "double jeopardy" rules of the NAFTA by characterizing different aspects of the same dispute as separate "matters." The United States may well contribute to the proliferation of parallel actions by filing Section 301 actions relating to the principal case, as in High Fructose Corn Syrup, even in circumstances where it is unlikely that such unilateral approaches will be pursued. In this respect, Mexico and Canada are at a tactical disadvantage because their laws incorporate no equivalent to Section 301.

Even where the NAFTA and WTO legal provisions are equivalent, there may be political advantages in using the multilateral over the trilateral procedures because of the likelihood of attracting support from other WTO members through peer pressure, including, but not limited to, joining the action or reserving third party rights. On the other hand, a NAFTA Party may be more willing to reach a negotiated settlement if the settlement need be implemented only with regard to a single nation rather than for multiple plaintiffs.

Finally, a Party's track record within each forum may be a relevant consideration in choosing a new forum. Canada and Mexico have each won the sole case pursued by them to binational panel resolution under Chapter 20,.... The United States has, of course, lost both cases. Whether this experience will prejudice the official views of the American government against the Chapter 20 process, when and if new matters arise that could be brought in either forum, remains to be seen....

The experience of the NAFTA Parties at the WTO has been generally positive, but mixed.... It does not appear, however, that the experience of any of the three countries before the WTO is so far superior to its experience under Chapter 20 that this factor alone should determine forum choices in future disputes.

Questions and Comments

1. When Canada and Mexico considered a response to the Helms–Burton, there were other alternatives to a NAFTA Chapter 20 procedure, and there were other actions which did not depend upon or relate to NAFTA. One action, which both nations took, was the enactment of domestic laws which illustrated the nation's displeasure with Helms–Burton. Canada amended its Foreign Extraterritorial Measures Act, and Mexico enacted the Law for the Protection of Commerce and Investment from Foreign Laws that Contravene International Law, both "blocking" laws which attempt to prevent and counter the extraterritorial affect of the Helms–Burton (and similar) laws. With regard to pursuing a claim under NAFTA, Canada and Mexico had the alternative of initiating a claim under the WTO. The European Union did so in February, 1997, but suspended the action when the U.S. made promises to seek amendments to the Helms–Burton (which it failed to undertake). The U.S. indicated that it would raise the national security defense and not appear at a panel. Prof. Gantz offers a few comments on the NAFTA/WTO alternatives, and what influences party choices.

2. The stages prior to a panel include consultations under Art. 2006, and use of the good offices of the Commission under Art. 2007. They were unsuccessful in the *Broom Corn Brooms* case. Might we have expected either to be successful with regard to the Helms–Burton law? Prof. Lopez and Prof. Gantz each outline some of the experience under Chapter 20 in initiating a

proceeding. When are these early stages likely to be most effective? Why did it not work with *Broom Corn Brooms,* even though few who viewed that case as it progressed agreed with the ITC's conclusion that plastic and broom corn brooms were not like or directly competitive products? After all, they look alike, and are used for exactly the same purpose. Are these first stages useless?

3. Why did the Parties select an English (*Dairy Products, Cross–Border Trucking Services*) or an Australian (*Broom Corn Brooms*) jurist to chair the Chapter 20 panels? If they wanted to avoid using a national or a party to the dispute, why not keep it inside NAFTA and select a national of the party not involved?. In all three cases, the two U.S. panelists joined to make the panel unanimous, and to rule against the U.S. Any lessons to be learned? If panelists appear to be "too" independent, how might this affect the process of selecting persons for the roster, and persons for the panels? The Parties initially tried to keep even the names of the panelists secret, but abandoned that practice by 1999; why?

4. All Parties before NAFTA Chapter 20 panels have regularly cited the GATT and WTO panel decisions for support of their positions. Is that permitted under NAFTA for a Chapter 20 panel? Should it be? This raises at least two issues, the relevance of GATT/WTO jurisprudence in NAFTA, and the use of cases, if not as formal precedent, at least as persuasive authority. The relevance seems obvious in some cases. For example, if a NAFTA Chapter 20 panel for the first time is seeking to interpret the scope of the "national treatment" provisions in articles 1102 and 1202 (*Cross-border trucking services*), why not look to the enormous volume of GATT/WTO determinations under Article III (non-discrimination)? All three governments, their counsel, and the five panelists thought this jurisprudence was highly relevant. Moreover, in all Chapter 20 panels to date, at least three panelists (five in *Dairy Products*) were common law attorneys, trained from the first day of law school to look first to the case law for guidance. Mexico, the lone national civil law jurisdiction in North America, relies on a Canadian law firm as counsel in Chapter 20 (and Chapter 11) proceedings.

5. Many panel decisions, under Chapter 19 or 20, include some specific reference to the required *standard of review. Broom Corn Brooms* discusses this in terms of NAFTA Art. 803 and Annex 803.3, which outline the process that must be followed for safeguards matters. Mexico believed that the ITC failed to adequately support its findings on commercial interchangeability (corn brooms and the more common plastic brooms), using only a confidential ITC telephone survey which could not be challenged. What is the standard of review? Mexico concedes that the panel does not undertake a *de novo* review, but wants more than the United States. How rigorous a review is proper? Should it be as narrow as for Chapter 19 panels, as discussed in Problem 9.3? Note that in *Dairy Products* and *Cross-Border Trucking*, there could only be *de novo* review, since only a government action (or inaction) was before the tribunal.

6. Prof. Picker discusses the issuance of initial and final reports. Do you agree with his analysis as to why the initial report remains confidential outside the disputing parties? (The initial report in his case, *Dairy Products,* was leaked immediately; the initial reports were kept confidential in the

other two cases.) Is the final report really an appeal? If the initial report is only part of a work product leading to the final report, why not call it a draft for circulation among the disputing parties rather than an initial report? Does circulation of the interim report provide an opportunity for further settlement discussions that would be absent otherwise? For the application of political pressures? To give the tribunal an opportunity to correct factual and legal errors and interpretations, even if the final result is not changed? The interim report process is used by WTO panels, but not by the Appellate Body. Among the many proposed revisions to the WTO's dispute resolution procedures in the course of the Doha Round negotiations would be to require the Appellate Body to circulate an interim report to the disputing parties as well.

7. Prof. Picker comments on establishing a permanent tribunal in place of the Chapter 20 panels. Are his arguments sound? Why not a NAFTA court similar to the European Union Court of Justice? Is the political acceptability of a supranational "court" as much or more a function of the desired level of integration than of practical and legal factors?

8. The U.S. Trade Representative Charlene Barshefsky [1997–2000] stated soon after the *Broom Corn Brooms* decision that the decision had "virtually no effect" on the U.S. ability to impose sanctions under the safeguard provisions, that the panel did not rule on the substance of the ITC's finding, or on the safeguard measures taken by the President. She said she was pleased that the decision only found a "narrow, technical flaw in the ITC's injury decision." The measures taken by the U.S. President, and the countermeasures taken by Mexico, were not reviewed. Should they have been? What was the role of the panel—to review the determination of the ITC, or the President, or both? Note that when President Bush terminated steel safeguard in December 2003, a few weeks after they had been ruled illegal by the WTO's Dispute Settlement Body and the EU and others were threatening massive trade sanctions, the WTO ruling was not mentioned as one of the reasons for the change in policy.

9. Prof. Gantz' comments on the advantages and disadvantages of NAFTA versus the WTO may draw objections; several years after the article was written the pros and cons remain unclear. For example, does debate over the qualifications of a roster name necessarily take much less time than presenting names and debating them when there is no roster, or a roster with no names, as is the case of Chapter 20? (In fact, an informal, non-public roster of five individuals from each of the NAFTA nations *has* existed among the NAFTA trade ministries for at least six years, including during the panel selection process for *Cross-Border Trucking Services*.) Is the *experience* in complying (or not complying) the real measure? (In *Dairy Products*, there was no compliance issue because Canada prevailed. The United States complied with the decision in *Broom Corn Brooms* in nine months. Compliance in *Trucks* has required more than three and a half years.) Prof. Gantz does not indicate a clear preference for the WTO use of disinterested nationals, versus the NAFTA use of interested nationals (the latter almost mandatory with only three Parties). He is also uncertain about the suggested higher predictability of the WTO. Agree with him or not, his comments offer much to think about.

10.   One of the mysteries of the delay problem under Chapter 20 is why similar provisions seem to have assured very prompt panel selection and decisions under CFTA, Chapter 18. In the five cases brought under CFTA, the period required to complete the panel process averaged about six months, with panel selection taking from a few days to several months. With the three NAFTA cases, panel selection required from around six months to sixteen months, and the complete process from the panel request to circulation of the interim report to the Parties required from eleven months to two years and two months, with another six to eight weeks for the final report. Nor is the 90 day period from selection of the panelists to the interim report at all realistic. In *Broom Corn Brooms*, for example, the Parties required 82 days to complete the briefing process after panel selection, and a hearing could not be scheduled for an additional three weeks. In a system where the panelists live in multiple time zones, have full-time jobs, and in some cases are not all fluent in English, a period for rendering the interim report of at least six months or more would be appropriate. See Gantz, Government to Government Dispute Resolution Under NAFTA: A Commentary on the Process, 11 Am. Rev. Int'l Arb. 481, 503–05 (2002). Under the WTO's Dispute Settlement Understanding, panels have up to nine months to render a report, and most panel decisions are routinely requiring a year. (The WTO's Appellate Body, with a permanent roster of seven members and no panel selection issues, has consistently rendered its decisions within the 60–90 day period provided in the DSU.)

11.   Chapter 20 of CAFTA, and Chapters 21–22 of the U.S.–Chile FTA, contain language closely following NAFTA's Chapter 20, as do other recent U.S. FTAs.

PART B. THE HELMS–BURTON CHALLENGE

Having considered the structure of Chapter 20, and the procedure before a panel, we now turn to our hypothetical and consider how the challenge brought by Canada and Mexico against Title IV of the U.S. Helms–Burton Act might fare. While *Broom Corn Brooms* and *Cross-Border Trucking* involved a determination of the meaning of some specific language—"like or directly competitive" and "in like circumstances," respectively—our hypothetical is quite different. The challenges are broader, and there appear to be no prior NAFTA, CFTA or GATT/WTO decisions which help. This hypothetical also adds an untested *defense*, that of national security under Art. 2102.

LOWENFELD, AGORA: THE CUBAN LIBERTY AND DEMOCRATIC SOLIDARITY (LIBERTAD) ACT
90 Am.J.Int'l L. 419 (1996)*

* * *

HELMS-BURTON AND THE EFFECTS DOCTRINE

The authors of the Helms–Burton Act were prepared for criticism that they were engaged in extraterritorial legislation. They included in the Findings on which the operative portions of the Act are based, the statement:

> International law recognizes that a nation has the ability to provide for rules of law with respect to conduct outside its territory that has or is intended to have substantial effect within its territory. (Section 301(9))

This is, of course, a statement derived—indeed almost quoted—from the *Restatement of Foreign Relations Law*. But the "almost" is significant. . . .

* * *

I submit that the effort by the authors of Helms–Burton to build on the *Restatement* is flawed—fundamentally flawed—in two respects. *First,* the effect against which the legislation is directed—even if one can locate it in the United States—was caused by the Government of Cuba, not by the persons over whom jurisdiction is sought to be exercised. Thus, even leaving aside the thirty-six year interval between conduct and effect on the one hand, and exercise of prescriptive jurisdiction on the other, the effort to place Helms–Burton within the effects doctrine is no more than a play on words. It does not withstand analysis, and it would carry the effects doctrine farther than it has ever been carried before.

Second, the effort to impose United States policy on third countries or their nationals in the circumstances here contemplated is unreasonable by any standard. I need not here go through the criteria for evaluating reasonableness set out in the *Restatement;* different writers and courts have formulated or understood the criteria in different ways. I think for present purposes the most persuasive way to look at the legislation is to ask how Americans would react if the tables were turned.

The General Assembly of the Organization of American States, by Resolution of June, 1996, directed the Inter–American Juridical Committee of the OAS "to examine and decide upon the validity under international law" of the Helms–Burton Law, and to do so "as a matter of priority." The Juridical Committee rendered a unanimous 11%, including the U.S. member) opinion. It is a non-binding opinion, and addressed two areas, property rights and the issue of extraterritoriality. The opinion included the following:

OPINION OF THE INTER–AMERICAN JURIDICAL COMMITTEE IN RESPONSE TO RESOLUTION AG/DOC. 3375/96 OF THE GENERAL ASSEMBLY OF THE ORGANIZATION, ENTITLED "FREEDOM OF TRADE AND INVESTMENT IN THE HEMISPHERE"

* * *

B. EXTRATERRITORIALITY AND THE LIMITS IMPOSED BY INTERNATIONAL LAW ON THE EXERCISE OF JURISDICTION

7. The Committee understands that the legislation would result in the exercise of legislative or judicial jurisdiction over acts performed abroad by aliens on the basis of a concept termed "trafficking in confiscated properties."

8. The Committee has also examined the applicable norms of international law in respect of the exercise of jurisdiction by States and its limits on such exercise. In the opinion of the Committee, these norms include the following:

a) All States are subject to international law in their relations. No State may take measures that are not in conformity with international law without incurring responsibility.

b) All States have the freedom to exercise jurisdiction but such exercise must respect the limits imposed by international law. To the extent that such exercise does not comply with these limits, the exercising State will incur responsibility.

c) Except where a norm of international law permits, the State may not exercise its power in any form in the territory of another State. The basic premise under international law for establishing legislative and judicial jurisdiction is rooted in the principle of territoriality.

d) In the exercise of its territorial jurisdiction a State may regulate an act whose constituent elements may have occurred only in part in its territory: for example an act initiated abroad but consummated within its territory ("objective territoriality") or conversely an act initiated within its territory and consummated abroad ("subjective territoriality").

e) A State may justify the application of the laws of its territory only insofar as an act occurring outside its territory has a direct, substantial and foreseeable effect within its territory and the exercise of such jurisdiction is reasonable.

f) A State may exceptionally exercise jurisdiction on a basis other than territoriality only where there exists a substantial or otherwise significant connection between the matter in question and the State's sovereign authority, such as in the case of the exercise of jurisdiction over acts performed abroad by its nationals and in certain specific cases of the protection objectively necessary to safeguard its essential sovereign interests.

9. The Committee examined the provisions of the legislation that establish the exercise of jurisdiction on bases other than those of territoriality, and concluded that the exercise of such jurisdiction over acts of "trafficking in confiscated property" does not conform with the norms established by international law for the exercise of jurisdiction in each of the following respects:

a) A prescribing State does not have the right to exercise jurisdiction over acts of "trafficking" abroad by aliens unless specific conditions are fulfilled which do not appear to be satisfied in this situation.

b) A prescribing State does not have the right to exercise jurisdiction over acts of "trafficking" abroad by aliens under circumstances where neither the alien nor the conduct in question has any connection with its territory and where no apparent connection exists between such acts and the protection of its essential sovereign interests.

Therefore, the exercise of jurisdiction by a State over acts of "trafficking" by aliens abroad, under circumstances whereby neither the alien nor the conduct in question has any connection with its territory and there is no apparent connection between such acts and the protection of its essential sovereign interests, does not conform with international law.

Conclusion

10. For the above reasons the Committee concludes that in the significant areas described above the bases and potential application of the legislation which is the subject of this Opinion are not in conformity with international law.

GORDON, THE CONFLICT OF UNITED STATES SANCTIONS WITH OBLIGATIONS UNDER THE NORTH AMERICAN FREE TRADE AGREEMENT
27 Stetson L.Rev. 1259 (1998).*

* * *

The National Security Defense Under the NAFTA as an Obstacle to a Ruling on the Legitimacy of United States Sanctions

The legitimacy of sanctions like those described above is questionable under several theories. But those theories may never be tested. Article 2102 of the NAFTA allows a Party to enact laws for national security reasons. The WTO Agreement contains a similar provision. The United States has stated it will use these provisions in response to any challenge under either the WTO or the NAFTA. If, in a NAFTA proceeding, the United States formally claims that Cuba is a threat to its national security,[55] a view which has little support in the United States,[56] the challenging party might not be able to counter because each Party reserves the right to determine what actions "it considers necessary."[57] The Party appears to be the only judge of its own actions. This means a NAFTA or WTO panel might not consider the arguments, explored below, relating to United States sanctions laws and their impact on such NAFTA and WTO obligations as most-favored-nation treatment and nondiscrimination, if the panel first concluded the national security defense foreclosed it. But the panel might decide to examine each argument, then that, regardless of conclusions on the specific provisions, the national security defense precluded a final ruling against the United States. The United States might refuse to participate beyond its presentation of the defense. That action would be consistent with the United States refusal to participate in the Nicaraguan case before the International Court of Justice after the United States lost on the issue of jurisdiction.[59] Using the national security defense in the WTO to defend the LIBERTAD Act, especially in view of the United States experience as of early 1998 (seventeen wins and one loss), would both increase the ill feeling toward the United States regarding its attitude on interpreting trade provisions as foreign policy issues, and jeopardize the future success of the WTO for dealing with trade issues. National security could come to include vague meanings of "economic security," which might be used in future WTO cases like those the United States has won, such as beef hormones and the E.U., and publishing and Canada. Even bananas could assume national security proportions.

ALTERNATIVE APPROACHES TO UNITED STATES SANCTIONS LAWS AS IN CONFLICT WITH THE NAFTA

Assuming either that the United States does not raise the national security defense in a NAFTA challenge, or that the defense is not found to prevent consideration of possible violations of the NAFTA by the United States sanctions laws, there are at least three approaches with

55. Such threat is admitted in a specific provision in the LIBERTAD Act, regarding "international peace and security." *See* 22 U.S.C.A. § 6021(14).

56. The meaning of "national security" in either the NAFTA or the WTO does not suggest that the nations be on the brink of war, nor does it suggest that no other nation has the right to have an armed force. Perhaps the most likely claim would be that an "emergency in international relations" exists, but any reasonable interpretation of that provision ought to require some legitimate threat to the Party raising the defense. *Id.* Cessation of diplomatic relations should not constitute an emergency in international relations, especially when the nations maintain relations through special interest sections with staffs similar to what they would have were diplomatic relations to be restored.

57. The same language appears in both the NAFTA and WTO national security provisions. NAFTA, art. 2102(1)(b); GATT/WTO, art. XXI(b).

59. Case Concerning Military and Paramilitary Activities in and Against Nicaragua (Nicar. v. U.S.), 1986 I.C.J. 14 (June 27)....

respect to challenging United States sanctions laws under the NAFTA. First is that these laws constitute a violation of international law, thereby violating the NAFTA under Article 102(2). Second is that the entire tenor of the NAFTA is to further open trade where not specifically restricted, and that sanctions laws such as the LIBERTAD Act violate the "objectives" of Articles 101 and 102(2). Third is that there are specific violations of several trade provisions of the NAFTA, such as national treatment or nullification and impairment provisions, or rules on the transit of business persons, in the application of the sanctions laws. Secondary considerations include which of the above theories is most likely to be enforced, and whether the NAFTA dispute process was intended to address either of the first two concepts.

INTERNATIONAL LAW AND SANCTIONS LAW
Customary International Law

* * *

To what rules of customary international law might the Parties be subject, even in the absence of any reference to them in the NAFTA? Customary international law has two elements, recognition as a general practice and acceptance as a rule of law. Canada and Mexico are likely to argue that it applies to two aspects of sanctions law, the excessive extraterritorial effect, and the secondary boycott characteristics. Both of these might also be part of a more general charge of interference with the sovereignty of Canada and Mexico. . . .

* * *

The first customary international law argument likely to be presented in a NAFTA challenge is that the United States sanctions laws exceed permissible limits of the exercise of extraterritorial jurisdiction. The idea is more often referred to as the principle of territoriality, and often joined with a discussion of the nationality principle. Jurisdiction of one nation's laws to govern conduct abroad was earlier more closely linked with territory than it is today. The critical issue has become at what point in the extraterritorial exercise of either legislative or enforcement jurisdiction a nation so conflicts with another state's sovereignty as to constitute a breach of customary international law. Unfortunately, many American jurists tend to espouse as principles of international law the United States Restatement of Foreign Relations, or theories advanced by American scholars. This practice is obviously inconsistent both with the theory of the nature of international law in general, and with the evolution of customary international law.

The principal international case dealing with extraterritorial jurisdiction is the Permanent Court of International Justice's *Lotus* decision.[81] The court stated that one nation may not "exercise its power in any form in the territory of another State." But the court was unwilling

---

81. The S.S. Lotus (Fr. v. Turk.), 1927 P.C.I.J. (ser. A) No. 10 (Sept. 7).

to find a general prohibition in international law disallowing states from extending their laws and the jurisdiction of their courts to persons, property, and acts outside the nation's territory. Finding the law to be undeveloped at the time of the case (1927), the court allowed states some latitude to develop rules which a state regarded as "best and most suitable." Resting permission to exercise extraterritorial jurisdiction on a nation's sovereignty, the *Lotus* decision has been the basis for limited extraterritorial jurisdiction. The case is of marginal use in defining current customary international law, as nations in the last seven decades have expanded their activities across borders with new technology. With permission to exercise limited extraterritoriality a generally accepted principle, the task for a NAFTA panel is to determine the current status of those limits.

Does the *magnitude* of the expropriations by Cuba justify a greater extraterritorial application of United States law than otherwise would be permitted? However intriguing this argument may be, it has no support in international law. Perhaps one might argue that customary international law requires the use of proportionality in reacting to foreign acts, but that means *limiting* one's actions, not expanding them. With regard to boycotts, sometimes referred to as retorsion or measures of self-help, international law allows a nation to retaliate in response to an unfriendly act. What that response may be is the question. Expulsion of diplomats or even breaking diplomatic relations are viewed as acceptable. Unilateral economic sanctions are, for the most part, thought to be short of the kind of aggression condemned by the U.N. Charter, unless they raise serious questions of human rights. Nations tend to believe they have an absolute right to terminate trade as retaliation for any disputed act. The United States is probably on good ground in refusing to trade with Cuba, especially since it has left some small openings for humanitarian trade in food and medical supplies. But the extension of this retaliation to a secondary boycott is a very different situation. It intersects and perhaps merges with the above discussion of the permissible limits of extraterritorial laws.

* * *

Might it be argued that Cuba has no right to respond to the United States' acts of extraterritoriality because of Cuba's extensive violation of international law in expropriating property? But it is not Cuba that is the principal complainant regarding the sanctions laws, it is other nations, such as Canada and Mexico and the European Union. The fact that the other state is not Cuba, but third nations subject to the LIBERTAD Act, is often overlooked. Canada and Mexico are not complaining that Cuba is being improperly treated, they are complaining that Canada and Mexico are improperly the subject of the extraterritorial application of the United States sanctions laws. Attempting to justify the United States law by references to balancing United States interests with Cuban interests or self-help against Cuba for its unlawful expropriations overlooks the real issue of the impact on third nations. To argue that third nations are aiding Cuba and thus assuming the mantle of international pariahs is to carry the argument beyond what any respectable international jurist would accept.

If the effects test may be used to justify extraterritorial application of a nation's laws, what direct, substantial, and foreseeable effect occurs in the United States when, for example, a Canadian company doing business in Cuba has been assigned to use as its administrative offices a house expropriated from a Cuban citizen who emigrated and became a United States citizen? Any effect in the sense of economic loss to the Cuban individual arose from the Cuban act, not from the subsequent, incidental Canadian use. Too often the Cuban acts of expropriation are assumed to have had no impact on the title to the property. When an expropriation is not followed by proper compensation, to assume that title has not passed may be incorrect. But that view is at the heart of the LIBERTAD Act and the arguments of its few supporters. Only if the property has remained owned by its pre-expropriation owners do the arguments that a later user is a trafficker in stolen property have any merit. But if the property is viewed to have passed to the expropriating government, with proper compensation an outstanding and unresolved issue, then any users of expropriated property in Cuba cannot be charged as traffickers.

* * *

OBJECTIVES OF THE NAFTA AS A WHOLE AND THEIR RELATION TO SANCTIONS

Articles 101 and 102

... [T]he progression toward freer trade that was in place among Canada, Mexico, and the United States, and was furthered by the NAFTA, constitutes a movement in a direction in contrast to that taken by the unilateral United States sanctions against Cuba enacted after forming the NAFTA. The Cuban sanctions are both trade restrictive and unilateral clashes with the concept of a free trade area embodied in Article 101 of the NAFTA, and with the stated objectives of the NAFTA in Article 102.

None of Article 102's objectives specifically refer to one Party's obligations to another Party with respect to non-NAFTA nations, but it may be fair to view these objectives as including an implied obligation not to interfere with another Party's trade with non-NAFTA nations. Further, this "Objective" Article 102 states that the provisions of the Agreement are to be interpreted in light of the stated objectives *and* "in accordance with the applicable rules of international law." This suggests that any interpretation of provisions of the Agreement that might relate to and affect the use of sanctions, ought to be consistent with international law principles applicable to sanctions.

NAFTA's Specific Provisions and Unilateral Sanctions

* * *

Provisions of the NAFTA Relating to Trade in Goods

Article 301 requires one Party to "accord national treatment to the goods of another Party," following Article III of the General Agreement on Tariffs and Trade (GATT). While it does not so state, the implication and negotiating history suggests that the goods referred to are goods flowing *between* NAFTA Parties, not goods traded, for example, between Canada and Cuba. The NAFTA provisions apply, however, when the Canadian–Cuban trade includes the acquisition by a Canadian company of Cuban parts, which are then included in goods manufactured in Canada for export to the United States. If the content from Cuba is sufficient so that, under the NAFTA Chapter Four Rules of Origin, the manufactured goods would not qualify as "goods of another Party," national treatment would not apply. But even if the goods qualify as Canadian under the NAFTA rules, they may conflict with section 110 of the LIBERTAD Act, which prohibits the importation into the United States of any product that "is made or derived in whole or in part of any article which is the growth, produce, or manufacture of Cuba." Foreseeing this problem, the drafters of the LIBERTAD Act included a provision that states: "The Congress notes that United States accession to the NAFTA does not modify or alter the United States sanctions against Cuba." The provision incorporates a portion of the United States statement of administrative action that accompanied the NAFTA Implementation Act. That statement, which represents the United States view of its commitment under the NAFTA, states the NAFTA "will not affect the Cuban sanctions program." That statement must be read to mean the sanctions program as it existed when the NAFTA was adopted. The LIBERTAD Act had not yet been enacted. Nothing in the NAFTA suggests that a Party might unilaterally modify its NAFTA obligations, nor impose upon other Parties a mandate to participate in the secondary boycott provisions of the Cuban sanctions program as developed in the LIBERTAD Act after the creation of the NAFTA.

The same LIBERTAD Act section continues with a statement that Article 309(3) of the NAFTA grants the United States authority to "ensure that Cuban products or goods made from Cuban materials" are not brought into the United States from Canada or Mexico. Article 309(3) states that the NAFTA allows a boycott by a Party that prohibits the use of another Party's territory to circumvent the boycott. But Article 309(3) refers to "goods" and does not include the reference to "parts" contained in the LIBERTAD Act section 110(a)(3). The LIBERTAD Act section 110(b)(2) attempts to add to the language of NAFTA Article 309(3) "goods made from Cuban materials." It would seem reasonable to assume that the NAFTA Parties intended Article 309(3) to allow a Party to prohibit products to qualify under the Rules of Origin as a good of a NAFTA Party when much of the content of that good was from a boycotted country. But it probably was not intended to prohibit the entry of a good when the quantity of Cuban origin is de minimis, e.g., the bolt holding the bumper of an auto made in Mexico. As a practical matter, it would be difficult to determine origin in such a manner. The bolts may have been obtained by the Mexican auto manufacturer from a bolt distributor who in turn obtained them from many sources, including Cuba.

Canada and Mexico do not have very strong arguments that United States sanctions in the form of the primary boycott under the rules incorporated in the pre-NAFTA Cuban Assets Control Regulations and the Cuban Democracy Act violate United States obligations under NAFTA Chapter Three, in view of Article 309(3). There is little difficulty with goods imported into the United States, although some imports may have some Cuban content. A greater problem exists with goods imported into Cuba from Canada or Mexico which are wholly United States made, partly United States and partly Canadian or Mexican, or fully Canadian or Mexican but using United States technology. Goods made in the United States and entering Cuba through Canada or Mexico may or may not violate United States law. If the goods are merely transshipped to Cuba through Canada or Mexico, the United States exporter is subject to penalties. But if the goods are exported to Canada or Mexico with the expectation they will be sold and consumed in Canada or Mexico, but are then purchased by a Cuban government organization purchasing agent and shipped to Cuba, the United States exporter ought not be concerned. If the goods are partly made in Canada or Mexico with United States components, additional issues are raised such as who owns the facility in Canada or Mexico that finishes the production. Where goods are fully made in a third nation, but from United States technology, the issue is likely to depend on the nature of technology. Visitors to Cuba drink Coca–Cola bottled in many nations other than the United States. The foreign bottling companies are locally owned, but use United States technology. While proponents of the trade embargo favor interpreting the laws to prohibit any products of any United States origin, technology included, from reaching Cuba, the language of the laws is sufficiently vague to raise doubt about concluding that any United States product available in Cuba has arrived there by some illegal process.

Any arguments that Canada or Mexico might make that relate to most-favored-nation, quantitative restrictions, or other NAFTA provisions that affect the flow of goods will confront the same Article 309(3) defenses discussed above. . . .

* * *

TEMPORARY ENTRY FOR BUSINESS PERSONS UNDER NAFTA CHAPTER 16

NAFTA Article 1603 requires that "[e]ach Party shall grant temporary entry to business persons who are otherwise qualified for entry under applicable measures relating to health and safety and national security." Annex 1603 requires that temporary entry be granted as long as the person "otherwise complies with existing" immigration laws. "Existing" immigration laws refers to those in effect on January 1, 1994, with respect to Mexico, and on January 1, 1989, with respect to Canada. The LIBERTAD Act postdates both. Section 401 of Title IV of the

LIBERTAD Act requires the United States to prohibit visas to persons who have trafficked in confiscated property. But it is not an absolute prohibition. A party is allowed to obtain entry rights upon ceasing to traffic in confiscated property.

The NAFTA ought not be read to suggest that a Party may not alter its immigration laws in any manner. Certainly, national security interests would justify denying visas to other Parties' nationals. Supporters of the LIBERTAD Act may argue that "existing" immigration laws allow denial of entry to persons accused of crimes, and that all the LIBERTAD Act does is deny visas to such persons. But it does much more. First, not one of the corporate officials of the two Canadian and Mexican firms that have been denied rights to visas because their enterprises are thought to be trafficking has been charged with any crime. More troublesome is the denial of visas to their families, a guilt by association uncommon to American legal thought.

The OAS Juridical Committee did not address the form of visa denial contained in Title IV of the LIBERTAD Act. International law does not entitle free movement of peoples from one nation to another. A nation may establish its own concepts of immigration. The LIBERTAD Act Title IV visa denial provisions may be lawful under the law of nations, however angry it may make other nations. But in participating in the NAFTA, the United States relinquished some authority to restrict business travel by persons from the other Parties. If a NAFTA panel rejected Title III of the LIBERTAD Act, ruling the trafficking provisions inconsistent with NAFTA commitments, the support for Title IV would vanish. If a person cannot be a trafficker, that person cannot be denied entry under Title IV. If Title III were upheld, however, the Title IV provisions would have to be tested under the Article 1603 language of the NAFTA stated above, with attention to the permissible alteration of immigration laws in view of the "existing" law provisions.

Questions and Comments

1.   Title IV is one of two titles of the Helms–Burton Act which has been the subject of criticism. The other is Title III, which is the more controversial, but the right to bring actions under Title III has been deferred every six months by Presidents Bill Clinton and George W. Bush, under authority contained in the Act. Title III allows an action in U.S. courts by U.S. nationals who claim that their property was taken by Cuba and that the foreign party charged is now "trafficking" in such property. The President is not allowed to defer the implementation of Title IV, and the consequence has been considerable pressure on the President from some in Congress to list many more companies engaged in trade with and investment in Cuba.

2.   Title IV may prohibit the entry of officers, principals, or shareholders with a controlling interest in any entity trafficking in confiscated property, and includes a spouse, minor child or agent of the excludable persons. The U.S. first denied visa privileges to both the Sherritt International Corp., in Canada, and to Grupo Domos in Mexico. Sherritt has participated in a nickel project at Moa Bay, once owned by the United States

Freeport McMoRan company. Grupo Domos planned to participate in a telecommunications project which allegedly would use expropriated properties of IT&T. Visa denials have also been issued against an Israel owned citrus company. Some Congressional leaders have urged the president to use Title IV against the Spanish hotel company Melia.

3. The Canadian challenge, joined by Mexico, includes action taken by the President in listing persons under Title IV. (Involving possible questions of immigration, this could not have been raised in an action brought to the WTO.) Could Canada and Mexico have challenged Title IV prior to any such action, solely because of the *existence* of the provisions? The answer is important to any challenge to Title III, because an argument might be made that any action may not be challenged until there has been a judgment in a United States court upon which execution is sought against Canadian or Mexican property in the U.S. But the language in Section B of Chapter 20 speaks to the "interpretation or application of this Agreement," and the "avoidance or settlement of all disputes." (Art. 2004). The NAFTA action is dormant; it has not proceeded to the panel stage, presumably by mutual consent of the Parties.

4. A principal argument that Canada and Mexico would make is that the Helms–Burton law has an extraterritorial effect beyond what is permitted under international law. Article 102(2) requires the Parties to "interpret and apply the provisions of this Agreement . . . in accordance with applicable rules of international law." Prof. Lowenfeld, a strong advocate of the *Restatement of Foreign Relations Law*, is troubled by the findings upon which the Helms–Burton law was based. He believes they represent a flawed interpretation of the *Restatement*. Would a NAFTA panel refer to the *Restatement* in a search for international law? What sources would the panel use? Is the OAS Inter–American Juridical Committee opinion more relevant? Does it consider the Helms–Burton law to exceed permissible limits of extraterritorial jurisdiction? What does the OAS Opinion use as authority for its conclusions?

The OAS Opinion was unanimous that the U.S. went beyond what is a reasonable extraterritorial application of its laws. The few instances where foreign courts have considered U.S. extraterritoriality have not been favorable to the U.S. See Compagnie Européenne des Petroles S.A. v. Sensor Nederland B.V., Case 82/716 Rechtspraak van de Week 167 (Dist. Ct. Neth.), reprinted in 22 I.L.M. 66 (1983); Fruehauf Corp. v. Massardy, Court of Appeals of Paris, 14th Chamber (May 22, 1965 France), reprinted in 5 I.L.M. 476 (1966). Neither the OAS nor the *Sensor* or *Freuhauf* decisions included any reference to the Restatement, relying instead on such theories as the territorial and nationality principles.

5. The national security defense is most certainly to be tested if Canada and Mexico go forward. If you were to read Art. 2102 without having read the hypothetical, would you have thought that the kind of issues raised in the hypothetical were intended to result in the use of the national security defense? What if the U.S. refused to participate in the selection of a panel— could a panel nevertheless be formed? Would it be a good idea for Canada and Mexico to proceed if the U.S. refused to participate at this point? One concern of the U.S. is that if it fails to participate, it has no say in how the

proceedings will evolve. What would you recommend to the U.S. as its position? What if the U.S. claims national security, and immediately the EU claims national security in the banana dispute and the meat growth hormone dispute? Does an unreasonable use of the national security defense jeopardize the entire trade agreement structure, the NAFTA or the WTO?

6. Consider the Articles 101 and 102 "objectives" argument by Canada and Mexico. Is the language of these provisions sufficient on which to build a case against the visa denial? What proof would you offer in support of the argument? Is it better to focus on another argument, with the objectives provisions used for support in the way of how the panel ought to lean when there is more than one interpretation possible? If you were involved with drafting the proposed Free Trade Area of the Americas, and concerned with the U.S.-Cuban experience, might you try to include a provision such as the following:

> Parties shall be prohibited from imposing upon any other Party any actions which are intended to require the other Party to comply with, further or support any boycott fostered or imposed by the Party against a country which is friendly to the other Party.

If this appears familiar it is because it is adapted from the U.S. antiboycott provisions of the Export Administration Act, adopted to prevent U.S. companies from assisting in the Arab boycott of Israel, just as Canada and Mexico do not wish their companies to assist the U.S. in the boycott of Cuba.)

7. The extraterritorial argument is important. The OAS Committee did not specifically address Title IV. It was more concerned with Title III. But a Title IV argument is much stronger if the panel rules that the "trafficking" theory is a violation of international law, since the denial of visas is based on trafficking. What if the visa denial was merely based on the Canadian or Mexican company trading with Cuba? Can't a nation deny entry for any reason? The argument would seem to shift to the NAFTA movement of business persons provisions.

8. Canada and Mexico need to avoid challenging the relations between the U.S. and *Cuba*, and concentrate on the relations between the U.S. and Canada and Mexico which result from U.S. laws which may appear to be directed solely at Cuba. The U.S. was clearly addressing third nations with the Helms–Burton Act, having already seemingly exhausted sanctions levied directly against Cuba, which have been ineffective for four decades in achieving the intended goal, the downfall of Fidel Castro. Few deny the unlawfulness of the Cuban expropriations of U.S. property. Canada and Mexico will argue that however unlawful those expropriations were, the Helms–Burton Act does too much—it carries what is a permissible extraterritorial application of law in certain instances to an impermissible extreme. Note also that a NAFTA Party (e.g., the United States) may, under Article 1113, deny the benefits of Chapter 11 under certain circumstances:

> 1. A Party may deny the benefits of this Chapter to an investor of another Party that is an enterprise of such Party and to investments of such investor if investors of a non-Party own or control the enterprise and the denying Party: (a) *does not maintain diplomatic relations with the non-Party*; or (b) adopts or maintains measures with respect to the non-Party that prohibit transactions with the enterprise or that would

be violated or circumvented if the benefits of this Chapter were accorded to the enterprise or the investment. (Emphasis added)

9.   At first glance, it might seem that the U.S. actions violate the Art. 301 national treatment requirement. If goods are exported to the U.S. from Canada or Mexico which contain some Cuban content, but which remain classified as Canadian or Mexican goods under the rules of origin, how can the U.S. exclude them?

10.   What about goods going the other way, from Canada or Mexico to Cuba, which contain some U.S. content? Do the same provisions apply as in #9 above?

11.   The temporary entry of business persons provisions in NAFTA Chapter 16 did not contemplate the type of problem presented in this case. The Title IV denials in our hypothetical reach both persons who might be in the U.S. for business (i.e., officers of the Mexican company), but in our case all the persons were in the U.S. on holiday (Mexican company) or for school (Canada). Does the provision in Helms–Burton that allows persons entry once they stop trafficking mean that their denial is self-induced? But that would apply only to the business persons who make the business decisions, not to most of the employees, and certainly not to their families. Is the issue of who is permitted to enter a nation so much a part of national sovereignty that Title IV is impossible to challenge?

12.   Conflicts between the United States and its NAFTA partners regarding Cuba are likely to continue, as new restrictions affecting Cuba appear. For example, in June 2004, the Bush Administration further restricted U.S. citizen travel to Cuba, even where no financial transactions are involved. See Office of Foreign Assets Controls, Changes to Cuban Assets Control Regulations, Jun. 16, 2004, available at http://www.ustreas.gov/offices/eotffc/ofac/actions/index.html. These changes may affect Mexico and Canada only indirectly, rather than directly as with Helms–Burton; many American citizens who travel to Cuba, with or without U.S. government authorization, do so via Mexican or Canadian carriers. Would NAFTA permit the U.S. government to make it illegal for a Mexican carrier to transport U.S. citizens to Cuba when the citizen does not have a valid license for such travel issued by the Treasury Department?

PROBLEM 9.5 PRIVATE COMMERCIAL DISPUTE SETTLEMENT: FUNGICIDE MADE IN CANADA AND THE U.S. AND SOLD IN MEXICO

SECTION I.   THE SETTING

GROWFAST CHEMICALS, INC. (GROWFAST) is a Delaware chartered corporation with principal administrative offices in Dallas. It has manufacturing facilities in Texas, and in British Columbia, Canada (GROWCAN). It also has a wholly owned subsidiary in Mexico (GROWMEX). GROWFAST manufactures many different pesticides and fungicides used by commercial growers of ornamental plants. One of the fungicides is Sollate™. For nearly two decades Sollate™ has been used extensively by commercial and home growers of many tropical plants. It has long been considered the only successful fungicide to control several serious fungi.

The Commercial Claims

GROWFAST has sold Sollate™ throughout Latin America. Until recently all the Sollate™ sold in Latin America was manufactured in Texas or British Columbia and shipped direct. Several years ago, unknown to GROWFAST, the Sollate™ which was sold to growers throughout Mexico from both the Texas and British Columbia plants contained some chemicals poisonous to plants. The result was that many Mexican commercial growers lost their entire stocks of ornamental plants. The Sollate™ which caused the damage was purchased using standard documentary transactions, and each included a provision that the goods were sold "as is, with all faults", and the contract would be governed by the law of Texas (whether made in the U.S. or Canada). The name GROWFAST appeared on the invoices. GROWFAST believes that the Sollate™ was both mixed improperly and misapplied by the growers, and therefore that the growers are responsible. At minimum, GROWFAST believes that *force majeure* should be applied to excuse GROWFAST from responsibility. Assume that the only claims that are brought are based on breach of contract grounds. While there may be product liability raising tort/delict issues, product liability will be the subject of the separate problem below. The claims considered under this part of the problem address such contractual issues as the "suitability" of the delivered Sollate™.

The Tort Claims

Wholly unrelated to the facts giving rise to the contract issues above, a serious accident occurred at the GROWMEX, S.A., plant in Veracruz. This plant only recently began to make Sollate™. While transferring Sollate™ concentrate, obtained from the U.S. and Canadian plants, into vats for dilution and packaging, supervised by both Mexican employees and two technicians "on loan" from GROWFAST in Texas, an unexplained explosion occurred. One of the U.S. technicians and 35 Mexican employees were killed. Serious injury was suffered by dozens of other employees. The smoke from the explosion drifted over Veracruz and adjacent towns, causing serious burns to several hundred more people, including two United States tourists.

The Following Civil Claims Have Been Filed.

A. Contract Action Initiated in the United States

Some of the Mexican commercial growers who purchased the Sollate™ which allegedly caused the loss of plants have sued GROWFAST for breach of contract in federal district court in Brazoria, Texas.

B. Contract Actions Initiated in Mexico

The remaining Mexican commercial growers who purchased the Sollate™ have sued GROWFAST in state court in Veracruz, and in federal court in Mexico City. The new GROWMEX plant is in the state of Veracruz, but the company has offices in Mexico City.

C. Tort Actions Initiated in the United States

1. The two U.S. citizens who were tourists, and the personal representative of the U.S. citizen who was a GROWFAST employee, killed in the plant by the explosion, have both filed suits against GROWFAST in state court in the south Texas city where GROWFAST has a plant.

2. Some of the nearly 100 Mexicans (employees and area residents) that were injured, and some of the representatives of the 35 that were killed, have filed suit against GROWFAST in the same state court in south Texas.

The lawsuits filed in the United States all ask for the application of United States law, seek extensive discovery, request jury trials, and demand punitive damages. They all have been filed by attorneys that have signed contingent fee contracts with their clients.

D. Tort Action Initiated in Mexico

The remainder of the nearly 100 Mexicans (employees and area residents) that were injured, and the remainder of the representatives of the 35 that were killed, being the parties who did not file suit in Texas, have filed suit against GROWFAST and GROWMEX, in Veracruz, Mexico. They have asked for compensatory damages, and for moral damages in an amount which would be equivalent to punitive damages in the United States.

SECTION II. FOCUS OF CONSIDERATION

NAFTA Article 2022 is the sole provision in the Agreement which refers to the resolution of *private commercial* disputes. There is no provision which relates to *tort* litigation arising from commercial transactions. Article 2022 urges the Parties to "the maximum extent possible," to use arbitration and other means of alternative dispute resolution to settle international commercial disputes between *private parties*. NAFTA has generated more trade, and more trade means more disputes. The NAFTA negotiators did not attempt to do any more than add the above suggestion, but they also foresaw the possibility of developing mechanisms to improve the resolution of private commercial disputes by establishing the Advisory Committee on Private Commercial Disputes to formulate recommendations "on general issues referred to it by the Commission respecting the availability, use and effectiveness of arbitration and other procedures for the resolution of such disputes in the free trade area." But litigation will not wait for future developments. The parties to our hypothetical must make decisions now. You have been educated in both the Mexican and U.S. legal systems, and have been asked to provide opinions on a number of issues.

Part A will address issues regarding obtaining a judgment in one of the Parties. Part B will consider enforcement of such a domestic court judgment, and Part C will explore the NAFTA recommendation to use arbitration as an alternative dispute resolution method.

SECTION III.   READINGS, QUESTIONS AND COMMENTS

PART A. ACTIONS IN THE DOMESTIC COURTS

This Part assumes the parties have decided to use the domestic courts of the NAFTA Parties, rather than seek resolution of the disputes by means of some form of alternative dispute resolution, such as arbitration.

BARRAGÁN, HIGHLIGHTS OF MEXICAN LAW CONCERNING CONTRACTUAL AND PROCEDURAL FORMALITIES

Doing Business in Mexico 1.06(1).*

THE DIFFERENCES BETWEEN CIVIL AND COMMERCIAL CONTRACTS

The Mexican legal system maintains a dual legislation, one which regulates contracts of a civil nature and another which regulates contracts of a commercial nature. Therefore, it is always necessary to determine when a contract is of a civil nature and when it is of a commercial nature, in order to determine the applicable legislation.

The Commercial Code provides a list of acts or contracts which have a commercial nature, although such list is not exhaustive. In addition, the Commercial Code, in order to determine the commercial nature of certain acts, looks into the intent of the parties and regards certain acts or contracts as of a commercial nature when they are entered into for the purpose of business. . . .

Among the acts and activities considered to be of a commercial nature which are listed in the Commercial Code, are the following: purchases, sales and leases of personal property made for business purposes; . . .

In addition, there are cases in which a contract may be of a commercial nature for one of the parties and of a civil nature for the other. Such is the case of a person who buys from an established merchant (a department store or the like) some merchandise for his personal use. The merchant, when carrying out the sale of such merchandise, is doing so as part of his usual activities for the purpose of business, while the private party, when buying such merchandise, is doing so with the intent of satisfying a personal need. Furthermore, there are contracts which, regardless of the nature of the parties to them and the intent with which any of such parties enters into these agreements, always are of a civil nature. Such is the case in lease contracts of real estate, due to the fact that neither Article 75 of the Commercial

Code, nor any other laws contain a provision establishing that a lease of real estate is an act of a commercial nature.... According to the foregoing, in order to find out if an act or contract is of a commercial nature, it is necessary to determine whether an act or contract is one or other according to the Commercial Code or other commercial laws, or if the purpose with which the parties entered into such a contract was for business purposes.

* * *

In connection with those contracts in which, for one of the parties, the transaction was of a civil nature, and for the other, a commercial nature, the Commercial Code provides that in the event of default, the nature of the defendant is the one that determines the applicable legislation, which includes the substantive and related law. ...

VARGAS, TORT LAW IN MEXICO
2 Mexican Law 209 (1998).*

Unlike the United States, the principles governing tort law in Mexico have remained schematic, archaic and uninteresting for legal practitioners. When an injury occurs, Mexicans rely on a non-confrontational arrangement, instead of the more litigious avenue so common in the U.S., Mexican culture dictates that the tortfeasor is to provide the necessary assistance to the victim, covering the resulting medical and hospital expenses, and all material deterioration suffered by the victim's property, as well as any lost wages and any incapacities as calculated in the Federal Labor Act. The Mexican legal system does not allow punitive damages or compensation for pain and suffering....

Under the Civil Law of Mexico, there are three different types of liability: (1) contractual liability; (2) "objective liability;" and (3) the so-called "extra-contractual liability."

First, the most common and best known form of liability is contractual liability. Contractual liability is based upon Articles 1792 and 1793 of the Federal Civil Code**, which provide that "[A]n agreement is the accord between two or more individuals to create, transfer, modify or extinguish obligations," and that contracts are "those agreements that create or transfer obligations and rights," respectively. ...

Second, the Mexican notion of "objective liability" closely resembles the notion of strict liability for a U.S. practitioner. Objective liability

** Authors' note: The Civil Code discussed by Professor Vargas in this article is the former civil code for the Federal District and Throughout the Nation in Federal Matters. It was much the same as the various state civil codes. But in 2000, this code was divided into two civil codes, first a Federal Civil Code, and second a civil code for the Federal District. The substance of Vargas' discussion remains valid but it is important to note that some provisions differ among state civil codes, or between a state code and the Federal Code. That is especially true of "moral damages." What is a federal matter is the subject continuing debate in Mexico.

results from the commission of an illegal act which was precipitated by the use of mechanisms or inherently dangerous equipment or apparatus, animals and tangible things, regardless of the existence of fault or negligence. The only requirement the victim needs to prove to receive the corresponding indemnity is the existence of damage (or injury) and the causal relationship. Under Mexican Civil Law it is not necessary to prove fault or negligence.

The Mexican legal notion of "created risk" is also associated with this type of liability. Created risk refers to those damages or injuries resulting from the handling, use or operation of certain machines, equipment, instruments or apparatus which are inherently dangerous. In this regard, Article 1913 of the Federal Civil Code provides:

> If a person employs mechanisms, instruments, equipment or substances which by themselves are dangerous, or because of the speed they develop, their explosive nature and inflammable characteristics, or by the intensity of the electric current, or similar causes, he is liable for the damage or injuries they cause even though he is using them licitly, *unless he can prove that the damage was caused by the fault or inexcusable negligence of the victim.*

Third, Articles 1910–1934 of the Federal Civil Code apply to "extra-contractual liability," statutorily defined as the liability that derives from illicit acts (*i.e., De las obligaciones que nacen de los actos lícitos*). This form of liability is not derived from a contractual relationship, which in Mexico is considered the usual or basic source of liability. Rather, it results from an illicit act committed by one individual against another, or as a consequence of a created risk *(Riesgo creado)*. Whereas contractual liability finds its source in a given contract and materializes when that contract is breached, or when a specific contractual obligation is not fulfilled, extra-contractual liability exists even in the absence of any contractual relationship or legal link between the parties. Accordingly, it may be said that extra-contractual civil liability stems from the will of the drafters of the Civil Code.

Since there is virtually no tort law in Mexico, it becomes necessary to provide the reader with a legal overview on how "tort law cases" are handled in that country. Under Mexican law, tortious acts are governed by two separate kinds of legislation: (1) the Civil Code, and (2) the Federal Labor Act.

The Civil Code is at the center of Mexico's civil practice and litigation. Under the larger category of obligations, this code governs all matters in the civil legal realm, ranging from the civil status of individuals, family law, assets, possession and property, to successions, wills, inheritances and, in particular, contracts. Tortious acts appear under the category of: "Obligations which arise from illegal acts," commonly referred to as "Extra-contractual liability." There are two different kinds of civil codes in Mexico.

The Federal Civil Code applies to the Federal District (Mexico City) in ordinary matters and to the entire nation in federal matters....

Articles 1910–1934 of the Federal Civil Code (and the corresponding articles in the respective state codes) govern the civil liability generated by tortious acts under Mexican law, including: (a) "Fault liability" *(Responsabilidad por culpa);* (b) "Objective or absolute liability" *(Responsabilidad objectiva o absoluta);* (c) the economic compensation resulting from damages and losses; and (d) vicarious liability.

The Republic of Mexico is composed of 31 States, each of which has its own Constitution and Civil code. . . . Each state code governs civil law questions which take place within its territory. In general, each of these codes is a replica of the Federal Civil Code, with few and insignificant changes. . . .

* * *

Following the ideas advanced by French and Spanish doctrinarians, Mexican specialists consider that the source of extra-contractual liability derives from illegal enrichment, illegal acts and a created risk.

"Fault liability" occurs when an individual or a legal entity commits an illegal act by fault that causes damage or inflicts injury to another individual. Articles 1910 and 1913 of the Federal Civil Code govern this kind of liability. In this case, the tortfeasor is liable because of his/her fault or negligence.

Articles 1910 and 1915 of the Federal Civil Code establish the two most fundamental principles that govern extra-contractual liability cases (*i.e.,* tortious acts) in Mexico.

> He who acting illegally or against good customs causes damage to another, is obliged to repair it, unless he proves that the damage occurred in consequence of the fault or inexplicable negligence of the victim. [Art. 1910]

Pursuant to this article, "fault or inexplicable negligence of the victim" provides a complete bar to the plaintiff's recovery. From the viewpoint of a U.S. legal practitioner, this bar results from the plaintiff's comparative contributory negligence.

> The repair of the damage shall consist, at the election of the injured party, in the restoration of the status previously existing, when this is possible, or in the payment of damages and losses.

> When the damage is caused to persons and produces death, total permanent, partial permanent, total temporary or partial temporary incapacity, the amount of the indemnity shall be determined by the Federal Labor Act *(Ley Federal del Trabajo).* To calculate the appropriate indemnity one shall take as the base four times the minimum daily salary which is the highest in force in the region and shall be multiplied by the number of days indicated in the Federal Labor Law for each of the incapacities mentioned. In case of death, the indemnity shall correspond to the heirs of the victim.

The indemnity credits, when the victim is a salaried person, are not transferable and shall be covered preferably in one exhibit, save agreement between the parties. . . . [Art. 1915]

Mexican jurists agree that reparation of the damage is directed at placing the victim in the situation that existed before the occurrence of the tortious act. Only when this is not possible, or when the act causes a corporal or moral injury, does the resulting obligation convert into the payment of an indemnity to compensate for the material or moral damage inflicted to the victim. This indemnity should cover both damages and losses, as defined by the Federal Civil Code in Articles 2108 and 2109. Thus, the notion of civil liability includes not only the duty to repair or restitute for the damage caused but also the obligation to pay an indemnity, derived as a consequence of an illegal act or a created risk, which is typical of extra-contractual liability.

To calculate the damages and losses, the Federal Civil Code expressly refers this question to the pertinent legal principles contained in Mexico's Federal Labor Act.

In Mexico, the notion of civil liability is instantly associated with a contractual relationship. This is logical when one considers that, under Mexican civil law, a contract is the only legal avenue for creating, transferring, modifying or extinguishing obligations. In a sense, this provision establishes the most fundamental principle that governs civil liability in Mexico.

Accordingly, any civil liability derived from a different legal source, such as a tortious act, where no contract is in place, is only addressed in a cursory manner by the Federal Civil Code. For example, whereas the Code devotes close to 1,200 sections to obligations and contracts, and the corresponding civil liabilities associated with them, only 25 sections address civil liabilities from illegal acts. This explains the need confronted by the drafters of the Federal Civil Code to find more detailed legal principles elsewhere within the Mexican legal system to supplement the sparse provisions in this code. That supplementary legislation, as mandated by Article 1915 of the Federal Civil Code, is the Federal Labor Act.

. . . Given the few extra-contractual liability cases decided by civil courts in Mexico, it is not entirely clear to what degree civil judges apply the provisions of the Federal Labor Act. Unquestionably, civil judges apply the basic principles enumerated by the Federal Labor Act. However, the same degree of certainty does not exist with respect to the factual or technical details that may be present in a civil case, allowing judges to exercise some discretion. Occasionally, the application of Federal Labor Act provisions to extra-contractual liability cases poses serious challenges and difficulties to civil courts. This is especially evident when one considers that these two sets of rules were formulated to address two different legal areas.

* * *

It may be surprising for legal practitioners in the U.S. or Canada to learn that Mexico does not have any legal standards applicable to negligence or fault. Moreover, the Mexican legal system has not produced a statutory definition of "negligence" or "fault," nor any explicit legislative distinctions between "negligence" and "inexcusable negligence." ...

Since very few cases resulting from tortious actions are decided by trial courts (*Tribunales de Primera Instancia*) in Mexico, not to mention those rare cases that reach the appellate court level, it is understandable that, rather than enacting domestic legislation on this matter, Mexico has opted for the more practical avenue of allowing judges to use their ample discretion in deciding these rather unusual cases.

As enunciated by Article 1915, the fundamental principle of the Federal Civil Code provides that the repair of damages consist, at the election of the injured party, of the restoration of their prior status, when possible, or the payment of damages and losses.

... In general, "damages" may be equated to "out-of-pocket expenses." These expenses include:

1) Medical and surgical assistance;

2) Rehabilitation;

3) Hospitalization, when the case so requires;

4) Medication and medical materials; and

5) Any prosthetic and orthopedic devices.

* * *

It is evident that the Mexican legal system, contrary to ours, does not recognize punitive damages, or compensation for pain and suffering and emotional distress. Although the Federal Civil Code, in Article 1916, refers to "moral damages," this legal notion applies only to the injury caused to a person's "feelings, affections, beliefs, honor, decorum, reputation, privacy, image and physical appearance," or how that person "is perceived in the opinion of others." For this reason, moral damages in Mexico are construed now as "non-physical damages" or "defamatory injuries."

Moral damages is a legal notion that has been recently added to Mexico's Civil Law. It tends to be associated with libel and defamation, as well as with injuries resulting from the use of "mechanisms, instruments, equipment and substances," as enunciated by Article 1913 of the Federal Civil Code in cases involving the so-called "objective liability." So far, very few legal actions have been filed in Mexico based on this novel concept.

VARGAS, CONFLICT OF LAWS
2 Mexican Law 241 (1998).*

Until very recently, decisions involving conflict of law questions between the United States and Mexico were virtually nonexistent. This was due to several factors: (1) the "absolute territorialist" policy adopted by Mexico in its Civil Code for District and Federal Territories of 1932; (2) the fact that Mexico, for almost a century, maintained itself in an "isolationist cocoon" which kept it away from the codificatory developments taking place between 1889 and 1971, in private international law, particularly at the Inter–American level; and (3) the lack of interest of the Mexican government to systematize and simplify its conflict of law rules to put it in symmetry with the developments accomplished at the international level.

* * *

Not until December, 1988 did Mexico change its territorialist approach, adopting a new domestic legislative policy in symmetry with internationally recognized trends in private international law. This change was accomplished by means of three presidential decrees that amended, first, the Civil Code of the Federal District, second, the Code of Civil Procedure for the Federal District and lastly, the Federal Code of Civil Procedure. These amendments created Mexico's most profound reform in private international law during this century. The 1988 amendments covered five major legal areas, namely: (1) application and proof of foreign law in Mexico; (2) letters rogatory; (3) international cooperation on evidentiary questions, and (4) enforcement of judgments.

* * *

A New Limited Territorialism

Article 12 of Mexico's Civil Code for the Federal District introduces for the first time in the contemporary legal history of Mexico a rather "limited" type of territorialism. The amended text of this article reads:

> The Mexican laws apply to all the persons located in the Republic, as well as to the acts and factual situations which have taken place within its territory or jurisdiction, and to those who have submitted to said laws, save when those laws provide for the application of a foreign law and save, also, what is provided by the treaties and conventions to which Mexico has become a party.

* * *

As of today, only a very limited number of "Mexican laws" allow for the application of foreign law. All of these domestic statutes—particularly a few articles in the Civil Code—, are the direct result of the 1988 reform. . . .

* * *

Article 14 of Mexico's Civil Code provides that Mexican judges apply foreign law "as the corresponding foreign judge would do it", allowing judges to take judicial notice of foreign law. . . .

Article 14, paragraph V, deserves a special commentary because of its innovative nature: it provides that when different aspects of the same juridical relationship are governed by different foreign laws, the Mexican judge should apply all of them harmoniously. However, in difficult cases, the judge is allowed to turn to the notion of equity, a rather unprecedented step for judges that belong to the civil legal tradition. Mexican scholars have validly said that this provision constitutes the principal novelty of the 1988 reform.

* * *

Finally, the recent amendments to the Federal Civil Code established two universally recognized exceptions to the application of foreign law: (1) when fundamental principles of Mexican law have been evaded artificiously (*i.e., Fraude au loi*); and (2) when foreign law interferes with Mexico's "public interest" (*i.e.,* "Orden público Mexicano" or *Ordre public).*

WEINTRAUB, CHOICE OF LAW FOR PRODUCTS LIABILITY: DEMAGNETIZING THE UNITED STATES FORUM
52 Arkansas L. Rev. 157 (1999).*

* * *

The United States is a magnet forum for product liability litigation. When a foreign plaintiff injured abroad sues a United States manufacturer, a common defense tactic is a motion for *forum non conveniens* dismissal. This motion asserts that another forum, typically at the plaintiff's home, is a more appropriate site for the litigation in the light of the private and public factors that should determine a court's ruling on the motion.[6] Sometimes this tactic works[7] and sometimes it does not.[8]

Moreover, some states have *forum non conveniens* doctrines that permit dismissal in far fewer cases than does the federal doctrine. Federal courts exercising diversity or alienage jurisdiction have applied

---

* Copyright © Russell J. Weintraub. Reprinted with permission. (Russell J. Weintraub is a professor of law at the University of Texas Law School.)

6. Gulf Oil Corp. v. Gilbert, 330 U.S. 501 (1947), contains the classic list of these private and public factors. Private interests of the defendant focus on the practical difficulties of defense in a forum far removed from the site of injury, such as lack of access to evidence and witnesses. *Id.* at 508. Public factors guide the inquiry as to whether the forum has a sufficient interest in expending the governmental resources necessary to provide a forum for a foreign plaintiff, particularly if the necessity of determining and applying foreign law increases that cost. *Id.* at 508–09.

7. *See* Piper Aircraft Co. v. Reyno, 454 U.S. 235 (1981) (discussed *infra* note 9).

8. *See* Lony v. E.I. Du Pont de Nemours & Co., 935 F.2d 604, 613 (3d Cir.1991) (refusing dismissal in suit brought by German company that resold defendant's product); Picketts v. International Playtex, Inc., 576 A.2d 518, 525 (Conn.1990) (reversing dismissal of action for wrongful death of Canadian who used product in Canada).

the federal rather than state version of the *forum non conveniens* doctrine. Plaintiffs attempt to defeat dismissal by suing in a state court in a jurisdiction whose *forum non conveniens* doctrine is less robust than the federal version. These plaintiffs then prevent removal to federal court by joining a defendant domiciled in that state or of the same citizenship as a plaintiff. Defendants respond to these tactics by either removing to federal court and contending that the defendants whose presence would bar diversity jurisdiction should be dismissed as improperly joined, or by combing Title 28 of the United States Code to find some basis other than diversity for removal to federal court.

Therefore, *forum non conveniens* motions are not reliable bases for protecting United States manufacturers from foreign plaintiffs. Changing the choice-of-law doctrines that encourage suits in United States courts is more direct and more effective. It is a fair question whether any changes are desirable. If the quality of justice administered in United States courts is so high that the afflicted and aggrieved of the world flock here, perhaps that should be a point of pride rather than a reason for reexamining what we are doing. . . .

* * *

It would greatly diminish the attractiveness of the United States as a forum in product liability cases if all United States courts applied the law of the victim's home country when that law is less favorable to recovery than American law. In the light of current decisions, it is an uphill battle to convince a court to adopt this choice-of-law position. Another possibility is to argue that although United States law determines liability, damages should be quantified under the standards of the victim's home country. It is the injured person's habitual residence, its standard of living, its social services, that should determine whether, for example, one thousand dollars or one million dollars is appropriate compensation for pain and suffering. Thus, United States law would determine liability but foreign law would determine the proper level of damages. The label for this process of applying one law to some issues in the case and another law to other issues is *dépeçage*. This splitting up of the applicable law was possible even under the now largely displaced territorial choice-of-law rules. The new conflicts analysis increases the likelihood of *dépeçage* because that analysis gives separate consideration to each issue. Applying *dépeçage* will be especially difficult in view of the fact that courts have traditionally considered quantification of damages "procedural," so that the forum's standards apply even though another state's law governs liability.

LOPERENA AND GORDON, RESOLUTION OF COMMERCIAL DISPUTES: MEXICO AND THE UNITED STATES

[The following material is adapted from materials prepared by the authors for symposiums in Chicago, New York, Los Angeles and Santa Fe. The hypothetical used was similar to that in this Problem, but dealt with insulation sold by "National" to "Jalapa" from New York and possibly Ontario, not fungicides.]

* * *

CHOICE OF LAW

A. CHOICES. Although the procedural law to be applied during the trial will be the law of the forum, the court must determine in an international transaction whether the law of the plaintiff or the defendant (or some other law) will apply. As first noted above, Jalapa will not necessarily wish to argue for the application of Mexican law, if U.S. law clearly favors Jalapa's position. Having researched the substantive law, each party will argue for the application of the most favorable law to its position. . . .

As a matter of fact, Mexican courts usually do not apply foreign law. There are some Mexican lawyers who will argue under Mexican law only, even if they consider foreign law to be applicable in the case, because they consider it useless to argue on the basis of foreign law.

Mexico has substantive contract laws which may apply. They are rules contained in the Mexican Commercial Code or possibly in the Mexican Civil Code. The U.S. rules will be state law, probably rules based on the Uniform Commercial Code. But, as we will see, there may be a false conflict. Both the United States and Mexico are parties to the United Nations Convention on Contracts for the International Sale of Goods (CISG), which offers substantive contract rules which may apply in our dispute. For the moment we will assume that application of the CISG is uncertain, and we must go through the process of determining whether Mexican or United States law applies.

The choice of law conflicts rules which the forum applies will almost certainly be the forum's own conflicts rules. That means a Mexican court will apply Mexican conflicts rules to determine what substantive contract law applies, while a U.S. court will apply U.S. conflicts rules to determine what substantive contract law applies. Where are we? Consider the possibilities.

1. The New York court rules that a contract provision appearing to apply New York law was not part of the contract, but then rules that New York law nevertheless applies under New York conflicts principles.

2. The New York court rules the same regarding the provision that New York law applies, but then rules that Mexican law applies under New York conflicts principles.

3. The New York court rules that the provision applying New York law applies and therefore applies New York law.

4. The Mexican court rules that the provision applying New York law does not apply because it was not part of the contract, but then rules that New York law nevertheless applies under Mexican conflicts principles.

5. The Mexican court rules the same regarding the provision that New York law applies, but then rules that Mexican law applies under Mexican conflicts principles.

6. The Mexican court rules that the provision applying New York law applies and therefore applies New York law.

There may also be a ruling on the defendant's request to move the matter to a more appropriate forum.

1. The New York court rules that Mexican law applies and that a Mexican court would be a better forum to apply that law.

2. The New York court rules that Mexican law applies and proceeds to apply Mexican law.

3. The New York court rules that New York law applies and proceeds to apply that law.

4. The Mexican court rules that New York law applies and that a New York court would be a better forum to apply that law.

5. The Mexican court rules that New York law applies and proceeds to apply that law.

Application of a foreign law creates some very special problems. The foreign law may be in a different language. This means that there must either be acceptable translations of the applicable laws, or the court must accept an expert witness to state the foreign law. Relatively little Mexican law has been translated into English, and relatively little United States law has been translated into Spanish. What is available is often descriptive of the law, rather than a direct and literal translation. Finally, foreign law may constitute facts which must be proved, while domestic law is accepted by the court.

The parties no longer bear the burden of proof of foreign laws. The statutes provide that once the court finds foreign law applicable, it must decide the case applying that law. This may be more theory than practice.

B. CHOICE OF LAW IN THE UNITED STATES. If the issue is before a U.S. court, the court will probably turn to the New York Uniform Commercial Code. Section 1–105(1) allows the parties to choose what law applies.

The New York UCC further states that in the absence of a choice New York law should be applied to "transactions bearing an appropriate relation to this state." What constitutes "an appropriate relation" is not defined, and the court will have to look at the Comments to the UCC, or New York case law, or perhaps the case law of other states which have adopted the same language. The court may consider some of the many scholarly writings on the UCC. If the court is nevertheless uncertain about the UCC test, it might decide to look at the Restatement of the Conflict of Laws. The concept of the Restatement may be difficult to explain to our Mexican colleagues. Indeed, there is much debate in the United States over its accuracy in stating what U.S. law is as opposed to what its drafters would like it to be. Section 6 of the Restatement allows the parties to choose what law applies, similar to the UCC. If the parties have not so chosen, than § 6 goes on to list seven "factors" relevant to the choice of law, such as "the needs of the interstate and international systems." Section 188 states that the applicable law is that which bears the "most significant relationship to the transaction and the parties," under the seven § 6 stated factors, and further lists five "contacts" to be considered, such as the "place of contracting." While these "factors" and "contacts" may appear to offer guidance, they may also create more confusion. The "place of contracting" has been debated for years. How much weight ought to be given to any of the factors or contacts?

Applying either the UCC or Restatement rules does not lead to any clear result. It is the authors' view that under either the UCC or Restatement standard the law of Mexico would be preferred, but others may strongly disagree.

C. CHOICE OF LAW IN MEXICO. A Mexican court will not turn to the UCC or Restatement, but to Mexican conflicts rules. The Mexican court will turn to the Mexican Civil Code. The Civil Code will be the source of conflicts rules, but if Mexican law is determined to apply, the court will look to the Code of Commerce for the substantive law rules.

The provisions of the Civil Code may appear rather abstract and formal to a United States attorney. It is indeed difficult for a common law trained lawyer to fully understand the nature of a civil code in a civil law tradition legal system.

* * *

D. CHOICE OF LAW—A FALSE CONFLICT. The substantive rules of contract in Mexico, found principally in the Civil Code and the Code of Commerce, are quite different from the substantive rules of contract in the United States, found in the UCC of the applicable state law, and in the case law. But if the substantive rules of Mexico and the United States were the same, there might be little reason to go through the process of determining what law applies. There would be what is called a "false conflict." We are perhaps fortunate. Both Mexico and the United States are parties to the United Nations Convention on Contracts for the International Sale of Goods. The parties to an international commercial contract will be governed by the CISG, unless they have elected not to have the Convention apply. There is no suggestion that our parties have elected not to have the CISG apply, unless the statement that New York law is to apply is part of the contract and means that the New York UCC is to apply, not the CISG which is U.S. law. I doubt that a Mexican court would reach that conclusion, and suspect the same would be true in a New York court. I believe that either court would conclude that the CISG is applicable.

If the above belief that the CISG would apply means that it does not matter whether the issue is in a Mexican or New York court, we need to look further. Articles 14 through 19 relate to the issue of the formation of a contract. If a Mexican court is searching for the meaning of offer and acceptance under Article 19, where will it turn? To any sources that differ from sources were the same issue before a New York court? A Mexican court may proceed as it traditionally does in a contract matter under the Civil Code or Code of Commerce, that is it may attempt to rely upon an interpretation of the statute with little assistance other than the writings of Mexican scholars. A U.S. court may look for decisions in any courts in the United States which have interpreted the article. A more adventuresome court in either nation might seek assistance in the way of judicial decisions or writings in **any** nation which is a party to the Convention. Such assistance will be dependent upon the ability to locate such decisions, interpret them if necessary, and convince the court of their application, or non-application. Thus, which nations' court is to apply the CISG is not unimportant, it indeed may be critical to a favorable outcome for one's client.

Questions and Comments

Issues Raised by the Various Actions

A.   In the Commercial and Tort Actions in the United States

1.   What is your thinking from a *strategy* perspective on attempting to remove these suits to Mexico under the theory of *forum non conveniens*? If removal is granted, how will you control the case in Mexico, or do you just forget about it? If the U.S. court conditions removal on submission to Mexican personal jurisdiction, do you agree? What if the court conditions the removal on your agreeing to pay any judgment rendered in Mexico? That might be unwise if the Mexican court applied U.S. law and granted very large damages, or applied Mexican law but interpreted it to allow such damages.

2.   Weintraub suggests that there are obstacles to remove the matter to Mexico—the *Gilbert* case he cites notes *private* and *public* interests to be considered, and the court will have to be assured that the foreign forum is *adequate* and *available*. What are the interests involved in our case? Is Mexico an adequate forum for litigation if there is such a concern about avoiding Mexican courts that arbitration is often sought out by the disputing parties?

3.   Would the court apply the same legal reasoning for such a removal request as it would to a request to remove a matter from one state to

another within the United States? Certainly some of the factors which ought to have been identified in #2 above do not exist with other states, such as language obstacles, or different discovery rules. Would the courts be more likely to grant removal where the plaintiffs are Mexican than where they are U.S. citizens? When the matter is tort versus contract?

4. Assume removal on *forum non conveniens* grounds is granted. But Mexico has adopted a law that states that when a Mexican plaintiff, with a choice of initiating a suit in Mexico or abroad, initiates the suit abroad, if there is a dismissal on *forum non conveniens* grounds that action may not thereafter be commenced in Mexico. The plaintiffs apply to reinstate the case in Texas because there is no *available* and adequate forum in Mexico. What result? There are such laws in Ecuador and Guatemala.

5. Assuming removal is not requested or if requested is not granted by the court, should GROWFAST ask the court to apply Mexican law? What are the considerations the court is likely to face and wish to discuss before it rules on this choice of law issue? GROWFAST would only want Mexican law to apply if it is more favorable to GROWFAST than U.S. law. How might it be more favorable?

6. In proving Mexican law in the United States court, who would you seek as experts? Who might the court prefer to have appear as experts? The parties will obtain their own experts in the United States. In Mexico, the court will appoint the experts, which is usual in civil law nations. Which provides a fairer outcome?

7. If the U.S. court applies Mexican law, could it nevertheless grant punitive damages? Professor Weintraub notes the division between applying domestic or foreign law for liability, and domestic or foreign law for damages? Which rule makes more sense? What is behind your reasoning-what role are you trying to have damages play?

8. In the commercial actions, if the court rules that U.S. law applies, what is the source of that law? The UCC? The CISG?

9. In the same suits, if the court rules that Mexican law applies, what is the source of that law? A Mexican civil code? The Mexican federal commercial code? The CISG—(all three Parties to NAFTA are signatories)?

10. In the tort actions, if the court rules that U.S. law applies, what is the source of that law? Your courses in tort law made this rather clear. There is a vast body of tort case law, and some product liability statutes.

11. In the same tort actions, if the court rules that Mexican law applies, what is the source of that law? Professor Vargas makes it clear that there is no similar body of tort case law in Mexico. Does than mean any Mexican case law will be useless?

B. In the Commercial and Tort Actions in Mexico

1. Would you recommend to GROWFAST that it ignore the suits, leaving the defense and liability to GROWMEX, knowing that GROWMEX has few assets and believing GROWFAST would not be responsible for a judgment against GROWMEX? Mexico might not even find jurisdiction over GROWFAST; there is no developed veil piercing theory in Mexico.

2. Should you know anything about the federal and state court structure of Mexico? What Mexican courts might have jurisdiction? Does it matter? We know from the readings that the commercial case will be subject to federal law, but the tort case will be subject to one of the civil codes, either a state civil code or the civil code for the federal district. Most state civil codes follow the civil code for the federal district. But the latter allows moral damages with no specific limitation, while most (perhaps all?) state civil codes limit moral damages.

3. What law would a Mexican court apply? Our readings suggest that the answer is almost certain to be Mexican law, unless one finds a specific law or international agreement which allows application of foreign law.

4. Does Mexican commercial and tort law roughly parallel that in the United States? Commercial law may be almost the same, if the CISG applies. But the tort law is different. The basic premise of tort law is much the same, however, persons are responsible for their actions, and sometimes for strict liability. What differs most are damages, both what damages are available and the level of damages that the law permits.

5. Does the fact that there were "workers" involved affect the tort litigation? Workers raises the possible application of the federal labor law, which has some special damage provisions.

6. Would Mexico grant punitive damages? It is tempting to say that punitive damages are not available under civil law in *any* circumstances. It may be inevitable that change will come, but we do not want our case to be the first. For our case, the question will be "are moral damages under Mexican law the same as punitive damages?" As Professor Vargas has indicated, the answer is no.

7. How would a Mexican court determine moral damages? Are they available in both the commercial and tort cases? If the U.S. court is applying Mexican law and the issue of damages arises, would you try to insist that the plaintiffs produce examples of Mexican courts actually granting moral damages of the amount asked for?

PART B. ENFORCEMENT OF A DOMESTIC JUDGMENT RENDERED IN ONE NAFTA PARTY IN THE COURTS OF ANOTHER NAFTA PARTY

Obtaining a judgment may be of little real value if that judgment proves to be unenforceable. The U.S. Constitutional assurance of full faith and credit may comfort the plaintiffs if they have obtained a judgment in one state and wish it enforced in another. But if they have obtained a judgment in one NAFTA Party's courts and want it enforced in another Party's courts, no full, faith and credit assurance is present. In this Part we briefly explore judgment enforcement, and assume judgments have been rendered against GROWFAST in the United States (and perhaps GROWCAN in Canada), and against GROWFAST and GROWMEX (and perhaps GROWCAN) in Mexico.

Comment on Judgment Enforcement in the U.S. and Mexico

If the plaintiffs have a Mexican judgment which they cannot enforce in Mexico because the defendants have no assets in Mexico and refuse to pay the judgment, the plaintiffs will likely attempt to enforce it in the United States. Both nations acknowledge the appropriateness of enforcing another nation's judgments, but both nations address the issue quite differently.

ENFORCEMENT IN THE UNITED STATES. The plaintiffs' lawyers will quickly discover that enforcement of foreign judgments in the United States is complex. Whether the enforcement action is brought in a state or federal court, state law will apply. The various states have taken different approaches. Many base their law on the 1895 U.S. Supreme Court *Hilton v. Guyot* decision. 159 U.S. 113, 16 S.Ct. 139, 40 L.Ed. 95 (1895). In that case, a French judgment was not enforced because France would not enforce United States judgments. This is the use of "mutuality and reciprocity." But the Court also stated that it would consider whether (1) the defendant had a full and fair opportunity, (2) before a court of competent jurisdiction, (3) the trial was conducted with regular proceedings, (4) there was due citation or voluntary appearance of the defendant, (5) under an impartial system of justice, and (6) there was no prejudice or fraud. U.S. courts have consistently referred to the *Hilton* decision, but have not consistently applied its reasoning. Many courts have moved away from the application of reciprocity to a view on one or more of the six noted criteria in *Hilton*.

Currently about 28 states plus the District of Columbia have adopted the Uniform Foreign Money Judgments Recognition Act. This Act rejects the use of reciprocity but adopts many of the *Hilton* factors. The courts have not consistently applied the UFMJRA, leaving the law in the United States unpredictable and certainly confusing to the plaintiffs' lawyers.

The United States did participate in drafting the Inter–American Convention on the Jurisdiction in the International Sphere for the Extraterritorial Validity of Foreign Judgments, but has neither signed nor ratified it.

ENFORCEMENT IN MEXICO. Enforcement in Mexico may depend upon whether federal or state rules apply. There has long been some thought that since foreign judgments affect international relations, the matter is federal. But this is not fully accepted. Mexico appears to continue to apply reciprocity first, but because some United States decisions have enforced Mexican judgments, the reciprocity requirement appears to have been met. The Mexican court is likely to turn to the several conditions included in the applicable code for granting enforcement (*exequatur*). There were significant amendments in 1988 to the rules in the Code of Civil Procedure of the Federal District, as well as to the rules in the Federal Code of Civil Procedure. Some of the conditions for granting enforcement bear resemblance to those noted above in the United States *Hilton* decision, and in the UFMJRA, such as service of process.

Mexico is a party to the above mentioned Inter–American Convention on Jurisdiction in the International Sphere for the Extraterritorial Validity of Foreign Judgments. Absent United States participation, the Convention may not be applicable for the enforcement in Mexico of United States judgments. Mexico is also a party to the Inter–American Convention for the Extraterritorial Validity of Foreign Judgments and Arbitral Awards. The United States is not a party. If there is no applicable treaty and the losing party proves a lack of reciprocity, enforcement is denied.

VARGAS, ENFORCEMENT OF JUDGEMENTS AND ARBITRAL AWARDS

2 Mexican Law 275 (1998).*

* * *

The legal regime established by the Federal Code of Civil Procedure for the enforcement of judgments.... appear[s] to have been inspired by (a) the Inter–American Convention on the Extraterritorial Validity of Foreign Judgments and Arbitral Awards, and (b) by the few and concise provisions contained in the Code of Civil Procedure for the Federal District prior to the 1988 amendment....

Article 569 provides:

Judgments, private arbitral awards and other foreign jurisdictional resolutions shall have validity and be recognized in the Republic [of Mexico] in everything which is not contrary to the internal public order in the terms established by this code and other applicable laws, save what is provided by the treaties and conventions to which Mexico is a party.

* * *

... Article 571 adds the conditions that must be complied with to obtain "executive force" when foreign judgments are to be enforced in Mexico co-actively, in the proceedings known as *"Exequatur"* or *"Homologación."*

... Even when each of these conditions are fully complied with, this does not automatically guarantee the enforcement of the foreign judgement. A Mexican judge is empowered to deny the requested enforcement when it is proven, at his/her discretion, that similar foreign judgments are not enforced in the country of origin....

... Although the notion of reciprocity continues to attract some criticisms, Vázquez Pando points out that this notion was attenuated by three factors: (1) it is not necessary to prove the existence of reciprocity before a Mexican judge to obtain the enforcement, but to prove the lack of it to enjoin such enforcement; (2) the absence of reciprocity is only relevant when applied to similar cases; and (3) the Mexican judge is not obligated, but rather "empowered" (*i.e., facultado*), to deny the enforcement....

It must be stressed that, in accordance with Article 575, neither the trial court (*i.e., Tribunal de primera instancia*), nor the court of appeals may examine or decide over the justice or injustice of the [foreign] judgment, its rationale or the factual or legal grounds, but must limit their role to the examination of the authenticity of said judgement and determining whether it should be enforced in conformity with the applicable Mexican domestic legislation.

SOUTHWEST LIVESTOCK AND TRUCKING COMPANY, INC. v. RAMON

United States Court of Appeals, Fifth Circuit, 1999.
169 F.3d 317.

EMILIO M. GARZA, Circuit Judge:

Defendant–Appellant, Reginaldo Ramon, appeals the district court's grant of summary judgment in favor of Plaintiffs–Appellees, Southwest Livestock & Trucking Co., Inc., Darrel Hargrove and Mary Jane Hargrove. Ramon contends that the district court erred by not recognizing a Mexican judgment, that if recognized would preclude summary judgment against him. We vacate the district court's summary judgment and remand.

I

Darrel and Mary Jane Hargrove (the "Hargroves") are citizens of the United States and officers of Southwest Livestock & Trucking Co., Inc. ("Southwest Livestock"), a Texas corporation involved in the buying and selling of livestock. In 1990, Southwest Livestock entered into a loan arrangement with Reginaldo Ramon ("Ramon"), a citizen of the Republic of Mexico. Southwest Livestock borrowed $400,000 from Ramon. To accomplish the loan, Southwest Livestock executed a "pagare"—a Mexican promissory note—payable to Ramon with interest within thirty days. Each month, Southwest Livestock executed a new pagare to cover the outstanding principal and paid the accrued interest. Over a period of four years, Southwest Livestock made payments towards the principal, but also borrowed additional money from Ramon. In October of 1994, Southwest Livestock defaulted on the loan. With the exception of the last pagare executed by Southwest Livestock, none of the pagares contained a stated interest rate. Ramon, however, charged Southwest Livestock interest at a rate of approximately fifty-two percent. The last pagare stated an interest rate of forty-eight percent, and under its terms, interest continues to accrue until Southwest Livestock pays the outstanding balance in full.

After Southwest Livestock defaulted, Ramon filed a lawsuit in Mexico.... The Mexican court ... ordered Southwest Livestock to satisfy its debt and to pay interest at forty-eight percent....

After Ramon filed suit in Mexico, but prior to the entry of the Mexican judgment, Southwest Livestock brought suit in United States District Court, alleging that the loan arrangement violated Texas usury laws. Southwest Livestock then filed a motion for partial summary judgment, claiming that the undisputed facts established that Ramon charged, received and collected usurious interest in violation of Texas law. Ramon also filed a motion for summary judgment. By then the Mexican court had entered its judgment, and Ramon sought recognition of that judgment. He claimed that, under principles of collateral estoppel and res judicata, the Mexican judgment barred Southwest Livestock's suit. The district court judge referred both motions to a magistrate judge.

The magistrate judge recommended that the district court grant Southwest Livestock's motion for summary judgment as to liability under Texas usury law, and recommended that it hold a trial to determine damages. In reaching her decision, the magistrate judge first addressed whether the Texas Uniform Foreign Country Money–Judgment Recognition Act (the "Texas Recognition Act") required the district court to recognize the Mexican judgment. . . . The magistrate judge concluded that, contrary to Southwest Livestock's position, the Mexican court properly acquired personal jurisdiction over Southwest Livestock, and therefore, lack of jurisdiction could not constitute a basis for nonrecognition. Nonetheless, according to the magistrate judge, "the district court would be well within its discretion in not recognizing the Mexican judgment on the grounds that it violates the public policy of the state of Texas." Thus, the magistrate judge decided that the Mexican judgment did not bar Southwest Livestock's suit. The magistrate judge then addressed whether the district court should apply Texas or Mexican law to its resolution of Southwest Livestock's usury claim. The magistrate judge concluded that, under Texas choice of law rules, the district court should apply Texas law. Under Texas law, Ramon undisputably charged usurious interest.

The district court adopted the magistrate judge's recommendation, granting Southwest Livestock's motion for summary judgment as to liability under Texas usury law, and denying Ramon's motion for summary judgment. The district court agreed that the Mexican judgment violated Texas public policy, and that Texas law applied. The district court then heard evidence on the question of damages and granted $5,766,356.93 to Southwest Livestock. . . . Ramon appealed.

Ramon asks us to reverse the district court's grant of summary judgment in favor of Southwest Livestock. He contends that the district court erred by failing to recognize the Mexican judgment. He also argues that the district court erred by applying Texas law. According to Ramon, the district court should have applied Mexican law because the pagares executed by Southwest Livestock designated Mexico as the place of payment, and Mexico has the most significant relationship to the loan transaction. Ramon also objects to the district court's continuing charge for usury. . . .

Southwest Livestock asks us to affirm the district court. . . . It contends that the district court properly withheld recognition of the Mexican judgment and properly applied Texas law . . .

II

We must determine first whether the district court properly refused to recognize the Mexican judgment. . . .

Under the Texas Recognition Act, a court must recognize a foreign country judgment assessing money damages unless the judgment debtor establishes one of ten specific grounds for nonrecognition.... Southwest Livestock contends that it established a ground for nonrecognition. It notes that the Texas Constitution places a six percent interest rate limit on contracts that do not contain a stated interest rate.... It also points to a Texas statute that states that usury is against Texas public policy.... Thus, according to Southwest Livestock, the Mexican judgment violates Texas public policy, and the district court properly withheld recognition of the judgment....

... In reviewing the district court's decision, we note that the level of contravention of Texas law has "to be high before recognition [can] be denied on public policy grounds." Hunt v. BP Exploration Co. (Libya) Ltd., 492 F.Supp. 885, 900 (N.D.Tex.1980). The narrowness of the public policy exception reflects a compromise between two axioms—res judicata and fairness to litigants—that underlie our law of recognition of foreign country judgments....

To decide whether the district court erred in refusing to recognize the Mexican judgment on public policy grounds, we consider the plain language of the Texas Recognition Act.... Section 36.005(b)(3) of the Texas Recognition Act permits the district court not to recognize a foreign country judgment if "the cause of action on which the judgment is based is repugnant to the public policy" of Texas.... This subsection of the Texas Recognition Act does not refer to the judgment itself, but specifically to the "cause of action on which the judgment is based." Thus, the fact that a judgment offends Texas public policy does not, in and of itself, permit the district court to refuse recognition of that judgment....

In this case, the Mexican judgment was based on an action for collection of a promissory note. This cause of action is not repugnant to Texas public policy.... Under the Texas Recognition Act, it is irrelevant that the Mexican judgment itself contravened Texas's public policy against usury. Thus, the plain language of the Texas Recognition Act suggests that the district court erred in refusing to recognize the Mexican judgment.

Southwest Livestock, however, argues that we should not interpret the Texas Recognition Act according to its plain language. Southwest Livestock contends that Texas courts will not enforce rights existing under laws of other jurisdictions when to do so would violate Texas public policy.... Southwest Livestock argues ... that the law governing usury constitutes a fundamental policy in Texas, and that to recognize the Mexican judgment would transgress that policy.

To be sure, it is the underlying policy of each state's usury laws to protect necessitous borrowers within its borders. Yet, as we have noted, we have found no Texas cases that have invalidated a party choice of law on grounds that the application of a foreign usury statute would violate public policy.

* * *

We are especially reluctant to conclude that recognizing the Mexican judgment offends Texas public policy under the circumstances of this case. The purpose behind Texas usury laws is to protect unsophisticated borrowers from unscrupulous lenders.... Such laws are based upon a universally recognized public policy that protects necessitous borrowers from the exaction of exorbitant interest from unscrupulous lenders). This case, however, does not involve the victimizing of a naive consumer. Southwest Livestock is managed by sophisticated and knowledgeable people with experience in business. Additionally, the evidence in the record does not suggest that Ramon misled or deceived Southwest Livestock. Southwest Livestock and Ramon negotiated the loan in good faith and at arms length. In short, both parties fully appreciated the nature of the loan transaction and their respective contractual obligations.

Accordingly, in light of the plain language of the Texas Recognition Act, and ... and the purpose behind Texas public policy against usury, we hold that Texas's public policy does not justify withholding recognition of the Mexican judgment. The district court erred in deciding otherwise.

III

For the foregoing reasons, we VACATE the district court's summary judgment, and REMAND for further proceedings.

Questions and Comments

1. Enforcement of a judgment in the United States against GROW-FAST should not be difficult due to full faith and credit requirements. There is little opportunity for the courts of one state to inquire beyond the judgment. Enforcing the judgment in other nations depends upon the rules of those nations, which may vary from no enforcement at all, to enforcement only when there is a bilateral or multilateral treaty, to enforcement based on reciprocity, to enforcement without reciprocity. Enforcement of a punitive damages award is another matter. Other courts may refuse to enforce any part of the judgment because there were punitive damages awarded, or enforcement of all but the punitive damages. The *homologación* or *exequatur* procedure is typical of civil law legal systems.

2. Where the judgments against GROWFAST are in Mexico, the question regarding enforcement in the United States is a *state* law matter. If GROWFAST has most of its assets, but not all, in a state where there is a disinclination to enforce foreign judgments, what might the plaintiffs do? Could they obtain a judgment in a state where GROWFAST has some assets and will enforce the Mexican judgment, and then use that U.S. judgment as the basis for enforcement in the state with most of the assets? Enforcement in a third nation again depends upon the law of that nation. The *Southwest*

Livestock and Trucking Company, Inc. v. Ramón case is a recent Texas foreign judgment enforcement case dealing with a Mexican judgment. Do you agree with the public policy argument?

3. If a U.S. judgment were to be taken to Mexico for enforcement, Professor Vargas notes the changes which allow a greater opportunity for enforcement. But there is yet no significant indication that Mexican courts are actually enforcing foreign judgments on a consistent or predictable basis.

PART C. NAFTA ENCOURAGED ALTERNATIVES—MEDIATION AND ARBITRATION

This Part focuses on arbitration, which the NAFTA suggests as an appropriate method for the settlement of international private commercial disputes.

Comment on NAFTA Article 2022— Alternative Dispute Resolution

This four part article encourages each Party to use arbitration and other forms of alternative dispute resolution to settle international commercial disputes between *private* parties in the free trade area. Interestingly, it does not limit such encouragement to private parties which are nationals of one of the NAFTA Parties, but applies to *all* international commercial disputes "in the free trade area." A commercial conflict occurring in Mexico between a German supplier of a Brazilian wholly owned Mexican subsidiary, is also the target of such encouragement of the use of ADR.

All three of the NAFTA Parties are parties to the 1958 United Nations Convention on the Recognition and Enforcement of Foreign Arbitral Awards (the New York Convention). 21 U.S.T 2517, 330 U.N.T.S. 3; Mexican Diario Oficial June 22, 1971. Mexico and the United States are the only Parties that have signed the 1975 Inter–American Convention on International Commercial Arbitration (the Panama Convention). 104 Stat. 449, Pan–Am. T.S. 42; Mexican Diario Oficial April 27, 1978. The Panama Convention is very nearly identical to the New York Convention. Participation in either (and remaining in compliance) fulfills the Article's mandate that each Party provide "appropriate procedures to ensure observance of agreements to arbitrate and for the recognition and enforcement of arbitral awards in such disputes."

The last part of Article 2022 requires the Commission to establish an Advisory Committee on Private Commercial Disputes. That has been accomplished. The Committee is to "report and provide recommendations to the Commission on general issues referred to it by the Commission respecting the availability, use and effectiveness of arbitration and other procedures for the resolution of such disputes in the free trade area." The NAFTA Commission's joint statement of Ministers issued April 23, 1999, "Five Years of Achievement", had little to report on ADR. It endorsed progress towards a voluntary, industry driven private commercial dispute resolution system for trade in some specific perishable agricultural products, and applauded the recent agreement among industry representatives from the three Parties to establish five industry-led working groups to put the dispute resolution system in place.

In ten years the 2022 Committee has met fourteen times, but has produced little in the way of new initiatives. However, with the encouragement of the State Department, the Committee (or individual members thereof) have participated in a series of seminar presentations on ADR issues. A website providing detailed information on arbitration and other forms of ADR, to be hosted by the NAFTA Secretariat website, was in its final stages of implementation by the Committee in late 2004. It may well be that the most productive function of the 2022 Committee will be through such outreach functions.

WRIGHT, MEDIATION OF PRIVATE UNITED STATES–MEXICO COMMERCIAL DISPUTES: WILL IT WORK?
26 New Mexico L. Rev. 57 (1996).*

* * *

Advocates of a direct transfer of U.S. mediation models to Mexico may have the best of intentions, but they also may fail to understand that the models are based on cultural assumptions not generally accepted in Latin American countries, including Mexico....

Certain cultural assumptions concerning conflict and its resolution are at the core of the mediation models used in the United States. Cultural assumptions are beliefs so completely accepted within a group that "they do not need to be stated, questioned, or defended." When members of a group consider certain beliefs to be fundamental, they may assume the beliefs are universally held. In fact, the beliefs may not be accepted beyond the confines of the group.

* * *

A. INDIVIDUALIST AND COLLECTIVIST CULTURES IN MEXICO

Mexicans' dominant cultural values, like those of other Latin Americans, are collectivist. Mexicans value their relationships within groups, particularly within their extended families. Consensus and harmony are treasured in most social and business organizations. Because conflict is viewed as a threat to overall harmony, there is a reluctance to confront interpersonal differences directly. And because criticism usually is taken personally, it often occurs in private, to avoid a loss of face for the recipient.

When a disagreement does arise, great effort is made to prevent it from escalating into an open confrontation. To that end, and to preserve each party's dignity, insiders are asked to be conduits for communications and negotiations between disputants.... In business disputes, close business associates may be approached for advice and intercession. Negotiations may take place without the disputants ever speaking directly to each other. The dominant negotiating style appears to be based on deductive reasoning. The parties first attempt to agree on basic principles, then they apply the principles to the facts at hand. In most cases, "win/win" resolutions of disputes are preferred. . . .

* * *

Mexican society, while traditional, is far from static. Economic reforms in Mexico during the last decade have begun to change Mexicans' customary relationships with their government, their employers, and each other. The passage of NAFTA is expected to hasten this process as Mexican businesses attempt to compete with companies from the United States and Canada. Economic pressures, combined with a likely increase in Canadian and United States cultural influences, could have the effect of enlarging the individualist component of Mexican society.

Observers of Mexico already have noticed that the upper and middle classes exhibit certain individualist traits. This trend may be attributable to the concentration of the upper and middle classes in the urban, industrialized areas of Mexico, their exposure to United States cultural values through travel, movies and television, and the tendency of many well-educated Mexicans to obtain some part of their higher educations in the United States or Europe, where low-context cultural attitudes prevail. On a regional basis, similarities to United States culture have been detected in the northern industrial state of Nuevo Leon, its capital Monterrey, and in the cities along Mexico's border with the United States.

* * *

Modifications of U.S. mediation models may be necessary in dealing with the more collectivist sectors of Mexican society. . . . For example, in the more collectivist areas of Mexico, it may be necessary to identify and provide mediation training to respected "insiders" whom members of local society will trust. It also may be appropriate to conduct certain types of mediations in settings other than business offices. Instead of requiring the disputants to speak and negotiate directly with each other in joint sessions, it may be necessary to conduct an entire mediation through a series of private meetings between the mediator and one of the disputants. Conceivably, the parties may never speak to each other until a negotiation is successfully concluded. In disputes of sufficient size or complexity, co-mediators from the United States and Mexico may be warranted. . . .

SIQUEIROS, INTERNATIONAL COMMERCIAL ARBITRATION
2 Mexican Law 1 (1998).*

DEVELOPMENT OF ARBITRATION IN MEXICO
* * *

As in most civil law countries, there is a difference between *commercial arbitration* and *civil arbitration*; the former is regulated on the federal level by Article 1415 of the Commercial Code and the latter by the Codes of Civil Procedure of each of the individual states, including the Code of Civil Procedure for the Federal District.... The Civil Codes and the Federal Code of Civil Procedure do not contain any provisions governing arbitration, except the general treatment of enforcement of arbitral awards. Thus, pursuant to Article 2 of the Commercial Code, when this Code is silent with respect to any particular issue, ordinary (civil) substantive law will apply. Likewise, in matters of arbitral procedure, when the parties have not agreed to a specific procedure, the Code of Civil Procedure of the respective state regarding arbitral proceedings will apply.

Currently, Article 609 of the Code of Civil Procedure for the Federal District establishes that the parties to a dispute have the right to subject their dispute to arbitration. Article 620 ... provides that the obligation (understood as an arbitration clause contained in a contract or an agreement subsequent to the initiation of the controversy) requires that while the arbitration is active, neither party may attempt to advance the matter in a court of ordinary jurisdiction. Article 2 of the Law Governing the Justice Tribunals of General Jurisdiction of the Federal District recognizes the competence of arbitrators. The Law clarifies that the voluntary arbitrators are not vested with public authority, but confirms that, according to the terms of the arbitration agreement, they may resolve the civil matter to which the interested parties have entrusted him. It is clear that the arbitrator has jurisdictional authority to resolve and effectuate a disposition of the conflict. This notion was affirmed recently by the "Tribunales Colegiados" resolving that the parties in an arbitration proceeding submit the resolution of the litigation to the arbitrator in an identical fashion as if the resolution was submitted to a judge in a formal judicial proceeding. Article 634.... establishes that ordinary judges are required to utilize their jurisdiction to assist the arbitrators. Thus, there exists a synergy between the arbitration process and the Judicial Branch.

The Commercial Code became effective on January 1, 1890. For its first ninety-nine years the statute was practically silent regarding arbitration matters. Fortunately, there have been two recent changes in the panorama. The Commercial Code was amended on January 4, 1989, adding articles 1415 to 1437, and again on July 22, 1993 to add and perfect a completely new title that modernizes and updates the arbitration field. The 1993 decree amended the Commercial Code and several articles of the Federal Code of Civil Procedure in order to establish consistency in matters regarding recognition and enforcement of foreign awards. Additionally, the Commercial Code's older rules regulating "special commercial proceedings" were amended to differentiate between the procedure agreed to by the parties which is to be followed before the courts and that which is to govern the arbitral proceedings.

The 1993 decree enacted by the Mexican Congress amended Book V, Title Four of the Commercial Code entitled "Commercial Arbitration," substantially incorporating the UNCITRAL Model Law on International Commercial Arbitration and certain principles selected from the UNCITRAL Arbitration Rules on matters of procedure and costs of arbitration. As stated before, pursuant to article 2 of the Commercial Code, matters not regulated in the amended Commercial Code regarding specific regulation of arbitral proceedings are dealt with by the applicable rules of the respective Code of Civil Procedure at the arbitral situs.

As stated in the Exposition des Motifs submitted by the President of Mexico to the Congress, the principal purpose of the new legislation is to modernize and update the legal framework of commercial arbitration through the embodiment of the most advanced norms on the subject, thus achieving harmonization of the arbitral procedural rules oriented to the specific needs of dispute resolution in international commercial practice.

The previous text of Title Four of the Commercial Code (now abrogated) already incorporated some principles of the UNCITRAL Model Law, as well as other rules taken from the New York and Panama Conventions. However, the 1989 amendments were insufficient, as the Commercial Code nonetheless retained several provisions (articles 609–636) also contained in the C.P.C.D.F., which were plainly obsolete and inconsistent with the more advanced principles of commercial arbitration procedure.

The recent changes were also brought about by an apparent dichotomy prevailing in Mexican arbitration law. Ever since the country acceded to the New York Convention in 1971, ratified the Panama Convention in 1978, and also ratified the Inter–American Convention on Extraterritorial Validity of Foreign Judgments and Arbitral Awards in 1987, commercial arbitration had been governed by two different sets of rules. Arbitration cases with an international component were regulated (as to substance and procedure) by Mexican international law, while domestic cases were still conducted and governed by the old provisions of the Commercial Code and local Codes of Civil Procedure. Although the Model Law is specifically geared to international arbitration, in order not to have two legal regimes concerning arbitration coexisting within Mexico, the legislature made the necessary technical changes, thus providing that the new statute should apply to both domestic disputes and to international cases when the arbitral proceedings take place in national territory.

New Title Four of Book V of the Commercial Code closely follows the guidelines of the Model Law. Although it is not a verbatim adoption of its articles, comparison reveals only some two dozen variances, most editorial, some apparently typographical. The legislature deemed it proper to adjust the terminology to the Mexican legislative technique embodied in the rest of the Code, but the essence of the Model Law's basic principles remains unchanged. However, aside from cosmetic modifications, there are several deviations from the Model Law's text, including changes in the provisions for default appointment of arbitrators and the default rule of law applicable to the merits. In addition, while adopting the basic rules of Chapters VII and VIII of the Model Law concerning setting aside of and recognition and enforcement of awards, article 1463 of the Code nevertheless diverges from the Model Law by providing for a brief *exequatur* proceeding (*incidente*) in case the charged party opposes enforcement of the award. A similar type of proceeding is provided for setting aside the award in article 1457 of the Commercial Code....

* * *

Enforcement of foreign commercial arbitral awards has been made substantially easier than the enforcement of foreign judgments. Basically, enforcement of foreign commercial awards is subject to treaties and conventions to which Mexico is a party, supplemented by the provisions contained in articles 1461–1463 of the Commercial Code or applicable rules in the arbitration agreement.

In a significant liberalization of prior law and practice, article 1463 of Chapter IX of the Commercial Code provides an exclusive, accelerated, non-appealable procedure (*incidente*) in the nature of *exequatur* for the recognition and enforcement of all foreign as well as domestic commercial awards under article 360 of the Federal Code of Civil Procedure. Article 1461 of the Commercial Code closely follows article IV of the New York Convention and article 35 of the UNCITRAL Model Law.

The improved enforcement procedure approved in article 1462, applies equally to countries not a party to treaties with Mexico, providing recognition and enforcement of an arbitral award "whatever the country in which it was handed down." No special time limits, *exequatur* in the issuing country reciprocity, or letters rogatory are required. The grounds for denial are essentially those listed in article V of the New York Convention. Although the law provides no time limit for making a request for recognition and enforcement, article 360 of the C.F.P.C. fixes accelerated time limits once the procedure is commenced.

OGARRIO, THE ROLE OF NAFTA'S ADVISORY COMMITTEE ON PRIVATE COMMERCIAL DISPUTES PRACTICING LAW IN THE ERA OF NAFTA

San Antonio, Texas March 18, 1999.

* * *

ENFORCEMENT IN ARBITRATION

Subcommittee IV has surveyed conventions, laws, court decisions and related literature and practice in each NAFTA country concerning the enforcement of agreements to arbitrate and final foreign arbitral awards. It also sought to identify other legal issues that might be impediments to the enforcement of arbitration agreements and arbitral awards and has prepared a draft of a document on the subject, which is the basis for my comments. The Subcommittee noted that intra-NAFTA enforcement of arbitral awards appears to be somewhat easier than enforcement of foreign judicial judgments, which do not share the benefits of treaty obligations and a common legal framework.

* * *

1. Enforcement in Canada

In 1986, Canada acceded to the New York Convention, and adopted UNCITRAL Model Law legislation, including Article 8 which requires a court before which an action is brought in any matter that is the subject of an arbitration agreement to refer the parties to arbitration unless it finds that the agreement is null and void, inoperative or incapable of being performed.

The UNCITRAL Model Law as enacted in Canada applies to all international commercial arbitrations, with the word "commercial" interpreted expansively.

Canadian courts have expressed in strong terms the need to shake off what previously was seen as judicial hostility to arbitration and the courts' former unwillingness to cede jurisdiction to arbitral tribunals. They have also expressed a willingness to support the objective of giving effect to the intention of the parties in choosing to submit to arbitration, to facilitate predictability in the resolution of international commercial disputes, to foster consistency between jurisdictions in the resolution of international commercial disputes, and to encourage the use of international commercial arbitration as a dispute resolution alternative, thereby encouraging international commercial activity.

In enforcing foreign arbitral awards, Canadian courts have endorsed a liberal interpretation of pro-arbitration principles and objectives by narrowly limiting the grounds for not recognizing and enforcing such awards. For example, judicial decisions have made clear that arguments directed to the jurisdiction and authority of arbitral tribunals ought not to be left until the time of attempted enforcement but should be made earlier, either to the arbitral tribunal or before a court where the arbitration is taking place. The Canadian judiciary has also generally rejected attempts to resist enforcement of such awards on grounds of public policy and has restricted such a defense to situations where the principles of justice and fairness are offended in a fundamental way, and in a way which the parties could attribute to the fact that the award was made in another jurisdiction where the procedural or substantive rules diverge markedly from those of Canada, or where there was ignorance or corruption on the part of the tribunal which could not be seen to be tolerated by Canadian courts.

Generally, it can be said that Canadian law recognizes a strong public policy that where parties have agreed by contract that they will have arbitrators decide their claims, instead of resorting to the courts, the parties should be held to their contract.

2. *Enforcement in Mexico*

Enforcement of foreign commercial arbitral awards in Mexico has been made substantially easier than the enforcement of foreign court judgments, because the former are subject to treaties and conventions to which Mexico is a party, supplemented by the provisions of the Commercial Code.

However, an arbitral award does not have executory force until clothed with the *fiat execulio* of a court as a result of an *exequatur* proceeding. Chapter IX, Book Five of the Commercial Code governs recognition and enforcement, and Article 1461 (following Article 35 of the UNCITRAL Model Law) provides that the party seeking enforcement need only present the original award, duly authenticated, or a certified copy thereof, and the original of the arbitral agreement, or a certified copy thereof, to the court, with a Spanish translation if necessary.

In a significant liberalization of prior law and practice, Chapter IX of the Commercial Code provides an exclusive, accelerated, non-appealable procedure (*incidente*) in the nature of *exequatur* for the recognition and enforcement of all foreign as well as domestic commercial awards under Article 360 of the Federal Code of Civil Procedure.

* * *

The decision rendered by the court is not appealable except by way of the writ of *amparo*. The writ of amparo is a writ requesting a federal district court to enjoin or otherwise remedy a violation of the guarantees of the Mexican Constitution, particularly those provided by Articles 14 and 16 insuring due process of law and the legality, in this situation, of a judicial order or act recognizing or enforcing an arbitral award. There is at least one precedent denying a writ of amparo against the leave for enforcement issued by the court having jurisdiction. The view expressed by members of the Committee was that arbitrators should not be considered "authorities" for purposes of mounting an amparo challenge, and that their award should not be reviewable.

3. *Enforcement in the United States*

The United States has enacted a federal statute to implement the New York Convention, and a number of court decisions have enforced agreements to arbitrate and awards made by foreign arbitral tribunals.

Section 201 of the Federal Arbitration Act (the "FAA") provides for the enforcement of the New York Convention in the federal courts, and Section 202 defines arbitration agreements and awards that fall within the scope of the New York Convention as those "arising out of a legal relationship, whether contractual or not, which is considered as commercial", including relationships entirely between U.S. citizens if the relationship involves property located abroad, contemplates performance or enforcement abroad, or has some other reasonable relation with one or more foreign states.

If a party to an agreement containing an arbitration clause refuses to submit to arbitration, the other party may move in court to compel that party to participate. So long as it finds that there is valid agreement to arbitrate, the court will issue an order requiring the resisting party to submit to the arbitration. Similarly, if a party to an agreement containing an arbitration clause attempts to initiate a court action instead of proceeding with arbitration, the other party may move in court for an order dismissing the action or staying it pending the arbitration. In upholding a federal policy that generally favors arbitration, United States courts have stated that, when an agreement to arbitrate exists, there is a presumption that the arbitration will proceed unless it is rebutted by strong evidence that the dispute in question was not intended by the parties to be covered by the arbitration clause.

Confirmation of an arbitral award is also straightforward under the FAA. Within three years after the award is made, any party to the arbitration may apply to any court having jurisdiction under Section 203 for an order confirming the award and making it a judgment against any other party to the arbitration. Unless the court finds one of the grounds specified in the New York Convention for refusal or deferral of recognition or enforcement of the award, the court is required to confirm the award.

Questions and Comments

1. NAFTA Article 2022 encourages arbitration and *other* forms of alternative dispute resolution. One "other" form is mediation, which is increasing in use in the United States for many forms of civil trials. Perhaps our parties might use mediation. If they do they might want to read Attorney Wright's extract, which suggests that mediation has certain cultural assumptions in different nations, and that Mexican assumptions might be very different than those in the U.S. But if the U.S. is a mix of cultures, with no single negotiating style, U.S. mediators must be familiar with facing cultural values. But are there dominant negotiating styles in the U.S. that might ignore Mexican cultural values? Mediation is usually done with a single mediator. Who would serve as a mediator in the disputes in our hypothetical?

2. Turning to arbitration, the dominant feature of Article 2022, perhaps our commercial conflicts could be resolved by arbitration. But the tort actions are much less likely to be arbitrated, unless the parties agreed *after* the injury to arbitrate. What then enters the parties minds?

3. Professor and Licenciado Siqueiros is Mexico's most prominent arbitration expert. He has long been an arbitrator and an advocate of arbitration. He must be pleased with the progress in Mexico in acknowledging the usefulness of arbitration. Does his extract make you more comfortable about providing for arbitration in a commercial agreement?

4. The NAFTA Advisory Committee on Private Commercial Disputes has created a number of subcommittees to study different aspects of their

charge—to advise the NAFTA Commission on the availability, use and effectiveness of arbitration and other procedures for the resolution of private international commercial disputes in the free trade area. What should they consider? One important subcommittee is studying "enforcement in arbitration." It has noted a possible problem with enforcement in Mexico, and the possibility of an *amparo* challenge.

5. In August 2004, the Mexican Supreme Court rendered an opinion in an *amparo* challenge to an arbitration proceeding. The challenge asserted that Article 1435 of the Mexican law permitting arbitral procedures was in violation of the due process protections of Articles 1, 14, 16 and 17 of the Mexican Constitution. The Supreme Court effectively rejected the challenge, and in doing so confirmed the constitutionality of arbitration in Mexico. (Amparo en Revisión 759/2003, Aug. 20, 2004) While some Mexican attorneys view this decision as many years overdue, it is regarded by others as a strong endorsement of arbitration by the Mexican Supreme Court.

6. What other activities might the NAFTA 2022 Committee undertake to further support the objectives of Article 2022? Keep in mind that financing of the Committee by the NAFTA Parties is limited.

7. The Commercial Arbitration and Mediation Center for the Americas (CAMCA) is a collaborative effort organized by the American Arbitration Association, the British Colombia International Commercial Arbitration Centre, the Cámara Nacional de Comercio de la Ciudad de México, and the Centre d'arbitrage commercial National et international du Québec. CAMCA was created in direct response to NAFTA. It has its own mediation and arbitration rules.

*

Part Three

THE NAFTA SIDE AGREEMENTS

Chapter 10

LABOR

10.0   INTRODUCTION: THE LABOR SIDE AGREEMENT

The decision to trade, as well as the decision not to trade, has consequences for a nation's labor force. In the short term, a government that pursues a policy of protectionism shields existing labor arrangements from the disruptions that foreign competition can entail. Over the longer term, if the government is unable to sustain closed borders, protectionism may so weaken domestic industries that the turmoil wrought by liberalized trade and altered trade flows is more sudden and severe than otherwise might have been the case. Similarly, rapid and comprehensive free trade can generate widespread and politically unacceptable labor dislocations, cripple culturally-important industries, and even threaten national security.

Governments long have understood that labor disruption is a rational and inevitable consequence of free trade premised upon comparative advantage theory.[1] Nevertheless, relatively few international trade accords directly address these consequences. This reality may reflect a desire on the part of all governments concerned to avoid labor fallout and (particularly) its political content. For example, none of the dozens of trade agreements administered by the World Trade Organization addresses labor issues, although there is an ongoing dialogue aimed at doing so. One of the key issues in this dialogue is whether International Labor Organization (ILO) standards are effective. The ILO has been promoting international labor standards for many decades, and has been particularly influential in Europe, but has had relatively little impact in North America.[2]

In creating the Common Market, the Europeans have directly and steadfastly addressed labor issues. Indeed, in the European Union work-

---

1. *See* Wesley A. Cann, Jr., *Internationalizing Our Views Toward Recoupment and Market Power: Attacking the Antidumping/Antitrust Dichotomy through WTO–Consistent Global Welfare Theory*, 17 U. Pa. J. Int'l Econ. L. 69, 82 (1996).

2. For further discussion of the ILO see R. Folsom, et al., International Trade and Investment in a Nutshell, Ch. 12 (2000).

ers enjoy what amounts to a Bill of Rights. For example, Article 48 of the Treaty of Rome provides for the freedom of movement for workers across national borders. Moreover, in 1989, the European Council adopted the Charter of Fundamental Social Rights for Workers which proclaimed extensive labor rights, including the rights to fair remuneration, improved living and working conditions, adequate social security benefits, free association in unions, equal treatment for women and men, and safe and healthy working conditions.[3] However, it may be more accurate to compare the European Union's extensive treatment of labor issues today to the United States, rather than to free trade agreements such as Mexico.

In the case of NAFTA, labor concerns were an afterthought rather than an initial negotiating objective. The fact that the North American Agreement on Labor Cooperation (NAALC) was an eleventh-hour supplement to NAFTA should not minimize the significance of its adoption. The CFTA agreement did not address labor issues at all. Under NAALC, Canada, Mexico and the United States agreed to permit one another to investigate, second-guess, and report on a partner's failure to enforce its own labor laws. The general contours of the NAALC are described in the readings which follow.

LOWE, THE FIRST AMERICAN CASE UNDER THE NORTH AMERICAN AGREEMENT ON LABOR COOPERATION
51 U. Miami L. Rev. 481, 487–88 (1997).*

Political necessity gave birth to [the North American Agreement on Labor Cooperation (NAALC)]. Negotiation of NAFTA without any explicit provisions for labor standards provoked deep and spirited opposition among American labor unions and pro-labor politicians. United States congressional representatives opposing NAFTA argued alternatively for an agreement that would harmonize labor norms in all participating countries, sanction violations from these norms as "actionable unfair trade practice[s]," and create a dispute resolution mechanism that would enforce North American labor standards. Labor's opposition to NAFTA appeared to hinge on two ideas. First, labor feared that mutual elimination of tariffs and other trade barriers would lead to import surges from Mexico which would result in the loss of U.S. jobs. Second, labor feared Mexico's lack of enforcement of its labor laws would give Mexico a competitive advantage over the U.S. with a resulting loss of U.S. jobs. Conspicuously absent from the NAFTA debate was any discussion of U.S. labor laws themselves being rife with loopholes in their commitment to workers' organizational and collective bargaining rights.

The dynamics of the 1992 presidential campaign paved the way for NAALC. [Ross] Perot's vehement opposition to NAFTA countered Presi-

3. *See* R. FOLSOM, EUROPEAN UNION LAW IN A NUTSHELL, Chs. 4 & 5 (3d ed. 1999).

* Copyright © 1997 University of Miami Law Review and Sarah Lowe. Reprinted with permission.

dent Bush's wholesale endorsement of the treaty he shepherded. Candidate Bill Clinton positioned himself between the two extremes. He supported NAFTA conditionally–he insisted upon negotiation of side accords by the signatory countries. Once President, Clinton negotiated labor and environmental side accords, an agreement of these issues was reached on August 13, 1993. Although the agreement addressed some of labor's concern, it hardly stemmed all of labor's opposition to NAFTA. Many labor leaders and pro-labor politicians continued to assail Clinton for his support of NAFTA and lobbied heavily against its passage. In late November 1993, however, Congress passed the North American Free Trade Agreement Implementation Act, which Clinton signed on December 8, 1993.

U.S. NATIONAL ADMINISTRATIVE OFFICE, NORTH AMERICAN AGREEMENT ON LABOR COOPERATION: A GUIDE

<www.dol.gov/dol/ilab/media/reports/nao/naalcgd.htw> (April 1998).

The main objective of the NAALC is to improve working conditions and living standards in the United States, Mexico, and Canada as the North American Free Trade Agreement (NAFTA) promotes more trade and closer economic ties among the three countries. The preferred approach of the Agreement to reach this objective is through cooperation–exchanges of information, technical assistance, consultations–a concept that is explicitly recognized in the very title of the instrument. The Agreement also provides some oversight mechanisms to ensure that labor laws are being enforced in all three countries. These oversight mechanisms are aimed at promoting a better understanding by the public of labor laws and at enhancing transparency of enforcement. The Agreement does provide the ability to invoke trade sanctions as a last resort for non-enforcement of labor law by a Party.

STRUCTURE

The Agreement creates both international and domestic institutions. The international institution is the Commission for Labor Cooperation, consisting of a Council supported by a Secretariat. The domestic institutions are the National Administrative Offices (NAOs), located in each of the countries, and national or governmental advisory committees.

- The *Council*, which is composed of the three Cabinet-level labor officials, is the governing body of the Commission.

    > It has a broad mandate to work cooperatively on labor issues, including occupational safety and health, child labor, benefits for workers, minimum wages, industrial relations, legislation on the formation of unions and the resolution of labor disputes.

- An independent *Secretariat*, which is headed by an Executive Director appointed by consensus of the three Parties for a fixed term, provides technical support to the Council.

Among the functions of the Secretariat are to report periodically to the Council on a wide range of labor issues, including labor law and administrative procedures, trends and administrative strategies related to enforcement of labor law, labor market conditions, and human resource development issues.

- *National Administrative Offices* were created by each country to implement the Agreement and to serve as points of contact between Commission entities and national governments.

- NAOs can consult with each other and exchange information on labor matters.

   Each country has a right to determine the functions and powers of its own NAO and how it will be staffed.

- The Agreement also allows for each country to establish national and governmental advisory committees to their NAOs.

- The National Advisory Committee for the North American Agreement on Labor Cooperation was established in 1995 to provide advice to the U.S. NAO on issues arising under the NAALC, and other matters as they arise in the course of administering the Agreement. The committee is comprised of 12 members, four representing the labor community, four representing the business community, two representing academia and two representing the public at large.

COVERAGE

Labor law is defined broadly in the Agreement, to include laws and regulations, or provisions thereof, directly related to:

- freedom of association and protection of the right to organize;

- the right to bargain collectively;

- the right to strike;

- prohibition of forced labor;

- labor protections for children and young persons;

- minimum employment standards, such as minimum wages and over-time pay, covering wage earners, including those not covered by collective agreements;

- elimination of employment discrimination on the basis of race, religion, age, sex, or other grounds as determined by each country's domestic laws;

- equal pay for men and women;

- prevention of occupational injuries and illnesses;

- compensation in cases of occupational injuries and illnesses; and

- protection of migrant workers.

OBLIGATIONS

The Agreement obligates each Party to:

- ensure that its labor laws and regulations provide for high labor standards and to continue to strive to improve those standards;

- promote compliance with and effectively enforce its labor law through appropriate government action;

- ensure that persons with a legally recognized interest have appropriate access to administrative, quasi-judicial, judicial, or labor tribunals for enforcement of its labor law and that proceedings for the enforcement of its labor law are fair, equitable and transparent;

- ensure that its labor laws, regulations, procedures, and administrative rulings of general application are promptly published or otherwise made available to the public and promote public awareness of its labor law.

COMPA, NAFTA'S LABOR SIDE ACCORD: A THREE-YEAR ACCOUNTING
3 NAFTA: L. & Bus. Rev. Americas 6 (1997).*

STRUCTURE AND FUNCTIONING

To understand the NAALC one must see what it is not.

First, the NAALC is not an agreement that sets forth new standards to which countries must conform by harmonizing their laws or their standards and regulations. Instead, the NAALC stresses sovereignty in each country's internal labor affairs, recognizing "the right of each Party to establish its own domestic labor standards." Second, the NAALC does not create a new labor rights enforcement agency to supplant the domestic authorities of each country. NAALC negotiators took pains to declare that "nothing in this Agreement shall be construed to empower a Party's authorities to undertake law enforcement activities in the territory of another Party." Third, the NAALC does not create a supranational tribunal to receive evidence in order to decide the guilt or innocence of employers involved in labor disputes or to order remedies against violators. Domestic authorities retain this power. Instead, the NAALC countries created a system for mutual review of labor matters and labor law enforcement in defined areas of labor law. These reviews are conducted first by each other, and then, depending on the subject area, by independent, non-governmental evaluation committees or arbitral panels.

The core obligation assumed by each of the NAALC parties is to "effectively enforce its labor law." This notion of "effective enforcement" of domestic labor law is the heart of the NAALC. While the countries have not yielded sovereignty with respect to the content of their laws or the authorities and procedures for enforcing them, they have transcended traditional notions of sovereignty by opening themselves to critical international and independent reviews, evaluations, and even arbitrations over their performance in enforcing their labor laws. In three key areas–minimum wage, child labor, and occupational safety and health–the countries created a prospect of fines or loss of NAFTA trade benefits for a persistent pattern of failure to effectively enforce domestic law.

The significance of this acquiescence to outside scrutiny should not be deprecated. Countries traditionally shield domestic sovereignty over labor law and labor-management relations. Indeed, labor law usually reflects a balance of forces resulting from decades of social struggle. The hybrid approach taken by the NAALC countries—preserving sovereignty over the levels of labor laws and standards, but submitting to reviews by each other by independent, non-governmental bodies—extends as far as countries can advance in fashioning the first labor accord connected to an international trade agreement. This is especially true where the United States dominates the economic relationship among the three NAFTA countries, where both Mexico and Canada see their own labor laws as more protective of workers than those of the United States and where smaller countries resist any move toward harmonization that would be influenced by the gravitational pull of U.S. economic power. A fear already exists among labor rights advocates in Mexico and Canada that the U.S. de-regulatory model of labor relations is advancing in their countries.

* * *

STAGES OF TREATMENT AND SCOPE OF REVIEW

NAO Review and Ministerial Consultations

Subtle but important distinctions emerge in the scope of review in the various stages of treatment of labor matters under the NAALC and in the ability to trigger the next stage of treatment. The scope of initial review by an NAO and ministerial consultations is extremely wide. For NAO review, the scope includes "labor law matters arising in the territory of another Party" while ministerial consultations review covers "any matter within the scope of this Agreement". The matter need not be related to NAFTA or to trade. Furthermore, failure to effectively enforce domestic law is not a necessary element for NAO review.

NAO review also does not contain any "standing" requirement to file a complaint. Any citizen or organization of any country, alone or in coalition, may file a complaint with an NAO. The complaining party need not demonstrate harm or interest in the matter in order to have standing. The NAO must respond to the complaint either by accepting the complaint for review or, if it does not accept the complaint for review, by explaining in writing to the complainant the reasons for non-acceptance.

Beyond NAO review, however, the process becomes government-driven. Only the NAO may recommend ministerial consultations and only a minister can accept the recommendation and request consultations. Furthermore, one minister may initiate the formation of an Evaluation Committee of Experts (ECE) while two ministers are necessary to initiate the formation of an arbitral panel. In this context, lobbying skills and political pressure are needed for the private parties to push their complaints forward through the process.

ECE

Two new elements are needed for complaints to move to review by an ECE. First, the matter must be "trade-related," involving companies engaged in NAFTA trade or competing with traded goods or service from a NAFTA partner. Second, the matter must be covered by "mutually recognized labor laws" meaning both countries have laws on the matter. For example, a U.S. or Canadian request for ECE review on a matter involving Mexico's law, which requires profit-sharing by all firms, might fail because no such law exists in the United States or Canada.

The scope of an ECE's evaluation is narrower than that of an NAO review or ministerial consultation. Assuming that the matters are trade-related and covered by mutually recognized labor law, the NAALC specifies that the Committee "shall analyze, in the light of the objectives of this Agreement and in a non-adversarial manner, patterns of practice by each Party in the enforcement of its ... technical labor standards [Labor Principles 4–11]." This introduces three additional factors: 1) the exclusion of Labor Principles 1, 2 and 3 from ECE treatment, 2) the need to examine "patterns of practice" rather than "labor law matters" or "any matter", and 3) the need to examine "enforcement" rather than "labor law matters" or "any matter".

Dispute Resolution

Dispute resolution by an arbitral panel entails the same requirements for trade-relatedness and mutually recognized labor laws. However, the NAALC contains an important new formulation of the scope of treatment by an arbitral panel: the "alleged persistent pattern of failure to effectively enforce occupational safety and health, child labor or minimum wage technical labor standards." This new formulation makes only 3 labor principles susceptible to dispute resolution. It also introduces the concept of a "persistent pattern of failure to effectively enforce ... labor standards." Issues characterized simply as "labor law matters" or "any matter" for NAO reviews and ministerial consultations, or "patterns of practice" and "enforcement" for ECE evaluation, face new, higher hurdles with arbitral review requiring findings of a "persistent pattern" and "failure to enforce" to obtain an arbitral panel ruling in favor of workers' rights.

Note on the Application of the NAALC in Canada

The approach to legislating and implementing labor law varies in the three NAFTA countries. In Mexico, labor law is exclusively federal in nature. Mexican state governments are afforded a role in implementing labor law in limited contexts (*e.g.*, in matters relating to state employees and industries of a purely local nature); however, the federal government in Mexico is the dominant force in internal labor dealings. In the United States, although the fifty state governments have developed bodies of state labor law and play an important role in labor matters, the state role clearly is secondary to that of the federal government in the creation and implementation of laws regulating employer-employee relations. In contrast, in Canada labor law is left primarily to regulation by the ten provinces and, in only limited contexts, to the federal government. "Federal labor law is applicable to individuals working for the federal government and Crown corporations . . . [and] to certain industries such as communications, railroads, airlines and trucking insofar as they operate on a national or international basis. Any matter which does not fall in the federal sphere is subject to provincial legislation."[1] Thus, in Canada, one encounters numerous distinct sources of labor law.

The differing approaches to labor law in North America required that the implementation of the NAALC be specially adapted to the Canadian system. Thus, the NAALC was designed to apply comprehensively in Mexico and the United States once those governments ratified the accord but only incrementally in Canada as each governmental unit individually adopted it. Consequently, the NAALC is not in force in all jurisdictions in Canada. Each jurisdiction signals its adoption of the NAALC by signing the Canadian Intergovernmental Agreement Regarding the North American Agreement on Labour Cooperation. The federal government adopted the NAALC in this manner in May 1995. As of 2004 four provinces had signed the Intergovernmental Agreement: Alberta (May 1995), Manitoba (January 1997), Quebec (February 1997), and Prince Edward Island (October 1998).

The incremental adoption of the NAALC in Canada is governed by Annex 46 to the Agreement. Pursuant to Annex 46, a province cannot initiate NAALC proceedings if it has not ratified the accord. Further, Canada cannot initiate NAALC proceedings unless: (1) the matter at issue is one of federal jurisdiction or (2) the matter at issue is one of provincial jurisdiction and the federal government and provinces that have ratified the NAALC account for at least thirty-five percent of the country's total labor force. According to the Canadian National Administrative Office, the federal government and four provinces that had signed the Intergovernmental Agreement as of December 1999 account for forty percent of the country's labor force.

The fact that, as of late 2004, nearly eleven years into NAFTA, two of Canada's largest provinces (Ontario and British Columbia) had not yet elected to participate in the NAALC has important implications for Canadian labor. Although "[i]n seventeen of the twenty-two categories of manufacturing found in Canada, the province with the largest share of

1.   Gary E. Murg & John C. Fox, Labor Relations Law: Canada, Mexico, and Western Europe 89 (1978).

the national workforce is Ontario,"[2] these workers are not eligible to benefit from the Agreement. This includes eighty-two percent of Canada's auto industry workers, all of whom are based in Ontario. The combined absence of Ontario and British Columbia further limits the NAALC's application in Canada. "[I]t is no small matter that the non-participation of Ontario and British Columbia would prevent the federal government from using the Accord process for ten industries that comprised almost sixty-three percent of Canadian manufacturing employment in 1993."[3]

PROBLEM 10.1 LABOR ORGANIZATION: FREEDOM OF ASSOCIATION IN MEXICO AND PLANT CLOSINGS IN THE UNITED STATES

PART A. MEXICO

SECTION I. THE SETTING

Vidrios Mexicanos, S.A. de C.V., manufactures glass and fine glass products (glassware, bottles, stained glass, *etc.*) at its plant in the City of Toluca in the State of Mexico. Its products are sold throughout the world. For nearly forty years, the Union of Mexican Artisans (UMA), an affiliate of the Confederation of Mexican Workers (CTM), has controlled the collective bargaining agreement with Vidrios. The agreement covers all 600 Vidrios employees, regardless of whether or not they are UMA members.

Working conditions at the Vidrios facility are not entirely safe. Employees are exposed to hot, moving, or sharp machine parts and to hazardous substances, including lead and solvents. Vidrios provides no protective gear and does not monitor contamination levels. After appeals to UMA officials failed to improve matters, employees invited representatives of the CTM's main rival, the Authentic Labor Front (ALF), to undertake a union organizing drive at the plant. Under Mexican law, the ALF would supplant the UMA as the collective bargaining representative if it wins the support of a majority of Vidrios workers.

After several months of organizing activity, the ALF felt it had enough support to win a representation election (*recuento*) and petitioned the federal Conciliation and Arbitration Board (CAB) in Toluca to conduct an election. At this point a campaign of intimidation against the ALF and its supporters began within the plant. Several employees were dismissed, several were pressured by Vidrios management to reveal the identities of ALF supporters, others were warned that there would be consequences if the ALF won the representation election.

2. Ian Robinson, *The NAFTA Labour Accord in Canada: Experience, Prospects, and Alternatives*, 10 Conn. J. Int'l L. 475, 477 (1995).

3. *Id.* at 482.

The CAB took five months simply to schedule a representation election. When the ALF notified the CAB of continuing intimidation at Vidrios, CAB representatives initiated an investigation that included "confidential" interviews with twenty workers. Within days of the interviews, twelve of these workers were fired.

The representation election ultimately went forward as scheduled. The company stationed off-duty police officers armed with rifles at the plant entrance and on the plant floor. Members of the competing unions took positions outside the plant entrance, some carrying metal pipes and sticks. Despite protests by the ALF that the environment was too hostile to permit a fair election, CAB officials refused to suspend the election or permit employees to vote by secret ballot. The final vote tally was 492 for the UMA and 75 for the ALF.

Following the election, the ALF and three workers petitioned the CAB to void the results. The CAB dismissed the ALF from the petition on the grounds that it was not a proper party but allowed the workers to go forward *pro se*. At the hearing on the matter, the CAB refused to allow the ALF to present evidence. The three individual petitioners were illiterate and unable to effectively articulate their objections to the representation election. Three months later, the CAB issued a decision, finding no violations of Mexican law, that the petitioners had failed to establish any improprieties, and that the ALF did not have the support of a majority of workers. The CAB ruled that the UMA continued to hold the collective bargaining agreement at Vidrios.

SECTION II.   FOCUS OF CONSIDERATION

As of mid–2004, roughly eighteen of the twenty-eight submissions filed under the NAALC dealt with issues of freedom of association. This included thirteen freedom of association complaints against Mexico, four against the United States, and one against Canada. The explanation for the frequency of freedom of association submissions against the Mexican government is a subject of some controversy.

One view is that this phenomenon is due to circumstances inside Mexico. Such circumstances include politics and the state of labor organization activity in Mexico. Control of labor (and, therefore, of labor organization) is a linchpin of the PRI's control of Mexican politics and society, even after the election of a conservative PAN candidate, Vincente Fox, in 2000. The formation of truly independent unions would diminish the number of workers within the PRI's control and, in that way, strikes at the very heart of Mexican politics. In short, it serves the interests of the PRI, which still has a plurality in the Mexican Congress and holds the governorships of many Mexican states, to discourage the formation of independent unions.

Furthermore, most labor organization activity in contemporary Mexico is not in the form of new union formation or membership drives in plants where no union exists but rather involves so-called "title disputes"—attempts by one union to displace another as the collective bargaining representative of the workers. The Commission for Labor Cooperation reported that eighty-five percent (85%) of Mexican establishments with over 100 workers are unionized. During the early 1990s, the Mexican government issued an average of only twenty-five new union registrations per year in industries within the federal jurisdiction. In contrast, there were an average of over 600 title disputes per year in the same industries. In these cases, the central issue is the freedom of Mexican workers to associate with a union other than the one possessing the collective bargaining agreement. Because a government-affiliated union ordinarily is the existing union, this boils down to the right of workers to associate with a non-government-affiliated union. A challenger wins the right to act as the collective bargain representative of workers in a plant if it wins a representation election administered by the CAB. It is here that the government has an opportunity and incentive, through subtle methods, to defeat the formation of independent unions.

A competing view is that the frequency of freedom of association claims against Mexico is attributable to the tactics of U.S. labor organizations and internal political agenda of the U.S. government. Under this view, unions including the AFL–CIO have set out to use the NAALC to put the Mexican government, Mexican labor tribunals, and Mexican labor law in a very negative light. Doing so turns public opinion in the United States against trade with Mexico and, in that way, protects U.S. jobs. This abuse of the NAALC, it is alleged, serves the protectionists interests of the U.S. government. (*See* Luis Medina, A Dissenting Opinion, Review of the North American Agreement on Labor Cooperation (1998) [available at http://www.naalc.org/].)

As you study the readings which follow, assume that the ALF is considering filing a submission under the NAALC alleging violations of the principle of freedom of association by the Mexican government. Try to assess whether such a submission is permissible, what specific claims might be alleged, what stages of the NAALC consultation and dispute resolution processes might the submission reach, and whether such proceedings ultimately would accomplish any worthwhile objectives.

The NAALC is essential to an analysis of this problem. It is found in the Documents Supplement.

SECTION III.   READINGS, QUESTIONS AND COMMENTS

Labor in Mexico

HANSEN, THE POLITICS OF MEXICAN DEVELOPMENT
(Johns Hopkins Univ. Press 1982).*

With a few exceptions strong and independent labor unions do not exist in Mexico. One reason for this pattern is the fact that ever since the revolution the Mexican government has been active in the affairs of organized labor; so too have labor leaders been widely engaged in Mexican politics. In the unstable years between 1910 and 1930 labor bosses were often able to mobilize support for various revolutionary political factions; in return political leaders who controlled the government were in a position to sponsor and support the organizational activities of favored labor groups. The search for mutually advantageous alliances continued throughout the years of the revolution and the chaotic decade of the 1920s that followed.

* * *

What happened was that most of the leaders of the labor and *campesino* movements behaved much like their military counterparts: regardless of initial intentions, they eventually used their organizations for their own socioeconomic mobility. In doing so they undercut not only the manifest goals of the revolution but also the opportunity to broaden the bases of social solidarity and the capacity for cooperative action. Within the labor movement unions were "continuously the instruments, and almost as often the victim" of political intrigue and personal ambition. The fault was not solely that of the labor leaders; they, like their unions, were often the pawns of the period's military politicians. Presidential support or opposition could make or break national labor confederations, as could the inclinations of the powerful *caudillos* at the regional level. But the union leadership contributed greatly to the process by joining the game for personal advantage and forsaking the development of anything resembling labor movement solidarity.

Nowhere has this praetorian behavior better exemplified than within the largest and by far the most favored confederation of the 1920s, the *Confederación Regional de Obreros Mexicanos* [CROM]. How did the leaders of the confederation use their power? First, to crush as many competing confederations and independent labor unions as possible. As a result "rival unions soon learned to hate each other far more bitterly than any of them hated the capitalists." Second, to amass personal fortunes. An "immense majority" of the CROM leaders literally bathed in affluence by the end of the 1920s.

> They built themselves a magnificent country estate, with swimming pools, and a steel-girded fronton court ... became the owners of hotels and even, through intermediaries, of factories. Morones [the chief of the CROM who served several years as minister of industry] himself acquired the habit of wearing expensive diamond rings which, he explained to critics, he was keeping as a reserve fund which the working class could use in time of need.

> As Gruening noted, life for Morones and his CROM associates was lifted "to a plane of luxury unequaled except by millionaires" country clubs in the United States."

* * *

CROM leaders softened their commitment to the manifest goals of the revolution as they climbed the socio-economic ladder. By the late 1920s they too were calling for an end to "radical" reforms and for collaboration with the business community in building a new Mexico. Their prescription for Mexican development may well have been correct, but their private behavior mocked their public statesmanship, shattered the beginnings of labor solidarity and laid the groundwork for the captive labor movement that emerged within the official party in the following decades.

* * *

Between 1934 and 1940, ... Lazaro Cárdenas ... began to reunite and strengthen those same labor and agrarian mass organizations which Calles had fragmented earlier. He encouraged the formation of militant labor and peasant unions, and the grouping of each into national organizations.... Most of the reformist and radical labor unions were organized and centralized in the Workers Confederation of Mexico (CTM).

Having developed these bases of support, Cárdenas proceeded to reconstruct the official party. In 1938 the old National Revolutionary Party, based on a geographical and individual membership structure, was replaced by the Party of the Mexican Revolution (PRM). The new party was organized into four sectors: labor, agrarian, military and popular. The CTM, the largest of Mexico's labor confederations, represented the bulk of the labor movement within the party.... The popular sector of the party consisted primarily of government employees who had organized their own labor confederation, the FSTSE.

* * *

Thus the paradox of Mexican development emerges. By 1940 the social goals of the revolution were finally being implemented, and at a dramatic pace. Organized labor and the rural masses were directly represented in the official party, and were numerically the most important of that party's four sectors. The vast majority of the Mexican population was at long last beginning to share in the distribution of Mexican wealth.

Since 1940 two patterns can be observed in the relationship between union leaders and the government. One is the cooptive pattern, in which labor officials collaborate closely with the government. One commentator wrote of this group several years ago, "For two decades, the union boss has kept the rank and file in line, loyal to the Revolutionary regimes. His reward, besides the permanence of his tenure, sometimes comes in the form of a legislative office." For thirty years the leaders of the biggest confederation, the CTM, have regularly been given seats in the federal legislature by the Mexican president. Since consecutive terms in either the Chamber of Deputies or the Senate are prohibited in Mexico, this CTM clique has rotated offices but never relinquished them. While retaining his place in the national legislature, Fidel Velázquez has also held the secretary generalship of the CTM since 1949.

The second pattern of union-government relations might best be called repressive, and was most clearly evidenced during the years of Aleman's presidency. Perhaps the best description of the period would be one of total intervention by the government in union affairs. The government held wage increases in check while prices were rising at more than 10 percent a year, and labor opposition to Aleman's policies simply was not tolerated. The army was used to crush strikes, and government recognition of certain leftist unions was withdrawn. Many labor leaders openly critical of the regime were jailed, and others were forced to resign their offices. Then the government imposed its own union "leadership," a practice that Mexicans labeled "Charrismo Sindical" to emphasize the fact that the new officials represented the interests not of the union membership but of those who had chosen and imposed them.

Throughout these years of repression and imposed leadership the coopted union bosses of the CTM, led by Fidel Velázquez and the others in the group that Mexicans refer to as "the five little wolves," held the line for Aleman's policies and, not incidentally, their own sinecures. As a result, the number of strikes declined, and the unity of the labor movement achieved under Cardenas was fractured. By 1956 there were eight major federations and several independent industrial unions, all but one or two completely dominated by the government.

Since the mid–1950s a third pattern in union-government relations has emerged. There are some unions, like the electrical workers union, which have refused to join the government-oriented Workers' Unity Bloc, yet manage to be among the highest paid union workers in Mexico. In contrast, the members of many unions whose leaders belong to the Bloc and always support the government receive wages which barely match the legal minimums. It has been argued that some of the privileged unions whose leaders retain some independence from the government have achieved their status through a complex set of relationships including presidential favor, dynamic union leadership and the strategic nature of the industrial activity involved. Like most other attempts to fathom the workings of the Mexican political system, this observation cannot be clearly substantiated; nevertheless it seems to offer the best explanation we have at present.

What is clear is that the Mexican government will still not tolerate much union opposition. Since the late 1950s the army has been utilized to suppress strikes, union leaders have been and continue to be imprisoned, and new leaders are imposed when dissidents are removed. The range of tolerated opposition is perhaps growing, but the seeming inconsistency in government has led one Mexican scholar to argue that independent leaders are now never sure whether their labor demands will be met by government support or repression.

ENGLEHART, WITHERED GIANTS: MEXICAN AND U.S. ORGANIZED LABOR AND THE NORTH AMERICAN AGREEMENT ON LABOR COOPERATION

29 Case West. Res. J. Int'l L. (1997).*

Organized Labor's Ascent

* * *

At present, the PRI's labor bloc is organized under the *Congreso de Trabajo* (Congress of Labor, or CT), whose most influential members are the CTM and the *Confederación Regional de Obreros Mexicanos* (Regional Confederation of Mexican Workers, or CROM). The CT primarily functions as a coordinating body and wields little if any power, requiring of affiliates not much more than their participation in CT councils. The forum supplied by the CT acts as a safety valve for union leaders who wish to publicly proclaim their outrage against government austerity policies that they actually support. Since Cárdenas, the CTM has sustained a dominating influence within the CT and the labor bloc and thus within the party. Because of this proximity, the CTM has developed a philosophy that may be described as the defense and promotion of party and government policy as construed by the president in power. The CTM alternately has supported the labor-friendly policies of the leftists and the centrists as well as the policies of rightist presidents closely aligned with business interests and capital.

Organized Labor's Decline

Corruption

Corruption is threatening the PRI as Mexico attempts to enter mainstream twentieth century commerce as a modern nation.

* * *

Corruption also infects the CABs, the federal and local boards charged with hearing labor disputes. The CABs are staffed by representatives from labor and management sitting in equal numbers with one government representative, but most of the labor seats on the CAB are gifts of political patronage from the CTM. The CTM's stature as the PRI-backed confederation of official unions and its influence over CAB personnel cannot be denied. Most independent non-CTM unions are apolitical and thus tolerated, but others are leftist and considered a destabilizing force. Repression is not unknown. Due to the dominance of CTM appointees on the boards, CAB decisions resolving conflicts between a radical independent union and an apolitical independent union or between a radical independent union and a CTM affiliate, will disfavor the radical if possible, prompting legitimate charges of bias and corruption. The U.S. Embassy reports that while charges of corruption, strong-arm tactics, sweetheart deals, and the active frustration of true union organizing efforts have some validity, they are not the predominant pattern. The Embassy also reports that the government and the major labor confederations neither encourage nor sanction such acts, but instead work to eliminate them. A less systemic CAB problem is bribery, where the incentive is not political but pecuniary, and which may be instigated by either management or union at the expense of the aggrieved worker.

CONSTITUTION OF THE UNITED MEXICAN STATES

Article 9. The right to assemble or associate peaceably for any lawful purpose cannot be restricted; but only citizens of the Republic may exercise this right to take part in the political affairs of the country. No armed deliberative meeting is authorized.

Article 123. All persons have a right to dignified and socially useful work ... (A) With respect to relations between workers, day laborers, domestic servants, artisans and, in a general manner, all labor contracts ... XVI. Both employers and workers shall have the right to organize for the defense of their respective interests, by forming unions, professional associations, etc.... XX. Differences or disputes between capital and labor shall be subject to the decisions of a Conciliation and Arbitration Board, consisting of an equal number of representatives of workers and employers, and one from the government.

Article 133. This Constitution, the laws of the Congress of the Union that emanate therefrom, and all treaties that have been made and shall be made in accordance therewith by the President of the Republic, with the approval of the Senate, shall be the Supreme Law of the whole Union. The judges of each State shall conform to the said Constitution, laws, and treaties, in spite of any contradictory provisions that may appear in the constitutions or laws of the States.

FEDERAL LABOR LAW OF MEXICO

Article 6. The laws and treaties which are executed and approved under the terms of article 133 of the Constitution shall apply to employment relations insofar as they benefit the worker, from the date of their effectiveness.

Article 17. In the absence of an express provision in the Constitution, this law or its regulations, or in the treaties referred to in article 6, consideration shall be given to other provisions of such laws which govern similar cases, the general principles arising therefrom, general legal principles, general principles of social justice arising under article 123 of the Constitution, binding case law, custom, and equity.

Article 133. It shall be unlawful for an employer: ... IV. To obligate workers, through coercion or through any other means, to affiliate themselves with, or to withdraw from, a union or association to which they may belong, or that they vote for a specific candidate; V. To intervene in any manner in the internal governance of the union; ... VII. To engage in any activity which may impair the rights given to workers under the laws; . . . .

Article 354. The law recognizes the freedom of workers and employers to form coalitions.

Article 357. Workers and employers have the right to organize unions, without previous authorization.

Article 358. No one shall be obliged to participate in a union or abstain from such participation. Any agreement which establishes a contractual penalty for withdrawing from a union, or which impairs in any way the provisions contained in the preceding paragraph, shall have no effect.

Article 707. Representatives of the Government, of workers, or of employers on the [Conciliation and Arbitration] Board and its assistants are prohibited from participating in proceedings that arise, when: ... III. They have a direct or indirect personal interest in the proceeding; ... VI. They are a member, tenant, worker, owner, or economic dependent of any of the parties or of their representatives; ...

Article 728. The Chairmen of the Boards and the Assistants, may impose disciplinary measures in order to maintain good order in the hearings or proceedings, and may demand that due respect and consideration be kept therein.

Article 729. The disciplinary measures that may be imposed by order of the Board are: I. Admonition; II. Fine not in excess of seven times the general minimum wage in effect in the place and time in which the violation is committed; and III. Expulsion from the Board's premises; the person who refuses to comply with an order shall be evicted from the premises with the assistance of law enforcement.

Article 931. If a recount of the workers is offered as evidence, the following rules shall be observed: I. The Board shall fix a place, date and hour in which it must be effectuated; II. Only workers employed in the enterprise who are present when the recount is taken shall have the right to vote; III. Workers fired after the date of presentation of the notice of intention to strike shall be considered to be employees of the enterprise; IV. The votes of workers in positions of trust and workers hired after the date of presentation of the notice of intention to strike shall not be counted; and V. Objections to the workers present at the recount must be recorded in the minutes of the proceedings, in which case the Board shall arrange a meeting for the submission and presentation of proof.

INTERNATIONAL TREATY OBLIGATIONS

ILO CONVENTION 87 ON FREEDOM OF ASSOCIATION
AND PROTECTION OF THE RIGHT TO ORGANIZE

Article 2: Workers and employers, without distinction whatsoever, shall have the right to establish and, subject only to the rules of the organization concerned, to join organizations of their own choosing without previous authorization.

Article 3: 1. Workers' and employers' organizations shall have the right to draw up their constitutions and rules, to elect their representatives in full freedom, to organize their administration and activities and to formulate their programs. 2. The public authorities shall refrain from any interference which would restrict this right or impede the lawful exercise thereof.

INTERNATIONAL COVENANT ON CIVIL AND POLITICAL RIGHTS

Article 22: 1. Everyone shall have the right to freedom of association with others, including the right to form and join trade unions for the protection of his interests. 2. No restrictions may be placed on the exercise of this right other than those which are prescribed by law and which are necessary in a democratic society in the interests of national security and public safety, public order (*ordre public*), the protection of public health or morals or the protection of the rights and freedoms of others.

UNIVERSAL DECLARATION OF HUMAN RIGHTS

Article 23: Everyone has the right to form and to join trade unions for the protection of his interests.

AMERICAN CONVENTION ON HUMAN RIGHTS

Article 16: 1. Everyone has the right to associate freely for ideological, religious, political, economic, labour, social, cultural, sports, or other purposes. 2. The exercise of this right shall be subject only to such restrictions established by law as may be necessary in a democratic society, in the interests of national security, public safety or public order, or to protect public health or morals or the rights and freedoms of others.

HUMAN RESOURCES DEVELOPMENT CANADA, REVIEW OF PUBLIC COMMUNICATION CAN 98–1 (PT. I)

<www.labour-travail.hrdc-drhc.gc.ca> (1998).

AUTHORITY TO POSTPONE OR SUSPEND RECUENTOS

[The Conciliation and Arbitration Board (CAB)] can stop an election if it sees coercion. Furthermore, [CAB] agents* can warn the parties that

---

* The agents of the [CAB] who conduct the *recuento* are called actuaries, and their role is to tally the vote and make a record of any events which occur.

the vote may be suspended if there is violence and must report to the [CAB] with the reasons for their decision. The [CAB] can request the intervention of the police or request police presence during the *recuento* for security purposes. [CAB] agents are also responsible for ensuring there is no electioneering on the voting site.

DUE PROCESS

In Article 356 of the [Ley Federal del Trabajo (LFT)], a "trade union" is defined as "an association of workers or employers set up for the study, aim and defense of their respective interests." ... A registered union in Mexico ... is entitled to act as representative of its members in dealings with competent government authorities.

The legal status of trade unions is set out in Article 374 which reads:

> Every lawfully constituted trade union shall have legal personality and have capacity to: I. acquire ownership over movable goods or chattels; II. acquire ownership over the real and immovable property immediately and directly intended for the purposes of the union; III. defend its rights in dealings with authority and institute the corresponding legal proceedings.

The role of the union in representing the interest of members is outlined in Article 375 as follows: "[t]rade unions shall represent their members in defending the individual rights of the latter, without prejudice to the worker's right to act or intervene directly; in the latter case [a] trade union shall cease to act on behalf of the worker if the worker so requests."

Trade unions enjoy full legal personality and are recognized as representative of groups of workers, though workers may choose to defend their own rights in some cases.

For the purposes of proceedings before the [CAB], parties are defined, in Article 689, as "the individuals or legal entities furnishing evidence that they have a legal interest in the proceedings and bringing suits or entering a defense on that account."

Since trade unions are defined in the LFT as legal entities, they can appear as parties in proceedings before the [CAB] and there are many sections of the statute which clearly contemplate the participation of a trade union in the proceedings.

The LFT contains a number of signals indicating that proceedings before the CAB are to be conducted in a way which adequately provides the parties to those proceedings with the opportunity to bring forward evidence of various kinds, to make legal argument, to respond to their adversary, and to raise procedural questions.

The nature of the proceedings before the [CAB] is generally outlined in Article 685 as follows:

> Labour dispute proceedings shall be public, free of charge, expeditious and predominantly oral and shall be instituted at the request of any party concerned. Boards must take the necessary steps to ensure that proceedings are conducted with a maximum of economy, concentration and simplicity.

Article 690 provides that other parties "who are likely to be affected by the decision taken on a dispute may take part in the proceedings on furnishing evidence that they have a legal interest in the dispute, or may be summoned to appear, if so decided by the Board."

The LFT provides that the [CAB] has jurisdiction over both collective and individual disputes. This is indicated in, for example, Article 870 of the LFT, which states that the "ordinary proceedings" outlined in that part of the statute will apply to both collective and individual conflicts.

> . . . the [CAB] is accustomed to dealing with unions as entities which appear before them.

The nature of the proceedings under the LFT, like other proceedings in Mexican law, is an inquisitorial one, and does not follow the adversarial model which is seen in common law countries. The LFT does contemplate, however, that both parties will be given an opportunity to participate in the hearing at which a claim is considered.

Procedural Time Limits

There are a number of points indicated in the LFT to provide for time restrictions on the taking of certain steps in order to prevent unwarranted delays. For instance, in Article 910.IV, there is a time limit of 48 hours for workers to raise any objection to the involvement of particular members of the [CAB], or the legal status of the parties, following the receipt of the first reply of an employer. This Article also gives the [CAB] 24 hours to decide these questions.

Article 883 provides that, if all of the evidence cannot be presented in one hearing, further hearings may be held, but these should be held within 30 days. Following the end of the hearing, the officials of the [CAB] have, according to Article 885, a period of ten days to prepare a proposed disposition of the case. This is forwarded to the members of the [CAB], who have a further five days to state their views on this decision, and to suggest that further input from the parties may be needed. Within ten days after the five days permitted for members to state their views, or after any further hearing, the [CAB] is convened to vote on the disposition. The result of the case is to be declared at the end of this session, though it is possible for the [CAB] to suggest amendment or corrections before it is signed.

Article 890 stipulates that "[o]nce [an] award is elaborated, the Secretary shall have the members of the Board who voted on the case sign it, and once they are obtained shall turn the file over to the adviser, for the immediate personal notification of the award to the parties."

Article 889 specifies that the provisions of the LFT governing ordinary proceedings shall apply to special proceedings as appropriate, and this seems to include the procedures for making decisions.

ELECTION PROCEDURES

Apart from Article 25 of the International Covenant on Civil and Political Rights (ICCPR), which was incorporated into domestic law following its ratification by Mexico as provided for by Article 133 of the Constitution, there seems to be nothing in Mexican labour law specifically requiring that a *recuento* be conducted by secret ballot or in a neutral location.

Article 25 of the ICCPR states that "[e]very citizen shall have the right and the opportunity ... without unreasonable restrictions ... to vote and to be elected at genuine periodic elections which shall be by universal and equal suffrage and shall be held by secret ballot, guaranteeing the free expression of the will of the electors...."

Article 931 does not speak directly to the voting procedure in a *recuento*. However, its implication is that a *recuento* is a proceeding which is conducted under the authority of the [CAB], and, given the care which is taken throughout the LFT to ensure that the parties are given ample opportunity to express their views, and to ensure that the rights of workers are protected, it can be concluded that the [CAB] has a responsibility to ensure the procedural propriety of any vote which is conducted under its authority.

In practice, voters can cast secret votes in a *recuento* if both unions agree or if imposed by a [CAB].

While there is nothing in the LFT, and Article 931 in particular, which requires that *recuentos* be held on the premises of the employer, that is where they usually take place for reasons of convenience.

U.S. NATIONAL ADMINISTRATIVE OFFICE, PUBLIC REPORT OF REVIEW OF NAO SUBMISSION NO. 9702 (HAN YOUNG)

<www.dol.gov/dol/ilab/public/media/reports/> (Apr. 28, 1998).

SUMMARY OF SUBMISSION 9702

Case Summary

According to the submitters, beginning in April 1997, workers at the Han Young maquiladora plant in Tijuana, Baja California, Mexico, began to organize an independent union. The submitters state that the workers wanted a union to address issues of safety and health, job classifications and wage scales, low wages, annual bonuses, profit sharing, lack of dining facilities, and the lack of a company doctor in the plant. Among the cited health and safety concerns of the workers was the frequent occurrence of injuries such as burns and broken bones. They also expressed concern about respiratory illnesses, hearing loss, and loss of vision. . . .

The workers elected a union executive committee on May 31, 1997, and presented a petition listing demands to the plant management. After the election of the executive committee, Han Young management arranged for the workers to meet with a representative of a union that was already present at the plant and had previously entered into a collective bargaining agreement with the company. This local union (*Union de Trabajadores de Oficios Varios "José Maria Larroque"*) was affiliated with the Revolutionary Confederation of Workers and Peasants (*Confederación Revolucionaria de Obreros y Campesinos*—CROC). The CROC is affiliated with the Labor Congress (*Congreso del Trabajo*—CT) which groups together union organizations aligned with Mexico's dominant political party, the Institutional Revolutionary Party (*Partido Revolucionario Institucional*—PRI). . . .

. . . On July 15, 1997, the workers temporarily suspended their efforts to organize an independent union and elected to affiliate with the already registered STIMAHCS. Though STIMAHCS already possessed registration, it had, at that time, no membership in the maquiladoras and is not affiliated to the CT. The submitters indicated that STIMAHCS is considered to be more responsive to the interest of workers, compared to the unions affiliated to the major confederations.

* * *

On August 6, 1997, STIMAHCS filed for collective bargaining representation (*titularidad*) with the local CAB, in effect, challenging the CROC union for exclusive bargaining rights at the plant. . . .

* * *

A hearing to verify the credentials of the contending parties, hear challenges, and set a date for a representation election, was scheduled to be held on September 3, 1997, by the CAB. According to the CAB, this hearing was postponed to September 25 because of a clerical error. The submitters assert the actual reason was to allow the company more time to campaign against the union. At the September 25 meeting, the CAB heard arguments, reviewed the credentials of the parties, and set the representation election date for October 6, 1997, despite efforts by the CROC union to further postpone the proceedings. At this hearing, the CAB overruled objections by the CROC union that STIMAHCS lacked the appropriate certification to represent the Han Young workers in Baja California.

As the date of the election approached, the submitters claim that management continued its campaign of intimidation against STIMAHCS supporters and threatened workers with the loss of their jobs if that union won the election. Shortly prior to the election, the president of the local CAB, who had agreed to conduct the election, submitted his resignation. The submitters maintain, but do not substantiate, that this occurred at the instigation of the CROC and was intended to ensure an election outcome favorable to that organization.

On October 6, 1997, the representation election took place as scheduled at the offices of the CAB.... The submitters allege that the company transported a group of thirty-five workers, including supervisory personnel and new hires, to the voting site, where they were allowed to cast their ballots. According to the submitters, none of these people were eligible to vote but STIMAHCS representatives and supporters were prevented from checking the credentials of voters, whereas the credentials of STIMAHCS supporters were carefully scrutinized. Following the balloting, it was announced that STIMAHCS had won the election by a vote of 54–34 over the CROC.

* * *

At a CAB hearing on October 16, both STIMAHCS and the CROC challenged a number of the ballots cast at the representation election. The CAB then announced that it had concluded its proceedings in this case and would certify the result of the election after reviewing the evidence. However, on November 10, the CAB issued a ruling that nullified the election results on the grounds that STIMAHCS had failed to adequately substantiate that it had the support of the majority of the workers at the plant and that it lacked the proper registration to represent the workers at Han Young. Union representation remained with the CROC union....

Following considerable publicity on the case, the Mexican Federal Government intervened and mediated an agreement among the parties. The agreement called for a new representation election, to be conducted under the supervision of state and federal authorities. ...

The second representation election at Han Young took place on December 16, 1997. An affiliate of the CTM took part in this three-way election. The election was won again by STIMAHCS, by a vote of 30 for STIMAHCS, 26 for the CTM affiliate, and two for the CROC union.... On January 12, 1998, STIMAHCS was recognized by the CAB as the collective bargaining representative at the plant....

... Finally, the submitters allege that the company has hired additional workers as part of an effort to defeat STIMAHCS in a new representation election and that the CTM, in alliance with the CROC, has filed a petition for a new union election. The CAB has scheduled a hearing for May 21, 1998, at which a date for a new representation election will be set.

* * *

ANALYSIS

Freedom of Association

* * *

Mexican law provides that a representation election may be used to determine the majority preference when two or more unions contest for representation in the same workplace. A representation election took place on October 6. There is considerable testimonial evidence that the election was plagued with irregularities including changing the election date with little notice, threats to the workers supporting STIMAHCS, and the ability of persons without proper credentials to enter the voting premises and cast ballots.

[Federal Labor Law] Article 931(IV) provides that workers recruited after the date of the petition for union representation may not participate in the election. Neither may "employees of trust" (*trabajadores de confianza*). STIMAHCS filed for representation on August 8, 1997, and workers hired by Han Young after that date should not have been permitted to vote. The submitters assert, and workers testified, that ineligible workers were brought in by management in support of the CROC union, and were allowed, by CAB officials, to take part in the voting, despite the objections of STIMAHCS representatives. In addition to the testimony of the workers, it was reported by the print media that international observers present at the election recounted similar irregularities with the election process.

Despite considerable irregularities designed to influence the workers and the voting process, STIMAHCS won a convincing victory in the election. However, the CAB nullified the vote, ruling that STIMAHCS failed to demonstrate that it had the support of a majority of the workers in the workplace. The CAB stated that the representation election only showed the sympathies of the workers toward STIMAHCS during a given moment in time and was insufficient to prove that STIMAHCS had majority support. The CAB cited decisions by appeals courts and the Supreme Court dated 1969, 1971, 1972, 1973, and 1974 in support of this position. The CAB did not specify how a union was expected to demonstrate that it had majority support.

The CAB also ruled that STIMAHCS was registered before the Registrar of Associations of the Secretariat of Labor and Social Welfare as a national industrial union in the metallurgical sector, rather than the automotive sector, and could not, therefore, represent Han Young automobile workers in the state of Baja California. The CAB cited FLL Article 360 in support of this argument.

Contrary to the reasoning by the CAB that the election results were an insufficient basis for determining the bargaining representative, the Mexican NAO had previously informed the U.S. NAO that the Supreme Court of Mexico had, in 1979, ruled that the representation election (*recuento*) was the most effective way of determining the union preference of the majority of workers in a workplace. . . .

In nullifying the October 6 election results, the CAB also decided that STIMAHCS lacked the proper registration to represent workers at Han Young. The CAB's decision, reversing its earlier recognition of STIMAHCS as a registered union for the purpose of the representation election, seems inexplicable. Mexican labor law requires that a union or union organization be registered before the appropriate authorities, be they of the Federal Government or the state government. FLL Article 527 places a number of industries, including the metal and steel industry, under the jurisdiction of the Federal Government. Once registration is granted, the registered organization is authorized to represent itself and its members before state and Federal authorities. STIMAHCS was registered with the Federal Government and, according to the express language of FLL Articles 368 and 374, should have been recognized as a registered union before the Baja California CAB. Moreover, in arguing that the representation election, in itself, was not sufficient to determine the majority union, the CAB did not explain on what basis it chose to return representation to the CROC, which received fewer votes than STIMAHCS.

* * *

Moreover, the CAB verified STIMAHCS' credentials at the hearing held on September 25 before allowing the representation vote, rejecting at that time a challenge put forward by the CROC union that STIMAHCS lacked the legal authority to represent maquiladora workers in the state of Baja California. The decision of the CAB overturning the election result made no mention of this earlier decision which allowed the vote to take place and offered no explanation for the reversal.

* * *

FLL Article 387 requires an employer to enter into a collective bargaining agreement with the union in the establishment. If more than one union exists in the workplace, the employer must negotiate with the union that has representation rights (*titularidad*). Pablo Kang, Han Young Human Resources Director, testified at the February 18 hearing that he had not received official notice of the election results, ... Though FLL Article 890 requires the CAB to immediately notify the parties of its decisions, the employer was not officially notified of the results of the representation election until March 2, 1998, although the outcome had been common knowledge....

* * *

The irregularities that the Tijuana CAB permitted to take place during the first representation election, its reasoning in not recognizing STIMAHCS as the bargaining representative, and its delay in formally notifying Han Young of the results of the December 16 representation election, raise questions about its enforcement of those provisions of Mexico's FLL that govern procedures for determining union representation. These actions also raise questions about the impartiality of the CAB, particularly with regard to its duty to enforce the provisions of the FLL protecting workers from employer retaliation for the exercise of their freedom of association rights, and from employer interference in the establishment of a union.

Procedural Guarantees

Article 5.1 of the NAALC commits the Parties to ensure that labor tribunal proceedings are fair, equitable and transparent. Article 5.1(d) obligates the Parties to ensure that such proceedings are not unnecessarily complicated and do not entail unwarranted delays. Article 5.2(b) requires that final decisions in labor proceedings be made available without undue delay. Article 5.4 requires each Party to ensure that its labor tribunals are impartial, independent, and do not have a substantial interest in the outcome of the proceedings before it.

Submission 9702 raises the issue of compliance by Mexico with its procedural obligations under Article 5 of the NAALC. Namely, the submitters argue (1) that in permitting irregularities to occur during the representation election in favor of the CROC union, the CAB demonstrated that its proceedings are not fair and equitable, in violation of Article 5.1; (2) that in delaying the processing of workers' claims for unjustified dismissal and postponing the September 3 hearing, the CAB caused unwarranted delays in the case, in violation of Article 5.1(d); (3) that in failing to officially notify the parties to the representation election of the outcome, the CAB failed to make available, without undue delay, its final decision in the case, in violation of Article 5.2(b); and (4) that the failure to protect workers from dismissal for their union activities, the sudden change in the presidency of the CAB, the delay in certifying the election results, the earlier finding that STIMAHCS lacked the proper registration, and other actions by the CAB, demonstrate that it is not impartial and independent and is therefore in violation of Article 5.4.

COMPLIANCE WITH NAALC ARTICLES 5.1 AND 5.2

* * *

The Parties to the NAALC have a duty to promote labor rights by ensuring not only accessibility to tribunals but also that tribunals are impartial, independent and fair in applying the law. It is difficult to conceive of a legitimate reason why the CAB delayed until March 2 to officially inform the parties of the January 12 finding confirming the December 16 election result. This action by the CAB is troubling, especially when viewed within the context of its earlier decision of November 10 and the reasoning it provided for not recognizing STIMAHCS after the October 6 election.

COMPLIANCE BY MEXICO WITH NAALC ARTICLE 5.4

* * *

In its report on ministerial consultations on Submission No. 940003, the U.S. NAO made a number of findings on the union registration process in Mexico and the role of the CABs. Of relevance to Submission No. 9702 are the following:

. . .

The composition of the labor boards often complicates the registration of an independent union. The CABs are hybrid organizations that are administratively under the executive branch and dependent on the executive branch for their funding. However, they also fulfill a judicial role and, in the case of union registration, they have an administrative function. The labor representative on the CAB generally represents the incumbent or majority union, usually a CTM affiliate. Therefore, at least one member of the CAB has a competing interest with any independent union seeking registration.

Questions and Comments

1.   What allegations does the NAALC require for a submission to be accepted by a NAO? Refer to NAALC Article 16. How is the term "labor law" defined? Refer to Article 49, Compa.

2.   Against whom will the ALF's submission be brought? Vidrios, the employer? The CTM and its agents? The Mexican government? All three?

3.   What are some of the claims the ALF might make in its submission? Is there any claim that, on these facts, Mexico has violated its duty under NAALC Article 2 to "ensure that its labor law and regulations provide for high labor standards"? Refer to the foregoing provisions of Mexican and international law. Is there any claim that Mexico has violated its obligations under NAALC Articles 3, 4, or 5? Refer to Englehart, Human Resources Development Canada, and the NAO's Han Young Report. Has Mexico, in this problem, failed to enforce its own labor laws? Does that matter? Which laws?

4.   Does the language in NAALC Article 49.1 concerning the reasonable exercise of discretion or *bona fide* decisions concerning the allocation of resources alter your initial assessment of possible claims under Article 3? Can a NAFTA government enact laws that provide for high labor standards and then decline to enforce those laws with impunity under the NAALC on the grounds that it is concentrating its resources on other labor matters? Or does the NAALC create some baseline duty to fund the enforcement of labor laws one enacts?

5.   Does the ALF's submission present the type of controversy that could proceed from NAO consultations to ministerial consultations? Refer to NAALC Article 22. What does the term "any matter within the scope of this Agreement" mean?

6.   Is this the type of controversy that could proceed from ministerial consultations to review by an Evaluation Committee of Experts (ECE)? to consultations pursuant to NAALC Article 27? to an Article 29 arbitral panel? If not, why not? Refer to Compa.

7.   Can the ALF file a submission with the Mexican NAO? Why not? Which of the available forums, the U.S. NAO or Canadian NAO, would be the best place to file the ALF's submission? Is there any advantage to filing the submission in both countries? On what types of matters may one NAO request to consult with another NAO? Must such consultations occur? Refer to NAALC Article 21.

8. What is the best result that the ALF could hope for under the NAALC? Refer to Compa, Hansen.

9. Under the Labor Side Agreement, submissions by groups of non-governmental organizations (NGOs) that have banded together are frequent. Is there some advantage to making submissions as a group of NGOs as opposed to a single organization? Should the ALF join forces with other labor unions in Mexico and/or the United States in filing a submission under the NAALC?

10. Labor groups, by and large, have been disappointed with the NAALC. For example, "NAFTA's Labor Side Agreement: Fading Into Oblivion," published by the UCLA Center for Labor Research and Education, finds a significant benefit: "The NAALC has exposed violations of worker health and safety regulations—the sunshine effect—and the impact on the health of immigrant workers in the U.S. and on that of Mexican maquiladora workers." However, "The NAALC has failed to protect workers' rights to safe jobs. . . ." The number of cases has tapered off during the past several years, most likely due to the conclusion by the NGOs that usually filed the "public communications" on labor law violations that the process was not very effective, rather than to a general improvement in labor conditions or elsewhere in NAFTA. It is notable that the Commission on Labor Cooperation has not published an annual report for 2002 or any subsequent year.

11. In the U.S.–Chile FTA and CAFTA, a very different approach was taken to labor issues. In the Chile FTA, for example, labor is incorporated into the body of the agreement (Chapter 18). Violation of the principal, but circumscribed, labor obligation—"A Party shall not fail to effectively enforce its labor laws, through a sustained or recurring course of action or inaction, in a manner affecting trade between the Parties. . . ."—is enforceable under the general dispute resolution provisions of the agreement (Chapter 22). However, no trade sanctions but only monetary penalties are available for labor (or environmental) violations of the Chile FTA (Article 22.16), and the maximum penalty is US$15 million per year, which is to be paid into a fund for "appropriate labor or environmental initiatives." Perhaps most important in light of the UCLA Center comment, above, there is no NAO and no explicit provisions for "public submissions" by NGOs or private parties raising possible violations of the labor provisions. These provisions were accepted by the Congressional majorities that approved the Chile FTA, but some members have indicated that they would oppose CAFTA approval unless the labor (and environmental) provisions are strengthened.

PART B. THE UNITED STATES

SECTION I. THE SETTING

ChipCorp, Inc., one of the leading producers of micro machined multi-fiber array chips, micro-optics, and fiber optics, has plants in San Jose, California; Boston, Massachusetts; and Tijuana, Baja California,

Mexico. ChipCorp's products are distributed within the United States and exported to Asia and Latin America.

The company's workforce of about 1,200 is spread evenly among its three facilities. None of the employees at ChipCorp belongs to a union. Consequently, the employees tend to be paid less than other workers in the industry and do not receive health and retirement benefits that have become standard in the industry. Nonetheless, ChipCorp employees generally are happy with the company and have a strong sense of loyalty to it.

The Boston plant is the oldest and least profitable of the company's facilities, having lost money in some years. Moreover, Boston is no longer a rational company site considering the shift of activity to the West Coast and increased dealings with Asia. Although it made financial sense to close the Boston facility for a few years, ChipCorp kept it open for various reasons, including loyalty to long-term employees at the plant and the Boston community, the lack of a consensus within management to close the plant, and the substantial investment of capital and equipment made at the facility. Still, a sizeable minority of the company's directors consistently has pushed for closure. In contrast, the Tijuana facility was opened about two years after NAFTA took effect and rapidly has become the most profitable of the facilities. The company's overhead and expenses in Tijuana are low and, due to ChipCorp's investment in state of the art equipment, the workers' productivity is high.

Once rumors began to circulate that the company was considering closing the Boston facility, several employees from the plant approached the Technology Workers of America (TWA), hoping that unionization might forestall closure. Management first learned of the union activity when the TWA openly began soliciting support from ChipCorp employees. One manager commented to several workers: "If a union exists at our plant, the plant will fail. The cancer will eat us up and we will fall by the wayside. I'm not making a threat. I'm stating a fact." At a meeting convened to discuss unionization with the employees, the plant manager said: "It would be inappropriate for your company to comment on what it will or will not do if the plant is unionized. Whether this facility stays open or doesn't will depend on economics. We at ChipCorp are fortunate to have a growing operation in Mexico where we are able to produce when we become non-competitive here. I hope you will think very seriously before you take any action that will make your job a union job." As they ate lunch after the meeting, another manager joked with several employees: "I hope you guys are ready to pack up and move to Mexico."

In a matter of weeks, a majority of workers in the Boston plant had indicated a desire to join the union. The TWA petitioned the National Labor Relations Board (NLRB) to schedule a representation election at the Boston facility. Eight days before the election was to occur, ChipCorp's Board of Directors met and voted to shut down production of the micro-optics product line in Boston and layoff fifty workers. The company plans to relocate micro-optics production to Tijuana and, thereby, cut labor costs and increase profits.

To its surprise, the TWA ended up losing the representation election. It then filed unfair labor practice charges with the NLRB arguing that the statements and actions of ChipCorp management constituted intimidation of employees by means of an unlawful plant closing threat. Despite substantial legal precedent in favor of the TWA's position, the NLRB ruled that the union's arguments lacked merit. The NLRB held that the statements by ChipCorp managers were lawful predictions of a noncoercive nature or were jokes and not threats, and that the discontinuation of the micro-optics product line was motivated by economics, not anti-union animus. Further, the NLRB refused to adopt the TWA's view that *any* statements by management in the midst of a union organization campaign concerning unionization are threats *per se* and, therefore, constitute unfair labor practices.

Independent of the TWA's action, several of the laid off workers attempted to obtain relief under the federal Worker Adjustment and Retraining Notification Act (WARN). They were rebuffed by officials at the local NLRB office on the grounds that WARN benefits can be enforced only by filing suit in federal court. The workers were advised to consult private attorneys. In view of the cost of legal representation and delay involved in federal litigation, the workers dropped the matter.

SECTION II. FOCUS OF CONSIDERATION

One of the most common tactics used by employers in the United States to obstruct labor organization is the threat of plant closings. According to the Bureau of Labor Statistics, the primary cause of worker dislocation in the United States from 1991 to 1995 was plant closings. Of the millions of workers displaced in this way, nearly nine out of every ten were non-unionized. Total plant closures occur but are uncommon. Far more common are employer threats of closure should unionization succeed and partial closures through relocation of product lines, partial layoffs, and subcontracting. Plant closure can be a particularly effective anti-union strategy in companies with multiple plants where partial closure at one facility is used to send a message to employees at other facilities.

The body of labor law dealing with sudden or partial plant closings focuses on two issues: (1) what was the employer's motivation for completely or partially closing a plant and (2) distinguishing an employer's lawful expression of its views concerning unionization from unlawful threats of reprisal. The issues are complex because, in many cases, economic justification for a closing arguably is present, but so too is anti-union animus. Similarly, a manager's honest prediction of what may come to pass following unionization might reasonably be interpreted by workers as a threat.

Under the NAALC, the focus in this area of labor law is on whether the government has adopted laws that provide for high labor standards and, if so, whether in some instances the government's failure to find in favor of unions and against employers constitutes a failure to effectively enforce such laws. Consider these issues as you study the readings which follow.

SECTION III.   READINGS, QUESTIONS AND COMMENTS

LOWE, THE FIRST AMERICAN CASE UNDER THE NORTH AMERICAN AGREEMENT FOR LABOR COOPERATION
51 U. Miami L. Rev. 481 (1997).*

On June 14, 1994 La Conexion Familiar, Inc. ("LCF"), a subsidiary of Sprint corporation located in San Francisco, California, terminated its business due to alleged financial difficulties within eight days of a union certification election that promised to be the first successful representation drive among Sprint's long distance operators. LCF telemarketed long distance services, targeting recent Hispanic immigrants by providing all services and correspondence in Spanish. Notably, Sprint has no long distance employees represented by a union, although eighteen thousand employees are employed in their long distance division. In the face of what appeared to be a successful representation drive by the Communication Workers of America (CWA), LCF supervisors threatened plant closure should the union drive succeed; this despite the fact that such threats employed by management during election drives are illegal. In addition, many other unfair labor practices abounded at LCF, including the interrogation of employees concerning union activities, requests by supervisors that employees distribute anti-union buttons, management's solicitation of grievances of employees and the creation of the impression that management was conducting surveillance of employees' union activities.

Sprint maintained that LCF was closed because of its financial standing. While it is uncontroverted that LCF was performing poorly financially, the contention that financial status was the predominant factor motivating the LCF board of directors in its decision to close the company is vigorously disputed. The union asserts that a discriminatory union avoidance strategy motivated the decision to close LCF in violation of the statutory guarantees of the National Labor Relations Act (NLRA)—specifically, the rights contained in Section 8(a)(3) and, by necessary implication, Section 7.

The union points to evidence that, in spite of Sprint's assertions that it closed LCF due to its poor financial condition, Sprint was committed to retaining LCF as a going concern, a commitment that included giving the business time to implement a turn-around plan. This evidence includes the purchase of new expensive equipment, the expansion of office space, continued workforce training and the hiring of a new president one month before the decision to close. Additionally, the union argues that a falsely dated letter produced by a top Sprint labor official, memorializing a conversation that allegedly concerned placement of the soon-to-be terminated LCF employees, is circumstantial evidence of the company's anti-union sentiment. The union argues that such action demonstrates that Sprint was building a paper trail defense to the charge of discriminatory closing of the plant. The union additionally contends that Sprint's choice of paying terminated employees for sixty days pay rather giving them sixty days notice prior to the closing of certain categories of business, as required by the Worker Adjustment and Retraining Act, as is Sprint's usual pattern, demonstrates an unwillingness to risk the unionization of its workforce. This charge is buttressed by the fact that Sprint was forced to hire additional workers at its Dallas facility, where calls were routed following LCF's closing.

Sprint argues, however, that financial considerations rather than anti-union sentiment dictated closing LCF. Sprint further contends that the decision to close LCF was all but made at a board of directors' meeting held before the company was aware of the pending union organization drive. Sprint also argues that a consistently smaller customer base each month precluded the operation of LCF as a profitable business. Sprint counters the circumstantial evidentiary value of its decision to hire Maury Rosas, a new President for LCF, one month before closing by suggesting that Rosas had value as a potential employee of Sprint, irrespective of LCF's viability. Sprint also presented evidence that closing in July rather than waiting until the end of the fiscal year resulted in net savings of four million dollars. In summary, Sprint argued and continues to argue that the decision to close LCF stemmed from its poor financial performance rather than a union avoidance strategy.

The NLRA grants eligible employees the statutory right to organize and form unions for the purpose of collective bargaining. Section 7 of the NLRA guarantees workers, "the right to self-organization, to form, join, or assist labor organizations, to bargain collectively through representatives of their own choosing, and to engage in other concerted activities for the purpose of collective bargaining or other mutual aid or protection." Other statutory provisions of the NLRA are intended to safeguard the fundamental rights granted in Section 7. Section 8 of the NLRA includes as unfair labor practices, activities which interfere with Section 7. Specifically, Section 8(a)(3) prohibits "discrimination in regard to hire or tenure of employment or any term or condition of employment to encourage or discourage membership in any labor organization." An employer closing shop to avoid unionization of its workforce ostensibly violates the protective language of Section 8(a)(3), and by extension, the fundamental rights granted in Section 7.

American case law, however, has mitigated the clear mandate of these provisions. An employer may with impunity close its entire business simply to avoid unionization of its workforce, despite the statutory language of Sections 7 and 8. Only when an employer closes part of a larger enterprise in a discriminatory manner is the decision properly scrutinized under the standard of Section 8(a)(3). If, however, the plant is part of a larger concern, an employer's decision to close one of the shops is shielded from statutory remedies if it demonstrates that it had other "legitimate" motives, even where an anti-union motive exists. Therefore, legal decisions interpreting the mandate of section 8(a)(3) have injured the actual rights of American workers to organize into unions, delineated in Section 7.

This statutory structure, and, more importantly, its interpretation in case law, provided the framework through which the LCF closing was analyzed in the American legal system. Implicit to this analysis is the philosophic underpinning that capital should be able to freely and without impediment close shop, which in turn largely trumps the statutory rights granted in Section 7 of the NLRA. Because the doctrine governing partial closings is settled law, the philosophic assumptions underlying the law are largely veiled from judicial scrutiny. Adherence to precedent in the American judicial system precludes significant reordering of the values embedded in the doctrine governing Section 8(a)(3) closings.

Recently, however, a new forum has opened for challenges to labor doctrines that are inimical to the broad statutory rights ostensibly granted in the express language of the NLRA. The North American Agreement on Labor Cooperation (NAALC), the supplemental agreement to the North American Free Trade Agreement (NAFTA), provides a new venue in which to mount challenges to enforcement and implementation of American labor law.

Although designed with marked deference for the sovereignty of each nation, NAALC allows for complaints against other member nations for non-enforcement of their own labor laws. The result of political forces that threatened NAFTA's defeat, the labor accords were touted as an ameliorative response to poor Mexican working conditions and the downward pull they may exact on the American labor norm. The purpose of the labor agreements was to provide a model of transnational labor relations whereby each party could monitor and spur enforcement of the other party's internal labor policy.

The international forum available under NAALC does not require that domestic labor law remedies be exhausted, merely that actions and remedies to enforce domestic labor laws have been initiated. Thus, the NAALC forum may function as a concurrent alternative to the remedy sought in any of the member nations so long as there is some credible allegation that a signatory country is not enforcing its domestic labor laws. Labor groups in the U.S., initially among the most vehement detractors of NAFTA and NAALC, and who conceived of NAALC as the barest and flimsiest of protections, have begun to employ the process implemented by the labor accords to further effectuate enforcement of American labor principles embodied in the NLRA, in addition to enforcing Mexican labor law.

The LCF case may, and arguably should, become a prototype for a new type of labor case. Major areas of American labor law are settled in ways that preclude or significantly limit judicial challenges and meaningful remedies. The procedures that NAALC has put into place offer labor activists a way to challenge some of the implicit philosophic assumptions firmly embedded in American labor law. This Comment will focus upon the LCF case as it has and continues to proceed through the two track system contemplated by NAALC. This process will illuminate what are the beginnings of an emerging international strategy by labor unions to challenge domestic enforcement of American labor law.

LCF, INC. v. NATIONAL LABOR RELATIONS BOARD
129 F.3d 1276 (D.C. Cir.1997).

ANALYSIS

Terminating employees because of their union activity violates section 8(a)(3) and (1) of the National Labor Relations Act. ...Moreover, accelerating the timing of a management action that results in the termination of employees is also unlawful if done in response to union activity, even if the employer would have taken the same action at a later time.

Under the framework that the Supreme Court approved in *NLRB v. Transportation Management Corp.*, 462 U.S. 393, 399–403 (1983), *overruled in part on other grounds Dep't of Labor v. Greenwich Collieries*, 512 U.S. 267, 276–78 (1994), the NLRB's General Counsel must first establish that protected union activity "was a substantial or motivating factor" in the employer's closure decision. If the General Counsel meets that burden, then the employer may present the "affirmative defense" that it would have closed its facility at the same time, even in the absence of protected union activity and the employer's antiunion motivation. *Id.* at 401 ("[T]he [NLRB]'s construction of the statute permits an employer to avoid being adjudicated a violator by showing what his actions would have been regardless of his forbidden motivation. It extends to the employer what the Board considers to be an affirmative defense but does not change or add to the elements of the unfair labor practice that the General Counsel has the burden of proving under § 10(c).")....

This court's review of the NLRB's factual conclusions is highly deferential. We reject NLRB factual findings only if there is no substantial evidence in the record as a whole to support them. ..."So long as the Board's findings are reasonable, they may not be displaced on review even if the court might have reached a different result had the matter been before it de novo." ... However, this court's analysis "consider[s] not only the evidence supporting the Board's decision but also 'whatever in the record fairly detracts from its weight.' " ...

"The court's review of the Board's determination with respect to motive is even more deferential. Motive is a question of fact that may be inferred from direct or circumstantial evidence. In most cases only circumstantial evidence of motive is likely to be available. Drawing such inferences from the evidence to assess an employer's ... motive involves the experience of the Board, and consequently, the court gives substantial deference to inferences the Board has drawn from the facts, including inferences of impermissible motive." ...

This case presents the question of whether there is substantial evidence to support the first prong of the *Transportation Management Corp.* test, *i.e.*, NLRB's finding that antiunion animus "was a substantial or motivating factor" in Sprint's decision to close LCF. ... Locating direct evidence of antiunion motivation in a plant closure is often impossible, and here the NLRB's General Counsel has acknowledgedly amassed some relevant circumstantial evidence pointing to such motivation. In particular, the illegal antiunion campaign that LCF officials conducted in the spring of 1994 is an important piece of evidence.

The NLRB found that Sprint had decided at the May 6 board meeting to keep LCF open indefinitely; since nothing significant happened between then and the July 6 meeting–except for the scheduling of a representation election and the emergence of evidence that union victory was likely–it inferred that the changing labor situation at LCF explained Sprint's new course. The NLRB's conclusion that Sprint acted out of antiunion animus, however, ultimately lacks substantial evidence in the record. Simply put, the enormous body of financial data and testimony recording LCF's extremely serious financial decline dominates the record and indicates that, as the ALJ concluded, "Sprint had valid and compelling economic reasons for closing LCF."

Indeed, the ALJ's factual findings, based on fourteen days of hearings and voluminous documentary evidence, demonstrate that LCF's prospects were grim. By March 1994, Vice President Meyer's financial projections indicated that LCF would make $12 million less in 1994 than Sprint had expected, losing $4 million in the year rather than earning its anticipated $8 million annual profit. This "ominous forecast," *id.* at 13, was predicated on the basis of a number of troubling economic indicators. LCF's "churn rate," the percentage of its customer base lost each month, was 20.5% in January 1994, 18.5% in February, and 22.5% in March. In addition, LCF's telemarketers were unable to attract enough new customers to even keep the customer base stable. The rate of sales per hour for LCF's telemarketers declined by approximately 50% between January and March. By May, LCF was losing 1.41 customers for every customer that it was acquiring; LCF lost about 16,000 customers in May and June alone. By June 30, LCF's customer base had declined to about 85,000 customers, down from 130,000 in January. By July 14, when LCF closed its doors, LCF had just 76,532 customers.

This evidence of LCF's severe and continuing financial decline overwhelms the circumstances on which the NLRB relies. In fact, it renders NLRB's characterization of the May 6 meeting, which is the cornerstone of the NLRB's decision, implausible. The mere fact that the LCF board decided on May 6 to reconvene in sixty days after fully considering all of its options does not suggest, in light of all the other record evidence, that the board was then "inclined toward the option of keeping the business going for at least long enough to allow the turn-around initiatives to take hold" and only changed its collective mind at some point on or before July 6. The decision to hire Mr. Rosas ultimately does not alter the tenor of this meeting. Sprint may have mistreated Mr. Rosas by hiring him and giving him the go-ahead to manage LCF for five weeks without telling him that the board was considering closing LCF. But one of Sprint's largest concerns about LCF was that its lack of a full-time, on-site manager required Vice President Meyer to devote approximately one day a week to a small, failing, and geographically distant part of the business under his jurisdiction. Moreover, if, as seems more natural, the May 6 board decision is read as a sign that the board was already seriously concerned about LCF, then the NLRB's focus on the lack of change in LCF's finances during the sixty days between the May meeting and the July meeting no longer makes sense: LCF may not have been losing money and customers at a faster rate between May and July, but it was surely plummeting downward on its unprofitable course.

* * *

Finally, the timing of Sprint's actions is not sufficient to compensate for the other evidentiary deficiencies in the NLRB's decision. To be sure, the LCF board voted twenty-two days before the scheduled representation election to close LCF. Sprint's further decision to dismiss the LCF employees immediately and pay them for sixty days, rather than giving the LCF employees advance notice and requiring them to work during that period, conveniently terminated the LCF employees just eight days before the representation election that CWA was expected to win. But the July 6 meeting had been planned since May 6, well before CWA filed its representation petition. Moreover, the General Counsel and CWA have put forth no evidence of antiunion animus in the days after July 6, except for the bare fact of Sprint's timing. Sprint, in turn, has articulated a number of legitimate business reasons for its decision to terminate the LCF employees immediately, including the recognition that there was no point in having the LCF telemarketers continue to sell a product that would no longer be available. In a stronger case, the timing of Sprint's actions, particularly after July 6, might have taken the General Counsel's case over the edge. But here timing is not enough to make an otherwise unpersuasive NLRB decision survive judicial scrutiny.

COMMISSION FOR LABOR COOPERATION, PLANT
CLOSINGS AND LABOR RIGHTS
<www.naalc.org/english/reports.html> (1997).

Decisions of the National Labor Relations Board (NLRB or the Board) and federal courts have established the following basic principles in cases involving plant closings or threats of plant closing in connection with workers' organizing efforts:

1. An employer may not close a plant to avoid dealing with a union, to retaliate against workers for forming a union, or to discourage union organizing at another facility of the employer. Such an unfair labor practice may be remedied by an order to reopen the plant and rehire the employees. However, an employer may lawfully decide to go completely out of business and cease operating altogether, even for an anti-union motivation.

2. An employer may close a plant for legitimate economic considerations if the closing is not motivated by anti-union considerations.

3. An employer may not threaten to close a plant in reprisal for union activity.

4. An employer may express any views, argument, or opinion about plant closings or other possible consequences of unionization, as long as such expression contains no threat of reprisal or force, or promise of benefit.

The cases that arise in U.S. labor law posing issues of plant closings or threats of plant closing in connection with the workers' right to organize are among the most difficult and complex in labor jurisprudence. There is no "rule" for such cases, because proving motivation (anti-union versus economic), or proving whether certain statements amount to an unlawful threat or a lawful expression of views, argument, or opinion, is always a matter of interpretation of the evidence.

* * *

ELEMENTS OF THE U.S. LEGAL FRAMEWORK

Common Law Rights of Ownership

As a general principle, the common law places no restrictions on an owner's power to dispose of means of production through sale, lease, transfer, relocation, shutdown, or other form of alienability because of such a transaction's effects on workers. Until passage of the National Labor Relations Act of 1935 (NLRA or "Wagner Act," after the name of its author in the U.S. Senate) and its upholding by the U.S. Supreme Court in 1937, U.S. employers enjoyed unfettered power to close a plant in response to unionization drives by their employees, or to threaten plant closings if their employees chose union representation.

Notwithstanding this, much of U.S. heavy industry was unionized in the 1930s and 1940s through mass organizing drives and "sit down" strikes. An actual closing was not so easy at large-scale industrial plants representing huge investments, which characterized the period of the early 20th century. Many of these plants in the steel, auto, electrical, rubber, aircraft, and other mass production industries were relatively new, vertically integrated, and highly productive, so employers could not easily "walk away" from them, or credibly threaten to close them, if workers unionized.

The NLRA

The NLRA changed the law regarding plant closings and threats of plant closing related to workers' organizing efforts. The Wagner Act affirmed workers' freedom of association, defined certain anti-union conduct as an "unfair labor practice," and prohibited such conduct.

Section 7 of the NLRA extended to most private sector employees "the right to self-organization, to form, join, or assist labor organizations, to bargain collectively through representatives of their own choosing, and to engage in other concerted activities for the purpose of collective bargaining or other mutual aid or protection."

The Wagner Act also created a means to protect these rights by defining unfair labor practices in Sections 8(a)(1) and 8(a)(3) of the NLRA. An unfair labor practice violates the law and is subject to the remedies provided by the Act.

An anti-union plant closing, or a threat to close a plant in reprisal for workers' organizing activity, violates Section 8(a)(1) of the NLRA, which makes it an unfair labor practice to "interfere with, restrain, or coerce employees in the exercise of the rights guaranteed in Section 7." The Act empowers the NLRB to issue "cease-and-desist" orders and other remedial steps to prevent 8(a)(1) violations.

The Act provides for reinstatement and back pay (or other "make-whole" remedies) for workers who are discharged or otherwise discriminated against for such activity. For workers affected by a plant closing, the remedy may include an order to reopen the plant and re-employ the workers. The Act also empowers the Labor Board to set aside an election and order a new election if plant closing threats destroyed "laboratory conditions" for employee free choice of representation, whether or not an unfair labor practice charge is filed.

The Employer Free Speech Clause of the Taft–Hartley Act

While the Wagner Act of 1935 has been described as "Labor's Magna Carta," the 1947 Labor Management Relations Act (LMRA or "Taft–Hartley Act," after its legislative sponsors) reflected management interests. Opposed by U.S. unions as an anti-labor law while supported by management as a restoration of balance in the law, the LMRA added a new clause, Section 8(c), known as the "employer free speech" provision. It states that :

> The expressing of any views, argument, or opinion, or the dissemination thereof, whether in written, printed, graphic or visual form, shall not constitute or be evidence of an unfair labor practice under any of the provisions of this Act, if such expression contains no threat of reprisal or force or promise of benefit.

Section 8(c) codified a trend in court rulings that established the employer's right to communicate its views on unionization to employees. In the decades since then, the NLRB and the courts have introduced complicated and often shifting rules about how strongly, directly, or aggressively employers may speak out against unionization, including through such devices as "captive audience meetings" where workers are required to hear management speeches against union organization. Under these rules, employers are allowed to discuss with employees the possible consequences of unionization, including plant closings, as long as the employer's statements do not contain a "threat of reprisal or force or promise of benefit."

Critics have long argued that management's ability to discuss plant closings, however apparently neutral the discussion may be, inherently amounts to a threat of reprisal given the employer's acknowledged power to close a facility. Defenders of 8(c) argue that management cannot be denied its free speech rights to convey its opposition to unionization and to objectively discuss issues, including plant closings, as long as the discussion does not amount to a threat. Since this is a matter of interpretation of management statements, the NLRB and the courts closely scrutinize such statements in the overall context of company actions in an organizing campaign. The result is that the Board or the courts might find the same words permissible in one case and an unlawful threat in another case. Each case rises and falls on its own unique facts and circumstances as to whether employer statements stop short of a threat, or cross the line and become a threat.

Significantly, the Taft–Hartley Act did not diminish Section 7 rights or change the Wagner Act's definitions of unfair labor practices by employers. Sections 8(a)(1) and (3) of the Act remained intact. The statute preserved the unlawfulness of threats to close a plant to discourage union activity, and of the actual closing of a plant in reprisal for union activity.

Plant Closings: The Wright Line Test

In plant closing cases, the issue of motivation is paramount. Did the employer close for legitimate economic reasons or for unlawful anti-union reasons? This issue is even more difficult in "mixed motive" cases where both considerations are present.

The NLRB and the courts apply the same test to plant closing cases that they apply to unfair labor practice cases whereby they allege the discriminatory discharge of an individual employee for attempting to form a union. The employer usually responds that the employee was terminated for legitimate reasons such as absenteeism, misconduct, poor performance, and so on. Such cases can be either a "pretext" case, alleging that the employer's excuse is completely false and fabricated, or a "mixed motive" case, where there is some evidence of employee wrongdoing as well as evidence of anti-union motivation of the employer.

The test for such cases was elaborated in the NLRB's *Wright Line* decision. Under this ruling, the NLRB General Counsel first has the burden of proving that the employee's union activity was a motivating factor in the employer's action. If the General Counsel establishes a case of apparent anti-union motivation, the burden of proof shifts to the employer to demonstrate that the discharge was for legitimate, job-related causes. If the employer fails to prove any legitimate cause, it is a pretext case, and the employee is reinstated regardless of the degree of unlawful anti-union motivation. If the employer succeeds in proving some level of legitimate, business-related motivation, it is a mixed motive case. The employer must prove that the employee would have been terminated even in the absence of an anti-union motivation.

Plant closing cases usually pose the issue even more starkly. An employer can nearly always present some legitimate business reason for closing a plant, which is a much weightier action than discharging an individual employee. Thus, these cases usually present the mixed motive posture. The General Counsel first has the burden of showing that anti-union motivation is an element in the decision to close. Evidence could include such matters as the timing of the closing in relation to the union organizing effort, or statements by managers and supervisors suggesting that the closing is related to the unionization. The burden then shifts to the employer to show that the decision to close would have been made anyway, and to provide evidence of business, accounting, marketing, or other economic considerations motivating the decision.

Threats of Plant Closing: The Gissel Balancing Test

In the landmark *Gissel* case, the U.S. Supreme Court established the standards for balancing an employer's right to express any views, argument, or opinion on plant closings with the employees' right to organize. The court stated that balancing those rights "must take into account the economic dependence of the employees on their employers" and the "necessary tendency" of employees to perceive implied threats in statements "that might be more readily dismissed by a more disinterested ear."

An employer may make a prediction as to the precise effect he believes unionization will have, but such a prediction must be carefully phrased on the basis of objective fact involving demonstrably probable consequences beyond his control. If there is any implication that the employer may take action for reasons unrelated to economic necessity, the statement is an unlawful threat.

Remedies

The NLRB normally views an order to reopen the plant and rehire the workers as the proper remedy for an anti-union plant closing, unless the employer can demonstrate that reopening would endanger its continued viability. In this case, remedies are usually limited to back pay. The Board may order the employer to offer employment to affected workers at other facilities of the employer and to pay workers' the costs of moving to a new location. It should be recalled, however, that such remedies apply only when the employer relocates work or maintains operations elsewhere. Under the *Darlington* doctrine, there is no remedy when an employer goes entirely out of business for anti-union motivations.

NLRB decisions are routinely appealed to the federal courts. While generally the courts maintain a doctrine of "deference" to the Board's specialized expertise in labor relations matters, federal courts may reverse or modify Board decisions. In plant closing cases, some federal courts make the test one of "undue burden" on the employer rather than the viability of the enterprise. Under this standard, NLRB orders to reopen a plant are sometimes overturned by the federal court reviewing the Board's decision.

The remedy for plant closing threats is different from the remedy for a closing. The normal remedy for plant closing threats is a "cease-and-desist" order. The NLRB orders the employer (1) to cease and desist from threatening to close the plant, and (2) to repudiate the earlier threats by posting a notice at the workplace promising not to repeat the threat. In some cases the Board orders the employer to repudiate the threat in the same manner that the threat was made—in a letter to employees' homes, for example, or in a meeting with employees.

Critics argue that the mere posting of a notice or other promise not to repeat the threat is an empty remedy. They maintain that the effect of the threat remains, despite the employer's new statements to the contrary, as ordered by the NLRB, because of the employer's inherent power to carry out the threat. This argument is not accepted in U.S. labor law jurisprudence. However, U.S. law does provide that in extraordinary cases where plant closing threats are part of a pattern of massive unfair labor practices that would destroy a union's majority support and make a fair election impossible, the NLRB is empowered to issue an order to the employer to recognize and bargain with the union, either without an election or even if the union lost the election. This is also based on the *Gissel* ruling of the U.S. Supreme Court.

* * *

EARLY WARNING AND SUDDENNESS OF PLANT CLOSINGS

* * *

The Worker Adjustment and Retraining Notification Act (WARN) was enacted in 1988 to improve the adjustment prospects for displaced workers by providing workers and communities advance warning of impending dislocations. Under the WARN Act, certain firms are required to provide 60 days' advance notice to workers prior to a mass layoff or plant closing that will last more than 6 months and affect at least 50 workers.

In addition to the WARN Act, which is a federal requirement, numerous states have enacted advance warning legislation. Nine states enacted plant closing laws prior to the WARN Act enactment, and several others have since enacted such laws. The state requirements vary, with some exceeding the WARN Act 60–day requirement and others offering other improvements to the federal legislation.

Two exceptions to the WARN Act allow reduced notice requirements that are particularly relevant to this study. Given that the "intent" or "cause" of a plant closing is a key concern of this study, i.e., whether a plant closing was motivated by economic or anti-union reasons, exceptions to the WARN Act are useful to analyze.

The first exception is the so called "faltering company" exception, which applies only to plant closings. Under the Act, companies are allowed to provide less than the required 60–day notice in situations in which the announcement of a closing would adversely affect the company's ability to gain financing or new business that may keep the company afloat. Specifically, the exception applies if the company (1) is actively seeking capital or business at the time the 60–day notice would have been required, (2) possesses a realistic opportunity to obtain the financing or business sought, (3) has the ability to demonstrate that business sought would be sufficient to enable the employer to avoid or postpone the shutdown, and (4) believes in good faith that giving notice would preclude the employer from obtaining the needed capital or business.

A second important exception to the WARN Act's 60–day requirement is the "unforeseeable business circumstances" exception, applied to a sudden, unexpected action or condition outside the employer's control, such as the loss of a major contract, a strike at a major supplier of the employer, or a sudden dramatic economic downturn. Exceptions are also granted for temporary projects or facilities and strike or lockout situations.

Except for those employers who meet the requirements for the exceptions allowed under the Act, employers that do not provide the required 60–day notice are liable for monetary damages to employees who should have been notified under the Act. Such employees are eligible for damages including 1 day's pay plus benefits for each day that notice was not provided, for up to 60 days. In addition, employers are liable to the local government for damages of up to $500 a day for each day without notice.

A recent Supreme Court ruling reaffirmed the right of unions to file suit on behalf of employees to recover damages under the Act. This right had been questioned by some employers, who argued that only individual workers had standing to file these suits.

A 1993 study by the U.S. General Accounting Office (GAO) and related academic research since then have highlighted some of the shortcomings of the WARN Act. According to the GAO report, the

WARN Act, in its current form, excludes 98 percent of American businesses and leaves 64 percent of U.S. workers unprotected against sudden plant closings and mass layoffs. The flaws result primarily from the Act's narrow requirements, which cover only the following: (1) businesses with a total workforce of 100 or more employees; (2) plant closings that affect 50 or more workers; (3) mass layoffs of 50 or more workers, where those workers represent at least one-third of the workforce at that site; (4) mass layoffs where 500 or more workers are affected; and (5) full-time workers (i.e. part-time workers are not covered). The 1993 GAO report found that more than 10,000 WARN Act notice violations have occurred since its enactment, but only some 100 lawsuits for WARN violations have been filed.

Questions and Comments

1. Does the TWA have any NAALC claim it can assert against the United States government in a public submission? Refer to NAALC Articles 2, 3, 4 and 5; Lowe.

2. Assume that a group of several U.S. labor organizations is interested in making WARN Act damages more accessible to workers injured by sudden plant closings. Using the case of the laid off ChipCorp workers who desired relief under the WARN Act as an example, what are some of the claims that might be made in a NAALC submission on behalf of such workers? Refer to NAALC Article 4. Would you recommend that they file with the Canadian or Mexican NAO or both? Why?

3. Does the language in NAALC Article 49.1 concerning the reasonable exercise of discretion or *bona fide* decisions concerning the allocation of resources bar the assertion of an Article 4 claim?

4. Assuming the Mexican NAO were to accept a submission on behalf of the laid off workers seeking WARN Act relief, what might consultations between that NAO and the U.S. NAO look like? Does the NAALC provide for the direct participation of private parties in those consultations? Now suppose the workers at the Boston plant are largely Hispanic? Does that change your thinking?

5. Assuming the workers seeking WARN Act relief filed a submission with the *Canadian* NAO that subsequently advanced to ministerial consultations, what does consultation at the ministerial level add to the equation that was not present in the preceding NAO-to-NAO consultations?

6. Is this the type of controversy that could proceed from ministerial consultations to review by an Evaluation Committee of Experts (ECE)? If not, why not?

7. What is the best result that the workers seeking WARN Act relief could hope for under the NAALC? In this respect, is this CLC Report on "Plant Closings and Labor Rights" encouraging?

PROBLEM 10.2 DISCRIMINATION IN THE WORK- PLACE: FARM–WORKERS IN THE UNITED STATES AND PREGNANCY DISCRIMINATION IN MEXICO

PART A. THE UNITED STATES

SECTION I. THE SETTING

A recent report by the Association of Farmworker Opportunity Programs concluded: "Whether a farm worker is an adult or a child, a migrant or a seasonal worker, no other people in our society work harder, with as little protections from exploitation, and in return for so few opportunities or benefits. The farm worker adult and child make tremendous sacrifices in health, education, housing, and financial security in order to help provide the abundant supply of low-cost food that we as a nation take for granted."

Currently (2002–2004), an estimated five million people are employed as farm workers in U.S. fields stretching from California's Central Valley, to the Midwest, to Florida. Their labor is essential to the success of U.S. agriculture. Migrant farm workers spend the growing season traveling from worksite to worksite, living in makeshift housing along the way. The ranks of farm workers include U.S. citizens, legally resident foreign nationals, and undocumented aliens. Most migrant farm workers are Hispanic. The largest groups of migrants come from Texas' lower Rio Grande Valley and Mexico.

The National Safety Council classifies agricultural labor as the third most dangerous occupation in the country, behind mining and construction. One reason for this is that migrants work long hours (up to 100 hours a week), usually under the open sun in hot fields with little access to drinking water and sanitation. Because many are paid a "piece" rate (per bushel or basket) rather than a minimum hourly wage, farm worker incomes are very low. The average total annual income for farm worker families is less than $7,000. Farm workers frequently are exposed to toxic pesticides in violation of federal occupational safety and health regulations. In fields and canning facilities, migrant farm workers often are seriously injured as a result of exposure to unguarded machinery with sharp moving parts. According to the U.S. Center for Disease Control, the average life expectancy of migrant farm workers is twenty years less than that of the average American. Housing supplied by employers ordinarily consists of a one-room cabin per family and sometimes is substandard in condition, with dangerous and exposed live electrical wiring, insect infestations, rodents and other pests, and no bathroom facilities.

Perhaps the most alarming labor problem in U.S. commercial agriculture is the widespread use of child labor. It is estimated that from

300,000 (GAO) to 800,000 (United Farm Workers) children are working in U.S. agriculture annually. Exemptions under federal child labor laws permit children under twelve years of age to work in agriculture in excess of forty hours per week. Authorities have discovered children as young as six years-old working in fields. Families feel compelled to put young children to work to generate additional income. It is not surprising that school dropout rates for migrant children are nearly double the national average. By disrupting the children's education, such work ensures that the cycle of poverty is perpetuated. Added to this is the fact that young children are even more vulnerable than adults to serious injury from tractors and other farm machinery.

Farm worker advocacy groups have amassed an impressive body of evidence establishing systematic violations of federal and state labor laws, and filed numerous complaints with federal and state labor authorities. The claims asserted range from wage and hour complaints, to hazardous working conditions, to child labor violations. Often, government officials have expressed an inability to respond due to severe under funding. In San Francisco, for example, there are a total of only seven federal inspectors to patrol agricultural producers in a ten-county area that encompasses over 2,000 farms, vineyards, and other agricultural sites–and only one of the inspectors speaks Spanish. As a result of backlogs, the Department of Labor is unable to begin investigating wage claims for eighteen months. When advocates approached an OSHA investigator to initiate a complaint, he discouraged them from proceeding, saying it takes so long to investigate. Even when inspections are conducted and violations are found, employer fines and penalties are minimal. In most cases, it is cheaper for the employer to pay OSHA than it is to comply with the law in the first instance. The situation at the state level is even worse. The California Human Rights Commission, for example, often takes up to five years to investigate and decide employment-related claims.

As you read the excerpts which follow, assume that you are a recent law school graduate working on a fellowship with the United Farmworkers of America (UFA) in California and that the UFA wishes to lead a coalition of farm worker organizations in making a submission under the NAALC.

SECTION II. FOCUS OF CONSIDERATION

History confirms that the U.S.-Mexico border is merely a temporary impediment to inevitable and continuous human migration flows. Such migration serves important economic and political functions both in Mexico and the United States. For example, migrants can solve temporary labor shortages in U.S. agriculture and, simultaneously, serve as an important source of income for family members remaining in Mexico. Although migrants fulfill such critical functions, it is politically easy to disregard the needs of foreign workers or to concentrate scarce public resources on the enforcement of labor protections in other areas. In many instances, the immediate needs of the migrants for security, fair treatment, safe working conditions, and appropriate pay are sacrificed to serve the larger needs of governments and national economies.

The case of migrant farm workers in the United States touches upon three of the NAALC's central concerns–labor protections for children and young persons, prevention of occupational injuries and illnesses, and protection of migrant workers. The confluence of these NAALC priorities in one workplace setting serves as an excellent test for the strength of the U.S. commitment to carry out the Agreement in a meaningful sense. By entering the NAALC, did the U.S. government commit to undertake sweeping and expensive new labor law enforcement campaigns in sectors such as agriculture, or does the NAALC imply a less substantial obligation? If the U.S. government were to persist in failing to effectively enforce U.S. labor law in migrant farm worker settings, does the NAALC make possible the imposition of meaningful sanctions or is the NAALC merely a paper tiger? Consider these points as you read the excerpts which follow.

SECTION III. READINGS, QUESTIONS AND COMMENTS

LEHRFELD, PATTERNS OF MIGRATION: THE REVOLVING DOOR FROM WESTERN MEXICO TO CALIFORNIA AND BACK AGAIN

8 La Raza L.J. 209 (1995).*

THE CHANGING ATTITUDES TOWARD MEXICAN IMMIGRATION: 1930–1964

The second phase of immigration policies included both xenophobia and reactionism on the part of the U.S. government as well as an agreement between the U.S. and Mexican governments for an official temporary worker program. In response to the Great Depression, the U.S. government had reversed their open border policy toward Mexican migrants. The Great Depression created massive unemployment and desperation. During the Depression, Mexicans migrants fared much worse than any other group because, as temporary foreign workers, they were the most vulnerable. In fact, when immigrants and migrants were laid off from their jobs, they were not permitted the same economic relief granted to U.S. citizens. When Mexicans were finally expelled from the United States, 85,000 left voluntarily and 415,000 were forcibly repatriated. Unemployment and nativist sentiments seem the most likely explanation of this policy shift.

Gradually, however, this antipathy towards immigrants softened. One example can be seen in the New Deal legislation that provided education to the children of immigrants thereby making settlement in the U.S. more enticing. Moreover, when the labor shortages of World War II became apparent, the U.S. government once again encouraged migration.

* Copyright © 1995 La Raza Law Journal. Reprinted with permission.

During this same period in Mexico, the government of President Lázaro Cárdenas enacted the *Reparto Agrario*. The *Reparto Agrario* broke up the hacienda system and established the communal land system also known as the *ejido* system. Cárdenas responded to the needs of returnees by offering them agricultural incentives. However, the regime that succeeded Cárdenas supported the interests of large, private, export-oriented agriculture. "Through its manipulation of credit markets, irrigation projects and control of agricultural innovation and diffusion, [the Mexican government] encouraged the exploitation of the richest and most productive agricultural areas of the country by large firms." Consequently, the agricultural industry managed to appropriate much of the *ejidatorio*'s land. Rural landholders were left with low quality land that could not compete in the market. Eventually, the Mexican government reasoned that migrant income actually subsidized agricultural production in the Western Meso Central. Thus, they began to appreciate the benefits of a "safety valve that alleviated the poverty in some Mexican regions."

Mexico and the U.S. agreed to the Bracero Accord, a temporary agricultural worker program designed to fulfill the increasing labor demand in the U.S. and provide an outlet for the abundant labor supply in rural Mexico. It reflected a new "pragmatic approach to immigration" from both sides of the border. The Mexican government appreciated the benefits and manipulated the Bracero Program to calm social unrest in certain areas. Mexican officials distributed 50% of the Bracero contracts to areas that had strong counterrevolutionary movements, such as the *Sinarquista* movement. For its part, the U.S. government set the established standards for the wages and working conditions of temporary guest workers.

After legalizing and systematizing a pattern of temporary immigration for over 20 years, in 1964, the Bracero Program finally ended. In total, "4.5 million Mexicans worked as braceros in the United States, and at its height in the late 50s, more than 400,000 migrated each year." These workers came mostly from the states of Jalisco, Michoacan, Guanajuato and Zacatecas. One of the reasons cited for the termination of the program was the mechanization of certain agricultural crops in the U.S. Another reason cited was the activism of Chicanos who had convinced Congress that Mexican contract laborers were admitted to the U.S. in order "to oversupply the labor market to depress wages and to break strikes."

RESTRICTIONISM VERSUS LAISSEZ–FAIRE: 1965–PRESENT

The end of the Bracero Program in 1964 marks the beginning of a third period of U.S.-Mexico immigration policy. In 1965, the U.S. government acted once again to modify immigration laws. These amendments altered the Immigration and Nationality Act of 1952 by emphasizing family reunification over desirable labor market skills. "These amendments were later modified to eliminate separate hemispheric quotas and establish a worldwide ceiling for visas subject to numerical limitation."

Yet despite these modifications, the family members of Mexicans residing in the U.S. continued to be exempt from the National Origins Act country quotas.

In the 1970s, various groups began to pressure the U.S. government to restrict immigration. One of the most influential of these groups was the Federation for American Immigration Reform (FAIR). The pressure finally resulted in the compromise legislation of the 1986 Immigration Reform and Control Act (IRCA). This act stressed a three-pronged approach to combating illegal immigration: 1) Granting amnesty to undocumented migrants; 2) Prohibiting the hiring of subsequent undocumented migrants; and 3) Increasing border enforcement. However, IRCA has proved difficult to enforce, particularly against employers who benefit from undocumented migrant labor. As a way to avoid fines, employers simply began to rely on farm labor contractors who could recruit Mexican workers and who would vouch for the documented status of their recruits. It made no difference to the U.S. employers if the workers were documented since the contractors would bear the burden of any fines.

During this same period, the Green Revolution penetrated the Mexican agricultural sector. The Green Revolution modernized agriculture by introducing new seed varieties and chemical fertilizers. Small landholders shifted away from subsistence crops to cash crops while, at the same time, incorporating the new technology and mechanization. As a consequence, agricultural productivity rose while demand for day laborers decreased. Fortunately for the unemployed, migrant networks were well established in both countries by that point, thereby increasing the accessibility of jobs in the U.S. In total, from 1965 to 1985, approximately 1.5 million persons arrived in the U.S. from Mexico and of that number only 300,000 were undocumented.

Simultaneously, the Mexican government initiated the Border Industrialization Program to develop industry on the border and substitute for the lost bracero employment. The government established special trade zones that could liberally import and export without tariffs. As a result, *maquiladora* factories began appearing to manufacture and assemble products for an international market. However, since maquiladora employers preferred to hire young women, maquiladora employment has never served as a substitute for the bracero program.

In the 1980s, an economic crisis in Mexico created an additional economic force that would propel migrants northward. The crisis followed the rapid growth that had been generated by the Mexican government borrowing large amounts of foreign capital. When oil prices fell, Mexico was heavily indebted. In 1982, the gross domestic product fell by 4.7%, unemployment rates rose to 8% in three major cities, and wages fell 25% between 1981 and the summer of 1983. To make matters worse, the inflation rate reached 480%. As a consequence of these dire circumstances, documented migration grew 29% while undocumented migration increased by 82% from 1982–1987.

For all of these reasons, Mexico depended heavily on U.S. migration as a safety valve. As a consequence, the Mexican government did not want to risk a closed border with the United States. The Mexican government eased their earlier vigilant pressure on the U.S. government to protect migrants. They feared that any pressure would prompt an increase in restrictions rather than facilitate their goal of increasing migrant worker safeguards. In fact, the Mexican government excused itself entirely from the debate concerning the 1986 passage of IRCA. Overall, this reluctance to criticize U.S. policy toward Mexican migrants marked the beginning of the Mexican government's "laissez-faire approach" to Mexico–U.S. migration.

During this period, the Mexican government supported migration because Mexican officials recognized the economic benefit of migrant income sent home to Mexico. It had proved an invaluable supplement to rural income during periods of growth and change. Moreover, income remittances to the home communities helped pay for infrastructure development and increased the standard of living for families who had sent a member abroad. In 1990, "the money migrant workers sent to Mexico (including Social Security payments) represented 1.5% of Mexico's gross domestic product for that year and exceeded the value of agricultural and livestock exports and foreign investment the same year."

U.S. DEPARTMENT OF AGRICULTURE, MIGRANT AND SEASONAL AGRICULTURAL WORKER PROTECTION ACT

<www.usda.gov/oce/oce/labor-affairs/mspasumm.htm> (1992).

The Migrant and Seasonal Agricultural Worker Protection Act (MSPA), passed in 1983, was designed to provide migrant and seasonal farmworkers with protections concerning pay, working conditions, and work-related conditions, to require farm labor contractors to register with the U.S. Department of Labor, and to assure necessary protections for farmworkers, agricultural associations, and agricultural employers.

SUMMARY

The MSPA is the major Federal law that deals exclusively with agricultural employment. It was enacted to protect migrant and seasonal farmworkers on matters of pay and working and work-related conditions, to require farm labor contractors to register with the U.S. Department of Labor, and to assure necessary protections for farmworkers, agricultural associations, and agricultural employers.

The major requirements of MSPA are:

1. farm labor contractors and each of their employees who will be performing farm labor contractor activities must obtain a certificate of registration from the U.S. Department of Labor before they can start farm labor contractor activities,

2. farm labor contractors, agricultural employers, and agricultural associations must disclose to migrant and seasonal agricultural workers information about wages, hours, and other working conditions, and about housing when provided,

3. workers must be provided with written statements of earnings and deductions,

4. if transportation is provided, vehicles used must be safe and properly insured, and

5. if housing is provided, it must meet safety and health standards.

The law requires people who use the services of a farm labor contractor to take reasonable steps to determine that the contractor has a valid certificate of registration. This information can be verified by calling the U.S. Department of Labor's toll-free number (1–800–800–0235). The law designates criminal and civil penalties and administrative sanctions against anyone who violates it.

REQUIREMENTS

The law contains several major requirements for agricultural employers.

First, farm labor contractors and each of their employees who will be performing farm labor contractor activities must obtain a certificate of registration from the U.S. Department of Labor before they can start farm labor contractor activities.

Farm labor contractors who furnish worker transportation and housing must also:

• furnish proof to the U.S. Department of Labor that their transportation vehicles meet safety requirements,

• furnish proof to the U.S. Department of Labor that their transportation vehicles are insured for the amounts specified in the statute and regulations, and

• identify the housing that will be used and show that it meets State and Federal safety and health standards and is approved for occupancy.

Second, farm labor contractors, agricultural employers, and agricultural associations must provide written information to their workers on wages, hours, other working conditions, and housing when they recruit.

Third, farm labor contractors, agricultural employers, and agricultural associations must make and preserve written payroll records. They must also provide each employee with a written statement of earnings, deductions (plus reasons for deductions), and net pay.

FULFILLING THE REQUIREMENTS OF CONDITIONS OF EMPLOYMENT

A major requirement of employers and contractors under the MSPA is to provide workers with a statement of the conditions of their employment. This law requires that each farm labor contractor, agricultural employer, and agricultural association that recruits any migrant or day-haul workers must provide the following information in writing to each worker:

- Place of employment,
- Wage rates to be paid,
- Crops and kinds of activities in which the worker is to be employed,
- Period of employment,
- Transportation, housing, and any other employee benefits to be provided and any costs to be charged to workers,
- Existence of any strike, work stoppage, slowdown or interruption of operations by employees at the place of employment, and
- Whether anyone is paid a commission for items that may be sold to workers while they are employed.

This same information must be provided in writing to any seasonal workers, but only if they request it. The information must be provided in the language common to the farmworker if they are not fluent in English as necessary and reasonable.

Each farm labor contractor, agricultural employer, and agricultural association that employs any migrant or seasonal worker (including each day-haul worker) must make the following records for each employee and preserve them for 3 years:

- Basis on which wages are paid,
- Number of piecework units earned, if paid on a piecework basis,
- Number of hours worked,
- Total earnings,
- Specific sums withheld and the purpose of each sum withheld, and
- Net pay.

Workers must be paid every 2 weeks or twice a month. Each employee must be provided with an itemized written statement of the information listed above for each pay period. The information furnished to employees must be in a language common to workers.

Farm labor contractors must also furnish wage records to each agricultural employer and agricultural association for which the contractor provides workers. The agricultural employers and agricultural associations who receive these records are required to keep them for 3 years from the end of the employment period.

Enforcement

Violations of MSPA carry criminal and civil penalties and administrative sanctions. MSPA also permits people to bring legal action against alleged violators. The agency responsible for enforcing MSPA is the Wage and Hour Division of the U.S. Department of Labor.

SANCTIONS

Under the criminal sanctions, anyone knowingly and willfully violating MSPA or its regulations may be fined not more than $1,000 or sentenced to prison for not more than 1 year, or both, for first violations. Subsequent violations carry a fine of not more than $10,000 or a prison sentence of not more than 3 years, or both. An unregistered farm labor contractor who employs an illegal alien may be fined not more than $10,000 or sentenced to prison for not more than 3 years, or both.

Under civil sanctions, any person who commits a violation of MSPA or any regulations under it may be assessed a civil money penalty of not more than $1,000 for each violation.

Under administrative sanctions, farm labor contractors who violate MSPA or any of its regulations may be subject to having their current certificate revoked and/or future applications for certificates denied.

PRIVATE RIGHT OF ACTION

A unique feature of MSPA is that it permits anyone aggrieved by a violation of any provision by a farm labor contractor, agricultural employer, agricultural association, or other person to file suit in any Federal District Court having jurisdiction over the parties. The suits may be filed regardless of the amount in controversy, regardless of the citizenship of the parties, and regardless of whether all administrative remedies the act provides have been exhausted. The court may appoint an attorney for the complainant. Finally, the court may award up to $500 per plaintiff per violation, or other equitable relief when violations are intentional.

EXEMPTIONS

Farm labor contractor registration. Farm labor contractors and each of their employees who will perform farm labor contractor activities must obtain a certificate of registration from the U.S. Department of Labor before they can start farm labor contractor activities. Those exempt from the registration requirement include:

1. Agricultural employers and associations or their employees.

2. Farm labor contractors who work within a 25–mile intrastate radius of their permanent residence for less than 13 weeks per year.

3. Custom combine, hay harvesting, or sheep shearing operations.

4. Seed production operations.

5. Custom poultry operations.

6. Common carriers.

7. Labor organizations.

8. Nonprofit charitable or educational institutions.

9. Persons hiring or recruiting students or other nonagricultural employees for employment in seed production or in stringing and harvesting shade-grown tobacco.

Migrant and seasonal agricultural workers protection. Farm labor contractors, agricultural employers, and agricultural associations must provide migrant and seasonal agricultural workers with information on wages, hours, and other working conditions. In the case of housing, housing providers must provide migrant and seasonal agricultural workers with information on housing. Those exempt from these provisions include:

1. All those listed above except number 1, (agricultural employers and associations or their employees).

2. Individuals or immediate family members who engage in farm labor contracting activities on behalf of their exclusively owned or operated enterprise.

3. Any person (for example, a farm operator), except a farm labor contractor, who qualifies for the 500–man-days exemption under the Fair Labor Standards Act.

GOLDSTEIN, ET AL., ENFORCING FAIR LABOR STANDARDS IN THE MODERN AMERICAN SWEATSHOP: REDISCOVERING THE STATUTORY DEFINITION OF EMPLOYMENT

46 UCLA L. Rev. 983 (1999).*

Congress had concluded in 1963 that the "plight of the migrant laborer in this country is an inexcusable and cancerous sore in the body politic." Farmworkers' "transportation and living conditions are far below the general standard of living–are indeed inhuman, the very worst conditions of human life in this country, totally unacceptable for human beings." At the same time, Congress noted that few of the "protective measures of federal law enjoyed by other workers are extended to migratory laborers." Secretary of Labor Willard Wirtz testified that neither state nor federal law safeguarded migrant workers: "It is an anomaly that the workers who stand in the greatest need of social and economic protection are the ones who have been denied such protection."

As a result of congressional hearings, the [Farm Labor Contractor Registration Act (FLCRA)] was enacted to stem the tide of "exploitation and abuse" of migrant workers at the hands of the farm labor contractors or crew leaders who transported and managed the workers for farmers. The focus of the new legislation was solely on the crew leader, who was required to obtain a certificate of registration from the [Department of Labor (DOL)] as a condition of engaging in the activities of a farm labor contractor. Grounds for revocation of the certificate included giving false or misleading information to migrant workers concerning the terms of agricultural employment. Crew leaders were also subject to a fine for willful violations of the act.

Three years later, in 1966, Congress for the first time extended some of the benefits and protections of the FLSA [Farm Labor Standards Act] to some agricultural workers. Congress found that the exclusion of farmworkers from minimum-wage protections was inequitable and inconsistent with the act's purpose. In extending the act's protections to farmworkers, Congress specifically recognized that questions would arise as to whether they were employees of the farmer or of the farm labor contractor. The Senate Labor and Public Welfare Committee endorsed the approach taken by the Supreme Court in *Rutherford Food Corp. v. McComb*, which refused to rely on isolated factors, looking instead to "the circumstances of the whole activity." The *Rutherford* Court emphasized the many ways in which the operations of an alleged independent contractor were integrated into the business operations of the slaughterhouse, which thus was the employer of the workers.

In 1973, a DOL study concluded that 73% of farm labor contractors were violating the FLCRA's worker protections. Moreover, in the entire decade since its enactment, only four FLCRA cases had been referred to the Justice Department for prosecution. Accordingly, by 1974 Congress had concluded that the FLCRA's exclusive regulatory focus on the crew leader had been an abject failure:

> It has become clear that the provisions of the Act cannot be effectively enforced. Noncompliance by those whose activities the Act were [sic] intended to regulate has become the rule rather than the exception. ... It is quite evident that the Act in its present form provides no real deterrent to violations.

The 1974 FLCRA amendments created a private right of action as a means of encouraging enforcement against these noncompliant labor contractors.

Nevertheless, by 1982 it became clearer still that the twenty-year effort under the FLCRA to reform the farm labor market by regulating farm labor contractors had "failed to reverse the historical pattern of abuse and exploitation of migrant and seasonal farmworkers." To redress these problems, Congress enacted the [Migrant and Seasonal Agricultural Workers Protection Act (AWPA)]. Although the AWPA repealed the FLCRA in its entirety, in most respects the AWPA merely renamed and reenacted FLCRA's provisions. The only sense in which the AWPA took a "completely new approach" to the issue of farmworker abuse was in abandoning the FLCRA's attempt to enforce its requirements through the single locus of the often-transient crew leader.

Thus, the AWPA regulates, in addition to crew leaders, a full range of "agricultural employers," including "any person who owns or operates a farm, ranch, processing establishment, cannery, gin, packing shed or nursery, or who produces or conditions seed." These businesses were made directly responsible for the act's substantive worker protections when they employ a migrant or seasonal farmworker.

Combining the new responsibilities placed on agricultural employers with the expansive scope of the AWPA's definition of "employ" prompted the AWPA's sponsor to explain:

> [I]n order to adequately insure ... the protections afforded migrant and seasonal workers under this or any act, you must tie the responsibility for protecting the workers to the person which has the ability to correct the hazard or control the abuse.... Agricultural employees will ... know who is responsible for their protections, by fixing the responsibility on those who ultimately benefit from their labors—the agricultural employer.

FOO, THE VULNERABLE AND EXPLOITABLE IMMIGRANT WORKFORCE AND THE NEED FOR STRENGTHENING WORKER PROTECTIVE LEGISLATION

103 Yale L.J. 2179 (1994).*

THE PROBLEMS WITH DWINDLING FIELD ENFORCEMENT

If the DOL and state labor agencies are so understaffed that they cannot bring lawsuits to enforce these tougher labor laws and collect the stiffer penalties, chronic violators will not be deterred. Statistics make clear that understaffing in labor enforcement will continue for years to come. Under President Carter, the DOL had 1600 wage and hour inspectors to police ninety million workers. Under President Reagan, the number was slashed to 700, and has increased only to 800 during President Clinton's tenure. Thus, while the FLSA "hot goods" law potentially is one of the DOL's most effective weapons, particularly for compelling payment of minimum wages by garment manufacturers when their subcontractors disappear, it is rarely used. The DOL simply does not have enough investigators.

The New York State Apparel Industry Task Force has only five inspectors to monitor 2000 garment shops. "Once they cite a factory for a violation, the task force rarely reinspects to ensure continued compliance." Similarly, in California, general budget cuts have reduced the staffing of the state Division of Labor Standards Enforcement (DLSE) from a high of over 430 in 1982–1983 down to 342.9 in 1993–1994. As a result, in 1988, the California State Labor Commissioner corrected 111,452 labor law violations, but by 1992 that number had dropped to 64,275. Between 1980 and 1991, the number of garment workers increased by one-third, from 106,500 to 137,600, and the number of workers in sewing shops increased from 3708 to 6132. Similarly, the number of hospitality workers increased from 113,100 to 189,100. Because the DLSE has suffered cutbacks in staffing and has shifted its focus from garment to other higher-wage industries, such as public works, inspections by the DLSE remained virtually constant, at just over 1200 a year, despite the increases in workers in these sweatshop industries. At this rate, the Labor Commissioner will not be able to reinspect a shop to ensure continuing compliance until four years after the initial inspection.

Before the DOL, or state labor agencies can recover minimum wages, overtime compensation or civil penalties for an entire workforce, they need the necessary resources, including a staff of attorneys. The enforcement agencies' legal staff is as overwhelmed as the field inspectors and can bring only a handful of lawsuits. Thus, there is a dire need to pass legislation that will encourage private plaintiffs and the private bar to become active in the enforcement of labor laws.

LUNA, AN INFINITE DISTANCE?: AGRICULTURAL EXCEPTIONALISM AND AGRICULTURAL LABOR

1 U. Pa. J. Lab. & Employment L. 487 (1998).*

Children comprise another group of farm workers because public law provides that lower age groups may work in agriculture. Estimates of farm worker children in agricultural fields range between 800,000 and 1.5 million. Agriculture's exemption from child welfare legislation permits ten and eleven-year-olds to work in hand-harvested commodities. In some instances, young children pick cucumbers and tomatoes. Other children prune grapes, harvest strawberries, lettuce, asparagus, citrus fruits, and pistachios. Children are in the fields because the lack of childcare facilities requires them to accompany their parents or because they are needed to supplement family incomes. Without supervision, children are injured in machinery-related accidents causing the loss of limbs, and some die from drowning in agricultural ditches.

Children suffer from multiple forms of chronic stress resulting from their migratory lifestyle. Migrating into other states to work, or accompanying their parents in the fields, plagues the childhood of farm children by leaving them little experience with a permanent home or with owning possessions. Farm worker children are in high health risk categories for child maltreatment, immunization difficulties, inadequate dietary intake, iron deficiencies, tuberculosis, and parasitic diseases. Researchers report farm worker children are ostracized from other school children and experience low self-esteem, academic, and self-concept problems. Inadequate medical and social services prevent improved health for farm worker children.

MULL, RECOMMENDATIONS FOR THE ELIMINATION
OF CHILD LABOR IN THE U.S.
<www.afop.org>.*

Since 1990, the Department of Labor's Wage and Hour Divisions' level of enforcement activities related to child labor has fluctuated from year to year. Yet, consistently the investment has been in a downward trend. The Department of Labor should establish a strategic plan for the implementation of its enforcement responsibilities, establish a higher commitment of resources for the enforcement of child labor laws, and maintain the investment consistently over the long term. Currently, Wage and Hour relies on a compliant driven mechanism for the reporting of violations before inspections are conducted. This approach will not work effectively in the agricultural sector. Given the economic problems experienced by the parents, service providers' sympathy because of the plight of the farmworker families, Cooperative Extension and Department of Agriculture's concerns for farmers and the industry, any expectations for complaints to be generated in a small, rural agricultural community are unrealistic. Only persistent, repeated, unannounced, full-scope investigations on all farms, regardless of the number of workers reported, is essential. The number of inspectors must be increased relative to the size and scope of the problem. Increasing inspectors on a seasonal basis during peak harvest seasons may prove to be somewhat more cost effective than hiring full-time inspectors.

We encourage raising monetary penalties for violators to a level that creates a significant disincentive, with the provision of serving time in prison for multiple violations or repeat offenders. Given the Department's modest fines and lack of success in collecting fines levied against child labor violators, we recommend that if an industry is found to be in violation of the law, the first time offender pays no less than a $10,000 fine per violation. Failure to pay such fines on time will result in the loss of their business license until such fine is paid. For a second violation, the industry loses all rights of access under the law to any federal or state employment exemptions, federal or state benefits or tax breaks afforded industry, or subsidy existing in law or enacted for a period up to five years. This includes prohibiting the employer from using guestworkers or other federal or state subsidized employment agents or services. Should a third violation occur or a pattern of practice be evident, the employer loses all rights for a period of ten years. Likewise it should be made clear that on farms where farm labor contractors are used as the employment agent for hiring workers, responsibility for the farm labor contractor's failure to comply with the child labor law lies with the farm owner. After a second violation, the farm owner is restricted from using any guestworkers or outside employment agents for the purpose of hiring workers and all penalties, restrictions and fines are shared by the farm owner.

Department of Labor educational initiatives that are targeted to prevent child labor in the agricultural sector should be developed and customized for the population. Glitzy campaigns for urban, educated populations are ineffective with the farmworker community. Special efforts must be undertaken to ensure that materials, messages, and media approaches are appropriately field tested with the population and are conducted by groups with special expertise in this area working with the farmworker population. To do otherwise, is a waste of valuable resources and time.

Questions and Comments

1. The total projected budget for the U.S. Department of Labor in Fiscal Year 2005 is $57.3 billion. The budgets for DOL's two main labor rights and safety enforcement agencies, the Employment Standards Administration (ESA) and Occupational Safety and Health Administration (OSHA), will be $528 million and $462 million, respectively. In addition, the DOL will spend an estimated $6 million specifically addressing violations of child labor laws in the agricultural sector. As a practical matter, what additional commitment in financial resources would be required for the United States to "effectively enforce" labor law protections in the hundreds of workplaces in the country in which migrant workers are present in significant numbers? Refer to Foo, Luna, and Mull. In ratifying the NAALC, did the U.S. government actually commit to make such expenditures? Refer also to NAALC Article 49.

2. What are some of the claims that might be made in a submission by the UFA on behalf of the migrant farm workers? Refer to Goldstein, Foo, and Mull. Is there any claim that, on these facts, the United States has violated NAALC Article 2? Article 3? Article 4?

3. NAO consultations would be available in this instance because a farm worker submission would involve "labor law" as defined in the NAALC. Ministerial consultations also would be proper in that protection of migrant workers is within the scope of the Agreement. If the matter were not resolved after ministerial consultations, could the submission advance to review by an Evaluation Committee of Experts (ECE)?

4. Could a farm worker submission by the UFA advance to Article 27 consultations?

5. Would a submission by the UFA be within the subject matter authority of an Article 29 arbitral panel?

6. Who is authorized to serve as a NAALC panelist? Refer to Article 30. What process will the governments follow in selecting five panelists? Refer to Article 32.

7. If an arbitral panel were to determine that, with regard to migrant farm workers, there exists a persistent pattern of failure by the United States to effectively enforce its occupational safety and health standards, and child labor standards, what elements might be included in an "action plan" designed by Mexico and the United States? Refer to U.S. Department of Agriculture, Foo, Luna and Mull.

8. If the United States were to refuse to agree to an action plan and the reconvened arbitral panel were to determine that a monetary enforcement assessment is warranted, what factors would the panel consider in determining the amount of the assessment? To whom would the assessment

be paid and how would it be spent? Refer to NAALC Annex 39. For purposes of answering these questions, assume that total trade in goods between the three NAFTA countries equaled $620 billion (2002).

9. The NAALC authorizes the suspension of NAFTA benefits in the event that the United States fails to pay the monetary enforcement assessment discussed in the prior question. How would a suspension of benefits by Mexico work in practice? Refer to NAALC Annex 41B.

10. Would pressing the submission to the advanced stages of NAALC dispute resolution serve the political interests of the Mexican government? Refer to Lehrfeld.

PART B. MEXICO

SECTION I. THE SETTING

Mexico's elementary and secondary school system is composed of a large number of government-funded public schools and a much smaller number of private schools. Generally speaking, the private schools have a reputation for academic excellence. While a few of these schools have substantial financial resources, most struggle to make ends meet. In the past decade, private schools owned and operated by religious groups based in the United States have begun to appear in Mexico at an increasing rate. Because these foreign-owned schools tend to be well-funded, they represent a competitive threat to traditional Mexican private schools.

Most teachers in Mexican schools are women, regardless of whether the schools are public or private. Mexican law provides significant benefits for female employees who become pregnant. Under the Federal Labor Law, a pregnant employee is entitled to twelve weeks maternity leave at full pay, to reinstatement to the employee's prior job upon returning from maternity leave, and to special accommodations if nursing. Most of the private primary and secondary schools faithfully comply with these requirements even though such accommodations add to their expenses. To minimize pregnancy-related costs, many private schools (but none of the foreign-owned schools) have adopted the practice of denying employment to women who are pregnant *at the time they apply* for a teaching position. Whether, in fact, schools save much money as a result of this practice is questionable.

Although the practice clearly is widespread and open, the way in which this exclusion is carried out varies from school to school. Many schools simply ask applicants to verify on the job application form that they are not pregnant. Women who disclose that they are pregnant are not hired. In other schools, pregnancy screening occurs during job interviews or medical examinations. Applicants sometimes are asked fairly intrusive questions concerning their sexual activity, last menstruation, methods of birth control, and number of children. In a minority of schools, female teaching applicants are required to produce urine samples for pregnancy testing.

Most of the women denied employment on the basis of their pregnancy status are not financially capable of pursuing legal action against the schools that deny them work. Job applicants who have attempted to file discrimination complaints with local labor tribunals, labor inspectors, or the Office for the Defense of Labor have been turned away on the grounds that pre-hiring pregnancy discrimination is legal under existing Mexican law. According to the government's interpretation, Mexico's Federal Labor Law prohibits employment discrimination only if an employer-employee relationship exists. A *prospective* employer owes no legal duties to job applicants. Thus, under Mexican law, there exists no legal mechanism by which to pursue a claim of pre-hiring pregnancy discrimination.

The National Council of Teachers (NCT), an educator's organization in the United States, has learned of the pre-hiring pregnancy discrimination problem among teaching applicants in Mexico. As part of a general plan to expand its influence and membership into Mexico, the NCT is interested in submitting a claim under NAALC on behalf of women denied teaching jobs based on their pregnancy status. They intend to allege that the Mexican government is aware of this widespread practice among private elementary and secondary schools and countenances such discrimination.

SECTION II. FOCUS OF CONSIDERATION

Pregnancy discrimination is an international problem, not just a Mexican problem. Although laws prohibiting pregnancy discrimination exist in the United States, substantial controversy remains over whether such laws are appropriate and effective. The NAALC allows one to view pregnancy discrimination not merely as improper interpersonal conduct but also as a form of anti-trade or protectionist activity. Such discrimination by Mexican private schools arguably gives them a small but still unfair competitive advantage over foreign-owned schools that do not discriminate in this manner.

Pregnancy discrimination is merely one of many gender discrimination issues arising with increasing frequency as the presence of women grows in the Mexican workforce. Expanded trade under NAFTA is one force adding to the number of female workers. For example, Mexico's maquiladora industry burgeoned from only twelve plants in 1965 to over 3,000 plants in 2000 with an estimated 1.4 million employees, although the total employment in 2004 is probably closer to 1.1 million. Nearly sixty percent of the production workers in maquiladoras are women (See U.S. NAO, Public Report of Review of Submission No. 9701, 13 (1998).) The employment-discrimination concerns of female maquiladora workers go unheeded for a variety of reasons. First, these women tend to be poorly educated and entirely dependent on their relatively small wages. Second, male-dominated unions and government agencies tend to discount the concerns of such women.

As you review the readings which follow, consider whether Mexico's existing employment discrimination laws are adequate to address pregnancy discrimination in the pre-hiring context and what role, if any, the NAALC can play in resolving this politically-sensitive but important labor issue.

SECTION III. READINGS, QUESTIONS AND COMMENTS

GRIMM, THE NORTH AMERICAN AGREEMENT ON LABOR COOPERATION AND ITS EFFECTS ON WOMEN WORKING IN MEXICAN MAQUILADORAS

48 Amer. U. L. Rev. 179 (1998).*

... a recent U.S. NAO public report of review addressed maquiladora hiring and employment practices that discriminate against female workers on the basis of pregnancy. Unlike the other maquiladora-related submissions, this case explicitly raised the issue of sex-based employment discrimination. The submission alleged that, in order to avoid government-mandated maternity leave costs, maquiladora managers required female applicants and employees to take pregnancy tests, submit to physical exams, and answer questions about their sexual activity, menstrual schedules, and use of birth control. The petition further stated that maquiladora managers refuse to hire pregnant applicants and attempt to coerce female employees who become pregnant into resigning by giving them work that is physically demanding and by requiring unpaid overtime.

The U.S. NAO held public hearings and released its report on January 12, 1998. The NAO focused its analysis on the legality of pregnancy discrimination under Mexican law, because the NAALC does not apply unless a violation of the law occurs. It found that employment discrimination against pregnant workers violates Mexican labor laws that prohibit dismissal or discrimination against pregnant current employees. Although some women obtained relief for illegal dismissals through CABs, the NAO found that the available venues for reporting violations are not widely accessible to maquiladora workers, who are often incapacitated by little education, poverty, and the fear of being labeled as troublemakers by maquiladora managers. The NAO's findings about discrimination against pregnant women were less decisive, due to conflicting opinions about the legality of practice. Although job applicants are not formally protected by Mexican labor laws because they lack contracts, the U.S. NAO looked to international agreements and Mexican governmental bodies that have questioned the validity of the practice. In order to further investigate the legality of pre-hire pregnancy testing and to more thoroughly examine the availability of redress for illegally dismissed pregnant women, the U.S. NAO recommended Ministerial Consultations.

This decision is especially significant for female maquiladora workers because of its focus on an aspect of maquiladora employment that specifically affects women. The U.S. NAO's attentive handling of the case, especially its willingness to look beyond Mexican federal law to international law documents and non-legal Mexican sources for opinions about pre-hire pregnancy discrimination, demonstrates that the NAO system can be responsive to problems of gender discrimination. This decision also shows that advocacy groups are responsive enough to female workers' concerns to file submissions on women's behalf. As with the maquiladora submissions concerning freedom of association, however, the lack of sanctions available under NAALC procedures for cases of gender discrimination may hinder truly effective enforcement of labor laws in the NAFTA free trade zone. In addition, the NAO's difficulty with the legality of pre-hire pregnancy discrimination, because Mexican labor laws do not clearly prohibit this practice, indicates the hazards of relying on an individual country's laws for enforcement of the workers' rights standards that the NAALC protects.

U.S. NATIONAL ADMINISTRATIVE OFFICE, PUBLIC REPORT OF REVIEW OF NAO SUBMISSION NO. 9701 (GENDER)

<www.dol.gov/dol/ilab/public/media/reports/nao/> (Jan. 12, 1998)

SUBMISSION SUMMARY

In March 1995, a HRW mission traveled to the cities of Tijuana, Baja California State, Chihuahua, Chihuahua State, and Matamoros, Reynosa and Rio Bravo, Tamaulipas State. The purpose of the mission was to investigate possible discrimination against women job applicants and women workers employed in the maquiladora sector, who were pregnant or who may become pregnant. The mission conducted interviews with women's rights activists, maquiladora personnel, labor rights advocates, Mexican Government officials, community organizers, and women workers.

The results of the interviews were released in a report in August, 1996. "HRW reported that pregnancy-based gender discrimination takes three forms: (1) testing and interviewing of job applicants during the hiring process to determine their pregnancy status; (2) denial of employment to pregnant applicants; and (3) dismissal of pregnant workers or the mistreatment of pregnant workers in an effort to bring about their resignation.

According to the submitters, the report showed that pregnancy testing by maquiladora employers is widespread. HRW alleged the use of pregnancy testing or other methods of determining the pregnancy status of job applicants in thirty-eight companies in the five cities. These other methods include direct and intrusive questioning of applicants by personnel officers on whether the applicant is sexually active, when she last menstruated, and the type of contraceptive(s) she uses. In some cases, the questions were included in the written job application. On some occasions, doctors, nurses, or other maquiladora personnel allegedly informed job applicants that if they were found to be pregnant they would not be hired. In other companies, personnel officers reportedly informed workers that if they became pregnant after they began work, they would lose their jobs.

HRW found that after a worker became pregnant, she could be subject to pressure to resign or harassment and mistreatment for becoming pregnant. It was alleged that working conditions were applied arbitrarily and punitively against pregnant workers in order to persuade them to resign. Such conditions were reported to included reassignment to more difficult tasks; alteration of work shifts on a weekly basis; being forced to stand instead of being offered a seat; and being obliged to work overtime hours without compensation as a condition for keeping their employment. Further, pregnant workers reported that maquiladora employers frequently use probationary contracts of thirty to ninety days as a mechanism to refuse permanent positions to pregnant workers. Finally, a number of the women interviewed reported that they were coerced and intimidated into submitting resignations after they were discovered to be pregnant.

The submitters assert that women who are subject to the treatment described are not afforded relief in Mexico, either through the appropriate administrative labor tribunals or the courts. They allege that the Inspectors of Labor (*Inspectores de Trabajo*) and the Office for the Defense of Labor (*Procraduría de la Defensa del Trabajo*) lack jurisdiction on the issue of pre-employment pregnancy-based discrimination and are unresponsive to complaints on the issue. They also allege that the Conciliation and Arbitration Boards (*Juntas de Conciliación y Arbitraje*—CABs), which are the primary bodies charged with the investigation and adjudication of labor disputes, are ineffective in dealing with gender discrimination issues.

According to the submitters, many of the women employed in the maquiladoras come from rural backgrounds, are poor, and have limited formal education. They are in need of employment and are not always aware of their rights under the law. This makes them particularly vulnerable to the actions described. Many of the workers lack confidence in the official institutions and mechanisms in place for the enforcement of the law and the protection of their rights.

* * *

Relevant Mexican Law

Equality between the sexes before the law is ensured in the Political Constitution of the United Mexican States (hereinafter, the Mexican Constitution), Article 4, which was enacted in 1974, and states, in relevant part: "Man and woman are equal before the law. This will protect the organization and development of the family." Article 4 goes on to state "[a]ll persons have the right to decide in a free, responsible and informed manner, on the number and spacing of their children." Article 5 of the Constitution states "[n]o person shall be prevented from pursuing the profession, trade, business, or work of their choice, provided it is legal."

Article 123(A) of the Mexican Constitution governs labor standards and labor-management relations. Paragraph V establishes protection for pregnant workers. Paragraph VII addresses equal pay for equal work, without regard to sex or nationality.

Article 123(A) is implemented by the Federal Labor Law (*Ley Federal del Trabajo*, hereinafter the FLL). Article 3 of the FLL states: "[t]here shall not be established distinctions among workers for [reason] of race, sex, age, religious creed, political doctrine or social position."

Title V of the FLL deals with the employment of women. Article 133 of that title lists prohibited practices by employers. Article 133 (I) states that employers may not "[r]efuse to accept workers for reason of age or sex...."

Article 164 states "[w]omen enjoy the same rights and have the same obligations as men."

Article 170 of Title V addresses pregnancy and maternity and states that working mothers shall have the following rights:

(I) during the period of pregnancy they shall not perform work demanding considerable strength, which is dangerous for their health in relation to the gestation period, such as lifting, dragging or pushing heavy weights, that which produces rapid vibrations, remaining in a standing position for long periods or that which may alter their mental or emotional state;

(II) they shall be entitled to maternity leave of six weeks duration before and after [delivery];

(III) the maternity leave referred to in the preceding item is extended by the time necessary if it is impossible for the woman to return to work on account of her pregnancy or confinement;

(IV) during the period of lactation the woman shall be entitled to two extra breaks each day of one half hour's duration each to breast feed her infant, in suitable hygienic premises designated by the enterprise;

(V) during the maternity leave referred to in item II the woman shall be entitled to her full wages. In case of the extended maternity leave referred to in item II, the woman shall be entitled to half pay for a period not exceeding sixty days....

FLL Title II, Chapter IV, Articles 46–52 and Chapter V, Articles 53–55 addresses the termination of the labor relationship. Article 47 lists fifteen causes for justified termination of the labor relationship, none of which includes pregnancy.

Article 38 of the FLL allows temporary contracts for a fixed term only when necessary due to the nature of the work, when temporarily replacing another worker, or as otherwise provided in the law. Mexican labor law does not provide for probationary or trial periods of employment to determine a person's ability and proficiency to perform a job, or for any other reason. There appear to be no provisions in Mexican labor law that would permit the use of temporary contracts to refuse permanent positions to pregnant workers, which practice the submitters refer to in the submission.

The Law of Social Security (*Ley de Seguiridad Social*), Mexican Federal Law 93, established the social security system in Mexico and created the Mexican Institute of Social Security (*Instituto Mexicano de Seguridad Social*) to implement and regulate the law. To be entitled to paid maternity leave, a worker must have participated and made payments to the Social Security Fund for at least thirty weeks during the twelve-month period prior to receiving the benefit. Workers who do not qualify for coverage by social security are entitled to the same rights and protections under FLL Article 170 at the expense of the employer.

ENFORCEMENT BODIES

Three Mexican Government entities appear to have jurisdiction in cases involving allegations of employment discrimination on the basis of sex.

1. The Federal and Local Conciliation and Arbitration Boards (CABs) adjudicate most individual and collective disputes between labor and management. FLL Article 604 establishes the Federal Conciliation and Arbitration Board (CAB) and empowers it to hear and decide labor disputes between workers and their employers. Article 621 establishes the Local Conciliation and Arbitration Boards (CABs) and empowers them to adjudicate disputes that do not fall within the jurisdiction of the Federal CABs.

FLL Article 604 states that "[t]he Federal Conciliation and Arbitration Board shall hear and decide labor disputes arising between workers and employers or between workers only or employers only, arising out of the labor relationships or acts closely connected with such relations. . . ."

Article 621 of the FLL states that "[l]ocal Conciliation and Arbitration Boards shall operate in each of the States of the Federation. They shall hear and settle labor disputes which do not fall within the competence of the Federal Conciliation and Arbitration Board."

The Mexican NAO asserts that there is no mechanism to bring cases of pre-employment pregnancy screening as both Article 123(A) of the Mexican Constitution and the Mexican Federal Labor Law protect only the rights of those parties already engaged in a labor relationship. Documented interviews with officers of the CABs, in which these officers gave similar responses on the non-application of the FLL and the absence of jurisdiction of the CABs in pre-employment issues, were included in both the *HRW Report* and in Submission No. 9701.

On post-hire pregnancy discrimination, there is general agreement that the CABs have the authority and jurisdiction to act under FLL Articles 46–55. In such cases, the action would be against unjustified dismissal. The submitters provided information at the public hearing that the CAB and the Office for the Defense of Labor in Juarez, Chihuahua, handle approximately one case per month of unjustified dismissal, some of which involved dismissal for pregnancy, and that favorable rulings for the workers have been obtained. The Secretariat of Labor and Social Welfare (STPS) estimates that the federal CABs heard over 53,000 cases in 1996, most of them individual cases. More than 9,000 of the CAB decisions were appealed to the courts using the *amparo* process. The NAO has no information on how many of these cases involved pregnancy discrimination or other forms of employment discrimination.

2.   The Inspectorate of Labor is primarily charged with workplace inspections. FLL Article 540 specifies the functions of the Inspectorate of Labor as follows:

(I) to ensure fulfillment of labor [standards];

(II) to provide technical information and advise workers and employers as to the most effective manner for fulfilling the labor [standards];

(III) to report to [the authorities] any failure to observe, and violations of, the labor [standards] it discovers in enterprises and establishments;

(IV) to make such studies and collect such data as may be required by the authorities and those which it deems necessary to achieve harmony in the relations between workers and employers; and

(V) such other functions as may be assigned to it by law.

Article 541 states that labor inspectors will have the following powers and duties:

(I) to ensure that the labor [standards] are observed, in particular those prescribing the rights and obligations of workers and employers, those concerning the prevention of employment injuries, safety and health;

(II) to inspect enterprises and establishments during the hours of work (day or night) on producing [appropriate] identification;

(III) to put questions to workers and employers, in the presence or in the absence of witnesses, on any matter connected with the application of the labor [standards];

(IV) to require the [presentation] of any books, registers or other documents required to be kept by the labor [standards];

(V) to suggest that any non-observance of the employment conditions be corrected;

(VI) to suggest that any duly ascertained defects in plans and methods of work be put right if they constitute a violation of the labor [standards] or a danger to the workers' safety or health, and the adoption of immediate measures in the case of any imminent danger;

(VII) to examine the substances and materials used in enterprises and establishments in the case of dangerous work; and

(VIII) any other powers and duties assigned to them by law.

The submitters maintain that the inspectors lack authority, support, and resources to effectively discharge their responsibilities. On the other hand, the Mexican NAO provided information that during 1997 STPS conducted 809 inspections of 437 maquiladoras and found that they were substantially in compliance with the law. In those cases where violations were detected, corrective action was taken which, in some cases, could include the application of sanctions against those companies found to be in violation of the law. The plants that were inspected reportedly employed 138,712 workers, of whom 3,414 were pregnant and 484 were nursing. In another memorandum, the Mexican NAO stated that approximately 48,000 worksite inspections are conducted annually in Mexico. According to the Mexican NAO, very few of the inspections revealed the violation of maternity protection laws.

The Mexican NAO has stated that STPS maintains an ongoing dialogue with the National Council of the Maquiladora Industry (CNIME), which cooperates in securing the compliance of its member companies with labor laws and standards and in correcting deficiencies. Further, since 1996, STPS has reportedly conducted a program of consciousness awareness among maquiladora employers on discrimination against women employed in the maquiladoras.

3. The Office for the Defense of Labor has the following functions, as outlined by FLL Article 530:

(I) to advise workers and their trade unions or represent them [before] any authority whenever requested, in matters connected with the application of the labor [standards];

(II) to bring ordinary and extraordinary appeals which may arise on behalf of a worker or trade union; and

(III) to propose [negotiated] solutions to the parties concerned for the settlement of their disputes and make official reports of the results thereof.

The submitters argue that the Office for the Defense of Labor is ineffective in discharging its obligations in pre-employment pregnancy cases because it is legally restricted to addressing only post-hire cases. On post-hire cases, the submitters allege that some of the attorneys of that agency are inaccessible to workers and lack the necessary material and human resources to effectively advocate on their behalf. On the other hand, in testimony at the public hearing, the submitters indicated that in Juarez, Chihuahua, the Attorney for the Defense of Labor did take up and win cases of post-hire dismissal for pregnancy before the CAB. The Mexican NAO has indicated that very few of the unspecified number of requests for assistance to the Office for the Defense of Labor involved complaints of violations of the FLL against pregnant or nursing women.

Mexico's courts entertain *amparo* appeals through which an individual or legal entity may seek protection against the violation of constitutional guarantees by the government or its agents. *Amparos*, however, must be filed against an action by the government or its agent. Further, according to the Mexican NAO, unless an action is prohibited by law, the *amparo* process may not be used to seek redress against the action. The *amparo* has been used with some success against decisions by the CABs in labor cases. As noted previously, over 9000 *amparo* appeals against CAB decisions were filed during 1996. There is no indication, however, that affected workers have availed themselves of the *amparo* process in gender discrimination cases.

Human Rights Commission

The Human Rights Commission of the Federal District is an autonomous body that derives its statutory authority from Article 102, Part B of the Mexican Constitution. Article 102, Part B, authorizes the National Congress and the State legislatures to establish bodies to protect those human rights that are covered by Mexican law. Their essential function is the investigation of administrative acts or omissions on the part of any governmental authority or individual that may violate human rights. The recommendations of the bodies created under the law are not binding and they are precluded from ruling on matters properly within the jurisdiction of the courts. Further, they are explicitly precluded from becoming involved in electoral, labor and jurisdictional issues.

* * *

Beginning on February 15, 1995, the Commission for the Federal District conducted an investigation of allegations that women in Mexico's Federal District were required to undergo pregnancy testing or provide certificates attesting to their non-pregnancy before being accepted for employment in a number of federal agencies located in the Federal District. The agencies included in the investigation were the Department of the Federal District, the Superior Court and Judicial Council of the Federal District, and the Office of the Attorney General for the Federal District. This case was considered a human rights case, not a labor case, and was, therefore, within the jurisdiction of the Commission. The Commission issued its report and recommendations on June 1, 1995, finding that such practices did occur, that they did discriminate against women, and that they were in violation of Articles 4 and 5 of the Mexican Constitution. The Commission cited Article 11(1) of the Convention on the Elimination of All Forms of Discrimination Against Women (CEDAW) in support of its conclusions and recommended that the federal entities that were engaging in this practice cease doing so.

The Mexican NAO has provided information stating that the recommendations of the Commission were accepted and implemented in their entirety.

SEDILLO LOPEZ, TWO LEGAL CONSTRUCTS OF MOTHERHOOD: "PROTECTIVE" LEGISLATION IN MEXICO AND THE UNITED STATES
1 S. Cal. Rev. L. & Women's Stud. 239 (1992).*

The Mexican constitution requires equal wages for equal work regardless of sex or nationality. Both the federal Mexican labor law and the Mexican constitution require state and federal governments to provide pregnant women with a six-week paid maternity leave prior to birth and a six-week paid maternity leave after birth. Further, under the federal labor law, non-government employers are also required to provide a six-week pre-birth paid maternity leave and a six-week after-birth paid maternity leave. After the child's birth, the law allows for two additional breaks a day in order to allow a nursing mother to continue nursing when she is at work. The employer must provide an adequate and sanitary place for this lactation period.

During maternity leave, women are to receive full salary for the mandatory period; if they take an extension of the mandatory period. They are also entitled to fifty percent of their salary for up to sixty days. They are entitled to return to their jobs if they return within a year after their child's birth. Their maternity leave periods are included in computations of seniority. Employers are directed to adopt measures to "ensure the greatest possible guarantee for the health and safety of workers" and, in the case of pregnant workers, for their unborn children. Pregnant women are prohibited from working in jobs which would endanger the health of the woman or of her fetus and from working after ten in the evening. In addition, a woman may not work over-time when her health or the health of her fetus is in danger. The labor law also requires that sufficient chairs or seats be provided for pregnant working women to use. Additionally, child care services are to be provided by the Mexican Institute of Social Security. Mexicans are quite proud of these special protections for women.

When employers comply with their legal obligations, pregnant women may use these protections to tend to their traditional family role as child-bearer and nurturer. However, some problems exist. First, not all women want or need these provisions. Many working women do not have children. Even among women who have children, not all of them would choose to use the protections afforded them. Second, Mexico does not have legislation prohibiting employment discrimination in hiring based on sex, pregnancy, or potential for pregnancy. Accordingly, some employers concerned with the potentially high cost of employing women who might need these mandatory benefits discriminate against women. In addition, some companies require women to state that they are infertile on job applications. If a woman becomes pregnant after stating she is infertile, she may be fired for lying on the job application. Thus, protective legislation has a negative effect on women's employment opportunities.

In Mexico, protective legislation furthers a concept of the family in which the husband is the head of the household and their wives are their dependents and the bearers and nurturers of their children. Protective legislation is viewed by many Mexicans as progress in improving most women's lives. The fact that protective legislation may reduce employment opportunities for women is viewed by some as positive support for the traditional family. Further, some feminists in Mexico advocate for enforcement of protective legislation such as day care and pregnancy leaves. Others are aware of its negative impact on women's employment opportunities.

EICHNER, SQUARE PEG IN A ROUND HOLE: PARENTING POLICIES AND LIBERAL THEORY
59 Ohio St. L.J. 133 (1998).*

Newspapers, public opinion polls, and political speeches all trumpet the view that Americans strongly support children and believe in the importance of good parenting. However, Americans are, in overwhelming numbers, concerned that they are failing their children. They are particularly concerned that they have too little time to spend with their children. It is therefore surprising that where parenting responsibilities conflict with work—unquestionably the activity that most limits parenting activities—this groundswell of support for children and parenting has resulted in very little legal support for working parents. There is, in fact, less support than in any of 151 other industrialized countries. The absence of legal support is especially surprising given the large number of Americans who support government help in meeting children's needs.

This Article challenges this curious state of affairs. I ask the reader to consider why our society appears to value parenting so much and to be so concerned about its condition, yet provides so little support for working parents. At least part of the answer, I contend, derives from contestable assumptions—about individuals, the relationships between individuals, and the role of the state—that are part of the dominant liberal philosophy in the United States. These assumptions, I argue, prevent formulation of a coherent legal framework able to cognize and support parenting and the goods associated with it.

* * *

PARENTING AND THE LAW

Employees whose work and parenting responsibilities conflict generally have two different avenues of legal protection: Title VII of the Civil Rights Act of 1964, and the Family and Medical Leave Act. On their face, the two statutes are very different: Title VII is concerned with eliminating employment discrimination from the workplace, while the FMLA provides protection for employees requiring time off work to attend to serious family needs. Yet both share certain features: they are extremely limited in the protection they provide working parents, they selectively focus on particular interests at stake in parenting at the same time as they obscure others, and they share a particular, narrow interpretation of what it means to parent.

Antidiscrimination Law as a Framework

In a society whose rhetoric is steeped in the value of families but which remains ambivalent about the value of sexual equality, it is paradoxical that the dominant legal framework through which the relation between parenting and the workplace has been negotiated is sex discrimination law. Yet because until passage of the FMLA in 1993 no other law provided protection for working parents, and because of the limited scope of the FMLA since that time, those seeking protection for parenting activities have generally litigated their claims under Title VII. That Act encompasses both a general prohibition on sex discrimination in employment and an amendment, the Pregnancy Discrimination Act of 1978 (PDA), which declares discrimination on the basis of pregnancy or childbirth-related conditions to be sex discrimination. The result of trying to fit the multiple needs and aspirations at stake in parenting into the antidiscrimination framework constructed by Title VII and the PDA is like the proverbial act of trying to fit a square peg into a round hole: in order to make it fit, such a large portion of the peg needs to be pared away that it becomes virtually unrecognizable.

Title VII

Title VII makes it unlawful for an employer "to fail or refuse to hire or to discharge any individual, or otherwise to discriminate against any individual ... because of ... sex." In order to fit parenting and work conflicts into a form cognizable by the statute, the complex of needs, aspirations, and goods at stake in parenting is pared down to two specific sets of interests–those of the employer and those of the employee as an employee. In this regard, Title VII applies only when the employee/parent's employment has been or will be affected by parenting responsibilities, and then only if this conflict can be linked to sex discrimination. Title VII does not apply when the employee/parent's parenting has been or will be affected by work responsibilities. Hence, Title VII excludes from consideration the importance to the employee of fulfilling child rearing responsibilities, raising well-balanced children, and being part of a healthy, happy family. Further, sex discrimination law completely ignores the needs of the child in receiving adequate parenting, the needs and aspirations of the family, and the interests of communities in ensuring that their members are raised adequately.

Moreover, by virtue of its limited goal of eliminating discrimination in the workplace, Title VII cannot ground any larger normative vision for the role of parenting. Sex discrimination law provides only the same level of protection to the act of parenting that it provides to other ways in which women may be disadvantaged relative to men: if all women were miserable parents and simply attended to work responsibilities while leaving their children unsupervised, the conditions of the sex discrimination framework would be satisfied. In other words, treating parenting within an antidiscrimination framework protects parenting only insofar as it is necessary to avoid discrimination. It does not support parenting because of the goods parenting makes available to parents, children, and communities, including allowing children to become healthy, competent people; parents to fulfill self-identified moral responsibilities to parent; and communities to have a sound citizenry. The problem is not chiefly that antidiscrimination law is failing to fulfill the function intended by Congress, but that its function, by nature, is limited, and that no other framework exists within United States' law that provides adequate protection to the broader spectrum of interests at stake in work-and-parenting conflicts.

The Pregnancy Discrimination Act

Despite the clear link between parenting and women's inequality, the only place in which Title VII provides any explicit protection for parenting is in the PDA. The PDA provides that "women affected by pregnancy, childbirth, or related medical conditions shall be treated the same for all employment-related purposes . . . as other persons not so affected but similar in their ability or inability to work." Even here, however, the enactment takes an extremely narrow view of the interests at issue.

First, in keeping with the broader antidiscrimination framework of which it is a part, the PDA pares down the issues at stake. It considers only the employment interests of the pregnant employee by focusing on her ability or inability to work. It does not consider the broader range of goods realized through parenting for the employee, children, and communities. Thus, in the only portion of federal antidiscrimination law that explicitly considers issues relating to parenting, the only feature of parenting deemed appropriate for legal cognizance is the mother's ability or inability to work, rather than the goods contributed by parenting to parents, children, and the community.

Second, the PDA protects only the medical aspects of pregnancy. A pregnancy-related condition is limited to "incapacitating conditions for which medical care or treatment is usual and normal." All non-medical circumstances that accompany pregnancy and childbirth are excluded from consideration under the statute.

Third, the PDA requires no accommodation for pregnancy and childbearing unless such accommodations are made for other medical conditions. The PDA therefore rejects the notion that the act of bringing children into the world is an activity for which a greater level of protection or support should be required than for medical conditions that lead to similar levels of ability or disability to work. As the Supreme Court stated in *Wimberly v. Labor and Industrial Relations Commission*, under the PDA, "the State cannot single out pregnancy for disadvantageous treatment, but it is not compelled to afford preferential treatment."

* * *

LIBERAL THEORY AND PARENTING

What has prevented the development of a legal framework that can adequately support the complex of needs and aspirations implicated in parenting, despite the general public support for parenting protections? I argue here that the answer derives in part from a particular view of the world that is widely shared within the United States–by members of Congress responsible for passing laws, by judges who interpret laws, by theorists who analyze them, and by citizens who hold such beliefs even while they support broader parenting policies. This world view is composed of a loosely related set of beliefs that derive from, in Charles Taylor's words, "a family of theories of liberalism that is now very popular, not to say dominant, in the English-speaking world."

According to this world view, society is composed of a collection of discrete, autonomous individuals engaged in the pursuit of diverse, equally acceptable plans of life. The state's role in this scheme is to prevent incursions on individuals' liberty to pursue their individual life plans, rather than to further any particular vision of the good life. Under this view, individuals have no obligations to one another unless they freely consent to them. Several features of this account prevent the law from grasping and supporting the fundamentally social and interdependent nature of parenting.

* * *

In summary, several elements of liberal ideology work together to hinder support for parenting. The conception of individuals as autonomous and existing prior to freely chosen obligations and relationships obscures the way in which individuals can be defined by their relationships with others, misconceives conditions of dependency and the need for care, and prevents recognition that individuals may need more support to realize their goals than simply the right to be left alone. The liberal demarcation between the public and private realms legitimizes the view that parenting responsibilities have no place in the realm of work and that government has no business instituting family policies in the employment realm. The conception of the state as simply a neutral arbiter of rights impedes the state from actively supporting parenting.

Finally, the liberal tradition's emphasis on liberty and autonomy obscures the more complex range of goods associated with parenting.

The current legal treatment of the intersection between work and parenting mirrors this liberal philosophy. Title VII replicates liberal theory in framing work-and-parenting issues solely in terms of the right of employers to conduct their business freely and the interests in equality of female employees, conceived apart from relationships with children. In keeping with the liberal view of the state as enforcing the right to fair procedures, the law then construes the employee's interest in equality as the right to be free from sex discrimination, rather than the right to substantive equality. In doing so, it precludes consideration of ways in which the law might affirmatively support parenting responsibilities. The employee's commitment to fulfill parenting responsibilities remains uncomprehended and unprotected in this analysis. Similarly, the needs of children and the benefits to the community realized through parenting go unrecognized. Child rearing, in this view, is conceived solely in voluntarist terms and is valued only as another lifestyle choice. While employees are allowed the right to choose to bear and rear children, they are not supported in securing the conditions that will enable them to combine a productive work life with the bearing and rearing of these children.

Questions and Comments

1. The NAALC's definition of "labor law" expressly includes laws relating to employment discrimination on the basis of sex. Does discrimination on the basis of one's pregnancy status constitutes sex discrimination?

2. Assume that pre-hiring pregnancy discrimination in fact is legal in Mexico. Does the NAALC in any way deprive Mexico of the right, as a sovereign, to decide whether such discrimination shall be legal or illegal under its own domestic labor laws? Does Mexico's failure to specifically declare such a practice illegal violate its duty under NAALC Article 2 to "ensure that its labor laws and regulations provide for high labor standards"?

3. Should pre-hiring pregnancy discrimination be illegal? To what degree is your answer to this question a function of U.S. culture or, as Eichner puts it, of the "dominant liberal philosophy in the United States." Does "protective legislation" such as a federal law prohibiting pre-hiring pregnancy discrimination negatively affect the interests of women? Refer to Sedillo Lopez. Which approach—the U.S. approach of prohibiting pre-hiring pregnancy discrimination or the Mexican approach of permitting pre-hiring pregnancy discrimination—is best for preserving the "traditional" family? Is it appropriate for one country to use the NAALC to criticize the cultural priorities of another country?

4. A suit filed in a Mexican court alleging pre-hiring pregnancy discrimination would be dismissed on the grounds that Mexican law does not recognize any such cause of action. Does the failure of Mexican law to prohibit pre-hiring pregnancy discrimination therefore also constitute a

violation of Mexico's obligation under NAALC Article 4 to ensure "appropriate access to administrative, quasi-judicial, judicial or labor tribunals"?

5.   NCT's proposed submission clearly is proper subject matter for NAO consultations and ministerial consultations. Could the submission advance from ministerial consultations to review by an ECE? Refer to NAALC Article 23. Who makes the determination of whether a matter is trade-related or covered by mutually recognized labor laws? Refer to NAALC Annex 23.

6.   Assuming the matter advances to review by an ECE, what will proceedings before the ECE look like? What type of work product will the ECE generate? Refer to Articles 24–26.

7.   Assuming the ECE concludes its work, can the controversy advance to Article 27 consultations?

8.   Suppose that the facts and the national laws are the same, but the country is Chile and the applicable agreement is the United States–Chile FTA. How would an action go forward, if at all? (Consult Chapters Eighteen and Twenty–Two of the FTA, in the Documents Supplement.)

Chapter 11

THE ENVIRONMENT

11.0 INTRODUCTION: THE ENVIRONMENTAL SIDE AGREEMENT

NAFTA is designed to promote economic development by facilitating the expansion of trade in goods and services in North America. Increased trade unavoidably has environmental and ecological consequences. In a report issued in 1999, the Commission for Environmental Cooperation–one of the international institutions spawned by NAFTA's adoption–grouped NAFTA's potential environmental effects into four broad categories: (1) production, management and technology effects, (2) effects upon physical infrastructure used for transportation and related services, (3) social organization, and (4) government policy. (*See* COMMISSION FOR ENVIRONMENTAL COOPERATION, ASSESSING ENVIRONMENTAL EFFECTS OF THE NORTH AMERICAN FREE TRADE AGREEMENT (NAFTA): AN ANALYTIC FRAMEWORK (PHASE II) AND ISSUE STUDIES 6, 27–36 (1999).)

The first category encompasses the environmental effects which flow from the production of goods and provision of services under NAFTA. These include the effects of the extraction and use of natural resources, the application of technology and management techniques, and the pollution resulting from such processes. The second category, physical infrastructure for transportation and related services, includes the pollution and other environmental consequences resulting from heightened use of "the transportation grid of highways, railways, and ports and public water and sewage treatment facilities" in North America. Infrastructure initially is implicated as inputs are transported to manufacturing plants and later as goods are shipped to market. The third category, social organization, is premised on the notion that NAFTA will have the positive effect of leading to the formation of new entities—*e.g.*, community groups, consumer and environmental coalitions, pollution prevention firms—to press for the redress of environmental concerns. In part, it is thought that new trilateral transnational coalitions will form and will support the creation of conservation measures such as voluntary environmental standards for industry. The final category encompasses all aspects of government activity that may reinforce or offset NAFTA-related environmental effects. Such activity includes government's enforcement of or failure to enforce environmental laws and provision of financial support for environmental protection and conservation programs.

In 1993, after NAFTA had been fully negotiated and signed, the United States, Mexico and Canada took the unprecedented step of negotiating a side agreement on the environment, the North American Agreement on Environmental Cooperation (NAAEC). The NAAEC represents the governments' attempt to reconcile the inherent tension between increased international trade and environmental protection. Because environmental degradation along the U.S.-Mexico border was an especially serious concern to environmental groups and inhabitants of the region, the United States and Mexico entered an additional environmental accord related to NAFTA–the Agreement Between the Government of the United States of America and the Government of the United Mexican States Concerning the Establishment of a Border Environment Cooperation Commission and a North American Development Bank.

This chapter examines the provisions of the various environmental agreements related to NAFTA, as well as the experience of the NAFTA governments in implementing those accords since January 1994.

CEC, THE NORTH AMERICAN MOSAIC: A STATE OF THE ENVIRONMENT REPORT*

INTERNATIONAL COOPERATION

The three nations in North America have been dealing with transboundary environmental issues for decades. The 1909 Boundary Waters Treaty between Canada and the United States provides the principles and mechanisms to help resolve and prevent disputes concerning the quantity and quality of boundary waters. The International Joint Commission was created and given quasi-judicial powers and other responsibilities to assist the governments in implementing the treaty. Another early treaty is The Convention for Migratory Birds in Canada and the United States, which was signed in 1916.

Since then, Canada and the United States have entered into numerous other environmental agreements, including the Great Lakes Water Quality Agreement, first signed in 1972 and since updated, and the 1991 Air Quality Agreement. The latter aims to reduce the transboundary movement of acid deposition precursors by providing assessment, notification, and mitigation of air pollution problems.

The 1944 Treaty Relating to the Utilization of Waters of the Colorado and Tijuana Rivers and of the Rio Grande is considered the centerpiece of the US–Mexican legal framework for managing transboundary waters. It established the International Boundary and Water Com-

* Report of the Commission for Environmental Cooperation, 2002, at 9–10; references omitted, *available at* http:// www.cec.org/files/PDF/PUBLICATIONS/soe _en.pdf. Copyright © 2002, CEC. Reprinted with Permission.

mission as a binational commission with many responsibilities, including the allocation of transboundary water resources, management of reclamation works, and development of joint sewage and sanitation facilities.

Growing concerns about environmental quality in the border region have resulted in the creation of several recent binational institutions. The United States–Mexico Border Environmental Cooperation Agreement (the La Paz Agreement) of 1983 established a process to reduce and prevent various forms of pollution in the border area. The Border Environment Cooperation Commission (BECC) and the North American Development Bank (NADBank) were created in 1994, under the auspices of NAFTA, to address problems related to water supply wastewater treatment and municipal solid waste management in the border region, which is defined in the Charter as the area within 100 kilometers (62 miles) north and south of the international boundary between the two countries. The BECC was established to address shortcomings in environmental infrastructure along the border by overseeing initial project development, while the NADB is responsible for implementing long-term oversight of projects. Another US–Mexico binational arrangement is the "consultative mechanism," created to fulfill commitments under the La Paz Agreement. It commits both countries to publicly disclose information about all existing and proposed hazardous or radioactive waste sites, as well as recycling, treatment and incineration facilities within 100 km of the border. The Integrated Border Environmental Plan (or Border XXI), another recent binational initiative, promotes intergovernmental cooperation and public involvement in sustainable development in the border area.

An example of the commitment to address problems that affect shared ecosystems in North America is the North American Waterfowl Management Plan, a partnership between the three federal governments, other local governmental agencies, NGOs, the private sector, and landowners. An agreement between Canada and the United States was signed in 1986 to help reverse a decline in waterfowl populations, mainly by maintaining and expanding critical wetland habitats in North America. In 1994, the plan was expanded to include Mexico.

Improved scientific understanding of North America's ecological interdependencies has contributed to an accelerated regional convergence of environmental policies. Following the 1992 Earth Summit, and since the North American Free Trade Agreement came into force in 1994, the number of cooperative efforts is growing, many of them involving the Commission for Environmental Cooperation.

Important international agreements and action plans that affect North America include the Montreal Protocol on Substances that Deplete the Ozone Layer, the Convention on Biological Diversity, the Convention on International Trade in Endangered Species of Wild Fauna and Flora (CITES), the Basel Convention (on the transboundary movement of hazardous waste), and the Ramsar Convention on Wetlands. Several of these treaties have yet to be ratified in each of the three countries, however, raising concerns that North American governments may have trouble honoring some of their international commitments. Canada and the United States have not yet been able to stabilize greenhouse gas emissions at 1990 levels, as called for in the 1992 UN Framework Convention on Climate Change. A 1997 agreement with targets for reducing greenhouse gas emissions—the Kyoto Protocol—is still to be ratified by any industrial country and has run into serious resistance in the United States.

* * *

CEC REVIEW COMMITTEE, TEN YEARS OF NORTH AMERICAN ENVIRONMENTAL COOPERATION
Report of the Ten-year Review and Assessment Committee, Jun. 15, 2004*

Ten years ago, Canada, the United States and Mexico negotiated the largest free trade agreement in the world at the time, the North American Free Trade Agreement. NAFTA created a marketplace of 400 million people and a combined GDP in excess of $7 trillion.

A separate international agreement, the North American Agreement on Environmental Cooperation (NAAEC), created a trilateral institution, the Commission for Environmental Cooperation (CEC). This Commission is led by a Council comprising Canada's Minster of Environment, Mexico's Secretary of the Environment and the Administrator of the United States Environmental Protection Agency. The Commission was the first of its kind in the world in linking environmental cooperation with trade relations.

Last fall, the CEC Council mandated our review committee, composed of two representatives from each of the three NAFTA countries, to assess NAAEC's implementation over its first decade and provide recommendations for the future. We have concluded as follows.

The CEC was and remains a unique, innovative and important institution. The CEC has helped both to demonstrate that North America is a collection of linked ecosystems and to create a sense of regional environmental consciousness. The CEC has also facilitated more fluid cooperation among the Parties (Canada, the United States and Mexico) and their various stakeholder groups by broadening their relationships and increasing the number and range of their contacts.

As well as promoting regional environmental cooperation, the CEC plays an important role in addressing the issues around environment and trade. Its work in this area provides the basis for proactive policies to mitigate the possible negative environmental effects of market integration and enhance its possible beneficial effects.

The CEC has pursued both its environmental cooperation agenda and its environment and trade agenda in active collaboration with civil

* Executive Summary, at ix-xi. Copyright
© 2004. Reprinted with permission.

society. It has involved the public of all three countries in its research work, promotional dialogue and information exchange through North American networks of individuals sharing the same interests and created an increasingly valuable body of knowledge of North American environmental issues.

The three Parties have benefitted significantly from the NAAEC. While Mexico has already revised its environmental legislation prior to the NAAEC, the Agreement facilitated progress in a number of areas, including pesticide and pollution prevention. Environmental awareness and the government's commitment to the environment have both grown, driven in part by the public participation process the CEC has introduced.

More specifically:

- The CEC has been an extraordinarily active organization, with a broad range of successful environmental cooperation activities in areas such as the sound management of chemicals, the conservation of biodiversity, the enforcement of environmental regulations and green trade.

- It has helped create a North American environmental community that provides the moral and scientific authority for the three governments to address issues of North American importance.

- The CEC has achieved substantial results on key North American issues such as chemicals management and set the basis for progress on the conservation of North American biodiversity.

- The CEC has built substantial environmental capacities, largely in Mexico but also in the United States and Canada.

- The CEC has advanced our understanding of trade-environment linkages and has provided useful information on the North American environment to a range of audiences.

- The CEC has successfully promoted citizen engagement or environmental issues and increased government accountability regarding the enforcement of environmental laws.

We have also found a number of issues that need attention if the CEC is to realize its full potential to act on the North American environmental agenda. These relate to:

- The need to engage more fully the environment ministers of the three countries. Ministers need to renew their commitment to the CEC as the premier body for trilateral environmental cooperation and for assessing the environmental implications of trade.

- The governance of the CEC. The Parties need to clarify the roles and responsibilities of the CEC's three main bodies–its ministerial Council, the Secretariat and the Joint Public Advisory Committee– as they relate to the cooperative agenda and the citizens' submission process.

- More effective outreach to key stakeholders and the mobilization of the CEC's diverse constituency across the three countries. The CEC must respond to the calls from business, indigenous peoples and academics to engage them more actively in the activities of the CEC while maintaining the active engagement of environmental NGOs.

- A sharper programming focus reflecting the CEC's priorities, its financial resources and increased demands for demonstrated results. Governments and key stakeholders would reap substantial benefits from the CEC playing its convening and research catalyst roles to bring credible information to bear on current key environment and sustainable development issues, for example related to energy and water.

- Establishing an adequate funding basis for the future. In order to continue delivering on its mandate, the CEC will need renewed funding from the three Parties and the ability to leverage additional resources through voluntary contributions and partnerships.

- A continued focus on integrating capacity building into the CEC's activities with an emphasis on helping Mexican government institutions and private organizations strengthen the implementation of environmental laws and policies.

* * *

RAUSTIALA, THE POLITICAL IMPLICATIONS OF THE ENFORCEMENT PROVISIONS OF THE NAFTA ENVIRONMENTAL SIDE AGREEMENT: THE CEC AS A MODEL FOR FUTURE ACCORDS

25 Envtl. L. 31 (1995).*

HISTORY OF THE ENVIRONMENTAL SIDE AGREEMENT

From the outset, environmental concerns plagued the NAFTA negotiations. In response to early congressional concern about the level and thoroughness of Mexican environmental regulation, the U.S. General Accounting Office conducted a survey of Mexican environmental law. The survey concluded, surprisingly, that Mexican environmental regulations were formally as strong as U.S. regulations in nearly all areas. This finding, however, did not assuage the worries of American environmental groups; rather, it refocused their attention on issues of enforcement and monitoring. Recognizing that formal Mexican law, though strict, was ineffective by itself, environmental groups sought to ensure compliance with those laws through a powerful and responsive supranational body to which they had access. This body was to be created in a side agreement devoted solely to environmental issues.

The first official statement mentioning the possibility of such an environmental side agreement appeared in May 1991 when the Bush Administration attempted to address growing concerns. This emphasized the importance the Administration placed on retaining high environmental standards, committed American negotiators to avoid weakening U.S. regulations, and indicated the Administration's intent to seek parallel agreements to NAFTA focused on labor and environmental concerns.

On August 12, 1992, at 1:00 a.m., the trade ministers of the United States, Canada, and Mexico [concluded] the NAFTA accord, just as the American presidential election campaign was gathering steam. Attacks on the agreement ensued immediately from many quarters. The major U.S. environmental groups in particular showed a keen, and generally negative, interest. One month after the signing of NAFTA, the environmental ministers of Canada and Mexico, Jean Chavest and Luis Donaldo Colosio, and the head of the U.S. Environmental Protection Agency, William Reilly, issued a joint statement endorsing the concept of a new trilateral North American Commission on the Environment (NACE). In October of the same year, then-presidential candidate Bill Clinton declared in a campaign speech in Raleigh, North Carolina, that an "Environmental Protection Commission" must be created before implementing any NAFTA. Clinton continued to curry favor with environmental groups throughout the last days of the campaign, stating that if he were elected, NAFTA would be revised to allow private groups to petition the government to bring enforcement actions against objectionable practices.

Most U.S. environmental groups remained skeptical and opposed to NAFTA. Joining with labor unions, they began to campaign against the accord while simultaneously seeking extensive changes that would render NAFTA more environmentally friendly. Their focus was primarily on enforcement matters. Upon taking office President Clinton began to subtly change his rhetoric on NAFTA, affirming his support–though still qualified–in stronger terms than during the campaign. In February, five months after the idea of an environmental commission was first officially proposed, the National Wildlife Federation released a detailed proposal for the NACE. The proposal emphasized the need for powerful enforcement mechanisms and open access to interested private parties in each of the three member states. On March 4, 1993 the Sierra Club, the Humane Society, Friends of the Earth, and twenty-one other environmental groups wrote to new U.S. Trade Representative (USTR) Mickey Kantor stating that a NACE must be empowered to levy sanctions to ensure compliance with national environmental laws.

The enforcement issue, and specifically the use of trade sanctions as a tool of enforcement, proved to be the crucial point around which the NAFTA environmental debate turned. Staking out the opposite position from the environmental lobby, a majority of Republican Senators sent a letter to President Clinton in the spring of 1993 lending their support to

NAFTA, but strongly opposing the creation of new environmental bureaucracies with enforcement powers. Kantor then rejected the notion of
granting enforcement powers to any supranational panel, primarily on
the grounds that it would be unnecessary: "The mere fact of making
[problems] public usually persuades the government to react properly."
Thus, great divisions existed on the issue of environmental enforcement
through trade sanctions both within the U.S. government and without,
as Canada, Mexico, and the GOP firmly opposed the notion.

Preliminary negotiations were finally initiated on the environmental
side agreement on March 17, 1993, concurrently with the supplemental
labor negotiations. The environmental lobby in the United States continued to push hard for the NACE, in the belief that Kantor's more
sanguine view of Mexican compliance was dangerously without basis. By
April 1993, after much debate and discussion within their own ranks and
with government officials, some of the major environmental groups
formally lent their qualified support to NAFTA. Negotiators for NAFTA
convened in Ottawa in May 1993 to begin the first round of serious
discussions on the proposed supplemental accords. Meanwhile, the
breakaway organizations announced that their full support would be
forthcoming if the proposed trinational panel had the power to arbitrate
environmental disputes. Buoyed by this show of support, the Clinton
Administration moved to push with greater alacrity for enforcement
powers. The then-current plan proposed to create two three-member
panels, one for environmental issues and one for labor. The panels
would, after appropriate arbitration proceedings, have the power to
impose trade sanctions by a two-to-one vote. While many Democratic
legislators welcomed this idea, most Republicans criticized the plan for
going too far; Senator John Danforth (R.-Mo.) called it "a disastrous
principle."

Canada and Mexico shared this view of the Clinton plan. Canadian
officials feared that the power to sanction, though clearly directed at
Mexico, could be used arbitrarily against Canada. The precursor to
NAFTA, the U.S.-Canadian Free Trade Agreement, does not contain
provisions for trade sanctions; rather, it allowed each nation to apply its
own trade laws in determining whether imports from the other country
hurt domestic producers. The Canadians had hoped to continue this
system. The negotiations stalled over this issue, and the sanctions
controversy would reemerge persistently over the course of the negotiations as the key stumbling block to agreement. Mexican officials argued
that sanctions would violate Mexican sovereignty, while Canadian
spokespersons called the proposed sanctioning powers too adversarial.
Canadian Trade Minister Michael Wilson suggested, furthermore, that
trade sanctions were fundamentally at odds with the spirit and purpose
of NAFTA as a free trade accord.

Within the United States, many Democrats insisted on a commission
with sanctioning powers while Republicans strongly objected to what
they saw as the creation of unnecessary and unwieldy multilateral
bureaucracies with little accountability. The fifth round of talks began in

July 1993. Though many observers and insiders felt that Mexico had finally come to accept the political necessity of sanctions, discussions of sanctions were postponed until the next round. The Wall Street Journal, meanwhile, reported that the Clinton Administration was backing away from its sanctions proposal just as Mexico was allegedly coming to accept it. The Journal reported an anonymous U.S. negotiator as stating, "[w]e don't expect the Secretariat or the trilateral commission to be imposing fines, sanctions or penalties." Naturally, this position was widely and virulently criticized by environmental interests. Kantor denied the Journal report of U.S. backsliding on the sanctions issue, and went on to state: "We have not changed our position at all.... We want real teeth, real enforcement."

On August 13, 1993, the trade ministers of the United States, Canada, and Mexico announced that they had completed the environmental and labor side agreements. Canada succeeded in its bid to keep trade sanctioning power inert for Canada; the agreements allowed for the imposition of fines by domestic Canadian courts, rather than sanctions declared by the proposed trinational commissions. Mexico backed down and accepted the trade sanctions rather than jeopardize the trade pact any further. With House Majority Whip David Bonior (D.-Mich.) leading the Democratic opposition to the trade pact, Mexico correctly perceived NAFTA's future as precarious.

THE NAFTA DENOUEMENT

In the final months of 1993, the national debate over NAFTA became increasingly virulent, though the vast majority of the commentary revolved around issues of jobs and wages. The environmental community seemed polarized by the final side agreement, with many of the mainstream groups pleased with the outcome, or at least in quiet acquiescence, and more radical groups still fundamentally opposed to NAFTA. The internal debate in the United States over NAFTA reached a fever pitch with the nationally-televised debate between Vice President Al Gore and self-appointed NAFTA nemesis H. Ross Perot on "Larry King Live."

NAFTA had transmogrified from a fairly technical trade and investment agreement, aimed at facilitating the emergence of a freer North American market, to a lightning rod for all complaints and fears of future shifts in the global economy, as well as a symbol for the decline of the American manufacturing job. The pact became a sort of modern-day Shiva, believed to be capable of massively creating and destroying jobs by turns. The environmental issues were increasingly crowded out in the mainstream press, though they continued to garner some limited attention. In the closing weeks, while the job-creating or job-destroying aspects of NAFTA were debated at length within the U.S., little debate occurred over either the terms or the likely long-run effects of the environmental side agreement.

DA SILVA, NAFTA AND THE ENVIRONMENTAL SIDE AGREEMENT: DISPUTE RESOLUTION IN THE COZUMEL PORT TERMINAL CONTROVERSY

21 Environs Envtl. L & Pol'y J. 43 (1998).*

GOALS AND OBJECTIVES

The Environmental Side Agreement sets forth a broad array of goals and objectives in Article I. Specifically, the Agreement aims to ensure that governments properly implement their own environmental laws. The Agreement establishes mechanisms to investigate allegations of environmental wrongdoing, arbitrate environmental disputes, and occasionally to sanction countries that fail to adequately respond to corrective measures. The Agreement's goals include promoting sustainable development based on cooperation, encouraging conservation, avoiding trade distortions or new trade barriers, preventing pollution, and increasing public participation. The objectives emphasize the need for nations to balance environmental protection against numerous countervailing concerns, including ecology, economics, intergenerational equity, and sovereignty.

STRUCTURE OF THE COMMISSION FOR ENVIRONMENTAL COOPERATION

The Environmental Side Agreement establishes the North American Commission for Environmental Cooperation (CEC) and authorizes the CEC to implement its objectives. The CEC, located in Canada, is the heart of the Agreement. The CEC relies on a Council, an Environmental Secretariat, and a Joint Public Advisory Committee to review allegations of environmental wrongdoing.

The CEC Council (Council) is comprised of cabinet-level or comparable representatives from each of the parties to the Agreement. The Council, which convenes at least once a year, implements the Agreement by establishing committees to address specific issues. The Agreement specifies that all decisions of the Council are public unless otherwise dictated. The Council committees deliberate environmental issues and recommend solutions to environmental disputes.

The CEC Secretariat serves as an independent body subject only to the authority of the Council. An Executive Director heads the Secretariat and serves for a three-year term subject to one additional renewal period. The Executive Director appoints and supervises the staff of the Secretariat in accordance with general standards established by the Council. The Council, by a two-thirds vote, may reject any appointment that does not meet these standards. The Secretariat prepares an annual report on CEC activities and the status of Party compliance with Agreement provisions. The Secretariat's basic function, in conjunction with the Council, is to provide public access to environmental information.

The Joint Public Advisory Commission ("Commission") consists of fifteen representatives selected from the public and non-governmental organizations. The Commission's job is to advise both the Council and the Secretariat. Specifically, the Commission ensures that the Council and Secretariat are properly apprized on technical issues and public perspectives regarding individual disputes.

<small>DISPUTE RESOLUTION OF NON-ENFORCEMENT AND ENFORCEMENT MATTERS</small>

The Agreement divides disputes into enforcement and non-enforcement matters. The procedures and duties of the Council and the Secretariat differ depending on which category governs a particular dispute.

Enforcement Matters

The Agreement characterizes a dispute as an enforcement matter when a government is accused of failing to effectively enforce environmental laws. The Agreement further divides enforcement matters according to the nature and timing of the government's alleged nonperformance. If a complaint simply alleges that a government has failed to adequately enforce environmental laws, Articles 14 and 15 supply the procedures for resolving the dispute. However, if a complaint also alleges that the government has established a pattern of continuous, negligent execution of environmental laws for an extensive period of time, then Articles 22 through 36 regulate the dispute.

Article 14

Under Article 14, non-governmental organizations and individuals residing in the appropriate territory may initiate dispute resolution by petitioning the Secretariat. This petition, commonly called a "submission," must not exceed fifteen pages and must clearly identify the Submitters. The Secretariat evaluates the submission to determine if it needs to prepare a response or to compile a factual record. The Council reviews the Secretariat's evaluation and may instruct the Secretariat to create a factual record and/or publicly disclose the final record, if the decision is supported by a two-thirds vote. The record, which includes public comments, may influence the government's perception of the controversy. However, Article 14 does not provide any binding method for settling disputes or enforcing environmental obligations.

Article 22

Article 22 of the Environmental Side Agreement governs disputes in which a party alleges that a government subject to NAFTA continuously and persistently fails to enforce environmental laws. The Article 22 process begins when any party requests consultation. If the parties do not settle the dispute, or settle it inappropriately, any participant may then request the Council to intervene. The Agreement requires the Council to hold a special session within twenty days of the request, unless other arrangements are made. The process incorporates the expertise of CEC members, but Article 22 also allows the Council to consult non-governmental experts.

If the special session does not resolve the dispute after sixty days, Article 22 allows NAFTA parties to utilize a Council-supervised arbitration panel. Any party to the allegation may request the services of an arbitration panel, but the Council must agree to use the panel by a two-thirds vote. The panel is composed of five arbitrators selected from a roster of governmental and non-governmental experts. The panel's duty is to review the complaint to determine if there is a consistent pattern of non-enforcement. Article 22 mandates that submissions must be in writing to provide parties with notice. It also guarantees a hearing so that all parties have the opportunity to participate in the process.

The panel must report its conclusions within 180 days of convening. The panel's report must include specific findings and recommendations. The parties may submit written comments during a sixty-day period before the panel publishes its final report. If the final report validates the allegations, then the parties should implement the resolutions offered in the final report. The parties may resolve the dispute in three different ways. First, the parties may agree to implement the panel's specific plan. Second, the parties may agree to implement certain aspects of the plan. Third, the parties may fail to agree on any plan. If the parties implement the plan partially or not at all, then Article 22 requires further enforcement procedures.

If the parties do not fully resolve the dispute, the panel may reconvene upon request. If the parties agree on only certain aspects of the plan, and fail to adequately implement that plan, the panel must reconvene within sixty days of a formal request. If the panel agrees that implementation is deficient, it can impose a monetary enforcement assessment against the deficient party. If that party neglects to pay the assessment, the council can suspend any NAFTA benefits held by the offending party up to the assessment amount. If the parties do not adopt any plan at all, then the panel, upon request, will reconvene within ninety days and impose a monetary enforcement assessment at that time. If the parties continue to neglect their duty to fulfill the assessment, the Council may suspend their NAFTA benefits. The Council may impose trade sanctions as a last resort.

Non-Enforcement Matters

The Agreement characterizes complaints that do not implicate enforcement of environmental laws as non-enforcement matters. Article 13 of the Agreement governs non-enforcement matters. This section allows the Secretariat to investigate the charges and prepare a report, which the Council supervises. The Council may instruct the Secretariat not to investigate particular charges. When the Secretariat does investigate, the Council may choose to publicly disclose the final report. Generally, the dispute resolution process for non-enforcement matters is less detailed than the process required for enforcement matters.

MAGRAW, NAFTA AND THE ENVIRONMENT: SUBSTANCE AND PROCESS
Environment Magazine (Mar. 1994).*

In October 1993, to strengthen bilateral cooperation along their border, Mexico and the United States entered into the Agreement Between the Government of the United States of America and the Government of the United Mexican States Concerning the Establishment of a Border Environment Cooperation Commission and a North American Development Bank. These institutions will provide additional mechanisms for the two governments to work towards resolving the serious environmental problems that exist along the border. Initially, attention will focus on the most serious public health and environment needs in the border region: providing clean drinking water, treating wastewater, and managing hazardous waste. Problems outside the border region may also be addressed under the Agreement if they have significant transboundary environmental effects.

The Border Environment Cooperation Commission (BECC) will work with affected state and local governments and with the public to develop and coordinate solutions to environmental problems. It will provide environmental, technical, and financial expertise to projects, but it will not develop or manage projects itself. It will also certify projects for financing by the North American Development Bank (NADBank), provided they meet appropriate environmental, technical, and financial criteria. The BECC will be governed by a binational Board of Directors–a majority of whose members will come from the border region–that represent federal, state and local governments and the public. An Advisory Council and certain procedures and requirements will ensure input from affected communities and the larger public.

The NADBank will finance environmental infrastructure projects certified by the BECC. It will be governed and capitalized by the two governments and will make available approximately $2 billion to $3 billion in loans and guarantees. The NADBank will supplement existing sources of funding and support the ability of governments and investors to raise capital from other sources. Taking into account these new funds as well as existing sources of financing, it is estimated that a total of $7 billion to $8 billion in financing will be available over the next decade for environmental infrastructure projects along the U.S.-Mexican border.

BECC, JOINT STATUS REPORT, SEPTEMBER 2004**

Assistance Programs

More than US$30.69 million has been allocated by BECC's Technical Assistance Program to aid in the development of 225 environmental infrastructure projects related to water, sewage, and municipal waste in 131 communities on both sides of the U.S.-Mexico border. Through its technical assistance programs, the NADB has authorized more than US$14.4 million in grant funding to carry out 163 institutional strengthening and project development studies for 77 border communities.

Project Development and Certification

To date, the BECC has certified 105 environmental infrastructure projects which will cost an estimated US$2.41 billion to build. Sixty-nine certified projects are located in the United States; 36 are located in Mexico. The NADB is working with the sponsors of 92 certified projects who have requested financial assistance. NADB participation in these projects is estimated at almost US$753.7 million, with 51 percent going to projects in Mexico and 49 percent to projects in the United States. As of September 30, 2004, the NADB has authorized just over US$689.2 million in loans and/or grant resources to partially finance 83 infrastructure projects estimated to cost a total of US$2.33 billion.

MORENO, ET AL., FREE TRADE AND THE ENVIRONMENT: THE NAFTA, THE NAAEC, AND IMPLICATIONS FOR THE FUTURE

12 Tulane Envtl. L.J. 405 (1999).*

* * *

One project certified by the BECC is the construction of a $25.8 million water treatment facility in the City of Brawley, California. This facility is designed to bring the city into compliance with existing federal and state water quality standards. NADBank's financing package helped Brawley (an unrated community) access funds from private sector institutional investors.

While some of the BECC-certified projects have focused on bringing a community or other entities into compliance with existing law, other projects have sought to move beyond mere compliance. Three such projects are the $99.6 million South Bay Reclamation Plant in San Diego, California, the $11.7 million Wastewater Reuse Project in El Paso, Texas, and the $170,000 Ecoparque project in Tijuana, Baja California. These facilities will treat wastewater for reuse in irrigation and, in some cases, for industrial use. In addition, these projects will reduce both the amount of waste discharged into nearby bodies of water, and the number of primary water sources used for irrigation and industrial purposes.

The efforts of the BECC and the NADBank have been subject to some criticism. Much of the criticism of these two institutions flows from the perception that the BECC has been too slow to certify projects and the NADBank has been too slow to provide financing. The BECC has generally attributed any delays to its constituency's inability to develop projects that are technically sustainable, while the NADBank found the projects to be financially unsustainable. Both organizations, however, have taken steps to address these concerns. For its part, the BECC has established a Technical Assistance Program to assist communities in developing technically and financially sustainable projects. The NADBank has established an Institutional Development Cooperation Program (IDP) to help eligible communities operate their water, wastewater, and municipal solid-waste management services effectively and efficiently. The NADBank has also established the Border Environment Infrastructure Fund (BEIF) to make environmental infrastructure projects affordable to border communities by combining grant finds with loans or guarantees for projects that would otherwise be financially unfeasible.

The BECC–NADBank agreement demonstrates the possibility of negotiating bilateral environmental agreements in conjunction with multilateral trade agreements as a mechanism for furthering the protection of the environment. These agreements are important to the development of infrastructure and capacity in economically disadvantaged regions that may not otherwise be equipped to address environmental concerns arising from increased development.

PROBLEM 11.1 CANADIAN ENFORCEMENT: SPORT FISHING, FISH TOXICANTS AND FIRST NATIONS

SECTION I.   THE SETTING

The Canadian province of Manitoba, which borders the states of North Dakota and Minnesota, is a world-famous sport fishing paradise. Manitoba's more than 100,000 lakes, rivers and streams offer wildlife enthusiasts over twenty-eight species of fish, including walleye, northern pike, several varieties of trout, smallmouth bass, carp, and lake sturgeon. The sport fishing industry, which includes 105 lodge and outfitter operations, generates a significant share of the Province's total tourism revenue.

Manitoba also is the home of many Native American tribes or "First Nations," including the Buffalo Point, Canupawakpa, Opaskwayak, Sagkeeng, and Sioux Valley First Nations. The ancestors of these and other First Nations fished the waters of the region for many generations before Europeans arrived in North America. Although Canadian law long has recognized the right of aboriginal peoples to fish for food, tension remains due to the competing interests of the First Nations and the sport fishing industry. On one hand, the First Nations seek to preserve their traditional fish stocks and protect the Canadian wilderness from depletion caused by tourism. On the other hand, the sport fishing industry contends that tourism and environmental conservation are compatible objectives.

A controversy between the groups that has been brewing in recent years centers around the use of fish toxicants–pest control products introduced into a body of water to eliminate undesirable ("pest") fish species so that highly prized sport fish can flourish. The Canadian Fisheries Act, a federal law, governs the management of fisheries resources, habitats and conservation throughout the country. Federal Fish Toxicant Regulations delegate to the provincial governments the authority to deposit fish toxicants in provincially-managed lakes, rivers and streams. Canadian federal law prohibits private parties from using fish toxicants and requires the provinces to investigate and prosecute claims that private parties are using such toxicants.

According to the First Nations, the Manitoban government does not exercise appropriate care in regulating the use of fish toxicants. As a result, the First Nations claim, essential fish stocks and fish species that are part of their traditional diets are being destroyed. The First Nations charge that the provincial government has authorized the use of toxicants when they were not necessary and refused to penalize members of the sport fishing industry found to possess and use fish toxicants. Appeals by the First Nations to the federal Department of Fisheries and Oceans for action have proven futile.

Members of the First Nations of Manitoba (FNM), a coalition of tribes within the Province, have read about the NAAEC in the popular media and on the internet and wish to pursue whatever relief or action may be available to them under the Agreement. They approach you, the Director of the Aboriginal Rights Clinic at Queen's College of Law in Winnipeg, Manitoba for assistance. As you consider the readings, comments and questions which follow, try to formulate advice for the First Nations on how they should proceed under the NAAEC.

SECTION II. FOCUS OF CONSIDERATION

The NAAEC is innovative in that it permits participation by non-governmental organizations and even ordinary citizens in international environmental controversies. However, some have criticized the NAAEC's citizen submission process because the standing requirements to make a public submission are unduly strict, citizens have no real participation in the process after a submission has been filed, there are no time limits on action by the Secretariat, and the process leads not to a binding judgment against a government but merely to the preparation of a "factual record." It is important to assess whether such criticisms are accurate by coming to understand how the citizen submission process works in practice.

The NAAEC also has been criticized for containing major exclusions or exceptions. As we will come to see, the fact that the NAAEC is not in effect in most of Canada has significant implications. For example, citizens in Canadian provinces are precluded from challenging the environmental actions or omissions of their provincial governments unless those governments have formally acceded to the NAAEC. Critics also have been quick to point out that the "natural resources exclusion" set forth in Article 45.2(b) of the NAAEC precludes inquiry into a substantial portion of North America's most pressing environmental concerns. These exclusions may defeat the ability of private parties to resort to the NAAEC institutions for aid in rectifying environmental wrongs by one or more of the NAFTA governments.

The NAAEC and Guidelines for Submissions on Enforcement Matters Under Articles 14 and 15 of the NAAEC are essential to an analysis of this problem. They are found in the Documents Supplement.

SECTION III. READINGS, QUESTIONS AND COMMENTS

PAIGE, H2OH NO!

Insight Magazine, Vol. 14, No. 22 (June 15, 1998).*

Nestled in the foot-hills of the snow-capped Sierra Nevadas, the sparkling waters of California's Davis Lake may look pure enough to drink. But don't, unless you like your Perrier laced with poison.

Contrary to its pristine appearance, everything in Davis Lake is dead, and its waters, which once quenched thirsts in the nearby town of Portola, are off limits. Why? Because, in arrogant disregard of local opposition, the California Department of Fish and Wildlife dumped poison into the lake seven months ago in an effort to kill off the northern pike. The aggressive, non-indigenous species was introduced to the area and posed a serious threat to other species, according to officials.

But in killing the pike the state also tainted the lake, which contrary to reassurances from Fish and Wildlife, continues to contain traces of the poison three months after it was supposed to return to normal. Portola is without a source of drinking water, and its town fathers are not happy. They reportedly are thinking of suing the state for negligence.

LANDERS, CALIFORNIA ICE ANGLERS CAN TAP DAVIS REVIVAL

Field & Stream (Jan. 1, 1999).**

After eight months without, Davis Lake once again became a fishing destination when the hatchery trucks pulled up to the shoreline in July. Since then more than 1.2 million trout have been stocked, making the reservoir a good winter angling destination.

Fishing was stalled last year after a chemical treatment in October, 1997, by the California Department of Fish and Game (CDFG) intended to remove the nonnative northern pike that threatened to devastate other downstream fisheries was botched. The non-trout fish species were eliminated, but an overdose of chemical forced the agency to bring in alternate water supplies for residents who depended on the reservoir's water. Fish could not be stocked as planned, and the entire county suffered from the loss of a premier fishery on the 7–mile-long reservoir.

The department rallied with a massive plant of 900,000 trout in July, followed by additional plants through the fall of trout ranging from fingerlings to lunkers weighing 15 pounds.

"Davis became a great trout fishery—and a great trophy fishery— the day after we stocked it," said Bruce Barngrover, CDFG regional hatchery supervisor.

PAIGE, CALIFORNIA POISONS LAKE TO KILL THE NORTHERN PIKE

Insight Magazine, Vol. 15, No. 24 (June 28, 1999).*

In 1997 the state of California purposely poisoned beautiful little Davis Lake, a pristine pool of blue cradled in the High Sierras, in a scorched-water effort to exterminate the northern pike, an aggressive, non-indigenous species that the Fish and Game Department said posed a threat to nearby rivers. The lake quickly would bounce back, "professionals" with the state assured skeptical locals, who rely on the lake as a tourist draw and source of water. But the deadened lake didn't rebound as predicted, resulting in financial hardships, lawsuits, criminal charges against the state and a recent $10 million settlement paid by California to the community.

But this spring the pike came bouncing back along with the rest of Davis Lake, and state officials again are skulking around (albeit with a lower profile). Locals are wondering if it's deadly deja vu all over again. "Oh, no, here we go again," one local said.

The discovery several weeks ago of two mature pike in the lake has state officials wondering how the pike survived the last poisoning or if they purposely were reintroduced by someone to the lake. "What we're trying to do is to establish whether we have a self-sustaining population of pike. If we do, then we're going to have to sit down with the community and discuss what to do," said a spokesman for California Fish and Game.

But the community—once burned, twice shy—is understandably reluctant again to place its fate in the hands of Fish and Game. "It's ridiculous," one local businessman told the Associated Press. "We've all suffered. My business went down to nothing. There have been pike all over the Midwest, all over the country. They are good game fish. Why not just go catch 'em?"

STIENSTRA, PIKE PROBLEM AT LAKE DAVIS WON'T GO AWAY

San Francisco Examiner (Aug. 4, 1999).*

The Department of Fish and Game again finds itself in a hell of a mess over Lake Davis.

Not only were another 28 pike caught last week, but the surprise appearance of tons of baby catfish over the weekend makes it near certain that the poisoning of Davis was completely botched by the DFG.

So, now what?

"Lake Davis is one of our favorite places," said Paulette Kenyon, visiting with her family from Pleasanton. "We too noticed the baby catfish, and as far as we know, no catfish were replanted. If they are alive, the pike may have pulled through as well. What are they going to do? It really is heartbreaking. There is so much wildlife up here, birds, deer and such. It's just sickening. Now what?"

Pending the results of DNA testing, the logic being advanced privately by DFG biologists is that the springs at the bottom of Lake Davis created "safe spots" during the 1997 poisoning. That would explain how breeding populations of pike and catfish could have survived the poisoning. That will be confirmed with the DNA tests at UCLA, which will document the origin of the pike, either from a new illegal plant or from the pre-poison population.

"There appears to be a self-sustaining, spawning population of pike in Lake Davis," said Dennis Lee, senior fisheries biologist for the DFG. He said the size of the pike, 6 to 9 inches, are the size of fish spawned this past spring.

So, now what?

The DFG has not publicly figured its options, and the latest news has reopened scars with the local community, which vehemently opposed the poisoning and then tried to prosecute DFG personnel when they went through with it.

Every state and federal fishery biologist in the West believes it would be Armageddon for Bay–Delta salmon and other fisheries if pike slipped over the spillway at Grizzly Dam at Davis, swim down the Feather River to Lake Oroville, then pass downstream below the outlet and then enter the Sacramento River.

Pike are a vicious predator with the ability to overwhelm other species, especially trout and salmon, then reproduce to the point that they become stunted and appear nothing more than a huge mouth connected to a tail. Pat O'Brien, senior biologist for the DFG, called the pike the ultimate "time bomb."

So, now what?

The options are extremely limited:

Screen the outlet and leave the lake alone: This would involve the Department of Water Resources building a device that would work as a permanent screen and fish grinder, killing any fish that slipped over the Davis spillway and into Grizzly Creek. This is the cheapest solution but involves a high degree of risk. What if the device wasn't 100–percent effective? It would also mean that the DFG would tolerate the pike fishery at Davis, making other lakes vulnerable to the fish being transported and spread illegally.

Re-poison the lake: Because poisoning was a success at Frenchman Lake near Chilcoot when pike were discovered there in the 1980s, it is always an option. But the poisoning of Davis cost an estimated $5 million in overhead, employee costs, fish restocking and fines, the equivalent of the sale of 175,000 fishing licenses. In addition, any proposal to try poison again would set off something like a Civil War in Plumas County.

Drain the lake and kill the pike: This sounds simple at first, but it is no simple feat. It would require removing the dam at Grizzly Creek, then while the water is drained into Lake Oroville, somehow keeping the pike from passing downstream. There is no precedent that this would be successful. Every such assumption the DFG has made in this debacle has proved wrong.

Davis Lake is about 50 miles northwest of Reno in southern Plumas County, set at 5,775 feet in the Sierra Nevada. It has always been a special place, with the richest aquatic biology of any lake in the mountains, with an abundant food chain that produces beautiful, bright-spotted rainbow trout, huge by Sierra lake standards.

I was here over the first week in September 1994, when the first pike was caught. It immediately sent shock waves through the local community—as well as among biologists across the United States.

At the time, Al Bruzza, who owns the Sportsmen's Den in Quincy, correctly predicted the entire debacle. "You know they're going to propose poisoning Davis," said Bruzza that weekend in '94. "But Davis isn't your normal lake. There's no guarantee that they'll get them all, and there's no guarantee that whoever put the pike there in the first place just doesn't do it again."

DUSSIAS, ASSERTING A TRADITIONAL ENVIRONMENTAL ETHIC: RECENT DEVELOPMENTS IN ENVIRONMENTAL REGULATION INVOLVING NATIVE AMERICAN TRIBES

33 New England L. Rev. 653 (1999).*

The effects that the increasing tribal role in environmental regulation will have on the environment may well be determined, at least in part, by Native Americans' perspective on nature and the environment. Native Americans traditionally have had a very different relationship with "client nature" than have most regulators; they are, we might say, "old friends." Native Americans are longstanding close observers of the effects of human activities on the environment.

Nature plays a very special role in the traditional Native American world view. Although we must be careful to avoid over-generalizing, over-simplifying, and over-romanticizing the relationship between Native Americans and nature, I think that it is safe to say that respect for nature plays a more central role in Native American society, culture, and religion than it does in Euro–American society, culture, and religion. Native Americans have traditionally enjoyed an intense interrelationship with the forms and forces of the environment. All natural forms are considered sacred. As one Native American scholar has put it, "seeing the universe through the eyes of a contemporary Native American is to see it as a complex whole of natural forces and spiritual beings–animal, human, and supernatural–woven together in a delicate, intricate, and indivisible web." Human beings have a special role as guardians of the natural world, while still sharing a "oneness of essence" with animals, rather than being wholly superior to them. In the words of White Mountain Apache Tribe Chairman Ronnie Lupe, "the land and its fruits have never been simply for the taking but are elements of our responsibility for stewardship of the lands that the Creator has provided to us. Our people have always been taught to respect the land and living things."

During the nineteenth century, federal government officials established a variety of programs aimed at destroying Native American culture and religion and assimilating Native Americans into Euro–American society. Native Americans' nature-centered beliefs and ceremonies were viewed as childish superstitions and as evidence of general tribal backwardness. These beliefs were to be replaced, the government hoped, with Christianity and with a new understanding of the land as an individually owned commodity. From this perspective, the various elements of nature were viewed simply as raw materials ripe for human exploitation. Thus, to the extent that a Native American environmental ethic exists today, its continued existence evidences the failure of government efforts to completely destroy the traditional Native American world view.

COMMISSION FOR ENVIRONMENTAL COOPERATION, SUMMARY OF ENVIRONMENTAL LAW IN CANADA

<www.cec.org/infobases/law>.*

The federal Fisheries Act is another important piece of federal legislation for the protection of the Canadian environment. Under the

Fisheries Act, it is an offence for anyone to carry on any works or undertaking that result in the harmful alteration, disruption, or destruction of fish habitat. Furthermore, it is an offence to deposit or permit the deposit of any type of deleterious substance in "water frequented by fish". The Fisheries Act is administered by Fisheries and Oceans Canada (DFO) and Environment Canada. DFO is responsible for fisheries management and the protection of fish habitats. Environment Canada is responsible for water quality aspects of fish habitats. In addition, there are a number of federal-provincial agreements and memoranda of understanding delegating certain fisheries powers to particular provincial governments.

The Fisheries Act has significant penalties for contravening its provisions, and the courts can order the violator to refrain from engaging in the activity which is the cause of a discharge or deposit into waters frequented by fish.

FISHERIES ACT, R.S.C. c. F–14*

Section 35. (1) No person shall carry on any work or undertaking that results in the harmful alteration, disruption or destruction of fish habitat.

(2) No person contravenes subsection (1) by causing the alteration, disruption or destruction of fish habitat by any means or under any conditions authorized by the Minister or under regulations made by the Governor in Council under this Act.

Section 36. (3) Subject to subsection (4), no person shall deposit or permit the deposit of a deleterious substance of any type in water frequented by fish or in any place under any conditions where the deleterious substance or any other deleterious substance that results from the deposit of the deleterious substance may enter any such water.

(4) No person contravenes subsection (3) by depositing or permitting the deposit in any water or place of: ... (b) a deleterious substance of a class, in a quantity or concentration and under conditions authorized by or pursuant to regulations applicable to that water or place or to any work or undertaking or class thereof, made by the Governor in Council....

Section 38. (3) An inspector may, at any reasonable time, enter any place, premises, vehicle or vessel, other than a private dwelling-place or any part of any place, premises, vehicle or vessel used as a permanent or temporary private dwelling-place, where the inspector believes on reasonable grounds that any work or undertaking resulting or likely to result in the deposit of a deleterious substance in water frequented by fish or in any place under any conditions referred to in subsection 37(1) is being, has been or is likely to be

* Updated through April 30, 2004. Available at http://laws.justice.gc.ca/en/F–14/60370.html.

carried on, and the inspector may, for any purpose related to the enforcement of this section, conduct inspections, including examining any substance or product found therein, taking samples thereof and conducting tests and measurements.

Section 40. (1) Every person who contravenes subsection 35(1) is guilty of

(a) an offense punishable on summary conviction and liable, for a first offence, to a fine not exceeding three hundred thousand dollars and, for any subsequent offence, to a fine not exceeding three hundred thousand dollars or to imprisonment for a term not exceeding six months, or to both; or

(b) an indictable offense and liable, for a first offence, to a fine not exceeding one million dollars and, for any subsequent offence, to a fine not exceeding one million dollars to imprisonment for a term not exceeding three years, or both.

(2) Any person who contravenes subsection 36(1) or (3) is guilty of [same as (a) and (b) above]

Section 42. (1) Where there occurs a deposit of a deleterious substance in water frequented by fish that is not authorized under section 36 or a serious and imminent danger thereof by reason of any condition, the persons who at any material time: (a) own the deleterious substance or have the charge, management or control thereof, or (b) are persons other than those described in paragraph (a) who cause or contribute to the causation of the deposit or danger thereof, are, subject to subsection (4) in the case of the persons referred to in paragraph (a) and to the extent determined according to their respective degrees of fault or negligence in the case of the persons referred to in paragraph (b), jointly and severally liable for all costs and expenses incurred by Her Majesty in right of Canada or a province, to the extent that those costs and expenses can be established to have been reasonably incurred in the circumstances, of and incidental to the taking of any measures to prevent any such deposit or condition or to counteract, mitigate or remedy any adverse effects that result or may reasonably be expected to result therefrom.

(2) All the costs and expenses referred to in subsection (1) are recoverable by Her Majesty in right of Canada or a province with costs in proceedings brought or taken therefor in the name of Her Majesty in any such right in any court of competent jurisdiction.

. . .

(4) The liability of any person described in paragraph (1)(a) is absolute and does not depend on proof of fault or negligence but no such person is liable for any costs and expenses pursuant to subsection (1) or loss of income pursuant to subsection (3) if he establishes that the occurrence giving rise to the liability was wholly caused by: (a) an act of war, hostilities, civil war, insurrection or a natural

phenomenon of an exceptional, inevitable and irresistible character; or (b) an act or omission with intent to cause damage by a person other than a person for whose wrongful act or omission he is by law responsible.

(5) Nothing in this section limits or restricts any right of recourse that any person who is liable pursuant to this section may have against any other person.

(6) No proceedings may be commenced under subsections (1) to (3) at any time later than two years after the occurrence to which the proceedings relate could reasonably be expected to have become known to Her Majesty in right of Canada or a province or to any licensed commercial fisherman, as the case may be.

* * *

FISH TOXICANT REGULATIONS SOR/88–258

1. These Regulations may be cited as the Fish Toxicant Regulations.

2. In these Regulations,

"Act" means the Fisheries Act;

"fish toxicant" means a pest control product that conforms to the requirements of the Pest Control Products Act and the Pest Control Products Regulations and that is used for the purpose of destroying any fish that is a pest as defined in section 2 of that Act.*

3. For the purposes of ... the Act, fish toxicants are hereby prescribed as deleterious substances that are authorized to be deposited.

4. For the purposes of ... the Act, the waters where fish toxicants are authorized to be deposited are the waters of the provinces of Saskatchewan and Alberta and the non-tidal waters of the provinces of Ontario, Quebec and Manitoba.

5. For the purposes of ... the Act and subject to section 6, the following persons are prescribed as persons who may, in the absence of any other authority, authorize the deposit of any fish toxicant: ... (c) in relation to the Province of Manitoba, the Minister of Natural Resources for that Province....

6. For the purposes of ... the Act, the prescribed conditions for granting the authorization referred to in section 5 are the following: (a) the Minister or the chief fishery officer is satisfied that the eradication of any fish that is a pest by the use of fish toxicants in any waters set out in section 4 and the subsequent restocking of those waters will enhance fishing in those waters; and (b) the authorization is given in writing.

* The Pest Control Products Act defines "pest" to mean "any injurious, noxious or troublesome insect, fungus, bacterial organism, virus, weed, rodent or other plant or animal pest...."

7.   For the purposes of . . . the Act, the condition under which fish toxicants are authorized to be deposited in the waters referred to in section 4 is that the deposit does not adversely affect fish in the waters adjacent to the waters where the deposit is made.

ANSSON, THE NORTH AMERICAN AGREEMENT ON ENVIRONMENTAL COOPERATION AND NATIVE AMERICAN TRIBES: HOW CAN TRIBAL INTERESTS BEST BE PROTECTED?

66 UMKC L. Rev. 837 (1998).*

. . . A tribe in its political capacity is not an individual or a nongovernmental organization (such as a corporation).** As a result, a tribe in its political capacity has no recourse under the Side Agreement if NAFTA negatively impacts the tribe. . . .

* * *

. . . only a Party to the agreement, an individual, or a non-governmental organization may participate in the dispute resolution process set up by the Environmental Side Agreement. An Indian tribe in its political capacity is none of these and may not participate in the processes designed to resolve disputes about environmental degradation caused by or linked to the North American Free Trade Agreement. So why were tribal entities not included as an entity that could rightfully bring a claim under the Side Agreement?

The Parties to the Agreement simply failed to afford Indian tribes the opportunity to bring claims under the Environmental Side Agreement. Mexico's failure to promote a tribal government's right to bring a claim in a multinational forum is not surprising since Mexico has rarely acknowledged tribal rights within their own country. However, the United States and Canada also failed to advocate that tribes in their political capacity should be afforded the opportunity to bring claims under the Side Agreement. This is curious since the United States and Canada have allowed natives to participate in other international environmental forums.

Note on the Application of the NAAEC in Canada

In Canada, environmental matters largely are within the jurisdiction of the provincial governments. Therefore, as is true with respect to the Labor Side Agreement, the scope of Canada's participation in the Environmental Side Agreement mostly is a function of provincial adoption of an intergovernmental agreement—the Canadian Intergovernmental Agreement Regard-

** A tribe in its political capacity is a sovereign entity with its own government. *Worcester v. Georgia,* 31 U.S. (6 Pet.) 515, 559–61 (1832). As such, a tribe is not within the Side Agreement's definition of a non-governmental organization. . . .

ing the North American Agreement on Environmental Cooperation. *See* Annex 41. As of 2004, only the federal government, Quebec, Manitoba, and Alberta had signed the Intergovernmental Agreement. Two of Canada's largest and economically-important provinces, Ontario and British Columbia, had not yet signed. Unfortunately, then, the following article is still generally accurate eleven years after NAFTA itself entered into force.

CANADIAN PROVINCES VIRTUALLY EXEMPT FROM PACT'S ENVIRONMENTAL SIDE ACCORD

17 BNA Int'l Env. Rep. 50 (Jan. 25, 1994).*

VANCOUVER, British Columbia (BNA)—Provisions in the supplemental agreement on the environment under the North American Free Trade Agreement virtually exempt Canadian provinces from cooperating on environmental issues related to the trade deal, according to environmentalists and government officials.

Canada's tenuous commitment to the [Commission for Environmental Cooperation] recently became increasingly apparent as the federal government in Ottawa began the process of choosing which city would host the commission's secretariat, the location of which was awarded to Canada when the deal was signed.

Alex Manson, director of North American and global strategies at Environment Canada, speaking from his office in Hull, Quebec, Jan. 12 told BNA that provisions in the side agreement require Canada to indicate which provinces adhere to the side agreement, since provinces are not automatically bound by federal approval of the accord. Canadian Prime Minister Jean Chrétien announced Dec. 2, 1993, that he would proclaim legislation to bring NAFTA into effect on the Jan. 1 agreed-upon date.

In Canada, responsibility for the environment is a shared jurisdiction, Manson said.

The extent of Canada's obligations as outlined in Annex 41 of the North American Agreement on Environmental Cooperation are circumscribed by provincial jurisdiction over most environmental laws.

Provinces that do not sign the agreement and fail to enforce their own environmental laws are not bound under the agreement, according to Section 4 of the annex.

PROVINCES' PARTICIPATION VOLUNTARY

Daniel Seligman, Washington representative for trade and environmental programs for the Sierra Club, said Jan. 18 that the lack of constitutional authority at the federal level in Canada makes provincial participation voluntary, a situation which could give Canadian industries a competitive advantage.

Seligman said the exclusion of natural resources from the agreement, 'essentially done at Canada's behest, to shield the timber industry,' renders the document of little interest to Canadian environmentalists.

This 'carving out' of natural resources also disturbs the even playing field NAFTA was designed to create, he said.

'The fact that the provinces can opt out of it suggests that they can take advantage of trade provisions,' Seligman said. 'If they choose to under-enforce environmental laws for competitive reasons, there would be no recourse for anyone in the United States,' he said.

Individual provincial governments must accede to the accord if Canada is to play a significant role under the agreement, according to the text of Annex 41.

Canada is precluded from taking action against the United States or Mexico for non-enforcement of those countries' laws unless the matter would come under federal jurisdiction if it were to arise in Canada, according to Section 4 of the annex.

Should the matter, were it to arise in Canada, fall under provincial jurisdiction, Canada is obliged to muster support for the agreement from enough provinces to account for at least 55 percent of Canada's gross domestic product, according to Section 4(b).

In addition, where the matter concerns a specific industry or sector, the provincial support for the agreement must constitute at least 55 percent of total Canadian production in that industry or sector, according to Section 4(c).

ACCEPTANCE FAR FROM ASSURED

Provincial acceptance of the pact is far from assured, according to Manson, who admitted 'some provinces indicated they were not completely happy or completely satisfied with NAFTA or the side agreements.'

'We certainly hope they will sign on,' he said, 'but if a province says no way, then a province says no way.... There's no recourse on it.'

Both Canadian and American environmentalists expressed grave doubts that enough provinces would come on board to give the agreement any teeth in Canada.

Provinces 'have very few incentives' to accede to the pact, according to Seligman. 'They have all the benefits of trade under NAFTA already, where as for Mexico, signing onto the environmental side agreement was a condition for signing onto NAFTA. There is little incentive for provinces to subject themselves to outside scrutiny.'

Michelle Swenarchuk, executive director of counsel for the Canadian Environmental Law Association in Toronto said Jan. 17 that 'a number of provinces are vehemently opposed' to the environmental commission.

* * *

B.C. Unlikely To Sign

British Columbia, one of Canada's wealthiest provinces, is unlikely to sign the agreement, according to provincial government officials. British Columbia is the leader in economic growth in Canada, has the largest forest sector, and boasts the country's third largest city, Vancouver.

'It's very much in the air whether B.C. will sign onto the side accord,' said an official with the provincial Environment Ministry. The source, who spoke on condition of anonymity Jan. 11, said the government of British Columbia, in addition to questioning the usefulness of the side accords, 'had serious reservations about the whole NAFTA process.'

* * *

Possible Holdouts

British Columbia and Ontario, which together account for about half of Canada's gross national product and industrial activity, according to Greasely, could 'hold out for a considerable length of time,' preventing Canada from having a viable role under the terms of the accord.

The British Columbia government's dissatisfaction with NAFTA and doubt about the commission's effectiveness in local matters was echoed repeatedly by environmental groups based in the province.

Greg MacDade, a lawyer with the Sierra Legal Defense Fund in Vancouver, Jan. 13 said, 'We agree generally with the British Columbia government's position on NAFTA.' Vicky Husband, spokeswoman for the Western Canada chapter of the Sierra Club in Victoria Jan. 13 said she personally questioned the usefulness of the side deal because of 'serious problems' with the NAFTA agreement itself.

Adriane Carr, executive director, Western Canada Wilderness Committee in Vancouver, Jan. 13 told BNA, 'Our position is to increase local control over management of the resource base, rather than to accede to international trade directives.' The organization, an umbrella for a score of environmental groups, is opposed to NAFTA because of the tendency of trade agreements to lower standards to the lowest common denominator,' Carr said.

She cited concern about the export of British Columbia water as another impediment to public and governmental support for the pact.

Leonard Fraser, spokesman for the Canadian Earthcare Society in Victoria, an organization with membership in the transborder Cascades International Alliance, Jan. 13 told BNA it was 'no secret that Canadian groups are not particularly enamored of the agreement.'

Questions and Comments

1. Article 14 of the NAAEC opens by stating that the Secretariat may consider a submission by any "non-governmental organization or person."

How is the term "non-governmental organization" defined for purposes of Article 14? *See* NAAEC Art. 45.1. The FNM members ask you whether the affected tribes or "First Nations" could initiate a submission in their formal capacities as tribes. What is your advice on this point? *See* Ansson. If you conclude that the tribes could not proceed in their capacities as sovereigns, who in this problem would qualify under Article 14 to file a submission? *See* Guideline 2. What action will the Secretariat take if it receives an Article 14 submission from an ineligible party? *See* Guideline 6.

2. Article 14.1 limits the subject matter of citizen submissions to assertions that a Party is failing to effectively enforce its "environmental law." How is the term "environmental law" defined for purposes of Article 14? *See* Art. 45.2. Assume that the Canadian government enacted a law that permitted unlimited commercial fishing throughout Canada to the point that traditional First Nation fish stocks became depleted, would this new law qualify as "environmental law" for purposes of an Article 14 submission? Based on the facts in this problem and the definition of "environmental law" in Article 45.2, do the Fisheries Act and Fish Toxicant Regulations constitute "environmental law"?

3. An Article 14 submission must charge that a NAFTA government is "failing to effectively enforce" its environmental law. How is this phrase defined for purposes of Article 14? *See* Art. 45.1. What claims could the FNM make that, with respect to fish toxicants use in Manitoba, the Canadian government is failing to effectively enforce its environmental law?

4. Does Article 14 allow for the submission of a claim asserting that the government of Manitoba is failing to effectively enforce its environmental law? *See* Annex 41.1. Assume that Manitoba strictly complies with the Fisheries Act and Fish Toxicant Regulations but that its neighboring provinces, Saskatchewan and Ontario, do not; consequently, toxicants illegally deposited in rivers in those provinces flow into Manitoba, killing large numbers of fish. In view of the refusal of Saskatchewan and Ontario to adopt the Intergovernmental Agreement, can an Article 14 submission properly be brought against those provinces contesting their failure to effectively enforce the Fisheries Act and Fish Toxicant Regulations? *See* Note on the Application of the NAAEC in Canada.

5. Assume that your Aboriginal Rights Clinic will serve as counsel on a submission filed on behalf of the FNM setting forth the claims discussed in Questions 3 and 4. What further Article 14.1 requirements must the submission meet to be accepted by the Secretariat? *See* Article 14.1; Guidelines 3–5.

6. After the Secretariat accepts a submission under Article 14.1, it must determine whether to request a response from the government complained against. What are the criteria for making this determination? *See* Article 14.2 and Guideline 7. What happens to the submission if the Secretariat determines that no response from the Party is merited? *See* Guidelines 7.2 & 8. If the Aboriginal Rights Clinic was to bring the submission on its own behalf, would it matter that the Aboriginal Rights Clinic is not the person directly harmed? Does the fish toxicant submission raise matters whose further study would advance the goals of the NAAEC? *See* Article 1. Would it matter if the FNM failed to pursue remedies available

to it before filing the submission? Is the fish toxicant submission drawn "exclusively" from mass media reports?

7.   Assume that the Secretariat concludes that a response from the governments of Canada and Manitoba is merited. Article 14.3(a) permits a Party to, in effect, terminate the proceeding if it can show that the matter is the subject of a pending "judicial or administrative proceeding." What constitutes a pending "judicial or administrative proceeding" for purposes of Article 14.3? *See* Art. 45.3. What is the rationale for terminating NAAEC proceedings simply because parallel judicial or administrative proceedings are ongoing?

8.   Assuming the Secretariat requests a response from the governments of Canada and Manitoba, is the filing of a response mandatory? What type of information will the governments' response(s) include? *See* Guideline 9.

9.   Assuming the Secretariat requests and receives a Party response in the fish toxicant matter, what happens next? *See* Article 15.1; Guidelines 9 & 10.

10.   The Ten Year Review is of course a product of the CEC and the NAFTA Parties; thus, one would not expect it to be overly critical. Reading between the lines, particularly in the "issues that need attention" section, how would you describe the problems with the system?

PROBLEM 11.2 MEXICAN ENFORCEMENT: MOUNTING BORDER POLLUTION PROBLEMS AND SCARCE ENFORCEMENT RESOURCES

SECTION I.   THE SETTING

In eleven years, NAFTA has proven to be extraordinarily successful at what it was principally intended to do, *i.e.*, increasing trade between the United States, Canada and Mexico. But along with significant gains in North American trade have come the pitfalls of increased production, particularly for the millions living along the 1,600 mile border shared by Mexico and the United States.

Environmental problems in the border region that pre-dated NAFTA have grown worse. Supplies of fresh water have declined due to increasing demands by agriculture, business, industry, and inhabitants. On a daily basis, hundreds of millions of gallons of untreated industrial and municipal sewage flow into the Pacific Ocean, Tijuana River, and Rio Grande River. Government testing confirms the presence of alarming levels of fecal coliform, fertilizers, pesticides and other pollutants in border water sources. Air quality also has suffered. Rising demand for electrical power adds to the emissions of millions of tons of sulfur dioxide by the coal-burning power plants on the Mexican side of the border. The lack of an adequate hazardous waste disposal system in Mexico leads to the contamination of landfills. Mexican industry located along the border produces over 100,000 tons of hazardous waste per month. The biggest offenders are the electronics, chemical and furniture industries which use large amounts of industrial solvents and paints. Studies show that perhaps as many as two-thirds of the hazardous waste generated by the maquiladoras is disposed of in compliance with Mexican laws; other studies, however, suggest that the compliance rate is much higher. In any event, the health consequences of mounting water, air and soil pollution are startling. Border residents are experiencing higher incidents of birth defects and pollution-related illnesses, including asthma, tuberculosis, lead-poisoning, cancer, auto-immune disorders, and hepatitis.

Although it was anticipated that expanded trade would have some negative effects on the border environment, few expected those effects to arise so rapidly and in such great magnitude. Since 1994 when NAFTA entered into force, Mexican enforcement of environmental laws in the border region largely has been sporadic at best. This is true despite substantial pressure on the Mexican government by domestic and international forces to tend to environmental matters.

Fearful of the health threat posed by the worsening environmental crisis along the border and furious with the Mexican government for its failure to address the crisis, 2 million citizens in sister-cities and towns stretching from Brownsville/Matamoros to San Diego/Tijuana formed the Coalition for a Clean and Healthy Border (CCHB). The objective of the CCHB, working with attorneys from numerous U.S. and Mexican environmental groups, is to prosecute the largest citizen submission in the history of the NAAEC touching on a sweeping array of border environmental problems and including thousands of specific instances of Mexico's failure to effectively enforce its environmental laws.

Some months ago, CCHB representatives personally delivered a 15–page submission (accompanied by boxes of supporting documents) to the Secretariat in Montreal. Although it took seven months to decide, the Secretariat concluded that the submission meets the requirements of Article 14.1 and Article 14.2, and requested a response from the Mexican government. After eleven months, Mexico submitted a 250–page response, asserting numerous technical objections to the submission, rebutting each allegation of nonfeasance, and concluding with the statement: "Mexico is in full compliance with its obligations under the NAAEC."

The CCHB now awaits the decisions of the Secretariat and Council on whether to prepare a factual record pursuant to NAAEC Article 15. You are a law student intern at the Environmental Secretariat in Montreal, Canada and have been asked to draft a memo on whether to proceed to a factual record. What is your conclusion?

SECTION II. FOCUS OF CONSIDERATION

The initial focus here is on the so-called "Mexican problem." The NAAEC came to pass mostly due to environmental concerns related to Mexico. The fact that the United States effectively imposed the NAAEC on Mexico caused tremendous resentment in that country. As late as

1998 the NAAEC Independent Review Committee reported that: "The perception that the CEC was designed mainly to watch over Mexico has not faded. . . . even though more citizen submissions have been directed at Canadian rather than Mexican environmental enforcement, a perception of institutional imbalance persists and is difficult to shake."*

Mexico's environmental laws, as written, are at least as strict as those of the United States. Thus, controversy concerning Mexico centers on what is the fundamental cause of the country's failure to effectively enforce its environmental laws. One obvious factor is the lack of adequate enforcement resources. The disparity of economic development and wealth between Mexico and the United States makes it unrealistic (and perhaps unfair) to expect Mexico to reach similar levels of environmental enforcement. Still, some maintain that Mexico's lack of environmental justice is not a resources problem but is a product of deeper political and social ills in the country—ills that NAFTA and the NAAEC certainty cannot be expected to solve.

Article 15 of the NAAEC provides for the preparation and public disclosure of "factual records" in cases initiated under Article 14. After receiving a Party response to a citizen submission, the Secretariat recommends that a factual record should (or should not) be prepared. If the Council authorizes the preparation of a factual record, the Secretariat then proceeds to prepare it. Upon the Council's approval, the final factual record may be made public. The Article 15 process has been subject to attack on a number of grounds. Critics argue that the process fails to set time limits on the actions of the Council and Secretariat, does not provide objective criteria for decisions by those institutions, and does not culminate in a binding resolution against a Party found to have failed to effectively enforce its environmental laws. An analysis of the "Mexico problem" in the context of the border environmental crisis allows us to judge the value of the Article 15 process and assess the validity of such criticisms.

NAAEC Article 15 and Guidelines 10 through 13 are essential to an analysis of this problem. They are found in the Documents Supplement.

SECTION III.   READINGS, QUESTIONS AND COMMENTS
NOTE ON MEXICAN ENVIRONMENTAL LAW AND AUTHORITIES

Mexico adopted its first comprehensive federal environmental law, the General Law of Ecological Balance and Environmental Protection ("Ecology Law"), in 1988. The Ecology Law contains stringent regulations concerning air pollution, hazardous waste, water quality, soil use and conservation, and related matters. The Ecology Law also provides for civil and criminal liability for violations. Violators may be fined, temporary or permanently closed, and/or imprisoned for up to six years.

---

* Independent Review Committee, Four–Year Review of the North American Agreement on Environmental Cooperation: Report of the Independent Review Committee, at ¶ 3.1 (June 1998), available at <http://www.cec.org/>.

"The Ecology Law is complemented by a number of media-specific laws and regulations in the areas of water, occupational health and safety, pesticides, fertilizers and toxic substances, fisheries, forestry, hunting, mining, agriculture, energy, and transportation of hazardous materials."*

Mexico's central environmental authority is the Secretariat of the Environment and Natural Resources (SEMARNAT). SEMARNAT formulates national environmental policy; coordinates all activities relating to the protection of natural resources; issues Official Mexican Standards (NOMs) for waste water discharges, hazardous wastes and other substances; and evaluates environmental impact assessments (EIAs) of proposed construction projects.

SEMARNAT includes, *inter alia*, three major decentralized agencies, the National Institute of Ecology (INE), Federal Attorney General for Environmental Protection (PROFEPA), and National Water Commission (CNA). The INE implements environmental protection programs. The PROFEPA, working through its headquarters in Mexico City and state delegations, enforces environmental laws, conducts inspections, and coordinates enforcement activities with state and local enforcement authorities. The CNA regulates and monitors wastewater discharges into federal waterways.

All thirty-one Mexican states have their own environmental laws and authorities who act on matters not within the exclusive jurisdiction of the federal government. Environmental matters not reserved to the federal government or the states are handled by municipal authorities.

"In sum, the common perception of Mexican environmental regulation as a permissive body of law no longer holds true. Instead, current Mexican environmental law provides a strict regime of environmental protection through its incorporation of modern environmental legal requirements and penalties."**

Mexico is no longer a one-party system. President Vincente Fox, a member of the PAN, who took office in December 2002, was the first Mexican leader in 71 years that was not a member of the PRI. A number of state governors have also been members of PAN. PAN's lack of a majority in the Mexican congress has been blamed in part for Fox's difficulties in governing. Many of Szekely's criticisms of the Mexican political system remain valid today, some five years after the following article was written.

---

* Commission for Environmental Cooperation, Summary of Environmental Law in Mexico, at ¶ 4.1 <www.cec.org/infobases/law/>.

** Nicolas Kublicki, *The Greening of Free Trade: NAFTA, Mexican Environmental Law, and Debt Exchanges for Mexican Environmental Infrastructure Development*, 19 COLUM. J. ENVTL. L. 59, 89 (1994).

SZÉKELY, DEMOCRACY, JUDICIAL REFORM, THE RULE OF LAW, AND ENVIRONMENTAL JUSTICE IN MEXICO
21 Hous. J. Int'l L. 385 (1999).*

By the end of 1997, political developments in the country seemed to hold the promise for a change in the basic foundations underlying the more-than-questionable record of compliance and enforcement of environmental legislation and, for that matter, of the national legislation as a whole.

This is due to the fact that the problem of environmental justice in Mexico is closely linked to and the unquestionable result of numerous political realities in Mexico. The lack of environmental justice is part and parcel of the precarious situation of democracy in the country, the bitter realities of the non-empire, the ineffectiveness of the rule of law, and the extremely poor quality of administration of justice in the country.

* * *

How could one expect a decent record of environmental legislative compliance and enforcement in a country where the contravention of the law is the daily rule rather than the exception and where the legal system in general is and has been historically plagued by the following:

a) A persistent, systematic, and generalized pattern of institutionalized official corruption at all levels and branches of government. Throughout the national territory, widespread influence peddling, graft, racketeering, bribery, payoffs, kickbacks, and abuse of authority exists, which makes it the sixth most corrupt country in the world after Nigeria, Bolivia, Colombia, Russia, and Pakistan, according to a report by Transparency International;

b) Prevailing impunity and the lack of transparency and accountability on the part of public officials. This impunity is at times acknowledged by some high officials and for others, such as Dr. Clemente Valdes, has even been "legalized" by the governing class through laws designed in such a way that those officials simply do not have to account for or respond to anyone for the ways in which they govern, much less for the manner in which they use and abuse public funds;

c) A simulated division of powers that still exists in the letter of the law, but in practice has been virtually eliminated;

d) A Congress that, historically, has been nothing more than a mere rubber stamp mechanism to quasi-legitimize the decisions of the executive branch and has amended more than two-thirds of the articles of the constitution, blindly and obediently following the dictates of the President;

e) State Governors who even today, in the case of a majority of them, to a large degree serve at the pleasure of the President, despite the federal system of government provided for by the constitution;

f) Ineffective public institutions that have become dysfunctional to the point of causing a breakdown in governance;

g) A notorious lack of independence in the judiciary, coupled with prosecutorial incompetence and dishonesty;

h) Discrimination, inequality, and a systematic denial of justice to the poor majorities, particularly the indigenous peoples, and at the same time, a system of justice that is often up for sale to whoever can pay for it and accessible only to the privileged few;

i) Systematic police brutality, extra-judicial executions, deplorable incarceration conditions, and widespread torture and violation of fundamental human rights which are establishing a worrisome pattern, despite the increasing activity of non-governmental organizations, which are sanitized by the government;

j) Governmental cooption of the various sectors of society, such as the professional and workers' unions, forming a corporate system of social control that breeds corruption; and

k) The largely unchallenged reign, for more than sixty years, of a single political party that has operated as a so-called "rotating dictatorship," staying in power through electoral fraud, that generates favors, and thrives on all of the above.

As if all of that was not enough, the country's precarious rule of law has been further shattered by the following:

a) The scourge of drug trafficking and its role in organized crime;

b) The use of political assassinations by the system, such as those in 1994 of PRI Presidential Candidate Luis Donaldo Colosio, PRI General Secretary Jose Francisco Ruiz Massieu, and of hundreds of opposition party members;

c) The widespread lack of security and reign of violence in the country, the legal uncertainty in most transactions, and the inability of the institutions to cope with crime, which is increasingly recognized by the government itself and exasperating the public. The proliferation of incidents of lynching and self help, thus prompting some hard-line sectors to demand the reinstatement of the death penalty and even the suspension of basic rights to criminals;

d) The operation of death squads (such as the infamous *Paz y Justicia* in Chiapas), of especially violent police groups (such as the Zorros and the Jaguares in Mexico City) and of other paramilitary groups that participate in rural and urban massacres (such as those in the Ejido Morelia in Taniperlas, Acteal in Chiapas, and Aguas Blancas and El Charco in Guerrero), and the increasing use of army intervention in civil police matters; and

e) The proliferation of white collar crimes and official financial scandals. . . .

How could there be a good record of environmental observance in such a "fundamentally flawed" system of justice where, according to Jorge Camil, the rule of law is nowhere to be found?

* * *

In the midst of such legal realities, go ahead and try as a concerned citizen of Mexico to challenge and stop the construction of a large tourist development project in a coastal area that is also the habitat of an endangered species of flora and fauna protected by the law. Try to stop the dumping of nuclear or hazardous wastes in a site located on top of aquifers and near a rural community. Try to stop a highly-polluting industrial project in a zone where the permitted land use is "ecological preservation" and where the land serves as a recharge area for the water supply of a neighboring town.

Try to ensure compliance by a powerful and influential entrepreneur who belongs to or supports the political or financial establishment. Try to make the Mexican government enforce environmental legislation in one of the many projected activities that will cancel the availability and enjoyment, for present and future generations of Mexicans, of the already scarce natural resources. These projects involve the commission of crimes typified in existing laws, often with the tolerance or negligence of competent authorities.

Finally, try in the current situation of the rule of law in Mexico and as a well meaning environmental authority to overcome the hard political resistance of the trade bureaucracy. The trade bureaucracy is supported at the highest levels of government. Try to secure the badly needed implementation of legally-mandated environmental modalities and restrictions on the exploitation of resources, the production of goods, or the rendering of services, which are alleged to keep the country competitive in international trade.

MORENO, ET AL., FREE TRADE AND THE ENVIRONMENT: THE NAFTA, THE NAAEC, AND IMPLICATIONS FOR THE FUTURE

12 Tulane Envtl. L.J. 405 (1999).*

One of the primary concerns with the NAFTA negotiations was Mexico's ability and/or willingness to enforce its existing environmental law. Also of concern was the perceived disparity between the degree of environmental protection afforded by Mexican environmental law and that afforded by United States and Canadian laws. Recent events, however, suggest that Mexico is making a greater effort in its enforcement program than critics anticipated. "From 1992 to 1996, Mexico conducted 12,347 inspection and compliance verification visits in the border area; partially or totally closing 548 facilities and fining 9,844 facilities. As a result, Mexico report[ed] a seventy-two percent reduction in serious violations in the maquiladora industries from 1993 to 1996, and a forty-three percent increase in the number of maquiladora facilities in complete compliance." Mexico's efforts have also included participation in cooperative efforts to increase its enforcement capacity through training in criminal enforcement of environmental laws, hazardous waste inspection, water discharge inspection, and investigatory sampling techniques.

In 1992, the Mexican government instituted an auditing program to promote industry leadership in voluntary compliance. As of April, 1997, 617 facilities had completed environmental audits through this program. In addition, 404 facilities had signed action plans in which they agreed to implement improvements to their facilities and/or procedures in order to attain, continually assure, and exceed compliance. These action plans have resulted in the commitment of at least $800 million U.S. dollars to environmental improvement projects in Mexico.

Since becoming a signatory to the NAAEC in 1994, Mexico has also taken steps to maintain high levels of environmental protection by amending its organic environmental law, the 1988 General Law on Ecological Balance and Environmental Protection (LGEEPA). In general, the 1996 Amendments are premised on a "new" environmental policy based on the principle of sustainable development. The Amendments strengthen environmental planning tools and provide for greater public participation. Additionally, the Amendments provide for: (1) greater specificity for the conduct of environmental impact assessments of private activities; (2) increased sanctions for recidivism; (3) more specific emergency injunctive authority; and (4) tighter hazardous waste control. The Amendments also add forfeiture and permit revocation as administrative penalties, and codify Mexico's environmental auditing program to promote self-regulation. While there has been some internal debate in Mexico regarding whether the decentralization of certain responsibilities and the new provisions for environmental impact assessments will be more protective of the environment, it is significant that Mexico has taken steps to improve its organic law to provide for better enforcement. Government officials have also publicly affirmed their political will to apply the new provisions vigorously and effectively. This will be crucial to improvements in the environment in Mexico and in the border area of the United States.

SCHILLER, GREAT EXPECTATIONS: THE NORTH AMERICAN COMMISSION ON ENVIRONMENTAL COOPERATION REVIEW OF THE COZUMEL PIER SUBMISSION

28 U. Miami Inter–Am. L. Rev. 437 (1997).*

Although some Mexican environmental legislation resembles U.S. laws, the Mexican government has historically failed to effectively enforce its environmental laws. Recently, Mexico has exhibited a commitment to higher environmental standards and a willingness to correct pollution problems, particularly along the Texas–Mexico border. In 1992, Mexico began serious efforts to enforce its environmental laws with the establishment of the federal office of the Environmental Attorney General. Notwithstanding the improving Mexican enforcement record and the new Secretariat of the Environment's continuing commitment to enforcement, the effectiveness and quality of Mexican enforcement effort significantly lags behind that of Canada and the United States.

Mexico's lack of financial resources significantly inhibits enforcement of its environmental laws. Government inspectors are few, and their salaries and morale are low. However, recent plant closings, the hiring of additional inspectors, and joint Mexican–U.S. enforcement efforts demonstrate Mexico's recent resolve to enforce its environmental law.

Although the Mexican government has established over 5000 health, safety, and environmental standards pursuant to the Ecology Law, limited public notification and lack of procedure to ensure private sector participation have resulted in a vague system of establishing standards and technical regulations.

COMMISSION FOR ENVIRONMENTAL COOPERATION, THE DEMAND FOR ENVIRONMENTAL EDUCATION AND TRAINING IN MEXICO
<www.cec.org> (1997).**

Mexico's economic climate is a major barrier to both the supply and demand of environmental education and training today because the resources to pay for employees attending classes are scarce. Nevertheless, the demand for environmental education in the industrial sector has grown dramatically in recent years. Today, over 250 higher education programs are offered annually in Mexico, in addition to more than 200 diplomado courses and over 600 short courses, most of which were begun in the past decade. Industrial participation in these programs serves to reinforce prior comments noting the interest of the industrial sector in environmental education and training, especially for executives and technical staff.

Prior studies and survey results all indicate that increased awareness of regulations and enforcement actions has the effect of increasing demand in specific sectors.

* * *

One point that clearly emerges from the survey is the lack of a regional influence in the demand picture; differences in relation to size and sector were noted but large, medium-size, and small companies all showed the same three areas of highest priority:

• Standards and legislation,

• Pollution prevention programs, and

• Wastewater treatment.

Another important point is the great variability in the awareness levels of the different industrial sectors. Demand appears to vary drastically among respondents as a function of their awareness, skills, regulatory knowledge and other factors. Many respondents are at a stage where they desire basic information rather than skill-set development.

Two points worth noting are that the size of the market is sufficiently large to attract numerous training institutions and that demand appears to be the highest where companies perceive a direct economic benefit. "Ecoefficiency" then, must be at the core of any incentive program to foster and promote environmental programs in both short and long terms. It is clear, however, that companies are willing to pay very little to train each worker, thus leading to the conclusion that fewer workers will be trained in the short term than indicated by the respondents. It does seem, though, that worker training will increase, especially in an improved economic climate, as better environmental training programs are put into place and executives and technical staff are trained.

The short-term demand for environmental education and training is characterized by three basic points:

• Although there is interest in environmental training, it is for low-cost programs and primarily in areas pushed by regulators or where environmental action has favorable economic consequences.

• Certain sectors, for instance the chemical, plastics, and state-owned companies, have a greater degree of environmental awareness than other sectors and therefore desire more detailed, skill-oriented environmental training programs.

• While all sectors need awareness training, some are ready for skill-based training. "Train the trainer" programs are needed to promote more rapid progress.

One of the problems with the development of both short-and long-term environmental training and education strategies is the fact that most of the higher education programs are concentrated in the Federal District while only 13 percent are offered in the southern and southeastern parts of the country. An analysis of programs by geographical distribution shows that two-thirds of the programs are offered in only six states plus the Federal District. These six states (Baja California, Coahuila, the State of Mexico, Jalisco, Nuevo León and Veracruz) and the Federal District have institutions of higher education that represent, in each state, a diversity of over ten different environmental programs.

One-third of the baccalaureate programs, 45 percent of the masters' programs and 64 percent of the doctoral programs are offered by institutions located in the Federal District and surrounding states. On the other hand, the southern region of the country offers only 8 percent of the baccalaureate and 2 percent of graduate education programs. Also concentrated in urban areas are diplomado courses, 40 percent of which are offered by institutions in the Federal District, where over 60 percent of short courses are also offered.

The apparent lack of environmental education and training infrastructure outside the Federal District and a few select areas of the country creates problems for companies without easy access to a sufficient diversity of programs. The expansion of environmental training programs beyond the few locations where they are offered today is a necessary step in the development of Mexico's environmental conscience. This needed program expansion presents opportunities for regional cooperation between the three neighbors in North America.

* * *

The process of economic globalization constitutes the most important driving force influencing the development of a long-range environmental education and training framework. In developing such a framework, it is important that production practices be modified to take into consideration the process of globalization and the environmental management standards demanded by production in a global market. The manufacture of products in Mexico must incorporate the environmental protection measures expected from both the national and international buying public; however, the fact that countries such as Mexico lack qualified human resources to implement global standards in both the public and private sectors must also be taken into consideration when such measures are developed.

While the industrial sector has some resources to support environmental training, and does use them, especially in those areas calculated to improve productivity and efficiency, the real challenge is to convince companies of the benefit of being "environmentally friendly," not only by reducing costs but also by improving community relations. One way to involve companies more intimately could be to document successful experiences in order to showcase the benefits of investing in environmental education and training.

It is probably not realistic to expect that large subsidies or multilateral credits will be available in the short term. Instead, the modest program recommended herein perhaps represents the best alternative.

The most difficult challenge, especially in the short term, is attracting smaller companies to participate in environmental education and training programs. With this in mind, the following suggestions are offered:

- Increase the number of awareness-building programs, including brochures and pamphlets. These include free or low-cost programs which apply directly to the needs of the smaller companies.

- Continue environmental audit and inspection programs aimed at smaller companies in order to reinforce awareness.

- In association with the industrial associations, develop environmental education programs of a general nature at low cost.

* * *

RECOMMENDATION OF THE SECRETARIAT TO COUNCIL FOR THE DEVELOPMENT OF A FACTUAL RECORD IN ACCORDANCE WITH ARTICLES 14 AND 15 OF THE NAAEC, NO. SEM–96–001

<www.cec.org> (June 7, 1996).*

In accordance with Article 15.1, and considering the possibility of a present failure to effectively enforce environmental law, the Secretariat recommends to Council that a Factual Record be prepared. The preparation of a Factual Record would shed light on both submitters' allegations of non-enforcement and the government of Mexico's important contentions in this matter.

A Factual Record would consider all of the information relevant to the issue of whether the Mexican environmental authorities' conduct in not requiring the submission of an [environmental impact assessment (EIA)] on the totality of works contemplated in the Cozumel Port Terminal project may constitute a failure to enforce existing law. For the most part, these considerations turn on facts relating to the definition of a "port terminal" under the Law of Ports ("Ley de Puertos") and the relevance of this issue to the matter under consideration, the extent to which the project or projects have been "authorized", and the facts relative to the documentation generated after January 1, 1994.

Given the concerns discussed above, the Secretariat does not advocate the examination of acts or conduct which occurred prior to the entering into force of the NAAEC for the purposes of evaluating any alleged failures to enforce law at that time, including for example the EIA prepared in 1990 for the Cozumel pier.

Finally, the Secretariat considers that the preparation of a Factual Record in this matter will promote the objectives stated in Article 1(g) and 1(f) of the NAAEC, which include "enhanc[ing] compliance with, and enforcement of, environmental laws and regulations" and "strengthen[ing] cooperation on the development and improvement of environmental laws, regulations, procedures, policies and practices".

MODEL LETTERS SENT BY THE SECRETARIAT, FINAL FACTUAL RECORD OF THE CRUISE SHIP PIER PROJECT IN COZUMEL, QUINTANA ROO
<www.cec.org> (1997).*

NAME

POSITION

This is to inform you that on August 2 of this year the Council of the Commission for Environmental Cooperation (CEC) instructed the Secretariat to prepare a Factual Record pursuant to the submission filed by three Mexican Non-governmental Organizations pertaining to "the failure to effectively enforce environmental legislation by Mexican authorities in regard to the port terminal project in Playa Paraíso, Cozumel, Quintana Roo."

In preparing the Factual Record, the Secretariat, in accordance with the provisions of Section 15.4 of the North American Agreement on Environmental Cooperation, "shall consider any information furnished by a Party, and may consider any relevant technical, scientific or other information that: a) is publicly available; b) submitted by interested non-governmental organizations or persons; c) submitted by the Joint Public Advisory Committee; or d) developed by the Secretariat or by independent experts."

Considering that the institution under your responsibility might have relevant information for the preparation of this Factual Record, the CEC Secretariat will be contacting you through Beatriz Bugeda, Chief of the Mexican Liaison Office, to whom you may also forward any information that might be relevant for the preparation of the said Record. . . .

I wish to thank you for the attention you will be giving to this matter and avail myself of this occasion to send you my warm regards.

Sincerely,

Victor Lichtinger

Executive Director

* * *

NAME

POSITION

As you already know, the Secretariat of the Commission for Environmental Cooperation (CEC), under instructions from its Council composed of the Secretaries and Ministers of the Environment of the United States, México and Canada, is preparing a Factual Record pursuant to the submission filed by three Mexican Non-governmental Organizations pertaining to "the failure to effectively enforce environmental legislation by Mexican authorities in regard to the port terminal project in Playa Paraíso, Cozumel, Quintana Roo."

In accordance with the provisions of Section 15.4 of the North American Agreement on Environmental Cooperation, the information to be considered by the Secretariat includes, among other sources, that which is "submitted by interested non-governmental organizations or persons."

Given that you or your organization have explicitly stated your interest in the case under consideration, we are inviting you to submit to this Secretariat, as soon as possible, the information that you might have and that, in your opinion, should be included in the referred to Factual Record. We would be most thankful should you be kind enough to forward this information in writing to Beatriz Bugeda, Chief of the Mexican Liaison Office, to whom you may also forward any information that might be relevant for the preparation of the said Record. . . .

I avail myself of this opportunity to send you my warm regards.

Sincerely,

Victor Lichtinger

Executive Director

BUGEDA, IS NAFTA UP TO ITS GREEN EXPECTATIONS? EFFECTIVE LAW ENFORCEMENT UNDER THE NORTH AMERICAN AGREEMENT ON ENVIRONMENTAL COOPERATION

32 U. Richmond L. Rev. 1591 (1999).*

The Cozumel submission represents a good example of both the potential that Article 14 has as a means to promote environmental law enforcement in North America, as well as the loopholes and limitations that the mechanism suffers from in practice.

The submission dealt with an alleged failure of enforcement of environmental laws in Mexico. Three Mexican non-governmental organizations, the Mexican Center for Environmental Law, the Committee for the Protection of Natural Resources, and the International Group of One Hundred presented the submission to the Secretariat of the CEC on

January 18, 1996. These organizations alleged failure on the part of the Mexican environmental authorities to effectively enforce environmental impact assessment law with regard to a port terminal project on the island of Cozumel.

According to the submitters, the failure to enforce environmental laws was harming the Paraiso coral reef. The Secretariat of the CEC requested a response to the submission from the Government of Mexico, and in light of this response, informed the Council that the submission warranted developing a factual record. The *Final Factual Record of the Cruise Ship Pier Project in Cozumel, Quintana Roo* was released to the public on October 24, 1997.

* * *

Undoubtedly, one of the major aspects of the NAAEC is the opportunity it creates, through Articles 14 and 15, for non-governmental organizations and individual citizens with no specific affiliation, to demand that their respective governments effectively enforce environmental laws, and to publicly denounce those governments when such enforcement does not occur. Through this procedure, the Secretariat of the CEC is empowered, within significant limits, to investigate the diligence of the parties in enforcing domestic environmental legislation. The Citizen's Submission process is undoubtedly an interesting and innovative procedure that allows citizens, NGOs, and even residents of North America to perform a role as watchdogs of the environmental performance of the three governments. However, this procedure suffers from many of the flaws emphasized by its critics. Because it does not provide for any private direct action and entails no actual enforcement, its efficiency is limited to the political pressure generated by the press and the public. Its role may be to embarrass governments into compliance.

The Cozumel Submission, the first such submission that resulted in a factual record, is a good example for measuring the practical impact of the Citizen's Submission process. When the submission was presented, and particularly when the Secretariat requested a response from the Mexican government, it captured the attention of the media in the three countries. The media attention may have been due to two facts: it was the first submission to generate a factual record, and it dealt with an alleged failure of enforcement by Mexico. During the negotiations of the NAFTA and the NAAEC, different parties severely questioned both Mexican environmental laws and their enforcement by the government.

Later, Mexico's thirty-six page response to the submission captured the attention of environmental groups, legal specialists, and the media. This created a spirited debate over Mexico's allegations that the agreement could not be applied "retroactively," that the submission exceeded the jurisdiction of the CEC, and that the submitters did not certify the damages they suffered nor exhaust local remedies.

In fact, some environmental groups believe that the declaration of the Cozumel Reef as a protected natural area was a direct result of the submission. The Mexican government severely questioned the role of the Secretariat, both in its response to the submission and in press conferences held by environmental authorities, including the Minister. When the three members of the Council cast the official vote, however, the Mexican government declared that it would act in a spirit of solidarity and cooperation, and joined the United States and Canada in instructing the Secretariat to develop a factual record.

The submission was presented in January of 1996, and almost two years passed before the final *Cozumel Factual Record* was released to the public in October of 1997. By then, the initial interest of environmental groups and the media had all but vanished. Very few newspapers in North America covered the release of the report or the reaction by the parties involved. In Mexico, it practically went unnoticed.

The submitters held a press conference and distributed a document with their interpretation of the *Cozumel Factual Record*, alleging that "it proved failure by the part of the Mexican environmental authorities to effectively enforce environmental law." On the other hand, some Mexican officials have said off-the-record that they are "pleased" with the *Cozumel Factual Record* because they believe that, even if it reaches no conclusions, it supports their position. Meanwhile, the JPAC has said nothing, and the Council remains silent to this day. For the CEC, with the release of the *Cozumel Factual Record*, the process is terminated.

One might wonder whether the procedure served its purpose and if the public is better informed as a result. The truth is that the procedure had very little impact on the environmental community, and none whatsoever on the tourist project in Cozumel that led to the submission.

The fact that the record does not provide any judgment or evaluation regarding the allegations made by the submitters might have disappointed the public. Indeed, the efficiency of the procedure was compromised as the political momentum faded during the long process. In any case, the critics of the CEC who claimed that it was born with no teeth seem to have scored a point.

BOLINGER, ASSESSING THE CEC ON ITS RECORD TO DATE
28 Law & Pol'y Int'l Bus. 1107 (1997).*

The NAAEC and its implementing institution, the CEC, were much criticized by many in the environmental community as weak political constructs that would fail to adequately address the environmental problems that would stem from the liberalization of trade represented by NAFTA. In the wake of the CEC's activities to date, such criticism has not abated and has indicted the institution on several counts: (1) the CEC is insufficiently independent and therefore has to "pull its punches" when reporting on environmental problems or investigating failures to enforce; (2) it is a "toothless" institution with no power to enforce its recommendations; and (3) its procedures are suspect and provide for inadequate transparency and public participation. This Part addresses each of these contentions and concludes that while the naysayers make some valid points, the CEC has the potential to be effective. If its potential is maximized, and if it can operate in conjunction with a stronger border infrastructure development policy, the CEC is a vital step forward for international trade agreements that will ultimately deliver on a promise to "do no further harm" to the environment.

CRITICISMS

The Political Issue

Critics contend that the CEC is "strapped into a political straight-jacket" because its Council is comprised of political appointees who are necessarily limited in their ability to respond to citizen complaints. This critique assumes that an independent Council and Secretariat could more aggressively address claims of non-enforcement of environmental laws. These critics' worst fears were realized, they would argue, when the Secretariat's Silva Reservoir Report determined that botulism, and not heavy metals, was the primary cause of the mass mortality of water birds at the Silva Reservoir: the report pulled punches and "covered up" the true cause of the bird deaths to protect those politically accountable. Furthermore, critics argued that the Secretariat's [Endangered Species Act] and Timber decisions were political decisions, not legal ones. Jay Tutchton, the author of the [Endangered Species Act] petition, has stated that "there may have been some desire at the Secretariat not to do anything against the U.S. Congress, which could zero out [the Secretariat's] funding."

However, by placing full power in political representatives of the Parties, the NAAEC preserves internationally accepted notions of national sovereignty, democratic accountability, and the ability of the institution's creators and fund suppliers to manage their creation. Political accountability need not be considered a weakness in international organizations; rather, the governments of Mexico, Canada, and the United States have ensured their own accountability by establishing the CEC. Thus, if the independent scientific panel appointed by the Secretariat to review the Silva die-off misconstrued the true cause of the die-off as botulism rather than emphasizing the presence of heavy metals in the birds, their scientific findings and reasoning are available for review and attack by the scientific community. If this attack indicates that the findings are specious or in any way inaccurate, then the Secretariat, the Council, and the represented governments will be held accountable by their domestic constituencies and ultimately will be censured.

* * *

Amid the sniping about "political straight-jackets" and the lack of a truly independent CEC, critics forget to acknowledge what the NAAEC and its institutions have actually brought to the table. In particular, the Silva Reservoir Report sent an international team of scientists to Mexico to investigate a bird die-off that otherwise would have received little public recognition or analysis and which arguably brings greater accountability for the poor state of Mexico's environment. Furthermore, the fact that even Mexico voted in favor of an investigation of the Cozumel pier situation as a failure to enforce its own environmental laws, and subsequently halted the pier project, shows that the CEC is not operating in a political straight-jacket. Instead, these decisions evidence the willingness of the environmental ministers who make up the Council to examine their own countries' environmental enforcement efforts.

As former Quebec Premier Pierre Marc Johnson has suggested, the credibility and relevancy of the CEC and the NAAEC rest on continuing cooperation among the NAFTA Parties, which in turn is "driven by domestic political accountability." The CEC and its Secretariat have thus far shown that their activities are not hamstrung by a lack of complete autonomy. Rather than acting as a hindrance, political accountability ensures that these institutions remain accountable to the very critics themselves.

Teeth?

The Secretariat's Canadian director has said that "[i]f the critics expect this to be an enforcement agency; they are right to be disappointed.... As a supernational agency, we're not it." Many feel that a lack of enforcement power renders the CEC worthless, and bemoan the fact that if a factual record developed under Articles 14 and 15 indicates a failure of effective enforcement, citizens can only depend upon another Party to pursue sanctions against the offending Party. Such criticism ignores the fact that even the formalized moral power of the CEC provides a benefit for the environment and a tool for environmentalists. Never before have U.S. citizens had the opportunity to challenge environmental enforcement activities in Mexico (or vice versa). Perhaps even more important is the fact that Mexican citizens now have an extremely accessible formal means to attack weak enforcement efforts in their own country—as evidenced by the Cozumel submission—to which they have never really had access.

* * *

Furthermore, it is not entirely clear that a CEC with strong enforcement powers would be beneficial for the environment. In fact, it has even been suggested that a strengthened CEC would necessarily alter the complex interaction between the legislature, the executive, and the judiciary behind U.S. regulation and result in a "reduction in agency-and technology-forcing statutes and a lessening of the substantive scope of environmental legislation." Environmental regulation, it is posited, is an interactive process whereby "the legislature sets sweeping but ambiguous standards, the executive agencies employ limited and sporadic application of the statutes, and environmental and industry groups challenge the legislation and its enforcement in the courts." If a supernational body such as the CEC were to step into this process with a strong enforcement hand, and, for example, aggressively sanction the United States for a persistent pattern of non-enforcement of air quality standards in Los Angeles, it is feared that environmental statutes would lessen in substantive scope in order to bring regulation in line with actual outcomes and to increase the total degree of enforcement. For the same reasons, Congress might institute lesser regulatory standards, such as "regulating in the public interest," in lieu of more protective ones, and technology-forcing statutes would become less common. Thus, it is possible that sharper teeth for the CEC could actually diminish environmental quality.

Transparency and Public Participation

The environmental NGO community generally believes that public input is important for bringing about political decision-making that will account for the environment. Several factors, including the lack of public input, an inability for NGOs to be heard, secret dispute resolution procedures, and the "unavailability of even basic documentation" have given other international agreements such as the World Trade Organization (WTO) a bad reputation among environmentalists. In this context, NAAEC needed to meet a very high standard of openness. While it succeeds to a great degree and represents a tremendous step forward from prior trade agreements, there is room for further improvement.

The NAAEC provides unprecedented access to international decision-making institutions through the Article 13 and 14 mechanisms. A key element to this open scheme is a public registry of submissions and responses. Furthermore, the Council must hold public meetings; the Secretariat's annual report must be made public; and a voice for NGOs is provided by the Joint Public Advisory Committee.

Prior to its enactment, critics contended that Article 14 placed strict limitations on citizen complaints. The record to date shows that there is little truth to this contention. No petitioner has yet failed the Article 14.1 threshold requirements, and the Cozumel petition indicates that very little is required in terms of standing to petition. It appears that so long as some degree of harm is asserted, the submission is not drawn exclusively from mass media reports, submitters have utilized the legal means available to them, and the claim of a failure to enforce is not derived from a legislative act, the Secretariat shall request a response from the Party alleged to have failed to enforce their environmental laws.

Although it is true that there is little reason not to impose time constraints on the Secretariat's review of citizen submissions or responses from Parties under Article 14, the NAAEC need not leave this up to the Secretariat's "unfettered discretion." In practice, the lack of time constraints in the enforcement petition process has not been abused by the Secretariat, which has responded quickly and effectively to submissions. Rather than the "long and arduous affair" complained of, the Secretariat dispatched with the [Endangered Species Act] submission in under five months, including appeals. More specifically, in the Silva situation, the Secretariat received a request in June, appointed a panel to investigate by July, and issued a very thorough report based on its findings in October, a turnaround applauded by petitioner National Audubon Society. Therefore, while the NAAEC mandates no time constraints, in practice the Secretariat has expeditiously handled submissions and requests. Certainly it is under the microscope of its natural constituency, environmental groups, and ultimately remains politically accountable to them.

Another aspect of the NAAEC that troubles many is the ability of the Council to block public access to factual records unless supported by a two-thirds vote. This would appear to be cautious drafting, because it is hard to imagine a situation in which the Council would refuse to make such information public; political accountability would dictate that they not do so without a significant and valid reason. In practice, it has yet to be an issue, though Mexico sought to block access to the Article 13 report on the Silva Reservoir.

Despite complaints to the contrary, the CEC has thus far shown itself to be extremely accessible to the public, and it is ironic that the complaints about accessibility have come from those environmental groups that have been able to utilize the CEC as an international forum in which to bring attention to the environmentally adverse practices of their governments. . . .

DE MESTRAL, THE SIGNIFICANCE OF THE NAFTA SIDE AGREEMENTS ON ENVIRONMENTAL AND LABOUR COOPERATION
15 Ariz. J. Int'l & Comp. L. 169 (1998).*

The complaint process can be seen as both something of a novelty and something of a success. The Commission has been extremely prudent, some would say too prudent, in its approach to responding to complaints and to conducting inquiries into complaints. However, those complaints which the Commission has followed up have resulted in solid and interesting analysis of the environmental problem and its causes. These reports have been the source of some embarrassment of the governments involved and have allowed members of the public to highlight issues of concern to them and to put pressure upon their governments in a way not otherwise open to them under domestic law. The originality of the process is that it provides an international forum which is directed to the implementation of domestic law. Because in many cases it is the implementation of domestic law as much as any trans-boundary impact which is the issue of fundamental concern, this would indicate that the complaint process is in fact fulfilling a useful role.

The Commission has been very discreet in the number of studies which it has undertaken independently. However, the same thing that has been said above with respect to the complaint process is equally true with respect to the reporting function. Both procedures provide the Commission with a small but nevertheless clear measure of autonomy as an independent and international body. Both procedures also allow the Commission to put the spotlight upon governmental action in a way which requires reflection upon the need to protect the environment of North America as a whole. Thus, the Commission has potential to focus attention upon the North American environment as a totality and to home in on individual problems which may well reflect issues of wider social and political concern.

BLOCK, THE NORTH AMERICAN COMMISSION FOR ENVIRONMENTAL COOPERATION AND THE ENVIRONMENTAL EFFECTS OF NAFTA: A DECADE OF LESSONS LEARNED AND WHERE THEY LEAVE US*

From the beginning, implementing the CEC's mandate to assess the environmental impacts of NAFTA has been a challenging, and at times controversial, undertaking. Yet, despite taking a while to find its feet, increasingly the work of the CEC in this area has begun to yield real world policy results and to stimulate others outside the institution to pursue related research and analysis. Indeed, in the last few years CEC work in this area has matured considerably and is receiving growing attention from scholars and others examining trade and environment, the NAFTA, and the effectiveness of the CEC. Paradoxically, the "big-picture" issues revealed by this body of work does not appear to be influencing the content of recent trade agreements in any appreciable way.

In general, the CEC's steady progress on developing, refining and testing a framework for assessing the environmental impacts of trade has supported and influenced similar efforts undertaken by the U.S. and Canadian governments, by researchers in Mexico and by other international organizations such as the O.E.C.D. and UNEP. The initiative has helped re-frame the question from whether assessing such impacts can be done at all, to how to conduct the inquiry in a way that yields meaningful public policy results. In fact, the CEC work has all but muted the most outspoken skeptics of assessing the environmental impacts of trade by demonstrating that impacts and causality form a continuum, with direct and fairly simple trade/environment linkages on one end, to more complex, contingent and indirect relationships on the other.

Nonetheless, when measured against the North American Agreement on Environmental Cooperation ("NAAEC") mandate to consider on an "ongoing basis" the environmental effects of the NAFTA, and high public expectations in this area, the initiative remains very modest in scope, and is not well insulated from budget or programmatic swings within the CEC workplan. In addition to "institutionalizing" its trade-environment linkages program, the CEC could improve its efforts to disseminate and call attention to its work in this area, as well as to conduct follow-up and tracking on key issues shown to contain a strong trade-economy-environment nexus.

While its overall relevance to informing and improving trade and environmental policy remains open to debate, the manner in which the CEC has developed an independent, open and inclusive process with a publically-driven agenda stands as a highwater mark for the institution and represents a notable achievement in its own right. For those international organizations striving to create meaningful opportunities for public participation, the CEC's trade and environment linkages program offers a practical means of involving the public in the work of a regional organization.

* * *

Questions and Comments

1. Article 15.1 provides that the Secretariat shall determine whether a submission warrants developing a factual record. What criteria will the Secretariat consider in making this determination in the CCHB submission? *See* Recommendation to Council and Guideline 10.1. Does Article 15 set a time limit on the Secretariat's completion of this task? Do private parties such as the CCHB play any role at this stage of the proceedings?

2. Article 15.2 provides that the Secretariat shall prepare a factual record if the Council, by at least a two-thirds vote, instructs it to do so. What criteria will the Council consider in deciding whether to authorize the preparation of a factual record concerning border environmental problems? Does Article 15 set a time limit on the Council's completion of this task? Do private parties such as the CCHB play any role at this stage of the proceedings?

3. Assuming the Council instructs the Secretariat to prepare a factual record concerning the border environmental dispute, what process will the Secretariat follow in preparing a draft factual record? *See* Art. 15.4, Guideline 11, and the Model Letters. Does Article 15 set a time limit on the Secretariat's completion of this task? Can the CCHB play any role at this stage of the proceedings?

4. What information or material is included in a factual record? *See* Guidelines 11.1 & 12, and Bugeda.

5. Article 15.7 provides that the Council may, by a two-thirds vote, make a final factual record "publicly available." What criteria will the

Council consider in deciding whether to make public the factual record in the CCHB case? *See* Guideline 13. Does Article 15 set a time limit on the Council's completion of this task?

6. Assuming a final factual record concerning Mexico's failure to effectively enforce its environmental laws in the border region is prepared and made public, what happens next? *See* Bugeda.

7. Considering that preparation and publication of a factual record in the CCHB case does not lead to a finding that Mexico is guilty of wrongdoing or require that Mexico take any particular action to address deficiencies in its border environmental enforcement, what is the value of a factual record and the Article 15 proceedings? *See* Bolinger and de Mestral. Is there any value to the process from Székely's point of view? What is the value of the process from the perspective of Moreno, *et al.*, Block and Schiller? After your study of this Problem 11.2, do you consider the assessments of the CEC and of its Review Committee (in the introduction to this chapter) reasonably objective, overly optimistic or a mix of the two?

PROBLEM 11.3 U.S. ENFORCEMENT: PETROCHEMICAL POLLUTION AND NATIONAL SOVEREIGNTY

SECTION I. THE SETTING

The production of petrochemical products, such as gasoline, involves three-stages: drilling, refining and disposal of resulting wastes. Air, water and soil pollution can occur at all three stages. Oil spills, such as the famous 1989 mishap involving the Exxon Valdez, are an example of pollution during the drilling phase of production. Equally devastating pollution can take place during the refining process.

Oil refineries are present in all parts of the country, including California, Texas, Louisiana, Mississippi, Minnesota, Ohio, Kentucky and West Virginia. The largest petrochemical complex in the world is in the Port of Houston. Twenty percent of the nation's gasoline is produced in a series of oil refineries located between New Orleans and Baton Rouge. Although some refineries are independent, most are owned by major oil companies such as Chevron USA, Shell, Exxon, Phillips Petroleum, Unocal, Mobile Oil and Texaco. Oil refineries tend to be major employers and a key source of tax revenue in the communities in which they are based.

A rotten-egg odor often is the first sign that one is approaching an oil refinery. For those living near refineries other forms of air contamination are a more serious concern. The refining process generates air pollutants including benzene (a known carcinogen), toluene (which has been linked to central nervous system dysfunctions), and xylene (which may cause respiratory problems). Although the scientific data remains in dispute, some medical research confirms that refinery pollution causes colon-cancer, lung-cancer, bladder-cancer, brain tumors, and respiratory infections.

The federal clean air standards regulating refinery emissions are clear and the technology required to effectively detect and mitigate such emissions is expensive but exists. According to one recent study, the strict enforcement of pollution controls in the refining industry would have a number of serious consequences. The significant additional expense of pollution control technology would be passed on to consumers in the form of substantially higher gasoline prices. In California alone the average price of a gallon of gasoline would jump from around $2.00 per gallon in late 2004 to perhaps $2.50. U.S. oil companies would be expected to close older refineries and shift petrochemical production to facilities abroad. The resulting losses in employment and demand for unemployment benefits would mean added costs for taxpayers. It is estimated that, as a result of enforcement, U.S. output of petrochemical products would drop by over 3 million barrels per day of capacity and oil imports would have to be increased by an equivalent amount.

For these reasons, most states and cities lack the political will necessary to fully enforce the applicable environmental laws. Local officials routinely permit refinery emissions to exceed federal standards. Environmental groups in many communities have called upon the federal Environmental Protection Agency (EPA) to compel enforcement by the states or to create a "federal implementation plan" and act unilaterally. To date, the EPA has been unwilling to respond.

The failure of federal and state officials to effectively enforce clean air standards governing the petrochemical refining process in the United States is no secret. Reeling from the negative publicity generated by the CCHB proceeding examined in Problem 11.2, the Mexican government has decided to turn the international environmental spotlight on this weakness of the United States government. As it is entitled to do, Mexico requests consultations with the United States pursuant to NAAEC Article 22. It is the intent of the Mexican government to make full use of the dispute resolution mechanism contained in Part Five of the NAAEC, Articles 22 through 36. What are its prospects?

SECTION II.   FOCUS OF CONSIDERATION

Two central themes of this study of the NAAEC are the NAFTA governments' concerns about preserving their sovereignty and the criticism of some commentators that the NAAEC is "toothless" or otherwise flawed. The sovereignty concern is reflected in that portion of the Preamble to the NAAEC expressly reaffirming "the sovereign right of States" to exploit their own natural resources as they deem appropriate. The role of several articles—e.g., Article 3 (which acknowledges the right of each Party to set its own levels of environmental protection), Article 37 (which prohibits enforcement activities by one Party in the territory of another Party), and Article 42 (which deals with national security)–is to confirm the supremacy of national decisions and interests. Criticisms of the NAAEC, such as that the Agreement fails to require harmonized environmental standards and that the CEC is powerless to punish environmental violations, are a byproduct of the governments' sovereignty needs.

The dispute resolution mechanism contained in Articles 22 through 36 has more "teeth" than does the Article 14 citizen submission process. For example, it allows government-to-government disputes to be decided by an international panel of arbitrators who are authorized to impose an "action plan" and, if necessary, a financial penalty on a government guilty of a persistent pattern of failure to effectively enforce its environmental law. Still, this dispute resolution process defers to the sovereign authority of the Parties in important ways. It respects the right of the governments to formulate their own environmental laws. It allows controversies to advance to arbitral panels only after diplomatic consultations and intervention by the Council have failed. Moreover, it permits the above-mentioned financial penalty to be collected only through the suspension of trade benefits rather than through a direct levy against a Party's treasury. After nearly eleven years, the arbitration mechanism under Articles 22–26 has never been utilized.

The focus here is on what a more powerful supranational environmental enforcement agency for North America might mean for national sovereignty and environmental protection. What might such an institution look like? To what degree would national sovereignty be sacrificed and what level of environmental protection would be gained? Are state and local officials willing to forego the loss of state sovereignty implicit in the creation of a North American Environmental Protection Agency? Perhaps most important of all, is the average American willing to bear the economic and political consequences that would flow from "effective" enforcement of domestic environmental laws? The Mexican Article 22 complaint concerning petrochemical pollution in the United States may reveal that, contrary to the wishes of NAAEC critics, American society would not favor a powerful and aggressive international environmental enforcement agency.

NAAEC Articles 22 through 36 are essential to an analysis of this problem. They are found in the Documents Supplement.

SECTION III.   READINGS, QUESTIONS AND COMMENTS

LOPEZ, DISPUTE RESOLUTION UNDER NAFTA: LESSONS FROM THE EARLY EXPERIENCE

32 Tex. Int'l L.J. 163 (1997).*

The dispute resolution system utilized when a NAFTA party engages in a persistent pattern of failure to effectively enforce its environmental law is far more intricate [than Article 14's citizen submission process]. Pursuant to Article 22, if a NAFTA party engages in a persistent pattern of failure to effectively enforce its environmental law, any other party may request consultations with the offending party. If the consulting parties fail to reach a mutually satisfactory resolution within sixty days of the request for consultation, any disputant may request a special session of the Council. Unless it decides otherwise, the Council shall meet within twenty days of the request and "shall endeavor to resolve the dispute promptly." The Council may use technical advisers or experts and make recommendations.

If the Council fails to settle the controversy within sixty days after convening, "the Council shall, on the written request of any consulting Party and by a two-thirds vote, convene an arbitral panel to consider the matter. . . ." The environmental panels consist of five arbitrators who are selected from a preformed roster of up to forty-five experts in environmental law, environmental law enforcement, international dispute resolution, or related scientific and technical fields. . . .

The narrow task of the environmental panel is "[t]o examine, in light of the relevant provisions of the [Environmental Side] Agreement . . . whether there has been a persistent pattern of failure by the Party complained against to effectively enforce its environmental law, and to make findings, determinations and recommendations. . . ." [E]nvironmental panels may seek advice from experts, and the disputants are guaranteed the right to at least one hearing before the panel and to make written submissions.

Within 180 days after the final panelist is selected, the panel shall present to the disputing parties an initial report containing findings of fact, a determination of whether the party complained against has engaged in a persistent pattern of failure to enforce its environmental law, and appropriate recommendations. Ordinarily, the panel's recommendations should be in the form of a proposed "action plan" that the offending party is to adopt and implement. The initial report is to be followed by written comments from the disputants (within thirty days of its issuance) and a final report by the panel (within sixty days of the initial report's issuance). "The final report of the panel shall be published five days after it is transmitted to the Council."

Where a panel finds that there is a persistent pattern of failure by a disputant to effectively enforce its environmental law, the final role of the environmental dispute resolution process is to implement the panel's final report. At least three situations may arise during the implementation stage. First, the disputants may agree on a "mutually satisfactory action plan" that the offending party proceeds to fully implement. Second, the disputants may agree on an action plan but the offending party may fail to fully implement it. Third, the disputants may be altogether unable to agree on an action plan.

If the first situation occurs, the controversy ends and no further oversight is required. If the second situation arises, the complaining party may, no earlier than 180 days after the action plan was established, request that the environmental panel be reconvened. The Council "shall" reconvene the panel. Within sixty days after it is reconvened, the panel shall determine whether the action plan is being fully implemented and, if it is not, shall impose a "monetary enforcement assessment" upon the offending party. Any such assessment may be "no greater than .007% of total trade in goods between the Parties during the most recent year for which data are available" and is to be paid in the currency of the offending party into a special fund, the proceeds of which will be spent at the Council's direction "to improve or enhance the environment or environmental law enforcement in the Party complained against, consistent with its law." The panel's imposition of a monetary enforcement assessment is deemed "final." In the event a party fails to pay a monetary enforcement assessment within 180 days after it is imposed, the complaining party may suspend as to the offending party "NAFTA benefits in an amount no greater than that sufficient to collect the monetary enforcement assessment."

If the third situation arises (i.e., the disputants cannot agree on an action plan) then the complaining party may, no earlier than sixty days after the date of the panel's final report, request that the panel be reconvened. Within ninety days after the Council reconvenes the panel, the panel is to establish an action plan "sufficient to remedy the pattern of non-enforcement" and may impose a monetary enforcement assessment on the offending party. Ultimately, noncompliance with the action plan and/or nonpayment of the monetary enforcement assessment may lead to the suspension of trade benefits.

CAMPBELL–MOHN, ET AL., SUSTAINABLE ENVIRONMENTAL LAW, III. ENERGY, CHAPTER 15. PETROLEUM
Sustain. Envtl. L. § 15.2 (1993).*

LAWS GOVERNING THE REFINING PROCESS

The second step in taking petroleum from the ground to using its various products in the home and workplace is refining. Refiners separate the petroleum into its constituent elements by thermal distillation, which vaporizes the elements at different temperatures and separates them. Alternatively, the heated crude can be pumped into a distillation tower where the elements segregate by weight. To obtain higher quality products, the molecules of the constituents are then "cracked," or "converted," through complex chemical processes. A fluid catalytic cracker breaks large hydrocarbon molecules into commercially desirable sizes using heat, pressure, and a catalyst. In the reactor, a catalytically induced reaction cracks the molecules, covering the catalyst particles with coke. The coke-covered catalyst flows into the regenerator, where the coke is burned off. The catalyst then flows back into the reactor. This separates crude into fractions and burns off excess molecules. Finally, additives may be introduced to the product.

* * *

The primary externalities from refineries are air emissions and wastewater. Air emissions produced during cracking include hydrogen sulfide, the gaseous precursor of sulfur oxide; carbon monoxide; hydrocarbon gases; nitrogen oxides; and catalyst dust. Catalytic cracking produces more air pollutants than other refining processes.

Other sources of air pollution include hydrocarbon vapors that escape from tanks containing gasoline or crude oil. Compressor stations release nitrogen oxide and sulphur dioxide. Hydrocarbons are emitted from improperly sealed storage tanks or leak from the valves, pipes, and hoses. Finally, when the crude is combusted, it releases sulfur oxides, nitrogen oxides, and carbon monoxide.

Air emissions are regulated under the [Clean Air Act (CAA)] and its amendments. Depending on their location, operators must use either "reasonably available control measures" or "best available control measures" to limit releases of nontoxic emissions. For toxic releases, EPA promulgates regulations governing categories of operators, which must use the "maximum achievable control technology." Refineries must limit their sulphur dioxide emissions by 3 percent per year by 1997 in serious, severe, and extreme areas as defined by ambient standards. Under the CAA, EPA has authority to develop regulations to allow industries to delay compliance with the toxic reduction requirements if they implement early, voluntary reductions in hazardous pollutants. Under Title I of the 1990 CAA amendments, new refineries must obtain offsets before they can locate in particular areas and must make steady progress in reducing emissions.

ADLER, INTEGRATED APPROACHES TO WATER POLLUTION: LESSONS FROM THE CLEAN AIR ACT

23 Harv. Envtl. L. Rev. 203 (1999).*

THE CLEAN AIR ACT

The Nature of Air Quality Standards

In the [Clean Air Act (CAA)], ambient environmental standards are known as "National Ambient Air Quality Standards" ("NAAQS"). The statute directs EPA to identify and to publish a list of pollutants "[the] emissions of which ... cause or contribute to air pollution which may reasonably be anticipated to endanger public health or welfare." Within one year after identification of any such pollutants, EPA is required to issue air quality criteria that "accurately reflect the latest scientific knowledge useful in indicating the kind and extent of all identifiable effects on public health and welfare." The Act further requires EPA to promulgate NAAQS for all pollutants for which it has issued air quality criteria. In spite of congressional expectations that more NAAQS would be forthcoming, however, EPA has only promulgated NAAQS for six air pollutants (the so-called "criteria air pollutants"). The scope of the [State Implementation Plan (SIP)] process and, in turn, regulation under the Act as a whole are therefore somewhat limited.

Designation of Air Quality Control Regions

Attainment and maintenance of the NAAQS is governed by an integrated and comprehensive statutory program, bound together largely by the state implementation planning process. All airsheds in the country are to be assessed for compliance with standards for each of the six criteria pollutants. States must then develop plans to ensure future compliance, either through programs to correct existing violations or through prevention programs designed to maintain air quality in clean areas.

Each State shall have the primary responsibility for assuring air quality within the entire geographic area comprising such State by submitting an implementation plan for such State which will specify the manner in which national primary and secondary ambient air quality standards will be achieved and maintained within each air quality control region in such State. This general requirement must be met by dividing each state (and hence the entire country) into separate air quality control regions ("AQCRs"). The State and EPA must then designate each AQCR as "nonattainment," "attainment" or "unclassifiable" for each criteria pollutant. Once an area is designated nonattainment, strict, uniform national rules govern any effort to redesignate the region to attainment status. Through this comprehensive system, the compliance status of each AQCR throughout the country is supposed to be known with respect to each criteria pollutant, according to a uniform national set of criteria and rules for monitoring and for interpreting those criteria. The "unclassifiable" designation, however, which is supposed to be limited to areas with inadequate data to ascertain attainment status, apparently has been abused to avoid more stringent source controls, and has provided an incentive to avoid collecting the data needed to determine attainment.

* * *

IMPLEMENTATION OF AIR QUALITY STANDARDS

The State Implementation Plan Process

Section 110 of the CAA requires each state to "adopt and submit to [EPA] ... a plan which provides for implementation, maintenance, and enforcement" of primary and secondary NAAQS in each AQCR of the state (*i.e.*, SIPs). In theory, states are given tremendous flexibility to choose whatever mix of controls they deem appropriate to meet local economic and environmental conditions, so long as the standards are attained and maintained. As discussed later, however, the statute and regulations became more prescriptive as deadlines passed with continuing NAAQS violations around the country. Ultimately, a state's failure to submit an approvable plan is supposed to result in promulgation of a Federal Implementation Plan ("FIP") by EPA.

The SIP requirements are immensely detailed and complex and are beyond the scope of this Article. Nevertheless, the most important aspects of the SIP process can be summarized fairly readily.... Most fundamentally, each SIP must provide sufficient pollution controls for all sources in an airshed emitting a particular pollutant to ensure attainment and maintenance of the NAAQS. This demands a structured, quantitative approach whereby the State must evaluate existing air quality; develop a "detailed inventory of emissions from point and area sources," including measured or estimated (where data are unavailable) emissions from all sources; and develop an inventory of emissions projected to continue after implementation of the plan's control measures. Based on these projections and the use of air quality models, each SIP must demonstrate that the combination of selected controls is sufficient to attain and maintain the applicable standard in a timely fashion. By regulation, the SIP must include expeditious deadlines for attainment of the standards, although extensions are available both by rule and by statute. The SIPs must include demonstrations of attainment for areas that fail to meet the standard, maintenance of air quality in regions currently in attainment, and preventive controls for threatened airsheds. Finally, once approved by EPA, all elements of a SIP—whether they pertain to stationary, area, or mobile sources—become legally enforceable, by governments and citizens alike, as a matter of federal law.

Specific Requirements for Prevention of Significant Deterioration Areas and Nonattainment Areas

* * *

Additional requirements for nonattainment SIPs are prescribed in detail in Title I, Part D of the statute, with even more detail added in the pollutant-specific amendments adopted in 1990. Most fundamentally, the statute requires that nonattainment SIPs must "provide for attainment" of the primary standards, according to specific interim and final deadlines. This entails a quantitative demonstration that identified control measures will succeed in meeting the standard by the applicable attainment date, according to specified annual increments known as "reasonable further progress." In each SIP, states must develop a rigorous emissions inventory that calculates total emissions from all existing sources, and that projects future emissions from major new and modified sources after implementation of identified control strategies, which must be "consistent with the achievement of reasonable further progress" and attainment and subsequent maintenance of the standards.

Timely attainment was to be achieved through implementation of "all reasonably available control measures," including minimum technology-based requirements for major stationary sources, along with "enforceable emissions limitations, and ... other control measures, means or techniques," and contingency measures in the event that the initial plans do not succeed. Emissions limitations for major existing and new or modified stationary sources must be implemented through permits designed to ensure compliance both with the minimum technology-based requirements of the Act, and with a system of "offsetting emissions reductions" for new and modified sources under which any new emissions must be offset by emissions reductions from other sources sufficient to attain the standards. This system accommodates economic growth in nonattainment areas as long as the net result is adequate progress towards attainment. The law places the responsibility for finding (or purchasing) such offsets squarely on the shoulders of the potential new sources, however, in ways that theoretically encourage economically efficient strategies for air pollution control.

In the 1990 Clean Air Act Amendments, Congress significantly augmented the requirements for nonattainment SIPs, adopting extraordinarily detailed new requirements specific to individual criteria pollutants and to different degrees of nonattainment. . . . The very fact that Congress elected to add so much more detail, however, indicates that it took careful note of the areas in which the less detailed pre–1990 provisions failed to attain the standards and adopted what it viewed as appropriate midcourse corrections. Although some states may believe that such detailed requirements constitute unreasonable and inflexible federal micro management of the SIP process, Congress apparently believed that states, left to their own devices, had not made sufficient progress towards attainment of the NAAQS on a national level.

MCGARITY, REGULATING COMMUTERS TO CLEAR THE AIR: SOME DIFFICULTIES IN IMPLEMENTING A NATIONAL PROGRAM AT THE LOCAL LEVEL

27 Pac. L.J. 1521 (1996).*

INTRODUCTION

For the twenty years preceding the enactment of the Clean Air Act Amendments of 1970, the history of pollution control in the United States was one of increasing federal assumption of power and responsibility. The next twenty years witnessed huge battles over attempts by the federal government to compel, cajole, or otherwise induce state and local governments to deal seriously with urban pollution. For most of the nation's polluted cities, this was a period of standoff in which state and local governments did little to bring about any serious changes in urban lifestyles and the federal government took only modest action to force auto manufacturers, petroleum producers and marketers to implement technologies aimed at reducing pollution at the source. As a consequence, polluted urban areas saw very few of the promised improvements. The 1990 Amendments to the Clean Air Act, which represented the culmination of years of intense legislative deliberation, took a longer view toward attaining air quality goals in the most severely polluted cities, but required stringent technological controls and sought to induce state and local governments to begin seriously to address necessary reductions in commuter traffic. Unfortunately, the familiar process of reaction and retrenchment began to set in almost as soon as the 1990 Amendments became law, and the complicated state/federal implementation scheme is coming unraveled once again.

From the outset, the modern Clean Air Act has contained the hortatory congressional finding that "air pollution prevention ... and air pollution control at its source is the primary responsibility of States and local governments." The history of the implementation of the Clean Air Act in urban areas, however, demonstrates that the relevant state and local governments have failed to meet their responsibilities. Although the federal government in the early 1970s attempted to force the state and local governments to meet their responsibilities, concerns for federalism in the courts and Congress blunted that initial effort. Since the mid–1970s, the history of the implementation of the Clean Air Act has been one of federal nudging, cajoling, and sometimes threatening to administer sanctions or to take over state programs, all of which resulted in very little serious effort at the state and local levels. To be sure, air quality in most urban areas is much healthier than it was twenty-five years ago, and the nation can take pride in this progress, most of which has taken place in the last five years. This Article will maintain, however, that nearly all of that progress is attributable to source control requirements directly or effectively imposed at the federal level and by lawsuits filed by affected citizens and environmental groups aimed at forcing federal, state, and local agencies to fulfill their statutory responsibilities. As a corollary, this Article will conclude that current efforts to accelerate the "devolution" of federal power to the states, if directed to urban pollution control, could very easily reverse the encouraging trend of the last five years and ensure that millions of American citizens never breathe clean air.

* * *

The Collapse of the 1990 Inspection and Maintenance Regime

Progress Under the 1990 Amendments

Congress hoped that the exceedingly complex, but relatively stringent 1990 Amendments would bring about relatively rapid improvements in air quality in less polluted areas and significant progress over a fairly short period in more heavily polluted areas. In 1991, just after the amendments were signed, there were ninety-eight nonattainment areas for photochemical oxidants and forty-two areas that did not meet the standards for carbon monoxide. The statute envisioned that all but one of the carbon monoxide nonattainment areas would be in attainment by

December 31, 1995, and that seventy-four of the ninety-eight ozone nonattainment areas would attain the standards by November 15, 1996.

* * *

Despite significant progress in some states, others are making very little progress. A 1995 report prepared by Clean Air Network found that little or no progress was being made in Michigan, Missouri, Montana, Texas, and Virginia, and that fifteen other states were making only minimal progress. The bottom line is that despite significant progress, more than 90 million people live in counties that are in nonattainment for carbon monoxide and photochemical oxidants, and many of those counties are still experiencing days during which pollution levels are quite high. At the same time, some areas that have been in attainment for years or that have been nearly in attainment are now at risk of going nonattainment. . . .

State Reactions to the 1994 Elections

The 1994 elections did not just change the landscape of Congress. Soon after the 104th Congress convened, representatives of several state organizations, including the National Governors' Association and the Environmental Council of the States, drafted a long list of sixty-five proposals for "improving" the implementation of the Clean Air Act. Among other things, the sixty-five proposals included (1) a two year moratorium on the initiation of any sanctions against any state for failure to meet its obligations when the state acted in good faith, (2) EPA approval of "committal SIPs" that adopted controls sufficient to produce a "substantial portion" of emissions reductions and promised to adopt additional controls in the future, and (3) revisions in the enhanced [inspection and maintenance (I/M)] requirements to do away with the preference for centralized test-only facilities and to allow states to adopt as enhanced I/M programs that were "only slightly more stringent" than basic I/M.

Under the leadership of Governors George Allen of Virginia and Christine Todd Whitman of New Jersey, representatives of several states met with EPA Assistant Administrator Mary Nichols on January 18, 1995 to present their proposals. After an all-day meeting, EPA officials essentially declared an unconditional surrender. State officials expressed their pleasure with EPA's new-found flexibility. The head of the State and Territorial Air Pollution Program Administrators and Association of Local Air Pollution Control Officials reported that the "states were extremely pleased with the level of cooperation and responsiveness that EPA provided at the meeting."

EPA Administrator Browner denied that EPA was sacrificing clean air goals in its attempts to be more flexible with respect to the states: "We tried to give state officials as much flexibility as possible in reaching the goals set under the act. But we did not relax a single standard for improving air quality. We are not backtracking on the objectives of the statute." Browner hoped that by avoiding a showdown with those who would gut the Clean Air Act, the agency's strategic retreat would avoid disastrous amendments. The retreat, however, quickly became a rout. From that date forward, EPA backed down from virtually every confrontation with state officials.

* * *

Unwillingness of the States to Undertake Adequate Implementation Efforts

The history of federal I/M programs plainly demonstrates that the states are entirely unwilling to implement such programs voluntarily. The states often couch resistance to implementing federal programs in the rhetoric of state sovereignty, and it is no doubt true that federal officials have at times paid insufficient attention to legitimate state concerns about the usurpation of their jealously guarded powers. It is also true that some states have occasionally gone out of their way to assert their independence, even when cooperation would not sacrifice any important state interests. For example, during the late 1993 face-off between California and EPA over whether a centralized test-only enhanced I/M program would go into effect in Los Angeles, a California lobbyist reported that: "Some legislators are just itching for a fight with the EPA, saying: 'We dare you to impose sanctions.'"

The fierce resistance in many states, however, is more complex than simplistic appeals to "states rights." Left to their own devices, the states would have achieved very little of the substantial progress that the country has made toward attaining health-based goals for urban air quality. And, it is painfully clear that if the states are again given primary responsibility for reaching those goals, they will never be achieved, and air quality in most urban areas will decline. There are several explanations for state resistance that go beyond simple "turf consciousness," including disagreement with basic implementation goals, lack of political will at the state level to accomplish environmental goals, competitive pressures among states, and local demagoguery.

* * *

CONCLUSION: UNCOOPERATIVE FEDERALISM AND THE ABSENCE OF CONSEQUENCES

Perhaps the clearest lesson of the history of state implementation of I/M programs is that there are generally no adverse consequences for states that thumb their noses at EPA and refuse to take the appropriate implementation steps. One California legislator noted during the collapse of the 1977 regulatory regime that EPA's sanctions lacked credibility because EPA almost never invoked them. Almost two decades later, a Texas legislator complained: "Citizens in Texas see that other states are not being punished for not following along with the EPA and they write to my office saying that, in actuality, Texans are being punished more for doing what they were supposed to do.''

When EPA asserted the power to compel state officials to take affirmative implementation steps under threat of civil and criminal penalties, Congress intervened even before the courts held that EPA lacked that power. The states that refused to put I/M programs into effect suffered no adverse consequences, and the states that in good faith attempted to write plans that at least set things moving in the right direction wound up stuck with exceedingly ambitious plans for the next two decades.

When Congress in the 1977 Amendments adopted the ''modified carrot'' approach and merely promised to take away highway funds and to impose a construction moratorium on states that did not request an extension until 1987, the states that were the most recalcitrant and refused even to request extensions suffered absolutely no adverse consequences. Congress dutifully provided appropriations riders prohibiting EPA from imposing the threatened sanctions. Later, when the extended 1987 deadline for attainment of the carbon monoxide and photochemical oxidant standards came and went, Congress once again obligingly placed a hold on the sanctions.

Administrator Browner in early 1995 assured Congress that ''the development of . . . state-based approaches will allow states like Colorado and Arizona to get the full environmental credit they deserve for moving forward with strong I/M programs, and will provide the flexibility needed by other states to ultimately achieve the emissions reductions necessary for clean air.'' But the agency, by yielding every time to state recalcitrance, sent precisely the opposite message to the states that went to the effort and expense of implementing a centralized high-tech program. As the Texas program was collapsing in the state legislature, one legislator who was an active participant in the state legislative debates testified to Congress that ''EPA's unequal treatment of the states has led to the massive public outcry against the IM–240 testing program implemented in Texas, and I for one cannot disagree with a single voice out there who refuses to take such treatment from the federal government.''

When EPA finally draws the line, Congress invariably steps in and takes recalcitrant states off the hook. Just as it did not escape the attention of drivers in Houston that drivers in California were able to avoid centralized I/M, it cannot escape the attention of drivers in Denver and Phoenix that drivers in Houston still do not have to undergo the basic I/M that was absolutely required by the 1977 Amendments and that Houston has not suffered a single sanction for its continued failure to implement an adequate I/M regime. At the end of the day, states like Colorado and Arizona did not get the credit they deserved for implementing effective I/M programs, and states like California and Texas got credit they did not deserve.

The lessons seem reasonably clear. It is almost impossible for the federal government to induce the states to press local populations to take action aimed at reducing pollution when there is no price to be paid for failure to engage in cooperative federalism. It is not clear that some state pollution control officials seriously believe that attaining the National Ambient Air Quality Standards is a desirable goal. Texas Natural Resource Conservation Commissioner, Ralph Marquez, for example, testified to Congress that, in his opinion, the game was not worth the candle. Yet in the face of active resistance by state officials who question the value of the entire federal enterprise, EPA has steadfastly refused to use the one tool that it does possess—the power to write a Federal Implementation Plan for the state.

It may be that the only credible way for EPA to send a message to recalcitrant states that the Federal Clean Air Act cannot be ignored is to take over the air quality planning process for a major metropolitan area. For example, EPA, not the state, could write the contracts with centralized I/M companies and send a strike force of federal officials to the area to exercise the federal government's authority to write field citations of up to $5000 to individual drivers who do not demonstrate proof of having successfully passed a biennial I/M test. The federal government will, of course, encounter resistance at the local level, as it did when it attempted to implement the federal civil rights laws in the 1960s. But most people will comply with the law, even at the cost of some personal inconvenience, if they are convinced that the law is being administered evenly in all states.

An aggressive show of federal determination to implement the federal law in a major urban area will no doubt precipitate attempts to amend the Clean Air Act to take away the power to write FIPs or to remove the centralized I/M requirement for heavily polluted areas....

If EPA fails to adopt an aggressive stance, it is safe to predict that states containing many of the nation's most heavily polluted urban areas will fail to make the demonstrations of hydrocarbon emissions reductions (6% by 1996 and 3% per year after that) and the "reasonable further progress" demonstrations required by the statute at the end of 1996. It is also safe to predict that those states will suffer no adverse consequences. The statutory consequences are plain, but in the real world they will never happen. EPA will first struggle to come up with innovative interpretations of the statute that provide sufficient wiggle room to let states off the hook or Congress will, as it has in the past, amend the statute in slight, behind-the-scenes ways to cushion or eliminate the impact of the required sanctions. This is not an especially comforting prospect from the perspective of the citizens who continue to breathe polluted air. It is, unfortunately, a realistic one.

LE PRIOL–VREJAN, THE NAFTA ENVIRONMENTAL SIDE AGREEMENT AND THE POWER TO INVESTIGATE VIOLATIONS OF ENVIRONMENTAL LAWS

23 Hofstra L. Rev. 483 (1994).*

THE EUROPEAN COMMUNITY INVESTIGATORY MODEL

In contrast to the weaknesses in the NAAEC which have been described, the European Commission is entitled to investigate on its own initiative or on the basis of complaints filed by the public, information received from the Parliament, or information supplied by Member States. The ramifications of this power demonstrate the crucial role the European Community ("EC" or "Community") plays in the enforcement of environmental laws and establishes guidelines that could serve as a model for the CEC.

Independent investigative power provides greater assurance of enforcement because the Community is able to bypass Member State inaction and demand compliance with Community directives. For example, in 1990 a European Parliament investigative team conducted an inspection of all 12 Member States, taking scientific samples to determine the status of compliance with Community environmental laws. The Parliament acted because it was dissatisfied with the level of Member State deference to Community environmental directives. It hoped that its investigation would "focus public attention on the lack of compliance with EC environmental standards, and [would] spur the Commission and the Member States on to actually do something about it." The Chairman of the European Parliament's Environment Committee discussing the report that prompted the 12 Member State investigation stated: "This report proves just how much we are at the mercy of bureaucrats in the Member States regarding the accuracy of the information and how up-to-date it is." If the CEC is faced with a similar situation, it will be unable to send out inspectors like the European Parliament, but rather will be forced to rely on a NAAEC Party bringing a complaint. However, such a complaint would probably never have been made. All the Member States investigated in 1990 were violating environmental requirements, and a Member State is not likely to demand an inspection because it would risk revealing its own non-compliance. Similarly, a complaint by a NAAEC Party is just as unlikely because it will subject its own environmental practices to intense scrutiny.

Secondly, the action of the EC Member States indicates that Parties to an international agreement will not always comply with a request for information despite an obligation to cooperate and act in good faith. Article 5 of the EEC Treaty requires that the Parties facilitate the Community's task in attaining the objectives of the treaty. Moreover, the

Vienna Convention imposes upon all members to all international agreements the obligation to perform in good faith. Nonetheless, "[a] large number of Member States do not respond, or respond only as briefly as possible, to the Commission's request for information." The Commission has even been refused permission to send experts to conduct investigations.

Finally, the difficulty encountered by the European Community in enforcing compliance with its environmental norms despite its broad investigative power provides guidance in tailoring the power of the CEC to avoid similar difficulties. The power of the Community has enabled it to bring enforcement proceedings against the Member States. Unfortunately, until ratification of the Maastricht Treaty, the scheme of Community law provided weak measures to ensure Member State compliance with enforcement action. Such a deficiency can render broad investigative power ineffective since it may not result in greater enforcement of environmental laws.

Conversely, the NAAEC has already established a detailed penalty system to ensure that a Party complies with a proposed remedial action plan if a Party fails to enforce its environmental laws. However, unlike the Community, the CEC, because of its limited investigative powers, does not have the power to bring enforcement proceedings effectively, which, in turn, render the goals of the NAAEC less obtainable. An ideal model would therefore combine the independent investigative power of the European Community model with the efficient enforcement measures incorporated in the NAAEC.

RAUSTIALA, THE POLITICAL IMPLICATIONS OF THE ENFORCEMENT PROVISIONS OF THE NAFTA ENVIRONMENTAL SIDE AGREEMENT: THE CEC AS A MODEL FOR FUTURE ACCORDS

25 Envtl. L. 31 (1995).*

Assume that a powerful CEC or CEC-type body does engage in extensive fact-finding, enforcement, and sanctioning activities. The immediate effects would include the introduction of new turmoil into the regulatory process and possibly costly sanctions or fines which would bring new actors into the regulatory arena. Besides these immediate effects, what sort of second-order effects can be predicted? In response, we might expect to see changes in the way environmental legislation is composed in the United States. . . .some preliminary hypotheses can be generated about the effects the introduction of a new institutional actor like the CEC would engender. If the CEC or a CEC-like body effectively engaged in enforcement proceedings, and used its powers of sanctioning, the analysis here suggests the following outcomes.

ENVIRONMENTAL STATUTES WILL LESSEN IN SUBSTANTIVE SCOPE

Rather than attempting to regulate broad classes of substances, Congress might be expected to regulate more narrowly, in line with the capabilities of the executive branch. In the past, broad-based legislation has overwhelmed the rule-making capacity of the agencies, resulting in regulation of many substances being delayed until well past their supposed statutory deadlines, or forgotten. In an era of tight budgets, Congress is far more likely to respond with narrowed laws than with agency funding substantially increased to the level necessary to meet these new demands. Finely-grained categories of substances are easier to regulate than broad classes; thus, by regulating "less," the agencies can actually carry out the CEC's version of congressional mandates.

Standards and deadlines will likely be relaxed. Again, this moves formal legislation closer to actual outcomes, raising the aggregate level of enforcement. Compliance will be easier to achieve. Sweeping congressional claims will become less frequent, and environmental legislation increasingly narrow. In the past, basic issues such as feasibility were not salient parts of the formal legislative process. For example, in *American Petroleum Institute v. Costle*, the D.C. Circuit upheld the EPA's standard on tropospheric ozone levels, despite challenges from all directions. Among the challengers was the City of Houston, which maintained that the natural levels of ozone in the Houston area and other physical traits of the local geography prevented the city from meeting the federal standard. The court ruled that "attainability and feasibility were not relevant considerations in setting National Ambient Air Quality Standards." In contrast, under a CEC-type structure feasibility would become a relevant, if not paramount, consideration.

New classes of substances that would be ignored in early, very narrow legislation can be addressed as regulations, standards, and deadlines are developed over time; thus, regulation would become more incremental, with more steps, more information flow, and more rule-making proceedings. This sort of process would be slower, with less regulatory "throughput," requiring more time and resources spent setting ultimately fewer and possibly lower standards.

CONGRESS WILL FAVOR WEAKER STANDARDS, SUCH AS "REGULATING
IN THE PUBLIC INTEREST," OVER MORE EXTENSIVE ONES

If a transnational environmental commission like the CEC is active and successful in pursuing persistent patterns of nonenforcement, Congress may respond by delegating more discretion for standard-and-deadline-setting to the relevant agencies, allowing standards to emerge from the more information-rich environment of an agency rule-making process. In the past twenty-five years Congress has frequently written standards and timetables right into the legislation it produces; for example, between 1970 and 1980 Congress included more than 300 specific deadlines in the fifteen environmental laws it enacted. Many if not most of these deadlines were missed, and subsequent amendments rolled them back, often several times. This practice continues today, if not in the same volume.

If persistent failure to enforce becomes the criterion against which performance is measured and sanctions meted out, future legislation might contain fewer of these mandated actions. Formal law might only require that standards be developed along vague lines (perhaps "in order to safeguard human health" or some variant thereof). The actual development of the standard would be delegated to the relevant agency. This change will likely cause formal environmental legislation to be enforced by shifting the act of standard-setting back to the executive branch.

This should result in standards which bear a closer resemblance to what is technically feasible, and therefore would be more enforceable and attainable at an acceptable cost. However, the balance of power and modes of redress for disaffected parties will be changed. A shift away from congressional standard-setting would enhance executive agency discretion and power. This is particularly true in the post-*Chevron* world, where agency actions appear essentially unchallengeable so long as they adhere to a reasonable interpretation of the statutory language. The ability of citizen groups to exploit citizen-suit provisions to rein in controversial agency policies would be seriously curtailed.

Additionally, such a shift would enhance the position of the regulated firms, who possess the best information on feasibility. With agencies setting more standards, agency-industry relations will play a greater role. Fear of agency capture was one of the motivating forces behind the shift away from broad agency discretion, but to the degree that regulator "capture" occurs, it should happen with greater frequency under this altered scheme.

TECHNOLOGY-AND AGENCY-FORCING REGULATIONS WILL BECOME LESS COMMON

With enhanced CEC-style enforcement, use of technology-and agency-forcing measures should occur less frequently. Such regulation is risky from an enforcement point of view, since outcomes are unknown and unpredictable. "Forcing" measures create incentives (in theory) that force innovation, but learning curves and rates of future technological change are unknown and difficult to predict with accuracy. Since agency- and technology-forcing regulation is inherently uncertain, and oftentimes fails to achieve the goals set forth, enforcement envisioned under the CEC scheme would be problematic. The barriers must be set high enough to stimulate real innovation; but the corollary to this is frequent failure to meet them. For this reason, lessening the reliance upon these measures would be the most likely effect of extensive CEC enforcement.

Agency-forcing measures might also diminish in frequency. In the 1990 Clean Air Act Amendments, agency-forcing provisions, including "hammers" to force timely action, abounded. In the words of Representative Waxman, one of the chief architects in 1990, the amendments contain "very detailed mandatory directives" and "statutory deadlines . . . to assure that required actions are taken in a timely fashion. More than two hundred rule-making actions are mandated in the first several years of the 1990 Amendments' implementation." Yet the same concerns militating against use of technology-forcing measures–that compliance with such measures is fraught with uncertainty–is no less applicable to agency-forcing measures, and will have the same tendency to discourage their use.

A move away from agency- and technology-forcing provisions is not necessarily bad. Such a move may further stimulate the current interest in market-based regulatory instruments, such as fees and tradeable-emissions permit schemes. These instruments, by establishing property rights and markets or levying taxes, allow markets to allocate production and avoid the uncertainty problems inherent in "forcing" legislation. Depending on one's perspective, this may or may not be a positive development. Most environmental groups in the United States have tended to resist the introduction of such measures into environmental legislation, though some, most notably the Environmental Defense Fund, have actively promoted them.

In sum, an active CEC or CEC-type body as envisioned by most mainstream U.S. environmental groups would have the effect of tightening statute-writing, diminishing the use of agency- and technology-forcing regulations, increasing agency discretion, and decreasing congressional standard- and deadline-setting within the originating legislation. Compliance will be heightened, but at the expense of more ambitious and possibly effective legislation. Whether these postulated effects are favorable, from an environmental perspective, is hardly a foregone conclusion. It seems more likely that these effects would have a negative influence, in the sense of diminishing environmental quality, than a positive one. The main exception would be a move towards further reliance upon market-based mechanisms.

In general, this argument illustrates the pitfalls of an undue focus on compliance with formal rules. Compliance with the law is important, but it must be remembered that compliance is an artifact of the standards and rules contained in the law. Compliance in the abstract may be better than noncompliance (though some have argued otherwise), but the promotion of compliance on its own is insufficient to ensure the protection of the environment in any real sense, arguably the side agreement's primary purpose. Most analysts recognize this, and for this reason the NAFTA contains language aimed at restricting a downward movement in regulatory standards. But shifts in the structure and process of regulation, by empowering and disempowering various actors, can result in changes in standards and levels of protection as well, without these changes ever being formally promulgated in the legislative process. It is this pathway of change that has been insufficiently recognized. In part, this is because the CEC is still such a weak body. But it also reflects a misinterpretation of the complexity of the American regulatory process. By focusing unduly on formal law and compliance, the CEC as it now stands reflects an incomplete vision of the regulatory process, one that could be counter-productive from an environmental perspective if the CEC were to be strengthened. It falsely separates enforcement from the lawmaking process, and, by granting enforcement powers to supranational expert panels, diminishes democratic accountability.

JOHNSON, COMMENTARY: TRADE SANCTIONS AND ENVIRONMENTAL OBJECTIVES IN THE NAFTA
5 Geo. Int'l Envtl. L. Rev. 577 (1993).*

Many of us favor environmentally sustainable development, and regard the economic growth which comes with liberalized trade and investment as a critical element in achieving it. In debating the contents of the environmental side agreement to the NAFTA and the scope of the [Commission for Environmental Cooperation (CEC)], there is a fuzzy, but still useful, distinction between the role of what is called "hard law" and "soft law."

Most of the proposals to date on behalf of various environmental groups represent examples of a "hard law" approach. They seek a very formalistic and process-oriented CEC that relies heavily on the creation of detailed adversarial and prosecutorial procedures, binding obligations, and trade sanctions to ensure environmentally sustainable trade and investment. Such an approach risks creating a new lawyers' relief act at great cost and with limited environmental benefits.

We agree on the goal, but not on the means to achieve it. I favor a different framework centered on a coordinated, "soft law" approach that pays more attention to the sticks that get results—like sunshine laws, consumer awareness, flexible institutional arrangements, and the need to respond to market-oriented forces—rather than emphasizing clubs like trade sanctions that are too cumbersome to swing cleanly and that may only serve to replace one market distortion undercutting sustainable development with another.

We should be wary of a sweeping mandate for the CEC and the use of trade sanctions to ensure adequate and effective environmental enforcement for a number of reasons:

First, the CEC, in effect, would become a supranational enforcement agency if the side agreement authorizes broad investigations of corporate practices or the imposition of trade sanctions for individual violations. As such, it would be an outside body second-guessing enforcement decisions made by local governments, by states or provinces, and by the federal governments of the United States, Canada and Mexico.

Significant other problems are associated with a prosecutorial-style CEC with broad powers and wide-ranging investigatory tools. The bureaucracy required to implement an independent trinational secretariat would be huge. It might deprive U.S. entities of due process guaranteed under the Constitution. Legitimate concerns also arise about the accountability of its bureaucrats and the CEC's authority to direct environmental priorities that may preempt national and local ones.

* * *

Second, sweeping investigations and trade sanctions are not likely to produce the desired improvement in environmental policies. Environmental policies involve sensitive political issues within each society which must be resolved by striking a balance on a case-by-case basis. They are subject to strong national and local pressures that overwhelm the influence of trade sanctions, especially on specific business operations. Historically, trade sanctions generally have not succeeded in pressuring other nations to accommodate U.S. noncommercial policy objectives.

Third, trade sanctions of any type will impose serious costs on U.S. companies, undercutting the gains in competitiveness, tariff reductions, protection of intellectual property rights, and the other anticipated benefits which have garnered business support for NAFTA. Perhaps more important than the trade disruptions caused by the actual imposition of sanctions is the chilling effect of and uncertainty about possible disruptions in market access, supply sources, and plant operations, which would negate the main value of the agreement to business: codification of a normalized, efficient commercial relationship.

These effects are made even more acute if the side agreements permit broad allegations about practices that are not directly related to the NAFTA, such as efforts to protect the global commons, or which have no demonstrable effect outside the borders of a single country. Moreover, they lend themselves to abuses by special interest groups seeking commercial protection in the guise of environmental protection. One of the lessons that should have been learned from international trade policy in the 1980s is that excessive bureaucratic discretion and litigious approaches to trade agreements tend give a disproportionate benefit to economically inefficient and environmentally unsustainable companies.

Fourth, the specter of trade sanctions in the CEC also risks putting more emphasis on the sticks than on the carrots. It will deflect time, attention, and resources that would be better used by the CEC in serving as the principal forum for technical assistance and for the regional coordination of environmental programs and infrastructure. It also will divert attention from the far more pressing problems associated with funding border cleanup and new, environmentally sustainable infrastructure.

If our objective really is enhanced environmental quality and sustainable development, then focusing the debate on trade sanctions misses the mark in several critical respects. In many instances, the root causes for the inadequate implementation of environmental standards are a lack of technical capacity, poor management, and a lack of affordable credit to finance cleaner production processes and pollution control equipment. The underlying environmental need, therefore, is pragmatic, result-oriented approaches to remediation of environmental degradation, to pollution prevention, and to adequate accounting for environmental costs and consequences.

* * *

Fifth, the NAFTA's environmental side agreement likely will have significant consequences beyond the trilateral implementation of the NAFTA. It will serve either as the benchmark or the starting point from which future bilateral or multilateral negotiations involving any of the three contracting parties will commence. The NAFTA also may be extended to embrace much of the Western Hemisphere during the next decade.

The elements of the environmental side agreement, therefore, must take account of the likelihood that they will be applied beyond the initial context of the NAFTA. The risk is that what is politically expedient now for obtaining ratification of the NAFTA may be ill-suited for other situations, but will be used as a blueprint for all future agreements and insisted on as a condition for accession.

Sixth, the approach taken to the NAFTA's environmental side agreement also should be sensitive to the realpolitik effects of unequal leverage created by the asymmetrical nature of trade among the three nations. Mexico and Canada depend heavily on trade with the United States. Trade with the United States totals 15% of Mexico's GNP and 20% of Canada's. By contrast, Canadian trade accounts for only 2% of the U.S. GNP, and Mexican trade, only 0.5%.

Policy makers need to recognize that dispute resolution or enforcement provisions in the side agreement that rely heavily on investigations and trade sanctions will not be applied equally among the parties. In practice, trade sanctions probably will not be an effective policy tool for Canada or Mexico to threaten or use against the United States, because such pressure likely will not force the United States to adhere to its obligations. Prior U.S.-Canadian environmental disputes suggest that this outcome is even more likely when the American enforcement shortcoming results from a disagreement between the Administration and Congress, or between the federal government and the states, over environmental policy or funding. At the same time, if U.S. complaints start producing trade sanctions, Mexican or Canadian domestic tribunals likely will start to penalize U.S. imports for "violations" of something.

In sum, current "hard law" proposals present significant problems. However, there are other models for a NAFTA environmental structure that could achieve the same or better results, but without infringing national sovereignty, without creating a massive new bureaucracy, without raising serious constitutional concerns, and without creating an unduly adversarial and litigious framework that puts new opportunities for lawyers ahead of both economic growth and the environment.

LOPEZ, DISPUTE RESOLUTION UNDER NAFTA: LESSONS FROM THE EARLY EXPERIENCE

32 Tex. Int'l L.J. 163 (1997).*

POLITICS AND NAFTA's DISPUTE RESOLUTION SYSTEMS

The early dispute resolution experience under NAFTA and the side agreements confirms that, even though the parties were serious in creating comprehensive and sophisticated dispute settlement processes, in some instances those processes must be overridden or disregarded to serve a government's internal political needs. For example, early events demonstrate that the NAFTA parties will violate the Agreement under sufficient pressure from domestic political forces. Certainly this is the case in the U.S.-Mexico trucking dispute (which is the product of pressure by the U.S. trucking industry) and the Helms–Burton Act case (which is a result of legislation designed to satisfy the demands of Cuban–Americans during an election year). Arguably, each instance involves a fairly clear violation of NAFTA inspired by domestic political interests.

A NAFTA Party could take a hard line approach to another country's politically motivated breaches of the Agreement by immediately demanding consultations and rapidly escalating the dispute to panel proceedings; however, the early NAFTA experience shows that that is not what is happening. Rather, the NAFTA parties have displayed tremendous sensitivity to the domestic electoral pressures faced by their fellow trading partners. Additionally, in the labor context, the United States may have defined narrowly the role of its NAO so as to avoid diplomatically unpleasant challenges to the labor structure that underlies the Mexican political establishment. In short, in approaching dispute settlement, the NAFTA countries focus on the overall NAFTA relationship but not on case-specific issues as a private person or entity may be apt to do.

Why are the parties willing to ignore NAFTA violations by one another that clearly would be proper matters for the Agreement's dispute resolution systems? One pragmatic reason may be that, as a general matter, NAFTA is improving the economic fortunes of all three countries. Since NAFTA took effect in 1994, annual trade between the parties has grown from under $300 billion to [over $600 billion]. Apparently, a lot of isolated trade conflicts can be overlooked for average revenue increases of $40 billion annually. Moreover, at some level, all three NAFTA parties need NAFTA to succeed.

Questions and Comments

1. Article 22 permits one NAFTA Party to request consultations with any other NAFTA Party regarding whether there has been a "persistent

pattern" of failure by the other Party to effectively enforce its environmental law. How is the term "persistent pattern" of failure defined for purposes of Article 22? *See* Article 45. Is there a persistent pattern of failure by the United States to effectively enforce the Clean Air Act and standards governing the petrochemical refining process? Is the term "to effectively enforce its environmental law" defined differently for purposes of Article 22 than it is for purposes of Article 14? *See* Article 45.

2. Article 22.4 requires the consulting governments to make every attempt to arrive at a mutually satisfactory resolution of the matter through consultations. Assume that, for reasons explained previously, no resolution short of full enforcement of standards regulating oil refineries will satisfy Mexico. Can the Mexican government unilaterally advance the dispute to a special session of the Council? *See* Articles 9 & 23. What would a special session of the Council concerning Mexico's complaint involve?

3. Assume that the Council is unsuccessful in resolving Mexico's complaint. Can the Mexican government unilaterally advance the dispute to an arbitral panel? *See* Article 24. Article 24.1 requires that a complaint relate to a situation involving workplaces, firms, companies or sectors that produce goods or provide services traded between the territories of the Parties or that compete, in the United States, with goods or services produced or provided by persons of another Party. Does Mexico's complaint meet this requirement?

4. Who may serve as NAAEC panelists? *See* Articles 25 & 26. How many panelists will preside over Mexico's complaint and how will they be selected? *See* Article 27. What will be the panel's assignment or "terms of reference"? *See* Article 28. How will the initial report produced by the panel differ from an Article 15 factual record? *Compare* Article 31 *with* Guideline 12. Does the Council have any discretion to withhold the publication of the panel's final report? *See* Article 32.

5. Assuming the Article 24 panel concludes that there has been a persistent pattern of failure by the United States to effectively enforce federal environmental standards relating to oil refinery emissions, the NAAEC envisions that, next, the United States and Mexico will attempt to agree on a mutually satisfactory "action plan." What is the action plan likely to provide or contain? *See* Article 33. How can Mexico assure that an agreed upon action plan is fully implemented by the United States? *See* Article 34.

6. Assuming the United States fails to implement the action plan and the panel imposes a monetary enforcement assessment (MEA) pursuant to Article 34.5, how much can it be and what criteria will the panel consider in determining the amount of the MEA? *See* Annex 34. What does it mean to say, in Article 34.6, that the panel's MEA provision or ruling "shall be final"?

7. Assuming the United States refuses to pay the MEA assessed by the panel, what recourse does Mexico have under the NAAEC? *See* Article 36 and Annex 36. Once the funds are collected, where and how are they supposed to be spent? *See* Annex 34.

8. In what ways does the dispute resolution process examined in Questions 1 through 7 satisfy the sovereignty concerns of the NAFTA

Parties? In what ways does this process come at the expense of some of the sovereignty of the NAFTA Parties?

9.   What might a supranational North American Environmental Protection Agency look like? *See* Le Priol–Vrejan, Raustiala, and Johnson. Do you think most Americans (or even the average American) would be willing to give up a substantial degree of national sovereignty to a supranational agency in the hope of raising the level of environmental enforcement in the United States? What about the president and Congress?

10.   The United States–Chile Free Trade Agreement takes a different approach to relating freer trade to protection of the environment. Under the FTA, the environmental provisions (like the labor provisions) are part of the Agreement, rather than relegated to a side agreement, as in NAFTA. (U.S.–Chile FTA, Chapter 19.) Also, violations are the environmental obligations are subject to the general dispute settlement provisions of Chapter 22. However, environmental (and labor) violations are punished not through trade sanctions, but through a fine of up to US$15 million per year. (Article 22.16) The proceeds from such fines are to be paid into a fund to be administered by the trade commissioners," and expended for "appropriate labor or environmental initiatives.... Most significantly, in the U.S.–Chile FTA there is no equivalent of the NAFTA Commission on Environmental Cooperation or permanent Secretariat, although each Party is required to "ensure that judicial, quasi-judicial or administrative proceedings are available under its law to sanction or remedy violations of its environmental laws." (Article 19.8) Thus, there is no mechanism for receiving citizen complaints, other than through national legal processes. (The environmental provisions of the U.S.—Chile FTA are reproduced in the Documents Supplement.)

11.   However, a more NAFTA-like approach is taken in the United States FTA with the Central American nations and the Dominican Republic. In many respects the CAFTA follows Chile, in the inclusion of the environmental provisions in the body of the agreement, making violations subject to the general dispute settlement provisions, and limiting the sanctions to US$15 million annual fines. Nevertheless, the CAFTA contemplates a separate agreement to implement its Article 17.7—Submissions on Enforcement Matters—which may create a secretariat and a mechanism for citizen complaints in many respects similar to the CEC under the NAAEC.

12.   Based on your study of the implementation of the NAAEC, what elements are most important in future FTAs to assure a reasonably effective environmental protection mechanism? Application of the same dispute settlement mechanism and penalties as for other violations of the Agreement? Minimum standards for national environmental protection legislation? The existence of a mechanism and process (CEC and NAAEC secretariat) that reviews citizen complaints, amasses factual records, issues reports and in general sheds public light on national environmental law compliance?

Part Four

BEYOND NAFTA

Chapter 12

FREE TRADE AND THE AMERICAS

12.0 INTRODUCTION: NAFTA'S ROLE IN HEMISPHERIC IN-TEGRATION

The opening chapters focused on the lengthy and sometimes quite bumpy path taken by Canada, the United States and Mexico to get to NAFTA. As we emphasized, NAFTA is in part a product of trade liberalization efforts which preceded it. The Canada–United States Free Trade Agreement (FTA) and the General Agreement on Tariffs and Trade (GATT) (particularly the slow-moving Uruguay Round of GATT negotiations) were particularly important influences on NAFTA. In the same way that NAFTA was shaped by prior accords, NAFTA itself has been viewed by many as a key element in the drive toward global commerce premised upon free trade. In the 1990s, a free trade zone encompassing all of the Americas seemed to be the next rational step in the evolution. By late 2004, however, the promise of a Free Trade Agreement of the Americas (FTAA) had faded, and the most intense activity was focused on sub-regional free trade agreements, most being negotiated either by the United States, Mexico or the Southern Cone Common Market (Mercosur) group.

Nevertheless, NAFTA is shaping other trade accords in the Americas in two significant ways. First, NAFTA includes a number of innovative provisions that are being duplicated–albeit often with significant modifications-by more recent free trade agreements. For example, NAFTA incorporates a new approach to rules of origin that broke with the longstanding and hopelessly complicated U.S. "substantial transformation" doctrine, while substituting other complexities. NAFTA was the first trade agreement to adopt provisions for eliminating restrictions on trade in services. To encourage foreign investment, NAFTA draws on prior bilateral investment treaties to extend new forms of security to North American investors, including a grant of standing to investors to directly challenge the actions of a NAFTA government before independent international arbitrators. With respect to intellectual property protection, NAFTA is the first international trade agreement to include coverage of trade secrets. NAFTA provides for binational and trinational dispute resolution mechanisms that displace domestic judicial processes in certain trade controversies. Finally, NAFTA was the first major trade agreement to involve side agreements relating to labor and the environment and permitting the submission of complaints by private citizens and non–governmental organizations. In the view of many, these NAFTA innovations have set new standards for what should be contained in a comprehensive free trade accord, and have influenced the content of free trade agreements to which the NAFTA parties are not even party.

Second, the experience of the Parties in implementing NAFTA has greatly influenced subsequent trade liberalization efforts. Several of the preceding chapters have focused on the way in which various features of the Agreement have operated in the eleven years since January 1994. As we have seen, implementation has not always proceeded smoothly. Perhaps this is due, in part, to inherent difficulties in integrating North America's economies. For example, NAFTA attempts to merge two highly developed economies with a relatively underdeveloped and much poorer economy. NAFTA also attempts to combine very distinct common law and civil law jurisdictions in a mutual legal endeavor. To succeed, current and future trade agreements involving the United States (or Canada) and Latin American nations will have to account for precisely the same types of difficulties.

At first glimpse, NAFTA's important role in the progression toward free trade and its many groundbreaking elements, along with the broad enthusiasm surrounding its passage, suggested that expanding NAFTA would have been an appropriate and straightforward means of extending free trade to the entire Western Hemisphere. Indeed, the three NAFTA governments contemplated at the time the Agreement was negotiated that other countries would be permitted to join the free trade area. In 1994, the addition of Chile as NAFTA's fourth member appeared to be an inevitable course of expansion. With Chile in the NAFTA fold, the eventual incorporation of other key South American economies (Argentina and Brazil) and later the Central American and Caribbean nations into a single free trade area appeared possible, even if difficult. Few expected that, during the late–1990s, the United States would prove incapable of facilitating Chile's accession to NAFTA and, in this way, eliminate any realistic possibility that NAFTA would be expanded. Problem 12.1 examines the issue of Chile's accession to NAFTA, the problems caused by the lack of U.S. fast track authority (later "Trade Promotion Authority") and, ultimately, the negotiation and conclusion of a bilateral FTA by the United States and Chile, several years after separate FTAs were concluded with Chile by Mexico and Canada. It also discusses briefly the United States–Central American FTA, signed in June and August 2004.

NAFTA–accession, of course, was only one of several possible paths toward hemispheric integration. The most recent FTAA approach—a separate agreement that would leave existing trade agreements such as NAFTA, Mercosur and the Central American Common Market agreement intact—nevertheless would likely have incorporated much of the

NAFTA approach had the negotiations been successful. NAFTA's adoption sparked renewed vigor in the drive for hemispheric free trade and, in December 1994, generated sufficient confidence among the hemisphere's political leaders for them to declare that a Free Trade Area of the Americas (FTAA) would become a reality by 2005. That deadline was not met and enthusiasm has largely dissipated, for reasons discussed in Problem 12.2.

Problem 12.2 also examines many of the key issues relating to broader economic integration in the Americas. Perhaps the most fundamental controversy is whether hemispheric integration is an appropriate goal in the first place, and whether the major nations of the region—particularly the United States and Brazil—will ever be willing to make the compromises that would be required for a comprehensive FTAA. By committing personnel and other resources to the massive proposition of negotiating an FTAA, nations in the Western Hemisphere may be foregoing opportunities to accelerate global trade liberalization through the World Trade Organization, to reach trade accords with Europe or Asia that could ultimately prove to be more beneficial than an FTAA, or to strengthen sub-regional hemispheric free trade (as between Mercosur and other South American nations or the United States and Central America). Whether the current proliferation of FTAs will ultimately complement or replace the FTAA concept is also an open question.

Finally, Problem 12.2, Part C, examines regional economic integration in the South American continent, focusing on Mercosur and Mercosur's apparently successful efforts to conclude FTAs with Chile, Bolivia and, more recently, the other members of the Andean Group. Even though the initial Mercosur agreements preceded NAFTA by several years, NAFTA's success has undoubtedly influenced the South American integration process as well.

PROBLEM 12.1 CHILE'S ACCESSION TO NAFTA AND THE U.S. FAST TRACK DILEMMA

SECTION I. THE SETTING

The United States Congress approved NAFTA on December 8, 1993 by a vote of 234–200 in the House and 61–38 in the Senate. In the weeks leading up to the vote, as Congress was embroiled in debate, the government of Chile contemplated the possibility that, if NAFTA passed, Chile would be first in line to join the United States, Canada and Mexico as members of the largest free trade area in the world. With Chile on board, NAFTA would include a total of more than 400 million consumers, the most open developing country economy in the Hemisphere (Chile), and be the hands down choice as the model for a future Free Trade Area of the Americas. Such a prospect promised great prestige for Chile as well as significant economic and business gains. Chile's accession to NAFTA would sustain Chile's already impressive record of economic growth and ensure that the country stayed the course toward freer trade and true democratic rule. For good reason, by early 1994 Chile's single most important foreign policy objective was accession to NAFTA.

The Chileans understood that entry into NAFTA hinged on the Clinton Administration's ability to obtain "fast track" authority from Congress to negotiate with Chile. The bruising battle that Congress and President Clinton endured to secure NAFTA's passage left Chilean officials concerned that congressional approval of fast track authority would prove to be difficult. For this reason, the government of Chile retained a prominent Washington, D.C. law and lobbying firm to make Chile's case for accession to NAFTA with members of Congress, to assist Chile in working with the Clinton Administration and Bush Administrations on this mutual goal and, ultimately, to assist in the negotiations of the U.S.—Chile Free Trade Agreement that finally entered into force January 1, 2004.

As you consider the readings and questions which follow, assume that you are a member of the legal/lobbying team hired by Chile to work on matters related to establishing Chile's free trade relationship with the United States. Your client will rely on you to explain to it developments in Congress between 1994 and 2002 relating to fast track and the concerns of Republican and Democratic members of Congress, including whether fast-track authority is indispensable to concluding an FTA with the United States. Among the issues for Chile during the 1994—2002 period, when neither President Clinton nor President Bush had fast-track authority, was whether Chile might better have devoted its trade liberalization efforts to countries in Europe, Asia and the Western Hemisphere other than the United States. Now that the United States—Chile FTA is in force, you will be consulted as to your views regarding what further agreements the Chilean government should seek with its trading partners.

SECTION II. FOCUS OF CONSIDERATION

NAFTA is unusual as a subregional trade agreements in the Western Hemisphere in that it provides for accession by other countries. (For a list of the other regional agreements, see Chapter 4.) The NAFTA accession process itself is straightforward. However, nations have been reluctant to negotiate with the United States absent fast track authority, whether in the GATT/WTO global context or regionally. Fast track ensures that key congressional players will be involved in shaping trade agreements before they are ever presented to Congress for approval. In this way, effective use of the fast track process can help to ensure that the votes in Congress necessary for passage are in place and, most significantly, that Congress will not try to change the bargain once the FTA is before it for approval

If any Latin American country appeared to be prepared to accede to NAFTA, that country was Chile. Yet, eleven years after NAFTA entered into force, no nation has acceded to NAFTA, and no such accession is likely in the future. Why not? For the most part, the answer lies in the failure of the Clinton Administration and Congress to reach agreement on legislation that would grant the President fast track authority to negotiate NAFTA accession, and the preference of the Bush Administration and its then U.S. Trade Representative, Robert Zoellick, for bilateral FTAs over the risks of reopening the national debate over NAFTA in the process of bringing in new members. Problem 12.1 focuses on the evolution of U.S. trade policy from expanding NAFTA to seeking separate, albeit similar FTAs, and the continuing importance of fast-track authority (now Trade Promotion Authority) in implementing this policy.

This problem also provides an opportunity to examine the broader implications of the Clinton Administration's inability to obtain fast track authority. This shortcoming, for which the Congress as well as President Clinton deserves much of the blame, deprived the United States of the ability to assume a leadership role in economic integration efforts in the Western Hemisphere during the second Clinton Administration. The reduced influence of the United States in free trade matters made it possible for other countries, including Brazil and the European nations, to gain greater influence in the hemisphere and trade concessions at the expense of U.S. interests. (Chile, for example, has concluded FTAs with Mercosur, the European Union and South Korea, among others.) Even our own NAFTA partners, Canada and Mexico, did not stand by while the United States faltered on Chilean accession. Both countries entered accords with Chile that duplicate NAFTA in important ways, and Mexico concluded an FTA with the European Union.

SECTION III.　READINGS, QUESTIONS AND COMMENTS

PART A: THE UNITED STATES, NAFTA, TPA AND CHILE

BAYER, EXPANSION OF NAFTA: ISSUES AND OBSTACLES REGARDING ACCESSION BY LATIN AMERICAN STATES AND ASSOCIATIONS

26 Ga. J. Int'l & Comp. L. 615 (1997).*

ACCESSION CLAUSE

The text of NAFTA allows for the possibility of accession, but gives few concrete guidelines for the procedure to be followed. Article 2204 states:

1.　Any country or group of countries may accede to this Agreement subject to such terms and conditions as may be agreed between such country or countries and the Commission and following approval in accordance with the applicable legal procedures of each country.

2. This Agreement shall not apply as between any Party and any acceding country or group of countries if, at the time of accession, either does not consent to such application.

PROCEDURE FOR ACCESSION

The general procedure for accession involves three steps–a formal invitation by the members of NAFTA to begin accession negotiations, negotiations between the applying county and representatives of the NAFTA members, and approval of the completed agreement by the three member countries and the acceding country. The first two steps are ad hoc in nature; the NAFTA members decide when and how to extend a formal invitation, after which they and the invitee agree on the logistics of the negotiations. The third step, however, must follow the domestic laws of each state.

In Mexico, international agreements must be ratified by a two-thirds majority of the Mexican Senate, and the implementing legislation must be approved by the Mexican Senate and the House of Deputies. In Canada, the agreement must first be approved by the Canadian Cabinet, then be introduced into the Canadian House of Commons and follow the normal parliamentary process in the Canadian House and Senate.

In the United States, accession requires Congressional approval and the passage of implementing legislation. Under section 108(b) of the legislation implementing NAFTA, by May 1, 1994, and again by May 1, 1997, the U.S. Trade Representative is required to submit a report to the President and the Ways and Means and Finance Committees of the Congress. This report lists the countries that either (1) currently provide fair and equitable market access to U.S. exports, or (2) have made significant progress in opening their markets to U.S. exports, and the further opening of whose markets has the greatest potential to increase U.S. exports. The President must then report to the committees on the countries with which the United States should seek to negotiate free trade agreements and the objectives for such negotiations.

An important feature of U.S. Congressional approval of international agreements generally is the "fast-track" procedure. Under this procedure, prior to the start of negotiations the Congress gives the President "fast-track" negotiating authority. When the agreement is completed and comes before Congress for consideration, Congress cannot amend any part of it, but can only approve or defeat the entire agreement. Although this authority is not required for the completion of a trade agreement, the lack of it significantly hinders both the negotiation and the approval of such agreements.

CRITERIA FOR ACCESSION

Article 2204 of NAFTA also does not prescribe the substantive criteria that a country must meet in order to accede. The requirements, however, are to be economic and non-economic criteria developed by the governments of the United States, Canada, and Mexico. The members of NAFTA have yet to put forth any official, specific requirements for accession, and a continuing lack of clear guidelines for accession complicates any expansion of NAFTA.

Although the criteria have never been officially announced, some generally recognized standards were articulated in the [Enterprise of the Americas Initiative] as "indicators of readiness"—(1) the economic and institutional capacity to fulfill long-term, serious commitments, (2) a stable macroeconomic environment and market-oriented policies, (3) progress in achieving open trade regimes, and (4) membership in the General Agreement on Tariffs and Trade (GATT). More recently, protection of intellectual property and investment has gained importance as a generally recognized requirement for admission into NAFTA.

MILLER, WILL THE CIRCLE BE UNBROKEN? CHILE'S ACCESSION TO THE NAFTA AND THE FAST–TRACK DEBATE

31 Val. U. L. Rev. 153 (1996).*

The original framers of the United States Constitution created a unique democracy in which each of the three branches of government may fulfill its own responsibilities and duties, free from the influence and interference of the other branches. At the same time, however, the Constitution permits one branch to seek assistance from another branch in meeting its duties. This interdependence, therefore, results in an often combative atmosphere. For example, both the legislative and executive branches are endowed with the authority to participate in the negotiation of international trade agreements. Article I of the Constitution provides Congress with the power to "regulate commerce with foreign nations." At the same time, Article II views the President as the United States' representative in all international matters and bestows upon the executive the authority to enter treaties. Therefore, the process of negotiating and concluding international trade agreements mandates cooperation between the two, often opposing, branches of government.

The use of fast-track procedures is a product of modern times. Before the advent of modern fast-track procedures, the President submitted international trade agreements to Congress for approval. However, without the efficiency provided by the fast-track process, Congress often took considerable time to approve and to implement the necessary legislation since it was not bound by a restrictive timetable. In addition, both the House of Representatives and the Senate were entitled to attach amendments or to redact portions of the agreement. Thus, not only were the original intentions of the parties to the agreement severely compromised by such practices of Congress, but the credibility of the United States in the eyes of its trading partners was diminished as well.

Fast-track authority, on the other hand, expedites the congressional approval process by ensuring that Congress deals with a trade agreement as a complete package.

Prior to 1934, Congress played a dominant role in the formulation of international trade agreements and the execution of foreign trade policy. The President, on the other hand, was restricted to the fulfillment of inconsequential responsibilities. Congressional dominance in the area of international trade, however, was short-lived. In 1930, despite the warnings of leading economists, Congress enacted the Smoot–Hawley Tariff Act which was aimed at sustaining the economic prosperity enjoyed by the United States in the years following World War I. This Act set tariffs at their highest level in the history of the United States and has been attributed as a primary cause of the [ ] Great Depression. As a result, Congress, having been publicly condemned for its traditional adherence to protectionist trade policies, enthusiastically turned the reins of international trade policy-making over to the executive branch in the Reciprocal Trade Agreements Act of 1934. This Act gave the President, for a certain period of time, wide latitude in unilaterally negotiating trade agreements, thereby insulating Congress from further political disasters.

In 1962, Congress attempted to take back some of the power previously granted to the executive branch in negotiating international trade agreements by enacting the Trade Expansion Act, which required the President to seek congressional approval for all trade agreements. This Act was intended to provide Congress with greater control over the content of international trade agreements. However, as a glaring illustration of the distrust and lack of cooperation that exists between Congress and the executive branch, President Johnson refused to abide by the Trade Expansion Act during the negotiations of the Kennedy Round of the General Agreement on Tariffs and Trade (GATT), and entered the GATT with neither congressional authorization nor approval. As a result, Congress enacted domestic legislation which, in effect, nullified President Johnson's agreement. In addition, Congress refused to grant any further unilateral negotiating authority to the executive until 1974.

THE BIRTH OF FAST-TRACK AUTHORITY

The Trade Act of 1974, which addressed the United States' involvement in the Tokyo Round of the GATT negotiations, marked the beginning of a new tool in formulating international trade agreements: fast-track authority. In addition to being granted advance authority to negotiate trade agreements, the President was given the responsibility of consulting with the Senate Finance Committee, the House Ways and Means Committee, and any other committees impacted by the proposed agreements. The President was also required to notify both houses of Congress ninety days before actually concluding the agreement, and to seek input from relevant government departments and agencies, the private sector, and Congress as well. In return, Congress modified the House and Senate Rules to provide for an up-or-down vote on the final draft of the agreement without amendments or redactions. Fast-track authority facilitated a greater cooperation between the legislative and executive branches by allowing Congress to have more access and input into trade agreements, and by ensuring that the President would retain his credibility and status as the United States' primary representative in the eyes of other negotiating nations.

Within the last fifteen years, fast-track authority has been a staple for the United States in the negotiation of international trade agreements. The Uruguay Round of the GATT and the North American Free Trade Agreement are the two most recent and significant trade agreements formulated under fast-track procedures. The multilateral negotiations for the Uruguay Round of the GATT began in 1986. The final GATT Ministerial Meetings, signifying the conclusion of the agreement, were scheduled for 1990; however, these meetings were stalled as a result of a dispute between the United States and the European Union regarding agricultural subsidies. Had the Uruguay Round been completed as scheduled in 1990, President Bush could have submitted the agreement to Congress under fast-track procedures within the requisite time frame. The disagreement between the United States and the European Union prevented the agreement from falling within the fast-track parameters, thereby forcing President Bush to seek an extension of fast-track authority from Congress.

When the conclusion of the GATT was immeasurably delayed, the United States turned its attention to bilateral trade agreements. "During the summer of 1990, President Salinas of Mexico requested bilateral negotiations with the United States for a free trade agreement." President Bush notified Congress of his intention to enter negotiations with Mexico, later amending this notification by including Canada in the negotiations. However, as in the case of the Uruguay Round of the GATT, the time frame for fast-track authority, which was set forth in the 1988 Act, was no longer applicable to the negotiation of the NAFTA. Therefore, President Bush was required to seek an extension of fast-track procedures from Congress.

On March 1, 1991, President Bush included both the GATT and the NAFTA in his request for the extension of fast-track authority. This request was supported by a comprehensive review of the Uruguay Round negotiations, a detailed report by the Advisory Committee for Trade Policy and Negotiations, and other materials which further illustrated the need for fast-track authority. Nevertheless, the extension request was not warmly received by Congress, and an explosive debate regarding the extension of fast-track authority ensued.

Two primary arguments arose against the extension of fast-track authority in Congress. First, many members of Congress opposed the concept of fast-track authority in general. This opposition was based largely on the premise that an extension of fast-track authority would signify a surrender of congressional power. Not only were these opponents distrusting of both the executive and the substantive content of the NAFTA, but they also asserted their belief that Congress ought to exercise more control over the process of negotiating and concluding international trade agreements. Second, many members of Congress, having been pressured by lobbying constituent groups, opposed the extension of fast-track authority for the NAFTA based on labor and environmental concerns. In terms of labor, Congress feared that companies in the United States would move to Mexico in order to take advantage of lower wage rates, thereby resulting in job losses and worker dislocation in the United States. In addition, Congress worried that labor dislocation, in the absence of adequate worker adjustment and retraining programs, would have a detrimental effect on the United States economy. With regard to the environment, Congress asserted that the health and safety standards of the United States might be attacked as non-tariff barriers to trade. Congress also warned of the possibility that United States companies would relocate to Mexico in order to avoid mandatory compliance with the strict environmental standards of the United States. In addition, Congress predicted that transboundary pollution along the border between the United States and Mexico would increase as a direct result of United States companies moving south. Therefore, because of the opposition to the NAFTA by many politicians, Congress threatened to reject the request for the extension of fast-track authority by issuing a procedural disapproval resolution.

In response to the threat of a procedural disapproval resolution by Congress, President Bush instituted an Action Plan, in which several promises were made in exchange for the extension of fast-track authority. First, President Bush committed his administration to maintaining a close relationship with Congress throughout the negotiation process. Next, the President promised to work with Congress to ensure that an effective worker retraining and assistance program would be implemented for dislocated American workers. Finally, the executive agreed to develop a joint program with Mexico to protect the environment. Ultimately, Congress rejected its procedural disapproval resolution.

* * *

In August of 1992, President Bush concluded the NAFTA negotiations and submitted the final agreement to Congress. Despite congressional outcries that the NAFTA was unsatisfactory for the United States, President Bush asserted that the executive branch had met its obligations to Congress under both the Action Plan and the Gephardt–Rostenkowski Resolution. Thus, the NAFTA became a highly controversial political issue during the 1992 Presidential elections. Upon taking office, President Clinton tried both to appease Congress' aversion to the NAFTA and to avoid offending Canada and Mexico. Clinton kept the final agreement as it was negotiated and addressed the labor and environmental issues of Congress through the negotiation of supplemental agreements, which were ultimately folded into the NAFTA. Thus, the struggle between Congress and the executive over the application of fast-track procedures to the negotiations of the GATT and the NAFTA illustrates the steady weakening of the fast-track process.

TIEFER, "ALONGSIDE" THE FAST TRACK: ENVIRONMENTAL AND LABOR ISSUES IN FTAA

7 Minn. J. Global Trade 329 (1998).*

THE EMERGENCE OF ENVIRONMENTAL AND LABOR ISSUES ON THE FAST TRACK

The 1974 arrangement lasted through the 1970s and 1980s, until the rise of new trade problems and a third phase of trade agreement structuring. When Mexico proposed negotiation of NAFTA in 1990, new, sensitive issues were raised. Previously, the major trade agreements had largely concerned relationships between developed countries. Creating a trade agreement between the developed United States and the less-developed Mexico, however, posed new tensions. For example, members of Congress, particularly House Democrats from "rust-belt" states, believed that the relocation of assembly plants to Mexico under the maquiladora program would hurt their constituents unfairly.

The Bush Administration initially opposed inclusion of environmental and labor issues in the negotiations. In 1990–91, however, these issues achieved prominence in Congressional hearings. The chairs of the House Ways and Means and Senate Finance Committees formally wrote President Bush in March 1991, asking him to comment on environmental and labor issues before Congress voted on fast track. President Bush's formal response proposed a "parallel track" for environmental issues related to NAFTA, thereby partly ushering in the current era of including such issues alongside, if not entirely on, the fast track system.

The second development in the emergence of environmental and labor issues on the fast track occurred the following year. President Bush had been accused of insensitivity to environmental issues concerning the Western Hemisphere. In submitting the main body of NAFTA to Congress in August 1992, President Bush had demonstrated only limited concern with environmental and labor issues. In contrast, then-candidate Clinton elaborated a new approach in a key campaign address in October 1992 in North Carolina. He advocated a middle path between the two extremes of completely accepting the NAFTA main body as negotiated by President Bush, and calling for its renegotiation. Following up his new campaign approach, President Clinton asked his trade representative to negotiate stronger environmental and labor protections in side agreements, which allowed him to win Congressional approval of NAFTA in 1994.

The new position of including these issues, but addressing them in side agreements, remained the consistent Administration position through the upheavals of the subsequent few years. . . .

* * *

How "Alongside" Works: The 1997 Proposed Legislation for Inclusion of Environmental and Labor Issues

In 1997, the Clinton Administration proposed legislation to Congress that would provide for environmental and labor issues to be included in the creation of trade agreements. Section 2(a) of the proposed legislation calls for the establishment of "overall trade negotiating objectives," which include "those aspects of foreign government policies and practices regarding labor, the environment, and other matters that are directly related to trade. . . ." Similarly, section 2(b) requires that the President establish "principal trade negotiating objectives," relating to the World Trade Organization and the International Labor Organization (ILO), as to "worker rights and protection of the environment."

* * *

The Rejected Alternatives

The "alongside" orientation is best understood by comparison with the alternatives rejected on the way to the 1997 debate and beyond. More specifically, comparing the "alongside" orientation with the rejected "off" the fast track approach, as proposed by the 1995 Republican Congress, and the recent 1997 debate proposals, best illuminates the form that the "alongside" approach ultimately is taking.

1995 Republican Congressional Position: "Off" the Fast Track

When the 1994 elections produced a Republican majority in both the House and the Senate, the new Congress opposed fast track treatment of environmental and labor matters. From the start of the 104th Congress, the new majority expressed a desire for "avoidance of the use of environmental objectives as a protectionist device." In a famous statement, House Speaker Newt Gingrich declared that "[f]ast track was not designed to circumvent regular legislative procedures with respect to matters unrelated to trade agreements."

At a House hearing in May 1995, the House majority party clashed with the Administration on this point. House Republicans persisted in developing a draft fast track bill with "a restrictive approach to the trade and labor/environment link." In September 1995, the House Ways and Means Committee reported a fast track bill supported by committee Republicans over the objections of the Administration and committee Democrats. As reported, the negotiating objectives listed in the bill omitted mention of environmental and labor goals. The bill only allowed the fast track procedure to be used to implement provisions "necessary" to carry out the trade agreement, rejecting the previously used broader formula of "necessary or appropriate." Deadlock on the issue persisted.

Chile provided a concrete focus for the issue. In December of 1995, Congress considered the plan of renewing fast track just for Chile's accession to NAFTA. Since the new majority in Congress opposed the inclusion of environmental and labor concerns, this plan did not get presidential support, and fell through. Chile had indicated willingness to join NAFTA if the United States had fast track ready, but its hopes were dashed when Congress and Clinton were unable to reach an agreement on fast track authority.

Thereafter, the issue became one for the 1996 presidential campaign. Senator Dole repeated opposition to "adding 'extraneous' issues such as labor and environmental protection to trade agreements." Nothing further happened in 1996, as observers noted, because the two sides had to see who would become President.

With President Clinton's victory in the election, Congressional Republicans effectively abandoned the position they had maintained since 1995. In 1997, the Clinton Administration made clear that it would insist on inclusion of such issues in fast track trade negotiations, notably through the President's statements during a May 1997 trip to Mexico. In May 1997, and again in July 1997, Congressional Republicans floated, but pulled back from the formula ultimately used, in which they relented to allow inclusion of trade and environmental issues that were "trade-related." The fast track debate that ensued further illuminates how Congress and the Clinton Administration resolved the issue of fast track.

1997 Debate on Fast Track Extension

In September 1997, President Clinton submitted his formal request regarding fast track extension, with the proposed bill language previously described. After hearings, Senate and House committees reported their own versions, which subtly drew back from the level of inclusion of environmental and labor issues which the Administration proposed. The Committee Reports provided some detail on environmental and labor issues which helped concretize what the term "trade-related" would mean. The Senate committee reported a negotiating objective opposing "the use of foreign government regulation and other government practices, including the lowering of, or derogation from, existing labor (including child labor), health and safety, or environmental standards, for the purpose of attracting investment or inhibiting United States exports." While such an objective did provide a way for the trade agreement to address environmental and labor issues, it fell short of the variety of goals which advocates desired to strive for in such agreements. The House committee reported a similar negotiating objective....

As the matter moved from the Congressional committees to the floor, the Senate critics of the proposed legislation attempted a filibuster. Among other arguments, they faulted its failure to include sufficiently strong environmental and labor protections. They also cited the opposition position of national environmental groups. The Senate ultimately overcame the filibuster, but the much needed boost that Senate approval was expected to provide the legislation in the House never developed.

Rather, House critics of the fast track extension maintained a steady drumbeat of opposition on many grounds, including, as in the Senate, its failure to include sufficiently strong environmental and labor protections. As Minority Leader Gephardt stated:

> Now, right now, the President is asking us for fast track negotiating authority to get new free trade agreement with, say Brazil or Argentina or Chile or other countries across the world, and just as in 1991, I voted for fast track for then-President Bush, I am quite prepared to vote for fast track for President Clinton because obviously I think he shares my values on these issues much more than President Bush did, but I do not want again to go to a set of negotiations without the Congress being very clear about what we expect in macro terms to be in these agreements. I did that once; I do not want to do that again. . . .

> I do not want the Brazilians to be misled as to what we will require in the Congress in these treaties. We want labor and environmental enforcement of their laws in the core trade treaty with trade sanctions in order to enforce it.

HUFBAUER & SCHOTT, WESTERN HEMISPHERE ECONOMIC INTEGRATION

(1994).*

READINESS INDICATORS

History holds few examples of developed and developing countries successfully entering reciprocal free trade agreements; hence the North American Free Trade Agreement (NAFTA) sets a notable precedent. Before it could embark on free trade negotiations with the United States and Canada, Mexico had to undergo a rigorous reform and adjustment process to prepare Mexican industries and workers for intense competition with their northern neighbors. And the United States and Canada had to think through the problems of economic integration with a country that has much less-developed social and environmental conditions.

The prospect of Western Hemisphere economic integration poses a similar challenge for the countries of North and South America. Within the Western Hemisphere, language differences are great, and more importantly, income disparities are huge. Large income disparities between North and South America do not foreclose the possibility of future integration, but they greatly complicate the process. Competitiveness in poor countries suffers from weak economic infrastructure, which for some industries may completely offset any cost advantage derived from lower wages. But for other industries, the comparative advantage of low wages may be decisive. Under these circumstances, the result of freer trade can be a dramatic contraction or expansion of certain firms and industries both in the poorer countries and in the richer countries.

Moreover, low income closely correlates with poor social conditions: for example, weak minimum wage legislation, inadequate health and safety rules for the workplace, missing social safety nets (old age, health, and welfare assistance), poor environmental controls, and low educational standards. Yawning differences in social conditions between the United States and Canada on the one hand and Latin America on the other are sure to create political resistance in North America as the process of hemispheric economic integration goes forward. . . .

In short, when income disparities and social conditions between trade partners are great, the trauma of economic integration is bound to be large. The economic playing field looks distinctly slanted, and for different reasons each country feels threatened by the economic standing of its partner.

* * *

There is no simple test that indicates when a country is ready to pursue closer economic integration with its neighbors. Strong trade and investment linkages provide the obvious starting point. Trade and investment interdependence determine a "natural region" for integration efforts and establish the raison d'etre for the negotiations—that is, to expand access in the known markets of the partner country and to boost investment. . . . Our analysis indicated that the prerequisite trade and investment linkages exist for integration efforts within subregions of Latin America and, to a lesser extent, for integration of the Western Hemisphere as a whole.

In addition, much depends on the political will to accept the "creative destruction" of local industries and jobs, the sort of destruction that Schumpeter (1942) identified as the lifeblood of a capitalist economy. Each country has a different threshold of economic pain and different means of sharing that pain across social groups. Those thresholds and mechanisms will inevitably govern the inauguration and the pace of economic integration.

The postwar experience of integration episodes yields some useful guideposts with regard to economic and political conditions in the prospective partner countries. This history suggests certain indicators of readiness for economic integration. Macroeconomic indicators include price stability, budget deficits, external debt, and exchange rate variability. Microeconomic indicators include market-oriented policies and fiscal reliance on trade taxes. The final indicator is the presence of a functioning democracy. While necessarily qualitative, this attribute is becoming increasingly important.

* * *

CHILE

The Chilean case is noteworthy in two respects. First, economic liberalization preceded political liberalization by more than a decade. In this respect, Chile was like Korea, Taiwan and Thailand. By contrast, economic liberalization was contemporaneous with, or even led by, political liberalization in other Latin countries. The second noteworthy aspect is that, while not yet a member of any trade group, Chile has been a pioneer advocate of freer trade and a textbook practitioner of unilateral liberalization.

Chile began modest market reforms in the 1960s under President Eduardo Frei and became an original signatory of the Cartagena Declaration that created the Andean Group in 1969. In 1970, Chilean policy reversed course under newly elected President Salvador Allende, who embarked on a program of nationalization and drastic import substitution. In 1973, General Augusto Pinochet seized control from President Allende in a bloody coup. Chile instituted an economic stabilization and liberalization program the next year, reversing both the macro and the microeconomic policies of the Allende regime.

In 1976, Chile dropped out of the Andean Group. By 1980, the new Chilean policies resulted in the privatization of more than 460 companies and the reduction of tariffs from an average of 105 to 10 percent.

The move toward liberalization stalled temporarily in early 1982 when Chile faced severe internal and external pressures. To avoid a financial sector collapse, the banking industry was nationalized in 1983. Tariff levels were initially raised to 35 percent to stimulate the manufacturing sector but later were gradually cut to 15 percent by 1988.

In 1985, Pinochet refocused economic policy. His new minister of finance, Hernan Büchi, concentrated on stimulating public investment, reprivatizing the financial sector, using monetary policy to target interest rates, and devaluing the exchange rate via a crawling peg. These measures spurred economic growth, which averaged 6.3 percent annually from 1985 to 1989.

In contrast to its Latin American neighbors, Chile was at least moderately successful in dealing with external debt during the mid–1980s. In 1985, the Pinochet regime instituted a debt conversion program and a debt-equity swap program, both administered by the Chilean Central Bank. The conversion program allowed Chilean investors to buy their own foreign liabilities in the secondary market. The swap program allowed foreign creditors to obtain equity stakes in Chilean companies in return for the reduction of foreign–currency debt. Critics argued that the debt–equity swap program implied a subsidy of some 30 percent to foreign investors. Nevertheless, the two programs together enabled Chile to cut its external debt in half from 1985 to 1990.

General Pinochet relinquished control of the government, while remaining chief of the army, when Patricio Aylwin was elected president in March 1990. In his initial economic program, Aylwin sought to allay the fears of foreign observers that a democratically elected government would succumb to internal redistributive pressures. In the first two years of his administration, Aylwin successfully balanced macroeconomic stability against social demands. His economic program continued the process of price liberalization. It also stressed a stable real exchange rate and low tariff levels. In early 1991, Aylwin unilaterally cut tariffs by a further 27 percent, to a uniform rate of 11 percent.

While keeping spending and inflation under control, Aylwin was successful in implementing a more liberal social policy. The Tax Reform of 1990, designed to fund social expenditures, temporarily increased corporate taxes and made the individual tax system more progressive. A labor reform act was passed in 1991, limiting the power of employers to discharge and lock out employees.

Under Aylwin, Chile complemented active participation in the Uruguay Round of GATT negotiations with a spate of new bilateral trade initiatives designed to cement internal reforms and to position Chile as a Latin American and Pacific nerve center. The first two bilateral agreements were signed in October 1990: a framework agreement with the United States under the Enterprise for the Americas Initiative (EAI) and a pact with Venezuela pledging to negotiate a free trade agreement.

In August 1991, Chile signed a framework agreement with Argentina to facilitate trade and promote investment between the two countries. In September 1991, Chile signed a bilateral agreement with Mexico; in April 1993, one with Venezuela; and in December 1993, one with Colombia. In their free trade agreement, Chile and Mexico pledged to reduce and eventually eliminate tariffs, starting in January 1992, on some 94 percent of the bilateral trade between the two countries by 1996. The agreements with Venezuela and Colombia will phase out tariffs by 1999. At the same time, Chile explored possible ties with the Mercosur group but did not go forward, judging that MERCOSUR's prospective common external tariff would likely be too high.

In February 1992, Chile signed an agreement with the United States to establish an EAI Environmental Fund. In May, Chile and Argentina began to integrate their mining sectors, allowing freer exchange of people, goods, and services in the industry. Also in May, Presidents Bush and Aylwin agreed to inaugurate free trade negotiations once the United States completed its negotiations with Canada and Mexico on a North American FTA. The Clinton Administration has recently confirmed that it intends to negotiate Chile's accession to NAFTA by late 1995.

Late in 1992, Chile signed four bilateral agreements with Malaysia. Under the agreements, the maximum duty will be 11 percent, and all tariffs on bilateral trade will be eliminated after five years.

Chile implemented a patent and trademark law in September 1991. The new law provides protection for pharmaceuticals, but it provides neither "pipeline" protection nor protection for plant and animal varieties. Patent protection lasts for 15 years, and copyright protection (revised in 1992) extends for the life of the author plus 50 years.

Chile is relatively open to foreign investment. However, foreign investors want a still better regime, and current restrictions are all targets of negotiations.

Chile's overall score for the readiness indicators is 4.4, with figures of 5 on budgetary discipline, external debt, currency stability, and market orientation. In fact, Chile has enjoyed budget surpluses since 1987. Chile's lowest score, 3, is for price stability: in 1992, inflation was still 15 percent.

In terms of overall readiness, Chile's scores come closer to those of the United States and Canada than the scores of any other Latin American country. In terms of political willingness, Chile is fully committed to strike a free trade deal with its northern neighbors as soon as possible.

MILLER, WILL THE CIRCLE BE UNBROKEN? CHILE'S ACCESSION TO THE NAFTA AND THE FAST–TRACK DEBATE
31 Val. U. L. Rev. 153 (1996).*

REASONS FOR DELAY

Despite the "Spirit of Miami" and the pledged commitment by the nations in the Americas to work toward free trade, many roadblocks have been thrown in front of the accession of Chile to the NAFTA. Unfortunately, it appears that all of these obstacles have been erected by the United States alone. Generally, the United States is responsible for three basic impediments to the expansion of the NAFTA at this time.

First, the United States' previously enthusiastic outlook on free trade in the Americas has dimmed in recent months as a result of the economic crisis in Mexico and its $20 billion bailout of the Mexican government. [Authors' Note: Less than two years later, Mexico repaid the entire loan, with interest.] Resulting from this diminished enthusiasm for free trade is the renewed belief in isolationism held by some members of Congress and various political candidates for the 1996 presidential election. These isolationists range from the extremists, who are pushing for the United States to pull out of the World Trade Organization and the NAFTA, to those in Congress who are seeking a moratorium on new trade agreements and who have refused to support the extension of fast-track authority for Chile's accession to the NAFTA. The proponents of isolationism fail to realize that the world has undergone significant changes since the 1930s. In today's economy, trade is carried on between different regional blocs, and individual nations are finding that they "are less masters of their own houses." That is, countries no longer engage in foreign trade based solely upon the formulation of a national trade policy; instead, multinational trading blocs are largely becoming the primary players in the international economy.

The second obstacle impeding Chile's entry into the NAFTA consists of Congress' and the Clinton Administration's failure to agree on the proper scope of the extension of fast-track authority. The Republican-controlled Congress refuses to extend fast-track authority to the Clinton Administration as long as provisions regarding labor and the environment are part of the negotiating process. They argue that such an extension of fast-track authority would allow the Clinton Administration to place undue restraints on foreign imports in the interest of social policy. On the other hand, just as matters regarding labor and the environment were part of the NAFTA negotiations with Mexico, the executive branch insists that they must be included in future negotiations with Chile. The Clinton Administration asserts that the inclusion of these issues in future fast-track negotiations regarding the NAFTA will enable the United States to enforce labor and environmental agreements with sanctions, as is the norm in other areas of trade.

Finally, Chile's accession to the NAFTA has been obstructed by the purely irrelevant and ulterior motives of party politics. As the 1996 presidential election approaches, politicians on both sides of the free trade debate have placed greater value on partisan campaign strategies, rather than on the United States' trade policy. For the Clinton Administration, the grant of fast-track authority, including the ability to negotiate labor and environmental standards, would be well received by labor and environmental groups, which constitute significant portions of the voting public. In the other partisan camp, Republican campaign strategies will hardly suffer if the trade agreement with Chile is never brought to fruition. Free trade is an extremely divisive issue for the Republican party; therefore, refusing to grant fast-track authority to the Clinton administration would convey a two-fold benefit to the Republican party. While keeping the matter of Chile's entry into the NAFTA and the issue of free trade, in general, out of the election, the Republican party would also prevent President Clinton from achieving a major trade victory during an election year.

PINE & HOOK, CLINTON PULLS TRADE BILL RATHER THAN RISK DEFEAT
L.A. Times A1 (Nov. 10, 1997).*

President Clinton was forced to withdraw his embattled "fast-track" trade bill from the House floor early today to avoid an embarrassing legislative defeat, in all likelihood killing the measure for the year.

* * *

Rejection of fast-track by Congress would be a stunning victory for organized labor and environmentalists, who vigorously opposed the legislation. The AFL–CIO waged a million-dollar television campaign against the measure, and threatened to target House and Senate lawmakers who supported it.

... GOP leaders were counting between 160 and 170 of the House's 228 Republicans as supporters of the bill, along with 42 of the 205 Democrats. A total of 218 votes would have been needed to assure passage if all members of the House were present.

As has been the case throughout the fast-track debate, Clinton's biggest problem was with his own party. While Republicans garnered a handful of additional votes on Sunday, Democratic support actually shrank. The erosion of support reflected widespread distrust among liberal Democrats who complained that Clinton had not kept promises made in previous trade debates.

In the end, Republican strategists said they advised the president that it would be better for him to pull the bill entirely than to risk having the House proceed with the vote and formally defeat it.

* * *

Although Congress has given fast-track authority to all U.S. presidents since 1974, organized labor has opposed the bill vehemently, threatening to help defeat any lawmaker who supports the measure this time around.

Labor leaders and environmentalists contend the bill would hurt American jobs, depress wages and pollute the environment. They want Congress to require the administration to include more safeguards in trade accords.

O'KEEFE, THE EVOLUTION OF CHILEAN TRADE POLICY IN THE AMERICAS: FROM LONE RANGER TO TEAM PLAYER

5 Sw. J. L. & Trade Am. 251 (1998).*

THE CANADA–CHILE FREE TRADE AGREEMENT

On November 5, 1996, Canada and Chile signed a free trade agreement (Canada–Chile F.T.A.) that went into effect in June of 1997. The agreement immediately lifted duties on about 90% of Chilean goods traditionally exported to Canada, and approximately 75% of Canadian items traditionally exported to Chile. A gradually decreasing preferential tariff rate will affect all remaining goods and will culminate in 0% duties by 2003. The big exceptions consist mostly of agricultural goods (*e.g.*, rice, vegetable oil, sugar, non-durum wheat and flour) on which the Chileans have imposed even longer phase-out periods of 10 (*i.e.*, pork, corn, sugar beet, etc.), 15 (*i.e.*, beef), 16 (*i.e.*, sugar), or 18 years (*i.e.*, non-durum wheat and flour). Dairy products and poultry are also subject to quota restrictions in both countries, and Canada has put permanent restrictions on the importation of Chilean tree trunks while Chile has done the same for Canadian used cars.

The Canada–Chile F.T.A. is very similar to the NAFTA, opening up, inter alia, the services sector to providers from each country. The agreement also eliminates nationality (except in the legal profession), minimal levels of production, and physical location requirements within the territory where the service is being offered. Excluded from coverage are services offered by governmental agencies, air transport, and financial services. The F.T.A. also requires the Chileans to offer Canadian business travelers a special business visa (instead of the standard tourist visa which, technically, prohibits the holder from conducting any type of remunerative activities while in the country), and eliminates additional requirements for obtaining employment authorization prior to conducting business activities within Chile. A social security agreement was signed in conjunction with the F.T.A. which allows Canadians living in Chile to be covered under the Canadian social security system, and not have to pay into a Chilean private sector social security fund or AFP. Further, it ensures that Chileans living in Canada have access to their social security proceeds. Both governments have also made a commitment to sign an agreement preventing double taxation "within a reasonable time after this agreement [*i.e.*, the F.T.A.] comes into force."

* * *

The Chile–Mexico Free Trade Agreement

* * *

In April of 1998, the Chilean and Mexican governments signed a new, and more expansive free trade agreement during the Second Summit of the Americas. The new Chile–Mexico Free Trade Agreement (T.L.C. Chile–Mexico) is very similar to the NAFTA, with the text divided into some 20 Chapters. In contrast to NAFTA there are no chapters covering financial services and government procurement. However, both countries made specific commitments to begin negotiating an additional chapter on financial services no later than June 30, 1999, as well as one on government procurement no later than the first anniversary of the agreement's effective date. Both governments have also committed themselves to negotiating the elimination of antidumping duties on imports within a year after the T.L.C. Chile–Mexico comes into effect.

Once it becomes effective, the T.L.C. Chile–Mexico will supersede A.C.E. No. 17 [a pre-existing trade liberalization accord] in the event of any discrepancies between the two treaties and the T.L.C. will be incorporated into the ALADI framework with a new A.C.E. number. Any products not already subject to bilateral free trade as of the date the agreement enters into force, will be accorded immediate duty-free treatment. The exceptions to this general rule are few and include apples (which are subject to quotas and gradually decreasing tariffs until 2006), certain Mexican seafood, grapes, vegetable-based oils, petroleum, and natural gas, as well as Chilean powdered milk, cheese, and flour. The importation of used vehicles is restricted by both countries, and Mexico can also restrict the importation of used machinery and computer equipment from Chile until 2004.

BREVETTI, CHILE READY TO START TALKS ON FREE–TRADE PACT, OFFICIAL SAYS

16 Int'l Trade Rep. 1333 (Aug. 11, 1999).*

"Chile is ready to work with the United States to undertake the analysis needed for negotiation of a bilateral free-trade agreement despite the lack of fast-track trade negotiating authority," Chilean Foreign Minister Juan Gabriel Valdes said Aug. 10.

The analysis Chile is proposing would focus on what areas should be negotiated, what the impact of the negotiations would be, and what tensions in the negotiating process can be expected, he said. "The matter of the fast track could be postponed and decided in a moment in which we have already achieved agreement in all topics," he added.

"Working groups could be formed in the areas of market access, rules of origin, investment, customs, services, intellectual property, and government procurement," Valdes said. "The working groups would exchange information, but the exercise will not constitute a negotiation. Nonetheless, the work will be very close to a negotiation," he said.

LANGMAN, AMERICAS ENVOY MACKAY OPTIMISTIC ABOUT CHILE'S PROPOSAL FOR FREE TRADE TALKS

16 Int'l Trade Rep. 1390 (Aug. 25, 1999).**

Kenneth H. "Buddy" MacKay Jr., President Clinton's special envoy for the Americas, said Aug. 23 that while it is too early to make a definitive statement on Chile's proposal to begin negotiations on a bilateral free trade agreement, he is optimistic that the negotiations can happen.

"We don't want to raise expectations that suddenly American politics is no longer complicated, but we welcome this initiative, and it seems to me that this was a carefully thought out, very realistic initiative," MacKay told BNA in an interview.

The United States will formally respond to the proposal from Chile at the Oct. 5–6 meeting of the U.S.–Chile Joint Commission on Trade and Investment, he said.

The proposal for a U.S.-Chile Free Trade Agreement gained momentum on Aug. 10 when Chile's Foreign Minister Juan Gabriel Valdes said Chile was proposing to start preliminary work on a bilateral FTA without U.S. fast-track negotiating authority.

"The proposal is to try and set up working groups and try to work through the feasibility of it. But I think . . . we have got to do it with diligence. Everybody wants to be sure that we don't leave Chile hanging out again. So we have got to touch base with it. Right now it has not been possible to do that," MacKay said.

In 1995, Chile withdrew from talks with the United States on accession to the North American Free Trade Agreement because of the lack of fast track authority.

MacKay said that the next step will take place at the September meeting of the Asia–Pacific Economic Cooperation forum in Auckland, New Zealand, where U.S. Trade Representative Charlene Barshefsky and Valdes will discuss the proposal informally.

MacKay began an eight-day trip to South America Aug. 22 to discuss trade and investment, encouraging institutional transparency and anti-corruption efforts, and working toward economic integration, according to a White House statement issued Aug. 19.

Separately, Chile's Secretary General to President Jose Miguel Insulza said at a press conference Aug. 23 that Chile is cautiously optimistic an agreement could be reached before 2004 . . . .

But MacKay said at some point fast track may still be necessary to conclude the negotiations. "I think the realities are that at some point in the negotiations you need to have a vote of confidence or no confidence, and so I think that fast track at some point is necessary. But in the [World Trade Organization] negotiations, the fast-track thing came basically at the end. If you have good communications with the Congress as you go along I think you can do it realistically," MacKay said.

TALKS PATTERNED AFTER FTAA

Alicia Frohmann, the chief of the North America department of the Chilean Ministry of Foreign Affairs' Bureau of International Economic Affairs, told BNA Aug. 23 that Chile is proposing bilateral negotiations similar to the Free Trade Area of the Americas negotiating pattern, with working groups, for example, in the areas of market access, rules of origin, investment, customs, services, intellectual property, and government procurement.

"NAFTA has somehow become a kind of 'four-letter word' in the United States, and other countries joining NAFTA isn't very popular. But we really don't care how we do it," Frohmann said. "FTAA is also very similar to the NAFTA. Basically what we have proposed is to anticipate at the bilateral level what we are trying to achieve within the FTAA process, but at a more expeditious pace. Also, the FTAA framework has a certain legitimacy within the administration and within the Congress, so we felt it wouldn't be seen as a threat because it is already being done within the FTAA context."

Earlier this month, a spokeswoman for the Office of the U.S. Trade Representative told BNA that it is premature to comment on issues involving scope, timing, and modalities. She said that such issues would be decided after a consultation process among interested parties and with Congress.

Value-Added Tariff Phase-out

Frohmann said that in a free trade negotiation with the United States, Chile would be especially interested in a phase-out of tariff escalation on its exports of value-added products.

"Basically tariffs in the U.S. are already very low, but for example, with copper cathodes we feel discriminated [against] because we have a 1 percent tariff and our competitors from Mexico, Canada, and Peru have a zero tariff," Frohmann said. "Also, what we would like is to phase out tariff escalation on our exports with a greater value-added content. We export fresh fruit, for example, but if we want to export canned peaches or peach juice or peach pie, we find an increasing tariff."

Labor/Environment Model

Frohmann said Chile is willing to sign on to the NAFTA environment and labor side agreements or to discuss a new type of trade agreement on labor and environmental issues, but so far the United States has not revealed how they want to deal with these issues.

"Chile is the only country in Latin America which is really willing to address these issues," Frohmann said. "Nobody wants to. That is also why we think the U.S., if it finds a country willing to address these issues, well this would definitely be a model of approaching these issues with other countries."

"But we don't know what the U.S. wants. We have asked the U.S. government what is it that you want regarding these issues, but we have never received answer. But we would certainly be willing to address them," said Frohmann.

MacKay said that if bilateral free trade negotiations do commence between the United States and Chile, it could become a model for other such agreements regarding environmental and labor issues.

BREVETTI, CHILE AND U.S. OFFICIALLY LAUNCH NEGOTIATIONS ON FREE TRADE PACT

17 Int'l Trade Rep. 1899 (Dec. 14, 2000)*

Achieving a free trade agreement with Chile will accelerate the Free Trade Area of the Americas process and help set very high standards for those talks, U.S. Trade Representative Charlene Barshefsky said Dec. 6, after officially launching U.S.-Chile negotiations. "That is a very important reason for moving forward now to make sure that the U.S. and Chile can be in a leadership role as [a] draft of the FTAA emerges," she said. Barshefsky, in remarks to reporters after meeting with Chile's foreign minister, said she expected a "very active effort" on both sides in negotiating the FTA. "Both of our presidents have indicated they want us to move rapidly," Barshefsky said, flanked by Chilean Foreign Minister Soledad Alvear, when questioned about the FTA timing.

Chile and the United States—along with 32 other Western Hemisphere democracies—are also involved in negotiating an FTAA. The time frame for completion of the FTAA talks is 2005 but some countries are pushing for an earlier conclusion. The USTR added that the pact will be comprehensive but declined to comment on specific issues. No specific date has been set for completion, Barshefsky said.

BREVETTI, BUSH SIGNS TPA BILL AFTER SENATE APPROVAL, WILL PURSUE FREE TRADE WITH OTHER NATIONS

19 Int'l Trade Rep. 1378 (Aug. 8, 2002)**

President Bush Aug. 6 signed major new trade legislation (H. Rept. 107–624, H.R. 3009) renewing trade promotion authority as well as providing first-time language for new health care benefits for workers displaced by trade, following Senate approval of the package Aug. 1. "We'll move quickly to build free trade relationships with individual nations such as Chile and Singapore and Morocco," the president said. "We'll explore free trade relationships with others such as Australia. The United States will negotiate a Free Trade Area of the Americas and pursue regional agreements with the nations of Central America and the Southern African Customs Union." U.S. Trade Representative Robert B. Zoellick told reporters Aug. 1 he hoped that both the Chile and Singapore free trade agreement negotiations could be concluded in a matter of months. Both chambers of Congress approved a conference report containing TPA before adjourning for the August recess—the Senate on Aug. 1 by a 64–34 bipartisan vote and the House in the early morning hours of July 27 by a 215–212 vote with mostly GOP support (19 ITR 1334, 8/1/02). The bill passed the Senate with the support of 20 Democrats, 43 Republicans, and one independent. Twenty-nine Democrats and five Republicans voted against it.

The East Room signing ceremony marked the culmination of an 18–month struggle by the Bush administration to get TPA renewed. TPA supporters said that it would help the United States regain its leadership role in trade negotiations. The Bush administration views TPA as critical to its ambitious trade agenda. TPA expired some eight years ago and efforts to renew it in the previous administration failed, largely due to differences over the treatment of labor and environmental standards in trade agreements. The conference report included TPA, new trade adjustment assistance benefits, Customs Service reauthorization provisions, and renewals of the Generalized System of Preferences and the Andean Trade Preference Act. Under TPA, trade agreements brought back to Congress will be subject to an up-or-down vote with no amendments. The conference report extends TPA to June 1, 2005 with an automatic two-year extension unless Congress adopts a disapproval resolution.

* * *

Trolling for Votes

The authority, which used to be called fast track, was used for congressional approval of the North American Free Trade Agreement and the Uruguay Round agreement under the General Agreements on Tariffs and Trade. However, Lori Wallach, director of Public Citizen's Global Trade Watch, said that future trade pacts face an "uncertain fate" as evidenced by the fact that a wartime president had to "come to Capitol Hill to personally troll for votes before a trade bill stalled for two years could be rammed through Congress by a 2–vote margin in the middle of the night." TPA passed in the House by 215–212 in the early morning hours of July 27 after Bush made a personal appeal to the GOP conference at the Capitol building.

The Business Roundtable Aug. 6 welcomed the signing of the conference report. "TPA enables the U.S. to engage in trade agreements that will make an enormous contribution to the U.S. export economy— directly benefitting our workers, farmers, businesses and communities," BRT Chairman John Dillon said in a press statement.

Zoellick's Running Shoes

Bush, who had repeatedly called on Congress to pass the bill before adjourning, said after the Senate vote Aug. 1 that his administration would immediately put the new authority to use. Bush congratulated Baucus, Sen. Charles Grassley (R–Iowa), Senate Minority Leader Trent Lott (R–Miss.), Zoellick, and Commerce Secretary Donald Evans in a conference call immediately after the Senate passed the measure. "We've now given you the authority so we're expecting you to negotiate these strong trade agreements." Baucus remarked. Bush said that Zoellick now has "his running shoes on—he's going to hit the ground running—and bring us some good trade agreements and I appreciate that very much."

* * *

USTR, U.S. AND CHILE CONCLUDE HISTORIC FREE TRADE AGREEMENT

USTR Press Release, Dec. 12, 2002*

The United States and Chile reached agreement today on an historic and comprehensive Free Trade Agreement (FTA) designed to strip away barriers and facilitate trade and investment between both countries. U.S. Trade Representative Robert B. Zoellick and Chilean Foreign Minister Soledad Alvear said they expect to sign the Agreement and submit it to their Congresses for approval next year. The U.S.-Chile FTA will be the first comprehensive trade agreement between the United States and a South American country. Both ministers expect this Agreement will encourage progress on negotiations of the Free Trade Area of the Americas (FTAA), to meet its goal of completion by 2005, as well as the ongoing global trade negotiations. "This is an excellent agreement that cuts tariffs and opens markets for American workers, farmers, investors and consumers. It's a win-win state of the art FTA for the modern economy—it not only slashes tariffs, it reduces barriers for services, protects leading-edge intellectual property, keeps pace with new technologies, ensures regulatory transparency and provides effective labor and environmental enforcement," said Zoellick. "The U.S.-Chile FTA really is a partnership for growth, a partnership in creating economic opportunity for the people of both countries. Chile is an ideal free trade partner for the United States because of its sound macroeconomic policies and commitment to free trade. The U.S.-Chile free trade partnership extends beyond this agreement—we are both working hard together to advance global trade negotiations and the Free Trade Area of the Americas." "I want to thank my Chilean counterparts, Foreign Minister Soledad Alvear, and Finance Minister Nicolas Eyzaguirre for their leadership and persistent pursuit of opening markets with this agreement. I also want to thank our lead negotiators, Regina Vargo for the United States and Osvaldo Rosales for Chile, and the hardworking negotiating teams of both countries for their perseverance and success, and Chilean Ambassador Andres Bianchi who helped in the closing days," said Zoellick. "In the final round, over 90 Chilean and 140 U.S. negotiators representing 19 U.S. agencies worked for nine straight days to reach agreement."

American workers, consumers, investors and farmers will enjoy preferential access to one of the world's fastest growing economies, enabling products and services to flow back and forth from the United States and Chile with no tariffs and under streamlined customs procedures. Under the Trade Act of 2002, the Administration must notify Congress at least 90 days before signing the agreement. The Administration will continue to consult with the Congress on the agreement during the waiting period and expects early next year to notify Congress of its intent to sign the FTA.

Two-way trade in goods and services (exports plus imports) between the United States and Chile totaled $8.8 billion in 2001. Trade in services amounted to $2.2 billion, with the United States in surplus by $472 million in services trade with Chile. Trade in goods totaled $6.6 billion, with the United States in deficit by $424 million in goods trade with Chile. In the seven years to 2001, U.S. goods trade with Chile expanded by 44% and services trade by 37%.

Background: The United States and Chile began bilateral negotiations on an FTA in December 2000, holding a series of 14 negotiating rounds with teams of specialists, alternating between Santiago, Chile and cities in the United States, including Miami, Atlanta and Washington, DC. Free Trade Agreements with the United States are comprehensive and provide unparalleled market access for the countries involved. The United States has only four FTA partners: Canada and Mexico (within the North American Free Trade Agreement, or NAFTA), Israel and Jordan. In November, Ambassador Zoellick announced conclusion of the substance of an FTA with Singapore. The Administration has notified Congress of its intent to launch negotiations with Australia, five Central American countries, Morocco and the South African Customs Union (SACU-South Africa, Namibia, Lesotho, Swaziland and Botswana).The United States views the U.S.-Chile FTA as a key way to increase U.S. market access for goods and services and provide strong protections for U.S. investors in Chile.

Some of the key provisions the FTA would provide follow: New Opportunities for U.S. Workers and Manufacturers: More than 85% of bilateral trade in consumer and industrial products becomes tariff-free immediately, with most remaining tariffs eliminated within four years. Key U.S. export sectors benefit, such as agricultural and construction equipment, autos and auto parts, computers and other information technology products, medical equipment, and paper products. Expanded markets for U.S. Farmers and Ranchers: About three-quarters of both U.S. and Chilean farm goods will be tariff-free within four years, with all tariffs and quotas phased out within 12 years. American agriculture wants to expand and compete into new markets, and Chile represents one of the fastest growing economies. U.S. farmers' access to Chilean markets will be as good or better than the European Union or Canada, both of which already have FTAs with Chile. Without this agreement U.S. farmers face higher tariffs than farmers from Canada or the EU. Farmers will gain duty-free treatment within four years for important U.S. products such as pork and pork products, beef and beef products, soybeans and soybean meal, durum wheat, feed grains, potatoes, and processed food products such as french fries, pasta, distilled spirits and breakfast cereals. This FTA will promote U.S. efforts to create markets for U.S. farmers and global competition for liberalization in the World Trade Organization (WTO), FTAA and bilaterally.

Access to a Fast–Growing Chilean Services Market: The agreement offers new access for U.S. banks, insurance companies, telecommunications companies, securities firms, express delivery companies, and professionals. U.S. firms may offer financial services to participants in Chile's highly successful privatized pension system. A Trade Agreement for the Digital Age: State-of-the-art protections and non-discriminatory treatment are provided for digital products such as U.S. software, music, text, and videos. Protections for U.S. patents, trademarks and trade secrets exceeds past trade agreements. Strong Protections for U.S. Investors: The Agreement establishes a secure, predictable legal framework for U.S. investors in Chile. Open and Fair Government Procurement: Ground-breaking anti-corruption measures in government contracting. U.S. firms are guaranteed a fair and transparent process to sell goods and services to a wide range of Chilean government entities, including airports and seaports. Strong Protections for Labor and Environment: Both parties commit to effectively enforce their domestic labor and environmental laws. An innovative enforcement mechanism includes monetary assessments to enforce commercial and labor and environmental obligations. Cooperative projects will help protect wildlife, reduce environmental hazards and promote internationally recognized labor rights.

PART B: THE UNITED STATES' FTA PROGRAM

Comment on the Proliferation of FTAs

As the USTR Press Release quoted above indicates, completion of the negotiations with Chile (and Singapore) begun by the Clinton Administration were only the beginning for the Bush Administration under the guidance of Ambassador Zoellick. Prior to the enactment of Trade Promotion Authority (fast-track), an FTA with Jordan was concluded (by the Clinton Administration) in October 2000, and approved by Congress a year later, with that approval due in large part to the political and strategic significance of this first FTA with an Arab nation. Between 2002 and late 2004, USTR concluded FTAs with the Central American nations; the Dominican Republic; Morocco; and Australia. FTA negotiations were under way with Colombia, Ecuador, Peru and Panama, Bahrain and the members of the South African Customs Union, among others. All of these, if successfully completed, are likely to be comprehensive agreements patterned after NAFTA. For example, all those concluded to date except the Australia FTA include comprehensive provisions for the resolution of investment disputes through binding international arbitration.

The flurry of bilateral trade agreement negotiations by the United States is probably driven in large part by the failure of the global trade negotiations to move forward promptly, and, in the Western Hemisphere, disappointment over the stalled FTAA negotiations. As Ambassador Zoellick stated after the failure of the WTO Doha Development Round negotiations in Cancun in September, 2003:

> Many countries—developing and developed—were dismayed by the transformation of the WTO [at Cancun] into a forum for the politics of protest. Some withstood pressure to join the strife from larger developing neighbours. Of course, negotiating positions differed. But the key division at Cancun was between the can-do and the won't-do. For over two years, the US has pushed to open markets globally, in our hemisphere, and with subregions or individual countries. As WTO members ponder the future, the US will not wait: we will move toward free trade with can-do countries.*

As indicated in the Press Release on the Chile FTA, the United States expects the conclusion of bilateral FTAs to put pressure on Brazil, Argentina, Venezuela and other Western Hemisphere nations which have been perceived as dragging their feet on the FTAA (and Doha) negotiations. The WTO Doha negotiations show some signs of movement, after agreement July 1, 2004, on a new work program, but few observers believe that those negotiations can be concluded before mid–2006 at the earliest. The conclusion of the FTAA negotiations, if it occurs at all, will likely be much later. Thus, for the time being the FTA negotiations are the only game in town. (Mercosur activity is discussed in Part C of Problem 12.2.) However, these sub-regional agreements go significantly beyond the principle that some free trade is probably better than no free trade.

GANTZ, THE FREE TRADE AGREEMENT OF THE AMERICAS: AN IDEA
Whose Time Has Come—And Gone?**

CAFTA presumably represents the latest thinking in United States views of the appropriate content of FTAs with developing nations in the Western Hemisphere. Much of CAFTA is derived from NAFTA and from U.S. proposals for the FTAA. The departures from NAFTA represent both ten years' experience with NAFTA and with shifting priorities. Central America/Dominican Republic—United States trade is not insignificant, over $31 billion per year in exports and imports, and will undoubtedly increase once CAFTA goes into force. However, increased trade is not the only major focus of CAFTA. Rather, CAFTA is probably as much a vehicle for economic development as it is for trade expansion *per se*, more so than NAFTA or any other earlier FTA, in such areas as rule of law, "trade capacity building," customs procedures, regulatory transparency, private property rights, competition, "civil society" partic-

---

* Zoellick, America will not Wait for the Won't Do Countries, quoted in the Financial Times, Sep. 22, 2003, London ed., at 23. Copyright © 2003 Financial Times.

** Adapted from 1 Loyola Int'l L. Rev. 179 (2004); Copyright © 2004 David A. Gantz and Loyola International Law Review. Reprinted with permission.

ipation, environmental protection, and labor law. More than forty years after the General Treaty on Central American Economic Integration was concluded, in 1960, the CAFTA, along with promised negotiations in 2004 or 2005 of an FTA with the European Union, may provide the necessary impetus for the Central American nations to complete the customs union and harmonization of commercial law that was agreed to long ago. Certainly, CAFTA does not go as far as one might hope in this direction. For example, CAFTA creates various "unfunded mandates" but does not necessarily provide the massive technical assistance to implement the CAFTA nations' new obligations. The U.S. government provided over $61 million in trade capacity building assistance in 2003 (roughly $12 million per Central American nation), and the Inter–American Development Bank has approved over $320 million in "CAFTA-related operations." These amounts reflect a general Bush Administration commitment to increased "trade capacity building" assistance made at the time of the October 2002 FTAA Ministerial meeting in Quito, Ecuador.

* * *

USTR, FREE TRADE WITH CENTRAL AMERICA: SUMMARY OF THE U.S.–CENTRAL AMERICA FREE TRADE AGREEMENT*

New Market Access for U.S. Consumer and Industrial Products: More than 80 percent of U.S. exports of consumer and industrial products to Central America will be duty-free immediately upon entry into force of the Agreement, and 85 percent will be duty free within five years. All remaining tariffs will be eliminated within ten years. Key U.S. exports, such as information technology products, agricultural and construction equipment, paper products, chemicals, and medical and scientific equipment will gain immediate duty-free access to Central America. Guatemala, Honduras and Nicaragua will soon join the WTOs Information Technology Agreement (ITA), which removes tariff and non-tariff barriers to IT products. Costa Rica and El Salvador are already participants. Under the U.S. Caribbean Basin Trade Partnership Act, many products from Central America already enter the United States duty-free. The CAFTA will consolidate those benefits and make them permanent, so that nearly all consumer and industrial products made in Central America will enter the U.S. duty free immediately on effectiveness of the agreement.

New Opportunities for U.S. Farmers and Ranchers: More than half of current U.S. farm exports to Central America will become duty-free immediately, including high quality cuts of beef, cotton, wheat, soybeans, key fruits and vegetables, processed food products, and wine, among others. Tariffs on most U.S. farm products will be phased out within 15

* Trade Facts, Dec. 17, 2003; Copyright ©
2003, USTR. The full text of CAFTA is
available at http://www.ustr.gov.

years. U.S. farm products that will benefit from improved market access include pork, beef, poultry, rice, fruits and vegetables, corn, processed products and dairy products. U.S. farmers and ranchers will have access to Central American countries that is generally better than suppliers in Canada, Europe and South America. The U.S. and Central America will work to resolve sanitary and phytosanitary barriers to agricultural trade, in particular problems and delays in food inspection procedures for meat and poultry. Central America will move toward recognizing export eligibility for all plants inspected under the U.S. food safety and inspection system.

Textiles and apparel will be duty-free and quota-free immediately if they meet the Agreement's rule of origin, promoting new opportunities for U.S. and Central American fiber, yarn, fabric and apparel manufacturing. The agreement's benefits for textiles and apparel will be retroactive to January 1, 2004. An unprecedented provision will give duty-free benefits to some apparel made in Central America that contains certain fabrics from NAFTA partners Mexico and Canada. This new provision encourages integration of the North and Central American textile industries, and is a step to prepare for an increasingly competitive global market. Apparel containing certain fabrics and materials in "short supply" in the U.S. and Central America may also qualify for duty-free treatment. An expanded list of such "short supply" materials was developed in consultation with industry in the U.S. and Central America. U.S. yarn and fabric will receive reciprocal treatment in Central American apparel entering Mexico and Canada. A "de minimis" provision will allow limited amounts of third-country content to go into CAFTA apparel, giving producers in both the US and Central America needed flexibility.

Open Services Markets Across the Region: The Central American countries will accord substantial market access across their entire services regime, subject to very few exceptions, using the so-called "negative list" approach. Central American countries have agreed to dismantle significant distribution barriers. Changes in the "dealer protection regimes" will loosen restrictions that lock U.S. firms into exclusive or inefficient distributor arrangements. Such laws have been used to ban imports of U.S. products when a dispute arose with a local distributor. Market access commitments apply across all sectors....

[The Agreement] removes most local residency requirements, which had imposed significant barriers to U.S. professionals. Central America will allow U.S.-based firms to supply insurance on a cross-border basis, including reinsurance; reinsurance brokerage; marine, aviation and transport (MAT) insurance; and other insurance services. Central America will allow U.S.-based firms to offer services cross-border to Central Americans in areas such as financial information and data processing, and financial advisory services. In addition, Central American mutual funds will be able to use foreign-based portfolio managers. The commitments in services cover both cross-border supply of services (such as services supplied through electronic means, or through the travel of nationals) as well as the right to invest and establish a local services presence. Market access to services is supplemented by requirements for regulatory transparency. Regulatory authorities must use open and transparent administrative procedures, consult with interested parties before issuing regulations, provide advance notice and comment periods for proposed rules, and publish all regulations. The financial services chapter includes core obligations of non-discrimination, most favored nation treatment, and additional market access obligations. It also includes additional provisions on transparency of domestic regulatory regimes.

E–Commerce: Free Trade in the Digital Age: Central America and the United States agreed to provisions on e-commerce that reflect the issue's importance in global trade and the importance of supplying services by electronic means as a key part of a vibrant e-commerce environment. All Parties committed to non-discriminatory treatment of digital products; agreed not to impose customs duties on such products and to cooperate in numerous policy areas related to e-commerce.

Important New Protections for U.S. Investors in the Region: The agreement will establish a secure, predictable legal framework for U.S. investors operating in the Central American countries. All forms of investment are protected under the Agreement, including enterprises, debt, concessions, contracts and intellectual property. U.S. investors enjoy in almost all circumstances the right to establish, acquire and operate investments in the Central American countries on an equal footing with local investors, and with investors of other countries, unless specifically stated otherwise. Pursuant to U.S. Trade Promotion Authority, the agreement draws from U.S. legal principles and practices to provide U.S. investors in the Central American countries a basic set of substantive protections that Central American investors currently enjoy under the U.S. legal system. Among the rights afforded to U.S. investors (consistent with those found in U.S. law) are due process protections and the right to receive a fair market value for property in the event of an expropriation. Investor rights are backed by an effective, impartial procedure for dispute settlement that is fully transparent. Submissions to dispute panels and panel hearings will be open to the public, and interested parties will have the opportunity to submit their views.

[Discussion of intellectual property and government procurement provisions omitted]

Groundbreaking Customs Procedures and Rules of Origin: Comprehensive rules of origin will ensure that only U.S. and Central American goods benefit from the Agreement. Rules are designed to be easier to administer. Agreement requires transparency and efficiency in administering customs procedures, including the CAFTA rules of origin. Central American countries commit to publish laws and regulations on the Internet, and will ensure procedural certainty and fairness. Both parties agree to share information to combat illegal trans-shipment of goods. In addition, the Agreement contains language designed to facilitate the rapid clearance through customs of express delivery shipments.

CAFTA fully meets the labor objectives set out by Congress in the Trade Promotion Act of 2002 and makes labor obligations a part of the core text of the trade agreement. [It seeks to improve working conditions through ensuring effective enforcement of existing labor laws; working with the ILO to improve existing labor laws and enforcement; and building local capacity to improve worker rights. The] Agreement fully meets the environmental objectives set out by Congress in the TPA. Environmental obligations are part of the core text of the agreement. CAFTA includes provisions for developing a "robust public submissions process ... bench-marking of environmental cooperation activities" and "enhancing the mutual supportiveness of multilateral environmental agreements and the free trade agreement."

Dispute Settlement: Tools to Enforce the CAFTA: Core obligations of the Agreement, including labor and environment provisions, are subject to the dispute settlement provisions of the Agreement. Dispute panel procedures set high standards of openness and transparency:

● Open public hearings;

● Public release of legal submissions by parties;

● Special labor or environment expertise for disputes in these areas;

● Opportunities for interested third parties to submit views.

Emphasis is on promoting compliance through consultation, joint action plans and trade-enhancing remedies. An innovative enforcement mechanism includes monetary penalties to enforce commercial, labor and environmental obligations of the trade agreement.

Trade Capacity–Building: Development and Trade Together: In a first for any free trade agreement, CAFTA will include a Committee on Trade Capacity Building, in recognition of the importance of such assistance in promoting economic growth, reducing poverty, and adjusting to liberalized trade. The trade capacity building committee will build on work done during the negotiations to enhance partnerships with international institutions (Inter–American Development Bank, World Bank, Organization of American States, ECLAC, and the Central American Bank for Economic Integration), non-governmental organizations, and the private sector. This year, in response to the needs identified by the Central American countries, the U.S. Government provided more than $61 million in trade capacity building (TCB) assistance. Since the launch of negotiations, the Inter–American Development Bank has approved more than $320 million in CAFTA-related operations. Private and non-government organizations joined in the effort on trade capacity building....

Questions and Comments

1. For an international trade agreement involving the United States to enter into force, Congress must approve the agreement and pass appropriate implementing legislation. What is the importance of "fast track procedure"

(Trade Promotion Authority) within the context of congressional approval of international trade agreements? What advantages does the TPA procedure have over Congress' traditional process for reviewing international agreements? What are some drawbacks to the TPA process? Refer to Miller.

2. The Trade Promotion Authority/fast track process significantly reduces Congress' flexibility in reviewing a proposed international agreement. Chilean officials ask you to explain why Congress would be willing to accept such limitations on its authority. In other words, what would Congress stand to gain by authorizing TPA in the context of the U.S.–Chile FTA, other FTAs and the WTO's Doha Development Round?

3. The Chilean government became frustrated and disenchanted with fast track developments in the years after NAFTA's passage. Why did Congress refuse to provide fast track authority to the Clinton Administration? Why did congressional Republicans oppose the fast track legislation submitted by President Clinton? Why did many congressional Democrats oppose the same legislation? Refer to Tiefer, Hufbauer & Schott. What changed to make it possible for President Bush to obtain TPA in 2002?

4. Even before NAFTA entered into force, a consensus existed that, of all of the countries in Latin America, Chile should be the next country to be incorporated into NAFTA or the subject of an FTA. Why? Is there any strong rational basis for Congressional opposition to a free trade relationship with Chile? (The Chile FTA was approved by overwhelming margins, 270–156 in the U.S. House of Representatives, 66–31 in the U.S. Senate, in 2003.)

5. Did the absence of TPA/fast-track from 1994–2002 do any lasting damage to U.S. international economic policies? Is it likely that the Clinton Administration would have negotiated more trade agreements during its second term than in the absence of fast-track? Note that an effort was made in Seattle in November 1999 to initiate a new round of WTO negotiations, which failed because of disagreements between the U.S., the European Union and Japan, and the developing country members, on the agenda for the negotiations.

6. Your client had told you (and has represented publicly) that environmental and labor issues should not be viewed as an obstacle to NAFTA accession because Chile is willing to commit to the obligations set forth in the NAAEC and NAALC. Refer to Langman. What are the pros and cons of separate agreements such as the NAAEC and NAALC compared to inclusion of the labor and environmental provisions in the agreement itself? Are the environmental and labor concerns of those members of Congress who have opposed fast track and trade promotion authority on these grounds likely to be satisfied in either event? Were Congressional concerns over labor and environmental issues regarding Chile likely as intense as those regarding Mexico under NAFTA?

7. Is it appropriate for the United States to use its economic power and size to attempt to dictate to other countries what their environmental and labor laws should provide and to what degree such laws must be enforced? Is it proper for the United States to include labor and environmental issues in trade agreements? If so, to what extent and in what ways?

8. Does the negotiation of various FTAs in the Western Hemisphere put any significant pressure on Brazil, Argentina et al to move toward an FTAA? To cooperate more fully in the WTO Doha Development Round negotiations? Why or why not? What arguments against negotiation of a multitude of FTAs can you suggest, to your Chilean clients or to the U.S. Congress? Is the TPA approval process for an FTAA likely to be significantly easier than for a broader agreement, such as the FTAA?

9. Based on the USTR's "Trade Facts," what are the major innovations in CAFTA compared to NAFTA? What trade facilitation elements were incorporated in NAFTA? To what extent were the Central American countries and the Dominican Republic likely to have been able to demand changes in agreement provisions offered by the United States? Is the sovereignty of the five Central American nations compromised if the completion of the Central American Common Market (after more than 40 years) is effectively a condition precedent for CAFTA? As of late 2004, progress continues, but a full customs union–with elimination of duties and charges at the internal borders and a single duty collection system for goods proceeding from outside the region–is probably at least several years away. Costa Rica, which has been ambivalent about Central American economic integration for many decades, is still holding back in several key areas. Also, the establishment of a full customs union has been impeded by weak communications infrastructure—including the inability of all of the customs posts in a given country to communicate electronically with each other or their counterparts in the neighboring countries—and by severe shortages of computers and telecommunications equipment. A single duty collection system is complicated by the fact that the Central American nations each have different value added tax rates to be collected in addition to import duties at any common border customs posts.

10. Considering Chile's geographical location, what other nations would be appropriate FTA partners, beyond South Korea, the European Union, the United States, Canada and Mexico? Japan? China? (Chile announced in September 2004 that it would in fact pursue FTA negotiations with both countries.) What trade sectors would you expect to be most difficult to negotiate with Japan?

PROBLEM 12.2 THE FREE TRADE AREA OF THE AMERICAS AND WESTERN HEMISPHERIC INTEGRATION

SECTION I.   THE SETTING

The Organization of American States (OAS), which is based in Washington, D.C., includes as active members all of the nations of the Western Hemisphere (except Cuba) and serves as a regional forum for multilateral dialogue and action. Founded in 1948, the objectives of the OAS are to strengthen democracy, advance human rights, promote peace and security, expand trade and tackle complex problems caused by poverty, drugs and corruption in the Americas. Historically, the OAS has been criticized by some for accomplishing little if anything of a concrete nature; however, the reviews of its supporting work related to the formation of the Free Trade Area of the Americas (FTAA) are positive.

In 1995, the OAS created a Trade Unit. The Trade Unit assists OAS member countries with matters related to trade and economic integration in the Western Hemisphere and, in particular, with their efforts to establish an FTAA. The Trade Unit has monitored trade developments which followed the first Summit of the Americas in December 1994. For example, the Trade Unit's staff has witnessed the rise and implementation of new trade accords such as the NAFTA and the Canada–Chile Free Trade Agreement, observed the increasing influence in the hemisphere of trading blocs from outside the hemisphere (including especially the European Union), and confirmed a growing tendency on the part of Latin American nations to look to Europe and Asia for new trade deals. The Trade Unit has prepared documents important to the FTAA process, including the "Analytical Compendium of Western Hemisphere Trade Arrangements (see Chapter 4)," "Toward Free Trade in the Americas" and various technical reports on specific economic integration issues. In 1998, after the Santiago Summit, the Trade Unit began providing technical support to several of the many FTAA Negotiating Groups.

Although the economic advancement of Latin American nations in general is important to the OAS, the organization has had a particular interest in seeing that Western Hemispheric integration—the integration of all democratic nations in the Western Hemisphere into a single free trade zone stretching from Alaska to Patagonia—becomes a reality. Initially, analysts at the OAS viewed accession into NAFTA as the best and most viable path to hemispheric integration. Chile's failed efforts to join NAFTA, and subsequent FTAA negotiating sessions, have shifted the focus to the negotiation of an entirely new free trade agreement.

As you read the materials and consider the questions which follow, assume that you are a consultant working in the OAS's Trade Unit. You have been given the following assignments: (1) identify the economic integration formula you conclude is most likely to succeed in unifying the Americas, (2) provide a frank assessment of whether hemispheric integration is possible or even worth pursuing, and (3) assess the pros and cons of FTAs between countries of the Western Hemisphere and the nations of Europe and Asia. While Brazil would likely never consult with the OAS, it is important, nevertheless, for the OAS to assess the impact of Brazil's effort, through MERCOSUR, of creating a unified South American trade bloc.

SECTION II.   FOCUS OF CONSIDERATION

NAFTA's birth in 1994 made economic integration in the Western Hemisphere seem more possible than at any other time in history. NAFTA spawned much of the enthusiasm evident at the Miami Summit for the Free Trade Area of the Americas. Understandably, therefore, since 1994 the governments of the Western Hemisphere have made economic integration a priority. Problem 12.2 calls upon the reader to rethink whether a free trade zone encompassing the entire American continent is a worthwhile objective, particularly if the most that could be achieved would be an "FTAA-lite" without the comprehensive coverage of NAFTA and more recent FTAs. Should the governments continue to expend their limited time and resources on such an endeavor? Is the FTAA movement destined to become just another one of the region's many failed attempts at integration? As a practical matter, is a single comprehensive trade accord feasible? What might the technical features of a hemispheric free trade agreement look like? In what ways, if any, will NAFTA shape such an agreement? Would efforts be better directed at trade liberalization with Japan or Europe, or within the Hemisphere?

These questions arise because Latin America's past is littered with unsuccessful drives to integrate the various economies. Part of this failure is attributable to the great political, social, historical and cultural diversity the exists in Latin America and to global economic and political forces beyond Latin America's control. One issue of great concern in the integration context is whether advanced economies (such as that of the United States) can be joined in a free trade accord with relatively underdeveloped economies (such as that of Nicaragua) or tiny economies (such as that of Antigua and Barbuda). Add to this mix the fact that political officials in the United States, having achieved TPA, have been unable to reach agreement in principle with the other heavyweight in the Hemisphere, Brazil, on the essential elements of an agreement.

Recent years have witnessed a flurry of new trade agreements between Latin American nations and countries outside of the Western Hemisphere. For example, the MERCOSUR countries have been focusing for several years on trade talks with the European Union, although such efforts were foundering in late 2004 due to disagreements over MERCO-SUR's access to the European Union for its agricultural products. Chile successfully concluded an FTA with South Korea and the European Union, and has negotiated with Singapore and New Zealand. Mexico concluded an FTA with the European Union in 2000 and with Japan in 2004. Peru has announced its intention to negotiate FTAs with Singapore, Thailand and possibly China in 2005. The Central American nations are seeking an FTA with the European Union. Do these extra-hemispheric initiatives threaten the success of the FTAA negotiations, or are they complementary? Do such initiatives by the Latin Americans suggest that it would be in the United States' best interests to adopt the same approach, focusing trade liberalization efforts on a massive economy such as that of Japan? Or, would it make more sense for the nations in the Western Hemisphere—all WTO members—to refocus on the Doha Development Round of global trade negotiations?

Your analysis of the issues discussed in this problem will be facilitated by a review of the Baker article in Chapter 4.

Relevant Provisions of the MERCOSUR treaties of Asuncion, Ouro Preto and Olivos are essential to an analysis of Part C of this Problem. The are included in the Documents Supplement.

SECTION III. READINGS, QUESTIONS AND COMMENTS

PART A: SEEKING THE FTAA

BARSHEFSKY, KEYNOTE ADDRESS

30 L. & Pol'y Int'l Bus. 1 (1999).*

The FTAA is both the result of and a contributor to a broader shift in the hemisphere. And we can begin to understand this shift by asking the basic question: why have we embarked on this effort? To this there are three mutually supporting answers. The first two of them are permanent facts of life. One is geography. The countries of the Western Hemisphere are our neighbors. They will always be our neighbors. And it is plainly in our national interest to have the best possible trade relationship with our neighbors. The other is the interest of our citizens. The Western Hemisphere is our largest and fastest-growing market and we are the largest and fastest-growing market for our neighbors. Broadening and deepening this trade relationship will help working people, firms, farmers, ranchers, and service providers everywhere to find new opportunities.

* * *

The lessons of this experience are clear. Trade integration has created growth and mutual benefit in North America, in the Caribbean Basin, and in South America. Trade integration has both benefitted from and strengthened peace, freedom, democracy and the rule of law throughout the hemisphere. And the Free Trade Area of the Americas will improve, strengthen, and transcend all of this. It will create the world's largest free trade area—uniting 34 countries and almost 800 million people; geographically stretching from Point Barrow to Patagonia, Hawaii to Recife, Easter Island to Newfoundland—through fair, transparent rules, and impartial dispute settlement procedures. And thus it will open new opportunities for prosperity to workers, businesses and farmers everywhere in the hemisphere.

* * *

This is the vision before us as the talks begin. A community of common interests in prosperity, jobs, and economic growth. A community of common aspirations for better health, environmental protection, and cultural exchange. And a community of common values, in a hemisphere united by democracy, freedom, social justice, and the rule of law. For the first time in two centuries, it is within our grasp. We must not let it slip away.

HUFBAUER & SCHOTT, WESTERN HEMISPHERE ECONOMIC INTEGRATION
(1994).*

LATIN AMERICAN GROWTH AND TRADE PROSPECTS

. . . if Latin American nations liberalize their economies and adopt outward-looking policies, higher trade-to-GDP ratios could potentially add $56 billion to total Latin American exports and boost import levels by $92 billion during the 1990's. . . . Policy-induced trade expansion of these magnitudes would powerfully stimulate Latin American GDP growth, bringing a second round of trade growth.

* * *

. . . we calculate that this degree of trade liberalization, complemented by other reforms (the WHFTA scenario), could enable Latin America to increase its annual real GDP growth rate by 1.5 percentage points in the 1990's as compared with our baseline scenario, which we label the continuing-reform scenario. The additional real GDP growth on account of policy liberalization would yield an annual increment in Latin American GDP of about $273 billion in the year 2002, or about $525 per capita.

Owing to the interaction between trade growth and GDP growth, the real level of Latin American exports would be $87 billion higher in the year 2002, and real imports would be $104 billion greater than in the continuing-reform scenario. The ambitious course of economic policy reform envisaged in the WHFTA scenario would thus add about $191 billion to the level of two-way Latin American trade by the year 2002.

* * *

US EXPORT AND IMPORT GAINS

The base-year level (average 1989–91) of US exports to Latin America was $24 billion. By 2002, US exports to Latin America are projected to reach a level of $70 billion (expressed in 1990 prices) under the continuing-reform scenario and $106 billion under the WHFTA scenario. The WHFTA scenario would thus increase US exports to Latin America in the year 2002 by about $36 billion above levels that might by reached under the continuing-reform scenario.

On the import side, the base-year level (average 1989–91) of US imports from Latin America was $30 billion. By 2002, US imports from Latin America are projected to reach $65 billion (expressed in 1990 prices) under the continuing-reform scenario and $92 billion under the WHFTA scenario. Thus, the WHFTA scenario entails an annual level of US imports from Latin America in 2002 that is about $28 billion greater than might be reached under the continuing-reform scenario. A WHFTA would enable the United States to reach a merchandise trade surplus with Latin America by the year 2002 that would be about $9 billion higher than under the continuing-reform scenario. In our view, this number represents a responsibly high estimate of the balance of trade impact of a successful Western Hemisphere Free Trade Area.

JOB EFFECTS AND WAGE LEVELS

Because the US trade balance with Latin America improves in both scenarios, the calculated net impact on US jobs will be positive. The WHFTA scenario shows a net increase of 60,800 US jobs in the year 2002 by comparison with the continuing-reform scenario.

* * *

Based on our calculations, the impact of different trade scenarios on US wage rates by worker groups is as follows. In the year 2002, wages for the highest-wage group with by far the larger number of employees– 63.5 million members, making up more than half the US workforce–are calculated to rise under a continuing-reform scenario by 0.52 percent as a result of expanded trade with Latin America. Under the WHFTA scenario, the rise would be 1.03 percent. In terms of weekly wages, the difference between the two scenarios (0.51 percent) translates into weekly wage gains of about $2.41, or annual wage gains of about $125, for more than half the US work force. However, the two lowest-wage groups lose ground. The hardest hit is the fourth group, with 6.7 million workers. This group suffers a wage loss of 8.71 percent in the WHFTA scenario, by comparison with a loss of 3.69 percent in the continuing-reform scenario. The additional loss (5.02 percent) translates into $16.70 per week, or about $868 per year, for this 6 percent of the US workforce.

These wage and job calculations can be summarized in the following way. By adopting counterfactual and pessimistic—but not outlandish—assumptions, it is possible to project small job losses and somewhat lower wages for lower skilled US workers as a consequence of expanded trade with Latin America. Net job losses for these workers are not significant relative to the size of the US work force (about 120 million) or the number of US employees dislocated annually for all reasons (nearly 2 million). For the US work force as a whole, expanded trade with Latin America implies slightly more jobs and slightly higher wages.

BAKER, INTEGRATION OF THE AMERICAS: A LATIN RENAISSANCE OR A PRESCRIPTION FOR DISASTER?
11 Temple Int'l & Comp. L.J. 309 (1997).*

... Currently, there are already a number of subregional and regional agreements in Latin America: (1) MERCOSUR, (2) the Group of

Three, (3) the Andean Pact, (4) the Caribbean Community ("CARI-COM"), (5) the Central American Common Market ("CACM"), (6) the Association of Caribbean States ("ACS"), and (7) the Latin American Integration Association ("LAIA"). A brief summary of these pacts will reveal the multifaceted character of their make-up.

(1) MERCOSUR—In 1991, Brazil, Argentina, Uruguay, and Paraguay signed the Asuncion Agreement, which calls for the creation of a free-trade zone and customs union modeled on the lines of the European Union ("EU"). "Known as MERCOSUR in Spanish, this 'market of the south' covers two-thirds of South America's economic activity." If MERCOSUR were a single country, it would be the world's second in land mass with 7 million square miles, fourth in population with 190 million people, and seventh in gross domestic product ("GDP") with $746 billion. Since the signing of the Asuncion Treaty of 1991, commerce between the four members has increased annually from $3.4 billion in 1991 to more than $10 billion in 1994. In addition to eliminating all tariffs within the bloc by the year 2000, MERCOSUR hopes to "recognize each others' university degrees, standardize their monetary systems, create a Southern Cone currency, and improve long-ignored trade routes."

In December of 1994, the four presidents from the member states of MERCOSUR met in Ouro Preto, Brazil, and signed the Ouro Preto Protocol, an annex to the Treaty of Asuncion. This annex established MERCOSUR as an "international legal entity" and allows MERCOSUR to negotiate on behalf of the four members with other foreign nations and other trade organizations, such as the EU and NAFTA. MERCOSUR's success readily attracted the attention of Chile, Bolivia, the Andean Pact, and the European Community. In addition, the Ouro Preto Protocol might be one method by which MERCOSUR can eventually integrate into NAFTA.

(2) Group of Three—Mexico, Colombia, and Venezuela, known as the Group of Three, form the second largest trade block in Latin America. The three nations agreed to erase all tariffs and quotas over the next decade; however, they did provide special exceptions for vulnerable sectors such as agriculture. On January 1, 1995, the Group of Three had an economy with a gross national product of $348 billion, with a market of 136 million potential consumers. Trade among the three countries reached $1.6 billion in 1992.

(3) Andean Pact—As typified by the 1970 Decision 24 of the Cartagena Agreement, Bolivia, Chile, Columbia, Ecuador, and Peru signed the Cartagena Agreement in 1969 to form the Andean Pact. Throughout its existence, numerous studies have been done regarding the Andean Pact in the field of foreign investments. During the early years of its existence, the Andean Pact centered on sub-regional economic development and was wary of foreigners. This early policy caused Chile to withdraw from membership in 1976. Today the Andean Pact consists of

Bolivia, Colombia, Ecuador, Peru, and Venezuela. In 1993, the five member nations had a total population of approximately 100 million and an overall GDP of $142 billion. Intra-group trade grew from $112 million in 1970 to $2.88 billion in 1993.

(4) CARICOM—The Caribbean Community ("CARICOM") is a common market between thirteen English-speaking Caribbean countries.* CARICOM was formed in 1973 and, after a slow start, has been steadily expanding. The purpose for CARICOM's existence is to address long-standing problems of the region: (1) to improve economic performance and standards of living through economic integration, and (2) to promote functional cooperation among the member states. CARICOM's goals are designed to be met "by accelerated, coordinated and sustained economic development, particularly through the exercise of permanent sovereignty over their natural resources, . . . and by presenting a common front to the external world." During the 1980s, member nations of CARICOM experienced severe recessions and a collapse of the regional payments system. Despite their troubles, in 1984, CARICOM members agreed to establish a Common External Tariff ("CET"), which is only partially implemented. The implementation of a CET should provide leverage in trade negotiations between CARICOM and other trade organizations. However, one study has also cautioned that CARICOM must take steps to reduce tariffs.

(5) CACM—The Central American Common Market ("CACM") was established in 1960. By 1969, almost all trade within the CACM region had achieved duty free status. Nevertheless, CACM witnessed declining trade during the 1970s because of economic, political, and ideological differences. CACM continues to face such problems today. In 1992, the value of intra-regional exports was forty percent below the 1980 level. The revival of intra-regional trade has been delayed by the uneven pace of adjustment among the member countries. One individual has characterized the CACM's adjustment policy as a "minimalist approach" producing "erratic and poorly" coordinated results. In July 1991, the CACM countries agreed to re-establish the common market.

(6) ACS—On July 24, 1994, CARICOM (consisting of thirteen members), twelve other Latin American countries, and other Caribbean nations formed the Association of Caribbean States ("ACS"). With a potential market of 200 million consumers, the ACS became the fourth-largest trading bloc in the world.

(7) LAIA—The Latin American Integration Association ("LAIA") consists of Argentina, Bolivia, Brazil, Chile, Colombia, Ecuador, Mexico, Paraguay, Peru, Uruguay, and Venezuela and was formed in 1980, replacing the Latin America Free Trade Association, which had been created in 1960. This agreement exists only on paper and has no schedule for more formal implementation.

* The CARICOM nations consist of Antigua and Barbuda, the Bahamas, Barbados, Belize, Dominica, Grenada, Guyana, Jamaica, Montserrat, St. Kitts and Nevis, St. Lucia, St. Vincent and the Grenadines, and Trinidad and Tobago.

LOPEZ–AYLLON, MEXICO'S EXPANDING MATRIX OF TRADE AGREEMENTS—A UNIFYING FORCE?

5 NAFTA L. & Bus. Rev. Am. 241 (1999).*

What will NAFTA's role be during the [FTAA negotiating] process? In other words, will NAFTA be able to serve as an agreement around which the negotiation process can be structured at the continental level? The answer to this question is, in principle, no. This does not, however, mean that NAFTA will not have an impact on the future of negotiations.

* * *

From this perspective, even if the NAFTA model is not implemented, the agreement does, however, contain significant improvements that could be used in the continental approach. Foremost among these is the relationship between investment and services, which is undoubtedly a more liberal and efficient approach than that which exists in the multilateral model. Other aspects in which the NAFTA can be used as a model is in the issue of government procurement and technical standards.

As regards rules of origin, an enormously complex yet crucial aspect, NAFTA offers a flexible scheme whose extension, with the appropriate modifications, could serve as the basis for the determination and application of regional preferences, as long as there is no consensus as regards multilateral negotiations.

Finally, one should consider the issues related to dispute settlement. It is generally accepted that the WTO's dispute settlement mechanism has proved effective. For this reason, and to ensure compatibility between multilateral and regional rules, it would be worth considering that the multilateral forum would be an appropriate forum for settling disputes in areas covered by WTO agreements. For those aspects not covered by the WTO, however, the NAFTA model could serve as a model for the creation of a flexible yet effective dispute settlement mechanism. Chapter XIX binational process review does not seem likely to be extended to a continental agreement. Instead substantive disciplines regarding antidumping/countervailing duty and competition policies may be developed in the FTAA.

In short, the complexity of the regional integration process, particularly in light of negotiations concerning the FTAA and regional integration agreements, make it unlikely that NAFTA will become the hub of the American system currently being created. This is due as much to the peculiarities of NAFTA itself as to the technical difficulties involved in a process of FTAA's scope.

Nevertheless, NAFTA will be an inevitable point of reference for at least the following three reasons. First, because NAFTA is a significantly more sophisticated and complete model than the majority of existing agreements in the region as regards both coverage and disciplines. Second, because this model has already been accepted in negotiations within the region and, with modifications, has become an element that integrates the system of regional accords. Third, because the negotiators who form part of the North American region will have the NAFTA model in mind as a parameter. These negotiators will obviously play a specific, crucial role in the process. Apropos of this, it will be extremely interesting to see the results of the interaction between the European model and the NAFTA model in the negotiations shortly to be initiated between the European Union and Mexico.

* * *

GANTZ, THE UNITED STATES AND THE EXPANSION OF WESTERN HEMISPHERE FREE TRADE: PARTICIPANT OR OBSERVER?

14 Ariz. J. Int'l & Comp. L. 381 (1997).*

Apart from the adverse political climate in the U.S., it is becoming increasingly evident that the NAFTA as presently structured is too complex and ponderous an instrument to expand to a large group of additional state parties. The problems include not only the difficulty of dealing with labor and environmental issues in a trade agreement, a concept which elicits little enthusiasm among hemispheric nations, but such basic aspects of the NAFTA as more than a dozen different tariff phase-out schedules eliminating tariffs immediately or over periods as long as fifteen years, multiple schedules for phasing in market access for services, and an enormously complex set of rules of origin. These provisions are functioning adequately with three member nations, but it is difficult to imagine a NAFTA of five, ten, or more members in which each pair of members has a separate set of tariff schedules and phase-outs.

The rules of origin are of particular concern because of the complexity of demonstrating compliance, particularly where regional value calculations are required. Moreover, such a complex system can be viewed as discriminating in favor of those countries–primarily the U.S. and Canada–whose customs services have the necessary sophistication and resources to ensure compliance. There are few other governments in the hemisphere that can hope to adequately issue rulings and conduct compliance audits. The U.S. and Canada can thus assure that only qualifying goods receive NAFTA benefits, but most other countries cannot. The rules in operation consequently favor the U.S. and Canada at the expense of their trading partners. It is thus not surprising that negotiation of acceptable rules of origin was one of the major hurdles facing Canada and Chile in their bilateral negotiations, although ultimately Canada apparently prevailed in convincing Chile to adopt the NAFTA rules. MERCOSUR rules of origin are less complicated and more liberal and, in any event, different, in part because a common external tariff eliminates much of the concern over trans-shipment of goods, by eliminating the incentive to enter the goods initially into the member country with the lowest tariff.

Given that the Free Trade Area of the Americas implies a merging, or at least linking, of the NAFTA and MERCOSUR countries, and perhaps the Andean Group nations as well, additional structural concerns arise. The NAFTA is a free trade area, in which the three nations remain free to set their own external tariffs, subject only to GATT/WTO limitations. MERCOSUR contemplates a customs union, vastly more difficult to achieve politically, in which the member states apply a uniform common external tariff to all imports from outside the group. The two are not compatible, yet MERCOSUR apparently has no intention of abandoning the common external tariff that had been negotiated with extreme difficulty over more than four years, even though it has not yet been implemented. The NAFTA could of course adopt a common external tariff, but for GATT reasons (avoiding an increase of duties), this would require Canada and Mexico to reduce most of their import duties, Canada modestly, Mexico by a substantial degree. Even with that understanding, U.S. tariffs–which will average about 3.5% after the Uruguay Round reductions are fully implemented in the year 2000–will be substantially lower than those of the other nations of the hemisphere. (The Andean Group agreements include arrangements both for elimination of most internal tariffs and for establishment of a common external tariff, but apparently neither has been fully implemented to date). One veteran U.S. official has suggested that the negotiation of a Free Trade Agreement of the Americas should contemplate eventual status as a customs union with a common external tariff, precisely to eliminate some of these difficulties. Ultimately, this approach, or a "hybrid" system in which a common external tariff applies to trade in major product sectors, may be essential to avail otherwise impossible conflicts.

Other differences between the NAFTA and MERCOSUR would also make conforming the two a difficult legal task. For example, NAFTA Chapter 11 incorporates a comprehensive set of investment protections, including binding international arbitration of disputes between foreign investors and host countries; MERCOSUR does not. At the urging of Mexico, the trade ministers of the hemisphere have agreed to create a working group on dispute settlement mechanisms for the FTAA in 1997. While the lack of investment protection provisions would not be a problem for Argentina, which has a bilateral investment treaty with the U.S. with provisions substantially similar to NAFTA Chapter 11, or for Chile, with its acceptance of similar provisions in the Canada–Chile Free Trade Agreement, many other Latin American nations will be reluctant to accept binding international arbitration of investment disputes. Yet it is difficult to envision the U.S. accepting a FTAA without the equivalent of Chapter 11. MERCOSUR also lacks comprehensive government-to-government dispute settlement mechanisms such as those found in the NAFTA. Nor does MERCOSUR deal with government procurement (market access for sales to government entities for foreign sellers), services generally, financial services, or telecommunications, all of which are treated under the NAFTA. As Canadian Trade Minister Art Eggleton has suggested, "these two agreements have fundamentally different objectives and could not be merged without one or the other dispensing with its core objectives." Canada apparently favors negotiation of a separate, thirty-four-nation agreement that would be less comprehensive than the NAFTA but which would contain more extensive obligations than the WTO agreements.

Yet another important potential problem is treatment of anti-dumping and countervailing duty actions. Despite strong Canadian and Mexican pressure, the U.S. refused to eliminate unfair trade actions within the NAFTA, or even to provide special, more lenient rules for the NAFTA partners. Canada continues to view reducing disputes over anti-dumping or countervailing duties as unfinished NAFTA business. Special treatment under the NAFTA is largely procedural: review of national administrative decisions under the anti-dumping and subsidies laws is by binational arbitral panels rather than national courts, but the substantive law of the importing country continues to apply. A working group was created as part of the NAFTA to develop a more acceptable framework for application of anti-dumping and countervailing duty laws within the NAFTA, but to date has failed to agree on any reforms.

* * *

KENNEDY, THE FTAA NEGOTIATIONS: A MELODRAMA IN FIVE ACTS

Loyola University Chicago Int'l Law Review, pp.121–138 (2004)*

On December 31, 2003, the North American Free Trade Agreement (NAFTA) marked its tenth anniversary. Another tenth anniversary in free trade also took place at the end of 2003, but this was an anniversary that went largely unnoticed, namely, the tenth anniversary of formal talks on a Free Trade Area of the Americas (FTAA). The FTAA was officially launched in Miami in 1994 at the first of four Summits of the Americas, and ten years later a renewed, albeit watered-down, commitment to completing those negotiations took place at the eighth and latest FTAA Ministerial Meeting in November 2003, again in Miami. Whether what occurred at the Miami Ministerial Meeting is cause for celebration or cause for frustration depends, of course, upon one's views about economic integration and globalization....

* 1 Loyola U. Chi. Int'l Law Rev. 121 (2004). Copyright © 2004 Kevin C. Kennedy [Professor of Law, Michigan State University College of Law] and the Loyola University Chicago International Law Review. Reprinted with permission. (Footnotes omitted.)

Background on the FTAA (and the Dramatis Personae)

A proposal to integrate the economies of the countries in the Western Hemisphere was launched by President George H.W. Bush in 1990 in his Enterprise for the Americas Initiative. This piece of unfinished business was championed by the Clinton administration and restyled as the Free Trade Area of the Americas. The goal of the FTAA, as articulated at the first Summit of the Americas held in Miami in December 1994, and renewed at the third FTAA Ministerial Meeting at Belo Horizonte, Brazil, in May 1997, was a free trade area stretching from Alaska to Tierra del Fuego by 2005. That far-sighted vision turned myopic at the eighth Ministerial Meeting held in Miami in November 2003.

The 34 heads of the democratic nations in the Western Hemisphere (all countries in the hemisphere with the exception of Cuba) launched FTAA negotiations at the 1994 Summit of the Americas in Miami, calling for the completion of an FTAA by 2005. The leaders committed themselves to integrate the patchwork quilt of bilateral and regional trade agreements (at least seven regional trade arrangements and more than twenty-five bilateral trade agreements) that exist in the Western Hemisphere. Upon its completion, the FTAA will integrate a population of over 850 million people into a $13 trillion market.

Act I: The 1994 Miami Summit of the Americas

The 1994 Miami Summit Action Plan called on the trade ministers of the 34 FTAA participants to meet in 1995 to draft a more complete plan for FTAA negotiations and to meet again in 1996 to develop a timetable for future work. To that end, trade ministers met in Denver in June 1995, and issued a Joint Declaration and Work Plan. The ministers agreed to set up nine FTAA working groups–subsequently renamed "negotiating groups" at the 1998 San Jose Ministerial Meeting–on investment; agriculture; subsidies, antidumping and countervailing duties; market access; services; competition policy; government procurement; intellectual property; and dispute settlement. It is noteworthy that negotiating groups have not been established for labor and the environment, notwithstanding a call in the Miami Summit Action Plan to "further secure the observance and promotion of worker rights" and to make trade liberalization and environmental policies "mutually supportive." Several Latin American representatives, as well as private groups, voiced concerns over a U.S. proposal to include the labor and environment ministers in the FTAA process. Opposition to the U.S. proposal was mounted on the ground that neither issue merits inclusion in the immediate action plan required to advance the FTAA process. Moreover, some participants argued that the proposed U.S. language on labor and the environment departed from the more vaguely worded language on labor and the environment in the Miami Summit Action plan. Sources monitoring the pre-Denver consultations reported that the United States agreed to soften its proposed language in order to achieve consensus at the June ministerial.

That June 1995 ministerial meeting in Denver failed to resolve two key points of disagreement about the future direction of FTAA negotiations: (1) the scope of the FTAA negotiations, and (2) the approach to be used to achieve the FTAA. Former U.S. Trade Representative Mickey Kantor and former Canadian Trade Minister MacLaren both viewed the FTAA as a two-track integration process—the newly established FTAA negotiating groups as one track, and the deepening and strengthening of existing sub-regional trade agreements as the other track. Under this view, the negotiating group discussions and the existing sub-regional agreements would be mutually reinforcing and would ultimately converge. A middle approach envisioned FTAA negotiations modeled after the Uruguay Round "single undertaking" approach. This scenario envisioned a multilateral forum open to all 34 countries in which they would simultaneously negotiate all aspects of the FTAA and in which all participants would accede to all of the agreements negotiated rather than adopt an "à la carte" approach as had been done in the Tokyo Round.

At the opposite end of the spectrum, former Brazilian Foreign Minister Luiz Felipe Lampreia advocated an approach that would have widened and deepened existing sub-regional agreements. The sub-regional accords would become "building blocks" for broader hemispheric economic integration along a path that ultimately would lead to bloc-to-bloc negotiations. But is this a "building block" or a "bloc building" approach? A constant concern about regionalism is that RTAs that create trade blocs may end up being trade diverting rather than trade creating because they close market access to more efficient producers from outside the bloc in favor of less efficient producers within the bloc. Advocates of the building block approach maintained that by capturing the gains and building on the progress already made in the sub-regional trade blocs, FTAA objectives would be realized more quickly than under the Uruguay Round's single-undertaking model. However, critics of the "building block" approach argued that much time could be lost in efforts to harmonize a diverse group of sub-regional arrangements ranging from free-trade areas, such as NAFTA, to common markets, such as MERCO-SUR.

At the March 1996 ministerial meeting in Cartagena, the trade ministers agreed on "the importance of further observance and promotion of worker rights and the need to consider appropriate processes in this area, through our respective governments." The lack of significant movement forward at this juncture can be explained in part by the incessant Brazilian–American sparring. While the United States would have preferred that an FTAA be a WTO "plus" agreement that would broaden the legal commitments made in the Uruguay Round, the early Brazilian model envisioned an FTAA that would first deepen existing sub-regional trade agreements before broadening them into an FTAA. The Brazilian vision would carry the day at the Cartegena ministerial meeting. As events would unfold, the Brazilians would ultimately win the argument over the future of FTAA negotiations.

Act II, Scene 1: The 1997 Belo Horizonte Ministerial Meeting

The glacial pace of FTAA negotiations was accelerated slightly at the 1997 Belo Horizonte ministerial meeting in Brazil. In their Joint Declaration, the trade ministers reiterated:

- the FTAA negotiations will be completed no later than 2005;

- the FTAA will be consistent with GATT Article XXIV and GATS Article V on regional trade agreements; and

- the FTAA will be trade creating, not trade diverting.

The 34 trade ministers also agreed on the following points: (1) decision-making is to be by consensus, (2) an FTAA must be a comprehensive undertaking, (3) countries may accede individually or as members of an RTA, and (4) a Secretariat is to be established to support the negotiations. As is explained below, the comprehensive undertaking goal of FTAA negotiations ultimately would be rejected at the November 2003 Ministerial Meeting in Miami.

Act II, Scene 2: The San Jose Ministerial Meeting

The participants in the FTAA negotiations held their fourth ministerial meeting in San Jose, Costa Rica, in March 1998. The 34 ministers of trade issued a joint declaration recommending to their respective heads of state that they formally launch negotiations on the FTAA at their second summit in Santiago, Chile. The ministers outlined the structure and organization of the negotiations into nine negotiating groups: market access; investment; services; government procurement; dispute settlement; agriculture; intellectual property rights; subsidies, antidumping, and countervailing duties; and competition policy. The trade ministers also reaffirmed their commitment "to make concrete progress by the year 2000. We direct the negotiating groups to achieve considerable progress by that year." Of course, 2000 came and went with no concrete progress having been made. Significantly, NGOs representing labor, environmental, and academic groups were invited to submit contributions to the FTAA ministerial meeting to be held in Canada in October 1999. A Committee of Government Representatives on the Participation of Civil Society is responsible for receiving and distributing submissions from civil society in the FTAA process. The participation of civil society has been ongoing, but whether or not it will have any impact remains to be seen.

Act II, Scene 3: The Santiago Summit

At the Second Summit of the Americas held in Santiago, Chile, in April 1998, the 34 heads of state accepted the recommendations made by their trade ministers in San Jose and officially launched negotiations on a Free Trade Area of the Americas. The Santiago Declaration reiterates the negotiators' commitment to complete FTAA negotiations by 2005. The Declaration also states that the FTAA will be balanced, comprehensive, WTO-consistent, and will constitute a single undertaking (i.e., will be an all-or-nothing, package deal).

* * *

THE INTERMISSION: INTERVENING MINISTERIAL MEETINGS BEFORE THE 2001 QUEBEC CITY SUMMIT

Every play has an intermission, but the melodrama that is the FTAA negotiations was especially long. Fast-track negotiating authority had expired in 1993. In the absence of a renewal of fast-track negotiating authority, the United States' ability to negotiate effectively was completely hamstrung. As a result, the three intervening Ministerial Meetings between the 1998 Santiago Summit and the 2001 Quebec City Summit were largely exercises in reaffirming the principles announced in the Santiago Summit Declaration: the FTAA would be balanced, comprehensive, WTO-consistent, and a single undertaking, i.e., an all-or-nothing, package deal. As will be explained shortly, the 2003 Ministerial Meeting was to depart dramatically from these consistently stated goals of the FTAA negotiations.

ACT III, SCENE 1: A DRAFT TEXT EMERGES (THE PLOT THICKENS)

In an effort to improve transparency, and at the same time to quell rumors and correct misinformation about what was being negotiated, it was agreed at the third Summit of the Americas held in Quebec City in April 2001 that a draft FTAA text would be made public. A preliminary first draft was published on July 3, 2001. Slightly revised versions were published in 2002 and again in November 2003.

Practically every line in the draft text is bracketed. Although I have not actually counted, I have heard that there are over 7,000 brackets in the draft text. There clearly is much work to be done and many differences to be bridged. A quick review of the text–if such a thing is possible, considering that the text is several hundred pages long–raises many intriguing questions. The following is a small sample:

• Chapter V calls for special and differential (S & D) treatment of countries in the hemisphere "that takes into account levels of development and size of the economies of the Parties...." But will S & D treatment mean extended transition periods for implementing obligations, as was the case in most of the Uruguay Round agreements, or will there be a substantive dimension as well? For example, under the WTO Agreement on Agriculture developed countries were obligated to reduce their export and domestic agricultural subsidies by percentages greater than those required of developing countries.

• Chapters VI and VII on the environment and labor, respectively, are completely bracketed, even their titles, meaning that provisions on environment and labor might not be included in any final agreement. An introductory sentence in both Chapters states that environmental and labor commitments "shall not be utilized as conditionalities or subject to disciplines, the non-compliance of which can be subject to trade restrictions or sanctions." In other words, no trade penalties may be imposed for a country's failure to enforce domestic labor and environmental standards.

● Chapters X and XI on rules of origin and certificates of origin are disturbingly reminiscent of NAFTA's labyrinthine rules of origin, including the nightmarish regional value methodologies of transaction value and net cost. These methodologies are truly the trade lawyers' revenge on the tax lawyers. I am hard pressed to cite a more efficient non-tariff barrier to trade adopted in the name of free trade. Will small and medium-size enterprises, both here and in the rest of the hemisphere, have the resources to comply with the record keeping that will be necessary to complete and substantiate a certificate of origin to the satisfaction of the U.S. Customs Service? We shall see, but I am skeptical.

● Chapter XVII on investment mirrors much of NAFTA Chapter 11 on investment, but with important clarifications, including a provision that, except in rare circumstances, government regulation for public health, safety, and environmental reasons does not amount to an indirect expropriation.

● Chapter XXIII on dispute settlement is a hybrid of NAFTA Chapter 20 on government-to-government dispute settlement and the WTO Dispute Settlement Understanding (DSU). Like NAFTA Chapter 20, Chapter XXIII permits the complaining party to choose either the FTAA dispute settlement mechanism or the WTO DSU in cases where the responding country's measures violate both FTAA and WTO obligations. Dispute settlement panelists may not be citizens of any of the disputing parties, reflecting Article 8.3 of the DSU. Chapter XXIII would also create a seven-member, standing Appellate Body, again mirroring the WTO DSU.

ACT III, SCENE 2: THE CANCÚN MEETING OF THE WTO
MINISTERIAL CONFERENCE AND THE FALLOUT

On September 14, 2003, the fifth meeting of the WTO Ministerial Conference was held at Cancún. As everyone knows, that meeting collapsed when developed and developing countries could not strike a compromise on the so-called Singapore issues, i.e., trade facilitation, investment, competition policy, and transparency in government procurement. A subtext was the inability of the European Union and the United States to achieve any breakthroughs on agricultural subsidies or market access for agricultural goods. No consensus emerged in the immediate aftermath of the Cancún failure as to what the impact, if any, would be on the FTAA negotiations. At least one U.S. negotiator offered the opinion, in Solomon-like fashion, that the failed Cancún ministerial meeting "could cut either way" as far as its impact on the FTAA negotiations, while Deputy USTR Peter Allgeier stated that the 2005 deadline for concluding the FTAA was still achievable. One activist predicted that the Cancun failure would have a negative impact on the

FTAA negotiations. Apprehensive over the negative impact that the Cancún collapse might have on the FTAA, the U.S. business community urged U.S. negotiators not to retreat from a comprehensive agreement in the FTAA negotiations. Participants in the FTAA negotiations, including the two key players of Argentina and Brazil, warned—perhaps presciently, perhaps in a self-fulfilling prophecy—that disagreement over agricultural subsidies and market access for agricultural products (the same issues that have divided the WTO members not only at Cancún but also in the entire Doha Development Round) could also derail the FTAA negotiations.

In the weeks leading up to the FTAA Miami Ministerial Meeting in November 2003, Brazil made rumblings that the FTAA's goal of reaching a comprehensive agreement would have to be cut back. Brazil argues that if agricultural subsides and antidumping rules were to be negotiated exclusively in the WTO as part of the Doha Round—the U.S. position—then so too would investment, competition policy, and government procurement. Brazil's vision, at least as I understand it, is an FTAA agreement basically limited to trade in goods, i.e., issues related to tariffs, customs procedures, market access, rules of origin, and dispute settlement, with other issues—investment, intellectual property, government procurement, competition policy, and agricultural subsidies—being moved either to bilateral negotiations or to the WTO in the Doha Round. Matters came to a head in the running Brazil–U.S. battle for the hearts and minds of the FTAA participants less than a month before the Miami Ministerial Meeting when Brazil accused the United States of "systematic arrogance" for allegedly trying to isolate Brazil in the FTAA negotiations. This was a truly melodramatic moment. The stage was now set for abandoning the comprehensive, single-undertaking package deal consistently sought by the United States in the FTAA negotiations.

ACT IV, SCENE 1: THE 2003 MIAMI MINISTERIAL MEETING (THE DÉNOUEMENT)

At the November 2003 Ministerial Meeting in Miami, the FTAA trade ministers apparently bowed to the inevitable, namely, a scaled-back FTAA. In a sharp departure from its earlier trajectory, the FTAA negotiations will no longer be a comprehensive, single undertaking as had been announced and reiterated over the previous nine years. Dubbed "FTAA-lite" by its critics, the U.S. business community put the best face on the situation, observing that the outcome of the Miami Ministerial was better than a total collapse of the negotiations.

The Miami Ministerial Declaration left a few observers scratching their heads. For example, the Declaration at one point states, "The Ministers reaffirm their commitment to a comprehensive and balanced FTAA ..." in all nine negotiating groups. Two paragraphs later, however, that same Declaration states, "Ministers recognize that countries may assume different levels of commitments.... One possible course of action would be for these countries to conduct plurilateral negotiations within the FTAA...." The scope of the FTAA negotiations have thus shifted from a single-undertaking approach to a two-tiered–or perhaps a multi-tiered–approach. The one prior commitment that was reaffirmed was to conclude the negotiations by January 1, 2005, with a new and earlier deadline of September 30, 2004 set for concluding the market access negotiations.

The details of the negotiations have yet to be worked out, but that process was scheduled to begin at a meeting of deputy trade ministers in Puebla, México, in early February, 2004 (after reaching an impasse the Puebla meeting was recessed until March 2004). Exactly what the direction of the FTAA negotiations will be in the aftermath of the Miami Ministerial Meeting is anyone's guess. Does it mean an FTAA on trade in goods and services without any linkages to the other negotiating groups, e.g., investment or government procurement, which seems to be Brazil's position? Does it mean an FTAA with baseline commitments in all nine negotiating groups, but with trade benefits on trade in goods being reduced if a country does not make significant commitments, for example, on investment, a "you get what you pay for" approach, which seems to be the U.S. position? Does it mean an FTAA with significant commitments in all nine negotiating groups, with obligations being phased in over time depending on a country's level of development but with all participants eventually assuming the same level of obligations, which seems to be the Canadian and Chilean position? As one Mexican official warned, the FTAA negotiators could find themselves "negotiating a process instead of a deal."

ACT IV, SCENE 2: THE "SPECIAL" SUMMIT OF THE AMERICAS (FTAA NEGOTIATIONS DERAILED?)

Perhaps realizing that the FTAA negotiations were close to being put on life support, a "special" Summit of the Americas was held in Monterrey, México, on January 13, 2004. The heads of state of the 34 participating countries engaged in a rather dull and hollow one-day meeting. In the words of Hugo Chavez, President of Venezuela, "We arrive, we greet each other, make speeches, sign a declaration, take some photos, smile, eat and go." Those are hardly the words of someone truly committed to the FTAA process. Despite President Chavez's apparent disenchantment, the Monterrey Declaration does make a commitment to the FTAA, but puts an unbelievable spin on the outcome of the Miami Ministerial Meeting—a meeting that may very well have dealt a mortal blow to the FTAA process. The Monterrey participants issued a rambling and essentially vacuous declaration that had the following to say regarding the FTAA negotiations:

> We welcome the progress achieved to date toward the establishment of a Free Trade Area of the Americas (FTAA) and take note with satisfaction of the balanced results of the VIII Ministerial Meeting of the FTAA held in Miami in November 2003. We support the agreement of ministers on the framework and calendar adopted for concluding the negotiations for the FTAA in the established timetable, which will most effectively foster economic growth, the reduction of poverty, development, and

integration through trade liberalization, contributing to the achievement of the broad Summit objectives.

My questions are these: Exactly what "progress has been achieved to date" after five years of negotiations? What "balanced results" are they referring to? What "framework for concluding the negotiations" was adopted at Miami? Is it significant that the Declaration fails to make an explicit reference to the January 2005 deadline for concluding negotiations? Some observers think it is. Reportedly, there was a fight at the Summit over this very question. The Monterrey Declaration also dropped this ominous footnote:

> Venezuela enters a reservation with respect to the paragraph on the Free Trade Area of the Americas (FTAA) because of questions of principle and profound differences regarding the concept and philosophy of the proposed model and because of the manner in which specific aspects and established time frames are addressed. We ratify our commitment to the consolidation of a regional fair trade bloc as a basis for strengthening levels of integration. This process must consider each country's particular cultural, social, and political characteristics; sovereignty and constitutionality; and the level and size of its economy, in order to guarantee fair treatment.

One is forced to wonder whether or not this statement portends disaster, but trouble is definitely brewing. Within a week after the "special" Monterrey Summit, the February 2004 Puebla meeting of deputy trade ministers was threatened with cancellation after Brazil learned that Chile had organized a pre-Puebla preparatory meeting to which only a hand-picked group of countries was invited—the United States, Canada, Mexico, and Costa Rica, all of which had supported a broad FTAA agreement. [Authors' Note: as of December 2004, the deputy trade ministers meeting had not been rescheduled.]

PART B: AGREEMENTS WITH NON–WESTERN HEMISPHERE NATIONS

LANGMAN, EU–MERCOSUR TRADE TALKS MAY BEGIN BY END OF 1999, BRAZILIAN OFFICIAL SAYS
16 Int'l Trade Rep. 820 (May 12, 1999).*

Brazilian Minister of Foreign Relations Luiz Felipe Lampreia May 7 told the Southern Common Market (MERCOSUR) Economic Summit that negotiations between the bloc and the European Union on a free-trade agreement may begin before the end of this year. Lampreia said he hoped the June 28–29 EU–MERCOSUR summit in Rio de Janeiro will formally launch the negotiations. "I cannot accept the concept that the EU would not want an agreement with MERCOSUR. Their interests in having an agreement outweigh their agricultural protectionism," Lampreia told the closing session of the May 5–7 summit, organized by the World Economic Forum in Santiago. The EU has been slow to embrace the free-trade negotiations because of concerns about opening its market to cheaper MERCOSUR agricultural exports. "I think we can start with other issues," Lampreia told BNA May 7. "This will be a long negotiation; it is not necessary to start it off with agriculture."

Skepticism on EU–MERCOSUR Talks

However, other officials in the MERCOSUR trading bloc—which comprises Brazil, Argentina, Paraguay, Uruguay, and associate members Chile and Bolivia—remain skeptical of reaching an agreement on free-trade negotiations with the EU. Felix Peña, undersecretary of foreign trade for Argentina's Ministry of Economy and Public Works, said that if there is not a positive result at the Rio Summit in June, it will not be the fault of MERCOSUR. "I hope the June meeting is not frustrating, and we can start the negotiations," Peña said at a May 6 conference panel.

"Obviously the MERCOSUR region has a strong interest in obtaining access to the European markets for our agricultural goods," Peña told BNA May 6. "And I think the European citizens will be glad to have us there because it will be very expensive for them to maintain their agricultural policy. We are also buying billions of dollars worth of capital goods in the MERCOSUR region. But perhaps maybe we will have to change our strategies and focus instead on agreements with the [Free Trade Area of the Americas], South Africa, New Zealand, Israel, and others."

Portugal's Minister of Finance Antonio Sousa Franco acknowledged at the May 6 EU–MERCOSUR panel session that preparations for the summit with the EU were moving slowly.

"The preparations for the summit are not fruitful at the moment. We don't even have a draft agenda yet. The blame for this should be on both sides," he said. "However, we, the heads of states, should be able to rise above this and craft an agenda in time to create a clear mandate at the Rio Summit for beginning negotiations in the first semester of 2000, as well as the issues that need to be negotiated."

Lack of Reciprocal Interests?

Jose Augusto Coelho Fernandes, executive director of the National Confederation of Industries in Brazil, said that there is a lack of well-defined interests and reciprocal understanding between MERCOSUR and the EU. He told the meeting he was concerned that the dialogue in an eventual negotiation would result in a "hierarchical mother-daughter relationship."

The EU is MERCOSUR's largest trading partner, and MERCOSUR is the EU's largest trading partner in Latin America. In 1997, the EU absorbed 23 percent of MERCOSUR's worldwide exports and supplied 26 percent of the bloc's total imports. The EU also is the largest foreign investor in the MERCOSUR region.

In another May 6 panel session, much of the discussion focused on the commitment of the United States to the FTAA. Thomas "Mack" McLarty, the Clinton administration's former special ambassador to Latin America, said the FTAA remains a high priority for the United States despite the absence of fast-track negotiating authority for the president.

"The lack of fast track has made things difficult, but we can move forward on some steps regarding trade with or without fast-track authority," McLarty said. Fast-track authority would allow the president to negotiate trade accords that were not subject to amendment in Congress.

McLarty said that the U.S. role in the region should include continued support for the so-called "second-generation reforms" mandated at the FTAA's April 1998 summit—democracy, justice, labor reform, and education. He also said that the United States ought to re-energize the FTAA process.

"A sustained engagement in the region is critical for the U.S. Latin Americans are the U.S.'s most dependable allies and major trading partners," McLarty said.

Mercosur First

But Paraguay's Minister of Industry and Trade Guillermo Caballero Vargas told BNA May 5 that MERCOSUR should first work to deepen integration within the region before entering into agreements with the FTAA or EU. "It is more important for us to equalize the opportunities between our countries and to promote an open discussion about our macroeconomic policies to correct situations like the sudden devaluation of the Brazilian currency," Vargas said.

The future of MERCOSUR was the central focus for many of the government officials speaking at the conference. Chile's President Eduardo Frei told the opening session that MERCOSUR needs to create new "supranational" regional institutions. Frei pointed to services as a regional issue in need of a regulating institution. "Chile's banks and pension funds operate in MERCOSUR countries, but we have no mechanisms for the resolution of potential conflicts in these areas," Frei said. Frei also told the conference that Chile is not a full member of MERCOSUR because the bloc's common external tariff is much higher than Chile's low (and still decreasing) uniform tariff rate. But Frei said, "We are working fully with MERCOSUR."

Broader Mandate for MERCOSUR?

Chile pushed repeatedly at the summit for MERCOSUR to widen its horizons and become more of a political body. "The problem with MERCOSUR is that it has to develop into something beyond a tariff accord," Chile's Foreign Minister Jose Miguel Insulza told a press conference May 5. "If it is just based on customs tariffs, it does not interest Chile. That is enough for us to remain an associate member for the moment." Insulza said that Chile would be a full member in the MERCOSUR only if the customs union widens its scope to include agreements on services, investment, transportation integration, electrical integration, consultation on macroeconomic policies, and other issues.

Many government officials at the meeting also mentioned that Bolivia should become a full member of MERCOSUR. However, Bolivia's Minister of Foreign Trade and Investment Jorge Crespo Velasco said at a press conference May 5 that the country is more interested at the moment in arranging a free-trade deal in 2000 between MERCOSUR and the Andean Pact nations. The Andean Pact includes Bolivia as a full member, along with Colombia, Ecuador, Venezuela, and Peru.

ACCORD WITH ANDEAN PACT

Alfredo Morelli, undersecretary for economic integration at Argentina's Ministry of Foreign Affairs, told BNA May 6 that a "limited" free-trade agreement between MERCOSUR and the Andean Pact could likely be completed by the middle of 2000. "An agreement with the Andean countries will depend a lot on how our negotiations with the EU and FTAA are going," Morelli said. "But in some ways it is better for the region if we coordinate before we start the FTAA."

TAYLOR, EUROPEAN UNION, MERCOSUR SUSPEND TALKS ON FREE TRADE AGREEMENT OVER KEY ISSUES

21 Int'l Trade Rep. 1381 (Aug. 19, 2004)*

Three days of talks between representatives of the European Union and the Southern Common Market (Mercosur) ended in failure Aug. 12 when the two sides suspended negotiations on a free trade accord. This was the second consecutive negotiating round to be suspended due to the inability of the two blocs to overcome impasses on key issues. The EU and Mercosur, a customs union comprising Argentina, Brazil, Paraguay, and Uruguay, have been engaged in talks on a free trade agreement for over two years and the final accord should be ready to be signed in October. The latest suspension, however, has now placed that deadline in real jeopardy. . . .

"If we want to sign an accord in October, it is necessary that they [the EU] put on the table a comprehensive proposal, clear and precise in its offers," said Brazil's Regis Arslanian, the head of the Mercosur negotiating team. Arslanian added that the Mercosur would not accept a piecemeal approach to the negotiations and accused the EU of presenting one proposal at the time. In relation to the EU offer to increase the MERCOSUR's beef quota, Arslanian said, "We receive this offer in a positive manner—it indicates that the negotiations are moving ahead—

* Excerpted with permission from the *International Trade Reporter,* Vol. 21, No. 34, p. 1381 (Aug. 19, 2004). Copyright 2004 by the Bureau of National Affairs, Inc. (800-372-1033) http://www.bna.com.

but we need the full picture of what is the agriculture package." Other Brazilian diplomats told BNA Aug. 12 that the Mercosur was prepared to increase its offers for market access and government procurement but only after the EU came up with a broad proposal for agriculture. If this did not occur, they stated, the talks would be suspended.

* * *

HASKEL, BUOYED BY RENEWED PROGRESS, EU, MERCOSUR SET UP PERMANENT FREE TRADE WORKING GROUP

21 Int'l Trade Rep. 1956 (Oct. 21, 2004)*

"Latin American nations should give better protection to European investments in the fields of public services and other areas," while "Europe should relinquish certain degree of agricultural protectionism and open wider its markets to Latin America," said [ex-Italian Premier Massimo] D'Alema, who was heading a European delegation participating in the seventh joint commission of EU and Mercosur lawmakers.

Softening of EU Position Seen. "Negotiations have reached a very advanced stage; what is needed now is strong political will from both sides," which should be made easier by the new permanent parliamentarian working group, he said. Help could also come from new European Trade Commissioner Peter Mandelson, who has decided to assign high priority to the free trade deal, D'Alema said. Argentine officials stressed that the visitor's calls for mutual concessions marked a stark contrast with previous EU's demands that Mercosur offer the Europeans a better deal in the industrial and financial products, investments, and government procurement areas.

Mercosur's head Eduardo Duhalde, a former president of Argentina, said after talks with D'Alema that he trusted the free trade—deal originally due to be concluded on Jan. 1. 2005, but postponed due to lingering differences—would be ready for signing in March. Yet he repeated Mercosur's complaints about the EU's "very strong subsidies" to its farmers. Mercosur EU free trade talks have had their ups and downs over the years due to mutual recriminations of lack of political will to further lift trade and nontrade barriers to each other's goods and services. The latest upbeat mood follows a series of recent setbacks that forced the two sides to put off their deadline for signing off the deal.

* * *

NAGEL, PROGRESS MADE IN EU–MEXICO TALKS, BUT MORE IS NEEDED ON RULES OF ORIGIN

16 Int'l Trade Rep. 1302 (Aug. 4, 1999).*

Negotiations toward a free-trade agreement between Mexico and the European Union advanced during the seventh round of negotiations ending July 23 in Brussels, but rules of origin remain a difficult point that will require further effort when the parties meet again in September, according to Mexico's ambassador to the EU, Jaime Zabludovsky. Speaking in a July 23 telephone interview with Mexican reporters, Zabludovsky said that significant progress was made in Brussels and that working group discussions have been completed on dispute resolution, safeguards, and phytosanitary issues. Progress was also made on financial services, government procurement, and investment. A transcript of the interview was made available to BNA.

Autos, Textiles Main Issues

However, rules of origin remain a controversial point that is holding up negotiations on tariff phase-outs, Zabludovsky said. Mexico touched on the issue of tariff phase-outs in Brussels, Zabludovsky said, but more information on rules of origin will be necessary in order to advance in that area. "Mexico said that to continue talking on a calendar for tariff phase-outs, we need to have information on the other side of the coin, which are rules of origin, and since we don't have rules of origin defined, it is difficult to evaluate the tariff package and continue working on these subjects," the Mexican ambassador said. Zabludovsky said that preliminary agreements have been reached on tariff phase-outs and rules of origin for some 1,000 tariff classifications, but that negotiations are pending on some 200 others. He said the auto, textile, and shoe industries are the main sectors affected by pending negotiations over rules of origin.

The EU is currently evaluating Mexico's position regarding rules of origin and consulting with member countries, Zabludovsky said, adding that he hoped that those consultations could be concluded by Sept. 27, when the eighth round of negotiations begins in Mexico City.

"There have been additional advances in rules of origin in the past weeks," Zabludovsky said. "We have been able to limit the pending package to 20 percent to 30 percent, which means that we have preliminary agreements on 70 percent to 80 percent of rules of origin. But obviously, nothing is agreed to until everything is agreed to, and we will have to keep working on this." Zabludovsky said the phytosanitary chapter "is very important for the agricultural sector, in that it recognizes that the parties have the right to impose restrictions or demands on agricultural producers to guarantee the health of the human population, but also plant and animal health" when the measures are justified and do not create unnecessary trade barriers.

Dispute Resolution

Zabludovsky said that dispute resolution procedures under a Mexico–EU pact will be similar to those of the North American Free Trade Agreement. The dispute resolution chapter "is the legal heart of the accord, the chapter that permits the oversight of administration of the agreement and . . . when there are violations of any of the commitments under the accord, it establishes consultation mechanisms and panels to resolve these differences. It is a very important chapter because it is one of the permanent elements of the accord and it guarantees the legal integrity of the accord while it is in effect," Zabludovsky said. Panels convened under the dispute resolution procedures will have three members, in order to allow them to be organized quickly. Otherwise, the dispute resolution procedures are very similar to those under NAFTA and other accords, he said.

NAFTA–Like Safeguards

The EU–Mexico pact's safeguard procedures to protect domestic industries will also be similar to those in the NAFTA. "In principle, we have agreed that there has to be compensation because when a country removes, even when justifiable, the benefits of trade liberalization to protect a sector, to put discipline in this instrument there must be a compensation. If the compensation is not acceptable for the country which has been affected by the safeguard, then this country can have the possibility of taking reprisals, which was a case very similar to what happened with the controversy over broom-corn brooms in the United States," Zabludovsky said.

End of 1999 a Target Date

Concluding the talks during 1999 is a high priority for the administration of Mexican President Ernesto Zedillo, the ambassador said. "This is a priority, because the EU is our second-largest trade partner, our second-largest source of foreign investment, and in the sense that Mexico can achieve a successful negotiation and corresponding agreement, as we have insisted on, Mexico will have a privileged and unique strategic position, being the country with preferential access to the two most important markets in the world." Zabludovsky added: "I think it is realistic that we will conclude negotiations this year, but this of course will depend on the advances in the negotiations and the type of solutions that we can find to issues that are still pending."

KIRWIN, EU, MEXICO SIGN FREE–TRADE AGREEMENT: ALL INDUSTRIAL TARIFFS TO BE LIFTED BY 2007

17 Int'l Trade Rep. 532 (Mar. 30, 2000)*

The European Union and Mexico signed a free-trade agreement March 23 that the 15 EU member states hope will help reverse the loss in exports that occurred in the 1990s due to the North American Free Trade Agreement. The deal, the largest trade agreement ever negotiated by the EU, will go into effect July 1 when 48 percent of EU exports and 82 percent of Mexican industrial exports will have duty-free access to each other's market. By 2003, the maximum tariff on all products, except agriculture goods, will be 5 percent. By 2007, all industrial tariffs will be lifted. Precise rules of origin to ensure that products from the United States or Canada do not get exported to the EU duty-free and vice versa are also part of the free trade agreement. "The EU–Mexico Free Trade Agreement levels the playing field for Mexican and European firms against those in the United States and Canada," said European Commission President Romano Prodi. "The agreement gives both sides preferential access to their goods and services markets and increases certainty for investment flows." In addition, competition policy, intellectual property, sanitary and phytosanitary standards, and a dispute settlement mechanism are part of the agreement.

The EU–Mexico free trade agreement was formally signed on the margins of an EU summit on economic reform. Negotiations between the EU and Mexico concluded last November. Since 1991, the EU's share of total Mexican trade has decreased from 10.6 percent to 6.5 percent in 1999, the European Commission said. In 1999, EU–Mexico trade totaled approximately $18 billion and EU exports faced an average duty of 8.7 percent to enter the Mexican market, with tariffs as high as 35 percent for some products, the Commission said. "In contrast, the tariffs paid by the U.S. and Canadian exporters to the Mexican market is approaching zero as the NAFTA tariff phase out period comes to an end," the Commission said in a statement.

* * *

YERKEY, SOUTH KOREA, CHILE ANNOUNCE PLAN TO NEGOTIATE FTA, OTHERS FOLLOW
16 Int'l Trade Rep. 1472 (Sept. 15, 1999).*

Kim Dae-jung and Eduardo Frei, the presidents of South Korea and Chile, announced Sept. 11 that their governments will begin negotiations on a bilateral free-trade agreement. It was the fourth such announcement at this year's leaders' meeting of the 21–nation Asia–Pacific Economic Cooperation (APEC) forum, after Singapore unveiled plans to pursue FTAs with New Zealand, Chile, and Mexico. Some critics here suggested that the APEC countries were having to resort to bilateral deals because APEC was failing to deliver on its promise of open regional trade. But officials from the countries involved in the new bilateral agreements defended their actions—even as they conceded that the APEC process may require some push forward to ensure success. A press release issued by the Singapore government, for instance, said that the FTA with Mexico would be designed to accelerate the pace of trade liberalization in APEC and would be "fully consistent" with WTO rules. "This decision reflects the desire of Mexico and Singapore to catalyze APEC into realizing its [goals] of free trade and investment," the statement said.

Chilean Foreign Minister Juan Gabriel Valdes said that an FTA between South Korea and Chile, like other such agreements, could act as a "catalyst" to jump-start the APEC plan to achieve free and open trade and investment in the Asia–Pacific region by 2010 for developed country members and 2020 for developing APEC nations. "The idea is to liberalize our economies bilaterally," Valdes told reporters. "We think that an exercise [like the Chile–South Korea FTA] can be a catalyst for the [APEC trade liberalization process]. We don't feel that there is a contradiction between bilateral initiatives and multilateral initiatives." Other officials said that Chile and New Zealand were also discussing on the sidelines of the APEC meetings in Auckland the possibility of negotiating a bilateral free-trade agreement. Terms of reference for the talks were being worked out, the officials said. [Authors' Note: A free trade agreement negotiated by Chile and South Korea entered into force in 2004.]

YERKEY, MEXICO, JAPAN AGREE TO LAUNCH TALKS ON INVESTMENT ACCORD, CONSIDER TRADE PACT
16 Int'l Trade Rep. 1471 (Sept. 15, 1999).**

Mexican Commerce Secretary Herminio Blanco announced Sept. 11 that Mexico and Japan have decided to begin negotiations this month on an agreement aimed at protecting and promoting investment between the two countries. He said that Mexico and Japan have also agreed to consider negotiating a bilateral free-trade agreement. "This means that, in Japan, we have attained a very special place," Blanco said, adding that Japan has agreed to negotiate an investment-protection pact with only one other country–South Korea. He said that the investment agreement would be particularly beneficial to small and medium-sized Japanese companies supplying Japanese maquiladoras in Mexico.

* * *

ARITAKE, JAPAN, MEXICO WORK OUT FINAL DETAILS FOR 2005 IMPLEMENTATION OF BILATERAL FTA
21 Int'l Trade Rep. 1471 (Sep. 9, 2004)*

Japan and Mexico have worked out final details of their bilateral Economic Partnership Agreement that incorporates a free trade agreement, paving the way for its implementation as early as next April, a senior Japanese government official said Sept. 1. "We've worked out all details, leaving only treaty issues to be worked out," the official told BNA. A formal definitive announcement of the bilateral FTA, the second FTA for Japan after the one with Singapore in 2002, will be made jointly by Prime Minister Junichiro Koizumi and Mexican President Vicente Fox when Koizumi visits Mexico and signs the agreement in late September, the official said.

A Japanese Foreign Ministry official said Koizumi's visit is being coordinated between the two governments and has yet to be finalized. The Japan–Mexico FTA was to be signed in November 2003 when Fox visited Japan, but it was not finalized because of Mexico's demand for quota increases for pork, citrus products, and other farm produce, as well as Japan's demand for progressive lowering of import tariffs on steel, autos, and other products. The two countries recently agreed that Mexico would abolish steel tariffs in phases over the next 10 years, according to Japanese government officials.

LAWRENCE, JAPAN TRADE RELATIONS AND IDEAL FREE TRADE PARTNERS: WHY THE UNITED STATES SHOULD PURSUE ITS NEXT FREE TRADE AGREEMENT WITH JAPAN, NOT LATIN AMERICA

20 Md. J. Int'l L. & Trade 61 (1996)**

This study posits that pursuing a WHFTA and aggressive unilateralism with Japan are not the best trade policies for the United States (or the world trading system). The United States is wise to encourage Latin American regional cooperation and improvement, but Latin America as a whole does not fit the criteria of an ideal free trade partner and few Latin American countries have liberalized sufficiently to expect that a WHFTA will be long-lasting. The potential benefit to the Unites States of a WHFTA, therefore, is questionable. Since forming a WHFTA encourages the digression of the world trade order into one of competing blocs, it is unwise for the United States to focus its policy in this direction.

The United States should focus its efforts to build an institutionalized and cooperative relationship with Japan, its most important trade partner and a state vital to U.S. efforts to maintain a stable security environment in East Asia. Japan fits the criteria of an ideal free trade partner very well. Rather than engaging in quarrelsome debates over market access targets and threatening to impose Section 301 sanctions, a threat which, by its mere assertion, further deteriorates U.S.-Japan relations and revives images of the ugly American, the United States ought to pursue building a cooperative framework with Japan through an FTA. Such an agreement would fundamentally alter U.S.-Japan relations by institutionalizing the means for the two countries to cooperate and lead the world in economic policy matters. It would fill the trust gap and, by doing so, make easier the task of establishing a more vibrant security alliance. Also, whereas U.S. influence over Japan is currently declining, a Japan–United States FTA (JUSFTA) would enshrine its influence, providing the United States a far greater amount of leverage with Japan in the future than it would otherwise possess.

* * *

JAPAN VERSUS LATIN AMERICA

President Bush presented the EAI as the starting point for the negotiation of a WHFTA. Ever since, the focus for the next U.S. FTA has been on Latin America. . . . Is Latin America, on the whole, an ideal free trade partner? Are any of the countries within it even ready for an FTA with the NAFTA members? If not, then who is? The significant trade relationship the United States has with Japan (as well as the European Union) indicates that it might be an ideal partner. How, then, do Japan and Latin America compare?

* * *

The First Tier—Comparison of Trade Characteristics

To review, the characteristics are: one, the significance of the trading partner; two, whether the partner is a principal market and a principal supplier; three, the competitiveness of the economies; and four, the wealth of the partner.

Trade Characteristic 1—Trading Partner Significance

By comparison, how significant are Latin America and Japan as U.S. trade partners? . . .

From the numbers, Japan is clearly a more significant trading partner than Latin America. Japan is 1.4 times a better customer for U.S. exports, and it is 2.9 times a better provider of U.S. imports. Thus if the United States liberalized trade in goods with all twenty countries included in Latin America's figures, it still would not be liberalizing more than it trades with Japan. If compared at a level below Latin America, Japan is 4.3 times a better customer than the Andean Group (the best sub-regional grouping customer and provider), and it is 7.0 times better the provider. Also, Japan is 8.3 times a better customer than Brazil (the best country customer), and 11.5 times a better provider than Venezuela (the best country provider). In comparison with Chile, Japan is 19.4 times a better customer and 61.2 times the better provider.

These findings show how much more significant U.S.-Japan trade relationship is than the U.S.-Latin America trade relationship in terms of dollar amounts. They suggest, therefore, that an FTA between the United States and Japan will lead primarily (if not exclusively) to trade creation. The reason is simple: an FTA will only reinforce the two countries' existing relationship and pattern of comparative advantage. Meanwhile, the relative insignificance of Latin America as a U.S. trading partner suggests that an FTA with it will lead to some modest degree of trade diversion.

* * *

Trade Characteristic 3—Competitiveness of the Economies

A good way to determine if two economies are competitive is to compare their revealed comparative advantage indices. This involves calculating the ratio of a country's share in world exports of a particular good to the country's share in total world exports. . . .

* * *

. . . the United States and Japan are competitive in six of the top U.S. exports, while Latin America is only competitive in three. Also, of the goods in which Japan is not very similar to the United States, both Japan and the United States have a comparative advantage in two. Therefore, while the two economies may not be very similar in these goods, they are somewhat comparable. Meanwhile, Latin America has a comparative advantage in none of the goods in which it is dissimilar to the United States. . . . Overall, these findings strongly suggest that, at least for the goods which the United States exports the most, Latin America's economy is very dissimilar to the U.S. economy, whereas Japan's economy is very similar to that of the U.S.

* * *

. . . in their most important exports, the United States and Latin America are not competitive. In other words, the two economies are very dissimilar, and if they were integrated, then one might expect trade diversion to ensue. Even if trade diversion did not occur, the integration of the two economies would not enhance their possibilities for specialization in production. In other words, integration would not provide much in the way of increased efficiency. What, then, from an economic point of view, would be the point of integrating the two economies through an FTA rather than through the multilateral process?

* * *

Trade Characteristic 4—Proportion of the World's Wealth

... The Japan–U.S. share of world wealth is a staggering 41.6%. With a 12.2% greater share of the world's wealth, Japan's is approximately 4.3 times wealthier than Latin America. It is 6.0 times wealthier than the Mercosur grouping (the wealthiest sub-grouping) and is 10.2 times wealthier than Brazil (the wealthiest country). In comparison to Chile—the next likely U.S. free trade partner—it is 88.9 times wealthier! When one considers the fact that, on average, individual Japanese are $15,039 wealthier than Latin Americans in general, $11,270 wealthier than Venezuelans (the richest of the Latin Americans), and $12,330 wealthier than Chileans, it becomes apparent that Japan and Latin America, just like the United States and Latin America, have very different purchasing powers. Indeed, while U.S. integration with Latin America would increase the size of the market to which U.S. firms have free access by approximately 14.3%, integration with Japan would increase it by over 62%. Thus while integration with Latin America would increase the possibilities for economies of scale for industries like high-technology manufacturing, integration with Japan would travel much farther towards this goal. Overall, the sheer size of the Japanese economy makes the scope for trade creation through integration far greater than that possible through integration with Latin America.

* * *

The Second Tier—Comparison of Readiness
Factors and Levels of Democracy

Recall that the second tier of this ideal free trade partner model is to be employed if and only if the potential partner fits the ideal trade characteristics. Strong performance on the readiness indicators, absent a similar performance on the trade characteristics, is not a justification for an FTA. The trade characteristics are primary. Therefore, since under this model's first tier analysis Latin America is not ideal, it should not be examined further. However, despite this observation, the United States is in actuality pursuing a WHFTA. Therefore, it is worthwhile for the purposes of this study to include Latin America nevertheless. The reader should keep in mind, however, that this is not in keeping with the model's prescribed methodology and that, based on the trade characteristics, Japan is an ideal free trade partner, whereas Latin America is not.

* * *

To review, the six readiness factors are price stability, real effective exchange rates, reliance on trade taxes, the extent of market-oriented policies, social conditions, and the level of democracy (freedom). This study scores the readiness factors on an 11 point scale (10 to 0), with 10 being the best possible score. It calculates the overall regional and sub-regional scores by adding the individual country scores together and dividing by the number of countries. This scale method allowed for an average score on readiness factors to be given.

* * *

OVERALL SCORES

Table 23 compiles the overall scores for the readiness factors and level of freedom. Japan received the highest score with a 9.43. Latin America received a 5.88. The difference of 3.55 points is quite significant. Overall, Latin America is not as ready for economic integration as is Japan.

Table 23: Performance Scores on Readiness Factors

	Price Stability	Currency Stability	Market Policies	Trade Tax Reliance	Social Conditions	Stable Democracy	Avg.
Japan	10.0	9.0	9.0	10.0	10.0	8.6	9.43
Latin America	4.13	8.3	6.0	4.07	5.6	7.19	5.88
Chile	7.0	9.0	10.0	6.0	7.0	8.6	7.93
Mercosur	2.25	7.25	7.0	6.25	6.0	7.5	6.04
Argentina	0.0	7.0	10.0	5.0	7.0	7.9	6.15
Brazil	0.0	6.0	6.0	10.0	5.0	7.1	5.68
Paraguay	6.0	9.0	6.0	4.0	5.0	6.4	6.07
Uruguay	3.0	7.0	6.0	6.0	7.0	8.6	4.60
Andean Group	3.8	9.4	6.8	4.8	5.0	6.86	6.11
Bolivia	7.0	10.0	8.0	6.0	3.0	7.9	6.98
Columbia	6.0	9.0	8.0	4.0	6.0	6.4	6.57
Ecuador	1.0	10.0	6.0	4.0	5.0	7.9	6.98
Peru	0.0	9.0	4.0	4.0	4.0	5.0	4.33
Venezuela	5.0	9.0	8.0	6.0	7.0	7.1	7.02
CACM	5.4	7.8	3.6	1.2	5.6	6.98	5.10
Costa Rica	7.0	9.0	6.0	0.0	9.0	9.3	6.72
El Salvador	7.0	9.0	4.0	1.0	5.0	7.1	5.52
Guatemala	6.0	5.0	2.0	0.0	4.0	5.0	3.67
Honduras	7.0	10.0	4.0	0.0	5.0	7.1	5.52
Nicaragua	0.0	6.0	2.0	5.0	5.0	6.4	4.07

At the sub-regional grouping level, the findings are similar; no grouping can confidently claim readiness. The CACM, with an overall score of 5.1, is the least ready. It has a dismal score of 1.2 on trade tax reliance and only a 3.6 score for the extent of market-oriented policies. The Andean Group and MERCOSUR are about equal with overall scores of 6.11 and 6.04 respectively. Both scored very poorly on price stability and fair to poor on trade tax reliance and social conditions. These group findings suggest that if NAFTA wishes to expand into a WHFTA, it might be necessary to do so on an individual, country-by-country basis. Nonetheless, the Andean Group is not as unprepared as its score suggests. Without Peru, its score increases from a 6.11 to a 6.89. Indeed, of its members, every country except Peru—that is, Bolivia, Colombia,

Ecuador, and Venezuela—can claim some degree of readiness. The only other countries that can do so are Costa Rica and Chile. Among the Latin American countries which are ready, Chile is the most prepared with an overall score of 7.93. Based on these figures it makes sense, then, for the first new member in NAFTA (en route to the WHFTA) to be this state. However, Japan proved to be the most ready, scoring an impressive 9.43.

CONCLUSION OF JAPAN VERSUS LATIN AMERICA

The comparison of Latin America and Japan demonstrates two things. From the point of view of the ideal free trade partner model employed here, Japan is an ideal free trade partner for the United States; Latin America is not. It is doubtful, then, that hemispheric free trade would be the panacean windfall U.S. trade policy-makers may desire it to be. . . .

* * *

Instead of focusing the expertise of its limited number of trade negotiators and analysts on a small gain like a WHFTA, the United States should use its limited resources more efficiently by pursuing a JUSFTA. . . . Moreover, continuing to ignore the core problems which have been weakening the U.S.-Japan alliance over the past two decades only insures that these problems will continue the alliance's deterioration. For a nation which wishes to maintain its current level of influence in world affairs into the twenty-first century, allowing its most important economic relationship to remain unattended is not wise policy. The United States should maintain its power by repairing, fortifying, and building upon its most important economic relationship, not by building a new one to counter it.

* * *

HUFBAUER & SCHOTT, WESTERN HEMISPHERE ECONOMIC INTEGRATION (1994)*

Economic logic suggests that the expansion of NAFTA in an Asian direction is just as desirable as its expansion in a Latin American direction. The Asia–Pacific region buys 24 percent of North America's exports while Latin America buys 6 percent. . . .

Despite the strong and growing commercial ties across the Pacific, we think that over the next decade formal links between the NAFTA and Asia will be limited by several considerations. First, regional pacts tend to grow out of political or economic necessity. Asia is booming without the benefit of an institutional superstructure. Second, the inclusion of environment and labor issues as essential components—from the US standpoint—for NAFTA enlargement has already caused some Asian countries to question direct links with the NAFTA.

* * *

In our view, NAFTA negotiations with Asia should differ sharply from NAFTA negotiations with Latin America.* In large measure, this conclusion reflects the economic, political, and cultural diversity of the Asia–Pacific region. In addition, it recognizes the complex trade and investment relationships that have already evolved among these countries because of the market-driven opportunities in their dynamic, high-growth economies.

The greater institutional and social differences between North America and Asia commend a topic-by-topic approach to a subset of negotiable questions. For the time being, disparities on environment, labor, human rights, and democracy issues may be too large to be bridged within the NAFTA context. However, a great deal can be accomplished if negotiations between NAFTA and Asia focus on framework rules both for specific functional areas such as investment and product standards and for specific commercial sectors such as financial services, telecommunications, and civil aviation. A rule-making agenda may not, in the first instance, achieve dramatic liberalization. However, it will set the stage for liberalization when underlying conditions are propitious.

Questions and Comments

1. Baker argues that, instead of following the path the European Union took toward economic integration, "Latin America must find a method which will work best under Latin conditions." What integration paths does Latin American history suggest should be avoided? What path(s) should Latin America follow? Refer to Baker, Lopez–Ayllon.

2. What justifications (legal, economic, political, social) exist for Western Hemispheric economic integration? Refer to Barshefsky, Hufbauer and Schott.

3. Leaders of the thirty-four democracies in the Western Hemisphere met in Miami in December 1994 at the first Summit of the Americas. What did the leaders attending the Miami Summit commit their nations to do? Why have the negotiations stalled after ten years? Refer to Kennedy.

4. The nations of the Western Hemisphere initially agreed that the document creating the FTAA would be comprehensive. As reflected by the Nine FTAA Negotiating Groups, the agreement would include provisions on market access, investment, services, government procurement, dispute settlement, agriculture, intellectual property rights, subsidies, antidumping and

---

* One possible exception: NAFTA might be enlarged in the next decade to include Korea. US–Korean commercial disputes are modest, not major; Korea is rapidly establishing an array of democratic institutions; and Korea is not now a member of another regional group. According to our calculations, the readiness indicator for Korea is 4.3 compared to a score of 3.9 for Mexico at the time NAFTA was signed.

countervailing duties, and competition policy. Why did the focus shift instead, in November 2003, to a much more modest "FTAA–Lite"? What influence, if any, is NAFTA likely to have on the technical aspects of the hemispheric trade agreement if there ultimately is one? Refer to Lopez–Ayllon, Gantz, Kennedy.

5. During the past ten years, several Latin American nations have aggressively sought to expand trade relations beyond the Western Hemisphere. This trend accelerated in 2004, with the Mexico–Japan and Chile–South Korea FTAs. South Korea, Singapore and China in Asia, and Chile, Peru, Brazil and Argentina, in South America, are among the nations seeking expanded Asian trade through FTAs most aggressively. China's apparently limitless appetite for agricultural products such as soybeans, iron ore, steel and industrial raw materials, has resulted in a strong interest in deeper trade and investment relations with the continent. How are such efforts likely to affect the likelihood of concluding an FTAA? U.S. economic dominance of South America? For example, is Chile, by concluding multiple trade agreements not only with the NAFTA Parties, but with Korea and perhaps other Asian nations, diluting the benefits of those earlier agreements for the NAFTA Parties?

6. The EU and Japanese negotiations with Mexico were successful, but, to date at least, not those with MERCOSUR. Refer to Kirwin, Haskell. What do the Latin American countries gain by strengthening their extra-hemispheric trade ties? What are the primary stumbling blocks to the culmination of free trade agreements between the Latin Americans and the Europeans and Asians? Refer to Langman, Nagel. What do the Latin American nations sacrifice in focusing their attention on free trade agreements with the FTAA and EU as opposed to sub-regional integration? Refer to Langman. Does the growing number of trade accords involving Latin American countries and countries in Europe and Asia make hemispheric integration more difficult to accomplish? Also, in August 2004, Canada announced that it would pursue closer trade relations with the EU.

7. Lawrence makes a strong economic case for the United States to abandon efforts toward an FTAA in favor of efforts toward a Japan–United States Free Trade Agreement (JUSFTA). Outline Lawrence's argument. Hufbauer and Schott agree that "economic logic" suggests that NAFTA ought to expand East rather than South; nonetheless, they do not believe that the expansion of NAFTA to include Asian nations is possible under present circumstances. Explain Hufbauer and Schott's contentions. Do you agree with Lawrence that it makes more sense for the United States to abandon hemispheric integration efforts in favor of free trade with Japan? Note that despite various proposals in recent years, and the persuasive arguments of some economists, there has never been serious consideration of a U.S.–Japan FTA at high political levels of the U.S. government. Why? Why would the U.S. seek agreements with Singapore? Jordan? Bahrain? The South African Customs Union States? Very preliminary discussions of a possible U.S. FTA with South Korea took place in 2004; to date, the United States appears unwilling to proceed until Korea indicates a greater willingness to the Korean domestic market to more U.S. foreign investment.

8. Considering the full mosaic of prior economic integration efforts in Latin America, the contemporary justifications for hemispheric integration, existing trade arrangements in the Western Hemisphere, FTAA developments since the 1994 Summit of the Americas, the lack of U.S. leadership, and the growing tendency of Latin American nations to look for trade partnerships among European and Asian nations, do you conclude that hemispheric integration is possible or even worth pursuing? What integration formula do you believe is most likely to succeed in unifying the Americas?

9. The proceedings of a comprehensive February 2004, Loyola University Chicago School of Law symposium, "The Free Trade Area of the Americas: Implications of a Hemispheric Marketplace," are available in 1 Loyola Univ. Chicago Int'l L. Rev. 119 2004.

PART C: MERCOSUR AND THE INTEGRATION OF SOUTH AMERICA

Comment On MERCOSUR

After NAFTA, MERCOSUR is clearly the most important regional trade regime in the Western Hemisphere, largely because it incorporates two of the largest economic powers of the region, Brazil and Argentina. On paper at least, it is more ambitious than NAFTA, because MERCOSUR contemplates a customs union/common market with a common external tariff (see Chapter One for the differences between FTAs and customs unions). Also, it creates a series of new institutions which resemble those of the European Union more than those of NAFTA. Despite the inability of the MERCOSUR members to meet their internal trade-freeing commitments on a timely basis, and to conclude an FTA with the European Union, the group has been initially successful (politically if not economically) in its efforts (led by Brazil) to create a South American regional economic bloc, first through FTAs with Chile, Bolivia and mor recently with the Andean Pact nations. (FTA negotiations with Panama and Mexico were announced in mid–2004.) In this manner, the MERCOSUR group has been able to establish itself, to some extent at least, as a counterweight to the United States' economic dominance of the hemisphere. In the longer term, success will depend on the implementation of the various agreements.

PORRATA–DORIA, MERCOSUR: THE COMMON MARKET OF THE SOUTHERN CONE*

MERCOSUR, the "Common Market of the Southern Cone," was created in March 1990 by the Treaty of Asuncion and was meant to create a common market among its four signatories (Argentina, Brazil, Paraguay, and Uruguay) by December 31, 1994. This common market

* Carolina Academic Press (2004). Copyright © 2004 Carolina Academic Press. Reprinted with permission; footnotes omitted.

(Professor Rafael A Porrata–Doria is Professor of Law at Temple University.)

would include the graduated elimination of all customs duties among its signatories, the creation of a common external tariff, the adoption of a common trade policy, and the harmonization of economic policies. The Treaty of Asuncion, and its supplementary Ouro Preto Protocol, created a number of institutions to assist in the implementation of these goals. Since its founding in 1990, MERCOSUR has generated many major achievements, more than its predecessor, the Latin American Free Trade Association (LAFTA) or any other economic integration organization in Latin America. It has formalized and expanded cooperation and trading relationships among Brazil, Argentina, Paraguay, and Uruguay, and has developed these relationships into a viable and vibrant economic integration organization. For a substantial period of time, its members enjoyed unprecedented expanded trade and greater prosperity. Trade and exports among its member states have increased exponentially. It became the third-largest trading block in the world, after the North American Free Trade Agreement (NAFTA) and the European Union (EU).

In 1996, the international press described MERCOSUR as a powerhouse and a potential future competitor to the EU and NAFTA. MERCOSUR seemed to be on its way to becoming "the Common Market of the Twenty–First Century." Institutionally, MERCOSUR agreed on a common external tariff covering eighty-five percent of imports currently being traded by its members and on a substantial number of trade matters. It has adopted many directives and resolutions seeking to eliminate barriers to free trade and to harmonize the legal and regulatory systems of the member states, as well as to form the basis of a system of community law. It generated a substantial amount of excitement among the elites of its members states, who now seem to view the idea of economic integration as both feasible and desirable. It acquired two additional members, Bolivia and Chile, in 1996, and entered into an extensive and substantial cooperative relationship with the EU, as well as with a number of other organizations and countries. It has an agenda for the future and is working towards its implementation. Commentators in the member states had been talking about more integration, macroeconomic policy harmonization, and even a single currency. This optimistic environment has changed since 1999. Severe economic difficulties since 1999, first in Brazil, then in Argentina and the other member states, have had a dramatic effect on MERCOSUR and its development.

* * *

The MERCOSUR Four: An Inevitable Marriage?

The idea that the nations of Latin America should undertake political and economic integration is not recent. As early as 1797, immediately after the independence of most Latin American nations from Spain, and throughout the nineteenth century, a number of conferences and negotiations undertook several attempts to create confederations or similar arrangements among the various states of Central and South America.

For a number of reasons, these efforts have tended to be unsuccessful in the past. Many Latin American countries who have attempted economic or political integration have had little in common with each other. Argentina, Brazil, Chile and Uruguay, on the other hand, seem unusually complementary to each other, politically, economically and historically. They have many things in common, starting with geography: three out of the four (Paraguay, Argentina and Brazil) share extensive common borders, as do Brazil and Uruguay. Uruguay and Argentina were actually once politically united. The political systems of all four countries had undergone recent substantial democratization and had taken part in the process of economic liberalization that took place in the region in the 1970s and 1980s. All four countries actually traded with each other, and had a history of economic cooperation, including joint administration of transnational infrastructure projects.

In spite of prior cooperation between them in the construction of the Corpus and Itaipu dams in the late 1970s, relations in the early 1980s between Brazil and Argentina were difficult. Argentine military governments tended to foster rivalry with Brazil and their foreign policy towards that country tended to stress competition rather than cooperation. Brazilian governments, on the other hand, retorted with strong protectionist measures aimed at Argentine exports, whose quantity and value had fallen greatly since 1980. This situation changed after the military regimes of Argentina and Brazil were replaced by democratic governments in the mid–1980s. Both the Brazilian and Argentine governments began to see the advantages of further cooperation and integration and a series of agreements between them were signed in quick succession. It can be argued that this turn of events was unavoidable. The relationship between Argentina and Brazil has been described as similar to that of France and Germany at the time of the creation of the European Economic Community: both countries had a long history of (sometimes hostile) interrelationships, and the exports of one (France, or in this case, Argentina) tended to be primarily agricultural, while those of the other (Germany, or in this case, Brazil) tended to be primarily industrial.

This complementarity becomes striking upon examination of certain economic characteristics. To begin with, Brazil and Argentina are the largest countries, in territory and population, in South America and each has large and highly developed consumer markets. Argentina is rich in natural resources, and has a highly developed export-oriented agricultural sector, which produces a variety of products. Argentina's industrial sector also produces a variety of products. Argentina also has a very large service sector, which accounted for sixty-six percent of GDP in 2001. Its exports, which were estimated at $26.5 billion in 2000, included edible oils, fuels and energy, cereals, feed, and motor vehicles. Its imports, which totaled $23.8 billion in 2000, chiefly included machinery and equipment, motor vehicles, chemicals, metal manufactures, and plastics. Argentina's principal trading partners in 2000, for both exports and imports, included Brazil, the United States, Chile, Spain, China, and

Germany, with Brazil being both its principal import and export partner. Argentina also exported 3.7 billion kWh and imported 7.5 billion kWh of electricity in 2000.

Brazil, on the other hand, has a much larger economy than Argentina does, and has large and well-developed agricultural, mining, manufacturing, and service sectors. Its principal agricultural products include coffee, soybeans, wheat, rice, corn, sugarcane, cocoa, citrus, and beef. Principal industrial products include textiles, shoes, chemicals, cement, lumber, iron ore, tin, steel, aircraft, motor vehicles, and other machinery and equipment. Its exports, which totaled $57.8 billion in 2001, are principally manufactured goods, iron ore, soybeans, footwear, coffee, and autos. Its imports, which totaled $57.7 billion in 2001, include machinery and equipment, chemical products, oil, electricity, autos, and auto parts. Brazil's principal trading partners in 2001, for both exports and imports, included the United States, Argentina, Germany, Japan, Italy, and the Netherlands. The United States and Argentina were Brazil's principal trading partners. Brazil also imported 42.3 billion kWh of electricity from Paraguay in 2000.

Uruguay, with a much smaller land mass and population than either Brazil or Argentina, has as the largest sector of its economy a well-developed services industry. Its agricultural sector, which principally produces rice, wheat, corn, barley, livestock, and fish, is extensive and export-oriented. Uruguay's industrial sector involves food processing, electrical machinery, transportation equipment, petroleum products, textiles, chemicals, and beverages. Its exports, which totaled $2.24 billion in 2001, included meat, rice, leather products, wool, vehicles, and dairy products. Its imports, which totaled $2.9 billion in 2001, chiefly included machinery, chemicals, road vehicles, and crude petroleum. Its principal trading partners in 2001, for both exports and imports, were the MERCOSUR countries, the EU, and the United States, with the MERCOSUR countries representing Uruguay's primary trading partners.

Paraguay, on the other hand, has a very different economy from the others. Its informal sector, which includes both re-export of imported consumer goods to neighboring countries and the activities of thousands of micro-enterprises and urban street vendors, is extremely large and important. A large percentage of the population derives their living from agricultural activity, often on a subsistence basis. Paraguay grows cotton, sugarcane, soy beans, corn, wheat, tobacco, tapioca, fruits, vegetables, beef, pork, eggs, milk, and timber. It has an industrial sector which produces cement, textiles, beverages, and wood products. A principal export industry is that of electricity generation, which accounted for substantial exports in 2000. Its principal exports, which totaled $2.2 billion in 2001, include electricity, soybeans, feed, cotton, meat, and edible oils. Its principal imports included road vehicles, consumer goods, tobacco, petroleum products, and electrical machinery. Paraguay's principal trading partners included Argentina, Brazil, and Uruguay.

Although there are a few areas of competition among them (such as the automotive industry), a number of natural economic connections among them surface from the brief descriptions set forth above. Thus, Brazil's extensive manufacturing sector has a natural market among Argentina's, Uruguay's, and Paraguay's populations. Argentina's (and to a lesser degree Paraguay's) extensive natural resources and agricultural sectors also have ready made markets in Brazil. Uruguay has had extensive economic connections with Argentina for many years. Its services industry (especially its financial services sector) also has many potential customers across the Rio de la Plata in Argentina. Lastly, Paraguay's electrical generation industry very profitably supplements Argentina's and Brazil's massive energy needs. These economic connections and long history of interaction among Brazil, Argentina, Uruguay, and Paraguay make successful integration efforts among them more likely to happen. Thus, MERCOSUR is a consummation of a likely, if not inevitable, economic marriage.

B. FORMALIZING THE RELATIONSHIP

The first step on the path of greater cooperation between Brazil and Argentina was taken in the Iguazu Declaration, signed by Presidents Alfonsin of Argentina and Sarncy of Brazil, on November 29, 1985. In this declaration, both presidents indicated joint positions on a number of economic and foreign policy issues. The most important parts of this Declaration, however, were the agreement that cooperation, harmonization, and integration of a number of sectors of the economy were desirable and the creation of an implementation mechanism. The presidents then announced the creation of a Joint Commission that would explore and make recommendations for bilateral cooperation and integration.

Eight months later, the negotiations started by the Iguazu Declaration resulted in an Agreement on Argentine–Brazilian Integration. The Integration Agreement created an Integration and Economic Cooperation Program between Brazil and Argentina. This program would involve a number of economic sectors and would seek to achieve economic cooperation and integration in a flexible and gradual fashion. Specific guidelines for individual economic areas were set forth in twelve protocols. Between 1986 and 1988, Argentina and Brazil signed twelve more protocols covering other economic sectors. This program was to be established and implemented by an Implementation Commission which would meet every six months and whose membership would consist of senior cabinet ministers from both countries.

During this time period, Uruguay was also involved with economic integration efforts with Brazil and Argentina. It had signed economic cooperation agreements with Argentina (known as CAUCE agreements, for their Spanish acronym) in 1974 and 1985, and commercial expansion treaties (known as PEC agreements for their Spanish acronym) in 1975 and 1986. These bilateral agreements gave Uruguay substantial tariff concessions for exports to Argentina and Brazil, effectively granting it preferential access to their markets. Not surprisingly, trade between Uruguay and Brazil and Argentina increased substantially. Further negotiations between Argentina and Brazil resulted in the Act of Buenos Aires, where both countries agreed in principle to establish a common market between them. This common market would be implemented by December 31, 1994.

C. CREATING A COMMON MARKET: PARTIAL SCOPE AGREEMENT 14

This agreement in principle was fleshed out in Partial Scope Agreement 14 (PSA 14) signed in Montevideo on December 20, 1990. PSA 14 set forth a number of concepts that would later be incorporated in the Treaty of Asuncion, which created MERCOSUR. First, the parties agreed to eliminate all customs duties, tariffs and restrictions between them by December 31, 1994. During the transition period before this date, all previously agreed tariff preferences between both countries would be maintained. This elimination of customs duties applied to all products, with the exception of those excepted by the parties in Annexes III and IV to the Agreement. Tariffs on these products were to be eliminated at the rate of twenty percent a year. Second, the parties agreed, as a necessary adjunct to the elimination of all tariffs, on the harmonization of all macroeconomic policies, especially those linked to the flow of commerce. The parties also agreed on rules of origin for products originating in their territory. These rules of origin were also included in the treaty as an Annex.

During the transition period (until December 31, 1994), each country could request the application of safeguard clauses against the importation of goods from the other. When an importing nation felt that the increase in imports of a particular good would cause great damage to its markets, it could solicit consultations on how to minimize this damage. These consultations could result in agreement on the imposition of a "safeguard clause," which would limit or otherwise place restrictions on imports of that good into the other country for a period of up to one year. The parties also agreed to promote and adopt more measures to integrate their economies and correct any temporary distortions in their markets caused by increased trade. The agreement would be administered and implemented by the Argentina–Brazil Common Market Group, which had been created by the Act of Buenos Aires.

After the signature of the Act of Buenos Aires, Paraguay and Uruguay expressed a strong interest in joining the Argentina–Brazil common market and negotiations began on an agreement to create a common market among all four countries. For Uruguay, this represented a natural "next step" from its prior negotiations and agreements with Brazil and Argentina. For Paraguay, which saw itself as a supplier of energy to its large neighbors, this too represented a natural progression from its prior cooperation on hydroelectric matters with Argentina and Brazil. Three months after the signature of PSA 14, on March 20, 1990, the negotiations among Argentina, Brazil, Paraguay, and Uruguay resulted in the signing of the Treaty of Asuncion, which created MERCO-

SUR. As shall be seen below, a whole new era of Latin American integration had begun.

D.   The Treaty of Asuncion, Its Protocols, and the Common Market

An analysis of MERCOSUR's legal and institutional foundation must begin with four key documents: the Treaty of Asuncion and its five Annexes, Ouro Preto, the Brasilia Protocol on the Resolution of Controversies, and the Olivos Protocol for the Resolution of Controversies. These documents form the backbone of the MERCOSUR legal system. The Treaty of Asuncion borrows a large number of concepts from PSA 14 and looks very similar to that agreement. Its purpose is to create a common market among its four signatories (Argentina, Brazil, Paraguay, and Uruguay) by December 31, 1994. This is the same date that PSA 14 sets for the elimination of all tariff barriers among its signatories. Like PSA 14, the Treaty of Asuncion calls for the graduated elimination of customs duties among its signatories at the rate of twenty percent a year (with certain exceptions for Paraguay and Uruguay), the exception of certain mutually agreed-upon areas from these tariff reductions, the harmonization of economic policies, the creation of rules of origin very similar to those of PSA 14, and the continuation of the safeguard clause system. Unlike PSA 14, the Treaty of Asuncion calls for a common external tariff and for the adoption of a common trade policy. Ouro Preto creates a number of additional MERCOSUR institutions and further enumerates and expands the roles of all of these institutions. Brasilia and Olivos augment the perfunctory provisions set forth in the Treaty of Asuncion and Ouro Preto for the resolution of disputes among member states and individuals. The major provisions of the latter documents will be discussed in some detail below.

E.   The MERCOSUR Institutions

Under the Treaty, Ouro Preto, and Olivos, seven institutions are charged with implementing MERCOSUR's principles and purposes. They include the Council of the Common Market (Council), the Common Market Group (Group), the MERCOSUR Commerce Commission (MCC), the Joint Parliamentary Commission, the Economic and Social Consultative Forum (Forum), the Administrative Secretariat (Secretariat), and the Permanent Appellate Tribunal (Tribunal).

The Council consists of the Foreign Relations and Economics Ministers of the four member states. Its presidency rotates among the member states, in alphabetical order, every six months. The Council is responsible for the political leadership of the integration process and for making decisions to ensure the implementation of the objectives of the Treaty of Asuncion. In addition, the Council is the legal representative of MERCOSUR, entitled to sign agreements with third-party countries, groups of countries, or international organizations. It supervises the other MERCOSUR institutions, and can modify or eliminate them. It also acts on policy proposals sent to it by the Group and has the power to designate the Director of the Secretariat. The Council acts by means of "Decisions," which, according to Ouro Preto, are "obligatory for the member states." The Council is the most important and powerful MERCOSUR institution.

The Group has four alternate representatives from each member state designated by their governments. Representatives from the economics and foreign ministries and central bank must be included in each member state's delegation. Each member state's delegates are coordinated by its minister of foreign relations. The Group's principal responsibilities include monitoring compliance with the Treaty of Asuncion, proposing policy for consideration by the Council and ensuring compliance with Council decisions. Analysis and recommendations on proposals or recommendations submitted by other MERCOSUR institutions are also part of the Group's responsibilities. It may, if authorized by the Council, become MERCOSUR's representative in negotiating agreements with non-member countries, groups of countries, or international organizations. Administratively, the Group approves the MERCOSUR budget, the Secretariat's annual expenditures, and supervises the Secretariat staff and Council meetings. The Group has its own internal regulations and can create "working subgroups" to assist it in its work. The Group's "Resolutions" are "binding on the member states."

The Council and the Group bear a superficial resemblance to the EU's Council and Commission. In both organizations, the Council is controlled by the member states and has the power to create policy or "community law," while the other institutions, the Commission in the EU and the Group in MERCOSUR, represent the proposer and implementer of policy. The European Commission and the Group are, however, very different institutions. The former is a supranational institution whose members are independent of the member states and which controls a substantial permanent staff. It has a substantial independent power base. The latter is controlled by the member states, whose senior civil servants serve as its members. It has no staff and no independent power base. Its role seems to be primarily administrative, rather than that of a planning and policy-making entity.

The MCC, a creature of Ouro Preto, has four representatives and four alternates from each member state. It implements the common commercial policy agreed to by the member states and monitors its application. Decisions regarding the administration and application of the common external tariff, as well as proposals relating to changes to the common external tariff and the common commercial policy, are also part of its responsibilities. The MCC also provides information to the Group on the evolution and application of the common commercial policy. It considers and decides applications submitted to it by the member states regarding the administration of MERCOSUR's common external tariff and common commercial policies. It monitors matters dealing with common commercial policies, intra-MERCOSUR trade, and trade relations between MERCOSUR and non-member states. It has internal regulations which regulate its proceedings. Furthermore, it also has the power to create Sub–Working Groups to examine and make proposals regarding different specific areas related to the common external tariff and the common commercial policy. It also has, under Olivos, the power to consider claims by individuals relating to member state violations of the Treaty and community law. The MCC issues either "Directives" or "Proposals," with the former being "binding on the member states." The MCC, with its specialized personnel, is a technical body whose principal task involves the analysis of areas of policy and the preparation of proposals relating thereto.

The Joint Parliamentary Commission, another Ouro Preto creation, serves as a representative of the legislatures of the member states. Each member state has an equal number of delegates who are designated by their parliaments. Its principal missions include planning and setting the stage for the creation of a future MERCOSUR parliament. It is also meant to be an institution to assist MERCOSUR in the implementation of its policies and in the harmonization of national legislation therewith. It has an advisory function at this point. Under Ouro Preto, the Forum's members represent the various sectors of economic and social life, such as merchants, consumers and workers. Its functions are purely advisory and this advice takes the form of "Recommendations" to the Group and other MERCOSUR institutions. It is meant to "cooperate actively" to promote economic and social progress within MERCOSUR, analyze and evaluate the social and economic impact of the various integration policies and their implementation, recommend economic and social norms and policies relating to integration, and perform studies and research on economic and social matters relevant to MERCOSUR.

The Secretariat is the only institution within MERCOSUR to have a permanent staff. It is permanently headquartered in Montevideo, Uruguay, and, at present, its staff consists of approximately twenty-seven persons. Its proposed 2002 budget was approximately $980,000. The Secretariat's responsibilities include translation of documents, logistical support for all of the other institutions, editing the MERCOSUR Official Gazette, gathering information for the other institutions, and handling communications with the member states. The Secretariat also has the task of monitoring and reporting on the implementation of all the MERCOSUR norms by each of the member states into its national legal system. Furthermore, the Secretariat manages the panel of arbitrators established by Brasilia and Olivos to resolve disputes arising out of the Treaty of Asuncion and its implementation. The Secretariat appears to have no substantive decision-making power. Again, the member states of MERCOSUR have clearly sought to ensure that control over the integration process remains in the hands of the member states and not in a group of independent international civil servants. The Secretariat is headed by a director which is appointed by the Group. The MERCOSUR Secretariat is divided into four major sections: Documents and Communications, Norms, Administration, and Information Technology.

* * *

O'KEEFE, A RESURGENT MERCOSUR: CONFRONTING
ECONOMIC CRISES AND NEGOTIATING TRADE
AGREEMENTS*

MERCOSUR's Dispute Resolution System

MERCOSUR's institutional framework based, inter alia, on a strong
intergovernmental bias and the absence of an independent judicial body
"gave governments a high degree of control over the process, ensuring
graduality and flexibility." This institutional model was very effective at
the initial stages, when interdependence was low and commitment was
high, and it proved quite resilient for nearly a decade. It also made the
integration process flexible and cost-effective at the initial stages. After
all, the primary purpose of MERCOSUR (especially for its two largest
members Argentina and Brazil) was to increase trade rather than to
administer its effects.

With the maxi-devaluation of the Brazilian real in January of 1999,
however, the shortcomings of MERCOSUR's minimalist institutional
framework became apparent. National governments attempted to impose
unilateral trade barriers to thwart alleged import surges that were illegal
under MERCOSUR, while private parties that had been detrimentally
affected found there were no institutional bodies within MERCOSUR
that could quickly redress their grievances. Reformers focused their
efforts on revamping what was perceived as MERCOSUR's weak dispute
resolution mechanism. Many of them claimed that what was needed was
a permanent Tribunal of Justice akin to that found in the European
Union and the Andean Community. The creation of such a court in the
MERCOSUR context would allow a venue for aggrieved parties to turn
to for decisions that would create binding precedents on the member
states. Demands for a more effective dispute resolution system were
eventually taken up by the national governments of the smaller member
states, who lacked sufficient political leverage to insure unrestricted
access to the larger subregional market for their national producers, as a
result of unilateral rule changes imposed by the bigger MERCOSUR
countries.

* * *

[T]here are two basic systems for dispute resolution in the formal
MERCOSUR framework. One system for resolving disputes between
private investors and a government is found in the "Protocol of Colonia
for the Promotion and Reciprocal Protection of Investments from within
the MERCOSUR" and the "Protocol for the Promotion and Reciprocal
Protection of Investments from outside the MERCOSUR. The second
dispute resolution system deals with disputes that may arise between

state parties or between an individual or company and (a) state party(ies) over the application or interpretation of norms and obligations arising out of the integration process. In discussing dispute resolution mechanisms within MERCOSUR, it is also important to note that a third option is available to private parties outside the formal MERCOSUR framework. To the extent that they have jurisdiction over the subject matter, private parties may also resort to the national court system to complain about a state party's failure to adhere to its MERCOSUR obligations. Unfortunately, it is not possible to comment on the first dispute resolution system's ability to handle conflicts between a private sector investor and a government because it has not yet entered into force. Neither protocol has been ratified, as of this writing. Accordingly, this paper will focus on the second formal MERCOSUR system for dispute resolution.

The Protocol of Brasilia

In December 1991, the presidents of the four MERCOSUR countries signed the Protocol of Brasilia for the Solution of Controversies. This Protocol replaced a temporary, three-step system found in Annex III to the Treaty of Asunción (the agreement signed on March 26, 1991, that formally brought MERCOSUR into existence). Interestingly, Annex III made no provisions for resolving disputes that might arise between private parties and a state party. In contrast, the Protocol of Brasilia not only provides a procedure for resolving disputes that might arise among state parties, but a second procedure exists for disputes between a private party and a state party(ies). The Protocol of Brasilia was designed to be temporary and eventually was to be replaced by a permanent system. With respect to disputes arising among state parties, the Protocol of Brasilia requires that the dispute must concern "the interpretation, application or non-compliance of the dispositions contained in the Treaty of Asunción, of the agreements celebrated within its framework, as well as any Decisions of the Common Market Council and the Resolutions of the Common Market Group." As a first step, the state parties should attempt to resolve their differences through direct negotiations within 15 working days, unless the parties extend that time limit. If this proves unsuccessful, then the matter is referred to the Common Market Group. The Common Market Group normally has 30 days within which to issue its recommendations for resolving the dispute. In formulating these recommendations, the Group is allowed to turn to a panel of experts for advice.

If the Common Market Group is also unable to resolve the dispute successfully, then the matter can be submitted at the request of a state party to a three-person, ad hoc arbitration panel. The arbitrators are limited to a maximum of 90 days to resolve a dispute and make an award. They are explicitly allowed to issue preliminary provisional measures to prevent severe and irreparable damages. Any decision they make is by majority vote, is binding on the parties, and cannot be appealed. The actual vote tally is kept confidential, and no dissenting opinions are allowed. The losing party generally has a maximum of 30 days to comply with a decision, unless this time period is briefly suspended in the event further clarification of the decision or an interpretation as to how it should be applied is sought. Failure to adhere to a decision allows the winning party(ies) the right to adopt temporary compensatory measures, such as the suspension of preferential tariff treatment or other concessions, in order to force compliance. The system established under the Protocol of Brasilia limits the right of an aggrieved private party to complain of the application by a state party or parties "of legal or administrative measures which have a restrictive, discriminatory or unfairly competitive effect, in violation of the Treaty of Asunción, of the agreements celebrated within its framework, the Decisions of the Common Market Council or the Resolutions of the Common Market Group." In other words, private parties are limited to complaining about the affirmative actions of a state and not any omissions, such as the failure of a state party to comply with its MERCOSUR obligations. Another major difference is that a private party complaint can never move beyond the Common Market Group to the third level of binding arbitration unless a state adopts the private party complaint as its own.

MODIFICATIONS INTRODUCED BY THE PROTOCOL OF OURO PRETO

December 1994, the presidents of the four MERCOSUR countries signed the Protocol of Ouro Preto, which introduced important modifications to the institutional structure of the MERCOSUR. These modifications also affected MERCOSUR's dispute resolution mechanism as established by the Protocol of Brasilia, in that the newly created MERCOSUR Trade Commission was now authorized to "consider the complaints presented by the National Sections of the MERCOSUR Trade Commission originating with the State Parties or private parties ... [that] fall within its jurisdiction." The main task of the MERCOSUR Trade Commission is to insure the application of common trade policy instruments with respect to intraregional and global trade. The Protocol of Ouro Preto also added the Directives of the MERCOSUR Trade Commission as additional legal norms upon which a party using the dispute system could base its complaint.

In terms of the procedural rules established by the Protocol of Ouro Preto for resolving complaints filed by a state party with the MERCOSUR Trade Commission, Annex I to the Protocol requires that the complaint be filed with the president pro-tempore of the full MERCOSUR Trade Commission. If the Commission cannot resolve the matter at its next regular meeting, then it is forwarded to one of seven permanent technical committees that assist the Trade Commission in its work. The relevant technical committee has 30 days to make a recommendation or, if there is a difference of opinion, to forward the conclusions of the different experts. If the MERCOSUR Trade Commission cannot resolve the matter, then the dispute with the different proposed experts' remedies are forwarded to the full Common Market Group for it to make a decision within 30 days. If the Common Market Group, in turn, cannot make a final determination or if an errant state party refuses to accept the Group's decision or the earlier decision of the MERCOSUR Trade Commission (if one were forthcoming at that level) within a reasonable time limit, then the aggrieved state party can proceed to binding arbitration under the Protocol of Brasilia.

Common Market Decision 17/98

In December 1998, the Common Market Council, MERCOSUR's highest institutional body, issued Decision 17/98, which contains the Regulations for fully implementing the Protocol of Brasilia for the Solution of Controversies. With the regulations in place, the final level of MERCOSUR's dispute resolution mechanism involving a three-person arbitration panel could now be utilized. Although the Protocol of Brasilia had been signed in 1991, the long delay in making the system fully effective can be explained, in part, by a Latin American cultural trait of allowing one's adversary in a conflict a face-saving way to retreat gracefully. In addition, during MERCOSUR's early days, commercial disputes were often used by member states as a means of obtaining other concessions from a culpable party rather than actually resolving the problem before them. Both these goals would be frustrated by a system in which the decisions of the arbitral panels are binding and no appeals are permitted.

C.M.C. Decision 17/98 did not make dramatic substantive changes to the provisions found in the Protocol of Brasilia (a shortcoming according to some analysts), but rather further expanded and explained in greater detail the procedural rules established in the earlier Protocol, such as those dealing with the selection of arbitrators. It also reemphasized the changes introduced through the Protocol of Ouro Preto that state-to-state disputes over the interpretation, application, or non-compliance with Directives of the MERCOSUR Trade Commission could be referred to the formal dispute resolution mechanism, as could disputes by private parties against a state party for enforcement of a legal or administrative measure in violation of a Directive.

The Protocol of Olivos for the Resolution of Controversies in MERCOSUR

On February 18, 2002, the presidents and foreign ministers of the MERCOSUR countries signed the Protocol of Olivos that, once it comes into effect, will contain the new transitional dispute resolution mechanism for MERCOSUR. [Authors' Note: The Olivos Protocol, reproduced in the Documentary Supplement, became effective February 10, 2004.] It is designed to replace the 1991 Protocol of Brasilia (and its implementing regulations found in Common Market Council Decision 17/98), although not the innovations introduced to MERCOSUR's dispute resolution system under the 1994 Protocol of Ouro Preto. Before the Protocol of Olivos can enter into force, however, it must be ratified by all four member states. In addition, the Common Market Group must also draft implementing regulations before the new system comes into effect. As was true of the Protocol of Brasilia, the new Protocol of Olivos is temporary in nature and is subject to replacement by a Permanent Dispute Resolution System before the common market aspect of the MERCOSUR project is fully implemented (now scheduled for January 1, 2006). The Protocol of Olivos addresses some of the criticisms long lodged against MERCOSUR's current dispute resolution system. Although it retains most of the procedural and institutional features of the Protocol of Brasilia, it grants the arbitral panels greater oversight capabilities to help ensure compliance with past decisions they have issued. In addition, it provides state parties with a faster route to the final stage of the dispute resolution system, binding arbitration, by allowing disputes to bypass the heavily politicized Common Market Group.

The most important innovation of the Protocol of Olivos is the establishment of a Permanent Tribunal of Review that is designed to "guarantee the correct interpretation, application and fulfillment of the fundamental instruments of the integration process" and MERCOSUR norms "in a consistent and systematic manner." The Permanent Tribunal of Review will have the power to "confirm, modify or revoke the legal basis and decisions" of an ad hoc arbitral panel and the Tribunal's decisions take precedence over those of the ad hoc body. Furthermore, state parties may request review by the Permanent Tribunal of Review of any dispute that falls within its subject matter jurisdiction if they are unable to resolve fully the matter through direct negotiations (bypassing the Common Market Group and ad hoc arbitration). Finally, the Common Market Council is authorized to establish regulations permitting advisory opinions from the Tribunal.

* * *

GENERAL SECRETARIAT, THE ANDEAN COMMUNITY, WHO ARE WE?*

The Andean Community is a subregional organization endowed with an international legal status, which is made up of Bolivia, Colombia, Ecuador, Peru and Venezuela and the bodies and institutions comprising the Andean Integration System (AIS). Located in South America, the five Andean countries together have 120 million inhabitants living in an area of 4 700 000 square kilometers, whose Gross Domestic Product in 2002 amounted to 260 billion dollars.

Objectives: The key objectives of the Andean Community (CAN) are: to promote the balanced and harmonious development of the member countries under equitable conditions, to boost their growth through integration and economic and social cooperation, to enhance participation in the regional integration process with a view to the progressive

* Adapted from information at http://www.comunidadandina.org/ingles/un-   ion.htm. Copyright © 2004 the Andean Community. Reprinted with permission.

formation of a Latin American common market, and to strive for a steady improvement in the standard of living of their inhabitants.

Background: The early beginnings of the Andean Community date back to 1969, when a group of South American countries signed the Cartagena Agreement, also known as the Andean Pact, for the purpose of establishing a customs union within a period of ten years. Over the next three decades, Andean integration passed through a series of different stages. A basically closed conception of inward-looking integration based on the import substitution model gradually gave way to a scheme of open regionalism.

Political boost: The direct intervention of the Presidents in the leadership of the process within the new model spurred integration and made it possible to attain the main objectives set by the Cartagena Agreement, such as the liberalization of trade in goods in the subregion, the adoption of a common external tariff, and the harmonization of foreign trade instruments and policies and economic policy, among others. The progress of integration and the emergence of new challenges stemming from global economic change brought to the fore the need for both institutional and policy reforms in the Cartagena Agreement. These were accomplished through the Protocols of Trujillo and Sucre, respectively.

Institutional reforms: The institutional reforms gave the process political direction and created the Andean Community and the Andean Integration System. The policy reforms, for their part, extended the scope of integration beyond the purely trade and economic areas. The Andean Community started operating on August 1, 1997 with a General Secretariat, whose headquarters are in Lima (Peru), as its executive body. The Council of Presidents and the Council of Foreign Ministers were formally established as new policy-making and leadership bodies.

Free Trade Area, Customs Union and Common Market: The Andean Free Trade Area was formed in February 1993, when Bolivia, Colombia, Ecuador, and Venezuela finished eliminating their customs tariffs and opened their markets to each other, while maintaining their own individual tariffs for third parties. Peru became a part of that area in July 1997 and since then has been gradually deregulating its trade with its Andean partners. Thus far, it has advanced more than 90% in this undertaking. The trade in goods between Bolivia, Colombia, Ecuador, and Venezuela is fully deregulated, which means that goods originating in any one of those countries can enter the territory of the others duty-free. As a result, these four countries have a free trade area that Peru is becoming a part of through a Liberalization Program. The efforts of the Andean countries are aimed at managing and perfecting this enlarged market and bringing about its efficient operation. The rules of origin, technical regulations, and measures for preventing and correcting practices that distort free competition all point in that direction.

The Andean Community is a Customs Union because the goods of its member countries circulate unimpededly throughout its territory free of duties of any sort, while imports from outside the Subregion pay a common tariff. The Andean Customs Union has been in operation since 1995, when the Common External Tariff (CET) approved by Colombia, Ecuador and Venezuela at the basic levels of 5, 10, 15 and 20 percent came into effect. Bolivia enjoys preferential treatment and only applies levels of 5 and 10 percent, while Peru did not sign that agreement. In the Santa Cruz Declaration of January 2002, the Andean Presidents stipulated that "Bolivia, Colombia, Ecuador, Peru and Venezuela will apply a common external tariff by December 31, 2003, at the latest." Accordingly, the Ministers of Foreign Affairs, Economy and the Treasury, Foreign Trade and Agriculture of the five CAN member countries on October 14, 2002 decided on the CET that is shown in Annex I to Decision 535. On April 14, 2003, the Andean countries put the finishing touches to the agreements for the adoption of a CET, thus bringing an important stage in the integration process to an end.

The countries of the Andean Community have assumed the commitment to establish a Common Market by 2005, at the latest. This is the highest phase of integration and is characterized by the free circulation of goods, services, capital, and people. What is being sought through its creation is to form a single internal market that will constitute a sole economic territory capable of multiplying the opportunities for trade, investment, and employment of entrepreneurs and workers from the Andean and third countries and to guarantee that the Subregion will have a stronger position in the world economy.

Trade in Services: The Andean countries, knowing that it is essential to gradually and progressively eliminate measures that restrict trade in services in the subregion, in order to create the Common Market by 2005, are currently working to do so. In order to boost this process, the Commission on October 31 approved Decision 510 "Adoption of the Inventory of Measures Restricting the Trade in Services." This Decision allows the citizens of an Andean country to provide in any of the four other subregional members any service, except for those listed in the Inventory, which will be progressively phased out by the year 2005. A general framework of principles and provisions (Decision 439) guides this entire process.

Court of Justice: This is the judicial body of the Andean Community, which is comprised of five Judges, each representing one of the Member Countries, and has territorial jurisdiction in the five countries, with permanent headquarters in Quito, Ecuador. The Court ensures the legality of Community provisions through nullity actions, interprets Andean Community laws to ensure that they are applied uniformly in the territories of the Member Countries, and settles disputes. The Protocol of Modification of the Treaty Establishing the Court of Justice of the Andean Community, approved in May 1996, and which came into force in August 1999, assigns new spheres of competence to this institution of the Andean Integration System (AIS), including Appeals for Omission or Inaction, Arbitration and Labor Jurisdiction. Its new By-laws, which update and detail the procedures carried out in this Court, were approved on June 22, 2001 by the Andean Council of Foreign Ministers.

* * *

HASKEL, MERCOSUR, ANDEAN COUNTRIES SIGN AGREEMENT ON FREE TRADE AREA HAILED AS ANSWER TO FTAA

21 Int'l Trade Rep. 1729 (Oct. 21, 2004)*

South America's two major trading blocs finally managed to overcome most of their lingering differences and on Oct. 18 signed a deal to set up a free trade area covering virtually the whole continent—a move some officials there are calling a Latin American answer to the United States' proposed Free Trade Area of the Americas among the 34 Western Hemisphere democracies. Foreign affairs ministers from the four Southern Common Market (Mercosur) partners—Argentina, Brazil, Paraguay, and Uruguay—and from the Andean Community of Nations (CAN), comprising Bolivia, Colombia, Ecuador, Peru, and Venezuela, inked the deal at a meeting of the Latin American Integration Association (ALADI) held in Montevideo.

The two sides formally launched the overall process last December and were originally expected to iron out several sticky points by last July. But some issues—including differences between Paraguay and some Andean nations over Paraguay's request for more market access for its soybeans, and Peruvian farmers' misgivings over Mercosur agricultural products—caused a three-month delay. The agreement now triggers a 60–day period during which it needs to win congressional ratification in each of the nine South American nations involved. It also sets off a 10–year timetable to gradually eliminate tariffs between the two blocs, with an extra five years for the most sensitive items.

SOUTH AMERICAN COMMUNITY OF NATIONS

But officials from both groups believe the effect should be felt immediately, taking bilateral trade from $31 billion now to $50 billion by 2007. The deal covers 98 percent of South America's territory and population, leaving out only tiny Guyana, Suriname, and French Guiana, which have traditionally opted out of regional integration movements.

Some Latin officials were also portraying the Mercosur–CAN pact as a Latin American answer to Washington's proposed FTAA among the 34 Western Hemisphere democracies.... "The signing of this pact [between Mercosur and CAN] is a clear step toward the South American Community of Nations," Brazilian Foreign Minister Celso Amorim—whose country currently holds the rotating Mercosur presidency as well as the co-chairmanship of the FTAA negotiations—told the meeting of

* Excerpted with permission from the *International Trade Reporter*, Vol. 21, No. 42, p. 1729 (Oct. 21, 2004). Copyright 2004 by the Bureau of National Affairs, Inc. (800-372-1033) http://www.bna.com.

ALADI, which comprises all Mercosur and CAN members plus Mexico, Chile, and Cuba.

* * *

Questions and Comments

1. Contrast NAFTA, and its trade-liberalizing achievements in ten years, to MERCOSUR. Why has MERCOSUR been less successful in achieving the elimination of intra-regional tariffs and non-tariff barriers? To what extent are the problems due to the fact that NAFTA is a combination of developed and developing nations, while all of the members of MERCOSUR are developing countries? How has the integration process been facilitated in MERCOSUR by the willingness of the members to conclude new treaties and protocols to deal with deficiencies or changing conditions, as contrasted to NAFTA, where amendment of the agreement has been politically impossible? Refer to Porrata–Doria.

2. How do the institutions of MERCOSUR differ from those of NAFTA? O'Keefe notes that the dispute settlement procedures have been modified extensively. There have been at least six arbitral decisions under these provisions. How does the process established in Olivos differ from NAFTA's Chapter 20? How is the Tribunal of Review (established under the Protocol of Olivos) likely to affect the dispute settlement process? Should the NAFTA Parties consider a similar institution to review decisions under Chapters 11, 19 and/or 20?

3. What factors are likely responsible for the failure of the MER-COSUR parties to ratify the Protocol of Colonia, the only Chapter 11–like investment protection language in the MERCOSUR treaties? After all, there is substantial intra-regional foreign investment, e.g., by Argentine investors in Brazil and vice-versa.

4. To what extent is the failure of the FTAA process responsible for the movement toward South American economic integration? Or is that movement at least partially responsible for the failure of the FTAA process? Recall that Chile already has FTAs with the United States, Canada and Mexico, and that the U.S. is currently (2004–2005) negotiating free trade agreements with Peru, Colombia, Ecuador and Panama, in addition to NAFTA and CAFTA. What are the risks that in the absence of an FTAA the United States will again lose interest in Latin America, as it did after the Kennedy/Johnson Alliance for Progress and Nixon's Spirit of Tlateloco?

5. Assuming that MERCOSUR's FTA with Venezuela, Colombia, Ecuador and Peru is promptly ratified and enters into force, along with the existing FTAs with Bolivia and Chile, what practical legal problems are likely to affect the trade within South America? What recommendations would you have made to the parties with regard to such prosaic legal/administrative matters as rules of origin and customs provisions?

6. Haskell reports that the MERCOSUR—Andean Community agreement will initiate a ten year schedule to eliminate tariffs of 80% of

all goods traded. Duties on some sensitive products, such as Andean textile, steel and paper products, and MERCOSUR wheat, soybeans and automobiles, will not be eliminated for 15 years, as in NAFTA. See Haskell, Mercosur, Andean Nations Agree to Launch Free Trade Pact July 1 (21 Int'l Trade Rep. 619 (Apr. 8, 2004).) Assuming that the total coverage is 80% of all intra-regional trade, would the FTA meet the requirements of GATT Article XXIV? (See Chapter 1).

*

Index

References are to Pages Unless Otherwise Noted

†

0–314–15397—7

90000

9 780314 153975